Tax Formula for Individu

Income (broadly conceived)	$xx,xxx
Less: Exclusions	(x,xxx)
Gross income	$xx,xxx
Less: Deductions *for* adjusted gross income	(x,xxx)
Adjusted gross income	$xx,xxx
Less: The greater of—	
Total itemized deductions *or* standard deduction	(x,xxx)
Personal and dependency exemptions	(x,xxx)
Taxable income	$xx,xxx

Basic Standard Deduction Amounts

	Standard Deduction Amount	
Filing Status	**1997**	**1998**
Single	$4,150	$4,250
Married, filing jointly	6,900	7,100
Surviving spouse	6,900	7,100
Head of household	6,050	6,250
Married, filing separately	3,450	3,550

Amount of Each Additional Standard Deduction

Filing Status	**1997**	**1998**
Single	$1,000	$1,050
Married, filing jointly	800	850
Surviving spouse	800	850
Head of household	1,000	1,050
Married, filing separately	800	850

Personal and Dependency Exemption

1997	**1998**
$2,650	$2,700

West's Federal Taxation

INDIVIDUAL INCOME TAXES

1999 Edition

General Editors

William H. Hoffman, Jr., J.D., Ph.D., C.P.A.   **James E. Smith,** Ph.D., C.P.A.

Eugene Willis, Ph.D., C.P.A.

Contributing Authors

James H. Boyd
Ph.D., C.P.A.
Arizona State University

William H. Hoffman, Jr.
J.D., Ph.D., C.P.A.
University of Houston

W. Eugene Seago
J.D., Ph.D., C.P.A.
*Virginia Polytechnic Institute
and State University*

D. Larry Crumbley
Ph.D., C.P.A.
Louisiana State University

David M. Maloney
Ph.D., C.P.A.
University of Virginia

James E. Smith
Ph.D., C.P.A.
College of William and Mary

Steven C. Dilley
J.D., Ph.D., C.P.A.
Michigan State University

William A. Raabe
Ph.D., C.P.A.
Samford University

Eugene Willis
Ph.D., C.P.A.
*University of Illinois
at Urbana*

Mary Sue Gately
Ph.D., C.P.A.
Texas Tech University

Boyd C. Randall
J.D., Ph.D.
Brigham Young University

WEST/SOUTH-WESTERN College Publishing

An International Thomson Publishing Company

Accounting Team Director: Richard Lindgren
Acquisitions Editor: Alex von Rosenberg
Developmental Editor: Esther Craig
Production Editor: Rebecca Glaab
Copyediting: Patricia A. Lewis
Production House: Peggy Williams with Texterity
Index: Catalyst Communication Arts
Cover Design: Matulionis Design
Internal Design: LightSource Images
Marketing Manager: Maureen L. Riopelle

TurboTax is a registered trademark of Intuit Inc.
Thomson World Class Learning is a trademark used herein under license.

ISBN: 0–538–88574–2

1 2 3 4 5 6 7 8 9 C 5 6 5 4 3 2 1 0 9 8

Printed in the United States of America

Library of Congress Cataloging-in-Publication Data

Main entry under title:
  West's Federal Taxation.
  Includes index.
    1. Income tax—United States—Law
I. Hoffman, William H.   III.   Willis, Eugene

ISBN 0–538–88574–2, 0–538–88892–X
KF6335.H63   343'.73'04   77–54355

ISSN 0272–0329
1999 ANNUAL EDITION

I⟨T⟩P®
WEST/South-Western College Publishing
An International Thomson Publishing Company

PREFACE

The publication of the 1999 Edition marks the twenty-second year of *West's Federal Taxation* (WFT). From a single textbook on Corporations, Partnerships, Estates, and Trusts with an accompanying solutions manual, the WFT series has grown to five major textbooks and a package of more than 50 ancillaries. During this period, WFT has made every effort to improve the quality of the materials and has consistently added attractive innovations. With sales surpassing the one million level, WFT looks forward to continued success in the future in serving you.

This textbook is intended as a basis for a first course in Federal taxation for undergraduate or graduate accounting, business, and law students. With certain modifications in the coverage of the materials, the textbook may be used in a survey course on Federal taxation for undergraduate or graduate students. The materials may also be valuable as a tool for self-study, since they contain numerous clarifying examples adaptable to such an approach.

Tax policy considerations and historical developments are introduced in the textbook only to the extent that they shed light on the reason for a particular rule. The many simple and straightforward examples further clarify the materials by showing how a particular tax rule applies in an actual situation.

Since the original edition was issued in 1978, we have followed a policy of annually revising the text material to reflect statutory, judicial, and administrative changes in the Federal tax law and to correct any errors or other shortcomings. Not only do we encourage user input, we actively seek the advice of users as the basis for improving the textbook.

Tax legislation may be enacted in 1998 or early 1999. If any significant tax legislation is enacted during this period, we will provide you with supplements on a timely basis.

Though the primary emphasis of the textbook is on the income taxation of individuals, Chapter 20 provides an overview of the Federal taxation of other forms of business organization (corporations and partnerships). This chapter could be of particular significance to students who do not plan to take a second course in Federal taxation. For others, Chapter 20 may serve as a lead-in to *West's Federal Taxation: Corporations, Partnerships, Estates, and Trusts*.

ENHANCED PEDAGOGICAL PLAN

In the 1999 edition, we have continued to enhance the pedagogy to assist the student in the learning process and to address the recommendations of the Accounting Education Change Commission (AECC).

- *Learning Objectives*. Each chapter begins with student learning objectives for the chapter. These behavioral objectives provide the students with guidance in learning the key concepts and principles.

- *Chapter Outline*. The learning objectives are followed by a topical outline of the material in the chapter. Page references appear in the outline to provide the student with ready access to each topic.
- *Chapter Introductions*. The introductions link the material in the current chapter to previous chapters and demonstrate its relevance. Frequently, the chapter introduction includes a "real-world" illustration to help convey the relevance of the material.
- *Margin Notes*. Each of the learning objectives appears in the margin where the related material is introduced and helps to guide the student through the chapter.
- *Tax in the News*. Tax in the News items appear in each chapter as a boxed feature to enliven the text discussion. These items are drawn from today's business press and present current issues that are relevant to the chapter material.
- *Ethical Considerations*. Ethical Considerations features appear in each chapter presenting thought-provoking issues related to the chapter topics. In response to the recommendations of the AECC, they also demonstrate that many issues do not have a single correct answer. The questions raised in the Ethical Considerations were selected to provoke discussion and provide opportunities for debate (oral communication) based on the student's value system rather than to provide a defensible answer. To assist the professor in providing guidance for the discussion, the *Instructor's Guide with Lecture Notes* includes material on each Ethical Consideration. This material identifies the issues raised in the Ethical Consideration and, where appropriate, recommends a solution or alternate solutions.
- *Key Terms*. Located before the Problem Materials in each chapter is a list of key terms to assist student learning. When the key term is introduced in the chapter, it appears in bold print. The list of key terms includes page references to the chapter coverage. In addition, each key term is defined in the Glossary (Appendix C).
- *Communication Assignments*. In recognition of the increasing emphasis in accounting and tax education on communication, identified items in the Problem Materials now include a written communication component. Selected Problems, Cumulative Problems, and Research Problems are identified as communication assignments with a "scroll" icon. These problems ask the student to prepare a tax client letter, a memorandum for the tax files, or other written materials. The discussion of the tax research process in Chapter 2 includes an illustration of the client letter and the memo.

- *Decision-Making Problems*. The Problem Materials include decision-making problems that are designed to enhance the student's analytical skills. These problems are identified with a "scales" icon.

- *Issue Recognition Questions*. The Problem Materials include questions that are designed to require the student to identify tax issues. With this issues orientation, such questions can be multifaceted and have no single right answer. These questions are identified with a "lightbulb" icon.
- *Team Projects: Arthur Andersen Tax Challenge Cases*. This feature at the end of the Problem Materials gives students experience working as a team to solve complex, real world tax issues. The two cases referenced in the text, along with two additional cases and the solutions, are available to adopters in a separate manual. Instructors may make copies of this material for classroom use; no additional permission is required. Case Notes for the instructor can be found in the *Instructor's Guide*.

- The Research Problems heading now includes a CD-ROM icon to emphasize that solutions to all the research problems can now be prepared using the RIA OnPoint System 4 Student Version CD-ROM available with this text.
- *Internet exercises.* Included as part of the Research Problems for each chapter are questions which require the use of the tax resources of the Internet. These exercises are identified with a globe and computer mouse icon.

SPECIAL FEATURES

A variety of other pedagogical devices are used to assist the student in the learning process. We recognize the importance of readability and continue to strive to make our textbook and supplements even more readable and understandable. The following features enhance the readability of the text:

- Including three levels of headings to aid in organization.
- Using bold print in the text to identify key terms the first time each term is used. Key terms are defined in the Glossary (Appendix C).
- Italicizing other key words to emphasize their importance to the student.
- Avoiding legal terminology except where it is beneficial.
- Using Concept Summaries to synthesize important concepts in chart or tabular form.
- Using Exhibits, Figures, and Tables to enhance presentations.
- Organizing the material in lists with bullets rather than presenting it in lengthy sentences.
- Using examples frequently to help the student understand the tax concept being discussed.
- Using a larger page size to provide a more open, accessible, and student-friendly textbook.

Once knowledge of the tax law has been acquired, it needs to be used. The tax minimization process, however, normally requires careful planning. Because we recognize the importance of planning procedures, most chapters include a separate section (called *Tax Planning Considerations*) illustrating the applications of these procedures to specific areas. While tax planning applications and suggestions appear *throughout* the chapter, this separate section at the end of the chapter calls the student's attention to the importance of tax planning.

We believe that any basic course in Federal taxation should offer the reader the opportunity to learn and utilize the methodology of tax research. This knowledge is requisite in today's environment with its increased emphasis on the concept of "learning to learn." Chapter 2 and Appendix E are devoted to this methodology. Also, most chapters contain *Research Problems* that require the use of research tools. Solutions to these Research Problems can be found in the *Instructor's Guide.* The effectiveness of the text does not, however, depend on the coverage of tax research procedures. Consequently, the treatment of this subject may be omitted without impairing the continuity of the remaining textual materials.

Although it is not our purpose to approach taxation from the standpoint of preparing tax returns, some familiarity with forms is necessary. Because 1998 forms will not be available until later in the year, most tax return problems in this edition are written for tax year 1997. For the reader's convenience, Appendix B contains a full reproduction of most of the 1997 tax forms frequently encountered in actual practice. The 1997 problems may be solved manually, or many may be solved using the tax return preparation software (*TurboTax®*) that may be purchased by students who use this textbook.

Appendix F contains two comprehensive tax return problems written for tax year 1997. Each of these problems lends itself for use as a term project because of the sophistication required for satisfactory completion. Solutions to the problems in Appendix F appear in the *Instructor's Guide*.

Most tax textbooks are published in the spring, long before tax forms for the year of publication are available from the government. We believe that students should be exposed to the most current tax forms. As a result, we develop some new problems and provide adopters with reproducible copies of these problems, along with blank tax forms and solutions on the new forms. Shortly after the beginning of 1999, adopters will receive a *Forms Problems Supplement* containing these tax return problems solved on 1998 forms.

RIA ONPOINT SYSTEM 4, STUDENT VERSION, CD-ROM

As a result of a partnership with RIA and West/South-Western College Publishing, this ultimate tax research tool is now available for student use. RIA OnPoint System 4, Student Version, offers an abbreviated version of this extensive and respected tax database. The OnPoint System 4, Student Version, offers detailed analysis and coherent explanation of the tax law by RIA's in-house experts, treatises written by renowned outside authors, primary source materials, practice aids, and more!

RIA OnPoint lets you access a complete and fully integrated tax law database with accuracy, precision, and ease. Check out these additional features:

- Over 600 watershed court cases and private letter rulings.
- The Federal Tax Coordinator.
- In-depth analysis, expert commentary and practical guidance for income, estate and gift tax, excises taxes, employment taxes, and U.S. taxation of foreign income.
- Internal Revenue Code, including complete legislative history since 1954.
- Treasury Regulations, including proposed regulations.
- Code arranged Committee Reports.
- Revenue Rulings, Procedures and Notices from 1954 to present, with head-notes and Internal Revenue Code classifications.
- Full text of current year American Federal Tax Reports (AFTR) cases.
- Over 230 of the most frequently requested IRS publications.

This item can be shrinkwrapped with the text and used by students to conduct computerized tax research.

SUPPLEMENTS

West is continuing to publish the Arthur Andersen Tax Challenge Cases, a set of four capstone cases and their solutions provided to the instructor for classroom use. The cases encompass both tax compliance and tax planning and provide an opportunity for a team approach in solving tax issues and recommending tax strategies. As a technique for further integrating the cases with the textbook coverage of the tax topics in the cases, page references to two of the cases appear at the end of each chapter.

Other products in our 1999 instructional package include the following:

- The *Instructor's Guide with Lecture Notes* contains lecture notes for each chapter, materials on the Ethical Considerations found in the textbook, materials on the two Arthur Andersen Tax Challenge Cases that are page referenced to the textbook, and solutions to Research Problems and Comprehensive Tax Return problems found in the textbook. The lecture notes consist of a lecture outline that the professor can use as the basis for his or her classroom presentation. These lecture notes include not only material covered in the textbook, but also cases and other relevant material and teaching aids. The lecture notes are also available on disk and on our Web site.

- A *Solutions Manual* that has been carefully checked to ensure that it is error-free. The problems are arranged in accordance with the sequence of the material in the chapter. All problems are labeled by topical coverage in a matrix that also indicates which problems are new, modified, or unchanged in the new edition. The matrix also includes the problem number for the unchanged and modified problems in the prior edition. Approximately 20 percent of the problems in the 1999 edition are new or modified. The solutions are referenced to pages in the textbook. The solutions manual is also available on disk and on our Web site.

- A *Test Bank* with questions and solutions referenced to pages in the textbook. The questions are arranged in accordance with the sequence of the material in the chapter. To assist the professor in selecting questions for an examination, all questions are labeled by topical coverage in a matrix that also indicates which questions are new, modified, or unchanged in the new edition. The matrix includes the question number for the unchanged and modified questions in the prior edition. Approximately 20 percent of the questions in the 1999 edition are new or modified.

- ITP World Class Test™, a microcomputer test generation program for IBM PCs and compatibles.

- A *Student Study Guide* prepared by Gerald E. Whittenburg, San Diego State University, includes a chapter review of key concepts and self-evaluation tests with solutions that are page referenced to the textbook.

- *Solutions Transparency Masters* for selected complex and cumulative problems, with a larger typeface for greater readability.

- *PowerPoint Presentation Software* allows qualified adopters to create interactive lectures and manipulate graphs, charts, and figures during in-class lectures. The package contains approximately 30 transparency masters per chapter consisting of alternate figures, outlines, and key points.

- *Teaching Transparency Acetates* contain the key charts and tables from the *PowerPoint* package for instructors who wish to use traditional overheads.

- *Arthur Andersen Tax Challenge: Cases and Solutions* is a separate manual that includes four of the Arthur Andersen Tax Challenge cases and their solutions. This manual is available to adopters with permission to copy the cases for classroom use as Team Projects (found at the end of Problem Materials).

- *WFT Individual Practice Sets*, 1998-99 edition, prepared by Mark Nixon, Bentley College, is designed to cover all the common forms that a tax practitioner would use for the average client.

- Limited free use to qualified adopters of WESTLAW, a computer-assisted tax and legal research service that provides access to hundreds of valuable information sources.

- *West's Internal Revenue Code of 1986 and Treasury Regulations: Annotated and Selected 1999 Edition* by James E. Smith, College of William and Mary. This provides the opportunity for the student to be exposed to the Code and the Regulations in a single-volume book, which also contains useful annotations that help the student work with and understand the Code.

- The WFT WEB SITE puts the most current information and supplements in the user's hands as soon as it is available. Adopters can log onto the web site (swcollege.com or wft.swcollege.com) and gain access to key information and supplements before they are available in print. The web site also includes extra problem materials and quizzes, topical news items, the latest news of West's Federal Tax supplements and publications, and more.

TAX PREPARATION SOFTWARE

The trend toward using the computer as an essential tool in tax practice has accelerated. To ensure that the *West's Federal Taxation* instructional package continues to set the pace in this important area, the following tax software product is available to be used with the 1999 edition:

- *TurboTax®* for Windows 97.01 by Intuit is a commercial tax preparation package. It teaches students how to prepare over 80 forms, schedules, and worksheets, and automatically performs all mathematical calculations and data transfers. The *TurboTax* package, available for student purchase, includes the software bound with a 200-page workbook containing exercises and problems. The software runs on IBM PCs and compatibles.

This software product is powerful, easy to learn, and easy to use. We believe that tax education can be raised to a higher level through the use of computers and well-designed software. This software package takes the drudgery out of performing the complex computations required to solve difficult tax problems.

To enable students to take advantage of this software product, the 1999 edition contains numerous tax return problems. Problems that lend themselves to computerized solutions are identified by a computer symbol.

ACKNOWLEDGMENTS

We are most appreciative of the many suggestions that we have received for revising the textbook, many of which have been incorporated in past editions and in the 1999 edition. We would also like to thank the people who have painstakingly worked through all the problems and text questions and generally acted as problem checkers to ensure the accuracy of the book and ancillary package. They are Tracey A. Anderson, Indiana University at South Bend; Caroline K. Craig, Illinois State University; Frank Linton, University of Scranton; Mark B. Persellin, St. Mary's University; Debra L. Sanders, Washington State University; Randall K. Serrett, Fort Lewis College; Thomas Sternburg, University of Illinois at Urbana; and Raymond F. Wacker, Southern Illinois University at Carbondale.

Finally, this 1999 edition would not have been possible without the technical assistance of and manuscript review by Bonnie Hoffman, CPA, Freda Mulhall, CPA, Nora Smith, M.Ed., and Ralph Traylor, CPA. We are indebted to them for their efforts.

William H. Hoffman, Jr.
James E. Smith
Eugene Willis

April 1, 1998

ABOUT THE EDITORS

William H. Hoffman, Jr., earned B.A. and J.D. degrees from the University of Michigan and M.B.A. and Ph.D. degrees from The University of Texas. He is a licensed CPA and attorney in Texas. His teaching experience includes: The University of Texas (1957–1961), Louisiana State University (1961–1967), and the University of Houston (1967 to present). Professor Hoffman has addressed many tax institutes and conferences and has published extensively in academic and professional journals. His articles appear in *The Journal of Taxation, The Tax Adviser, Taxes—The Tax Magazine, The Journal of Accountancy, The Accounting Review*, and *Taxation for Accountants*.

James E. Smith is the John S. Quinn Professor of Accounting at the College of William and Mary. He has been a member of the Accounting Faculty for twenty-eight years. He received his Ph.D. degree from the University of Arizona.

Jim has served as a discussion leader for Continuing Professional Education programs for the AICPA, Federal Tax Workshops, and various state CPA societies. He has conducted programs in over 40 states for approximately 25,000 CPAs. He has been the recipient of the AICPAs' Outstanding Discussion Leader Award.

Other awards received by Jim include the Virginia Society of CPAs' Outstanding Accounting Educator Award and the James Madison University's Outstanding Accounting Educator Award. He was the President of the Administrators of Accounting Programs Group (AAPG) in 1991–1992. He was the faculty adviser for the William and Mary teams that received first place in the Arthur Andersen Tax Challenge in 1994, 1995, and 1997.

Eugene Willis is the Arthur Andersen Alumni Professor of Accountancy at the University of Illinois (Urbana-Champaign). He joined the Illinois faculty in 1975 after receiving his Ph.D. from the University of Cincinnati. He serves as Head of the department. His articles have appeared in leading academic and professional journals, including the *Accounting Review, The Journal of the American Taxation Association, The Journal of Accountancy*, and *The Journal of Taxation*. Professor Willis is co-director of the National Tax Education Program, a continuing education program co-sponsored by the American Institute of CPAs and the University of Illinois.

CONTENTS IN BRIEF

CONTENTS

▼ PART III
DEDUCTIONS

P A R T IV
SPECIAL TAX COMPUTATION METHODS, PAYMENT PROCEDURES, AND TAX CREDITS

▼

PART V
PROPERTY TRANSACTIONS

PART VI

ACCOUNTING PERIODS, ACCOUNTING
METHODS, AND DEFERRED
COMPENSATION

CHAPTER 18
Accounting Periods and Methods   **18–1**

APPENDIXES

I

INTRODUCTION AND BASIC TAX MODEL

Part I provides an introduction to taxation in the United States. Although the primary orientation of this text is income taxation, other types of taxes are also discussed briefly. The purposes of the Federal tax law are examined, and the legislative, administrative, and judicial sources of Federal tax law, including their application to the tax research process, are analyzed. Part I concludes with the introduction of the basic tax model for the individual taxpayer.

AN INTRODUCTION TO TAXATION AND UNDERSTANDING THE FEDERAL TAX LAW

LEARNING OBJECTIVES

After completing Chapter 1, you should be able to:

1. Understand some of the history, including trends, of the Federal income tax.

2. Know some of the criteria for selecting a tax structure and understand the components of a tax structure.

3. Identify the different taxes imposed in the United States at the Federal, state, and local levels.

4. Understand the administration of the tax law including the audit process utilized by the IRS.

5. Appreciate some of the ethical guidelines involved in tax practice.

6. Recognize the economic, social, equity, and political considerations that justify various aspects of the tax law.

7. Describe the role played by the IRS and the courts in the evolution of the Federal tax system.

The primary objective of this chapter is to provide an overview of the Federal tax system. Among the topics discussed are the following:

- A brief history of the Federal income tax.
- The different types of taxes imposed at the Federal, state, and local levels.
- Some highlights of tax law administration.
- Tax concepts that help explain the reasons for various tax provisions.
- The influence that the Internal Revenue Service (IRS) and the courts have had in the evolution of current tax law.

Why does a text devoted primarily to the Federal individual income tax discuss state and local taxes? A simple illustration shows the importance of non-Federal taxes.

EXAMPLE 1

Rick is employed by Flamingo Corporation in San Antonio, Texas, at a salary of $54,000. Rick's employer offers him a chance to transfer to its New York City office at a salary of $60,000. Neither Texas nor San Antonio imposes an income tax, but New York State and New York City do. A quick computation indicates that the additional income taxes (Federal, state, and local) involved approximate $5,000. ▼

Although Rick must consider many nontax factors before he decides on a job change, he should also evaluate the tax climate. How do state and local taxes compare? In this case, what appears to be a $6,000 pay increase is only $1,000 when the additional income taxes of $5,000 are taken into account.

HISTORY OF U.S. TAXATION

EARLY PERIODS

1 ▼ LEARNING OBJECTIVE
Understand some of the history, including trends, of the Federal income tax.

The concept of an income tax can hardly be regarded as a newcomer to the Western Hemisphere. An income tax was first enacted in 1634 by the English colonists in the Massachusetts Bay Colony, but the Federal government did not adopt this form of taxation until 1861. In fact, both the Federal Union and the Confederate States of America used the income tax to raise funds to finance the Civil War. Although modest in its reach and characterized by broad exemptions and low rates, the income tax generated $376 million of revenue for the Federal government during the Civil War.

When the Civil War ended, the need for additional revenue disappeared, and the income tax was repealed. As was true before the war, the Federal government was able to finance its operations almost exclusively from customs duties (tariffs). It is interesting to note that the courts held that the Civil War income tax was not contrary to the Constitution.

When a new Federal income tax on individuals was enacted in 1894, its opponents were prepared to and did again challenge its constitutionality. The U.S. Constitution provided that ". . . No Capitation, or other direct, Tax shall be laid, unless in Proportion to the Census or Enumeration herein before directed to be taken." In *Pollock v. Farmers' Loan and Trust Co.*,[1] the U.S. Supreme Court found that the income tax was a direct tax that was unconstitutional because it was not apportioned among the states in proportion to their populations.

A Federal corporate income tax, enacted by Congress in 1909, fared better in the judicial system. The U.S. Supreme Court found this tax to be constitutional because it was treated as an excise tax.[2] In essence, it was a tax on the right to do business in the corporate form. As such, it was likened to a form of the franchise tax.[3] The corporate form of doing business had been developed in the late nineteenth century and was an unfamiliar concept to the framers of the U.S. Constitution. Since a corporation is an entity created under law, jurisdictions possess the right to tax its creation and operation. Using this rationale, many states still impose franchise taxes on corporations.

The ratification of the Sixteenth Amendment to the U.S. Constitution in 1913 sanctioned both the Federal individual and corporate income taxes and, as a consequence, neutralized the continuing effect of the *Pollock* decision.

REVENUE ACTS

Following ratification of the Sixteenth Amendment, Congress enacted the Revenue Act of 1913. Under this Act, the first Form 1040 was due on March 1, 1914. The law allowed various deductions and personal exemptions of $3,000 for a single individual and $4,000 for married taxpayers. Rates ranged from a low of 2 percent to a high of 6 percent. The 6 percent rate applied only to taxable income in excess of $500,000![4]

Various revenue acts were passed between 1913 and 1939. In 1939, all of these revenue laws were codified into the Internal Revenue Code of 1939. In 1954, a similar codification of the revenue law took place. The current law is entitled the Internal Revenue Code of 1986, which largely carries over the provisions of the 1954 Code. To date, the Code has been amended several times since 1986. This matter is discussed further in Chapter 2 under Origin of the Internal Revenue Code.

HISTORICAL TRENDS

The income tax has proved to be a major source of revenue for the Federal government. Figure 1–1, which contains a breakdown of the major revenue sources,[5]

---

[1] 3 AFTR 2602, 15 S.Ct. 912 (USSC, 1895). See Chapter 2 for an explanation of the citations of judicial decisions.

[2] *Flint v. Stone Tracy Co.*, 3 AFTR 2834, 31 S.Ct. 342 (USSC, 1911).

[3] See the discussion of state franchise taxes later in the chapter.

[4] This should be contrasted with the highest current tax rate of 39.6%, which applies once taxable income exceeds $278,450.

[5] Budget of the United States Government for Fiscal Year 1998, Office of Management and Budget (Washington, D.C.: U.S. Government Printing Office, 1997).

▼ **FIGURE 1–1**
Federal Budget Receipts—1998

Individual income taxes	41%
Corporation income taxes	11
Social insurance taxes and contributions	33
Excise taxes	4
Borrowing	7
Other	4
	100%

demonstrates the importance of the income tax. *Estimated* income tax collections from individuals and corporations amount to 52 percent of the total receipts.

The need for revenues to finance the war effort during World War II converted the income tax into a *mass tax*. For example, in 1939, less than 6 percent of the U.S. population was subject to the Federal income tax. In 1945, over 74 percent of the population was subject to the Federal income tax.[6]

Certain changes in the income tax law are of particular significance in understanding the Federal income tax. In 1943, Congress passed the Current Tax Payment Act, which provided for the first pay-as-you-go tax system. A pay-as-you-go income tax system requires employers to withhold for taxes a specified portion of an employee's wages. Persons with income from other than wages must make periodic (e.g., quarterly) payments to the taxing authority (the Internal Revenue Service) for estimated taxes due for the year.

One trend that has caused considerable concern has been the increasing complexity of the Federal income tax laws. Often, under the name of tax reform, Congress has added to this complexity by frequently changing the tax laws. The recent enactment of the Taxpayer Relief Act (TRA) of 1997 continues this trend. Increasingly, this complexity forces many taxpayers to seek the assistance of tax professionals. At this time, therefore, substantial support exists for tax law simplification.

CRITERIA USED IN THE SELECTION OF A TAX STRUCTURE

▼
2 LEARNING OBJECTIVE
Know some of the criteria for selecting a tax structure and understand the components of a tax structure.

In the eighteenth century, Adam Smith identified the following *canons of taxation*, which are still considered when evaluating a particular tax structure:[7]

- *Equality.* Each taxpayer enjoys fair or equitable treatment by paying taxes in proportion to his or her income level. Ability to pay a tax is the measure of how equitably a tax is distributed among taxpayers.
- *Convenience.* Administrative simplicity has long been valued in formulating tax policy. If a tax is easily assessed and collected and its administrative costs are low, it should be favored. An advantage of the withholding (pay-as-you-go) system is its convenience for taxpayers.

---

[6]Richard Goode, *The Individual Income Tax* (Washington, D.C.: The Brookings Institution, 1964), pp. 2–4.

[7]*The Wealth of Nations*, Book V, Chapter II, Part II (New York: Dutton, 1910).

- *Certainty.* A tax structure is *good* if the taxpayer can readily predict when, where, and how a tax will be levied. Individuals and businesses need to know the likely tax consequences of a particular type of transaction.
- *Economy.* A *good* tax system involves only nominal collection costs by the government and minimal compliance costs on the part of the taxpayer. Although the government's cost of collecting Federal taxes amounts to less than one-half of 1 percent of the revenue collected, the complexity of our current tax structure imposes substantial taxpayer compliance costs.

By these canons, the Federal income tax is a contentious product. *Equality* is present as long as one accepts ability to pay as an ingredient of this component. *Convenience* exists due to a heavy reliance on pay-as-you-go procedures. *Certainty* probably generates the greatest controversy. In one sense, certainty is present since a mass of administrative and judicial guidelines exists to aid in interpreting the tax law. In another sense, however, certainty does not exist since many questions remain unanswered and frequent changes in the tax law by Congress lessen stability. *Economy* is present if only the collection procedure of the IRS is considered. Economy is not present, however, if one focuses instead on taxpayer compliance efforts and costs.

THE TAX STRUCTURE

TAX BASE

A tax base is the amount to which the tax rate is applied. In the case of the Federal income tax, the tax base is *taxable income.* As noted later in the chapter (Figure 1–2), taxable income is gross income reduced by certain deductions (both business and personal).

TAX RATES

Tax rates are applied to the tax base to determine a taxpayer's liability. The tax rates may be proportional or progressive. A tax is *proportional* if the rate of tax remains constant for any given income level.

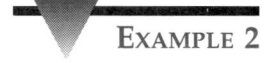

EXAMPLE 2   Bill has $10,000 of taxable income and pays a tax of $3,000, or 30%. Bob's taxable income is $50,000, and the tax on this amount is $15,000, or 30%. If this constant rate is applied throughout the rate structure, the tax is proportional. ▼

A tax is *progressive* if a higher rate of tax applies as the tax base increases. The Federal income tax, Federal gift and estate taxes, and most state income tax rate structures are progressive.

EXAMPLE 3   If Cora, a married individual filing jointly, has taxable income of $10,000, her tax for 1998 is $1,500 for an average tax rate of 15%. If, however, Cora's taxable income is $50,000, her tax will be $8,495 for an average tax rate of 16.99%. The tax is progressive since higher rates are applied to greater amounts of taxable income. ▼

INCIDENCE OF TAXATION

The degree to which various segments of society share the total tax burden is difficult to assess. Assumptions must be made concerning who absorbs the burden for paying the tax. For example, since dividend payments to shareholders are not deductible by a corporation and are generally taxable to shareholders, the same income is subject to a form of double taxation. Concern over double taxation is valid to the extent that corporations are *not* able to shift the corporate tax to the consumer through higher commodity prices. Many research studies have shown a high degree of shifting of the corporate income tax. When the corporate tax can be shifted, it becomes merely a consumption tax that is borne by the ultimate purchasers of goods.

The progressiveness of the U.S. Federal income tax rate structure for individuals has varied over the years. As late as 1986, for example, there were 15 rates, ranging from 0 to 50 percent. These later were reduced to two rates of 15 and 28 percent. Currently, there are five rates, ranging from 15 to 39.6 percent.

MAJOR TYPES OF TAXES

PROPERTY TAXES

3 LEARNING OBJECTIVE
Identify the different taxes imposed in the United States at the Federal, state, and local levels.

Normally referred to as **ad valorem taxes** because they are based on value, property taxes are a tax on wealth, or capital. In this regard, they have much in common with death taxes and gift taxes discussed later in the chapter. Although property taxes do not tax income, the income actually derived (or the potential for any income) may be relevant insofar as it affects the value of the property being taxed.

Property taxes fall into *two* categories: those imposed on realty and those imposed on personalty. Both have added importance since they usually generate a deduction for Federal income tax purposes (see Chapter 10).

Ad Valorem Taxes on Realty.   Property taxes on realty are exclusively within the province of the states and their local political subdivisions (e.g., cities, counties, school districts). They represent a major source of revenue for *local* governments, but their importance at the *state* level has waned over the past few years. Some states, for example, have imposed freezes on the upper revaluations of residential housing.

How realty is defined can have an important bearing on which assets are subject to tax. This is especially true in jurisdictions that do not impose ad valorem taxes on personalty. Primarily a question of state property law, **realty** generally includes real estate and any capital improvements that are classified as fixtures. Simply stated, a *fixture* is something so permanently attached to the real estate that its removal will cause irreparable damage. A built-in bookcase might well be a fixture, whereas a movable bookcase would not be a fixture. Certain items such as electrical wiring and plumbing cease to be personalty when installed in a building and become realty.

The following are some of the characteristics of ad valorem taxes on realty:

- Property owned by the Federal government is exempt from tax. Similar immunity usually is extended to property owned by state and local governments and by certain charitable organizations.
- Some states provide for lower valuations on property dedicated to agricultural use or other special uses (e.g., wildlife sanctuaries).
- Some states partially exempt the homestead portion of property from taxation. Modern homestead laws normally protect some or all of a personal residence (including a farm or ranch) from the actions of creditors pursuing claims against the owner.

- Lower taxes may apply to a residence owned by an elderly taxpayer (e.g., age 65 and older).
- When non-income-producing property (e.g., a personal residence) is converted to income-producing property (e.g., a rental house), typically the appraised value increases.
- Some jurisdictions extend immunity from tax for a specified period of time (a *tax holiday*) to new or relocated businesses.

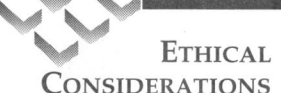

ETHICAL CONSIDERATIONS

Is Ownership Important?

Cynthia, a widow, dies at the age of 70. Andy, her son and sole heir, takes possession of the few assets she owned. He converts Cynthia's personal residence to a rental house and immediately leases it to an elderly couple.

The city and county are not aware of the ownership change and continue to send all tax notices to Cynthia. Since Andy pays these taxes, he sees no reason to have himself listed as the owner of the property. As long as the taxes are paid, what difference does it make who owns the property?

Comment on Andy's actions. Are his perceptions correct?

Unlike the ad valorem tax on personalty (see below), the tax on realty is difficult to avoid. Since real estate is impossible to hide, a high degree of taxpayer compliance is not surprising. The only avoidance possibility that is generally available is associated with the assessed value of the property. For this reason, the assessed value of the property—particularly, a value that is reassessed upward—may be subject to controversy and litigation.

Four methods are currently in use for assessing the value of real estate:

1. Actual purchase or construction price.
2. Contemporaneous sales prices or construction costs of comparable properties.
3. Cost of reproducing a building, less allowance for depreciation and obsolescence from the time of actual construction.
4. Capitalization of income from rental property.

Because all of these methods suffer faults and lead to inequities, a combination of two or more is not uncommon. For example, when real estate values and construction costs are rising, the use of actual purchase or construction price (method 1) places the purchaser of a new home at a definite disadvantage compared with an owner who acquired similar property years before. As another illustration, if the capitalization of income (method 4) is used for property subject to rent controls (e.g., New York City), the property may be undervalued.

The history of the ad valorem tax on realty has been marked by inconsistent application due to a lack of competent tax administration and definitive guidelines for assessment procedures. In recent years, however, some significant improvements have occurred. Some jurisdictions, for example, have computerized their reassessment procedures so they will have an immediate effect on all property located within the jurisdiction. Nevertheless, the property tax area continues to be controversial.

TAX IN THE NEWS

DOES BILL GATES HAVE A FANCY PAD, OR WHAT?

The county where Bill Gates built his new house assessed the value of the house at approximately $53 million, the cost of its construction. With this assessment, Gates pays annual ad valorem taxes of $600,000. Gates considered disputing the use of construction cost as the measure of value. He feels that because the house is unique, it would be difficult to sell. Consequently, he thinks the assessed value should be discounted for lack of marketability.

Incidentally, the residence is situated on a five-acre wooded lakefront tract near Seattle. The main manor has 40,000 square feet (with a separate, 1,700-square-foot guest house), a 60-foot pool, a sauna, two spas, a 20-seat theater, a reception hall for 100 people, an arcade, a boat dock for water skiing, and a library. Surely, Bill would have no difficulty finding a buyer for this property!

Ad Valorem Taxes on Personalty.   **Personalty** can be defined as all assets that are not realty. It may be helpful to distinguish between the *classification* of an asset (realty or personalty) and the *use* to which it is put. Both realty and personalty can be either business use or personal use property. Examples include a residence (realty that is personal use), an office building (realty that is business use), surgical instruments (personalty that is business use), and regular wearing apparel (personalty that is personal use).[8]

Personalty can also be classified as tangible property or intangible property. For ad valorem tax purposes, intangible personalty includes stocks, bonds, and various other securities (e.g., bank shares).

The following generalizations may be made concerning the ad valorem taxes on personalty:

- Particularly with personalty devoted to personal use (e.g., jewelry, household furnishings), taxpayer compliance ranges from poor to zero. Some jurisdictions do not even attempt to enforce the tax on these items. For automobiles devoted to personal use, many jurisdictions have converted from value as the tax base to arbitrary license fees based on the weight of the vehicle. Some jurisdictions also consider the vehicle's age (e.g., automobiles six years or older are not subject to the ad valorem tax because they are presumed to have little, if any, value).
- For personalty devoted to business use (e.g., inventories, trucks, machinery, equipment), taxpayer compliance and enforcement procedures are measurably better.
- Which jurisdiction possesses the authority to tax movable personalty (e.g., railroad rolling stock) always has been and continues to be a troublesome issue.
- A few states levy an ad valorem tax on intangibles such as stocks and bonds. Taxpayer compliance may be negligible if the state lacks means of verifying security transactions and ownership.

---

[8]The distinction, important for ad valorem and for Federal income tax purposes, often becomes confused when personalty is referred to as "personal" property to distinguish it from "real" property. This designation does not give a complete picture of what is involved. The description "personal" residence, however, is clearer, since a residence can be identified as being realty. What is meant, in this case, is realty that is personal use property.

TRANSACTION TAXES

Transaction taxes, which characteristically are imposed at the manufacturer's, wholesaler's, or retailer's level, cover a wide range of transfers. Like many other types of taxes (e.g., income taxes, death taxes, and gift taxes), transaction taxes usually are not within the exclusive province of any level of taxing authority (Federal, state, local government). As the description implies, these levies place a tax on transfers of property and normally are determined by multiplying the value involved by a percentage rate.

Federal Excise Taxes.   Long one of the mainstays of the Federal tax system, Federal **excise taxes** had declined in relative importance until recently. In recent years, Congress substantially increased the Federal excise taxes on such items as tobacco products, fuel and gasoline sales, telephone usage, and air travel. Other Federal excise taxes include the following:

- Manufacturers' excise taxes on trucks, trailers, tires, firearms, sporting equipment, coal, and the gas guzzler tax on automobiles.[9]
- Alcohol taxes.
- Luxury tax on automobiles. For 1998, the tax is 7 percent of the retail price in excess of $36,000 (adjusted each year for inflation). The tax originally was 10 percent and is scheduled to be phased out in yearly increments by year 2003.
- Miscellaneous taxes (e.g., the tax on wagering).

The list of transactions covered, although seemingly impressive, has diminished over the years. At one time, for example, there was a Federal excise tax on admission to amusement facilities (e.g., theaters) and on the sale of such items as leather goods, jewelry, furs, and cosmetics.

When reviewing the list of both Federal and state excise taxes, one should recognize the possibility that the tax laws may be trying to influence social behavior. For example, the gas guzzler tax is intended as an incentive for the automobile companies to build cars that are fuel efficient. Since many consider alcohol and tobacco to be harmful to a person's health, why not increase their cost by imposing excise taxes and thereby discourage their use? Unfortunately, the evidence of the level of correlation between the imposition of an excise tax and consumer behavior is mixed.

State Excise Taxes.   Many state and local excise taxes parallel the Federal version. Thus, all states tax the sale of gasoline, liquor, and tobacco products; however, the rates vary significantly. For gasoline products, for example, compare the 39 cents per gallon imposed by the state of Connecticut with the 8 cents per gallon levied by the state of New York. For tobacco sales, contrast the 2.5 cents per pack of cigarettes in effect in Virginia with the $1.00 per pack applicable in Alaska. Given the latter situation, is it surprising that the smuggling of cigarettes for resale elsewhere is so widespread?

Other excise taxes found at some state and local levels include those on admission to amusement facilities; hotel occupancy and the rental of various other facilities; and the sale of playing cards, oleomargarine products, and prepared foods. Most states impose a transaction tax on the transfer of property that requires the

---

[9]The gas guzzler tax is imposed on the manufacturers of automobiles and progresses in amount as the mileage ratings per gallon of gas decrease.

recording of documents (e.g., real estate sales).[10] Some extend the tax to the transfer of stocks and other securities.

General Sales Taxes. The distinction between an excise tax and a general **sales tax** is easy to make. One is restricted to a particular transaction (e.g., the 18.4 cents per gallon Federal excise tax on the sale of gasoline), while the other covers a multitude of transactions (e.g., a 5 percent tax on *all* retail sales). In actual practice, however, the distinction is not always that clear. Some state statutes exempt certain transactions from the application of the general sales taxes (e.g., sales of food to be consumed off the premises, sales of certain medicines and drugs). Also, it is not uncommon to find that rates vary depending on the commodity involved. Many states, for example, allow preferential rates for the sale of agricultural equipment or apply different rates (either higher or lower than the general rate) to the sale of automobiles. With many of these special exceptions and classifications of rates, a general sales tax can take on the appearance of a collection of individual excise taxes.

A **use tax** is an ad valorem tax, usually at the same rate as the sales tax, on the use, consumption, or storage of tangible property. The purpose of a use tax is to prevent the avoidance of a sales tax. Every state that imposes a general sales tax levied on the consumer also has a use tax. Alaska, Delaware, Montana, New Hampshire, and Oregon have neither tax.

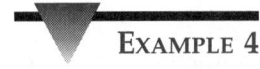

EXAMPLE 4

Susan resides in a jurisdiction that imposes a 5% general sales tax but lives near a state that has no sales or use tax at all. Susan purchases an automobile for $10,000 from a dealer located in the neighboring state. Has she saved $500 in sales taxes? The state use tax is designed to pick up the difference between the tax paid in another jurisdiction and what would have been paid in the state in which Susan resides. ▼

The use tax is difficult to enforce for many purchases and is therefore often avoided. In some cases, for example, it may be worthwhile to make purchases through an out-of-state mail-order business. In spite of shipping costs, the avoidance of the local sales tax that otherwise might be incurred could make the price of such products as computer components cheaper. Some states are taking steps to curtail this loss of revenue. For items such as automobiles (refer to Example 4), the use tax probably will be collected when the purchaser registers the item in his or her home state.

Local general sales taxes, over and above those levied by the state, are common. It is not unusual to find taxpayers living in the same state but paying different general sales taxes due to the location of their residence.

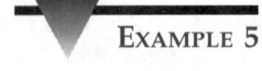

EXAMPLE 5

Pete and Sam both live in a state that has a general sales tax of 3%. Sam, however, resides in a city that imposes an additional general sales tax of 2%. Even though Pete and Sam live in the same state, one is subject to a rate of 3%, while the other pays a tax of 5%. ▼

Severance Taxes. **Severance taxes** are an important source of revenue for many states. These transaction taxes are based on the notion that the state has an interest in its natural resources (e.g., oil, gas, iron ore, coal). Therefore, a tax is imposed when the natural resources are extracted.

---

[10]This type of tax has much in common with the stamp tax levied by Great Britain on the American colonies during the pre-Revolutionary War period in U.S. history.

DEATH TAXES

A **death tax** is a tax on the right to transfer property or to receive property upon the death of the owner. Consequently, a death tax falls into the category of an excise tax. If the death tax is imposed on the right to pass property at death, it is classified as an **estate tax.** If it taxes the right to receive property from a decedent, it is termed an **inheritance tax.** As is typical of other types of excise taxes, the value of the property transferred provides the base for determining the amount of the death tax.

The Federal government imposes only an estate tax. State governments, however, levy inheritance taxes, estate taxes, or both.

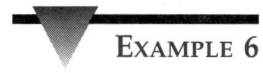
EXAMPLE 6

At the time of her death, Wilma lived in a state that imposes an inheritance tax but not an estate tax. Mary, one of Wilma's heirs, lives in the same state. Wilma's estate is subject to the Federal estate tax, and Mary is subject to the state inheritance tax. ▼

The Federal Estate Tax.   The Revenue Act of 1916 incorporated the estate tax into the tax law. Never designed to generate a large amount of revenue, the tax was originally intended to prevent large concentrations of wealth from being kept within a family for many generations. Whether this objective has been accomplished is debatable. Like the income tax, estate taxes can be reduced through various planning procedures.

The gross estate includes property the decedent owned at the time of death. It also includes life insurance proceeds when paid to the estate or when paid to a beneficiary other than the estate if the deceased-insured had any ownership rights in the policy. Quite simply, the gross estate represents property interests subject to Federal estate taxation.[11] All property included in the gross estate is valued as of the date of death or, if the alternate valuation date is elected, six months later.[12]

Deductions from the gross estate in arriving at the taxable estate include funeral and administration expenses, certain taxes, debts of the decedent, casualty losses[13] incurred during the administration of the estate, transfers to charitable organizations, and, in some cases, the marital deduction. The *marital deduction* is available for amounts actually passing to a surviving spouse (a widow or widower).

Once the taxable estate has been determined and certain taxable gifts have been added to it, the estate tax can be computed. From the amount derived from the appropriate tax rate schedules, various credits should be subtracted to arrive at the tax, if any, that is due.[14] Although many other credits are also available, probably the most significant is the *unified transfer tax credit*. The main reason for this credit is to eliminate or reduce the estate tax liability for modest estates. For 1998, the amount of the credit is $202,050. Based on the estate tax rates, the credit covers a tax base of $625,000.

EXAMPLE 7

Ned made no taxable gifts before his death in 1998. If Ned's taxable estate amounts to $625,000 or less, no Federal estate tax is due because of the application of the unified transfer tax credit. Under the tax law, the estate tax on a taxable estate of $625,000 is $202,050. ▼

---

[11]For further information on these matters, see *West's Federal Taxation: Corporations, Partnerships, Estates, and Trusts.*

[12]See the discussion of the alternate valuation date in Chapter 14.

[13]For a definition of casualty losses, see the Glossary of Tax Terms in Appendix C.

[14]For tax purposes, it is always crucial to appreciate the difference between a deduction and a credit. A *credit* is a dollar-for-dollar reduction of tax liability. A *deduction*, however, only benefits the taxpayer to the extent of his or her tax bracket. An estate in a 50% tax bracket, for example, would need $2 of deductions to prevent $1 of tax liability from developing. In contrast, $1 of credit neutralizes $1 of tax liability.

Because the effect of inflation was causing an increasing number of decedents to incur a Federal estate tax, the TRA of 1997 has scheduled further increases in the unified transfer tax credit. These are to be phased in over a period of years until the credit reaches $345,800 in 2006. This amount covers a taxable estate (or taxable gift) of $1 million.

State Death Taxes. As noted earlier, states usually levy an inheritance tax, an estate tax, or both. The two forms of death taxes differ according to whether the tax is imposed on the heirs or on the estate.

Characteristically, an inheritance tax divides the heirs into classes based on their relationship to the decedent. The more closely related the heir, the lower the rates imposed and the greater the exemption allowed. Some states completely exempt from taxation amounts passing to a surviving spouse.

GIFT TAXES

Like a death tax, a **gift tax** is an excise tax levied on the right to transfer property. In this case, however, the tax is imposed on transfers made during the owner's life and not at death. Also, a gift tax applies only to transfers that are not supported by full and adequate consideration.

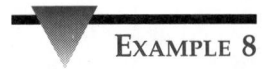

EXAMPLE 8

Carl sells property worth $20,000 to his daughter for $1,000. Although property worth $20,000 has been transferred, only $19,000 represents a gift, since this is the portion not supported by full and adequate consideration. ▼

The Federal Gift Tax. First enacted in 1932, the Federal gift tax was intended to complement the estate tax. In the absence of a tax applicable to lifetime transfers by gift, it would be possible to avoid the estate tax and escape taxation entirely.

Only taxable gifts are subject to the gift tax. For this purpose, a taxable gift is measured by the fair market value of the property on the date of transfer less the *annual exclusion of $10,000 per donee* and, in some cases, less the *marital deduction*, which allows tax-free transfers between spouses. Each donor is allowed an annual exclusion of $10,000 for each donee.[15]

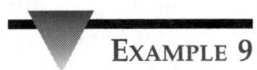

EXAMPLE 9

On December 31, 1997, Vera (a widow) gives $10,000 to each of her four married children, their spouses, and her eight grandchildren. On January 3, 1998, she repeats the same procedure. Due to the annual exclusion, Vera has not made a taxable gift, although she transferred $160,000 [$10,000 × 16 (number of donees)] in 1997 and $160,000 [$10,000 × 16 (number of donees)] in 1998 for a total of $320,000 ($160,000 + $160,000). ▼

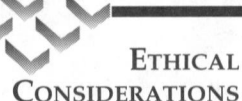

ETHICAL
CONSIDERATIONS

The Annual Exclusion for Gifts

A rlene, a wealthy widow, would like to transfer $20,000 of cash to her son, Wilbur, in 1998 without exceeding the $10,000 per donee annual exclusion. To achieve this result, Arlene devises the following scheme: she gives $10,000 to Wilbur and $10,000 to her brother, George, who gives $10,000 to Wilbur.

Will Arlene's scheme succeed? What could go wrong?

---

[15]The purpose of the annual exclusion is to avoid the need to report and pay a tax on *modest* gifts. Without the exclusion, the IRS could face a real problem of taxpayer noncompliance. After 1998, the annual exclusion of $10,000 will be indexed for inflation.

A special election applicable to married persons allows one-half of the gift made by the donor-spouse to be treated as being made by the nondonor-spouse (*gift splitting*). This election to split the gifts of property made to third persons has the effect of increasing the number of annual exclusions available. Also, it allows the use of the nondonor-spouse's unified transfer tax credit and may lower the tax brackets that will apply.

The gift tax rate schedule is the same as that applicable to the estate tax. The schedule is commonly referred to as the *unified transfer tax schedule*.

The Federal gift tax is *cumulative* in effect. What this means is that the tax base for current taxable gifts includes past taxable gifts. Although a credit is allowed for prior gift taxes, the result of adding past taxable gifts to current taxable gifts is to force the donor into a higher tax bracket.[16] Like the Federal estate tax rates, the Federal gift tax rates are progressive (see Example 3 earlier in this chapter).

The unified transfer tax credit is available for all taxable gifts, and as with the Federal estate tax, the amount of this credit for 1998 is $202,050. There is, however, only one unified transfer tax credit, and it applies both to taxable gifts and to the Federal estate tax. In a manner of speaking, therefore, once the unified transfer tax credit has been exhausted for Federal gift tax purposes, it is no longer available to insulate a decedent from the Federal estate tax.

In summary, transfers by gift and transfers by death are subject to the unified transfer tax. The same rates and credits apply. Further, taxable gifts are added to the taxable estate in arriving at the tax base for applying the unified transfer tax at death.

State Gift Taxes.   The states currently imposing a state gift tax are Connecticut, Delaware, Louisiana, New York, North Carolina, and Tennessee. Most of the laws provide for lifetime exemptions and annual exclusions. Like the Federal gift tax, the state taxes are cumulative in effect. But unlike the Federal version, the amount of tax depends on the relationship between the donor and the donee. Like state inheritance taxes, larger exemptions and lower rates apply when the donor and donee are closely related to each other.

INCOME TAXES

Income taxes are levied by the Federal government, most states, and some local governments. The trend in recent years has been to place greater reliance on this method of taxation. This trend is not consistent with what is happening in other countries, and in this sense, our system of taxation is somewhat different.

Income taxes generally are imposed on individuals, corporations, and certain fiduciaries (estates and trusts). Most jurisdictions attempt to assure the collection of income taxes by requiring certain pay-as-you-go procedures (e.g., withholding requirements for employees and estimated tax prepayments for other taxpayers).

Federal Income Taxes.   Chapters 3 through 19 deal with the application of the Federal income tax to individuals. The procedure for determining the Federal income tax applicable to individuals is summarized in Figure 1–2.

The application of the Federal corporate income tax does not require the computation of adjusted gross income (AGI) and does not provide for the standard deduction and personal and dependency exemptions. All allowable deductions of a corporation fall into the business-expense category. In effect, therefore, the taxable

---

[16]For further information on the Federal gift tax, see *West's Federal Taxation: Corporations, Partnerships, Estates, and Trusts.*

▼ **FIGURE 1–2**

Formula for Federal Income
Tax on Individuals

Income (broadly conceived)	$ xx,xxx
Less: Exclusions (income that is not subject to tax)	(x,xxx)
Gross income (income that is subject to tax)	$ xx,xxx
Less: Certain business deductions (usually referred to as deductions *for* adjusted gross income)	(x,xxx)
Adjusted gross income	$ xx,xxx
Less: The greater of certain personal and employee deductions (usually referred to as *itemized deductions*) *or* The standard deduction (including any additional standard deduction) *and*	(x,xxx)
Less: Personal and dependency exemptions	(x,xxx)
Taxable income	$ xx,xxx
Tax on taxable income (see Tax Rate Schedules in Appendix A)	$ x,xxx
Less: Tax credits (including Federal income tax withheld and other prepayments of Federal income taxes)	(xxx)
Tax due (or refund)	$ xxx

income of a corporation is the difference between gross income (net of exclusions) and deductions.

Chapter 20 summarizes the rules relating to corporations. For an in-depth treatment of the Federal income tax as it affects corporations, estates, and trusts, see *West's Federal Taxation: Corporations, Partnerships, Estates, and Trusts*, 1999 Edition, Chapters 2 through 9, 12, and 19.

State Income Taxes.   All but the following states impose an income tax on individuals: Alaska, Florida, Nevada, South Dakota, Texas, Washington, and Wyoming.

Some of the characteristics of state income taxes are summarized as follows:

- With few exceptions, all states require some form of withholding procedures.
- Most states use as the tax base the income determination made for Federal income tax purposes.
- A minority of states go even further and impose a flat rate upon AGI as computed for Federal income tax purposes. Several apply a rate to the Federal income tax liability. This is often referred to as the piggyback approach to state income taxation. Although the term *piggyback* does not lend itself to precise definition, in this context, it means making use, for state income tax purposes, of what was done for Federal income tax purposes.
- Because of the tie-in to the Federal return, the state may be notified of any changes made by the IRS upon audit of a Federal return.
- Most states allow a deduction for personal and dependency exemptions. Some states substitute a tax credit for a deduction.
- A diminishing minority of states allow a deduction for Federal income taxes.
- Most states allow their residents some form of tax credit for income taxes paid to other states.
- The due date for filing generally is the same as for the Federal income tax (the fifteenth day of the fourth month following the close of the tax year).

VISITORS BEWARE! THE CITY AND STATE YOU VISIT MAY NOT BE ALL THAT FRIENDLY

Even if you are not a resident, you may be subject to local and state income taxes if you earn money in that jurisdiction. Besides the nonresident who commutes (e.g., a taxpayer who lives in Connecticut but works full-time in New York City), taxpayers who perform services on an itinerant basis may be vulnerable. For example, the Dallas Cowboys are subject to the city of Philadelphia income tax every time they are hosted by the Eagles. This must be particularly distressing to Troy Aikman, who lives in a city (Dallas) and a state (Texas) that do not have an income tax.

Although these situations are commonly referred to as the application of the "jock tax," other persons besides professional athletes get hit. Particularly susceptible are entertainers, doctors, lawyers, lecturers, and anyone who generates large fees and has a high profile. Ordinary professionals are not targeted because the amount of taxes involved would not justify the collection effort.

Is it any wonder that Las Vegas, which has no city or state income tax, is such a popular place to perform highly paid services (e.g., entertainment, prize fighting)?

Nearly all states have an income tax applicable to corporations. It is difficult to determine those that do not because a state franchise tax sometimes is based in part on the income earned by the corporation.[17]

Local Income Taxes.   Cities imposing an income tax include, but are not limited to, Baltimore, Cincinnati, Cleveland, Detroit, Kansas City (Mo.), New York, Philadelphia, and St. Louis. The application of a city income tax is not limited to local residents.

EMPLOYMENT TAXES

Classification as an employee usually leads to the imposition of **employment taxes** and to the requirement that the employer withhold specified amounts for income taxes. The rules governing the withholding for income taxes are discussed in Chapter 13. The material that follows concentrates on the two major employment taxes: FICA (Federal Insurance Contributions Act—commonly referred to as the Social Security tax)—and FUTA (Federal Unemployment Tax Act). Both taxes can be justified by social and public welfare considerations: FICA offers some measure of retirement security, and FUTA provides a modest source of income in the event of loss of employment.

Employment taxes come into play only if two conditions are satisfied. First, is the individual involved an *employee* (as opposed to *self-employed*)? The differences between an employee and a self-employed person are discussed in Chapter 9.[18] Second, if the individual involved is an employee, is he or she covered under FICA or FUTA or both? The coverage of both of these taxes is summarized in Exhibit 13–2 in Chapter 13.[19]

---

[17]See the discussion of franchise taxes later in the chapter.
[18]See also Circular E, Employer's Tax Guide, issued by the IRS as Publication 15.

[19]Chapter 13 includes coverage on the self-employment tax (the Social Security and Medicare taxes for self-employed persons).

FICA Taxes.   The **FICA tax** rates and wage base have steadily increased over the years. It is difficult to imagine that the initial rate in 1937 was only 1 percent of the first $3,000 of covered wages. Thus, the maximum tax due was only $30!

Currently, the FICA tax has two components: Social Security tax (old age, survivors, and disability insurance) *and* Medicare tax (hospital insurance). The Social Security tax rate is 6.2 percent for 1997 and 1998, and the Medicare tax rate is 1.45 percent for these years. The base amount for Social Security is $65,400 for 1997 and $68,400 for 1998. There is no limit on the base amount for the Medicare tax. The employer must match the employee's portion for both the Social Security tax and the Medicare tax.

A spouse employed by another spouse is subject to FICA. However, children under the age of 18 who are employed in a parent's trade or business are exempted.

FUTA Taxes.   The purpose of the **FUTA tax** is to provide funds that the states can use to administer unemployment benefits. This leads to the somewhat unusual situation of one tax being handled by both Federal and state governments. The end result of such joint administration is to compel the employer to observe a double set of rules. Thus, state and Federal returns must be filed and payments made to both governmental units.

In 1998, FUTA applies at a rate of 6.2 percent on the first $7,000 of covered wages paid during the year to each employee. The Federal government allows a credit for FUTA paid (or allowed under a merit rating system) to the state. The credit cannot exceed 5.4 percent of the covered wages. Thus, the amount required to be paid to the IRS could be as low as 0.8 percent (6.2% − 5.4%).

States follow a policy of reducing the unemployment tax on employers who experience stable employment. Thus, an employer with little or no employee turnover might find that the state rate drops to as low as 0.1 percent or, in some states, even to zero. The reason for the merit rating credit is that the state has to pay fewer unemployment benefits when employment is steady.

FUTA differs from FICA in the sense that the incidence of taxation falls entirely upon the employer. A few states, however, levy a special tax on employees to provide either disability benefits or supplemental unemployment compensation, or both.

OTHER U.S. TAXES

To complete the overview of the U.S. tax system, some missing links need to be covered that do not fit into the classifications discussed elsewhere in this chapter.

Federal Customs Duties.   One tax that has not yet been mentioned is the tariff on certain imported goods.[20] Generally referred to as customs duties or levies, this tax, together with selective excise taxes, provided most of the revenues needed by the Federal government during the nineteenth century. In view of present times, it is remarkable to note that tariffs and excise taxes alone paid off the national debt in 1835 and enabled the U.S. Treasury to pay a surplus of $28 million to the states.

In recent years, tariffs have served the nation more as an instrument for carrying out protectionist policies than as a means of generating revenue. Thus, a particular U.S. industry might be saved from economic disaster, so the argument goes, by placing customs duties on the importation of foreign goods that can be sold at

---

[20]Less-developed countries that rely principally on one or more major commodities (e.g., oil, coffee) are prone to favor *export* duties as well.

lower prices. Protectionists contend that the tariff therefore neutralizes the competitive edge held by the producer of the foreign goods.[21]

Protectionist policies seem more appropriate for less-developed countries whose industrial capacity has not yet matured. In a world where a developed country should have everything to gain by encouraging international free trade, such policies may be of dubious value. History shows that tariffs often lead to retaliatory action on the part of the nation or nations affected.

Miscellaneous State and Local Taxes. Most states impose a franchise tax on corporations. Basically, a **franchise tax** is levied on the right to do business in the state. The base used for the determination of the tax varies from state to state. Although corporate income considerations may come into play, this tax most often is based on the capitalization of the corporation (either with or without certain long-term indebtedness).

Closely akin to the franchise tax are **occupational taxes** applicable to various trades or businesses, such as a liquor store license, a taxicab permit, or a fee to practice a profession such as law, medicine, or accounting. Most of these are not significant revenue producers and fall more into the category of licenses than taxes. The revenue derived is used to defray the cost incurred by the jurisdiction in regulating the business or profession in the interest of the public good.

PROPOSED U.S. TAXES

Considerable dissatisfaction with the U.S. Federal income tax has led to several recent proposals that, to say the least, are rather drastic in nature. One proposal would retain the income tax but with substantial change. Two other proposals would replace the Federal income tax with an entirely different system of taxation.

The Flat Tax. Representative Dick Armey (R, Texas) has proposed a **flat tax** that would replace the current graduated income tax with one rate, 17 percent. Large personal exemptions (e.g., approximately $30,000 for a family of four) would allow many low- and middle-income taxpayers to pay no tax. All other deductions would be eliminated, and no tax would be imposed on income from investments.

Various other versions of the flat tax have been suggested that would retain selected deductions (e.g., interest on home mortgages and charitable contributions) and not exclude all investment income from taxation.

The major advantage of the flat tax is its simplicity. Everyone agrees that the current Federal income tax is unbelievably complex. Consequently, compliance costs are disproportionately high.

Value Added Tax. The **value added tax (VAT)** is one of two proposals that would replace the Federal income tax. Under the VAT, a business would pay the tax (approximately 17 percent) on all of the materials and services required to manufacture its product. In effect, the VAT taxes the increment in value as goods move through production and manufacturing stages to the marketplace. Moreover, the VAT paid by the producer will be reflected in the selling price of the goods. Thus, the VAT is a tax on consumption.

Several other countries (e.g., European Union countries) use the VAT either as a supplement to or a replacement for an income tax.

---

[21]The North American Free Trade Agreement (NAFTA), enacted in 1993, substantially reduced the tariffs on trade between Canada, Mexico, and the United States. The General Agreement on Tariffs and Trade (GATT) legislation enacted in 1994 also reduced tariffs on selected commodities among 124 signatory nations.

Sales Tax. A **national sales tax** is favored by Representative Bill Archer (R, Texas), who is the current chairman of the House Ways and Means Committee. This tax differs from a VAT in that it would be collected on the final sale of goods and services. Consequently, it is collected from the consumer and not from businesses that add value to the product. Like the VAT, the national sales tax is intended to replace the Federal income tax.

Critics contend that consumption taxes (both a VAT and a national sales tax) impose more of a burden on low-income taxpayers because they must spend larger proportions of their incomes on essential purchases. Representative Archer's proposal would attempt to remedy this inequity by granting some sort of credit or exemption to low-income taxpayers.

TAX ADMINISTRATION

INTERNAL REVENUE SERVICE

4 LEARNING OBJECTIVE
Understand the administration of the tax law including the audit process utilized by the IRS.

The responsibility for administering the Federal tax laws rests with the Treasury Department. Administratively, the IRS is part of the Department of the Treasury and is responsible for enforcing the tax laws. The Commissioner of Internal Revenue is appointed by the President and is responsible for establishing policy and supervising the activities of the entire IRS organization.

The field organization of the IRS includes the following:

- Service Centers (10) that are primarily responsible for processing tax returns, including the selection of returns for audit. The Service Center having proper jurisdiction is where taxpayers must file their Federal tax returns.
- District Directors (33) who are responsible for audits and for the collection of delinquent taxes. Some states have no District Director (e.g., Idaho, Wyoming) while others have more than one (e.g., California, New York).

THE AUDIT PROCESS

Selection of Returns for Audit. Due to budgetary limitations, only a small minority of returns are audited. For the fiscal year ending September 30, 1996, for example, the IRS audited only 1.63 percent of the total returns.

The IRS utilizes mathematical formulas and statistical sampling techniques to select tax returns that are most likely to contain errors and to yield substantial amounts of additional tax revenues upon audit.

Though the IRS does not openly disclose all of its audit selection techniques, the following observations may be made concerning the probability of selection for audit:

- Certain groups of taxpayers are subject to audit much more frequently than others. These groups include individuals with gross income in excess of $50,000, self-employed individuals with substantial business income and deductions, and taxpayers with prior tax deficiencies. Also vulnerable are cash businesses (e.g., cafes and small service businesses) where the potential for tax avoidance is high.

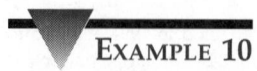
EXAMPLE 10

Jack owns and operates a liquor store on a cash-and-carry basis. Since all of Jack's sales are for cash, he might well be a prime candidate for an audit by the IRS. Cash transactions are easier to conceal than those made on credit. ▼

TAX IN THE NEWS

THE "SNITCH FEE": SOME MISCONCEPTIONS AND PITFALLS

Although the IRS does pay a 10 percent informant fee, this fee is not awarded automatically. To be eligible, the snitcher must furnish evidence that actually leads to the collection of delinquent taxes. Even if this occurs, moreover, the reward need not be a full 10 percent of the amount collected. After the first $75,000 collected, the 10 percent rate is reduced to 5 percent for the next $25,000 and 1 percent for further amounts. In no event, may the reward paid exceed $100,000. Most tips are not specific enough to generate a reward. In 1996, for example, only 650 of the 9,350 informants qualified, and the average payout was just $5,431.

On occasion, a tip can hurt the tipster. This result is particularly likely when a tipster seeks revenge on an ex-spouse. Suppose, for example, an ex-wife tells the IRS about an income tax return filed by her ex-husband. Were they married during the period involved? If so, did they file a joint return that the informant signed? In this case and by virtue of the joint and several liability, the informant could also be vulnerable for any taxes evaded.

Equally adverse, a conviction of the ex-spouse for tax fraud could lead to loss of earning power and cut off (or reduce) future alimony and child support payments.

[Note: A recent change has increased the maximum rate to 15 percent.]

SOURCE: Adapted from J. Novack, "Boomerang!" *Forbes*, July 7, 1997, pp. 42, 43.

- If information returns (e.g., Form 1099, Form W–2) are not in substantial agreement with reported income, an audit can be anticipated.
- If an individual's itemized deductions are in excess of norms established for various income levels, the probability of an audit is increased.
- Filing of a refund claim by the taxpayer may prompt an audit of the return.
- Certain returns are selected on a random sampling basis under the Taxpayer Compliance Measurement Program (TCMP). The TCMP is used to develop, update, and improve the mathematical formulas and statistical sampling techniques used by the IRS. For the present, the TCMP has been suspended due to a lack of congressional funding.
- Information obtained from other sources (e.g., informants, news items) may lead to an audit. The tax law permits the IRS to pay rewards to persons who provide information that leads to the detection and punishment of those who violate the tax laws. The rewards may not exceed 15 percent (formerly 10 percent) of the taxes, fines, and penalties recovered as a result of such information.

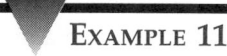

EXAMPLE 11

After 15 years of service, Rita is discharged by her employer, Dr. Smith. Shortly thereafter, the IRS receives an anonymous letter informing it that Dr. Smith keeps two separate sets of books, one of which substantially understates his cash receipts. ▼

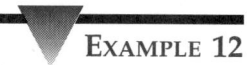

EXAMPLE 12

During a divorce proceeding, it is revealed that Leo, a public official, kept large amounts of cash in a shoe box at home. This information is widely disseminated by the news media and comes to the attention of the IRS. Needless to say, the IRS would be interested in knowing whether these funds originated from a taxable source and, if so, whether they were reported on Leo's income tax returns. ▼

Types of Audits. Once a return is selected for audit, the taxpayer is notified accordingly. If the issue involved is minor, the matter often can be resolved simply by correspondence (a **correspondence audit**) between the IRS and the taxpayer.

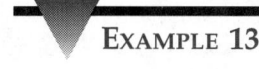

EXAMPLE 13

During 1996, Janet received dividend income from Green Corporation. In early 1997, Green Corporation reported the payment on Form 1099–DIV (an information return for reporting dividend payments), the original being sent to the IRS and a copy to Janet. When preparing her income tax return for 1996, Janet apparently overlooked this particular Form 1099–DIV and failed to include the dividend on Schedule B, Interest and Dividend Income, of Form 1040. In 1998, the IRS sends a notice to Janet calling her attention to the omission and requesting a remittance for additional tax, interest, and penalty. Janet promptly mails a check to the IRS for the requested amount, and the matter is closed. ▼

Other examinations are generally classified as either office audits or field audits. An **office audit** usually is restricted in scope and is conducted in the facilities of the IRS. In contrast, a **field audit** involves an examination of numerous items reported on the return and is conducted on the premises of the taxpayer or the taxpayer's representative.

Upon the conclusion of the audit, the examining agent issues a Revenue Agent's Report (RAR) that summarizes the findings. The RAR will result in a refund (the tax was overpaid), a deficiency (the tax was underpaid), or a *no change* (the tax was correct) finding.

Settlement Procedures. If an audit results in an assessment of additional tax and no settlement is reached with the IRS agent, the taxpayer may attempt to negotiate a settlement with the IRS. If an appeal is desired, an appropriate request must be made to the Appeals Division of the IRS. In some cases, a taxpayer may be able to obtain a percentage settlement or a favorable settlement of one or more disputed issues. The Appeals Division is authorized to settle all disputes based on the *hazard of litigation* (the probability of favorable resolution of the disputed issue or issues if litigated).

If a satisfactory settlement is not reached within the administrative appeal process, the taxpayer may wish to litigate the case in the Tax Court, a Federal District Court, or the Court of Federal Claims. However, litigation is recommended only as a last resort because of the legal costs involved and the uncertainty of the final outcome. Tax litigation considerations are discussed more fully in Chapter 2.

STATUTE OF LIMITATIONS

A **statute of limitations** is a provision in the law that offers a party a defense against a suit brought by another party after the expiration of a specified period of time. The purpose of a statute of limitations is to preclude parties from prosecuting stale claims. The passage of time makes the defense of such claims difficult since witnesses may no longer be available or evidence may have been lost or destroyed. Found at the state and Federal levels, such statutes cover a multitude of suits, both civil and criminal.

For our purposes, the relevant statutes deal with the Federal income tax. The two categories involved cover both the period of limitations applicable to the assessment of additional tax deficiencies by the IRS and the period that deals with claims for refunds by taxpayers.

Assessment by the IRS. Under the general rule, the IRS may assess (impose) an additional tax liability against a taxpayer within *three years* of the filing of the income tax return. If the return is filed early, the three-year period begins to run from the due date of the return (usually April 15 for a calendar year individual taxpayer).

If a taxpayer omits an amount of gross income in excess of 25 percent of the gross income reported on the return, the statute of limitations is increased to six years.

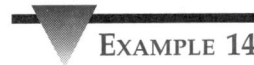

EXAMPLE 14   For 1993, Mark, a calendar year taxpayer, reported gross income of $400,000 on a timely filed income tax return. If Mark omitted more than $100,000 (25% × $400,000), the six-year statute of limitations would apply to the 1993 tax year. ▼

The six-year provision on assessments by the IRS applies only to the omission of income and does not cover other factors that might lead to an understatement of tax liability (e.g., overstatement of deductions and credits).

There is *no* statute of limitations on assessments of tax if *no return* is filed or if a *fraudulent* return is filed.

Limitations on Refunds. If a taxpayer believes that an overpayment of Federal income tax was made, a claim for refund should be filed with the IRS. A *claim for refund*, therefore, is a request to the IRS that it return to the taxpayer the excessive income taxes paid.[22]

A claim for refund generally must be filed within *three years* from the date the return was filed *or* within *two years* from the date the tax was paid, whichever is later. Income tax returns that are filed early are deemed to have been filed on the date the return was due.

INTEREST AND PENALTIES

Interest rates are determined quarterly by the IRS based on the existing Federal short-term rate. The rates for tax refunds (overpayments) are 1 percent below those applicable to assessments (underpayments). For the first quarter (January 1–March 31) of 1998, the rates were 8 percent for refunds and 9 percent for assessments.[23]

For assessments of additional taxes, the interest begins running on the unextended due date of the return. With refunds, however, no interest is allowed if the overpayment is refunded to the taxpayer within 45 days of the date the return is filed. For this purpose, returns filed early are deemed to have been filed on the due date.

The tax law provides various penalties for lack of compliance by taxpayers. Some of these penalties are summarized as follows:

- For a *failure to file* a tax return by the due date (including extension—see Chapter 3), a penalty of 5 percent per month (up to a maximum of 25 percent) is imposed on the amount of tax shown as due on the return. Any fraction of a month counts as a full month.
- A penalty for a *failure to pay* the tax due (as shown on the return) is imposed in the amount of 0.5 percent per month (up to a maximum of 25 percent). Again, any fraction of a month counts as a full month. During any month in which both the failure to file penalty and the failure to pay penalty

---

[22]Generally, an individual filing a claim for refund should use Form 1040X.

[23]The rates applicable after March 31, 1998, were not available when this text went to press.

apply, the failure to file penalty is reduced by the amount of the failure to pay penalty.

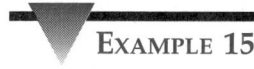

EXAMPLE 15

Adam files his tax return 18 days after the due date of the return. Along with the return, he remits a check for $1,000, which is the balance of the tax he owed. Disregarding the interest element, Adam's total penalties are as follows:

Failure to pay penalty (0.5% × $1,000)		$ 5
Plus:		
Failure to file penalty (5% × $1,000)	$ 50	
Less failure to pay penalty for the same period	(5)	
Failure to file penalty		45
Total penalties		$ 50

Note that the penalties for one full month are imposed even though Adam was delinquent by only 18 days. Unlike the method used to compute interest, any part of a month is treated as a whole month. ▼

- A *negligence* penalty of 20 percent is imposed if any of the underpayment was for intentional disregard of rules and regulations without intent to defraud. The penalty applies to just that portion attributable to the negligence.

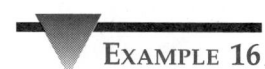

EXAMPLE 16

Cindy underpaid her taxes for 1997 in the amount of $20,000, of which $15,000 is attributable to negligence. Cindy's negligence penalty is $3,000 (20% × $15,000). ▼

- Various fraud penalties may be imposed. *Fraud* is a deliberate action on the part of the taxpayer evidenced by deceit, misrepresentation, concealment, etc. For possible fraud situations, refer to Examples 11 and 12. The burden of proving fraud is on the IRS. This is in contrast to the usual deficiency assessment made by the IRS, where the burden is on the taxpayer to show that he or she does not owe any additional tax.

TAX PRACTICE

The area of tax practice is largely unregulated. Virtually anyone can aid another in complying with the various tax laws. If a practitioner is a member of a profession, such as law or public accounting, he or she must abide by certain ethical standards. Furthermore, the Internal Revenue Code imposes penalties upon the preparers of Federal tax returns who violate proscribed acts and procedures.

5 LEARNING OBJECTIVE
Appreciate some of the ethical guidelines involved in tax practice.

Ethical Guidelines.   The American Institute of CPAs has issued numerous guides for CPAs engaged in tax practice. Called "Statements on Responsibilities in Tax Practice," some of these are summarized below.

- Do not take questionable positions on a client's tax return in the hope that the return will not be selected for audit by the IRS. Any positions taken should be supported by a good-faith belief that they have a realistic chance of being sustained if challenged. The client should be fully advised of the risks involved and of the penalties that would result if the position taken is not successful.
- A practitioner can use a client's estimates if they are reasonable under the circumstances. If the tax law requires verification (e.g., receipts), the client should be so advised. In no event should an estimate be given the appearance

of greater accuracy than is the case. For example, an estimate of $1,000 should not be deducted on a return as $999.

- Every effort should be made to answer questions appearing on tax returns. A question need not be answered if the information requested is not readily available, the answer is voluminous, or the question's meaning is uncertain. The failure to answer a question on a return cannot be justified on the grounds that the answer could prove disadvantageous to the taxpayer.
- Upon learning of an error on a past tax return, advise the client to correct it. Do not, however, inform the IRS of the error. If the error is material and the client refuses to correct it, consider withdrawing from the engagement. This will be necessary if the error has a carryover effect and prevents the current year's tax liability from being determined correctly.

Statutory Penalties Imposed on Tax Return Preparers.   In addition to ethical constraints, a tax return preparer may be subject to certain statutorily sanctioned penalties, including the following:

- Various penalties involving procedural matters. Examples include failing to furnish the taxpayer with a copy of the return; endorsing a taxpayer's refund check; failing to sign the return as a preparer; failing to furnish one's identification number; and failing to keep copies of returns or maintain a client list.
- Understatement of a tax liability based on a position that lacks any realistic possibility of being sustained. If the position is not frivolous, the penalty can be avoided by disclosing it on the return.
- Any willful attempt to understate taxes. This usually results when a preparer disregards or makes no effort to obtain pertinent information from a client.
- Failure to exercise due diligence in determining eligibility for, or the amount of, an earned income tax credit.

UNDERSTANDING THE FEDERAL TAX LAW

6   LEARNING OBJECTIVE
Recognize the economic, social, equity, and political considerations that justify various aspects of the tax law.

The Federal tax law is a mosaic of statutory provisions, administrative pronouncements, and court decisions. Anyone who has attempted to work with this body of knowledge would have to admit to its complexity. For the person who has to trudge through a mass of rules to find the solution to a tax problem, it may be of some consolation to know that the law's complexity can generally be explained. Whether sound or not, there is a reason for the formulation of every rule. Knowing these reasons, therefore, is a considerable step toward understanding the Federal tax law.

The Federal tax law has as its *major objective* the raising of revenue. But although the fiscal needs of the government are important, other considerations explain certain portions of the law. Economic, social, equity, and political factors also play a significant role. Added to these factors is the marked impact the IRS and the courts have had and will continue to have on the evolution of Federal tax law. These matters are treated in the remainder of the chapter, and, wherever appropriate, the discussion is referenced to subjects covered later in the text.

REVENUE NEEDS

The foundation of any tax system has to be the raising of revenue to cover the cost of government operations. Ideally, annual outlays should not exceed anticipated revenues, thereby leading to a balanced budget with no resulting deficit. Many states have achieved this objective by passing laws or constitutional amendments precluding deficit spending. Unfortunately, the Federal government has no such conclusive prohibition, and annual deficits have become an increasing concern for many. Legislation enacted in 1997 is supposed to alleviate this problem.

When enacting tax legislation, a deficit-conscious Congress often has been guided by the concept of **revenue neutrality.** The concept means that the changes made will neither increase nor decrease the net result reached under the prior rules. Revenue neutrality does not mean that any one taxpayer's tax liability will remain the same. Since the circumstances involved will differ, one taxpayer's increased tax liability could be another's tax savings. Although revenue-neutral tax reform does not reduce deficits, at least it does not aggravate the problem.

In addition to making changes in the tax law revenue neutral, several other procedures can be taken to reduce the revenue loss. When tax reductions are involved, the full impact of the legislation can be phased in over a period of years. Or, as an alternative, the tax reduction can be limited to a period of years. When the period expires, Congress can then renew or not renew the provision in light of budget considerations.[24]

ECONOMIC CONSIDERATIONS

Using the tax system in an effort to accomplish economic objectives has become increasingly popular in recent years. Generally, proponents of this goal use tax legislation to amend the Internal Revenue Code and promote measures designed to help control the economy or encourage certain activities and businesses.

Control of the Economy.   Congress has used depreciation write-offs as a means of controlling the economy. Theoretically, shorter asset lives and accelerated methods should encourage additional investment in depreciable property acquired for business use. Conversely, longer asset lives and the required use of the straight-line method of depreciation dampen the tax incentive for capital outlays.

A change in the tax rate structure has a more immediate impact on the economy. With lower tax rates, taxpayers are able to retain additional spendable funds. If lower tax rates are accompanied by the elimination of certain deductions, exclusions, and credits, however, the overall result may not be lower tax liabilities.

Encouragement of Certain Activities.   Without passing judgment on the wisdom of any such choices, it is quite clear that the tax law does encourage certain types of economic activity or segments of the economy. For example, the favorable treatment allowed research and development expenditures can be explained by the desire to foster technological progress. Under the tax law, such expenditures can be either deducted in the year incurred or capitalized and amortized over a period of 60 months or more. In terms of the timing of the tax savings, these options usually are preferable to capitalizing the cost with a write-off over the estimated useful life of the asset created. If the asset developed has an indefinite useful life, no write-off would be available without the two options allowed by the tax law.

Is it desirable to encourage the conservation of energy resources? Considering the world energy situation and our own reliance on foreign oil, the answer to this question has to be yes. The concern over energy usage was a prime consideration

---

[24]An example of a gradual phase-in is the increase in the unified transfer tax credit (discussed earlier in this chapter), which does not become fully implemented at $1 million until year 2006. An example of a temporary tax reduction is the exclusion from gross income of employer-provided educational assistance benefits (discussed in Chapter 5), which are scheduled to expire during year 2000.

in the enactment of legislation to make various tax savings for energy conservation expenditures available to taxpayers.

Is preserving the environment a desirable objective? Ecological considerations explain why the tax law permits a 60-month amortization period for costs incurred in the installation of pollution control facilities.

Is it wise to stimulate U.S. exports of goods and services? Considering the pressing and continuing problem of a deficit in the U.S. balance of payments, the answer should be clear. Along this line, Congress has created Foreign Sales Corporations (FSCs), which are designed to encourage domestic exports of goods. The FSC provisions exempt a percentage of profits from export sales from the Federal income tax. Also in an international setting, Congress has deemed it advisable to establish incentives for U.S. citizens who accept employment overseas. Such persons receive generous tax breaks through special treatment of their foreign-source income and certain housing costs.

Is saving desirable for the economy? Saving leads to capital formation and thereby makes funds available to finance home construction and industrial expansion. The tax law encourages saving by according preferential treatment to private retirement plans. Not only are contributions to Keogh (H.R. 10) plans and certain Individual Retirement Accounts (IRAs) deductible, but income from the contributions accumulates free of tax. As noted below, the encouragement of private-sector pension plans can also be justified under social considerations.

Encouragement of Certain Industries.   No one can question the proposition that a sound agricultural base is necessary for a well-balanced national economy. Undoubtedly, this can explain why farmers are accorded special treatment under the Federal tax system. Among the benefits are the election to expense rather than capitalize certain soil and water conservation expenditures and fertilizers and the election to defer the recognition of gain on the receipt of crop insurance proceeds.

Encouragement of Small Business.   At least in the United States, a consensus exists that what is good for small business is good for the economy as a whole. Whether valid or not, this assumption has led to a definite bias in the tax law favoring small business.

In the corporate tax area, several provisions can be explained by the desire to benefit small business. One provision permits the shareholders of a small business corporation to make a special election that generally will avoid the imposition of the corporate income tax.[25] Furthermore, such an election enables the corporation to pass through its operating losses to its shareholders.

SOCIAL CONSIDERATIONS

Some provisions of the Federal tax law, particularly those dealing with the income tax of individuals, can be explained by social considerations. Some notable examples and their rationales include the following:

- Certain benefits provided to employees through accident and health plans financed by employers are nontaxable to employees. Encouraging such plans is considered socially desirable since they provide medical benefits in the event of an employee's illness or injury.
- Most premiums paid by an employer for group term insurance covering the life of the employee are nontaxable to the employee. These arrangements

---

[25]Known as the S election, it is discussed in Chapter 20.

can be justified on social grounds in that they provide funds for the family unit to help it adjust to the loss of wages caused by the employee's death.

- A contribution made by an employer to a qualified pension or profit sharing plan for an employee receives special treatment. The contribution and any income it generates are not taxed to the employee until the funds are distributed. Such an arrangement also benefits the employer by allowing a tax deduction when the contribution is made to the qualified plan. Private retirement plans are encouraged to supplement the subsistence income level the employee otherwise would have under the Social Security system.[26]
- A deduction is allowed for contributions to qualified charitable organizations. The deduction attempts to shift some of the financial and administrative burden of socially desirable programs from the public (the government) to the private (the citizens) sector.
- A tax credit is allowed for amounts spent to furnish care for certain minor or disabled dependents to enable the taxpayer to seek or maintain gainful employment. Who could deny the social desirability of encouraging taxpayers to provide care for their children while they work?
- Various tax credits, deductions, and exclusions that are designed to encourage taxpayers to obtain additional education.[27]
- A tax deduction is not allowed for certain expenditures deemed to be contrary to public policy. This disallowance extends to such items as fines, penalties, illegal kickbacks, bribes to government officials, and gambling losses in excess of gains. Social considerations dictate that the tax law should not encourage these activities by permitting a deduction.

Many other examples could be cited, but the conclusion would be unchanged. Social considerations do explain a significant part of the Federal tax law.

EQUITY CONSIDERATIONS

The concept of equity is relative. Reasonable persons can, and often do, disagree about what is fair or unfair. In the tax area, moreover, equity is most often tied to a particular taxpayer's personal situation. To illustrate, compare the tax positions of those who rent their personal residences with those who own their homes. Renters receive no Federal income tax benefit from the rent they pay. For homeowners, however, a large portion of the house payments they make may qualify for the Federal interest and property tax deductions. Although renters may have difficulty understanding this difference in tax treatment, the encouragement of home ownership can be justified on both economic and social grounds.

In the same vein, compare the tax treatment of a corporation with that of a partnership. Although the two businesses may be of equal size, similarly situated, and competitors in the production of goods or services, they are not treated comparably under the tax law. The corporation is subject to a separate Federal income tax; the partnership is not. Whether the differences in tax treatment can be justified logically in terms of equity is beside the point. The point is that the tax law can and does make a distinction between these business forms.

Equity, then, is not what appears fair or unfair to any one taxpayer or group of taxpayers. It is, instead, what the tax law recognizes. Some recognition of equity does exist, however, and explains part of the law. The concept of equity appears in tax provisions that alleviate the effect of multiple taxation and postpone the

[26]The same rationale explains the availability of similar arrangements for self-employed persons (the H.R. 10, or Keogh, plan). See Chapter 19.

[27]These provisions can also be justified under the category of economic considerations. No one can take issue with the conclusion that a better educated workforce carries a positive economic impact.

recognition of gain when the taxpayer lacks the ability or wherewithal to pay the tax. Provisions that mitigate the effect of the application of the annual accounting period concept and help taxpayers cope with the eroding results of inflation also reflect equity considerations.

Alleviating the Effect of Multiple Taxation.   The income earned by a taxpayer may be subject to taxes imposed by different taxing authorities. If, for example, the taxpayer is a resident of New York City, income might generate Federal, state of New York, and city of New York income taxes. To compensate for this apparent inequity, the Federal tax law allows a taxpayer to claim a deduction for state and local income taxes. The deduction does not, however, neutralize the effect of multiple taxation, since the benefit derived depends on the taxpayer's Federal income tax rate. Only a tax credit, rather than a deduction, would eliminate the effects of multiple taxation on the same income.

Equity considerations can explain the Federal tax treatment of certain income from foreign sources. Since double taxation results when the same income is subject to both foreign and U.S. income taxes, the tax law permits the taxpayer to choose between a credit and a deduction for the foreign taxes paid.

The Wherewithal to Pay Concept.   The **wherewithal to pay** concept recognizes the inequity of taxing a transaction when the taxpayer lacks the means with which to pay the tax. It is particularly suited to situations in which the taxpayer's economic position has not changed significantly as a result of the transaction.

An illustration of the wherewithal to pay concept is the provision of the tax law dealing with the treatment of gain resulting from an involuntary conversion. An involuntary conversion occurs when property is destroyed by casualty or taken by a public authority through condemnation. If gain results from the conversion, it need not be recognized if the taxpayer replaces the property within a specified period of time. The replacement property must be similar or related in service or use to that involuntarily converted.

EXAMPLE 17

Ron, a rancher, has some of his pasture land condemned by the state for use as a game preserve. The condemned pasture land cost Ron $120,000, but the state pays him $150,000 (its fair market value). Shortly thereafter, Ron buys more pasture land for $150,000. ▼

In Example 17, Ron has realized gain of $30,000 [$150,000 (condemnation award) – $120,000 (cost of land)]. It would be inequitable to force Ron to pay a tax on this gain for two reasons. First, without disposing of the property acquired (the new land), Ron would be hard-pressed to pay the tax. Second, his economic position has not changed.

A warning is in order regarding the application of the wherewithal to pay concept. If the taxpayer's economic position changes in any way, tax consequences may result.

EXAMPLE 18

Assume the same facts as in Example 17, except that Ron reinvests only $140,000 of the award in new pasture land. Now, Ron has a taxable gain of $10,000. Instead of ending up with only replacement property, Ron now has $10,000 in cash. ▼

Mitigating the Effect of the Annual Accounting Period Concept.   For purposes of effective administration of the tax law, all taxpayers must report to and settle with the Federal government at periodic intervals. Otherwise, taxpayers would remain uncertain as to their tax liabilities, and the government would have difficulty judging revenues and budgeting expenditures. The period selected for final settlement of most tax liabilities, in any event an arbitrary determination, is one year. At the close of each year, therefore, a taxpayer's position becomes complete for that particular year. Referred to as the annual accounting period concept, its effect is to divide each taxpayer's life, for tax purposes, into equal annual intervals.

The finality of the annual accounting period concept could lead to dissimilar tax treatment for taxpayers who are, from a long-range standpoint, in the same economic position.

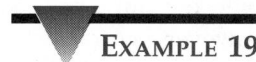

EXAMPLE 19

José and Alicia, both sole proprietors, have experienced the following results during the past four years:

Profit (or Loss)		
Year	José	Alicia
1996	$50,000	$150,000
1997	60,000	60,000
1998	60,000	(40,000)

Although José and Alicia have the same profit of $170,000 over the period from 1996 to 1998, the finality of the annual accounting period concept places Alicia at a definite disadvantage for tax purposes. The net operating loss procedure offers Alicia some relief by allowing her to apply some or all of her 1998 loss to the earlier profitable years (in this case, 1996). Thus, with a net operating loss carryback, Alicia is in a position to obtain a refund for some of the taxes she paid on the $150,000 profit reported for 1996. ▼

The same reasoning used to support the deduction of net operating losses can explain the special treatment the tax law accords to excess capital losses and excess charitable contributions.[28] Carryback and carryover procedures help mitigate the effect of limiting a loss or a deduction to the accounting period in which it was realized. With such procedures, a taxpayer may be able to salvage a loss or a deduction that might otherwise be wasted.

The installment method of recognizing gain on the sale of property allows a taxpayer to spread tax consequences over the payout period.[29] The harsh effect of taxing all the gain in the year of sale is thereby avoided. The installment method can also be explained by the wherewithal to pay concept since recognition of gain is tied to the collection of the installment notes received from the sale of the property. Tax consequences, then, tend to correspond to the seller's ability to pay the tax.

Coping with Inflation.   Because of the progressive nature of the income tax, a wage adjustment to compensate for inflation can increase the income tax bracket of the recipient. Known as *bracket creep*, its overall impact is an erosion of purchasing power. Congress recognized this problem and began to adjust various income tax components, such as tax brackets, standard deduction amounts, and personal and dependency exemptions, through an indexation procedure. Indexation is based upon the rise in the consumer price index over the prior year.

[28]The tax treatment of these items is discussed in Chapters 7, 10, and 16.
[29]Under the installment method, each payment received by the seller represents both a recovery of capital (the nontaxable portion) and profit from the sale (the taxable portion). The tax rules governing the installment method are discussed in Chapter 18.

POLITICAL CONSIDERATIONS

A large segment of the Federal tax law is made up of statutory provisions. Since these statutes are enacted by Congress, is it any surprise that political considerations influence tax law? For purposes of discussion, the effect of political considerations on the tax law is divided into the following topics: special interest legislation, political expediency situations, and state and local government influences.

Special Interest Legislation.   There is no doubt that certain provisions of the tax law can largely be explained by the political influence some pressure groups have had on Congress. Is there any other realistic reason that, for example, prepaid subscription and dues income are not taxed until earned while prepaid rents are taxed to the landlord in the year received?

A recent example of special interest legislation was a provision attached to the House of Representatives's version of the TRA of 1997. The provision would have exempted "bakery drivers" from being classified as employees. Since the drivers would have become self-employed independent contractors, the baking companies would no longer have needed to cover them under Social Security, Medicare, and FUTA. The representative who originated the provision is from Nebraska and represents the district that is the home of Pepperidge Farm and Interstate Bakeries (maker of Wonder bread).

Special interest legislation is not necessarily to be condemned if it can be justified on economic, social, or some other utilitarian grounds. At any rate, it is an inevitable product of our political system.

Political Expediency Situations.   Various tax reform proposals rise and fall in favor with the shifting moods of the American public. That Congress is sensitive to popular feeling is an accepted fact. Therefore, certain provisions of the tax law can be explained by the political climate at the time they were enacted.

Measures that deter more affluent taxpayers from obtaining so-called preferential tax treatment have always had popular appeal and, consequently, the support of Congress. Provisions such as the alternative minimum tax, the imputed interest rules, and the limitation on the deductibility of interest on investment indebtedness can be explained on this basis.[30]

Other changes explained at least partially by political expediency include the lowering of individual income tax rates, the increase in the personal and dependency exemptions, and the increase in the amount of the earned income credit. One of the expressed objectives of legislation enacted in 1993 was to increase taxes levied on wealthy individuals by instituting new 36 and 39.6 percent rates on higher-income brackets.

State and Local Government Influences.   Political considerations have played a major role in the nontaxability of interest received on state and local obligations. In view of the furor that has been raised by state and local political figures every time any modification of this tax provision has been proposed, one might well regard it as next to sacred.

Somewhat less apparent has been the influence state law has had in shaping our present Federal tax law. Such was the case with community property systems. The nine states with community property systems are Louisiana, Texas, New Mexico, Arizona, California, Washington, Idaho, Nevada, and Wisconsin. The rest of

---

[30]See Chapters 4, 10, and 12.

the states are classified as common law jurisdictions. The difference between common law and community property systems centers around the property rights possessed by married persons. In a common law system, each spouse owns whatever he or she earns. Under a community property system, one-half of the earnings of each spouse is considered owned by the other spouse.

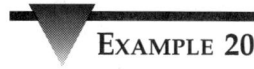

EXAMPLE 20

Al and Fran are husband and wife, and their only income is the $60,000 annual salary Al receives. If they live in New Jersey (a common law state), the $60,000 salary belongs to Al. If, however, they live in Arizona (a community property state), the $60,000 is divided equally, in terms of ownership, between Al and Fran. ▼

At one time, the tax position of the residents of community property states was so advantageous that many common law states actually adopted community property systems. Needless to say, the political pressure placed on Congress to correct the disparity in tax treatment was considerable. To a large extent this was accomplished in the Revenue Act of 1948, which extended many of the community property tax advantages to residents of common law jurisdictions.

The major advantage extended was the provision allowing married taxpayers to file joint returns and compute the tax liability as if the income had been earned one-half by each spouse. This result is automatic in a community property state, since half of the income earned by one spouse belongs to the other spouse. The income-splitting benefits of a joint return are now incorporated as part of the tax rates applicable to married taxpayers. See Chapter 3.

INFLUENCE OF THE INTERNAL REVENUE SERVICE

7 LEARNING OBJECTIVE
Describe the role played by the IRS and the courts in the evolution of the Federal tax system.

The influence of the IRS is apparent in many areas beyond its role in issuing the administrative pronouncements that make up a considerable portion of our tax law. In its capacity as the protector of the national revenue, the IRS has been instrumental in securing the passage of much legislation designed to curtail the most flagrant tax avoidance practices (to close *tax loopholes*). In its capacity as the administrator of the tax law, the IRS has sought and obtained legislation to make its job easier (to attain administrative feasibility).

The IRS as Protector of the Revenue.   Innumerable examples can be given of provisions in the tax law that stem from the direct influence of the IRS. Usually, such provisions are intended to prevent a loophole from being used to avoid the tax consequences intended by Congress. Working within the letter of existing law, ingenious taxpayers and their advisers devise techniques that accomplish indirectly what cannot be accomplished directly. As a consequence, legislation is enacted to close the loopholes that taxpayers have located and exploited. Some tax law can be explained in this fashion and is discussed in the chapters to follow.

In addition, the IRS has secured from Congress legislation of a more general nature that enables it to make adjustments based on the substance, rather than the formal construction, of what a taxpayer has done. One such provision permits the IRS to make adjustments to a taxpayer's method of accounting when the method used by the taxpayer does not clearly reflect income.[31]

---

[31]See Chapter 18.

EXAMPLE 21

Tina, a cash basis taxpayer, owns and operates a pharmacy. All drugs and other items acquired for resale (e.g., cosmetics) are charged to the purchases account and written off (expensed) for tax purposes in the year of acquisition. As this procedure does not clearly reflect income, it would be appropriate for the IRS to require that Tina establish and maintain an ending inventory account. ▼

Administrative Feasibility.   Some of the tax law is justified on the grounds that it simplifies the task of the IRS in collecting the revenue and administering the law. With regard to collecting the revenue, the IRS long ago realized the importance of placing taxpayers on a pay-as-you-go basis. Elaborate withholding procedures apply to wages, while the tax on other types of income may be paid at periodic intervals throughout the year. The IRS has been instrumental in convincing the courts that accrual basis taxpayers should pay taxes on prepaid income in the year received and not when earned. The approach may be contrary to generally accepted accounting principles, but it is consistent with the wherewithal to pay concept.

Of considerable aid to the IRS in collecting revenue are the numerous provisions that impose interest and penalties on taxpayers for noncompliance with the tax law. Provisions such as the penalties for failure to pay a tax or to file a return that is due, the negligence penalty for intentional disregard of rules and regulations, and various penalties for civil and criminal fraud serve as deterrents to taxpayer noncompliance.

One of the keys to an effective administration of our tax system is the audit process conducted by the IRS. To carry out this function, the IRS is aided by provisions that reduce the chance of taxpayer error or manipulation and therefore simplify the audit effort that is necessary. An increase in the amount of the standard deduction, for example, reduces the number of individual taxpayers who will choose the alternative of itemizing their personal deductions.[32] With fewer deductions to check, the audit function is simplified.[33]

The audit function of the IRS has also been simplified by provisions of the tax law dealing with the burden of proof. Suppose, for example, the IRS audits a taxpayer and questions a particular deduction. Who has the burden of proving the propriety of the deduction? The so-called presumption of correctness that attaches in favor of any deficiency assessed by the IRS can be explained by the nature of our tax system. The Federal income tax is a *self-assessed tax*, which means that each taxpayer is responsible for rendering an accounting to the IRS of all of his or her transactions during the year. A failure to do so means that any doubts will be resolved in favor of the IRS. Only in the case of fraud (which could involve fines and penal sanctions) does the IRS carry the burden of proof.

INFLUENCE OF THE COURTS

In addition to interpreting statutory provisions and the administrative pronouncements issued by the IRS, the Federal courts have influenced tax law in two other respects.[34] First, the courts have formulated certain judicial concepts that serve as

---

[32]For a discussion of the standard deduction, see Chapter 3.

[33]The same justification was given by the IRS when it proposed to Congress the $100 limitation on personal casualty and theft losses. Imposition of the limitation eliminated many casualty and theft loss deductions and, as a consequence, saved the IRS considerable audit time. Later legislation, in addition to retaining the $100 feature, limits

deductible losses to those in excess of 10% of a taxpayer's adjusted gross income. See Chapter 7.

[34]A great deal of case law is devoted to ascertaining congressional intent. The courts, in effect, ask: What did Congress have in mind when it enacted a particular tax provision?

guides in the application of various tax provisions. Second, certain key decisions have led to changes in the Internal Revenue Code.

Judicial Concepts Relating to Tax.

A leading tax concept developed by the courts deals with the interpretation of statutory tax provisions that operate to benefit taxpayers. The courts have established the rule that these relief provisions are to be narrowly construed against taxpayers if there is any doubt about their application.

Important in this area is the *arm's length* concept. Particularly in dealings between related parties, transactions may be tested by looking to whether the taxpayers acted in an arm's length manner. The question to be asked is: Would unrelated parties have handled the transaction in the same way?

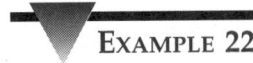

EXAMPLE 22

Rex, the sole shareholder of Silver Corporation, leases property to the corporation for a yearly rent of $6,000. To test whether the corporation should be allowed a rent deduction for this amount, the IRS and the courts will apply the arm's length concept. Would Silver Corporation have paid $6,000 a year in rent if it had leased the same property from an unrelated party (rather than from Rex)? Suppose it is determined that an unrelated third party would have paid an annual rent for the property of only $5,000. Under these circumstances, Silver Corporation will be allowed a deduction of only $5,000. The other $1,000 it paid for the use of the property represents a nondeductible dividend. Accordingly, Rex will be treated as having received rent income of $5,000 and dividend income of $1,000. ▼

Judicial Influence on Statutory Provisions.

Some court decisions have been of such consequence that Congress has incorporated them into statutory tax law. For example, many years ago the courts found that stock dividends distributed to the shareholders of a corporation were not taxable as income. This result was largely accepted by Congress, and a provision in the tax statutes now covers the issue.

On occasion, however, Congress has reacted negatively to judicial interpretations of the tax law.

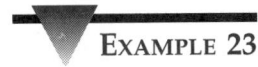

EXAMPLE 23

Nora leases unimproved real estate to Wade for 40 years. At a cost of $200,000, Wade erects a building on the land. The building is worth $100,000 when the lease terminates and Nora takes possession of the property. Does Nora have any income either when the improvements are made or when the lease terminates? In a landmark decision, a court held that Nora must recognize income of $100,000 upon the termination of the lease. ▼

Congress felt that the result reached in Example 23 was inequitable in that it was not consistent with the wherewithal to pay concept. Consequently, the tax law was amended to provide that a landlord does not recognize any income either when the improvements are made (unless made in lieu of rent) or when the lease terminates.

SUMMARY

In addition to its necessary revenue-raising objective, the Federal tax law has developed in response to several other factors:

- *Economic considerations*. The emphasis here is on tax provisions that help regulate the economy and encourage certain activities and types of businesses.
- *Social considerations*. Some tax provisions are designed to encourage (or discourage) certain socially desirable (or undesirable) practices.

- *Equity considerations.* Of principal concern in this area are tax provisions that alleviate the effect of multiple taxation, recognize the wherewithal to pay concept, mitigate the effect of the annual accounting period concept, and recognize the eroding effect of inflation.
- *Political considerations.* Of significance in this regard are tax provisions that represent special interest legislation, reflect political expediency, and exhibit the effect of state and local law.
- *Influence of the IRS.* Many tax provisions are intended to aid the IRS in the collection of revenue and the administration of the tax law.
- *Influence of the courts.* Court decisions have established a body of judicial concepts relating to tax law and have, on occasion, led Congress to enact statutory provisions to either clarify or negate their effect.

These factors explain various tax provisions and thereby help in understanding why the tax law developed to its present state. The next step involves learning to work with the tax law, which is the subject of Chapter 2.

KEY TERMS

Ad valorem tax, 1–6

Correspondence audit, 1–20

Death tax, 1–11

Employment taxes, 1–15

Estate tax, 1–11

Excise tax, 1–9

FICA tax, 1–16

Field audit, 1–20

Flat tax, 1–17

Franchise tax, 1–17

FUTA tax, 1–16

Gift tax, 1–12

Inheritance tax, 1–11

National sales tax, 1–18

Occupational tax, 1–17

Office audit, 1–20

Personalty, 1–8

Realty, 1–6

Revenue neutrality, 1–24

Sales tax, 1–10

Severance tax, 1–10

Statute of limitations, 1–20

Use tax, 1–10

Value added tax (VAT), 1–17

Wherewithal to pay, 1–27

PROBLEM MATERIALS

DISCUSSION QUESTIONS

1. Irene, a middle management employee, is offered a pay increase by her employer. As a condition of the offer, Irene must move to another state. What tax considerations should Irene weigh before making a decision on whether to accept the offer?

2. Before the passage of the Sixteenth Amendment to the Constitution, there was no income tax in the United States. Please comment.

3. Did the passage of the Sixteenth Amendment to the U.S. Constitution have any effect on the income tax imposed on corporations? Explain.

4. A tax law that was enacted in 1953 would be part of which Internal Revenue Code (i.e., 1939, 1954, or 1986)? Explain.

5. How does the pay-as-you-go procedure apply to wage earners? To persons who have income from other than wages?

6. Analyze the Federal income tax in light of Adam Smith's canons of taxation.

7. Is the Medicare tax component of FICA a *proportional* or a *progressive* tax? Explain.

8. When Gull Company constructs a climate-controlled warehouse, it is very careful to keep many of the components portable. Thus, the sprinkler system is detachable, air conditioning and heating are provided by window units, and the interior walls can be removed. What is Gull trying to accomplish?

9. Several years ago, Jim and Martha purchased their personal residence from St. Andrew's Methodist Church. The property had previously been used by the church as a parsonage for its minister. Since the purchase, Jim and Martha have received no property tax bills from either the city or the county where the residence is located. Is there a plausible explanation?

10. Al is considering starting a new business that will require the construction of a manufacturing facility. Jefferson County, one of the geographic locations Al is considering, has proposed a tax holiday. What does this mean?

11. Matt buys a new home for $150,000, its cost of construction plus the usual profit margin for the builder. The new home is located in a neighborhood largely developed 10 years ago when the homes sold for approximately $50,000 each. Assuming the homes of his neighbors are worth (in current values) in the vicinity of $150,000, could Matt be at a disadvantage with regard to the ad valorem tax on realty?

12. Recently, one of your friends successfully challenged a reappraisal of his personal residence by the county board of real estate tax assessors. He remarks to you that this should put him "in good shape for the next five years." What does he mean?

13. A taxpayer owns an apartment building in a community where rent controls exist. If these controls are lifted (i.e., rescinded), could this change the amount of the ad valorem tax on the property? Why or why not?

14. The tax on tobacco products and the gas guzzler tax have a common objective. Elaborate.

15. While out of town on business, Paul stays at a motel with an advertised room rate of $80 per night. When checking out, Paul is charged $88. What would be a plausible reason for the extra $8 Paul had to pay?

16. Julia lives in a jurisdiction that imposes a 5% general sales tax. On a recent trip to the supermarket, she spent $100 but paid only $4 in sales tax. The store where Julia shops is a full-line market and sells prepared foods and drugs in addition to groceries. What is a possible explanation as to why Julia paid only $4 in sales tax and not $5 (5% × $100)?

17. At a recent social gathering, Carrie and Daryl were discussing some recent catalog purchases from out-of-state firms. Carrie was surprised to learn that her purchase was subject to use tax while Daryl's was not. Is there a realistic explanation for the difference?

18. Jean lives in Smithville (the major city in Smith County). She does all of her shopping in Madisonville (the major city in Madison County). If the cities' retail outlets are comparable, why does Jean go out of her way to shop?

19. Alaska has no general sales tax and no income tax. Further, Alaska is a large oil producer. What, if any, is the connection between these factors?

20. What was the original justification for the Federal estate tax?

21. Explain the difference between an inheritance tax and an estate tax.

22. A decedent who leaves all of his property to his surviving spouse and to qualified charitable organizations is not subject to a Federal estate tax. Explain.

23. Why was the Federal gift tax enacted?

24. In 1996, Horace makes a taxable gift of $250,000 upon which he pays a Federal gift tax of $70,800. In 1998, Horace makes another taxable gift of $250,000. Will the 1998 taxable gift result in the same gift tax as the 1996 gift? Why or why not?

25. How much property can Herman, a widower, give to his four married children, their spouses, and eight grandchildren over a period of 10 years without making a taxable gift?

26. When married persons elect to split a gift, what tax advantages do they enjoy?

27. Contrast the major differences between the Federal income tax schemes applicable to individuals and to corporations.

28. John, a nationally known vocalist, lives in Nevada. John's agent has been trying to convince him to go on tour to increase his record sales. John, however, refuses to perform anywhere but in Las Vegas clubs. What might explain John's attitude?

29. When a state uses a "piggyback" approach for its state income tax, what is the state doing?

30. Chee lives in a state that imposes an income tax. His Federal income tax return for 1996 is audited in 1998, and, as a result of several adjustments made by the IRS, Chee has to pay additional Federal income tax. Several months later, Chee is notified that his 1996 state income tax return is to be audited. Are these two incidents a coincidence or does a reasonable explanation exist?

31. As to those states that impose an income tax on individuals, comment on the following:
    a. Use of withholding procedures.
    b. Treatment of Federal income taxes paid.
    c. Due date for filing.
    d. Handling of personal and dependency exemptions.

32. Each year, the base amount for the FICA tax is changed. Comment on the validity of this statement.

33. Keith, a sole proprietor, owns and operates a grocery store. Keith's wife and his 17-year-old son work in the business and are paid wages. Will the wife and son be subject to FICA? Explain.

34. Dan, the owner and operator of a construction company that builds outdoor swimming pools, releases most of his construction personnel during the winter months. Should this hurt Dan's FUTA situation? Why or why not?

35. Compare FICA and FUTA in connection with each of the following:
    a. Incidence of taxation.
    b. Justification for taxation.
    c. Rates and base involved.

36. What is a "flat tax"? What is its major advantage?

37. One of your friends contends that a value added tax (VAT) is the same as a national sales tax. Do you agree or disagree and why?

38. Hollis is married and is the sole proprietor of a dry-cleaning business. His sister, Phoebe, is single and is a management-level employee at IBM. Although both earn about the same income each year, Hollis has been audited by the IRS on three different occasions, while Phoebe has never been audited. Is there a rational explanation for the difference in treatment?

39. Elsie notifies the IRS that her ex-husband cheats on his income tax. Elsie is motivated by spite and also hopes to collect an informant's reward. Has Elsie acted wisely?

40. What is the difference between an "office" audit and a "field" audit?

41. As a result of an audit by the IRS of her Federal income tax return, Sophy receives an RAR. What does this mean?

42. On a Federal income tax return filed five years ago, Andy inadvertently omitted a large amount of gross income.
    a. Andy seeks your advice as to whether the IRS is barred from assessing additional income tax in the event he is audited. What is your advice?
    b. Would your advice differ if you are the person who prepared the return in question? Explain.
    c. Suppose Andy asks you to prepare his current year's return. Would you do so? Explain.

43. Jill files her income tax return 45 days after the due date of the return without obtaining an extension from the IRS. Along with the return, she remits a check for $4,000, which

is the balance of the tax she owes. Disregarding the interest element, what are Jill's penalties for failure to file and for failure to pay?

44. Ed overstated deductions on his Federal income tax return for 1997. Upon audit by the IRS, it is determined that the overstatement was partially the result of negligence. As a result, Ed owes additional income taxes of $10,000 ($8,000 attributable to the negligence). What is Ed's penalty?

45. In March 1998, Jim asks you to prepare his Federal income tax returns for tax years 1995, 1996, and 1997. In discussing this matter with him, you discover that he also has not filed for tax year 1994. When you mention this fact, Jim tells you that the statute of limitations precludes the IRS from taking any action as to this year.
    a. Is Jim correct about the application of the statute of limitations? Why?
    b. If Jim refuses to file for 1994, should you prepare returns for 1995 through 1997?

46. You are preparing Ellen's Federal income tax return for 1997. Although she has no records, she estimates that she has given cash of about $500 to various charities during the year. She suggests that it would "look better" if you listed $501 as charitable contributions. What should you do?

47. What is meant by revenue-neutral tax reform?

48. How does the tax law foster technological progress?

49. Discuss the probable justification for the following provisions of the tax law:
    a. The election permitting certain corporations to avoid the corporate income tax.
    b. A provision that excludes from gross income certain benefits furnished to employees through accident and health plans financed by employers.
    c. Nontaxable treatment for an employee for premiums paid by an employer for group term insurance covering the life of the employee.

50. The tax law encourages private retirement plans and contributions to charitable organizations. In terms of nonrevenue objectives, what is the common justification for this special tax treatment?

51. What purpose is served by allowing a deduction for home mortgage interest and property taxes?

52. Allowing a taxpayer a deduction for Federal income tax purposes for state income taxes paid eliminates the double taxation of the same income. Do you agree? Why or why not?

53. Wilma, a cattle rancher, has a pasture condemned by the State Parks Commission for use as a recreational facility. The pasture cost Wilma $30,000, and the state paid her its appraised value of $100,000. Shortly thereafter, Wilma purchases additional pasture land for $80,000. Can Wilma avoid the tax on any of the gain under the wherewithal to pay concept? Explain.

54. In what manner does the tax law mitigate the effect of the annual accounting period concept for a net operating loss?

55. How does the tax law cope with the impact of inflation?

56. Forcing accrual basis taxpayers to recognize prepaid income when received (as opposed to when earned) accomplishes what objective?

57. On his income tax return for the year, Henry claims as a deduction certain charitable contributions that he did not make. When you question him about this, he responds:
    a. "How is the IRS going to prove that I did not make these contributions?"
    b. "Even if the IRS disallows the deductions, the worst that can happen is that I will owe the same amount of tax I would have paid anyway."

    Comment on Henry's misconceptions about the tax law.

58. Edward leases real estate to Janet for a period of 20 years. Janet makes capital improvements to the property. When the lease expires, Edward reclaims the property, including the improvements made by Janet.

    a. Under current law, at what point does Edward recognize income as a result of Janet's improvements?

    b. Has the law in (a) always been the rule?

    c. What is the justification, if any, for the current rule?

TEAM PROJECT: ARTHUR ANDERSEN TAX CHALLENGE CASES

Arthur Andersen & Co. has provided two of the cases that have been used in the Arthur Andersen Tax Challenge for use in *West's Federal Taxation: Individual Income Taxes* (or *West's Federal Taxation: Comprehensive Volume*). The Tax Challenge is a nationwide university competition to stimulate student interest in tax careers. The case studies are based on Federal tax issues confronting an individual or family with their own business, with investments made by the individual, compensation matters, itemized deductions, and related issues that affect the taxpayer's filing status and tax profile.

    The Tax Challenge is a team competition with four members on each team. Thus, the cases are excellent materials for team projects in tax classes. We suggest that team members read assigned cases in their entirety at this point in the course. Because the cases require the application of knowledge gained throughout the course, it is not possible to prepare a solution early in the course. However, the length and complexity of the cases dictate that students must spend some time working on them during the entire course. To facilitate this course-long effort, we have identified topics related to each chapter and placed instructions regarding these topics in the end-of-chapter problem materials as appropriate.

    Information related to tax issues and problems that are discussed in this chapter may be found in the

Day and Ball case on pages 11, 12, 25, and 26
Fence case on pages 39, 40, 52, and 55

Read and analyze the case you have been assigned and *identify* any issues and problems that are related to material covered in this chapter. If the information provided in the case is complete, prepare answers for this part of the case at this time. If you need information that is contained in later parts of the case, write a memo summarizing the questions or problems so you can prepare a complete answer at a later date.

WORKING WITH THE TAX LAW

LEARNING OBJECTIVES

After completing Chapter 2, you should be able to:

1. Distinguish between the statutory, administrative, and judicial sources of the tax law and understand the purpose of each source.

2. Locate and work with the appropriate tax law sources.

3. Understand the tax research process.

4. Communicate the results of the tax research process in a client letter and a tax file memorandum.

5. Apply tax research techniques and planning procedures.

6. Have an awareness of electronic tax research.

TAX SOURCES

1 LEARNING OBJECTIVE
Distinguish between the statutory, administrative, and judicial sources of the tax law and understand the purpose of each source.

Understanding taxation requires a mastery of the sources of the *rules of tax law*. These sources include not only legislative provisions in the form of the Internal Revenue Code, but also congressional Committee Reports, Treasury Department Regulations, other Treasury Department pronouncements, and court decisions. Thus, the *primary sources* of tax information include pronouncements from all three branches of government: legislative, executive, and judicial.

In addition to being able to locate and interpret the sources of the tax law, a tax professional must understand the relative weight of authority within these sources. The tax law is of little significance, however, until it is applied to a set of facts and circumstances. This chapter, therefore, both introduces the statutory, administrative, and judicial sources of tax law and explains how the law is applied to individual and business transactions. It also explains how to apply research techniques and use planning procedures effectively.

A large part of tax research focuses on determining the intent of Congress. Although Congress often claims simplicity as one of its goals, a cursory examination of the tax law indicates that it has not been very successful in achieving this objective. Commenting on his 48-page tax return, James Michener, the author, said "it is unimaginable in that I graduated from one of America's better colleges, yet I am totally incapable of understanding tax returns." David Brinkley, the television news commentator, observed that "settling a dispute is difficult when our tax regulations are all written in a foreign tongue whose language flows like damp sludge leaking from a sanitary landfill."

Frequently, uncertainty in the tax law causes disputes between the Internal Revenue Service (IRS) and taxpayers. Due to these *gray areas* and the complexity of the tax law, a taxpayer may have more than one alternative for structuring a business transaction. In structuring business transactions and engaging in other tax planning activities, the tax adviser must be cognizant that the objective of tax planning is not necessarily to minimize the tax liability. Instead a taxpayer should maximize his or her after-tax return, which may include maximizing nontax as well as noneconomic benefits.

SMALL IS BEAUTIFUL?

In income tax history, 1913 was an important year. In that year, the Sixteenth Amendment to the Constitution was ratified:

The Congress shall have power to tax and collect taxes on incomes, from whatever source derived, without apportionment among the several States, and without regard to any census or enumeration.

The first income tax legislation that definitely was constitutional was passed that same year.

Since 1913, Congress has enacted hundreds of tax bills. The Internal Revenue Code is now more than 2,200 pages in length. Of course, this seems short when compared to a tax service such as CCH's *Standard Federal Tax Reporter* and *RIA's United States Tax Reporter*, which fill up library shelves. As an example of how the size and complexity of the income tax have changed, consider that when CCH published its first tax guide in 1913, it was only 400 pages long.

STATUTORY SOURCES OF THE TAX LAW

Origin of the Internal Revenue Code. Before 1939, the statutory provisions relating to Federal taxation were contained in the individual revenue acts enacted by Congress. Because dealing with many separate acts was inconvenient and confusing, in 1939 Congress codified all of the Federal tax laws. Known as the Internal Revenue Code of 1939, the codification arranged all Federal tax provisions in a logical sequence and placed them in a separate part of the Federal statutes. A further rearrangement took place in 1954 and resulted in the Internal Revenue Code of 1954, which continued in effect until 1986 when it was replaced by the Internal Revenue Code of 1986. Although Congress did not recodify the law in the Tax Reform Act (TRA) of 1986, the magnitude of the changes made by TRA of 1986 did provide some rationale for renaming the Federal tax law the Internal Revenue Code of 1986.

The following observations help clarify the codification procedure:

- With some exceptions, neither the 1939 nor the 1954 Code substantially changed the tax law existing on the date of its enactment. Much of the 1939 Code, for example, was incorporated into the 1954 Code; the major change was the reorganization and renumbering of the tax provisions.
- Although the 1986 Code resulted in substantial changes, only a minority of the statutory provisions were affected.[1]
- Statutory amendments to the tax law are integrated into the Code. For example, the Technical and Miscellaneous Revenue Act of 1988, the Revenue Reconciliation Act of 1989, the Revenue Reconciliation Act of 1990, the Revenue Reconciliation Act of 1993, the Small Business Job Protection Act of 1996, and the Taxpayer Relief Act of 1997 all became part of the Internal Revenue Code of 1986. Considering the tax legislation

---

[1]This point is important in assessing judicial decisions interpreting provisions of the Internal Revenue Code of 1939 and the Internal Revenue Code of 1954. If the same provision was included in the Internal Revenue Code of 1986 and has not been subsequently amended, the decision has continuing validity.

enacted in recent years, it appears that the tax law will continue to be amended frequently.

The Legislative Process.   Federal tax legislation generally originates in the House of Representatives, where it is first considered by the House Ways and Means Committee. Tax bills originate in the Senate when they are attached as riders to other legislative proposals.[2] If acceptable to the House Ways and Means Committee, the proposed bill is referred to the entire House of Representatives for approval or disapproval. Approved bills are sent to the Senate, where they are considered by the Senate Finance Committee. The next step is referral from the Senate Finance Committee to the entire Senate. Assuming no disagreement between the House and Senate, passage by the Senate results in referral to the President for approval or veto. If the bill is approved or if the President's veto is overridden, the bill becomes law and part of the Internal Revenue Code of 1986.

When the Senate version of the bill differs from that passed by the House, the Joint Conference Committee, which includes members of both the House Ways and Means Committee and the Senate Finance Committee, is called upon to resolve the differences. Major tax bills frequently have differing versions. One reason bills are often changed in the Senate is that each individual senator has considerable latitude to make amendments when the Senate as a whole is voting on a bill referred to it by the Senate Finance Committee.[3] In contrast, the entire House of Representatives either accepts or rejects what is proposed by the House Ways and Means Committee, and changes from the floor are rare. The deliberations of the Joint Conference Committee usually produce a compromise between the two versions, which is then voted on by both the House and the Senate. If both bodies accept the bill, it is referred to the President for approval or veto.

Effective January 1, 1997, the President has the line-item veto power to delete objectional clauses in tax and spending laws rather than being required to veto the entire bill. In August 1997, President Clinton used this authority to veto a tax shelter for financial firms, another one for sellers of food-processing plants, and a provision that allowed the state of New York more than its fair share of Federal health subsidies. Congress did not override these line-item vetoes.

Referrals from the House Ways and Means Committee, the Senate Finance Committee, and the Joint Conference Committee are usually accompanied by Committee Reports. Because these Committee Reports often explain the provisions of the proposed legislation, they are a valuable source for ascertaining the *intent of Congress*. What Congress had in mind when it considered and enacted tax legislation is, of course, the key to interpreting such legislation by taxpayers, the IRS, and the courts. Since Regulations normally are not issued immediately after a statute is enacted, taxpayers often look to legislative history materials to determine congressional intent.

The typical legislative process for dealing with tax bills is summarized as follows:

---

[2]The Tax Equity and Fiscal Responsibility Act of 1982 originated in the Senate, and its constitutionality was unsuccessfully challenged in the courts. The Senate version of the Deficit Reduction Act of 1984 was attached as an amendment to the Federal Boat Safety Act.

[3]During the passage of the Tax Reform Act of 1986, Senate leaders tried to make the bill *amendment proof* to avoid the normal amendment process.

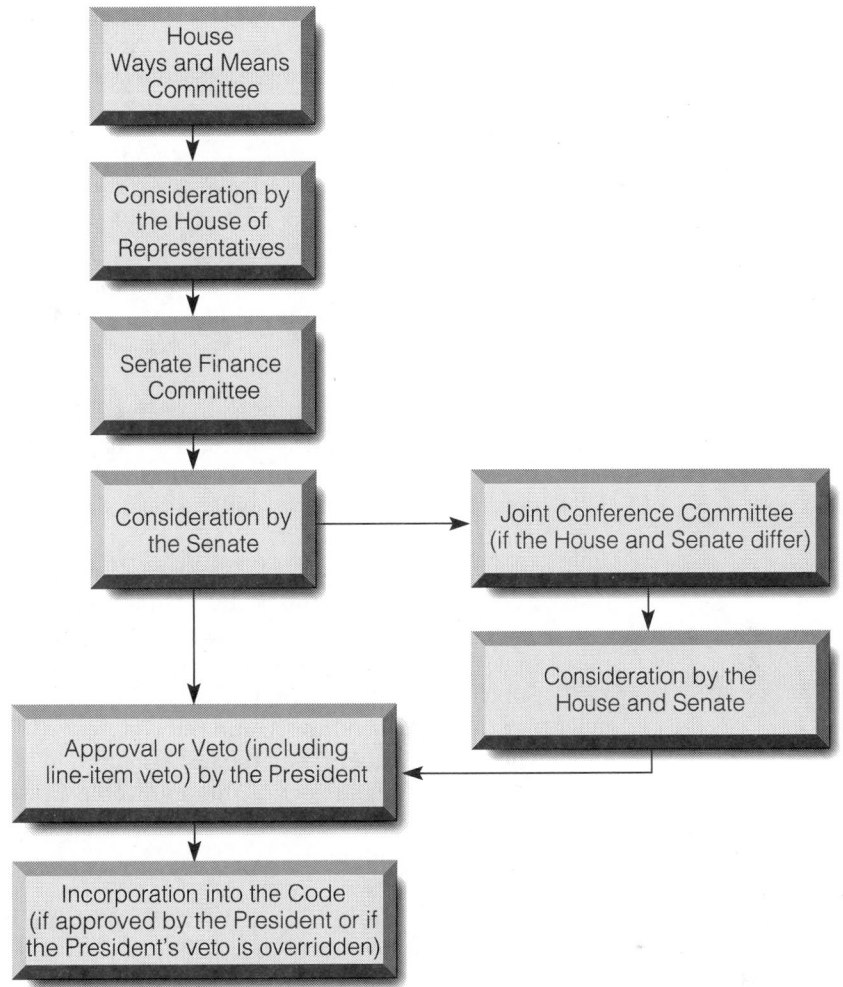

The role of the Joint Conference Committee indicates the importance of compromise in the legislative process. As an example of the practical effect of the compromise process, consider what happened to a limitation on contributions by employees to their education Individual Retirement Accounts in the Taxpayer Relief Act of 1997 (TRA of 1997).

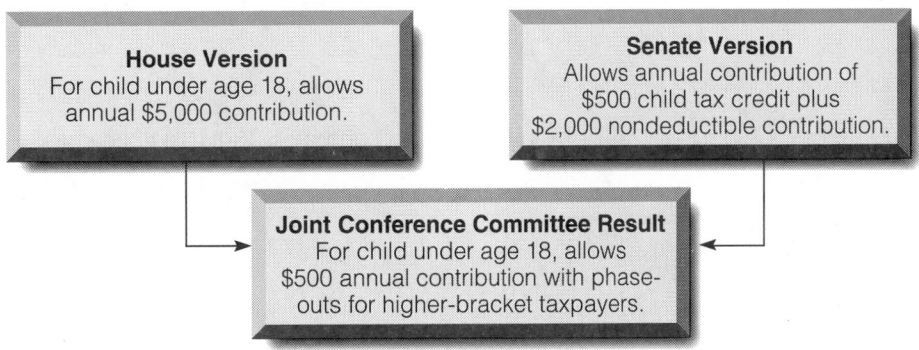

Arrangement of the Code.   The Internal Revenue Code of 1986 is found in Title 26 of the U.S. Code. In working with the Code, it helps to understand the format. Note, for example, the following partial table of contents:

> Subtitle A. Income Taxes
> > Chapter 1. Normal Taxes and Surtaxes
> > > Subchapter A. Determination of Tax Liability
> > > > Part I. Tax on Individuals
> > > > > Sections 1–5
> > > > Part II. Tax on Corporations
> > > > > Sections 11–12

* * *

In referring to a provision of the Code, the *key* is usually the Section number. In citing Section 2(a) (dealing with the status of a surviving spouse), for example, it is unnecessary to include Subtitle A, Chapter 1, Subchapter A, Part I. Merely mentioning Section 2(a) will suffice, since the Section numbers run consecutively and do not begin again with each new Subtitle, Chapter, Subchapter, or Part. Not all Code Section numbers are used, however. Notice that Part I ends with Section 5 and Part II starts with Section 11 (at present there are no Sections 6, 7, 8, 9, and 10).[4]

Tax practitioners commonly refer to some specific areas of income tax law by their Subchapters. Some of the more common Subchapter designations include Subchapter C ("Corporate Distributions and Adjustments"), Subchapter K ("Partners and Partnerships"), and Subchapter S ("Tax Treatment of S Corporations and Their Shareholders"). In the last situation in particular, it is much more convenient to describe the subject of the applicable Code provisions (Sections 1361–1379) as S corporation status rather than as the "Tax Treatment of S Corporations and Their Shareholders."

Citing the Code.   Code Sections often are broken down into subparts.[5] Section 2(a)(1)(A) serves as an example.

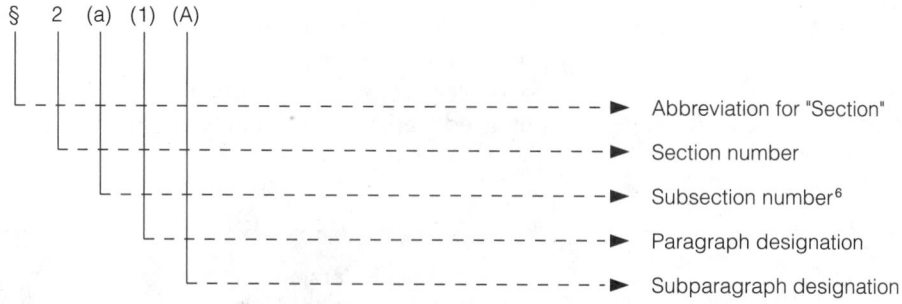

Broken down by content, § 2(a)(1)(A) becomes:

---

[4]When the 1954 Code was drafted, some Section numbers were intentionally omitted so that later changes could be incorporated into the Code without disrupting its organization. When Congress does not leave enough space, subsequent Code Sections are given A, B, C, etc., designations. A good example is the treatment of §§ 280A through 280H.

[5]Some Code Sections do not require subparts. See, for example, §§ 211 and 241.

[6]Some Code Sections omit the subsection designation and use the paragraph designation as the first subpart. See, for example, §§ 212(1) and 1221(1).

§ 2 ——————————————→ Definitions and special rules (relating to the income tax imposed on individuals)

(a) ——————————————→ Definition of a surviving spouse

(1) ——————————————→ For purposes of § 1 (the determination of the applicable rate schedule), a surviving spouse must meet certain conditions.

(A) ——————————————→ One of the conditions necessary to qualify as a surviving spouse is that the taxpayer's spouse must have died during either of his or her two taxable years immediately preceding the present taxable year.

Throughout the remainder of the text, references to the Code Sections are in the form given above. The symbols "§" and "§§" are used in place of "Section" and "Sections." Unless otherwise stated, all Code references are to the Internal Revenue Code of 1986. The following table summarizes the format that will be used:

Complete Reference	Text Reference
Section 2(a)(1)(A) of the Internal Revenue Code of 1986	§ 2(a)(1)(A)
Sections 1 and 2 of the Internal Revenue Code of 1986	§§ 1 and 2
Section 2 of the Internal Revenue Code of 1954	§ 2 of the Internal Revenue Code of 1954
Section 12(d) of the Internal Revenue Code of 1939[7]	§ 12(d) of the Internal Revenue Code of 1939

Effect of Treaties.   The United States signs certain tax treaties (sometimes called tax conventions) with foreign countries to render mutual assistance in tax enforcement and to avoid double taxation. The Technical and Miscellaneous Revenue Act of 1988 provided that neither a tax law nor a tax treaty takes general precedence. Thus, when there is a direct conflict, the most recent item will take precedence. A taxpayer must disclose on the tax return any position where a treaty overrides a tax law.[8] There is a $1,000 penalty per failure to disclose for individuals and a $10,000 per failure penalty for corporations.[9]

ADMINISTRATIVE SOURCES OF THE TAX LAW

The administrative sources of the Federal tax law can be grouped as follows: Treasury Department Regulations, Revenue Rulings and Revenue Procedures, and other administrative pronouncements (see Exhibit 2–1). All are issued by either the U.S. Treasury Department or one of its instrumentalities (e.g., the IRS or a District Director).

---

[7]§ 12(d) of the Internal Revenue Code of 1939 is the predecessor to § 2 of the Internal Revenue Code of 1954 and the Internal Revenue Code of 1986. Keep in mind that the 1954 Code superseded the 1939 Code and the 1986 Code has superseded the 1954 Code. Footnote 1 of this chapter explains why references to the 1939 or 1954 code are included.

[8]§ 7852(d).

[9]Reg. §§ 301.6114–1 and 301.6712–1.

▼ **EXHIBIT 2–1**
Administrative Sources

Source	Location	Authority**
Regulations	*Federal Register**	Force and effect of law.
Temporary Regulations	*Federal Register** *Internal Revenue Bulletin* *Cumulative Bulletin*	May be cited as a precedent.
Proposed Regulations	*Federal Register** *Internal Revenue Bulletin* *Cumulative Bulletin*	Preview of final Regulations.
Revenue Rulings Revenue Procedures Action on Decision	*Internal Revenue Bulletin* *Cumulative Bulletin*	Do not have the force and effect of law.
General Counsel's Memoranda Technical Advice Memoranda	*Tax Analysts' Tax Notes*; RIA's *Internal Memoranda of the IRS*; CCH's *IRS Position Reporter*	May not be cited as a precedent.
Letter Rulings	Research Institute of America and Commerce Clearing House loose-leaf services	Applicable only to taxpayer addressed. No precedential force.

*Finalized, Temporary, and Proposed Regulations are published in soft-cover form by several publishers.
**Each of these sources may be substantial authority for purposes of the accuracy-related penalty in § 6662.
  Notice 90–20, 1990–1 C.B. 328.

Treasury Department Regulations.   Regulations are issued by the U.S. Treasury Department under authority granted by Congress.[10] Interpretive by nature, they provide taxpayers with considerable guidance on the meaning and application of the Code. Regulations may be issued in *proposed, temporary*, or *final* form. Regulations carry considerable weight and are an important factor to consider in complying with the tax law.

Since Regulations interpret the Code, they are arranged in the same sequence as the Code. A number is added at the beginning, however, to indicate the type of tax or administrative, procedural, or definitional matter to which they relate. For example, the prefix 1 designates the Regulations under the income tax law. Thus, the Regulations under Code § 2 are cited as Reg. § 1.2 with subparts added for further identification. The numbers of these subparts often do not correspond to the numbers of the Code subsections. The prefix 20 designates estate tax Regulations; 25 covers gift tax Regulations; 31 relates to employment taxes; and 301 refers to procedure and administration. This list is not all-inclusive.

New Regulations and changes to existing Regulations are usually issued in proposed form before they are finalized. The interval between the proposal of a Regulation and its finalization permits taxpayers and other interested parties to comment on the propriety of the proposal. **Proposed Regulations** under Code § 2, for example, are cited as Prop.Reg. § 1.2. The Tax Court indicates that Proposed Regulations carry no more weight than a position advanced in a written brief prepared by a litigating party before the Tax Court. **Finalized Regulations** have the force and effect of law.[11]

---

[10]§ 7805.
[11]*F. W. Woolworth Co.*, 54 T.C. 1233 (1970); *Harris M. Miller*, 70 T.C.
  448 (1978); and *James O. Tomerlin Trust*, 87 T.C. 876 (1986).

TAX IN THE NEWS

A POTPOURRI OF NEWS ABOUT THE IRS

- The Tax Reform Act of 1997 includes a provision that allows the Federal government to accept credit cards and debit cards for the payment of Federal income taxes. An interesting feature of the legislation is that it prohibits the IRS from paying the discount rate (typically 1 to 2 percent) that merchants normally pay banks to process their credit-card transactions.
- New IRS Regulations will allow more people to qualify for rewards that helps the IRS collect taxes people have not paid. The new finders fee can be as large as 15 percent of the amount collected excluding interest.
- Most disputes with the IRS are resolved without litigation. Only about 25,000 to 30,000 Tax Court petitions are filed each year. Most of these are settled, so the Tax Court actually tries and decides only about 1,200 to 1,500 cases each year.
- For 1996, the top 10 percent of taxpayers in terms of adjusted gross income paid 63 percent of the total Federal income tax.

Sometimes the Treasury Department issues **Temporary Regulations** relating to elections and other matters where speed is important. These Regulations are issued without the comment period required for Proposed Regulations. Temporary Regulations have the same authoritative value as final Regulations and may be cited as precedents. Temporary Regulations must now also be issued as Proposed Regulations and automatically expire within three years after the date of issuance.[12] Temporary Regulations and the simultaneously issued Proposed Regulations carry more weight than traditional Proposed Regulations. An example of a Temporary Regulation is Temp.Reg. § 1.417(e)–1T(d), which contains provisions for determining the present value of an employee's benefits under a defined benefit retirement plan.

Proposed, Temporary, and final Regulations are published in the *Federal Register* and are reproduced in major tax services. Final Regulations are issued as Treasury Decisions (TDs).

Regulations may also be classified as *legislative, interpretive*, or *procedural*. This classification scheme is discussed under Assessing the Validity of a Treasury Regulation later in the chapter.

Revenue Rulings and Revenue Procedures. **Revenue Rulings** are official pronouncements of the National Office of the IRS.[13] Like Regulations, they are designed to provide interpretation of the tax law. However, they do not carry the same legal force and effect as Regulations and usually deal with more restricted problems. In addition, Regulations are approved by the Secretary of the Treasury, whereas Revenue Rulings are not. Both Revenue Rulings and Revenue Procedures serve an important function by providing *guidance* to IRS personnel and taxpayers in routine tax matters. Revenue Rulings and Revenue Procedures generally apply retroactively and may be revoked or modified by subsequent rulings or procedures, Regulations, legislation, or court decisions.

---

[12]§ 7805(e).

[13]§ 7805(a).

Although letter rulings (discussed below) are not the same as Revenue Rulings, a Revenue Ruling often results from a specific taxpayer's request for a letter ruling. If the IRS believes that a taxpayer's request for a letter ruling deserves official publication because of its widespread impact, the holding will be converted into a Revenue Ruling and issued for the information and guidance of taxpayers, tax practitioners, and IRS personnel. Names, identifying descriptions, and money amounts are changed to disguise the identity of the taxpayer. In addition to resulting from taxpayer requests, Revenue Rulings arise from technical advice to District Offices of the IRS, court decisions, suggestions from tax practitioner groups, and various tax publications.

Revenue Procedures are issued in the same manner as Revenue Rulings, but deal with the internal management practices and procedures of the IRS. Familiarity with these procedures can increase taxpayer compliance and help the IRS administer the tax laws efficiently. A taxpayer's failure to follow a Revenue Procedure can result in unnecessary delay or cause the IRS to decline to act in a discretionary situation on behalf of the taxpayer.

Revenue Rulings and Revenue Procedures are published weekly by the U.S. Government in the *Internal Revenue Bulletin* (I.R.B.). Semiannually, the bulletins for a six-month period are gathered together, reorganized by Code Section classification, and published in a bound volume called the *Cumulative Bulletin* (C.B.).[14] The proper form for citing Revenue Rulings and Revenue Procedures depends on whether the item has been published in the *Cumulative Bulletin* or is only available in I.R.B. form. Consider, for example, the following transition:

Temporary Citation
{
Rev.Rul. 97–8, I.R.B. No. 7, 4.
Explanation: Revenue Ruling Number 8, appearing on page 4 of the 7th weekly issue of the *Internal Revenue Bulletin* for 1997.

Permanent Citation
{
Rev.Rul. 97–8, 1997–1 C.B. 326.
Explanation: Revenue Ruling Number 8, appearing on page 326 of Volume 1 of the *Cumulative Bulletin* for 1997.

Since the first volume of the 1997 *Cumulative Bulletin* was not published until December of 1997, the I.R.B. citation had to be used until that time. After the publication of the *Cumulative Bulletin*, the C.B. citation is proper. The basic portion of both citations (Rev.Rul. 97–8) indicates that this document was the 8th Revenue Ruling issued by the IRS during 1997.

Revenue Procedures are cited in the same manner, except that "Rev.Proc." is substituted for "Rev.Rul." Some recent Revenue Procedures had the following effects:

- Specified the procedures for requesting consent to changes in accounting methods.
- Issued guidance on the deadline for amending qualified plans to comply with changes made by the Small Business Job Protection Act of 1996.
- Announced a new procedure for relief for late S corporation elections.

---

[14]Usually, only two volumes of the *Cumulative Bulletin* are published each year. However, when Congress has enacted major tax legislation, other volumes may be published containing the congressional Committee Reports supporting the Revenue Act. See, for example, the two extra volumes for 1984 dealing with the Deficit Reduction Act of 1984. The 1984–3 *Cumulative Bulletin*, Volume 1, contains the text of the law itself; 1984–3, Volume 2, contains the Committee Reports. There are a total of four volumes of the *Cumulative Bulletin* for 1984: 1984–1; 1984–2; 1984–3, Volume 1; 1984–3, Volume 2.

Letter Rulings. Individual **letter rulings** are issued for a fee upon a taxpayer's request and describe how the IRS will treat a proposed transaction for tax purposes. They apply only to the taxpayer who asks for and obtains the ruling, but post-1984 letter rulings may be substantial authority for purposes of the accuracy-related penalty.[15] The IRS issues about 40 letter rulings each week. Though this procedure may sound like the only real way to carry out effective tax planning, the IRS limits the issuance of individual rulings to restricted, preannounced areas of taxation. The main reason the IRS will not rule in certain areas is that they involve fact-oriented situations. Thus, a ruling may not be obtained on many of the problems that are particularly troublesome for taxpayers.[16]

The law now requires the IRS to make individual rulings available for public inspection after identifying details are deleted.[17] Published digests of private letter rulings can be found in *Private Letter Rulings* (published by RIA), BNA *Daily Tax Reports,* and Tax Analysts & Advocates *Tax Notes. IRS Letter Rulings Reports* (published by Commerce Clearing House) contains both digests and full texts of all letter rulings. *Letter Ruling Review* (published by Tax Analysts) is a monthly publication that selects and discusses the more important of the approximately 160 letter rulings issued each month.

Letter rulings receive multidigit file numbers, which indicate the year and week of issuance as well as the number of the ruling during that week. Consider, for example, Ltr.Rul. 9730032, which deals with unsolicited contributions to a health care charity:

97	30	032
Year 1997	30th week of issuance	Number of the ruling issued during the 30th week

Other Administrative Pronouncements. *Treasury Decisions* (TDs) are issued by the Treasury Department to promulgate new Regulations, amend or otherwise change existing Regulations, or announce the position of the Government on selected court decisions. Like Revenue Rulings and Revenue Procedures, TDs are published in the *Internal Revenue Bulletin* and subsequently transferred to the *Cumulative Bulletin.*

The IRS publishes other administrative communications in the *Internal Revenue Bulletin* such as Announcements, Notices, LRs (Proposed Regulations), and Prohibited Transaction Exemptions.

Like letter rulings, **determination letters** are issued at the request of taxpayers and provide guidance on the application of the tax law. They differ from letter rulings in that the issuing source is the District Director rather than the National Office of the IRS. Also, determination letters usually involve completed (as opposed to proposed) transactions. Determination letters are not published and are made known only to the party making the request.

The following examples illustrate the distinction between letter rulings and determination letters:

---

[15]Notice 90–20, 1990–1 C.B. 328. In this regard, letter rulings differ from Revenue Rulings, which are applicable to *all* taxpayers. Letter rulings may later lead to the issuance of a Revenue Ruling if the holding involved affects many taxpayers. In its Agents' Manual, the IRS indicates that letter rulings may be used as a guide with other research materials in formulating a District Office position on an issue. The IRS is required to charge a taxpayer a fee for letter rulings, determination letters, etc.

[16]Rev.Proc. 98–3, I.R.B. No. 1, 100 contains a list of areas in which the IRS will not issue advance rulings. From time to time, subsequent Revenue Procedures are issued that modify or amplify Rev.Proc. 98–3.

[17]§ 6110.

TAX IN THE NEWS

TAX FREEDOM DAY SETS A NEW RECORD

According to the Tax Foundation, the average American had to work 128 days in 1997 to pay off his or her total tax bill. In other words, a taxpayer only earned tax freedom on the 129th day, or May 9, 1997. Tax Freedom Day, says the Tax Foundation, is the day that the average American is free to spend his or her income on other goods and services.

The majority of the tax burden—82 days—stems from individual income taxes and social insurance taxes. On average, Americans spent 2 hours and 49 minutes of each working day laboring to pay for the various government services and programs.

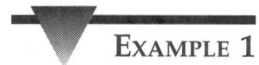

EXAMPLE 1

The shareholders of Red Corporation and Green Corporation want assurance that the consolidation of the corporations into Blue Corporation will be a nontaxable reorganization. The proper approach would be to request the National Office of the IRS to issue a letter ruling concerning the income tax effect of the proposed transaction. ▼

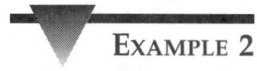

EXAMPLE 2

Chris operates a barber shop in which he employs eight barbers. To comply with the rules governing income tax and payroll tax withholdings, Chris wants to know whether the barbers working for him are employees or independent contractors. The proper procedure would be to request a determination letter on their status from the appropriate District Director. ▼

The National Office of the IRS releases **Technical Advice Memoranda (TAMs)** weekly. Although TAMs and letter rulings both give the IRS's determination of an issue, they differ in several respects. Letter rulings deal with proposed transactions and are issued to taxpayers at their request. In contrast, TAMs deal with completed transactions and are often requested in relation to exempt organizations and employee plans. Futhermore, TAMs arise from questions raised by IRS personnel during audits and are issued by the National Office of the IRS to its field personnel rather than to taxpayers. TAMs are not officially published and may not be cited or used as precedent.[18] They are assigned file numbers according to the same procedure used for letter rulings. For example, TAM 9728005 refers to the 5th TAM issued during the 28th week of 1997.

Several internal memoranda that constitute the working law of the IRS now must be released. These General Counsel Memoranda (GCMs) and Technical Advice Memoranda (TAMs) are not officially published, and the IRS indicates that they may not be cited as precedents by taxpayers.[19] However, these working documents do explain the IRS's position on various issues.

---

[18]§ 6110(j)(3). Post-1984 TAMs may be substantial authority for purposes of avoiding the accuracy-related penalty. Notice 90–20, 1990–1 C.B. 328.

[19]These are unofficially published by the publishers listed in Exhibit 2–1. Such internal memoranda for post-1984 may be substantial authority for purposes of the accuracy-related penalty. Notice 90–20, 1990–1 C.B. 328.

▼ **FIGURE 2–1**
Federal Judicial System

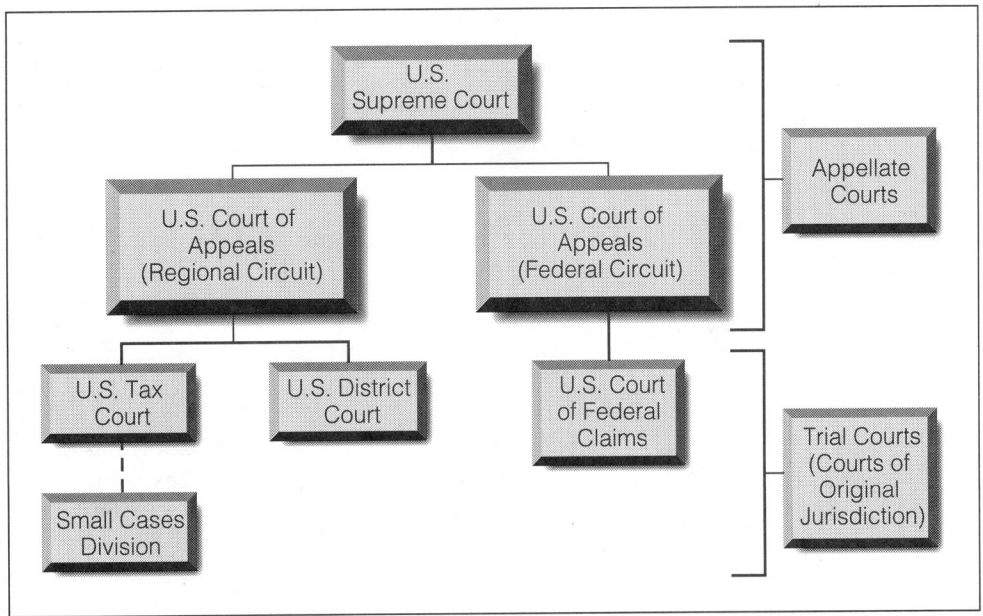

JUDICIAL SOURCES OF THE TAX LAW

The Judicial Process in General.   After a taxpayer has exhausted some or all of the remedies available within the IRS (i.e., no satisfactory settlement has been reached at the agent or at the Appeals Division level), the dispute can be taken to the Federal courts. The dispute is first considered by a **court of original jurisdiction** (known as a trial court) with any appeal (either by the taxpayer or the IRS) taken to the appropriate appellate court. In most situations, the taxpayer has a choice of any of *four trial courts:* a **Federal District Court,** the **U.S. Court of Federal Claims,** the **U.S. Tax Court,** or the **Small Cases Division** of the U.S. Tax Court. The trial and appellate court scheme for Federal tax litigation is illustrated in Figure 2–1.

The broken line between the U.S. Tax Court and the Small Cases Division indicates that there is no appeal from the Small Cases Division. The jurisdiction of the Small Cases Division is limited to cases involving amounts of $10,000 or less. The proceedings of the Small Cases Division are informal (e.g., no necessity for the taxpayer to be represented by a lawyer or other tax adviser). Special trial judges rather than Tax Court judges preside over these proceedings. The decisions of the Small Cases Division are not precedents for any other court decision and are not reviewable by any higher court. Proceedings can be more timely and less expensive in the Small Cases Division.

American law, following English law, is frequently *made* by judicial decisions. Under the doctrine of *stare decisis*, each case (except in the Small Cases Division) has precedential value for future cases with the same controlling set of facts. Most Federal and state appellate court decisions and some decisions of trial courts are published. More than 4 million judicial opinions have been published in the United States; over 130,000 cases are published each year.[20] Published court decisions are organized by jurisdiction (Federal or state) and level of court (trial or appellate).

---

[20]Jacobstein, Mersky, and Dunn, *Fundamentals of Legal Research,* 6th
  ed. (Westbury, N.Y.: The Foundation Press, 1994), p. 11.

A decision of a particular court is called its holding. Sometimes a decision includes dicta or incidental opinions beyond the current facts. Such passing remarks, illustrations, or analogies are not essential to the current holding. Although the holding has precedential value under *stare decisis*, dicta are not binding on a future court.

Trial Courts.   The various trial courts (courts of original jurisdiction) differ in several respects:

- *Number of courts.* There is only one Court of Federal Claims and only one Tax Court, but there are many Federal District Courts. The taxpayer does not select the District Court that will hear the dispute but must sue in the one that has jurisdiction.
- *Number of judges.* Each District Court has only 1 judge, the Court of Federal Claims has 16 judges, and the Tax Court has 19 regular judges. The entire Tax Court, however, will review a case (the case is sent to court conference) only when more important or novel tax issues are involved. Most cases will be heard and decided by one of the 19 judges.
- *Location.* The Court of Federal Claims meets most often in Washington, D.C., whereas a District Court meets at a prescribed seat for the particular district. Each state has at least one District Court, and many of the more populous states have more than one. Therefore, the inconvenience and expense of traveling (present with many suits in the Court of Federal Claims) for the taxpayer and his or her counsel are largely eliminated. Although the Tax Court is officially based in Washington, D.C., the various judges travel to different parts of the country and hear cases at predetermined locations and dates. Although this procedure eases the distance problem for the taxpayer, it may mean a delay before the case comes to trial and is decided.
- *Jurisdiction of the Court of Federal Claims.* The Court of Federal Claims has jurisdiction over any claim against the United States that is based upon the Constitution, any Act of Congress, or any regulation of an executive department. Thus, the Court of Federal Claims hears nontax litigation as well as tax cases. This forum appears to be more favorable for issues having an equitable or pro-business orientation (as opposed to purely technical issues) and for those requiring extensive discovery.[21]
- *Jurisdiction of the Tax Court and District Courts.* The Tax Court hears only tax cases and is the most popular forum. The District Courts hear nontax litigation as well as tax cases. Some Tax Court justices have been appointed from IRS or Treasury Department positions. For these reasons, some people suggest that the Tax Court has more expertise in tax matters.
- *Jury trial.* The only court in which a taxpayer can obtain a jury trial is a District Court. But since juries can only decide questions of fact and not questions of law, even taxpayers who choose the District Court route often do not request a jury trial. In that event, the judge will decide all issues. Note that a District Court decision is controlling only in the district in which the court has jurisdiction.
- *Payment of deficiency.* For the Court of Federal Claims or a District Court to have jurisdiction, the taxpayer must pay the tax deficiency assessed by the

---

[21]T. D. Peyser, "The Case for Selecting the Claims Court to Litigate a Federal Tax Liability," *The Tax Executive* (Winter 1988): 149.

IRS and sue for a refund. A taxpayer who wins (assuming no successful appeal by the Government) recovers the tax paid plus appropriate interest. For the Tax Court, however, jurisdiction is usually obtained without first paying the assessed tax deficiency. In the event the taxpayer loses in the Tax Court (and does not appeal or an appeal is unsuccessful), the deficiency must be paid with appropriate interest. With the elimination of the deduction for personal (consumer) interest, the Tax Court route of delaying payment of the deficiency can become expensive. For example, to earn 11 percent after tax, a taxpayer with a 39.6 percent marginal tax rate would have to earn 18.2 percent. By paying the tax, a taxpayer limits underpayment interest and penalties on the underpayment.

- *Termination of running of interest.* A taxpayer who selects the Tax Court may deposit a cash bond to stop the running of interest. The taxpayer must deposit both the amount of the tax and any accrued interest. If the taxpayer wins and the deposited amount is returned, the Government does not pay interest on the deposit.
- *Appeals.* Appeals from a District Court or a Tax Court decision are to the appropriate U.S. Court of Appeals. Appeals from the Court of Federal Claims go to the Court of Appeals for the Federal Circuit.
- *Bankruptcy.* When a taxpayer files a bankruptcy petition, the IRS, like other creditors, is prevented from taking action against the taxpayer. Sometimes a bankruptcy court may settle a tax claim.

For a summary, see Concept Summary 2–1.

Appellate Courts.   The losing party can appeal a trial court decision to a **Circuit Court of Appeals.** The 11 geographical circuits, the circuit for the District of Columbia, and the Federal Circuit[22] appear in Figure 2–2. The appropriate circuit for an appeal depends upon where the litigation originated. For example, an appeal from New York goes to the Second Circuit.

If the Government loses at the trial court level (District Court, Tax Court, or Court of Federal Claims), it need not (frequently does not) appeal. The fact that an appeal is not made, however, does not indicate that the IRS agrees with the result and will not litigate similar issues in the future. The IRS may decide not to appeal for a number of reasons. First, the current litigation load may be heavy, and as a consequence, the IRS may decide that available personnel should be assigned to other, more important cases. Second, the IRS may determine that this is not a good case to appeal. Perhaps the taxpayer is in a sympathetic position or the facts are particularly strong in his or her favor. In that event, the IRS may wait to test the legal issues involved with a taxpayer who has a much weaker case. Third, if the appeal is from a District Court or the Tax Court, the Court of Appeals of jurisdiction could have some bearing on whether the IRS chooses to go forward with an appeal. Based on past experience and precedent, the IRS may conclude that the chance for success on a particular issue might be more promising in another Court of Appeals. If so, the IRS will wait for a similar case to arise in a different jurisdiction.

---

[22]The Court of Appeals for the Federal Circuit was created, effective October 1, 1982, by P.L. 97–164 (4/2/82) to hear decisions appealed from the Claims Court (now the Court of Federal Claims).

CONCEPT SUMMARY 2–1

Federal Judicial System: Trial Courts

Issue	U.S. Tax Court	U.S. District Court	U.S. Court of Federal Claims
Number of judges per court	19*	1	16
Payment of deficiency before trial	No	Yes	Yes
Jury trial available	No	Yes	No
Types of disputes	Tax cases only	Most criminal and civil issues	Claims against the United States
Jurisdiction	Nationwide	Location of taxpayer	Nationwide
IRS acquiescence policy	Yes	Yes	Yes
Appeal route	U.S. Court of Appeals	U.S. Court of Appeals	U.S. Court of Appeals for the Federal Circuit

*There are also 14 special trial judges and 9 senior judges.

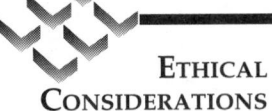

ETHICAL CONSIDERATIONS

Choosing Cases for Appeal

The U.S. Government loses a tax case against a prominent citizen in the U.S. District Court of Iowa. The taxpayer, a minister, had set up three separate trusts for each of his three children (i.e., a total of nine trusts). The Government argued that under Reg. § 1.641(a)–0(c) these trusts should be consolidated and treated as three trusts to stop the taxpayer from mitigating the progressive tax structure (e.g., 39.6 percent top tax bracket).

The IRS has decided to appeal a case in this multiple trust area. As one of the attorneys for the Government, you must choose between the Iowa case and a similar multiple trust conflict in the U.S. District Court of Virginia. Here the taxpayer is a CPA who has established four separate trusts for her two children (i.e., a total of eight trusts). See *Estelle Morris Trusts*, 51 T.C. 20 (1968). Factors you are considering are the potential sympathy associated with the minister's profession and a lack thereof associated with the CPA, the facts indicating that the attempt at tax avoidance is more egregious in the Iowa case, and a colleague's opinion that the Virginia case is winnable. Which case will you select? Comment on the fairness of the Government's ability and willingness to select a case to appeal in this fashion.

With the establishment of the Federal Circuit at the appellate level, a taxpayer has an alternative forum to the Court of Appeals of his or her home circuit for the appeal. Appeals from both the Tax Court and the District Court go to a taxpayer's home circuit. Now, when a particular circuit has issued an adverse decision, the taxpayer may wish to select the Court of Federal Claims route, since any appeal will be to the Federal Circuit.

District Courts, the Tax Court, and the Court of Federal Claims must abide by the **precedents** set by the Court of Appeals of jurisdiction. A particular Court of

▼ **FIGURE 2–2**
The Federal Courts of Appeals

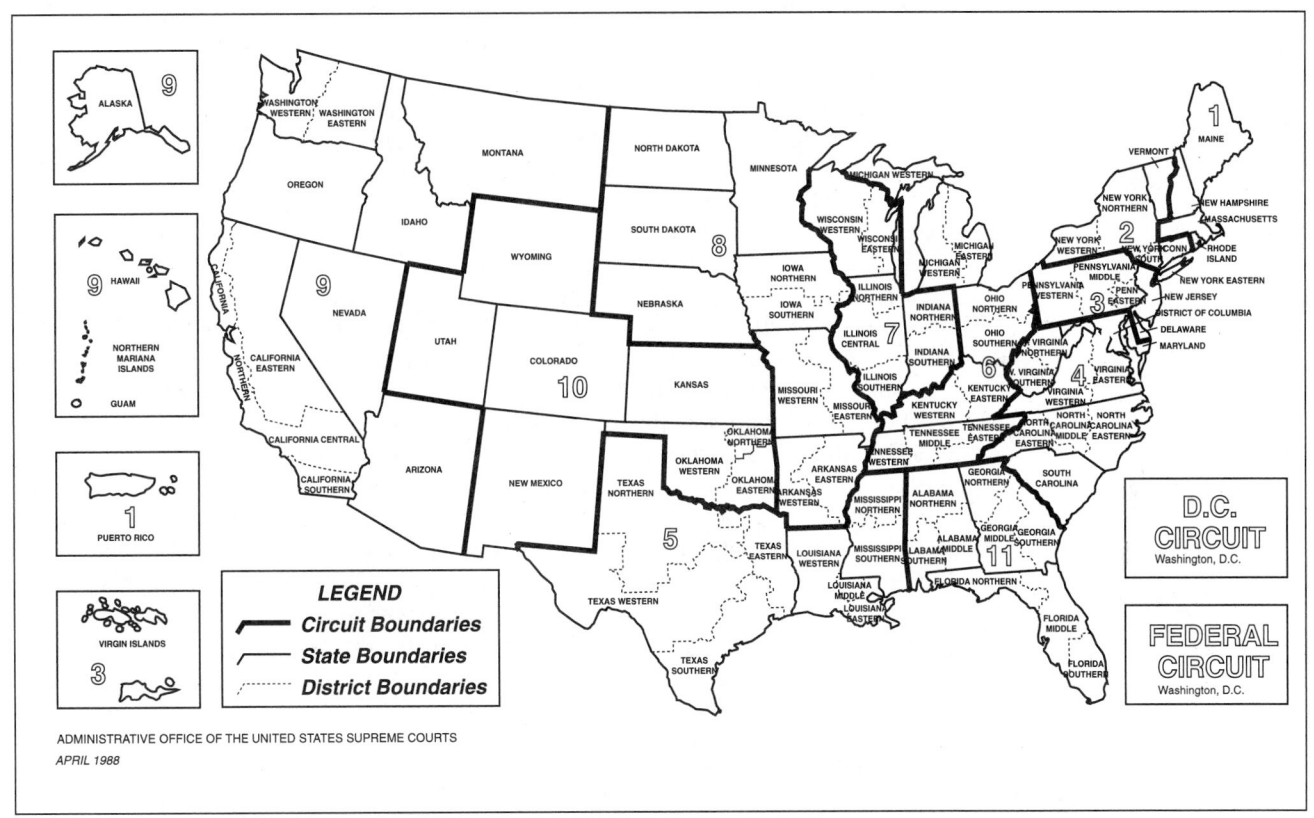

ADMINISTRATIVE OFFICE OF THE UNITED STATES SUPREME COURTS
APRIL 1988

Appeals need not follow the decisions of another Court of Appeals. All courts, however, must follow the decisions of the **U.S. Supreme Court.**

Because the Tax Court is a national court (it hears and decides cases from all parts of the country), the observation made in the previous paragraph has caused problems. For many years, the Tax Court followed a policy of deciding cases based on what it thought the result should be, even though its decision might be appealed to a Court of Appeals that had previously decided a similar case differently. A number of years ago this policy was changed in the *Golsen*[23] decision. Now the Tax Court will decide a case as it feels the law should be applied *only* if the Court of Appeals of appropriate jurisdiction has not yet passed on the issue or has previously decided a similar case in accord with the Tax Court's decision. If the Court of Appeals of appropriate jurisdiction has previously held otherwise, the Tax Court will conform under the *Golsen* rule even though it disagrees with the holding.

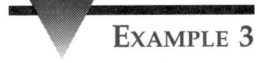
EXAMPLE 3

Emily lives in Texas and sues in the Tax Court on Issue A. The Fifth Court of Appeals is the appellate court of appropriate jurisdiction. The Fifth Court of Appeals has already decided, in a case involving similar facts but a different taxpayer, that Issue A should be resolved against the Government. Although the Tax Court feels that the Fifth Court of Appeals is wrong, under its *Golsen* policy it will render judgment for Emily. Shortly thereafter, Rashad, a resident of New York, in a comparable case, sues in the Tax Court on Issue A.

---

[23]*Jack E. Golsen*, 54 T.C. 742 (1970).

Assume that the Second Court of Appeals, the appellate court of appropriate jurisdiction, has never expressed itself on Issue A. Presuming the Tax Court has not reconsidered its position on Issue A, it will decide against Rashad. Thus, it is entirely possible for two taxpayers suing in the same court to end up with opposite results merely because they live in different parts of the country. ▼

Appeal to the U.S. Supreme Court is by **Writ of Certiorari.** If the Court accepts jurisdiction, it will grant the Writ *(Cert. Granted)*. Most often, it will deny jurisdiction *(Cert. Denied)*. For whatever reason or reasons, the Supreme Court rarely hears tax cases. The Court usually grants certiorari to resolve a conflict among the Courts of Appeals (e.g., two or more appellate courts have assumed opposing positions on a particular issue) or where the tax issue is extremely important. The granting of a Writ of Certiorari indicates that at least four members of the Supreme Court believe that the issue is of sufficient importance to be heard by the full Court.

The *role* of appellate courts is limited to a review of the record of trial compiled by the trial courts. Thus, the appellate process usually involves a determination of whether the trial court applied the proper law in arriving at its decision. Rarely will an appellate court disturb a lower court's fact-finding determination.

Both the Code and the Supreme Court indicate that Federal appellate courts are bound by findings of facts unless they are clearly erroneous.[24] This aspect of the appellate process is illustrated by a decision of the Court of Appeals for the District of Columbia involving whether a taxpayer was engaged in an activity for profit under § 183.[25] This appeals court specifically held that the "Tax Court's findings of facts are binding on Federal courts of appeals unless clearly erroneous." The Court applauded the Tax Court for the thoroughness of its factual inquiry but could "not place the stamp of approval upon its eventual legal outcome." In reversing and remanding the decision to the Tax Court, the appellate court said that "the language of § 183, its legislative history and the applicable Treasury regulation combine to demonstrate that the court's [Tax Court's] standard is erroneous as a matter of law." The appeals court held that this taxpayer's claims of deductibility were to be evaluated by proper legal standards.

An appeal can have any of a number of possible outcomes. The appellate court could approve (affirm) or disapprove (reverse) the lower court's finding, or it could send the case back for further consideration (remand). When many issues are involved, a mixed result is not unusual. Thus, the lower court could be affirmed *(aff'd)* on Issue A and reversed *(rev'd)* on Issue B, while Issue C is remanded *(rem'd)* for additional fact finding.

When more than one judge is involved in the decision-making process, disagreements are not uncommon. In addition to the majority view, one or more judges may concur (agree with the result reached but not with some or all of the reasoning) or dissent (disagree with the result). In any one case, of course, the majority view controls. But concurring and dissenting views can have an influence on other courts or, at some subsequent date when the composition of the court has changed, even on the same court.

Knowledge of several terms is important in understanding court decisions. The term *plaintiff* refers to the party requesting action in a court, and the *defendant* is the party against whom the suit is brought. Sometimes a court uses the terms *petitioner* and *respondent*. In general, "petitioner" is a synonym for "plaintiff," and "respondent" is a synonym for "defendant." At the trial court level, a taxpayer is

---

[24]§§ 7482(a) and (c). *Comm. v. Duberstein*, 60–2 USTC ¶9515, 5 AFTR2d 1626, 80 S.Ct. 1190 (USSC, 1960). See Rule 52(a) of the Federal Rules of Civil Procedure.

[25]*Dreicer v. Comm.*, 81–2 USTC ¶9683, 48 AFTR2d 5884, 665 F.2d 1292 (CA–DC, 1981).

normally the plaintiff (or petitioner), and the Government is the defendant (or respondent). If the taxpayer wins and the Government appeals as the new petitioner (or appellant), the taxpayer becomes the new respondent.

2 ▶ LEARNING OBJECTIVE
Locate and work with the appropriate tax law sources.

Judicial Citations—General.   Having concluded a brief description of the judicial process, it is appropriate to consider the more practical problem of the relationship of case law to tax research. As previously noted, court decisions are an important source of tax law. The ability to cite and locate a case is, therefore, a must in working with the tax law. Judicial citations usually follow a standard pattern: case name, volume number, reporter series, page or paragraph number, and court (where necessary).

Judicial Citations—The U.S. Tax Court.   A good starting point is with the Tax Court. The Tax Court issues two types of decisions: Regular and Memorandum. The Chief Judge decides whether the opinion is issued as a Regular or Memorandum decision. The distinction between the two involves both substance and form. In terms of substance, *Memorandum* decisions deal with situations necessitating only the application of already established principles of law. *Regular* decisions involve novel issues not previously resolved by the Court. In actual practice, however, this distinction is not always preserved. Not infrequently, Memorandum decisions will be encountered that appear to warrant Regular status and vice versa. At any rate, do not conclude that Memorandum decisions possess no value as precedents. Both represent the position of the Tax Court and, as such, can be relied upon.

The Regular and Memorandum decisions issued by the Tax Court also differ in form. Memorandum decisions are officially published in mimeograph form only. Regular decisions are published by the U.S. Government in a series entitled *Tax Court of the United States Reports*. Each volume of these *Reports* covers a six-month period (January 1 through June 30 and July 1 through December 31) and is given a succeeding volume number. But, as was true of the *Cumulative Bulletin*, there is usually a time lag between the date a decision is rendered and the date it appears in bound form. A temporary citation might be necessary to aid the researcher in locating a recent Regular decision. Consider, for example, the temporary and permanent citations for *Sprint Corporation and Subsidiaries*, a decision filed on April 30, 1997:

Temporary ⎰ *Sprint Corporation and Subsidiaries,* 108 T.C. ___, No. 4 (1997).
Citation   ⎱ *Explanation:* Page number left blank because not yet known.

Permanent ⎰ *Sprint Corporation and Subsidiaries,* 108 T.C. 384 (1997).
Citation   ⎱ *Explanation:* Page number now available.

Both citations tell us that the case will ultimately appear in Volume 108 of the *Tax Court of the United States Reports*. But until this volume is bound and made available to the general public, the page number must be left blank. Instead, the temporary citation identifies the case as being the 4th Regular decision issued by the Tax Court since Volume 107 ended. With this information, the decision can easily be located in either of the special Tax Court services published by Commerce Clearing House (now owned by the Dutch company Wolter Klower) or Research Institute of America (formerly by Prentice-Hall). Once Volume 108 is released, the permanent citation can be substituted and the number of the case dropped.

Before 1943, the Tax Court was called the Board of Tax Appeals, and its decisions were published as the *United States Board of Tax Appeals Reports* (B.T.A.). These 47 volumes cover the period from 1924 to 1942. For example, the citation *Karl Pauli,* 11 B.T.A. 784 (1928) refers to the 11th volume of the *Board of Tax Appeals Reports,* page 784, issued in 1928.

If the IRS loses in a decision, it may indicate whether it agrees or disagrees with the results reached by the court by publishing an **acquiescence** ("A" or "Acq.") or **nonacquiescence** ("NA" or "Nonacq."), respectively. Until 1991, acquiescences and nonacquiescences were published only for certain Regular decisions of the Tax Court, but the IRS has expanded its acquiescence program to include other civil tax cases where guidance is helpful. The acquiescence or nonacquiescence is published in the *Internal Revenue Bulletin* and the *Cumulative Bulletin* as an *Action on Decision*. The IRS can retroactively revoke an acquiescence.

Most often the IRS issues nonacquiescences to adverse decisions that are not appealed. A nonacquiescence provides a warning to taxpayers that a similar case cannot be settled administratively. A taxpayer will incur fees and expenses appealing within the IRS even though the IRS may be unwilling to litigate a fact pattern similar to a nonacquiesce decision.[26]

Although Memorandum decisions are not published by the U.S. Government, they are published by Commerce Clearing House (CCH) and Research Institute of America (RIA [formerly by Prentice-Hall]). Consider, for example, the three different ways that *Jack D. Carr* can be cited:

> *Jack D. Carr,* T.C.Memo. 1985–19
> > The 19th Memorandum decision issued by the Tax Court in 1985.
>
> *Jack D. Carr,* 49 TCM 507
> > Page 507 of Vol. 49 of the CCH *Tax Court Memorandum Decisions.*
>
> *Jack D. Carr,* RIA T.C.Mem.Dec. ¶85,019
> > Paragraph 85,019 of the RIA *T.C. Memorandum Decisions.*

Note that the third citation contains the same information as the first. Thus, ¶85,019 indicates the following information about the case: year 1985, 19th T.C. Memo. decision.[27] Although the RIA citation does not specifically include a volume number, the paragraph citation indicates that the decision can be found in the 1985 volume of the RIA Memorandum decision service.

Judicial Citations—The U.S. District Court, Court of Federal Claims, and Courts of Appeals.

District Court, Court of Federal Claims, Court of Appeals, and Supreme Court decisions dealing with Federal tax matters are reported in both the CCH *U.S. Tax Cases* (USTC), and the RIA *American Federal Tax Reports* (AFTR) series. Federal District Court decisions, dealing with *both* tax and nontax issues, also are published by West Publishing Company in its *Federal Supplement Series*. The following examples illustrate three different ways of citing a District Court case:

> *Simons-Eastern Co. v. U.S.,* 73–1 USTC ¶9279 (D.Ct.Ga., 1972).
>
> *Explanation:* Reported in the first volume of the *U.S. Tax Cases* (USTC) published by Commerce Clearing House for calendar year 1973 (73–1) and located at paragraph 9279 (¶9279).
>
> *Simons-Eastern Co. v. U.S.,* 31 AFTR2d 73–640 (D.Ct.Ga., 1972).
>
> *Explanation:* Reported in the 31st volume of the second series of the *American Federal Tax Reports* (AFTR2d) published by RIA and beginning on page 640. The "73" preceding the page number indicates the year the case was published but is a designation used only in recent decisions.
>
> *Simons-Eastern Co. v. U.S.,* 354 F.Supp. 1003 (D.Ct.Ga., 1972).
>
> *Explanation:* Reported in the 354th volume of the *Federal Supplement Series* (F.Supp.) published by West Publishing Company and beginning on page 1003.

---

[26]G. W. Carter, "Nonacquiescence: Winning by Losing," *Tax Notes* (September 19, 1988): 1301–1307.

[27]In this text, the RIA citation for Memorandum decisions of the U.S. Tax Court is omitted. Thus, *Jack D. Carr* would be cited as 49 TCM 507, T.C.Memo. 1985–19.

In all of the preceding citations, note that the name of the case is the same (Simons-Eastern Co. being the taxpayer), as is the reference to the Federal District Court of Georgia (D.Ct.Ga.) and the year the decision was rendered (1972).[28]

Decisions of the Court of Federal Claims[29] and the Courts of Appeals are published in the USTCs, AFTRs, and a West Publishing Company reporter called the *Federal Second Series* (F.2d). Volume 999, published in 1993, is the last volume of the *Federal Second Series*. It is followed by the *Federal Third Series* (F.3d). Beginning with October 1982, the Court of Federal Claims decisions are published in another West Publishing Company reporter entitled the *Claims Court Reporter*. Beginning with Volume 27 on October 30, 1992, the name of the reporter changed to the *Federal Claims Reporter* (abbreviated as *Fed.Cl.*). The following examples illustrate the different forms:

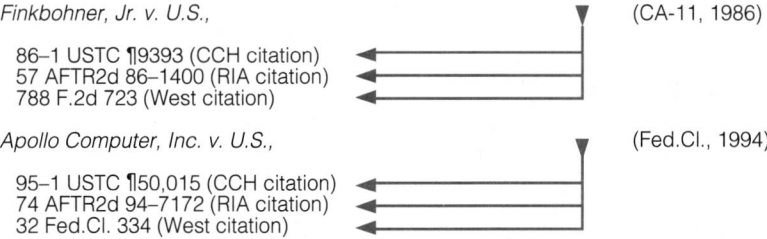

Note that *Finkbohner, Jr.* is a decision rendered by the Eleventh Court of Appeals in 1986 (CA–11, 1986), while *Apollo Computer, Inc.* was issued by the Court of Federal Claims in 1994 (Fed.Cl., 1994).

Judicial Citations—The U.S. Supreme Court.

Like all other Federal tax decisions (except those rendered by the Tax Court), Supreme Court decisions are published by Commerce Clearing House in the USTCs and by RIA (formerly by Prentice-Hall) in the AFTRs. The U.S. Government Printing Office also publishes these decisions in the *United States Supreme Court Reports* (U.S.) as does West Publishing Company in its *Supreme Court Reporter* (S.Ct.) and the Lawyer's Co-operative Publishing Company in its *United States Reports, Lawyer's Edition* (L.Ed.). The following illustrates the different ways the same decision can be cited:

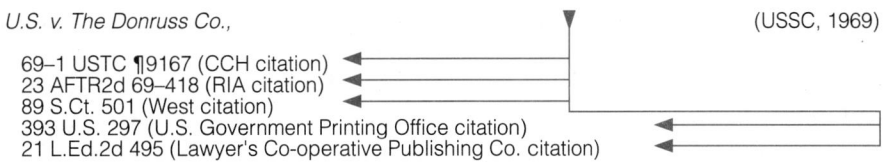

The parenthetical reference (USSC, 1969) identifies the decision as having been rendered by the U.S. Supreme Court in 1969. In this text, the citations of Supreme

---

[28]In this text, the case would be cited in the following form: *Simons-Eastern Co. v. U.S.*, 73–1 USTC ¶9279, 31 AFTR2d 73–640, 354 F.Supp. 1003 (D.Ct.Ga., 1972). Prentice-Hall Information Services is now owned by Research Institute of America. Although recent volumes contain the RIA imprint, many of the older volumes continue to have the P-H imprint.

[29]Before October 29, 1992, the Court of Federal Claims was called the Claims Court. Before October 1, 1982, the Court of Federal Claims was called the Court of Claims.

Judicial Sources

Court	Location	Authority
U.S. Supreme Court	S.Ct. Series (West) U.S. Series (U.S. Gov't.) L.Ed. (Lawyer's Co-op.) AFTR (RIA) USTC (CCH)	Highest authority
U.S. Courts of Appeal	Federal 3d (West) AFTR (RIA) USTC (CCH)	Next highest appellate court
Tax Court (Regular decisions)	U.S. Govt. Printing Office, RIA/CCH separate services	Highest trial court*
Tax Court (Memorandum decisions)	RIA T.C.Memo. (RIA) TCM (CCH)	Less authority than Regular T.C. decision
U.S. Court of Federal Claims**	Federal Claims Reporter (West) AFTR (RIA) USTC (CCH)	Similar authority as Tax Court
U.S. District Courts	F.Supp. Series (West) AFTR (RIA) USTC (CCH)	Lowest trial court
Small Cases Division of Tax Court	Not published	No precedent value

*Theoretically, the Tax Court, Court of Federal Claims, and District Courts are on the same level of authority. But some people believe that since the Tax Court hears and decides tax cases from all parts of the country (it is a national court), its decisions may be more authoritative than a Court of Federal Claims or District Court decision.
**Before October 29, 1992, the U.S. Claims Court.

Court decisions will be limited to the CCH (USTC), RIA (AFTR), and West (S.Ct.) versions. For a summary, see Concept Summary 2–2.

WORKING WITH THE TAX LAW— TAX RESEARCH

3 LEARNING OBJECTIVE
Understand the tax research process.

Tax research is the method by which a tax practitioner, student, or professor determines the best available solution to a situation that possesses tax consequences. In other words, it is the process of finding a competent and professional conclusion to a tax problem. The problem may originate from completed or proposed transactions. In the case of a completed transaction, the objective of the research is to determine the tax result of what has already taken place. For example, was the expenditure incurred by the taxpayer deductible or not deductible for tax purposes? When dealing with proposed transactions, the tax research process is directed toward the determination of possible tax consequences. To the extent that tax research leads to a choice of alternatives or otherwise influences the future actions of the taxpayer, it becomes the key to effective tax planning.

▼ **FIGURE 2–3**
Tax Research Process

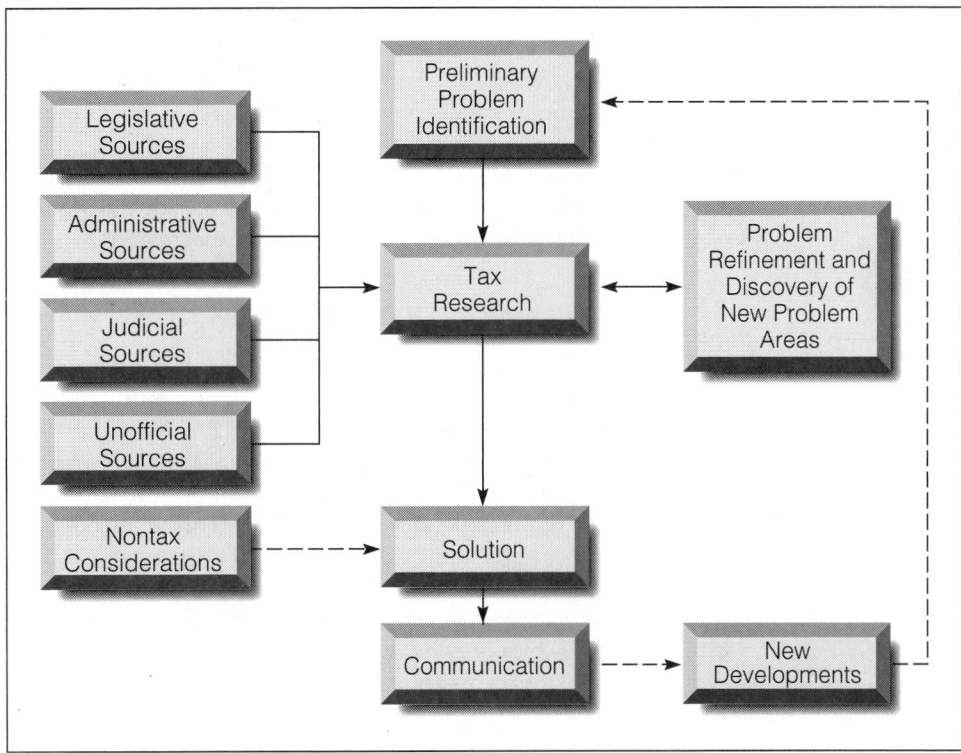

Tax research involves the following procedures:

- Identifying and refining the problem.
- Locating the appropriate tax law sources.
- Assessing the validity of the tax law sources.
- Arriving at the solution or at alternative solutions with due consideration given to nontax factors.
- Effectively communicating the solution to the taxpayer or the taxpayer's representative.
- Following up on the solution (where appropriate) in light of new developments.

These procedures are diagrammed in Figure 2–3. The broken lines reflect the steps of particular interest when tax research is directed toward proposed, rather than completed, transactions.

IDENTIFYING THE PROBLEM

Problem identification must start with a compilation of the relevant facts involved.[30] In this regard, *all* of the facts that may have a bearing on the problem must be gathered because any omission could modify the solution to be reached. To illustrate, consider what appears to be a very simple problem.

---

[30]For an excellent discussion of the critical role of facts in carrying out tax research, see Ray M. Sommerfeld and G. Fred Streuling, *Tax Research Techniques*, Tax Study No. 5 (New York: The American Institute of Certified Public Accountants, 1981), Chapter 2.

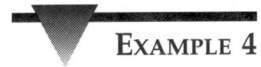

EXAMPLE 4

Early in December, Fred and Megan review their financial and tax situation with their son, Sam, and daughter-in-law, Dana. Fred and Megan are in the 28% tax bracket. Both Sam and Dana are age 21. Sam, a student at a nearby university, owns some publicly traded stock that he inherited from his grandmother. A current sale would result in approximately $7,000 of gross income. At this point, Fred and Megan provide about 55% of Sam and Dana's support. Although neither is now employed, Sam has earned $960 and Dana has earned $900. The problem: Should the stock be sold, and would the sale prohibit Fred and Megan from claiming Sam and Dana as dependents? ▼

REFINING THE PROBLEM

Initial reaction is that Fred and Megan in Example 4 could *not* claim Sam and Dana as dependents if the stock is sold, since Sam would then have earned more than the exemption amount under § 151(d).[31] However, Sam is a full-time student, and § 151(c)(1)(B) allows a son or daughter who is a full-time student and is under age 24 to earn more than the exemption amount without penalizing the parents with the loss of the dependency exemption. Thus, Sam could sell the stock without penalizing the parents with respect to the gross income test. However, the $7,000 income from the sale of the stock might lead to the failure of the greater-than-50 percent support test, depending on how much Sam spends for his (or Dana's) support.

Assume, however, that further fact gathering reveals the following additional information:

- Sam does not really need to spend the proceeds from the sale of the stock.
- Sam receives a sizable portion of his own support from a scholarship.

With these new facts, additional research leads to § 152(d) and Reg. § 1.152–1(c), which indicate that a scholarship received by a student is not included for purposes of computing whether the parents furnished more than one-half of the child's support. Further, if Sam does not spend the proceeds from the sale of stock, the unexpended amount is not counted for purposes of the support test. Thus, it appears that the parents would not be denied the dependency exemptions for Sam and Dana.

LOCATING THE APPROPRIATE TAX LAW SOURCES

Once the problem is clearly defined, what is the next step? Although the next step is a matter of individual judgment, most tax research begins with the index volume of the tax service, a keyword search on an on-line tax service, or a CD-ROM search (see the subsequent discussion of Electronic Tax Research). If the problem is not complex, the researcher may bypass the tax service or on-line service and turn directly to the Internal Revenue Code and Treasury Regulations. For the beginner, the latter procedure saves time and will solve many of the more basic problems. If the researcher does not have a personal copy of the Code or Regulations, resorting to the appropriate volume(s) of a tax service will be necessary.[32] The major tax services available are as follows:

Standard Federal Tax Reporter, Commerce Clearing House.

United States Tax Reporter, Research Institute of America (entitled *Federal Taxes* prior to July 1992).

---

[31]See the related discussion in Chapter 3.

[32]Several of the major tax services publish paperback editions of the Code and Treasury Regulations that can be purchased at modest prices. These editions are usually revised twice each year. For an annotated and abridged version of the Code and Regulations that is published annually, see James E. Smith, *West's Internal Revenue Code of 1986 and Treasury Regulations: Annotated and Selected* (St. Paul, Minn.: West Publishing Company, 1998).

Federal Tax Coordinator 2d, Research Institute of America.

Tax Management Portfolios, Bureau of National Affairs.

Rabkin and Johnson, *Federal Income, Gift and Estate Taxation*, Matthew Bender, Inc.

CCH's Federal Tax Service, Commerce Clearing House.

Mertens Law of Federal Income Taxation, Callaghan and Co.

Working with the Tax Services. In this text, it is not feasible to teach the use of any particular tax service; this ability can be obtained only by practice.[33] However, several important observations about the use of tax services cannot be overemphasized. First, never forget to check for current developments. The main text of any service is not revised frequently enough to permit reliance on that portion as the *latest* word on any subject. Where current developments can be found depends, of course, on which service is being used. Commerce Clearing House's *Standard Federal Tax Reporter* service contains a special volume devoted to current matters. Both RIA's *U.S. Tax Reporter* and *Federal Tax Coordinator 2d* integrate the new developments into the body of the service throughout the year. Second, when dealing with a tax service synopsis of a Treasury Department pronouncement or a judicial decision, remember there is no substitute for the original source.

To illustrate, do not base a conclusion solely on a tax service's commentary on *Simons-Eastern Co. v. U.S.*[34] If the case is vital to the research, look it up. The facts of the case may be distinguishable from those involved in the problem being researched. This is not to say that the case synopsis contained in the tax service is wrong; it might just be misleading or incomplete.

Tax Periodicals. The various tax periodicals are another source of tax information. The best way to locate a journal article pertinent to a tax problem is through Commerce Clearing House's *Federal Tax Articles*. This multivolume service includes a subject index, a Code Section number index, and an author's index. The RIA (formerly P-H) tax service also has a topical "Index to Tax Articles" section that is organized using the RIA paragraph index system. Also, beginning in 1992, *The Accounting & Tax Index* is available in three quarterly issues plus a cumulative year-end volume covering all four quarters. The original *Accountant's Index* started in 1921 and ended in 1991.

The following are some of the more useful tax periodicals:

The Journal of Taxation
Warren, Gorham and Lamont
31 St. James Avenue
Boston, MA 02116

The International Tax Journal
Panel Publishers
14 Plaza Road
Greenvale, NY 11548

Tax Law Review
Warren, Gorham and Lamont
31 St. James Avenue
Boston, MA 02116

TAXES—The Tax Magazine
Commerce Clearing House, Inc.
2700 Lake Cook Road
Riverwood, IL 60015

Trusts and Estates
6151 Powers Ferry Road NW
Atlanta, GA 30339

National Tax Journal
5310 East Main Street
Columbus, OH 43213

---

[33]The representatives of the various tax services are prepared to provide the users of their services with printed booklets and individual instruction on the use of the materials.

[34]Refer to Footnote 28.

Oil, Gas, and Energy Quarterly
Matthew Bender & Co.
2 Park Avenue
New York, NY 10016

The Practical Accountant
11 Penn Plaza
New York, NY 10001

Estate Planning
Warren, Gorham and Lamont
31 St. James Avenue
Boston, MA 02116

Taxation for Accountants
Warren, Gorham and Lamont
31 St. James Avenue
Boston, MA 02116

The Tax Executive
1001 Pennsylvania Avenue NW
Suite 320
Washington, D.C. 20004

Tax Notes
6830 Fairfax Drive
Arlington, VA 22213

The Tax Adviser
AICPA
1211 Avenue of the Americas
New York, NY 10036

Journal of Taxation for Individuals
Warren, Gorham and Lamont
31 St. James Avenue
Boston, MA 02116

The Tax Lawyer
American Bar Association
750 N. Lake Shore Drive
Chicago, IL 60611

Journal of the American Taxation Association
American Accounting Association
5717 Bessie Drive
Sarasota, FL 34233

Journal of Corporate Taxation
Warren, Gorham and Lamont
31 St. James Avenue
Boston, MA 02116

ASSESSING THE VALIDITY OF THE TAX LAW SOURCES

Once a source has been located, the next step is to assess it in light of the problem at hand. Proper assessment involves careful interpretation of the tax law with consideration given to its relevance and validity. In connection with validity, an important step is to check for recent changes in the tax law.

Interpreting the Internal Revenue Code.   The language of the Code can be extremely difficult to comprehend fully. For example, a subsection [§ 341(e)] relating to collapsible corporations contains *one* sentence of more than 450 words (twice as many as in the Gettysburg Address). Within this same subsection is another sentence of 300 words. Research has shown that in one-third of the conflicts reaching the Tax Court, the Court could not discern the intent of Congress by simply reading the statute. Yet the overriding attitude of the Tax Court judges is that the statute comes first. Even when the statute is unworkable, the Court will not rewrite the law.[35]

Assessing the Validity of a Treasury Regulation.   It is often stated that Treasury Regulations have the force and effect of law. This statement is certainly true for most Regulations, but some judicial decisions have held a Regulation or a portion thereof invalid. When a court holds a Regulation invalid, it usually does so on the ground that the Regulation is contrary to the intent of Congress when it enacted a particular Code Section. Most often the courts do not question the

---

[35]T. L. Kirkpatrick and W. B. Pollard, "Reliance by the Tax Court on the Legislative Intent of Congress," *The Tax Executive* (Summer 1986): 358–359.

INTERNAL REVENUE CODE: INTERPRETATION PITFALLS

One author has noted 10 common pitfalls in interpreting the Code:

1. Determine the limitations and exceptions to a provision. Do not permit the language of the Code Section to carry greater or lesser weight than was intended.
2. Just because a Section fails to mention an item does not necessarily mean that the item is excluded.
3. Read definitional clauses carefully.
4. Do not overlook small words such as *and* and *or*. There is a world of difference between these two words.
5. Read the Code Section completely; do not jump to conclusions.
6. Watch out for cross-referenced and related provisions, since many Sections of the Code are interrelated.
7. At times Congress is not careful when reconciling new Code provisions with existing Sections. Conflicts among Sections, therefore, do arise.
8. Be alert for hidden definitions; terms in a particular Code Section may be defined in the same Section or in a separate Section.
9. Some answers may not be found in the Code; therefore, a researcher may have to consult the Regulations and/or judicial decisions.
10. Take careful note of measuring words such as *less than 50 percent*, *more than 50 percent*, and *at least 80 percent*.

SOURCE: Adapted by permission from Henry G. Wong, "Ten Common Pitfalls in Reading the Internal Revenue Code," *Journal of Business Strategy*, July–August 1972, pp. 30–33. Reprinted with permission by Faulkner & Gray, Inc., 11 Penn Plaza, New York, NY 10001.

validity of Regulations because of the belief that "the first administrative interpretation of a provision as it appears in a new act often expresses the general understanding of the times or the actual understanding of those who played an important part when the statute was drafted."[36]

Keep the following observations in mind when assessing the validity of a Regulation:

- IRS agents must give the Code and the Regulations issued thereunder equal weight when dealing with taxpayers and their representatives.
- Proposed Regulations provide a preview of future final Regulations, but they are not binding on the IRS or taxpayers.
- In a challenge, the burden of proof is on the taxpayer to show that the Regulation is wrong. However, a court may invalidate a Regulation that varies from the language of the statute and has no support in the Committee Reports.
- If the taxpayer loses the challenge, a 20 percent negligence penalty may be imposed.[37] This accuracy-related penalty applies to any failure to make a reasonable attempt to comply with the tax law and any disregard of rules and regulations.[38]

[36]*Augustus v. Comm.*, 41–1 USTC ¶9255, 26 AFTR 612, 118 F.2d 38 (CA–6, 1941).

[37]§§ 6662(a) and (b)(1).
[38]§ 6662(c).

- Final Regulations tend to be legislative, interpretive, or procedural. **Procedural Regulations** neither establish tax laws nor attempt to explain tax laws. Procedural Regulations are *housekeeping-type instructions* indicating information that taxpayers should provide the IRS as well as information about the internal management and conduct of the IRS itself.
- Some **interpretive Regulations** merely reprint or rephrase what Congress stated in the Committee Reports that were issued when the tax legislation was enacted. Such Regulations are *hard* and *solid* and almost impossible to overturn because they clearly reflect the intent of Congress. An interpretive Regulation is given less deference than a legislative Regulation, however. The Supreme Court has told lower courts to analyze Treasury Regulations carefully before accepting the Treasury's interpretation.[39]
- In some Code Sections, Congress has given the *Secretary or his delegate* the authority to prescribe Regulations to carry out the details of administration or to otherwise complete the operating rules. Under such circumstances, it could almost be said that Congress is delegating its legislative powers to the Treasury Department. Regulations issued pursuant to this type of authority truly possess the force and effect of law and are often called **legislative Regulations** (e.g., consolidated return Regulations).
- Courts tend to apply a legislative reenactment doctrine. A particular Regulation is assumed to have received congressional approval if the Regulation was finalized many years earlier and Congress has not amended the Code Section pertaining to that Regulation.

Assessing the Validity of Other Administrative Sources of the Tax Law. Revenue Rulings issued by the IRS carry less weight than Treasury Department Regulations. Revenue Rulings are important, however, in that they reflect the position of the IRS on tax matters. In any dispute with the IRS on the interpretation of tax law, therefore, taxpayers should expect agents to follow the results reached in any applicable Revenue Rulings. A 1986 Tax Court decision, however, indicated that Revenue Rulings "typically do not constitute substantive authority for a position."[40] Most Revenue Rulings apply retroactively unless a specific statement indicates the extent to which a ruling is to be applied without retroactive effect.[41]

Actions on Decisions further tell the taxpayer the IRS's reaction to certain court decisions and Revenue Rulings. Recall that the IRS follows a practice of either acquiescing (agreeing) or nonacquiescing (not agreeing) with selected decisions. A nonacquiescence does not mean that a particular court decision is of no value, but it does indicate that the IRS will continue to litigate the issue involved.

Assessing the Validity of Judicial Sources of the Tax Law. The judicial process as it relates to the formulation of tax law has already been described. How much reliance can be placed on a particular decision depends upon the following variables:

- The level of the court. A decision rendered by a trial court (e.g., a Federal District Court) carries less weight than one issued by an appellate court (e.g., the Fifth Court of Appeals). Unless Congress changes the Code, decisions by the U.S. Supreme Court represent the last word on any tax issue.

---

[39]*U.S. v. Vogel Fertilizer Co.*, 82–1 USTC ¶9134, 49 AFTR2d 82–491, 102 S.Ct. 821 (USSC, 1982); *National Muffler Dealers Assn., Inc.*, 79–1 USTC ¶9264, 43 AFTR2d 79–828, 99 S.Ct. 1304 (USSC, 1979).

[40]*Nelda C. Stark*, 86 T.C. 243 (1986). See also *Ann R. Neuhoff*, 75 T.C. 36 (1980). For a different opinion, however, see *Industrial Valley Bank & Trust Co.*, 66 T.C. 272 (1976).

[41]Rev.Proc. 87–1, 1987–1 C.B. 503.

- The legal residence of the taxpayer. If, for example, a taxpayer lives in Texas, a decision of the Fifth Court of Appeals means more than one rendered by the Second Court of Appeals. This result occurs because any appeal from a U.S. District Court or the Tax Court would be to the Fifth Court of Appeals and not to the Second Court of Appeals.[42]
- A Tax Court Regular decision carries more weight than a Memorandum decision since the Tax Court does not consider Memorandum decisions to be binding precedents.[43] Furthermore, a Tax Court *reviewed* decision carries even more weight. All of the Tax Court judges participate in a reviewed decision.
- A Circuit Court decision where certiorari has been requested and denied by the U.S. Supreme Court carries more weight than a Circuit Court decision that was not appealed. A Circuit Court decision heard *en banc* (all the judges participate) carries more weight than a normal Circuit Court case.
- Whether the decision represents the weight of authority on the issue. In other words, is it supported by the results reached by other courts?
- The outcome or status of the decision on appeal. For example, was the decision appealed and, if so, with what result?

In connection with the last two variables, the use of a citator is invaluable to tax research.[44] Citators and their use are discussed in Appendix E.

Assessing the Validity of Other Sources. *Primary sources* of tax law include the Constitution, legislative history materials, statutes, treaties, Treasury Regulations, IRS pronouncements, and judicial decisions. In general, the IRS considers only primary sources to constitute substantial authority. However, a researcher might wish to refer to *secondary materials* such as legal periodicals, treatises, legal opinions, General Counsel Memoranda, and written determinations. In general, secondary sources are not authority.

Until 1990, the IRS considered only primary sources to constitute substantial authority. In Notice 90–20,[45] the IRS expanded the list of substantial authority *for purposes of* the accuracy-related penalty in § 6662 to include a number of secondary materials (e.g., letter rulings, General Counsel Memoranda, the Bluebook). As under former § 6661, "authority" does not include conclusions reached in treatises, legal periodicals, and opinions rendered by tax professionals.

A letter ruling or determination letter is substantial authority only for the taxpayer to whom it is issued, except as noted above with respect to the accuracy-related penalty.

Upon the completion of major tax legislation, the staff of the Joint Committee on Taxation (in consultation with the staffs of the House Ways and Means and Senate Finance Committees) often will prepare a General Explanation of the Act, commonly known as the Bluebook because of the color of its cover. The IRS will not accept this detailed explanation as having legal effect, except as noted above with respect to the accuracy-related penalty. The Bluebook does, however, provide valuable guidance to tax advisers and taxpayers until Regulations are issued, and some letter rulings and General Counsel Memoranda of the IRS cite its explanations.

ARRIVING AT THE SOLUTION OR AT ALTERNATIVE SOLUTIONS

Example 4 raised the question of whether a taxpayer would be denied dependency exemptions for a son and a daughter-in-law if the son sold some stock

---

[42]Before October 1, 1982, an appeal from the then-named U.S. Court of Claims (the other trial court) was directly to the U.S. Supreme Court.

[43]*Severino R. Nico, Jr.*, 67 T.C. 647 (1977).

[44]The major citators are published by Commerce Clearing House, RIA, and Shepard's Citations, Inc.

[45]1990–1 C.B. 328; see also Reg. § 1.6661–3(b)(2).

near the end of the year. A refinement of the problem supplies additional information:

- Sam was a full-time student during four calendar months of the year.
- Sam and Dana anticipate filing a joint return.

Additional research leads to Regulation § 1.151-3(b), which indicates that to qualify as a student, Sam must be a full-time student during each of *five* calendar months of the year at an educational institution. Thus, proceeds from Sam's sale of the stock would cause his parents to lose at least one dependency exemption because Sam's gross income would exceed the exemption amount. The parents still might be able to claim Dana as an exemption if the support test is met.

Section 151(c)(2) indicates that a supporting taxpayer is not permitted a dependency exemption for a married dependent if the married individual files a joint return. Initial reaction is that a joint return by Sam and Dana would be disastrous to the parents. However, more research uncovers two Revenue Rulings that provide an exception if neither the dependent nor the dependent's spouse is required to file a return but does so solely to claim a refund of tax withheld. The IRS asserts that each spouse must have gross income of less than the exemption amount.[46] Therefore, if Sam sells the stock and he and Dana file a joint return, the parents would lose the dependency exemption for both Sam and Dana.

If the stock is not sold until January, both exemptions may still be available to the parents. However, under § 151(d)(2) a personal exemption is not available to a taxpayer who can be claimed as a dependent by another taxpayer (whether actually claimed or not). Thus, if the parents can claim Sam and Dana as dependents, Sam and Dana would lose their personal exemptions on their tax return.

COMMUNICATING TAX RESEARCH

4   LEARNING OBJECTIVE
Communicate the results of the tax research process in a client letter and a tax file memorandum.

Once satisfied that the problem has been researched adequately, the researcher may need to prepare a memo, letter, or oral presentation setting forth the result. The form such a communication takes could depend on a number of considerations. For example, does an employer or professor recommend a particular procedure or format for tax research memos? Is the memo to be given directly to the client or will it first go to the researcher's employer? Who is the audience for the oral presentation? How long should you talk? Whatever form it takes, a good tax research communication should contain the following elements:

- A clear statement of the issue.
- In more complex situations, a short review of the fact pattern that raises the issue.
- A review of the controlling tax law sources (e.g., Code, Regulations, Revenue Rulings, judicial authority).
- Any assumptions made in arriving at the solution.
- The solution recommended and the logic or reasoning supporting it.
- The references consulted in the research process.

In short, a good tax research communication should tell the audience what was researched, the results of that research, and the justification for the recommendation made.[47]

---

[46]Rev.Rul. 54–567, 1954–2 C.B. 108; Rev.Rul. 65–34, 1965–1 C.B. 86.
[47]See Chapter 6 of the publication cited in Footnote 30. For oral presentations, see W.A. Raabe and G.E. Whittenburg, "Talking Tax: How to Make a Tax Presentation," The Tax Adviser (March, 1997): 179-182.

Illustrations of the memos for the tax file and the client letter associated with Example 4 appear in Figures 2–4, 2–5, and 2–6.

▼ **FIGURE 2–4**
Tax File Memorandum

August 16, 1998

TAX FILE MEMORANDUM

FROM: John J. Jones

SUBJECT: Fred and Megan Taxpayer
           Engagement: Issues

Today I talked to Fred Taxpayer with respect to his August 14, 1998 letter requesting tax assistance. He wishes to know if his son, Sam, can sell stock worth $19,000 (basis = $12,000) without the parents losing the dependency exemptions for Sam and Sam's wife, Dana.

Fred Taxpayer is married to Megan, and Sam is a full-time student at a local university. Sam inherited the stock from his grandmother about five years ago. If he sells the stock, he will save the proceeds from the sale. Sam does not need to spend the proceeds if he sells the stock because he receives a $3,000 scholarship that he uses for his own support (i.e., to pay for tuition, books, and fees). Fred and Megan are in the 28% tax bracket and furnish approximately 55% of Sam and Dana's support.

ISSUE: If the stock is sold, would the sale prohibit Fred and Megan from claiming Sam and Dana as dependents? I told Fred that we would have an answer for him within two weeks.

▼ **FIGURE 2–5**
Tax File Memorandum

August 26, 1998

TAX FILE MEMORANDUM

FROM: John J. Jones

SUBJECT: Fred and Megan Taxpayer
           Engagement: Conclusions

Section 152(a) provides that in order for a taxpayer to take a dependency exemption, the taxpayer must provide over 50% of the support of the potential dependent. Fred and Megan provide about 55% of the support of their son, Sam, and their daughter-in-law, Dana. If Sam should sell the stock in 1998, he would not need to spend the proceeds for support purposes (i.e., would save the proceeds). Thus, the stock sale would not affect his qualifying for the support test. In calculating the percentage of support provided by Fred and Megan, a $3,000 scholarship received by Sam is not counted in determining the amount of support Sam provides for himself [see Reg. § 1.152–1(c)].

Section 151(c)(1) provides that in order to qualify for a dependency exemption, the potential dependent's gross income must be less than the exemption amount (i.e., $2,700 in 1998). Without the stock sale, the gross income of both Sam ($960) and Dana ($900) will be below the exemption amount in 1998. The $3,000 Sam receives as a scholarship is excluded from his gross income under § 117(a) because he uses the entire amount to pay for his tuition, books, and fees at a local university.

The key issue then is whether the stock, which will generate $7,000 gain for Sam, will cause the gross income test to be violated. The gain will increase Sam's gross income to $7,960 ($7,000 + $960). However, § 151(c)(1)(B) permits a child's gross income to exceed the exemption amount if the child is a student under the age of 24. Under Reg. § 1.151–3(b), to qualify as a student, the person must be a full-time student during each of five calendar months. A telephone call to Megan provided the information that Sam was a student for only four months in 1998. Thus, since Sam is not eligible for the student exception, the sale of the stock by Sam in 1998 would result in Fred and Megan losing the dependency exemption for Sam.

The stock sale would also result in the loss of the dependency exemption for Dana if Sam and Dana file a joint return for 1998 [see § 151(c)(2)].

From a tax planning perspective, Sam should not sell the stock until 1999. This will enable Fred and Megan to claim dependency exemptions on their 1998 return for Sam and Dana. Note, however, that neither Sam nor Dana will be permitted to take a personal exemption deduction on their 1998 tax return since they are claimed as dependents on someone else's return [see § 151(d)(2)]. However, this will not produce any negative tax consequences since their tax liability will be zero if the stock is not sold in 1998.

▼ **FIGURE 2–6**
Client Letter

Hoffman, Smith, and Willis, CPAs
5101 Madison Road
Cincinnati, Ohio 45227

August 30, 1998

Mr. and Ms. Fred Taxpayer
111 Boulevard
Williamsburg, Virginia 23185

Dear Mr. and Ms. Taxpayer:

This letter is in response to your request for us to review your family's financial and tax situation. Our conclusions are based upon the facts as outlined in your August 14th letter. Any change in the facts may affect our conclusions.

You provide over 50% of the support for your son, Sam, and his wife, Dana. The scholarship Sam receives is not included in determining support. If the stock is not sold, you will qualify for a dependency exemption for both Sam and Dana.

However, if the stock is sold, a gain of approximately $7,000 will result. This amount will result in the gross income requirement being violated (i.e., potential dependent's gross income must not exceed $2,700) for Sam. Therefore, you will not qualify to receive a dependency exemption for Sam. In addition, if Sam sells the stock and he and Dana file a joint return, you also will not qualify for a dependency exemption for Dana.

From a tax planning perspective, Sam should not sell the stock in 1998. Delaying the stock sale will enable you to claim dependency exemptions for both Sam and Dana. If the stock is sold, Sam and Dana should not file a joint return. This will still enable you to qualify for a dependency exemption for Dana.

Should you need more information or need to clarify our conclusions, do not hesitate to contact me.

Sincerely yours,

John J. Jones, CPA
Partner

WORKING WITH THE TAX LAW— TAX PLANNING

5   LEARNING OBJECTIVE
Apply tax research techniques and planning procedures.

Tax research and tax planning are inseparable. The *primary* purpose of effective *tax planning* is to reduce the taxpayer's total tax bill. This statement does not mean that the course of action selected must produce the lowest possible tax under the circumstances. The minimization of tax liability must be considered in context with the legitimate business goals of the taxpayer.

A *secondary* objective of effective tax planning is to reduce or defer the tax in the current tax year. Specifically, this objective aims to accomplish one or more of the following: eradicating the tax entirely; eliminating the tax in the current year; deferring the receipt of income; converting ordinary income into capital gains; converting active to passive income; converting passive to active expense; proliferating taxpayers (i.e., forming partnerships and corporations or making lifetime gifts to family members); eluding double taxation; avoiding ordinary income; or creating, increasing, or accelerating deductions. However, this second objective should be approached with considerable reservation and moderation. For example, a tax election in one year may reduce taxes currently, but saddle future years with a disadvantageous tax position.

NONTAX CONSIDERATIONS

There is an honest danger that tax motivations may take on a significance that does not correspond to the true values involved. In other words, tax considerations may impair the exercise of sound business judgment by the taxpayer. Thus, the tax planning process can become a medium through which to accomplish ends that are socially and economically objectionable. All too often, planning seems to lean toward the opposing extremes of placing either too little or too much emphasis on tax considerations. The happy medium—a balance that recognizes the significance of taxes, but not beyond the point where planning detracts from the exercise of good business judgment—turns out to be the promised land that is too infrequently reached.

The remark is often made that a good rule is to refrain from pursuing any course of action that would not be followed were it not for certain tax considerations. This statement is not entirely correct, but it does illustrate the desirability of preventing business logic from being *sacrificed at the altar of tax planning*.

TAX AVOIDANCE AND TAX EVASION

A fine line exists between legal tax planning and illegal tax planning—tax avoidance versus tax evasion. **Tax avoidance** is merely tax minimization through legal techniques. In this sense, tax avoidance is the proper objective of all tax planning. Tax evasion, while also aimed at the elimination or reduction of taxes, connotes the use of subterfuge and fraud as a means to an end. Popular usage—probably because of the common goals involved—has so linked these two concepts that many individuals are no longer aware of the true distinctions between them. Consequently, some taxpayers have been deterred from properly taking advantage of planning possibilities. The now classic words of Judge Learned Hand in *Commissioner v. Newman* reflect the true values the taxpayer should have:

> Over and over again courts have said that there is nothing sinister in so arranging one's affairs as to keep taxes as low as possible. Everybody does so, rich or poor; and all do right, for nobody owes any public duty to pay more than the law demands: taxes are enforced extractions, not voluntary contributions. To demand more in the name of morals is mere cant.[48]

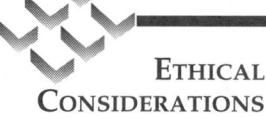

ETHICAL CONSIDERATIONS

Tax Avoidance

In a speech class, a philosophy student argues that tax advisers are immoral because they help people cheat the government. Each time a tax adviser shows a taxpayer a tax planning idea that reduces the client's liability, all other taxpayers have to pay more taxes. Society would be better off if all tax advisers would work at improving our environment or living conditions in the inner cities.

An accounting student argues that the primary purpose of tax planning is to reduce a taxpayer's overall liability. This advisory process can result in avoiding, deferring, or postponing the tax burden until the future. There is nothing illegal or immoral about tax avoidance.

[48]*Comm. v. Newman,* 47–1 USTC ¶9175, 35 AFTR 857, 159 F.2d 848 (CA–2, 1947).

Taxpayers have every legal right to be concerned about tax avoidance and to arrange their affairs so as to pay no more taxes than the law demands. There is no difference between reducing a tax expense through the help of a tax adviser and reducing a cost of operating a business with the aid of a cost accountant.

Comment on each student's position.

FOLLOW-UP PROCEDURES

Because tax planning usually involves a proposed (as opposed to a completed) transaction, it is predicated upon the continuing validity of the advice based upon the tax research. A change in the tax law (either legislative, administrative, or judicial) could alter the original conclusion. Additional research may be necessary to test the solution in light of current developments (refer to the broken lines at the right in Figure 2–3).

TAX PLANNING—A PRACTICAL APPLICATION

Returning to the facts of Example 4, what could be done to protect the dependency exemptions for the parents? If Sam and Dana were to refrain from filing a joint return, both could be claimed by the parents. This result assumes that the stock is not sold.

An obvious tax planning tool is the installment method. Could the securities be sold using the installment method under § 453 so that most of the gain is deferred into the next year? Under the installment method, certain gains may be postponed and recognized as the cash proceeds are received. The problem is that the installment method is not available for stock traded on an established securities market.[49]

A little more research, however, indicates that Sam might be able to sell the stock and postpone the recognition of gain until the following year by selling short an equal number of substantially identical shares and covering the short sale in the subsequent year with the shares originally held. Selling short means that Sam sells borrowed stock (substantially identical) and repays the lender with the stock held on the date of the short sale. This *short against the box* technique would allow Sam to protect his $7,000 profit and defer the closing of the sale until the following year.[50] However, additional research indicates that TRA of 1997 provides that the short against the box technique will no longer produce the desired postponement of recognized gain. That is, at the time of the short sale, Sam will have a recognized gain of $7,000 from a constructive sale. Note the critical role of obtaining the correct facts in attempting to resolve the proper strategy for the taxpayers.

Throughout this text, most chapters include observations on Tax Planning Considerations. Such observations are not all-inclusive but are intended to illustrate some of the ways in which the material covered can be effectively utilized to minimize taxes.

---

[49]See Chapter 18 for a discussion of installment sales.
[50]§§ 1233(a) and 1233(b)(2). See Chapter 16 for a discussion of short sales.

ELECTRONIC TAX RESEARCH

6 LEARNING OBJECTIVE
Have an awareness of electronic tax research.

Computer-based tax research tools now hold a prominent position in tax practice. Electronic tax resources allow the tax library to reflect the tax law itself, including its dynamic and daily changes. Nevertheless, using electronic means to locate tax law sources cannot substitute for developing and maintaining a thorough knowledge of the tax law or for logical and analytical review in addressing open tax research issues.

Accessing tax documents through electronic means offers several important advantages over a strictly paper-based approach:

- Materials generally are available to the practitioner faster through an electronic system, as delays related to typesetting, proofreading, production, and distribution of the new materials are streamlined.
- Some tax documents, such as so-called slip opinions of trial-level court cases and interviews with policymakers, are available only through electronic means.
- Commercial subscriptions to electronic tax services are likely to provide, at little or no cost, additional tax law sources to which the researcher would not have access through stand-alone purchases of traditional material. For example, the full text of private letter rulings are quite costly to acquire in a paper-based format, but electronic publishers may bundle the rulings with other materials for a reasonable cost.

Strict cost comparisons of paper and electronic tax research materials are difficult to construct, especially when the practitioner uses hardware, including workstations and communications equipment, that is already in place and employed elsewhere in the practice. Over time, though, the convenience, cost, and reliability of electronic research tools clearly will make them the dominant means of finding and analyzing the law in tax practice.

Using Electronic Services.   Tax researchers often use electronic means to find sources of the tax law. Usually, the law is found using one of the following strategies:

- *Search* various databases using keywords that are likely to be found in the underlying documents, as written by Congress, the judiciary, or administrative sources.
- *Link* to tax documents for which all or part of the proper citation is known.
- *Browse* the tax databases, examining various tables of contents and indexes in a traditional manner or using cross-references in the documents to jump from one tax law source to another.

Virtually all of the major commercial tax publishers and some of the primary sources of the law itself, such as the Supreme Court and some of the Courts of Appeals, now provide tax materials in electronic formats. Competitive pressures are forcing computer literacy upon tax practitioners, and the user-friendliness of the best of the tax search software is of great benefit to both the daily and the occasional user.

CD-ROM Services.   The CD has been a major source of electronic tax data for about a decade. Data compression techniques continue to allow more tax materials to fit on a single disk every year. CCH, RIA, WESTLAW and others offer vast tax libraries to the practitioner, often in conjunction with a subscription to traditional paper-based resources or accompanied by newsletters, training seminars, and ongoing technical support.

CD Tax Service	Description
CCH ACCESS	Includes the CCH tax service, primary sources including treatises, and other subscription materials. Ten to twenty disks.
RIA OnPoint	Includes the RIA topical *Coordinator* and the annotated tax service formerly provided by Prentice-Hall. The Citator has elaborate document-linking features, and major tax treatises also are provided. One to ten disks.
WESTLAW	Code, Regulations, *Cumulative Bulletins*, cases, citator, and editorial material. About a dozen disks.
Kleinrock's	A single disk with all tax statutory, administrative, and judicial law. Another single disk provides tax forms and instructions for Federal and state jurisdictions.

On-Line Service	Description
LEXIS/NEXIS	Federal and state statutory, administrative, and judicial material. Extensive libraries of newspapers, magazines, patent records, and medical and economic databases, both U.S. and foreign-based.
RIA	Includes the RIA tax services, major tax treatises, federal and state statutes, administrative documents, and court opinions. Extensive citator access, editorial material, and practitioner aids.
CCH	Includes the CCH tax service, primary sources including treatises, and other subscription materials. Tax and economic news sources, extensive editorial material, and practitioner support tools.
WESTLAW	Federal and state statutes, administrative documents, and court opinions. Extensive citator access, editorial material, and gateways to third-party publications. Extensive government document databases.

At its best, a CD-based tax library provides the archival data that make up a permanent, core library of tax documents. For about $200 a year, the tax CD is updated quarterly, providing more comprehensive tax resources than the researcher is ever likely to need. The CD is comparable in scope to a paper-based library of a decade ago costing perhaps $20,000 to establish and $5,000 per year in perpetuity to maintain. If the library is contained on a small number of disks, it also can offer portability through use on laptop computers. Exhibit 2–2 summarizes the most popular of the CD tax services on the market today.

On-Line Systems. An on-line research system allows a practitioner to obtain virtually instantaneous use of tax law sources by accessing the computer of the service provider. On-line services generally employ price-per-search cost structures, which can average close to $200 per hour, significantly higher than the cost of CD services. Thus, unless a practitioner can pass along related costs to clients or others, on-line searching generally is limited to the most important issues and to the researchers with the most experience and training in search techniques.

▼ **EXHIBIT 2–4**
The IRS *Digital Daily*

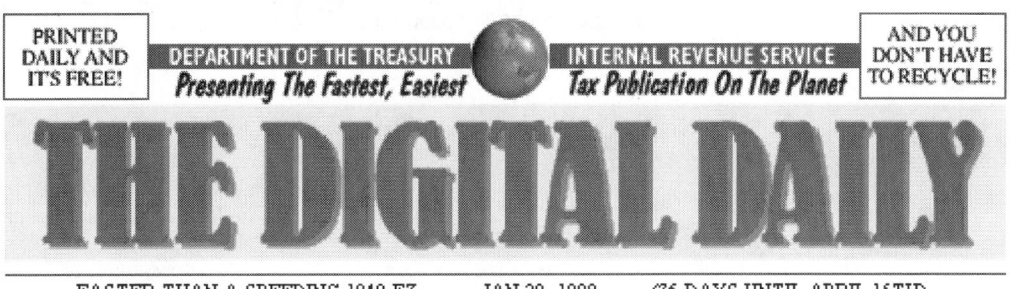

[Text Only Version]

IN TODAY'S ISSUE
....
Employment Opportunities

Famous Physicist Finds Fabulous Formula For E-File

Perhaps the best combination of electronic tax resources is to conduct day-to-day work on a CD system, so that the budget for the related work is known in advance, and augment the CD search with on-line access where it is judged to be critical. Exhibit 2–3 lists the most commonly used commercial on-line tax services.

The Internet. The Internet provides a wealth of tax information in several popular forms, sometimes at no direct cost to the researcher. Using so-called browser software that often is distributed with new computer systems and their communication devices, the tax professional can access information provided around the world that can aid the research process.

- *Home pages (sites) on the World Wide Web (WWW)* are provided by accounting and consulting firms, publishers, tax academics and libraries, and governmental bodies as a means of making information widely available or of soliciting subscriptions or consulting engagements. The best sites offer links to other sites and direct contact to the site providers. One of the best sites available to the tax practitioner is the Internal Revenue Service's *Digital Daily*, as illustrated in Exhibit 2–4. This site offers downloadable forms and

▼ **EXHIBIT 2–5**
Tax-Related Web Sites

Web Site	WWW Address at Press Date (Usually preceded by http://www.)	Description
Internal Revenue Service	**irs.gov/cover.html**	News releases, downloadable forms and instructions, tables, and E-mail
Court opinions	The site at **law.emory.edu/FEDCTS/** allows the researcher to link to the site of the jurisdiction (other than the Tax Court) that is the subject of the query (see Exhibit 2–6).	
Discussion groups moderated by Tax Analysts	**tax.org/notes**	Policy-oriented discussions of tax laws and proposals to change the law, links to student tax clinics, excerpts from the Tax Notes newsletter, and a tax calendar
Tax Sites Directory	**taxsites.com/**	References and links to tax sites on the Internet, including state and Federal tax sites, academic and professional pages, tax forms, and software
Tax laws on-line	Regulations are at **access.gpo.gov/nara/cfr/cfr-table-search.html**, and the Code is at **fourmilab.ch/ustax/ustax.html**	
Tax World	**omer.actg.uic.edu**	References and links to tax sites on the Internet, including property tax and international tax links
Commercial tax publishers	For instance, **riatax.com** and **cch.com**	Information about products and services available by subscription, newsletter excerpts
Large accounting firms and professional organizations	For instance, the AICPA's page is at **aicpa.org.**, an Ernst and Young Tax Services page is at **ey.com/default.stm**, and KPMG Peat Markwick is at **kpmg.com**	Tax planning newsletters, descriptions of services offered and career opportunities, and exchange of data with clients and subscribers
South-Western College Publishing	**swcollege.com/tax/tax.html**	Informational updates, newsletters, support materials for subscribers and adopters, and continuing education

Note: Caution: addresses change frequently.

instructions, "plain English" versions of Regulations, and news update items. Exhibit 2–5 lists some of the Web sites that may be most useful to tax researchers and their Internet addresses as of press date.

- *Newsgroups* provide a means by which information related to the tax law can be exchanged among taxpayers, tax professionals, and others who subscribe to the group's services. Newsgroup members can read the exchanges among other members and offer replies and suggestions to inquiries as desired. Discussions address the interpretation and application of existing

▼ **EXHIBIT 2–6**
The Emory *Federal Courts Finder*

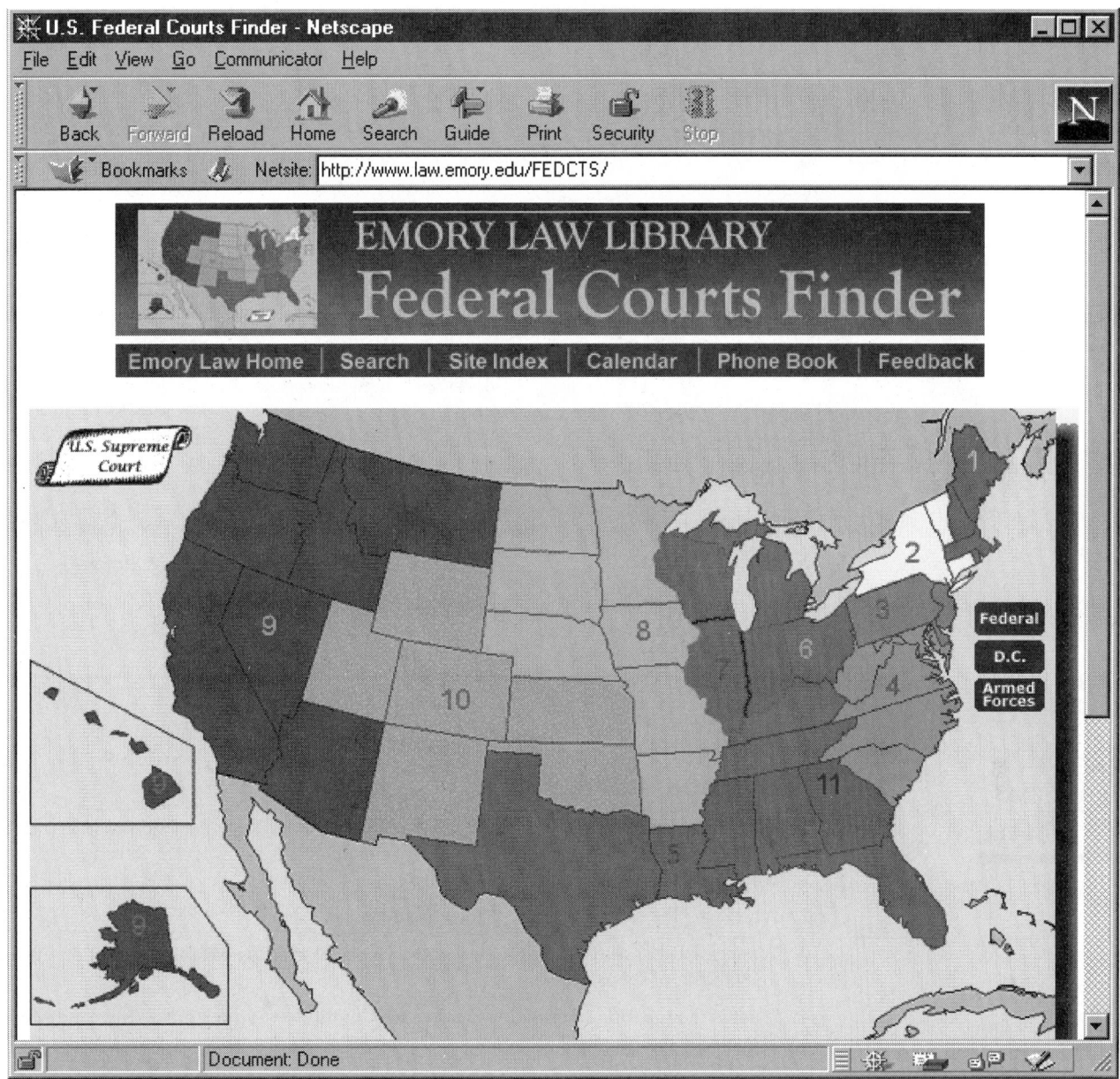

law, analysis of proposals and new pronouncements, and reviews of tax software.

- *E-mail capabilities* are available to most tax professionals through an employer's equipment or by a subscription providing Internet access at a low and usually fixed cost for the period. E-mail allows for virtually instantaneous sending and receiving of messages, letters, tax returns and supporting data, spreadsheets, and other documents necessary to solve tax problems.

In many situations, solutions to research problems will benefit from, or require, the use of various electronic tax research tools. A competent tax professional must become familiar and proficient with these tools and be able to use them to meet the expectations of clients and the necessities of work in the modern world.[51]

KEY TERMS

Acquiescence, 2–20

Circuit Court of Appeals, 2–15

Court of original jurisdiction, 2–13

Determination letters, 2–11

Federal District Court, 2–13

Finalized Regulations, 2–8

Interpretive Regulations, 2–28

Legislative Regulations, 2–28

Letter rulings, 2–11

Nonacquiescence, 2–20

Precedents, 2–16

Procedural Regulations, 2–28

Proposed Regulations, 2–8

Revenue Procedures, 2–10

Revenue Rulings, 2–9

Small Cases Division, 2–13

Tax avoidance, 2–33

Tax research, 2–22

Technical Advice Memoranda (TAMs), 2–12

Temporary Regulations, 2–9

U.S. Court of Federal Claims, 2–13

U.S. Supreme Court, 2–17

U.S. Tax Court, 2–13

Writ of Certiorari, 2–18

PROBLEM MATERIALS

DISCUSSION QUESTIONS

1. Judicial decisions interpreting a provision of the Internal Revenue Code of 1939 or 1954 are no longer of any value in view of the enactment of the Internal Revenue Code of 1986. Assess the validity of this statement.

2. When was the last time Congress codified the tax laws?

3. Tax legislation normally originates in the House Ways and Means Committee. Assess the validity of this statement.

4. What is the function of the Joint Conference Committee of the House Ways and Means Committee and the Senate Finance Committee?

5. Why are certain Code Section numbers missing from the Internal Revenue Code (e.g., §§ 6, 7, 8, 9, 10)?

6. Paul Jacobs operates a small international firm named Teal, Inc. A new treaty between the United States and Ukraine conflicts with a Section of the Internal Revenue Code. Paul asks you for advice. If he follows the treaty position, does he need to disclose this on his tax return? If he is required to disclose, are there any penalties for failure to disclose? Prepare a letter in which you respond to Paul. Teal's address is 100 International Drive, Tampa, FL 33620.

7. Interpret this Regulation citation: Reg. § 1.274–2(a)(1)(i).

---

[51]For a more detailed discussion of the use of electronic tax research in the modern tax practice, see W.A. Raabe, G.E. Whittenburg, and J. C. Bost, *West's Federal Tax Research,* 4th ed (St. Paul, Minn.: West Publishing Co., 1997).

8. Distinguish between legislative, interpretive, and procedural Regulations.

9. Distinguish between:
   a. Treasury Regulations and Revenue Rulings.
   b. Revenue Rulings and Revenue Procedures.
   c. Revenue Rulings and letter rulings.
   d. Letter rulings and determination letters.

10. Rank the following items from the highest authority to the lowest in the Federal tax law system:
    a. Interpretive Regulation.
    b. Legislative Regulation.
    c. Letter ruling.
    d. Revenue Procedure.
    e. Internal Revenue Code.
    f. Proposed Regulation.

11. Interpret each of the following citations:
    a. Rev.Rul. 65–235, 1965–2 C.B. 88.
    b. Rev.Proc. 87–56, 1987–2 C.B. 674.
    c. Ltr.Rul. 9046036.

12. Michelle Zull calls you on the phone. She says that she has found a 1988 letter ruling that agrees with a position she wishes to take on her tax return. She asks you about the precedential value of a letter ruling. Draft a memo for the tax files outlining what you told Michelle.

13. Edith is considering writing the IRS to determine if a proposed divisive reorganization would be tax-free. Outline some relevant tax issues Edith faces in making this decision.

14. a. What are Treasury Decisions (TDs)?
    b. What purpose do they serve?
    c. Where are they published?

15. What are the major differences between letter rulings and determination letters?

16. What is a Technical Advice Memorandum (TAM)?

17. Caleb receives a ninety-day letter after his discussion with an appeals officer. He is not satisfied with the $92,000 settlement offer. Identify the relevant tax research issues facing Caleb.

18. Which of the following would be considered advantages of the Small Cases Division of the Tax Court?
    a. Appeal to the U.S. Tax Court is possible.
    b. A hearing of a deficiency of $12,000 is considered on a timely basis.
    c. Taxpayer can handle the litigation without using a lawyer or certified public accountant.
    d. Taxpayer can use other Small Cases Division decisions for precedential value.
    e. The actual hearing is conducted informally.
    f. Travel time will probably be reduced.

19. List an advantage and a disadvantage of using a U.S. District Court as the trial court for Federal tax litigation.

20. Sam Brown is considering litigating a tax deficiency of approximately $317,000 in the court system. He asks you to provide him with a short description of his alternatives indicating the advantages and disadvantages of each. Prepare your response to Sam in the form of a letter. His address is 200 Mesa Drive, Tuscon, AZ 85714.

21. List an advantage and a disadvantage of using the U.S. Court of Federal Claims as the trial court for Federal tax litigation.

22. A taxpayer lives in Michigan. In a controversy with the IRS, the taxpayer loses at the trial court level. Describe the appeal procedure under the following different assumptions:

    a. The trial court was the Small Cases Division of the U.S. Tax Court.
    b. The trial court was the U.S. Tax Court.
    c. The trial court was a U.S. District Court.
    d. The trial court was the U.S. Court of Federal Claims.

23. Suppose the U.S. Government loses a tax case in the U.S. District Court of South Carolina but does not appeal the result. What does the failure to appeal signify?

24. Because the U.S. Tax Court is a national court, it always decides the same issue in a consistent manner. Assess the validity of this statement.

25. For the U.S. Tax Court, U.S. District Court, and the U.S. Court of Federal Claims, indicate the following:
    a. Number of regular judges per court.
    b. Availability of a jury trial.
    c. Whether the deficiency must be paid before the trial.

26. In which of the following states could a taxpayer appeal the decision of a U.S. District Court to the Ninth Court of Appeals?
    a. Alaska.
    b. Arkansas.
    c. New York.
    d. South Carolina.
    e. Utah.

27. Explain the fact-finding determination of a Federal Court of Appeals.

28. What is the Supreme Court's policy on hearing tax cases?

29. In assessing the validity of a prior court decision, discuss the significance of the following on the taxpayer's issue:
    a. The decision was rendered by the U.S. District Court of Wyoming. Taxpayer lives in Wyoming.
    b. The decision was rendered by the U.S. Court of Federal Claims. Taxpayer lives in Wyoming.
    c. The decision was rendered by the Second Court of Appeals. Taxpayer lives in California.
    d. The decision was rendered by the U.S. Supreme Court.
    e. The decision was rendered by the U.S. Tax Court. The IRS has acquiesced in the result.
    f. Same as (e) except that the IRS has issued a nonacquiescence as to the result.

30. The IRS may acquiesce or nonacquiesce to what court decisions? Can an acquiescence be withdrawn retroactively?

31. What is the difference betwen a Regular and a Memorandum decision of the U.S. Tax Court?

32. Answer the following questions based upon this citation: *Schuster's Express, Inc.*, 66 T.C. 588 (1976), *aff'd* 562 F.2d 39 (CA–2, 1977), *nonacq.*
    a. In which court did this decision first appear?
    b. Who was the plaintiff?
    c. Who was the respondent?
    d. Did the appellate court agree or disagree with the trial court?
    e. Does the Government agree with the position of the court?

33. Interpret each of the following citations:
    a. 54 T.C. 1514 (1970).
    b. 408 F.2d 1117 (CA–2, 1969).
    c. 69–1 USTC ¶9319 (CA–2, 1969).
    d. 23 AFTR2d 69–1090 (CA–2, 1969).
    e. 293 F.Supp. 1129 (D.Ct. Miss., 1967).
    f. 67–1 USTC ¶9253 (D.Ct. Miss., 1967).
    g. 19 AFTR2d 647 (D.Ct. Miss., 1967).
    h. 56 S.Ct. 289 (USSC, 1935).

    i. 36–1 USTC ¶9020 (USSC, 1935).
    j. 16 AFTR 1274 (USSC, 1935).
    k. 422 F.2d 1336 (Ct.Cls., 1970).

34. Explain the following abbreviations:
    a. CA-2   i. USTC
    b. Fed.Cl.   j. AFTR
    c. *aff'd.*   k. F.3d
    d. *rev'd.*   l. F.Supp.
    e. *rem'd.*   m. USSC
    f. *Cert. Denied*   n. S.Ct.
    g. *acq.*   o. D.Ct.
    h. B.T.A.

35. Give the Commerce Clearing House citation for the following courts:
    a. Small Cases Division of the Tax Court.
    b. Federal District Court.
    c. U.S. Supreme Court.
    d. U.S. Court of Federal Claims.
    e. Tax Court Memorandum decision.

36. Where can you locate a published decision of the U.S. Court of Federal Claims?

37. Which of the following items can probably be found in the *Cumulative Bulletin*?
    a. Revenue Ruling.
    b. Small Cases Division of the U.S. Tax Court decision.
    c. Letter ruling.
    d. Revenue Procedure.
    e. Proposed Regulation.
    f. District Court decision.
    g. Senate Finance Committee Report.
    h. Acquiescences to Tax Court decisions.
    i. Tax Court Memorandum decision.

38. As part of her course work for a Masters of Tax degree, Ann is required to prepare a 30-page term paper about limited liability partnerships. Identify some relevant research steps Ann may take.

39. Since a Regulation has the force and effect of tax law, can a Regulation be overturned by a court?

40. Determine the level of authority for a Tax Court Memorandum decision, a Tax Court Regular decision, and a Tax Court reviewed decision.

41. Which of the following would be considered differences between the Research Institute of America and Commerce Clearing House citators?
    a. Distinguishes between the various issues in a particular court decision.
    b. Lists all court decisions that cite the court decision being researched.
    c. Allows a researcher to determine the validity of a Revenue Ruling.
    d. Indicates whether a court decision is explained, criticized, followed, or overruled by a subsequent decision.
    e. Pinpoints the exact page on which a decision is cited by another case.

42. You inherit a tax problem that was researched five months ago. You believe the answer is correct, but you are unfamiliar with the general area. How would you find some recent articles dealing with the subject area? How do you evaluate the reliability of the authority cited in the research report? How do you determine the latest developments pertaining to the research problem?

43. Budgetwise, how can electronic tax resources best be combined for day-to-day tax research?

PROBLEMS

44. Tom, an individual taxpayer, has just been audited by the IRS and, as a result, has been assessed a substantial deficiency (which has not yet been paid) in additional income taxes. In preparing his defense, Tom advances the following possibilities:
    a. Although a resident of Kentucky, Tom plans to sue in a U.S. District Court in Oregon that appears to be more favorably inclined toward taxpayers.
    b. If (a) is not possible, Tom plans to take his case to a Kentucky state court where an uncle is the presiding judge.
    c. Since Tom has found a B.T.A. decision that seems to help his case, he plans to rely on it under alternative (a) or (b).
    d. If he loses at the trial court level, Tom plans to appeal either to the U.S. Court of Federal Claims or to the U.S. Second Court of Appeals because he has relatives in both Washington, D.C., and New York. Staying with these relatives could save Tom lodging expense while his appeal is being heard by the court selected.
    e. Whether or not Tom wins at the trial court or appeals court level, he feels certain of success on an appeal to the U.S. Supreme Court.

    Evaluate Tom's notions concerning the judicial process as it applies to Federal income tax controversies.

45. Using the legend provided, identify the governmental unit that produces the following tax sources:

    Legend

    T = U.S. Treasury Department
    NO = National Office of the IRS
    DD = District Director of the IRS
    NA = Not applicable

    a. Proposed Regulations.
    b. Revenue Procedures.
    c. Letter rulings.
    d. Determination letters.
    e. Technical Advice Memoranda.
    f. Treasury Decisions.
    g. Revenue Rulings.

46. Using the legend provided, classify each of the following statements (more than one answer per statement may be appropriate):

    Legend

    D = Applies to the U.S. District Court
    T = Applies to the U.S. Tax Court
    C = Applies to the U.S. Court of Federal Claims
    A = Applies to the U.S. Court of Appeals
    U = Applies to the U.S. Supreme Court
    N = Applies to none of the above

    a. Decides only Federal tax matters.
    b. Decisions are reported in the F.3d Series.
    c. Decisions are reported in the USTCs.
    d. Decisions are reported in the AFTRs.
    e. Appeal is by Writ of Certiorari.
    f. Court meets most often in Washington, D.C.
    g. A jury trial is available.
    h. Trial court.

i. Appellate court.
j. Appeal is to the Federal Circuit and bypasses the taxpayer's particular circuit court.
k. Has a Small Cases Division.
l. The only trial court where the taxpayer does not have to pay the tax assessed by the IRS first.

47. Using the legend provided, classify each of the following citations as to the type of court:

Legend

T = Applies to the U.S. Tax Court
D = Applies to the U.S. District Court
C = Applies to the U.S. Court of Federal Claims
A = Applies to the U.S. Court of Appeals
U = Applies to the U.S. Supreme Court
N = Applies to none of the above

a. 241 F.2d 197 (CA–4, 1957).
b. 90 T.C. 1 (1988).
c. 54 S.Ct. 8 (USSC, 1933).
d. 3 B.T.A. 1042 (1926).
e. T.C.Memo. 1954–141.
f. 597 F.2d 760 (Ct.Cl., 1979).
g. Ltr.Rul. 9414051.
h. 354 F.Supp. 1003 (D.Ct. Ga., 1972).
i. Rev.Rul. 74–164.

48. Using the legend provided, classify each of the following tax sources:

Legend

P = Primary tax source
S = Secondary tax source
B = Both
N = Neither

a. Sixteenth Amendment to the Constitution.
b. Tax treaty between the United States and France.
c. Revenue Rulings.
d. General Counsel Memoranda (1988).
e. Tax Court Memorandum decision.
f. *Yale Law Review* article.
g. Temporary Regulations (issued 1994).
h. District Court decision.
i. Small Cases Division of the U.S. Tax Court decision.
j. Senate Finance Committee report.

49. Using the legend provided, classify each of the following citations as to publisher:

Legend

RIA = Research Institute of America
CCH = Commerce Clearing House
W = West Publishing Company
U.S. = U.S. Government
O = Others

a. 83–2 USTC ¶9600.
b. 52 AFTR2d 83–5954.
c. 67 T.C. 293 (1976).
d. 39 TCM 32 (1979).
e. 416 U.S. 938.
f. RIA T.C.Memo. ¶80,582.
g. 89 S.Ct. 501.
h. 2 Cl.Ct. 600.
i. 415 F.2d 488.
j. 592 F.Supp. 18.
k. Rev.Proc. 77–37, 1977–2 C.B. 568.
l. 21 L.Ed.2d 495.
m. S.Rep. No. 1622, 83rd Cong., 2d Sess. 42 (1954).

50. Using the legend provided, classify each of the following statements:

Legend

A = Tax avoidance
E = Tax evasion
N = Neither

---

a. Terry writes a $250 check as a charitable contribution on December 28, 1998, but does not mail the check to the charitable organization until January 10, 1999. She takes a deduction in 1998.
b. Robert decides not to report interest income from a bank because the amount is only $11.75.
c. Jim pays property taxes on his home in December 1997 rather than waiting until February 1998.
d. Jane switches her investments from taxable corporate bonds to tax-exempt municipal bonds.
e. Ted encourages his mother to save most of her Social Security benefits so that he will be able to claim her as a dependent.

RESEARCH PROBLEMS

*Note: Use the **RIA OnPoint System 4 Student Version CD-ROM**, which is available to accompany this text, in preparing solutions to the Research Problems. Alternatively, tax research materials found in a standard tax library can be used.*

Research Problem 1.   When the same word is used at different places in the Internal Revenue Code, does the word mean the same thing?

Research Problem 2.   Determine what is covered in the following subchapters in Chapter 1. Subtitle A of the Internal Revenue Code of 1986:
a. B.
b. D.
c. F.
d. K.
e. P.

Research Problem 3.   A particular Code Section, which was passed in 1986, conflicts with a treaty between the United States and France, which was signed in 1991. Which source controls? Where can a researcher find tax treaties?

Research Problem 4.   Determine how the term *person* is defined in the Internal Revenue Code of 1986.

Research Problem 5.   Go to page 44,274 of the August 25, 1995, issue of the *Federal Register*. What action was taken by the IRS, and what was the subject matter?

Research Problem 6. What do acquiescence, acquiescence in result only, and nonacquiescence mean? What position did the IRS take with respect to *Zabolotny v. Comm.*, 7 F.3d 774 (CA–8, 1993)?

Research Problem 7. Locate the following tax services in your library and indicate the name of the publisher and whether the service is organized by topic or Code Section:
  a. *United States Tax Reporter.*
  b. *Standard Federal Tax Reporter.*
  c. *Federal Tax Coordinator 2d.*
  d. *Mertens Law of Federal Income Taxation.*
  e. *Tax Management Portfolios.*
  f. Rabkin & Johnson, *Federal Income, Gift & Estate Taxation.*
  g. *Federal Tax Service.*

Research Problem 8. In the Tax Publications Matrix below, place an X if a court decision can be found in the publication. There may be more than one X in a row for a particular court.

Court	U.S. Govt. Printing Office	West Publishing Company				Research Institute of America			Commerce Clearing House	
		Federal Supp.	Federal 3d	Federal Claims Reporter	S.Ct.	BTA Memo	TC Memo	AFTR	TC Memo	USTC
U.S. Supreme Court										
Court of Appeals										
Court of Federal Claims										
District Court										
Tax Court (Regular decisions)										
Tax Court (Memo decisions)										
Board of Tax Appeal										
BTA Memo										

Research Problem 9. With respect to the changes in the maximum amounts to be expensed under § 179 in 1998 and 1999, what was the House's position, the Senate's position, and the Conference Agreement in the Small Business Job Protection Act of 1996?

Research Problem 10. Complete the following citations:
  a. *Foxman v. Comm.*, 352 F.2d 466 (CA–3, ___).
  b. Rev.Rul. 79–___, 1979–1 C.B. 144.
  c. *Clark v. Comm.*, 489 U.S. ___ (1989).
  d. Rev.Proc. 92–89, 1992–2 C.B. ___.
  e. *U.S. v. Catto*, 223 F.Supp. 663 (W.D. Tex., ___).
  f. *Korn Industries, Inc., v. U.S.*, 532 F.2d ___ (Ct.Cl., 1976).
  g. *Miller v. Comm.*, 45 B.T.A. ___ (1941).

Research Problem 11. Answer the following questions:
  a. Has Prop.Reg. § 1.482–2 been finalized?
  b. What happened to *Golconda Mining Corp.*, 58 T.C. 736 (1972) on appeal?
  c. Does Rev. Rul. 69–185 still represent the position of the IRS on the issue involved?

Research Problem 12. Determine the disposition of the following decisions:
  a. *Kimbell-Diamond Milling Co.*, 14 T.C. 74 (1950).
  b. *U.S. v. Catto*, 223 F.Supp. 663 (W.D. Tex., 1963).
  c. *Schuster's Express, Inc.*, 66 T.C. 588 (1976).

Research Problem 13. Determine the reliability of the following items:
  a. *Simpson v. U.S.*, 261 F.2d 497 (CA–7, 1958).

b. Rev.Proc. 83–78, 1983–2 C.B. 595.

c. *Estate of Grace E. Lang,* 64 T.C. 404 (1975).

Research Problem 14.   During 1998, Frank lived with and supported a 20-year-old woman who was not his wife. He resides in a state that has a statute that makes it a misdemeanor for a man and woman who are not married to each other to live together. May Frank claim his *friend* as a dependent assuming he satisfies the normal tax rules for the deduction? Should Frank consider moving to another state?

Partial list of research aids:

§ 152(b)(5).

John T. Untermann, 38 T.C. 93 (1962).

S.Rept. 1983, 85th Cong., 2d Sess., reprinted in the 1958 Code Cong. & Adm. News 4791, 4804.

Research Problem 15.   Using the 1985–1989 volume of CCH's *Federal Tax Articles,* locate Code Section 636, article .012. Who are the authors, in what journal does the article appear, and what principle is discussed in the article?

Use the tax resources of the Internet to address the following questions. Do not restrict your search to the World Wide Web, but include a review of newsgroups and general reference materials, practitioner sites and resources, primary sources of the tax law, chat rooms and discussion groups, and other opportunities.

Research Problem 16.   Go to each of the following Internet locations.

a. Several primary sources of the tax law, including the U.S. Supreme Court, a circuit Court of Appeal, the Internal Revenue Service, and final Regulations.

b. Sources of proposed Federal tax legislation.

c. A collection of tax rules for your state.

Research Problem 17.   Go to each of the following Internet locations.

a. Several newspapers and magazines, such as *USA Today,* the *New York Times,* the *Washington Post, Newsweek* magazine, your local newspaper, and a local television station.

b. Other news sources such as *CNN Interactive,* Newspapers OnLine, and a collection of on-line versions of magazines.

Research Problem 18.   Go to each of the following Internet locations.

a. The American Institute of CPAs, the American Taxation Association, several tax-related newsgroups, and tax information provided by enrolled agents.

b. *Tax World,* the *Tax Prophet, Taxing Times,* and Dennis Schmidt's Internet tax index. Home pages for the professor of your course, Price Waterhouse LLP, Ernst & Young LLP, Deloitte & Touche LLP, a local tax consulting firm, and a local tax law firm.

3

TAX DETERMINATION; PERSONAL AND DEPENDENCY EXEMPTIONS; AN OVERVIEW OF PROPERTY TRANSACTIONS

LEARNING OBJECTIVES

After completing Chapter 3, you should be able to:

1. Understand and apply the components of the Federal income tax formula.

2. Apply the rules for arriving at personal and dependency exemptions.

3. Use the proper method for determining the tax liability.

4. Identify and work with kiddie tax situations.

5. Recognize the filing requirements and the proper filing status.

6. Possess an overview of property transactions.

7. Identify tax planning opportunities associated with the individual tax formula.

Individuals are subject to Federal income tax based on taxable income. This chapter explains how taxable income and the income tax of an individual taxpayer are determined.

To compute taxable income, it is necessary to understand the tax formula in Figure 3–1. Although the tax formula is rather simple, determining an individual's taxable income can be quite complex. The complexity stems from the numerous provisions that govern the determination of gross income and allowable deductions.

After computing taxable income, the appropriate rates must be applied. This requires a determination of the individual's filing status, since different rates apply for single taxpayers, married taxpayers, and heads of household. The basic tax rate structure is progressive, with rates ranging from 15 percent to 39.6 percent.[1] For

▼ **FIGURE 3–1**
Tax Formula

Income (broadly conceived)	$ xx,xxx
Less: Exclusions	(x,xxx)
Gross income	$ xx,xxx
Less: Deductions *for* adjusted gross income	(x,xxx)
Adjusted gross income	$ xx,xxx
Less: The greater of—	
Total itemized deductions *or* the standard deduction	(x,xxx)
Personal and dependency exemptions	(x,xxx)
Taxable income	$ xx,xxx

---

[1]The 1998 Tax Table was not available from the IRS at the date of publication of this text. The Tax Table for 1997 and the Tax Rate Schedules for 1997 and 1998 are reproduced in Appendix A. For quick reference, the 1997 and 1998 Tax Rate Schedules are also reproduced inside the front cover of this text.

comparison, the lowest rate structure, which was in effect in 1913–1915, ranged from 1 to 7 percent, and the highest, in effect during 1944–1945, ranged from 23 to 94 percent.

Once the individual's tax has been computed, prepayments and credits are subtracted to determine whether the taxpayer owes additional tax or is entitled to a refund.

When property is sold or otherwise disposed of, a gain or loss may result, which can affect the determination of taxable income. Although property transactions are covered in detail in Chapters 14–17, an understanding of certain basic concepts helps in working with some of the materials to follow. The concluding portion of this chapter furnishes an overview of property transactions, including the distinction between realized and recognized gain or loss, the classification of such gain or loss (ordinary or capital), and treatment for income tax purposes.

TAX FORMULA

1 LEARNING OBJECTIVE
Understand and apply the components of the Federal income tax formula.

Most individuals compute taxable income using the tax formula shown in Figure 3–1. Special provisions govern the computation of taxable income and the tax liability for certain minor children who have unearned income in excess of specified amounts. These provisions are discussed later in the chapter.

Before illustrating the application of the tax formula, a brief discussion of its components is helpful.

COMPONENTS OF THE TAX FORMULA

Income (Broadly Conceived). This includes all the taxpayer's income, both taxable and nontaxable. Although it is essentially equivalent to gross receipts, it does not include a return of capital or receipt of borrowed funds.

EXAMPLE 1

Dave needed money to purchase a house. He sold 5,000 shares of stock for $100,000. He had paid $40,000 for the stock. In addition, he borrowed $75,000 from a bank. Dave has income that is taxable of $60,000 from the sale of the stock ($100,000 selling price − $40,000 return of capital). He has no income from the $75,000 borrowed from the bank because he has an obligation to repay that amount. ▼

Exclusions. For various reasons, Congress has chosen to exclude certain types of income from the income tax base. The principal income exclusions are discussed in Chapter 5. A partial list of these exclusions is shown in Exhibit 3–1.

Gross Income. The Internal Revenue Code defines gross income broadly as "except as otherwise provided . . ., all income from whatever source derived."[2] The "except as otherwise provided" refers to exclusions. Gross income includes, but is not limited to, the items in the partial list in Exhibit 3–2. It does not include unrealized gains. Gross income is discussed in Chapters 4 and 5.

---

[2]§ 61(a).

▼ EXHIBIT 3-1
Partial List of Exclusions from
Gross Income

Accident insurance proceeds

Annuities (cost element)

Bequests

Child support payments

Cost-of-living allowance (for military)

Damages for personal injury or sickness

Gifts received

Group term life insurance, premium paid by employer (for coverage up to $50,000)

Inheritances

Interest from state and local (i.e., municipal) bonds

Life insurance paid on death

Meals and lodging (if furnished for employer's convenience)

Military allowances

Minister's dwelling rental value allowance

Railroad retirement benefits (to a limited extent)

Scholarship grants (to a limited extent)

Social Security benefits (to a limited extent)

Veterans' benefits

Welfare payments

Workers' compensation benefits

▼ EXHIBIT 3-2
Partial List of Gross Income
Items

Alimony

Annuities (income element)

Awards

Back pay

Bargain purchase from employer

Bonuses

Breach of contract damages

Business income

Clergy fees

Commissions

Compensation for services

Death benefits

Debts forgiven

Director's fees

Dividends

Embezzled funds

Employee awards (in certain cases)

Employee benefits (except certain fringe benefits)

Estate and trust income

Farm income

Fees

Gains from illegal activities

Gains from sale of property

Gambling winnings

Group term life insurance, premium paid by employer (for coverage over $50,000)

Hobby income

Interest

Jury duty fees

Living quarters, meals (unless furnished for employer's convenience)

Mileage allowance

Military pay (unless combat pay)

Notary fees

Partnership income

Pensions

Prizes

Professional fees

Punitive damages

Rents

Rewards

Royalties

Salaries

Severance pay

Strike and lockout benefits

Supplemental unemployment benefits

Tips and gratuities

Travel allowance (in certain cases)

Wages

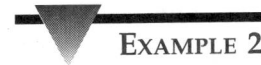

EXAMPLE 2

Beth received the following amounts during the year:

Salary	$30,000
Interest on savings account	900
Gift from her aunt	10,000 *— Not taxable*
Prize won in state lottery	1,000
Alimony from ex-husband	12,000
Child support from ex-husband	6,000
Damages for injury in auto accident	25,000 *— Not taxable*
Increase in the value of stock held for investment	5,000 *— Not taxable*

Review Exhibits 3–1 and 3–2 to determine the amount Beth must include in the computation of taxable income and the amount she may exclude. Then check your answer in footnote 3.[3] ▼

Deductions for Adjusted Gross Income.   Individual taxpayers have two categories of deductions: (1) deductions *for* adjusted gross income (deductions to arrive at adjusted gross income) and (2) deductions *from* adjusted gross income.

Deductions *for* adjusted gross income (AGI) include ordinary and necessary expenses incurred in a trade or business, one-half of self-employment tax paid, alimony paid, certain payments to an Individual Retirement Account and Medical Savings Accounts, moving expenses, forfeited interest penalty for premature withdrawal of time deposits, the capital loss deduction, and others.[4] The principal deductions *for* AGI are discussed in Chapters 6, 7, 8, 9, and 11.

Adjusted Gross Income (AGI).   AGI is an important subtotal that serves as the basis for computing percentage limitations on certain itemized deductions, such as medical expenses and charitable contributions. For example, medical expenses are deductible only to the extent they exceed 7.5 percent of AGI, and charitable contribution deductions may not exceed 50 percent of AGI. These limitations might be described as a 7.5 percent *floor* under the medical expense deduction and a 50 percent *ceiling* on the charitable contribution deduction.

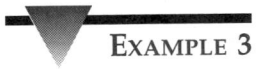

EXAMPLE 3

Keith earned a salary of $23,000 in the current tax year. He contributed $2,000 to his Individual Retirement Account (IRA) and sustained a $1,000 capital loss on the sale of Wren Corporation stock. His AGI is computed as follows:

Gross income		
Salary		$ 23,000
Less: Deductions *for* AGI		
IRA contribution	$2,000	
Capital loss	1,000	(3,000)
AGI		$ 20,000

▼

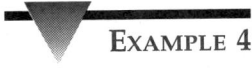

EXAMPLE 4

Assume the same facts as in Example 3, and that Keith also had medical expenses of $1,800. Medical expenses may be included in itemized deductions to the extent they exceed 7.5% of AGI. In computing his itemized deductions, Keith may include medical expenses of $300 [$1,800 medical expenses − $1,500 (7.5% × $20,000 AGI)]. ▼

---

[3]Beth must include $43,900 in computing taxable income ($30,000 salary + $900 interest + $1,000 lottery prize + $12,000 alimony). She can exclude $41,000 ($10,000 gift from aunt + $6,000 child support + $25,000 damages). The unrealized gain on the stock held for investment also is not included in gross income. Such gain will be included in gross income only when it is realized upon disposition of the stock.
[4]§ 62.

Itemized Deductions.   As a general rule, personal expenditures are disallowed as deductions in arriving at taxable income. However, Congress has chosen to allow specified personal expenses as **itemized deductions.** Such expenditures include medical expenses, certain taxes and interest, and charitable contributions.

In addition to these personal expenses, taxpayers are allowed itemized deductions for expenses related to (1) the production or collection of income and (2) the management of property held for the production of income.[5] These expenses, sometimes referred to as *nonbusiness expenses*, differ from trade or business expenses (discussed previously). Trade or business expenses, which are deductions *for* AGI, must be incurred in connection with a trade or business. Nonbusiness expenses, on the other hand, are expenses incurred in connection with an income-producing activity that does not qualify as a trade or business. Such expenses are itemized deductions.

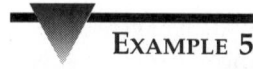

EXAMPLE 5   Leo is the owner and operator of a video game arcade. All allowable expenses he incurs in connection with the arcade business are deductions *for* AGI. In addition, Leo has an extensive portfolio of stocks and bonds. Leo's investment activity is not treated as a trade or business. All allowable expenses that Leo incurs in connection with these investments are itemized deductions. ▼

Itemized deductions include, but are not limited to, the expenses listed in Exhibit 3–3. See Chapter 10 for a detailed discussion of itemized deductions.

Standard Deduction.   The **standard deduction,** which is set by Congress, is a specified amount that depends on the filing status of the taxpayer. The effect of the standard deduction is to exempt a taxpayer's income, up to the specified amount, from Federal income tax liability. In the past, Congress has attempted to

▼ EXHIBIT 3–3
Partial List of Itemized Deductions

Medical expenses in excess of 7.5% of AGI

State and local income taxes

Real estate taxes

Personal property taxes

Interest on home mortgage

Investment interest (to a limited extent)

Charitable contributions (within specified percentage limitations)

Casualty and theft losses in excess of 10% of AGI

Miscellaneous expenses (to the extent such expenses exceed 2% of AGI)

    Union dues

    Professional dues and subscriptions

    Certain educational expenses

    Tax return preparation fee

    Investment counsel fees

    Unreimbursed employee business expenses (after a percentage reduction for meals and entertainment)

---

[5]§ 212.

set the tax-free amount represented by the standard deduction approximately equal to an estimated poverty level,[6] but it has not always been consistent in doing so.

The standard deduction is the sum of two components: the *basic* standard deduction and the *additional* standard deduction.[7] Table 3–1 lists the basic standard deduction allowed for taxpayers in each filing status. All taxpayers allowed a *full* standard deduction are entitled to the applicable amount listed in Table 3–1. The standard deduction amounts are subject to adjustment for inflation each year.

Certain taxpayers are not allowed to claim *any* standard deduction, and the standard deduction is *limited* for others. These provisions are discussed later in the chapter.

A taxpayer who is age 65 or over *or* blind qualifies for an *additional standard deduction* of $850 or $1,050, depending on filing status (see amounts in Table 3–2). Two additional standard deductions are allowed for a taxpayer who is age 65 or over *and* blind. The additional standard deduction provisions also apply for a qualifying spouse who is age 65 or over or blind, but a taxpayer may not claim an additional standard deduction for a dependent.

To determine whether to itemize, the taxpayer compares the *total* standard deduction (the sum of the basic standard deduction and any additional standard deductions) with total itemized deductions. Taxpayers are allowed to deduct the *greater* of itemized deductions or the standard deduction. Taxpayers whose itemized deductions are less than the standard deduction compute their taxable income using the standard deduction rather than itemizing.

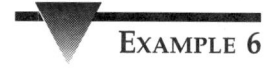

EXAMPLE 6

Sara, who is single, is 66 years old. She had total itemized deductions of $5,100 during 1998. Her total standard deduction is $5,300 ($4,250 basic standard deduction plus $1,050 additional standard deduction). Sara should compute her taxable income for 1998 using the standard deduction ($5,300), since it exceeds her itemized deductions ($5,100). ▼

▼ **TABLE 3–1**
Basic Standard Deduction
Amounts

Filing Status	Standard Deduction Amount	
	1997	**1998**
Single	$4,150	$4,250
Married, filing jointly	6,900	7,100
Surviving spouse	6,900	7,100
Head of household	6,050	6,250
Married, filing separately	3,450	3,550

▼ **TABLE 3–2**
Amount of Each Additional
Standard Deduction

Filing Status	1997	1998
Single	$1,000	$1,050
Married, filing jointly	800	850
Surviving spouse	800	850
Head of household	1,000	1,050
Married, filing separately	800	850

---

[6]S.Rep. No. 92–437, 92nd Cong., 1st Sess., 1971, p. 54. Another purpose of the standard deduction was discussed in Chapter 1 under Influence of the Internal Revenue Service—Administrative Feasibility. The size of the standard deduction has a direct bearing on the number of taxpayers who are in a position to itemize deductions.

Reducing the number of taxpayers who itemize also reduces the audit effort required from the IRS. Currently, about 70% of all individual taxpayers choose to use the standard deduction.
[7]§ 63(c)(1).

Personal and Dependency Exemptions. Exemptions are allowed for the taxpayer, for the taxpayer's spouse, and for each dependent of the taxpayer. The exemption amount is $2,650 in 1997 and $2,700 in 1998.

APPLICATION OF THE TAX FORMULA

The tax formula shown in Figure 3–1 is illustrated in Example 7.

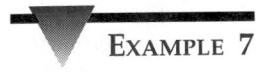

EXAMPLE 7

Grace, age 25, is single and has no dependents. She is a high school teacher and earned a $20,000 salary in 1998. Her other income consisted of a $1,000 prize won in a sweepstakes contest and $500 interest on municipal bonds received as a graduation gift in 1995. During 1998, she sustained a deductible capital loss of $1,000. Her itemized deductions are $4,400. Grace's taxable income for the year is computed as follows:

Income (broadly conceived)		
Salary		$ 20,000
Prize		1,000
Interest on municipal bonds		500
		$ 21,500
Less: Exclusion—		
Interest on municipal bonds		(500)
Gross income		$ 21,000
Less: Deduction *for* adjusted gross income—		
Capital loss		(1,000)
Adjusted gross income		$ 20,000
Less: The greater of—		
Total itemized deductions	$4,400	
or the standard deduction	$4,250	(4,400)
Personal and dependency exemptions (1 × $2,700)		(2,700)
Taxable income		$ 12,900

The structure of the individual income tax return (Form 1040, 1040A, or 1040EZ) differs somewhat from the tax formula in Figure 3–1. On the tax return, gross income generally is the starting point in computing taxable income. With few exceptions, exclusions are not reported on the tax return.

INDIVIDUALS NOT ELIGIBLE FOR THE STANDARD DEDUCTION

The following individual taxpayers are ineligible to use the standard deduction and must therefore itemize:[8]

- A married individual filing a separate return where either spouse itemizes deductions.
- A nonresident alien.
- An individual filing a return for a period of less than 12 months because of a change in the annual accounting period.

[8]§ 63(c)(6).

SPECIAL LIMITATIONS FOR INDIVIDUALS WHO CAN BE CLAIMED AS DEPENDENTS

Special rules apply to the standard deduction and personal exemption of an individual who can be claimed as a dependent on another person's tax return.

When filing his or her own tax return, a *dependent's* basic standard deduction in 1998 is limited to the greater of $700 or the sum of the individual's earned income for the year plus $250.[9] However, if the sum of the individual's earned income plus $250 exceeds the normal standard deduction, the standard deduction is limited to the appropriate amount shown in Table 3–1. These limitations apply only to the basic standard deduction. A dependent who is 65 or over or blind or both is also allowed the additional standard deduction amount on his or her own return (refer to Table 3–2). These provisions are illustrated in Examples 8 through 11.

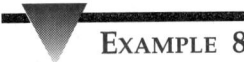

EXAMPLE 8   Susan, who is 17 years old and single, is claimed as a dependent on her parents' tax return. During 1998, she received $1,200 interest (unearned income) on a savings account. She also earned $300 from a part-time job. When Susan files her own tax return, her standard deduction is $700 (the greater of $700 or the sum of earned income of $300 plus $250). ▼

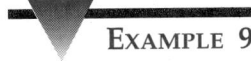

EXAMPLE 9   Assume the same facts as in Example 8, except that Susan is 67 years old and is claimed as a dependent on her son's tax return. In this case, when Susan files her own tax return, her standard deduction is $1,750 [$700 (the greater of $700 or the sum of earned income of $300 plus $250) + $1,050 (the additional standard deduction allowed because Susan is 65 or over)]. ▼

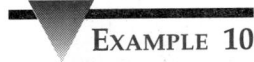

EXAMPLE 10   Peggy, who is 16 years old and single, earned $600 from a summer job and had no unearned income during 1998. She is claimed as a dependent on her parents' tax return. Her standard deduction is $850 (the greater of $700 or the sum of $600 earned income plus $250). ▼

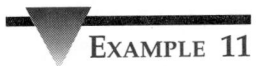

EXAMPLE 11   Jack, who is a 20-year-old, single, full-time college student, is claimed as a dependent on his parents' tax return. He worked as a musician during the summer of 1998, earning $4,300. Jack's standard deduction is $4,250 (the greater of $700 or the sum of $4,300 earned income plus $250, but limited to the $4,250 standard deduction for a single taxpayer). ▼

A taxpayer who claims an individual as a dependent is allowed to claim an exemption for the dependent. The dependent cannot claim a personal exemption on his or her own return. Based on the tax formula, Jack in Example 11 would have taxable income of $50, determined as follows:

Gross income	$ 4,300
Less: Standard deduction	(4,250)
Personal exemption	(–0–)
Taxable income	$ 50

---

[9] § 63(c)(5). The $700 amount is subject to adjustment for inflation each year. The amount was $650 for 1997. The $250 amount is adjusted for inflation beginning in 1999. The $250 amount is newly created by the Taxpayer Relief Act of 1997.

PERSONAL AND DEPENDENCY EXEMPTIONS

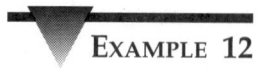

2 **LEARNING OBJECTIVE**
Apply the rules for arriving at personal and dependency exemptions.

The use of exemptions in the tax system is based in part on the idea that a taxpayer with a small amount of income should be exempt from income taxation. An exemption frees a specified amount of income from tax ($2,650 in 1997 and $2,700 in 1998). The exemption amount is indexed (adjusted) annually for inflation. An individual who is not claimed as a dependent by another taxpayer is allowed to claim his or her own personal exemption. In addition, a taxpayer may claim an exemption for each dependent.

EXAMPLE 12

Bonnie, who is single, supports her mother and father, who have no income of their own, and claims them as dependents on her tax return. Bonnie may claim a personal exemption for herself plus an exemption for each dependent. On her 1998 tax return, Bonnie may deduct $8,100 for exemptions ($2,700 per exemption × 3 exemptions). ▼

PERSONAL EXEMPTIONS

The Code provides a **personal exemption** for the taxpayer and an exemption for the spouse if a joint return is filed. However, when separate returns are filed, a married taxpayer cannot claim an exemption for his or her spouse *unless* the spouse has no gross income and is not claimed as the dependent of another taxpayer.

The determination of marital status generally is made at the end of the taxable year, except when a spouse dies during the year. Spouses who enter into a legal separation under a decree of divorce or separate maintenance before the end of the year are considered to be unmarried at the end of the taxable year. The following table illustrates the effect of death or divorce upon marital status:

	Marital Status for 1998
• Walt is the widower of Helen who died on January 3, 1998.	Walt and Helen are considered to be married for purposes of filing the 1998 return.
• Bill and Jane entered into a divorce decree that is effective on December 31, 1998.	Bill and Jane are considered to be unmarried for purposes of filing the 1998 return.

DEPENDENCY EXEMPTIONS

As indicated in Example 12, the Code allows a taxpayer to claim a dependency exemption for each eligible individual. A **dependency exemption** may be claimed for each individual for whom the following five tests are met:

- Support.
- Relationship or member of the household.
- Gross income.
- Joint return.
- Citizenship or residency.

A person who dies during the year can still be claimed as a dependent if all of the tests are met. In such a case, no proration is necessary, and the full amount of the exemption is allowed.

Support Test. Over one-half of the support of the individual must be furnished by the taxpayer. Support includes food, shelter, clothing, medical and dental care, education, etc. However, a scholarship received by a student is not included for purposes of computing whether the taxpayer furnished more than half of the child's support.[10]

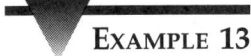

EXAMPLE 13

Hal contributed $3,400 (consisting of food, clothing, and medical care) toward the support of his son, Sam, who earned $1,500 from a part-time job and received a $2,000 scholarship to attend a local university. Assuming that the other dependency tests are met, Hal can claim Sam as a dependent since he has contributed more than half of Sam's support. The $2,000 scholarship is not included as support for purposes of this test. ▼

If the individual does not spend funds that have been received from any source, the unexpended amounts are not counted for purposes of the support test.

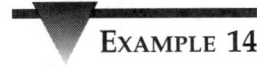

EXAMPLE 14

Emily contributed $3,000 to her father's support during the year. In addition, her father received $2,400 in Social Security benefits, $200 of interest, and wages of $600. Her father deposited the Social Security benefits, interest, and wages in his own savings account and did not use any of the funds for his support. Thus, the Social Security benefits, interest, and wages are not considered as support provided by Emily's father. Emily may claim her father as a dependent if the other tests are met. ▼

Capital expenditures for items such as furniture, appliances, and automobiles are included in total support if the item does, in fact, constitute support.[11]

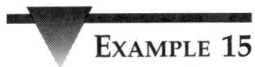

EXAMPLE 15

Norm purchased a television set costing $150 and gave it to his minor daughter. The television set was placed in the child's bedroom and was used exclusively by her. Norm should include the cost of the television set in determining the support of his daughter. ▼

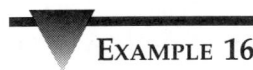

EXAMPLE 16

Mark paid $6,000 for an automobile that was titled and registered in his name. Mark's minor son is permitted to use the automobile equally with Mark. Since Mark did not give the automobile to his son, the $6,000 cost is not includible as a support item. However, out-of-pocket operating expenses incurred by Mark for the benefit of his son are includible as support. ▼

One exception to the support test involves a **multiple support agreement.** A multiple support agreement permits one of a group of taxpayers who furnish more than half of the support of an individual to claim a dependency exemption for that individual even if no one person provides more than 50 percent of the support.[12] Any person who contributed *more than 10 percent* of the support is entitled to claim the exemption if each person in the group who contributed more than 10 percent files a written consent. This provision frequently enables one of the children of aged dependent parents to claim an exemption when none of the children meets the 50 percent support test. Each person who is a party to the multiple support agreement must meet all other requirements (except the support requirement) for claiming the exemption. A person who does not meet the relationship or member-of-household requirement, for instance, cannot claim the dependency exemption under a multiple support agreement. It does not matter if he or she contributes more than 10 percent of the individual's support.

---

[10]Reg. § 1.152–1(c).
[11]Rev.Rul. 57–344, 1957–2 C.B. 112; Rev.Rul. 58–419, 1958–2 C.B. 57.

[12]§ 152(c).

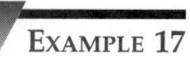

EXAMPLE 17

Wanda, who resides with her son, Adam, received $6,000 from various sources during 1998. This constituted her entire support for the year. She received support from the following:

	Amount	Percentage of Total
Adam, a son	$2,880	48
Bob, a son	600	10
Carol, a daughter	1,800	30
Diane, a friend	720	12
	$6,000	100

If Adam and Carol file a multiple support agreement, either may claim the dependency exemption for Wanda. Bob may not claim Wanda because he did not contribute more than 10% of her support. Bob's consent is not required in order for Adam and Carol to file a multiple support agreement. Diane does not meet the relationship or member-of-household test and cannot be a party to the agreement. The decision as to who claims Wanda rests with Adam and Carol. It is possible for Carol to claim Wanda, even though Adam furnished more of Wanda's support. ▼

Each person who qualifies under the more-than-10 percent rule (except for the person claiming the exemption) must complete Form 2120 (Multiple Support Declaration) waiving the exemption. The person claiming the exemption must attach all Forms 2120 to his or her own return.

A second exception to the 50 percent support requirement can occur for a child of parents who are divorced or separated under a decree of separate maintenance. For decrees executed after 1984, the custodial parent is allowed to claim the exemption unless that parent agrees in writing not to claim a dependency exemption for the child.[13] Thus, claiming the exemption is dependent on whether or not a written agreement exists, *not* on meeting the support test.

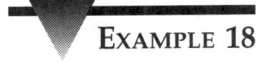

EXAMPLE 18

Ira and Rita obtain a divorce decree in 1990. In 1998, their two children are in Rita's custody. Ira contributed over half of the support for each child. In the absence of a written agreement on the dependency exemptions, Rita (the custodial parent) is entitled to the exemptions in 1998. However, Ira may claim the exemptions if Rita agrees in writing. ▼

For the noncustodial parent to claim the exemption, the custodial parent must complete Form 8332 (Release of Claim to Exemption for Child of Divorced or Separated Parents). The release can apply to a single year, a number of specified years, or all future years. The noncustodial parent must attach a copy of Form 8332 to his or her return.

Relationship or Member-of-the-Household Test.   To be claimed as a dependent, an individual must be either a relative of the taxpayer or a member of the taxpayer's household. The Code contains a detailed listing of the various blood and marriage relationships that qualify. Note, however, that the relationship test is met if the individual is a relative of either spouse. Once established by marriage, a relationship continues regardless of subsequent changes in marital status.

The following individuals may be claimed as dependents of the taxpayer if the other tests for dependency are met:[14]

- A son or daughter of the taxpayer or a descendant of either, such as a grandchild.
- A stepson or stepdaughter of the taxpayer.
- A brother, sister, stepbrother, or stepsister of the taxpayer.
- The father or mother of the taxpayer or an ancestor of either, such as a grandparent.
- A stepfather or stepmother of the taxpayer.
- A nephew or niece of the taxpayer.
- An uncle or aunt of the taxpayer.
- A son-in-law, daughter-in-law, father-in-law, mother-in-law, brother-in-law, or sister-in-law of the taxpayer.
- An individual who, for the entire taxable year of the taxpayer, has as his or her principal place of abode the home of the taxpayer and is a member of the taxpayer's household. This does not include an individual who, at any time during the taxable year, was the spouse of the taxpayer.

The following rules are also prescribed in the Code:[15]

- A legally adopted child is treated as a natural child.
- A foster child qualifies if the child's principal place of abode is the taxpayer's household.

---

[13] § 152(e).

[14] § 152(a). However, under § 152(b)(5), a taxpayer may not claim someone who is a member of his or her household as a dependent if their relationship is in violation of local law. For example, the dependency exemption was denied because the taxpayer's relation-ship to the person claimed as a dependent constituted *cohabitation*, a crime under applicable state law. *Cassius L. Peacock, III*, 37 TCM 177, T.C.Memo. 1978–30.

[15] § 152(b)(2).

Gross Income Test.   The dependent's gross income must be less than the exemption amount ($2,700 in 1998).[16] The gross income test is measured by income that is taxable. In the case of scholarships, for example, it excludes the nontaxable portion (e.g., amounts received for books and tuition) but includes the taxable portion (e.g., amounts received for room and board).

A parent may claim a dependency exemption for his or her child, even when the child's gross income exceeds $2,700, if the parent provided over half of the child's support and the child, at year-end, is under age 19 or is a full-time student under age 24. If the parent claims a dependency exemption, the dependent child may not claim a personal exemption on his or her own income tax return.

A child is defined as a son, stepson, daughter, stepdaughter, adopted son, or adopted daughter and may include a foster child.[17] For the child to qualify as a student for purposes of the dependency exemption, he or she must be a full-time student at an educational institution during some part of five calendar months of the year.[18] This exception to the gross income test for dependent children who are under age 19 or full-time students under age 24 permits a child or college student to earn money from part-time or summer jobs without penalizing the parent with the loss of the dependency exemption.

Joint Return Test.   If a dependent is married, the supporting taxpayer (e.g., the parent of a married child) generally is not permitted a dependency exemption if the married individual files a joint return with his or her spouse.[19] The joint return rule does not apply, however, if the following conditions are met:

- The reason for filing is to claim a refund for tax withheld.
- No tax liability would exist for either spouse on separate returns.
- Neither spouse is required to file a return.

See Table 3–4 later in the chapter and the related discussion concerning income level requirements for filing a return.

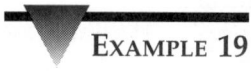

EXAMPLE 19

Paul provides over half of the support of his son Quinn. He also provides over half of the support of Vera, who is Quinn's wife. During the year, both Quinn and Vera had part-time jobs. In order to recover the taxes withheld, they file a joint return. If Quinn and Vera are not required to file a return, Paul is allowed to claim both as dependents. ▼

Citizenship or Residency Test.   To be a dependent, the individual must be either a U.S. citizen, a U.S. resident, or a resident of Canada or Mexico for some part of the calendar year in which the taxpayer's tax year begins.

ETHICAL CONSIDERATIONS

How to Generate More Dependency Exemptions

Raul is a citizen of Honduras but a resident of California. He furnishes most of the support for his family (i.e., parents and grandparents) who are citizens and residents of Honduras. In December 1998, Raul has his family move to Mexico and establish legal residence there. On his income tax return for calendar year 1998, Raul claims four dependency exemptions for his family. Has Raul acted properly? Why?

---

[16]§ 151(c)(1).
[17]Reg. § 1.151–3(a).

[18]Reg. §§ 1.151–3(b) and (c).
[19]§ 151(c)(2).

Phase-out of Exemptions.   Several provisions of the tax law are intended to increase the tax liability of more affluent taxpayers who might otherwise enjoy some benefit from having some of their taxable income subject to the lower income tax brackets (e.g., 15 percent, 28 percent). One such provision phases out personal and dependency exemptions as AGI exceeds specified threshold amounts. For 1997 and 1998, the phase-out *begins* at the following threshold amounts:

	1997	**1998**
Joint returns/surviving spouse	$181,800	$186,800
Head of household	151,500	155,650
Single	121,200	124,500
Married, filing separately	90,900	93,400

These threshold amounts are indexed for inflation each year.

Exemptions are phased out by 2 percent for each $2,500 (or fraction thereof) by which the taxpayer's AGI exceeds the threshold amounts. For a married taxpayer filing separately, the phase-out is 2 percent for each $1,250 or fraction thereof.

The allowable exemption amount can be determined with the following steps:

1. AGI – threshold amount = excess amount
2. Excess amount ÷ $2,500 = reduction factor [rounded up to the next whole increment (e.g., 18.1 = 19)] × 2 = phase-out percentage
3. Phase-out percentage (from step 2) × exemption amount = amount of exemptions phased out
4. Exemption amounts – phase-out amount = allowable exemption deduction

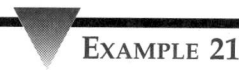
EXAMPLE 20

Frederico is married but files a separate return. His AGI is $113,400. He is entitled to one personal exemption.

1. $113,400 – $93,400 = $20,000 excess amount
2. [($20,000 ÷ $1,250) × 2] = 32% (phase-out percentage)
3. 32% × $2,700 = $864 amount of exemption phased out
4. $2,700 – $864 = $1,836 allowable exemption deduction ▼

Note that the exemption amount is completely phased out when the taxpayer's AGI exceeds the threshold amount by more than $122,500 ($61,250 for a married taxpayer filing a separate return), calculated as follows:

$122,501 ÷ $2,500 = 49.0004, rounded to 50 and multiplied by 2 = 100% (phase-out percentage)

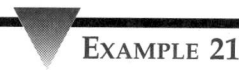
EXAMPLE 21

Bill and Isabella file a joint return claiming two personal exemptions and one dependency exemption for their child. Their AGI equals $310,800.

$310,800 – $186,800 = $124,000 excess amount

Since the excess amount exceeds $122,500, the exemptions are completely phased out. ▼

TAX DETERMINATION

TAX TABLE METHOD

3 LEARNING OBJECTIVE
Use the proper method for
determining the tax liability.

Most taxpayers compute their tax using the **Tax Table.** Eligible taxpayers compute taxable income (as shown in Figure 3–1) and *must* determine their tax by reference to the Tax Table. The following taxpayers, however, may not use the Tax Table method:

- An individual who files a short period return (see Chapter 18).
- Individuals whose taxable income exceeds the maximum (ceiling) amount in the Tax Table. The 1997 Tax Table applies to taxable income below $100,000 for Form 1040.
- An estate or trust.

The 1998 Tax Table was not available at the date of publication of this text. Therefore, the 1997 Tax Table will be used to illustrate the tax computation using the Tax Table method.

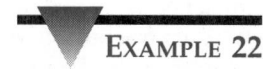

EXAMPLE 22

Pedro, a single taxpayer, is eligible to use the Tax Table. For 1997, he had taxable income of $25,025. To determine Pedro's tax using the Tax Table (see Appendix A), find the $25,000 to $25,050 income line. The first column to the right of the taxable income column is for single taxpayers. Pedro's tax for 1997 is $3,803. ▼

TAX RATE SCHEDULE METHOD

The **Tax Rate Schedules** contain rates of 15, 28, 31, 36, and 39.6 percent. Separate schedules are provided for the following filing statuses: single, married filing jointly, married filing separately, and head of household. The rate schedules for 1997 and 1998 are reproduced inside the front cover of this text and also in Appendix A.

The rate schedules are adjusted for inflation each year. Comparison of the 1997 and 1998 schedules for single taxpayers shows that the top amount to which the 15 percent bracket applies rose from $24,650 in 1997 to $25,350 in 1998. Thus, inflation allowed $700 ($25,350 − $24,650) more taxable income to be subject to the lowest 15 percent rate. The 1998 rate schedule for single taxpayers is reproduced in Table 3–3. This schedule is used to illustrate the tax computations in Examples 23, 24, and 25.

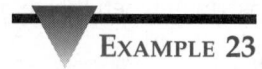

EXAMPLE 23

Pat is single and had $18,000 of taxable income in 1998. His tax is $2,700 ($18,000 × 15%). ▼

▼ **TABLE 3–3**
1998 Tax Rate Schedule for
Single Taxpayers

If Taxable Income Is			Of the Amount
Over	But Not Over	The Tax Is:	Over
$ –0–	$ 25,350	15%	$ –0–
25,350	61,400	$ 3,802.50 + 28%	25,350
61,400	128,100	13,896.50 + 31%	61,400
128,100	278,450	34,573.50 + 36%	128,100
278,450		88,699.50 + 39.6%	278,450

Several terms are used to describe tax rates. The rates in the Tax Rate Schedules are often referred to as *statutory* (or nominal) rates. The *marginal* rate is the highest rate that is applied in the tax computation for a particular taxpayer. In Example 23, the statutory rate and the marginal rate are both 15 percent.

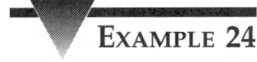

EXAMPLE 24

Chris is single and had taxable income of $41,450 in 1998. Her tax is $8,310.50 [$3,802.50 + 28%($41,450 − $25,350)]. ▼

The *average* rate is equal to the tax liability divided by taxable income. In Example 24, Chris has statutory rates of 15 percent and 28 percent, and a marginal rate of 28 percent. Chris's average rate is 20.05 percent ($8,310.50 tax liability ÷ $41,450 taxable income).

Note that $3,802.50, which is the starting point in the tax computation in Example 24, is 15 percent of the $25,350 taxable income in the first bracket. Income in excess of $25,350 is taxed at a 28 percent rate. This reflects the *progressive* (or graduated) rate structure on which the U.S. income tax system is based. A tax is progressive if a higher rate of tax applies as the tax base increases.

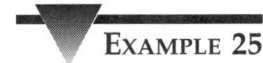

EXAMPLE 25

Carl is single and had taxable income of $81,900 in 1998. His tax is $20,251.50 [$13,896.50 + 31%($81,900 − $61,400)]. Note that the effect of this computation is to tax part of Carl's income at 15%, part at 28%, and part at 31%. An alternative computational method provides a clearer illustration of the progressive rate structure:

Tax on $25,350 at 15%	$ 3,802.50
Tax on $61,400 − $25,350 at 28%	10,094.00
Tax on $81,900 − $61,400 at 31%	6,355.00
Total	$20,251.50

▼

A special computation limits the effective tax rate on mid-term capital gain and long-term capital gain. The beneficial tax treatment of mid-term capital gain and long-term capital gain is discussed in detail in Chapter 16.

COMPUTATION OF NET TAXES PAYABLE OR REFUND DUE

The pay-as-you-go feature of the Federal income tax system requires payment of all or part of the taxpayer's income tax liability during the year. These payments take the form of Federal income tax withheld by employers or estimated tax paid by the taxpayer or both.[20] The payments are applied against the tax from the Tax Table or Tax Rate Schedules to determine whether the taxpayer will get a refund or pay additional tax.

Employers are required to withhold income tax on compensation paid to their employees and to pay this tax over to the government. The employer notifies the employee of the amount of income tax withheld on Form W–2 (Wage and Tax Statement). The employee should receive this form by January 31 after the year in which the income tax is withheld.

If taxpayers receive income that is not subject to withholding or income from which not enough tax is withheld, they must pay estimated tax. These individuals must file Form 1040–ES (Estimated Tax for Individuals) and pay in quarterly installments the income tax and self-employment tax estimated to be due (see Chapter 13 for a thorough discussion).

---

[20]§ 3402 for withholding; § 6654 for estimated payments.

The income tax from the Tax Table or the Tax Rate Schedules is reduced first by the individual's tax credits. There is an important distinction between tax credits and tax deductions. Tax credits reduce the tax liability dollar-for-dollar. Tax deductions reduce taxable income on which the tax liability is based.

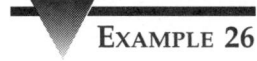

EXAMPLE 26

Gail is a taxpayer in the 28% tax bracket. As a result of incurring $1,000 in child care expenses (see Chapter 13 for details), she is entitled to a $200 child care credit ($1,000 child care expenses × 20% credit rate). She also contributed $1,000 to the American Cancer Society and included this amount in her itemized deductions. The child care credit results in a $200 reduction of Gail's tax liability for the year. The contribution to the American Cancer Society reduces taxable income by $1,000 and results in a $280 reduction in Gail's tax liability ($1,000 reduction in taxable income × 28% tax rate). ▼

Tax credits are discussed in Chapter 13. The following are several of the more common credits:

- Earned income credit.
- Credit for child and dependent care expenses.
- Credit for the elderly.
- Foreign tax credit.
- Child tax credit.

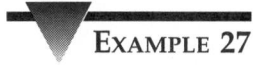

EXAMPLE 27

Kelly, age 30, is a head of household with a disabled and dependent mother living with him. During 1998, Kelly had the following: taxable income, $30,000; income tax withheld, $3,950; estimated tax payments, $600; and credit for dependent care expenses, $200. Kelly's net tax payable is computed as follows:

Income tax (from 1998 Tax Rate Schedule, Appendix A)		$ 4,500
Less: Tax credits and prepayments—		
Credit for dependent care expenses	$ 200	
Income tax withheld	3,950	
Estimated tax payments	600	(4,750)
Net taxes payable or (refund due if negative)		$ (250)

▼

UNEARNED INCOME OF CHILDREN UNDER AGE 14 TAXED AT PARENTS' RATE

4 **LEARNING OBJECTIVE**
Identify and work with kiddie tax situations.

At one time, a dependent child could claim an exemption on his or her own return even if claimed as a dependent by the parents. This enabled a parent to shift investment income (such as interest and dividends) to a child by transferring ownership of the assets producing the income. The child would pay no tax on the income to the extent that it was sheltered by the child's exemption.

Also, an additional tax motivation existed for shifting income from parents to children. Although a child's unearned income in excess of the exemption amount was subject to tax, it was taxed at the child's rate, rather than the parents' rate.

To reduce the tax savings that result from shifting income from parents to children, the net **unearned income** (commonly called investment income) of certain minor children is taxed as if it were the parents' income.[21] Unearned income includes such income as taxable interest, dividends, capital gains, rents, royalties, pension

---
[21]§ 1(g).

and annuity income, and income (other than earned income) received as the beneficiary of a trust. This provision, commonly referred to as the **kiddie tax,** applies to any child for any taxable year if the child has not reached age 14 by the close of the taxable year, has at least one living parent, and has unearned income of more than $1,400. The *kiddie tax* provision does not apply to a child age 14 or older. However, the limitation on the use of the standard deduction and the unavailability of the personal exemption do apply to such a child as long as he or she is eligible to be claimed as a dependent by a parent.

Net Unearned Income.   Net unearned income of a dependent child is computed as follows:

Unearned income
Less: $700
Less: The greater of
  • $700 of the standard deduction *or*
  • The amount of allowable itemized deductions directly connected with the production of the unearned income
Equals: Net unearned income

If net unearned income is zero (or negative), the child's tax is computed without using the parent's rate. If the amount of net unearned income (regardless of source) is positive, the net unearned income is taxed at the parent's rate. The $700 amounts in the preceding formula are subject to adjustment for inflation each year (refer to footnote 9).

Tax Determination.   If a child under age 14 has net unearned income, there are two options for computing the tax on the income. A separate return may be filed for the child, or the parents may elect to report the child's income on their own return. If a separate return is filed for the child, the tax on net unearned income (referred to as the *allocable parental tax*) is computed as though the income had been included on the parents' return. Form 8615 (reproduced in Appendix B) is used to compute the tax. The steps required in this computation are illustrated below.

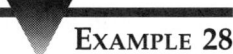

EXAMPLE 28

Olaf and Olga have a child, Hans (age 10). In 1998, Hans received $2,900 of interest and dividend income and paid investment-related fees of $200. Olaf and Olga had $70,000 of taxable income, not including their child's investment income. Olaf and Olga do not make the parental election.

1. Determine Hans's net unearned income

Gross income (unearned)	$ 2,900
Less: $700	(700)
Less: The greater of	
• $700 or	
• Investment expense ($200)	(700)
Equals: Net unearned income	$ 1,500

2. Determine allocable parental tax

Parents' taxable income	$ 70,000
Plus: Hans's net unearned income	1,500
Equals: Revised taxable income	$ 71,500
Tax on revised taxable income	$ 14,515
Less: Tax on parents' taxable income	(14,095)
Allocable parental tax	$ 420

3. Determine Hans's nonparental source tax

Hans's AGI	$ 2,900
Less: Standard deduction	(700)
Less: Personal exemption	(–0–)
Equals: Taxable income	$ 2,200
Less: Net unearned income	(1,500)
Nonparental source taxable income	$ 700
Equals: Tax ($700 × 15% rate)	$ 105

4. Determine Hans's total tax liability

Nonparental source tax (step 3)	$ 105
Allocable parental tax (step 2)	420
Total tax	$ 525

▼

Election to Claim Certain Unearned Income on Parent's Return. If a child under age 14 is required to file a tax return and meets all of the following requirements, the parent may elect to report the child's unearned income that exceeds $1,400 on the parent's own tax return:

- Gross income is from interest and dividends only.
- Gross income is more than $700 but less than $7,000.
- No estimated tax has been paid in the name and Social Security number of the child, and the child is not subject to backup withholding (see Chapter 13).

If the parental election is made, the child is treated as having no gross income and then is not required to file a tax return.

The parent(s) must also pay an additional tax equal to the smaller of $105 or 15 percent of the child's gross income over $700. Parents who have substantial itemized deductions based on AGI (see Chapter 10) may find that making the parental election increases total taxes for the family unit. Taxes should be calculated both with the parental election and without it to determine the appropriate choice.

Other Provisions.   If parents have more than one child subject to the tax on net unearned income, the tax for the children is computed as shown in Example 28 and then allocated to the children based on their relative amounts of income. For children of divorced parents, the taxable income of the custodial parent is used to determine the allocable parental tax. This parent is the one who may elect to report the child's unearned income. For married individuals filing separate returns, the individual with the greater taxable income is the applicable parent.

FILING CONSIDERATIONS

5 **LEARNING OBJECTIVE**
Recognize the filing requirements and the proper filing status.

Under the category of filing considerations, the following questions need to be resolved:

- Is the taxpayer required to file an income tax return?
- If so, which form should be used?
- When and how should the return be filed?
- In computing the tax liability, which column of the Tax Table or which Tax Rate Schedule should be used?

The first three questions are discussed under Filing Requirements, and the last is treated under Filing Status.

▼ **TABLE 3–4**
Filing Levels

Filing Status	1997 Gross Income	1998 Gross Income
Single		
Under 65 and not blind	$ 6,800	$ 6,950
Under 65 and blind	6,800	6,950
65 or older	7,800	8,000
Married, filing joint return		
Both spouses under 65 and neither blind	$12,200	$12,500
Both spouses under 65 and one or both spouses blind	12,200	12,500
One spouse 65 or older	13,000	13,350
Both spouses 65 or older	13,800	14,200
Married, filing separate return		
All—whether 65 or older or blind	$ 2,650	$ 2,700
Head of household		
Under 65 and not blind	$ 8,700	$ 8,950
Under 65 and blind	8,700	8,950
65 or older	9,700	10,000
Qualifying widow(er)		
Under 65 and not blind	$ 9,550	$ 9,800
Under 65 and blind	9,550	9,800
65 or older	10,350	10,650

FILING REQUIREMENTS

General Rules.   An individual must file a tax return if certain minimum amounts of gross income have been received. The general rule is that a tax return is required for every individual who has gross income that equals or exceeds the sum of the exemption amount plus the applicable standard deduction.[22] For example, a single taxpayer under age 65 must file a tax return in 1998 if gross income equals or exceeds $6,950 ($2,700 exemption plus $4,250 standard deduction). Table 3–4 lists the income levels[23] that require tax returns under the general rule and under certain special rules.

The additional standard deduction for being age 65 or older is considered in determining the gross income filing requirements. For example, note in Table 3–4 that the 1998 filing requirement for a single taxpayer age 65 or older is $8,000 ($4,250 basic standard deduction + $1,050 additional standard deduction + $2,700 exemption). However, the additional standard deduction for blindness is not taken into account. The 1998 filing requirement for a single taxpayer under age 65 and blind is $6,950 ($4,250 basic standard deduction + $2,700 exemption).

A self-employed individual with net earnings of $400 or more from a business or profession must file a tax return regardless of the amount of gross income.

Even though an individual has gross income below the filing level amounts and therefore does not owe any tax, he or she must file a return to obtain a tax refund of amounts withheld. A return is also necessary to obtain the benefits of the earned income credit allowed to taxpayers with little or no tax liability. Chapter 13 discusses the earned income credit.

---

[22]The gross income amounts for determining whether a tax return must be filed are adjusted for inflation each year.

[23]§ 6012(a)(1).

Filing Requirements for Dependents.   Computation of the gross income filing requirement for an individual who can be claimed as a dependent on another person's tax return is subject to more complex rules. Such an individual must file a return if he or she has *either* of the following:

- Earned income only and gross income that is more than the total standard deduction (including any additional standard deduction) that the individual is allowed for the year.
- Unearned income only and gross income of more than $700 plus any additional standard deduction that the individual is allowed for the year.
- Both earned and unearned income and gross income of more than the larger of $700 or the sum of earned income plus $250 (but limited to the applicable basic standard deduction), plus any additional standard deduction that the individual is allowed for the year.

Thus, the filing requirement for a dependent who has no unearned income is the total of the *basic* standard deduction plus any *additional* standard deduction, which includes both the additional deduction for blindness and the deduction for being age 65 or older. For example, the 1998 filing requirement for a single dependent who is under 65 and not blind is $4,250, the amount of the basic standard deduction for 1998. The filing requirement for a single dependent under 65 and blind is $5,300 ($4,250 basic standard deduction + $1,050 additional standard deduction).

Selecting the Proper Form.   The 1998 tax forms had not been released at the date of publication of this text. The following comments apply to 1997 forms. It is possible that some provisions will change for the 1998 forms.

Individual taxpayers file a return on either Form 1040 (the long form), Form 1040A (the short form), or Form 1040EZ. Taxpayers who cannot use either Form 1040EZ or Form 1040A must use Form 1040. These forms are reproduced in Appendix B. Examine the forms to determine which form is appropriate for a particular taxpayer.

When and Where to File.   Tax returns of individuals are due on or before the fifteenth day of the fourth month following the close of the tax year. For the calendar year taxpayer, the usual filing date is on or before April 15 of the following year.[24] When the due date falls on a Saturday, Sunday, or legal holiday, the last day for filing falls on the next business day. If the return is mailed to the proper address with sufficient postage and is postmarked on or before the due date, it is deemed timely filed. The Code enables the IRS to prescribe rules governing the filing of returns using various private parcel delivery services (e.g., Airborne Express, DHL, FedEx, UPS).[25]

If a taxpayer is unable to file the return by the specified due date, a four-month extension of time can be obtained by filing Form 4868 (Application for Automatic Extension of Time to File U.S. Individual Income Tax Return).[26] Further extensions may be granted by the IRS upon a showing of good cause by the taxpayer. For this purpose, Form 2688 (Application for Extension of Time to File U.S. Individual Income Tax Return) should be used. An extension of more than six months will not be granted if the taxpayer is in the United States.

Although obtaining an extension excuses a taxpayer from a penalty for failure to file, it does not insulate against the penalty for failure to pay. If more tax is owed, the filing of Form 4868 should be accompanied by an additional remittance

---

[24]§ 6072(a).
[25]§ 7502(f). See, for example, Notice 97–50, I.R.B. No. 37, 21.
[26]Reg. § 1.6081–4.

IS ALLOWING THE USE OF PLASTIC TO PAY TAXES A GOOD IDEA?

A provision in the Taxpayer Relief Act of 1997 permits the IRS to accept credit, debit, or charge cards for the payment of Federal income taxes. Although the provision is intended to benefit taxpayers, one can argue that it may cause more harm than good. Some feel that the easy accessibility of credit sources has resulted in many Americans becoming overburdened with credit card debt. Allowing the cards to be used for paying taxes will certainly further worsen the situation.

Other potential problems come to mind. What happens if the taxpayer charges the taxes and later refuses to pay the bill? Who gets stuck—the IRS or the credit card company? If the latter, is it desirable to have as a tax collector someone other than the IRS? A further problem is who absorbs the discount rate that merchants pay banks to process credit card transactions? Also, will credit card companies extend current incentives (e.g., cash rebates, frequent flyer miles) to holders who use the cards to pay Federal income taxes?

---

to cover the balance due. The failure to file and failure to pay penalties are discussed in Chapter 1.

The return should be sent or delivered to the Regional Service Center of the IRS for the area where the taxpayer lives.[27]

If an individual taxpayer needs to file an amended return (e.g., because of a failure to report income or to claim a deduction or tax credit), Form 1040X is filed. The form generally must be filed within three years of the filing date of the original return or within two years from the time the tax was paid, whichever is later.

FILING STATUS

The amount of tax will vary considerably depending on which Tax Rate Schedule is used. This is illustrated in the following example.

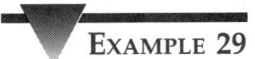

EXAMPLE 29

The following amounts of tax are computed using the 1998 Tax Rate Schedules for a taxpayer (or taxpayers in the case of a joint return) with $40,000 of taxable income (see Appendix A).

Filing Status	Amount of Tax
Single	$7,904.50
Married, filing joint return	6,000.00
Married, filing separate return	8,447.25
Head of household	6,786.50

▼

Rates for Single Taxpayers.   A taxpayer who is unmarried or separated from his or her spouse by a decree of divorce or separate maintenance and does not qualify for another filing status must use the rates for single taxpayers. Marital

---

[27]The Regional Service Centers and the geographical area each covers can be found in *Your Federal Income Tax*, IRS Publication 17 for 1997 or at http://www.irs.ustreas.gov.

status is determined as of the last day of the tax year, except when a spouse dies during the year. In that case, marital status is determined as of the date of death. State law governs whether a taxpayer is considered married, divorced, or legally separated.

Under a special relief provision, however, married persons who live apart may be able to qualify as single. Married taxpayers who are considered single under the *abandoned spouse rules* are allowed to use the head-of-household rates. See the discussion of this filing status under Abandoned Spouse Rules later in the chapter.

Rates for Married Individuals.   The joint return (Tax Rate Schedule Y, Code § 1(a)) was originally enacted in 1948 to establish equity between married taxpayers in common law states and those in community property states. Before the joint return rates were enacted, taxpayers in community property states were in an advantageous position relative to taxpayers in common law states because they could split their income. For instance, if one spouse earned $100,000 and the other spouse was not employed, each spouse could report $50,000 of income. Splitting the income in this manner caused the total income to be subject to lower marginal tax rates. Each spouse would start at the bottom of the rate structure.

Taxpayers in common law states did not have this income-splitting option, so their taxable income was subject to higher marginal rates. This inconsistency in treatment was remedied by the joint return provisions. The progressive rates in the joint return Tax Rate Schedule are constructed based on the assumption that income is earned equally by the two spouses.

If married individuals elect to file separate returns, each reports only his or her own income, exemptions, deductions, and credits, and each must use the Tax Rate Schedule applicable to married taxpayers filing separately. It is generally advantageous for married individuals to file a joint return, since the combined amount of tax is lower. However, special circumstances (e.g., significant medical expenses incurred by one spouse subject to the 7.5 percent limitation) may warrant the election to file separate returns. It may be necessary to compute the tax under both assumptions to determine the most advantageous filing status.

When Congress enacted the rate structure available to those filing joint returns, it intended to favor married taxpayers. In certain situations, however, the parties would incur less tax if they were not married and filed separate returns. The additional tax that a joint return can cause, commonly called the **marriage penalty,** can develop when *both* spouses have larger taxable incomes.

EXAMPLE 30

John and Betty are employed, and each earns taxable income of $55,000. If they *are not married* and file separate returns, each has a tax liability of $12,105, or a total of $24,210 ($12,105 × 2). If they are married to each other, the filing of a joint return produces a tax of $25,526 on taxable income of $110,000 ($55,000 + $55,000). Thus, being married results in $1,316 ($25,526 − $24,210) more tax! ▼

Although some have suggested changes to lessen the impact of the marriage penalty, any remedy is apt to make the tax law more complex.

The Code places some limitations on deductions, credits, etc., when married individuals file separately. If either spouse itemizes deductions, the other spouse must also itemize. Married taxpayers who file separately cannot take either of the following:

- The credit for child and dependent care expenses (in most instances).
- The earned income credit.

TAX IN THE NEWS

LOW-INCOME TAXPAYERS ALSO SUFFER FROM THE MARRIAGE PENALTY

The inequity of the marriage penalty is not limited to taxpayers with high incomes (see Example 30).

Consider, for example, Albert and June, each of whom has one dependent child. During 1998, Albert and June both earn wages of $10,000. Neither has any deductions *for* AGI.

Situation A shows the income tax result if Albert and June are married and file a joint return. Situation B assumes Albert and June are not married, qualify for head-of-household status, and file accordingly, with each claiming one child as a dependent. Because the Tax Tables for 1998 were not yet available, the Tax Rate Schedules were used to compute the tax.

The harsh effect of the marriage penalty is apparent. Albert and June are $2,416 better off (refunds totaling $4,542 versus $2,126) by not being married. This result is remarkable when one considers that AGI of only $20,000 is involved!

Their Taxes:	Situation A	Situation B				
	If They Are Married	If They Are Not Married				
		Albert		June		Total
Adjusted gross income	$20,000	$10,000	+	$10,000	=	$20,000
Personal and dependency exemptions	10,800	5,400	+	5,400	=	10,800
Standard deduction	7,100	6,250	+	6,250	=	12,500
Taxable income	2,100	–0–	+	–0–	=	–0–
Taxes owed	315	–0–	+	–0–	=	–0–
Earned income tax credit*	2,126	2,271	+	2,271	=	4,542
Child tax credit*	315	–0–	+	–0–	=	–0–
Refund	$ 2,126	$ 2,271	+	$ 2,271	=	$ 4,542

*See Chapter 13 for a discussion of the earned income tax credit and the child tax credit. The credits above were calculated following the procedure utilized in Chapter 13.

The joint return rates also apply for two years following the death of one spouse, if the surviving spouse maintains a household for a dependent child.[28] This is referred to as **surviving spouse** status.

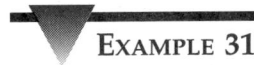

EXAMPLE 31

Fred dies in 1997 leaving Ethel with a dependent child. For the year of Fred's death (1997), Ethel files a joint return with Fred (presuming the consent of Fred's executor is obtained). For the next two years (1998 and 1999), Ethel, as a surviving spouse, may use the joint return rates. In subsequent years, Ethel may use the head-of-household rates if she continues to maintain a household as her home that is the domicile of the child. ▼

---

[28]§ 2(a).

Rates for Heads of Household.   Unmarried individuals who maintain a household for a dependent (or dependents) are entitled to use the **head-of-household** rates.[29] The tax liability using the head-of-household rates falls between the liability using the joint return Tax Rate Schedule and the liability using the Tax Rate Schedule for single taxpayers.

To qualify for head-of-household rates, a taxpayer must pay more than half the cost of maintaining a household as his or her home. The household must also be the principal home of a dependent relative.[30] As a general rule, the dependent must live in the taxpayer's household for over half the year.

There are two exceptions to these requirements. One exception is that an *unmarried child* (child also means grandchild, stepchild, or adopted child) need not be a dependent in order for the taxpayer to qualify as a head of household.

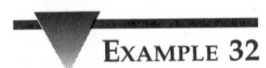

EXAMPLE 32   Nancy maintains a household where she and Dan, her nondependent unmarried son, reside. Since Dan is not married, Nancy qualifies for the head-of-household rates. ▼

Another exception to the general rule is that head-of-household status still may be claimed if the taxpayer maintains a *separate home* for his or her *parent or parents* if at least one parent qualifies as a dependent of the taxpayer.[31]

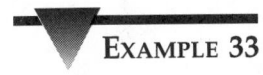

EXAMPLE 33   Rick, an unmarried individual, lives in New York City and maintains a household in Detroit for his dependent parents. Rick may use the head-of-household rates even though his parents do not reside in his New York home. ▼

Head-of-household status is not changed during the year by the death of the dependent. As long as the taxpayer provided more than half of the cost of maintaining the household prior to the dependent's death, head-of-household status is preserved.

Abandoned Spouse Rules.   When married persons file separate returns, several unfavorable tax consequences result. For example, the taxpayer must use the Tax Rate Schedule for married taxpayers filing separately. To mitigate such harsh treatment, Congress enacted provisions commonly referred to as the **abandoned spouse** rules. These rules allow a married taxpayer to file as a head of household if all of the following conditions are satisfied:

- The taxpayer does not file a joint return.
- The taxpayer paid more than one-half the cost of maintaining his or her home for the tax year.
- The taxpayer's spouse did not live in the home during the last six months of the tax year.
- The home was the principal residence of the taxpayer's child, stepchild, or adopted child for more than half the year.
- The taxpayer could claim the child, stepchild, or adopted child as a dependent.[32]

---

[29]§ 2(b).
[30]As defined in § 152(a). See § 2(b)(1)(A).
[31]§ 2(b)(1)(B).
[32]The dependency requirement does not apply, however, if the taxpayer could have claimed a dependency exemption except for the

fact that the exemption was claimed by the noncustodial parent under a written agreement. Refer to Example 18 and the related discussion.

GAINS AND LOSSES FROM PROPERTY TRANSACTIONS—IN GENERAL

6 **LEARNING OBJECTIVE**
Possess an overview of property transactions.

Gains and losses from property transactions are discussed in detail in Chapters 14 through 17. Because of their importance in the tax system, however, they are introduced briefly at this point.

When property is sold or otherwise disposed of, gain or loss may result. Such gain or loss has an effect on the income tax position of the party making the sale or other disposition when the *realized* gain or loss is *recognized* for tax purposes. Without realized gain or loss, generally, there can be no recognized gain or loss. The concept of realized gain or loss is expressed as follows:

$$\begin{array}{c} \text{Amount realized} \\ \text{from the sale} \end{array} - \begin{array}{c} \text{Adjusted basis of} \\ \text{the property} \end{array} = \begin{array}{c} \text{Realized gain} \\ \text{(or loss)} \end{array}$$

The amount realized is the selling price of the property less any costs of disposition (e.g., brokerage commissions) incurred by the seller. The adjusted basis of the property is determined as follows:

Cost (or other original basis) at date of acquisition[33]
Add: Capital additions
Subtract: Depreciation (if appropriate) and other capital recoveries
            (see Chapter 8)
Equals: Adjusted basis at date of sale or other disposition

All realized gains are recognized (taxable) unless some specific part of the tax law provides otherwise (see Chapter 15 dealing with certain nontaxable exchanges). Realized losses may or may not be recognized (deductible) for tax purposes, depending on the circumstances involved. Generally, losses realized from the disposition of personal use property (property neither held for investment nor used in a trade or business) are not recognized.

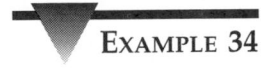

EXAMPLE 34

During the current year, Ted sells his sailboat (adjusted basis of $4,000) for $5,500. Ted also sells one of his personal automobiles (adjusted basis of $8,000) for $5,000. Ted's realized gain of $1,500 from the sale of the sailboat is recognized. On the other hand, the $3,000 realized loss on the sale of the automobile is not recognized and will not provide Ted with any deductible tax benefit. ▼

Once it has been determined that the disposition of property results in a recognized gain or loss, the next step is to classify the gain or loss as capital or ordinary. Although ordinary gain is fully taxable and ordinary loss is fully deductible, the same may not hold true for capital gains and capital losses.

GAINS AND LOSSES FROM PROPERTY TRANSACTIONS—CAPITAL GAINS AND LOSSES

The Taxpayer Relief Act of 1997 (TRA of 1997) made significant changes in the tax treatment of capital gains. Although highly beneficial for the taxpayers affected,

---

[33]Cost usually means purchase price plus expenses related to the acquisition of the property and incurred by the purchaser (e.g., brokerage commissions). For the basis of property acquired by gift or inheritance and other basis rules, see Chapter 14.

the price paid was to add further complexity to the Code. Some of these changes, for example, do not become effective until after the year 2000. Since this chapter is intended to present only an overview of capital gains and losses, refer to Chapter 16 for an in-depth treatment.

DEFINITION OF A CAPITAL ASSET

Capital assets are defined in the Code as any property held by the taxpayer *other than* property listed in § 1221. The list in § 1221 includes inventory, accounts receivable, and depreciable property or real estate used in a business. Thus, the sale or exchange of assets in these categories usually results in ordinary income or loss treatment (see Chapter 17).

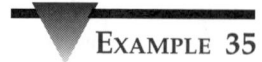

EXAMPLE 35

Kelly owns a pizza parlor. During the current year, he sells two automobiles. The first automobile, which had been used as a pizza delivery car for three years, was sold at a loss of $1,000. Because this automobile is an asset used in his business, Kelly has an ordinary loss deduction of $1,000, rather than a capital loss deduction. The second automobile, which Kelly had owned for two years, was his personal use car. It was sold for a gain of $800. The personal use car is a capital asset. Therefore, Kelly has a capital gain of $800. ▼

The principal capital assets held by an individual taxpayer include assets held for personal (rather than business) use, such as a personal residence or an automobile, and assets held for investment purposes (e.g., corporate securities and land). Capital assets generally include collectibles, which are subject to somewhat unique tax treatment. **Collectibles** include art, antiques, gems, metals, stamps, some coins and bullion, and alcoholic beverages that are held as investments.

TAXATION OF NET CAPITAL GAIN

Currently, *net capital gain* (as defined below) is subject to the following *maximum* rates:

	Maximum Rate
Short-term gains (held for 12 months or less)	39.6%
Mid-term gains (held for more than 12 and not more than 18 months)	28%
Long-term gains (held for more than 18 months)	20%

Collectibles, if the holding period requirement is satisfied, are always included in the mid-term category. In no event will a capital gain be taxed at a rate higher than the taxpayer's regular bracket for the year. Further, if a taxpayer has a long-term gain and his or her regular tax bracket for the year is 15 percent, the usual 20 percent rate is reduced to 10 percent.

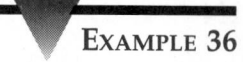

EXAMPLE 36

In 1998, Polly is in the 15% tax bracket and has the following capital gains for the year:

Robin Corporation stock (held for 6 months)	$1,000
Crow Corporation stock (held for 19 months)	1,000

Polly's tax on these transactions is $150 ($1,000 × 15%) as to Robin and $100 ($1,000 × 10%) as to Crow. ▼

DETERMINATION OF NET CAPITAL GAIN

In order to arrive at a net capital gain, capital losses must be taken into account. The capital losses are aggregated by holding period (short-term, mid-term, and long-term) and applied against the gains in that category. If excess losses result, they are then shifted to the category carrying the *highest* tax rate.

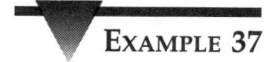

EXAMPLE 37

In 1998, Colin is in the 31% tax bracket and has the following capital transactions for the year:

Penguin Corporation stock (held for 7 months)	$1,000
Owl Corporation stock (held for 9 months)	(3,000)
Stamp collection (held for 4 years)	2,000
Land (held for 3 years)	4,000

The Penguin Corporation gain of $1,000 is offset by the Owl Corporation loss of $3,000. The net short-term capital loss of $2,000 is then applied against the stamp collection gain of $2,000. The end result is a net long-term capital gain of $4,000 from the land sale taxed at a 20% rate. Note that the stamp collection gain would have been taxed at a higher 28% rate had it not been offset by the excess short-term capital loss. ▼

TREATMENT OF NET CAPITAL LOSS

For individual taxpayers, net capital loss can be used to offset ordinary income of up to $3,000. Any remaining net capital loss is carried over indefinitely until exhausted. When carried over, the excess capital loss retains its classification (i.e., short-, mid- or long-term), except that both mid-term and long term are treated as mid-term.

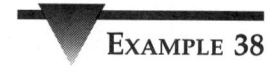

EXAMPLE 38

Tina has a short-term capital loss of $5,000 during the current year and no capital gains. She can deduct $3,000 of this amount as an ordinary loss. The remaining $2,000 is carried over to the next year as a short-term capital loss. ▼

TAX PLANNING CONSIDERATIONS

7 **LEARNING OBJECTIVE**
Identify tax planning opportunities associated with the individual tax formula.

TAKING ADVANTAGE OF TAX RATE DIFFERENTIALS

It is natural for taxpayers to be concerned about the tax rates they are paying. How does a tax practitioner communicate information about rates to clients? There are several possibilities.

The marginal rate (refer to Examples 23 through 25) provides information that can help a taxpayer evaluate a particular course of action or structure a transaction in the most advantageous manner. For example, a taxpayer who is in the 15 percent bracket this year and expects to be in the 31 percent bracket next year should, if possible, defer payment of deductible expenses until next year to maximize the tax benefit of the deduction.

A note of caution is in order with respect to shifting income and expenses between years. Congress has recognized the tax planning possibilities of such shifting and has enacted many provisions to limit a taxpayer's ability to do so. Some of these limitations on the shifting of income are discussed in Chapters 4, 5, and 18. Limitations that affect a taxpayer's ability to shift deductions are discussed in Chapters 6 through 11 and in Chapter 18.

A taxpayer's *effective rate* can be an informative measure of the effectiveness of tax planning. The effective rate is computed by dividing the taxpayer's tax liability by the total amount of income. A low effective rate can be considered an indication of effective tax planning.

One way of lowering the effective rate is to exclude income from the tax base. For example, a taxpayer might consider investing in tax-free municipal bonds rather than taxable corporate bonds. Although pre-tax income from corporate bonds is usually higher, after-tax income may be higher if the taxpayer invests in tax-free municipals.

Another way of lowering the effective rate is to make sure that the taxpayer's expenses and losses are deductible. For example, losses on investments in passive activities may not be deductible (see Chapter 11). Therefore, a taxpayer who plans to invest in an activity that will produce a loss in the early years should take steps to ensure that the business is treated as active rather than passive. Active losses are deductible while passive losses are not.

INCOME OF MINOR CHILDREN

Taxpayers can use several strategies to avoid or minimize the effect of the rules that tax the unearned income of certain minor children at the parents' rate. The kiddie tax rules do not apply once a child reaches age 14. Parents should consider giving a younger child assets that defer taxable income until the child reaches age 14. For example, U.S. government Series EE savings bonds can be used to defer income until the bonds are cashed in (see Chapter 4).

Growth stocks typically pay little in the way of dividends. However, the profit on an astute investment may more than offset the lack of dividends. The child can hold the stock until he or she reaches age 14. If the stock is sold then at a profit, the profit is taxed at the child's low rates.

Taxpayers in a position to do so can employ their children in their business and pay them a reasonable wage for the work they actually perform (e.g., light office help, such as filing). The child's earned income is sheltered by the standard deduction, and the parents' business is allowed a deduction for the wages. The kiddie tax rules have no effect on earned income, even if it is earned from the parents' business.

DEPENDENCY EXEMPTIONS

The Joint Return Test.   A married person can be claimed as a dependent only if that individual does not file a joint return with his or her spouse. If a joint return has been filed, the damage may be undone if separate returns are substituted on a timely basis (on or before the due date of the return).

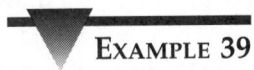

EXAMPLE 39

While preparing a client's 1997 income tax return on April 8, 1998, the tax practitioner discovered that the client's daughter filed a joint return with her husband in late January of 1998. Presuming the daughter otherwise qualifies as the client's dependent, the exemption is not lost if she and her husband file separate returns on or before April 15, 1998. ▼

An initial election to file a joint return must be considered carefully in any situation in which the taxpayers might later decide to amend their return and file separately. As indicated above, separate returns may be substituted for a joint return only if the amended returns are filed on or before the normal due date of the return. If the taxpayers in Example 39 attempt to file separate returns after April 15, 1998, the returns will not be accepted, and the joint return election is binding.[34]

---

[34]Reg. § 1.6013–1(a)(1).

Keep in mind that the filing of a joint return is not fatal to the dependency exemption if the parties are filing solely to recover all income tax withholdings, they are not required to file a return, and no tax liability would exist on separate returns.

The Gross Income Test.   The exception to the gross income test for a person under the age of 19 or a full-time student under the age of 24 applies only to a child of the taxpayer. The term *child* is limited to a son, stepson, daughter, stepdaughter, adopted son, or adopted daughter and may include a foster child.

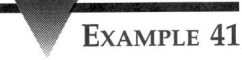
EXAMPLE 40

Austin provides more than 50% of the support of his son, Irvin, and his daughter-in-law, Donna, who live with him. Donna, age 22, is a full-time student and earns $3,000 from a part-time job. Irvin and Donna do not file a joint return. Austin may claim Irvin as a dependent but not Donna. Although students under the age of 24 are excepted from the gross income test, this applies only to a "child" of the taxpayer. Donna does not come within the exception because she is not Austin's child. ▼

Can the fact that the parties live in a community property state make a difference?

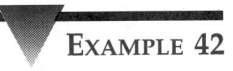
EXAMPLE 41

Assume the same facts as in Example 40 except that all parties live in Nevada, a community property jurisdiction. Now Austin can claim both Irvin and Donna as his dependents. Since Donna's income is only $1,500 (her half of the community), she now satisfies the gross income test (less than $2,700 for 1998). ▼

The Support Test.   Adequate records of expenditures for support should be maintained in the event a dependency exemption is questioned on audit by the IRS. The maintenance of adequate records is particularly important for exemptions arising from multiple support agreements.

Relationship to the Deduction for Medical Expenses.   Generally, medical expenses are deductible only if they are paid on behalf of the taxpayer, his or her spouse, and their dependents. Since deductibility may rest on dependency status, planning is important in arranging multiple support agreements.

EXAMPLE 42

During the year, Zelda will be supported by her two sons (Vern and Vito) and her daughter (Maria). Each will furnish approximately one-third of the required support. If the parties decide that the dependency exemption should be claimed by the daughter under a multiple support agreement, any medical expenses incurred by Zelda should be paid by Maria. ▼

In planning a multiple support agreement, take into account which of the parties is most likely to exceed the 7.5 percent limitation (see Chapter 10). In Example 42, for instance, Maria might be a poor choice if she and her family do not expect to incur many medical and drug expenses of their own.

ETHICAL CONSIDERATIONS   **Manipulating Deductions**

Jason and his two sisters furnish more than 50 percent of the support of their widowed mother. Their mother lives with Jason, and his sisters sign Form 2120 enabling him to claim her as a dependent. During the year, the mother incurred medical expenses that were paid by one of Jason's sisters.

In completing his income tax return for the tax year, Jason claims his mother's medical expenses along with his own. Although he did not pay the expenses, Jason reasons that he could have done so from the funds he furnished for his mother's support.

Comment on the propriety of what Jason has done.

One exception permits the deduction of medical expenses paid on behalf of someone who is not a spouse or a dependent. If the person could be claimed as a dependent *except* for the gross income or joint return test, the medical expenses are, nevertheless, deductible. For additional discussion, see Chapter 10.

KEY TERMS

Abandoned spouse, 3–26

Collectibles, 3–28

Dependency exemption, 3–10

Head of household, 3–26

Itemized deductions, 3–6

Kiddie tax, 3–19

Marriage penalty, 3–24

Multiple support agreement, 3–11

Personal exemption, 3–10

Standard deduction, 3–6

Surviving spouse, 3–25

Tax Rate Schedules, 3–16

Tax Table, 3–16

Unearned income, 3–18

PROBLEM MATERIALS

DISCUSSION QUESTIONS

1. A friend of yours remarks that the current top rate of 39.6% is the highest the Federal income tax has ever been. Please comment.

2. Rearrange the following components to show the formula for arriving at the amount of Federal taxable income:
   a. Deductions *for* AGI.
   b. The greater of the standard deduction or itemized deductions.
   c. Income (broadly conceived).
   d. Adjusted gross income.
   e. Exclusions.
   f. Personal and dependency exemptions.
   g. Gross income.

3. During the year, Ned inherits $5,000 from a great uncle. To help Ned come up with a $15,000 down payment on a condominium, Ned's mother lends him an additional $10,000. How do these transactions affect Ned's gross income for the year? No affect because this is not an income

4. During the year, Mildred's stock investment increased in value by $13,000. She also sold some stock for $4,500; the stock had cost $4,000. How do these facts affect Mildred's gross income?

5. Jason and Kara (both age 64) will itemize their deductions on a joint return for 1998. Since they will not have certain itemized deductions next year, they expect their income tax liability to increase. Comment on their expectation.

6. Al and Melissa are husband and wife, and both are employed. They do not live in a community property state. Since Melissa incurred most of their itemized deductions (e.g., medical, charitable), Al feels that they would save taxes if they filed separate returns. On such returns, Al would claim the standard deduction, and Melissa would itemize her deductions *from* AGI. Comment on this proposed course of action.

7. Discuss the marital status of the parties under the following circumstances:
   a. One spouse dies during the year.
   b. The spouses are divorced during the year.

8. If an individual who may qualify as a dependent does not spend funds that he or she has received (e.g., wages or Social Security benefits), are these unexpended amounts considered in applying the support test?

9. Freda purchased a stereo system for her son Wes, age 16. The stereo was placed in Wes's room and used exclusively by him. Freda also purchased a new sports car, titled and registered in her own name, that was used 90% of the time by Wes. Should the cost of these items be considered as support in determining whether Freda may claim Wes as a dependent?

10. Carol provided 75% of the support of Debra, her niece. Debra was a full-time student during the year and earned $3,800 from a part-time job. Can Carol claim Debra as a dependent?

11. Besides what he furnishes on his own, Walter receives support from his daughter (20%) and his son (25%). Can either the daughter or the son claim Walter as a dependent under a multiple support agreement? Why or why not?

12. After Hugh and Ashley were divorced, Ashley disappeared with their two children. Under the divorce decree (issued in 1997), Ashley is awarded custody, and Hugh is awarded the dependency exemptions for the two children. Does Hugh have a problem? Explain.

13. A taxpayer who is divorced continues to support his former mother-in-law. May he claim her as a dependent? Suppose she does not live with him. Does this make any difference?

14. Roberto, who is single, is a U.S. citizen and resident. He provides almost all of the support of his parents and two aunts, who are citizens and residents of Guatemala. Roberto's parents and aunts are seriously considering moving to and becoming residents of Mexico. Would such a move have any impact on Roberto? Why or why not?

15. What perceived abuse is the kiddie tax designed to correct?

16. A single individual age 65 or over and blind is required to file a Federal income tax return in 1998 if he or she has gross income of $8,000 or more (refer to Table 3–4).
   a. Explain how the $8,000 filing requirement was computed.
   b. In general, explain the effect of the additional standard deduction on the determination of the gross income requirement for filing.

17. Comment on the so-called marriage penalty in connection with the following:
   a. What it is.
   b. When it is likely to occur.
   c. What income level (i.e., low, modest, high) could be vulnerable.

18. Baron and Cheryl are both professionals who have held jobs since they graduated from college five years ago. For several years, they have been engaged to be married. Both would like to tie the knot, but Cheryl is hesitant because of a "marriage penalty" she has heard about. Baron feels Cheryl's fears are unfounded and says they should be able to avoid any such penalty by filing separate returns as married persons. Comment on Baron and Cheryl's situation.

19. In 1998, Ginger's husband dies. Ginger plans to file as a surviving spouse for tax years 1998 through 2000. Ginger's only dependent is her mother, who lives with her. Comment on any misconceptions Ginger may have regarding the tax law.

20. Jacob is single and lives alone in an apartment. He maintains the home where his parents live, but only his mother qualifies as Jacob's dependent. When Jacob files his own return, he chooses single status since *both* of his parents do not qualify as dependents. Comment on Jacob's filing status.

21. Several years ago, after a particularly fierce argument, Fran's husband moved out and has not been heard from or seen since. Because Fran cannot locate her husband, she has been using "married, filing separate" status when filing her income tax return. Comment on Fran's status.

22. During 1998, Andre had a short-term capital loss, a mid-term capital gain, and a long-term capital gain.
    a. To which category of capital gain (i.e., mid- or long-term) is the capital loss first applied?
    b. Is the approach taken in part (a) favorable or unfavorable to the taxpayer?

23. Are net long-term capital assets (i.e., those held for more than 18 months) always taxed at a rate of 20%? Explain.

24. For 1998, Ann's only capital transaction is a short-term loss of $4,000. How is this loss handled for tax purposes?

25. What are collectibles?
    a. How is the sale of collectibles handled for tax purposes?
    b. In connection with part (a), would it matter if the collectible had been held for more than 18 months? For one year or less?

26. Perry is divorced and has living with him his married daughter, Celia, and her husband, Clark. During the year, Celia earned $3,100 from a part-time job and filed a separate return to recover her withholdings. Clark has no income. Perry can prove that he provided more than 50% of Celia and Clark's support. Perry did not claim Celia as his dependent because he believed she failed the gross income test. Perry filed his return using single taxpayer status. All parties reside in California. Comment on Perry's tax position.

27. Erica and her two brothers equally furnish all of the support of their mother. Erica is married and has four children. Her brothers are single and claim the standard deduction. Erica's mother is not in good health. What suggestions can you make regarding the tax position of the parties?

PROBLEMS

28. Compute the taxpayer's taxable income for 1998 in each of the following cases:
    a. Jack is married and files a joint return with his wife Alice. Jack and Alice have two dependent children. They have AGI of $50,000 and $8,300 of itemized deductions.
    b. Pete is an unmarried head of household with two dependents. He has AGI of $45,000 and itemized deductions of $5,200.
    c. Iris, age 22, is a full-time college student who is claimed as a dependent by her parents. She earns $4,200 from a part-time job and has interest income of $1,500.
    d. Matt, age 20, is a full-time college student who is claimed as a dependent by his parents. He earns $2,500 from a part-time job and has interest income of $4,100. His itemized deductions related to the investment income are $800.

    Note: Problems 29 and 30 can be solved by referring to Figure 3–1, Exhibits 3–1 through 3–3, Tables 3–1 and 3–2, and the discussion under Deductions for Adjusted Gross Income in this chapter.

29. Compute taxable income for 1998 for Blake on the basis of the following information. His filing status is head of household.

Salary	$60,000
Alimony paid	1,200
Casualty loss (deductible portion)	7,500
Interest on home mortgage	4,200
Property taxes on home	2,200
State and local income taxes	1,500
Number of dependents (two children and both of Blake's parents)	4
Age	46

30. Compute taxable income for 1998 for Amber on the basis of the following information. Her filing status is single.

Inheritance received from mother	$29,000
Gift received from aunt	14,000
Cash dividends from stock investments	15,000
Interest income from savings accounts and money market deposits	11,000
Interest on state and local bonds	11,000
Lottery winnings	3,600
Cash charitable contributions	4,000
Age	66

31. Determine the amount of the standard deduction allowed for 1998 in the following independent situations. In each case, assume the taxpayer is claimed as another person's dependent.
    a. Mona, age 16, has income as follows: $710 interest from a savings account and $800 from a part-time job.
    b. Aaron, age 18, earns $4,300 from a part-time job.
    c. Irving, age 71 and single, has income as follows: $3,100 nontaxable Social Security benefits and $1,050 from a part-time job.
    d. Maureen, age 67, is single and blind and has cash dividends of $1,300 from a stock investment.

32. Determine the number of personal and dependency exemptions in the following independent situations:
    a. Wesley, age 45, provides all of the support of Doreen (age 70) who does not live with him. Doreen was Wesley's mother-in-law before his divorce.
    b. Carol, age 50, provides all of the support of two cousins, Rick and Jane. Jane lives with Carol but Rick does not.
    c. Ron, age 66, provides all of the support of Cynthia and Leona who live with him. Cynthia is Ron's wife, and Leona is unrelated but is a close friend of the family and a member of their church. Ron files a separate return. Neither Cynthia nor Leona has any income, and neither files a return.
    d. Nicole, age 60, provides all of the support of Alan, age 66 and blind, and Grace, age 89. Alan, Nicole's husband, died in February of the current year. Grace is Alan's mother and lives in a nursing home. Nicole files a separate return.

33. Compute the number of personal and dependency exemptions in the following independent situations:
    a. Roberto, a U.S. citizen and resident, contributes 100% of the support of his parents who are citizens of Mexico and live there.
    b. Pablo, a U.S. citizen and resident, contributes 100% of the support of his parents who are citizens of Guatemala. Pablo's father is a resident of Guatemala, and his mother is a legal resident of the United States.
    c. Marlena, a U.S. citizen and resident, contributes 100% of the support of her parents who are also U.S. citizens but are residents of Germany.

34. Determine the number of personal and dependency exemptions in each of the following independent situations:

a. Warren and Terri provide more than half of the support of their children, Demi and Paul. Demi, age 19, earns $3,200 from a part-time job. Paul, age 21, earns $2,800 from a part-time job.

b. Hortense, age 64 and widowed, furnishes more than half of the support of her father, age 88 and blind. The father receives Social Security benefits of $4,300, interest on a savings account of $2,400, and interest on tax-exempt bonds of $10,000.

c. Dennis and Ava provide more than half of the support of their son, Henry. Henry, age 25, is a full-time student in medical school. During the year, Henry receives $2,500 in dividends from stock investments.

d. Earl provides more than half of the support of his nephew, Brad, who lives with him. Brad, age 17 and a full-time student, earns $2,500 from a part-time job.

35. Caleb and Carrie are married and file a joint return. Their four children and Carrie's parents qualify as their dependents. If Caleb and Carrie's AGI is $210,000, what is their allowable exemption deduction for 1998?

36. Melvin and Sarah Turner are married and file a joint return. Transactions for 1998 are as follows:

Salaries ($42,000 for Melvin and $39,000 for Sarah)	$81,000
Lottery winnings	1,200
Inheritance from Melvin's father	30,000
Gift from Sarah's mother	10,000
Short-term capital loss from sale of stock held as an investment	3,000

The Turners provided all of the support of their 20-year-old married daughter, Maryanne, and her husband, Boyd. Maryanne and Boyd live with the Turners, and neither has any gross income. The Turners also furnish over half of the support of Sarah's aunt who lives in a nursing home. The aunt, age 76, has interest of $2,700 from State of Alabama bonds. Melvin is age 65, while Sarah is age 45. If the Turners have itemized deductions of $7,000, what is their taxable income for 1998?

37. Bob, age 13, is a full-time student supported by his parents who claim him on their tax return for 1998. Bob's parents present you with the following information and ask that you prepare Bob's Federal income tax return for the year:

Wages from summer job	$2,100
Interest on savings account at First National Bank	950
Interest on City of Chicago bonds Bob received as a gift from his grandfather two years ago	750
Dividend from Owl Corporation	200

a. What is Bob's taxable income for 1998?

b. Bob's parents file a joint return for 1998 on which they report taxable income of $66,000. Compute Bob's 1998 tax liability.

38. Walter and Nancy provide 70% of the support of their daughter (age 21) and son-in-law (age 22). The son-in-law (John) is a full-time student at a local university, while the daughter (Irene) holds various part-time jobs from which she earns $3,000. Walter and Nancy engage you to prepare their tax return for 1998. During a meeting with them in late March of 1999, you learn that John and Irene do not file a joint return. What tax advice would you give based on the following assumptions:

a. All parties live in Louisiana (a community property state).

b. All parties live in New Jersey (a common law state).

39. Don is a wealthy executive who had taxable income of $200,000 in 1998. He is considering transferring title in a duplex he owns to his son Sam, age 16. Sam has no other income and is claimed as a dependent by Don. Net rent income from the duplex is $10,000 a year, which Sam will be encouraged to place in a savings account. Will the family save income taxes in 1998 if Don transfers title in the duplex to Sam? Explain.

40. Compute the 1998 tax liability for each of the following taxpayers:
    a. Norm and Nancy, both age 46, are married, have two dependent children, and file a joint return. Their combined salaries totaled $66,000. They had deductions *for* AGI of $7,000 and total itemized deductions of $7,400.
    b. Clark, age 45, is single and has no dependents. He had a salary of $52,000, deductions *for* AGI of $3,000, and total itemized deductions of $4,200.
    c. David and Susan, both age 65, are married, have no dependents, and file a joint return. Their combined salaries were $92,000. They had deductions *for* AGI of $2,000 and itemized deductions of $8,500.

41. Dustin and Vicki are married and file a joint return. Dustin is age 70, and Vicki is age 65. Their income is as follows: $32,000 (cash dividends from stock investments); $12,000 (interest income on certificates of deposits); and $18,000 (interest income on City of Detroit bonds). In addition, they incur a long-term capital loss of $2,500 on the sale of stock held as an investment. They furnish more than half of the support of Vicki's cousin who does not live with them. If they have itemized deductions of $8,000, determine their taxable income for 1998.

42. Peter, age 12, is claimed as a dependent on his parents' 1998 Federal income tax return, on which they reported taxable income of $95,000. During the summer, Peter earned $2,500 from a job as a model. His only other income consisted of $1,700 in interest on a savings account. Compute Peter's taxable income and tax liability.

43. Carmen, who is 12 years old, is claimed as a dependent on her parents' tax return. During 1998, she received $12,200 in dividends and interest and had no investment expenses related to this income. She also earned $2,000 wages from a part-time job. Compute the amount of income that is taxed at Carmen's parents' rate.

44. Bruce Smith and Wanda Brown are young professionals who are employed in well-paying jobs. They have been dating each other for several years and are considering getting married in December 1998 or January 1999. For 1998, their respective AGIs are $65,000 and $68,000. They anticipate earning the same income in 1999. In both years, they will claim the standard deduction.

    Bruce and Wanda solicit your tax advice. Specifically, they wish to know what Federal income tax results from their getting married in 1998 or in 1999. Prepare a letter to Wanda (4339 Elm St., Apt. 39A, Cincinnati, OH 45221) setting forth the tax determination under each choice.

45. Which of the following individuals are required to file a tax return for 1998? Should any of these individuals file a return even if filing is not required? Why?
    a. Sam is married and files a joint return with his spouse, Lana. Both Sam and Lana are 67 years old. Their combined gross income was $14,000.
    b. Bobby is a dependent child under age 19 who received $4,000 in wages from a part-time job.
    c. Mike is single and is 67 years old. His gross income from wages was $6,700.
    d. Marge is a self-employed single individual with gross income of $4,500 from an unincorporated business. Business expenses amounted to $4,000.

46. Which of the following taxpayers must file a Federal income tax return for 1998?
    a. Bob, age 19, is a full-time college student. He is claimed as a dependent by his parents. He earned $4,100 wages during the year.
    b. Anita, age 12, is claimed as a dependent by her parents. She earned interest income of $1,200 during the year.
    c. Earl, age 16, is claimed as a dependent by his parents. He earned wages of $2,700 and interest of $1,100 during the year.
    d. Karen, age 16 and blind, is claimed as a dependent by her parents. She earned wages of $2,600 and interest of $1,200 during the year.
    e. Pat, age 17, is claimed as a dependent by her parents. She earned interest of $300 during the year. In addition, she earned $550 during the summer operating her own business at the beach, where she painted caricatures of her customers.

47. In each of the following situations, determine Darlene's filing status for tax year 1998:
   a. Darlene is a widow and maintains a household in which her two dependent children live. Darlene's husband died in 1996.
   b. Same as (a) except that Darlene's husband died in 1994 (not 1996).
   c. Darlene is single and lives alone. She maintains the household of her parents, only one of whom qualifies as her dependent.
   d. Darlene is married, but her husband disappeared for parts unknown in 1997. Darlene maintains the household in which she and her dependent children live.

48. In each of the following situations, determine Isaac's filing status for tax year 1998:
   a. Isaac lives alone. He has not seen or heard from his wife since 1997.
   b. Isaac's wife died in January 1998. He maintains the home in which he and his dependent child live.
   c. Isaac's wife died in 1994. He maintains the home in which he and his unmarried child live. The child does not qualify as Isaac's dependent.
   d. Isaac is divorced and lives alone. He also maintains a home in which his dependent child lives.

49. Henry died on January 1, 1996. He was survived by his wife, Sue, and their 19-year-old son, Mike, who was a college sophomore. Mike was a full-time student in 1997 and earned $3,000 for the year. In 1998, Mike reduced his school load and became a part-time student. He earned $5,200 in 1998. Mike continues to live with his mother, who provides over half of his support. What is Sue's filing status in 1996, 1997, and 1998?

50. Tracy, age 66, is a widow. Her husband died in 1996. Tracy maintains a home in which she and her 28-year-old son reside. Her son Gary is a piano player at a local nightclub, where he earned $12,000 during 1998. Gary contributed $3,000 of his income toward household expenses and put the remainder in a savings account that he used to return to college full-time to pursue a master's degree in music starting in August 1998. Tracy contributed $12,000 toward household expenses. What is the most favorable filing status available to Tracy for 1998, and how many exemptions may she claim?

51. During 1998, Hazel had the following gains from sales of capital assets:

Short-term (held one year or less)	$4,000
Mid-term (held more than one year but not more than 18 months)	2,000
Long-term (held more than 18 months)	5,000

   a. If Hazel is in the 31% tax bracket, how much income tax do these transactions generate?
   b. What if Hazel is in the 15% tax bracket?

52. During 1998, Cole had the following gains and losses from the sale of capital assets:

Loss on Pidgeon Corporation stock (held 9 months)	($4,000)
Gain on a painting (held for 3 years as an investment)	5,000
Gain on unimproved land (held for 3 years as an investment)	3,000

   a. If Cole is in the 36% tax bracket, how much income tax do these transactions generate?
   b. What if Cole is in the 15% tax bracket?

53. Gina, a cash basis taxpayer, is single and has no dependents. She provides you with the following estimates for 1997 and 1998:

	1997	1998
Adjusted gross income	$56,000	$60,000
Charitable contributions	2,200	2,400
Interest on home mortgage	1,000	850
Property taxes	700	700

Can Gina decrease taxable income over the two-year period by prepaying her 1998 charitable contributions in 1997?

CUMULATIVE PROBLEMS

54. Matt and Anita Huerta are married and live at 3486 International Blvd., El Paso, TX 79968. Both have full-time jobs. Matt's Social Security number is 433-22-1111, and Anita's is 437-00-1112. The Huertas have four children who live with them. Three of the children are their own, while the oldest is Anita's child from a prior marriage.

During 1998, the Huertas had the following receipts:

Salaries (Matt and Anita combined)	$71,000
Child support payments received by Anita from her former husband	3,600
Fees earned by Matt for jury duty service	90
Proceeds from garage sale	1,180
Gift of cash received from Matt's mother	4,000
Cash prize won for being the ninth caller on a radio talk show	1,000

Matt's employer withheld Federal income taxes of $2,600, and Anita's employer withheld $3,400. The garage sale involved used clothing, toys, appliances, furniture and other personal effects, and household goods. The Huertas estimate that the cost of the items was in excess of $4,000.

Expenses for 1998 are summarized below:

Interest on home mortgage	$5,600
Property taxes on home	3,400
Charitable contributions	4,200

The Huertas furnish all of the support of Anita's widowed mother, who lives with them. The mother, although a U.S. resident, is still a citizen of Mexico. The mother helps with the household chores and takes care of the children while Anita and Matt are at work. The Huertas also furnish all of the support of Anita's grandparents, who are over age 65. The grandparents live in Mexico and are citizens of Mexico.

Compute the Huertas' tax liability for 1998. Suggested software (if available): *TurboTax.*

55. Horace Fern, age 43, lives at 321 Grant Avenue, Cheyenne, WY 82002. Horace's mother Kate (age 65) lived with him until her death in August 1997. Up to the time of her death, Kate qualified as Horace's dependent. Horace maintained the household where he and his mother lived.

Horace is a manager for Bison Lumber Company at a yearly salary of $62,000. Because his job duties will be expanded, Bison plans to increase Horace's salary by 10% starting in 1998.

During 1997, Horace paid $3,300 ($300 each month) in alimony to Janet, his ex-wife. As Janet was remarried in late November, Horace's alimony obligation has terminated.

Besides his salary, Horace received interest income of $5,700 from Western Bank and $6,300 from First Savings Bank on $200,000 in certificates of deposit (CDs) he owns. Horace received the CDs as a gift from his mother several years ago.

Except as otherwise noted, Horace's expenditures for 1997 are summarized below:

Interest on home mortgage	$3,300
Property taxes on home	1,300
Charitable contributions	1,800

Relevant Social Security numbers are as follows:

Horace Fern	520–31–4596
Kate Fern	520–32–3214
Janet Fern	520–33–4432

Federal income taxes withheld from Horace's salary amounted to $10,900. He also paid estimated tax of $300 each quarter.

Part 1—Tax Computation

Compute Horace's net tax payable or refund due for 1997. Horace does not wish to contribute to the Presidential Election Campaign Fund. If he has overpaid, he wants the amount refunded. If you use tax forms for your computations, you will need Form 1040 and Schedules A and B. Suggested software (if available): *TurboTax*.

Part 2—Tax Planning

In addition to preparing the return for 1997, Horace has asked you to advise him regarding his tax situation for 1998. He is particularly concerned about the tax effects of the following:

• The death of Kate.

• The cessation of alimony payments due to Janet's remarriage.

• The salary increase.

• Interest income on the CDs.

Write a letter to Horace in which you summarize (in approximate amounts) how much more (or less) he will owe in income taxes for 1998. Also include recommendations on what can be done to mitigate the tax consequences resulting from the investment in CDs. Assume that Horace's itemized deductions will remain constant in 1998.

RESEARCH PROBLEMS

*Note: Use the **RIA OnPoint System 4 Student Version CD-ROM**, which is available to accompany this text, in preparing solutions to the Research Problems. Alternatively, tax research materials found in a standard tax library can be used.*

Research Problem 1. In the state of Texas, a lawsuit was instituted charging that the state schools for the mentally retarded furnished inadequate, unsafe, and improper care, treatment, and education. As part of the settlement of this suit, the Texas Department of Mental Health offered to pay a fixed daily amount to third-party providers of these services. Under this arrangement, the taxpayers received $16,425 during the year for the care of their mentally retarded daughter. This amount covered a daily per diem for food and board, medical expenses, cost of special food, clothing, transportation, special laundry, home repairs, and other living expenses. The daughter lived with the taxpayers and during the year attended classes at a special school operated by the local school district.

  Although the taxpayers did not pay for more than 50% of their daughter's support, they claimed her as a dependent for the year. The taxpayers contend that the amount they received from the state is a scholarship and, therefore, should not be taken into account in applying the support test. The IRS disagrees. What is the appropriate result?

Partial list of research aids:
§ 152(d).
Rev.Rul. 61–186, 1961–2 C.B. 30.
Rev.Rul. 64–221, 1964–2 C.B. 46.

Research Problem 2. Susan Carpenter, although married, lives alone. She maintains a household that includes her three-year-old son. Susan and her husband are not on good terms, but neither has ever bothered to file for legal separation or divorce. Susan is gainfully employed and provides all of the support for herself and her son. During the year, she utilizes the service of a day care center while she works.

Susan has contacted you regarding her tax situation. She is particularly interested in ascertaining her filing status and whatever deductions and credits are available.

a. Write a letter to Susan addressing her concerns. She lives at 3126 Kingsride Rd., Funston, UT 84602. Try to express yourself in nonlegal terms.

b. Prepare a memo containing legal substantiation for your position. The memo is for inclusion in your firm's files.

Research Problem 3. Judy and Greg married in 1989 and have since resided in California. In October 1995, Judy filed in state court to have her marriage to Greg annulled. The annulment was granted in May 1996. Under California law, an annulment voids the marriage and, in effect, treats it as if it never occurred.

Judy files her Federal income tax return for calendar year 1995 using "single" status. Upon audit of the return, the IRS contends that Judy's correct filing status is "married filing separate." Who is correct and why?

Partial list of research aids:
§ 7703(a)(1).
Reg. § 1.6013–4(a)(1).
Harold K. Lee, 64 T.C. 552 (1975).
Betty J. Shackelford, 70 TCM 945, T.C.Memo. 1995–484.

Use the tax resources of the Internet to address the following questions. Do not restrict your search to the World Wide Web, but include a review of newsgroups and general reference materials, practitioner sites and resources, primary sources of the tax law, chat rooms and discussion groups, and other opportunities.

Research Problem 4. Many tax advisers with materials on the Internet propose tax planning techniques for minimizing liabilities under the kiddie tax. Summarize the most effective of these proposals, and cite the providers of the information.

Research Problem 5. Find an Internet site that receives and answers technical tax questions from the public. Pose a question of the site with respect to whether a dependency exemption is available in a described situation, or whether head-of-household status can be used. How quickly did the site provider respond? Did it apply the law correctly to your query?

Research Problem 6. Find an Internet site that computes an individual's Federal income taxes at no charge. Submit a set of facts to the site using data from one of your assignment problems. Did the Internet tax calculator match the answer you had derived previously?

TEAM PROJECT: ARTHUR ANDERSEN TAX CHALLENGE CASES

For more information on the Arthur Andersen Tax Challenge Cases, refer to Chapter 1, page 1–37.

Information related to tax issues and problems that are discussed in this chapter may be found in the

Day and Ball case on pages 2, 3, 4, and 7
Fence case on pages 43, 47, and 61

Read and analyze the case you have been assigned and *identify* any issues and problems that are related to material covered in this chapter. If the information provided in the case is complete, prepare answers for this part of the case at this time. If you need information that is contained in the later parts of the case, write a memo summarizing the questions or problems so you can prepare a complete answer at a later date.

II

GROSS INCOME

Part II presents the income component of the basic tax model. Included in this presentation are the determination of what is income and the statutory exclusions that are permitted in calculating gross income. Because the taxpayer's accounting method and accounting period affect when income is reported, an introductory discussion of these topics is also included.

GROSS INCOME: CONCEPTS AND INCLUSIONS

LEARNING OBJECTIVES

After completing Chapter 4, you should be able to:

1. Explain the concepts of gross income and realization and distinguish between the economic, accounting, and tax concepts of gross income.

2. Describe the cash and accrual methods of accounting and the related effects of the choice of taxable year.

3. Identify who should pay the tax on a particular item of income in various situations.

4. Apply the Internal Revenue Code provisions on alimony, loans made at below-market interest rates, annuities, prizes and awards, group term life insurance, unemployment compensation, and Social Security benefits.

5. Identify tax planning strategies for minimizing gross income.

OUTLINE

Mr. Zarin lost over $2,500,000 of his own money gambling. The casino then allowed him to gamble on credit. After several months, his liability to the casino totaled more than $3,400,000. Following protracted negotiations, the casino agreed to settle its claim against Mr. Zarin for a mere $500,000. Although Mr. Zarin had paid for gambling losses of $3,000,000, the IRS had the audacity to ask him to pay tax on $2,900,000, that is, the amount the casino marked down his account.[1] Mr. Zarin undoubtedly had difficulty understanding how he could be deemed to have income in this situation.

Given an understanding of the income tax formula, though, one can see how the "free" gambling Mr. Zarin enjoyed could constitute income. The starting point in the formula is the determination of gross income rather than "net income." Once gross income is determined, the next step is to determine the allowable deductions. In Mr. Zarin's way of thinking, these steps were collapsed.

This chapter is concerned with the first step in the computation of taxable income—the determination of gross income. Questions that are addressed include the following:

- What: What is income?
- When: In which tax period is the income recognized?
- Who: Who must include the item of income in gross income?

The Code provides an all-inclusive definition of gross income in § 61. Chapter 5 presents items of income that are specifically excluded from gross income (exclusions).

---

[1]*Zarin v. Comm.*, 90–2 USTC ¶50,530, 66 AFTR2d 90–5679, 916 F.2d
110 (CA–3, 1990).

GROSS INCOME—WHAT IS IT?

DEFINITION

1   **LEARNING OBJECTIVE**
Explain the concepts of gross income and realization and distinguish between the economic, accounting, and tax concepts of gross income.

Section 61(a) of the Internal Revenue Code defines the term **gross income** as follows:

> Except as otherwise provided in this subtitle, gross income means all income from whatever source derived.

This definition is derived from the language of the Sixteenth Amendment to the Constitution.

Supreme Court decisions have made it clear that all sources of income are subject to tax unless Congress specifically excludes the type of income received:

> The starting point in all cases dealing with the question of the scope of what is included in "gross income" begins with the basic premise that the purpose of Congress was to use the full measure of its taxing power.[2]

Although at this point we know that *income* is to be broadly construed, we still do not have a satisfactory definition of the term *income*. Congress left it to the judicial and administrative branches to thrash out the meaning of income. Early in the development of the income tax law, a choice was made between two competing models: economic income and accounting income.

ECONOMIC AND ACCOUNTING CONCEPTS

The term **income** is used in the Code but is not separately defined. Thus, early in the history of our tax laws, the courts were required to interpret "the commonly understood meaning of the term which must have been in the minds of the people when they adopted the Sixteenth Amendment to the Constitution."[3] In determining the definition of income, the Supreme Court rejected the economic concept of income.

Economists measure income (**economic income**) by first determining the fair market value of the individual's net assets at the beginning and end of the year (change in net worth). Then, to arrive at economic income, this change in net worth is added to the goods and services that person actually consumed during the period. Economic income also includes imputed values for such items as the rental value of an owner-occupied home and the value of food a taxpayer might grow for personal consumption.[4]

EXAMPLE 1

Helen's economic income is calculated as follows:

Fair market value of Helen's assets on December 31, 1998	$220,000	
Less liabilities on December 31, 1998	(40,000)	
Net worth on December 31, 1998		$180,000
Fair market value of Helen's assets on January 1, 1998	$200,000	
Less liabilities on January 1, 1998	(80,000)	
Net worth on January 1, 1998		(120,000)

---

[2] *James v. U.S.*, 61–1 USTC ¶9449, 7 AFTR2d 1361, 81 S.Ct. 1052 (USSC, 1961).

[3] *Merchants Loan and Trust Co. v. Smietanka*, 1 USTC ¶42, 3 AFTR 3102, 41 S.Ct. 386 (USSC, 1921).

[4] See Henry C. Simons, *Personal Income Taxation* (Chicago: University of Chicago Press, 1933), Ch. 2–3.

Increase in net worth	$ 60,000
Consumption	
Food, clothing, and other personal expenditures	25,000
Imputed rental value of the home Helen owns and occupies	12,000
Economic income	$ 97,000

▼

The need to value assets annually would make compliance with the tax law burdensome and would cause numerous controversies between the taxpayer and the IRS over valuation. In addition, using market values to determine income for tax purposes could result in liquidity problems. That is, the taxpayer's assets may increase in value even though they are not readily convertible into the cash needed to pay the tax (e.g., commercial real estate). Thus, the IRS, Congress, and the courts have rejected the economic concept of income as impractical.

In contrast, the accounting concept of income is founded on the realization principle.[5] According to this principle, income (**accounting income**) is not recognized until it is realized. For realization to occur, (1) an exchange of goods or services must take place between the accounting entity and some independent, external group, and (2) in the exchange the accounting entity must receive assets that are capable of being objectively valued. Thus, the mere appreciation in the market value of assets before a sale or other disposition is not sufficient to warrant income recognition. In addition, the imputed savings that arise when an individual creates assets for her own use (e.g., feed grown for a farmer's own livestock) are not income because no exchange has occurred. The courts and the IRS have ruled, however, that embezzlement proceeds and buried treasures found satisfy the realization requirement and, therefore, must be recognized as income.[6]

The Supreme Court expressed an inclination toward the accounting concept of income when it adopted the realization requirement in *Eisner v. Macomber*:

> Income may be defined as the gain derived from capital, from labor, or from both combined, provided it is understood to include profit gained through a sale or conversion of capital assets. . . . Here we have the essential matter: not a gain accruing to capital; not a *growth* or *increment* of value *in* investment; but a gain, a profit, something of exchangeable value, *proceeding from* the property, *severed from* the capital however invested or employed, and *coming in*, being *"derived"*—that is, *received* or *drawn by* the recipient for his separate use, benefit and disposal—*that is*, income derived from the property.[7]

In summary, *income* represents an increase in wealth recognized for tax purposes only upon realization.

COMPARISON OF THE ACCOUNTING AND TAX CONCEPTS OF INCOME

Although income tax rules frequently parallel financial accounting measurement concepts, differences do exist. Of major significance, for example, is the fact that unearned (prepaid) income received by an accrual basis taxpayer often is taxed in the year of receipt. For financial accounting purposes, such prepayments are not

---

[5] See the American Accounting Association Committee Report on the "Realization Concept," *The Accounting Review* (April 1965): 312–322.
[6] *Rutkin v. U.S.*, 52–1 USTC ¶9260, 41 AFTR2d 596, 72 S.Ct. 571 (USSC, 1952); Rev.Rul. 61, 1953–1 C.B. 17.

[7] 1 USTC ¶32, 3 AFTR 3020, 40 S.Ct. 189 (USSC, 1920).

TAX IN THE NEWS

IRS CALLS FOUL ON NBA REFEREES

Four NBA referees have been called for "tax fouls" and ejected from the game for not reporting income. The rules of the game were as follows:

- Through a travel agent, the referees would purchase first-class airline tickets to cities where they were officiating.
- The referees would then turn the tickets in to the travel agent in exchange for coach tickets and cash.
- The referees were reimbursed for the first-class tickets by the NBA.
- The referees chose not to include the cash differential received in their gross income.

The IRS filed criminal charges against the four referees (i.e., filing false Federal income tax returns). Three of the four have pleaded guilty.

---

treated as income until earned.[8] Because of this and other differences, many corporations report financial accounting income that is substantially different from the amounts reported for tax purposes (see Chapter 20, Reconciliation of Taxable Income and Accounting Income).

The Supreme Court provided an explanation for some of the variations between accounting and taxable income in a decision involving inventory and bad debt adjustments:

> The primary goal of financial accounting is to provide useful information to management, shareholders, creditors, and others properly interested; the major responsibility of the accountant is to protect these parties from being misled. The primary goal of the income tax system, in contrast, is the equitable collection of revenue. . . . Consistently with its goals and responsibilities, financial accounting has as its foundation the principle of conservatism, with its corollary that 'possible errors in measurement [should] be in the direction of understatement rather than overstatement of net income and net assets.' In view of the Treasury's markedly different goals and responsibilities, understatement of income is not destined to be its guiding light.
>   . . . Financial accounting, in short, is hospitable to estimates, probabilities, and reasonable certainties; the tax law, with its mandate to preserve the revenue, can give no quarter to uncertainty.[9]

FORM OF RECEIPT

Gross income is not limited to cash received. "It includes income realized in any form, whether in money, property, or services. Income may be realized [and recognized], therefore, in the form of services, meals, accommodations, stock or other property, as well as in cash."[10]

---

[8]Similar differences exist in the deduction area.

[9]*Thor Power Tool Co. v. Comm.*, 79–1 USTC ¶9139, 43 AFTR2d 79–362, 99 S.Ct. 773 (USSC, 1979).

[10]Reg. § 1.61–1(a).

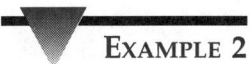

EXAMPLE 2   Ostrich Corporation allowed Bill, an employee, to use a company car for his vacation. Bill realized income equal to the rental value of the car for the time and mileage. ▼

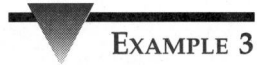

EXAMPLE 3   Terry owed $10,000 on a mortgage. The creditor accepted $8,000 in full satisfaction of the debt. Terry realized income of $2,000 from retiring the debt.[11] ▼

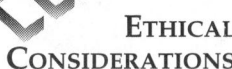

ETHICAL CONSIDERATIONS

Unreported Income

The roof of your office building recently experienced some damage as the result of a storm. You are negotiating with a carpenter who has quoted two prices for the repair work: $600 if you pay in cash ("folding money") and $700 if you pay by check. The carpenter observes that the IRS can more readily discover his receipt of a check. Thus, he hints that he will report the receipt of the check (but not the cash). The carpenter has a full-time job and will do the work after hours and on the weekend. He comments that he should be allowed to keep all he earns after regular working hours. Evaluate what you should do including whether you have an ethical obligation to pay the higher price.

RECOVERY OF CAPITAL DOCTRINE

The Constitution grants Congress the power to tax income but does not define the term. Because the Constitution does not define income, it would seem that Congress could simply tax gross receipts. Although Congress does allow certain deductions, none are constitutionally required. However, the Supreme Court has held that there is no income subject to tax until the taxpayer has recovered the capital invested.[12] This concept is known as the **recovery of capital doctrine.**

In its simplest application, this doctrine means that sellers can reduce their gross receipts (selling price) by the adjusted basis of the property sold.[13] This net amount, in the language of the Code, is gross income.

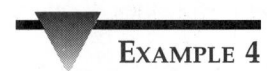

EXAMPLE 4   Dave sold common stock for $15,000. He had purchased the stock for $12,000. Dave's gross receipts are $15,000. This amount consists of a $12,000 recovery of capital and $3,000 of gross income. ▼

Collections on annuity contracts and installment payments received from sales of property must be allocated between recovery of capital and income. Annuities are discussed in this chapter, and installment sales are discussed in Chapter 18.

---

[11]Reg. § 1.61–12. See *U.S. v. Kirby Lumber Co.*, 2 USTC ¶814, 10 AFTR 458, 52 S.Ct. 4 (USSC, 1931). Exceptions to this general rule are discussed in Chapter 5.

[12]*Doyle v. Mitchell Bros. Co.*, 1 USTC ¶17, 3 AFTR 2979, 38 S.Ct. 467 (USSC, 1916).

[13]For a definition of adjusted basis, see the Glossary of Tax Terms in Appendix C.

YEAR OF INCLUSION

TAXABLE YEAR

The annual accounting period or **taxable year** is a basic component of our tax system.[14] Generally, an entity must use the *calendar year* to report its income. However, a *fiscal year* (a period of 12 months ending on the last day of any month other than December) can be elected if the taxpayer maintains adequate books and records. This fiscal year option generally is not available to partnerships, S corporations, and personal service corporations, as discussed in Chapter 18.[15]

Determining the particular year in which the income will be taxed is important for determining when the tax must be paid. But the year each item of income is subject to tax can also affect the total tax liability over the entity's lifetime. This is true for the following reasons:

- With a progressive rate system, a taxpayer's marginal tax rate can change from year to year.
- Congress may change the tax rates.
- The relevant rates may change because of a change in the entity's status (e.g., a person may marry or a business may be incorporated).
- Several provisions in the Code are dependent on the taxpayer's gross income for the year (e.g., whether the person can be claimed as a dependent, as discussed in Chapter 3).

ACCOUNTING METHODS

The year an item of income is subject to tax often depends upon which acceptable **accounting method** the taxpayer regularly employs.[16] The three primary methods of accounting are (1) the cash receipts and disbursements method, (2) the accrual method, and (3) the hybrid method. Most individuals use the cash receipts and disbursements method of accounting, whereas most corporations use the accrual method. The Regulations require the accrual method for determining purchases and sales when inventory is an income-producing factor.[17] Some businesses employ a hybrid method that is a combination of the cash and accrual methods of accounting.

In addition to these overall accounting methods, a taxpayer may choose to spread the gain from the sale of property over the collection periods by using the installment method of income recognition. Contractors may either spread profits from contracts over the periods in which the work is done (the percentage of completion method) or defer all profit until the year in which the project is completed (the completed contract method, which can be used only in limited circumstances).[18]

The IRS has the power to prescribe the accounting method to be used by the taxpayer. Section 446(b) grants the IRS broad powers to determine if the accounting method used *clearly reflects income:*

---

[14]See Accounting Periods in Chapter 18.
[15]§§ 441(a) and (d).
[16]See Accounting Methods in Chapter 18.
[17]Reg. § 1.446–1(c)(2)(i). Other circumstances in which the accrual method must be used are presented in Chapter 18.

[18]§§ 453 and 460. See Chapter 18 for limitations on the use of the installment method and the completed contract method.

Exceptions—If no method of accounting has been regularly used by the taxpayer, or *if the method used does not clearly reflect income, the computation of taxable income shall be made under such method as, in the opinion of the Secretary. . . does clearly reflect income.*

A change in the method of accounting requires the consent of the IRS.[19]

Cash Receipts Method.   Under the **cash receipts method,** property or services received are included in the taxpayer's gross income in the year of actual or constructive receipt by the taxpayer or agent, regardless of whether the income was earned in that year.[20] The income received need not be reduced to cash in the same year. All that is necessary for income recognition is that property or services received have a fair market value—a cash equivalent.[21] Thus, if a cash basis taxpayer receives a note in payment for services, he has income in the year of receipt equal to the fair market value of the note. However, a creditor's mere promise to pay (e.g., an account receivable), with no supporting note, is not usually considered to have a fair market value.[22] Thus, the cash basis taxpayer defers income recognition until the account receivable is collected.

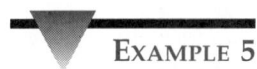

EXAMPLE 5

Dana, an accountant, reports her income by the cash method. In 1998, she performed an audit for Orange Corporation and billed the client for $5,000, which was collected in 1999. In 1998, Dana also performed an audit for Blue Corporation. Because of Blue's precarious financial position, Dana required Blue to issue an $8,000 secured negotiable note in payment of the fee. The note had a fair market value of $6,000. Dana collected $8,000 on the note in 1999. Dana's gross income for the two years is as follows:

	1998	1999
Fair market value of note received from Blue	$6,000	
Cash received		
From Orange on account receivable		$5,000
From Blue on note receivable		8,000
Less: Recovery of capital		(6,000)
Total gross income	$6,000	$7,000

Generally, a check received is considered a cash equivalent. Thus, a cash basis taxpayer must recognize the income when the check is received. This is true even if the taxpayer receives the check after banking hours.[23]

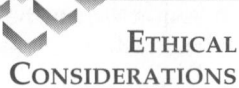

ETHICAL CONSIDERATIONS

Accounting Errors and Omissions

You have prepared Ted and Jane's tax return for the past five years. In the process of preparing the current year's return, you discover that you inadvertently omitted a $10,000 item of income from the previous year's return. Generally, the client does not examine the return in detail before filing it. As a result of your oversight, you are faced

---

[19]§ 446(e). See Chapter 18.
[20]*Julia A. Strauss,* 2 B.T.A. 598 (1925). See the Glossary of Tax Terms in Appendix C for a discussion of the terms "cash equivalent doctrine" and "constructive receipt."

[21]Reg. §§ 1.446–1(a)(3) and (c)(1)(i).
[22]*Bedell v. Comm.,* 1 USTC ¶359, 7 AFTR 8469, 30 F.2d 622 (CA–2, 1929).
[23]*Charles F. Kahler,* 18 T.C. 31 (1952).

with the following choices: (1) ignore the omission; (2) advise Ted and Jane that the previous year's return should be amended; (3) include the $10,000 in the current year's gross income and advise Ted and Jane of the previous omission; or (4) include the $10,000 in the current year's gross income and do not mention the adjustment to Ted and Jane.

Accrual Method.   Under the **accrual method,** an item is generally included in the gross income for the year in which it is earned, regardless of when the income is collected. The income is earned when (1) all the events have occurred that fix the right to receive such income and (2) the amount to be received can be determined with reasonable accuracy.[24]

Generally, the taxpayer's rights to the income accrue when title to property passes to the buyer or the services are performed for the customer or client.[25] If the rights to the income have accrued but are subject to a potential refund claim (e.g., under a product warranty), the income is reported in the year of sale, and a deduction is allowed in subsequent years when actual claims accrue.[26]

Where the taxpayer's rights to the income are being contested (e.g., when a contractor fails to meet specifications), the year in which the income is subject to tax depends upon whether payment has been received. If payment has not been received, no income is recognized until the claim is settled. Only then is the right to the income established.[27] However, if the payment is received before the dispute is settled, the court-made **claim of right doctrine** requires the taxpayer to recognize the income in the year of receipt.[28]

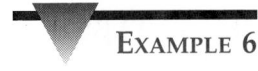

EXAMPLE 6

A contractor completed a building in 1998 and presented a bill to the customer. The customer refused to pay the bill and claimed that the contractor had not met specifications. A settlement with the customer was not reached until 1999. No income would accrue to the contractor until 1999. If the customer paid for the work and then filed suit for damages, the contractor could not defer the income (the income would be taxable in 1998). ▼

The measure of accrual basis income is generally the amount the taxpayer has a right to receive. Unlike the cash basis, the fair market value of the customer's obligation is irrelevant in measuring accrual basis income.

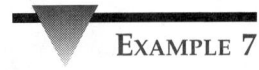

EXAMPLE 7

Assume the same facts as in Example 5, except Dana is an accrual basis taxpayer. Dana must recognize $13,000 ($8,000 + $5,000) income in 1998, the year her rights to the income accrued. ▼

Hybrid Method.   The **hybrid method** is a combination of the accrual method and the cash method. Generally, when the hybrid method is used, inventory is an income-producing factor. Therefore, the Regulations require that the accrual method be used for determining sales and cost of goods sold. In this circumstance, to simplify record keeping, the taxpayer accounts for inventory using the accrual method and uses the cash method for all other income and expense items (e.g., dividend and interest income). The hybrid method is primarily used by small businesses.

---

[24]Reg. § 1.451–1(a).

[25]*Lucas v. North Texas Lumber Co.,* 2 USTC ¶484, 8 AFTR 10276, 50 S.Ct. 184 (USSC, 1930).

[26]*Brown v. Helvering,* 4 USTC ¶1222, 13 AFTR 851, 54 S.Ct. 356 (USSC, 1933).

[27]*Burnet v. Sanford and Brooks,* 2 USTC ¶636, 9 AFTR 603, 51 S.Ct. 150 (USSC, 1931).

[28]*North American Oil Consolidated Co. v. Burnet,* 3 USTC ¶943, 11 AFTR 16, 52 S.Ct. 613 (USSC, 1932).

A FENDER-BENDER WITH THE IRS

Should used-car dealers be required to include in their gross income amounts they may never receive? They say no—doing so will drive them out of business. The IRS says yes—it is the law.

Creditors such as Credit Acceptance and National Auto Credit provide financing on used-car sales to buyers with poor credit ratings. This enables used-car dealers to sell more cars. But there is a catch. When a sale is financed through such a lender, the used-car dealer receives as little as half of the loan proceeds right away. To reduce their risk, the lenders turn over the rest of the money to the dealer only after they have collected it from the buyer. If the buyer defaults, the used-car dealer may not receive any of the remaining balance.

Dealers complain that having to record all the income at the time of the sale is driving them out of business. The amount involved is huge. For example, at the end of 1997, Credit Acceptance owed $469 million to nearly 5,400 dealers. The National Independent Automobile Dealers Association, which represents used-car dealers, is lobbying Congress for relief.

SOURCE: Adapted from Michael Selz, "Used-Car Dealers Face Fender-Benders with the IRS," *Wall Street Journal,* February 25, 1997, p. B2.

EXCEPTIONS APPLICABLE TO CASH BASIS TAXPAYERS

Constructive Receipt.   Income that has not actually been received by the taxpayer is taxed as though it had been received—the income is constructively received—under the following conditions:

- The amount is made readily available to the taxpayer.
- The taxpayer's actual receipt is not subject to substantial limitations or restrictions.[29]

The rationale for the **constructive receipt** doctrine is that if the income is available, the taxpayer should not be allowed to postpone the income recognition. For instance, a taxpayer is not permitted to defer income for December services by refusing to accept payment until January. However, determining whether the income is *readily available* and whether *substantial limitations or restrictions exist* necessitates a factual inquiry that leads to a judgment call.[30] The following are some examples of the application of the constructive receipt doctrine.

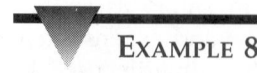

EXAMPLE 8

Ted is a member of a barter club. In 1998, Ted performed services for other club members and earned 1,000 points. Each point entitles him to $1 in goods and services sold by other members of the club; the points can be used at any time. In 1999, Ted exchanged his points for a new color TV. Ted must recognize $1,000 income in 1998 when the 1,000 points were credited to his account.[31] ▼

---

[29]Reg. § 1.451–2(a).
[30]*Baxter v. Comm.*, 87–1 USTC ¶9315, 59 AFTR2d 87–1068, 816 F.2d 493 (CA–9, 1987).

[31]Rev.Rul. 80–52, 1980–1 C.B. 100.

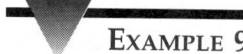

EXAMPLE 9

On December 31, an employer issued a bonus check to an employee but asked her to hold it for a few days until the company could make deposits to cover the check. The income was not constructively received on December 31 since the issuer did not have sufficient funds in its account to pay the debt.[32] ▼

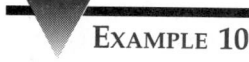

EXAMPLE 10

Rick owned interest coupons that matured on December 31. The coupons could be converted to cash at any bank at maturity. Thus, the income is constructively received on December 31.[33] ▼

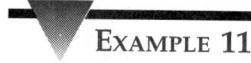

EXAMPLE 11

Dove Company mails dividend checks on December 31, 1998. The checks will not be received by shareholders until January. The shareholders do not realize income until 1999.[34] ▼

The constructive receipt doctrine does not reach income that the taxpayer is not yet entitled to receive even though the taxpayer could have contracted to receive the income at an earlier date.

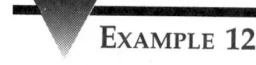

EXAMPLE 12

Sara offered to pay Ivan $100,000 for land in December 1998. Ivan refused but offered to sell the land to Sara on January 1, 1999, when he would be in a lower tax bracket. If Sara accepts Ivan's offer, the gain is taxed to Ivan in 1999 when the sale is completed.[35] ▼

Income set apart or made available is not constructively received if its actual receipt is subject to *substantial restrictions*. The life insurance industry has used substantial restrictions as a cornerstone for designing life insurance contracts with favorable tax features. Ordinary life insurance policies provide (1) current protection—an amount payable in the event of death—and (2) a savings feature—a cash surrender value payable to the policyholder if the policy is terminated during the policyholder's life. The annual increase in cash surrender value is not taxable because the policyholder must cancel the policy to actually receive the increase in value. Because the cancellation requirement is a substantial restriction, the policyholder does not constructively receive the annual increase in cash surrender value.[36] Employees often receive from their employers property subject to substantial restrictions. Generally, no income is recognized until the restrictions lapse.[37]

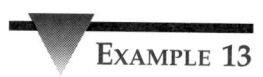

EXAMPLE 13

Carlos is a key employee of Red, Inc. The corporation gave stock with a value of $10,000 to Carlos. The stock could not be sold, however, for five years. Carlos will not be required to recognize income until the restrictions lapse at the end of five years. ▼

Original Issue Discount.   Lenders frequently make loans that require a payment at maturity of more than the amount of the original loan. The difference between the amount due at maturity and the amount of the original loan is actually interest but is referred to as **original issue discount.** Under the general rules of tax accounting, the cash basis lender would not report the original issue discount as interest income until the year the amount is collected, although an accrual basis borrower would deduct the interest as it is earned. However, the Code puts the lender and borrower on parity by requiring that the original issue discount be

---

[32]*L. M. Fischer*, 14 T.C. 792 (1950).
[33]Reg. § 1.451–2(b).
[34]Reg. § 1.451–2(b).
[35]*Cowden v. Comm.*, 61–1 USTC ¶9382, 7 AFTR2d 1160, 289 F.2d 20 (CA–5, 1961).

[36]*Theodore H. Cohen*, 39 T.C. 1055 (1963).
[37]§ 83(a). See also the discussion of Restricted Property Plans in Chapter 19.

TAX IN THE NEWS

ORIGINAL ISSUE DISCOUNT RULES MAY DAMPEN ENTHUSIASM FOR INFLATION-ADJUSTED BONDS

The U.S. Treasury Department is now issuing inflation-adjusted bonds. The bonds are aimed at small investors who want to be assured that inflation will not cause their savings to deteriorate. The interest paid each year and the principal are adjusted to reflect the inflation for the year. These bonds present some unique tax accounting issues.

In Temporary Regulation § 1.1275–7T, the Treasury Department concluded that in addition to the interest received each year, the taxpayer is required to include the change in the principal amount as original issue discount amortized during the year. For example, if the bond is issued for $1,000 when the index is 100, and the index at the end of the first year is 102, the bondholder is entitled to $1,020 at maturity assuming no further change in the price level between the end of the first year and the maturity date. The investor is required to include $20 in gross income for the increase in the principal that will not be received until maturity. Thus, inflation adjustments can create gross income before the cash has been received.

reported when it is earned, regardless of the taxpayer's accounting method.[38] The interest "earned" is calculated by the effective interest rate method.

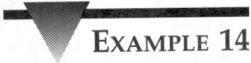

EXAMPLE 14

On January 1, 1998, Mark, a cash basis taxpayer, paid $82,645 for a 24-month certificate. The certificate was priced to yield 10% (the effective interest rate) with interest compounded annually. No interest was paid until maturity, when Mark received $100,000. Thus, Mark's gross income from the certificate is $17,355 ($100,000 – $82,645). Mark's income earned each year is calculated as follows:

1998 (.10 × $82,645) =	$ 8,264
1999 [.10 × ($82,645 + $8,264)] =	9,091
	$17,355

The original issue discount rules do not apply to U.S. savings bonds (discussed in the following paragraphs) or to obligations with a maturity date of one year or less from the date of issue.[39] See Chapter 16 for additional discussion of the tax treatment of original issue discount.

Series E and Series EE Bonds.   Certain U.S. government savings bonds (Series E before 1980 and Series EE after 1979) are issued at a discount and are redeemable for fixed amounts that increase at stated intervals. No interest payments are actually made. The difference between the purchase price and the amount received on redemption is the bondholder's interest income from the investment.

The income from these savings bonds is generally deferred until the bonds are redeemed or mature. Furthermore, Series E bonds can be exchanged within one year of their maturity date for Series HH bonds, and the interest on the Series E

---

[38]§§ 1272(a)(3) and 1273(a).

[39]§ 1272(a)(2).

bonds can be further deferred until maturity of the Series HH bonds.[40] Thus, U.S. savings bonds have attractive income deferral features not available with corporate bonds and certificates of deposit issued by financial institutions.

Of course, the deferral feature of government bonds issued at a discount is not an advantage if the investor has insufficient income to be subject to tax as the income accrues. In fact, the deferral may work to the investor's disadvantage if she has other income in the year the bonds mature or the bunching of the bond interest into one tax year creates a tax liability. Fortunately, U.S. government bonds have a provision for these investors. A cash basis taxpayer can elect to include in gross income the annual increment in redemption value.[41]

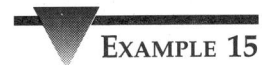

EXAMPLE 15   Kate purchases Series EE U.S. savings bonds for $500 (face value of $1,000) on January 2 of the current year. If the bonds are redeemed during the first six months, no interest is paid. At December 31, the redemption value is $519.60.

If Kate elects to report the interest income annually, she must report interest income of $19.60 for the current year. If she does not make the election, she will report no interest income for the current year. ▼

When a taxpayer elects to report the income from the bonds on an annual basis, the election applies to all such bonds the taxpayer owns at the time of the election and to all such securities acquired subsequent to the election. A change in the method of reporting the income from the bonds requires permission from the IRS.

Amounts Received under an Obligation to Repay.   The receipt of funds with an obligation to repay that amount in the future is the essence of borrowing. Because the taxpayer's assets and liabilities increase by the same amount, no income is realized when the borrowed funds are received. Because amounts paid to the taxpayer by mistake and customer deposits are often classified as borrowed funds, receipt of these funds is not a taxable event.

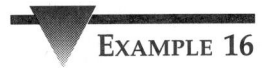

EXAMPLE 16   A landlord receives a damage deposit from a tenant. The landlord does not recognize income until the deposit is forfeited because the landlord has an obligation to repay the deposit if no damage occurs.[42] However, if the deposit is in fact a prepayment of rent, it is taxed in the year of receipt. ▼

EXCEPTIONS APPLICABLE TO ACCRUAL BASIS TAXPAYERS

Prepaid Income.   For financial reporting purposes, advance payments received from customers are reflected as prepaid income and as a liability of the seller. However, for tax purposes, the prepaid income often is taxed in the year of receipt.

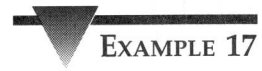

EXAMPLE 17   In December 1998, a tenant paid his January 1999 rent of $1,000. The accrual basis landlord must include the $1,000 in his 1998 income for tax purposes, although the unearned rent income is reported as a liability on the landlord's December 31, 1998, balance sheet. ▼

Taxpayers have repeatedly argued that deferral of income until it is actually earned properly matches revenues and expenses. Moreover, a proper matching of

---

[40]Treas. Dept. Circulars No. 1–80 and No. 2–80, 1980–1 C.B. 714, 715. Note that interest is paid at semiannual intervals on the Series HH bonds and must be included in income as received. Refer to Chapter 5 for a discussion of the savings bond interest exclusion.

[41]§ 454(a).
[42]*John Mantell*, 17 T.C. 1143 (1952).

income with the expenses of earning the income is necessary to clearly reflect income, as required by the Code. The IRS responds that § 446(b) grants it broad powers to determine whether an accounting method clearly reflects income. The IRS further argues that generally accepted financial accounting principles should not dictate tax accounting for prepaid income because of the practical problems of collecting Federal revenues. Collection of the tax is simplest in the year the taxpayer receives the cash from the customer or client.

Over 40 years of litigation, the IRS has been only partially successful in the courts. In cases involving prepaid income from services to be performed at the demand of customers (e.g., dance lessons to be taken at any time in a 24-month period), the IRS's position has been upheld.[43] In such cases, the taxpayer's argument that deferral of the income was necessary to match the income with expenses was not persuasive because the taxpayer did not know precisely when each customer would demand services and, thus, when the expenses would be incurred. However, taxpayers have had some success in the courts when the services were performed on a fixed schedule (e.g., a baseball team's season-ticket sales).[44] In some cases involving the sale of goods, taxpayers have successfully argued that the prepayments were mere deposits[45] or in the nature of loans.[46]

Against this background of mixed results in the courts, congressional intervention, and taxpayers' strong resentment of the IRS's position, in 1971 the IRS modified its prepaid income rules, as explained in the following paragraphs.

Deferral of Advance Payments for Goods. Generally, a taxpayer can elect to defer recognition of income from *advance payments for goods* if the method of accounting for the sale is the same for tax and financial reporting purposes.[47]

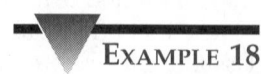
EXAMPLE 18

Brown Company will ship goods only after payment for the goods has been received. In December 1998, Brown received $10,000 for goods that were not shipped until January 1999. Brown can elect to report the income for tax purposes in 1999, assuming the company reports the income in 1999 for financial reporting purposes. ▼

Deferral of Advance Payments for Services. Revenue Procedure 71–21[48] permits an accrual basis taxpayer to defer recognition of income for *advance payments for services* to be performed by the end of the tax year following the year of receipt. No deferral is allowed if the taxpayer might be required to perform any services, under the agreement, after the tax year following the year of receipt of the advance payment. In addition, prepaid rent and prepaid interest cannot be deferred under this revenue procedure.

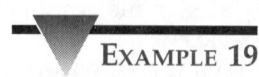
EXAMPLE 19

Yellow Corporation, an accrual basis taxpayer, sells its services under 12-month, 18-month, and 24-month contracts. The corporation provides services to each customer every month. In April of 1998, Yellow Corporation sold the following customer contracts:

[43]*American Automobile Association v. U.S.*, 61–2 USTC ¶9517, 7 AFTR2d 1618, 81 S.Ct. 1727 (USSC, 1961); *Schlude v. Comm.*, 63–1 USTC ¶9284, 11 AFTR2d 751, 83 S.Ct. 601 (USSC, 1963).

[44]*Artnell Company v. Comm.*, 68–2 USTC ¶9593, 22 AFTR2d 5590, 400 F.2d 981 (CA–7, 1968). See also *Boise Cascade Corp. v. U.S.*, 76–1 USTC ¶9203, 37 AFTR2d 76–696, 530 F.2d 1367 (Ct. Cls., 1976).

[45]*Veenstra & DeHavaan Coal Co.*, 11 T.C. 964 (1948).

[46]*Consolidated-Hammer Dry Plate & Film Co. v. Comm.*, 63–1 USTC ¶9494, 11 AFTR2d 1518, 317 F.2d 829 (CA–7, 1963); *Comm. v. Indian-*

apolis Power & Light Co., 90–1 USTC ¶50,007, 65 AFTR2d 90–394, 110 S.Ct. 589 (USSC, 1990).

[47]Reg. § 1.451–5(b). See Reg. § 1.451–5(c) for exceptions to this deferral opportunity. The financial accounting conformity requirement is not applicable to contractors who use the completed contract method.

[48]1971–2 C.B. 549.

Length of Contract	Total Proceeds
12 months	$6,000
18 months	3,600
24 months	2,400

Fifteen hundred dollars of the $6,000 may be deferred ($\frac{3}{12} \times$ $6,000), and $1,800 of the $3,600 may be deferred ($\frac{9}{18} \times$ $3,600) because those amounts will not be earned until 1999. However, the entire $2,400 received on the 24-month contracts is taxable in the year of receipt (1998), since a part of the income will still be unearned by the end of the tax year following the year of receipt (part will be earned in 2000). ▼

In summary, Revenue Procedure 71–21 will result in conformity of tax and financial accounting in a very limited number of prepaid income cases. It is not apparent why prepaid rents and interest may not be deferred, why revenues under some service contracts may be spread over two years, and why revenues under longer service contracts must be reported in one year. Although Revenue Procedure 71–21 has reduced the number of controversies involving prepaid income, a consistent policy has not yet evolved.

INCOME SOURCES

PERSONAL SERVICES

3 **LEARNING OBJECTIVE**
Identify who should pay the tax on a particular item of income in various situations.

It is a well-established principle of taxation that income from personal services must be included in the gross income of the person who performs the services. This principle was first established in a Supreme Court decision, *Lucas v. Earl*.[49] Mr. Earl entered into a binding agreement with his wife under which Mrs. Earl was to receive one-half of Mr. Earl's salary. Justice Holmes used the celebrated **fruit and tree metaphor** to explain that the fruit (income) must be attributed to the tree from which it came (Mr. Earl's services). A mere **assignment of income** does not shift the liability for the tax.

Services of an Employee. Services performed by an employee for the employer's customers are considered performed by the employer. Thus, the employer is taxed on the income from the services provided to the customer, and the employee is taxed on any compensation received from the employer.[50]

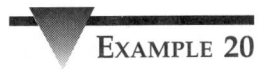 **EXAMPLE 20**

Dr. Shontelle incorporated her medical practice and entered into a contract to work for the corporation for a salary. All patients contracted to receive their services from the corporation, and those services were provided through the corporation's employee, Dr. Shontelle. The corporation must include the patients' fees in its gross income. Dr. Shontelle must include her salary in her gross income. The corporation will be allowed a deduction for the reasonable salary paid to Dr. Shontelle (see the discussion of unreasonable compensation in Chapter 6). ▼

---

[49]2 USTC ¶496, 8 AFTR 10287, 50 S.Ct. 241 (USSC, 1930).
[50]*Sargent v. Comm.*, 91–1 USTC ¶50,168, 67 AFTR2d 91–718, 929 F.2d 1252 (CA–8, 1991).

Services of a Child.   In the case of a child, the Code specifically provides that amounts earned from personal services must be included in the child's gross income. This result applies even though the income is paid to other persons (e.g., the parents).[51]

INCOME FROM PROPERTY

Income from property (interest, dividends, rent) must be included in the gross income of the *owner* of the property. If a father clips interest coupons from bonds shortly before the interest payment date and gives the coupons to his son, the interest will still be taxed to the father. A father who assigns rents from rental property to his daughter will be taxed on the rent since he retains ownership of the property.[52]

Often income-producing property is transferred after income from the property has accrued, but before the income is recognized under the transferor's method of accounting. The IRS and the courts have developed rules to allocate the income between the transferor and the transferee.

Interest.   According to the IRS, interest accrues daily. Therefore, the interest for the period that includes the date of the transfer is allocated between the transferor and transferee based on the number of days during the period that each owned the property.

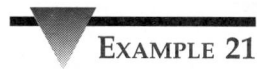

EXAMPLE 21

Floyd, a cash basis taxpayer, gave his son, Seth, bonds with a face amount of $10,000 and an 8% stated annual interest rate. The gift was made on January 31, 1998, and the interest was paid on December 31, 1998. Floyd must recognize $68 in interest income (8% × $10,000 × 31/365). Seth will recognize $732 in interest income ($800 – $68). ▼

When the transferor must recognize the income from the property depends upon the method of accounting and the manner in which the property was transferred. In the case of a gift of income-producing property, the donor must recognize his share of the accrued income at the time it would have been recognized had he continued to own the property.[53] However, if the transfer is a sale, the transferor must recognize the accrued income at the time of the sale. This results because the accrued interest will be included in the sales proceeds.

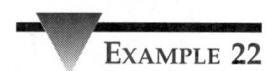

EXAMPLE 22

Assume the same facts as in Example 21, except the interest that was payable as of December 31 was not actually or constructively received by the bondholders until January 3, 1999. As a cash basis taxpayer, Floyd generally does not recognize interest income until it is received. If Floyd had continued to own the bonds, the interest would have been included in his 1999 gross income, the year it would have been received. Therefore, Floyd must include the $68 accrued income in his gross income as of January 3, 1999.

Further assume that Floyd sold identical bonds on the date of the gift. The bonds sold for $9,900, including accrued interest. On January 31, 1998, Floyd must recognize the accrued interest of $68 on the bonds sold. Thus, the selling price of the bonds is $9,832 ($9,900 – $68). ▼

---

[51]§ 73. For circumstances in which the child's unearned income is taxed at the parents' rate, see Unearned Income of Certain Minor Children Taxed at Parents' Rate in Chapter 3.

[52]*Galt v. Comm.*, 54–2 USTC ¶9457, 46 AFTR 633, 216 F.2d 41 (CA–7, 1954); *Helvering v. Horst*, 40–2 USTC ¶9787, 24 AFTR 1058, 61 S.Ct. 144 (USSC, 1940).

[53]Rev.Rul. 72–312, 1972–1 C.B. 22.

Dividends. A corporation is taxed on its earnings, and the shareholders are taxed on the dividends paid to them from the corporation's after-tax earnings. The dividend can take the form of an actual dividend or a constructive dividend (e.g., shareholder use of corporate assets).

Unlike interest, dividends do not accrue on a daily basis because the declaration of a dividend is at the discretion of the corporation's board of directors. Generally, dividends are taxed to the person who is entitled to receive them—the shareholder of record as of the corporation's record date.[54] Thus, if a taxpayer sells stock after a dividend has been declared but before the record date, the dividend generally will be taxed to the purchaser.

If a donor makes a gift of stock to someone (e.g., a family member) after the declaration date but before the record date, the Tax Court has held that the donor does not shift the dividend income to the donee. The *fruit* has sufficiently ripened as of the declaration date to tax the dividend income to the donor of the stock.[55] In a similar set of facts, the Fifth Court of Appeals concluded that the dividend income should be included in the gross income of the donee (the owner at the record date). In this case, the taxpayer gave stock to a qualified charity (a charitable contribution) after the declaration date and before the record date.[56]

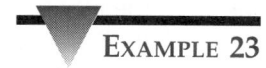

EXAMPLE 23

On June 20, the board of directors of Black Corporation declares a $10 per share dividend. The dividend is payable on June 30, to shareholders of record on June 25. As of June 20, Maria owned 200 shares of Black Corporation's stock. On June 21, Maria sold 100 of the shares to Norm for their fair market value and gave 100 of the shares to Sam (her son). Assume both Norm and Sam are shareholders of record as of June 25. Norm (the purchaser) will be taxed on $1,000 since he is entitled to receive the dividend. However, Maria (the donor) will be taxed on the $1,000 received by Sam (the donee) because the gift was made after the declaration date of the dividend. ▼

INCOME RECEIVED BY AN AGENT

Income received by the taxpayer's agent is considered to be received by the taxpayer. A cash basis principal must recognize the income at the time it is received by the agent.[57]

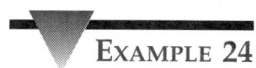

EXAMPLE 24

Jack, a cash basis taxpayer, delivered cattle to the auction barn in late December. The auctioneer, acting as the farmer's agent, sold the cattle and collected the proceeds in December. The auctioneer did not pay Jack until the following January. Jack must include the sales proceeds in his gross income for the year the auctioneer received the funds. ▼

INCOME FROM PARTNERSHIPS, S CORPORATIONS, TRUSTS, AND ESTATES

A **partnership** is not a separate taxable entity. Rather, the partnership merely files an information return (Form 1065), which serves to provide the data necessary for determining the character and amount of each partner's distributive share of the partnership's income and deductions. Each partner must then report her distributive share of the partnership's income and deductions for the partnership's tax year ending within or with her tax year. The income must be reported by each

---

[54]Reg. § 1.61–9(c). The record date is the cutoff for determining the shareholders who are entitled to receive the dividend.

[55]*M. G. Anton,* 34 T.C. 842 (1960).

[56]*Caruth Corporation v. U.S.,* 89–1 USTC ¶9172, 63 AFTR2d 89–716, 865 F.2d 644 (CA–5, 1989).

[57]Rev.Rul. 79–379, 1979–2 C.B. 204.

partner in the year it is earned, even if such amounts are not actually distributed to the partners. Because a partner pays tax on income as the partnership earns it, a distribution by the partnership to the partner is treated under the recovery of capital rules.[58]

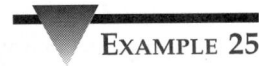

EXAMPLE 25

Tara owned a one-half interest in the capital and profits of T & S Company (a calendar year partnership). For tax year 1998, the partnership earned revenue of $150,000 and had operating expenses of $80,000. During the year, Tara withdrew from her capital account $2,500 per month (for a total of $30,000). For 1998, Tara must report $35,000 as her share of the partnership's profits [½ × ($150,000 − $80,000)] even though she received distributions of only $30,000. ▼

Contrary to the general provision that a corporation must pay tax on its income, a *small business corporation* may elect to be taxed similarly to a partnership. Thus, the shareholders, rather than the corporation, pay the tax on the corporation's income.[59] The electing corporation is referred to as an **S corporation.** Generally, the shareholder reports his proportionate share of the corporation's income and deductions for the year, whether or not the corporation actually makes any distributions to the shareholder.

The *beneficiaries of estates and trusts* generally are taxed on the income earned by the estates or trusts that is actually distributed or required to be distributed to them.[60] Any income not taxed to the beneficiaries is taxable to the estate or trust.

INCOME IN COMMUNITY PROPERTY STATES

General.   State law in Louisiana, Texas, New Mexico, Arizona, California, Washington, Idaho, Nevada, and Wisconsin is based upon a community property system. All other states have a common law property system. The basic difference between common law and community property systems centers around the property rights of married persons. Questions about community property income most frequently arise when the husband and wife file separate returns.

Under a **community property** system, all property is deemed either to be separately owned by the spouse or to belong to the marital community. Property may be held separately by a spouse if it was acquired before marriage or received by gift or inheritance following marriage. Otherwise, any property is deemed to be community property. For Federal tax purposes, each spouse is taxed on one-half of the income from property belonging to the community.

The laws of Texas, Louisiana, Wisconsin, and Idaho distinguish between separate property and the income it produces. In these states, the income from separate property belongs to the community. Accordingly, for Federal income tax purposes, each spouse is taxed on one-half of the income. In the remaining community property states, separate property produces separate income that the owner-spouse must report on his or her Federal income tax return.

What appears to be income, however, may really represent a recovery of capital. A recovery of capital and gain realized on separate property retain their identity as separate property. Items such as nontaxable stock dividends, royalties from

---

[58]§ 706(a) and Reg. § 1.706–1(a)(1). For further discussion, see Chapter 20.

[59]§§ 1361(a) and 1366. For further discussion, see Chapter 20.

[60]§§ 652(a) and 662(a). For further discussion of the taxation of income from partnerships, S corporations, trusts, and estates, see *West's*

Federal Taxation: Corporations, Partnerships, Estates, and Trusts, Chapters 10, 11, 12, and 19.

mineral interests, and gains and losses from the sale of property take on the same classification as the assets to which they relate.

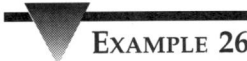

EXAMPLE 26

Bob and Jane are husband and wife and reside in California. Among other transactions during the year, the following occurred:

- Nontaxable stock dividend received by Jane on stock that was given to her after her marriage by her mother.
- Gain of $10,000 on the sale of unimproved land purchased by Bob before his marriage.
- Oil royalties of $15,000 from a lease Jane acquired after marriage with her separate funds.

Since the stock dividend was distributed on stock held by Jane as separate property, it also is her separate property. The same result occurs for the oil royalties Jane receives. All of the proceeds from the sale of unimproved land (including the gain of $10,000) are Bob's separate property. ▼

In all community property states, income from personal services (e.g., salaries, wages, income from a professional partnership) is generally treated as if one-half is earned by each spouse.

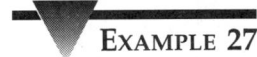

EXAMPLE 27

Fred and Wilma are married but file separate returns. Fred received $25,000 salary and $300 taxable interest on a savings account he established in his name. The deposits to the savings account were made from Fred's salary that he earned since the marriage. Wilma collected $2,000 taxable dividends on stock she inherited from her father. Wilma's gross income is computed as follows under three assumptions as to the state of residency of the couple:

	California	**Texas**	**Common Law States**
Dividends	$ 2,000	$ 1,000	$2,000
Salary	12,500	12,500	–0–
Interest	150	150	–0–
	$14,650	$13,650	$2,000

▼

Community Property Spouses Living Apart. The general rules for taxing the income from services performed by residents of community property states can create complications and even inequities for spouses who are living apart.

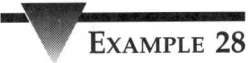

EXAMPLE 28

Cole and Debra were married but living apart for the first nine months of 1998 and were divorced as of October 1, 1998. In December 1998, Cole married Emily, who was married but living apart from Frank before their divorce in June 1998. Cole and Frank had no income from personal services in 1998.

Cole brought into his marriage to Emily a tax liability on one-half of Debra's earnings for the first nine months of the year. However, Emily left with Frank a tax liability on one-half of her earnings for the first six months of 1998. ▼

In circumstances such as those depicted in Example 28, the accrued tax liability could be factored into a property division being negotiated at a time when the parties do not need further complications. In other cases, an abandoned spouse could be saddled with a tax on income earned by a spouse whose whereabouts are unknown.

Congress has developed a simple solution to the many tax problems of community property spouses living apart. A spouse (or former spouse) is taxed only on his or her actual earnings from personal services if the following conditions are met:[61]

- The individuals live apart for the entire year.
- They do not file a joint return with each other.
- No portion of the earned income is transferred between the individuals.

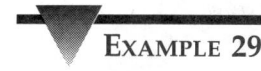
EXAMPLE 29

Jim and Lori reside in a community property state, and both are gainfully employed. On July 1, 1998, they separated, and on June 30, 1999, they were divorced. Assuming their only source of income is wages, one-half of such income for each year is earned by June 30, and they did not file a joint return for 1998, each should report the following gross income:

	Jim's Separate Return	Lori's Separate Return
1998	One-half of Jim's wages	One-half of Jim's wages
	One-half of Lori's wages	One-half of Lori's wages
1999	All of Jim's wages	All of Lori's wages

The results would be the same if Jim or Lori married another person in 1999, except the newlyweds would probably file a joint return. ▼

The IRS may absolve from liability an *innocent spouse* who does not live apart for the entire year and files a separate return but omits his or her share of the community income received by the other spouse. To qualify for the innocent spouse relief, the taxpayer must not know or must have no reason to know of the omitted community income.

ITEMS SPECIFICALLY INCLUDED IN GROSS INCOME

The general principles of gross income determination (discussed in the previous sections) as applied by the IRS and the courts have on occasion yielded results Congress found unacceptable. Consequently, Congress has provided more specific rules for determining the gross income from certain sources. Some of these special rules appear in §§ 71–90 of the Code.

ALIMONY AND SEPARATE MAINTENANCE PAYMENTS

4   **LEARNING OBJECTIVE**
Apply the Internal Revenue Code provisions on alimony, loans made at below-market interest rates, annuities, prizes and awards, group term life insurance, unemployment compensation, and Social Security benefits.

When a married couple divorce or become legally separated, state law generally requires a division of the property accumulated during the marriage. In addition, one spouse may have a legal obligation to support the other spouse. The Code distinguishes between the support payments (alimony or separate maintenance) and the property division in terms of the tax consequences.

    Alimony and separate maintenance payments are *deductible* by the party making the payments and are *includible* in the gross income of the party receiving the payments.[62] Thus, income is shifted from the income earner to the income beneficiary, who is better able to pay the tax on the amount received.

---

[61]§ 66.

[62]§§ 71 and 215.

EXAMPLE 30

Pete and Tina were divorced, and Pete was required to pay Tina $15,000 of alimony each year. Pete earns $31,000 a year. The tax law presumes that because Tina received the $15,000, she is better able than Pete to pay the tax on that amount. Therefore, Tina must include the $15,000 in her gross income, and Pete is allowed to deduct $15,000 from his gross income. ▼

A transfer of property *other than cash* to a former spouse under a divorce decree or agreement is not a taxable event. The transferor is not entitled to a deduction and does not recognize gain or loss on the transfer. The transferee does not recognize income and has a cost basis equal to the transferor's basis.[63]

EXAMPLE 31

Paul transfers stock to Rosa as part of a 1998 divorce settlement. The cost of the stock to Paul is $12,000, and the stock's value at the time of the transfer is $15,000. Rosa later sells the stock for $16,000. Paul is not required to recognize gain from the transfer of the stock to Rosa, and Rosa has a realized and recognized gain of $4,000 ($16,000 − $12,000) when she sells the stock. ▼

In the case of *cash payments*, however, it is often difficult to distinguish payments under a support obligation (alimony) and payments for the other spouse's property (property settlement). In 1984, Congress developed objective rules to classify the payments.

Post-1984 Agreements and Decrees. Payments made under post-1984 agreements and decrees are *classified as alimony* only if the following conditions are satisfied:

1. The payments are in cash.
2. The agreement or decree does not specify that the payments are not alimony.
3. The payor and payee are not members of the same household at the time the payments are made.
4. There is no liability to make the payments for any period after the death of the payee.[64]

Requirement 1 simplifies the law by clearly distinguishing alimony from a property division; that is, if the payment is not in cash, it must be a property division. Requirement 2 allows the parties to determine by agreement whether or not the payments will be alimony. The prohibition on cohabitation—requirement 3—is aimed at assuring the alimony payments are associated with duplicative living expenses (maintaining two households).[65] Requirement 4 is an attempt to prevent alimony treatment from being applied to what is, in fact, a payment for property rather than a support obligation. That is, a seller's estate generally will receive payments for property due after the seller's death. Such payments after the death of the payee could not be for the payee's support.

Front-Loading. As a further safeguard against a property settlement being disguised as alimony, special rules apply to post-1986 agreements if payments in the first or second year exceed $15,000. If the change in the amount of the payments exceeds statutory limits, **alimony recapture** results to the extent of the excess alimony payments. In the *third* year, the payor must include the excess alimony

---

[63]§ 1041, added to the Code in 1984 to repeal the rule of *U.S. v. Davis*, 62–2 USTC ¶9509, 9 AFTR2d 1625, 82 S.Ct. 1190 (USSC, 1962). Under the Davis rule, which applied to pre-1985 divorces, a property transfer incident to divorce was a taxable event.

[64]§ 71(b)(1). This set of alimony rules can also apply to pre-1985 agreements and decrees if both parties agree in writing. The rules applicable to pre-1985 agreements and decrees are not discussed in this text.

[65]*Alexander Washington*, 77 T.C. 601 (1981) at 604.

payments for the first and second years in gross income, and the payee is allowed a deduction for these excess alimony payments. The recaptured amount is computed as follows:[66]

$$R = D + E$$

$$D = B - (C + \$15,000)$$

$$E = A - \left(\frac{B - D + C}{2} + \$15,000\right)$$

R   =   amount recaptured in Year 3 tax return

D   =   recapture from Year 2

E   =   recapture from Year 1

A, B, C   =   payments in the first (A), second (B), and third (C) calendar years of the agreement or decree, where $D \geq 0$, $E \geq 0$

The recapture formula provides an objective technique for determining alimony recapture. Thus, at the time of the divorce, the taxpayers can ascertain the tax consequences. The general concept is that if the alimony payments decrease by more than $15,000 between years in the first three years, there will be alimony recapture with respect to the decrease in excess of $15,000 each year. This rule is applied for the change between Year 2 and Year 3 (D in the above formula). However, rather than making the same calculation for Year 2 payments versus Year 1 payments, the Code requires that the *average* of the payments in Years 2 and 3 be compared with the Year 1 payments (E in the above formula). For this purpose, revised alimony for Year 2 (alimony deducted for Year 2 minus the alimony recapture for Year 2) is used.

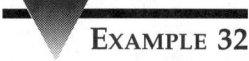

EXAMPLE 32

Wes and Rita were divorced in 1998. Under the agreement, Rita was to receive $50,000 in 1998, $20,000 in 1999, and nothing thereafter. The payments were to cease upon Rita's death or remarriage. In 2000, Wes must include an additional $32,500 in gross income for alimony recapture, and Rita is allowed a deduction for the same amount.

$$D = \$20,000 - (\$0 + \$15,000) = \$5,000$$

$$E = \$50,000 - \left(\frac{\$20,000 - \$5,000 + \$0}{2} + \$15,000\right) = \$27,500$$

$$R = \$5,000 + \$27,500 = \$32,500$$

Note that for 1998 Wes deducts alimony of $50,000 and Rita includes $50,000 in her gross income. For 1999, the amount of the alimony deduction for Wes is $20,000, and Rita's gross income from the alimony is $20,000.

If instead $50,000 were paid in 1998 and nothing is paid for the following years, $35,000 would be recaptured in 2000.

$$D = \$0 - (\$0 + \$15,000) = -\$15,000, \text{ but D must be} \geq \$0$$

$$E = \$50,000 - \left(\frac{\$0 - \$0 + \$0}{2} + \$15,000\right) = \$35,000$$

$$R = \$0 + \$35,000 = \$35,000 \qquad \blacktriangledown$$

Alimony recapture does not apply if the decrease in payments is due to the death of either spouse or the remarriage of the payee.[67] Recapture is not applicable because these events typically terminate alimony under state laws. In addition, the

[66]§ 71(f).   [67]§ 71(f)(5)(A).

CONCEPT SUMMARY 4–1

Tax Treatment of Payments and Transfers Pursuant to Post-1984 Divorce Agreements and Decrees

	Payor	Recipient
Alimony	Deduction from gross income.	Included in gross income.
Alimony recapture	Included in gross income of the third year.	Deducted from gross income of the third year.
Child support	Not deductible.	Not includible in gross income.
Property settlement	No income or deduction.	No income or deduction; basis for the property is the same as the transferor's basis.

recapture rules do not apply to payments where the amount is contingent (e.g., a percentage of income from certain property or a percentage of the payor spouse's compensation), the payments are to be made over a period of three years or longer (unless death, remarriage, or other contingency occurs), and the contingencies are beyond the payor's control.[68]

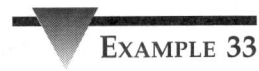

EXAMPLE 33

Under a 1998 divorce agreement, Ed was to receive an amount equal to one-half of Nina's income from certain rental properties for 1998–2001. Payments were to cease upon the death of Ed or Nina or upon the remarriage of Ed. Ed received $50,000 in 1998 and $50,000 in 1999; in 2000, however, the property was vacant, and Ed received nothing. Nina, who deducted alimony in 1998 and 1999, is not required to recapture any alimony in 2000 because the payments were contingent. ▼

Child Support. A taxpayer does not realize income from the receipt of child support payments made by his or her former spouse. This result occurs because the money is received subject to the duty to use the money for the child's benefit. The payor is not allowed to deduct the child support payments because the payments are made to satisfy the payor's legal obligation to support the child.

In many cases, it is difficult to determine whether an amount received is alimony or child support. If the amount of the payments would be reduced upon the happening of a contingency related to a child (e.g., the child attains age 21 or dies), the amount of the future reduction in the payment is deemed child support.[69]

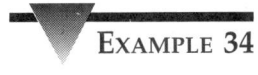

EXAMPLE 34

A divorce agreement provides that Matt is required to make periodic alimony payments of $500 per month to Grace. However, when Matt and Grace's child reaches age 21, marries, or dies (whichever occurs first), the payments will be reduced to $300 per month. Grace has custody of the child. Since the required contingency is the cause for the reduction in the payments, from $500 to $300, child support payments are $200 per month, and alimony is $300 per month. ▼

IMPUTED INTEREST ON BELOW-MARKET LOANS

As discussed earlier in the chapter, generally no income is recognized unless it is realized. Realization generally occurs when the taxpayer performs services or sells goods and thus becomes entitled to a payment from the other party. It follows that no income is realized if the goods or services are provided at no charge. Under this interpretation of the realization requirement, before 1984, interest-free loans were used to shift income between taxpayers.

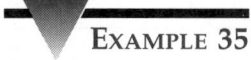

EXAMPLE 35

Veneia (daughter) is in the 20% tax bracket and has no investment income. Kareem (father) is in the 50% tax bracket and has $200,000 in a money market account earning 10% interest. Kareem would like Veneia to receive and pay tax on the income earned on the $200,000. Because Kareem would also like to have access to the $200,000 should he need the money, he does not want to make an outright gift of the money, nor does he want to commit the money to a trust.

Before 1984, Kareem could achieve his goals as follows. He could transfer the money market account to Veneia in exchange for her $200,000 non-interest-bearing note, payable on Kareem's demand. As a result, Veneia would receive the income, and the family's taxes would be decreased by $6,000.

Decrease in Kareem's tax—	
(.10 × $200,000).50 =	($10,000)
Increase in Veneia's tax—	
(.10 × $200,000).20 =	4,000
Decrease in the family's taxes	($ 6,000)

Under the 1984 amendments to the Code, Kareem in Example 35 is required to recognize **imputed interest** income.[70] Veneia is deemed to have incurred interest expense equal to Kareem's imputed interest income. Veneia's interest may be deductible on her return as investment interest if she itemizes deductions (see Chapter 10). To complete the fictitious series of transactions, Kareem is then deemed to have given Veneia the amount of the imputed interest she did not pay. The gift received by Veneia is not subject to income tax (see Chapter 5), although Kareem may be subject to the gift tax (unified transfer tax) on the amount deemed given to Veneia (refer to Chapter 1).

Imputed interest is calculated using the rate the Federal government pays on new borrowings and is compounded semiannually. This Federal rate is adjusted monthly and is published by the IRS.[71] Actually, there are three Federal rates: short-term (not over three years and including demand loans), mid-term (over three years but not over nine years), and long-term (over nine years).[72]

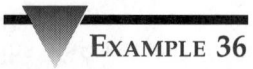

EXAMPLE 36

Assume the Federal rate applicable to the loan in Example 35 is 7% through June 30 and 8% from July 1 through December 31. Kareem made the loan on January 1, and the loan is still outstanding on December 31. Kareem must recognize interest income of $15,280, and Veneia has interest expense of $15,280. Kareem is deemed to have made a gift of $15,280 to Veneia.

Interest calculations	
January 1–June 30—	
.07($200,000) (½ year)	$ 7,000
July 1–December 31—	
.08($200,000 + $7,000) (½ year)	8,280
	$15,280

---

[70]§ 7872(a)(1).
[71]§§ 7872(b)(2) and (f)(2).

[72]§ 1274(d).

CONCEPT SUMMARY 4–2

Effect of Certain Below-Market Loans on the Lender and Borrower

Type of Loan		Lender	Borrower
Gift	Step 1	Interest income	Interest expense
	Step 2	Gift made	Gift received
Compensation-related	Step 1	Interest income	Interest expense
	Step 2	Compensation expense	Compensation income
Corporation to shareholder	Step 1	Interest income	Interest expense
	Step 2	Dividend paid	Dividend income

If interest is charged on the loan but is less than the Federal rate, the imputed interest is the difference between the amount that would have been charged at the Federal rate and the amount actually charged.

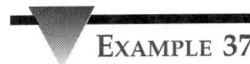

EXAMPLE 37

Assume the same facts as in Example 36, except that Kareem charged 6% interest, compounded annually.

Interest at the Federal rate	$15,280
Less interest charged (.06 × $200,000)	(12,000)
Imputed interest	$ 3,280

The imputed interest rules apply to the following *types* of below-market loans:[73]

1. Gift loans (made out of love, affection, or generosity, as in Example 35).
2. Compensation-related loans (employer loans to employees).
3. Corporation-shareholder loans (a corporation's loans to its shareholders).
4. Tax avoidance loans and other loans that significantly affect the borrower's or lender's Federal tax liability (discussed in the following paragraphs).

The effects of the first three types of loans on the borrower and lender are summarized in Concept Summary 4–2.

Tax Avoidance and Other Below-Market Loans. In addition to the three specific types of loans that are subject to the imputed interest rules, the Code includes a catchall provision for *tax avoidance loans* and other arrangements that have a significant effect on the tax liability of the borrower or lender. The Conference Report provides the following example of an arrangement that might be subject to the imputed interest rules.[74]

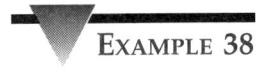

EXAMPLE 38

Annual dues for the Good Health Club are $400. In lieu of paying dues, a member can make a $4,000 deposit, refundable at the end of one year. The club can earn $400 interest on the deposit.

---

[73]§ 7872(c).   [74]H. Rep. No. 98–861, 98th Cong., 2d Sess., 1984, p. 1023.

If interest were not imputed, an individual with $4,000 could, in effect, earn tax-exempt income on the deposit. That is, rather than invest the $4,000, earn $400 in interest, pay tax on the interest, and then pay $400 in dues, the individual could avoid tax on the interest by making the deposit. Thus, income and expenses are imputed as follows: interest income and nondeductible health club fees for the club member; income from fees and interest expense for the club. ▼

Many commercially motivated transactions could be swept into this other below-market loans category. However, the temporary Regulations have carved out a frequently encountered exception for customer prepayments. If the prepayments are included in the recipient's income under the recipient's method of accounting, the payments are not considered loans and, thus, are not subject to the imputed interest rules.[75]

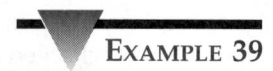

EXAMPLE 39

Landlord, a cash basis taxpayer, charges tenants a damage deposit equal to one month's rent on residential apartments. When the tenant enters into the lease, the landlord also collects rent for the last month of the lease.

The prepaid rent for the last month of the lease is taxed in the year received and thus is not considered a loan. The security deposit is not taxed when received and is therefore a candidate for imputed interest. However, no apparent tax benefit is derived by the landlord or the tenant, and thus the security deposit should not be subject to the imputed interest provisions. But if making the deposit would reduce the rent paid by the tenant, the tenant could derive a tax benefit, much the same as the club member in Example 38. ▼

Exceptions and Limitations. No interest is imputed on total outstanding *gift loans* of $10,000 or less between individuals, unless the loan proceeds are used to purchase income-producing property.[76] This exemption eliminates from these complex provisions immaterial amounts that do not result in apparent shifts of income. However, if the proceeds of such a loan are used to purchase income-producing property, the limitations discussed in the following paragraphs apply instead.

On loans of $100,000 or less between individuals, the imputed interest cannot exceed the borrower's net investment income for the year (gross income from all investments less the related expenses).[77] As discussed above, one of the purposes of the imputed interest rules is to prevent high-income taxpayers from shifting income to relatives in a lower marginal bracket. This shifting of investment income is considered to occur only to the extent the borrower has investment income. Thus, the income imputed to the lender is limited to the borrower's net investment income. As a further limitation, or exemption, if the borrower's net investment income for the year does not exceed $1,000, no interest is imputed on loans of $100,000 or less. However, these limitations for loans of $100,000 or less do not apply if a principal purpose of a loan is tax avoidance. In such a case, interest is imputed, and the imputed interest is not limited to the borrower's net investment income.[78]

---

[75]Prop.Reg. § 1.7872–2(b)(1)(i).
[76]§ 7872(c)(2).
[77]§ 7872(d).

[78]*Deficit Reduction Tax Bill of 1984: Explanation of the Senate Finance Committee* (April 2, 1984), p. 484.

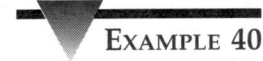

EXAMPLE 40

Vicki made interest-free gift loans as follows:

Borrower	Amount	Borrower's Net Investment Income	Purpose
Susan	$ 8,000	$ –0–	Education
Dan	9,000	500	Purchase of stock
Bonnie	25,000	–0–	Purchase of a business
Megan	90,000	15,000	Purchase of a residence
Olaf	120,000	–0–	Purchase of a residence

Assume that tax avoidance is not a principal purpose of any of the loans. The loan to Susan is not subject to the imputed interest rules because the $10,000 exception applies. The $10,000 exception does not apply to the loan to Dan because the proceeds were used to purchase income-producing assets. However, under the $100,000 exception, the imputed interest is limited to Dan's investment income ($500). Since the $1,000 exception also applies to this loan, no interest is imputed.

No interest is imputed on the loan to Bonnie because the $100,000 exception applies. Interest is imputed on the loan to Megan based on the lesser of (1) the borrower's $15,000 net investment income or (2) the interest as calculated by applying the Federal rate to the outstanding loan. None of the exceptions apply to the loan to Olaf because the loan was for more than $100,000.

Assume the relevant Federal rate is 10% and the loans were outstanding for the entire year. Vicki would recognize interest income, compounded semiannually, as follows:

Loan to Megan:
First 6 months (.10 × $90,000 × ½ year) $ 4,500
Second 6 months (.10 × $94,500 × ½ year) 4,725
$ 9,225

Loan to Olaf:
First 6 months (.10 × $120,000 × ½ year) $ 6,000
Second 6 months (.10 × $126,000 × ½ year) 6,300
$12,300
Total imputed interest ($9,225 + $12,300) $21,525

As with gift loans, there is a $10,000 exemption for *compensation-related loans* and *corporation-shareholder loans*. However, the $10,000 exception does not apply if tax avoidance is one of the principal purposes of a loan.[79] This vague tax avoidance standard makes practically all compensation-related and corporation-shareholder loans suspect. Nevertheless, the $10,000 exception should apply when an employee's borrowing was necessitated by personal needs (e.g., to meet unexpected expenses) rather than tax considerations.

These exceptions to the imputed interest rules are summarized in Concept Summary 4–3.

INCOME FROM ANNUITIES

Annuity contracts generally require the purchaser (the annuitant) to pay a fixed amount for the right to receive a future stream of payments. Typically, the issuer

[79]§ 7872(c)(3).

CONCEPT SUMMARY 4–3

Exceptions to the Imputed Interest Rules For Below-Market Loans

Exception	Eligible Loans	Ineligible Loans and Limitations
De minimis—aggregate loans of $10,000 or less	Gift loans	Proceeds used to purchase income-producing assets.
	Employer-employee	Principal purpose is tax avoidance.
	Corporation-shareholder	Principal purpose is tax avoidance.
Aggregate loans of $100,000 or less	Between individuals	Principal purpose is tax avoidance. For all other loans, interest is imputed to the extent of the borrower's net investment income (NII), if the borrower's NII exceeds $1,000.

of the contract is an insurance company and will pay the annuitant a cash value if the annuitant cancels the contract. The insurance company invests the amounts received from the annuitant, and the income earned serves to increase the cash value of the policy. No income is recognized by the annuitant at the time the cash value of the annuity increases because the taxpayer has not actually received any income. The income is not constructively received because, generally, the taxpayer must cancel the policy to receive the increase in value (the increase in value is subject to substantial restrictions).

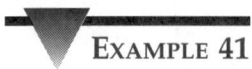

EXAMPLE 41

Jean, age 50, paid $30,000 for an annuity contract that is to pay her $500 per month beginning when she reaches age 65 and continuing until her death. If Jean should cancel the policy after one year, she would receive $30,200. The $200 increase in value is not includible in Jean's gross income as long as she does not actually receive the $200. ▼

The tax accounting problem associated with receiving payments under an annuity contract is one of apportioning the amounts received between recovery of capital and income.

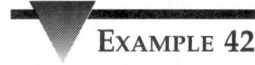

EXAMPLE 42

In 1998, Tom purchased for $15,000 an annuity intended as a source of retirement income. In 2000, when the cash value of the annuity was $17,000, Tom collected $1,000 on the contract. Is the $1,000 gross income, recovery of capital, or a combination of recovery of capital and income? ▼

The statutory solution to this problem depends upon whether the payments began before or after the annuity starting date and upon when the policy was acquired.

Collections before the Annuity Starting Date.   Generally, an annuity contract specifies a date on which monthly or annual payments will begin—the annuity starting date. Often the contract will also allow the annuitant to collect a limited amount before the starting date. The amount collected may be characterized as either an actual withdrawal of the increase in cash value or a loan on the policy. In 1982, Congress changed the rules applicable to these withdrawals and loans.

Collections (including loans) equal to or less than the post-August 13, 1982, increases in cash value must be included in gross income. Amounts received in excess of post-August 13, 1982, increases in cash value are treated as a recovery of capital until the taxpayer's cost has been entirely recovered. Additional amounts are included in gross income.[80]

The taxpayer may also be subject to a penalty on early distributions of 10 percent of the income recognized. The penalty generally applies if the amount is received before the taxpayer reaches age 59½ or is disabled.[81] The early distribution penalty is deemed necessary to prevent taxpayers from using annuities as a way of avoiding the original issue discount rules. That is, the investment in the annuity earns a return that is not taxed until it is collected under the annuity rules, whereas the interest on a certificate of deposit is taxed each year as the income accrues. Thus, the annuity offers a tax advantage (deferral of income) that Congress does not want exploited.

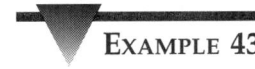

EXAMPLE 43   Jack, age 50, purchased an annuity policy for $30,000 in 1997. In 1999, when the cash value of the policy has increased to $33,000, Jack withdraws $4,000. He must recognize $3,000 of income ($33,000 cash value − $30,000 cost) and must pay a penalty of $300 ($3,000 × 10%). The remaining $1,000 is a recovery of capital and reduces Jack's basis in the annuity policy. ▼

Collections on and after the Annuity Starting Date. The annuitant can exclude from income (as a recovery of capital) the proportion of each payment that the investment in the contract bears to the expected return under the contract. The *exclusion amount* is calculated as follows:

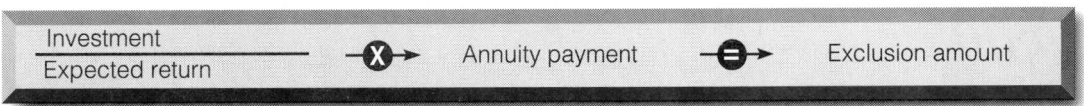

The *expected return* is the annual amount to be paid to the annuitant multiplied by the number of years the payments will be received. The payment period may be fixed (a *term certain*) or for the life of one or more individuals. When payments are for life, the taxpayer generally must use the annuity table published by the IRS to determine the expected return (see Table 4–1). This is an actuarial table that contains life expectancies.[82] The expected return is calculated by multiplying the appropriate multiple (life expectancy) by the annual payment.

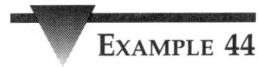

EXAMPLE 44   The taxpayer, age 54, purchased an annuity from an insurance company for $90,000. She was to receive $500 per month for life. Her life expectancy (from Table 4–1) is 29.5 years from the annuity starting date. Thus, her expected return is $500 × 12 × 29.5 = $177,000, and the exclusion amount is $3,051 [($90,000 investment/$177,000 expected return) × $6,000 annual payment]. The $3,051 is a nontaxable return of capital, and $2,949 is included in gross income. ▼

The *exclusion ratio* (investment ÷ expected return) applies until the annuitant has recovered her investment in the contract. Once the investment is recovered, the entire amount of subsequent payments is taxable. If the annuitant dies before

---

[80]§ 72(e)(3); Reg. § 1.72–9.

[81]§ 72(q).

[82]The life expectancies in Table 4–1 apply for annuity investments made on or after July 1, 1986. See *Pension and Annuity Income*, IRS

Publication 575 (Rev. Nov. 87), pp. 22–24 for the IRS table to use for investments made before July 1, 1986.

▼ **TABLE 4–1**
Ordinary Life Annuities:
One Life-Expected Return
Multiples

Age	Multiple	Age	Multiple	Age	Multiple
5	76.6	42	40.6	79	10.0
6	75.6	43	39.6	80	9.5
7	74.7	44	38.7	81	8.9
8	73.7	45	37.7	82	8.4
9	72.7	46	36.8	83	7.9
10	71.7	47	35.9	84	7.4
11	70.7	48	34.9	85	6.9
12	69.7	49	34.0	86	6.5
13	68.8	50	33.1	87	6.1
14	67.8	51	32.2	88	5.7
15	66.8	52	31.3	89	5.3
16	65.8	53	30.4	90	5.0
17	64.8	54	29.5	91	4.7
18	63.9	55	28.6	92	4.4
19	62.9	56	27.7	93	4.1
20	61.9	57	26.8	94	3.9
21	60.9	58	25.9	95	3.7
22	59.9	59	25.0	96	3.4
23	59.0	60	24.2	97	3.2
24	58.0	61	23.3	98	3.0
25	57.0	62	22.5	99	2.8
26	56.0	63	21.6	100	2.7
27	55.1	64	20.8	101	2.5
28	54.1	65	20.0	102	2.3
29	53.1	66	19.2	103	2.1
30	52.2	67	18.4	104	1.9
31	51.2	68	17.6	105	1.8
32	50.2	69	16.8	106	1.6
33	49.3	70	16.0	107	1.4
34	48.3	71	15.3	108	1.3
35	47.3	72	14.6	109	1.1
36	46.4	73	13.9	110	1.0
37	45.4	74	13.2	111	.9
38	44.4	75	12.5	112	.8
39	43.5	76	11.9	113	.7
40	42.5	77	11.2	114	.6
41	41.5	78	10.6	115	.5

recovering her investment, the unrecovered cost is deductible in the year the payments cease (usually the year of death).[83]

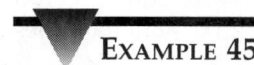

EXAMPLE 45   Assume the taxpayer in Example 44 received annuity payments for 30.5 years (366 months). For the last 12 months [366 − (12 × 29.5) = 12], the taxpayer would include $500 each month in gross income. If instead the taxpayer died after 36 months, she is eligible for a $80,847 deduction on her final tax return.

[83]§ 72(b).

▼ **TABLE 4–2**
Number of Anticipated
Monthly Annuity Payments
under the Simplified Method

Age	Number of Anticipated Monthly Payments
55 and under	360
56–60	310
61–65	260
66–70	210
71 and over	160

Cost of the contract	$90,000
Cost previously recovered $90,000/$177,000 × 36($500) =	(9,153)
Deduction	$80,847

▼

Simplified Method for Annuity Distributions from Qualified Retirement Plans. A simplified method is available for allocating basis to the annuity payments received under a qualified retirement plan. The portion of each annuity payment that is excluded as a return of capital is the employee's investment in the contract divided by the number of anticipated monthly payments determined in accordance with Table 4–2.[84]

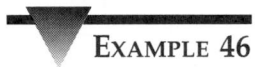

EXAMPLE 46

Andrea, age 62, receives an annuity distribution of $500 per month for life from her qualified retirement plan beginning in January 1998. Her investment in the contract is $100,100. The excludible amount of each payment is $385 ($100,100 investment/260 monthly payments). Thus, $115 ($500 – $385) of each annuity payment is included in Andrea's gross income. ▼

The rules for annuity payments received after the basis has been recovered by the annuitant and for the annuitant who dies before recovering his basis are the same as under the exclusion ratio method discussed earlier.

PRIZES AND AWARDS

The fair market value of prizes and awards (other than scholarships exempted under § 117, to be discussed subsequently) must be included in gross income.[85] Therefore, TV giveaway prizes, magazine publisher prizes, door prizes, and awards from an employer to an employee in recognition of performance are fully taxable to the recipient.

A narrow exception permits a prize or award to be excluded from gross income if *all* of the following requirements are satisfied:

- The prize or award is received in recognition of religious, charitable, scientific, educational, artistic, literary, or civic achievement (e.g., Nobel Prize, Pulitzer Prize).
- The recipient transfers the prize or award to a qualified governmental unit or nonprofit organization.
- The recipient was selected without any action on her part to enter the contest or proceeding.
- The recipient is not required to render substantial future services as a condition for receiving the prize or award.[86]

---

[84]§ 72(d).
[85]§ 74.

[86]§ 74(b).

CONCEPT SUMMARY 4–4

Taxation of Annuities: Exclusion Ratio Method

Term	Description	Formula
A	Amount of each annuity payment under the contract.	
N	Number of expected payments based on the expected life of the annuitant.	
V	Investment in the annuity contract.	
R	Number of annuity payments actually received.	
Expected return	Total amount the annuitant is expected to collect over the life of the contract based on his life expectancy.	$A \times N$
Exclusion percentage	Percentage of each annuity payment that is excluded from gross income.	$\dfrac{V}{A \times N}$
Inclusion percentage	Percentage of each annuity payment that is included in gross income.	$1 - \left(\dfrac{V}{A \times N}\right)$
Post-recovery of capital payments	Once R = N, the total cost has been recovered. The total amount of each subsequent payment is included in gross income.	
Annuitant's deductible loss	If the annuity payments cease before R = N, the annuitant can claim a loss.	$V - \left(\dfrac{V}{A \times N}\right) \times (A \times R)$

Because the transfer of the property to a qualified governmental unit or nonprofit organization ordinarily would be a charitable contribution (an itemized deduction as presented in Chapter 10), the exclusion produces beneficial tax consequences in the following situations:

- The taxpayer does not itemize deductions and thus would receive no tax benefit from the charitable contribution.
- The taxpayer's charitable contributions exceed the annual statutory ceiling on the deduction.
- Including the prize or award in gross income would reduce the amount of deductions the taxpayer otherwise would qualify for because of gross income limitations (e.g., the gross income test for a dependency exemption, the adjusted gross income limitation in calculating the medical expense deduction).

Another exception is provided for certain *employee achievement awards* in the form of tangible personal property (e.g., a gold watch). The awards must be made in recognition of length of service or safety achievement. Generally, the ceiling on the excludible amount for an employee is $400 per taxable year. However, if the award is a qualified plan award, the ceiling on the exclusion is $1,600 per taxable year.[87]

[87]§§ 74(c) and 274(j).

▼ **TABLE 4–3**
Uniform Premiums for $1,000
of Group Term Life
Insurance Protection

Attained Age on Last Day of Employee's Tax Year	Cost per $1,000 of Protection for One-Month Period
Under 30	$ .08
30–34	.09
35–39	.11
40–44	.17
45–49	.29
50–54	.48
55–59	.75
60–64	1.17
65–69	2.10
70 and over	3.76

GROUP TERM LIFE INSURANCE

For many years, the IRS did not attempt to tax the value of life insurance protection provided to an employee by the employer. Some companies took undue advantage of the exclusion by providing large amounts of insurance protection for executives. Therefore, Congress enacted § 79, which created a limited exclusion for **group term life insurance.** The premiums on the first $50,000 of group term life insurance protection are excludible from the employee's gross income.

The benefits of this exclusion are available only to employees. Proprietors and partners are not considered employees. Moreover, the Regulations generally require broad-scale coverage of employees to satisfy the *group* requirement (e.g., shareholder-employees would not constitute a qualified group). The exclusion applies only to term insurance (protection for a period of time but with no cash surrender value) and not to ordinary life insurance (lifetime protection plus a cash surrender value that can be drawn upon before death).

As mentioned, the exclusion applies to the first $50,000 of group term life insurance protection. For each $1,000 of coverage in excess of $50,000, the employee must include the amounts indicated in Table 4–3 in gross income.[88]

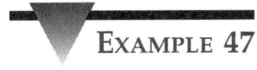

EXAMPLE 47

Finch Corporation has a group term life insurance policy with coverage equal to the employee's annual salary. Keith, age 52, is president of the corporation and receives an annual salary of $75,000. Keith must include $144 in gross income from the insurance protection for the year.

$$\frac{\$75,000 - \$50,000}{\$1,000} \times .48 \times 12 \text{ months} = \$144$$

▼

Generally, the amount that must be included in gross income, computed from Table 4–3, is much less than the price an individual would pay an insurance company for the same amount of protection. Thus, even the excess coverage provides some tax-favored income for employees when group term life insurance coverage in excess of $50,000 is desirable.

If the plan discriminates in favor of certain key employees (e.g., officers), the key employees are not eligible for the exclusion. In such a case, the key employees must include in gross income the *greater* of actual premiums paid by the employer or the amount calculated from the Uniform Premiums in Table 4–3. The other

---

[88]Reg. § 1.79–3(d)(2).

employees are still eligible for the $50,000 exclusion and continue to use the Uniform Premiums table to compute the income from excess insurance protection.[89]

UNEMPLOYMENT COMPENSATION

The unemployment compensation program is sponsored and operated by the states and Federal government to provide a source of income for people who have been employed and are temporarily (hopefully) out of work. In a series of rulings over a period of 40 years, the IRS exempted unemployment benefits from tax. These payments were considered social benefit programs for the promotion of the general welfare. After experiencing dissatisfaction with the IRS's treatment of unemployment compensation, Congress amended the Code to provide that the benefits are taxable.[90]

SOCIAL SECURITY BENEFITS

If a taxpayer's income exceeds a specified base amount, as much as 85 percent of Social Security retirement benefits must be included in gross income. The taxable amount of benefits is determined through the application of one of two formulas that utilize a unique measure of income—*modified adjusted gross income (MAGI)*.[91] MAGI is, generally, the taxpayer's adjusted gross income from all sources (other than Social Security) plus the foreign earned income exclusion and any tax-exempt interest income.

In the formulas, two sets of base amounts are established. The first set is as follows:

- $32,000 for married taxpayers who file a joint return.
- $0 for married taxpayers who do not live apart for the entire year but file separate returns.
- $25,000 for all other taxpayers.

The second set of base amounts is as follows:

- $44,000 for married taxpayers who file a joint return.
- $0 for married taxpayers who do not live apart for the entire year but file separate returns.
- $34,000 for all other taxpayers.

If MAGI plus one-half of Social Security benefits exceeds the first set of base amounts, but not the second set, the taxable amount of Social Security benefits is the *lesser* of the following:

- .50(Social Security benefits).
- .50[MAGI + .50(Social Security benefits) – first base amount].

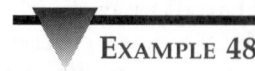

EXAMPLE 48

A married couple with adjusted gross income of $30,000, no tax-exempt interest, and $11,000 of Social Security benefits who file jointly must include $1,750 of the benefits in gross income. This works out as the lesser of the following:

1. .50($11,000) = $5,500.
2. .50[$30,000 + .50($11,000) – $32,000] = .50($3,500) = $1,750.

---

[89]§ 79(d).
[90]§ 85.

[91]§ 86.

If the couple's adjusted gross income were $15,000 and their Social Security benefits totaled $5,000, none of the benefits would be taxable, since .50[$15,000 + .50($5,000) – $32,000] is not a positive number. ▼

If MAGI plus one-half of Social Security benefits exceeds the second set of base amounts, the taxable amount of Social Security benefits is the *lesser* of 1 or 2 below:

1. .85(Social Security benefits).
2. Sum of:
   a. .85[MAGI + .50(Social Security benefits) – second base amount], and
   b. Lesser of:
      • Amount included through application of the first formula.
      • $4,500 ($6,000 for married filing jointly).

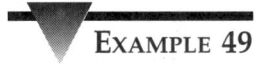

EXAMPLE 49

A married couple who file jointly have adjusted gross income of $72,000, no tax-exempt interest, and $12,000 of Social Security benefits. Their includible Social Security benefits would be $10,200.

Include the lesser of the following:

1. .85($12,000) = $10,200.
2. Sum of:
   a. .85[$72,000 + .50($12,000) – $44,000] = $28,900, and
   b. Lesser of:
      • Amount calculated by the first formula, which is the lesser of:
         • .50($12,000) = $6,000.
         • .50[$72,000 + .50($12,000) – $32,000] = $23,000.
      • $6,000.

The sum equals $34,900 ($28,900 + $6,000). Since 85% of the Social Security benefits received is less than this amount, $10,200 is included in the couples' gross income. ▼

**TAX PLANNING
CONSIDERATIONS**

5   LEARNING OBJECTIVE
Identify tax planning strategies
for minimizing gross income.

The materials in this chapter have focused on the following questions:

• What is income?
• When is the income recognized?
• Who is the taxpayer?

Planning strategies suggested by these materials include the following:

• Maximize economic benefits that are not included in gross income.
• Defer the recognition of income.
• Shift income to taxpayers who are in a lower marginal tax bracket.

Some specific techniques for accomplishing these strategies are discussed in the following paragraphs.

NONTAXABLE ECONOMIC BENEFITS

Home ownership is the prime example of economic income from capital that is not subject to tax. If the taxpayer uses her capital to purchase investments, but pays rent on a personal residence, she would pay the rent from after-tax income. However, if the taxpayer purchases a personal residence instead of the investments, she would give up gross income from the forgone investments in exchange for the rent savings. The savings in rent enjoyed as a result of owning the home are not subject to tax. Thus, the homeowner will have substituted nontaxable for taxable income.

TAX DEFERRAL

General. Since deferred taxes are tantamount to interest-free loans from the government, the deferral of taxes is a worthy goal of the tax planner. However, the tax planner must also consider the tax rates for the years the income is shifted from and to. For example, a one-year deferral of income from a year in which the taxpayer's tax rate was 28 percent to a year in which the tax rate will be 39.6 percent would not be advisable if the taxpayer expects to earn less than a 11.6 percent after-tax return on the deferred tax dollars.

The taxpayer can often defer the recognition of income from appreciated property by postponing the event triggering realization (the final closing on a sale or exchange of property). If the taxpayer needs cash, obtaining a loan by using the appreciated property as collateral may be the least costly alternative. When the taxpayer anticipates reinvesting the proceeds, a sale may be inadvisable.

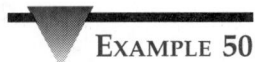

EXAMPLE 50

Ira owns 100 shares of Pigeon Company common stock with a cost of $20,000 and a fair market value of $50,000. Although the stock's value has increased substantially in the past three years, Ira thinks the growth days are over. If he sells the Pigeon stock, Ira will invest the proceeds from the sale in other common stock. Assuming Ira's marginal tax rate on the sale is 20%, he will have only $44,000 [$50,000 − .20($50,000 − $20,000)] to reinvest. The alternative investment must substantially outperform Pigeon in the future in order for the sale to be beneficial. ▼

Selection of Investments. Because no tax is due until a gain has been recognized, the law favors investments that yield appreciation rather than annual income.

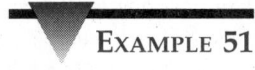

EXAMPLE 51

Vera can buy a corporate bond or an acre of land for $10,000. The bond pays $1,000 of interest (10%) each year, and Vera expects the land to increase in value 10% each year for the next 10 years. She is in the 40% (combined Federal and state) tax bracket for ordinary income and 26% for qualifying capital gains. Assuming the bond would mature or the land would be sold in 10 years and Vera would reinvest the interest at a 10% before-tax return, she would accumulate the following amount at the end of 10 years.

		Bond	Land
Original investment		$10,000	$10,000
Annual income	$1,000		
Less tax	(400)		
	$ 600		
Compound amount reinvested for 10 years at 6% after-tax	× 13.18	7,908	
		$17,908	
Compound amount, 10 years at 10%			× 2.59
			$25,900
Less tax on sale: 26%($25,900 − $10,000)			(4,134)
			$21,766

Therefore, the value of the deferral that results from investing in the land rather than in the bond is $3,858 ($21,766 – $17,908). ▼

Series E and EE bonds can also be purchased for long-term deferrals of income. As discussed in the chapter, Series E bonds can be exchanged for new Series HH bonds to further postpone the tax. In situations where the taxpayer's goal is merely to shift income one year into the future, bank certificates of deposit are useful tools. If the maturity period is one year or less, all interest is reported in the year of maturity. Time certificates are especially useful for a taxpayer who realizes an unusually large gain from the sale of property in one year (and thus is in a high tax bracket) but expects his income to be less the following year.

Cash Basis. The timing of income from services can often be controlled through the use of the cash method of accounting. Although taxpayers are somewhat constrained by the constructive receipt doctrine (they cannot turn their backs on income), seldom will customers and clients offer to pay before they are asked. The usual lag between billings and collections (e.g., December's billings collected in January) will result in a continuous deferring of some income until the last year of operations. A salaried individual approaching retirement may contract with her employer before the services are rendered to receive a portion of compensation in the lower tax bracket retirement years.

Prepaid Income. For the accrual basis taxpayer who receives advance payments from customers, the transactions should be structured to avoid payment of tax on income before the time the income is actually earned. Revenue Procedure 71–21 provides the guidelines for deferring the tax on prepayments for services, and Regulation § 1.451–5 provides the guidelines for deferrals on sales of goods. In addition, both cash and accrual basis taxpayers can sometimes defer income by stipulating that the payments are deposits rather than prepaid income. For example, a landlord should require an equivalent damage deposit rather than prepayment of the last month's rent under the lease.

SHIFTING INCOME TO RELATIVES

The tax liability of a family can be minimized by shifting income from higher- to lower-bracket family members. This can be accomplished through gifts of income-producing property. Furthermore, in many cases, income can be shifted with no negative effect on the family's investment plans.

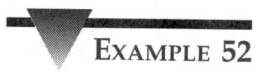

EXAMPLE 52

Adam, who is in the 28% tax bracket, would like to save for his children's education. All of the children are under 14 years of age. Adam could transfer income-producing properties to the children, and the children could each receive up to $700 of income each year (refer to Chapter 3) with no tax liability. The next $700 would be taxed at the child's tax rate. After a child has more than $1,400 income, there is no tax advantage to shifting more income to the child (because the income will be taxed at the parents' rate) until the child is 14 years old (when all income will be taxed according to the child's tax rate). ▼

The Uniform Gifts to Minors Act, a model law adopted by all states (but with some variations among the states), facilitates income shifting. Under the Act, a gift of intangibles (e.g., bank accounts, stocks, bonds, life insurance contracts) can be made to a minor but with an adult serving as custodian. Usually, a parent who makes the gift is also named as custodian. The state laws allow the custodian to sell or redeem and reinvest the principal and to accumulate or distribute the income, practically at the custodian's discretion provided there is no commingling of the child's income with the parent's property. Thus, the parent can give appreciated securities to the child, and the donor custodian can then sell the securities and reinvest the proceeds, thereby shifting both the gain and the annual income to the child. Such planning is limited by the tax liability calculation provision for a child under the age of 14 (refer to Chapter 3).

U.S. government bonds (Series E and EE) can be purchased by the parent for his children. When this is done, the children generally should file a return and elect to report the income on the accrual basis.

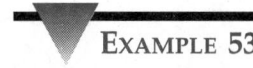

EXAMPLE 53

Abby pays $7,500 for Series EE bonds in 1998 and immediately gives them to Wade (her son), who will enter college the year of original maturity of the bonds. The bonds have a maturity value of $10,000. Wade elects to report the annual increment in redemption value as income for each year the bonds are held. The first year the increase is $250, and Wade includes that amount in his gross income. If Wade has no other income, no tax will be due on the $250 bond interest, since such an amount will be more than offset by his available standard deduction. The following year, the increment is $260, and Wade includes this amount in income. Thus, over the life of the bonds, Wade will include $2,500 in income ($10,000 − $7,500), none of which will result in a tax liability, assuming he has no other income. However, if the election had not been made, Wade would be required to include $2,500 in income on the bonds in the year of original maturity, if they were redeemed as planned. This amount of income might result in a tax liability. ▼

In some cases, it may be advantageous for the child not to make the accrual election. For example, a child under age 14 with investment income of more than $1,400 each year and parents in the 28, 31, 36, or 39.6 percent tax bracket would probably benefit from deferring the tax on the savings bond interest. The child would also benefit from the use of the usually lower tax rate (rather than subjecting the income to her parents' tax rate) if the bonds mature after the child is age 14 or older.

ACCOUNTING FOR COMMUNITY PROPERTY

The classification of income as community or separate property becomes important when either of two events occurs:

- Husband and wife, married taxpayers, file separate income tax returns for the year.
- Husband and wife obtain a divorce and therefore have to file separate returns for the year (refer to Chapter 3).

For planning purposes, it behooves married persons to keep track of the source of income (community or separate). To be in a position to do this effectively when income-producing assets are involved, it may be necessary to distinguish between separate and community property.[92]

ALIMONY

The person making the alimony payments favors a divorce settlement that includes a provision for deductible alimony payments. On the other hand, the recipient

---

[92]Being able to distinguish between separate and community property is crucial to the determination of a property settlement incident to a divorce. It also is vital in the estate tax area (refer to Chapter 1) since the surviving wife's or husband's share of the community property is not included in the gross estate of the deceased spouse.

prefers that the payments do not qualify as alimony. If the payor is in a higher tax bracket than the recipient, both parties may benefit by increasing the payments and structuring them so that they qualify as alimony.

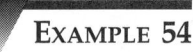

EXAMPLE 54

Carl and Polly are negotiating a divorce settlement. Carl has offered to pay Polly $10,000 each year for 10 years, but payments would cease upon Polly's death. Polly is willing to accept the offer, if the agreement will specify that the cash payments are not alimony. Carl is in the 36% tax bracket, and Polly's marginal rate is 15%.

If Carl and Polly agree that Carl will pay Polly $12,000 of alimony each year, both will have improved after-tax cash flows.

| | Annual Cash Flows | |
	Carl	Polly
Nonalimony payments	($10,000)	$10,000
Alimony payments	($12,000)	$12,000
Tax effects		
.36($12,000)	4,320	
.15($12,000)		(1,800)
After-tax cash flows	($ 7,680)	$10,200
Benefit of alimony option	$ 2,320	$ 200

Both parties benefit at the government's expense if the $12,000 alimony option is used. ▼

KEY TERMS

Accounting income, 4-4

Accounting method, 4-7

Accrual method, 4-9

Alimony and separate maintenance payments, 4-20

Alimony recapture, 4-21

Annuity, 4-27

Assignment of income, 4-15

Cash receipts method, 4-8

Claim of right doctrine, 4-9

Community property, 4-18

Constructive receipt, 4-10

Economic income, 4-3

Fruit and tree metaphor, 4-15

Gross income, 4-3

Group term life insurance, 4-33

Hybrid method, 4-9

Imputed interest, 4-24

Income, 4-3

Original issue discount, 4-11

Partnership, 4-17

Recovery of capital doctrine, 4-6

S corporation, 4-18

Taxable year, 4-7

PROBLEM MATERIALS

DISCUSSION QUESTIONS

1. The Internal Revenue Code contains a broad definition of gross income, but does not provide a listing of all possible types of income subject to tax. Would the tax law be improved if the Code included a complete listing of taxable sources of income?

2. Which of the following would be considered "income" for the current year by an economist but would not be gross income for tax purposes? Explain.

10,000 (1997) cost
1/1/98   12,000   FMC
12/31/98   13,000   FMC.

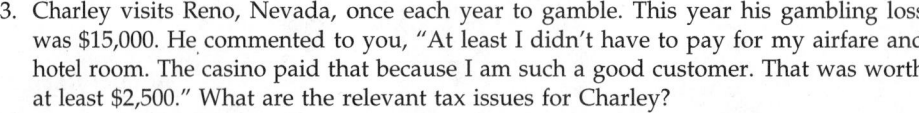

a. Securities acquired two years ago for $10,000 had a value of $12,000 at the beginning of the current year and a value of $13,000 at the end of the year. *No because it was sold*

b. An individual lives in the home he owns. *Yes opportunity costs because we rent it out*

c. A shareholder paid a corporation $3,000 for property valued at $5,000.

d. An individual owned property that was stolen. The cost of the property three years ago was $2,000, and an insurance company paid the owner $6,000 (the value of the property on the date of theft).

e. An individual found a box of seventeenth-century Spanish coins while diving off the Virginia coast.

3. Charley visits Reno, Nevada, once each year to gamble. This year his gambling loss was $15,000. He commented to you, "At least I didn't have to pay for my airfare and hotel room. The casino paid that because I am such a good customer. That was worth at least $2,500." What are the relevant tax issues for Charley?

4. Evaluate the following alternative proposals for taxing the income from property:

a. All assets would be valued at the end of the year, any increase in value that occurred during the year would be included in gross income, and any decrease in value would be deductible from gross income.

b. No gain or loss would be recognized until the taxpayer sold or exchanged the property.

c. Increases or decreases in the value of property traded on a national exchange (e.g., the New York Stock Exchange) would be reflected in gross income for the years the changes in value occurred. For all other assets, no gain or loss would be recognized until the property is sold or exchanged.

5. Lief owns 100 acres adjoining a national forest. Lief's cost of the land is $50,000. The park service decided to develop a hiking trail through the forest. To complete the trail, hikers would have to travel approximately 1,000 feet on Lief's property. The park service pays Lief $1,000 for an easement allowing the hikers to walk across his property. Is Lief required to recognize income from the receipt of the $1,000?

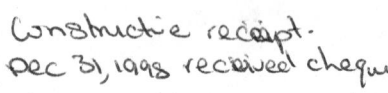

Constructive receipt.
Dec 31, 1998 received cheque

6. Sparrow, Inc., receives all of its income from repairing computers. The company reports its income by the cash method. On December 31, an employee went to a customer's office and repaired a computer. The customer gave Sparrow's employee a check for $300, but the employee did not remit the check to Sparrow until January of the following year. When is Sparrow required to recognize the income?

7. Lane is a self-employed consultant who reports his income by the cash method of accounting. In December 1998, Lane received a check for $5,000 from a client. Lane misplaced the check and did not find it until January 1999, when he deposited it in his bank account. Lane uses his deposit records to compute his income. Therefore, he included the $5,000 in his 1999 gross income.

a. In what year should Lane report the income?

b. Why does it matter whether Lane reports the income in 1998 or 1999, so long as he actually reports it?

8. Doug, a cash basis taxpayer, operated Craig's farm under an arrangement whereby Doug would receive one-half of the grain crop, less the cost of seed and fertilizer. The seed and fertilizer cost $8,000, which was paid during the year. In October Doug harvested the crop. A portion of the grain was sold for $28,000 cash in October, and Doug received $10,000 as his share of the $28,000 in November. Also in November, more of the grain was sold for $40,000. The grain was delivered to the purchaser in November, but payment was not to be received until January of the following year. Doug also used a portion of the grain for his personal use. The cost of the personal use grain was $1,200, but it could have been sold for $2,000. In February of the following year, Doug collected the balance Craig owed to him. Identify the relevant tax issues for Doug.

9. Olga, a cash basis taxpayer, sold a bond with accrued interest of $800 for $11,000. Olga's basis in the bond was $10,000. Compute Olga's income from this transaction.

10. Marlene, a cash basis taxpayer, purchased a 10-year zero coupon bond (no interest is paid annually) for $5,083 on January 2, 1998. The maturity value of the bond in 10 years is $10,000, which is the principal plus 7% interest compounded annually.
    a. What is Marlene's interest income from the bond for 1998?
    b. What is her basis for the bond on December 31, 1998?

11. Taupe Car Wash, an accrual basis taxpayer, sells certificates throughout the year that entitle the holder to a free car wash at any time during the next 24 months. At the end of 1998, certificates with a total face amount of $10,000 are outstanding. When is Taupe required to include the $10,000 in gross income?

12. Quinn (father) paid $200 for an automobile that needed repairs. He worked nights and weekends to restore the car. Several individuals offered to purchase the car for $2,800. Quinn gave the car and a list of potential buyers to Ron (son), whose college tuition was due in a few days. Ron sold the car for $2,800 and paid his tuition. Does Quinn have any taxable income from the transaction?

13. Tom Jr., a cash basis minor, performed services and was to be paid $100 in 1998. In 1998, the employer paid the $100 to Tom Sr., who deposited the money in his bank account. The following year, Tom Sr. used the $100 to buy his son a car.
    a. In whose gross income is the $100 included?
    b. When is the $100 included in gross income?

14. Isabella incorporated her law practice. She entered into an employee contract with the corporation, and all contracts with clients are between the client and Isabella's corporation. None of the clients would do business with the corporation if Isabella were not in fact doing all of the work. Who should report the income from the legal services?

15. Who pays the tax on (a) the income of an S corporation and on (b) the income of a partnership?

16. Ted and Alice were residents of a community property state. In 1998, Ted left Alice for parts unknown. Ted and Alice were still married at year-end. How will Ted's absence complicate Alice's 1998 tax return?

17. Hank and Elaine are negotiating their divorce agreement, which requires the division of their jointly owned property. Hank has proposed that he receive the couple's house (basis of $50,000 and fair market value of $75,000) while Elaine would receive (a) securities (basis of $10,000 and fair market value of $75,000) or (b) four annual payments of $22,644 each, which is equivalent to a $75,000 loan at 8% interest. Elaine will probably sell the securities if she receives them. Elaine does not want the house. Which option should she accept?

18. William and Abigail, who live in San Francisco, have been experiencing problems with their marriage. They have a three-year-old daughter, April, who stays with William's parents during the day since both William and Abigail are employed. Abigail worked to support William while he attended medical school, and now she has been accepted into medical school in Mexico. Abigail has decided to divorce William and attend medical school. April will stay in San Francisco because of her strong attachment to her grandparents and because they can provide her with excellent day care. Abigail knows that William will expect her to contribute to the cost of raising April. Abigail also feels that, to finance her education, she must receive cash for her share of the property they accumulated during their marriage. In addition, she feels she should receive some reimbursement for her contribution to William's support while he was in medical school. She expects the divorce proceedings will take several months. Identify the relevant tax issues for Abigail.

19. In the case of below-market loans between relatives, why is the lender deemed to have made a gift?

20. Elisha loaned $11,000 to Andy, her son, who used the money to buy a personal residence. This was the only outstanding loan between them. Elisha did not charge interest on

the loan, although the market rate of interest was 7%. Andy had $600 of net investment income for the year. Do the imputed interest rules apply?

21. In the case of a corporation's interest-free loan to its controlling shareholder who is also an employee of the corporation, why would the corporation prefer that the loan be classified as an employer-employee loan rather than a corporation-shareholder loan?

22. Brad is the president of the Yellow Corporation. He and other members of his family control the corporation. Brad has a temporary need for $50,000, and the corporation has excess cash. He could borrow the money from a bank at 9%, and Yellow is earning 6% on its temporary investments. Yellow has made loans to other employees on several occasions. Therefore, Brad is considering borrowing $50,000 from the corporation. He will repay the loan principal in two years plus interest at 5%. Identify the relevant tax issues for Brad and the Yellow Corporation.

23. Alfred, age 56, is a victim of corporate downsizing. After several months of unsuccessfully searching for a job, Alfred is forced to start drawing upon his annuity contract. The contract is part of a qualified retirement plan to which he contributed $6,200. Under the contract, Alfred is to receive $800 per month for the remainder of his life. How much of each monthly annuity payment is included in his gross income?

24. Gail is a full-time employee of Purple Corporation. One of the fringe benefits the company offers its employees is group term life insurance protection equal to the employee's annual salary. Gail is 45 years old, and her annual salary is $70,000. What is Gail's gross income from the life insurance protection for the year?

25. When a taxpayer is receiving Social Security benefits, could a $1,000 increase in income from services cause the taxpayer's adjusted gross income to increase by more than $1,000?

PROBLEMS

26. Determine the effects of the following on Anne's gross income for the year:
    a. Anne bought a used sofa for $25. After she took the sofa home, she discovered $15,000 in a secret compartment. Anne was unable to determine who placed the money in the sofa. Therefore, she put the money in her bank account.
    b. Anne also discovered oil on her property during the year, and the value of the land increased from $10,000 to $3 million.
    c. One year later, Anne found a diamond in the sofa she had purchased. Apparently, the diamond was in the sofa when Anne purchased it. The value of the diamond was $6,000. Under state law, the diamond became Anne's property when she purchased the sofa.
    d. Anne's bank charges a $3 per month service charge. However, the fee is waived if the customer maintains an average balance for the month of at least $1,000. Anne's account exceeded the minimum deposit requirement, and as a result she was not required to pay any service charges for the year.

27. Compute the taxpayer's (1) economic income and (2) gross income for tax purposes from the following events:
    a. The taxpayer sold securities for $10,000. The securities cost $6,000 in 1994. The fair market value of the securities at the beginning of the year was $9,000.
    b. The taxpayer sold his business and received $15,000 under a covenant not to compete with the new owner.
    c. The taxpayer used her controlled corporation's automobile for her vacation. The rental value of the automobile for the vacation period was $800.
    d. The taxpayer raised vegetables in her garden. The fair market value of the vegetables was $900, and the cost of raising them was $100. She ate some of the vegetables and gave the remainder to neighbors.
    e. The local government changed the zoning ordinances so that some of the taxpayer's residential property was reclassified as commercial. Because of the change, the fair market value of the taxpayer's property increased by $10,000.

f. During the year, the taxpayer borrowed $50,000 for two years at 9% interest. By the end of the year, interest rates had increased to 12%, and the lender accepted $49,000 in full satisfaction of the debt.

28. Kevin, a cash basis taxpayer, received the following from his employer during 1998:

- Salary of $75,000.

- Bonus of $10,000. In 1999, the company determined that the bonus had been incorrectly computed and required Kevin to repay $3,000.

- Use of a company car for his vacation. Rental value for the period would have been $900. Kevin paid for the gas.

- $4,000 advance for travel expenses. Kevin had spent only $3,400 at the end of the year.

Determine the effects of these items on Kevin's gross income.

29. Which of the following investments of $10,000 each will yield the greater after-tax value assuming the taxpayer is in the 40% tax bracket (combined Federal and state) for ordinary income and 26% for qualifying capital gains in all years and the investments will be liquidated at the end of five years?
   a. Land that will increase in value by 10% each year.
   b. A taxable bond yielding 10% before tax, and the interest can be reinvested at 10% before tax.

Prepare a brief speech for your tax class in which you explain why the future value of the land will exceed the future value of the taxable bond.

Given: Compound amount of $1 and compound value of annuity payments at the end of five years:

Interest Rate	$1 Compounded for 5 Years	$1 Annuity Compounded for 5 Years
6%	$1.33	$5.64
10%	1.61	6.10

30. Determine the taxpayer's income for tax purposes in each of the following cases:
   a. Zelda borrowed $30,000 from the First National Bank. She was required to deliver to the bank stocks with a value of $30,000 and a cost of $10,000. The stocks were to serve as collateral for the loan.
   b. Zelda owned a lot on Sycamore Street that measured 100 feet by 100 feet. The cost of the lot to her is $10,000. The city condemned a 10-foot strip of the land so that it could widen the street. Zelda received a $2,000 condemnation award.
   c. Zelda owned land zoned for residential use only. The land cost $5,000 and had a market value of $7,000. Zelda spent $500 and several hundred hours petitioning the county supervisors to change the zoning to A–1 commercial. When the county approved the zoning change, the value of the property immediately increased to $20,000.

31. Determine Amos Seagull's gross income in each of the following cases:
   a. In the current year, Seagull Corporation purchased an automobile for $25,000. The company was to receive a $1,500 rebate from the manufacturer. However, the corporation directed that the rebate be paid to Amos, the corporation's sole shareholder.
   b. Amos sold his corporation. In addition to the selling price of the stock, he received $50,000 for a covenant not to compete—an agreement that he will not compete with his former business for five years.
   c. Amos and his neighbor got into an argument over Amos's dog. The neighbor built a fence to keep the dog out of his yard. The fence added $1,500 to the value of Amos's property.

32. Al is an attorney who conducts his practice as a sole proprietor. During the year, he received cash of $100,000 for legal services. At the beginning of the year, he had receiv-

ables from clients of $45,000. At the end of the year, his receivables totaled $40,000. Compute Al's gross income from the practice for the year:
   a. Using the cash basis of accounting.
   b. Using the accrual basis of accounting.

33. The taxpayer began operating a grocery store during the year. Her only books and records are based on cash receipts and disbursements, but she has asked you to compute her gross profit from the business for tax purposes.

Sales of merchandise	$350,000
Purchases of merchandise	220,000

You determine that as of the end of the year the taxpayer has accounts payable for merchandise of $15,000 and accounts receivable from customers totaling $6,000. The cost of merchandise on hand at the end of the year was $9,000. Compute the grocery store's accrual method gross profit for the year.

34. Your client is a new partnership, Aspen Associates, which is an engineering consulting firm. Generally, Aspen bills clients for services at the end of each month. Client billings are about $50,000 each month. On average, it takes 45 days to collect the receivables. Aspen's expenses are primarily for salary and rent. Salaries are paid on the last day of each month, and rent is paid on the first day of each month. The partnership has a line of credit with a bank, which requires monthly financial statements. These must be prepared using the accrual method. Aspen's managing partner, Amanda Sims, has suggested that the firm should also use the accrual method for tax purposes and thus reduce accounting fees by $500. Write a letter to your client explaining why you believe it would be worthwhile for Aspen to file its tax return on the cash basis even though its financial statements are prepared on the accrual basis. Aspen's address is 100 James Tower, Denver, CO 80208.

35. Color Paint Shop, Inc., (459 Ellis Avenue, Harrisburg, PA 17111), is an accrual basis taxpayer that paints automobiles. During the year, the company painted Samuel's car and was to receive a $1,000 payment from his insurance company. Samuel was not satisfied with the work, however, and the insurance company refused to pay. In December 1998, Color and Samuel agreed that Color would receive $600 for the work, subject to final approval by the insurance company. In the past, Color had come to terms with customers only to have the insurance company negotiate an even lesser amount. In May 1999, the insurance company reviewed the claim and paid the $600 to Color. An IRS agent thinks that Color, as an accrual basis taxpayer, should report $1,000 of income in 1998, when the work was done and then deduct a $400 loss in 1999. Prepare a memo to Susan Apple, a tax partner for whom you are working, with the recommended treatment for the disputed income.

36. Determine the effect of the following on a cash basis taxpayer's gross income for 1998:
   a. Received his paycheck for $3,000 from his employer on December 31, 1998. He deposited the paycheck on January 2, 1999.   *effect*
   b. Received a bonus of $5,000 from his employer on January 10, 1999. The bonus was for the outstanding performance of his division during 1998.   *No effect*
   c. Received a dividend check from IBM on November 28, 1998. He mailed the check back to IBM in December requesting that additional IBM stock be issued to him under IBM's dividend reinvestment plan.   *Yes because it a cash dividend*

37. Mohammed owns a life insurance policy. The cash surrender value of the policy increased $800 during the year. He purchased a certificate of deposit on June 30 of the current year for $44,500. The certificate matures in two years when its value will be $50,000 (interest rate of 6%). However, if Mohammed redeems the certificate before the end of the first year, he receives no interest. Mohammed also purchased a Series EE U.S. government savings bond for $7,348. The maturity value of the bond is $10,000 in seven years (yield of 4.5%), and the redemption price of the bond increased by $380

during the year. Mohammed has owned no other savings bonds. What is Mohammed's current-year gross income from the above items?

38. Pelican, Inc., an accrual basis taxpayer, sells and installs consumer appliances. Determine the effects of each of the following transactions on the company's 1998 gross income:
    a. In December 1998, the company received a $1,200 advance payment from a customer. The payment was for an appliance that Pelican specially ordered from the manufacturer. The appliance had not arrived at the end of 1998.
    b. At the end of 1998, the company installed an appliance and collected the full price of $750 for the item. However, the customer claimed the appliance was defective and asked the company for a refund. The company conceded that the appliance was defective, but claimed that the customer should collect from the manufacturer. The dispute had not been settled by the end of 1998. In early 1999, it was determined that Pelican did not install the appliance properly, and the company was required to refund the full sales price.
    c. The company sold an appliance for $1,200 (plus a market rate of interest) and received the customer's note for that amount. However, because of the customer's poor credit rating, the value of the note was only $700.

39. Freda is a cash basis taxpayer. In 1998, she negotiated her salary for 1999. Her employer offered to pay her $20,000 each month—a total of $240,000 for the year. Freda countered that she would accept $20,000 each month for the first nine months of the year and the remaining $60,000 in January 2000. The employer accepted Freda's terms in 1999 and 2000.
    a. Did Freda actually or constructively receive $240,000 in 1999?
    b. What could explain Freda's willingness to spread her salary over a longer period of time?

40. The Heron Apartments requires its new tenants to pay the rent for the first and last months of the annual lease and a $400 damage deposit, all at the time the lease is signed. In December 1998, a tenant paid $800 for January 1999 rent, $800 for December 1999 rent, and $400 for the damage deposit. In January 2000, Heron refunded the tenant's damage deposit. What are the effects of these payments on Heron's taxable income for 1998, 1999, and 2000?
    a. Assume Heron is a cash basis taxpayer.
    b. Assume Heron is an accrual basis taxpayer.

41. Leo has asked you to review portions of his tax return. He provides you with the following information:

Gain on redemption of a 2-year 6% certificate of deposit		
Proceeds received June 30, 1998	$10,000	
Purchase price July 1, 1996	(8,900)	
Gain		$1,100
Gain on redemption of a 6-month 6% certificate of deposit		
Proceeds received March 31, 1998	$ 5,000	
Purchase price October 1, 1997	(4,855)	
Gain		145
Gain from 8% Series E savings bond		
Proceeds received September 30, 1998	$ 2,500	
Purchase price June 30, 1984	(780)	
Gain		1,720
Distributions from a family partnership		1,500

Leo's share of the partnership's earnings were $1,800. Determine Leo's 1998 gross income from the above.

42. a. Gus is a cash basis taxpayer. On September 1, 1998, Gus gave a corporate bond to his son, Hans. The bond had a face amount of $10,000 and paid $900 of interest each January 31. On December 1, 1998, Gus gave common stocks to his daughter, Dena. Dividends totaling $720 had been declared on the stocks on November 30, 1998, and were payable on January 15, 1999. Dena became the shareholder of record in time to collect the dividends. What is Gus's 1999 gross income from the bond and stocks?

    b. Gus's mother was unable to pay her bills as they came due. Gus, his employer, and his mother's creditors entered into an arrangement whereby the employer would withhold $500 per month from Gus's salary and pay the $500 to the creditors. Three thousand dollars were withheld from Gus's salary and paid to the creditors. Is Gus required to pay tax on the $3,000?

43. Tracy, a cash basis taxpayer, is employed by Eagle Corporation, also a cash basis taxpayer. Tracy is a full-time employee of the corporation and receives a salary of $60,000 per year. He also receives a bonus equal to 10% of all collections from clients he serviced during the year. Determine the tax consequences of the following events to the corporation and to Tracy:

    a. On December 31, 1998, Tracy was visiting a customer. The customer gave Tracy a $3,000 check payable to the corporation for appraisal services Tracy performed during 1998. Tracy did not deliver the check to the corporation until January 1999.

    b. The facts are the same as in (a), except that the corporation is an accrual basis taxpayer and Tracy deposited the check on December 31, but the bank did not add the deposit to the corporation's account until January 1999.

    c. The facts are the same as in (a), except the customer told Tracy to hold the check until January when the customer could make a bank deposit that would cover the check.

44. Eve, Fran, and Gary each have a one-third interest in the capital and profits of the EFG Partnership. At the beginning of the year, each partner had a $50,000 balance in his or her capital account. The partnership's gross income for the year was $300,000, and its total expenses were $60,000. During the year, Eve contributed an additional $10,000 to the partnership and did not have any withdrawals from her capital account. Fran withdrew $30,000, and Gary withdrew $24,000. Compute each partner's taxable income from the partnership for the year.

45. Diego and Carmen lived together for part of the year but were divorced on December 31, 1998. Diego earned $30,000 salary from his employer during the year. Carmen's salary was $16,000. Carmen also received $8,000 in taxable dividends from stock held as separate property.

    a. If Diego and Carmen reside in Texas, how much income should each report on their separate tax returns for 1998?

    b. If amounts are withheld from their salaries, how are these amounts reported on Diego and Carmen's separate returns?

    c. If Diego and Carmen reside in a common law state, how much income should each report on their separate returns?

46. Liz and Doug were divorced on July 1 of the current year after 10 years of marriage. Their current year's income received before the divorce was as follows:

Doug's salary	$18,000
Liz's salary	25,000
Rent on apartments purchased by Liz 15 years ago	6,000
Dividends on stock Doug inherited from his mother 4 years ago	1,200
Interest on a savings account in Liz's name funded with her salary	1,800

Allocate the income to Liz and Doug assuming they live in:
a. California.
b. Texas.

47. Nell and Kirby are in the process of negotiating their divorce agreement. What would be the tax consequences to Nell and Kirby if the following, considered individually, became part of the agreement:
    a. Nell and Kirby will continue as joint owners of the personal residence. Nell can continue to occupy the residence as long as she so desires. If she ever sells the residence, however, Kirby will receive one-half the proceeds. The fair rental value of the residence is $2,000 per month.
    b. Nell will receive $1,000 per month for 100 months, and Kirby will receive the $180,000 in securities (adjusted basis is $100,000) that were formerly owned jointly by the couple. If Nell dies before she receives all of the payments, Kirby is not required to continue the payments.
    c. Nell is to have custody of their 12-year-old son and is to receive $600 per month until (1) the child dies or (2) attains age 21 (whichever occurs first).

48. Under the terms of a post-1986 divorce agreement, Al is to receive payments from Karen as follows: $60,000 in Year 1, $45,000 in Year 2, and $20,000 each year for Years 3 through 10. Al is also to receive custody of their minor son. The payments will decrease by $5,000 per year if the son dies or when he attains age 21 and will cease upon Al's death.
    a. What will be Al's taxable alimony in Year 1?
    b. What will be the effect of the Years 2 and 3 payments on Al's taxable income?

49. Under the terms of their divorce agreement, Barry is to transfer common stock (cost of $25,000, market value of $60,000) to Sandra. Barry and Sandra have a 14-year-old child. Sandra will have custody of the child, and Barry is to pay $300 per month as child support. In addition, Sandra is to receive $1,000 per month for 10 years. However, the payments will be reduced to $750 per month when their child reaches age 21. In the first year under the agreement, Sandra receives the common stock and the correct cash payments for six months. How will the terms of the agreement affect Sandra's gross income?

50. Gus decides to buy a personal residence and goes to the bank for a $50,000 loan. The bank tells him he can borrow the funds at 8% if his father will guarantee the debt. Gus's father, Hal, owns certificates of deposit currently yielding 7%. The Federal rate is 6%. Hal is willing to do either of the following:

    • Cash in the certificates and lend Gus the funds at 7% interest.

    • Guarantee the loan for Gus.

    Hal will consider lending the funds to Gus at an even lower interest rate, depending on the tax consequences. Hal is in the 36% marginal tax bracket. Gus, whose only source of income is his salary, is in the 15% marginal tax bracket. The interest Gus pays on the mortgage will be deductible by him. Considering only the tax consequences, which option will maximize the family's after-tax wealth?

51. On June 30, 1998, Ridge borrowed $52,000 from his employer. On July 1, 1998, Ridge used the money as follows:

Interest-free loan to Ridge's controlled corporation (operated by Ridge on a part-time basis)	$21,000
Interest-free loan to Tab (Ridge's son)	11,000
National Bank of Grundy 6% certificate of deposit ($14,840 due at maturity, June 30, 1999)	14,000
National Bank of Grundy 6.25% certificate of deposit ($6,773 due at maturity, June 30, 2000)	6,000
	$52,000

Ridge's employer did not charge him interest. The applicable Federal rate was 8% throughout the relevant period. Tab had investment income of $800 for the year, and he used the loan proceeds to pay medical school tuition. There were no other outstanding loans between Ridge and Tab. What are the effects of the preceding transactions on Ridge's taxable income for 1998?

52. Indicate whether the imputed interest rules should apply in the following situations:
    a. Mitch is a cash basis attorney who charges his clients based on the number of hours it takes to do the job. The bill is due upon completion of the work. However, for clients who make an initial payment when the work begins, Mitch grants a discount on the final bill. The discount is equal to 10% interest on the deposit.
    b. Local Telephone Company requires that customers make a security deposit. The deposit is refunded after the customer has established a good record for paying the telephone bill. The company pays 6% interest on the deposits.
    c. Lynn asked Kelly for a $125,000 loan to purchase a new home. Kelly made the loan and did not charge interest. Kelly never intended to collect the loan, and at the end of the year Kelly told Lynn that the debt was forgiven.

53. Vito is the sole shareholder of Vito, Inc. He is also employed by the corporation. On June 30, 1998, Vito borrowed $8,000 from Vito, Inc., and on July 1, 1999, he borrowed an additional $3,000. Both loans were due on demand. No interest was charged on the loans, and the Federal rate was 10% for all relevant dates. Vito used the money to purchase stock, and he had no investment income. Determine the tax consequences to Vito and Vito, Inc., in each of the following situations:
    a. The loans are considered employer-employee loans.
    b. The loans are considered corporation-shareholder loans.

54. Albert purchased an annuity from an insurance company for $100,000 on January 1, 1998. The annuity was to pay him $6,000 per year for life starting in January 1998. At the annuity starting date, Albert was age 65.
    a. Determine Albert's gross income from the annuity in the first year.
    b. Assume Albert lives 25 years after purchasing the contract. What would be his gross income in the twenty-fourth year?
    c. Assume Albert died in 2001, after collecting a total of $20,000. What will be the effect of the annuity on his 2001 adjusted gross income?

55. For each of the following, determine the amount that should be included in gross income:
    a. Joe was selected as the most valuable player in the Super Bowl. In recognition of this, he was awarded a sports car worth $60,000 and $50,000 in cash.
    b. Wanda won the Mrs. America beauty contest. She received various prizes valued at $75,000.
    c. George was awarded the Nobel Peace Prize. He donated the $900,000 check he received to State University, his alma mater.

56. The LMN Partnership has a group term life insurance plan. Each partner has $200,000 protection, and each employee has protection equal to twice his or her annual salary. Employee Alice (age 44) had $110,000 insurance under the plan, and partner Kay (age 56) had $200,000 coverage. The cost of Alice's coverage for the year was $180, and the cost of Kay's protection was $1,500.
    a. Assuming the plan is nondiscriminatory, how much must Alice and Kay include in gross income from the insurance?
    b. Assuming the plan is discriminatory, how much must Kay include in her gross income from the insurance?

57. Herbert was employed for the first six months of the year and earned $60,000 in salary. During the next six months, he collected $7,800 of unemployment compensation, borrowed $6,000 (using his personal residence as collateral), and withdrew $1,000 from his savings account (including $60 interest). His luck was not all bad, for in December he won $800 in the lottery on a $5 ticket. Calculate Herbert's gross income.

58. Linda and Don are married and file a joint return. In 1998, they received $9,000 in Social Security benefits and $28,000 taxable pension benefits, interest, and dividends.
    a. Compute the couple's adjusted gross income on a joint return.
    b. Don would like to know whether they should sell for $100,000 a corporate bond (at no gain or loss) that pays 8% in interest each year and use the proceeds to buy a $100,000 nontaxable State of Virginia bond that will pay $6,000 in interest each year.

c. If Linda in (a) works part-time and earns $30,000, how much would Linda and Don's adjusted gross income increase?

59. Melissa and James are married and file a joint return. They receive $12,000 in Social Security benefits, $21,000 in pension benefits (all taxable), and $9,000 in taxable dividends. They are considering selling appreciated stock that they own. They purchased the stock three years ago for $8,000, and it now has a market value of $15,000. Melissa and James have asked you to explain the tax consequences of the sale including the effect on their adjusted gross income.

60. Donna does not think she has an income tax problem but would like to discuss her situation with you just to make sure she will not get hit with an unexpected tax liability. Base your suggestions on the following relevant financial information:
    a. Donna's share of the SAT Partnership income is $70,000, but none of the income can be distributed because the partnership needs the cash for operations.
    b. Donna's Social Security benefits totaled $8,400, but Donna loaned the cash received to her nephew.
    c. Donna assigned to a creditor the right to collect $1,200 interest on some bonds she owned.
    d. Donna and her husband lived together in California until September, when they separated. Donna has heard rumors that her husband had substantial gambling winnings since they separated.

Dependent

CUMULATIVE PROBLEMS

61. Dan and Freida Butler, husband and wife, file a joint return. The Butlers live at 625 Oak Street, Corbin, KY 27521. Dan's Social Security number is 482–61–1231, and Freida's is 162–79–1245.

    During 1998, Dan and Freida furnished over half of the total support of each of the following individuals:
    a. Gina, their daughter, age 22, a full-time student, who was married on December 21, 1998, has no income of her own, and for 1998 did not file a joint return with her husband, who earned $4,000 during 1998. *Yes Dependent*
    b. Sam, their son, age 20, who had gross income of $2,900 and who dropped out of college in February 1998. *No - because he dropped out of school 5 months*
    c. Ben Brow, Freida's brother, age 22, who is a full-time college student with gross income of $4,000. *No, because he is Freida broth*

    Dan, a radio announcer for WJJJ, earned a salary of $60,000 in 1998. Freida was employed part-time as a real estate salesperson by Corbin Realty and was paid commissions of $40,000 in 1998. Freida sold a house on December 30, 1998, and will be paid a commission of $1,500 (not included in the $40,000) on the January 10, 1999, closing date.

    $100,000

    Dan and Freida collected $15,000 on a certificate of deposit that matured on September 30, 1998. The certificate was purchased on October 1, 1996, for $13,102, and the yield to maturity was 7%.

    under cash basis

    Other income received consisted of the following:

Dividends on CSX stock → *Gift*	$2,200
Interest on savings account at Second Bank	1,500

    ← not taxable

    CSX had been instructed by Dan and Freida to pay the dividends directly to Freida's brother, Ben. CSX complied with their instructions.

    800 Freida is a 8% partner in the Green Partnership. Green reported taxable income of $100,000 for 1998 and made no distributions to any of the partners in 1998.

    Dan and Freida had itemized deductions as follows:

State income tax withheld	$3,600
Personal property taxes paid	300
Real estate taxes paid	2,800
Interest on home mortgage (paid to Corbin Savings and Loan)	5,900
Cash contributions to the Boy Scouts	620

Their employers withheld Federal income tax of $16,500 (Dan $10,400, Freida $6,100), and the Butlers paid estimated tax of $4,000.

Part 1—Tax Computation
Compute Dan and Freida's 1998 Federal income tax payable (or refund due). Suggested software (if available): *TurboTax.*

Part 2—Tax Planning
Dan plans to reduce his work schedule and work only halftime for WJJJ in 1999. He has been writing songs for several years and wants to devote more time to developing a career as a songwriter. Because of the uncertainty in the music business, however, he would like you to make all computations assuming he will have no income from songwriting in 1999. To make up for the loss of income, Freida plans to increase the amount of time she spends selling real estate. She estimates she will be able to earn $65,000 in 1999. Assume all other income and expense items will be approximately the same as they were in 1998. Will the Butlers have more or less disposable income (after Federal income tax) in 1999? Write a letter to the Butlers that contains your advice and prepare a memo for the tax files. Suggested software (if available): *TurboTax.*

62. Cecil C. Seymour is a 66-year-old widower. He had income for 1997 as follows:

Pension from former employer	$23,400
Interest income from Alto National Bank	6,500
Interest income on City of Alto bonds	2,000
Dividends received from AT&T	4,000
Collections on annuity contract he purchased from Great Life Insurance	4,800
Social Security benefits	12,000

The cost of the annuity was $36,000, and Cecil was expected to receive a total of 120 monthly payments of $400. Cecil has received 30 payments through 1997.

Cecil's 40-year-old daughter, Sarah C. Seymour, borrowed $40,000 from Cecil in 1996. She used the money to start a new business. Cecil does not charge her interest because she could not afford to pay it, but he does expect to eventually collect the principal. Sarah is living with Cecil until the business becomes profitable. Except for housing, Sarah provides her own support from her business and $1,500 in dividends on stocks that she inherited from her mother.

Other relevant information is presented below:

- Cecil's Social Security number: 259–83–4444

- Address: 3840 Springfield Blvd., Alto, GA 30754

- Sarah's Social Security number: 257–49–8862

- State income taxes paid: $1,300

- County personal property taxes paid: $1,900

- Payments on estimated 1997 Federal income tax: $6,500

- Charitable contributions of cash to Alto Baptist Church: $4,400

- Federal interest rate: 8%

Compute Cecil's 1997 Federal income tax payable (or refund due). If you use tax forms for your computations, you will need Form 1040 and Schedules A and B. Suggested software (if available): *TurboTax*.

RESEARCH PROBLEMS

*Note: Use the **RIA OnPoint System 4 Student Version CD-ROM**, which is available to accompany this text, in preparing solutions to the Research Problems. Alternatively, tax research materials found in a standard tax library can be used.*

Research Problem 1.   Edith Sanders gave common stock to her daughter, Joyce. The cost of the stock was $20,000, and its fair market value was $150,000. The uniform transfer tax on the gift was $30,000. Edith was liable for the transfer tax, but the gift was made on the condition that Joyce would pay the gift tax (i.e., a "net gift"). Joyce paid the $30,000 in accordance with the agreement.

The IRS agent contends that Edith must treat the transactions as part sale and part gift. That is, 20% of the stock ($30,000/$150,000 = .20) was sold, and the balance was given to Joyce. According to the agent, Edith must recognize taxable gain of $26,000 [$30,000 − (.20)($20,000)]. Edith is having difficulty understanding why she would be required to recognize any income since she made a gift of property and did not receive anything. Write a letter to the taxpayer that contains your advice and prepare a memo for the tax files. Edith's address is 400 Rock Street, Memphis, TN 38152.

Research Problem 2.   Ted owns a convertible bond issued by Blue Corporation. His original cost is $1,000, and the bond is convertible into 10 shares of Blue common stock. Two years after he purchased the bond, Ted is considering whether to exercise his conversion rights. The value of the Blue common stock is now $130 per share. Ted would like to know whether the conversion will result in a taxable gain.

Research Problem 3.   Debra is a cash basis taxpayer whose employer defers 10% of her annual salary until she reaches age 65. To assure that the company can pay the deferred compensation when it comes due, the company purchases an annuity policy that will be payable when Debra reaches retirement age. The company will continue to own the policy and will collect the proceeds and pay Debra. A revenue agent argues that Debra has constructively received the income as soon as her employer purchases the annuity contract. Is the revenue agent correct?

Partial list of research aids:
Rev.Rul. 72–25, 1972–1 C.B. 127; Rev.Rul 68–99, 1968–1 C.B. 193.

Research Problem 4.   The First Central Bank, an accrual basis taxpayer, has a credit card operation. Customers pay $30 per year for the right to use the card. If the customer decides to cancel the card during the year, the customer receives a refund of a prorated amount. The IRS position is that the amounts received are interest and thus are not eligible for deferral under Revenue Procedure 71–21. The taxpayer argues that the prepaid income is for services that are to be rendered over 12 months and thus the prepaid income can be amortized over the 12-month period. Determine the appropriate tax treatment.

Use the tax resources of the Internet to address the following questions. Do not restrict your search to the World Wide Web, but include a review of newsgroups and general reference materials, practitioner sites and resources, primary sources of the tax law, chat rooms and discussion groups, and other opportunities.

Research Problem 5.   Determine the applicable Federal rate for purposes of below-market loans. Use this figure to complete Problem 51 for this chapter.

Research Problem 6.   Go to the Web page of a consulting firm that offers counseling services to individuals as they negotiate the terms of a divorce. What specific tax-related services do these firms offer? Send an e-mail message to one of these firms suggesting that it add a specific service or revise its Web page to emphasize other tax-related services for its clients.

TEAM PROJECT: ARTHUR ANDERSEN TAX CHALLENGE CASES

For more information on the Arthur Andersen Tax Challenge Cases, refer to Chapter 1, page 1–37.

Information related to tax issues and problems that are discussed in this chapter may be found in the

Day and Ball case on pages 1, 2, 4, 11–17, 31, 34, 35, and 37
Fence case on pages 39, 40, 41, 47, 50, 58, 60, and 63

Read and analyze the case you have been assigned and *identify* any issues and problems that are related to material covered in this chapter. If the information provided in the case is complete, prepare answers for this part of the case at this time. If you need information that is contained in the later parts of the case, write a memo summarizing the questions or problems so you can prepare a complete answer at a later date.

GROSS INCOME: EXCLUSIONS

LEARNING OBJECTIVES

After completing Chapter 5, you should be able to:

1. Understand that statutory authority is required to exclude an item from gross income.

2. Identify the circumstances under which various items are excludible from gross income.

3. Determine the extent to which receipts can be excluded under the tax benefit rule.

4. Describe the circumstances under which income must be reported from the discharge of indebtedness.

5. Identify tax planning strategies for obtaining the maximum benefit from allowable exclusions.

ITEMS SPECIFICALLY EXCLUDED FROM GROSS INCOME

Chapter 4 discussed the concepts and judicial doctrines that affect the determination of gross income. If an income item is within the all-inclusive definition of gross income, the item can be excluded only if the taxpayer can locate specific authority for doing so. Chapter 5 focuses on the exclusions Congress has authorized. These exclusions are listed in Exhibit 5–1.

Tax advisers spend countless hours trying to develop techniques to achieve tax-exempt status for income. Employee benefits planning is greatly influenced by the availability of certain types of exclusions. Taxes play an important role in employee benefits, as well as in other situations, because attaining an exclusion is another means of enhancing after-tax income. For example, for a person whose combined Federal and state marginal tax rate is 40 percent, $1.00 of tax-exempt income is equivalent to $1.66 in income subject to taxation. The tax adviser's ideal is to attach the right labels or provide the right wording to render income nontaxable without affecting the economics of the transaction.

Consider the case of an employee who is in the 28 percent marginal tax bracket and is paying $3,000 a year for health insurance. If the employer provided this protection in a manner that qualified for exclusion treatment but reduced the employee's salary by $3,000, the employee's after-tax and after-insurance income would increase at no additional cost to the employer.

▼ **EXHIBIT 5–1**

Summary of Principal Exclusions
from Gross Income

1. Donative items
   Gifts, bequests, and inheritances (§ 102)
   Life insurance proceeds paid by reason of death (§ 101)
   Accelerated death benefits [§ 101(g)]
   Survivor benefits for public safety officer killed in the line of duty [§ 101(h)]
   Scholarships (§ 117)
2. Personal and welfare items
   Injury or sickness payments (§ 104)
   Public assistance payments (Rev.Rul. 71–425, 1971–2 C.B. 76)
   Amounts received under insurance contracts for certain living expenses (§ 123)
   Reimbursement for the costs of caring for a foster child (§ 131)
3. Wage and salary supplements
   a. Fringe benefits
      Accident and health benefits (§§ 105 and 106)
      Medical savings accounts [§ 106(b)]
      Lodging and meals furnished for the convenience of the employer (§ 119)
      Rental value of parsonages (§ 107)
      Employee achievement awards [§ 74(c)]
      Employer contributions to employee group term life insurance (§ 79)
      Cafeteria plans (§ 125)
      Educational assistance payments (§ 127)*
      Child or dependent care (§ 129)
      Services provided to employees at no additional cost to the employer (§ 132)
      Employee discounts (§ 132)
      Working condition and *de minimis* fringes (§ 132)
      Athletic facilities provided to employees (§ 132)
      Qualified transportation fringe (§ 132)
      Qualified moving expense reimbursement (§ 132)
      Tuition reductions granted to employees of educational institutions (§ 117)
      Child adoption expenses (§ 137)
      Long-term care insurance (§ 7702B)
   b. Military benefits
      Combat pay (§ 112)
      Housing, uniforms, and other benefits (§ 134)
   c. Foreign earned income (§ 911)
4. Investor items
   Interest on state and local government obligations (§ 103)
   Improvements by tenant to landlord's property (§ 109)
   Fifty percent exclusion for gain from sale of certain small business stock (§ 1202)
5. Benefits for the elderly
   Social Security benefits (except in the case of certain higher-income taxpayers)
      (§ 86)
6. Other benefits
   Income from discharge of indebtedness (§ 108)
   Recovery of a prior year's deduction that yielded no tax benefit (§ 111)
   Gain from the sale of personal residence (§ 121)
   Educational savings bonds (§ 135)
   Qualified state tuition program (§ 529)
   Lessee construction allowances for short-term leases (§ 110)

*Exclusion treatment applies for courses beginning before June 1, 2000.

Salary received to use to purchase health insurance	$ 3,000
Less: Taxes ($3,000 × 28%)	(840)
Cash available to purchase health insurance	$ 2,160
Less: Cost of health insurance	(3,000)
Excess of cost of health insurance over cash available	$ 840

Thus, the employee in this case is $840 better off with a salary reduction of $3,000 and employer-provided health insurance. The employee may still decide that the $3,000 salary is preferable. For example, if the employee has not been sick, he or she may feel that health insurance is no longer needed. Understanding the tax influence, however, does enable the employee to make a more informed choice.

STATUTORY AUTHORITY

1 **LEARNING OBJECTIVE**
Understand that statutory authority is required to exclude an item from gross income.

Sections 101 through 150 provide the authority for excluding specific items from gross income. In addition, other exclusions are scattered throughout the Code. Each exclusion has its own legislative history and reason for enactment. Certain exclusions are intended as a form of indirect welfare payments. Other exclusions prevent double taxation of income or provide incentives for socially desirable activities (e.g., nontaxable interest on certain U.S. government bonds where the owner uses the funds for educational expenses).

In some cases, Congress has enacted exclusions to rectify the effects of judicial decisions. For example, the Supreme Court held that the fair market value of improvements (not made in lieu of rent) made by a tenant to the landlord's property should be included in the landlord's gross income upon termination of the lease.[1] The landlord was required to include the value of the improvements in gross income even though the property had not been sold or otherwise disposed of. Congress provided relief in this situation by enacting § 109, which defers taxing the value of the improvements until the property is sold.[2]

GIFTS AND INHERITANCES

GENERAL

2 **LEARNING OBJECTIVE**
Identify the circumstances under which various items are excludible from gross income.

Beginning with the Income Tax Act of 1913 and continuing to the present, Congress has allowed the recipient of a gift to exclude the value of the property from gross income. The exclusion applies to gifts made during the life of the donor (*inter vivos* gifts) and transfers that take effect upon the death of the donor (bequests and inheritances).[3] However, as discussed in Chapter 4, the recipient of a gift of income-producing property is subject to tax on the income subsequently earned from the property. Also, as discussed in Chapter 1, the donor or the decedent's estate may be subject to gift or estate taxes on the transfer.

In numerous cases, gifts are made in a business setting. For example, a salesperson gives a purchasing agent free samples; an employee receives cash from his or her employer on retirement; a corporation makes payments to employees who were victims of a natural disaster; a corporation makes a cash payment to a deceased employee's spouse. In these and similar instances, it is frequently unclear whether the payment was a gift or whether it represents compensation for past, present, or future services.

The courts have defined a **gift** as "a voluntary transfer of property by one to another without adequate [valuable] consideration or compensation therefrom."[4]

---

[1]*Helvering v. Bruun*, 40–1 USTC ¶9337, 24 AFTR 652, 60 S.Ct. 631 (USSC, 1940).
[2]If the tenant made the improvements in lieu of rent, the value of the improvements is not eligible for exclusion.

[3]§ 102.
[4]*Estate of D. R. Daly*, 3 B.T.A. 1042 (1926).

If the payment is intended to be for services rendered, it is not a gift, even though the payment is made without legal or moral obligation and the payor receives no economic benefit from the transfer. To qualify as a gift, the payment must be made "out of affection, respect, admiration, charity or like impulses."[5] Thus, the cases on this issue have been decided on the basis of the donor's intent.

In a landmark case, *Comm. v. Duberstein,*[6] the taxpayer (Duberstein) received a Cadillac from a business acquaintance. Duberstein had supplied the businessman with the names of potential customers with no expectation of compensation. The Supreme Court concluded:

> . . . despite the characterization of the transfer of the Cadillac by the parties [as a gift] and the absence of any obligation, even of a moral nature, to make it, it was at the bottom a recompense for Duberstein's past service, or an inducement for him to be of further service in the future.

Duberstein was therefore required to include the fair market value of the automobile in gross income.

GIFTS TO EMPLOYEES

In the case of cash or other property *received by an employee* from his or her employer, Congress has eliminated any ambiguity. Transfers from an employer to an employee cannot be excluded as a gift unless the transfer fits into a statutory exclusion provision other than the one for gifts.[7]

EMPLOYEE DEATH BENEFITS

Frequently, an employer makes payments (**death benefits**) to a deceased employee's surviving spouse, children, or other beneficiaries. If the decedent had a nonforfeitable right to the payments (e.g., the decedent's accrued salary), the amounts are generally taxable to the recipient just the same as if the employee had lived and collected the payments. But where the employer makes voluntary payments, the gift issue arises. Generally, the IRS considers such payments to be compensation for prior services rendered by the deceased employee.[8] However, some courts have held that payments to an employee's surviving spouse or other beneficiaries are gifts if the following are true:[9]

- The payments were made to the surviving spouse and children rather than to the employee's estate.
- The employer derived no benefit from the payments.
- The surviving spouse and children performed no services for the employer.
- The decedent had been fully compensated for services rendered.
- Payments were made pursuant to a board of directors' resolution that followed a general company policy of providing payments for families of deceased employees (but not exclusively for families of shareholder-employees).

When all of the above conditions are satisfied, the payment is presumed to have been made *as an act of affection or charity.* When one or more of these conditions is

---

[5]*Robertson v. U.S.,* 52–1 USTC ¶9343, 41 AFTR 1053, 72 S.Ct. 994 (USSC, 1952).
[6]60–2 USTC ¶9515, 5 AFTR2d 1626, 80 S.Ct. 1190 (USSC, 1960).
[7]§ 102(c).

[8]Rev.Rul. 62–102, 1962–2 C.B. 37.
[9]*Estate of Sydney J. Carter v. Comm.,* 72–1 USTC ¶9129, 29 AFTR2d 332, 453 F.2d 61 (CA–2, 1972), and the cases cited there.

not satisfied, the surviving spouse and children may still be deemed the recipients of a gift if the payment is made in light of the survivors' financial needs.[10]

LIFE INSURANCE PROCEEDS

GENERAL RULE

Life insurance proceeds paid to the beneficiary because of the death of the insured are exempt from income tax.[11]

EXAMPLE 1

Mark purchased an insurance policy on his life and named his wife Linda as the beneficiary. Mark paid $24,000 in premiums. When he died, Linda collected the insurance proceeds of $60,000. The $60,000 is exempt from Federal income tax. ▼

Congress chose to exempt life insurance proceeds for the following reasons:

- For family members, life insurance proceeds serve much the same purpose as a nontaxable inheritance.
- In a business context (as well as in a family situation), life insurance proceeds replace an economic loss suffered by the beneficiary.

EXAMPLE 2

Gold Corporation purchased a life insurance policy to cover its key employee. If the proceeds were taxable, the corporation would require more insurance coverage to pay the tax as well as to cover the economic loss of the employee. ▼

Thus, in general, Congress concluded that making life insurance proceeds exempt from income tax was a good policy.

ACCELERATED DEATH BENEFITS

Generally, if the owner of a life insurance policy cancels the policy and receives the cash surrender value, the taxpayer must recognize gain equal to the excess of the amount received over premiums paid on the policy (a loss is not deductible). The gain is recognized because the general exclusion provision for life insurance proceeds applies only to life insurance proceeds paid upon the death of the insured. If the taxpayer cancels the policy and receives the cash surrender value, the life insurance policy is treated as an investment by the insured.

In 1996, Congress decided that in some cases it is appropriate to allow the insured to receive the benefits of the life insurance contract without having to include the gain in gross income. Under the **accelerated death benefits** provisions, exclusion treatment is available for insured taxpayers who are either terminally ill or chronically ill.[12] A terminally ill taxpayer can collect the cash surrender value of the policy from the insurance company or assign the policy proceeds to a qualified third party. The resultant gain, if any, is excluded from the insured's gross income. A *terminally ill* individual is one whom a medical doctor certifies as having an illness that is reasonably expected to cause death within 24 months.

In the case of a chronically ill patient, no gain is recognized if the proceeds of the policy are used for the long-term care of the insured. A person is *chronically ill* if he or she is certified as being unable to perform without assistance certain

---

[10]*Simpson v. U.S.*, 58–2 USTC ¶9923, 2 AFTR2d 6036, 261 F.2d 497 (CA–7, 1958), *cert. denied*, 79 S.Ct. 724 (USSC, 1958).

[11]§ 101(a).
[12]§ 101(g).

activities of daily living. These exclusions for the terminally ill and the chronically ill are available only to the insured. Thus, a person who purchases a life insurance policy from the insured does not qualify.

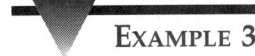

EXAMPLE 3

Tom owned a term life insurance policy at the time he was diagnosed as having a terminal illness. After paying $5,200 in premiums, he sold the policy to Amber Benefits, Inc., a company that is authorized by the State of Virginia to purchase such policies. Amber paid Tom $50,000. When Tom died six months later, Amber collected the face amount of the policy, $75,000. Tom is not required to include the $44,800 gain ($50,000 – $5,200) on the sale of the policy in his gross income. Assume Amber pays additional premiums of $4,000 during the six-month period. When Amber collects the life insurance proceeds of $75,000, it must include the $21,000 gain ($75,000 proceeds – $50,000 cost – $4,000 additional premiums paid) in gross income. ▼

ETHICAL
CONSIDERATIONS

Investing in Death

Recent changes in the tax law allow a person with a terminal illness to sell his or her life insurance policy without recognizing gain. Limited partnerships have been formed to purchase the policies insuring AIDS patients. The shorter the patient's life span, the greater the investor's potential profit. When the Food and Drug Administration announces that a potential cure for AIDS cannot be marketed until it has been tested for several years, the market value of these partnership interests increases. Should the tax law be a participant in a system that allows individuals to profit from other people's misfortunes?

TRANSFER FOR VALUABLE CONSIDERATION

A life insurance policy (other than one associated with accelerated death benefits) may be transferred after it is issued by the insurance company. If the policy is *transferred for valuable consideration*, the insurance proceeds are includible in the gross income of the transferee to the extent the proceeds received exceed the amount paid for the policy by the transferee plus any subsequent premiums paid.

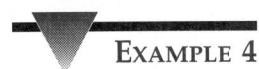

EXAMPLE 4

Adam pays premiums of $500 for an insurance policy in the face amount of $1,000 upon the life of Beth and subsequently transfers the policy to Carol for $600. On Beth's death, Carol receives the proceeds of $1,000. The amount that Carol can exclude from gross income is limited to $600 plus any premiums she paid subsequent to the transfer. ▼

The Code, however, provides four exceptions to the rule illustrated in the preceding example. These exceptions permit exclusion treatment for transfers to the following:

1. A partner of the insured.
2. A partnership in which the insured is a partner.
3. A corporation in which the insured is an officer or shareholder.
4. A transferee whose basis in the policy is determined by reference to the transferor's basis.

The first three exceptions facilitate the use of insurance contracts to fund buy-sell agreements.

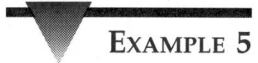
EXAMPLE 5

Rick and Sam are equal partners who have an agreement that allows either partner to purchase the interest of a deceased partner for $50,000. Neither partner has sufficient cash to actually buy the other partner's interest, but each has a life insurance policy on his own life in the amount of $50,000. Rick and Sam could exchange their policies (usually at little or no taxable gain), and upon the death of either partner, the surviving partner could collect tax-free insurance proceeds. The proceeds could then be used to purchase the decedent's interest in the partnership. ▼

The fourth exception applies to policies that were transferred pursuant to a tax-free exchange or were received by gift.[13]

Investment earnings arising from the reinvestment of life insurance proceeds are generally subject to income tax. Often the beneficiary will elect to collect the insurance proceeds in installments. The annuity rules (discussed in Chapter 4) are used to apportion the installment payment between the principal element (excludible) and the interest element (includible).[14]

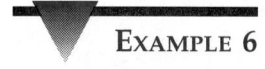
SCHOLARSHIPS

GENERAL INFORMATION

Payments or benefits received by a student at an educational institution may be (1) compensation for services, (2) a gift, or (3) a scholarship. If the payments or benefits are received as compensation for services (past or present), the fact that the recipient is a student generally does not render the amounts received nontaxable.[15]

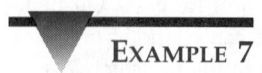
EXAMPLE 6

State University waives tuition for all graduate teaching assistants. The tuition waived is intended as compensation for services and is therefore included in the graduate assistant's gross income. ▼

As discussed earlier, gifts are not includible in gross income.

The **scholarship** rules are intended to provide exclusion treatment for education-related benefits that cannot qualify as gifts but are not compensation for services. According to the Regulations, "a scholarship is an amount paid or allowed to, or for the benefit of, an individual to aid such individual in the pursuit of study or research."[16] The recipient must be a candidate for a degree (either undergraduate or graduate) at an educational institution.[17]

EXAMPLE 7

Terry enters a contest sponsored by a local newspaper. Each contestant is required to submit an essay on local environmental issues. The prize is one year's tuition at State University. Terry wins the contest. The newspaper has a legal obligation to Terry (as contest winner). Thus, the benefits are not a gift. However, since the tuition payment aids Terry in pursuing her studies, the payment is a scholarship. ▼

A scholarship recipient may exclude from gross income the amount used for tuition and related expenses (fees, books, supplies, and equipment required for courses), provided the conditions of the grant do not require that the funds be

[13]See the discussion of gifts in Chapter 14 and tax-free exchanges in Chapters 15 and 20.
[14]Reg. §§ 1.72–7(c)(1) and 1.101–7T.
[15]Reg. § 1.117–2(a). See *C. P. Bhalla*, 35 T.C. 13 (1960), for a discussion of the distinction between a scholarship and compensation. See also *Bingler v. Johnson*, 69–1 USTC ¶9348, 23 AFTR2d 1212, 89 S.Ct. 1439 (USSC, 1969). For potential exclusion treatment, see the subsequent discussion of qualified tuition reductions.
[16]Prop.Reg. § 1.117–6(c)(3)(i).
[17]§ 117(a).

used for other purposes.[18] Amounts received for room and board are *not* excludible and are treated as earned income for purposes of calculating the standard deduction for a taxpayer who is another taxpayer's dependent.[19]

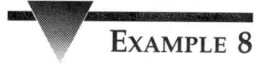

EXAMPLE 8

Kelly received a scholarship of $9,500 from State University to be used to pursue a bachelor's degree. She spent $4,000 on tuition, $3,000 on books and supplies, and $2,500 for room and board. Kelly may exclude $7,000 ($4,000 + $3,000) from gross income. The $2,500 spent for room and board is includible in Kelly's gross income.

The scholarship was Kelly's only source of income. Her parents provided more than 50% of Kelly's support and claimed her as a dependent. Kelly's standard deduction will equal her $2,500 gross income. Thus, she has no taxable income. ▼

TIMING ISSUES

Frequently, the scholarship recipient is a cash basis taxpayer who receives the money in one tax year but pays the educational expenses in a subsequent year. The amount eligible for exclusion may not be known at the time the money is received. In that case, the transaction is held *open* until the educational expenses are paid.[20]

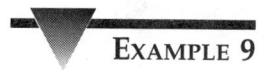

EXAMPLE 9

In August 1998, Sanjay received $10,000 as a scholarship for the academic year 1998–1999. Sanjay's expenditures for tuition, books, and supplies were as follows:

August–December 1998	$3,000
January–May 1999	4,500
	$7,500

Sanjay's gross income for 1999 includes $2,500 ($10,000 – $7,500) that is not excludible as a scholarship. None of the scholarship is included in his gross income in 1998. ▼

DISGUISED COMPENSATION

Some employers make scholarships available solely to the children of key employees. The tax objective of these plans is to provide a nontaxable fringe benefit to the executives by making the payment to the child in the form of an excludible scholarship. However, the IRS has ruled that the payments are generally includible in the gross income of the parent-employee.[21]

QUALIFIED TUITION REDUCTION PLANS

Employees (including retired and disabled former employees) of nonprofit educational institutions are allowed to exclude a tuition waiver from gross income, if the waiver is pursuant to a **qualified tuition reduction plan.**[22] The plan may not discriminate in favor of highly compensated employees. The exclusion applies to the employee, the employee's spouse, and the employee's dependent children. The exclusion also extends to tuition reductions granted by any nonprofit educational institution to employees of any other nonprofit educational institution (reciprocal agreements).

[18]§ 117(b).
[19]Prop.Reg. § 1.117–6(h).
[20]Prop.Reg. § 1.117–6(b)(2).

[21]Rev.Rul. 75–448, 1975–2 C.B. 55. *Richard T. Armantrout,* 67 T.C. 996 (1977).
[22]§ 117(d).

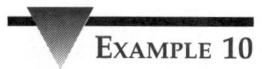

EXAMPLE 10

ABC University allows the dependent children of XYZ University employees to attend ABC University with no tuition charge. XYZ University grants reciprocal benefits to the children of ABC University employees. The dependent children can also attend tuition-free the university where their parents are employed. Employees who take advantage of these benefits are not required to recognize gross income. ▼

Generally, the exclusion is limited to *undergraduate* tuition waivers. However, in the case of teaching or research assistants, graduate tuition waivers may also qualify for exclusion treatment. According to the Proposed Regulations, the exclusion is limited to the value of the benefit in excess of the employee's reasonable compensation.[23] Thus, a tuition reduction that is a substitute for cash compensation cannot be excluded.

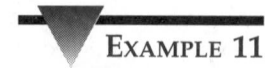

EXAMPLE 11

Susan is a graduate research assistant. She receives a $5,000 salary for 500 hours of service over a nine-month period. This pay, $10 per hour, is reasonable compensation for Susan's services. In addition, Susan receives a waiver of $6,000 for tuition. Susan may exclude the tuition waiver from gross income. ▼

COMPENSATION FOR INJURIES AND SICKNESS

DAMAGES

A person who suffers harm caused by another is often entitled to compensatory damages. The tax consequences of the receipt of damages depend on the type of harm the taxpayer has experienced. The taxpayer may seek recovery for (1) a loss of income, (2) expenses incurred, (3) property destroyed, or (4) personal injury.

Generally, reimbursement for a loss of income is taxed the same as the income replaced. The recovery of an expense is not income, unless the expense was deducted. Damages that are a recovery of the taxpayer's previously deducted expenses are generally taxable under the tax benefit rule, discussed later in this chapter.

A payment for damaged or destroyed property is treated as an amount received in a sale or exchange of the property. Thus, the taxpayer has a realized gain if the damage payments received exceed the property's basis. Damages for personal injuries receive special treatment under the Code.

Personal Injury.　The legal theory of personal injury damages is that the amount received is intended "to make the plaintiff [the injured party] whole as before the injury."[24] It follows that if the damage payments received were subject to tax, the after-tax amount received would be less than the actual damages incurred and the injured party would not be "whole as before the injury."

In terms of personal injury damages, a distinction is made between compensatory damages and punitive damages. Under specified circumstances, compensatory damages may be excluded from gross income. Under no circumstances may punitive damages be excluded from gross income.

Compensatory damages are intended to compensate the taxpayer for the damages incurred. Only those compensatory damages received on account of *physical personal injury or physical sickness* can be excluded from gross income.[25] Compensatory damages awarded on account of emotional distress are not received on account

[23]Prop.Reg. § 1.117–6(d).
[24]*C. A. Hawkins*, 6 B.T.A. 1023 (1928).

[25]§ 104(a)(2).

CONCEPT SUMMARY 5–1

Taxation of Damages

Type of Claim	Taxation of Award or Settlement
Breach of contract (generally loss of income)	Taxable.
Property damages	Recovery of cost, gain to the extent of the excess over basis. A loss is deductible for business property and investment property to the extent of basis over the amount realized. A loss may be deductible for personal use property (see discussion of casualty losses in Chapter 7).
Personal injury	
Physical	All compensatory amounts are excluded unless previously deducted (e.g., medical expenses). Amounts received as punitive damages are included in gross income.
Nonphysical	Compensatory damages and punitive damages are included in gross income.

---

of physical injury or physical sickness and thus cannot be excluded (except to the extent of any amount received for medical care) from gross income. Likewise, any amounts received for age discrimination or injury to one's reputation cannot be excluded.

Punitive damages are amounts the person who caused the harm must pay to the victim as punishment for outrageous conduct. Punitive damages are not intended to compensate the victim, but rather to punish the party who caused the harm. Thus, it follows that amounts received as punitive damages may actually place the victim in a better economic position than before the harm was experienced. Logically, punitive damages are thus included in gross income.

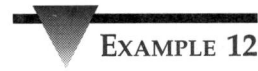

EXAMPLE 12

Tom, a television announcer, was dissatisfied with the manner in which Ron, an attorney, was defending the television station in a libel case. Tom stated on the air that Ron was botching the case. Ron sued Tom for slander, claiming damages for loss of income from clients and potential clients who heard Tom's statement. Ron's claim is for damages to his business reputation, and the amounts received are taxable.

Ron collected on the suit against Tom and was on his way to a party to celebrate his victory when a negligent driver, Norm, drove a truck into Ron's automobile, injuring Ron. Ron filed suit for the physical personal injuries and claimed as damages the loss of income for the period he was unable to work as a result of the injuries. Ron also collected punitive damages that were awarded because of Norm's extremely negligent behavior. Ron's wife also collected damages for the emotional distress she experienced as a result of the accident. Ron may exclude the amounts he received for damages, except the punitive damages. Ron's wife must include the amounts she received for damages in gross income because the amounts were not received because of physical personal injuries or sickness. ▼

WORKERS' COMPENSATION

State workers' compensation laws require the employer to pay fixed amounts for specific job-related injuries. The state laws were enacted so that the employee will not have to go through the ordeal of a lawsuit (and possibly not collect damages because of some defense available to the employer) to recover the damages. Although the payments are intended, in part, to compensate for a loss of future income, Congress has specifically exempted workers' compensation benefits from inclusion in gross income.[26]

ACCIDENT AND HEALTH INSURANCE BENEFITS

The income tax treatment of accident and health insurance benefits depends on whether the policy providing the benefits was purchased by the taxpayer or the taxpayer's employer. Benefits collected under an accident and health insurance policy *purchased by the taxpayer* are excludible. In this case, benefits collected under the taxpayer's insurance policy are excluded even though the payments are a substitute for income.[27]

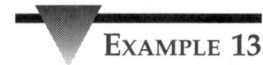 **EXAMPLE 13**

Bonnie purchased a medical and disability insurance policy. The insurance company paid Bonnie $200 per week to replace wages she lost while in the hospital. Although the payments serve as a substitute for income, the amounts received are tax-exempt benefits collected under Bonnie's insurance policy. ▼

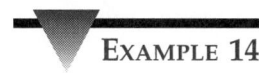 **EXAMPLE 14**

Joe's injury results in a partial paralysis of his left foot. He receives $5,000 for the injury from his accident insurance company under a policy he had purchased. The $5,000 accident insurance proceeds are tax-exempt. ▼

A different set of rules applies if the accident and health insurance protection was *purchased by the individual's employer*, as discussed in the following section.

EMPLOYER-SPONSORED ACCIDENT AND HEALTH PLANS

Congress encourages employers to provide employees, retired former employees, and their dependents with **accident and health benefits,** disability insurance, and long-term care plans. The *premiums* are deductible by the employer and excluded from the employee's income.[28] Although § 105(a) provides the general rule that the employee has includible income when he or she collects the insurance *benefits*, two exceptions are provided.

Section 105(b) generally excludes payments received for medical care of the employee, spouse, and dependents. However, if the payments are for expenses that do not meet the Code's definition of medical care,[29] the amount received must be included in gross income. In addition, the taxpayer must include in gross income any amounts received for medical expenses that were deducted by the taxpayer on a prior return.

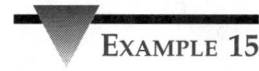 **EXAMPLE 15**

In 1998, Tab's employer-sponsored health insurance plan paid $4,000 for hair transplants that did not meet the Code's definition of medical care. Tab must include the $4,000 in his gross income for 1998. ▼

---

[26]§ 104(a)(1).
[27]§ 104(a)(3).

[28]§ 106, Reg. § 1.106–1, and Rev.Rul. 82–196, 1982–1 C.B. 106.
[29]See the discussion of medical care in Chapter 10.

Section 105(c) excludes payments for the permanent loss or the loss of the use of a member or function of the body or the permanent disfigurement of the employee, spouse, or a dependent. Payments that are a substitute for salary (e.g., related to the period of time absent) are includible.

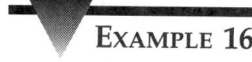
EXAMPLE 16

Jill lost an eye in an automobile accident unrelated to her work. As a result of the accident, Jill incurred $2,000 of medical expenses, which she deducted on her return. She collected $10,000 from an accident insurance policy carried by her employer. The benefits were paid according to a schedule of amounts that varied with the part of the body injured (e.g., $10,000 for loss of an eye, $20,000 for loss of a hand). Because the payment was for loss of a *member or function of the body*, the $10,000 is excluded from income. Jill was absent from work for a week as a result of the accident. Her employer provided her with insurance for the loss of income due to illness or injury. Jill collected $500, which is includible in gross income. ▼

MEDICAL REIMBURSEMENT PLANS

In lieu of providing the employee with insurance coverage for hospital and medical expenses, the employer may agree to reimburse the employee for these expenses. The amounts received through the insurance coverage (insured plan benefits) are excluded from income under § 105 (as previously discussed). Unfortunately in terms of cost considerations, the insurance companies that issue this type of policy usually require a broad coverage of employees. An alternative is to have a plan that is not funded with insurance (a self-insured arrangement). The benefits received under a self-insured plan can be excluded from the employee's income, if the plan does not discriminate in favor of highly compensated employees.[30]

Small employers (50 or fewer employees) have an alternative means of accomplishing a medical reimbursement plan. The employer can purchase a medical insurance plan with a high deductible (e.g., the employee is responsible for the first $2,000 of medical expenses) and then make contributions to the employee's **medical savings account (MSA)**.[31] The employer can make contributions each year up to the maximum contribution of 65 percent of the deductible amount for an individual or 75 percent of the deductible amount in the case of family coverage. Withdrawals from the MSA must be used to reimburse the employee for the medical expenses paid by the employee that are not covered under the high-deductible plan. The employee is not taxed on the employer's contributions to the MSA, the earnings on the funds in the account, or the withdrawals made for medical expenses.[32]

LONG-TERM CARE INSURANCE BENEFITS

Generally, **long-term care insurance,** which covers expenses such as the cost of care in a nursing home, is treated the same as accident and health insurance benefits. Thus, the employee does not recognize income when the employer pays the premiums. When benefits are received from the policy, whether the employer or the individual purchased the policy, the exclusion from gross income is limited to the greater of the following amounts:

---

[30]§ 105(h).
[31]These MSAs are part of a pilot program. They are available only to the first 750,000 participants each year from 1997 through 2000. See additional coverage in Chapter 10.

[32]§§ 106(b) and 220.

- $175 (to be indexed) for each day the patient receives the long-term care.
- The actual cost of the care.

The above amount is reduced by any amounts received from other third parties (e.g., damages received).[33]

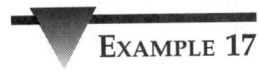

EXAMPLE 17

Hazel, who suffers from Alzheimer's disease, was a patient in a nursing home for the last 30 days of the year. While in the nursing home, she incurred total costs of $6,000. Medicare paid $3,200 of the costs. Hazel received $3,600 from her long-term care insurance policy (which paid $120 per day while she was in the facility).

The amount that Hazel may exclude is calculated as follows:

Greater of:		
Daily statutory amount of $175 ($175 × 30 days)	$5,250	
Actual cost of the care	6,000	$ 6,000
Less: Amount received from Medicare		(3,200)
Amount of exclusion		$ 2,800

Therefore, Hazel must include $800 ($3,600 − $2,800) of the long-term care benefits received in her gross income. ▼

The exclusion for long-term care insurance is not available if it is provided as part of a cafeteria plan or a flexible spending plan.

MEALS AND LODGING

FURNISHED FOR THE CONVENIENCE OF THE EMPLOYER

As discussed in Chapter 4, income can take any form, including meals and lodging. However, § 119 excludes from income the value of meals and lodging provided to the employee and the employee's spouse and dependents under the following conditions:[34]

- The meals and/or lodging are *furnished* by the employer, on the employer's *business premises*, for the *convenience of the employer*.
- In the case of lodging, the *employee is required* to accept the lodging as a condition of employment.

The courts have construed both of these requirements strictly.

Furnished by the Employer. The following two questions have been raised with regard to the *furnished by the employer* requirement:

- Who is considered an *employee*?
- What is meant by *furnished*?

The IRS and some courts have reasoned that because a partner is not an employee, the exclusion does not apply to a partner. However, the Tax Court and the Fifth Court of Appeals have ruled in favor of the taxpayer on this issue.[35]

---

[33]§ 7702B.

[34]§ 119(a). The meals and lodging are also excluded from FICA and FUTA tax. *Rowan Companies, Inc. v. U.S.*, 81–1 USTC ¶9479, 48 AFTR2d 81–5115, 101 S.Ct. 2288 (USSC, 1981).

[35]Rev.Rul. 80, 1953–1 C.B. 62; *Comm. v. Doak*, 56–2 USTC ¶9708, 49 AFTR 1491, 234 F.2d 704 (CA–4, 1956); but see *G. A. Papineau*, 16 T.C. 130 (1951); *Armstrong v. Phinney*, 68–1 USTC ¶9355, 21 AFTR2d 1260, 394 F.2d 661 (CA–5, 1968).

The Supreme Court held that a cash meal allowance was ineligible for the exclusion because the employer did not actually furnish the meals.[36] Similarly, one court denied the exclusion where the employer paid for the food and supplied the cooking facilities but the employee prepared the meal.[37]

On the Employer's Business Premises.   The *on the employer's business premises* requirement, applicable to both meals and lodging, has resulted in much litigation. The Regulations define business premises as simply "the place of employment of the employee."[38] Thus, the Sixth Court of Appeals held that a residence, owned by the employer and occupied by an employee, two blocks from the motel that the employee managed was not part of the business premises.[39] However, the Tax Court considered an employer-owned house across the street from the hotel that was managed by the taxpayer to be on the business premises of the employer.[40] Perhaps these two cases can be reconciled by comparing the distance from the lodging facilities to the place where the employer's business was conducted. The closer the lodging to the business operations, the more likely the convenience of the employer is served.

For the Convenience of the Employer.   The *convenience of the employer* test is intended to focus on the employer's motivation for furnishing the meals and lodging rather than on the benefits received by the employee. If the employer furnishes the meals and lodging primarily to enable the employee to perform his or her duties properly, it does not matter that the employee considers these benefits to be a part of his or her compensation.

The Regulations give the following examples in which the tests for excluding meals are satisfied:[41]

- A waitress is required to eat her meals on the premises during the busy lunch and breakfast hours.
- A bank furnishes a teller meals on the premises to limit the time the employee is away from his or her booth during the busy hours.
- A worker is employed at a construction site in a remote part of Alaska. The employer must furnish meals and lodging due to the inaccessibility of other facilities.

Required as a Condition of Employment.   The *employee is required to accept* test applies only to lodging. If the employee's use of the housing would serve the convenience of the employer, but the employee is not required to use the housing, the exclusion is not available.

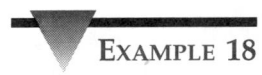

EXAMPLE 18

VEP, a utilities company, has all of its service personnel on 24-hour call for emergencies. The company encourages its employees to live near the plant so that the employees can respond quickly to emergency calls. Company-owned housing is available rent-free. Only 10 of the employees live in the company housing because it is not suitable for families.

Although the company-provided housing serves the convenience of the employer, it is not required. Therefore, the employees who live in the company housing cannot exclude its value from gross income. ▼

---

[36]*Comm. v. Kowalski*, 77–2 USTC ¶9748, 40 AFTR2d 6128, 98 S.Ct. 315 (USSC, 1977).

[37]*Tougher v. Comm.*, 71–1 USTC ¶9398, 27 AFTR2d 1301, 441 F.2d 1148 (CA–9, 1971).

[38]Reg. § 1.119–1(c)(1).

[39]*Comm. v. Anderson*, 67–1 USTC ¶9136, 19 AFTR2d 318, 371 F.2d 59 (CA–6, 1966).

[40]*J. B. Lindeman*, 60 T.C. 609 (1973).

[41]Reg. § 1.119–1(f).

In addition, if the employee has the *option* of cash or lodging, the *required* test is not satisfied.

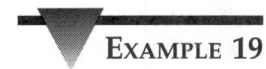

EXAMPLE 19

Khalid is the manager of a large apartment complex. The employer gives Khalid the option of rent-free housing (value of $6,000 per year) or an additional $5,000 per year. Khalid selects the housing option. Therefore, he must include $6,000 in gross income. ▼

OTHER HOUSING EXCLUSIONS

Employees of Educational Institutions.   An employee of an educational institution may be able to exclude the value of campus housing provided by the employer. Generally, the employee does not recognize income if he or she pays annual rents equal to or greater than 5 percent of the appraised value of the facility. If the rent payments are less than 5 percent of the value of the facility, the deficiency must be included in gross income.[42]

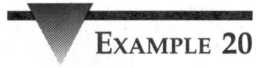

EXAMPLE 20

Swan University provides on-campus housing for its full-time faculty during the first three years of employment. The housing is not provided for the convenience of the employer. Professor Edith pays $3,000 annual rent for the use of a residence with an appraised value of $100,000 and an annual rental value of $12,000. Edith must recognize $2,000 gross income [.05($100,000) − $3,000 = $2,000] for the value of the housing provided to her. ▼

Ministers of the Gospel.   Ministers of the gospel can exclude (1) the rental value of a home furnished as compensation or (2) a rental allowance paid to them as compensation, to the extent the allowance is used to rent or provide a home.[43] The housing or housing allowance must be provided as compensation for the conduct of religious worship, the administration and maintenance of religious organizations, or the performance of teaching and administrative duties at theological seminaries.

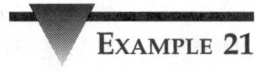

EXAMPLE 21

Pastor Bill is allowed to live rent-free in a house owned by the congregation. The annual rental value of the house is $6,000 and is provided as part of the pastor's compensation for ministerial services. Assistant Pastor Olga is paid a $4,500 cash housing allowance. She uses

---

[42]§ 119(d).   [43]§ 107 and Reg. § 1.107–1.

the $4,500 to pay rent and utilities on a home she and her family occupy. Neither Pastor Bill nor Assistant Pastor Olga is required to recognize gross income associated with the housing or housing allowance. ▼

Military Personnel.   Military personnel are allowed housing exclusions under various circumstances. Authority for these exclusions generally is found in Federal laws that are not part of the Internal Revenue Code.[44]

OTHER EMPLOYEE FRINGE BENEFITS

SPECIFIC BENEFITS

Congress has enacted exclusions to encourage employers to (1) finance and make available child care facilities, (2) provide athletic facilities for employees, (3) finance certain employees' education, and (4) pay or reimburse child adoption expenses. These provisions are summarized as follows:

- The employee does not have to include in gross income the value of child and dependent care services paid for by the employer and incurred to enable the employee to work. The exclusion cannot exceed $5,000 per year ($2,500 if married and filing separately). For a married couple, the annual exclusion cannot exceed the earned income of the spouse who has the lesser amount of earned income. For an unmarried taxpayer, the exclusion cannot exceed the taxpayer's earned income.[45]
- The value of the use of a gymnasium or other athletic facilities by employees, their spouses, and their dependent children may be excluded from an employee's gross income. The facilities must be on the employer's premises, and substantially all of the use of the facilities must be by employees and their family members.[46]
- Qualified employer-provided educational assistance (tuition, fees, books, and supplies) at the undergraduate level is excludible from gross income. The exclusion is subject to an annual employee statutory ceiling of $5,250.[47]
- The employee can exclude from gross income up to $5,000 of expenses incurred to adopt a child where the adoption expenses are paid or reimbursed by the employer under a qualified adoption assistance program.[48] The limit on the exclusion is increased to $6,000 if the child has special needs (is not physically or mentally capable of caring for himself or herself). The exclusion is phased out as adjusted gross income increases from $75,000 to $115,000.

CAFETERIA PLANS

Generally, if an employee is offered a choice between cash and some other form of compensation, the employee is deemed to have constructively received the cash even when the noncash option is elected. Thus, the employee has gross income regardless of the option chosen.

---

[44]H. Rep. No. 99–841, 99th Cong., 2d Sess., p. 548 (1986). See also § 134.

[45]§ 129. The exclusion applies to the same types of expenses that, if they were paid by the employee (and not reimbursed by the employer), would be eligible for the Credit for Child and Dependent Care Expense discussed in Chapter 13.

[46]§ 132(j)(4).

[47]§ 127. Exclusion treatment applies for courses that begin before June 1, 2000.

[48]§ 137.

An exception to this constructive receipt treatment is provided under the **cafeteria plan** rules. Under such a plan, the employee is permitted to choose between cash and nontaxable benefits (e.g., group term life insurance, health and accident protection, and child care). If the employee chooses the otherwise nontaxable benefits, the cafeteria plan rules enable the benefits to remain nontaxable.[49] Cafeteria plans provide tremendous flexibility in tailoring the employee pay package to fit individual needs. Some employees (usually the younger group) prefer cash, while others (usually the older group) will opt for the fringe benefit program. However, Congress excluded long-term care insurance from the excludible benefits that can be provided under a cafeteria plan.[50] Thus, the employer must provide these benefits separate from the cafeteria plan.

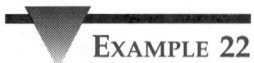 **EXAMPLE 22**

Hawk Corporation offers its employees (on a nondiscriminatory basis) a choice of any one or all of the following benefits:

Benefit	Cost
Group term life insurance	$ 200
Hospitalization insurance for family members	2,400
Child care payments	1,800
	$4,400

If a benefit is not selected, the employee receives cash equal to the cost of the benefit. Kay, an employee, has a spouse who works for another employer that provides hospitalization insurance but no child care payments. Kay elects to receive the group term life insurance, the child care payments, and $2,400 of cash. Only the $2,400 must be included in Kay's gross income. ▼

FLEXIBLE SPENDING PLANS

Flexible spending plans (often referred to as flexible benefit plans) operate much like cafeteria plans. Under these plans, the employee accepts lower cash compensation in return for the employer agreeing to pay certain costs that the employer can pay without the employee recognizing gross income. For example, assume the employer's health insurance policy does not cover dental expenses. The employee could estimate his or her dental expenses for the upcoming year and agree to a salary reduction equal to the estimated dental expenses. The employer then pays or reimburses the employee for the actual dental expenses incurred, with a ceiling of the amount of the salary reduction. If the employee's actual dental expenses are less than the reduction in cash compensation, the employee cannot recover the difference. Hence, these plans are often referred to as *use or lose* plans. As is the case for cafeteria plans, flexible spending plans cannot be used to pay long-term care insurance premiums.

GENERAL CLASSES OF EXCLUDED BENEFITS

An employer can confer numerous forms and types of economic benefits on employees. Under the all-inclusive concept of income, the benefits are taxable unless one of the provisions previously discussed specifically excludes the item from gross income. The amount of the income is the fair market value of the benefit. This

---

[49]§ 125.   [50]§ 125(f).

reasoning can lead to results that Congress considers unacceptable, as illustrated in the following example.

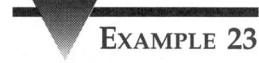
EXAMPLE 23

Vern is employed in New York as a ticket clerk for Trans National Airlines. He has a sick mother in Miami, Florida, but has no money for plane tickets. Trans National has daily flights from New York to Miami that often leave with empty seats. The cost of a round-trip ticket is $400, and Vern is in the 28% tax bracket. If Trans National allows Vern to fly without charge to Miami, under the general gross income rules, Vern has income equal to the value of a ticket. Therefore, Vern must pay $112 tax (.28 × $400) on a trip to Miami. Because Vern does not have $112, he cannot visit his mother, and the airplane flies with another empty seat. ▼

If Trans National in Example 23 will allow employees to use resources that would otherwise be wasted, why should the tax laws interfere with the employee's decision to take advantage of the available benefit? Thus, to avoid the undesirable results that occur in Example 23 and in similar situations, as well as to create uniform rules for fringe benefits, Congress established six broad classes of nontaxable employee benefits:[51]

- No-additional-cost services.
- Qualified employee discounts.
- Working condition fringes.
- *De minimis* fringes.
- Qualified transportation fringes.
- Qualified moving expense reimbursements.

No-Additional-Cost Services.   Example 23 illustrates the **no-additional-cost service** type of fringe benefit. The services will be nontaxable if all of the following conditions are satisfied:

- The employee receives services, as opposed to property.
- The employer does not incur substantial additional cost, including forgone revenue, in providing the services to the employee.
- The services are offered to customers in the ordinary course of the business in which the employee works.[52]

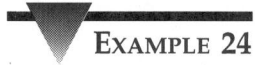
EXAMPLE 24

Assume that Vern in Example 23 can fly without charge only if the airline cannot fill the seats with paying customers. That is, Vern must fly on standby. Although the airplane may burn slightly more fuel because Vern is on the airplane and Vern may receive the same meal as paying customers, the additional costs would not be substantial. Thus, the trip could qualify as a no-additional-cost service.

On the other hand, assume that Vern is given a reserved seat on a flight that is frequently full. The employer would be forgoing revenue to allow Vern to fly. This forgone revenue would be a substantial additional cost, and thus the benefit would be taxable. ▼

Note that if Vern were employed in a hotel owned by Trans National, the receipt of the airline ticket would be taxable because Vern did not work in that line of business. However, the Code allows the exclusion for reciprocal benefits offered by employers in the same line of business.

---

[51]See, generally, § 132.   [52]Reg. § 1.132–2.

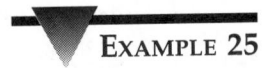

EXAMPLE 25

Grace is employed as a desk clerk for Plush Hotels, Inc. The company and Chain Hotels, Inc., have an agreement that allows any of their employees to stay without charge in either company's resort hotels during the off-season. Grace would not be required to recognize income from taking advantage of the plan by staying in a Chain Hotel. ▼

The no-additional-cost exclusion extends to the employee's spouse and dependent children and to retired and disabled former employees. In the Regulations, the IRS has conceded that partners who perform services for the partnership are employees for purposes of the exclusion.[53] (As discussed earlier in the chapter, the IRS's position is that partners are not employees for purposes of the § 119 meals and lodging exclusion.) However, the exclusion is not allowed to highly compensated employees unless the benefit is available on a nondiscriminatory basis.

Qualified Employee Discounts. When the employer sells goods or services (other than no-additional-cost benefits just discussed) to the employee for a price that is less than the price charged regular customers, the employee realizes income equal to the discount. However, the discount, referred to as a **qualified employee discount,** can be excluded from the gross income of the employee, subject to the following conditions and limitations:

- The exclusion is not available for real property (e.g., a house) or for personal property of the type commonly held for investment (e.g., common stocks).
- The property or services must be from the same line of business in which the employee works.
- In the case of *property*, the exclusion is limited to the *gross profit component* of the price to customers.
- In the case of *services*, the exclusion is limited to 20 percent of the customer price.[54]

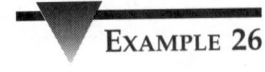

EXAMPLE 26

Silver Corporation, which operates a department store, sells a television set to a store employee for $300. The regular customer price is $500, and the gross profit rate is 25%. The corporation also sells the employee a service contract for $120. The regular customer price for the contract is $150. The employee must recognize $75 income.

Customer price for property	$ 500
Less: Gross profit (25%)	(125)
	$ 375
Employee price	(300)
Income	$ 75
Customer price for service	$ 150
Less: 20 percent	(30)
	$ 120
Employee price	(120)
Income	$ –0–

▼

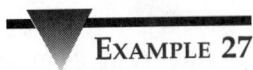

EXAMPLE 27

Assume the same facts as in Example 26, except the employee is a clerk in a hotel operated by Silver Corporation. Because the line of business requirement is not met, the employee must recognize $200 income ($500 – $300) from the purchase of the television and $30 income ($150 – $120) from the service contract. ▼

[53]Reg. § 1.132–1(b).   [54]§ 132(c).

As in the case of no-additional-cost benefits, the exclusion applies to employees (including service partners), employees' spouses and dependent children, and retired and disabled former employees. However, the exclusion does not apply to highly compensated individuals unless the discount is available on a nondiscriminatory basis.

Working Condition Fringes.   Generally, an employee is not required to include in gross income the cost of property or services provided by the employer if the employee could deduct the cost of those items if he or she had actually paid for them.[55] These benefits are called **working condition fringes.**

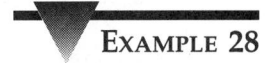

EXAMPLE 28

Mitch is a certified public accountant employed by an accounting firm. The employer pays Mitch's annual dues to professional organizations. Mitch is not required to include the payment of the dues in gross income because if he had paid the dues, he would have been allowed to deduct the amount as an employee business expense (as discussed in Chapter 9). ▼

In many cases, this exclusion merely avoids reporting income and an offsetting deduction. However, in two specific situations, the working condition fringe benefit rules allow an exclusion where the expense would not be deductible if paid by the employee:

- Automobile salespeople are allowed to exclude the value of certain personal use of company demonstrators (e.g., commuting to and from work).[56]
- The employee business expense would be eliminated by the 2 percent floor on miscellaneous deductions under § 67 (see Chapter 10).

Unlike the other fringe benefits discussed previously, working condition fringes can be made available on a discriminatory basis and still qualify for the exclusion.

De Minimis **Fringes.**   As the term suggests, *de minimis* **fringe** benefits are so small that accounting for them is impractical. The House Report contains the following examples of *de minimis* fringes:

- The typing of a personal letter by a company secretary, occasional personal use of a company copying machine, occasional company cocktail parties or picnics for employees, occasional supper money or taxi fare for employees because of overtime work, and certain holiday gifts of property with a low fair market value are excluded.
- Subsidized eating facilities (e.g., an employees' cafeteria) operated by the employer are excluded if located on or near the employer's business premises, if revenue equals or exceeds direct operating costs, and if nondiscrimination requirements are met.

When taxpayers venture beyond the specific examples contained in the House Report and the Regulations, there is obviously much room for disagreement as to what is *de minimis*. However, note that except in the case of subsidized eating facilities, the *de minimis* fringe benefits can be granted in a manner that favors highly compensated employees.

---

[55]§ 132(d).   [56]§ 132(j)(3).

Qualified Transportation Fringes. The intent of the exclusion for **qualified transportation fringes** is to encourage the use of mass transit for commuting to and from work. Qualified transportation fringes encompass the following transportation benefits provided by the employer to the employee:[57]

1. Transportation in a commuter highway vehicle between the employee's residence and the place of employment.
2. A transit pass.
3. Qualified parking.

Statutory dollar limits are placed on the amount of the exclusion. Categories (1) and (2) above are combined for purposes of applying the limit. In this case, the limit on the exclusion for 1998 is $65 per month. Category (3) has a separate limit. For qualified parking, the limit on the exclusion for 1998 is $175 per month. Both of these dollar limits are indexed annually for inflation.

A *commuter highway vehicle* is any highway vehicle with a seating capacity of at least 6 adults (excluding the driver). In addition, at least 80 percent of the vehicle's use must be for transporting employees between their residences and place of employment.

Qualified parking includes the following:

- Parking provided to an employee on or near the employer's business premises.
- Parking provided to an employee on or near a location from which the employee commutes to work via mass transit, in a commuter highway vehicle, or in a carpool.

Qualified transportation fringes may be provided directly by the employer or may be in the form of cash reimbursements.

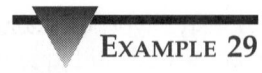

EXAMPLE 29

Gray Corporation's offices are located in the center of a large city. The company pays for parking spaces to be used by the company officers. Steve, a vice president, receives $250 of such benefits each month. The parking space rental qualifies as a qualified transportation fringe. Of the $250 benefit received each month by Steve, $175 is excludible from gross income. The balance of $75 is included in his gross income. The same result would occur if Steve paid for the parking and was reimbursed by his employer. ▼

Qualified Moving Expense Reimbursements. Qualified moving expenses that are reimbursed or paid by the employer are excludible from gross income. A qualified moving expense is one that would be deductible under § 217. See the discussion of moving expenses in Chapter 9.

Nondiscrimination Provisions. For no-additional-cost services and qualified employee discounts, if the plan is discriminatory in favor of highly compensated employees, these key employees are denied exclusion treatment. However, the non-highly compensated employees who receive benefits from the plan can still enjoy exclusion treatment for the no-additional-cost services and qualified employee discounts.[58]

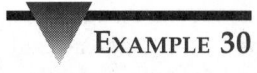

EXAMPLE 30

Dove Company's officers are allowed to purchase goods from the company at a 25% discount. Other employees are allowed only a 15% discount. The company's gross profit margin on these goods is 30%.

---

[57]§ 132(f).   [58]§ 132(j)(1).

Peggy, an officer in the company, purchased goods from the company for $750 when the price charged to customers was $1,000. Peggy must include $250 in gross income because the plan is discriminatory.

Leo, an employee of the company who is not an officer, purchased goods for $850 when the customer price was $1,000. Leo is not required to recognize income because he received a qualified employee discount. ▼

De minimis (except in the case of subsidized eating facilities) and working condition fringe benefits can be provided on a discriminatory basis. The *de minimis* benefits are not subject to tax because the accounting problems that would be created are out of proportion to the amount of additional tax that would result. A nondiscrimination test would simply add to the compliance problems. In the case of working condition fringes, the types of services required vary with the job. Therefore, a nondiscrimination test probably could not be satisfied, although usually there is no deliberate plan to benefit a chosen few. Likewise, the qualified transportation fringe and the qualified moving expense reimbursement can be provided on a discriminatory basis.

TAXABLE FRINGE BENEFITS

If the fringe benefits cannot qualify for any of the specific exclusions or do not fit into any of the general classes of excluded benefits, the taxpayer must recognize gross income equal to the fair market value of the benefits. Obviously, problems are frequently encountered in determining values. The IRS has issued extensive Regulations addressing the valuation of personal use of an employer's automobiles and meals provided at an employer-operated eating facility.[59]

If a fringe benefit plan discriminates in favor of highly compensated employees, generally those employees are not allowed to exclude the benefits they receive that other employees do not enjoy. However, the highly compensated employees, as well as the other employees, are generally allowed to exclude the nondiscriminatory benefits.[60]

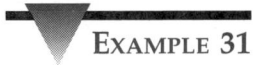

EXAMPLE 31

MED Company has a medical reimbursement plan that reimburses officers for 100% of their medical expenses, but reimburses all other employees for only 80% of their medical expenses. Cliff, the president of the company, was reimbursed $1,000 during the year for medical expenses. Cliff must include $200 in gross income [(1 − .80) × $1,000 = $200]. Mike, an employee who is not an officer, received $800 (80% of his actual medical expenses) under the medical reimbursement plan. None of the $800 is includible in his gross income. ▼

FOREIGN EARNED INCOME

A U.S. citizen is generally subject to U.S. tax on his or her income regardless of the income's geographic origin. The income may also be subject to tax in the foreign country, and thus the taxpayer must carry a double tax burden. Out of a sense of fairness and to encourage U.S. citizens to work abroad (so that exports might be

---

[59]Reg. § 1.61–2 T(j). Generally, the income from the personal use of the employer's automobile is based on the lease value of the automobile (what it would have cost the employee to lease the automobile). Meals are valued at 150% of the employer's direct costs (e.g., food and labor) of preparing the meals.

[60]§§ 79(d), 105(h), 127(b)(2), and 132(j)(1). See the discussion of the term "highly compensated employee" in Chapter 19.

CONCEPT SUMMARY 5–2

General Classes of Excluded Benefits

Benefit	Description and Examples	Coverage Allowed	Effect of Discrimination
1. No-additional-cost services	The employee takes advantage of the employer's excess capacity (e.g., free passes for airline employees).	Current, retired, and disabled employees; their spouses and dependent children; spouses of deceased employees. Partners are treated as employees.	No exclusion for highly compensated employees.
2. Qualified discounts on goods	The employee is allowed to purchase the employer's merchandise at a price that is not less than the employer's cost.	Same as (1) above.	Same as (1) above.
3. Qualified discounts on services	The employee is allowed a discount (maximum of 20%) on services the employer offers to customers.	Same as (1) above.	Same as (1) above.
4. Working condition fringes	Expenses paid by the employer that would be deductible if paid by the employee (e.g., a mechanic's tools). Also, includes auto salesperson's use of a car held for sale.	Current employees, partners, directors, and independent contractors.	No effect.
5. *De minimis* items	Expenses so immaterial that accounting for them is not warranted (e.g., occasional supper money, personal use of the copy machine).	*Any recipient* of a fringe benefit.	No effect.
6. Qualified transportation fringes	Transportation benefits provided by the employer to employees including commuting in a commuter highway vehicle, a transit pass, and qualified parking.	Current employees.	No effect.
7. Qualified moving expense reimbursements	Qualified moving expenses that are paid or reimbursed by the employer. A qualified moving expense is one that would be deductible under § 217.	Current employees.	No effect.

increased), Congress has provided alternative forms of relief from taxes on foreign earned income. The taxpayer can elect *either* (1) to include the foreign income in his or her taxable income and then claim a credit for foreign taxes paid or (2) to exclude the foreign earnings from his or her U.S. gross income (the **foreign earned income exclusion**).[61] The foreign tax credit option is discussed in Chapter 13, but as is apparent from the following discussion, most taxpayers will choose the exclusion.

---

[61]§ 911(a).

Foreign earned income consists of the earnings from the individual's personal services rendered in a foreign country (other than as an employee of the U.S. government). To qualify for the exclusion, the taxpayer must be either of the following:

- A bona fide resident of the foreign country (or countries).
- Present in a foreign country (or countries) for at least 330 days during any 12 consecutive months.[62]

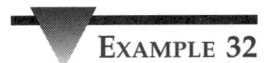
EXAMPLE 32

Sandra's trips to and from a foreign country in connection with her work were as follows:

Arrived in Foreign Country	Arrived in United States
March 10, 1997	February 1, 1998
March 7, 1998	June 1, 1998

During the 12 consecutive months ending on March 10, 1998, Sandra was present in the foreign country for at least 330 days (365 days less 28 days in February and 7 days in March 1998). Therefore, all income earned in the foreign country through March 10, 1998, is eligible for the exclusion. The income earned from March 11, 1998, through May 31, 1998, is also eligible for the exclusion because Sandra was present in the foreign country for 330 days during the 12 consecutive months ending on May 31, 1998. ▼

The exclusion is *limited* to $72,000 in 1998. For married persons, both of whom have foreign earned income, the exclusion is computed separately for each spouse. Community property rules do not apply (the community property spouse is not deemed to have earned one-half of the other spouse's foreign earned income). If all the days in the tax year are not qualifying days, then the taxpayer must compute the maximum exclusion on a daily basis ($72,000 divided by the number of days in the entire year and multiplied by the number of qualifying days).

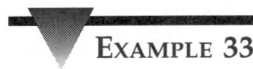
EXAMPLE 33

Keith qualifies for the foreign earned income exclusion. He was present in France for all of 1998. Keith's salary for 1998 is $90,000. Since all of the days in 1998 are qualifying days, Keith can exclude $72,000 of his $90,000 salary.

Assume instead that only 335 days were qualifying days. Then, Keith's exclusion is limited to $66,082, computed as follows:

$$\$72,000 \times \frac{335 \text{ days in foreign country}}{365 \text{ days in the year}} = \$66,082$$
▼

In addition to the exclusion for foreign earnings, the *reasonable housing costs* incurred by the taxpayer and the taxpayer's family in a foreign country in excess of a base amount may be excluded from gross income. The base amount is 16 percent of the U.S. government pay scale for a GS–14 (Step 1) employee, which varies from year to year.[63]

As previously mentioned, the taxpayer may elect to include the foreign earned income in gross income and claim a credit (an offset against U.S. tax) for the foreign tax paid. The credit alternative may be advantageous if the individual's foreign earned income far exceeds the excludible amount so that the foreign taxes paid exceed the U.S. tax on the amount excluded. However, once an election is made,

[62]§ 911(d). For the definition of resident, see Reg. § 1.871–2(b). Under the Regulations, a taxpayer is not a resident if he or she is there for a definite period (e.g., until completion of a construction contract).

[63]§ 911(c).

it applies to all subsequent years unless affirmatively revoked. A revocation is effective for the year of the change and the four subsequent years.

INTEREST ON CERTAIN STATE AND LOCAL GOVERNMENT OBLIGATIONS

At the time the Sixteenth Amendment was ratified by the states, there was some question as to whether the Federal government possessed the constitutional authority to tax interest on state and local government obligations. Taxing such interest was thought to violate the doctrine of intergovernmental immunity in that the tax would impair the state and local governments' ability to finance their operations.[64] Thus, interest on state and local government obligations was specifically exempted from Federal income taxation.[65] However, the Supreme Court recently concluded that there is no constitutional prohibition against levying a nondiscriminatory Federal income tax on state and local government obligations.[66] Nevertheless, currently the statutory exclusion still exists.

Obviously, the exclusion of the interest reduces the cost of borrowing for state and local governments. A taxpayer in the 36 percent tax bracket requires only a 5.12 percent yield on a tax-exempt bond to obtain the same after-tax income as a taxable bond paying 8 percent interest [5.12% ÷ (1 − .36) = 8%].

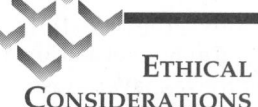

ETHICAL CONSIDERATIONS

Tax-Exempt Bonds: Any Redeeming Value?

The exclusion from Federal income tax of state and local bond interest is often criticized as creating a tax haven for the wealthy. These critics, however, often fail to take into account the effect of market forces. In recent months, the long-term tax-exempt rate has been 5.45 percent while the long-term taxable rate for bonds of comparable risk was approximately 6.4 percent.

On the other hand, the state or local governments enjoy a savings in interest costs. To date, Congress has concluded that the benefits gained by the states and municipalities and their residents outweigh any damage to our system of progressive taxation. Do you agree with the proponents or the opponents of the exclusion?

The lower cost for the state and local governments is more than offset by the revenue loss of the Federal government. Also, tax-exempt interest is considered to be a substantial loophole for the very wealthy. For these reasons, bills have been introduced in Congress calling for Federal government subsidies to state and local governments that voluntarily choose to issue taxable bonds. Under the proposals, the tax-exempt status of existing bonds would not be eliminated.

The current exempt status applies solely to state and local government bonds. Thus, income received from the accrual of interest on a condemnation award or

---

[64]*Pollock v. Farmer's Loan & Trust Co.*, 3 AFTR 2602, 15 S.Ct. 912 (USSC, 1895).

[65]§ 103(a).

[66]*South Carolina v. Baker III*, 88–1 USTC ¶9284, 61 AFTR2d 88–995, 108 S.Ct. 1355 (USSC, 1988).

an overpayment of state income tax is fully taxable.[67] Nor does the exemption apply to gains on the sale of tax-exempt securities.

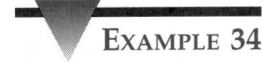

EXAMPLE 34

Megan purchases State of Virginia bonds for $10,000 on July 1, 1997. The bonds pay $400 interest each June 30th and December 31st. On March 31, 1998, Megan sells the bonds for $10,500 plus $200 accrued interest. Megan must recognize a $500 gain ($10,500 − $10,000), but the $200 accrued interest is exempt from taxation. ▼

State and local governments have developed sophisticated financial schemes to attract new industry. For example, local municipalities have issued bonds to finance the construction of plants to be leased to private enterprise. Because the financing could be arranged with low-interest municipal obligations, the plants could be leased at a lower cost than the private business could otherwise obtain. However, Congress has placed limitations on the use of tax-exempt securities to finance private business.[68]

DIVIDENDS

GENERAL INFORMATION

A *dividend* is a payment to a shareholder with respect to his or her stock. Dividends to shareholders are taxable only to the extent the payments are made from *either* the corporation's *current earnings and profits* (similar to net income per books) or its *accumulated earnings and profits* (similar to retained earnings per books).[69] Distributions that exceed earnings and profits are treated as a nontaxable recovery of capital and reduce the shareholder's basis in the stock. Once the shareholder's basis is reduced to zero, any subsequent distributions are taxed as capital gains (see Chapter 14).[70]

Some payments are frequently referred to as dividends but are not considered dividends for tax purposes:

- Dividends received on deposits with savings and loan associations, credit unions, and banks are actually interest (a contractual rate paid for the use of money).
- Patronage dividends paid by cooperatives (e.g., for farmers) are rebates made to the users and are considered reductions in the cost of items purchased from the association. The rebates are usually made after year-end (after the cooperative has determined whether it has met its expenses) and are apportioned among members on the basis of their purchases.
- Mutual insurance companies pay dividends on unmatured life insurance policies that are considered rebates of premiums.
- Shareholders in a mutual investment fund are allowed to report as capital gains their proportionate share of the fund's gains realized and distributed. The capital gain and ordinary income portions are reported on the Form 1099 that the fund supplies its shareholders each year.

---

[67]*Kieselbach v. Comm.*, 43–1 USTC ¶9220, 30 AFTR 370, 63 S.Ct. 303 (USSC, 1943); *U.S. Trust Co. of New York v. Anderson*, 3 USTC ¶1125, 12 AFTR 836, 65 F.2d 575 (CA–2, 1933).
[68]See § 103(b).

[69]§ 316(a).
[70]§ 301(c). See Chapter 4, *West's Federal Taxation: Corporations, Partnerships, Estates, and Trusts*, for a detailed discussion of corporate distributions.

STOCK DIVIDENDS

When a corporation issues a simple stock dividend (e.g., common stock issued to common shareholders), the shareholder has merely received additional shares that represent the same total investment. Thus, the shareholder does not realize income.[71] However, if the shareholder has the *option* of receiving either cash or stock in the corporation, the individual realizes gross income whether he or she receives stock or cash.[72] A taxpayer who elects to receive the stock could be deemed to be in constructive receipt of the cash he or she has rejected.[73] However, the amount of the income in this case is the value of the stock received, rather than the cash the shareholder has rejected. See Chapter 14 for a detailed discussion of stock dividends.

EDUCATIONAL SAVINGS BONDS

The cost of a college education has risen dramatically during the past 10 years, increasing at a rate almost twice the change in the general price level. The U.S. Department of Education estimates that by the year 2007, the cost of attending a publicly supported university for four years will exceed $60,000. For a private university, the cost is expected to exceed $200,000.[74] Consequently, Congress has attempted to assist low- to middle-income parents in saving for their children's college education.

The assistance is in the form of an interest income exclusion on **educational savings bonds.**[75] The interest on Series EE U.S. government savings bonds may be excluded from gross income if the bond proceeds are used to pay qualified higher education expenses. The exclusion applies only if both of the following requirements are satisfied:

- The savings bonds are issued after December 31, 1989.
- The savings bonds are issued to an individual who is at least 24 years old at the time of issuance.

The exclusion is not available for a married couple who file separate returns.

The redemption proceeds must be used to pay qualified higher education expenses. *Qualified higher education expenses* consist of tuition and fees paid to an eligible educational institution for the taxpayer, spouse, or dependent. In calculating qualified higher education expenses, the tuition and fees paid are reduced by excludible scholarships and veterans' benefits received. If the redemption proceeds (both principal and interest) exceed the qualified higher education expenses, only a pro rata portion of the interest will qualify for exclusion treatment.

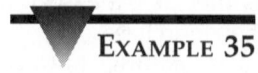
EXAMPLE 35

Tracy's redemption proceeds from qualified savings bonds during the taxable year were $6,000 (principal of $4,000 and interest of $2,000). Tracy's qualified higher education expenses were $5,000. Since the redemption proceeds exceed the qualified higher education expenses, only $1,667 [($5,000/$6,000) × $2,000] of the interest is excludible. ▼

The exclusion is limited by the application of the wherewithal to pay concept. That is, once the modified adjusted gross income exceeds a threshold amount, the phase-out of the exclusion begins. *Modified adjusted gross income (MAGI)* is adjusted

---

[71]*Eisner v. Macomber,* 1 USTC ¶32, 3 AFTR 3020, 40 S.Ct. 189 (USSC, 1920); § 305(a).

[72]§ 305(b).

[73]Refer to the discussion of constructive receipt in Chapter 4.

[74]See generally, Knight and Knight, "New Ways to Manage Soaring Tuition Costs," *Journal of Accountancy* (March 1989): 207.

[75]§ 135.

gross income prior to the § 911 foreign earned income exclusion and the educational savings bond exclusion. The threshold amounts are adjusted for inflation each year. For 1998, the phase-out begins at $52,250 ($78,350 on a joint return).[76] The phase-out is completed when MAGI exceeds the threshold amount by more than $15,000 ($30,000 on a joint return). The otherwise excludible interest is reduced by the amount calculated as follows:

$$\frac{\text{MAGI} - \$52{,}250}{\$15{,}000} \times \frac{\text{Excludible interest}}{\text{before phase-out}} = \frac{\text{Reduction in}}{\text{excludible interest}}$$

On a joint return, $78,350 is substituted for $52,250 (in 1998), and $30,000 is substituted for $15,000.

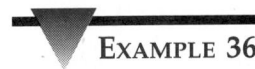

EXAMPLE 36

Assume the same facts as in Example 35, except that Tracy's MAGI for 1998 is $60,000. The phase-out will result in Tracy's interest exclusion being reduced by $861[($60,000 – $52,250)/ $15,000 × $1,667]. Therefore, Tracy's exclusion is $806 ($1,667 – $861). ▼

QUALIFIED STATE TUITION PROGRAMS

Several states have created programs whereby parents can in effect prepay their child's college tuition. The prepayment serves as a hedge against future increases in tuition. Generally, if the child does not attend college, the parents are refunded their payments plus interest. Upon first impression, these prepaid tuition programs resemble the below-market loans discussed in Chapter 4. That is, assuming the tuition increases, the parent receives a reduction in the child's tuition in exchange for the use of the funds. However, Congress has created an exclusion provision for these programs.[77]

Under a **qualified state tuition program,** the amounts contributed must be used for qualified higher education expenses. These expenses include tuition, fees, books, supplies, room and board, and equipment required for enrollment or attendance at a college, university, or certain vocational schools.

The difference between the amount contributed to the fund and the amount used to pay qualified higher education expenses is included in the gross income of the student (not the parent) using an annuity-type calculation to distinguish between contributions and income.

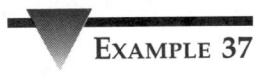

EXAMPLE 37

Agnes paid $15,000 into a qualified state tuition program associated with the future education of her son, Andrew. This amount prepaid four years of tuition ($3,750 per year). By the time Andrew attended college, the annual tuition had increased to $5,000. As Andrew utilizes the tuition prepayment, he must include $1,250 ($5,000 – $3,750) in his gross income each year. ▼

There are no tax consequences to the parent if the amount contributed is used for qualified higher education expenses of the child. If the parent receives a refund (e.g., child does not attend college), however, the excess of the amount refunded over the amount contributed by the parent is included in the parent's gross income.

---

[76]The indexed amounts for 1997 are $50,850 and $76,250.   [77]§ 529.

TAX BENEFIT RULE

3 ▼ LEARNING OBJECTIVE
Determine the extent to which receipts can be excluded under the tax benefit rule.

Generally, if a taxpayer obtains a deduction for an item in one year and in a later year recovers all or a portion of the prior deduction, the recovery is included in gross income in the year received.[78]

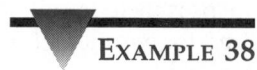
EXAMPLE 38

A taxpayer deducted as a loss a $1,000 receivable from a customer when it appeared the amount would never be collected. The following year, the customer paid $800 on the receivable. The taxpayer must report the $800 as income in the year it is received. ▼

However, the § 111 **tax benefit rule** provides that no income is recognized upon the recovery of a deduction, or the portion of a deduction, that did not yield a tax benefit in the year it was taken. If the taxpayer in Example 38 had no tax liability in the year of the deduction (e.g., itemized deductions and personal exemptions exceeded adjusted gross income), the recovery would be partially or totally excluded from income in the year of the recovery.[79]

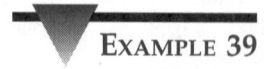
EXAMPLE 39

Before deducting a $1,000 loss from an uncollectible business receivable, Ali had taxable income of $200, computed as follows:

Adjusted gross income	$ 13,300
Itemized deductions and personal exemptions	(13,100)
Taxable income	$ 200

The business bad debt deduction yields only a $200 tax benefit. That is, taxable income is reduced by only $200 (to zero) as a result of the bad debt deduction. Therefore, if the customer

---

[78]§ 111(a).

[79]Itemized deductions are discussed in Chapter 10.

makes a payment on the previously deducted receivable in a subsequent year, only the first $200 is a recovery of a prior deduction and thus is taxable. Any additional amount collected is nontaxable because only $200 of the loss yielded a reduction in taxable income. ▼

INCOME FROM DISCHARGE OF INDEBTEDNESS

4 ▼ LEARNING OBJECTIVE
Describe the circumstances under which income must be reported from the discharge of indebtedness.

A transfer of appreciated property (fair market value is greater than adjusted basis) in satisfaction of a debt is an event that triggers the realization of income. The transaction is treated as a sale of the appreciated property followed by payment of the debt.[80] Foreclosure by a creditor is also treated as a sale or exchange of the property.[81]

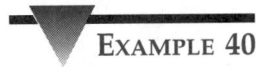

EXAMPLE 40

Juan owed the State Bank $100,000 on an unsecured note. Juan satisfied the note by transferring to the bank common stock with a basis of $60,000 and a fair market value of $100,000. Juan must recognize $40,000 gain on the transfer. Juan also owed the bank $50,000 on a note secured by land. When Juan's basis in the land was $20,000 and the land's fair market value was $50,000, the bank foreclosed on the loan and took title to the land. Juan must recognize a $30,000 gain on the foreclosure. ▼

In some cases, a creditor will not exercise his or her right of foreclosure and will even forgive a portion of the debt to assure the vitality of the debtor. In such cases, the debtor realizes income from discharge of indebtedness.

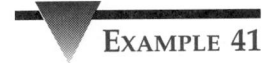

EXAMPLE 41

Brown Corporation is unable to meet the mortgage payments on its factory building. Both the corporation and the mortgage holder are aware of the depressed market for industrial property in the area. Foreclosure would only result in the creditor's obtaining unsalable property. To improve Brown Corporation's financial position and thus improve Brown's chances of obtaining the additional credit from other lenders necessary for survival, the creditor agrees to forgive all amounts past due and to reduce the principal amount of the mortgage. ▼

Generally, the income realized by the debtor from the forgiveness of a debt is taxable.[82] A similar debt discharge (produced by a different creditor motivation) associated with personal use property is illustrated in Example 42.

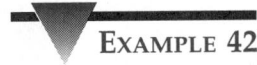

EXAMPLE 42

In 1993, Joyce borrowed $60,000 from National Bank to purchase her personal residence. Joyce agreed to make monthly principal and interest payments for 15 years. The interest rate on the note was 7%. In 1998, when the balance on the note had been reduced through monthly payments to $48,000, the bank offered to accept $45,000 in full settlement of the note. The bank made the offer because interest rates had increased to 11%. Joyce accepted the bank's offer. As a result, Joyce must recognize $3,000 ($48,000 – $45,000) income.[83] ▼

The following discharge of indebtedness situations are subject to special treatment:[84]

---

[80]Reg. § 1.1001–2(a).
[81]*Estate of Delman v. Comm.*, 73 T.C. 15 (1979).
[82]*U.S. v. Kirby Lumber Co.*, 2 USTC ¶814, 10 AFTR 458, 52 S.Ct. 4 (USSC, 1931), codified in § 61(a)(12).

[83]Rev.Rul. 82–202, 1982–1 C.B. 35.
[84]§§ 108 and 1017.

1. Creditors' gifts.
2. Discharges under Federal bankruptcy law.
3. Discharges that occur when the debtor is insolvent.
4. Discharge of the farm debt of a solvent taxpayer.
5. Discharge of **qualified real property business indebtedness.**
6. A seller's cancellation of the buyer's indebtedness.
7. A shareholder's cancellation of the corporation's indebtedness.
8. Forgiveness of loans to students.

If the creditor reduces the debt as an act of *love, affection or generosity*, the debtor has simply received a nontaxable gift (situation 1). Rarely will a gift be found to have occurred in a business context. A businessperson may settle a debt for less than the amount due, but as a matter of business expediency (e.g., high collection costs or disputes as to contract terms) rather than generosity.[85]

In situations 2, 3, 4, and 5, the Code allows the debtor to reduce his or her basis in the assets by the realized gain from the discharge.[86] Thus, the realized gain is merely deferred until the assets are sold (or depreciated). Similarly, in situation 6 (a price reduction), the debtor reduces the basis in the specific assets financed by the seller.[87]

A shareholder's cancellation of the corporation's indebtedness to him or her (situation 7) usually is considered a contribution of capital to the corporation. Thus, the corporation's paid-in capital is increased, and its liabilities are decreased by the same amount.[88]

Many states make loans to students on the condition that the loan will be forgiven if the student practices a profession in the state upon completing his or her studies. The amount of the loan that is forgiven (situation 8) is excluded from gross income.[89]

TAX PLANNING CONSIDERATIONS

The present law excludes certain types of economic gains from taxation. Therefore, taxpayers may find tax planning techniques helpful in obtaining the maximum benefits from the exclusion of such gains. Following are some of the tax planning opportunities made available by the exclusions described in this chapter.

5 **LEARNING OBJECTIVE**
Identify tax planning strategies for obtaining the maximum benefit from allowable exclusions.

LIFE INSURANCE

Life insurance offers several favorable tax attributes. As discussed in Chapter 4, the annual increase in the cash surrender value of the policy is not taxable (because no income has been actually or constructively received). By borrowing on the policy's cash surrender value, the owner can actually receive the policy's increase in value in cash but without recognizing income.

EMPLOYEE BENEFITS

Generally, employees view accident and health insurance, as well as life insurance, as necessities. Employees can obtain group coverage at much lower rates than individuals would have to pay for the same protection. Premiums paid by the

---

[85]*Comm. v. Jacobson*, 49–1 USTC ¶9133, 37 AFTR 516, 69 S.Ct. 358 (USSC, 1949).

[86]§§ 108(a), (c), (e), and (g). Note that § 108(b) provides that other tax attributes (e.g., net operating loss) will be reduced by the realized gain from the debt discharge prior to the basis adjustment unless the taxpayer elects to apply the basis adjustment first.

[87]§ 108(e)(5).
[88]§ 108(e)(6).
[89]§ 108(f).

TAX IN THE NEWS

WHEN PUBLIC HOUSING AND TAX POLICIES COLLIDE

n testimony before the House Banking Subcommittee on September 17, 1997, Kenneth Kies, chief of staff of the Joint Committee on Taxation, explained how efforts to rescue government-subsidized housing might be thwarted by the tax laws. The Department of Housing and Urban Development wanted to reduce the rent subsidy payments to landlords. However, many of the housing projects eligible for the payments were subject to large amounts of debt. The reduced payments would cause the project owners to default on their mortgages, which were guaranteed by the Federal government. The government did not want to become the landlord. Therefore, the House Banking Subcommittee was considering proposals to restructure the debt by reducing the principal.

Kies explained that altering the mortgages could create income from discharge of indebtedness to the landlord. This would be taxed as ordinary income in the year the debt was restructured. Thus, to prevent the Federal government from becoming a major landlord, a scheme that took into account the tax consequences would have to be developed.

---

employer can be excluded from the employees' gross income. Because of the exclusion, employees will have a greater after-tax and after-insurance income if the employer pays a lower salary but also pays the insurance premiums.

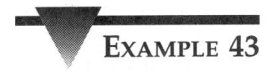

EXAMPLE 43

Pat receives a salary of $30,000. The company has group insurance benefits, but Pat was required to pay his own premiums as follows:

Hospitalization and medical insurance	$1,400
Term life insurance ($30,000 coverage)	200
Disability insurance	400
	$2,000

To simplify the analysis, assume Pat's tax rate on income is 28%. After paying taxes of $8,400 (.28 × $30,000) and $2,000 for insurance, Pat has $19,600 ($30,000 − $8,400 − $2,000) for his other living needs.

If Pat's employer reduced Pat's salary by $2,000 (to $28,000) but paid his insurance premiums, Pat's tax liability would be only $7,840 ($28,000 × .28). Thus, Pat would have $20,160 ($28,000 − $7,840) to meet his other living needs. The change in the compensation plan would save Pat $560 ($20,160 − $19,600). ▼

Similarly, employees must often incur expenses for child care and parking. The employee can have more income for other uses if the employer pays these costs for the employee but reduces the employee's salary by the cost of the benefits.

The use of cafeteria plans has increased dramatically in recent years. These plans allow employees to tailor their benefits to meet their individual situations. Thus, where both spouses in a married couple are working, duplications of benefits can be avoided and other needed benefits can often be added. If less than all of the employee's allowance is spent, the employee can receive cash.

The meals and lodging exclusion enables employees to receive from their employer what they ordinarily must purchase with after-tax dollars. Although the requirements that the employee live and take his or her meals on the employer's premises limit the tax planning opportunities, the exclusion is an important factor in the employee's compensation in certain situations, (e.g., hotels, motels, restaurants, farms, and ranches).

The employees' discount provision is especially important for manufacturers and wholesalers. Employees of manufacturers can avoid tax on the manufacturer's, wholesaler's, and retailer's markups. The wholesaler's employees can avoid tax on an amount equal to the wholesale and retail markups.

It should be recognized that the exclusion of benefits is generally available only to employees. Proprietors and partners must pay tax on the same benefits their employees receive tax-free. By incorporating and becoming an employee of the corporation, the former proprietor or partner can also receive these tax-exempt benefits. Thus, the availability of employee benefits is a consideration in the decision to incorporate.

INVESTMENT INCOME

Tax-exempt state and local government bonds are almost irresistible investments for many high-income taxpayers. To realize the maximum benefit from the exemption, the investor can purchase zero coupon bonds. Like Series EE U.S. government savings bonds, these investments pay interest only at maturity. The advantage of the zero coupon feature for a tax-exempt bond is that the investor can earn tax-exempt interest on the accumulated principal and interest. If the investor purchases a bond that pays the interest each year, the interest received may be such a small amount that an additional tax-exempt investment cannot be made. In addition, reinvesting the interest may entail transaction costs (broker's fees). The zero coupon feature avoids these problems.

Series EE U.S. government savings bonds can earn tax-exempt interest if the bond proceeds are used for qualified higher education expenses. Many taxpayers can foresee these expenditures being made for their children's educations. In deciding whether to invest in the bonds, however, the investor must take into account the income limitations for excluding the interest from gross income.

KEY TERMS

Accelerated death benefits, 5–6

Accident and health benefits, 5–12

Cafeteria plan, 5–18

Compensatory damages, 5–10

De minimis fringes, 5–21

Death benefits, 5–5

Educational savings bonds, 5–28

Flexible spending plan, 5–18

Foreign earned income exclusion, 5–24

Gift, 5–4

Life insurance proceeds, 5–6

Long-term care insurance, 5–13

Medical savings account (MSA), 5–13

No-additional-cost service, 5–19

Punitive damages, 5–11

Qualified employee discount, 5–20

Qualified real property business indebtedness, 5–32

Qualified state tuition program, 5–29

Qualified transportation fringes, 5–22

Qualified tuition reduction plan, 5–9

Scholarship, 5–8

Tax benefit rule, 5–30

Working condition fringes, 5–21

PROBLEM MATERIALS

DISCUSSION QUESTIONS

1. In 1995, Grape Corporation constructed a building on property it leased on a long-term basis. In 1997, Grape went bankrupt and forfeited the improvements to the owner of the land. In 1998, the owner sold the land and building. When does the landlord realize income from the improvements made by Grape?

2. Hazel made gifts to her three nephews. The first nephew, Al, received $10,000 cash during Hazel's lifetime. The second nephew, Bob, received $10,000 as a bequest when Hazel died. The third nephew, Carl, was the beneficiary of a $10,000 life insurance policy that Hazel purchased for $4,000. Are Al, Bob, and Carl required to include the amounts they received in gross income?

3. Violet Company gave $500 to each household in the community that had suffered a flood loss. The purpose of the payments was to help the flood victims. If some of the recipients are employees of Violet Company, can the employees exclude the payments from gross income?

4. Hannah, a cash basis taxpayer, died while employed by Purple Corporation. Purple paid Hannah's husband, Wade, $4,600 in sales commissions that Hannah had earned. The company also gave him an additional $3,000 to help with the expenses he had accumulated while caring for his wife in her final days. Are any of the amounts received by Wade includible in his gross income?

5. Matt's truck was stalled on the side of the road. Abby stopped to help and called Al, who agreed to repair the truck for $75. Matt paid Al $75 and Abby $25. The payment to Al was made because of a contractual obligation and therefore is not a gift. The payment to Abby was not made because of a contractual obligation. Does this mean that the payment Abby received is a gift?

6. Ted is diagnosed as having a terminal illness and has substantial liabilities he wants to pay prior to his death. Ted sells his guaranteed renewable term life insurance policy to Purple, Inc., a company that is a state-authorized dealer in such contracts. Ted receives $40,000, and he has paid $16,000 in premiums. Purple pays $3,000 in premiums before Ted dies. Purple collects the $60,000 face value of the policy. How much income are Ted and Purple required to recognize from these transactions?

7. Ed purchased a new tractor for his unincorporated trucking business. The seller, an accrual basis tractor dealer, financed the transaction. Under the financing terms, Ed is required to purchase a term life insurance policy. Ed is the owner of the policy, but he must name the seller as the beneficiary for the amount due on the note at the time of Ed's death. What are the tax consequences to Ed and to the seller if Ed dies and the seller collects from the insurance company an amount equal to the balance due on the note?

8. Black Corporation purchased a $1 million insurance policy on the life of the company's president. The company paid $100,000 of premiums, the president died, and the company collected the face amount of the policy. How much must Black Corporation include in gross income?

9. José is a graduate assistant at State University. He receives $7,000 a year in salary. In addition, tuition of $4,000 is waived. The tuition waiver is available to all full- and part-time employees. The fair market value of José's services is $11,000. How much is José required to include in his gross income?

10. Nancy was injured in an automobile accident caused by a drunk driver. Nancy suffered a broken arm and injuries to her spinal cord. She received damage awards as follows:

Medical expenses	$15,000
Loss of income	4,000
Punitive damages	40,000

None of the medical expenses has been deducted on her tax return. What is Nancy's gross income from the damage awards?

11. Sara was the victim of sexual harassment and collected the following from her employer: $15,000 for lost wages and $50,000 in punitive damages. How much of the damage award of $65,000 must Sara include in her gross income?

12. Holly works in a factory and earns $400 per week. Jill usually works in an office, but she was unable to work for one week because of an infected paper cut sustained at work. Jill collected $400 in workers' compensation as a result of her injury. Is the $400 Holly and Jill each received treated the same for income tax purposes?

13. Pam was hit by an automobile driven by a person under the influence of alcohol. Although Pam's injuries were minor (she did not go to the hospital or visit a doctor), she has recurring nightmares about the accident. Over the past 12 months, she has spent more than $6,000 for psychological therapy. Although she had problems before the accident, the recurring nightmares brought her to the realization that she needed professional help. Pam has not filed a lawsuit, but the driver of the automobile, who is very wealthy, "wants to do the right thing." The driver has offered Pam $30,000 as a settlement. He believes that this is more than she is entitled to under the law, but feels a great deal of remorse about all of the grief he has caused her. Pam is concerned about the tax consequences of the settlement offer. What are the relevant tax issues raised by these facts?

14. Wes purchases an accident and health insurance plan that was advertised in the Sunday newspaper. The annual premiums are $400. During the year, Wes received payments of $1,200 under the plan.
    a. How much of the $1,200 must Wes include in his gross income?
    b. Would the tax consequences differ if the $1,200 represented amounts paid by the insurance company to replace lost wages while Wes was hospitalized?

15. What nontaxable fringe benefits are available to employees that are not available to partners and proprietors?

16. Paula is employed by a telemarketing firm that pays a fixed amount for unlimited long-distance telephone calls. Employees are allowed to use the toll-free line for 5 minutes each month at no charge to the employee. The normal charge for the calls Paula made during the year was $75. How much is Paula required to include in gross income?

17. Gary is employed by Pelican, Inc., an automobile manufacturing company. Pelican sells Gary a new automobile at company cost of $12,000. A dealer would have been charged $14,000, and the retail price of the automobile is $17,000. What is Gary's gross income from the purchase of the automobile?

18. Eagle Life Insurance Company pays its employees $.25 per mile for driving their personal automobiles to and from work. The company reimburses each employee who rides the bus $45 a month for the cost of a pass. Tom collected $60 for his automobile mileage, and Ted received $45 as reimbursement for the cost of a bus pass.
    a. What are the effects of the above on Tom and Ted's gross income?
    b. Assume that Tom and Ted are in the 28% marginal tax bracket, and the actual before-tax cost for Tom to drive to and from work is $.25 per mile. What are Tom and Ted's after-tax costs of commuting to and from work? *included because it is not driving rule*

19. Zack works for Blue Pest Control, which offers a discount on its extermination services to its employees: officers receive a 50% discount, and all other employees receive a 30% discount. Zack, who is not an officer, had the company treat his home for termites and paid $280 for the service that is normally priced at $400. Zack's supervisor, an officer, had her home treated for carpenter ants and paid $500 for the service that is normally priced at $1,000. How much, if any, will Zack and his supervisor have to include in gross income for the services they received?

20. Several of Egret Company's employees have asked the company to create a hiking trail that employees could use during their lunch hours. The company owns vacant land that is being held for future expansion, but would have to spend approximately $50,000 if it were to make a trail. Nonemployees would be allowed to use the facility as part

of the company's effort to build strong community support. What are the relevant tax issues for the employees?

21. Marla worked for Robin Industries, Inc., and earned $80,000 in 1998. She spent 365 days out of the United States during 1998 working in a foreign country. Marla wants to exclude her foreign-earned income from U.S. taxation if possible. Does Marla qualify for doing so? If she does, how much of her income will be taxable in the United States?

22. Donna and George are married, file a joint return, and are in the 28% marginal tax bracket. They would like to save for their child's education. Currently, Amber, Inc. bonds are yielding 6%. Comparable Series EE U.S. government bonds are yielding 5%. Which investment would be preferable considering Donna and George's objective?

23. Maria, a cash method farmer, owns stock in a farmers' cooperative. During 1997, she purchased from the cooperative $80,000 of feed and fertilizer, which she expensed. This was a very good year for Maria's farm, which produced a $100,000 net profit. The farm was Maria's only source of income. The cooperative also had a very good year in 1997 and declared a patronage dividend that was distributed in early 1998. Maria's dividend was $5,000. What effect does the patronage dividend have on her gross income?

24. Arthur paid $20,000 to the Virginia State Tuition Program. Under the program, if Rachel, his daughter, enrolls in a state college or university, her tuition will be paid by the program. What are the tax consequences to Arthur and to Rachel of the program paying her tuition of $7,500 each year for four years?

25. In 1998, Mary received a $2,000 sales commission. However, in 1999, her employer discovered that Mary should have received only a $1,500 commission in 1998. Therefore, the employer withheld $500 from Mary's 1999 commission. Mary's standard deduction and personal exemption for 1998 exceeded her gross income. What effect would the tax benefit rule have on Mary's gross income for 1999?

26. Ida purchased a ranch. She gave the seller $50,000 cash and a 7% note for $200,000. When the principal on the note had been reduced to $180,000, the seller agreed to accept $165,000 in retirement of the debt. The creditor made the offer because interest rates had increased substantially. Ida was not undergoing bankruptcy and was not insolvent. Did Ida realize income from retiring the debt and, if so, is she required to include the amount in her gross income?

 27. Harry has experienced financial difficulties as a result of his struggling business. He has been behind on his mortgage payments for the last six months. The mortgage holder, who is a friend of Harry's, has offered to accept $80,000 in full payment of the $100,000 owed on the mortgage and payable over the next 10 years. The interest rate of the mortgage is 7%, and the market rate is now 8%. What tax issues are raised by the creditor's offer?

PROBLEMS

28. During the year, Wally received the following:
    - Gift of a car worth $32,000 from his fiancée.
    - Inheritance of stock worth $25,000 from his Aunt Jane's estate. Aunt Jane's basis for the stock was $10,000.
    - Proceeds (cash surrender value) of $20,000 from a life insurance policy he canceled to pay off credit-card debts. Wally had paid total premiums of $17,000.

    Determine the effect on Wally's gross income.

29. Determine the taxable life insurance proceeds in the following cases:
    a. When José died, his wife collected $50,000 on a group term insurance policy purchased by José's employer. José had never included the premiums in gross income.

b. The Cardinal Software Company purchased an insurance policy on the life of a key employee. The company paid $50,000 in premiums and collected $500,000 of insurance proceeds.

c. When Barbara died, she and her husband owed $15,000 on a loan. Under the terms of the loan, Barbara was required to purchase life insurance to pay the creditor the amount due at the date of Barbara's death. The creditor collected from the life insurance company the amount due at the time of Barbara's death. Is the creditor required to recognize income from the collection of the life insurance proceeds?

30. Laura was recently diagnosed as having a terminal case of cancer and has started chemotherapy treatments. She would like to pay all of her debts and make some charitable contributions prior to her death. This will require approximately $50,000. She is considering selling some stock she owns with a cost of $10,000 and a fair market value of $50,000. She also owns a term life insurance policy with a face amount of $100,000. The Viatical Benefits Company has announced that it will purchase any policy from a terminally ill patient for $.50 on the dollar. The company will then pay the premiums until death and will receive the face amount of the policy upon Laura's death. Laura is in the 28% marginal tax bracket. Laura has consulted you regarding the alternatives. What do you recommend?

31. Determine whether the taxpayer has gross income in each of the following situations:
   a. Jim is a waiter in a restaurant. The rule of thumb is that a customer should leave the waiter a tip equal to 15% of the customer's bill for food and beverages. Jim collected $6,000 in tips during the year.
   b. Tara works at a grocery store, bagging groceries and carrying them to the customers' automobiles. Her employer posts a sign saying that the employees are paid by the hour and the customer is not expected to tip them. Tara received $1,800 in tips from customers.
   c. Sheila worked at a hotel. Her home was damaged by a fire. Sheila's employer allowed her to stay at the hotel for no charge until she could return to her home. The normal charge for the room Sheila occupied during this period was $500, and the hotel had several vacant rooms.

32. Donald died at age 35. He was married and had four minor children. Donald's employer, Lark Painting Company, made payments to his wife as follows:

Donald's accrued salary at date of death	$4,000
A payment authorized by the board of directors to help his wife pay debts accumulated by Donald	7,000

   In addition, Donald's wife was the beneficiary of her husband's life insurance policy of $50,000. Lark Painting Company had paid for the policy. Donald had excluded all of the premiums paid by the employer from gross income as group term life insurance. His wife left the insurance proceeds with the insurance company and elected to receive an annuity of $4,000 each year for life. Her life expectancy is 40 years. She collected one $4,000 payment at the end of the current year. A joint return was filed in the year of Donald's death. Which of the above amounts must be included in gross income?

33. The Swan Partnership, a financial consulting company, has a cross-purchase agreement that requires the partnership to purchase a deceased partner's interest. The partner's interest is to be purchased from the deceased partner's estate with the price being 150% of the book value at the time of the partner's death. To finance the cross-purchase agreement, the partnership carries an insurance policy on the life of each of its partners. During the year, a partner died. The partnership collected the $250,000 face amount of the life insurance policy on the deceased partner and purchased her interest for $225,000. Swan had paid $100,000 in premiums on the policy. What are the tax consequences of these transactions for the deceased partner and for the partnership?

34. Walt made the all-state football team during his junior and senior years in high school. He accepted an athletic scholarship from State University. The scholarship provided the following:

Tuition and fees	$8,000
Room and board	7,500
Books and supplies	1,000

Determine the effect of the scholarship on Walt's gross income.

35. Alejandro was awarded an academic scholarship to State University. He received $5,000 in August and $6,000 in December 1998. Alejandro had enough personal savings to pay all expenses as they came due. Alejandro's expenditures for the relevant period were as follows:

Tuition, August 1998	$2,900
Tuition, December 1998	3,200
Room and board	
August–December 1998	3,000
January–May 1999	2,400
Books and educational supplies	
August–December 1998	800
January–May 1999	950

Determine the effect on Alejandro's gross income for 1998 and 1999.

36. Liz sued an overzealous bill collector and received the following settlement:

Damage to her automobile the collector attempted to repossess	$ 1,000
Physical damage to her arm caused by the collector	8,000
Loss of income while her arm was healing	6,000
Punitive damages	30,000

   a. What effect does the settlement have on Liz's gross income?
   b. Assume Liz also collected $40,000 of damages for slander to her personal reputation caused by the bill collector misrepresenting the facts to Liz's employer and other creditors. Is this $40,000 included in Liz's gross income?

37. Determine the taxpayer's taxable damages in each of the following cases:
   a. Orange Corporation collected $500,000 for damages to its business reputation.
   b. Don collected $100,000 in lost wages caused by age discrimination by his employer. Under the relevant law, a successful plaintiff can recover only lost wages.
   c. Kirby was injured in an automobile accident and collected $10,000 for loss of the use of his left arm, $15,000 for pain and suffering, $9,000 in lost wages, $5,000 for medical expenses, and $10,000 of punitive damages. Kirby had deducted none of the medical expenses.
   d. Nell received $10,000 of damages for invasion of her privacy by a photographer and $5,000 of punitive damages.
   e. Joanne received compensatory damages of $50,000 and punitive damages of $200,000 from a cosmetic surgeon who botched her nose job.

38. Rex, age 45, is an officer of Blue Company, which provided him with the following nondiscriminatory fringe benefits in 1998:
   a. Hospitalization insurance for Rex and his dependents. The cost of coverage for Rex was $450, and the additional cost for Rex's dependents was $400.
   b. Reimbursement of $700 from an uninsured medical reimbursement plan available to all employees.
   c. Group term life insurance protection of $120,000. (Each employee received coverage equal to twice his or her annual salary.)
   d. Salary continuation payments of $2,600 while Rex was hospitalized for an illness.

   While Rex was ill, he collected $1,600 on a salary continuation insurance policy he had purchased. Determine the amounts Rex must include in gross income.

39. The UVW Union and HON Corporation are negotiating contract terms. Assume the union members are in the 28% marginal tax bracket and all benefits are provided on a nondiscriminatory basis. Write a letter to the UVW Union members explaining the tax consequences of the options discussed below. The union's address is 905 Spruce Street, Washington, D.C. 20227.
    a. The company would impose a $100 deductible on medical insurance benefits. Most employees incur more than $100 each year in medical expenses.
    b. Employees would get an additional paid holiday with the same annual income (the same pay but less work).
    c. An employee who did not need health insurance (because the employee's spouse works and receives family coverage) would be allowed to receive the cash value of the coverage.

40. Sally and Bill are married and file a joint return. In 1998, Bill, an accountant, has a salary of $75,000, and Sally receives a salary of $25,000 as an apartment manager. What are the tax consequences of the following benefits that Bill and Sally's employers provide?
    a. Bill receives a reimbursement of $5,000 for child care expenses. Sally and Bill have three children who are not yet school age.
    b. Bill and Sally are provided a free membership at a local fitness and exercise club that allows them to attend three aerobic exercise sessions per week. The value of this type of membership is $1,600 per year.
    c. Bill is provided free parking at work. The value of the parking is $1,800 per year.
    d. Sally is provided with a free apartment. Living in this apartment is a condition of her employment. Similar apartments rent for $1,200 per month.

41. Determine the taxpayer's gross income for each of the following:
    a. Alice is the manager of a plant. The company owns a house one mile from the plant (rental value of $6,000) that Alice is allowed to occupy.
    b. Pam works for an insurance company that allows employees to eat in the cafeteria for $.50 a meal. Generally, the cost to the insurance company of producing a meal is $5.00, and a comparable meal could be purchased for $4.00. Pam ate 150 meals in the cafeteria during the year.
    c. Wade is a Methodist minister and receives a housing allowance of $600 per month from his church. Wade is buying his home and uses the $600 to make house payments ($450) and to pay utilities ($150).
    d. Floyd is a college professor and lives in campus housing. He is not charged rent. The fair market value of the house is $100,000, and the annual rental value is $7,200.

42. Does the taxpayer recognize gross income in the following situations?
    a. Ann is a registered nurse working in a community hospital. She is not required to take her lunch on the hospital premises, but she can eat in the cafeteria at no charge. The hospital adopted this policy to encourage employees to stay on the premises and be available in case of emergencies. During the year, Ann ate most of her meals on the premises. The total value of those meals was $750.
    b. Ira is the manager of a hotel. His employer will allow him to live in one of the rooms rent-free or to receive a $600 per month cash allowance for rent. Ira elected to live in the hotel.
    c. Seth is a forest ranger and lives in his employer's cabin in the forest. He is required to live there, and because there are no restaurants nearby, the employer supplies Seth with groceries that he cooks and eats on the premises.
    d. Rocky is a partner in the BAR Ranch (a partnership). He is the full-time manager of the ranch. BAR has a business purpose for Rocky's living on the ranch.

43. Betty is considering taking an early retirement offered by her employer. She would receive $2,000 per month, indexed for inflation. However, she would no longer be able to use the company's health facilities, and she would be required to pay her hospitalization insurance of $7,800 each year. Betty and her husband will file a joint return and take the standard deduction. She currently receives a salary of $40,000 a year, and her employer pays for all of her hospitalization insurance. If she retires, Betty would not be able to use her former employer's exercise facilities because of the commuting

distance. She would like to continue to exercise, however, and will therefore join a health club at a cost of $50 per month. Betty and her husband have other sources of income and are in and will remain in the 28% marginal tax bracket. She currently pays Social Security taxes of 7.65% on her salary, but her retirement pay would not be subject to this tax. She will earn about $11,000 a year from a part-time job. Betty would like to know whether she should accept the early retirement offer.

44. Sparrow, Inc., has a wide variety of fringe benefits available to its employees. However, not all of the employees actually need the benefits. For example, some employees have working spouses whose employers provide health insurance benefits for the employee's families. In addition, Sparrow reimburses up to $5,000 for child care costs, but not all of the employees have children. Some employees have expressed a strong interest in long-term care insurance. Sparrow's management has asked you to write a memo explaining how the company can accommodate the varying needs of its employees at the lowest after-tax cost to the employee. Sparrow's address is 300 Harbor Drive, Vermillion, SD 57069.

45. Thrush Corporation has 10 employees, three of whom are shareholders in the corporation. The company is considering adopting a group health insurance plan. Some of the employees have even expressed a willingness to take a cut in pay in order to obtain health insurance. Three of the employees are interested in long-term care insurance. Fred Thrush, the majority shareholder, has asked your advice about structuring insurance benefits in a favorable tax manner. He is vaguely familiar with flexible benefit plans and has read some articles on medical savings accounts. Write a letter to Mr. Thrush, explaining the possible tax features of a plan to suit the company's and employees' needs. Thrush's address is 500 Fern Avenue, Scranton, PA 18509.

46. Tara's employer provides a flexible benefits plan. Under the plan, medical and dental expenses incurred during the year that are not covered by the company's group health insurance plan will be paid by the flexible benefits plan. At the first of each year, the employee must set the amount to be covered by the plan. The employee's monthly salary is reduced by one-twelfth of the identified flexible benefit amount for the year. Tara thinks it is highly unlikely that she can accurately estimate her medical and dental expenses not covered by the company's group health insurance plan, but she feels these costs will probably be in the range of $1,500 to $2,500. She expects to be in the 28% marginal tax bracket. Tara would like your advice regarding how much she should reduce her salary in exchange for the expanded dental and medical benefits.

47. Snowbird Corporation would like you to review its employee fringe benefits program with regard to the effects of the plan on the company's president (Polly), who is also the majority shareholder:
    a. All employees receive free tickets to State University football games. Polly is seldom able to attend the games and usually gives her tickets to her nephew. The cost of Polly's tickets for the year was $75.
    b. The company pays all parking fees for its officers but not for other employees. The company paid $1,200 for Polly's parking for the year.
    c. Employees are allowed to use the copy machine for personal purposes as long as the privilege is not abused. Polly is president of a trade association and made extensive use of the copy machine to prepare mailings to members of the association. The cost of the copies was $900.
    d. The company is in the household moving business. Employees are allowed to ship goods without charge whenever there is excess space on a truck. Polly purchased a dining room suite for her daughter. Company trucks delivered the furniture to the daughter. Normal freight charges would have been $600.
    e. The company has a storage facility for household goods. Officers are allowed a 20% discount on charges for storing their goods. All other employees are allowed a 10% discount. Polly's discounts for the year totaled $400.

48. George, a U.S. citizen, is employed by Pelican, Inc., a global company. His salary for 1998 is $66,000 and his 1999 salary is $85,000. George's first foreign assignment is to St. Petersburg, Russia, and began on July 1, 1998. He works in St. Petersburg until

December 31, 1999. Being a workaholic, George did not take any vacation during this period.
  a. Compute George's 1998 salary that is includible in his gross income.
  b. Compute George's 1999 salary that is includible in his gross income.

49. Determine Hazel's gross income from the following receipts for the year:

Gain on sale of Augusta County bonds	$ 300
Interest on U.S. government savings bonds	700
Interest on state income tax refund	225
Interest on Augusta County bonds	800
Patronage dividend from Potato Growers Cooperative	1,200

The patronage dividend was received in March of the current year for amounts paid and deducted in the previous year as expenses of Hazel's profitable cash basis farming business.

50. Determine Jack's gross income from the following items:
  a. Jack owns 100 shares of Roadrunner Company common stock. The company has a dividend reinvestment plan. Under the plan, Jack can receive an $18 cash dividend or an additional share of stock with a fair market of $18. Jack elected to take the stock.
  b. Jack owns 100 shares of Bat Corporation. The company declared a dividend, and Jack was to receive an additional share of the company's common stock with a fair market value of $18. Jack did not have the option to receive cash. However, a management group announced a plan to repurchase all available shares for $18 each. The offer was part of a takeover defense.
  c. Jack also collected $125 on a corporate debenture. The corporation had been in bankruptcy for several years. Jack had correctly deducted the cost of the bond in a prior year because the bankruptcy judge had informed the bondholders they would not receive anything in the final liquidation. Later the company collected on an unanticipated claim and had the funds to make partial payment on the bonds.

51. Lynn Schwartz recently inherited $25,000. She is considering using the money to finance a college education for her 5-year-old son. She currently earns $45,000 a year. She asks your advice about tax-favored programs for college savings. Write a letter to Lynn advising her as to her options. Lynn's address is 100 Myrtle Cove, Fairfield, CT 06432.

52. Starting in 1990, Chuck and Luane have been purchasing Series EE bonds in their name to use for the higher education of their daughter (Susie who currently is age 18). During the year, they cash in $12,000 of the bonds to use for freshman year tuition, fees, and room and board. Of this amount, $5,000 represents interest. Of the $12,000, $8,000 is used for tuition and fees, and $4,000 is used for room and board. Their AGI, before the educational savings bond exclusion, is $85,000.
  a. Determine the tax consequences for Chuck and Luane, who will file a joint return, and for Susie.
  b. Assume that Chuck and Luane purchased the bonds in Susie's name. Determine the tax consequences for Chuck and Luane and for Susie.
  c. How would your answer for (a) change if Chuck and Luane file separate returns?

53. Carlos made payments to the Qualified State Tuition Program for the benefit of his son, Ramon. Carlos contributed $4,000 each year for a four-year period. This will satisfy Ramon's tuition and fees for four years of college. At the time of Ramon's freshman year, the tuition and fees have increased to $6,000 per year. Determine the effect on Carlos and Ramon's gross income for Ramon's freshman year.

54. How does the tax benefit rule apply in the following cases?
  a. In 1998, Wilma paid Vera $5,000 for locating a potential client. The deal fell through, and in 1999, Vera refunded the $5,000 to Wilma.
  b. In 1998, Wilma paid an attorney $300 for services in connection with a title search. Because the attorney was negligent, Wilma incurred some additional costs in acquiring the land. In 1999, the attorney refunded his $300 fee to Wilma.

c. In 1998, Wilma received a $90 dividend with respect to 1998 premiums on her life insurance policy.

d. In 1999, Wilma, a cash basis farmer, received a $400 patronage dividend with respect to 1998 purchases of cattle feed.

55. Mary and her two sisters, Cary and Gladys, were injured in a car accident in 1998, and each sustained injuries requiring $1,200 in medical expenses. Because the claim was not settled until 1999, each sister had completed her 1998 income tax return before the settlement. Mary does not itemize deductions. Cary does itemize deductions, but the $1,200 medical expense did not exceed the 7.5%-of-AGI threshold; consequently, the deduction did not result in a reduction of her tax liability. Gladys also itemizes deductions. Because of other medical expenses, the $1,200 expense pushed her $800 over the 7.5%-of-AGI threshold. Therefore, Gladys benefited from the deduction by having her taxes reduced. In 1999, each sister received a $1,200 insurance settlement for her injuries. How much of the $1,200 settlement received does each sister need to include in gross income?

56. Fran, who is in the 36% tax bracket, recently collected $100,000 on a life insurance policy she carried on her father. She currently owes $120,000 on her personal residence and $120,000 on business property. National Bank holds the mortgage on both pieces of property and has agreed to accept $100,000 in complete satisfaction of either mortgage. The interest rate on the mortgages is 8%, and both mortgages are payable over 10 years. What would be the tax consequences of each of the following alternatives, assuming Fran currently deducts the mortgage interest on her tax return?

a. Retire the mortgage on the residence.

b. Retire the mortgage on the business property.

Which alternative should Fran select?

57. Robin Company is experiencing financial troubles and is considering negotiating the following with its creditors. Determine the tax consequences to Robin of the following plan:

a. The Motor Finance Company will cancel $1,500 in accrued interest. Robin had deducted the interest in the prior year. Motor Finance Company will also reduce the principal on the note by $1,000. The note financed the purchase of equipment from a local dealer.

b. The Trust Land Company, which sold Robin land and buildings, will reduce the mortgage on the building by $15,000.

c. Ridge, the sole shareholder in the corporation, will cancel a $50,000 receivable from the corporation in exchange for additional stock.

CUMULATIVE PROBLEMS

58. Albert S. Moore (Social Security number 363–22–1141) is 35 years old and is married to Bonnie B. Moore (Social Security number 259–50–4284). The Moores live at 215 Harper's Road, Newport News, VA 23100. They file a joint return and have two dependent children (Bobby and Cindy). In 1998, Albert and Bonnie had the following transactions:

a. Albert received $90,000 in salary from Plum Steel Company. He worked on a construction project in Mexico from July 1, 1997, through December 31, 1998. Withholding for Federal income tax was $11,000. The proper amount of FICA taxes was withheld.

b. Albert and Bonnie received $1,200 of interest on U.S. government bonds and $600 of interest on Montgomery County School bonds.

c. Bonnie was involved in an automobile accident in 1997 and incurred $12,000 of medical expenses. Insurance paid $8,000 of the expenses, and Albert and Bonnie deducted the remaining $4,000 on their 1997 return. During 1998, Bonnie received a settlement from the other driver's insurance company. She received $12,000 for her medical expenses, $65,000 as compensatory damages for the physical injury, and $35,000 of punitive damages.

d. Bonnie received 10 shares of Cherry, Inc., as a stock dividend. The shares received had a fair market value of $360. Bonnie had the option of receiving cash equal to the value of the shares, but chose not to do so.

e. Albert paid $9,000 of alimony to his first wife, Rosa T. Monroe (Social Security number 800–60–2580).

f. Albert and Bonnie's itemized deductions were as follows:

- State income taxes paid and withheld totaled $2,400. In addition, a $600 overpayment for their 1997 state taxes (deducted on the 1997 Federal return) was applied to their 1998 liability.

- Real estate taxes on their principal residence were $1,500.

- Interest on their principal residence was $3,600.

- Cash contributions to the church were $2,200.

Part 1—Tax Computation
Compute the Moores' net tax payable (or refund due) for 1998. Suggested software (if available): *TurboTax.*

Part 2—Tax Planning
Assume the Moores provided you with the above information late in 1998. They are considering selling Orange, Inc., stock purchased in November 1998 for $6,000. The stock has a present and projected fair market value of $4,000. The sale could occur in late 1998 or early 1999. They do not expect any major changes in their income situation, except Albert's salary will increase to $125,000 and he will be working in the United States for the entire year. Write a letter to the Moores that contains your advice and prepare a memo for the tax files.

59. Alfred E. Old and Beulah Crane, each age 42, married on September 7, 1997. Alfred and Beulah will file a joint return for 1997. Alfred's Social Security number is 262–60–3815. Beulah's Social Security number is 259–68–4285, and she will adopt "Old" as her married name. They live at 211 Brickstone Drive, Atlanta, GA 30304.

Alfred was divorced from Sarah Old in March 1996. Under the divorce agreement, Alfred is to pay Sarah $800 per month for the next 10 years or until Sarah's death, whichever occurs first. Alfred pays Sarah $9,600 in 1997. In addition, in January 1997, Alfred pays Sarah $50,000, which is designated as being for her share of the marital property. Also, Alfred is responsible for all prior years' income taxes and is to receive any refund of overpaid taxes for prior years. Sarah's Social Security number is 444–10–2211.

Alfred's salary for 1997 is $62,000, and his employer, Cherry, Inc., provides him with group term life insurance equal to twice his annual salary. His employer withheld $10,300 for Federal income taxes, $3,000 for state income taxes, and the appropriate amount for FICA.

Beulah recently graduated from law school and is employed by Legal Aid Society, Inc., as a public defender. She receives a salary of $36,000 in 1997. Her employer withheld $5,200 for Federal income taxes, $2,100 for state income taxes, and the appropriate amount for FICA.

Beulah has $1,500 in dividends on Yellow Corporation stock she inherited. Beulah receives a $600 refund of 1996 state income taxes. She used the standard deduction on her 1996 Federal income tax return. Alfred receives a $1,100 refund of his 1996 state income taxes. He itemized deductions on his 1996 Federal income tax return. Alfred and Beulah pay $4,300 interest and $1,200 property taxes on their personal residence in 1997. Their charitable contributions total $800 (all to their church).

Compute the Olds' net tax payable (or refund due) for 1997. If you use tax forms for your solution, you will need Form 1040 and Schedules A and B. Suggested software (if available): *TurboTax.*

RESEARCH PROBLEMS

*Note: Use the **RIA OnPoint System 4 Student Version CD-ROM,** which is available to accompany this text, in preparing solutions to the Research Problems. Alternatively, tax research materials found in a standard tax library can be used.*

Research Problem 1.   David Hobson is the minister at the First Baptist Church. As part of his compensation, David receives an $800 per month housing allowance. David is purchasing his residence, and he uses the $800 each month to make mortgage and property tax payments. The mortgage interest and property taxes are deducted (as itemized deductions) on David's tax return. The examining IRS agent thinks David would be enjoying a double benefit if the housing allowance is excluded and the itemized deductions are allowed. In addition, the agent contends that the housing allowance exclusion should apply only where the church provides the residence or the minister uses the funds to pay rent. Therefore, the agent maintains that David should include in gross income the $800 received each month. David has asked your assistance in this matter. Write a letter to David that contains your advice and prepare a memo for the tax files. David's address is 982 Richmond Drive, Hollis, OK 73550.

Research Problem 2.   The Beige Real Estate Company borrowed $1,400,000 from the First National Bank to purchase a building. The loan was without recourse; that is, if Beige did not pay the mortgage, the bank could repossess the property. But if the fair market value of the property repossessed was less than the amount of the debt, Beige would not be responsible for the difference. When the fair market value of the property was $800,000 and the balance on the mortgage was $1,000,000, Beige was unable to make its monthly loan payment. After much negotiation, the bank reduced the principal to $800,000, which enabled Beige to make its payment in a timely manner. The IRS added $200,000 of income from discharge of indebtedness to Beige's taxable income for the year. Beige contends it has no gross income because the fair market value of the building is not more than the reduced principal of the debt. Advise Beige on who is correct.

Partial list of research aids:
Rev.Rul. 91–31, 1991–1 C.B. 19.

Research Problem 3.   Your client operates a well-known chain of retail stores. A shopping center developer has offered to rent space to your client at a very low price under a 10-year lease. Your client will be an "anchor tenant." While other tenants will lease a mere shell and be responsible for making the improvements necessary to operate their businesses, the developer has offered to make improvements with a maximum cost of $500,000 to meet specific needs of your client. These expenditures will be made as an inducement to your client to locate in the shopping center. Before deciding whether to accept the offer, your client asks your opinion about the tax consequences of receiving the $500,000 in improvements.

Research Problem 4.   Snipe Company is closing one of its plants. The company's management is very concerned about employee morale at other plants. To minimize the damage to employee relations, the company has decided to pay the costs of "outplacement services" for the employees of the plant to be closed. The services include the use of a consultant in writing resumés, identifying potential employers, and writing to those employers. The company has asked your advice as to whether the employees would be required to include the costs of the services in their gross incomes.

Use the tax resources of the Internet to address the following questions. Do not restrict your search to the World Wide Web, but include a review of newsgroups and general reference materials, practitioner sites and resources, primary sources of the tax law, chat rooms and discussion groups, and other opportunities.

Research Problem 5.   Go to the IRS site on the Internet and download instructions and regulations relative to educational savings bonds and qualified state tuition programs. Summarize one of the key provisions in these materials in outline format.

Research Problem 6.   Employers often use the Internet as a means of attracting applications from potential employees. Locate an Internet site offering employment opportunities, ideally one provided by a well-known corporation. How does the employer promote its fringe benefit and cafeteria plan packages? Contrast several such sites.

TEAM PROJECT: ARTHUR ANDERSEN TAX CHALLENGE CASES

For more information on the Arthur Andersen Tax Challenge Cases, refer to Chapter 1, page 1–37.

Information related to tax issues and problems that are discussed in this chapter may be found in the

Day and Ball case on pages 3, 5, 17, and 30
Fence case on pages: None

Read and analyze the case you have been assigned and *identify* any issues and problems that are related to material covered in this chapter. If the information provided in the case is complete, prepare answers for this part of the case at this time. If you need information that is contained in the later parts of the case, write a memo summarizing the questions or problems so you can prepare a complete answer at a later date.

6

DEDUCTIONS AND LOSSES: IN GENERAL

LEARNING OBJECTIVES

After completing Chapter 6, you should be able to:

1. Differentiate between deductions *for* and *from* adjusted gross income and understand the relevance of the differentiation.

2. Describe the cash and accrual methods of accounting.

3. Apply the Internal Revenue Code deduction disallowance provisions associated with the following: public policy limitations, political activities, excessive executive compensation, investigation of business opportunities, hobby losses, vacation home rentals, payment of others' expenses, personal expenditures, capital expenditures, related-party transactions, and expenses related to tax-exempt income.

4. Identify tax planning opportunities for maximizing deductions and minimizing the disallowance of deductions.

CLASSIFICATION OF DEDUCTIBLE EXPENSES

1 LEARNING OBJECTIVE
Differentiate between deductions *for* and *from* adjusted gross income and understand the relevance of the differentiation.

The tax law has an all-inclusive definition of income; that is, income from whatever source derived is includible in gross income. Income cannot be excluded unless there is a specific statement to that effect in the Internal Revenue Code.

Similarly, deductions are disallowed unless a specific provision in the tax law permits them. The inclusive definition of income and the exclusive definition of deductions may not seem fair to taxpayers, but it is the structure of the tax law.

The courts have held that whether and to what extent deductions are allowed depends on legislative grace.[1] In other words, any exclusions from income and all deductions are gifts from Congress!

It is important to classify deductible expenses as **deductions for adjusted gross income** (AGI) or **deductions from adjusted gross income.** Deductions *for* AGI can be claimed whether or not the taxpayer itemizes. Deductions *from* AGI result in a tax benefit only if they exceed the taxpayer's standard deduction. If itemized deductions (*from* AGI) are less than the standard deduction, they provide no tax benefit.

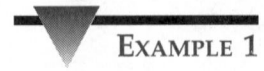
EXAMPLE 1

Steve is a self-employed CPA. Ralph is one of Steve's employees. During the year, Steve and Ralph incur the following expenses:

	Steve	Ralph
Dues to American Institute of CPAs and State Society of CPAs	$ 400	$ 300
Subscriptions to professional journals	500	200
Registration fees for tax conferences	800	800
	$1,700	$1,300

---

[1]*New Colonial Ice Co. v. Helvering,* 4 USTC ¶1292, 13 AFTR 1180, 54 S.Ct. 788 (USSC, 1934).

Steve does not reimburse any of his employees for dues, subscriptions, or educational programs.

Steve's expenses are classified as a deduction *for* AGI. Therefore, he can deduct the $1,700 on his Federal income tax return. Ralph's expenses are classified as deductions *from* AGI. Ralph will be able to benefit from the $1,300 of expenses on his Federal income tax return only if he itemizes deductions. If he takes the standard deduction instead, the $1,300 of expenses will have no effect on the calculation of his taxable income. Even if Ralph does itemize deductions, he must reduce the $1,300 of expenses, which are classified as miscellaneous itemized deductions, by 2% of his AGI. As this example illustrates, whether a deduction is classified as *for* AGI or *from* AGI can affect the benefit the taxpayer receives from the deduction. ▼

Deductions *for* AGI are also important in determining the *amount* of itemized deductions because many itemized deductions are limited to amounts in excess of specified percentages of AGI. Examples of itemized deductions that are limited by AGI are medical expenses and personal casualty losses. Itemized deductions that are deductible only to the extent that they exceed a specified percentage of AGI are increased when AGI is decreased. Likewise, when AGI is increased, these itemized deductions are decreased.

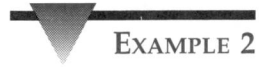
EXAMPLE 2

Tina earns a salary of $20,000 and has no other income. She itemizes deductions during the current year. Medical expenses for the year are $1,800. Since medical expenses are deductible only to the extent they exceed 7.5% of AGI, Tina's medical expense deduction is $300 [$1,800 − (7.5% × $20,000)]. If Tina had a $2,000 deduction *for* AGI, her medical expense deduction would be $450 [$1,800 − (7.5% × $18,000)], or $150 more. If the $2,000 deduction was *from* AGI, her medical expense deduction would remain $300 since AGI is unchanged. ▼

DEDUCTIONS FOR ADJUSTED GROSS INCOME

To understand how deductions of individual taxpayers are classified, it is necessary to examine the role of § 62. The purpose of § 62 is to classify various deductions as deductions *for* AGI. It does not provide the statutory authority for taking the deduction. For example, § 212 allows individuals to deduct expenses attributable to income-producing property. Section 212 expenses that are attributable to rents or royalties are classified as deductions *for* AGI. Likewise, a deduction for trade or business expenses is allowed by § 162. These expenses are classified as deductions *for* AGI.

If a deduction is not listed in § 62, it is an itemized deduction, *not* a deduction *for* AGI. Following is a *partial* list of the items classified as deductions *for* AGI by § 62:

- Expenses attributable to a trade or business carried on by the taxpayer. A trade or business does not include the performance of services by the taxpayer as an employee.
- Expenses incurred by a taxpayer in connection with the performance of services as an employee if the expenses are reimbursed and other conditions are satisfied.
- Deductions that result from losses on the sale or exchange of property by the taxpayer.
- Deductions attributable to property held for the production of rents and royalties.
- The deduction for payment of alimony.
- Certain contributions to pension, profit sharing, and annuity plans of self-employed individuals.
- The deduction for certain retirement savings allowed by § 219 (e.g., IRAs).

- The penalty imposed on premature withdrawal of funds from time savings accounts or deposits.
- The deduction for moving expenses.
- The deduction for interest paid on student loans.

These items are covered in detail in various chapters in the text.

ITEMIZED DEDUCTIONS

The Code defines itemized deductions as the deductions allowed other than "the deductions allowable in arriving at adjusted gross income."[2] Thus, if a deduction is not properly classified as a deduction *for* AGI, then it is classified as an itemized deduction.

Section 212 Expenses.   Section 212 allows deductions for ordinary and necessary expenses paid or incurred for the following:

- The production or collection of income.
- The management, conservation, or maintenance of property held for the production of income.
- Expenses paid in connection with the determination, collection, or refund of any tax.

Section 212 expenses related to rent and royalty income are deductions *for* AGI.[3] Expenses paid in connection with the determination, collection, or refund of taxes related to the income of sole proprietorships, rents and royalties, or farming operations are deductions *for* AGI. All other § 212 expenses are itemized deductions (deductions *from* AGI). For example, investment-related expenses (e.g., safe deposit box rentals) are deductible as itemized deductions attributable to the production of investment income.[4]

---

[2]§ 63(d).
[3]§ 62(a)(4).

[4]Reg. § 1.212–1(g).

Deductible Personal Expenses. Taxpayers are allowed to deduct certain expenses that are primarily personal in nature. These expenses, which generally are not related to the production of income, are deductions *from* AGI (itemized deductions). Some of the more frequently encountered deductions in this category include the following:

- Contributions to qualified charitable organizations (not to exceed a specified percentage of AGI).
- Medical expenses (in excess of 7.5 percent of AGI).
- Certain state and local taxes (e.g., real estate taxes and state and local income taxes).
- Personal casualty losses (in excess of an aggregate floor of 10 percent of AGI and a $100 floor per casualty).
- Certain personal interest (e.g., mortgage interest on a personal residence).

Itemized deductions are discussed in detail in Chapter 10.

TRADE OR BUSINESS EXPENSES AND PRODUCTION OF INCOME EXPENSES

Section 162(a) permits a deduction for all ordinary and necessary expenses paid or incurred in carrying on a trade or business. These include reasonable salaries paid for services, expenses for the use of business property, and one-half of self-employment taxes paid (see Chapter 13). Such expenses are deducted *for* AGI.

It is sometimes difficult to determine whether an expenditure is deductible as a trade or business expense. The term "trade or business" is not defined in the Code or Regulations, and the courts have not provided a satisfactory definition. It is usually necessary to ask one or more of the following questions to determine whether an item qualifies as a trade or business expense:

- Was the use of the particular item related to a business activity? For example, if funds are borrowed for use in a business, the interest is deductible as a business expense.
- Was the expenditure incurred with the intent to realize a profit or to produce income? For example, expenses in excess of the income from raising horses are not deductible if the activity is classified as a personal hobby rather than a trade or business.
- Were the taxpayer's operation and management activities extensive enough to indicate the carrying on of a trade or business?

Section 162 *excludes* the following items from classification as trade or business expenses:

- Charitable contributions or gifts.
- Illegal bribes and kickbacks and certain treble damage payments.
- Fines and penalties.

A bribe paid to a domestic official is not deductible if it is illegal under the laws of the United States. Foreign bribes are deductible unless they are unlawful under the Foreign Corrupt Practices Act of 1977.[5]

---

[5]§ 162(c)(1).

PAYING RETAINERS TO KEEP LAWYERS FROM RIVALS

In a recent Claims Court case, the IRS attempted to disallow a deduction for a taxpayer who paid a retainer to a law firm to ensure that the law firm would not do legal work for a hostile suitor. The taxpayer paid a retainer to the law firm for 16 years, even though the firm did little or no legal work for the taxpayer during that time.

The IRS's position was that the payments were not deductible because they were capital expenditures rather than ordinary and necessary business expenses deductible under § 162. The Claims Court concluded that the taxpayer's long history of paying an annual retainer established the payments as an ordinary and necessary business expense and thus they were currently deductible.

SOURCE: Adapted from Tom Herman, "Companies Can Deduct Retainers to Keep Lawyers from Rivals," *Wall Street Journal*, July 28, 1997, p. B8.

Ordinary and Necessary Requirement.   The terms **ordinary and necessary** are found in both §§ 162 and 212. To be deductible, any trade or business expense must be "ordinary and necessary." In addition, compensation for services must be "reasonable" in amount.

Many expenses that are necessary are *not* ordinary. Neither "ordinary" nor "necessary" is defined in the Code or Regulations. The courts have held that an expense is *necessary* if a prudent businessperson would incur the same expense and the expense is expected to be appropriate and helpful in the taxpayer's business.[6]

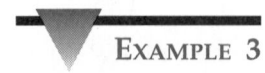

EXAMPLE 3

Pat purchased a manufacturing concern that had just been adjudged bankrupt. Because the business had a poor financial rating, Pat satisfied some of the obligations to employees and outside salespeople incurred by the former owners. Pat had no legal obligation to pay these debts, but felt this was the only way to keep salespeople and employees. The Second Court of Appeals found that the payments were necessary in that they were both appropriate and helpful.[7] However, the Court held that the payments were *not* ordinary but were in the nature of capital expenditures to build a reputation. Therefore, no deduction was allowed. ▼

An expense is *ordinary* if it is normal, usual, or customary in the type of business conducted by the taxpayer and is not capital in nature.[8] However, an expense need not be recurring to be deductible as ordinary.

EXAMPLE 4

Albert engaged in a mail-order business. The post office judged that his advertisements were false and misleading. Under a fraud order, the post office stamped "fraudulent" on all letters addressed to Albert's business and returned them to the senders. Albert spent $30,000 on legal fees in an unsuccessful attempt to force the post office to stop. The legal fees (though not recurring) were ordinary business expenses because they were normal, usual, or customary in the circumstances.[9] ▼

---

[6]*Welch v. Helvering*, 3 USTC ¶1164, 12 AFTR 1456, 54 S.Ct. 8 (USSC, 1933).

[7]*Dunn and McCarthy, Inc. v. Comm.*, 43–2 USTC ¶9688, 31 AFTR 1043, 139 F.2d 242 (CA–2, 1943).

[8]*Deputy v. DuPont*, 40–1 USTC ¶9161, 23 AFTR 808, 60 S.Ct. 363 (USSC, 1940).

[9]*Comm. v. Heininger*, 44–1 USTC ¶9109, 31 AFTR 783, 64 S.Ct. 249 (USSC, 1943).

For § 212 deductions, the law requires that expenses bear a reasonable and proximate relationship to (1) the production or collection of income or to (2) the management, conservation, or maintenance of property held for the production of income.[10]

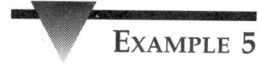

EXAMPLE 5

Wendy owns a small portfolio of investments, including 10 shares of Hawk, Inc., common stock worth $1,000. She incurred $350 in travel expenses to attend the annual shareholders' meeting at which she voted her 10 shares against the current management group. No deduction is permitted because a 10-share investment is insignificant in value in relation to the travel expenses incurred.[11] ▼

Reasonableness Requirement. The Code refers to **reasonableness** solely with respect to salaries and other compensation for services.[12] But the courts have held that for any business expense to be ordinary and necessary, it must also be reasonable in amount.[13]

What constitutes reasonableness is a question of fact. If an expense is unreasonable, the excess amount is not allowed as a deduction. The question of reasonableness generally arises with respect to closely held corporations where there is no separation of ownership and management.

Transactions between the shareholders and the closely held company may result in the disallowance of deductions for excessive salaries and rent expense paid by the corporation to the shareholders. The courts will view an unusually large salary in light of all relevant circumstances and may find that the salary is reasonable despite its size.[14] If excessive payments for salaries and rents are closely related to the percentage of stock owned by the recipients, the payments are generally treated as dividends.[15] Since dividends are not deductible by the corporation, the disallowance results in an increase in the corporate taxable income. Deductions for reasonable salaries will not be disallowed *solely* because the corporation has paid insubstantial portions of its earnings as dividends to its shareholders.

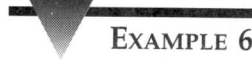

EXAMPLE 6

Sparrow Corporation, a closely held corporation, is owned equally by Lupe, Carlos, and Ramon. The company has been highly profitable for several years and has not paid dividends. Lupe, Carlos, and Ramon are key officers of the company, and each receives a salary of $200,000. Salaries for similar positions in comparable companies average only $100,000. Amounts paid the owners in excess of $100,000 may be deemed unreasonable, and, if so, a total of $300,000 in salary deductions by Sparrow is disallowed. The disallowed amounts are treated as dividends rather than salary income to Lupe, Carlos, and Ramon because the payments are proportional to stock ownership. Salaries are deductible by the corporation, but dividends are not. ▼

BUSINESS AND NONBUSINESS LOSSES

Section 165 provides for a deduction for losses not compensated for by insurance. As a general rule, deductible losses of individual taxpayers are limited to those incurred in a trade or business or in a transaction entered into for profit. Individuals are also allowed to deduct losses that are the result of a casualty. Casualty losses include, but are not limited to, fire, storm, shipwreck, and theft. See Chapter 7 for

[10]Reg. § 1.212–1(d).
[11]*J. Raymond Dyer*, 36 T.C. 456 (1961).
[12]§ 162(a)(1).
[13]*Comm. v. Lincoln Electric Co.*, 49–2 USTC ¶9388, 38 AFTR 411, 176 F.2d 815 (CA–6, 1949).

[14]*Kennedy, Jr. v. Comm.*, 82–1 USTC ¶9186, 49 AFTR2d 82–628, 671 F.2d 167 (CA–6, 1982), *rev'g* 72 T.C. 793 (1979).
[15]Reg. § 1.162–8.

a further discussion of this topic. Deductible personal casualty losses are reduced by $100 per casualty, and the aggregate of all personal casualty losses is reduced by 10 percent of AGI. A personal casualty loss is an itemized deduction. See Concept Summary 6–2 near the end of the chapter for the classification of expenses.

REPORTING PROCEDURES

All deductions *for* and *from* AGI wind up on pages 1 and 2 of Form 1040. All deductions *for* AGI are reported on page 1. The last line on page 1 is adjusted gross income.

The first item on page 2 is also adjusted gross income. Itemized deductions are entered next, followed by the deduction for personal and dependency exemptions. The result is taxable income.

Most of the deductions *for* AGI on page 1 originate on supporting schedules. Examples include business expenses (Schedule C) and rent, royalty, partnership, and fiduciary deductions (Schedule E). Other deductions *for* AGI, such as IRAs, Keogh retirement plans, and alimony, are entered directly on page 1 of Form 1040.

All itemized deductions on page 2 are carried over from Schedule A. Some Schedule A deductions originate on other forms. Examples include home mortgage interest, investment interest, noncash charitable contributions in excess of $500, casualty losses, and unreimbursed employee expenses.

Form 1040 becomes a summary of the detailed information entered on the other schedules and forms. See Figure 6–1.

Deductions and Losses—Timing of Expense Recognition

IMPORTANCE OF TAXPAYER'S METHOD OF ACCOUNTING

2   **LEARNING OBJECTIVE**
Describe the cash and accrual methods of accounting.

A taxpayer's **accounting method** is a major factor in determining taxable income. The method used determines when an item is includible in income and when an item is deductible on the tax return. Usually, the taxpayer's regular method of record keeping is used for income tax purposes.[16] The taxing authorities do not require uniformity among all taxpayers. They do require that the method used clearly reflect income and that items be handled consistently.[17] The most common methods of accounting are the cash method and the accrual method.

Throughout the portions of the Code dealing with deductions, the phrase "paid or incurred" is used. *Paid* refers to the cash basis taxpayer who gets a deduction only in the year of payment. *Incurred* concerns the accrual basis taxpayer who obtains the deduction in the year in which the liability for the expense becomes certain (refer to Chapter 4).

CASH METHOD REQUIREMENTS

The expenses of cash basis taxpayers are deductible only when they are actually paid with cash or other property. Promising to pay or issuing a note does not satisfy the actually paid requirement.[18] However, the payment can be made with borrowed funds. At the time taxpayers charge expenses on their credit cards, they

---

[16]§ 446(a).
[17]§§ 446(b) and (e); Reg. § 1.446–1(a)(2).

[18]*Page v. Rhode Island Trust Co., Exr.,* 37–1 USTC ¶9138, 19 AFTR 105, 88 F.2d 192 (CA–1, 1937).

▼ **FIGURE 6–1**
Format of Form 1040

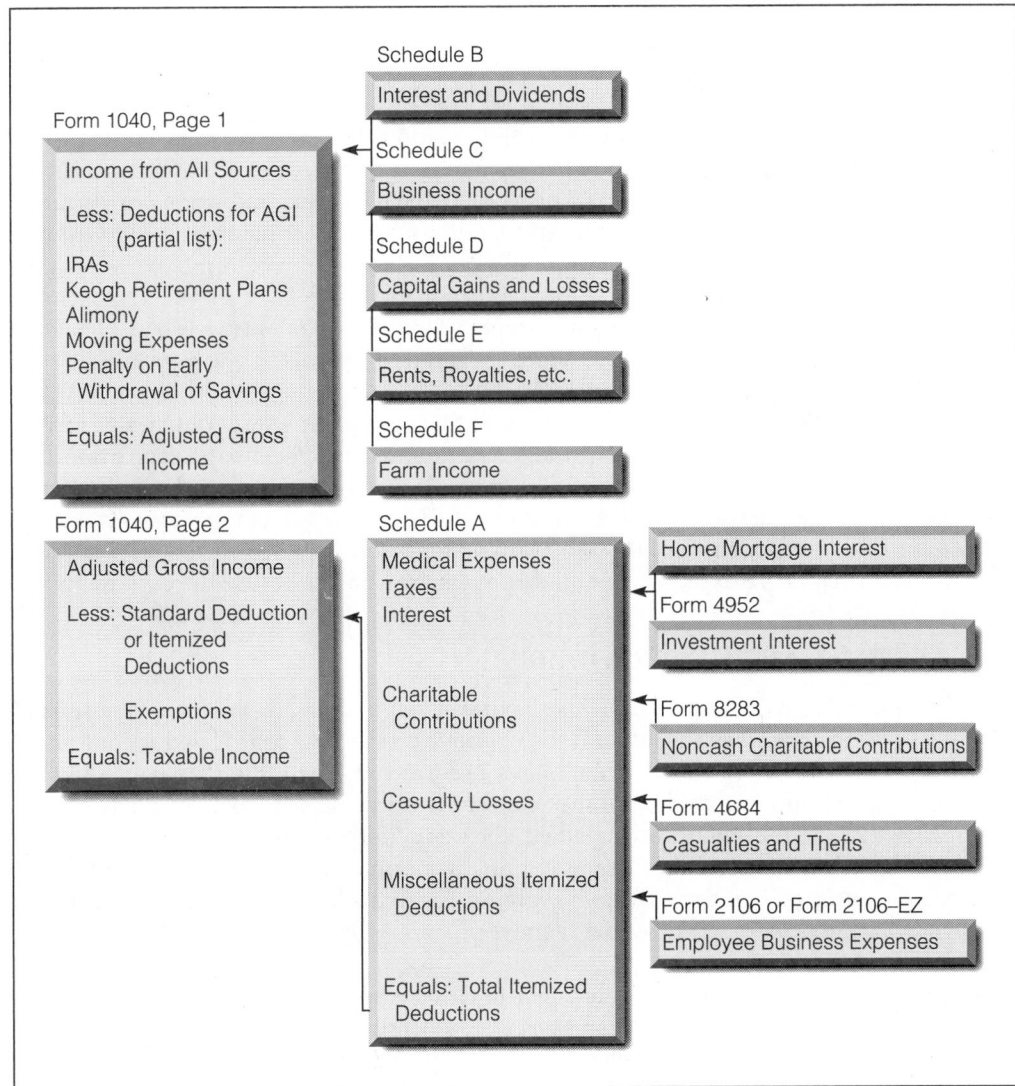

are allowed to claim the deduction. They are deemed to have simultaneously borrowed money from the credit card issuer and constructively paid the expenses.[19]

Although the cash basis taxpayer must have actually or constructively paid the expense, payment does not assure a current deduction. Cash basis and accrual basis taxpayers cannot take a current deduction for capital expenditures except through amortization, depletion, or depreciation over the life (actual or statutory) of the asset. The Regulations set forth the general rule that an expenditure that creates an asset having a useful life that extends substantially beyond the end of the tax year must be capitalized.[20]

[19]Rev.Rul. 78–39, 1978–1 C.B. 73. See also Rev.Rul. 80–335, 1980–2 C.B. 170, which applies to pay-by-phone arrangements.

[20]Reg. § 1.461–1(a).

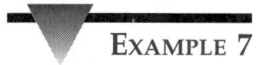

EXAMPLE 7

John, a cash basis taxpayer, rents property from Carl. On July 1, 1998, John paid $2,400 rent for the 24 months ending June 30, 2000. The prepaid rent extends 18 months after the close of the tax year—substantially beyond the year of payment. Therefore, John must capitalize the prepaid rent and amortize the expense on a monthly basis. His deduction for 1998 is $600. ▼

The Tax Court and the IRS took the position that an asset that will expire or be consumed by the end of the tax year following the year of payment must be prorated. The Ninth Court of Appeals held that such expenditures are currently deductible, however, and the Supreme Court apparently concurs (the one-year rule for prepaid expenses).[21]

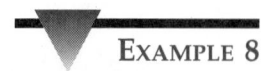

EXAMPLE 8

Assume the same facts as in Example 7 except that John was required to pay only 12 months' rent in 1998. He paid $1,200 on July 1, 1998. The entire $1,200 would be deductible in 1998. ▼

The payment must be required, not a voluntary prepayment, to obtain the current deduction under the one-year rule.[22] The taxpayer must also demonstrate that allowing the current deduction will not result in a material distortion of income. Generally, the deduction will be allowed if the item is recurring or was made for a business purpose rather than to manipulate income.[23]

As Chapter 18 explains, not all taxpayers are allowed to use the cash method.[24]

ACCRUAL METHOD REQUIREMENTS

The period in which an accrual basis taxpayer can deduct an expense is determined by applying the *all events test* and the *economic performance test*. A deduction cannot be claimed until (1) all the events have occurred to create the taxpayer's liability and (2) the amount of the liability can be determined with reasonable accuracy. Once these requirements are satisfied, the deduction is permitted only if economic performance has occurred. The economic performance test is met only when the service, property, or use of property giving rise to the liability is actually performed for, provided to, or used by the taxpayer.[25]

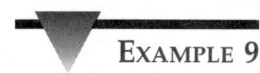

EXAMPLE 9

On December 22, 1998, Chris's entertainment business sponsored a jazz festival in a rented auditorium at a local college. His business is responsible for cleaning up the auditorium after the festival and for reinstalling seats that were removed so more people could attend the festival. Since the college is closed over the Christmas holidays, the company hired by Chris to perform the work did not begin these activities until January 2, 1999. The cost to Chris is $1,200. Chris cannot deduct the $1,200 until 1999, when the services are performed. ▼

An exception to the economic performance requirements allows certain *recurring items* to be deducted if the following conditions are met:

- The item is recurring in nature and is treated consistently by the taxpayer.
- Either the accrued item is not material, or accruing it results in better matching of income and expenses.

---

[21]*Zaninovich v. Comm.,* 80–1 USTC ¶9342, 45 AFTR2d 80–1442, 616 F.2d 429 (CA–9, 1980), *rev'g* 69 T.C. 605 (1978). Cited by the Supreme Court in *Hillsboro National Bank v. Comm.,* 83–1 USTC ¶9229, 51 AFTR2d 83–874, 103 S.Ct. 1134 (USSC, 1983).

[22]*Bonaire Development Co. v. Comm.,* 82–2 USTC ¶9428, 50 AFTR2d 82–5167, 679 F.2d 159 (CA–9, 1982).

[23]*Keller v. Comm.,* 84–1 USTC ¶9194, 53 AFTR2d 84–663, 725 F.2d 1173 (CA–8, 1984), *aff'g* 79 T.C. 7 (1982).

[24]§ 448.

[25]§ 461(h).

- All the events have occurred that determine the fact of the liability, and the amount of the liability can be determined with reasonable accuracy.
- Economic performance occurs within a reasonable period (but not later than 8½ months after the close of the taxable year).[26]

EXAMPLE 10

Rick, an accrual basis, calendar year taxpayer, entered into a monthly maintenance contract during the year. He makes a monthly accrual at the end of every month for this service and pays the fee sometime between the first and fifteenth of the following month when services are performed. The amount involved is immaterial, and all the other tests are met. The December 1998 accrual is deductible even though the service is performed on January 12, 1999. ▼

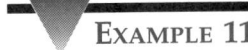

EXAMPLE 11

Rita, an accrual basis, calendar year taxpayer, shipped merchandise sold on December 30, 1998, via Greyhound Van Lines on January 2, 1999, and paid the freight charges at that time. Since Rita reported the sale of the merchandise in 1998, the shipping charge should also be deductible in 1998. This procedure results in a better matching of income and expenses. ▼

Reserves for estimated expenses (frequently employed for financial accounting purposes) generally are not allowed for tax purposes because the economic performance test cannot be satisfied.

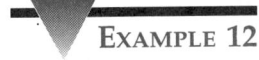

EXAMPLE 12

Blackbird Airlines is required by Federal law to test its engines after 3,000 flying hours. Aircraft cannot return to flight until the tests have been conducted. An unrelated aircraft maintenance company does all of the company's tests for $1,500 per engine. For financial reporting purposes, the company accrues an expense based upon $.50 per hour of flight and credits an allowance account. The actual amounts paid for maintenance are offset against the allowance account. For tax purposes, the economic performance test is not satisfied until the work has been done. Therefore, the reserve method cannot be used for tax purposes. ▼

DISALLOWANCE POSSIBILITIES

3 **LEARNING OBJECTIVE**
Apply the Internal Revenue Code deduction disallowance provisions associated with the following: public policy limitations, political activities, excessive executive compensation, investigation of business opportunities, hobby losses, vacation home rentals, payment of others' expenses, personal expenditures, capital expenditures, related-party transactions, and expenses related to tax-exempt income.

The tax law provides for the disallowance of certain types of expenses. Without specific restrictions in the tax law, taxpayers might attempt to deduct certain items that in reality are personal expenditures. For example, specific tax rules are provided to determine whether an expenditure is for trade or business purposes or related to a personal hobby.

Certain disallowance provisions are a codification or extension of prior court decisions. After the courts denied deductions for payments considered to be in violation of public policy, the tax law was changed to provide specific authority for the disallowance of these deductions. Discussions of specific disallowance provisions in the tax law follow.

PUBLIC POLICY LIMITATION

Justification for Denying Deductions.
The courts developed the principle that a payment that is in violation of public policy is not a necessary expense and

---
[26]§ 461(h)(3)(A).

is not deductible.[27] Although a bribe or fine may be appropriate, helpful, and even contribute to the profitability of an activity, the courts held that to allow such expenses would frustrate clearly defined public policy. A deduction would dilute the effect of the penalty since the government would be indirectly subsidizing a taxpayer's wrongdoing.

Accordingly, the IRS was free to restrict deductions if, in its view, the expenses were contrary to public policy. But since the law did not explain which actions violated public policy, taxpayers often had to go to court to determine whether or not their expense fell into this category.

Furthermore, the public policy doctrine could be arbitrarily applied in cases where no clear definition had emerged. To solve these problems, Congress enacted legislation that attempts to limit the use of the doctrine. Under the legislation, deductions are disallowed for certain specific types of expenditures that are considered contrary to public policy:

- Bribes and kickbacks including those associated with Medicare or Medicaid (in the case of foreign bribes and kickbacks, only if the payments violate the U.S. Foreign Corrupt Practices Act of 1977).
- Fines and penalties paid to a government for violation of law.

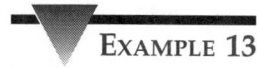

EXAMPLE 13

Brown Corporation, a moving company, consistently loads its trucks with weights in excess of the limits allowed by state law. The additional revenue more than offsets the fines levied. The fines are for a violation of public policy and are not deductible. ▼

- Two-thirds of the treble damage payments made to claimants resulting from violation of the antitrust law.[28]

To be disallowed, the bribe or kickback must be illegal under either Federal or state law and must also subject the payer to a criminal penalty or the loss of license or privilege to engage in a trade or business. For a bribe or kickback that is illegal under state law, a deduction is denied only if the state law is generally enforced.

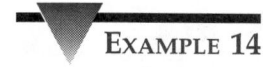

EXAMPLE 14

During the year, Keith, an insurance salesman, paid $5,000 to Karen, a real estate broker. The payment represented 20% of the commissions Keith earned from customers referred by Karen. Under state law, the splitting of commissions by an insurance salesperson is an act of misconduct that could warrant a revocation of the salesperson's license. Keith's $5,000 payments to Karen are not deductible provided the state law is generally enforced. ▼

ETHICAL CONSIDERATIONS

To Obey the Law

Clyde owns a trucking firm that operates in the Mid-Atlantic states. One of his major customers frequently ships goods between Charlotte and Baltimore. Occasionally, the customer sends last-minute shipments that are outbound for Europe on a freighter sailing from Baltimore. To satisfy the delivery schedule in these cases, Clyde's drivers must substantially exceed the speed limit. Clyde's business pays for any related speeding tickets. Twice within the past year, drivers have had their license suspended for 30 days for driving at such excessive speeds. Clyde's firm continues to pay the driver's salary during such suspension periods.

---

[27]*Tank Truck Rentals, Inc. v. Comm.,* 58–1 USTC ¶9366, 1 AFTR2d 1154, 78 S.Ct. 507 (USSC, 1958).

[28]§§ 162(c), (f), and (g).

Clyde believes that it is necessary to conduct his business in this manner if it is to be profitable, maintain the support of his drivers, and maintain the goodwill of his customers. Evaluate Clyde's business practices.

Legal Expenses Incurred in Defense of Civil or Criminal Penalties. To deduct legal expenses, the taxpayer must be able to show that the origin and character of the claim are directly related to a trade or business, an income-producing activity, or the determination, collection, or refund of a tax. Personal legal expenses are not deductible. Thus, legal fees incurred in connection with a criminal defense are deductible only if the crime is associated with the taxpayer's trade or business or income-producing activity.[29]

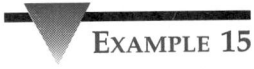

EXAMPLE 15

Debra, a financial officer of Blue Corporation, incurred legal expenses in connection with her defense in a criminal indictment for evasion of Blue's income taxes. Debra may deduct her legal expenses because she is deemed to be in the trade or business of being an executive. The legal action impairs her ability to conduct this business activity.[30] ▼

Deductible legal expenses associated with the following are deductible *for* AGI:

- Ordinary and necessary expenses incurred in connection with a trade or business.
- Ordinary and necessary expenses incurred in conjunction with rental or royalty property held for the production of income.

All other deductible legal expenses are deductible *from* AGI. For example, legal expenses generally are deductible *from* AGI if they are for fees for tax advice relative to the preparation of an individual's income tax return. Contrast this with the deduction *for* classification of legal fees for tax advice relative to the preparation of the portion of the tax return for a sole proprietor's trade or business (Schedule C) or an individual's rental or royalty income (Schedule E).

Expenses Relating to an Illegal Business. The usual expenses of operating an illegal business (e.g., a numbers racket) are deductible.[31] However, § 162 disallows a deduction for fines, bribes to public officials, illegal kickbacks, and other illegal payments.

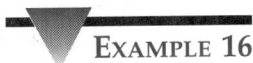

EXAMPLE 16

Sam owns and operates an illegal gambling establishment. In connection with this activity, he had the following expenses during the year:

Rent	$ 60,000
Payoffs to the police	40,000
Depreciation on equipment	100,000
Wages	140,000
Interest	30,000
Criminal fines	50,000
Illegal kickbacks	10,000
Total	$430,000

---

[29]*Comm. v. Tellier*, 66–1 USTC ¶9319, 17 AFTR2d 633, 86 S.Ct. 1118 (USSC, 1966).
[30]Rev.Rul. 68–662, 1968–2 C.B. 69.

[31]*Comm. v. Sullivan*, 58–1 USTC ¶9368, 1 AFTR2d 1158, 78 S.Ct. 512 (USSC, 1958).

All of the usual expenses (rent, depreciation, wages, and interest) are deductible; payoffs, fines, and kickbacks are not deductible. Of the $430,000 spent, $330,000 is deductible and $100,000 is not. ▼

An exception applies to expenses incurred in illegal trafficking in drugs.[32] *Drug dealers* are not allowed a deduction for ordinary and necessary business expenses incurred in their business. In arriving at gross income from the business, however, dealers may reduce total sales by the cost of goods sold.[33] In this regard, no distinction is made between legal and illegal businesses in calculating gross income. Treating cost of goods sold as a negative income item rather than as a deduction item produces the unseemly result that a drug dealer's taxable income is reduced by cost of goods sold.

POLITICAL CONTRIBUTIONS AND LOBBYING ACTIVITIES

Political Contributions.   Generally, no business deduction is permitted for direct or indirect payments for political purposes.[34] Historically, the government has been reluctant to accord favorable tax treatment to business expenditures for political purposes. Allowing deductions might encourage abuses and enable businesses to have undue influence upon the political process.

Lobbying Expenditures.   Lobbying expenses incurred in attempting to influence state or Federal legislation or the actions of certain high-ranking public officials (e.g., the President, Vice President, cabinet-level officials, and the two most senior officials in each agency of the executive branch) are not deductible.[35] The disallowance also applies to a pro rata portion of the membership dues of trade associations and other groups that are used for lobbying activities.

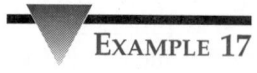

EXAMPLE 17   Egret Company pays a $10,000 annual membership fee to the Free Trade Group, a trade association for plumbing wholesalers. The trade association estimates that 70% of its dues are allocated to lobbying activities. Thus, Egret Company's deduction is limited to $3,000 ($10,000 × 30%). ▼

There are three exceptions to the disallowance of lobbying expenses. An exception is provided for influencing local legislation (e.g., city and county governments). Second, the disallowance provision does not apply to activities devoted solely to monitoring legislation. Third, a *de minimis* exception is provided for annual in-house expenditures (lobbying expenses other than those paid to professional lobbyists or any portion of dues used by associations for lobbying) if such expenditures do not exceed $2,000. If the in-house expenditures exceed $2,000, none of the in-house expenditures can be deducted.

EXCESSIVE EXECUTIVE COMPENSATION

The deduction of executive compensation is subject to two limitations. As discussed earlier in this chapter, the compensation of shareholder-employees of closely held corporations is subject to the reasonableness requirement. The second limitation, the

---

[32]§ 280E.

[33]Reg. § 1.61–3(a). Gross income is defined as sales minus cost of goods sold. Thus, while § 280E prohibits any deductions for drug dealers, it does not modify the normal definition of gross income.

[34]§ 276.

[35]§ 162(e).

so-called millionaires provision, applies to publicly held corporations (a corporation that has at least one class of stock registered under the Securities Act of 1934).[36]

The millionaires provision does not limit the amount of compensation that can be paid to an employee. Instead, it limits the amount the employer can deduct for the compensation of a covered executive to $1 million annually. Covered employees include the chief executive officer and the four other most highly compensated officers.

Employee compensation *excludes* the following:

- Commissions based on individual performance.
- Certain performance-based compensation based on company performance according to a formula approved by a board of directors compensation committee (comprised solely of two or more outside directors) and by shareholder vote. The performance attainment must be certified by this compensation committee.
- Payments to tax-qualified retirement plans.
- Payments that are excludible from the employees' gross income (e.g., certain fringe benefits).

INVESTIGATION OF A BUSINESS

Investigation expenses are expenses paid or incurred to determine the feasibility of entering a new business or expanding an existing business. They include such costs as travel, engineering and architectural surveys, marketing reports, and various legal and accounting services. How such expenses are treated for tax purposes depends on a number of variables, including the following:

- The current business, if any, of the taxpayer.
- The nature of the business being investigated.
- The extent to which the investigation has proceeded.
- Whether or not the acquisition actually takes place.

If the taxpayer is in a business the *same as or similar to* that being investigated, all investigation expenses are deductible in the year paid or incurred. The tax result is the same whether or not the taxpayer acquires the business being investigated.[37]

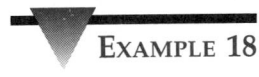

EXAMPLE 18

Terry, an accrual basis sole proprietor, owns and operates three motels in Georgia. In the current year, Terry incurs expenses of $8,500 in investigating the possibility of acquiring several additional motels located in South Carolina. The $8,500 is deductible in the current year whether or not Terry acquires the motels in South Carolina. ▼

When the taxpayer is *not* in a business that is the same as or similar to the one being investigated, the tax result depends on whether the new business is acquired. If the business is not acquired, all investigation expenses generally are nondeductible.[38]

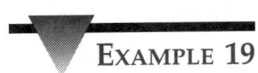

EXAMPLE 19

Lynn, a retired merchant, incurs expenses in traveling from Rochester, New York, to California to investigate the feasibility of acquiring several auto care centers. If no acquisition takes place, none of the expenses are deductible. ▼

---

[36]§ 162(m).

[37]§ 195. *York v. Comm.*, 58–2 USTC ¶9952, 2 AFTR2d 6178, 261 F.2d 421 (CA–4, 1958).

[38]Rev.Rul. 57–418, 1957–2 C.B. 143; *Morton Frank*, 20 T.C. 511 (1953); and *Dwight A. Ward*, 20 T.C. 332 (1953).

If the taxpayer is *not* in a business that is the same as or similar to the one being investigated and actually acquires the new business, the expenses must be capitalized. At the election of the taxpayer, the expenses may be amortized over a period of 60 months or more, beginning with the month in which the business is started.[39]

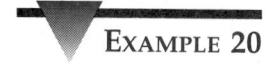

EXAMPLE 20

Tina owns and operates 10 restaurants located in various cities throughout the Southeast. She travels to Atlanta to discuss the acquisition of an auto dealership. In addition, she incurs legal and accounting costs associated with the potential acquisition. After incurring total investigation costs of $12,000, she acquires the auto dealership on October 1, 1998.

Tina must capitalize the $12,000 of investigation expenses for the auto dealership. If she elects to amortize the expenses over 60 months, she can deduct $600 ($12,000 × 3/60) in 1998. ▼

HOBBY LOSSES

Business or investment expenses are deductible only if the taxpayer can show that the activity was entered into for the purpose of making a profit. Certain activities may have either profit-seeking or personal attributes, depending upon individual circumstances. Examples include raising horses and operating a farm used as a weekend residence. While personal losses are not deductible, losses attributable to profit-seeking activities may be deducted and used to offset a taxpayer's other income. For this reason, the tax law limits the deductibility of **hobby losses.**

General Rules. If an individual can show that an activity has been conducted with the intent to earn a profit, losses from the activity are fully deductible. The hobby loss rules apply only if the activity is not engaged in for profit. Hobby expenses are deductible only to the extent of hobby income.[40]

The Regulations stipulate that the following nine factors should be considered in determining whether an activity is profit-seeking or a hobby:[41]

- Whether the activity is conducted in a businesslike manner.
- The expertise of the taxpayers or their advisers.
- The time and effort expended.
- The expectation that the assets of the activity will appreciate in value.
- The taxpayer's previous success in conducting similar activities.
- The history of income or losses from the activity.
- The relationship of profits earned to losses incurred.
- The financial status of the taxpayer (e.g., if the taxpayer does not have substantial amounts of other income, this may indicate that the activity is engaged in for profit).
- Elements of personal pleasure or recreation in the activity.

The presence or absence of a factor is not by itself determinative of whether the activity is profit-seeking or a hobby. Rather, the decision is a subjective one that is based on an analysis of the facts and circumstances.

Presumptive Rule of § 183. The Code provides a rebuttable presumption that an activity is profit-seeking if the activity shows a profit in at least three of any five prior consecutive years.[42] If the activity involves horses, a profit in at least two of seven consecutive years meets the presumptive rule. If these

---

[39]§ 195.
[40]§ 183(b)(2).

[41]Reg. §§ 1.183–2(b)(1) through (9).
[42]§ 183(d).

profitability tests are met, the activity is presumed to be a trade or business rather than a personal hobby. In this situation, the IRS bears the burden of proving that the activity is personal rather than trade or business related.

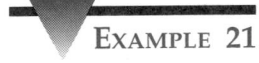

EXAMPLE 21

Camille, an executive for a large corporation, is paid a salary of $200,000. Her husband is a collector of antiques. Several years ago, he opened an antique shop in a local shopping center and spends most of his time buying and selling antiques. He occasionally earns a small profit from this activity but more frequently incurs substantial losses. If the losses are business related, they are fully deductible against Camille's salary income on a joint return. In resolving this issue, consider the following:

- Initially determine whether the antique activity has met the three-out-of-five years profit test.
- If the presumption is not met, the activity may nevertheless qualify as a business if the taxpayer can show that the intent is to engage in a profit-seeking activity. It is not necessary to show actual profits.
- Attempt to fit the operation within the nine criteria prescribed in the Regulations and listed above. These criteria are the factors considered in trying to rebut the § 183 presumption. ▼

Determining the Amount of the Deduction. If an activity is deemed to be a hobby, the expenses are deductible only to the extent of the gross income from the hobby. These expenses must be deducted in the following order:

- Amounts deductible under other Code sections without regard to the nature of the activity, such as property taxes and home mortgage interest.
- Amounts deductible under other Code sections if the activity had been engaged in for profit, but only if those amounts do not affect adjusted basis. Examples include maintenance, utilities, and supplies.
- Amounts that affect adjusted basis and would be deductible under other Code sections if the activity had been engaged in for profit.[43] Examples include depreciation, amortization, and depletion.

These deductions are deductible *from* AGI as itemized deductions to the extent they exceed 2 percent of AGI.[44] If the taxpayer uses the standard deduction rather than itemizing, all hobby loss deductions are wasted.

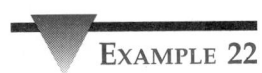

EXAMPLE 22

Jim, the vice president of an oil company, has AGI of $80,000. He decides to pursue painting in his spare time. He uses a home studio, comprising 10% of the home's square footage. During the current year, Jim incurs the following expenses:

Frames	$ 350
Art supplies	300
Fees paid to models	1,000
Home studio expenses:	
Total property taxes	900
Total home mortgage interest	10,000
Depreciation on 10% of home	500
Total home maintenance and utilities	3,600

---

[43]Reg. § 1.183–1(b)(1).

[44]Reg. § 1.67–1T(a)(1)(iv) and Rev.Rul. 75–14, 1975–1 C.B. 90.

During the year, Jim sold paintings for a total of $3,200. If the activity is held to be a hobby, Jim is allowed deductions as follows:

Gross income		$ 3,200
Deduct: Taxes and interest (10% of $10,900)		(1,090)
Remainder		$ 2,110
Deduct: Frames	$ 350	
Art supplies	300	
Models' fees	1,000	
Maintenance and utilities (10%)	360	(2,010)
Remainder		$ 100
Depreciation ($500, but limited to $100)		(100)
Net income		$ –0–

Jim includes the $3,200 of income in AGI, making his AGI $83,200. The taxes and interest are itemized deductions, deductible in full. The remaining $2,110 of expenses are reduced by 2% of his AGI ($1,664); so the net deduction is $446. Since the property taxes and home mortgage interest are deductible anyway, the net effect is a $2,754 ($3,200 less $446) increase in taxable income. ▼

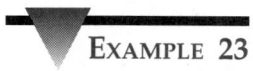

EXAMPLE 23   Assume that Jim's activity in Example 22 is held to be a business. The business is located in a small office building he owns. Expenses are property taxes of $90, mortgage interest of $1,000, frames of $350, art supplies of $300, models' fees of $1,000, maintenance and utilities of $360, and depreciation of $500. Under these circumstances, Jim could deduct expenses totaling $3,600. All these expenses would be trade or business expenses deductible *for* AGI. His reduction in AGI would be as follows:

Gross income		$ 3,200
Less: Taxes and interest	$ 1,090	
Other business expenses	2,010	
Depreciation	500	(3,600)
Reduction in AGI		($ 400)

▼

RENTAL OF VACATION HOMES

Restrictions on the deductions allowed for part-year rentals of personal **vacation homes** were written into the law to prevent taxpayers from deducting essentially personal expenses as rental losses. Many taxpayers who owned vacation homes had formerly treated the homes as rental property and generated rental losses as deductions *for* AGI. For example, a summer cabin would be rented for 2 months per year, used for vacationing for 1 month, and left vacant the rest of the year. The taxpayer would then deduct 11 months' depreciation, utilities, maintenance, etc., as rental expenses, resulting in a rental loss. Section 280A eliminates this treatment by allowing deductions on residences used primarily for personal purposes only to the extent of the income generated. Only a break-even situation is allowed; no losses can be deducted.

There are three possible tax treatments for residences used for both personal and rental purposes. The treatment depends upon the *relative time* the residence is used for personal purposes versus rental use.

TAX IN THE NEWS

IS A DREAM HOME IN THE MOUNTAINS OR AT THE BEACH FOR YOU?

Most of us have dreamed of having a second home in the mountains or at the beach. The general attitude is that we deserve a second home and that it would be a healthy environment for the kids. Then we encounter the reality of paying for it.

One frequently prescribed technique is to rent a vacation home to others when you are not using it. Supposedly, the second home will generate rent income to use for the mortgage payments and deductions (e.g., mortgage interest and property taxes) on your income tax return, while providing a vacation getaway.

Unfortunately, the dream can become a nightmare. More than likely, the vacation home will be subject to both the § 280A limitation on deducting expenses in excess of rent income and the § 469 passive activity loss provision (see Chapter 11). To make matters worse, the vacation home is unlikely to be self-sustaining (i.e., cash inflows including tax benefits do not at least equal cash outflows). Therefore, those who view the vacation home as a cool investment are likely to be disappointed.

Thomas Ochsenschlanger, a partner in the Washington office of Grant Thornton, recommends discussing the financial aspects of a vacation home with your accountant *before* buying the property.

SOURCE: Adapted from Scott R. Schmedel, "Dream Second Home Can Be a Tax-Return Nightmare," *Wall Street Journal*, March 8, 1996, pp. C1 and C15.

Primarily Personal Use. If the residence is *rented* for *fewer than 15 days* in a year, it is treated as a personal residence. The rent income is excluded from gross income, and mortgage interest and real estate taxes are allowed as itemized deductions, as with any personal residence.[45] No other expenses (e.g., depreciation, utilities, maintenance) are deductible. Although this provision exists primarily for administrative convenience, several bills have been introduced in Congress, including one in 1997, that would have repealed this exclusion from gross income.

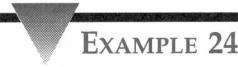
EXAMPLE 24

Dixie owns a vacation cottage on the lake. During the current year, she rented it for $1,600 for two weeks, lived in it two months, and left it vacant the remainder of the year. The year's expenses amounted to $6,000 mortgage interest expense, $500 property taxes, $1,500 utilities and maintenance, and $2,400 depreciation. Since the property was not rented for at least 15 days, the income is excluded, the mortgage interest and property tax expenses are itemized deductions, and the remaining expenses are nondeductible personal expenses. ▼

Primarily Rental Use. If the residence is *rented* for 15 days or more in a year and is *not used* for personal purposes for more than the greater of (1) 14 days or (2) 10 percent of the total days rented, the residence is treated as rental property.[46] The expenses must be allocated between personal and rental days if there are any personal use days during the year. The deduction of the expenses allocated to rental days can exceed rent income and result in a rental loss. The loss may be deductible under the passive activity loss rules (discussed in Chapter 11).

---

[45]§ 280A(g).   [46]§ 280A(d) and Prop.Reg. § 1.280A–3(c).

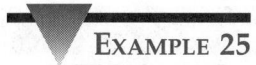

EXAMPLE 25

Assume instead that Dixie in Example 24 used the cottage for 12 days and rented it for 48 days for $4,800. Since she rented the cottage for 15 days or more but did not use it for more than 14 days, the cottage is treated as rental property. The expenses must be allocated between personal and rental days.

	Percentage of Use	
	Rental 80%	Personal 20%
Income	$ 4,800	$ –0–
Expenses		
Mortgage interest ($6,000)	($ 4,800)	($1,200)
Property taxes ($500)	(400)	(100)
Utilities and maintenance ($1,500)	(1,200)	(300)
Depreciation ($2,400)	(1,920)	(480)
Total expenses	($ 8,320)	($2,080)
Rental loss	($ 3,520)	$ –0–

Dixie deducts the $3,520 rental loss *for* AGI (assuming she meets the passive activity loss rules, discussed in Chapter 11). She also has an itemized deduction for property taxes of $100 associated with the personal use. The mortgage interest of $1,200 associated with the personal use is not deductible as an itemized deduction because the cottage is not a qualified residence (qualified residence interest) for this purpose (see Chapter 10). The portion of utilities and maintenance and depreciation attributable to personal use is not deductible. ▼

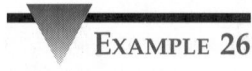

EXAMPLE 26

Assume instead that Dixie in Example 24 rented the cottage for 200 days and lived in it for 19 days. The cottage is primarily rental use since she rented it for 15 days or more and did not use it for personal purposes for more than 20 days (10% of the rental days). The expenses must be allocated between personal and rental days as illustrated in Example 25. ▼

Personal/Rental Use.   If the residence is rented for 15 days or more in a year *and* is used for personal purposes for more than the greater of (1) 14 days or (2) 10 percent of the total days rented, it is treated as a personal/rental use residence. The expenses must be allocated between personal days and rental days. Expenses are allowed only to the extent of rent income.

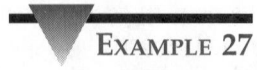

EXAMPLE 27

Assume instead that Dixie in Example 24 rented the property for 30 days and lived in it for 30 days. The residence is classified as personal/rental use property since she used it more than 14 days and rented it for 15 days or more. The expenses must be allocated between rental use and personal use, and the rental expenses are allowed only to the extent of rent income. ▼

If a residence is classified as personal/rental use property, the expenses that are deductible anyway (e.g., real estate taxes and mortgage interest) must be deducted first. If a positive net income results, otherwise nondeductible expenses that do not affect adjusted basis (e.g., maintenance, utilities, insurance) are allowed next. Finally, if any positive balance remains, depreciation is allowed.

Expenses must be allocated between personal and rental days before the limits are applied. The courts have held that real estate taxes and mortgage interest, which accrue ratably over the year, are allocated on the basis of 365 days.[47] The IRS, however, disagrees and allocates real estate taxes and mortgage interest on the basis of total days of use.[48] Other expenses (utilities, maintenance, depreciation, etc.) are allocated on the basis of total days used.

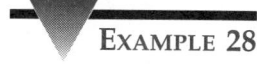

EXAMPLE 28

Jason rents his vacation home for 60 days and lives in the home for 30 days. The limitations on personal/rental use residences apply. Jason's gross rent income is $10,000. For the entire year (not a leap year), the real estate taxes are $2,190; his mortgage interest expense is $10,220; utilities and maintenance expense equals $2,400; and depreciation is $9,000. Using the IRS approach, these amounts are deductible in this specific order:

Gross income	$ 10,000
Deduct: Taxes and interest ($^{60}\!/\!_{90}$ × $12,410)	(8,273)
Remainder to apply to rental operating expenses and depreciation	$ 1,727
Deduct: Utilities and maintenance ($^{60}\!/\!_{90}$ × $2,400)	(1,600)
Balance	$ 127
Deduct: Depreciation ($^{60}\!/\!_{90}$ × $9,000 = $6,000 but limited to above balance)	(127)
Net rent income	$ –0–

The nonrental use portion of real estate taxes and mortgage interest ($4,137 in this case) is deductible if the taxpayer elects to itemize (see Chapter 10). The personal use portion of utilities, maintenance, and depreciation is not deductible in any case. Also note that the basis of the property is not reduced by the $5,873 depreciation not allowed ($6,000 – $127) because of the above limitation. (See Chapter 14 for a discussion of the reduction in basis for depreciation allowed or allowable.) ▼

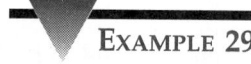

EXAMPLE 29

Using the court's approach in allocating real estate taxes and mortgage interest, Jason, in Example 28, would have this result:

Gross income	$ 10,000
Deduct: Taxes and interest ($^{60}\!/\!_{365}$ × $12,410)	(2,040)
Remainder to apply to rental operating expenses and depreciation	$ 7,960
Deduct: Utilities and maintenance ($^{60}\!/\!_{90}$ × $2,400)	(1,600)
Balance	$ 6,360
Deduct: Depreciation ($^{60}\!/\!_{90}$ × $9,000, but limited to $6,360)	(6,000)
Net rent income	$ 360

Jason can deduct $10,370 ($12,410 paid – $2,040 deducted as expense in computing net rent income) of personal use mortgage interest and real estate taxes as itemized deductions. ▼

Note the contrasting results in Examples 28 and 29. The IRS's approach (Example 28) results in no rental gain or loss and an itemized deduction for real estate taxes and mortgage interest of $4,137. In Example 29, Jason has net rent income of $360 and $10,370 of itemized deductions. The court's approach decreases his taxable income by $10,010 ($10,370 itemized deductions less $360 net rent income). The IRS's approach reduces his taxable income by only $4,137.

---

[47]*Bolton v. Comm.*, 82–2 USTC ¶9699, 51 AFTR2d 83–305, 694 F.2d 556 (CA–9, 1982).

[48]Prop.Reg. § 1.280A–3(d)(4).

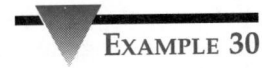

EXAMPLE 30

Assume instead that Jason in Example 28 had not lived in the home at all during the year. The house is rental property. The rental loss is calculated as follows:

Gross income	$ 10,000
Expenses	
Taxes and interest	($ 12,410)
Utilities and maintenance	(2,400)
Depreciation	(9,000)
Total expenses	($ 23,810)
Rental loss	($ 13,810)

Whether any of the rental loss would be deductible depends upon whether Jason actively participated in the rental activity and met the other requirements for passive activity losses (discussed in Chapter 11). ▼

Conversion to Rental Property.   A related issue is whether or not a taxpayer's *primary residence* is subject to the preceding rules if it is converted to rental property. If the vacation home rules apply, a taxpayer who converts a personal residence to rental property during the tax year, without any tax avoidance motive, could have the allowable deductions limited to the rent income. This would occur if the personal use exceeded the greater of 14 days or 10 percent of rental days test (a likely situation). The Code, however, provides that during a *qualified rental period*, any personal use days are not counted as personal use days in terms of classifying the use of the residence as *personal/rental use* rather than as *primarily rental use*.[49] In effect, the deduction for expenses of the property incurred during a qualified rental period is not subject to the personal use test of the vacation home rules. A qualified rental period is a consecutive period of 12 or more months. The period begins or ends in the taxable year in which the residence is rented or held for rental at a fair price. The residence must not be rented to a related party. If the property is sold before the 12-month period expires, the qualified rental period is the actual time rented.

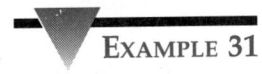

EXAMPLE 31

Rhonda converts her residence to rental property on May 1 and rents it for the remainder of 1998 for $5,600 and for all of 1999 for $8,400. The house would be classified as personal/rental use property (personal use days during 1998 are greater than both 14 days and 10% of rental days) except that this is a qualified rental period. Therefore, Rhonda's deduction for rental expenses is not limited to the gross income of $5,600 in 1998. ▼

See Concept Summary 6–1 for a summary of the vacation home rules.

EXPENDITURES INCURRED FOR TAXPAYER'S BENEFIT OR TAXPAYER'S OBLIGATION

An expense must be incurred for the taxpayer's benefit or arise from the taxpayer's obligation. An individual cannot claim a tax deduction for the payment of the expenses of another individual.

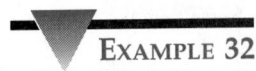

EXAMPLE 32

During the current year, Fred pays the interest on his son, Vern's, home mortgage. Neither Fred nor Vern can take a deduction for the interest paid. Fred is not entitled to a deduction because the mortgage is not his obligation. Vern cannot claim a deduction because he did

---

[49]§ 280A(d).

CONCEPT SUMMARY 6–1

Vacation/Rental Home

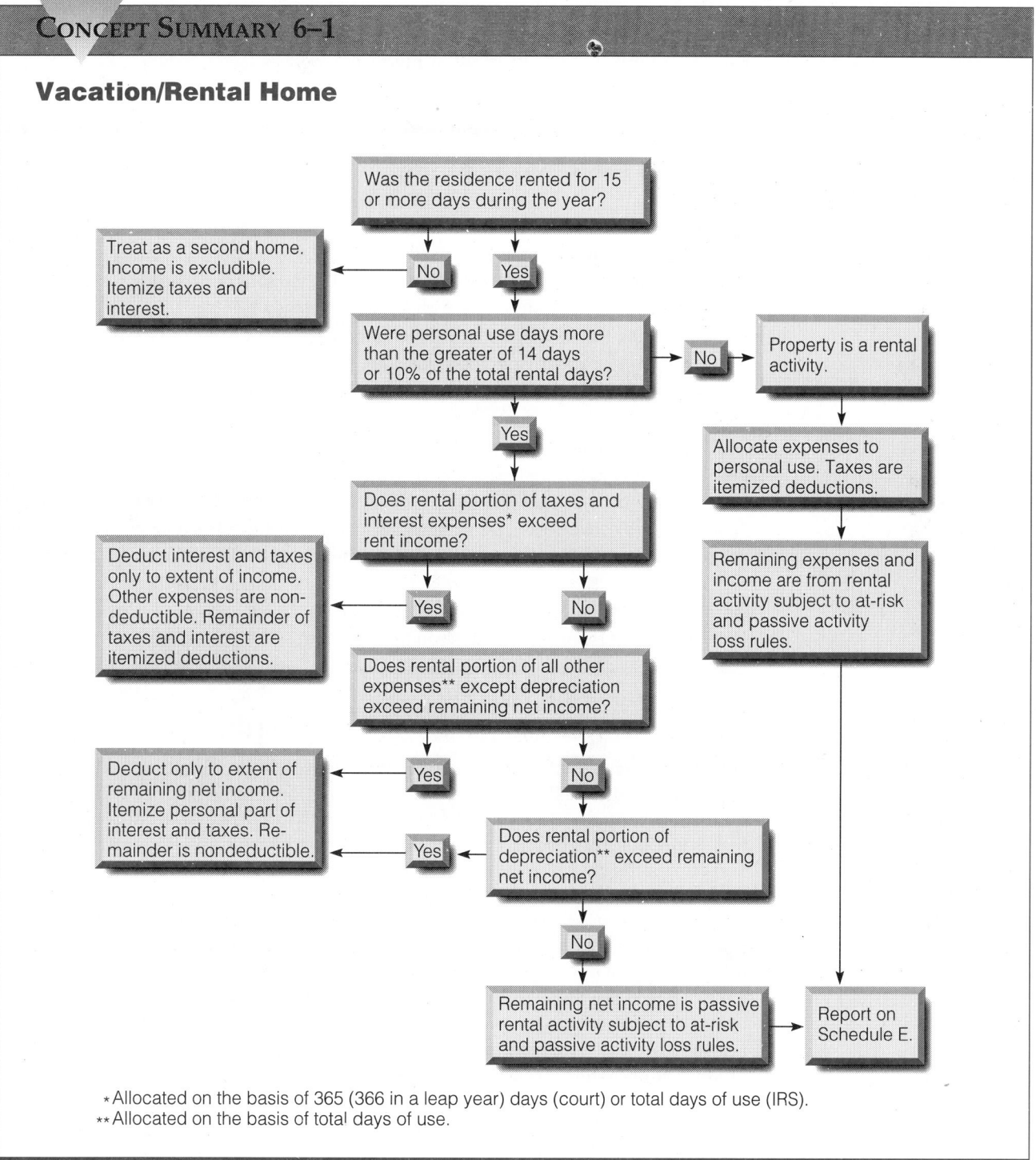

*Allocated on the basis of 365 (366 in a leap year) days (court) or total days of use (IRS).
**Allocated on the basis of total days of use.

not pay the interest. The tax result would have been more favorable had Fred made a cash gift to Vern and let him pay the interest. Then Vern could have deducted the interest, and Fred might not have been liable for any gift taxes depending upon the amount involved. A deduction would have been created with no cash difference to the family. ▼

One exception to this disallowance rule is the payment of medical expenses for a dependent. Such expenses are deductible by the payer subject to the normal rules that limit the deductibility of medical expenses (see Chapter 10).[50]

How the Payment Is Made

Dan and Jeff both have sons who graduated from college recently and are employed by the same company in a rural community where rental housing is not readily available. Each father lends his son $10,000; the sons combine their resources and use the $20,000 as a down payment on a house that they buy together.

During 1998, the sons make all the mortgage payments on their house until December when they are furloughed from their jobs. Dan gives his son $900 to use to pay his share of the mortgage payment, and Jeff pays $900 directly to the mortgage company for his son. In each of these $900 amounts, $800 represents interest on the mortgage.

Over lunch recently, Dan and Jeff were discussing their sons' real estate investment and the $900 mortgage payment each father had funded. Jeff indicated that since he had paid the mortgage payment directly, he was going to deduct the $800 of interest on his Form 1040. After this conversation, Dan concludes that, in substance, he and Jeff have done the same thing. Accordingly, Dan calls his son and tells him that he wants to deduct the $800 on his tax return. Though Dan's son is not pleased, he agrees to permit his father to take the deduction and says he will not deduct the mortgage interest on his own return.

Evaluate the propriety of the position taken by Dan.

DISALLOWANCE OF PERSONAL EXPENDITURES

Section 262 states that "except as otherwise expressly provided in this chapter, no deduction shall be allowed for personal, living, or family expenses." To justify a deduction, an individual must be able to identify a particular section of the Code that sanctions the deduction (e.g., charitable contributions, medical expenses). Sometimes the character of a particular expenditure is not easily determined.

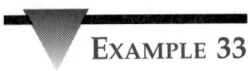

EXAMPLE 33

During the current year, Howard pays $1,500 in legal fees and court costs to obtain a divorce from his wife, Vera. Involved in the divorce action is a property settlement that concerns the disposition of income-producing property owned by Howard. In a similar situation, the Tax Court held that the taxpayer could not deduct any such costs.[51] "Although fees primarily related to property division concerning his income-producing property, they weren't ordinary and necessary expenses paid for conservation or maintenance of property held for production of income. Legal fees incurred in defending against claims that arise from a taxpayer's marital relationship aren't deductible expenses regardless of possible consequences on taxpayer's income-producing property." ▼

The IRS has clarified the issue of the deduction of legal fees incurred in connection with a divorce.[52] To be deductible, an expense must relate solely to tax advice in a divorce proceeding. For example, legal fees attributable to the determination of dependency exemptions of children are deductible if the fees are distinguishable

[50]§ 213(a).
[51]*Harry H. Goldberg*, 29 TCM 74, T.C.Memo. 1970–27.

[52]Rev.Rul. 72–545, 1972–2 C.B. 179.

from the general legal fees incurred in obtaining a divorce. Other examples are the costs of creating a trust to make periodic alimony payments and the determination of the tax consequences of a property settlement. Therefore, it is advisable to request an itemization of attorney's fees to substantiate a deduction for the tax-related amounts.

DISALLOWANCE OF DEDUCTIONS FOR CAPITAL EXPENDITURES

The Code specifically disallows a deduction for "any amount paid out for new buildings or for permanent improvements or betterments made to increase the value of any property or estate."[53] The Regulations further define capital expenditures to include those expenditures that add to the value or prolong the life of property or adapt the property to a new or different use.[54] Incidental repairs and maintenance of the property are not capital expenditures and can be deducted as ordinary and necessary business expenses. Repairing a roof is a deductible expense, but replacing a roof is a capital expenditure subject to depreciation deductions over its useful life. The tune-up of a delivery truck is an expense; a complete overhaul probably is a capital expenditure.

Capitalization versus Expense.   When an expenditure is capitalized rather than expensed, the deduction is at best deferred and at worst lost forever. Although an immediate tax benefit for a large cash expenditure is lost, the cost may be deductible in increments over a longer period of time.

If the expenditure is for a tangible asset that has an ascertainable life, it is capitalized and may be deducted as depreciation (or cost recovery) over the life of the asset (for depreciation) or over a statutory period (for cost recovery under either ACRS or MACRS).[55] Land is not subject to depreciation (or cost recovery) since it does not have an ascertainable life.

EXAMPLE 34   Stan purchased a prime piece of land located in an apartment-zoned area. Stan paid $500,000 for the property, which had an old but usable apartment building on it. He immediately had the building demolished at a cost of $100,000. The $500,000 purchase price and the $100,000 demolition costs must be capitalized, and the basis of the land is $600,000. Since land is a nondepreciable asset, no deduction is allowed. More favorable tax treatment might result if Stan rented the apartments in the old building for a period of time to attempt to establish that there was no intent to demolish the building. If Stan's attempt is successful, it might be possible to allocate a substantial portion of the original purchase price of the property to the building (a depreciable asset). When the building is later demolished, any remaining adjusted basis can be deducted as an ordinary (§ 1231) loss. (See Chapter 17 for a discussion of the treatment of § 1231 assets.) ▼

If the expenditure is for an intangible asset (e.g., copyright, patent, covenant not to compete, goodwill), the capitalized expenditure can be amortized, regardless of whether or not the intangible asset has an ascertainable life. Intangible assets, referred to as § 197 intangibles, are amortized over a 15-year statutory period using the straight-line method. See Chapter 8 for additional discussion of the amortization of intangibles.

---

[53]§ 263(a)(1).
[54]Reg. § 1.263(a)–1(b).

[55]See Chapter 8 for the discussion of depreciation and cost recovery.

TRANSACTIONS BETWEEN RELATED PARTIES

The Code places restrictions on the recognition of gains and losses from **related-party transactions.** Without these restrictions, relationships created by birth, marriage, and business would provide endless possibilities for engaging in financial transactions that produce tax savings with no real economic substance or change. For example, to create an artificial loss, a wife could sell investment property to her husband at a loss and deduct the loss on their joint return. Her husband could then hold the asset indefinitely, and the family would sustain no real economic loss. A complex set of laws has been designed to eliminate such possibilities.

Losses.   The Code provides for the disallowance of any "losses from sales or exchanges of property . . . directly or indirectly" between related parties.[56] When the property is subsequently sold to a nonrelated party, any gain recognized is reduced by the loss previously disallowed. Any disallowed loss not used by the related-party buyer to offset the recognized gain on a subsequent sale or exchange to an unrelated party is permanently lost.

EXAMPLE 35   Freida sells common stock with a basis of $1,000 to her son, Bill, for $800. Bill sells the stock several years later for $1,100. Freida's $200 loss is disallowed upon the sale to Bill, and only $100 of gain ($1,100 selling price – $800 basis – $200 disallowed loss) is taxable to him upon the subsequent sale. ▼

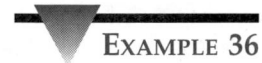

EXAMPLE 36   George sells common stock with a basis of $1,050 to his son, Ray, for $800. Ray sells the stock eight months later to an unrelated party for $900. Ray's gain of $100 ($900 selling price – $800 basis) is not recognized because of George's previously disallowed loss of $250. Note that the offset may result in only partial tax benefit upon the subsequent sale (as in this case). If the property had not been transferred to Ray, George could have recognized a $150 loss upon the subsequent sale to the unrelated party ($1,050 basis – $900 selling price). ▼

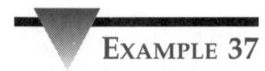

EXAMPLE 37   Pete sells common stock with a basis of $1,000 to an unrelated third party for $800. Pete's son repurchased the same stock in the market on the same day for $800. The $200 loss is not allowed because the transaction is an indirect sale between related parties.[57] ▼

Unpaid Expenses and Interest.   The law prevents related taxpayers from engaging in tax avoidance schemes where one related taxpayer uses the accrual method of accounting and the other uses the cash basis. An accrual basis, closely held corporation, for example, could borrow funds from a cash basis individual shareholder. At the end of the year, the corporation would accrue and deduct the interest, but the cash basis lender would not recognize interest income since no interest had been paid. Section 267 specifically defers the deduction of the accruing taxpayer until the recipient taxpayer must include it in income; that is, when it is actually paid to the cash basis taxpayer. This *matching* provision applies to interest as well as other expenses, such as salaries and bonuses.

This deduction deferral provision does not apply if both of the related taxpayers use the accrual method or both use the cash method. Likewise, it does not apply if the related party reporting income uses the accrual method and the related party taking the deduction uses the cash method.

---

[56]§ 267(a)(1).
[57]*McWilliams v. Comm.*, 47–1 USTC ¶9289, 35 AFTR 1184, 67 S.Ct. 1477 (USSC, 1947).

Relationships and Constructive Ownership. Section 267 operates to disallow losses and defer deductions only between related parties. Losses or deductions generated by similar transactions with an unrelated party are allowed. *Related parties* include the following:

- Brothers and sisters (whether whole, half, or adopted), spouse, ancestors (parents, grandparents), and lineal descendants (children, grandchildren) of the taxpayer.
- A corporation owned more than 50 percent (directly or indirectly) by the taxpayer.
- Two corporations that are members of a controlled group.
- A series of other complex relationships between trusts, corporations, and individual taxpayers.

Constructive ownership provisions are applied to determine whether the taxpayers are related. Under these provisions, stock owned by certain relatives or related entities is *deemed* to be owned by the taxpayer for purposes of applying the loss and expense deduction disallowance provisions. A taxpayer is deemed to own not only his or her stock but the stock owned by lineal descendants, ancestors, brothers and sisters or half-brothers and half-sisters, and spouse. The taxpayer is also deemed to own his or her proportionate share of stock owned by any partnership, corporation, estate, or trust of which he or she is a member. An individual is deemed to own any stock owned, directly or indirectly, by his or her partner. However, constructive ownership by an individual of the partnership's and the other partner's shares does not extend to the individual's spouse or other relatives (no double attribution).

EXAMPLE 38

The stock of Sparrow Corporation is owned 20% by Ted, 30% by Ted's father, 30% by Ted's mother, and 20% by Ted's sister. On July 1 of the current year, Ted loaned $10,000 to Sparrow Corporation at 8% annual interest, principal and interest payable on demand. For tax purposes, Sparrow uses the accrual basis, and Ted uses the cash basis. Both are on a calendar year. Since Ted is deemed to own the 80% owned by his parents and sister, he constructively owns 100% of Sparrow Corporation. If the corporation accrues the interest within the taxable year, no deduction can be taken until payment is made to Ted. ▼

SUBSTANTIATION REQUIREMENTS

The tax law is built on a voluntary system. Taxpayers file their tax returns, report income and take deductions to which they are entitled, and pay their taxes through withholding or estimated tax payments during the year. The taxpayer has the burden of proof for substantiating expenses deducted on the returns and must retain adequate records. Upon audit, the IRS will disallow any undocumented or unsubstantiated deductions. These requirements have resulted in numerous conflicts between taxpayers and the IRS.

Some events throughout the year should be documented as they occur. For example, it is generally advisable to receive a pledge payment statement from one's church, in addition to a canceled check (if available) for proper documentation of a charitable contribution.[58] In addition, for charitable contributions, a donor must obtain a receipt from the donee for contributions of $250 or more. Other types of deductible expenditures may require receipts or some other type of support.

---

[58]Rev.Proc. 92–71, 1992–2 C.B. 437, addresses circumstances where checks are not returned by a financial institution or where electronic transfers are made.

Specific and *more stringent* rules for deducting travel, entertainment, and gift expenses are discussed in Chapter 9. Certain mixed-use (both personal and business use) and listed property are also subject to the adequate records requirement (discussed in Chapter 8).

EXPENSES AND INTEREST RELATING TO TAX-EXEMPT INCOME

Certain income, such as interest on municipal bonds, is tax-exempt.[59] The law also allows the taxpayer to deduct expenses incurred for the production of income.[60] Deduction disallowance provisions, however, make it impossible to make money at the expense of the government by excluding interest income and deducting interest expense.[61]

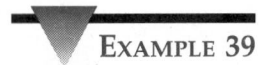

EXAMPLE 39

Sandy, a taxpayer in the 36% bracket, purchased $100,000 of 6% municipal bonds. At the same time, she used the bonds as collateral on a bank loan of $100,000 at 8% interest. A positive cash flow would result from the tax benefit as follows:

Cash paid out on loan	($8,000)
Cash received from bonds	6,000
Tax savings from deducting interest expense (36% of $8,000 interest expense)	2,880
Net positive cash flow	$ 880

To eliminate the possibility illustrated in Example 39, the Code specifically disallows as a deduction the expenses of producing tax-exempt income. Interest on any indebtedness incurred or continued to purchase or carry tax-exempt obligations also is disallowed.

Judicial Interpretations. It is often difficult to show a direct relationship between borrowings and investment in tax-exempt securities. Suppose, for example, that a taxpayer borrows money, adds it to existing funds, buys inventory and stocks, then later sells the inventory and buys municipal bonds. A series of transactions such as these can completely obscure any connection between the loan and the tax-exempt investment. One solution would be to disallow interest on any debt to the extent that the taxpayer holds any tax-exempt securities. This approach would preclude individuals from deducting part of their home mortgage interest if they owned any municipal bonds. The law was not intended to go to such extremes. As a result, judicial interpretations have tried to be reasonable in disallowing interest deductions.

In one case, a company used municipal bonds as collateral on short-term loans to meet seasonal liquidity needs.[62] The Court disallowed the interest deduction on the grounds that the company could predict its seasonal liquidity needs. The company could anticipate the need to borrow the money to continue to carry the tax-exempt securities. The same company *was* allowed an interest deduction on a building mortgage, even though tax-exempt securities it owned could have been sold to pay off the mortgage. The Court reasoned that short-term liquidity needs would have been impaired if the tax-exempt securities were sold. Furthermore, the Court ruled that carrying the tax-exempt securities bore no relationship to the long-term financing of a construction project.

---

[59]§ 103.
[60]§ 212.
[61]§ 265.

[62]*The Wisconsin Cheeseman, Inc. v. U.S.*, 68–1 USTC ¶9145, 21 AFTR2d 383, 388 F.2d 420 (CA–7, 1968).

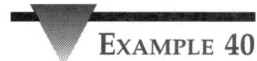

EXAMPLE 40

In January of the current year, Alan borrowed $100,000 at 8% interest. He used the loan proceeds to purchase 5,000 shares of stock in White Corporation. In July, he sold the stock for $120,000 and reinvested the proceeds in City of Denver bonds, the income from which is tax-exempt. Assuming the $100,000 loan remained outstanding throughout the entire year, Alan cannot deduct the interest attributable to the period in which he held the bonds. ▼

**TAX PLANNING
CONSIDERATIONS**

TIME VALUE OF TAX DEDUCTIONS

Cash basis taxpayers often have the ability to make early payments for their expenses at the end of the tax year. This permits the payments to be deducted currently instead of in the following tax year. In view of the time value of money, a tax deduction this year may be worth more than the same deduction next year. Before employing this strategy, the taxpayer must consider next year's expected income and tax rates and whether a cash-flow problem may develop from early payments. Thus, the time value of money as well as tax rate changes must be considered when an expense can be paid and deducted in either of two years.

4 **LEARNING OBJECTIVE**
Identify tax planning opportunities for maximizing deductions and minimizing the disallowance of deductions.

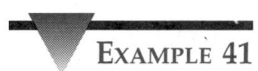

EXAMPLE 41

Jena pledged $5,000 to her church's special building fund. She can make the contribution in December 1998 or January 1999. Jena is in the 36% tax bracket in 1998, and in the 31% bracket in 1999. She itemizes in both years. Assume Jena's discount rate is 8%. If she takes the deduction in 1998, she saves $365 ($1,800 – $1,435), due to the decrease in the tax rates and the time value of money.

	1998	1999
Contribution	$5,000	$5,000
Tax bracket	.36	.31
Tax savings	$1,800	$1,550
Discounted @ 8%	1.0	.926
Savings in present value	$1,800	$1,435

▼

EXAMPLE 42

Assume the same facts as in Example 41, except that Jena is in the 31% bracket in both 1998 and 1999. By taking the deduction in 1998, Jena saves $115 ($1,550 – $1,435), due to the time value of money.

	1998	1999
Contribution	$5,000	$5,000
Tax bracket	.31	.31
Tax savings	$1,550	$1,550
Discounted @ 8%	1.0	.926
Savings in present value	$1,550	$1,435

▼

UNREASONABLE COMPENSATION

In substantiating the reasonableness of a shareholder-employee's compensation, an internal comparison test is sometimes useful. If it can be shown that nonshareholder-employees and shareholder-employees in comparable positions receive comparable compensation, it is indicative that compensation is not unreasonable.

CONCEPT SUMMARY 6–2

Classification of Expenses

Expense Item	Deductible For AGI	Deductible From AGI	Not Deductible	Applicable Code §
Investment expenses				
Rent and royalty	X			§ 62(a)(4)
All other investments		X[4]		§ 212
Employee expenses				
Commuting expenses			X	§ 262
Travel and transportation[1]		X[4,5]		§ 162(a)(2)
Reimbursed expenses[1]	X			§ 62(a)(2)(A)
Moving expenses	X			§ 62(a)(15)
Entertainment[1]		X[4,5]		§ 162(a)
All other employee expenses[1]		X[4,5]		§ 162(a)
Certain expenses of performing artists	X			§ 62(a)(2)(B)
Trade or business expenses	X			§§ 162 and 62(a)(1)
Casualty losses				
Business	X			§ 165(c)(1)
Personal		X[6]		§ 165(c)(3)
Tax determination				
Collection or refund expenses	X[8]	X[4]		§§ 212 and 62(a)(1) or (4)
Bad debts	X			§§ 166 and 62(a)(1) or (3)
Medical expenses		X[7]		§ 213
Charitable contributions		X		§ 170
Taxes				
Trade or business	X			§§ 162 and 62(a)(1)
Personal taxes				
Real property		X		§ 164(a)(1)
Personal property		X		§ 164(a)(2)
State and local income		X		§ 164(a)(3)
Investigation of a business[2]	X			§§ 162 and 62(a)(1)
Interest				
Business	X			§§ 162 and 62(a)(1)
Personal		X[3]	X[9]	§§ 163(a), (d), and (h)
All other personal expenses			X	§ 262

1. Deduction *for* AGI if reimbursed, an adequate accounting is made, and employee is required to repay excess reimbursements.
2. Provided certain criteria are met.
3. Subject to the excess investment interest and the qualified residence interest provisions.
4. Subject (in the aggregate) to a 2%-of-AGI floor imposed by § 67.
5. Only 50% of meals and entertainment are deductible.
6. Subject to a $100 floor per event and a 10%-of-AGI floor per tax year.
7. Subject to a 7.5%-of-AGI floor.
8. Only the portion relating to business, rental, or royalty income or losses.
9. Other personal interest is disallowed.

Another possibility is to demonstrate that the shareholder-employee has been underpaid in prior years. For example, the shareholder-employee may have agreed to take a less-than-adequate salary during the unprofitable formative years of the business. The expectation is that the "postponed" compensation would be paid in later, more profitable years. The agreement should be documented, if possible, in the corporate minutes.

Keep in mind that in testing for reasonableness, the *total* pay package must be considered. Look at all fringe benefits or perquisites, such as contributions by the corporation to a qualified pension plan. Even though those amounts are not immediately available to the covered shareholder-employee, they must be taken into account.

EXCESSIVE EXECUTIVE COMPENSATION

With the $1 million limit on the deduction of compensation of covered employees, many corporations and their executives must engage in additional tax planning. Previously, concerns over the deductibility of compensation related primarily to closely held corporations. The $1 million limit applies specifically to publicly held corporations. In many instances, it is now necessary for these corporations to restructure the compensation packages of their top executives in order to deduct payments in excess of $1 million. Opportunities include compensation payable on a commission basis, certain other performance-based compensation, payments to qualified retirement plans, and payments that are excludible fringe benefits.

SHIFTING DEDUCTIONS

Taxpayers should manage their obligations to avoid the loss of a deduction. Deductions can be shifted among family members, depending upon which member makes the payment. For example, a father buys a condo for his daughter and puts the title in both names. The taxpayer who makes the payment gets the deduction for the property taxes. If the condo is owned by the daughter only and her father makes the payment, neither is entitled to a deduction. In this case, the father should make a cash gift to the daughter who then makes the payment to the taxing authority.

HOBBY LOSSES

To demonstrate that an activity has been entered into for the purpose of making a profit, a taxpayer should treat the activity as a business. The business should engage in advertising, use business letterhead stationery, and maintain a business phone.

If a taxpayer's activity earns a profit in three out of five consecutive years, the presumption is that the activity is engaged in for profit. It may be possible for a cash basis taxpayer to meet these requirements by timing the payment of expenses or the receipt of revenues. The payment of certain expenses incurred before the end of the year might be made in the following year. The billing of year-end sales might be delayed so that collections are received in the following year.

Keep in mind that the three-out-of-five-years rule under § 183 is not absolute. All it does is shift the presumption. If a profit is not made in three out of five years, the losses may still be allowed if the taxpayer can show that they are due to the nature of the business. For example, success in artistic or literary endeavors can take a long time. Also, depending on the state of the economy, even full-time farmers and ranchers are often unable to show a profit. How can one expect a part-time farmer or rancher to do so?

Merely satisfying the three-out-of-five-years rule does not guarantee that a taxpayer is automatically home free. If the three years of profits are insignificant relative to the losses of other years, or if the profits are not from the ordinary operation of the business, the taxpayer is vulnerable. The IRS may still be able to establish that the taxpayer is not engaged in an activity for profit.

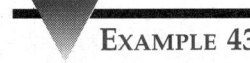
EXAMPLE 43

Ashley had the following gains and losses in an artistic endeavor:

1994	($50,000)
1995	(65,000)
1996	400
1997	200
1998	125

Under these circumstances, the IRS might try to overcome the presumption. ▼

If Ashley in Example 43 could show conformity with the factors enumerated in the Regulations or could show evidence of business hardships (e.g., injury, death, or illness), the government cannot override the presumption.[63]

CAPITAL EXPENDITURES

On the sale of a sole proprietorship where the sales price exceeds the fair market value of the tangible assets and stated intangible assets, a planning opportunity may exist for both the seller and the buyer. The seller's preference is for the excess amount to be allocated to goodwill. Goodwill is a capital asset whereas a covenant not to compete produces ordinary income treatment (see Chapter 16).

Because both a covenant and goodwill are amortized over a statutory 15-year period, the tax results of a covenant and goodwill are the same for the buyer. However, the buyer should recognize that an allocation to goodwill rather than a covenant may provide a tax benefit to the seller. Therefore, the seller and buyer, in negotiating the sales price, should factor in the tax benefit to the seller of having the excess amount labeled goodwill rather than a covenant not to compete. Of course, if the noncompetition aspects of a covenant are important to the buyer, part of the excess amount can be assigned to a covenant.

KEY TERMS

Accounting method, 6–8

Deductions *for* adjusted gross income, 6–2

Deductions *from* adjusted gross income, 6–2

Hobby losses, 6–16

Ordinary and necessary, 6–6

Reasonableness, 6–7

Related-party transactions, 6–26

Vacation home, 6–18

---

[63]*Faulconer, Sr. v. Comm.*, 84–2 USTC ¶9955, 55 AFTR2d 85–302, 748 F.2d 890 (CA–4, 1984), *rev'g* 45 TCM 1084, T.C.Memo. 1983–165.

PROBLEM MATERIALS

DISCUSSION QUESTIONS

1. "All income must be reported and all deductions are allowed unless specifically disallowed in the Code." Discuss.

2. Discuss the difference in the tax treatment of deductions *for* and deductions *from* AGI.

3. Does an expenditure that is classified as a deduction *from* AGI produce the same tax benefit as an expenditure that is classified as a deduction *for* AGI?

4. Classify each of the following expenditures as a deduction *for* AGI, a deduction *from* AGI, or not deductible:
   a. Allison pays qualified moving expenses of $3,000.
   b. Emalie gives $1,000 to the Girl Scouts.
   c. Amos pays alimony of $2,500 per month to his former spouse.
   d. Arnold pays $600 for real estate taxes levied by the county on his personal residence.
   e. April gives $1,000 to a family whose house was destroyed by a fire.

5. Classify each of the following expenditures as a deduction *for* AGI, a deduction *from* AGI, or not deductible:
   a. Amos contributes $500 to his H.R. 10 plan (i.e., a retirement plan for a self-employed individual).
   b. Keith pays $500 of child support to his former wife, Renee, for the support of their son, Chris.
   c. Judy pays $500 for professional dues that are reimbursed by her employer.
   d. Ted pays $500 as the monthly mortgage payment on his personal residence. Of this amount, $100 represents a payment on principal, and $400 represents an interest payment.
   e. Lynn pays $500 to a moving company for moving her household goods to Detroit where she is starting a new job.

6. Larry and Susan each invest $10,000 in separate investment activities. They each incur deductible expenses of $800 associated with their respective investments. Explain why Larry's expenses are properly classified as deductions *from* AGI (itemized deductions) and Susan's expenses are appropriately classified as deductions *for* AGI.

7. List the three items that § 162 specifically excludes from classification as a trade or business expense.

8. Wendy, a machinist employed by Silver Airlines, owns 25 shares of Silver Airlines stock. Silver has 900,000 shares of stock outstanding. Wendy spends $800 to travel to Chicago for Silver's annual meeting. Her expenses would have been $500 more, but she was permitted to fly free on Silver. She attended both days of the shareholders' meeting and actively participated. What are the tax consequences of the trip for Wendy?

9. Sam and Vera are the owners of a corporation. To reduce the corporation's taxable income, they pay a $1,000 salary each month to their 7-year-old daughter, Peg. Why is this salary disallowed as a deduction?

10. Which of the following losses are deductible?
   a. Loss on the sale of a factory building used in a trade or business.
   b. Loss on the sale of a truck held for personal use.
   c. Loss from the destruction by a tornado of a warehouse used in a trade or business.
   d. Loss on the destruction by fire of the taxpayer's residence.
   e. Loss on the sale of Lavender Corporation stock held as an investment.

11. Mary Kate owns a building that she leases to an individual who operates a grocery store. Rent income is $10,000 and rental expenses are $6,000. On what Form 1040 schedule or schedules are the income and expenses reported?

12. Distinguish between the timing for the recording of a deduction under the cash method versus the accrual method.

13. Landry, a cash basis taxpayer, decides to reduce his taxable income for 1998 by buying $10,000 worth of supplies on December 28, 1998. The supplies will be used up in 1999.

a. Can Landry deduct this expenditure in 1998?

b. Would your answer differ if Landry bought the supplies because a supplier was going out of business and had given him a significant discount on the supplies?

14. What is the significance of the all events and economic performance tests?

15. James provides a one-year warranty on the vacuum cleaners manufactured by his company. Claims under the warranty typically amount to 2% of sales. Can James use the reserve method to account for the warranty expense?

16. Lemon, Inc., is a soft-drink distributor. Lemon's delivery trucks frequently are required to park in "No Parking" zones in order to make their deliveries. Occasionally, the trucks are ticketed and Lemon pays the parking fine. Can Lemon deduct these fines?

17. Ted is an agent for an airline manufacturer and is negotiating a sale with a representative of the U.S. government and with a representative of a developing country. Ted's company has sufficient capacity to handle only one of the orders. Both orders will have the same contract price. Ted believes that if his employer will authorize a $500,000 payment to the representative of the foreign country, he can guarantee the sale. He is not sure that he can obtain the same result with the U.S. government. Identify the relevant tax issues for Ted.

18. Stuart, an insurance salesman, is arrested for allegedly robbing a convenience store. He hires an attorney who is successful in getting the charges dropped. Is the attorney's fee deductible?

19. Linda operates a drug-running operation. Which of the following expenses she incurs can reduce taxable income?
    a. Bribes paid to border guards.
    b. Salaries to employees.
    c. Price paid for drugs purchased for resale.
    d. Kickbacks to police.
    e. Rent on an office.

20. Gordon anticipates that being positively perceived by the individual who is elected mayor will be beneficial for his business. Therefore, he contributes to the campaigns of both the Democratic and the Republican candidates. The Republican candidate is elected mayor. Can Gordon deduct any of the political contributions he made?

21. Carmine, Inc., a tobacco manufacturer, incurs certain expenditures associated with political contributions and lobbying activities. Which of these expenditures can be deducted?

Payments to Washington, D.C. law firm to lobby members of Congress	$800,000
Payments to Washington, D.C. law firm to lobby the Vice President	200,000
Payments to Washington, D.C. law firm to lobby the head of the FDA	25,000
Payments to Richmond law firm to lobby members of the state legislature	50,000
Payments to Williamsburg law firm to lobby members of the Williamsburg City Council	5,000
Political contribution to the Democratic National Committee	300,000
Political contribution to the Republican National Committee	350,000
Political contribution to Committee to Re-elect the Mayor of Williamsburg	6,000

22. Agnes, an executive of a large corporation, receives a salary of $1.5 million. Taylor, who is an executive of another large corporation, receives a salary of $1.3 million. Agnes's corporation is permitted to deduct all of her salary while Taylor's corporation is permitted to deduct only part of his. Explain how this could happen. Assume both salaries are reasonable.

23. Ralph owns a restaurant in Baton Rouge. He is considering expanding into New Orleans by purchasing an existing restaurant there. As an alternative, he is considering purchasing an economy motel in New Orleans that does not offer food services. What are the

tax consequences to Ralph of the costs incurred investigating each of these business opportunities?

24. Amanda had been raising quarter horses for three years. Each year, her losses were about $15,000. She projects that her losses for the current year will be about $10,000. However, if she sells a promising mare before the end of the year, the $10,000 projected loss can be converted into a $4,000 projected profit. Without the perceived need to produce a current-year profit, Amanda would prefer to keep the mare for breeding purposes. Identify the relevant tax issues for Amanda.

25. Are there any circumstances under which a taxpayer can rent his or her personal residence and not be required to report the rent income received?

26. Karen and Andy own a beach house. They have an agreement with a rental agent to rent it up to 200 days per year. For the past three years, the agent has been successful in renting it for 200 days. Karen and Andy use the beach house for one week during the summer and one week during Thanksgiving. Their daughter, Sarah, a college student, has asked if she and some friends can use the beach house for the week of spring break. Advise Karen and Andy how they should respond and identify any relevant tax issues.

27. Hank was transferred from Phoenix to North Dakota on March 1 of the current year. He immediately put his home in Phoenix up for rent. The home was rented May 1 to November 30 and was vacant during the month of December. It was rented again on January 1 for six months. What expenses, if any, can Hank deduct on his return? Which deductions are *for* AGI and which ones are *from* AGI?

28. Erika would like to help her daughter Hillary and son-in-law James with what she hopes are short-term financial problems. This assistance will be in the form of paying their monthly mortgage payments for the past six months. If the payments are not made, the mortgage company will foreclose on their residence. Erika's preference is to make the payments directly to the mortgage company. However, she is willing to give the money to Hillary and James who then would pay the arrearages. Advise Erika on which option, if any, offers preferential tax treatment to her.

29. Explain which, if any, legal fees incurred obtaining a divorce are deductible. Are they deductible *for* or *from* AGI?

30. Igor repaired the roof on his factory at a cost of $1,500 in the current year. During the same year, Raisa replaced the roof on her small rental house for $1,500. Both taxpayers are on the cash basis. Are their expenditures treated the same on their tax returns? Why or why not?

31. Ella owns 60% of the stock of Peach. The stock has declined in value since Ella purchased it five years ago. She is going to sell 5% of her stock to a relative to pay her 12-year-old daughter's private school tuition. Ella is also going to make a gift of 10% of her stock to another relative. Identify the relevant tax issues for Ella.

32. Which of the following are related parties under § 267?
    - Mother
    - Sister
    - Nephew
    - Aunt
    - Cousin
    - Granddaughter
    - Corporation in which the shareholder owns 45% of the stock

PROBLEMS

33. Sandra is an attorney. She incurs the following expenses when she and her employee, Fred, attend the American Bar Association convention in San Francisco:

Conference registration:	
Sandra	$200
Fred	200
Airline tickets from Pittsburgh to San Francisco:	
Sandra	700
Fred	400
Lodging in San Francisco:	
Sandra	450
Fred	250

Calculate the effect of these expenses on Sandra's AGI.

34. Calvin received the following income and incurred and paid the following expenses during the current tax year:

Salary income	$60,000
Dividend income	4,000
Interest income	3,000
Contributions to First Church	2,500
Real estate taxes on personal residence	1,800
Alimony paid to former spouse	12,000
Retirement plan contribution	2,000
Mortgage interest on personal residence	6,000
State income taxes	3,500
Loss on the sale of stock	900

Calculate Calvin's AGI.

35. Drew and his wife Cassie own all of the stock of Thrush. Cassie is the president and Drew is the vice-president. Cassie and Drew are paid salaries of $400,000 and $300,000, respectively, each year. They consider the salaries to be reasonable based on a comparison with salaries paid for comparable positions in comparable companies. They project Thrush's taxable income for next year, before their salaries, to be $800,000. They decide to place their four teenage children on the payroll and to pay them total salaries of $100,000. The children will each work about five hours per week for Thrush.
    a. What are Drew and Cassie trying to achieve by hiring the children?
    b. Calculate the tax consequences of hiring the children on Thrush, and on Drew and Cassie's family.

36. Amber incurs the following losses during the current tax year:

Loss on the sale of Brown stock	$ 1,100
Theft loss of uninsured car used in Amber's business	1,500
Loss on the sale of Amber's personal use car	3,000
Loss on the sale of Amber's personal residence	12,000
Loss on sale of City of Norfolk bonds	900

Calculate Amber's deductible losses.

37. The income statement for Karl's business reported the following revenues and expenses for 1998, the initial year of operations:

Sales revenue (including $8,000 credit sales uncollected at year-end)	$60,000
Wage expenses ($1,000 unpaid at year-end)	22,000
Office expenses (supplies, copying, etc.)	2,000
Bad debt expense (consists of reserve established for $3,000 with write-offs of $500)	3,000
Utilities and telephone expense*	6,000
Insurance expense*	4,000
Rent expense (January 1, 1998–January 31, 1999)	9,750

*Amount incurred = amount paid.

  a. Calculate Karl's AGI using the accrual method.

  b. Calculate Karl's AGI using the cash method.

38. Doris is the owner of a sole proprietorship that uses the cash method. She leases an office building for $24,000 for an 18-month period on October 1, 1998. In order to obtain this favorable lease rate, she pays the $24,000 at the inception of the lease. How much rent expense may Doris deduct on her 1998 tax return?

39. Duck, an accrual basis corporation, sponsored a rock concert on December 29, 1998. Gross receipts were $300,000. The following expenses were incurred and paid as indicated:

Expense		Payment Date
Rental of coliseum	$ 25,000	December 21, 1998
Cost of goods sold:		
Food	30,000	December 30, 1998
Souvenirs	60,000	December 30, 1998
Performers	100,000	January 5, 1999
Cleaning of coliseum	10,000	February 1, 1999

Since the coliseum was not scheduled to be used again until January 15, the company with which Duck had contracted did not actually perform the cleanup until January 8–10, 1999.

Calculate Duck's net income from the concert for tax purposes for 1998.

40. Doug incurred and paid the following expenses during the year:

- $50 for a ticket for running a red light while he was commuting to work.
- $100 for a ticket for parking in a handicapped parking space.
- $200 to an attorney to represent him for the two above tickets.
- $500 to an attorney to draft a lease agreement with a tenant for a one-year lease on an apartment that Doug owns.

Determine the amount that Doug can deduct for each of these payments.

41. Marcia, an attorney with a leading New York law firm, is convicted of failing to file Federal income tax returns for 1994–1996. Her justification for failing to do so was the pressures of her profession (80–90 hour workweeks). She is assessed taxes, interest, and penalties of $90,000 by the IRS. In addition, she incurs related legal fees of $60,000. Determine the amount that Marcia can deduct, and classify it as a deduction *for* or a deduction *from* AGI.

42. David runs an illegal numbers racket. His gross revenues were $500,000. He incurred the following expenses:

Illegal kickbacks	$20,000
Salaries	80,000
Rent	24,000
Utilities and telephone	9,000
Bribes to police	25,000
Interest	6,000
Depreciation on equipment	12,000

    a. What is his net income from this business that is includible in taxable income?

    b. If the business was an illegal drug operation and cost of goods sold was $100,000, how would your answer differ?

43. Edward, an attorney, is hired by a major accounting firm to represent it and its clients in dealing with members of the U.S. Congress. The accounting firm is supporting liability reform that would limit the "joint and several" liability of professionals such as attorneys and CPAs. During the year, Edward is paid $10,000 for this representation. The firm also reimburses Edward $2,500 for meal and entertainment expenses incurred in meeting with members of Congress and their staffs. In addition, the firm pays Edward $5,000 for his work in opposing legislation that would adversely affect several of its major clients. What is the amount of these payments that the firm may deduct?

44. Amber, a publicly held corporation, currently pays its president an annual salary of $900,000. In addition, it contributes $20,000 annually to a defined contribution pension plan for him. As a means of increasing company profitability, the board of directors decides to increase the president's compensation. Two proposals are being considered. Under the first proposal, the salary and pension contribution for the president would be increased by 30%. Under the second proposal, Amber would implement a performance-based compensation program that is projected to provide about the same amount of additional compensation and pension contribution for the president.

    a. Evaluate the alternatives from the perspective of Amber, Inc.

    b. Prepare a letter to Amber's board of directors that contains your recommendations. Address the letter to the board chairperson, Agnes Riddle, whose address is 100 James Tower, Cleveland, OH 44106.

45. Vermillion, Inc., a publicly held corporation, pays the following salaries to its executives:

	Salary	Bonus	Retirement Plan Contribution
CEO	$2,000,000	$100,000	$80,000
Executive vice president	1,800,000	90,000	72,000
Treasurer	1,600,000	–0–	64,000
Marketing vice president	1,500,000	75,000	60,000
Operations vice president	1,400,000	70,000	56,000
Distribution vice president	1,200,000	60,000	48,000
Research vice president	1,100,000	–0–	44,000
Controller	800,000	–0–	32,000

Vermillion normally does not pay bonuses, but after reviewing the results of operations for the year, the board of directors decided to pay a 5% bonus to selected executives. What is the amount of these payments that Vermillion may deduct?

46. Jenny, the owner of a very successful restaurant chain, is exploring the possibility of expanding the chain into a city in the neighboring state. She incurs $20,000 of expenses associated with this investigation. Based on the regulatory environment for restaurants in the city, she decides not to do so. During the year, she also investigates opening a hotel that will be part of a national hotel chain. Her expenses for this are $15,000. The

hotel begins operations on December 1. Determine the amount that Jenny can deduct in the current year for investigating these two businesses.

47. Tim traveled to a neighboring state to investigate the purchase of two restaurants. His expenses included travel, legal, accounting, and miscellaneous expenses. The total was $12,000. He incurred the expenses in March and April 1998.
    a. What can Tim deduct in 1998 if he was in the restaurant business and did not acquire the two restaurants?
    b. What can Tim deduct in 1998 if he was in the restaurant business and acquired the two restaurants and began operating them on July 1, 1998?
    c. What can Tim deduct in 1998 if he did not acquire the two restaurants and was not in the restaurant business?
    d. What can he deduct in 1998 if he acquired the two restaurants, but was not in the restaurant business when he acquired them? Operations began on July 1, 1998.

48. Alfred, who is single, conducts an activity that is appropriately classified as a hobby. The activity produces the following revenues and expenses:

Revenue	$10,000
Property taxes	3,000
Materials and supplies	2,000
Utilities	1,000
Advertising	2,500
Insurance	500
Depreciation	4,000

    Without regard to this activity, Alfred's AGI is $40,000. Determine how much income Alfred must report, the amount of the expenses he is permitted to deduct, and his taxable income.

49. Sandra, an orthodontist, is single and has net earnings of $90,000 from her orthodontic practice. In addition, she collects antique books that she buys and sells at antique shows. She participates in six to eight weekend antique shows per year. Her income and expenses for the current year are as follows:

Revenue from sale of antique books	$22,000
Expenses	
Cost of goods sold	12,000
Show registration costs	3,000
Advertising	1,000
Dealer's license—annual fee	500
Insurance	900
Depreciation of display cases	1,200

    Sandra has no other items that would affect her AGI. Itemized deductions from taxes, interest, and charitable contributions are $19,000.
    a. Calculate Sandra's taxable income if the antique book activity is classified as a hobby.
    b. Calculate Sandra's taxable income if the antique book activity is classified as a business.

50. Ashley, who lives in a summer resort area, rented her personal residence for two weeks while she was visiting Paris. Rent income was $2,000. Related expenses for the year were as follows:

Real property taxes	$ 3,000
Mortgage interest	6,000
Utilities	2,400
Insurance	1,200
Repairs	600
Depreciation	12,000

Determine the effect on Ashley's AGI.

51. In 1998, Anna rented her vacation home for 60 days, used it personally for 20 days, and left it vacant for 285 days. She had the following income and expenses:

Rent income	$ 6,000
Expenses	
Real estate taxes	2,000
Interest on mortgage	9,000
Utilities	600
Repairs	1,000
Roof replacement	12,000
Depreciation	8,000

a. Compute Anna's net rent income or loss and the amounts she can itemize on her tax return, using the court's approach in allocating property taxes and interest.

b. How would your answer in (a) differ using the IRS's method of allocating property taxes and interest?

52. How would your answer in Problem 51 differ if Anna had rented the house for 90 days and had used it personally for 12 days?

53. Chee, single, age 40, had the following income and expenses in 1998:

Income	
Salary	$43,000
Rental of vacation home (rented 60 days, used personally 60 days, vacant 245 days)	4,000
Municipal bond interest	2,000
Dividend from General Motors	400
Expenses	
Interest	
On home mortgage	8,400
On vacation home	4,758
On loan used to buy municipal bonds	3,100
Taxes	
Property tax on home	2,200
Property tax on vacation home	1,098
State income tax	3,300
Charitable contributions	1,100
Tax return preparation fee	300
Utilities and maintenance on vacation home	2,600
Depreciation on rental 50% of vacation home	3,500

Calculate Chee's taxable income for 1998 before personal exemptions.

54. Velma and Clyde operate a retail sports memorabilia shop. For the current year, sales revenue is $50,000 and expenses are as follows:

Cost of goods sold	$19,000
Advertising	1,000
Utilities	2,000
Rent	4,000
Insurance	1,500
Wages to Boyd	7,000

Velma and Clyde pay $7,000 in wages to Boyd, a part-time employee. Since this amount is $1,000 below the minimum wage, Boyd threatens to file a complaint with the appropriate Federal agency. Although Velma and Clyde pay no attention to Boyd's threat, Chelsie (Velma's mother) gives Boyd a check for $1,000 for the disputed wages. Both Velma and Clyde ridicule Chelsie for wasting money when they learn what she has done. The retail shop is the only source of income for Velma and Clyde.
   a. Calculate Velma and Clyde's AGI.
   b. Can Chelsie deduct the $1,000 payment on her tax return?
   c. How could the tax position of the parties be improved?

55. Terry is purchasing a business from the estate of Anne. The amount being paid exceeds the fair market value of the identifiable assets of the business by $150,000. Advise Terry on the tax consequences of the $150,000 being allocated to goodwill versus it being allocated to a 10-year covenant not to compete.

56. Jay's sole proprietorship has the following assets

	Basis	Fair Market Value
Cash	$ 10,000	$ 10,000
Accounts receivable	18,000	18,000
Inventory	25,000	30,000
Patent	22,000	40,000
Land	50,000	75,000
	$125,000	$173,000

The building in which Jay's business is located is leased. The lease expires at the end of the year.

Jay is age 70 and would like to retire. He expects to be in the 36% tax bracket. Jay is negotiating the sale of the business with Lois, a key employee. They have agreed on the fair market value of the assets, as indicated above, and agree the total purchase price should be about $200,000.
   a. Advise Jay regarding how the sale should be structured.
   b. Advise Lois regarding how the purchase should be structured.
   c. What might they do to achieve an acceptable compromise?

57. Janet Saxon sold stock (basis of $40,000) to her brother, Fred, for $32,000.
   a. What are the tax consequences to Janet?
   b. What are the tax consequences to Fred if he later sells the stock for $42,000? For $28,000? For $36,000?
   c. Write a letter to Janet in which you inform her of the tax consequences if she sells the stock to Fred for $32,000 and explain how a sales transaction could be structured that would produce better tax consequences for her. Janet's address is 32 Country Lane, Lawrence, KS 66045.

58. The Robin Corporation is owned as follows:

Irene	20%
Paul, Irene's husband	20%
Sylvia, Irene's mother	15%
Ron, Irene's father	25%
Quinn, an unrelated party	20%

Robin is on the accrual basis, and Irene and Paul are on the cash basis. Irene and Paul each loaned the Robin Corporation $10,000 out of their separate funds. On December 31, 1998, Robin accrued interest at 7% on both loans. The interest was paid on February 4, 1999. What is the tax treatment of this interest expense/income to Irene, Paul, and Robin?

59. What is Kim's constructive ownership of Wren Corporation, given the following information?

Shares owned by Kim	900
Shares owned by Sam, Kim's uncle	600
Shares owned by Barbara, Kim's partner	30
Shares owned by Vera, Kim's granddaughter	670
Shares owned by unrelated parties	800

60. Chris has a brokerage account and buys on the margin, which resulted in an interest expense of $9,000 during the year. Income generated through the brokerage account was as follows:

Municipal interest	$35,000
Taxable dividends and interest	65,000

How much investment interest can Chris deduct?

61. Lee incurred the following expenses in the current tax year. Indicate, in the spaces provided, whether each expenditure is deductible for AGI, from AGI, or not deductible.

Expense Item	For AGI	From AGI	Not Deductible
a. Lee's personal medical expenses		✓	
b. Lee's dependent daughter's medical expenses		✓	
c. Real estate taxes on rental property	✓		
d. Real estate taxes on Lee's personal residence		✓	
e. Real estate taxes on daughter's personal residence			✓
f. Lee's state income taxes		✓	
g. Interest on rental property mortgage	✓		
h. Interest on Lee's personal residence mortgage		✓	
i. Interest on daughter's personal residence mortgage			✓
j. Interest on business loans	✓		
k. Charitable contributions		✓	
l. Depreciation on rental property	✓		
m. Utilities & maintenance on:			
(1) Rental property	✓		
(2) Lee's home			✓
(3) Daughter's home			✓

		Deductible		Not
	Expense Item	For AGI	From AGI	Deductible
n.	Depreciation on auto used in Lee's business	✓		
o.	Depreciation on Lee's personal auto	~~✓~~		✓
p.	Depreciation on daughter's personal auto			✓

CUMULATIVE PROBLEMS

62. John and Mary Jane Sanders are married, filing jointly. Their address is 204 Shoe Lane, Blacksburg, VA 24061. They are expecting their first two children (twins) in early 1999. John's salary in 1998 was $85,000, from which $11,000 of Federal income tax and $3,600 of state income tax were withheld. Mary Jane made $40,000 and had $4,000 of Federal income tax and $2,000 of state income tax withheld. The appropriate amount of FICA tax was withheld for John and for Mary Jane.

    John and Mary Jane are both covered by their employer's medical insurance policies with all of the premiums being paid by the employers. The premiums were $3,600 for John and $3,200 for Mary Jane. Mary Jane received medical benefits of $2,400 under the plan. John was not ill during 1998.

    John makes alimony payments of $30,000 per year to June, his former wife. He also makes child support payments of $12,000 for his son, Rod, who lives with June except for two months in the summer when he visits John and Mary Jane.

    Mary Jane's father lived with them until his death in October. His only sources of income were salary of $1,600, $500 of unemployment compensation benefits, and Social Security benefits of $3,200. Of this amount, he deposited $3,000 in a savings account. The remainder of his support, including funeral expenses of $5,000, was provided by John and Mary Jane.

    Other income received by the Sanders was as follows:

Interest on certificates of deposit	$ 900
Dividend income	600
Share of partnership taxable income (distributions from the partnership to Mary Jane were $200)	300
Award received by Mary Jane from employer for outstanding suggestion for cutting costs	1,000

    They made charitable contributions of $3,500 during the year and paid an additional $700 in state income taxes in 1998 upon filing their 1997 state income tax return. Their deductible home mortgage interest was $9,000, and their property taxes came to $2,400. They had no other deductible expenses.

Part 1—Tax Computation
Calculate their tax (or refund) due for 1998. Suggested software (if available): *TurboTax*.

Part 2—Tax Planning
Assume that they come to you for advice in December 1998. John has learned that he will receive a $15,000 bonus. He wants to know if he should take it in December 1998 or in January 1999. Mary Jane will quit work on December 31 to stay home with the twins. Their itemized deductions will decrease by $2,000 because Mary Jane will not have state income taxes withheld. Mary Jane does not expect to receive the employee award in 1999. She expects the medical benefits received to be $4,500. The Sanders expect all of their other income items to remain the same in 1999. Write a letter to John and Mary Jane that contains your advice and prepare a memo for the tax files. Suggested software (if available): *TurboTax*.

63. Helen Archer, age 30, is single and lives at 120 Sanborne Avenue, Springfield, IL 60740. Her Social Security number is 648–11–9981. Helen has been divorced from her former husband, Albert, for three years. She has a son, Jason, who is age 8. His Social Security number is 648–98–3471. Helen does not wish to contribute $3 to the Presidential Election Campaign Fund.

    Helen, an advertising executive, earned a salary of $80,000 in 1997. Her employer withheld $11,000 in Federal income tax, $3,500 in state income tax, and the appropriate amount of FICA tax.

    Helen has legal custody of Jason. Jason lives with his father during summer vacation. Albert indicates that his expenses for Jason are $10,000. Helen can document that she spent $4,500 for Jason's support during 1997.

    Helen's mother died on January 7, 1997. Helen inherited assets worth $200,000 from her mother. As the sole beneficiary of her mother's life insurance policy, Helen received insurance proceeds of $100,000. Her mother's cost basis for the life insurance policy was $40,000. Helen's favorite aunt gave her $10,000 for her thirtieth birthday in October.

    On November 8, 1997, Helen sells for $19,000 Amber stock that she had purchased for $20,000 from her first cousin, Walt, on December 5, 1991. His cost basis for the stock was $12,000, and the stock was worth $20,000 on December 5, 1991. On December 1, 1997, Helen sold Falcon stock for $15,000. She had acquired the stock on July 2, 1997, for $10,000.

    An examination of Helen's records reveals the following information:

    • Received interest income of $3,500 from First Savings Bank.

    • Received groceries valued at $500 from a local grocery store for being the 100,000th customer.

    • Received dividend income of $1,500 from Amber.

    • Received $2,200 of interest income on City of Springfield school bonds.

    • Received alimony of $20,000 from Albert.

    • Received a distribution of $2,000 from ST Partnership. Her distributive share of the partnership passive taxable income was $2,800.

    From her checkbook records, she determines that she made the following payments during 1997.

    • Charitable contributions of $1,500 to First Presbyterian Church and $1,100 to the American Red Cross.

    • Mortgage interest on her residence of $6,900.

    • Property taxes of $1,900 on her residence and $900 on her car.

    • Sales taxes of $1,700.

    • Estimated Federal income taxes of $10,300 and estimated state income taxes of $1,000.

    • Medical expenses of $4,000 for her and $500 for Jason. Eight hundred dollars of her medical expenses were reimbursed by her medical insurance policy in December.

    Calculate Helen's net tax payable or refund due for 1997. If you use tax forms, you will need Form 1040 and Schedules A, B, D, and E. Suggested software (if available): *TurboTax*.

RESEARCH PROBLEMS

Note: Use the **RIA OnPoint System 4 Student Version CD-ROM**, *which is available to accompany this text, in preparing solutions to the Research Problems. Alternatively, tax research materials found in a standard tax library can be used.*

Research Problem 1. Noel is an employee of the U.S. Immigration Service and is stationed at Dorval International Airport in Montreal. Noel received a Living Quarters Allowance (LQA) of $10,000. An LQA is a stipend provided to qualifying Federal employees stationed abroad who are not otherwise provided with housing and is excludible from gross income under § 912(1)(C).

Noel and Janet, his spouse, purchased a house in Montreal and lived in it during the tax year. They deducted mortgage interest of $9,000 and property taxes of $2,000. A Revenue Agent disallowed a portion of these deductions under § 265 (Expenses and Interest Relating to Tax-Exempt Income). The disallowed amount was the portion that was allocable to the tax-exempt LQA. Advise Noel on the appropriate treatment of the disallowed property taxes and mortgage interest.

Research Problem 2.   Gray Chemical Company manufactured pesticides that were toxic. Over the course of several years, the toxic waste contaminated the air and water around the company's plant. Several employees suffered toxic poisoning, and the Environmental Protection Agency cited the company for violations. In court, the judge found Gray guilty and imposed fines of $15 million. The company voluntarily set up a charitable fund for the purpose of bettering the environment and funded it with $8 million. The company incurred legal expenses in setting up the foundation and defending itself in court. The court reduced the fine from $15 million to $7 million.

Gray Chemical Company deducted the $8 million paid to the foundation and the legal expenses incurred. The IRS disallowed both deductions on the grounds that the payment was, in fact, a fine and in violation of public policy.

Gray's president, Ted Jones, has contacted you regarding the deductibility of the $7 million fine, the $8 million payment to the foundation, and the legal fees. Write a letter to Mr. Jones that contains your advice and prepare a memo for the tax files. Gray's address is 200 Lincoln Center, Omaha, NE 68182.

Partial list of research aids:
§§ 162(a) and (f).
Reg. § 1.162–21(b).

Research Problem 3.   Rex and Agnes Harrell purchased a beach house at Duck, North Carolina, in early 1996. Although they intended to use the beach house occasionally for recreational purposes, they also planned to rent it through the realty agency that had handled the purchase in order to help pay the mortgage payments, property taxes, and maintenance costs. Rex is a surgeon, and Agnes is a counselor.

The beach house was in need of substantial repairs. Rather than hiring a contractor, Rex and Agnes decided they would make the repairs themselves. During both high school and college, Rex had worked summers in construction. In addition, he had taken an advanced course in woodworking and related subjects from a local community college several years ago.

During 1996, according to a log maintained by the Harrells, they occupied the beach house on 38 days and rented it on 49 days. The log also indicated that on 24 of the 38 days that they occupied the beach house, one or both of them were engaged in work on the beach house. Their two teenage children were with them on all of these days, but did not help with the work being done. On their 1996 income tax return, Rex and Agnes, who filed a joint return, treated the beach house as a rental property and deducted a pro rata share of the property taxes, mortgage interest, utilities, maintenance and repairs, and depreciation in determining their net loss from the beach home. A Revenue Agent has limited the deductions to the rent income. He contends that the 14-day personal use provision was exceeded and that many of the alleged repairs were capital expenditures. Advise the Harrells on how they should respond to the IRS.

Research Problem 4.   Rick is a CPA who practices as a sole proprietor. In college, he majored in art and minored in accounting. His primary reason for leaving his prior accounting position and establishing his own accounting practice was to have time to develop as an artist while the accounting business "paid the rent."

Rick's income from his accounting practice for the past four years was as follows: $10,000, $17,000, $20,000, and $30,000. For the same period, his losses from his art activity were $8,000, $27,000, $27,000, and $28,000. A Schedule C was filed for each activity. Rick maintained only limited records associated with the art activity (i.e., a cash receipts journal and a shoe box full of credit card receipts).

According to Rick, each business had a positive effect on the other. Most of his accounting clients are acquaintances from the artist community, and his artist clients are attracted to his CPA practice because he is a fellow artist.

An IRS agent has classified Rick's art activity as a hobby. Rick contends that his art activity is a trade or business. Alternatively, he contends that the accounting practice and the art activity are a single trade or business. Rick has come to you for tax advice.

Research Problem 5.   Tom and Jane owned a second home in a resort area in Florida. During the year, they vacationed there for 27 days. Their vacation home was leased to the resort rental company under a 30-month lease. The rental agreement provided that the resort was to pay Tom and Jane a fixed annual rent of $21,000 plus 40% of rent income in excess of $52,500. For any day that Tom and Jane used the vacation home, they were required to pay the resort $10 (limited to four weeks). For any personal use in excess of four weeks, they were required to pay the resort 80% of the regular rental amount. The resort rental agent rented their vacation home to tourists for 200 days during the year.

Based on the rental agreement, Tom and Jane's accountant concluded that the vacation home should be classified as primarily rental use property rather than personal/rental use property. The accountant concluded that for § 280A purposes the vacation home was rented for 338 days (i.e., 365 days – 27 days) rather than for only 200 days. Therefore, Tom and Jane were able to take deductions on the vacation home in excess of the rent income. On audit, the IRS treated the property as personal/rental use property and disallowed the excess deductions.

Advise Tom and Jane on how they should respond to the IRS.

Use the tax resources of the Internet to address the following questions. Do not restrict your search to the World Wide Web, but include a review of newsgroups and general reference materials, practitioner sites and resources, primary sources of the tax law, chat rooms and discussion groups, and other opportunities.

Research Problem 6.   Locate and read a recent judicial or administrative ruling regarding the deductibility of hobby losses. Look for rulings that deal with horse breeding, professional sports teams, or art collecting activities. Which criteria did the ruling emphasize in upholding or reversing the taxpayer's deduction for such losses?

Research Problem 7.   The $1 million maximum compensation deduction does not seem to have deterred large corporations from remunerating their executives at very high levels. What techniques are being used to work around the millionaires provision? Are executives taking pay cuts, or are their salaries being deferred or changed in nature due to § 162(m)?

TEAM PROJECT: ARTHUR ANDERSEN TAX CHALLENGE CASES

For more information on the Arthur Andersen Tax Challenge Cases, refer to Chapter 1, page 1–37.

Information related to tax issues and problems that are discussed in this chapter may be found in the

Day and Ball case on pages 2, 3, 5, and 20–24
Fence case on pages 39, 40, 42, and 49

Read and analyze the case you have been assigned and *identify* any issues and problems that are related to material covered in this chapter. If the information provided in the case is complete, prepare answers for this part of the case at this time. If you need information that is contained in the later parts of the case, write a memo summarizing the questions or problems so you can prepare a complete answer at a later date.

DEDUCTIONS AND LOSSES: CERTAIN BUSINESS EXPENSES AND LOSSES

LEARNING OBJECTIVES

After completing Chapter 7, you should be able to:

1. Determine the amount, classification, and timing of the bad debt deduction.

2. Understand the tax treatment of worthless securities including § 1244 stock.

3. Distinguish between deductible and nondeductible losses of individuals.

4. Identify a casualty and determine the amount, classification, and timing of casualty and theft losses.

5. Recognize and apply the alternative tax treatments for research and experimental expenditures.

6. Determine the amount of the net operating loss and recognize the impact of the carryback and carryover provisions.

7. Identify tax planning opportunities in deducting certain business expenses, business losses, and personal losses.

Working with the tax formula for individuals requires the proper classification of items that are deductible *for* adjusted gross income (AGI) and items that are deductions *from* AGI (itemized deductions). Business expenses and losses, discussed in this chapter, are reductions of gross income to arrive at the taxpayer's AGI. Expenses and losses incurred in connection with a transaction entered into for profit and attributable to rents and royalties are deducted *for* AGI. All other expenses and losses incurred in connection with a transaction entered into for profit are deducted *from* AGI.

The situation of Robert P. Groetzinger provides an interesting insight into the importance of the proper classification for the individual taxpayer. In January 1978, Groetzinger terminated his employment with a private company and devoted virtually all of his working time to pari-mutuel wagering on dog races. He had no other profession or employment, and his only sources of income, apart from his gambling winnings, were interest, dividends, and sales from investments. During the tax year in question, he went to the track six days a week and devoted 60 to 80 hours per week to preparing and making wagers on his own account.

The tax question that this case presents is whether Groetzinger's gambling activities constitute a trade or business. If the gambling is a trade or business, his gambling losses are deductions *for* AGI. If the gambling activity is not a trade or business, the losses are itemized deductions, and Groetzinger's taxes increase by $2,142.[1]

Deductible losses on personal use property are deducted as an itemized deduction. Itemized deductions are deductions *from* AGI. While the general coverage of itemized deductions is in Chapter 10, casualty and theft losses on personal use property are discussed in this chapter.

In determining the amount and timing of the deduction for bad debts, proper classification is again important. A business bad debt is classified as a deduction *for* AGI, and a nonbusiness bad debt is classified as a short-term capital loss.

---

[1]*Groetzinger v. Comm.*, 85–2 USTC ¶9622, 56 AFTR2d 85–5683, 771 F.2d 269 (CA–7, 1985).

A BANK OR AN S&L? LOSS OF BAD DEBT RESERVE INFLUENCES DECISION

Robert McCarthy, Jr., chief executive of Parkvale Savings Bank, a savings and loan association, announced that Parkvale might convert to a commercial bank in 1997. One of the factors influencing this decision was the change in the federal law that removed a tax advantage thrifts enjoyed over banks. Under the old law, thrifts were allowed to take a bad debt deduction of up to 8 percent of their taxable income. Under the new law, thrifts won't get that yearly tax break and must pay back the last nine years of liabilities. Parkvale would be required to pay back $1.4 million.

SOURCE: Adapted from Thomas Olson, "Thrift Mulls Switch to Bank," *Tribune Review–Greensburg PA*, October 25, 1996, p. B3.

Other topics discussed in Chapter 7 are research and experimental expenditures and the net operating loss deduction.

BAD DEBTS

1 **LEARNING OBJECTIVE**
Determine the amount, classification, and timing of the bad debt deduction.

If a taxpayer sells goods or provides services on credit and the account receivable subsequently becomes worthless, a **bad debt** deduction is permitted only if income arising from the creation of the account receivable was previously included in income.[2] No deduction is allowed, for example, for a bad debt arising from the sale of a product or service when the taxpayer is on the cash basis because no income is reported until the cash has been collected. Permitting a bad debt deduction for a cash basis taxpayer would amount to a double deduction because the expenses of the product or service rendered are deducted when payments are made to suppliers and to employees, or at the time of the sale.

EXAMPLE 1

Tracy, an individual engaged in the practice of accounting, performed accounting services for Pat for which she charged $8,000. Pat never paid the bill, and his whereabouts are unknown.

If Tracy is an accrual basis taxpayer, the $8,000 is included in income when the services are performed. When it is determined that Pat's account will not be collected, the $8,000 is expensed as a bad debt.

If Tracy is a cash basis taxpayer, the $8,000 is not included in income until payment is received. When it is determined that Pat's account will not be collected, the $8,000 is not deducted as a bad debt expense since it was never recognized as income. ▼

A bad debt can also result from the nonrepayment of a loan made by the taxpayer or from purchased debt instruments.

SPECIFIC CHARGE-OFF METHOD

Taxpayers (other than certain financial institutions) may use only the **specific charge-off method** in accounting for bad debts. Certain financial institutions are allowed to use the **reserve method** for computing deductions for bad debts.

---

[2]Reg. § 1.166–1(e).

CONCEPT SUMMARY 7–1

Specific Charge-Off Method

Expense deduction and account write-off	The expense arises and the write-off takes place when a specific business account becomes either partially or wholly worthless or when a specific nonbusiness account becomes wholly worthless.
Recovery of accounts previously written off	If the account recovered was written off during the current taxable year, the write-off entry is reversed. If the account recovered was written off during a previous taxable year, income is created subject to the tax benefit rule.

A taxpayer using the specific charge-off method may claim a deduction when a specific business debt becomes either partially or wholly worthless or when a specific nonbusiness debt becomes wholly worthless.[3] For the business debt, the taxpayer must satisfy the IRS that the debt is partially worthless and must demonstrate the amount of worthlessness.

If a business debt previously deducted as partially worthless becomes totally worthless in a future year, only the remainder not previously deducted can be deducted in the future year.

In the case of total worthlessness, a deduction is allowed for the entire amount in the year the debt becomes worthless. The amount of the deduction depends on the taxpayer's basis in the bad debt. If the debt arose from the sale of services or products and the face amount was previously included in income, that amount is deductible. If the taxpayer purchased the debt, the deduction is equal to the amount the taxpayer paid for the debt instrument.

One of the more difficult tasks is determining if and when a bad debt is worthless. The loss is deductible only in the year of partial or total worthlessness for business debts and only in the year of total worthlessness for nonbusiness debts. Legal proceedings need not be initiated against the debtor when the surrounding facts indicate that such action will not result in collection.

EXAMPLE 2   In 1996, Ross loaned $1,000 to Kay, who agreed to repay the loan in two years. In 1998, Kay disappeared after the note became delinquent. If a reasonable investigation by Ross indicates that he cannot find Kay or that a suit against Kay would not result in collection, Ross can deduct the $1,000 in 1998. ▼

Bankruptcy is generally an indication of at least partial worthlessness of a debt. Bankruptcy may create worthlessness before the settlement date. If this is the case, the deduction may be taken in the year of worthlessness.

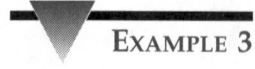

EXAMPLE 3   In Example 2, assume Kay filed for personal bankruptcy in 1997 and that the debt is a business debt. At that time, Ross learned that unsecured creditors (including Ross) were ultimately expected to receive 20¢ on the dollar. In 1998, settlement is made and Ross receives only $150. He should deduct $800 ($1,000 loan − $200 expected settlement) in 1997 and $50 in 1998 ($200 balance − $150 proceeds). ▼

If a receivable has been written off as uncollectible during the current tax year and is subsequently collected during the current tax year, the write-off entry is

---

[3]§ 166(a) and Reg. § 1.166.

reversed. If a receivable has been written off as uncollectible, the collection of the receivable in a later tax year may result in income being recognized. Income will result if the deduction yielded a tax benefit in the year it was taken. See Examples 38 and 39 in Chapter 5.

BUSINESS VERSUS NONBUSINESS BAD DEBTS

A **nonbusiness bad debt** is a debt unrelated to the taxpayer's trade or business either when it was created or when it became worthless. The nature of a debt depends on whether the lender was engaged in the business of lending money or whether there is a proximate relationship between the creation of the debt and the lender's trade or business. The use to which the borrowed funds are put by the debtor is of no consequence. Loans to relatives or friends are the most common type of nonbusiness bad debt.

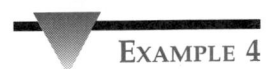
EXAMPLE 4

Jamil loaned his friend, Esther, $1,500. Esther used the money to start a business, which subsequently failed. Even though the proceeds of the loan were used in a business, the loan is a nonbusiness bad debt because the business was Esther's, not Jamil's. ▼

The distinction between a business bad debt and a nonbusiness bad debt is important. A **business bad debt** is deductible as an ordinary loss in the year incurred, whereas a nonbusiness bad debt is always treated as a short-term capital loss. Thus, regardless of the age of a nonbusiness bad debt, the deduction may be of limited benefit due to the capital loss limitations on deductibility in any one year. The maximum amount of a net short-term capital loss that an individual can deduct against ordinary income in any one year is $3,000 (see Chapter 16 for a detailed discussion). Although no deduction is allowed when a nonbusiness bad debt is partially worthless, the taxpayer is entitled to deduct the net amount of the loss upon final settlement.

The following example is an illustration of business bad debts adapted from the Regulations.[4]

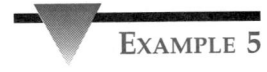
EXAMPLE 5

In 1997, Leif sold his business but retained a claim (note or account receivable) against Bob. The claim became worthless in 1998. Leif's loss is treated as a business bad debt because the debt was created in the conduct of his former trade or business. Leif is accorded business bad debt treatment even though he was holding the note as an investor and was no longer in a trade or business when the claim became worthless. ▼

The nonbusiness bad debt provisions are *not* applicable to corporations. It is assumed that any loans made by a corporation are related to its trade or business. Therefore, any bad debts of a corporation are business bad debts.

LOANS BETWEEN RELATED PARTIES

Loans between related parties (especially family members) raise the issue of whether the transaction was a *bona fide* loan or a gift. The Regulations state that a bona fide debt arises from a debtor-creditor relationship based on a valid and enforceable obligation to pay a fixed or determinable sum of money. Thus, individual circumstances must be examined to determine whether advances between related parties are gifts or loans. Some considerations are these:

---

[4]Reg. § 1.166–5(d).

- Was a note properly executed?
- Was there a reasonable rate of interest?
- Was collateral provided?
- What collection efforts were made?
- What was the intent of the parties?

EXAMPLE 6

Lana loans $2,000 to her widowed mother for an operation. Lana's mother owns no property and is not employed, and her only income consists of Social Security benefits. No note is issued for the loan, no provision for interest is made, and no repayment date is mentioned. In the current year, Lana's mother dies leaving no estate. Assuming the loan is not repaid, Lana cannot take a deduction for a nonbusiness bad debt because the facts indicate that no debtor-creditor relationship existed. ▼

ETHICAL CONSIDERATIONS

Writing Off a Loan to a Friend

Loans to family members and friends raise concerns with respect to whether a deductible bad debt exists. The fact that the debtor is a family member or friend does not preclude a deduction for a bad debt. However, evidence must show that the debt is bona fide and that it is in fact worthless.

Frank, an engineer, loans $8,000 to Chris, a friend from high school who is a musician. Chris uses the money to cut a record. The loan, which is evidenced by a formal written instrument, has a maturity date of three years and an 8 percent interest rate.

The record is unsuccessful, and at the maturity date, Chris does not repay the loan. Frank writes Chris twice requesting repayment. Frank hears from another friend that Chris is now divorced and has a drinking problem.

Frank decides to give up trying to collect the loan. Since Frank's combined Federal and state tax rate is 44 percent, he decides he can live without $4,480 ($8,000 × 56%). He deducts the $8,000 as a nonbusiness bad debt on his Federal and state tax returns.

Evaluate the financial and ethical aspects of what Frank has done.

LOSS ON DEPOSITS IN INSOLVENT FINANCIAL INSTITUTIONS

Qualified individuals can *elect* to deduct losses on deposits in qualified financial institutions as personal casualty losses in the year in which the amount of the loss can be reasonably estimated. If the election is made to treat a loss on a deposit as a personal casualty loss, no bad debt deduction for the loss is allowed.[5] As a personal casualty loss, the loss is subject to the $100 per event floor and the 10 percent-of-AGI aggregate floor. Both floors limiting casualty losses are explained later in the chapter. The amount of loss to be recognized under the election is the difference between (1) the taxpayer's basis in the deposit and (2) a reasonable estimate of the amount to be received.

A *qualified individual* is any individual other than:

- An owner of 1 percent or more of the value of the stock of the institution in which the loss was sustained.
- An officer of the institution.

[5]§ 165(l).

• Certain relatives and other persons who are tax-related to such owners and officers.

A *qualified financial institution* is a commercial bank, thrift institution, insured credit union, or any similar institution chartered and supervised under Federal or state law. A *deposit*, for purposes of this provision, is any deposit, withdrawal certificate, or withdrawable or repurchasable share of or in a qualified financial institution. The term *insolvent* generally denotes a situation where the liabilities exceed the fair market value of the assets.

If the individual does not elect to deduct the loss as a casualty loss, it is treated as a nonbusiness bad debt and, hence, as a short-term capital loss. As a short-term capital loss, it is subject to the capital loss limitation rules (see the discussion in Chapter 16).

WORTHLESS SECURITIES

2 **LEARNING OBJECTIVE**
Understand the tax treatment of worthless securities including § 1244 stock.

A loss is allowed for securities that become *completely* worthless during the year (**worthless securities**).[6] Such securities are shares of stock, bonds, notes, or other evidence of indebtedness issued by a corporation or government. The losses generated are treated as capital losses deemed to have occurred on the *last day* of the taxable year. By treating the loss as having occurred on the last day of the taxable year, a loss that would otherwise have been classified as short term (if the date of worthlessness was used) may be classified as a long-term capital loss. Capital losses may be of limited benefit due to the $3,000 capital loss limitation.

 EXAMPLE 7

Ali, a calendar year taxpayer, owns stock in Owl Corporation (a publicly held company). The stock was acquired as an investment on May 31, 1997, at a cost of $5,000. On April 1, 1998, the stock became worthless. Since the stock is deemed to have become worthless as of December 31 of 1998, Ali has a capital loss from an asset held for 19 months (a long-term capital loss). ▼

SMALL BUSINESS STOCK

The general rule is that shareholders receive capital gain or loss treatment upon the sale or exchange of stock. However, it is possible to receive an ordinary loss deduction if the loss is sustained on **small business stock (§ 1244 stock).** This loss could arise from a sale of the stock or from the stock becoming worthless. Only *individuals*[7] who acquired the stock *from* the corporation are eligible to receive ordinary loss treatment under § 1244. The ordinary loss treatment is limited to $50,000 ($100,000 for married individuals filing jointly) per year. Losses on § 1244 stock in excess of the statutory limits receive capital loss treatment.

The corporation must meet certain requirements for the loss on § 1244 stock to be treated as an *ordinary*—rather than a capital—loss. The major requirement is that the total amount of money and other property received by the corporation for stock as a contribution to capital (or paid-in surplus) does not exceed $1 million. The $1 million test is made at the time the stock is issued. Section 1244 stock can

---

[6]§ 165(g).
[7]The term "individuals" for this purpose includes a partnership but not a trust or an estate.

CONCEPT SUMMARY 7–2

Bad Debt Deductions

A ←— No —— Does a valid debt exist (a debtor-creditor relationship)?
↓ Yes

A ←— No —— Is the debt really worthless?
↓ Yes

Is the debt evidenced by a security? —— Yes ——→ See § 165(g) dealing with worthless securities (discussed on page 7–7)
↓ No

Is the creditor a corporation? —— Yes ——→ **C**
↓ No

Is the debt a deposit of a qualified individual in a qualified financial institution? —— Yes ——→ Is an election made to treat the loss as a personal casualty? —— Yes ——→ **D**
↓ No   ↓ No
                                                                                             B

Is the debt created or incurred in connection with the creditor's trade or business? —— No ——→
↓ Yes

C

—————— Legend to Tax Treatment ——————

A ↓   **B** ↓   **C** ↓   **D** ↓

No deduction allowed | Nonbusiness bad debt (treated as a short-term capital loss) | Business bad debt (treated as an ordinary deduction) | Personal casualty loss

---

be common or preferred stock. Section 1244 applies only to losses. If § 1244 stock is sold at a gain, the Section has no application, and the gain is capital gain.

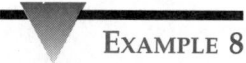

EXAMPLE 8 On July 1, 1996, Iris, a single individual, purchased 100 shares of Eagle Corporation common stock for $100,000. The Eagle stock qualified as § 1244 stock. On June 20, 1998, Iris sold all of the Eagle stock for $20,000. Because the Eagle stock is § 1244 stock, Iris would have $50,000 of ordinary loss and $30,000 of long-term capital loss. ▼

LOSSES OF INDIVIDUALS

3 LEARNING OBJECTIVE
Distinguish between deductible and nondeductible losses of individuals.

An individual may deduct the following losses under § 165(c):

- Losses incurred in a trade or business.
- Losses incurred in a transaction entered into for profit.
- Losses caused by fire, storm, shipwreck, or other casualty or by theft.

An individual taxpayer may deduct losses to property used in the taxpayer's trade or business or losses to property used in a transaction entered into for profit. Examples include a loss on property used in a proprietorship, a loss on property held for rent, or a loss on stolen bearer bonds. Note that an individual's losses on property used in a trade or business or on transactions entered into for profit are not limited to losses caused by fire, storm, shipwreck, or other casualty or by theft.

An individual taxpayer suffering losses from damage to nonbusiness property can deduct only those losses attributable to fire, storm, shipwreck, or other casualty or theft. Although the meaning of the terms *fire, storm, shipwreck,* and *theft* is relatively free from dispute, the term *other casualty* needs further clarification. It means casualties analogous to fire, storm, or shipwreck. The term also includes accidental loss of property provided the loss qualifies under the same rules as any other casualty. These rules are that the loss must result from an event that is (1) identifiable; (2) damaging to property; and (3) sudden, unexpected, and unusual in nature.

A *sudden event* is one that is swift and precipitous and not gradual or progressive. An *unexpected event* is an event that is ordinarily unanticipated and occurs without the intent of the individual who suffers the loss. An *unusual event* is one that is extraordinary and nonrecurring and does not commonly occur during the activity in which the taxpayer was engaged when the destruction occurred.[8] Examples include hurricanes, tornadoes, floods, storms, shipwrecks, fires, auto accidents, mine cave-ins, sonic booms, and vandalism. Weather that causes damages (drought, for example) must be unusual and severe for the particular region. Damage must be to the taxpayer's property to qualify as a **casualty loss.**

A taxpayer can take a deduction for a casualty loss from an automobile accident only if the damage was not caused by the taxpayer's willful act or willful negligence.

EXAMPLE 9

Ted parks his car on a hill and fails to set the brake properly and to curb the wheels. As a result of Ted's negligence, the car rolls down the hill and is damaged. The repairs to Ted's car should qualify for casualty loss treatment since Ted's act of negligence appears to be simple rather than willful. ▼

EVENTS THAT ARE NOT CASUALTIES

4 LEARNING OBJECTIVE
Identify a casualty and determine the amount, classification, and timing of casualty and theft losses.

Not all acts of God are treated as casualty losses for income tax purposes. Because a casualty must be sudden, unexpected, and unusual, progressive deterioration (such as erosion due to wind or rain) is not a casualty because it does not meet the suddenness test.

Examples of nonsudden events that generally do not qualify as casualties include disease and insect damages. When the damage was caused by termites over

[8]Rev.Rul. 72–592, 1972–2 C.B. 101.

a period of several years, some courts have disallowed a casualty loss deduction.[9] On the other hand, some courts have held that termite damage over periods of up to 15 months after infestation constituted a sudden event and was, therefore, deductible as a casualty loss.[10] Despite the existence of some judicial support for the deductibility of termite damage as a casualty loss, the current position of the IRS is that termite damage is not deductible.[11]

Other examples of events that are not casualties are losses resulting from a decline in value rather than an actual loss of the property. No loss was allowed where the taxpayer's home declined in value as a result of a landslide that destroyed neighboring homes but did no actual damage to the taxpayer's home.[12] Similarly, a taxpayer was allowed a loss for the actual flood damage to his property but not for the decline in market value due to the property's being flood-prone.[13]

THEFT LOSSES

Theft includes, but is not necessarily limited to, larceny, embezzlement, and robbery.[14] Theft does not include misplaced items.[15]

Theft losses are computed like other casualty losses (discussed in the following section), but the *timing* for recognition of the loss differs. A theft loss is deducted in the year of discovery, not the year of the theft (unless, of course, the discovery occurs in the same year as the theft). If, in the year of the discovery, a claim exists (e.g., against an insurance company) and there is a reasonable expectation of recovering the adjusted basis of the asset from the insurance company, no deduction is permitted.[16] If, in the year of settlement, the recovery is less than the asset's adjusted basis, a partial deduction may be available. If the recovery is greater than the asset's adjusted basis, gain may be recognized.

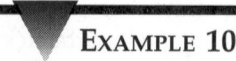

EXAMPLE 10

Keith's new sailboat, which he uses for personal purposes, was stolen from the storage marina in December 1996. He discovered the loss on June 3, 1997, and filed a claim with his insurance company that was settled on January 30, 1998. Assuming there is a reasonable expectation of full recovery, no deduction is allowed in 1997. A partial deduction may be available in 1998 if the actual insurance proceeds are less than the lower of the fair market value or the adjusted basis of the asset. (Loss measurement rules are discussed later in this chapter.) ▼

ETHICAL CONSIDERATIONS

Deducting a Theft Loss

Theft losses of personal use assets are itemized deductions in the year of discovery. The taxpayer must show that the property was actually stolen. Losses due to mislaying or losing property cannot be deducted. If there is no positive proof that a theft occurred, all of the details and evidence should be presented. If the reasonable inferences point to a theft, the Tax Court has allowed a deduction. If the inferences point to a mysterious (unexplained) disappearance, however, the deduction will be disallowed.

[9]*Fay v. Helvering*, 41–2 USTC ¶9494, 27 AFTR 432, 120 F.2d 253(CA–2, 1941); *U.S. v. Rogers*, 41–1 USTC ¶9442, 27 AFTR 423, 120 F.2d 244 (CA–9, 1941).
[10]*Rosenberg v. Comm.*, 52–2 USTC ¶9377, 42 AFTR 303, 198 F.2d 46 (CA–8, 1952); *Shopmaker v. U.S.*, 54–1 USTC ¶9195, 45 AFTR 758, 119 F.Supp. 705 (D.Ct.Mo., 1953).
[11]Rev.Rul. 63–232, 1963–2 C.B. 97.

[12]*H. Pulvers v. Comm.*, 69–1 USTC ¶9222, 23 AFTR2d 69–678, 407 F.2d 838 (CA–9, 1969).
[13]*S. L. Solomon*, 39 TCM 1282, T.C.Memo. 1980–87.
[14]Reg. § 1.165–8(d).
[15]*Mary Francis Allen*, 16 T.C. 163 (1951).
[16]Reg. §§ 1.165–1(d)(2) and 1.165–8(a)(2).

A taxpayer went shopping in a major city, riding the subway to and from the city. During the day, he purchased items using money from his wallet. When he arrived home, his wallet was missing. He is considering claiming a theft loss deduction for the wallet and the money it contained.

WHEN TO DEDUCT CASUALTY LOSSES

General Rule.   Generally, a casualty loss is deducted in the year the loss occurs. However, no casualty loss is permitted if a reimbursement claim with a *reasonable prospect of full recovery* exists.[17] If the taxpayer has a partial claim, only part of the loss can be claimed in the year of the casualty, and the remainder is deducted in the year the claim is settled.

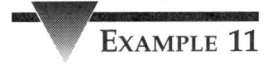

EXAMPLE 11

Brian's new sailboat was completely destroyed by fire in 1998. Its cost and fair market value were $10,000. Brian's only claim against the insurance company was on a $7,000 policy that was not settled by year-end. The following year, 1999, Brian settled with the insurance company for $6,000. He is entitled to a $3,000 deduction in 1998 and a $1,000 deduction in 1999. If Brian held the sailboat for personal use, the $3,000 deduction in 1998 would be reduced first by $100 and then by 10% of his 1998 AGI. The $1,000 deduction in 1999 would be reduced by 10% of his 1999 AGI (see the following discussion on the $100 and 10% floors). ▼

If a taxpayer receives reimbursement for a casualty loss sustained and deducted in a previous year, an amended return is not filed for that year. Instead, the taxpayer must include the reimbursement in gross income on the return for the year in which it is received to the extent that the previous deduction resulted in a tax benefit.

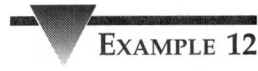

EXAMPLE 12

Fran had a deductible casualty loss of $5,000 on her 1997 tax return. Fran's taxable income for 1997 was $60,000. In June 1998, Fran was reimbursed $3,000 for the prior year's casualty loss. Fran would include the entire $3,000 in gross income for 1998 because the deduction in 1997 produced a tax benefit. ▼

Disaster Area Losses.   An exception to the general rule for the time of deduction is allowed for **disaster area losses,** which are casualties sustained in an area designated as a disaster area by the President of the United States.[18] In such cases, the taxpayer may *elect* to treat the loss as having occurred in the taxable year immediately *preceding* the taxable year in which the disaster actually occurred. The rationale for this exception is to provide immediate relief to disaster victims in the form of accelerated tax benefits.

If the due date, plus extensions, for the prior year's return has not passed, a taxpayer makes the election to claim the disaster area loss on the prior year's tax return. If the disaster occurs after the prior year's return has been filed, it is necessary to file either an amended return or a refund claim. In any case, the taxpayer must show clearly that such an election is being made.

Disaster loss treatment also applies in the case of a personal residence that has been rendered unsafe for use as a residence because of a disaster. This provision applies when, within 120 days after the President designates the area as a disaster area, the state or local government where the residence is located orders the taxpayer to demolish or relocate the residence.[19]

---

[17]Reg. § 1.165–1(d)(2)(i).
[18]§ 165(h).

[19]§ 165(k).

TAX IN THE NEWS

FILING RELIEF FOR DISASTER AREA VICTIMS

Federal revenue officials extended the deadline for filing tax returns from April 15 to May 30 for individuals and businesses in Minnesota counties that were declared a disaster area as a result of spring floods. The announcement informed individual taxpayers that they could claim uninsured flood casualty losses on either their 1996 or their 1997 returns. Those relying on this flood-related relief were to write "97 FLOODS" at the top of their returns.

SOURCE: Adapted from Conrad deFiebre, "Tax Deadline Extended to May 30 for Flood Victims," *Minneapolis Star Tribune*, April 11, 1997, p. 19A.

MEASURING THE AMOUNT OF LOSS

Amount of Loss.   The rules for determining the amount of a loss depend in part on whether business use, income-producing use, or personal use property was involved. Another factor that must be considered is whether the property was partially or completely destroyed.

If business property or property held for the production of income (e.g., rental property) is *completely destroyed*, the loss is equal to the adjusted basis of the property at the time of destruction.

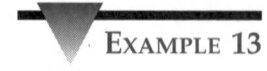

EXAMPLE 13

Vicki's automobile, which was used only for business purposes, was destroyed by fire. Vicki had unintentionally allowed her insurance coverage to expire. The fair market value of the automobile was $9,000 at the time of the fire, and its adjusted basis was $10,000. Vicki is allowed a loss deduction of $10,000 (the basis of the automobile). The $10,000 loss is a deduction *for* AGI. ▼

A different measurement rule applies for *partial destruction* of business property and income-producing property and for *partial* or *complete destruction* of personal use property. In these situations, the loss is the *lesser* of the following:

- The adjusted basis of the property.
- The difference between the fair market value of the property before the event and the fair market value immediately after the event.

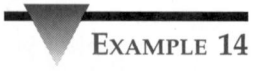

EXAMPLE 14

Kelly's uninsured automobile, which was used only for business purposes, was damaged in a wreck. At the date of the wreck, the fair market value of the automobile was $12,000, and its adjusted basis was $9,000. After the wreck, the automobile was appraised at $4,000. Kelly's loss deduction is $8,000 (the lesser of the adjusted basis or the decrease in fair market value). The $8,000 loss is a deduction *for* AGI. ▼

The deduction for the loss of property that is part business and part personal must be computed separately for the business portion and the personal portion.

Any insurance recovery reduces the loss for business, production of income, and personal use losses. In fact, a taxpayer may realize a gain if the insurance proceeds exceed the amount of the loss. Chapter 17 discusses the treatment of net gains and losses on business property and income-producing property.

A taxpayer is not permitted to deduct a casualty loss for damage to insured personal use property unless she files a *timely insurance claim* with respect to the damage to the property. This rule applies to the extent that any insurance policy provides for full or partial reimbursement for the loss.[20]

Generally, an appraisal before and after the casualty is needed to measure the amount of the loss. However, the *cost of repairs* to the damaged property is acceptable as a method of establishing the loss in value provided the following criteria are met:

- The repairs are necessary to restore the property to its condition immediately before the casualty.
- The amount spent for such repairs is not excessive.
- The repairs do not extend beyond the damage suffered.
- The value of the property after the repairs does not, as a result of the repairs, exceed the value of the property immediately before the casualty.[21]

Reduction for $100 and 10 Percent-of-AGI Floors.   The amount of the loss for personal use property must be further reduced by a $100 *per event* floor and a 10 percent-of-AGI *aggregate* floor.[22] The $100 floor applies separately to each casualty and applies to the entire loss from each casualty (e.g., if a storm damages both a taxpayer's residence and automobile, only $100 is subtracted from the total amount of the loss). The losses are then added together, and the total is reduced by 10 percent of the taxpayer's AGI. The resulting loss is the taxpayer's itemized deduction for casualty and theft losses.

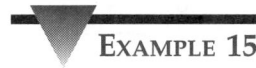

EXAMPLE 15

Rocky, who had AGI of $30,000, was involved in a motorcycle accident. His motorcycle, which was used only for personal use and had a fair market value of $12,000 and an adjusted basis of $9,000, was completely destroyed. He received $5,000 from his insurance company. Rocky's casualty loss deduction is $900 [$9,000 basis – $5,000 insurance – $100 floor – $3,000 (.10 × $30,000 AGI)]. The $900 casualty loss is an itemized deduction (*from* AGI). ▼

When a nonbusiness casualty loss is spread between two taxable years because of the *reasonable prospect of recovery* doctrine, the loss in the second year is not reduced by the $100 floor. This result occurs because this floor is imposed per event and has already reduced the amount of the loss in the first year. However, the loss in the second year is still subject to the 10 percent floor based on the taxpayer's second-year AGI (refer to Example 11).

Taxpayers who suffer qualified disaster area losses can elect to deduct the losses in the year preceding the year of occurrence. The disaster loss is treated as having occurred in the preceding taxable year. Hence, the 10 percent-of-AGI floor is determined by using the AGI of the year for which the deduction is claimed.[23]

Multiple Losses.   The rules for computing loss deductions where multiple losses have occurred are explained in Examples 16 and 17.

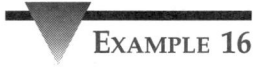

EXAMPLE 16

During the year, Tim had the following casualty losses:

Asset	Adjusted Basis	Fair Market Value of Asset		Insurance Recovery
		Before the Casualty	After the Casualty	
A	$900	$600	$–0–	$400
B	300	800	250	100

[20]§ 165(h)(4)(E).
[21]Reg. § 1.165–7(a)(2)(ii).
[22]§ 165(c)(3).
[23]§ 165(i).

Assets A and B were used in Tim's business at the time of the casualty. The following losses are allowed:

Asset A: $500. The complete destruction of a business asset results in a deduction of the adjusted basis of the property (reduced by any insurance recovery) regardless of the asset's fair market value.

Asset B: $200. The partial destruction of a business (or personal use) asset results in a deduction equal to the lesser of the adjusted basis ($300) or the decline in value ($550), reduced by any insurance recovery ($100).

Both Asset A and Asset B losses are deductions *for* AGI. The $100 floor and the 10%-of-AGI floor do not apply because the assets are business assets. ▼

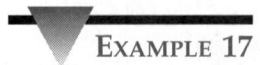
EXAMPLE 17

During the year, Emily had AGI of $20,000 and the following casualty losses:

Asset	Adjusted Basis	Fair Market Value of Asset		Insurance Recovery
		Before the Casualty	After the Casualty	
A	$ 900	$ 600	$ –0–	$200
B	2,500	4,000	1,000	–0–
C	800	400	100	250

Assets A, B, and C were held for personal use, and the losses to these three assets are from three different casualties. The loss for each asset is computed as follows:

Asset A: $300. The lesser of the adjusted basis of $900 or the $600 decline in value, reduced by the insurance recovery of $200, minus the $100 floor.

Asset B: $2,400. The lesser of the adjusted basis of $2,500 or the $3,000 decline in value, minus the $100 floor.

Asset C: $0. The lesser of the adjusted basis of $800 or the $300 decline in value, reduced by the insurance recovery of $250, minus the $100 floor.

Emily's itemized casualty loss deduction for the year is $700:

Asset A loss	$ 300
Asset B loss	2,400
Asset C loss	–0–
Total loss	$ 2,700
Less: 10% of AGI (10% × $20,000)	(2,000)
Itemized casualty loss deduction	$ 700

▼

STATUTORY FRAMEWORK FOR DEDUCTING LOSSES OF INDIVIDUALS

Casualty and theft losses incurred by an individual in connection with a trade or business are deductible *for* AGI.[24] These losses are not subject to the $100 per event and the 10 percent-of-AGI limitations.

[24]§ 62(a)(1).

Casualty and theft losses incurred by an individual in a transaction entered into for profit are not subject to the $100 per event and the 10 percent-of-AGI limitations. If these losses are attributable to rents or royalties, the deduction is *for* AGI.[25] However, if these losses are not connected with property held for the production of rents and royalties, they are deductions *from* AGI. More specifically, these losses are classified as other miscellaneous itemized deductions. An example of this type of loss would be the theft of a security. The aggregate of certain miscellaneous itemized deductions is subject to a 2 percent-of-AGI floor (explained in Chapter 9).

Casualty and theft losses attributable to personal use property are subject to the $100 per event and the 10 percent-of-AGI limitations. These losses are itemized deductions, but they are not subject to the 2 percent-of-AGI floor.[26]

PERSONAL CASUALTY GAINS AND LOSSES

If a taxpayer has personal casualty and theft gains as well as losses, a special set of rules applies for determining the tax consequences. A **personal casualty gain** is the recognized gain from a casualty or theft of personal use property. A **personal casualty loss** for this purpose is a casualty or theft loss of personal use property after the application of the $100 floor. A taxpayer who has both gains and losses for the taxable year must first net (offset) the personal casualty gains and personal casualty losses. If the gains exceed the losses, the gains and losses are treated as gains and losses from the sale of capital assets. The capital gains and losses are short term or long term, depending on the period the taxpayer held each of the assets. In the netting process, personal casualty and theft gains and losses are not netted with the gains and losses on business and income-producing property.

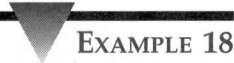
EXAMPLE 18

During the year, Cliff had the following personal casualty gains and losses (after deducting the $100 floor):

Asset	Holding Period	Gain or (Loss)
A	Three months	($ 300)
B	Three years	(2,400)
C	Two years	3,200

Cliff would compute the tax consequences as follows:

Personal casualty gain	$ 3,200
Personal casualty loss ($300 + $2,400)	(2,700)
Net personal casualty gain	$ 500

Cliff would treat all of the gains and losses as capital gains and losses and would have the following:

Short-term capital loss (Asset A)	$ 300
Long-term capital loss (Asset B)	2,400
Long-term capital gain (Asset C)	3,200

▼

If personal casualty losses exceed personal casualty gains, all gains and losses are treated as ordinary items. The gains—and the losses to the extent of gains—are

---

[25]§ 62(a)(4).   [26]§ 67(b)(3).

treated as ordinary income and ordinary loss in computing AGI. Losses in excess of gains are deducted as itemized deductions to the extent the losses exceed 10 percent of AGI.[27]

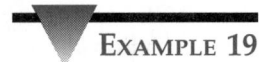

EXAMPLE 19

During the year, Hazel had AGI of $20,000 and the following personal casualty gain and loss (after deducting the $100 floor):

Asset	Holding Period	Gain or (Loss)
A	Three years	($2,700)
B	Four months	200

Hazel would compute the tax consequences as follows:

Personal casualty loss	($2,700)
Personal casualty gain	200
Net personal casualty loss	($2,500)

Hazel would treat the gain and the loss as ordinary items. The $200 gain and $200 of the loss would be included in computing AGI. Hazel's itemized deduction for casualty losses would be computed as follows:

Casualty loss in excess of gain ($2,700 – $200)	$ 2,500
Less: 10% of AGI (10% × $20,000)	(2,000)
Itemized deduction	$ 500

RESEARCH AND EXPERIMENTAL EXPENDITURES

5 LEARNING OBJECTIVE
Recognize and apply the alternative tax treatments for research and experimental expenditures.

Section 174 covers the treatment of research and experimental expenditures. The Regulations define **research and experimental expenditures** as follows:

> . . . all such costs incident to the development of an experimental or pilot model, a plant process, a product, a formula, an invention, or similar property, and the improvement of already existing property of the type mentioned. The term does not include expenditures such as those for the ordinary testing or inspection of materials or products for quality control or those for efficiency surveys, management studies, consumer surveys, advertising, or promotions.[28]

Expenses in connection with the acquisition or improvement of land or depreciable property are not research and experimental expenditures. Rather, they increase the basis of the land or depreciable property. However, depreciation on a building used for research may be a research and experimental expense. Only the depreciation that is a research and experimental expense (not the cost of the asset) is subject to the three alternatives discussed below.

The law permits the following *three alternatives* for the handling of research and experimental expenditures:

- Expensed in the year paid or incurred.
- Deferred and amortized.
- Capitalized.

---
[27]§ 165(h).   [28]Reg. § 1.174–2(a)(1).

CONCEPT SUMMARY 7–3

Casualty Gains and Losses

	Business Use or Income-Producing Property	Personal Use Property
Event creating the loss	Any event.	Casualty or theft.
Amount	The lesser of the decline in fair market value or the adjusted basis, but always the adjusted basis if the property is totally destroyed.	The lesser of the decline in fair market value or the adjusted basis.
Insurance	Insurance proceeds received reduce the amount of the loss.	Insurance proceeds received (or for which there is an unfiled claim) reduce the amount of the loss.
$100 floor	Not applicable.	Applicable per event.
Gains and losses	Gains and losses are netted (see detailed discussion in Chapter 17).	Personal casualty and theft gains and losses are netted.
Gains exceeding losses		The gains and losses are treated as gains and losses from the sale of capital assets.
Losses exceeding gains		The gains—and the losses to the extent of gains—are treated as ordinary items in computing AGI. The losses in excess of gains, to the extent they exceed 10% of AGI, are itemized deductions.

If the costs are capitalized, a deduction is not available until the research project is abandoned or is deemed worthless. Since many products resulting from research projects do not have a definite and limited useful life, a taxpayer should ordinarily elect to write off the expenditures immediately or to defer and amortize them. It is generally preferable to elect an immediate write-off of the research expenditures because of the time value of the tax deduction.

The law also provides for a research activities credit. The credit amounts to 20 percent of certain research and experimental expenditures.[29] (The credit is discussed more fully in Chapter 13.)

EXPENSE METHOD

A taxpayer can elect to expense all of the research and experimental expenditures incurred in the current year and all subsequent years. The consent of the IRS is not required if the method is adopted for the first taxable year in which such expenditures were paid or incurred. Once the election is made, the taxpayer must continue to expense all qualifying expenditures unless a request for a change is made to, and approved by, the IRS. In certain instances, a taxpayer may incur research and experimental expenditures before actually engaging in any trade or

---

[29]§ 41. See the information in Chapter 13 on the termination date for the research activities credit.

business activity. In such instances, the Supreme Court has applied a liberal standard of deductibility and permitted a deduction in the year of incurrence.[30]

DEFERRAL AND AMORTIZATION METHOD

Alternatively, research and experimental expenditures may be deferred and amortized if the taxpayer makes an election.[31] Under the election, research and experimental expenditures are amortized ratably over a period of not less than 60 months. A deduction is allowed beginning with the month in which the taxpayer first realizes benefits from the experimental expenditure. The election is binding, and a change requires permission from the IRS.

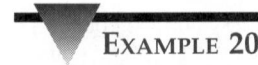

EXAMPLE 20

Gold Corporation decided to develop a new line of adhesives. The project was begun in 1998. Gold incurred the following expenses in 1998 in connection with the project:

Salaries	$25,000
Materials	8,000
Depreciation on machinery	6,500

Gold incurred the following expenses in 1999 in connection with the project:

Salaries	$18,000
Materials	2,000
Depreciation on machinery	5,700

The benefits from the project will be realized starting in March 2000. If Gold Corporation elects a 60-month deferral and amortization period, there will be no deduction prior to March 2000, the month benefits from the project begin to be realized. The deduction for 2000 would be $10,867, computed as follows:

Salaries ($25,000 + $18,000)	$43,000
Materials ($8,000 + $2,000)	10,000
Depreciation ($6,500 + $5,700)	12,200
Total	$65,200
$65,200 × (10 months/60 months) =	$10,867

The option to treat research and experimental expenditures as deferred expense is usually employed when a company does not have sufficient income to offset the research and experimental expenses. Rather than create net operating loss carryovers that might not be utilized because of the 20-year limitation on such carryovers, the deferral and amortization method may be used. The deferral of research and experimental expenditures should also be considered if the taxpayer expects higher tax rates in the future.

---

[30]*Snow v. Comm.*, 74–1 USTC ¶9432, 33 AFTR2d 74–1251, 94 S.Ct. 1876 (USSC, 1974).

[31]§ 174(b)(2).

NET OPERATING LOSSES

6   LEARNING OBJECTIVE
Determine the amount of the net
operating loss and recognize
the impact of the carryback and
carryover provisions.

The requirement that every taxpayer file an annual income tax return (whether on a calendar year or a fiscal year) may result in certain inequities for taxpayers who experience cyclical patterns of income or expense. Inequities result from the application of a progressive rate structure to taxable income determined on an annual basis. A **net operating loss (NOL)** in a particular tax year would produce no tax benefit if the Code did not provide for the carryback and carryforward of such losses to profitable years.

EXAMPLE 21

Juanita has a business and realizes the following taxable income or loss over a five-year period: Year 1, $50,000; Year 2, ($30,000); Year 3, $100,000; Year 4, ($200,000); and Year 5, $380,000. She is married and files a joint return. Hubert also has a business and has a taxable income pattern of $60,000 every year. He, too, is married and files a joint return. Note that both Juanita and Hubert have total taxable income of $300,000 over the five-year period. Assume there is no provision for carryback or carryover of NOLs. Juanita and Hubert would have the following five-year tax bills:

Year	Juanita's Tax	Hubert's Tax
1	$ 8,495	$11,295
2	–0–	11,295
3	22,495	11,295
4	–0–	11,295
5	124,084	11,295
	$155,074	$56,475

The computation of tax is made without regard to any NOL benefit.
Rates applicable to 1998 are used to compute the tax.

Even though Juanita and Hubert realized the same total taxable income ($300,000) over the five-year period, Juanita had to pay taxes of $155,074, while Hubert paid taxes of only $56,475. ▼

To provide partial relief from this inequitable tax treatment, a deduction is allowed for NOLs.[32] This provision permits NOLs for any one year to be offset against taxable income of other years. The NOL provision is intended as a form of relief for business income and losses. Thus, only losses from the operation of a trade or business (or profession), casualty and theft losses, or losses from the confiscation of a business by a foreign government can create an NOL. In other words, a salaried individual with itemized deductions and personal exemptions in excess of gross income is not permitted to deduct the excess amounts as an NOL. On the other hand, a personal casualty loss is treated as a business loss and can therefore create (or increase) an NOL for an individual.

CARRYBACK AND CARRYOVER PERIODS

General Rules.   An NOL must be applied initially to the two taxable years preceding the year of the loss (unless an election is made not to carry the loss back at all). It is carried first to the second prior year, and then to the immediately preceding tax year (or until used up). If the loss is not fully used in the carryback period, it must

---

[32]§ 172.

NET OPERATING LOSSES OF A BIOTECH COMPANY:
THE VALUABLE ASSET

Aprogenex, a Houston biotech company, announced that it will reduce its operations to a minimal level. The company spent $29 million trying to develop a new medical testing technology, but the business did not work out to the extent expected. The stock was delisted by the American Stock Exchange, and efforts to raise additional capital were unsuccessful.

Aprogenex does, however, possess substantial NOLs that could be valuable to other biotech companies. In its press release, the company stated that one of its goals was to preserve the loss carryforwards and other items that could benefit shareholders.

SOURCE: Adapted from Bill Mintz, "Aprogenex to Cut Back Operations," *Houston Chronicle*, August 29, 1997, p. 2 of Business section.

be carried forward to the first year after the loss year, and then forward to the second, third, etc., year after the loss year. The carryover period is 20 years. A loss sustained in 1998 is used in this order: 1996, 1997, 1999 through 2018.

A three-year carryback period is available for any portion of an individual's NOL resulting from a casualty or theft loss. The three-year carryback rule also applies to NOLs that are attributable to presidentially declared disasters and are incurred by a small business or a taxpayer engaged in farming. A small business is one whose average annual gross receipts for a three-year period are $5 million or less.

If the loss is being carried to a preceding year, an amended return is filed on Form 1040X, or a quick refund claim is filed on Form 1045. In any case, a refund of taxes previously paid is requested. When the loss is carried forward, the current return shows an NOL deduction for the prior year's loss.

Sequence of Use of NOLs.   Where there are NOLs in two or more years, the rule is always to use the earliest year's loss first until it is completely absorbed. The later years' losses can then be used until they also are absorbed or lost. Thus, one year's return could show NOL carryovers from two or more years. Each loss is computed and applied separately.

Election to Forgo Carryback.   A taxpayer can *irrevocably elect* not to carry back an NOL to any of the prior years. In that case, the loss is available as a carryover for 20 years. A taxpayer would make the election if it is to his or her tax advantage. For example, a taxpayer might be in a low marginal tax bracket in the carryback years but expect to be in a high marginal tax bracket in future years. Therefore, it would be to the taxpayer's advantage to use the NOL to offset income in years when the tax rate is high rather than use it when the tax rate is relatively low.

COMPUTATION OF THE NET OPERATING LOSS

Since the NOL provisions apply solely to business-related losses, certain adjustments must be made so that the loss more closely resembles the taxpayer's *economic* loss. The required adjustments for corporate taxpayers are usually insignificant because a corporation's tax loss is generally similar to its economic loss. However, in computing taxable income, individual taxpayers are allowed deductions for such items as personal and dependency exemptions and itemized deductions that do not reflect actual business-related economic losses.

To arrive at the NOL for an individual, taxable income must be adjusted by adding back the following items:[33]

1. No deduction is allowed for personal and dependency exemptions. These amounts do not reflect economic, or business, outlays and hence must be added back.

2. The NOL carryover or carryback from another year is not allowed in the computation of the current year's NOL.

3. Capital losses and nonbusiness deductions are limited in determining the current year's NOL. These limits are as follows:

   a. The excess of nonbusiness capital losses over nonbusiness capital gains must be added back.

   b. The excess of nonbusiness deductions over the sum of nonbusiness income and *net* nonbusiness capital gains must be added back. *Net nonbusiness capital gains* are the excess of nonbusiness capital gains over nonbusiness capital losses. *Nonbusiness income* includes such passive items as dividends and interest. It does not include such items as salaries, rents, and gains and losses on the sale or exchange of business assets. *Nonbusiness deductions* are total itemized deductions less personal casualty and theft losses.

   A taxpayer who does not itemize deductions computes the excess of nonbusiness deductions over nonbusiness income by substituting his or her standard deduction for total itemized deductions.

   c. The excess of business capital losses over the sum of business capital gains and the excess of nonbusiness income and net nonbusiness capital gains over nonbusiness deductions must be added back.

   d. The add-back for net nonbusiness capital losses and excess business capital losses does not include net capital losses not included in the current-year computation of taxable income because of the capital loss limitation provisions (discussed in Chapter 16).

The capital loss and nonbusiness deduction limits are illustrated in Examples 22 through 25.

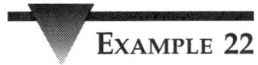

EXAMPLE 22

For 1998, taxpayer and spouse have $6,000 of nonbusiness capital losses and $4,000 of nonbusiness capital gains. They must add back $2,000 ($6,000 – $4,000) in determining the excess of nonbusiness capital losses over nonbusiness capital gains. ▼

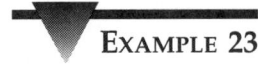

EXAMPLE 23

For 1998, taxpayer and spouse have $2,000 of nonbusiness capital gains, $1,000 of nonbusiness capital losses, $2,000 of interest income, and no itemized deductions. They must add back $4,100 {$7,100 standard deduction – [$2,000 interest income + $1,000 ($2,000 – $1,000) net nonbusiness capital gains]}. Note that, in this example, there is no excess of nonbusiness capital losses over nonbusiness capital gains. ▼

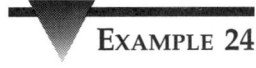

EXAMPLE 24

For 1998, taxpayer and spouse have $2,000 of nonbusiness capital gains, $1,000 of nonbusiness capital losses, $9,000 of interest income, $9,500 of itemized deductions (none of which are personal casualty and theft losses), $4,000 of business capital losses, and $1,000 of business capital gains. They must add back $2,500 {$4,000 business capital losses – [$1,000 business capital gains + ($9,000 nonbusiness income + $1,000 net nonbusiness capital gains – $9,500 nonbusiness deductions)]}. Note that, in this example, there is no excess of nonbusiness

---

[33]§ 172(d); Reg. § 1.172–3(a).

capital losses over nonbusiness capital gains, nor is there an excess of nonbusiness deductions over the sum of nonbusiness income and net nonbusiness capital gains. ▼

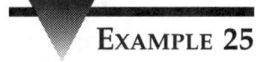

EXAMPLE 25

For 1998, taxpayer and spouse have $2,000 of nonbusiness capital gains, $3,000 of nonbusiness capital losses, $8,000 of interest income, $9,000 of itemized deductions (none of which are personal casualty and theft losses), $8,000 of business capital losses, and $4,000 of business capital gains. They must add back $1,000 ($9,000 – $8,000), the excess of nonbusiness deductions over nonbusiness income, and $3,000, the excess of combined capital losses. Because of the capital loss limitations, only $3,000 of the loss would have been used in computing taxable income for the year. ▼

Example 26 illustrates the computation of an NOL.

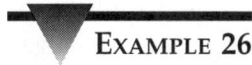

EXAMPLE 26

James opened a retail store in 1997 and experienced an NOL of $185 for that year. James had no taxable income for 1994, 1995, or 1996. James is married, has no dependents, and files a joint return. For 1998, James and his wife had the following taxable income:

Gross income from the business	$ 67,000	
Less: Business expenses	(71,000)	($ 4,000)
Salary from a part-time job		875
Interest on savings account		525
Nonbusiness long-term capital gain		1,000
NOL carryover from 1997		(185)
Net loss on rental property		(100)
Adjusted gross income		($ 1,885)
Less: Itemized deductions		
Interest expense	$ 3,000	
Taxes	4,300	
Casualty loss	2,000	
Total itemized deductions		(9,300)
Exemptions (2 × $2,700)		(5,400)
Taxable income		($16,585)

James's NOL is computed as follows:

Taxable income				($16,585)
Add:				
Net operating loss from 1997			$ 185	
Personal exemptions (2)			5,400	
Excess of nonbusiness deductions over nonbusiness income				
Total itemized deductions		$ 9,300		
Less: Casualty loss		(2,000)		
		$ 7,300		
Less: Interest	$ 525			
Less: Long-term capital gain	1,000	(1,525)	5,775	11,360
Net operating loss				($ 5,225)

The NOL can be thought of as follows:

Business loss	($4,000)
Rental loss	(100)
Casualty loss	(2,000)
Salary income	875
Net operating loss	($5,225)

RECOMPUTATION OF TAX LIABILITY FOR YEAR TO WHICH NET OPERATING LOSS IS CARRIED

When an NOL is carried back to a nonloss year, the taxable income and income tax for the carryback year must be recomputed by including the NOL as a deduction *for* AGI. Several deductions (such as medical expenses and charitable contributions) are based on the amount of AGI. When an NOL is carried back, all such deductions *except* the charitable contributions deduction must be recomputed on the basis of the new AGI after the NOL has been applied. The deduction for charitable contributions is determined without regard to any NOL carryback but with regard to any other modification affecting AGI. Furthermore, any tax credits limited by or based upon the tax must be recomputed, based on the recomputed tax.

EXAMPLE 27

Peggy sustained an NOL of $11,000 in 1999. Because Peggy had no taxable income in 1997, the loss is carried back to 1998. For 1998, the joint income tax return of Peggy and her husband was as follows:

Salary income		$ 10,000
Dividends		4,000
Net long-term capital gain		1,400
Adjusted gross income		$ 15,400
Itemized deductions		
Charitable contributions	$2,700	
Interest	4,800	
Taxes	1,420	(8,920)
Exemptions (2 × $2,700)		(5,400)
Taxable income		$ 1,080
Tax (married filing jointly)		$ 162

Peggy's new tax liability for the carryback year is computed as follows:

Adjusted gross income		$ 15,400
Less: Net operating loss		(11,000)
Recomputed adjusted gross income		$ 4,400
Itemized deductions		
Charitable contributions	$2,700	
Interest	4,800	
Taxes	1,420	(8,920)
Exemptions (2 × $2,700)		(5,400)
Recomputed taxable income		$ (9,920)
Tax		$ –0–
Tax originally paid and refund claim		$ 162

CALCULATION OF THE REMAINING NET OPERATING LOSS

After computing the amount of the refund claim for the initial carryback year, it is then necessary to determine the extent to which any NOL remains to carry over to future years. The amount of this carryover loss is the excess of the NOL over the taxable income of the year to which the loss is being applied. However, the taxable income of the year to which the loss is being applied must be determined with the following *modifications:*

- No deduction is allowed for excess capital losses over capital gains.
- No deduction is allowed for the NOL that is being carried back. However, deductions are allowed for NOLs occurring before the loss year.
- Any deductions claimed that are based on or limited by AGI must be determined after making the preceding adjustments. However, charitable contributions do not take into account any NOL carryback.
- No deduction is allowed for personal and dependency exemptions.

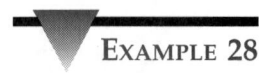

EXAMPLE 28

Referring to the facts in Example 27, the NOL carryover from 1998 available for future years would be ($4,520), computed as follows:

Salary income		$ 10,000
Dividends		4,000
Net long-term capital gain		1,400
Adjusted gross income		$ 15,400
Itemized deductions		
Charitable contributions	$ 2,700	
Interest	4,800	
Taxes	1,420	(8,920)
Exemptions (not allowed)		–0–
Modified taxable income		$ 6,480
Net operating loss		($ 11,000)
Modified taxable income		6,480
Net operating loss to carry forward		($ 4,520)

Since the ending figure is negative, it represents the NOL remaining to carry over to 2000 or later years.

TAX PLANNING CONSIDERATIONS

7   **LEARNING OBJECTIVE**
Identify tax planning opportunities in deducting certain business expenses, business losses, and personal losses.

TAX CONSEQUENCES OF THE *GROETZINGER* CASE

In the *Groetzinger* case discussed earlier in the chapter, the court established that the appropriate tests for determining if gambling is a trade or business are whether an individual engages in gambling full-time in good faith, with regularity, and for the production of income as a livelihood, and not as a mere hobby. The court held that Robert Groetzinger satisfied the tests because of his constant and large-scale effort. Skill was required and was applied. He did what he did for a livelihood, though with less than successful results. His gambling was not a hobby, a passing fancy, or an occasional bet for amusement. Therefore, his gambling was a trade or business, and hence, he was able to deduct his gambling losses *for* AGI. If the court had ruled that Groetzinger's gambling was not a trade or business, his gambling losses would have been limited to his gambling winnings and would have been classified as itemized deductions.

CONCEPT SUMMARY 7-4

Computation of Net Operating Loss

Taxable income shown on the return
Add back:

1. Personal and dependency exemptions.
2. Net operating loss carryover or carryback from another year.
3. The excess of nonbusiness capital losses over nonbusiness capital gains.
4. The excess of nonbusiness deductions over the sum of nonbusiness income plus *net* nonbusiness capital gains.
5. The excess of business capital losses over the sum of business capital gains plus the excess of nonbusiness income and *net* nonbusiness capital gains over nonbusiness deductions. The add-back from the total of items 3 and 5 will not exceed $3,000 because of the capital loss limitation rules.

Equals the net operating loss

DOCUMENTATION OF RELATED–TAXPAYER LOANS, CASUALTY LOSSES, AND THEFT LOSSES

Since non-bona fide loans between related taxpayers may be treated as gifts, adequate documentation is needed to substantiate a bad debt deduction if the loan subsequently becomes worthless. Documentation should include proper execution of the note (legal form) and the establishment of a bona fide purpose for the loan. In addition, it is desirable to stipulate a reasonable rate of interest and a fixed maturity date.

Since a theft loss is not permitted for misplaced items, a loss should be documented by a police report and evidence of the value of the property (e.g., appraisals, pictures of the property, newspaper clippings). Similar documentation of the value of property should be provided to support a casualty loss deduction because the amount of loss is measured, in part, by the decline in fair market value of the property.

Casualty loss deductions must be reported on Form 4684 (see Appendix B).

SMALL BUSINESS STOCK

Because § 1244 limits the amount of loss classified as ordinary loss on a yearly basis, a taxpayer might maximize the benefits of § 1244 by selling the stock in more than one taxable year. The result could be that the losses in any one taxable year would not exceed the § 1244 limits on ordinary loss.

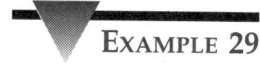

EXAMPLE 29

Mitch, a single individual, purchased small business stock in 1996 for $150,000 (150 shares at $1,000 per share). On December 20, 1998, the stock is worth $60,000 (150 shares at $400 per share). Mitch wants to sell the stock at this time. Mitch earns a salary of $80,000 a year, has no other capital transactions, and does not expect any in the future. If Mitch sells all of the small business stock in 1998, his recognized loss will be $90,000 ($60,000 − $150,000). The loss will be characterized as a $50,000 ordinary loss and a $40,000 long-term capital loss. In computing taxable income for 1998, Mitch could deduct the $50,000 ordinary loss but could deduct only $3,000 of the capital loss. The remainder of the capital loss could be carried over and used in future years subject to the $3,000 limitation if Mitch has no capital gains. If Mitch sells 82 shares in 1998, he will recognize an ordinary loss of $49,200 [82 × ($1,000 − $400)]. If Mitch then sells the remainder of the shares in 1999, he will recognize an ordinary loss of $40,800 [68 × ($1,000 − $400)]. Mitch could deduct the $49,200 ordinary loss in computing 1998 taxable income and the $40,800 ordinary loss in computing 1999 taxable income. ▼

CASUALTY LOSSES

A special election is available for taxpayers who sustain casualty losses in an area designated by the President as a disaster area. This election affects only the timing, not the calculation, of the deduction. The deduction can be taken in the year before the year in which the loss occurred. Thus, an individual can take the deduction on the 1997 return for a loss occurring between January 1 and December 31, 1998. The benefit, of course, is a faster refund (or reduction in tax). It will also be advantageous to carry the loss back if the taxpayer's tax rate in the carryback year is higher than the tax rate in the year of the loss.

To find out if an event qualifies as a disaster area loss, one can look in any of the major tax services, the Weekly Compilation of Presidential Documents, or the *Internal Revenue Bulletin*.

NET OPERATING LOSSES

In certain instances, it may be advisable for a taxpayer to elect not to carry back an NOL. For an individual, the benefits from the loss carryback could be scaled down or lost due to the economic adjustments that must be made to taxable income for the year to which the loss is carried. For example, a taxpayer should attempt to minimize the number of taxable years to which an NOL is carried. The more years to which the NOL is applied, the more benefits are lost from adjustments for items such as personal and dependency exemptions.

The election not to carry back the loss might also be advantageous if there is a disparity in marginal tax rates applicable to different tax years.

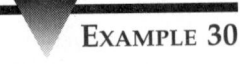

EXAMPLE 30

Abby sustained an NOL of $10,000 in Year 3. Her marginal tax bracket in Year 1 was 15%. In Year 4, however, she expects her bracket to be 39.6% due to a large profit she will make on a business deal. If Abby carries her loss back, her refund will be $1,500 (15% × $10,000). If she elects not to carry it back to Year 1 but chooses, instead, to carry it forward, her savings will be $3,960 (39.6% × $10,000). Even considering the time value of an immediate tax refund, Abby appears to be better off using the carryover approach. ▼

KEY TERMS

Bad debt, 7–3

Business bad debt, 7–5

Casualty loss, 7–9

Disaster area losses, 7–11

Net operating loss (NOL), 7–19

Nonbusiness bad debt, 7–5

Personal casualty gain, 7–15

Personal casualty loss, 7–15

Research and experimental expenditures, 7–16

Reserve method, 7–3

Section 1244 stock, 7–7

Small business stock, 7–7

Specific charge-off method, 7–3

Theft loss, 7–10

Worthless securities, 7–7

PROBLEM MATERIALS

DISCUSSION QUESTIONS

1. Explain whether a bad debt deduction is allowed for a debt arising from the sale of services by a cash basis taxpayer.

2. Discuss when a deduction may be taken for a business debt.

3. Discuss the tax treatment for the recovery of an account receivable previously written off as uncollectible.

4. Discuss the difference between business and nonbusiness bad debts. How is the distinction determined? How is each treated on the return?

5. What factors are to be considered in determining whether a bad debt arising from a loan between related parties is, in fact, a bad debt?

6. Sam used the cash method of accounting for Federal income tax purposes and filed a joint Federal income tax return for the current year. On February 27 of the current year, Sam instituted a civil lawsuit against Dave, alleging fraud in the handling of a real estate project in which Sam had invested. On June 19 of the current year, a default judgment was entered against Dave and in favor of Sam. Under its terms, Sam was to recover from Dave general damages of $20,000 and punitive damages of $50,000. During the current year, Sam did not recover from Dave any of either the general or the punitive damages. Identify the relevant tax issues for Sam.

7. Discuss a taxpayer's options for the tax treatment of a loss incurred on a deposit in a qualified financial institution. Also note the consequences of each option.

8. John purchased stock six years ago for $10,000. As of the close of the current tax year, John has determined that the stock is worth only $100. Discuss whether John may treat the stock as worthless securities and, hence, claim a capital loss of $9,900 ($100 − $10,000) on his current-year tax return.

9. Discuss the ordinary loss limitations on the sale of § 1244 stock and the advantages of such a characterization.

10. Jim discovers that his sea wall, which protects his personal residence from the ocean, has been extensively damaged by the ocean. Discuss whether he may take a deduction for the damage to the wall.

11. Discuss the provision for determining the year in which a theft loss is deductible.

12. Discuss the tax treatment when a casualty loss is deducted in a prior year and a reimbursement is received in the current year.

13. Discuss the treatment of a disaster area loss.

14. How is a personal casualty loss computed? A business casualty loss? What effect do insurance proceeds have on both types of losses?

15. Discuss the tax consequences of not making an insurance claim when insured business property is subject to a loss.

16. Discuss the circumstances under which the cost of repairs to the damaged property can be used to measure the amount of a casualty loss.

17. During May of the current year, personal use property was stolen from Jim's home. Later in the year, Jim's home and two personal use cars were damaged by a severe storm. Discuss how the $100 floor applies to these casualties.

18. Bonnie sustained a loss on a duplex damaged by fire. She owns the duplex and lives in one unit. She rents out the other unit to a tenant. Discuss the tax treatment of the loss on Bonnie's individual tax return.

19. When casualty losses exceed casualty gains, only the amount of the casualty loss in excess of casualty gains is subject to the 10%-of-AGI floor. Discuss the significance of netting losses against gains in this manner rather than having the entire casualty loss subject to the 10%-of-AGI floor.

20. Monte opened a personal savings account at First National Bank many years ago. Last year, First National's banking license was revoked. In January of this year, Monte was informed that First National had been put into compulsory liquidation. The liquidation was precipitated by the embezzlement of funds by First National's former president. In February Monte submitted a claim for $12,459 to the liquidators of First National. In May of the current year, the liquidators advised Monte that they would keep him informed as to the progress of the liquidation and his prospects of recovery. The letter also stated that claimants would be notified if the liquidators were unable to agree to their claims. In November of the current year, Monte was notified that at the present time the liquidators could not predict with any degree of certainty how much of their funds depositors might eventually recover. Identify the relevant tax issues for Monte.

21. Fred and Diane purchased their home many years ago. The property included a large black oak tree approximately 80 feet in height and about 100 years old. The tree was the dominant feature of the front yard, where it stood alone next to the street. Because of the age and stature of the tree, Fred and Diane had it inspected regularly by a tree expert. In August of the current year, Fred noticed that the entire top or crown of the tree had turned brown. Because none of the leaves on other trees in the area had turned brown, Fred called the tree expert to inspect the tree. The inspection showed that the tree had been attacked by woodborers and was beyond saving and effectively dead. Identify the relevant tax issues for Fred and Diane.

22. What kinds of expenditures qualify as research and experimental expenditures?

23. If a business does not elect to expense or amortize research expenditures, what is the possibility of writing off such expenditures?

24. Power and Light, a public utility company, planned a research and development project. To obtain a construction permit to expand its facilities, the company filed an application with state regulatory agencies and conducted various studies to support its application as required by the agencies. Because the taxpayer's expansion involved both the construction of a nuclear power plant and the installation of an ultrahigh voltage electric transmission line, the agencies required that the company conduct several types of environmental impact studies for site selection. The studies measured specific site conditions and the resulting environmental impact of the construction and operation of the project. The company conducted part of the studies directly and used a research organization to conduct the remainder of the studies on its behalf. Identify the relevant tax issues for Power and Light.

25. Discuss the types of losses that can create an NOL.

26. Discuss the periods to which an individual's NOL may be carried.

27. Why are such items as nonbusiness deductions and personal and dependency exemptions not allowed in computing the NOL?

28. If an individual has no nonbusiness capital transactions for the year, discuss the treatment of the excess of nonbusiness income over nonbusiness deductions with respect to the NOL.

29. Discuss the recomputation of the tax liability for the year to which an NOL is carried.

30. Discuss the calculation of the NOL remaining after a carryback to a particular tax year.

PROBLEMS

31. Several years ago John Johnson loaned his friend Sara $20,000 to help her make a business investment. In May of the current year, Sara filed for bankruptcy, and John was notified that he could expect to receive no more than 60 cents on the dollar. As of the end of the current year, John has not received any payments. John has contacted you about the possibility of taking a bad debt deduction of $8,000 for the current year.

Write a letter to John that contains your advice as to whether he can claim a bad debt deduction of $8,000 for the current year. Also, prepare a memo for the tax files. John's address is 100 Tyler Lane, Erie, PA 16563.

32. In 1996, Morgan loaned the Peach Company $50,000. In 1997, Morgan was told that he would probably receive $5,000 of the loan. In 1998, Morgan received $3,000 in final settlement on the loan. Determine Morgan's possible deductions with respect to the loan for 1996, 1997, and 1998.

33. In 1997, Wilma deposited $117,500 with a commercial bank. On July 1, 1998, Wilma was notified that the bank was insolvent, and subsequently she received only $100,000 of the deposit. Wilma also has a salary of $40,000, long-term capital gain of $12,000, and itemized deductions (other than casualty and theft) of $7,000. Determine whether Wilma should elect to treat the loss on the deposit as a personal casualty loss or as a bad debt.

34. Zenith, a single taxpayer, had the following items for 1998:

- Salary of $75,000.

- Gain of $19,000 on the sale of § 1244 stock acquired three years ago.

- Loss of $71,000 on the sale of § 1244 stock acquired two years ago.

- Stock acquired on June 20, 1997, for $2,500 became worthless on April 3, 1998.

Determine Zenith's AGI for 1998.

35. Mary, a single taxpayer, purchased 10,000 shares of § 1244 stock several years ago at a cost of $20 per share. In November of the current year, Mary received an offer to sell the stock for $12 per share. She has the option of either selling all of the stock now or selling half of the stock now and half of the stock in January of next year. Mary will receive a salary of $80,000 for the current year and $90,000 next year. Mary will have long-term capital gains of $8,000 for the current year and $10,000 next year. If Mary's goal is to minimize her AGI for the two years, determine whether she should sell all of her stock this year or half of her stock this year and half next year.

36. Upon returning from a night out, John, an antique collector, found that a fire had damaged his home and destroyed some of his antiques. John's home was covered by an insurance policy that had a 20% deductible clause. The antiques were insured for their fair market value. Information with respect to the damaged and destroyed assets is as follows:

Asset	Cost	FMV Before	FMV After	Insurance Recovery
Home	$250,000	$300,000	$175,000	$100,000
Antique clock	1,500	2,000	–0–	2,000
Antique table	4,000	3,000	–0–	3,000
Antique organ	15,000	20,000	–0–	20,000

If John's AGI is $80,000 before considering the effects of the fire, determine his deductible loss *from* AGI.

37. Olaf owns a 500-acre farm in Minnesota. A tornado hit the area and destroyed a farm building and some farm equipment and damaged a barn. Fortunately for Olaf, the tornado occurred after he had harvested his corn crop. Applicable information is as follows:

Item	Adjusted Basis	FMV Before	FMV After	Insurance Proceeds
Building	$80,000	$100,000	$ –0–	$60,000
Equipment	40,000	50,000	–0–	25,000
Barn	90,000	120,000	90,000	25,000

Because of the extensive damage caused by the tornado, the President designated the area as a disaster area.

Olaf, who files a joint return with his wife Anna, had $90,000 of taxable income last year. Their taxable income for the current year, excluding the loss from the tornado, is $220,000.

Determine the amount of Olaf and Anna's loss and the year in which they should take the loss.

38. On January 5 of the current year, Janice dropped off to sleep while driving home from a business trip. Luckily, she was only slightly injured in the resulting accident, but her car was completely destroyed.

Janice had purchased the car new two years ago and had driven it 42,000 miles at the time of the accident. Of these miles, 18,000 were business miles; the remaining miles were personal miles. The car cost $32,000 new. Janice has taken $3,400 of depreciation for the business use of the car. The fair market value at the time of the accident was $20,000. Janice carried collision insurance with a $5,000 deductible on the car. She made a claim on the policy and received a payment of $15,000.

After Janice was released from the hospital the day after the accident, she could not find her purse (cost $110, fair replacement value $30) or its contents, which included $350 in cash. She also was unable to locate the stone from her diamond ring. The stone cost $4,000 when it was purchased 10 years ago and was worth $7,500 at the time of the accident. If Janice's AGI is $54,000 before considering the effects of the accident, determine her deduction *for* AGI and her deduction *from* AGI as a result of the accident.

39. On November 1 of the current year, Sam Smith was involved in an accident with his personal use automobile. Sam had purchased the car for $25,000. The automobile had a fair market value of $19,000 before the accident and $12,000 after the accident. The car was covered by an insurance policy that had a $1,000 deductible clause. Sam is afraid that the policy will be canceled if he makes a claim for the damages. Therefore, he is considering not filing a claim. Sam believes that the casualty loss deduction will help mitigate the loss of the insurance reimbursement. Sam's AGI for the current year is $25,000.

Write a letter to Sam that contains your advice with respect to the tax consequences of filing versus not filing a claim for the insurance reimbursement for the damages to his car. Also, prepare a memo for the tax files. Sam's address is 450 Colonel's Way, Warrensburg, MO 64093.

40. Green Corporation, a manufacturing company, decided to develop a new line of fireworks. Because of the danger involved, Green purchased an isolated parcel of land for $300,000 and constructed a building for $1,220,000. The building was to be used for research and experimentation in creating the new fireworks. The project was begun in 1998. Green had the following expenses in connection with the project:

	1998	**1999**
Salaries	$160,000	$200,000
Utilities	20,000	30,000
Materials	40,000	40,000
Insurance	50,000	30,000
Cost of market survey to determine profit potential for new fireworks line	20,000	–0–
Depreciation on the building	30,000	31,000

The benefits from the project will be realized starting in June 2000.

a. If Green Corporation elects to expense research and experimental expenditures, determine the amount of the deduction for 1998, 1999, and 2000.

b. If Green Corporation elects a 60-month deferral and amortization period, determine the amount of the deduction for 1998, 1999, and 2000.

41. Sam and Sally, who file a joint return, had the following items for 1998:

Sam's salary	$20,000
Sally's salary	15,000
Interest income from State of Minnesota bonds	60,000
Itemized deductions (no casualty or theft)	32,000

    a. Determine Sam and Sally's taxable income for 1998.
    b. Determine Sam and Sally's NOL for 1998.

42. Bill, a single taxpayer, had the following items of income and expense during 1998:

Gross receipts from business	$170,000
Business expenses	200,000
Bill's salary	20,000
Itemized deductions (no casualty or theft)	3,000

    a. Determine Bill's taxable income for 1998.
    b. Determine Bill's NOL for 1998.

43. Gus, who is married and files a joint return, owns a grocery store. In 1998, his gross sales were $286,000 and operating expenses were $310,000. Other items on his 1998 return were as follows:

Nonbusiness capital gains (short-term)	$10,000
Nonbusiness capital losses (long-term)	9,000
Itemized deductions (no casualty or theft)	10,000
Ordinary nonbusiness income	4,000
Salary from part-time job	10,000

During the year 1996, Gus had no taxable income. In 1997, Gus had taxable income of $23,800 computed as follows:

Net business income		$ 60,000
Interest income		2,000
Adjusted gross income		$ 62,000
Less: Itemized deductions		
Charitable contributions of $40,000, limited to 50% of AGI	$31,000	
Medical expenses of $6,550, limited to the amount in excess of 7.5% of AGI ($6,550 − $4,650)	1,900	
Total itemized deductions		(32,900)
Exemptions (2 × 2,650)		(5,300)
Taxable income		$ 23,800

    a. What is Gus's 1998 NOL?
    b. Determine Gus's recomputed taxable income for 1997.

44. During 1998, Rick and his wife Sara had the following items of income and expense to report:

Gross receipts from business	$400,000
Business expenses	525,000
Interest income from bank savings accounts	8,000
Sara's salary	50,000
Long-term capital gain on stock held as an investment	4,000
Itemized deductions (no casualty or theft)	15,000

    a. Assuming Rick and Sara file a joint return, what is their taxable income for 1998?
    b. What is the amount of Rick and Sara's NOL for 1998?

45. Assume that in addition to the information in Problem 44, Rick had no taxable income for the year 1996 and $6,400 of taxable income for 1997 computed as follows:

Salary		$ 25,000
Capital loss		(1,000)
Adjusted gross income		$ 24,000
Less: Itemized deductions		
Charitable contributions of $20,000, limited to 50% of AGI	$12,000	
Medical expenses of $2,100, limited to the amount in excess of 7.5% of AGI ($2,100 – $1,800)	300	
Total itemized deductions		(12,300)
Exemptions (2 × $2,650)		(5,300)
Taxable income		$ 6,400

Determine the amount of Rick and Sara's 1998 NOL to be carried forward to 1999.

46. Robert and Susan Reid had an NOL of $20,000 in 1998. They had no taxable income for the year 1996 and $18,100 of taxable income for 1997 computed as follows:

Salary		$ 50,000
Capital loss		(2,000)
Adjusted gross income		$ 48,000
Less: Itemized deductions		
Charitable contributions of $40,000, limited to 50% of AGI	$24,000	
Medical expenses of $4,200, limited to the amount in excess of 7.5% of AGI ($4,200 – $3,600)	600	
Total itemized deductions		(24,600)
Exemptions (2 × $2,650)		(5,300)
Taxable income		$ 18,100

Write a letter to Robert and Susan informing them of the amount of the remaining NOL to be carried forward if the loss is applied against the 1997 taxable income. Also, prepare a memo for the tax files. Their address is 201 Jerdone Avenue, Conway, SC 29526.

47. Fran is single and had the following income and deductions for 1998:

Business receipts	$ 90,000
Business expenses	130,000
Dividends from domestic corporations	20,000
Interest received from bank savings account	6,000
Itemized deductions (no casualty or theft)	30,000
1997 NOL carried to 1998	20,000

a. What is Fran's taxable income for 1998?
b. What is Fran's NOL for 1998?

48. Soong, single and age 32, had the following items for the tax year 1998:

• Salary of $44,000.

• Interest income from U.S. government bonds of $2,000.

• Dividends from a foreign corporation of $500.

• Sale of small business § 1244 stock on October 20, 1998, for $10,000. The stock had been acquired two years earlier for $65,000.

• Business bad debt of $3,000.

• Nonbusiness bad debt of $5,000.

- Sale of small business § 1244 stock on November 12, 1998, for $4,000. The stock had been acquired on June 5, 1998, for $800.

- Sale of common stock on December 4, 1998, for $40,000. The stock was acquired four years ago for $18,000.

- Total itemized deductions of $8,000 (no casualty or theft).

Determine Soong's NOL for 1998.

49. Nell, single and age 38, had the following income and expense items in 1998:

Nonbusiness bad debt	$ 6,000
Business bad debt	2,000
Nonbusiness long-term capital gain	4,000
Nonbusiness short-term capital loss	3,000
Salary	40,000
Interest income	1,000

Determine Nell's AGI for 1998.

50. Assume that in addition to the information in Problem 49, Nell had the following items in 1998:

Personal casualty gain on an asset held for four months	$10,000
Personal casualty loss on an asset held for two years	1,000

Determine Nell's AGI for 1998.

51. Assume that in addition to the information in Problems 49 and 50, Nell had the following items in 1998:

Personal casualty loss on an asset held for five years	$50,000
Interest expense on home mortgage	3,000

Determine Nell's taxable income and NOL for 1998.

52. Jed, age 55, is married with no children. During 1998, Jed had the following income and expense items:
    a. Three years ago, Jed loaned a friend $10,000 to help him purchase a new car. In June of the current year, Jed learned that his friend had been declared bankrupt and had left the country. There is no possibility that Jed will ever collect any of the $10,000.
    b. In April of last year, Jed purchased some stock for $5,000. In March of the current year, the company was declared bankrupt, and Jed was notified that his shares of stock were worthless.
    c. Several years ago, Jed purchased some § 1244 stock for $120,000. This year, he sold the stock for $30,000.
    d. In July of this year, Jed sold some land that he had held for two years for $60,000. He had originally paid $42,000 for the land.
    e. Jed received $40,000 of interest income from State of Minnesota bonds.
    f. In September, Jed's home was damaged by an earthquake. Jed's basis in his home was $430,000. The value of the home immediately before the quake was $610,000. After the quake, the home was worth $540,000. Because earthquake damage was an exclusion on Jed's homeowners insurance policy, he received no insurance recovery.
    g. Jed received a salary of $80,000.
    h. Jed made a charitable contribution of $4,000.

If Jed files a joint return for 1998, determine his NOL for the year.

CUMULATIVE PROBLEMS

53. Alan Rice, age 45 and single, lives at 230 Wood Lane, Salt Lake City, UT 84201. His Social Security number is 885–33–3774. Alan had the following items for the year 1998:

    • Salary of $100,000.

    • Business bad debt of $8,000.

    • Nonbusiness bad debt of $7,000.

    • Sale of § 1244 stock resulting in a loss of $80,000. The stock was acquired two years earlier.

    • Dividends of $40,000 from domestic corporations.

    • Interest income of $10,000 from First Interstate Bank.

    • Long-term capital gain of $31,000.

    • NOL carryover from 1997 of $12,000.

    • On January 1, 1998, a fire severely damaged a two-story building owned by Alan, who occupied the second story of the building as a residence. He had recently opened a flower shop on the ground level. The following information is available with respect to the incident:

Asset	Adjusted Basis	Fair Market Value	
		Before	After
Building	$70,000	$130,000	$50,000
Inventory	35,000	55,000	None
Store equipment	3,000	2,500	None
Home furnishings	12,600	7,000	800
Personal auto	8,900	7,800	7,600

    • Alan's fire insurance policy paid the following amounts for damages covered by the policy:

Building	$50,000	(policy maximum)
Inventory	30,000	(policy maximum)
Store equipment	None	
Home furnishings	1,000	(policy maximum)
Personal auto	None	

    • Other itemized deductions of $3,500.

    • Alan's employer withheld $10,000 of Federal income tax.

    Compute Alan's 1998 Federal income tax payable (or refund due). Suggested software (if available): *TurboTax*.

54. Jane Smith, age 40, is single and has no dependents. She is employed as a legal secretary by Legal Services, Inc. She owns and operates Typing Services located near the campus of San Jose State University at 1986 Campus Drive. She is a cash basis taxpayer. Jane lives at 2020 Oakcrest Road, San Jose, CA 95134. Jane's Social Security number is 123-89-6666. Jane indicates that she wishes to designate $3 to the Presidential Election Campaign Fund. During 1997, Jane had the following income and expense items:
    a. $50,000 salary from Legal Services, Inc.
    b. $20,000 gross receipts from her typing services business.
    c. $700 cash dividend from Buffalo Mining Company, a Canadian corporation.
    d. $1,000 Christmas bonus from Legal Services, Inc.

e. $60,000 life insurance proceeds on the death of her sister.

f. $5,000 check given to her by her wealthy aunt.

g. $100 won in a bingo game.

h. Expenses connected with the typing service:

Office rent	$7,000
Supplies	4,400
Utilities and telephone	4,680
Wages to part-time typists	5,000
Payroll taxes	500
Equipment rentals	3,000

i. $9,000 interest expense on a home mortgage (paid to San Jose Savings and Loan).

j. $5,000 fair market value of silverware stolen from her home by a burglar on October 12, 1997. Jane had paid $4,000 for the silverware on July 1, 1988. She was reimbursed $1,500 by her insurance company.

k. Jane had loaned $2,100 to a friend, Joan Jensen, on June 3, 1994. Joan declared bankruptcy on August 14, 1997, and was unable to repay the loan.

l. Legal Services, Inc., withheld Federal income tax of $8,500 and the required amount of FICA tax.

m. Alimony of $10,000 received from her former husband, Ted Smith.

n. Interest income of $800 on City of San Jose bonds.

o. Jane made estimated tax payments of $1,000.

Part 1—Tax Computation

Compute Jane Smith's 1997 Federal income tax payable (or refund due). If you use tax forms for your computations, you will need Forms 1040 and 4684 and Schedules A, C, and D. Suggested software (if available): *TurboTax.*

Part 2—Tax Planning

In 1998, Jane plans to continue her job with Legal Services, Inc. Therefore, items a, d, and 1 will recur in 1998. Jane plans to continue her typing services business (refer to item b) and expects gross receipts of $26,000. She projects that all business expenses (refer to item h) will increase by 10%, except for office rent, which, under the terms of her lease, will remain the same as in 1997. Items e, f, g, j, and k will not recur in 1998. Items c, i, m, and n will be approximately the same as in 1997.

Jane would like you to compute the minimum amount of estimated tax she will have to pay for 1998 so that she will not have to pay any additional tax upon filing her 1998 Federal income tax return. Write a letter to Jane that contains your advice and prepare a memo for the tax files. Suggested software (if available): *TurboTax.*

RESEARCH PROBLEMS

Note: Use the **RIA OnPoint System 4 Student Version CD-ROM**, *which is available to accompany this text, in preparing solutions to the Research Problems. Alternatively, tax research materials found in a standard tax library can be used.*

Research Problem 1. While Ralph was in the process of obtaining a divorce, his wife, without Ralph's knowledge, had the furniture removed from his apartment. Discuss whether Ralph would be entitled to a tax deduction for the loss of the furniture.

Partial list of research aids:
Landis G. Brown, 30 TCM 257, T.C.Memo. 1971–60.
Jerry L. Goode, 42 TCM 1209, T.C.Memo. 1981–548.

Research Problem 2. Jed Johnson is the owner and president of Teal Bank. One day last year, he was having lunch with Hal Smith, a customer of the bank. During the conversation, Jed learned that Hal was interested in trying to acquire a particular line of business. Jed knew of such a business and shared this information with Hal.

Hal contacted the owners of the business and eventually acquired the company. Early this year, Hal sent Jed a check for $25,000 as a "finder's fee" for helping him locate the company that he acquired.

For the current year, Jed has a business loss of $40,000 that he wants to carry back and apply against previous years' income. He also has itemized deductions, none arising from casualty or theft losses, of $20,000. Discuss how the "finder's fee" should be treated and what effect it will have on any potential NOL carryback.

Research Problem 3. George Johnson, a Minnesota resident, parked his car on a lake while he was watching an iceboat race. During the race, the ice beneath his car unexpectedly gave way, and the car sank to the bottom of the lake. Write a letter to George advising him as to whether he can claim a casualty loss for the damage to the car. Also, prepare a memo for the tax files. George's address is 100 Apple Lane, St. Paul, MN 55123.

Research Problem 4. John Smith was engaged to be married to Nancy Brown. In contemplation of marriage, Nancy deposited $20,000 in a bank account for John, to be used after their marriage. Sometime thereafter, the engagement was broken off, and John used the $20,000 for himself. Nancy has attempted to collect the $20,000 from John without success, and now John has filed for bankruptcy. Discuss the possibility of Nancy's claiming the $20,000 as a nonbusiness bad debt on her income tax return.

Research Problem 5. John had $175,000 of personal savings on deposit in Swan Savings and Loan Association. During the current year, an employee embezzled large sums of money from Swan. As a result, Swan was declared insolvent. At the present, it appears that John will recover only $100,000 of his deposit. John was an officer of Swan for most of the current year. Just after Swan was declared insolvent and placed in conservatorship, John resigned his position as an officer. Evaluate the possibility of John taking the $75,000 loss as a theft or casualty loss on his tax return.

Use the tax resources of the Internet to address the following questions. Do not restrict your search to the World Wide Web, but include a review of newsgroups and general reference materials, practitioner sites and resources, primary sources of the tax law, chat rooms and discussion groups, and other opportunities.

Research Problem 6. Find a newspaper article that discusses tax planning for casualty losses when a disaster area designation is made. Does the article convey the pertinent tax rules correctly? Then list all of the locations identified by the President as Federal disaster areas in the last two years.

Research Problem 7. Scan several publications that are read by owners of small businesses. Some of the articles in these publications address tax-related issues such as how to structure a new business. Do these articles do an adequate job of conveying the benefits of issuing § 1244 small business stock? Prepare a short memo explaining the use of § 1244 stock and post it to a newsgroup that is frequented by inventors, engineers, and others involved in start-up corporations.

TEAM PROJECT: ARTHUR ANDERSEN TAX CHALLENGE CASES

For more information on the Arthur Andersen Tax Challenge Cases, refer to Chapter 1, page 1–37.

Information related to tax issues and problems that are discussed in this chapter may be found in the

Day and Ball case on pages: None
Fence case on pages: None

Read and analyze the case you have been assigned and *identify* any issues and problems that are related to material covered in this chapter. If the information provided in the case is complete, prepare answers for this part of the case at this time. If you need information that is contained in the later parts of the case, write a memo summarizing the questions or problems so you can prepare a complete answer at a later date.

CHAPTER

8

DEPRECIATION, COST RECOVERY, AMORTIZATION, AND DEPLETION

LEARNING OBJECTIVES

After completing Chapter 8, you should be able to:

1. Understand the rationale for the cost consumption concept and identify the relevant time periods for depreciation, ACRS, and MACRS.

2. Determine the amount of cost recovery under ACRS and MACRS.

3. Recognize when and how to make the § 179 expensing election, calculate the amount of the deduction, and apply the effect of the election in making the MACRS calculation.

4. Identify listed property and apply the deduction limitations on listed property and on luxury automobiles.

5. Determine when and how to use the alternative depreciation system (ADS).

6. Identify intangible assets that are eligible for amortization and calculate the amount of the deduction.

7. Determine the amount of depletion expense including being able to apply the alternative tax treatments for intangible drilling and development costs.

8. Perform the reporting procedures for cost recovery.

9. Identify tax planning opportunities for cost recovery, amortization, and depletion.

OUTLINE

1 LEARNING OBJECTIVE
Understand the rationale for the cost consumption concept and identify the relevant time periods for depreciation, ACRS, and MACRS.

The Internal Revenue Code provides for a deduction for the consumption of the cost of an asset through depreciation, cost recovery, amortization, or depletion. These deductions are applications of the recovery of capital doctrine (discussed in Chapter 4).

A distinction is made between tangible and intangible property. Tangible property is any property with physical substance (e.g., equipment, buildings), while intangible property lacks such substance (e.g., goodwill, patents).

The **depreciation** rules were completely overhauled by the Economic Recovery Tax Act of 1981 (ERTA). Hence, *most* property placed in service after December 31, 1980, is subject to the accelerated **cost recovery** system (ACRS). However, property placed in service before January 1, 1981, that is still in use, as well as *certain* property placed in service after December 31, 1980, is subject to the pre-ERTA depreciation rules. The Tax Reform Act (TRA) of 1986 completely revised the ACRS rules for property placed in service after December 31, 1986 (MACRS). Therefore, a knowledge of all of the depreciation and cost recovery rules may be needed as Example 1 illustrates.

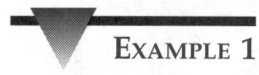

EXAMPLE 1

The Brown Company owns machinery purchased in 1980. The machinery has a 20-year useful life. The business also owns equipment purchased in 1986 that has a 15-year cost recovery life. In 1998, the business purchased a computer. To compute the depreciation and cost recovery for 1998, Brown will use the pre-ERTA depreciation rules for the machinery, the pre-TRA of 1986 cost recovery rules (ACRS) for the equipment, and the post-TRA of 1986 cost recovery rules (MACRS) for the computer. ▼

This chapter initially focuses on the ACRS and MACRS rules.[1] The chapter then concludes with a discussion of the amortization of intangible property and the depletion of natural resources.

ACRS was one of many provisions in ERTA that were intended to stimulate the economy. The following features of ACRS result in accelerated write-offs:

- Cost recovery periods are shorter than the estimated useful lives required under the pre-1981 depreciation system.
- The use of salvage value, required under the pre-1981 depreciation system, is eliminated under ACRS.

---

[1] § 168. Pre-ERTA depreciation rules under § 167 are covered in Appendix H.

CONCEPT SUMMARY 8-1

Depreciation and Cost Recovery: Relevant Time Periods

System	Date Property Is Placed in Service
§ 167 depreciation	Before January 1, 1981, and *certain* property placed in service after December 31, 1980.
Original accelerated cost recovery system (ACRS)	After December 31, 1980, and before January 1, 1987.
Modified accelerated cost recovery system (MACRS)	After December 31, 1986.

- For many assets, the methods for computing ACRS deductions are more generous than the allowable methods for computing depreciation.

For assets placed in service after 1986, ACRS is replaced with MACRS. The basic effect of MACRS is to somewhat dampen the economic stimulus effect of ACRS. MACRS cost recovery periods are generally longer than ACRS cost recovery periods. In addition, the cost recovery methods available under MACRS are, in most cases, not as generous as the methods available under ACRS.

OVERVIEW

Taxpayers may write off the cost of certain assets that are used in a trade or business or held for the production of income. A write-off may take the form of depreciation (or cost recovery), depletion, or amortization. Tangible assets, other than natural resources, are *depreciated*. Natural resources, such as oil, gas, coal, and timber, are *depleted*. Intangible assets, such as copyrights and patents, are *amortized*. Generally, no write-off is allowed for an asset that does not have a determinable useful life.

ACRS and MACRS provide separate cost recovery tables for realty (real property) and personalty (personal property). Realty generally includes land and buildings permanently affixed to the land. Write-offs are not available for land because it does not have a determinable useful life. Cost recovery allowances for real property, other than land, are based on recovery lives specified in the law. The IRS provides tables that specify cost recovery allowances for most types of realty.

Personalty is defined as any asset that is not realty.[2] Personalty includes furniture, machinery, equipment, and many other types of assets. Do not confuse personalty (or personal property) with *personal use* property. Personal use property is any property (realty or personalty) that is held for personal use rather than for use in a trade or business or an income-producing activity. Write-offs are not allowed for personal use assets.

In summary, both realty and personalty can be either business use/income-producing property or personal use property. Examples include a residence (realty that is personal use), an office building (realty that is business use), a dump truck (personalty that is business use), and regular wearing apparel (personalty that is personal use). It is imperative that this distinction between the *classification* of an asset (realty or personalty) and the *use* to which the asset is put (business or personal) be understood.

---

[2]Refer to Chapter 1 for a further discussion.

ACCELERATED COST RECOVERY SYSTEM (ACRS AND MACRS)

GENERAL CONSIDERATIONS

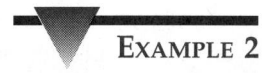

2 **LEARNING OBJECTIVE**
Determine the amount of cost recovery under ACRS and MACRS.

Under the **accelerated cost recovery system (ACRS),** the cost of an asset is recovered over a predetermined period that is generally shorter than the useful life of the asset or the period the asset is used to produce income. The ACRS system was designed to encourage investment, improve productivity, and simplify the law and its administration. However, the pre-ACRS depreciation rules will continue to apply in the following situations:

- Property placed in service after 1980 whose life is not based on years (e.g., units-of-production method).
- The remaining depreciation on property placed in service by the taxpayer before 1981.
- Personal property acquired after 1980 if the property was owned or used during 1980 by the taxpayer or a related person (antichurning rule).[3]
- Property that is amortized (e.g., leasehold improvements).

The basis for cost recovery generally is the adjusted cost basis used to determine gain if property is sold or otherwise disposed of. The basis is reduced by the amount of the cost recovery deducted.

Cost Recovery Allowed or Allowable.   The basis of cost recovery property must be reduced by the cost recovery allowed and by not less than the allowable amount. The *allowed* cost recovery is the cost recovery actually taken, whereas the *allowable* cost recovery is the amount that could have been taken under the applicable cost recovery method. If the taxpayer does not claim any cost recovery on property during a particular year, the basis of the property must still be reduced by the amount of cost recovery that should have been deducted (the allowable cost recovery).

EXAMPLE 2

On March 15, Jack paid $10,000 for a copier to be used in his business. The copier is five-year property. Jack elected to use the straight-line method of cost recovery, but did not take cost recovery in years 3 or 4. Therefore, the allowed cost recovery (cost recovery actually deducted) and the allowable cost recovery are as follows:

	Cost Recovery Allowed	**Cost Recovery Allowable**
Year 1	$1,000	$1,000
Year 2	2,000	2,000
Year 3	–0–	2,000
Year 4	–0–	2,000
Year 5	2,000	2,000
Year 6	1,000	1,000

If Jack sold the copier for $800 in year 7, he would recognize an $800 gain ($800 amount realized – $0 adjusted basis) because the adjusted basis of the copier is zero. ▼

---

[3]§ 168(f). The antichurning rules may also require the use of pre-TRA of 1986 ACRS rules on property placed in service after December 31, 1986 (property that otherwise would be subject to MACRS).

Cost Recovery Basis for Personal Use Assets Converted to Business or Income-Producing Use. If personal use assets are converted to business or income-producing use, the basis for cost recovery and for loss is the *lower* of the adjusted basis or the fair market value at the time the property was converted. As a result of this lower-of-basis rule, losses that occurred while the property was personal use property will not be recognized for tax purposes through the cost recovery of the property.

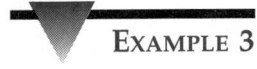

EXAMPLE 3

Hans acquires a personal residence for $120,000. Four years later, when the fair market value is only $100,000, he converts the property to rental use. The basis for cost recovery is $100,000, since the fair market value is less than the adjusted basis. The $20,000 decline in value is deemed to be personal (since it occurred while the property was held for personal use) and therefore nondeductible. ▼

ELIGIBLE PROPERTY UNDER ACRS OR MACRS

Assets used in a trade or business or for the production of income are eligible for cost recovery if they are subject to wear and tear, decay or decline from natural causes, or obsolescence. Assets that do not decline in value on a predictable basis or that do not have a determinable useful life (e.g., land, stock, antiques) are not eligible for cost recovery.

PERSONALTY: RECOVERY PERIODS AND METHODS

Classification of Property: ACRS. ACRS provides that the cost of eligible personalty (and certain realty) is recovered over 3, 5, 10, or 15 years. Property is classified by recovery period as follows:

3 years	Autos, light-duty trucks, R & D equipment, racehorses over 2 years old and other horses over 12 years old, and personalty with an ADR* midpoint life of 4 years or less.[4]
5 years	Most other equipment except long-lived public utility property. Also includes single-purpose agricultural structures and petroleum storage facilities, which are designated as § 1245 property under the law.
10 years	Public utility property with an ADR midpoint life greater than 18 but not greater than 25 years, burners and boilers using coal as a primary fuel if used in a public utility power plant and if replacing or converting oil- or gas-fired burners or boilers, railroad tank cars, mobile homes, and realty with an ADR midpoint life of 12.5 years or less (e.g., theme park structures).
15 years	Public utility property with an ADR midpoint life exceeding 25 years (except certain burners and boilers using coal as a primary fuel).

*ADR refers to the Asset Depreciation Range system.

Taxpayers who own 15-year ACRS property continue to compute cost recovery allowances under the ACRS rules. However, all cost has already been recovered on any 3-year, 5-year, or 10-year ACRS property.

Taxpayers had the choice of using (1) the straight-line method over the regular or optional (see below) recovery period or (2) a prescribed accelerated method over

---

[4]Rev.Proc. 83–35, 1983–1 C.B. 745 is the source for the ADR midpoint lives.

the regular recovery period. These two methods are both part of the ACRS system, but a convenient name is not provided for either method. Hereafter, the straight-line method will be referred to as the *optional* (or *elective*) *straight-line method*. The method using percentages prescribed in the Code will be referred to as the *statutory percentage method*.

The rates to be used in computing the deduction under the statutory percentage method are shown in Table 8–1 (all tables are located at the end of the chapter prior to the Problem Materials) and are based on the 150 percent declining-balance method, using the **half-year convention**[5] and an assumption of zero salvage value. The rates in the cost recovery tables at the end of the chapter reflect the relevant methods, conventions, and assumptions.

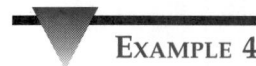

EXAMPLE 4

Green Utilities acquired 15-year public utility property in 1985 at a cost of $100,000. The property was placed in service on September 1, 1985. Green's cost recovery allowance for 1998 is determined from Table 8–1. The cost recovery percentage for 1998 (recovery year 14) is 6%, and the cost recovery allowance is $6,000 ($100,000 cost × 6%). ▼

Note that in 1985, Green got a half-year's cost recovery deduction (since the half-year convention is reflected in the percentages in Table 8–1) although it held the property only four months.

In the year that personal property is disposed of, no cost recovery is allowed.

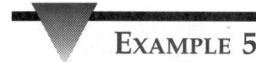

EXAMPLE 5

Assume the same facts as in the previous example and that the property is sold in May 1999. Green is not allowed a cost recovery deduction for the property in 1999. ▼

Reduction of Basis for Investment Tax Credit.   For personalty placed in service after 1982 and before January 1, 1986, taxpayers were required to reduce the basis of the property for the ACRS write-off by one-half the amount of the investment tax credit taken on the property.[6] The investment tax credit was not allowed on realty.

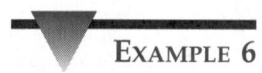

EXAMPLE 6

Beige Electric Company acquired property on September 4, 1985, for $100,000. The property was 15-year ACRS property, and Beige claimed a $10,000 investment tax credit ($100,000 × 10% investment tax credit rate). The basis of the property was reduced by $5,000 (one-half of the $10,000 investment tax credit). Therefore, the basis for cost recovery was $95,000. The cost recovery for 1998 is $5,700 [$95,000 × 6% (Table 8–1)]. ▼

As an alternative to reducing the basis of the property, a taxpayer could elect to take a *reduced* investment tax credit. Under this election, the investment tax credit was 8 percent (rather than 10 percent) for recovery property other than three-year property and 4 percent (instead of 6 percent) for three-year property. In Example 6, if the reduced investment tax credit election were made, Beige's cost recovery basis would be $100,000 rather than $95,000.

TRA of 1986 generally repealed the investment tax credit for property placed in service after December 31, 1985. Therefore, the reduction of basis for the investment tax credit does not apply to such property.

Classification of Property: MACRS.   The general effect of TRA of 1986 was to lengthen asset lives. The **modified accelerated cost recovery system (MACRS)** provides that the cost recovery basis of eligible personalty (and certain realty) is

---

[5]The half-year convention assumes all property is placed in service at mid-year and thus provides for a half-year's cost recovery.

[6]§ 48(q).

TAX IN THE NEWS

WHO GETS THE REFUND?

In October 1985, Ralston Purina Co. sold its subsidiary, Foodmaker, Inc., which owns and franchises Jack in the Box restaurants. At the time of the sale, several years of Foodmaker's tax returns were being audited by the IRS. The IRS was questioning accelerated depreciation deductions and investment tax credits that had been claimed on Jack in the Box restaurant buildings. Ralston and the buyers agreed that if the IRS decided Foodmaker was owed a refund, this money would be paid to Ralston. Likewise, if additional taxes were due, Ralston would reimburse the new owners.

In 1986, Foodmaker filed a return based on the assumption that the IRS's earlier tax claims would be proved wrong. In effect, this gave the $11.7 million refund to Foodmaker. Ralston claims that Foodmaker did not inform it of the refund claim associated with the 1986 tax return. In September 1996, Ralston learned that Foodmaker had claimed the refund 10 years earlier. Ralston now alleges that Foodmaker owes it at least $11 million plus interest from July 1986 and has filed a suit.

SOURCE: Adapted from Fred Faust, "Surprise! From Jack in the Box," *St. Louis Post-Dispatch*, June 2, 1997, Business Plus, p. 5.

recovered over 3, 5, 7, 10, 15, or 20 years. Property is classified by recovery period under MACRS as follows (see Exhibit 8–1 for examples):[7]

3-year 200% class . . . . ADR midpoints of 4 years and less.[8] Excludes automobiles and light trucks. Includes racehorses more than 2 years old and other horses more than 12 years old.

5-year 200% class . . . . ADR midpoints of more than 4 years and less than 10 years, adding automobiles, light trucks, qualified technological equipment, renewable energy and biomass properties that are small power production facilities, research and experimentation property, semiconductor manufacturing equipment, and computer-based central office switching equipment.

7-year 200% class . . . . ADR midpoints of 10 years and more and less than 16 years, adding single-purpose agricultural or horticultural structures and property with no ADR midpoint not classified elsewhere. Includes railroad track and office furniture, fixtures, and equipment.

10-year 200% class . . . . ADR midpoints of 16 years and more and less than 20 years.

15-year 150% class . . . . ADR midpoints of 20 years and more and less than 25 years, including sewage treatment plants, and telephone distribution plants and comparable equipment used for the two-way exchange of voice and data communications.

20-year 150% class . . . . ADR midpoints of 25 years and more, other than real property with an ADR midpoint of 27.5 years and more, and including sewer pipes.

[7]§ 168(e).
[8]Rev.Proc. 87–56, 1987–2 C.B. 674 is the source for the ADR midpoint lives.

▼ **EXHIBIT 8–1**
Cost Recovery Periods: MACRS

Class of Property	Examples
3-year	Tractor units for use over-the-road.
	Any horse that is not a racehorse and is more than 12 years old at the time it is placed in service.
	Any racehorse that is more than 2 years old at the time it is placed in service.
	Breeding hogs.
	Special tools used in the manufacturing of motor vehicles such as dies, fixtures, molds, and patterns.
5-year	Automobiles and taxis.
	Light and heavy general-purpose trucks.
	Buses.
	Trailers and trailer-mounted containers.
	Typewriters, calculators, and copiers.
	Computers and peripheral equipment.
	Breeding and dairy cattle.
7-year	Office furniture, fixtures, and equipment.
	Breeding and work horses.
	Agricultural machinery and equipment.
	Single-purpose agricultural or horticultural structures.
	Railroad track.
10-year	Vessels, barges, tugs, and similar water transportation equipment.
	Assets used for petroleum refining or for the manufacture of grain and grain mill products, sugar and sugar products, or vegetable oils and vegetable oil products.
15-year	Land improvements.
	Assets used for industrial steam and electric generation and/or distribution systems.
	Assets used in the manufacture of cement.
	Assets used in pipeline transportation.
	Electric utility nuclear production plant.
	Municipal wastewater treatment plant.
20-year	Farm buildings except single-purpose agricultural and horticultural structures.
	Gas utility distribution facilities.
	Water utilities.
	Municipal sewer.

Accelerated depreciation is allowed for these six MACRS classes of property. Two hundred percent declining-balance is used for the 3-, 5-, 7-, and 10-year classes, with a switchover to straight-line depreciation when it yields a larger amount. One hundred and fifty percent declining-balance is allowed for the 15-and 20-year classes, with an appropriate straight-line switchover.[9]

Taxpayers may *elect* the straight-line method to compute cost recovery allowances for each of these classes of property. Certain property is not eligible for accelerated cost recovery and must be depreciated under an alternative depreciation system (ADS). Both the straight-line election and ADS are discussed later in the chapter.

The original ACRS system gave the taxpayer a half-year of cost recovery for the tax year an asset was placed in service but allowed the taxpayer to recover the

[9]§ 168(b).

balance of the cost recovery basis over the years remaining in the property's recovery period. No cost recovery deduction was permitted for the year of disposition or retirement of the property. Thus, conceptually, the taxpayer was considered to have placed property in service at the beginning of the recovery period but was allowed only a half-year's worth of cost recovery for the year it was placed in service.

By contrast, MACRS views property as placed in service in the middle of the first year.[10] Thus, for example, the statutory recovery period for three-year property begins in the middle of the year an asset is placed in service and ends three years later. In practical terms, this means that taxpayers must wait an extra year to recover the cost of depreciable assets. That is, the actual write-off periods are 4, 6, 8, 11, 16, and 21 years. MACRS also allows for a half-year of cost recovery in the year of disposition or retirement.

The procedure for computing the cost recovery allowance under MACRS is the same as under the original ACRS method. The cost recovery basis is multiplied by the percentages that reflect the applicable cost recovery method and the applicable convention. The percentages are shown in Table 8–2.

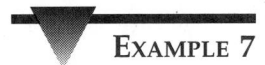

EXAMPLE 7

Kareem acquires a five-year class asset on April 10, 1998, for $30,000. Kareem's cost recovery deduction for 1998 is $6,000 [$30,000 × .20 (Table 8–2)]. ▼

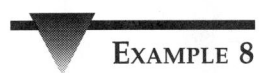

EXAMPLE 8

Assume the same facts as in Example 7, and that Kareem disposes of the asset on March 5, 2000. Kareem's cost recovery deduction for 2000 is $2,880 [$30,000 × ½ × .192 (Table 8–2)]. ▼

Mid-Quarter Convention. Under the original ACRS rules for personal property, the half-year convention was used no matter when property was acquired during the year. Thus, if a substantial dollar amount of assets was acquired late in the tax year, the half-year convention still applied. The law now contains a provision to curtail the benefits of such a tax strategy. If more than 40 percent of the value of property other than eligible real estate (see Realty: Recovery Periods and Methods: MACRS for a discussion of eligible real estate) is placed in service during the last quarter of the year, a **mid-quarter convention** applies.[11] Property acquisitions are then grouped by the quarter they were acquired for cost recovery purposes. Acquisitions during the first quarter are allowed 10.5 months of cost recovery; the second quarter, 7.5 months; the third quarter, 4.5 months; and the fourth quarter, 1.5 months. The percentages are shown in Table 8–3.

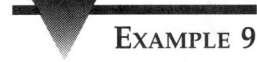

EXAMPLE 9

Silver Corporation acquires the following five-year class property in 1998:

Property Acquisition Dates	Cost
February 15	$ 200,000
July 10	400,000
December 5	600,000
Total	$1,200,000

If Silver Corporation uses the statutory percentage method, the cost recovery allowances for the first two years are computed as indicated below. Since more than 40% ($600,000/ $1,200,000 = 50%) of the acquisitions are in the last quarter, the mid-quarter convention applies.

[10]§ 168(d)(4)(A).   [11]§ 168(d)(3).

1998		
February 15	[$200,000 × .35 (Table 8–3)]	$ 70,000
July 10	($400,000 × .15)	60,000
December 5	($600,000 × .05)	30,000
Total		$160,000

1999		
February 15	[$200,000 × .26 (Table 8–3)]	$ 52,000
July 10	($400,000 × .34)	136,000
December 5	($600,000 × .38)	228,000
Total		$416,000

When property to which the mid-quarter convention applies is disposed of, the property is treated as though it were disposed of at the midpoint of the quarter. Hence, in the quarter of disposition, cost recovery is allowed for one-half of the quarter.

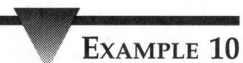

EXAMPLE 10

Assume the same facts as in Example 9, except that Silver Corporation sells the $400,000 asset on November 30 of 1999. The cost recovery allowance for 1999 is computed as follows:

February 15	[$200,000 × .26 (Table 8–3)]	$ 52,000
July 10	[$400,000 × .34 × (3.5/4)]	119,000
December 5	($600,000 × .38)	228,000
Total		$399,000

REALTY: RECOVERY PERIODS AND METHODS

ACRS.   Under the original ACRS rules, realty was assigned a 15-year recovery period. Real property other than low-income housing is depreciated using the 175 percent declining-balance method, with a switchover to straight-line depreciation when it yields a larger amount. Low-income housing is depreciated using the 200 percent declining-balance method, with an appropriate straight-line switchover. In either case, zero salvage value is assumed. Statutory percentages for real property are shown in Table 8–4, which contains rates for low-income housing as well as for other 15-year real estate. As explained later in the chapter, taxpayers were allowed to elect the straight-line method for real property.

The half-year convention does not apply to 15-year real property. As a result, Table 8–4 is structured differently from Tables 8–1 and 8–2. The cost recovery deduction for 15-year real property is based on the month the asset is placed in service rather than on the half-year convention. No cost recovery is allowed for the month in which an asset is disposed of if the asset is disposed of before the end of the recovery period.

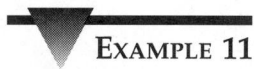

EXAMPLE 11

Alicia purchased a warehouse for $100,000 on January 1, 1984. The cost recovery allowance for the years 1984 through 1998, using the statutory percentage method, is as follows (see Table 8–4 for percentages).

1984—$12,000 (12% × $100,000)
1985—$10,000 (10% × $100,000)
1986—$9,000 (9% × $100,000)
1987—$8,000 (8% × $100,000)
1988—$7,000 (7% × $100,000)
1989—$6,000 (6% × $100,000)
1990—$6,000 (6% × $100,000)
1991—$6,000 (6% × $100,000)
1992—$6,000 (6% × $100,000)
1993—$5,000 (5% × $100,000)
1994—$5,000 (5% × $100,000)
1995—$5,000 (5% × $100,000)
1996—$5,000 (5% × $100,000)
1997—$5,000 (5% × $100,000)
1998—$5,000 (5% × $100,000)   ▼

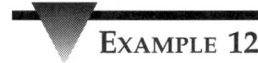

EXAMPLE 12   Assume the same facts as in Example 11, except the property is low-income housing. Cost recovery deductions using the statutory percentage method for 1984 through 1998 are as follows (see Table 8–4 for percentages):

1984—$13,000 (13% × $100,000)
1985—$12,000 (12% × $100,000)
1986—$10,000 (10% × $100,000)
1987—$9,000 (9% × $100,000)
1988—$8,000 (8% × $100,000)
1989—$7,000 (7% × $100,000)
1990—$6,000 (6% × $100,000)
1991—$5,000 (5% × $100,000)
1992—$5,000 (5% × $100,000)
1993—$5,000 (5% × $100,000)
1994—$4,000 (4% × $100,000)
1995—$4,000 (4% × $100,000)
1996—$4,000 (4% × $100,000)
1997—$4,000 (4% × $100,000)
1998—$4,000 (4% × $100,000)   ▼

The Deficit Reduction Act of 1984 changed the recovery period for real property to 18 years. This applies generally to property placed in service after March 15, 1984. However, the 15-year recovery period was retained for low-income housing as well as for other real property placed in service before March 16, 1984.

Eighteen-year real property placed in service after June 22, 1984, is subject to a **mid-month convention.**[12] This means that real property placed in service at any time during a particular month is treated as if it were placed in service in the middle of the month. This allows for one-half month's cost recovery for the month the property is placed in service. If the property is disposed of before the end of the recovery period, one-half month's cost recovery is permitted for the month of disposition regardless of the specific date of disposition. Statutory percentages for 18-year real property with a mid-month convention are shown in Table 8–5.

---

[12]A transitional rule, which provides for a full-month convention, is effective for property placed in service after March 15, 1984, and before June 23, 1984. The cost recovery tables for property placed in service during this period are not included in this chapter.

CONCEPT SUMMARY 8–2

Statutory Percentage Method under ACRS and MACRS

ACRS

	Personal Property	Real Property		
		15-Year	**18-Year**	**19-Year**
Convention	Half-year	Full-month	Mid-month	Mid-month
Cost recovery deduction in the year of disposition	None	Full-month up to month of disposition	Half-month for month of disposition	Half-month for month of disposition

MACRS

	Personal Property	Real Property*
Convention	Half-year or mid-quarter	Mid-month
Cost recovery deduction in the year of disposition	Half-year for year of disposition or half-quarter for quarter of disposition	Half-month for month of disposition

*Straight-line method must be used.

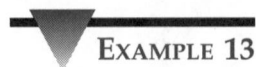

EXAMPLE 13

Rex purchased a building for $300,000 and placed it in service on August 21, 1984. The first year's cost recovery using the statutory percentage method is $12,000 [$300,000 × 4% (Table 8–5)]. ▼

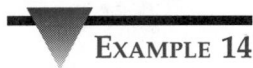

EXAMPLE 14

Assume the same facts as in Example 13 and that Rex disposes of the building on May 3, 1998. The cost recovery in the year of disposition is $4,500 ($300,000 × 4% × 4.5/12). ▼

Public Law 99–121 extended the minimum recovery period for real property (except low-income housing) from 18 years to 19 years. This applies to property placed in service after May 8, 1985, and before January 1, 1987. Statutory percentages for 19-year real property are shown in Table 8–6. Because the percentages are determined using a mid-month convention, the computation of cost recovery is mechanically the same as for 18-year property with the mid-month convention.

MACRS. Under MACRS, the cost recovery period for residential rental real estate is 27.5 years, and the straight-line method is used for computing the cost recovery allowance. **Residential rental real estate** includes property where 80 percent or more of the gross rental revenues are from nontransient dwelling units (e.g., an apartment building). Hotels, motels, and similar establishments are not residential rental property. Low-income housing is classified as residential rental real estate. Nonresidential real estate has a recovery period of 31.5 years (39 years for such property placed in service after May 12, 1993) and is also depreciated using the straight-line method.[13]

---

[13]§§ 168(b), (c), and (e).

Some items of real property are not treated as real estate for purposes of MACRS. For example, single-purpose agricultural structures are in the 7-year MACRS class. Land improvements are in the 15-year MACRS class.

All eligible real estate is depreciated using the mid-month convention. Regardless of when during the month the property is placed in service, it is deemed to have been placed in service at the middle of the month. In the year of disposition, a mid-month convention is also used.

Cost recovery is computed by multiplying the applicable rate (Table 8–7) by the cost recovery basis.

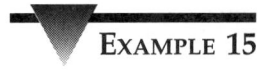

EXAMPLE 15 Alec acquired a building on April 1, 1994, for $800,000. If the building is classified as residential rental real estate, the cost recovery allowance for 1998 is $29,088 (.03636 × $800,000). If the building is classified as nonresidential real estate, the 1998 cost recovery allowance is $25,400 (.03175 × $800,000). (See Table 8–7 for percentages.) ▼

As part of the deficit reduction legislation of the Clinton administration (Revenue Reconciliation Act of 1993), nonresidential real estate placed in service after May 12, 1993, is subject to a 39-year recovery period. Property placed in service before 1994 that was subject to a binding contract to construct or purchase, as of May 12, 1993, may still be treated as 31.5-year property under the prior rules.

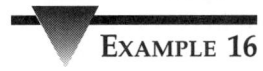

EXAMPLE 16 Assume the same facts as in Example 15, except that Alec acquired the nonresidential building on November 19, 1998. The 1998 cost recovery allowance is $2,568 [$800,000 × .00321 (Table 8–7)]. ▼

STRAIGHT-LINE ELECTION UNDER ACRS AND MACRS

ACRS. Under ACRS, taxpayers could *elect* to write off an asset using the straight-line method rather than the statutory percentage method. The straight-line recovery period could be the same as the prescribed recovery period under the statutory percentage method, or a longer period. The allowable straight-line recovery periods for each class of property are summarized as follows:

3-year property	3, 5, or 12 years
5-year property	5, 12, or 25 years
10-year property	10, 25, or 35 years
15-year property	15, 35, or 45 years
18-year real property and low-income housing (placed in service after March 15, 1984)	18, 35, or 45 years
19-year real property and low-income housing (placed in service after May 8, 1985)	19, 35, or 45 years

If the straight-line option was elected for personal property, the half-year convention applies in computing the cost recovery deduction. The effect of electing the straight-line method for personal property is to extend the statutory recovery period by one year (e.g., three to four and five to six years). There is no cost recovery deduction in the year of the disposition of the property.

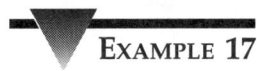

EXAMPLE 17 On May 6, 1986, Owl Utilities paid $100,000 for gas-fired boilers to replace coal-fired boilers (10-year property). Owl elected to compute the cost recovery allowance using the optional straight-line method and a 25-year cost recovery period. Owl's cost recovery allowance for 1986 was $2,000 ($100,000 basis × 4% straight-line rate × ½ year), which reflects the effect

of the half-year convention. The cost recovery allowance for 1998 is $4,000 ($100,000 basis × 4% straight-line rate). ▼

For each class of personal property, the straight-line election applied to *all* assets in a *particular class* that were placed in service during the year for which the election was made. The election applies for the entire recovery period of these assets. The election is not binding for personal property of the same class placed in service in another tax year.

Under the straight-line option for 15-year *real* property, the first year's cost recovery deduction and the cost recovery deduction for the year of disposition are computed on the basis of the number of months the property was in service during the year.

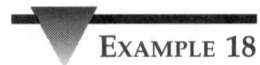

EXAMPLE 18

Kate acquired a store building on March 1, 1984, at a cost of $150,000. She elected the straight-line method using a recovery period of 15 years. Kate's cost recovery deduction for 1984 was $8,333 [($150,000 ÷ 15) × $^{10}/_{12}$]. ▼

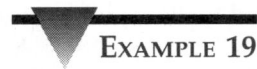

EXAMPLE 19

Assume the same facts as in Example 18 and that Kate disposes of the asset on January 31, 1998. Kate's cost recovery deduction for 1998 is $833 [($150,000 ÷ 15) × $^{1}/_{12}$]. ▼

Under the straight-line option for 18-year or 19-year real property, the cost recovery allowances in the year the property is placed in service and in the year of disposition are computed in the same manner (except for the use of different rates) as under the statutory percentage method. Note that 18-year and 19-year real property use a mid-month convention, whereas 15-year real property uses a full-month convention. Table 8–8 contains the applicable percentages to be used under the straight-line option for 19-year real property. (The tables that contain the percentages for 18-year real property using the straight-line method over 18, 35, and 45 years and 19-year real property using the straight-line method over 35 and 45 years are not reproduced in this text.)

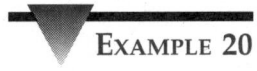

EXAMPLE 20

Ned acquired 19-year real property on October 1, 1986, at a cost of $150,000. He elected the straight-line method of cost recovery. Ned's cost recovery deduction for 1986 was $1,650 [$150,000 × 1.1% (Table 8–8)]. ▼

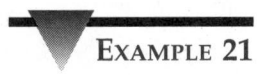

EXAMPLE 21

Assume the same facts as in Example 20 and that Ned disposes of the asset on September 20, 1998. Ned's cost recovery deduction for 1998 is $5,631 {[$150,000 × 5.3% × (8.5/12)] (Table 8–8)}. ▼

The straight-line election for 15-year, 18-year, or 19-year real property may be made on a *property-by-property* basis within the same year.

MACRS.　Although MACRS requires straight-line depreciation for all eligible real estate as previously discussed, the taxpayer may *elect* to use the straight-line method for personal property.[14] The property is depreciated using the class life (recovery period) of the asset with a half-year convention or a mid-quarter convention, whichever is applicable. The election is available on a class-by-class and year-by-year basis. The percentages for the straight-line election with a half-year convention appear in Table 8–9.

---

[14]§ 168(b)(5).

CONCEPT SUMMARY 8–3

Straight-Line Election under ACRS and MACRS

	Personal Property	ACRS		
		Real Property		
		15-Year	18-Year	19-Year
Convention	Half-year	Full-month	Mid-month	Mid-month
Cost recovery deduction in the year of disposition	None	Full-month up to month of disposition	Half-month for month of disposition	Half-month for month of disposition
Elective or mandatory	Elective	Elective	Elective	Elective
Breadth of election	Class by class	Property by property	Property by property	Property by property

	MACRS	
	Personal Property	Real Property*
Convention	Half-year or mid-quarter	Mid-month
Cost recovery deduction in the year of disposition	Half-year for year of dispositon or half-quarter for quarter of disposition	Half-month for month of disposition
Elective or mandatory	Elective	Mandatory
Breadth of election	Class by class	

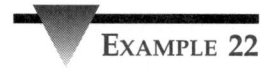

EXAMPLE 22

Terry acquires a 10-year class asset on August 4, 1998, for $100,000. He elects the straight-line method of cost recovery. Terry's cost recovery deduction for 1998 is $5,000 ($100,000 × .050). His cost recovery deduction for 1999 is $10,000 ($100,000 × .100). (See Table 8–9 for percentages.) ▼

ELECTION TO EXPENSE ASSETS

3 **LEARNING OBJECTIVE**
Recognize when and how to make the § 179 expensing election, calculate the amount of the deduction, and apply the effect of the election in making the MACRS calculation.

Section 179 (Election to Expense Certain Depreciable Business Assets) permits the taxpayer to elect to write off up to $18,500 in 1998[15] of the acquisition cost of *tangible personal property* used in a trade or business. Amounts that are expensed under § 179 may not be capitalized and depreciated. The **§ 179 expensing** election is an annual election and applies to the acquisition cost of property placed in service that year. The immediate expense election is not available for real property or for property used for the production of income.[16]

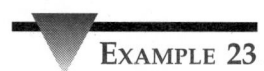

EXAMPLE 23

Kelly acquires machinery (five-year class) on February 1, 1998, at a cost of $40,000 and elects to expense $18,500 under § 179. Kelly's statutory percentage cost recovery deduction for 1998 is $4,300 [($40,000 cost − $18,500 expensed) × .200]. (See Table 8–2 for percentage.) Kelly's total deduction for 1998 is $22,800 ($18,500 + $4,300). ▼

[15]This amount was $10,000 for property placed in service in tax years beginning before January 1, 1993; $17,500 for property placed in service in tax years beginning after December 31, 1992, and before January 1, 1997; and $18,000 for property placed in service in tax years beginning in 1997.

[16]§§ 179(b) and (d). The amount shown is per taxpayer, per year. On a joint return, the statutory amounts apply to the couple. If the taxpayers are married and file separate returns, each spouse is eligible for 50% of the statutory amount.

For tax years beginning in 1997, an increase in the maximum § 179 amount is being phased in as follows:

Tax Year Beginning in	Maximum Expense Deduction
1997	$18,000
1998	18,500
1999	19,000
2000	20,000
2001 or 2002	24,000
2003 and thereafter	25,000

Annual Limitations. Two additional limitations apply to the amount deductible under § 179. First, the ceiling amount on the deduction is reduced dollar-for-dollar when property (other than eligible real estate) placed in service during the taxable year exceeds $200,000. Second, the amount expensed under § 179 cannot exceed the aggregate amount of taxable income derived from the conduct of any trade or business by the taxpayer. Taxable income of a trade or business is computed without regard to the amount expensed under § 179. Any § 179 expensed amount in excess of taxable income is carried forward to future taxable years and added to other amounts eligible for expensing (and is subject to the ceiling rules for the carryforward years).

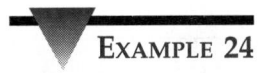

EXAMPLE 24

Jill owns a computer service and operates it as a sole proprietorship. In 1998, she will net $11,000 before considering any § 179 deduction. If Jill spends $204,000 on new equipment, her § 179 expense deduction is computed as follows:

§ 179 deduction before adjustment	$18,500
Less: Dollar limitation reduction ($204,000 − $200,000)	(4,000)
Remaining § 179 deduction	$14,500
Business income limitation	$11,000
§ 179 deduction allowed	$11,000
§ 179 deduction carryforward ($14,500 − $11,000)	$ 3,500

Effect on Basis. The basis of the property for cost recovery purposes is reduced by the § 179 amount after it is adjusted for property placed in service in excess of $200,000. This adjusted amount does not reflect any business income limitation.

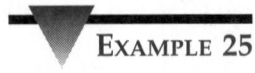

EXAMPLE 25

Assume the same facts as in Example 24 and that the new equipment is five-year class property. Jill's statutory percentage cost recovery deduction for 1998 is $37,900 [($204,000 − $14,500) × .200]. (See Table 8–2 for percentage.) ▼

Conversion to Personal Use. Conversion of the expensed property to personal use at any time results in recapture income (see Chapter 17). A property is converted to personal use if it is not used predominantly in a trade or business. Regulations provide for the mechanics of the recapture.[17]

---

[17]Reg. § 1.179-1(e).

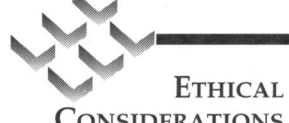

ETHICAL CONSIDERATIONS

Section 179 and Limited Personal Use

Sam, a salesman, purchased a new computer near the end of last year. He used the computer during the remainder of the year only in connection with his business. On his tax return for last year, Sam expensed the computer under § 179. During the current year, Sam has continued to use the computer in his business. However, he also allows his children to use the computer for their schoolwork. Sam has not maintained a log showing business and personal use of the computer for the current year. He feels that because the computer was expensed last year, no further accounting for it on his tax return is necessary. Do you agree?

BUSINESS AND PERSONAL USE OF AUTOMOBILES AND OTHER LISTED PROPERTY

4 LEARNING OBJECTIVE
Identify listed property and apply the deduction limitations on listed property and on luxury automobiles.

Limits exist on ACRS and MACRS deductions for automobiles and other listed property that are used for both personal and business purposes.[18] If the listed property is *predominantly used* for business, the taxpayer is allowed to use the statutory percentage method to recover the cost. In cases where the property is *not predominantly used* for business, the cost is recovered using the straight-line method.
Listed property includes the following:

- Any passenger automobile.
- Any other property used as a means of transportation.
- Any property of a type generally used for purposes of entertainment, recreation, or amusement.
- Any computer or peripheral equipment, with the exception of equipment used exclusively at a regular business establishment, including a qualifying home office.
- Any cellular telephone or other similar telecommunications equipment.
- Any other property specified in the Regulations.[19]

Automobiles and Other Listed Property Used Predominantly in Business. For listed property to be considered as predominantly used in business, its business usage must exceed 50 percent.[20] The use of listed property for production of income does not qualify as business use for purposes of the more-than-50 percent test. However, if the more-than-50 percent test is met, both production of income and business use percentages are used to compute the cost recovery deduction.

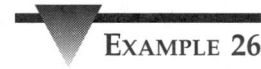

EXAMPLE 26

On September 1, 1998, Emma places in service listed five-year recovery property. The property cost $10,000. If Emma uses the property 40% for business and 25% for the production of income, the property is not considered as predominantly used for business. The cost is recovered using straight-line cost recovery. Emma's cost recovery allowance for the year is $650 ($10,000 × 10% × 65%). If, however, Emma uses the property 60% for business and 25% for the production of income, the property is considered as used predominantly for business. Therefore, she may use the statutory percentage method. Emma's cost recovery allowance for the year is $1,700 ($10,000 × .200 × 85%). ▼

---

[18]§ 280F.
[19]§ 280F(d)(4).

[20]§ 280F(b)(4).

The method for determining the percentage of business usage for listed property is specified in the Regulations. The Regulations provide that for automobiles a mileage-based percentage is to be used. Other listed property is to use the most appropriate unit of time (e.g., hours) the property is actually used (rather than available for use).[21]

The law places special limitations on the cost recovery deduction for passenger automobiles. These statutory dollar limits were imposed on passenger automobiles because of the belief that the tax system was being used to underwrite automobiles whose cost and luxury far exceeded what was needed for their business use.

A *passenger automobile* is any four-wheeled vehicle manufactured for use on public streets, roads, and highways with an unloaded gross vehicle weight rating of 6,000 pounds or less.[22] This definition specifically excludes vehicles used directly in the business of transporting people or property for compensation such as taxicabs, ambulances, hearses, and trucks and vans as prescribed by the Regulations.

The following limits apply to the cost recovery deductions for passenger automobiles for 1997:[23]

Year	Recovery Limitation*
1	$3,160
2	5,000
3	3,050
Succeeding years until the cost is recovered	1,775

*The indexed amounts for 1998 were not available at the time of this writing.

These limits are imposed before any percentage reduction for personal use. In addition, the limitation in the first year includes any amount the taxpayer elects to expense under § 179.[24] If the passenger automobile is used partly for personal use, the personal use percentage is ignored for the purpose of determining the unrecovered cost available for deduction in later years.

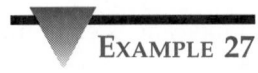

EXAMPLE 27

On July 1, 1998, Dan places in service an automobile that cost $20,000. The car is always used 80% for business and 20% for personal use. The cost recovery for the automobile would be as follows:

1998—$2,528 [$20,000 × 20% (limited to $3,160) × 80%]

1999—$4,000 [$20,000 × 32% (limited to $5,000) × 80%]

2000—$2,440 [$20,000 × 19.2% (limited to $3,050) × 80%]

2001—$1,420 [$20,000 × 11.52% (limited to $1,775) × 80%]

2002—$1,420 [$20,000 × 11.52% (limited to $1,775) × 80%]

2003—$1,420 [$5,240 unrecovered cost ($20,000 − $14,760*) (limited to $1,775) × 80%]

*($3,160 + $5,000 + $3,050 + $1,775 + $1,775). Although the statutory percentage method appears to restrict the deduction to $922 [$20,000 × 5.76% (limited to $1,775) × 80%], the unrecovered cost of $5,240 (limited to $1,775) multiplied by the business usage percentage is deductible. At the start of 2001 (year 4), there is an automatic switch to the straight-line cost recovery method. Under this method, the unrecovered cost up to the maximum allowable limit ($1,775) is deductible in the last year of the recovery period (2003 or year 6). Because the limit may restrict the deduction, any remaining unrecovered cost is deductible in the next or succeeding year(s), subject to the maximum allowable yearly limit ($1,775), multiplied by the business usage percentage.

The total cost recovery for the years 1998–2003 is $13,228. ▼

---

[21]Reg. § 1.280F-6T(e).

[22]§ 280F(d)(5).

[23]§ 280F(a)(2). The 1997 indexed amounts of $3,160, $5,000, $3,050, and $1,775 are used for the 1998 calculations that follow.

[24]§ 280F(d)(1).

The cost recovery limitations are maximum amounts. If the regular calculation produces a lesser amount of cost recovery, the lesser amount is used.

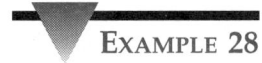

EXAMPLE 28

On April 2, 1998, Gail places in service an automobile that cost $10,000. The car is always used 70% for business and 30% for personal use. The cost recovery allowance for 1998 is $1,400 ($10,000 × 20% × 70%), which is less than $2,212 ($3,160 × 70%). ▼

Note that the cost recovery limitations apply *only* to passenger automobiles and not to other listed property.

Automobiles and Other Listed Property Not Used Predominantly in Business.   The cost of listed property that does not pass the more-than-50 percent business usage test in the year the property is placed in service must be recovered using the straight-line method.[25] The straight-line method to be used is that required under the alternative depreciation system (explained later in the chapter). This system requires a straight-line recovery period of five years for automobiles. However, even though the straight-line method is used, the cost recovery allowance for passenger automobiles cannot exceed the dollar limitations.

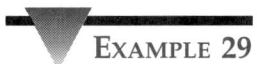

EXAMPLE 29

On July 27, 1998, Fred places in service an automobile that cost $20,000. The auto is used 40% for business and 60% for personal use. The cost recovery allowance for 1998 is $800 [$20,000 × 10% (Table 8–11) × 40%]. ▼

EXAMPLE 30

Assume the same facts as in Example 29, except that the auto cost $50,000. The cost recovery allowance for 1998 is $1,264 [$50,000 × 10% (Table 8–11) = $5,000 (limited to $3,160) × 40%]. ▼

If the listed property fails the more-than-50 percent business usage test, the straight-line method must be used for the remainder of the property's life. This applies even if at some later date the business usage of the property increases to more than 50 percent. Even though the straight-line method must continue to be used, however, the amount of cost recovery will reflect the increase in business usage.

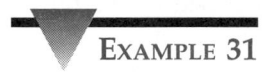

EXAMPLE 31

Assume the same facts as in Example 29, except that in 1999, Fred uses the auto 70% for business and 30% for personal use. Fred's cost recovery allowance for 1999 is $2,800 [$20,000 × 20% (Table 8–11) × 70%], which is less than 70% of the second-year limit. ▼

Change from Predominantly Business Use.   If the business use percentage of listed property falls to 50 percent or lower after the year the property is placed in service, the property is subject to *cost recovery recapture*. The amount required to be recaptured and included in the taxpayer's return as ordinary income is the excess cost recovery.

Excess cost recovery is the excess of the cost recovery deduction taken in prior years using the statutory percentage method over the amount that would have been allowed if the straight-line method had been used since the property was placed in service.[26]

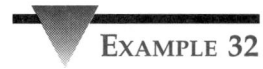

EXAMPLE 32

Seth purchased a car on January 22, 1998, at a cost of $20,000. Business usage was 80% in 1998, 70% in 1999, 40% in 2000, and 60% in 2001. Statutory percentage cost recovery deductions in 1998 and 1999 are $2,528 (80% × $3,160) and $3,500 (70% × $5,000), respectively. Seth's excess cost recovery to be recaptured as ordinary income in 2000 is $1,628, calculated as follows:

---

[25]§ 280F(b)(2).   [26]§ 280F(b)(3).

1998	
Statutory percentage allowance	$ 2,528
Straight-line ($20,000 × 10% × 80%)	(1,600)
Excess	$ 928

1999	
Statutory percentage allowance	$ 3,500
Straight-line ($20,000 × 20% × 70%)	(2,800)
1999 excess	$ 700
1998 excess	928
Total excess	$ 1,628

After the business usage of the listed property drops below the more-than-50 percent level, the straight-line method must be used for the remaining life of the property.

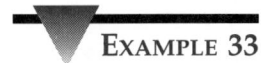

EXAMPLE 33   Assume the same facts as in Example 32. Seth's cost recovery allowance for the years 2000 and 2001 would be $1,220 and $1,065, computed as follows:

2000—$1,220   [($20,000 × 20%) limited to $3,050 × 40%]
2001—$1,065   [($20,000 × 20%) limited to $1,775 × 60%]

Leased Automobiles.   A taxpayer who leases a passenger automobile must report an *inclusion amount* in gross income. The inclusion amount is computed from an IRS table for each taxable year for which the taxpayer leases the automobile. The purpose of this provision is to prevent taxpayers from circumventing the cost recovery dollar limitations by leasing, instead of purchasing, an automobile.

The dollar amount of the inclusion is based on the fair market value of the automobile and is prorated for the number of days the auto is used during the taxable year. The prorated dollar amount is then multiplied by the business and income-producing usage percentage to determine the amount to be included in gross income.[27] The taxpayer deducts the lease payments, multiplied by the business and income-producing usage percentage. The net effect is that the annual deduction for the lease payment is reduced by the inclusion amount.

EXAMPLE 34   On April 1, 1998, Jim leases and places in service a passenger automobile worth $40,000. The lease is to be for a period of five years. During the taxable years 1998 and 1999, Jim uses the automobile 70% for business and 30% for personal use. Assuming the dollar amounts from the IRS table for 1998 and 1999 are $188 and $412, Jim must include $99 in gross income for 1998 and $288 for 1999, computed as follows:

1998 $188 × (275/365) × 70% = $99
1999 $412 × (365/365) × 70% = $288

In addition, Jim can deduct 70% of the lease payments each year because this is the business use percentage. ▼

---

[27]Reg. § 1.280F-7T(a).

SUBSTANTIATING A DEPRECIATION DEDUCTION

The IRS disallowed a depreciation deduction of $53,997 on the 1993 income tax return of Daniel Becnel, Jr. Becnel deducted the depreciation on 13 automobiles that he said were used strictly for business. Becnel claimed that the cars, nine of which were Mercedes-Benzes, were used to drive to states where his firm was handling lawsuits. The IRS disallowed the deduction claiming that Becnel didn't establish that the automobiles were used in a trade or business. Becnel has filed a petition with the U.S. Tax Court.

SOURCE: Adapted from Judi Russell and William Ringle, Jr., "Attorney Battles with IRS over Deduction for 13 Cars," City Business/New Orleans, Inc., June 23, 1997.

Substantiation Requirements. Listed property is now subject to the substantiation requirements of § 274. This means that the taxpayer must prove the business usage as to the amount of expense or use, the time and place of use, the business purpose for the use, and the business relationship to the taxpayer of persons using the property. Substantiation requires adequate records or sufficient evidence corroborating the taxpayer's statement. However, these substantiation requirements do not apply to vehicles that, by reason of their nature, are not likely to be used more than a *de minimis* amount for personal purposes.[28]

ALTERNATIVE DEPRECIATION SYSTEM (ADS)

5 LEARNING OBJECTIVE
Determine when and how to use the alternative depreciation system (ADS).

The **alternative depreciation system (ADS)** must be used for the following:[29]

- To calculate the portion of depreciation treated as an alternative minimum tax (AMT) adjustment for purposes of the corporate and individual AMT (see Chapters 12 and 20).
- To compute depreciation allowances for property for which any of the following is true:

  - Used predominantly outside the United States.
  - Leased or otherwise used by a tax-exempt entity.
  - Financed with the proceeds of tax-exempt bonds.
  - Imported from foreign countries that maintain discriminatory trade practices or otherwise engage in discriminatory acts.

- To compute depreciation allowances for earnings and profits purposes (see Chapter 20).

In general, ADS depreciation is computed using straight-line recovery without regard to salvage value. However, for purposes of the AMT, depreciation of personal property is computed using the 150 percent declining-balance method with an appropriate switch to the straight-line method.

The taxpayer must use the half-year or the mid-quarter convention, whichever is applicable, for all property other than eligible real estate. The mid-month convention is used for eligible real estate. The applicable ADS rates are found in Tables 8–10, 8–11, and 8–12.

[28]§§ 274(d) and (i). [29]§ 168(g).

CONCEPT SUMMARY 8–4

Listed Property Cost Recovery

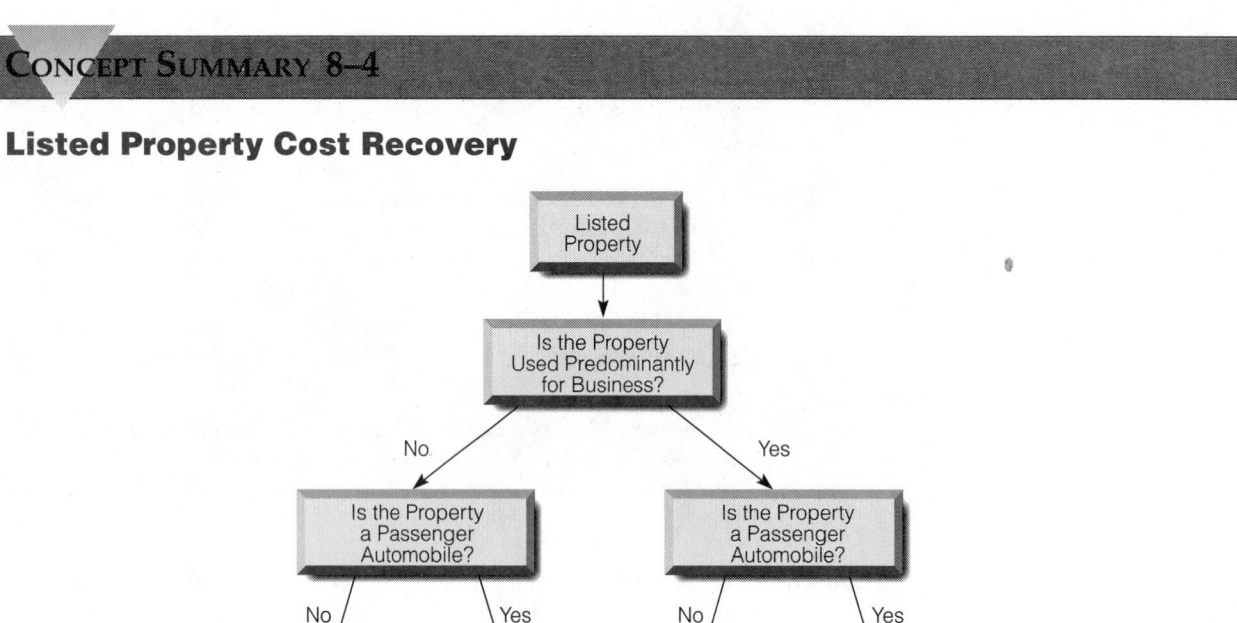

Legend to Tax Treatment

A   Straight-line cost recovery reduced by the personal use percentage.

B   Straight-line cost recovery subject to the recovery limitations ($3,160, $5,000, $3,050, $1,775) and reduced by the personal use percentage.

C   Statutory percentage cost recovery reduced by the personal use percentage.

D   Statutory percentage cost recovery subject to the recovery limitations ($3,160, $5,000, $3,050, $1,775) and reduced by the personal use percentage.

The recovery periods under ADS are as follows:[30]

- The ADR midpoint life for property that does not fall into any of the following listed categories.
- Five years for qualified technological equipment, automobiles, and light-duty trucks.
- Twelve years for personal property with no class life.
- Forty years for all residential rental property and all nonresidential real property.

Taxpayers may *elect* to use the 150 percent declining-balance method to compute the regular income tax rather than the 200 percent declining-balance method that is available for personal property. Hence, if the election is made, there will be no difference between the cost recovery for computing the regular income tax and the AMT. However, taxpayers who make this election must use the ADS recovery periods in computing the cost recovery for the regular income tax, and the ADS recovery periods generally are longer than the regular recovery periods under MACRS. For property placed in service after December 31, 1998, TRA of 1997

---

[30]The class life for certain properties described in § 168(e)(3) is specially determined under § 168(g)(3)(B).

provides that the regular income tax MACRS recovery periods can be used for both the regular income tax and the AMT rather than the longer ADS recovery periods.

The following are examples of the classification of property by class life for the ADS recovery periods:[31]

3-year . . . . . Special tools used in the manufacture of motor vehicles, breeding hogs.
5-year . . . . . Automobiles, light general-purpose trucks.
7-year . . . . . Breeding and dairy cattle.
9.5-year . . . . Computer-based telephone central office switching equipment.
10-year . . . . Office furniture, fixtures, and equipment, railroad track.
12-year . . . . Racehorses more than 2 years old at the time they are placed in service.

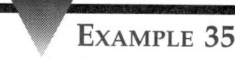

EXAMPLE 35

On March 1, 1998, Abby purchases computer-based telephone central office switching equipment for $80,000. If Abby uses statutory percentage cost recovery (assuming no § 179 election), the cost recovery allowance for 1998 is $16,000 [$80,000 × 20% (Table 8–2, 5-year class property)]. If Abby elects to use ADS 150% declining-balance cost recovery (assuming no § 179 election), the cost recovery allowance for 1998 is $6,312 [$80,000 × 7.89% (Table 8–10, 9.5-year class property)]. Note that if the equipment were placed in service in 1999, the 5-year recovery period could be used with the ADS 150% declining-balance cost recovery. ▼

In lieu of depreciation under the regular MACRS method, taxpayers may *elect* straight-line under ADS for property that qualifies for the regular MACRS method. The election is available on a class-by-class and year-by-year basis for property other than eligible real estate. The election for eligible real estate is on a property-by-property basis. One reason for making this election is to avoid a difference between deductible depreciation and earnings and profits depreciation.

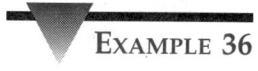

EXAMPLE 36

Polly acquires an apartment building on March 17, 1998, for $700,000. She takes the maximum cost recovery allowance for determining taxable income. Polly's cost recovery allowance for computing 1998 taxable income is $20,153 [$700,000 × .02879 (Table 8–7)]. However, Polly's cost recovery for computing her earnings and profits is only $13,853 [$700,000 × .01979 (Table 8–12)]. ▼

AMORTIZATION

6 **LEARNING OBJECTIVE**
Identify intangible assets that are eligible for amortization and calculate the amount of the deduction.

Taxpayers can claim an **amortization** deduction on intangible assets called "amortizable § 197 intangibles." The amount of the deduction is determined by amortizing the adjusted basis of such intangibles ratably over a 15-year period beginning in the month in which the intangible is acquired.[32]

An *amortizable § 197 intangible* is any § 197 intangible acquired after August 10, 1993, and held in connection with the conduct of a trade or business or for the production of income. Section 197 intangibles include goodwill and going-concern value, franchises (except sports franchises), trademarks, and trade names. Covenants not to compete, copyrights, and patents are also included if they are acquired in connection with the acquisition of a business. Generally, self-created intangibles are not § 197 intangibles. The 15-year amortization period applies regardless of the actual useful life of an amortizable § 197 intangible. No other depreciation or

---

[31]Rev.Proc. 87-56, 1987-2 C.B. 674 is the source for the recovery periods.   [32]§ 197(a).

amortization deduction is permitted with respect to any amortizable § 197 intangible except those permitted under the 15-year amortization rules.

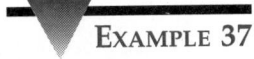

EXAMPLE 37 On June 1, 1998, Neil purchased and began operating the Falcon Cafe. Of the purchase price, $90,000 is correctly allocated to goodwill. The deduction for amortization for 1998 is $3,500 [($90,000/15) × (7/12)]. ▼

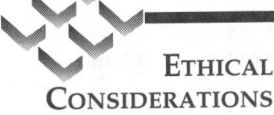

ETHICAL CONSIDERATIONS

Allocating Intangible Assets When a Business Is Sold

Marge and Stan are negotiating Stan's purchase of Marge's business. Both are in the 36 percent tax bracket. They have agreed that the tangible assets of the business are worth $100,000. Marge's adjusted basis for these assets is $70,000. The only other asset of the business is the going-concern value. Marge believes that this asset is worth about $50,000. Stan believes that it is worth somewhat less, probably about $40,000.

Marge and Stan are handling their own negotiations since they do not believe in wasting money on attorneys or CPAs when such professional services are not required. Stan knows from an MBA class he took five years ago that goodwill is not deductible, but that a covenant not to compete can be deducted over the covenant period. Stan believes that Marge, who is age 67 and in poor health, is going to retire. In order to maximize the tax benefits to himself, Stan increases his offer from $140,000 to $145,000 (i.e., "we'll split the difference") if Marge will agree to sign a five-year covenant with $45,000 of the $145,000 purchase price allocated to the covenant. Marge, who believes that the tax consequences of the sale ($145,000 amount realized – $70,000 adjusted basis = $75,000 recognized gain) will be the same regardless of whether the $45,000 is for goodwill or for a covenant, accepts the offer. Evaluate the decisions made by Marge and Stan.

▼ DEPLETION

7   LEARNING OBJECTIVE
Determine the amount of depletion expense including being able to apply the alternative tax treatments for intangible drilling and development costs.

Natural resources (e.g., oil, gas, coal, gravel, timber) are subject to **depletion,** which is simply a form of depreciation applicable to natural resources. Land generally cannot be depleted.

The owner of an interest in the natural resource is entitled to deduct depletion. An owner is one who has an economic interest in the property.[33] An economic interest requires the acquisition of an interest in the resource in place and the receipt of income from the extraction or severance of that resource. Like depreciation, depletion is a deduction *for* adjusted gross income.

Although all natural resources are subject to depletion, oil and gas wells are used as an example in the following paragraphs to illustrate the related costs and issues.

In developing an oil or gas well, the producer must make four types of expenditures:

---

[33]Reg. § 1.611-1(b).

- Natural resource costs.
- Intangible drilling and development costs.
- Tangible asset costs.
- Operating costs.

Natural resources are physically limited, and the costs to acquire them (e.g., oil under the ground) are, therefore, recovered through depletion. Costs incurred in making the property ready for drilling such as the cost of labor in clearing the property, erecting derricks, and drilling the hole are **intangible drilling and development costs (IDC).** These costs generally have no salvage value and are a lost cost if the well is dry. Costs for tangible assets such as tools, pipes, and engines are capital in nature. These costs must be capitalized and recovered through depreciation (cost recovery). Costs incurred after the well is producing are operating costs. These costs would include expenditures for such items as labor, fuel, and supplies. Operating costs are deductible when incurred (on the accrual basis) or when paid (on the cash basis).

The expenditures for depreciable assets and operating costs pose no unusual problems for producers of natural resources. The tax treatment of depletable costs and intangible drilling and development costs is quite a different matter.

INTANGIBLE DRILLING AND DEVELOPMENT COSTS (IDC)

Intangible drilling and development costs (IDC) can be handled in one of two ways at the option of the taxpayer. They can be *either* charged off as an expense in the year in which they are incurred *or* capitalized and written off through depletion. The taxpayer makes the election in the first year such expenditures are incurred either by taking a deduction on the return or by adding them to the depletable basis. No formal statement of intent is required. Once made, the election is binding on both the taxpayer and the IRS for all such expenditures in the future. If the taxpayer fails to make the election to expense IDC on the original timely filed return the first year such expenditures are incurred, an automatic election to capitalize them has been made and is irrevocable.

As a general rule, it is more advantageous to expense IDC. The obvious benefit of an immediate write-off (as opposed to a deferred write-off through depletion) is not the only advantage. Since a taxpayer can use percentage depletion, which is calculated without reference to basis (see Example 41), the IDC may be completely lost as a deduction if they are capitalized.

DEPLETION METHODS

There are two methods of calculating depletion: cost and percentage. Cost depletion can be used on any wasting asset (and is the only method allowed for timber). Percentage depletion is subject to a number of limitations, particularly for oil and gas deposits. Depletion should be calculated both ways, and generally the method that results in the *larger* deduction is used. The choice between cost and percentage depletion is an annual election.

Cost Depletion. **Cost depletion** is determined by using the adjusted basis of the asset.[34] The basis is divided by the estimated recoverable units of the asset (e.g., barrels, tons) to arrive at the depletion per unit. The depletion per unit then is multiplied by the number of units sold (*not* the units produced) during the year

---

[34]§ 612.

▼ **EXHIBIT 8–2**
Sample of Percentage Depletion
Rates

22% Depletion	
Cobalt	Sulfur
Lead	Tin
Nickel	Uranium
Platinum	Zinc
15% Depletion	
Copper	Oil and gas
Gold	Oil shale
Iron	Silver
14% Depletion	
Borax	Magnesium carbonates
Calcium carbonates	Marble
Granite	Potash
Limestone	Slate
10% Depletion	
Coal	Perlite
Lignite	Sodium chloride
5% Depletion	
Gravel	Pumice
Peat	Sand

to arrive at the cost depletion allowed. Cost depletion, therefore, resembles the units-of-production method of calculating depreciation.

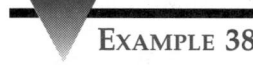

EXAMPLE 38

On January 1, 1998, Pablo purchased the rights to a mineral interest for $1,000,000. At that time, the remaining recoverable units in the mineral interest were estimated to be 200,000. The depletion per unit is $5 [$1,000,000 (adjusted basis) ÷ 200,000 (estimated recoverable units)]. If during the year 60,000 units were mined and 25,000 were sold, the cost depletion would be $125,000 [$5 (depletion per unit) × 25,000 (units sold)]. ▼

If the taxpayer later discovers that the original estimate was incorrect, the depletion per unit for future calculations must be redetermined based on the revised estimate.[35]

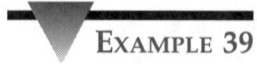

EXAMPLE 39

Assume the same facts as in Example 38. In 1999, Pablo realizes that an incorrect estimate was made. The remaining recoverable units now are determined to be 400,000. Based on this new information, the revised depletion per unit is $2.1875 [$875,000 (adjusted basis) ÷ 400,000 (estimated recoverable units)]. Note that the adjusted basis is the original cost ($1,000,000) reduced by the depletion claimed in 1998 ($125,000). If 30,000 units are sold in 1999, the depletion for the year would be $65,625 [$2.1875 (depletion per unit) × 30,000 (units sold)]. ▼

Percentage Depletion. **Percentage depletion** (also referred to as statutory depletion) is a specified percentage provided for in the Code. The percentage varies according to the type of mineral interest involved. A sample of these percentages is shown in Exhibit 8–2. The rate is applied to the gross income from the property,

---

[35]§ 611(a).

TAX IN THE NEWS

PERCENTAGE DEPLETION

On March 17, 1997, the U.S. Supreme Court declined to consider the IRS's appeal in a case against Exxon Corporation as to the proper way to calculate a depletion deduction. The disagreement involved the proper sales price of natural gas to be used in computing the percentage depletion deduction. The IRS argued that the depletion deduction for some natural gas sales should not be allowed to exceed the company's total income from those sales. Exxon argued that the law allows the use of a representative market price for natural gas in the field where it was produced, even if that price far exceeds the actual price received. At stake was about $1 billion in tax liability.

SOURCE: Adapted from Bloomberg News, "Supreme Court Declines to Hear IRS Appeal in Exxon Tax Fight," *Fort Worth Star-Telegram*, March 18, 1997, Business, p. 3.

---

but in no event may percentage depletion exceed 50 percent of the taxable income from the property before the allowance for depletion.[36]

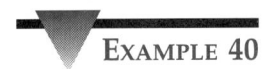

EXAMPLE 40

Assuming gross income of $100,000, a depletion rate of 22%, and other expenses relating to the property of $60,000, the depletion allowance is determined as follows:

Gross income	$100,000
Less: Other expenses	(60,000)
Taxable income before depletion	$ 40,000
Depletion allowance [the lesser of $22,000 (22% × $100,000) or $20,000 (50% × $40,000)]	(20,000)
Taxable income after depletion	$ 20,000

The adjusted basis of the property is reduced by $20,000, the depletion allowed. If the other expenses had been only $55,000, the full $22,000 could have been deducted, and the adjusted basis would have been reduced by $22,000. ▼

Note that percentage depletion is based on a percentage of the gross income from the property and makes no reference to cost. Thus, when percentage depletion is used, it is possible to deduct more than the original cost of the property. If percentage depletion is used, however, the adjusted basis of the property (for computing cost depletion) must be reduced by the amount of percentage depletion taken until the adjusted basis reaches zero.

Effect of Intangible Drilling Costs on Depletion.   The treatment of IDC has an effect on the depletion deduction in two ways. If the costs are capitalized, the basis for cost depletion is increased. As a consequence, the cost depletion is increased. If IDC are expensed, they reduce the taxable income from the property. This reduction may result in application of the provision that limits depletion to

---

[36]§ 613(a). Special rules apply for certain oil and gas wells under § 613A (e.g., the 50% ceiling is replaced with a 100% ceiling, and the percentage depletion may not exceed 65% of the taxpayer's taxable income from all sources before the allowance for depletion).

50 percent (100 percent for certain oil and gas wells) of taxable income before deducting depletion.

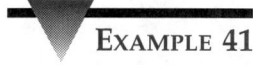 **EXAMPLE 41**

Iris purchased the rights to an oil interest for $1,000,000. The recoverable barrels were estimated to be 200,000. During the year, 50,000 barrels were sold for $2,000,000. Regular expenses amounted to $800,000, and IDC were $650,000. If the IDC are capitalized, the depletion per unit is $8.25 ($1,000,000 + $650,000 ÷ 200,000 barrels), and the following taxable income results:

Gross income	$2,000,000
Less: Expenses	(800,000)
Taxable income before depletion	$1,200,000
Cost depletion ($8.25 × 50,000) = $412,500	
Percentage depletion (15% × $2,000,000) = $300,000	
Greater of cost or percentage depletion	(412,500)
Taxable income	$ 787,500

If the IDC are expensed, the taxable income is $250,000, calculated as follows:

Gross income	$ 2,000,000
Less: Expenses, including IDC	(1,450,000)
Taxable income before depletion	$ 550,000
Cost depletion [($1,000,000 ÷ 200,000 barrels) × 50,000 barrels] = $250,000	
Percentage depletion (15% of $2,000,000 = $300,000, limited to 100% of $550,000 taxable income before depletion) = $300,000	
Greater of cost or percentage depletion	(300,000)
Taxable income	$ 250,000

For further restrictions on the use or availability of the percentage depletion method, see § 613.

REPORTING PROCEDURES

8   **LEARNING OBJECTIVE**
Perform the reporting procedures for cost recovery.

Sole proprietors engaged in a business should file a Schedule C, Profit or Loss from Business, to accompany Form 1040. Schedule C for 1997 is presented because the 1998 form was not yet available.

The top part of page 1 requests certain key information about the taxpayer (e.g., name, address, Social Security number) and the business methods involved (e.g., accounting method and inventory method used). Part I provides for the reporting of items of income. If the business requires the use of inventories and the computation of cost of goods sold (see Chapter 18 for when this is necessary), Part III must be completed and the cost of goods sold amount transferred to line 4 of Part I.

Part II allows for the reporting of deductions. Some of the deductions discussed in Chapters 7 and 8 and their location on the form are bad debts (line 9), depletion (line 12), and depreciation (line 13). Other expenses (line 27) include those items not already covered (see lines 8–26). An example would be research and experimental expenditures.

If depreciation is claimed, it should be supported by completing Form 4562. Form 4562 for 1997 is presented because the 1998 form was not yet available. The amount listed on line 21 of Form 4562 is then transferred to line 13 of Part II of Schedule C.

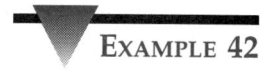

EXAMPLE 42

Thomas Andrews, Social Security number 123–45–6789, was employed as an accountant until July 1996, when he opened his own practice. His address is 279 Mountain View, Ogden, UT 84201. Andrews keeps his books on the accrual basis and had the following revenue and business expenses in 1997:

a. Revenue from accounting practice, $80,000.
b. Bad debts, $2,000.
c. Automobile expenses, $3,000.
d. Insurance, $800.
e. Office supplies, $4,000.
f. Rent, $12,000.
g. Furniture and fixtures acquired on July 15, 1996, for $6,000. Andrews used the statutory percentage cost recovery method.
h. Business automobile acquired on May 20, 1996, for $10,000. Andrews used the statutory percentage cost recovery method. The automobile, which was driven 12,000 miles during 1997, was used only for business purposes.
i. Microcomputer acquired on May 7, 1997, for $21,500. Andrews elects § 179 and uses the statutory percentage cost recovery method.
   (Remember that the statutory ceiling amount for § 179 expensing for 1997 is $18,000.)

Andrews would report the above information on Schedule C and Form 4562 as illustrated on the following pages. ▼

TAX PLANNING CONSIDERATIONS

COST RECOVERY

Cost recovery schedules should be reviewed annually for possible retirements, abandonments, and obsolescence.

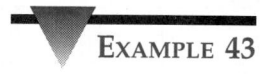

EXAMPLE 43

An examination of the cost recovery schedule of Eagle Company reveals the following:

- Asset A was abandoned when it was discovered that the cost of repairs would be in excess of the cost of replacement. Asset A had an adjusted basis of $3,000.
- Asset J became obsolete this year, at which point, its adjusted basis was $8,000.

Assets A and J should be written off for an additional expense of $11,000 ($3,000 + $8,000). ▼

9 ▼ **LEARNING OBJECTIVE**
Identify tax planning opportunities for cost recovery, amortization, and depletion.

Because of the deductions for cost recovery, interest, and ad valorem property taxes, investments in real estate can be highly attractive. In figuring the economics of such investments, one should be sure to take into account any tax savings that result.

Form **4562**

Department of the Treasury
Internal Revenue Service   (99)

Depreciation and Amortization
(Including Information on Listed Property)

▶ See separate instructions.   ▶ Attach this form to your return.

OMB No. 1545-0172

1997

Attachment
Sequence No. **67**

Name(s) shown on return	Business or activity to which this form relates	Identifying number
Thomas Andrews	*Accounting Services*	*123-45-6789*

Part I   **Election To Expense Certain Tangible Property (Section 179) (Note:** *If you have any "listed property,"* complete Part V before you complete Part I.)

1	Maximum dollar limitation. If an enterprise zone business, see page 2 of the instructions . .	**1**	$18,000
2	Total cost of section 179 property placed in service. See page 2 of the instructions	**2**	*$21,500*
3	Threshold cost of section 179 property before reduction in limitation	**3**	$200,000
4	Reduction in limitation. Subtract line 3 from line 2. If zero or less, enter -0-	**4**	*–0–*
5	Dollar limitation for tax year. Subtract line 4 from line 1. If zero or less, enter -0-. If married filing separately, see page 2 of the instructions	**5**	*$18,000*

(a) Description of property	(b) Cost (business use only)	(c) Elected cost	
6 *5-Year Class Prop.-Microcomputer*	*$21,500*	*$18,000*	

7	Listed property. Enter amount from line 27	**7**	
8	Total elected cost of section 179 property. Add amounts in column (c), lines 6 and 7 . . .	**8**	*$18,000*
9	Tentative deduction. Enter the smaller of line 5 or line 8	**9**	*$18,000*
10	Carryover of disallowed deduction from 1996. See page 3 of the instructions	**10**	
11	Business income limitation. Enter the smaller of business income (not less than zero) or line 5 (see instructions)	**11**	*$18,000*
12	Section 179 expense deduction. Add lines 9 and 10, but do not enter more than line 11 . .	**12**	*$18,000*
13	Carryover of disallowed deduction to 1998. Add lines 9 and 10, less line 12 ▶	**13**	

Note: *Do not use Part II or Part III below for listed property (automobiles, certain other vehicles, cellular telephones, certain computers, or property used for entertainment, recreation, or amusement). Instead, use Part V for listed property.*

Part II   **MACRS Depreciation For Assets Placed in Service ONLY During Your 1997 Tax Year (Do Not Include Listed Property.)**

Section A—General Asset Account Election

14   If you are making the election under section 168(i)(4) to group any assets placed in service during the tax year into one or more general asset accounts, check this box. See page 3 of the instructions . . . . ▶ ☐

Section B—General Depreciation System (GDS) (See page 3 of the instructions.)

(a) Classification of property	(b) Month and year placed in service	(c) Basis for depreciation (business/investment use only—see instructions)	(d) Recovery period	(e) Convention	(f) Method	(g) Depreciation deduction
15a 3-year property						
b 5-year property		*$3,500*	*5-Year*	*HY*	*200DB*	*700*
c 7-year property						
d 10-year property						
e 15-year property						
f 20-year property						
g 25-year property			25 yrs.		S/L	
h Residential rental property			27.5 yrs.	MM	S/L	
			27.5 yrs.	MM	S/L	
i Nonresidential real property			39 yrs.	MM	S/L	
				MM	S/L	

Section C—Alternative Depreciation System (ADS) (See page 6 of the instructions.)

16a Class life					S/L	
b 12-year			12 yrs.		S/L	
c 40-year			40 yrs.	MM	S/L	

Part III   **Other Depreciation (Do Not Include Listed Property.)** (See page 6 of the instructions.)

17	GDS and ADS deductions for assets placed in service in tax years beginning before 1997	**17**	*1,959*
18	Property subject to section 168(f)(1) election	**18**	
19	ACRS and other depreciation	**19**	

Part IV   **Summary** (See page 7 of the instructions.)

20	Listed property. Enter amount from line 26	**20**	*3,200*
21	**Total.** Add deductions on line 12, lines 15 and 16 in column (g), and lines 17 through 20. Enter here and on the appropriate lines of your return. Partnerships and S corporations—see instructions . .	**21**	*23,859*
22	For assets shown above and placed in service during the current year, enter the portion of the basis attributable to section 263A costs	**22**	

For Paperwork Reduction Act Notice, see the separate instructions.   Cat. No. 12906N   Form **4562** (1997)

Form 4562 (1997)

Part V	Listed Property—Automobiles, Certain Other Vehicles, Cellular Telephones, Certain Computers, and Property Used for Entertainment, Recreation, or Amusement

Note: *For any vehicle for which you are using the standard mileage rate or deducting lease expense, complete **only** 23a, 23b, columns (a) through (c) of Section A, all of Section B, and Section C if applicable.*

Section A—Depreciation and Other Information (Caution: *See page 8 of the instructions for limits for passenger automobiles.*)

23a Do you have evidence to support the business/investment use claimed? ☒ **Yes** ☐ **No** | **23b** If "Yes," is the evidence written? ☒ **Yes** ☐ **No**

(a) Type of property (list vehicles first)	(b) Date placed in service	(c) Business/ investment use percentage	(d) Cost or other basis	(e) Basis for depreciation (business/investment use only)	(f) Recovery period	(g) Method/ Convention	(h) Depreciation deduction	(i) Elected section 179 cost
24 Property used more than 50% in a qualified business use (See page 7 of the instructions.):								
Automobile	*5/20/96*	*100* %	*10,000*	*10,000*	*5-YR*	*200DB-HY*	*3,200*	
		%						
		%						
25 Property used 50% or less in a qualified business use (See page 7 of the instructions.):								
		%				S/L –		
		%				S/L –		
		%				S/L –		
26 Add amounts in column (h). Enter the total here and on line 20, page 1.						**26**	*3,200*	
27 Add amounts in column (i). Enter the total here and on line 7, page 1							**27**	

Section B—Information on Use of Vehicles

Complete this section for vehicles used by a sole proprietor, partner, or other "more than 5% owner," or related person.
If you provided vehicles to your employees, first answer the questions in Section C to see if you meet an exception to completing this section for those vehicles.

		(a) Vehicle 1		(b) Vehicle 2		(c) Vehicle 3		(d) Vehicle 4		(e) Vehicle 5		(f) Vehicle 6	
28	Total business/investment miles driven during the year (DO NOT include commuting miles)	*12,000*											
29	Total commuting miles driven during the year	*–0–*											
30	Total other personal (noncommuting) miles driven	*–0–*											
31	Total miles driven during the year. Add lines 28 through 30.	*12,000*											
		Yes	**No**	**Yes**	**No**	**Yes**	**No**	**Yes**	**No**	**Yes**	**No**	**Yes**	**No**
32	Was the vehicle available for personal use during off-duty hours?		*X*										
33	Was the vehicle used primarily by a more than 5% owner or related person?	*X*											
34	Is another vehicle available for personal use?	*X*											

Section C—Questions for Employers Who Provide Vehicles for Use by Their Employees

Answer these questions to determine if you meet an exception to completing Section B for vehicles used by employees who **are not** more than 5% owners or related persons.

		Yes	No
35	Do you maintain a written policy statement that prohibits all personal use of vehicles, including commuting, by your employees?		
36	Do you maintain a written policy statement that prohibits personal use of vehicles, except commuting, by your employees? See page 9 of the instructions for vehicles used by corporate officers, directors, or 1% or more owners		
37	Do you treat all use of vehicles by employees as personal use?		
38	Do you provide more than five vehicles to your employees, obtain information from your employees about the use of the vehicles, and retain the information received?		
39	Do you meet the requirements concerning qualified automobile demonstration use? See page 9 of the instructions		

Note: *If your answer to 35, 36, 37, 38, or 39 is "Yes," you need not complete Section B for the covered vehicles.*

Part VI	**Amortization**

(a) Description of costs	(b) Date amortization begins	(c) Amortizable amount	(d) Code section	(e) Amortization period or percentage	(f) Amortization for this year
40 Amortization of costs that begins during your 1997 tax year:					
41 Amortization of costs that began before 1997				**41**	
42 **Total.** Enter here and on "Other Deductions" or "Other Expenses" line of your return				**42**	

✳

SCHEDULE C
(Form 1040)

Department of the Treasury
Internal Revenue Service   (99)

Profit or Loss From Business
(Sole Proprietorship)

▶ Partnerships, joint ventures, etc., must file Form 1065.

▶ Attach to Form 1040 or Form 1041.   ▶ See Instructions for Schedule C (Form 1040).

OMB No. 1545-0074

1997

Attachment
Sequence No. **09**

Name of proprietor	Social security number (SSN)
Thomas Andrews	123 : 45 : 6789

A   Principal business or profession, including product or service (see page C-1)

      Accounting Services

B Enter principal business code
(see page C-6) ▶ | | | | |

C   Business name. If no separate business name, leave blank.

      Andrews Accounting Services

D Employer ID number (EIN), if any
| | : | | | | | |

E   Business address (including suite or room no.) ▶   *270 Mountain View*
City, town or post office, state, and ZIP code   *Ogden, UT 84201*

F   Accounting method: **(1)** ☐ Cash   **(2)** ☒ Accrual   **(3)** ☐ Other (specify) ▶ ....

G   Did you "materially participate" in the operation of this business during 1997? If "No," see page C-2 for limit on losses . ☒ **Yes**   ☐ **No**

H   If you started or acquired this business during 1997, check here . . . . ▶ ☐

Part I   Income

1	Gross receipts or sales. **Caution:** *If this income was reported to you on Form W-2 and the "Statutory employee" box on that form was checked, see page C-2 and check here* . . . . ▶ ☐	**1**	*80,000*	
2	Returns and allowances	**2**		
3	Subtract line 2 from line 1	**3**	*80,000*	
4	Cost of goods sold (from line 42 on page 2)	**4**		
5	**Gross profit.** Subtract line 4 from line 3	**5**	*80,000*	
6	Other income, including Federal and state gasoline or fuel tax credit or refund (see page C-2) . . .	**6**		
7	**Gross income.** Add lines 5 and 6 . . . . ▶	**7**	*80,000*	

Part II   Expenses. Enter expenses for business use of your home **only** on line 30.

8	Advertising	**8**		**19**	Pension and profit-sharing plans	**19**		
9	Bad debts from sales or services (see page C-3) . .	**9**	*2,000*	**20**	Rent or lease (see page C-4):			
					a Vehicles, machinery, and equipment .	**20a**		
10	Car and truck expenses (see page C-3)	**10**	*3,000*		**b** Other business property . .	**20b**	*12,000*	
11	Commissions and fees . .	**11**		**21**	Repairs and maintenance . .	**21**		
12	Depletion	**12**		**22**	Supplies (not included in Part III) .	**22**		
13	Depreciation and section 179 expense deduction (not included in Part III) (see page C-3) . .	**13**	*23,859*	**23**	Taxes and licenses	**23**		
				24	Travel, meals, and entertainment:			
					a Travel	**24a**		
14	Employee benefit programs (other than on line 19) . . .	**14**			**b** Meals and entertainment .			
15	Insurance (other than health) .	**15**	*800*		**c** Enter 50% of line 24b subject to limitations (see page C-4) .			
16	Interest:				**d** Subtract line 24c from line 24b .	**24d**		
	a Mortgage (paid to banks, etc.) .	**16a**		**25**	Utilities	**25**		
	b Other . . . . ▶	**16b**		**26**	Wages (less employment credits) .	**26**		
17	Legal and professional services . . . . . . ▶	**17**		**27**	Other expenses (from line 48 on page 2)	**27**		
18	Office expense	**18**	*4,000*					

28	**Total expenses** before expenses for business use of home. Add lines 8 through 27 in columns ▶	**28**	*45,659*	
29	Tentative profit (loss). Subtract line 28 from line 7	**29**	*34,341*	
30	Expenses for business use of your home. Attach **Form 8829**	**30**		
31	**Net profit or (loss).** Subtract line 30 from line 29. • If a profit, enter on **Form 1040, line 12,** and ALSO on **Schedule SE, line 2** (statutory employees, see page C-5). Estates and trusts, enter on Form 1041, line 3. • If a loss, you MUST go on to line 32.	**31**	*34,341*	
32	If you have a loss, check the box that describes your investment in this activity (see page C-5). • If you checked 32a, enter the loss on **Form 1040, line 12,** and ALSO on **Schedule SE, line 2** (statutory employees, see page C-5). Estates and trusts, enter on Form 1041, line 3. • If you checked 32b, you MUST attach **Form 6198.**	**32a** ☐ All investment is at risk. **32b** ☐ Some investment is not at risk.		

For Paperwork Reduction Act Notice, see Form 1040 instructions.   Cat. No. 11334P   Schedule C (Form 1040) 1997

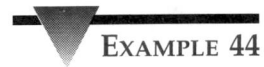

EXAMPLE 44

In early January 1997, Vern purchased residential rental property for $170,000 (of which $20,000 was allocated to the land and $150,000 to the building). Vern made a down payment of $25,000 and assumed the seller's mortgage for the balance. Under the mortgage agreement, monthly payments of $1,000 are required and are applied toward interest, taxes, insurance, and principal. Since the property was already occupied, Vern continued to receive rent of $1,200 per month from the tenant. Vern actively participates in this activity and hence comes under the special rule for a rental real estate activity with respect to the limitation on passive activity losses (refer to Chapter 11). Vern is in the 31% tax bracket.

During 1998, Vern's expenses were as follows:

Interest	$10,000
Taxes	800
Insurance	1,000
Repairs and maintenance	2,200
Depreciation ($150,000 × .03636)	5,454
Total	$19,454

The deductible loss from the rental property is computed as follows:

Rent income ($1,200 × 12 months)	$ 14,400
Less expenses (see above)	(19,454)
Net loss	($ 5,054)

But what is Vern's overall position for the year when the tax benefit of the loss is taken into account? Considering just the cash intake and outlay, it is summarized as follows:

Intake—		
Rent income	$14,400	
Tax savings [31% (income tax bracket) × $5,054 (loss from the property)]	1,567	$ 15,967
Outlay—		
Mortgage payments ($1,000 × 12 months)	$12,000	
Repairs and maintenance	2,200	(14,200)
Net cash benefit		$ 1,767

It should be noted, however, that should Vern cease being an active participant in the rental activity, the passive activity loss rules would apply, and Vern could lose the current period benefit of the loss.

AMORTIZATION

When a business is purchased, goodwill and covenants not to compete are both subject to a statutory amortization period of 15 years. Therefore, the purchaser does not derive any tax benefits when part of the purchase price is assigned to a covenant rather than to goodwill.

Thus, from the purchaser's perspective, bargaining for a covenant should be based on legal rather than tax reasons. Note, however, that from the seller's perspective, goodwill is a capital asset and the covenant is an ordinary income asset.

Since the amortization period for both goodwill and a covenant is 15 years, the purchaser may want to attempt to minimize these amounts if the purchase price can be assigned to assets with shorter lives (e.g., inventory, receivables, and personalty). Conversely, the purchaser may want to attempt to maximize these amounts if part of the purchase price will otherwise be assigned to assets with longer recovery periods (e.g., realty) or to assets not eligible for cost recovery (e.g., land).

DEPLETION

Since the election to use the cost or percentage depletion method is an annual election, a taxpayer can use cost depletion (if higher) until the basis is exhausted and then switch to percentage depletion in the following years.

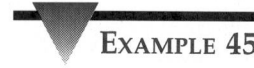

EXAMPLE 45

Assume the following facts for Melissa:

Remaining depletable basis	$ 11,000
Gross income (10,000 units)	100,000
Expenses (other than depletion)	30,000

Since cost depletion is limited to the basis of $11,000 and if the percentage depletion is $22,000 (assume a 22% rate), Melissa would choose the latter. Her basis is then reduced to zero. In future years, however, she can continue to take percentage depletion since percentage depletion is taken without reference to the remaining basis. ▼

The election to expense intangible drilling and development costs is a one-time election. Once the election is made to either expense or capitalize the intangible drilling and development costs, it is binding on all future expenditures. The permanent nature of the election makes it extremely important for the taxpayer to determine which treatment will provide the greatest tax advantage. (Refer to Example 41 for an illustration of the effect of using the two different alternatives for a given set of facts.)

TABLES

Summary of Tables

Table 8-1	Original ACRS statutory percentage table for personalty.
	Applicable depreciation method: 150 percent declining-balance switching to straight-line.
	Applicable recovery periods: 3, 5, 10, 15 years.
	Applicable convention: half-year.
Table 8-2	Modified ACRS statutory percentage table for personalty.
	Applicable depreciation methods: 200 or 150 percent declining-balance switching to straight-line.
	Applicable recovery periods: 3, 5, 7, 10, 15, 20 years.
	Applicable convention: half-year.

Table 8-3	Modified ACRS statutory percentage table for personalty.
	Applicable depreciation method: 200 percent declining-balance switching to straight-line.
	Applicable recovery periods: 3, 5, 7 years.
	Applicable convention: mid-quarter.
Table 8-4	Original ACRS statutory percentage table for realty.
	Applicable depreciation methods: 200 or 175 percent declining-balance switching to straight-line.
	Applicable recovery period: 15 years.
	Applicable convention: full-month.
Table 8-5	Original ACRS statutory percentage table for realty.
	Applicable depreciation method: 175 percent declining-balance switching to straight-line.
	Applicable recovery period: 18 years.
	Applicable convention: mid-month.
Table 8-6	Original ACRS statutory percentage table for realty.
	Applicable depreciation method: 175 percent declining-balance switching to straight-line.
	Applicable recovery period: 19 years.
	Applicable convention: mid-month.
Table 8-7	Modified ACRS straight-line table for realty.
	Applicable depreciation method: straight-line.
	Applicable recovery periods: 27.5, 31.5, 39 years.
	Applicable convention: mid-month.
Table 8-8	Original ACRS optional straight-line table for realty.
	Applicable depreciation method: straight-line.
	Applicable recovery period: 19 years.
	Applicable convention: mid-month.
Table 8-9	Modified ACRS optional straight-line table for personalty.
	Applicable depreciation method: straight-line.
	Applicable recovery periods: 3, 5, 7, 10, 15, 20 years.
	Applicable convention: half-year.
Table 8-10	Alternative minimum tax declining-balance table for personalty.
	Applicable depreciation method: 150 percent declining-balance switching to straight-line.
	Applicable recovery periods: 3, 5, 7, 9.5, 10, 12 years.
	Applicable convention: half-year.
Table 8-11	Alternative depreciation system straight-line table for personalty.
	Applicable depreciation method: straight-line.
	Applicable recovery periods: 5, 9.5, 12 years.
	Applicable convention: half-year.
Table 8-12	Alternative depreciation system straight-line table for realty.
	Applicable depreciation method: straight-line.
	Applicable recovery period: 40 years.
	Applicable convention: mid-month.

▼ **TABLE 8–1**
ACRS Statutory Percentages for Property Other Than 15-Year Real Property, 18-Year Real Property, or 19-Year Real Property Assuming Half-Year Convention

For Property Placed in Service after December 31, 1980, and before January 1, 1987

The Applicable Percentage for the Class of Property Is:

Recovery Year	3-Year	5-Year	10-Year	15-Year Public Utility
1	25	15	8	5
2	38	22	14	10
3	37	21	12	9
4		21	10	8
5		21	10	7
6			10	6
7			9	6
8			9	6
9			9	6
10			9	6
11				6
12				6
13				6
14				6
15				6

▼ **TABLE 8–2**
MACRS Accelerated Depreciation for Personal Property Assuming Half-Year Convention

For Property Placed in Service after December 31, 1986

Recovery Year	3-Year (200% DB)	5-Year (200% DB)	7-Year (200% DB)	10-Year (200% DB)	15-Year (150% DB)	20-Year (150% DB)
1	33.33	20.00	14.29	10.00	5.00	3.750
2	44.45	32.00	24.49	18.00	9.50	7.219
3	14.81*	19.20	17.49	14.40	8.55	6.677
4	7.41	11.52*	12.49	11.52	7.70	6.177
5		11.52	8.93*	9.22	6.93	5.713
6		5.76	8.92	7.37	6.23	5.285
7			8.93	6.55*	5.90*	4.888
8			4.46	6.55	5.90	4.522
9				6.56	5.91	4.462*
10				6.55	5.90	4.461
11				3.28	5.91	4.462
12					5.90	4.461
13					5.91	4.462
14					5.90	4.461
15					5.91	4.462
16					2.95	4.461
17						4.462
18						4.461
19						4.462
20						4.461
21						2.231

*Switchover to straight-line depreciation.

▼ **TABLE 8–3**
MACRS Accelerated
Depreciation for Personal
Property Assuming Mid-Quarter
Convention

For Property Placed in Service after December 31, 1986 (Partial Table*)

| | | *3-Year* | | |
Recovery Year	First Quarter	Second Quarter	Third Quarter	Fourth Quarter
1	58.33	41.67	25.00	8.33
2	27.78	38.89	50.00	61.11
		5-Year		
Recovery Year	First Quarter	Second Quarter	Third Quarter	Fourth Quarter
1	35.00	25.00	15.00	5.00
2	26.00	30.00	34.00	38.00
		7-Year		
Recovery Year	First Quarter	Second Quarter	Third Quarter	Fourth Quarter
1	25.00	17.85	10.71	3.57
2	21.43	23.47	25.51	27.55

*The figures in this table are taken from the official tables that appear in Rev.Proc.87–57, 1987–2 C.B. 687. Because of their length, the complete tables are not presented.

▼ **TABLE 8–4**
ACRS Statutory Percentages for
15-Year Real Property

For Property Placed in Service after December 31, 1980, and before January 1, 1987: 15-Year Real Property—Low-Income Housing

| If the Recovery Year Is: | And the Month in the First Recovery Year the Property Is Placed in Service Is: | | | | | | | | | | | |
	1	2	3	4	5	6	7	8	9	10	11	12
	The Applicable Percentage Is (Use the Column for the Month in the First Year the Property Is Placed in Service):											
1	13	12	11	10	9	8	7	6	4	3	2	1
2	12	12	12	12	12	12	12	13	13	13	13	13
3	10	10	10	10	11	11	11	11	11	11	11	11
4	9	9	9	9	9	9	9	9	10	10	10	10
5	8	8	8	8	8	8	8	8	8	8	8	9
6	7	7	7	7	7	7	7	7	7	7	7	7
7	6	6	6	6	6	6	6	6	6	6	6	6
8	5	5	5	5	5	5	5	5	5	5	6	6
9	5	5	5	5	5	5	5	5	5	5	5	5
10	5	5	5	5	5	5	5	5	5	5	5	5
11	4	5	5	5	5	5	5	5	5	5	5	5
12	4	4	4	5	4	5	5	5	5	5	5	5
13	4	4	4	4	4	4	5	4	5	5	5	5
14	4	4	4	4	4	4	4	4	4	5	4	4
15	4	4	4	4	4	4	4	4	4	4	4	4
16	—	—	1	1	2	2	2	3	3	3	4	4

▼ TABLE 8-4 (Continued)

For Property Placed in Service after December 31, 1980, and before March 16, 1984: 15-Year Real Property—Other Than Low-Income Housing

	12	11	10	9	8	7	6	5	4	3	2	1
1	12	11	10	9	8	7	6	5	4	3	2	1
2	10	10	11	11	11	11	11	11	11	11	11	12
3	9	9	9	9	10	10	10	10	10	10	10	10
4	8	8	8	8	8	8	9	9	9	9	9	9
5	7	7	7	7	7	7	8	8	8	8	8	8
6	6	6	6	6	7	7	7	7	7	7	7	7
7	6	6	6	6	6	6	6	6	6	6	6	6
8	6	6	6	6	6	6	5	6	6	6	6	6
9	6	6	6	6	5	6	5	5	5	6	6	6
10	5	6	5	6	5	5	5	5	5	5	6	5
11	5	5	5	5	5	5	5	5	5	5	5	5
12	5	5	5	5	5	5	5	5	5	5	5	5
13	5	5	5	5	5	5	5	5	5	5	5	5
14	5	5	5	5	5	5	5	5	5	5	5	5
15	5	5	5	5	5	5	5	5	5	5	5	5
16	—	—	1	1	2	2	3	3	4	4	4	5

▼ TABLE 8-5
ACRS Cost Recovery Table for
18-Year Real Property

For Property Placed in Service after June 22, 1984, and before May 9, 1985: 18-Year Real Property (18-Year 175% Declining Balance) (Assuming Mid-Month Convention)

	And the Month in the First Recovery Year the Property Is Placed in Service Is:											
If the Recovery Year Is:	1	2	3	4	5	6	7	8	9	10	11	12
	The Applicable Percentage Is (Use the Column for the Month in the First Year the Property Is Placed in Service):											
1	9	9	8	7	6	5	4	4	3	2	1	0.4
2	9	9	9	9	9	9	9	9	9	10	10	10.0
3	8	8	8	8	8	8	8	8	9	9	9	9.0
4	7	7	7	7	7	8	8	8	8	8	8	8.0
5	7	7	7	7	7	7	7	7	7	7	7	7.0
6	6	6	6	6	6	6	6	6	6	6	6	6.0
7	5	5	5	5	6	6	6	6	6	6	6	6.0
8	5	5	5	5	5	5	5	5	5	5	5	5.0
9	5	5	5	5	5	5	5	5	5	5	5	5.0
10	5	5	5	5	5	5	5	5	5	5	5	5.0
11	5	5	5	5	5	5	5	5	5	5	5	5.0
12	5	5	5	5	5	5	5	5	5	5	5	5.0
13	4	4	4	5	4	4	5	4	4	4	5	5.0
14	4	4	4	4	4	4	4	4	4	4	4	4.0
15	4	4	4	4	4	4	4	4	4	4	4	4.0
16	4	4	4	4	4	4	4	4	4	4	4	4.0
17	4	4	4	4	4	4	4	4	4	4	4	4.0
18	4	3	4	4	4	4	4	4	4	4	4	4.0
19		1	1	1	2	2	2	3	3	3	3	3.6

▼ **TABLE 8–6**
ACRS Cost Recovery Table for
19-Year Real Property

For Property Placed in Service after May 8, 1985, and before January 1, 1987
19-Year Real Property (19-Year 175% Declining Balance)
(Assuming Mid-Month Convention)

If the Recovery Year Is:	And the Month in the First Recovery Year the Property Is Placed in Service Is:											
	1	2	3	4	5	6	7	8	9	10	11	12
	The Applicable Percentage Is (Use the Column for the Month in the First Year the Property Is Placed in Service):											
1	8.8	8.1	7.3	6.5	5.8	5.0	4.2	3.5	2.7	1.9	1.1	0.4
2	8.4	8.5	8.5	8.6	8.7	8.8	8.8	8.9	9.0	9.0	9.1	9.2
3	7.6	7.7	7.7	7.8	7.9	7.9	8.0	8.1	8.1	8.2	8.3	8.3
4	6.9	7.0	7.0	7.1	7.1	7.2	7.3	7.3	7.4	7.4	7.5	7.6
5	6.3	6.3	6.4	6.4	6.5	6.5	6.6	6.6	6.7	6.8	6.8	6.9
6	5.7	5.7	5.8	5.9	5.9	5.9	6.0	6.0	6.1	6.1	6.2	6.2
7	5.2	5.2	5.3	5.3	5.3	5.4	5.4	5.5	5.5	5.6	5.6	5.6
8	4.7	4.7	4.8	4.8	4.8	4.9	4.9	5.0	5.0	5.1	5.1	5.1
9	4.2	4.3	4.3	4.4	4.4	4.5	4.5	4.5	4.5	4.6	4.6	4.7
10	4.2	4.2	4.2	4.2	4.2	4.2	4.2	4.2	4.2	4.2	4.2	4.2
11	4.2	4.2	4.2	4.2	4.2	4.2	4.2	4.2	4.2	4.2	4.2	4.2
12	4.2	4.2	4.2	4.2	4.2	4.2	4.2	4.2	4.2	4.2	4.2	4.2
13	4.2	4.2	4.2	4.2	4.2	4.2	4.2	4.2	4.2	4.2	4.2	4.2
14	4.2	4.2	4.2	4.2	4.2	4.2	4.2	4.2	4.2	4.2	4.2	4.2
15	4.2	4.2	4.2	4.2	4.2	4.2	4.2	4.2	4.2	4.2	4.2	4.2
16	4.2	4.2	4.2	4.2	4.2	4.2	4.2	4.2	4.2	4.2	4.2	4.2
17	4.2	4.2	4.2	4.2	4.2	4.2	4.2	4.2	4.2	4.2	4.2	4.2
18	4.2	4.2	4.2	4.2	4.2	4.2	4.2	4.2	4.2	4.2	4.2	4.2
19	4.2	4.2	4.2	4.2	4.2	4.2	4.2	4.2	4.2	4.2	4.2	4.2
20	0.2	0.5	0.9	1.2	1.6	1.9	2.3	2.6	3.0	3.3	3.7	4.0

PART III   Deductions

▼ **TABLE 8–7**
MACRS Straight-Line
Depreciation for Real Property
Assuming Mid-Month
Convention*

For Property Placed in Service after December 31, 1986: 27.5-Year Residential Real Property

The Applicable Percentage Is (Use the Column for the Month in the First Year the Property Is Placed in Service):

Recovery Year(s)	1	2	3	4	5	6	7	8	9	10	11	12
1	3.485	3.182	2.879	2.576	2.273	1.970	1.667	1.364	1.061	0.758	0.455	0.152
2–18	3.636	3.636	3.636	3.636	3.636	3.636	3.636	3.636	3.636	3.636	3.636	3.636
19–27	3.637	3.637	3.637	3.637	3.637	3.637	3.637	3.637	3.637	3.637	3.637	3.637
28	1.970	2.273	2.576	2.879	3.182	3.485	3.636	3.636	3.636	3.636	3.636	3.636
29	0.000	0.000	0.000	0.000	0.000	0.000	0.152	0.455	0.758	1.061	1.364	1.667

For Property Placed in Service after December 31, 1986, and before May 13, 1993: 31.5-Year Nonresidential Real Property

The Applicable Percentage Is (Use the Column for the Month in the First Year the Property Is Placed in Service):

Recovery Year(s)	1	2	3	4	5	6	7	8	9	10	11	12
1	3.042	2.778	2.513	2.249	1.984	1.720	1.455	1.190	0.926	0.661	0.397	0.132
2–19	3.175	3.175	3.175	3.175	3.175	3.175	3.175	3.175	3.175	3.175	3.175	3.175
20–31	3.174	3.174	3.174	3.174	3.174	3.174	3.174	3.174	3.174	3.174	3.174	3.174
32	1.720	1.984	2.249	2.513	2.778	3.042	3.175	3.175	3.175	3.175	3.175	3.175
33	0.000	0.000	0.000	0.000	0.000	0.000	0.132	0.397	0.661	0.926	1.190	1.455

For Property Placed in Service after May 12, 1993: 39-Year Nonresidential Real Property

The Applicable Percentage Is (Use the Column for the Month in the First Year the Property Is Placed in Service):

Recovery Year(s)	1	2	3	4	5	6	7	8	9	10	11	12
1	2.461	2.247	2.033	1.819	1.605	1.391	1.177	0.963	0.749	0.535	0.321	0.107
2–39	2.564	2.564	2.564	2.564	2.564	2.564	2.564	2.564	2.564	2.564	2.564	2.564
40	0.107	0.321	0.535	0.749	0.963	1.177	1.391	1.605	1.819	2.033	2.247	2.461

*The official tables contain a separate row for each year. For ease of presentation, certain years are grouped in these tables. In some instances, this will produce a difference of .001 for the last digit when compared with the official tables.

▼ **TABLE 8–8**
ACRS Cost Recovery Table for
19-Year Real Property: Optional
Straight-Line

For Property Placed in Service after May 8, 1985, and before January 1, 1987: 19-Year Real Property for Which an Optional 19-Year Straight-Line Method Is Elected (Assuming Mid-Month Convention)

And the Month in the First Recovery Year the Property Is Placed in Service Is:

If the Recovery Year Is:	1	2	3	4	5	6	7	8	9	10	11	12
	The Applicable Percentage Is (Use the Column for the Month in the First Year the Property Is Placed in Service):											
1	5.0	4.6	4.2	3.7	3.3	2.9	2.4	2.0	1.5	1.1	.7	.2
2	5.3	5.3	5.3	5.3	5.3	5.3	5.3	5.3	5.3	5.3	5.3	5.3
3	5.3	5.3	5.3	5.3	5.3	5.3	5.3	5.3	5.3	5.3	5.3	5.3
4	5.3	5.3	5.3	5.3	5.3	5.3	5.3	5.3	5.3	5.3	5.3	5.3
5	5.3	5.3	5.3	5.3	5.3	5.3	5.3	5.3	5.3	5.3	5.3	5.3
6	5.3	5.3	5.3	5.3	5.3	5.3	5.3	5.3	5.3	5.3	5.3	5.3
7	5.3	5.3	5.3	5.3	5.3	5.3	5.3	5.3	5.3	5.3	5.3	5.3
8	5.3	5.3	5.3	5.3	5.3	5.3	5.3	5.3	5.3	5.3	5.3	5.3
9	5.3	5.3	5.3	5.3	5.3	5.3	5.3	5.3	5.3	5.3	5.3	5.3
10	5.3	5.3	5.3	5.3	5.3	5.3	5.3	5.3	5.3	5.3	5.3	5.3
11	5.3	5.3	5.3	5.3	5.3	5.3	5.3	5.3	5.3	5.3	5.3	5.3
12	5.3	5.3	5.3	5.3	5.3	5.3	5.3	5.3	5.3	5.3	5.3	5.3
13	5.3	5.3	5.3	5.3	5.3	5.3	5.3	5.3	5.3	5.3	5.3	5.3
14	5.2	5.2	5.2	5.2	5.2	5.2	5.2	5.2	5.2	5.2	5.2	5.2
15	5.2	5.2	5.2	5.2	5.2	5.2	5.2	5.2	5.2	5.2	5.2	5.2
16	5.2	5.2	5.2	5.2	5.2	5.2	5.2	5.2	5.2	5.2	5.2	5.2
17	5.2	5.2	5.2	5.2	5.2	5.2	5.2	5.2	5.2	5.2	5.2	5.2
18	5.2	5.2	5.2	5.2	5.2	5.2	5.2	5.2	5.2	5.2	5.2	5.2
19	5.2	5.2	5.2	5.2	5.2	5.2	5.2	5.2	5.2	5.2	5.2	5.2
20	.2	.6	1.0	1.5	1.9	2.3	2.8	3.2	3.7	4.1	4.5	5.0

▼ **TABLE 8–9**
MACRS Straight-Line
Depreciation for Personal
Property Assuming Half-Year
Convention*

For Property Placed in Service after December 31, 1986

MACRS Class	% First Recovery Year	Other Recovery Years		Last Recovery Year	
		Years	%	Year	%
3-year	16.67	2–3	33.33	4	16.67
5-year	10.00	2–5	20.00	6	10.00
7-year	7.14	2–7	14.29	8	7.14
10-year	5.00	2–10	10.00	11	5.00
15-year	3.33	2–15	6.67	16	3.33
20-year	2.50	2–20	5.00	21	2.50

*The official table contains a separate row for each year. For ease of presentation, certain years are grouped in this table. In some instances, this will produce a difference of .01 for the last digit when compared with the official table.

▼ **TABLE 8–10**
Alternative Minimum Tax: 150%
Declining-Balance Assuming
Half-Year Convention

	For Property Placed in Service after December 31, 1986 (Partial Table*)					
Recovery Year	3-Year 150%	5-Year 150%	7-Year 150%	9.5-Year 150%	10-Year 150%	12-Year 150%
1	25.00	15.00	10.71	7.89	7.50	6.25
2	37.50	25.50	19.13	14.54	13.88	11.72
3	25.00**	17.85	15.03	12.25	11.79	10.25
4	12.50	16.66**	12.25**	10.31	10.02	8.97
5		16.66	12.25	9.17**	8.74**	7.85
6		8.33	12.25	9.17	8.74	7.33**
7			12.25	9.17	8.74	7.33
8			6.13	9.17	8.74	7.33
9				9.17	8.74	7.33
10				9.16	8.74	7.33
11					4.37	7.32
12						7.33
13						3.66

*The figures in this table are taken from the official table that appears in Rev.Proc. 87–57, 1987–2 C.B. 687. Because of its length, the complete table is not presented.
**Switchover to straight-line depreciation.

▼ **TABLE 8–11**
ADS Straight-Line for Personal
Property Assuming Half-Year
Convention

	For Property Placed in Service after December 31, 1986 (Partial Table*)		
Recovery Year	5-Year Class	9.5-Year Class	12-Year Class
1	10.00	5.26	4.17
2	20.00	10.53	8.33
3	20.00	10.53	8.33
4	20.00	10.53	8.33
5	20.00	10.52	8.33
6	10.00	10.53	8.33
7		10.52	8.34
8		10.53	8.33
9		10.52	8.34
10		10.53	8.33
11			8.34
12			8.33
13			4.17

*The figures in this table are taken from the official table that appears in Rev.Proc. 87–57, 1987–2 C.B. 687. Because of its length, the complete table is not presented. The tables for the mid-quarter convention also appear in Rev.Proc. 87–57.

▼ **TABLE 8–12**
ADS Straight-Line for Real
Property Assuming Mid-Month
Convention

For Property Placed in Service after December 31, 1986

| Recovery Year | Month Placed in Service | | | | | | | | | | | |
	1	2	3	4	5	6	7	8	9	10	11	12
1	2.396	2.188	1.979	1.771	1.563	1.354	1.146	0.938	0.729	0.521	0.313	0.104
2–40	2.500	2.500	2.500	2.500	2.500	2.500	2.500	2.500	2.500	2.500	2.500	2.500
41	0.104	0.312	0.521	0.729	0.937	1.146	1.354	1.562	1.771	1.979	2.187	2.396

KEY TERMS

Accelerated cost recovery system (ACRS), 8–4

Alternative depreciation system (ADS), 8–21

Amortization, 8–23

Cost depletion, 8–25 ·

Cost recovery, 8–2

Depletion, 8–24

Depreciation, 8–2

Half-year convention, 8–6

Intangible drilling and development costs (IDC), 8–25

Listed property, 8–17

Mid-month convention, 8–11

Mid-quarter convention, 8–9

Modified accelerated cost recovery system (MACRS), 8–6

Percentage depletion, 8–26

Residential rental real estate, 8–12

Section 179 expensing, 8–15

PROBLEM MATERIALS

DISCUSSION QUESTIONS

1. Discuss whether personal use property is subject to cost recovery.

2. Henry purchased a rental home for $67,000 from Amy. He made a down payment of $17,000 and borrowed $50,000 from James with a mortgage on the home as collateral. The note secured by the mortgage contained an acceleration clause, which provided that the loan would become due if Henry were to sell or convey the property. Several years later, Henry sold the house to John. To avoid triggering the acceleration clause, Henry and John wove a complicated web to deceive James. As part of this plan, the sales agreement provided that Henry would continue to claim the depreciation on his tax return. Henry also owned property where he maintained his office. Last year, because the property generated a loss, Henry did not deduct the depreciation on the property. During the current year, Henry sold this property at a gain. Identify the relevant tax issues for Henry.

3. If a personal use asset is converted to business use, why is it necessary to compute cost recovery on the lower of fair market value or adjusted basis at the date of conversion?

4. Discuss whether a painting is eligible for cost recovery.

5. Pale, an electric utility company, constructed and placed in service during the taxable year a hydroelectric dam. In connection with the dam, Pale was required under a Federal Power Commission license to construct and maintain various facilities for the

preservation of fish and for public recreational purposes. The fish preservation facilities constructed below the dam consisted of an entrance pool, a fish ladder, and a holding pool. The recreational facilities located above the dam included access roads, fixed wharves, landings, and other facilities. All of these facilities are tangible properties, some of which are inextricably associated with the land. Identify the relevant tax issues for Pale.

6. Discuss when the mid-quarter convention must be used.

7. Discuss the computation of cost recovery in the year of sale of an asset when the mid-quarter convention is being used.

8. Discuss the test for determining whether real property is residential rental real estate or nonresidential real estate.

9. Discuss the mid-month convention as it is used in the MACRS rules.

10. Alan is engaged in the sale of rental warehouse space and related services. When he sought a bank loan to expand one of his warehouses, the lender required Alan to abate the problem of exposed and damaged asbestos-containing pipe insulation in the warehouse. Accordingly, Alan incurred costs of $200,000 to employ an asbestos contractor to remedy the problem. The contractor rewrapped and encapsulated the damaged or punctured areas of asbestos-containing pipe insulation and removed insulation that was too damaged to be rewrapped. The pipes requiring encapsulation amounted to less than 25% of the total pipes in the warehouse. Identify the relevant tax issues for Alan.

11. Discuss the applicable conventions if a taxpayer elects to use straight-line cost recovery for property placed in service after December 31, 1986.

12. If a taxpayer makes a straight-line election under MACRS, discuss the possibility of taking a cost recovery deduction, for personal and real property, in the year of disposition.

13. Discuss the type of property that qualifies for limited expensing.

14. Discuss the maximum § 179 expensing amount.

15. Discuss the limitation on the § 179 amount that can be expensed and its impact on the basis of the property.

16. John was employed as a financial officer for an investment bank. By the middle of the year, John realized that he was going to be terminated by the bank. Therefore, he began preparing for a career in financial consulting as a sole practitioner. John became interested in consulting for a marina, but believing that boat owners formed a close fraternity, he decided that he could obtain such work only by acquiring a boat himself. Accordingly, he purchased a 23-foot Sea Ray Boat for $25,000. During the year, John used the boat only once to visit marinas on the lake to discuss potential employment as a consultant. A few days after this one excursion, John injured his back and was unable to use the boat for the remainder of the year. John was unsuccessful in his attempts to obtain a consulting position with any of the marinas.

At the beginning of the year, John also purchased a new car to be used for personal purposes. After John was terminated from the bank in September, he began using the car for business purposes.

Identify the relevant tax issues for John.

17. What are the tax consequences of listed property failing to meet the predominantly business use test?

18. Discuss the limits on cost recovery for a taxicab.

19. Discuss the tax consequences that result when a passenger automobile, which failed the more-than-50% business usage test during the first two years, satisfies the test for the third year.

20. Explain the reason for the inclusion amount with respect to leased passenger automobiles.

21. Explain how an inclusion amount is determined with respect to leased passenger automobiles.

22. Explain the amortization period of a § 197 intangible if the actual useful life is less than 15 years.

23. What is the amortization period for self-created goodwill?

24. Discuss the options for handling intangible drilling and development costs.

25. Briefly discuss the differences between cost depletion and percentage depletion.

PROBLEMS

26. On January 1, 1994, Black Company acquired an asset (three-year property) for $10,000 for use in its business. In the years 1994 and 1995, Black took $3,333 and $4,445 of cost recovery. The allowable cost recovery for the years 1996 and 1997 was $1,481 and $741, but Black did not take the deductions. In those years, Black had net operating losses, and the company wanted to "save" the deductions for later years. On January 1, 1998, the asset was sold for $2,000. Calculate the gain or loss on the sale of the asset in 1998.

27. Eve acquired a personal residence in 1992 for $180,000. In January 1998, when the fair market value was $160,000, she converted the residence to rental property.
    a. Calculate the amount of cost recovery that can be taken in 1998.
    b. What would your answer be if the property were worth $200,000 in 1998?

28. Jane acquired a seven-year class asset on March 1, 1998, for $100,000. She did not elect immediate expensing under § 179.
    a. Determine Jane's cost recovery for 1998.
    b. Determine Jane's cost recovery for 2001.

29. Walt purchased a tugboat for use in his business on March 15, 1998, for $500,000. He does not elect immediate expensing under § 179. On February 16, 2004, Walt sells the tug.
    a. Determine Walt's cost recovery for 1998.
    b. Determine Walt's cost recovery for 2004.

30. Juan acquires a five-year class asset on December 2, 1998, for $150,000. This is the only asset acquired by Juan during the year. He does not elect immediate expensing under § 179. On July 15, 1999, Juan sells the asset.
    a. Determine Juan's cost recovery for 1998.
    b. Determine Juan's cost recovery for 1999.

31. Debra acquired a building for $300,000 (exclusive of land) on January 1, 1984. Calculate the cost recovery using the statutory percentage method for 1984 and 1998 if:
    a. The real property is low-income housing.
    b. The real property is a factory building.

32. On December 2, 1984, Wade purchased and placed in service a warehouse. The warehouse cost $850,000. Wade used the statutory percentage cost recovery method. On July 7, 1998, Wade sold the warehouse.
    a. Determine Wade's cost recovery for 1984.
    b. Determine Wade's cost recovery for 1998.

33. On November 1, 1998, Terry purchases and places in service a building that is used as a warehouse. The cost of the building is $2 million. An appraisal determined that 20% of the total cost was attributed to the value of the land. Determine Terry's cost recovery for 1998.

34. Pat acquires a warehouse on November 1, 1998, at a cost of $4.5 million. On January 30, 2009, Pat sells the warehouse. Calculate Pat's cost recovery for 1998. For 2009.

35. Janice acquired an apartment building on June 4, 1998, for $1.4 million. The value of the land is $200,000. Janice sold the apartment building on November 29, 2004.
    a. Determine Janice's cost recovery for 1998.
    b. Determine Janice's cost recovery for 2004.

36. Lori, who is single, is thinking of acquiring a new copier (five-year class property) for $30,000 in either December of 1998 or January of 1999. Lori expects the taxable income derived from her business (without regard to the amount expensed under § 179) to always be about $100,000. Lori will elect immediate expensing under § 179. Lori acquired three-year property for $140,000 in March 1998 and does not want to elect § 179 for this property.

    a. Determine Lori's total deduction with respect to the copier if she acquires the copier in 1998.
    b. Determine her total deduction with respect to the copier if she acquires the copier in 1999.
    c. What is your advice to Lori?

37. Jack owns a small business that he operates as a sole proprietor. In 1998, Jack will net $10,000 of business income before consideration of any § 179 deduction. Jack spends $207,000 on new equipment in 1998. If Jack also has $3,000 of § 179 deduction carryforwards from 1997, determine his § 179 expense deduction for 1998 and the amount of any carryforward.

38. Olga is the proprietor of a small business. In 1998, her business income, before consideration of any § 179 deduction, is $7,500. Olga spends $202,000 on new equipment and furniture for 1998. If Olga elects to take the § 179 deduction on a desk that cost $20,000 (included in the $202,000), determine her total cost recovery for 1998 with respect to the desk.

39. On March 10, 1998, Yoon purchased three-year class property for $20,000. On December 15, 1998, Yoon purchased five-year class property for $50,000. He has net business income of $19,000 before consideration of any § 179 deduction.

    a. Calculate Yoon's cost recovery for 1998, assuming he does not make the § 179 election or use straight-line cost recovery.
    b. Calculate Yoon's cost recovery for 1998, assuming he does elect to use § 179 and does not elect to use straight-line cost recovery.
    c. Assuming Yoon's marginal tax rate is 36%, determine his tax benefit from electing § 179.

40. On July 1, 1998, Wilma places in service a computer (five-year class property). The computer cost $20,000. Wilma used the computer 65% for business. The remainder of the time she used the computer for personal purposes. If Wilma does not elect § 179, determine her cost recovery deduction for the computer for 1998.

41. John Johnson is considering acquiring an automobile at the beginning of 1998 that he will use 100% of the time as a taxi. The purchase price of the automobile is $25,000. John has heard of cost recovery limits on automobiles and wants to know how much of the $25,000 he can deduct in the first year. Write a letter to John in which you present your calculations. Also, prepare a memo for the tax files. John's address is 100 Morningside, Clinton, MS 39058.

42. On February 16, 1998, Ron purchased and placed into service a new car. The purchase price was $18,000. Ron drove the car 12,000 miles during the remainder of the year, 9,000 miles for business and 3,000 miles for personal use. Ron used the statutory percentage method of cost recovery. Calculate the total deduction Ron may take for 1998 with respect to the car.

43. On June 5, 1998, Leo purchased and placed in service a $19,000 car. The business use percentage for the car is always 100%. Compute Leo's cost recovery deduction in 2004.

44. On June 14, 1998, Helen purchased and placed in service a new car. The purchase price was $16,000. The car was used 75% for business and 25% for personal use in both 1998 and 1999. In 2000, the car was used 40% for business and 60% for personal use. Compute the cost recovery deduction for the car in 2000 and the cost recovery recapture.

45. In 1998, Paul purchased a computer (five-year property) for $120,000. The computer was used 60% for business, 20% for income production, and 20% for personal use. In

1999, the usage changed to 40% for business, 30% for income production, and 30% for personal use. Compute the cost recovery deduction for 1999 and any cost recovery recapture. Assume Paul did not make a § 179 election on the computer in 1998.

46. Sally purchased a computer (five-year property) for $4,000. Sally could use the computer 100% of the time in her business, or she could allow her family to also use the computer. Sally estimates that if her family uses the computer, the business use will be 45% and the personal use will be 55%. Determine the tax cost to Sally, in the year of acquisition, of allowing her family to use the computer. Assume that Sally would not elect § 179 limited expensing and that her marginal tax rate is 31%.

47. Midway through 1998, Abdel leases and places in service a passenger automobile. The lease will run for five years, and the payments are $430 per month. During 1998, Abdel uses the car 70% for business use and 30% for personal use. Assuming the inclusion dollar amount from the IRS table is $98, determine the tax consequences to Abdel from the lease for the year 1998.

48. Use the information given in Problem 47, but assume the inclusion dollar amount for 1999 is $180. Abdel uses the car 60% for business use and 40% for personal use in 1999. Determine Abdel's tax consequences from the lease in 1999.

49. Dennis Harding is considering acquiring an automobile that he will use 100% for business. The purchase price of the automobile would be $30,500. If Dennis leased the car for five years, the lease payments would be $350 per month. Dennis will acquire the car on January 1, 1998. The inclusion dollar amounts from the IRS table for the next five years are $129, $286, $423, $500, and $590. Dennis desires to know the effect on his adjusted gross income of purchasing versus leasing the car for the next five years. Write a letter to Dennis and present your calculations. Also, prepare a memo for the tax files. His address is 150 Avenue I, Memphis, TN 38112.

50. On March 5, 1998, Nell purchased equipment for $70,000. The equipment has an ADS midpoint of 9.5 years. Determine Nell's cost recovery deduction for computing 1998 taxable income using the straight-line method under ADS and assuming she does not make a § 179 election.

51. In 1998, Muhammad purchased a light-duty truck for $12,000. The truck is used 100% for business. Muhammad did not make a § 179 election with respect to the truck. If Muhammad uses the statutory percentage method, determine his cost recovery deduction for 1998 for computing taxable income and for computing his alternative minimum tax.

52. In June 1998, Cardinal, Inc., purchased and placed in service railroad track costing $600,000.
    a. Calculate Cardinal's cost recovery deduction for 1998 for computing taxable income, assuming Cardinal does not make the § 179 election or use straight-line cost recovery.
    b. Calculate Cardinal's cost recovery deduction for 1998 for computing taxable income, assuming Cardinal does not make the § 179 election but does elect to use ADS 150% declining-balance cost recovery.
    c. Assume that the railroad track was placed in service in June 1999. Calculate Cardinal's cost recovery deduction for 1999 for computing taxable income, assuming Cardinal does not make the § 179 election but does elect to use ADS 150% declining-balance cost recovery.

53. Jamie purchased $60,000 of office furniture for her business in June of the current year. Jamie understands that if she elects to use ADS to compute her regular income tax, there will be no difference between the cost recovery for computing the regular income tax and the AMT. Jamie wants to know the *regular* income tax cost, after three years, of using ADS rather than MACRS. Assume that Jamie does not elect § 179 limited expensing and that her marginal tax rate is 31%.

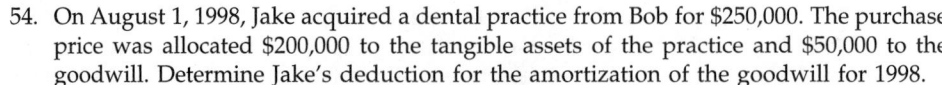

54. On August 1, 1998, Jake acquired a dental practice from Bob for $250,000. The purchase price was allocated $200,000 to the tangible assets of the practice and $50,000 to the goodwill. Determine Jake's deduction for the amortization of the goodwill for 1998.

55. Mike Saxon is negotiating the purchase of a business. The final purchase price has been agreed upon, but the allocation of the purchase price to the assets is still being discussed. Appraisals on a warehouse range from $1.2 to $1.5 million. If a value of $1.2 million is used for the warehouse, the remainder of the purchase price, $800,000, will be allocated to goodwill. If $1.5 million is allocated to the warehouse, goodwill will be $500,000. Mike wants to know what effect each alternative will have on cost recovery and amortization during the first year. Under the agreement, Mike will take over the business on January 1 of next year. Write a letter to Mike in which you present your calculations and recommendation. Also, prepare a memo for the tax files. Mike's address is 200 Rolling Hills Drive, Shavertown, PA 18708.

56. Wes acquired a mineral interest during the year for $5 million. A geological survey estimated that 250,000 tons of the mineral remained in the deposit. During the year, 80,000 tons were mined, and 45,000 tons were sold for $6 million. Other expenses amounted to $4 million. Assuming the mineral depletion rate is 22%, calculate Wes's lowest taxable income.

57. Chris purchased an oil interest for $2,000,000. Recoverable barrels were estimated to be 500,000. During the year, 120,000 barrels were sold for $3,840,000, regular expenses (including cost recovery) were $1,240,000, and IDC were $1,000,000. Calculate Chris's taxable income under the expensing and capitalization methods of handling IDC.

CUMULATIVE PROBLEMS

58. John Smith, age 31, is single and has no dependents. At the beginning of 1998, John started his own excavation business and named it Earth Movers. John lives at 1045 Center Street, Lindon, UT, and his business is located at 381 State Street, Lindon, UT. The zip code for both addresses is 84059. John's Social Security number is 321–09–6456, and the business identification number is 98–1234567. John is a cash basis taxpayer. During 1998, John had the following items in connection with his business:

Fees for services	$290,000
Building rental expense	36,000
Office furniture and equipment rental expense	6,000
Office supplies	2,500
Utilities	3,000
Salary for secretary	35,000
Salary for equipment operators	78,000
Payroll taxes	9,000
Fuel and oil for the equipment	20,000
Purchase of three front-end loaders on January 15, 1998, for $175,000. John made the election under § 179.	175,000
Purchase of a new dump truck on January 18, 1998	30,000

During 1998, John had the following additional items:

Interest income from First National Bank	$8,000
Dividends from Exxon	2,500
Quarterly estimated tax payments	11,500

On October 8, 1998, John inherited IBM stock from his Aunt Mildred. John had been her favorite nephew. According to the data provided by the executor of Aunt Mildred's estate, the stock had been valued for estate tax purposes at $90,000. John is considering selling the IBM stock for $95,000 on December 29, 1998, and using $60,000 of the proceeds to purchase an Acura NSX. He would use the car 100% for business. John wants to know what effect these transactions would have on his 1998 adjusted gross income.

Write a letter to John in which you present your calculations. Also, prepare a memo for the tax files. Suggested software (if available): *TurboTax*.

59. Janice Morgan, age 32, is single and has no dependents. She is a freelance writer. In January 1997, Janice opened her own office located at 2751 Waldham Road, Pleasantville, NM 17196. She called her business Writers Anonymous. Janice is a cash basis taxpayer. She lives at 132 Stone Avenue, Pleasantville, NM 17196. Her Social Security number is 789–57–6691. Janice desires to contribute to the Presidential Election Campaign Fund.

During 1997, Janice had the following income and expense items connected with her business:

Income from sale of articles	$110,000
Rent	18,000
Utilities	6,900
Supplies	1,300
Travel (including meals of $700)	2,500

Janice purchased and placed in service the following fixed assets for her business:

- Furniture and fixtures costing $15,000 on January 10, 1997.

- Computer equipment costing $20,000 on January 15, 1997.

Janice would like to deduct these costs as soon as possible.
Janice's itemized deductions are as follows:

State income tax	$2,000
Home mortgage interest paid to First Bank	4,800
Property taxes on home	1,100
Property taxes on car	500
Charitable contributions	1,200

Janice has interest income of $3,000 on certificates of deposit at Second Bank. Janice makes estimated tax payments of $19,000 for 1997.

Compute Janice Morgan's 1997 Federal income tax payable (or refund due). If you use tax forms for your computations, you will need Form(s) 1040 and 4562 and Schedules A, B, C, and SE. Suggested software (if available): *TurboTax*.

RESEARCH PROBLEMS

*Note: Use the **RIA OnPoint System 4 Student Version CD-ROM**, which is available to accompany this text, in preparing solutions to the Research Problems. Alternatively, tax research materials found in a standard tax library can be used.*

Research Problem 1. Harry Pickart, who is one of your clients, is considering building a golf course in the resort area of Sun River, Oregon. Because the land is unimproved, all of the sand traps, greens, fairways, and tees will need to be constructed. Write a letter to Harry that contains your advice on whether any deductions can be taken for the landscaping improvements. Also, prepare a memo for the tax files. His mailing address is P.O. Box 100, Sun River, OR 97600.

Research Problem 2. Doug operates a restaurant in a small town. In May of the current year, Doug had a new septic tank installed for the restaurant. The town plans to construct a sewage system in five years. At that time, Doug will be required to be connected to the town system, and his septic tank will be obsolete. Doug believes that depreciation should represent wear, tear, and obsolescence, and, hence, he believes he should use a five-year life for the depreciation of the septic tank. Discuss the proper period and method for depreciating the septic tank.

Partial list of research aids:
J. O. Miller, 56 TCM 1242, T.C.Memo. 1989–66.
Rev.Proc. 87–56, 1987–2 C.B. 674.

Research Problem 3. Sandra purchased the following personal property during 1998:

Date	Asset	Cost
June 1	Machine A	$20,000
July 10	Machine B	10,000
November 15	Machine C	25,000

Sandra elects to take the § 179 expense on Machine C. Discuss what convention Sandra must use to determine her cost recovery deduction for 1998.

Research Problem 4. Juan owns a business that acquires exotic automobiles that are high-technology, state-of-the-art vehicles with unique design features or equipment. The exotic automobiles are not licensed nor are they set up to be used on the road. Rather, the cars are used exclusively for car shows or related promotional photography. Juan would like to know whether he can take a cost recovery deduction with respect to the exotic automobiles on his Federal income tax return.

Research Problem 5. Alfred acquires $50,000 of machinery and equipment for his sole proprietorship. In addition, the Golden Partnership, in which Alfred is a 20% partner, acquires $100,000 of machinery and equipment during the year. Both Alfred's sole proprietorship and Golden Partnership would like to elect the maximum § 179 limited expensing for the tax year. The net income of the partnership is $300,000, and the sole proprietorship has net income of $150,000. Advise Alfred of the amount of § 179 deductions he can take on his income tax return and the source (i.e., sole proprietorship, partnership, or both).

 Use the tax resources of the Internet to address the following questions. Do not restrict your search to the World Wide Web, but include a review of newsgroups and general reference materials, practitioner sites and resources, primary sources of the tax law, chat rooms and discussion groups, and other opportunities.

Research Problem 6. Locate a financial calculator program that assesses the wisdom of buying versus leasing a new car. Install the program on your computer and become familiar with it. Use the program to work through Problem 49 in this chapter.

Research Problem 7. Changes to depreciation systems often are discussed by policy makers and observers of the tax system. Outline the terms and policy objectives of one of the changes currently proposed by the Treasury, a member of Congress, or a tax policy think tank.

TEAM PROJECT: ARTHUR ANDERSEN TAX CHALLENGE CASES

For more information on the Arthur Andersen Tax Challenge Cases, refer to Chapter 1, page 1–37.

Information related to tax issues and problems that are discussed in this chapter may be found in the

Day and Ball case on pages 7 and 20
Fence case on pages 40 and 59

Read and analyze the case you have been assigned and *identify* any issues and problems that are related to material covered in this chapter. If the information provided in the case is complete, prepare answers for this part of the case at this time. If you need information that is contained in the later parts of the case, write a memo summarizing the questions or problems so you can prepare a complete answer at a later date.

DEDUCTIONS: EMPLOYEE EXPENSES

LEARNING OBJECTIVES

After completing Chapter 9, you should be able to:

1. Distinguish between employee and self-employed status.

2. Recognize deductible transportation expenses.

3. Know how travel expenses are treated.

4. Determine the moving expense deduction.

5. Differentiate between deductible and nondeductible education expenses.

6. Understand how entertainment expenses are treated.

7. Identify other employee expenses.

8. Appreciate the difference between accountable and nonaccountable employee plans.

9. Work with the limitations on miscellaneous itemized deductions.

10. Develop tax planning ideas related to employee business expenses.

OUTLINE

Considering the large number of taxpayers affected, the tax treatment of job-related expenses is unusually complex. To resolve this matter in a systematic fashion, a number of key questions must be asked:

- Is the taxpayer an *employee* or *self-employed?*
- If an employee, what expenses *qualify* as deductions?
- How are the expenses that qualify *classified* for tax purposes?
- To the extent the expenses are classified as deductions *from* AGI, are they subject to any *limitation?*

Once these questions have been posed and answered, the chapter considers various planning procedures available to maximize the deductibility of employee expenses.

EMPLOYEE VERSUS SELF-EMPLOYED

1 LEARNING OBJECTIVE
Distinguish between employee and self-employed status.

When one person performs services for another, the person performing the service is either an employee or self-employed (an **independent contractor**). Failure to recognize employee status can have serious consequences. Not only can interest and penalties result, but a government career can be abruptly squelched. Such was the case with several persons that President Clinton nominated to his cabinet during his first term. Zoe Baird (Attorney General), Kimba Wood (Attorney General), and Retired Admiral Bobby Inman (Secretary of Defense) all had to withdraw from

---

TAX IN THE NEWS

ARE GOLF CLUBS IN TROUBLE WITH THE IRS?

For many years, the IRS has not questioned the tax classification of caddies as independent contractors. See, for example, Revenue Ruling 69–26 (1969–1 C.B. 251). This classification is consistent with the manner in which the services are performed. Most caddies work when they want, receive minimum training at their golf courses, and are paid "by the bag" (not by the hour). Further, they are paid by the golfer (not the club).

Recent actions by the IRS, however, indicate that it now regards caddies as employees. If the IRS maintains this position and pursues its enforcement, serious tax consequences could result. Golf clubs could find themselves liable for past Social Security payments and even income tax withholding. Even worse could be the prospect of future record-keeping and reporting requirements. The added compliance costs could convince clubs to ditch the caddie system and replace it with less troublesome electric carts.

SOURCE: Adapted from M. C. Fondo, "IRS Bogey-Man Threatens Caddies," *Wall Street Journal*, June 3, 1997, p. A22.

---

consideration when it was revealed that they had failed to report and pay payroll taxes on their household employees.

The problem is likely to intensify since businesses are increasingly relying on the services of self-employed persons for numerous reasons. Unlike employees, self-employed persons do not have to be included in various fringe benefit programs (e.g., group term life insurance) and retirement plans. Since they are not covered by FICA and FUTA (see Chapter 1), these payroll costs are avoided.

The IRS is very much aware of the tendency of businesses to wrongly classify workers as self-employed rather than as employees. In terms of tax consequences, employment status also makes a great deal of difference to the persons who perform the services. Expenses of self-employed taxpayers, to the extent allowable, are classified as deductions *for* AGI and are reported on Schedule C (Profit or Loss From Business) of Form 1040.[1] With the exception of reimbursement under an accountable plan (see later in the chapter), expenses of employees are deductions *from* AGI. They are reported on Form 2106 (Employee Business Expenses) and Schedule A (Itemized Deductions) of Form 1040.[2]

But when does an employer-employee relationship exist? Such a relationship exists when the employer has the right to specify the end result and the ways and means by which that result is to be attained.[3] An employee is subject to the will and control of the employer with respect not only to what shall be done but also to how it shall be done. If the individual is subject to the direction or control of another only to the extent of the end result but not as to the means of accomplishment, an employer-employee relationship does not exist. An example is the preparation of a taxpayer's return by an independent CPA.

Certain factors indicate an employer-employee relationship. They include (1) the right to discharge without legal liability the person performing the

---

[1] §§ 62(a)(1) and 162(a). See Appendix B for a reproduction of Schedule C.

[2] See Appendix B for a reproduction of Form 2106 and Schedule A.
[3] Reg. § 31.3401(c)–(1)(b).

service, (2) the furnishing of tools or a place to work, and (3) payment based on time spent rather than the task performed. Each case is tested on its own merits, and the right to control the means and methods of accomplishment is the definitive test. Generally, physicians, lawyers, dentists, contractors, subcontractors, and others who offer services to the public are not classified as employees.

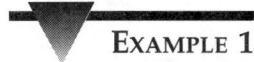

EXAMPLE 1

Arnold is a lawyer whose major client accounts for 60% of his billings. He does the routine legal work and income tax returns at the client's request. He is paid a monthly retainer in addition to amounts charged for extra work. Arnold is a self-employed individual. Even though most of his income comes from one client, he still has the right to determine how the end result of his work is attained. ▼

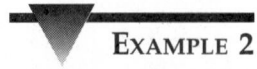

EXAMPLE 2

Ellen is a lawyer hired by Arnold to assist him in the performance of services for the client mentioned in Example 1. Ellen is under Arnold's supervision; he reviews her work and pays her an hourly fee. Ellen is an employee of Arnold. ▼

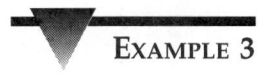

EXAMPLE 3

Frank is a licensed practical nurse who works as a private-duty nurse. He is under the supervision of the patient's doctor and is paid by the patient. Frank is not an employee of either the patient (who pays him) or the doctor (who supervises him). The ways and means of attaining the end result (care of the patient) are under his control. ▼

Employees in a special category are also allowed to file Schedule C to report income and deduct expenses *for* AGI. These employees are called **statutory employees** because they are not common law employees under the rules explained above. The wages or commissions paid to statutory employees are not subject to Federal income tax withholding but are subject to Social Security tax.[4]

EMPLOYEE EXPENSES—IN GENERAL

Once the employment relationship is established, employee expenses fall into one of the following categories:

- Transportation.
- Travel.
- Moving.
- Education.
- Entertainment.
- Other.

These expenses are discussed below in the order presented.

Keep in mind, however, that these expenses are not necessarily limited to employees. A deduction for business transportation, for example, is equally available to taxpayers who are self-employed.

---

[4]See Circular E, *Employer's Tax Guide* (IRS Publication 15), for further discussion of statutory employees.

TRANSPORTATION EXPENSES

QUALIFIED EXPENDITURES

2 LEARNING OBJECTIVE
Recognize deductible transportation expenses.

An employee may deduct unreimbursed employment-related transportation expenses as an itemized deduction *from* AGI. **Transportation expenses** include only the cost of transporting the employee from one place to another in the course of employment when the employee is *not* away from home *in travel status*. Such costs include taxi fares, automobile expenses, tolls, and parking.

Commuting Expenses. Commuting between home and one's place of employment is a personal, nondeductible expense. The fact that one employee drives 30 miles to work and another employee walks six blocks is of no significance.[5]

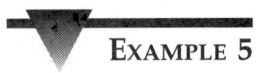

EXAMPLE 4

Geraldo is employed by Sparrow Corporation. He drives 22 miles each way to work. The 44 miles he drives each workday are nondeductible commuting expenses. ▼

The rule that disallows a deduction for commuting expenses has several exceptions. An employee who uses an automobile to transport heavy tools to work and who otherwise would not drive to work is allowed a deduction, but only for the additional costs incurred to transport the work implements. Additional costs are those exceeding the cost of commuting by the same mode of transportation without the tools. For example, the rental of a trailer for transporting tools is deductible, but the expenses of operating the automobile generally are not deductible.[6] The Supreme Court has held that a deduction is permitted only when the taxpayer can show that the automobile would not have been used without the necessity to transport tools or equipment.[7]

Another exception is provided for an employee who has a second job. The expenses of getting from one job to another are deductible. If the employee goes home between jobs, the deduction is based on the distance between jobs.

EXAMPLE 5

In the current year, Cynthia holds two jobs, a full-time job with Blue Corporation and a part-time job with Wren Corporation. During the 250 days that she works (adjusted for weekends, vacation, and holidays), Cynthia customarily leaves home at 7:30 A.M. and drives 30 miles to the Blue Corporation plant, where she works until 5:00 P.M. After dinner at a nearby cafe, Cynthia drives 20 miles to Wren Corporation and works from 7:00 to 11:00 P.M. The distance from the second job to Cynthia's home is 40 miles. Her deduction is based on 20 miles (the distance between jobs). ▼

If the taxpayer is required to incur a transportation expense to travel between work stations, that expense is deductible.

EXAMPLE 6

Thomas, a general contractor, drives from his home to his office, then drives to three building sites to perform his required inspections, and finally drives home. The costs of driving to his office and driving home from the last inspection site are nondeductible commuting expenses. The other transportation costs are deductible. ▼

---

[5]*Tauferner v. U.S.*, 69–1 USTC ¶9241, 23 AFTR2d 69–1025, 407 F.2d 243 (CA–10, 1969).
[6]Rev.Rul. 75–380, 1975–2 C.B. 59.

[7]*Fausner v. Comm.*, 73–2 USTC ¶9515, 32 AFTR2d 73–5202, 93 S.Ct. 2820 (USSC, 1973).

Likewise, the commuting costs from home to a temporary work station and from the temporary work station to home are deductible.[8]

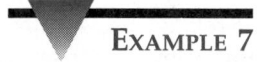

EXAMPLE 7

Vivian works for a firm in downtown Denver and commutes to work. She occasionally works in a customer's office. On one such occasion, Vivian drove directly to the customer's office, a round-trip distance from her home of 40 miles. She did not go into her office, which is a 52-mile round-trip. Her mileage for going to and from the temporary work station is deductible. ▼

Also deductible is the reasonable travel cost between the general working area and a temporary work station outside that area.[9] What constitutes the general working area depends on the facts and circumstances of each situation. Furthermore, if an employee customarily works on several temporary assignments in a localized area, that localized area becomes the regular place of employment. Transportation from home to these locations becomes a personal, nondeductible commuting expense.

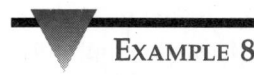

EXAMPLE 8

Sam, a building inspector in Minneapolis, regularly inspects buildings for building code violations for his employer, a general contractor. During one busy season, the St. Paul inspector became ill, and Sam was required to inspect several buildings in St. Paul. The expenses for transportation for the trips to St. Paul are deductible. ▼

COMPUTATION OF AUTOMOBILE EXPENSES

A taxpayer has two choices in computing automobile expenses. The actual operating cost, which includes depreciation (cost recovery), gas, oil, repairs, licenses, and insurance, may be used. Records must be kept that detail the automobile's personal and business use. Only the percentage allocable to business transportation and travel is allowed as a deduction. Complex rules for the computation of depreciation (discussed in Chapter 8) apply if the actual expense method is used.

Use of the **automatic mileage method** (also called the standard mileage method) is the second alternative. For 1998 the deduction is based on 32.5 cents per mile for all business miles.[10] Parking fees and tolls are allowed in addition to expenses computed using the automatic mileage method.

Generally, a taxpayer may elect either method for any particular year. However, the following restrictions apply:

- The vehicle must be owned or leased by the taxpayer.
- If two or more vehicles are in use (for business purposes) at the *same* time (not alternately), a taxpayer may not use the automatic mileage method.
- A basis adjustment is required if the taxpayer changes from the automatic mileage method to the actual operating cost method. Depreciation is considered allowed for the business miles in accordance with the following schedule for the most recent five years:

---

[8]Rev.Rul. 90–23, 1990–1 C.B. 28 as amplified by Rev.Rul. 94–47, 1994–2 C.B. 18.

[9]Rev.Rul. 190, 1953–2 C.B. 303 as amplified by Rev.Rul. 94–47, 1994–2 C.B. 18.

[10]Rev.Proc. 97–58, I.R.B. No. 52, 24. The rate was 31.5 cents a mile for 1997.

Year	Rate per Mile
1998	12 cents
1997	12 cents
1996	12 cents
1995	12 cents
1994	12 cents

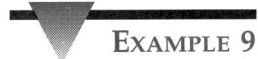

EXAMPLE 9

Tim purchased his automobile in 1995 for $15,000. It is used 90% for business purposes. Tim drove the automobile for 10,000 business miles in 1997; 8,500 miles in 1996; and 6,000 miles in 1995. At the beginning of 1998, the basis of the business portion is $10,560.

Cost ($15,000 × 90%)	$13,500
Less depreciation:	
1997 (10,000 miles × 12 cents)	(1,200)
1996 (8,500 miles × 12 cents)	(1,020)
1995 (6,000 miles × 12 cents)	(720)
Adjusted business basis 1/1/98	$10,560

- Use of the automatic mileage method in the first year the auto is placed in service is considered an election to exclude the auto from the MACRS method of depreciation (discussed in Chapter 8).
- A taxpayer may not switch to the automatic mileage method if the MACRS statutory percentage method or the election to expense under § 179 has been used.

TRAVEL EXPENSES

DEFINITION OF TRAVEL EXPENSES

3 LEARNING OBJECTIVE Know how travel expenses are treated.

An itemized deduction is allowed for unreimbursed travel expenses related to a taxpayer's employment. **Travel expenses** are more broadly defined in the Code than are transportation expenses. Travel expenses include transportation expenses and meals and lodging while away from home in the pursuit of a trade or business. Meals cannot be lavish or extravagant under the circumstances. Transportation expenses (as previously discussed) are deductible even though the taxpayer is not away from home. A deduction for travel expenses is available only if the taxpayer is away from his or her tax home. Travel expenses also include reasonable laundry and incidental expenses.

AWAY-FROM-HOME REQUIREMENT

The crucial test for the deductibility of travel expenses is whether or not the employee is away from home overnight. "Overnight" need not be a 24-hour period, but it must be a period substantially longer than an ordinary day's work and must require rest, sleep, or a relief-from-work period.[11] A one-day business trip is not travel status, and meals and lodging for such a trip are not deductible.

---
[11]*U.S. v. Correll*, 68–1 USTC ¶9101, 20 AFTR2d 5845, 88 S.Ct. 445 (USSC, 1967); Rev.Rul. 75–168, 1975–1 C.B. 58.

Temporary Assignments.   The employee must be away from home for a temporary period. If the taxpayer-employee is reassigned to a new post for an indefinite period of time, that new post becomes his or her tax home. *Temporary* indicates that the assignment's termination is expected within a reasonably short period of time. The position of the IRS is that the tax home is the business location, post, or station of the taxpayer. Thus, travel expenses are not deductible if a taxpayer is reassigned for an indefinite period and does not move his or her place of residence to the new location.

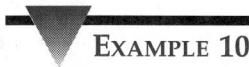

EXAMPLE 10   Malcolm's employer opened a branch office in San Diego. Malcolm was assigned to the new office for three months to train a new manager and to assist in setting up the new office. He tried commuting from his home in Los Angeles for a week and decided that he could not continue driving several hours a day. He rented an apartment in San Diego, where he lived during the week. He spent weekends with his wife and children at their home in Los Angeles. Malcolm's rent, meals, laundry, incidentals, and automobile expenses in San Diego are deductible. To the extent that Malcolm's transportation expense related to his weekend trips home exceeds what his cost of meals and lodging would have been, the excess is personal and nondeductible. ▼

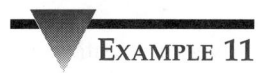

EXAMPLE 11   Assume that Malcolm in Example 10 was transferred to the new location to become the new manager permanently. His wife and children continued to live in Los Angeles until the end of the school year. Malcolm is no longer "away from home" because the assignment is not temporary. His travel expenses are not deductible. ▼

To curtail controversy in this area, the Code specifies that a taxpayer "*shall not be treated as temporarily away from home during any period of employment if such period exceeds 1 year.*"[12]

Determining the Tax Home.   Under ordinary circumstances, determining the location of a taxpayer's tax home does not present a problem. The tax home is the area in which the taxpayer derives his or her principal source of income. When the taxpayer has more than one place of employment, the tax home is based on the amount of time spent in each area.

It is possible for a taxpayer never to be away from his or her tax home. In other words, the tax home follows the taxpayer.[13] Thus, all meals and lodging remain personal and are not deductible.

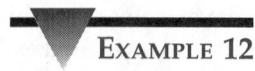

EXAMPLE 12   Bill is employed as a long-haul truck driver. He is single, stores his clothes and other belongings at his parents' home, and stops there for periodic visits. Most of the time, Bill is on the road, sleeping in his truck and in motels. It is likely that Bill is never in travel status, as he is not away from home. Consequently, none of his meals and lodging are deductible. ▼

RESTRICTIONS ON TRAVEL EXPENSES

The possibility always exists that taxpayers will attempt to treat vacation or pleasure travel as deductible business travel. To prevent such practices, the law contains restrictions on certain travel expenses.

---

[12]§ 162(a).

[13]*Moses Mitnick*, 13 T.C. 1 (1949).

Conventions.   For travel expenses to be deductible, a convention must be directly related to the taxpayer's trade or business.[14]

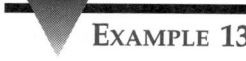
EXAMPLE 13

Dr. Hill, a pathologist who works for a hospital in Ohio, travels to Las Vegas to attend a two-day session on recent developments in estate planning. No deduction is allowed for Dr. Hill's travel expenses. ▼

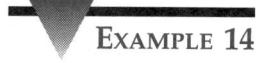
EXAMPLE 14

Assume the same facts as in Example 13 except that the convention deals entirely with recent developments in forensic medicine. Under these circumstances, a travel deduction is allowed. ▼

If the proceedings of the convention are videotaped, the taxpayer must attend convention sessions to view the videotaped materials along with other participants. This requirement does not disallow deductions for costs (other than travel, meals, and entertainment) of renting or using videotaped materials related to business.

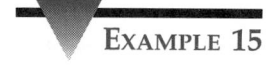
EXAMPLE 15

A CPA is unable to attend a convention at which current developments in taxation are discussed. She pays $200 for videotapes of the lectures and views them at home later. The $200 is an itemized deduction if the CPA is an employee. If she is self-employed, the $200 is a deduction *for* AGI. ▼

The Code places stringent restrictions on the deductibility of travel expenses of the taxpayer's spouse or dependent.[15] Generally, the accompaniment by the spouse or dependent must serve a bona fide business purpose, and the expenses must be otherwise deductible.

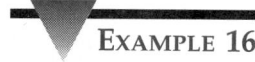
EXAMPLE 16

Assume the same facts as in Example 14 with the additional fact that Dr. Hill is accompanied by Mrs. Hill. Mrs. Hill is not employed, but possesses secretarial skills and takes notes during the proceedings. No deduction is allowed for Mrs. Hill's travel expenses. ▼

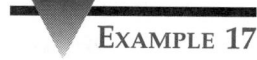
EXAMPLE 17

Modify the facts in Example 16 to make Mrs. Hill a nurse trained in pathology, who is employed by Dr. Hill as his assistant. Now, Mrs. Hill's travel expenses qualify as deductions. ▼

Education.   Travel as a form of education is not deductible.[16] If, however, the education qualifies as a deduction, the travel involved is allowed.

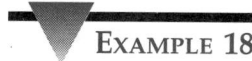
EXAMPLE 18

Greta, a German teacher, travels to Germany to maintain general familiarity with the language and culture. No travel expense deduction is allowed. ▼

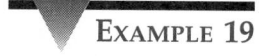
EXAMPLE 19

Jean-Claude, a scholar of French literature, travels to Paris to do specific library research that cannot be done elsewhere and to take courses that are offered only at the Sorbonne. The travel costs are deductible, assuming that the other requirements for deducting education expenses (discussed later in the chapter) are met. ▼

COMBINED BUSINESS AND PLEASURE TRAVEL

To be deductible, travel expenses need not be incurred in the performance of specific job functions. Travel expenses incurred in attending a professional convention are deductible by an employee if attendance is connected with services as an employee.

---

[14]§ 274(h)(1).
[15]§ 274(m)(3).

[16]§ 274(m)(2).

For example, an employee of a law firm can deduct travel expenses incurred in attending a meeting of the American Bar Association.

Domestic Travel. Travel deductions have been used in the past by persons who claimed a tax deduction for what was essentially a personal vacation. As a result, several provisions have been enacted to govern deductions associated with combined business and pleasure trips. If the business/pleasure trip is from one point in the United States to another point in the United States, the transportation expenses are deductible only if the trip is *primarily for business*.[17] If the trip is primarily for pleasure, no transportation expenses qualify as a deduction. Meals, lodging, and other expenses are allocated between business and personal days.

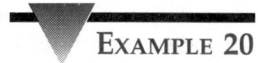

EXAMPLE 20

In the current year, Hana travels from Seattle to New York primarily for business. She spends five days conducting business and three days sightseeing and attending shows. Her plane and taxi fare amounts to $560. Her meals amount to $100 per day, and lodging and incidental expenses are $150 per day. She can deduct the transportation charges of $560, since the trip is primarily for business (five days of business versus three days of sightseeing). Meals are limited to five days and are subject to the 50% cutback (discussed later in the chapter) for a total of $250 [5 days × ($100 × 50%)], and other expenses are limited to $750 (5 days × $150). If Hana is an employee, the unreimbursed travel expenses are miscellaneous itemized deductions. ▼

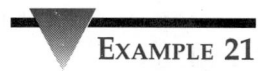

EXAMPLE 21

Assume Hana goes to New York for a two-week vacation. While there, she spends several hours renewing acquaintances with people in her company's New York office. Her transportation expenses are not deductible. ▼

Foreign Travel. When the trip is *outside the United States*, special rules apply.[18] Transportation expenses must be allocated between business and personal unless (1) the taxpayer is away from home for seven days or less *or* (2) less than 25 percent of the time was for personal purposes. No allocation is required if the taxpayer has no substantial control over arrangements for the trip or the desire for a vacation is not a major factor in taking the trip. If the trip is primarily for pleasure, no transportation charges are deductible. Days devoted to travel are considered business days. Weekends, legal holidays, and intervening days are considered business days, provided that both the preceding and succeeding days were business days.

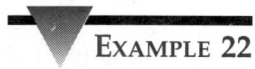

EXAMPLE 22

In the current year, Robert takes a trip from New York to Japan primarily for business purposes. He is away from home from June 10 through June 19. He spends three days vacationing and seven days conducting business (including two travel days). His airfare is $2,500, his meals amount to $100 per day, and lodging and incidental expenses are $160 per day. Since Robert is away from home for more than seven days and more than 25% of his time is devoted to personal purposes, only 70% (7 days business/10 days total) of the transportation is deductible. His deductions are as follows:

Transportation (70% × $2,500)		$1,750
Lodging ($160 × 7)		1,120
Meals ($100 × 7)	$ 700	
Less: 50% cutback (discussed later)	(350)	350
Total		$3,220

---

[17]Reg. § 1.162–2(b)(1).

[18]§ 274(c) and Reg. § 1.274–4.

If Robert is gone the same period of time but spends only two days (rather than three) vacationing, no allocation of transportation is required. Since the pleasure portion of the trip is less than 25% of the total, all of the airfare qualifies for the travel deduction. ▼

Certain restrictions are imposed on the deductibility of expenses paid or incurred to attend conventions located outside the North American area. The expenses are disallowed unless it is established that the meeting is directly related to a trade or business of the taxpayer. Disallowance also occurs unless the taxpayer shows that it is as reasonable for the meeting to be held in a foreign location as within the North American area.

The foreign convention rules do not operate to bar a deduction to an employer if the expense is compensatory in nature. For example, a trip to Rome won by a top salesperson is included in the gross income of the employee and is fully deductible by the employer.

MOVING EXPENSES

4 **LEARNING OBJECTIVE**
Determine the moving expense deduction.

Moving expenses are deductible for moves in connection with the commencement of work at a new principal place of work.[19] Both employees and self-employed individuals can deduct these expenses. To be eligible for a moving expense deduction, a taxpayer must meet two basic tests: distance and time.

DISTANCE TEST

To meet the distance test, the taxpayer's new job location must be at least 50 miles farther from the taxpayer's old residence than the old residence was from the former place of employment. In this regard, the location of the new residence is not relevant. This eliminates a moving deduction for taxpayers who purchase a new home in the same general area without changing their place of employment. Those who accept a new job in the same general area as the old job location are also eliminated.

EXAMPLE 23

Harry is permanently transferred to a new job location. The distance from Harry's former home to his new job (80 miles) exceeds the distance from his former home to his old job (30 miles) by at least 50 miles. Harry has met the distance test for a moving expense deduction. (See the following diagram.)

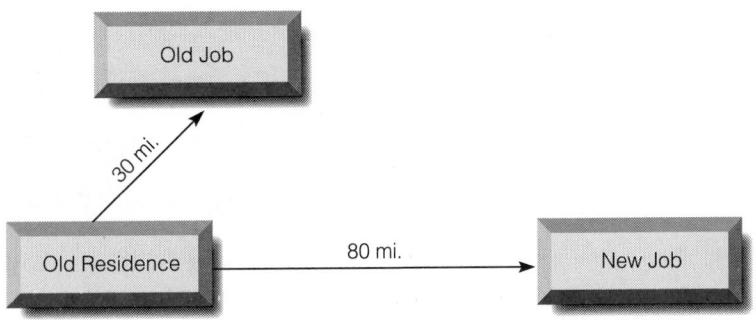

---

[19]§ 217(a).

If Harry is not employed before the move, his new job must be at least 50 miles from his former residence. In this instance, Harry has met the distance test if he was not previously employed. ▼

TIME TEST

To meet the time test, an employee must be employed on a full-time basis at the new location for 39 weeks in the 12-month period following the move. If the taxpayer is a self-employed individual, he or she must work in the new location for 78 weeks during the next two years. The first 39 weeks must be in the first 12 months. The time test is suspended if the taxpayer dies, becomes disabled, or is discharged or transferred by the new employer through no fault of the employee.

A taxpayer might not be able to meet the 39-week test by the due date of the tax return for the year of the move. For this reason, two alternatives are allowed. The taxpayer can take the deduction in the year the expenses are incurred, even though the 39-week test has not been met. If the taxpayer later fails to meet the test, either (1) the income of the following year is increased by an amount equal to the deduction previously claimed for moving expenses, or (2) an amended return is filed for the year of the move. The second alternative is to wait until the test is met and then file an amended tax return for the year of the move.

TREATMENT OF MOVING EXPENSES

What Is Included. "Qualified" moving expenses include *reasonable* expenses of:

- Moving household goods and personal effects.
- Traveling from the former residence to the new place of residence.

For this purpose, *traveling* includes lodging, but not meals, for the taxpayer and members of the household.[20] It does not include the cost of moving servants or others who are not members of the household. The taxpayer can elect to use actual auto expenses (no depreciation is allowed) or the automatic mileage method. In this case, moving expense mileage is limited in 1998 to 10 cents per mile (10 cents in 1997) for each car. These expenses are also limited by the reasonableness standard. For example, if one moves from Texas to Florida via Maine and takes six weeks to do so, the transportation and lodging must be allocated between personal and moving expenses.

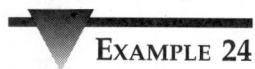

EXAMPLE 24

Jill is transferred by her employer from the Atlanta office to the San Francisco office. In this connection, she spends the following amounts:

Cost of moving furniture	$2,800
Transportation	700
Meals	200
Lodging	300

Jill's total qualified moving expense is $3,800 ($2,800 + $700 + $300). ▼

The moving expense deduction is allowed regardless of whether the employee is transferred by the existing employer or is employed by a new employer. It is allowed if the employee moves to a new area and obtains employment or switches from self-employed status to employee status (and vice versa). The moving expense

---

[20]§ 217(b).

deduction is also allowed if an individual is unemployed before obtaining employment in a new area.

How Treated. Qualified moving expenses that are paid (or reimbursed) by the employer are not reported as part of the gross income of the employee.[21] Moving expenses that are paid (or reimbursed) by the employer and are not qualified moving expenses are included in the employee's gross income and are not deductible. The employer is responsible for allocating the reimbursement between the qualified and nonqualified moving expenses. Reimbursed qualified moving expenses are separately stated on the Form W–2 given to the employee for the year involved. Qualified moving expenses that are not reimbursed and those of self-employed taxpayers are deductions *for* AGI.[22]

Form 3903 is used to report the details of the moving expense deduction if the employee is not reimbursed or a self-employed person is involved.

EDUCATION EXPENSES

GENERAL REQUIREMENTS

5 **LEARNING OBJECTIVE**
Differentiate between deductible and nondeductible education expenses.

An employee can deduct expenses incurred for education (**education expenses**) as ordinary and necessary business expenses provided the expenses are incurred for either of two reasons:

1. To maintain or improve existing skills required in the present job.
2. To meet the express requirements of the employer or the requirements imposed by law to retain his or her employment status.

Education expenses are *not* deductible if the education is for either of the following purposes:

1. To meet the minimum educational standards for qualification in the taxpayer's existing job.
2. To qualify the taxpayer for a new trade or business.[23]

Fees incurred for professional qualification exams (the bar exam, for example) and fees for review courses (such as a CPA review course) are not deductible.[24] If the education incidentally results in a promotion or raise, the deduction still can be taken as long as the education maintained and improved existing skills and did not qualify a person for a new trade or business. A change in duties is not always fatal to the deduction if the new duties involve the same general work. For example, the IRS has ruled that a practicing dentist's education expenses incurred to become an orthodontist are deductible.[25]

REQUIREMENTS IMPOSED BY LAW OR BY THE EMPLOYER FOR RETENTION OF EMPLOYMENT

Teachers are permitted to deduct education expenses if additional courses are required by the employer or are imposed by law. Many states require a minimum of a bachelor's degree and a specified number of additional courses to retain a

---

[21]§§ 132(a)(6) and (g).
[22]§ 62(a)(15).
[23]Reg. §§ 1.162–5(b)(2) and (3).

[24]Reg. § 1.212–1(f) and Rev.Rul. 69–292, 1969–1 C.B. 84.
[25]Rev.Rul. 74–78, 1974–1 C.B. 44.

teaching job. In addition, some public school systems have imposed a master's degree requirement and require teachers to make satisfactory progress toward a master's degree in order to keep their positions. If the required education is the minimum degree required for the job, no deduction is allowed.

A taxpayer classified as an Accountant I who went back to school to obtain a bachelor's degree was not allowed to deduct the expenses. Although some courses tended to maintain and improve his existing skills in his entry-level position, the degree was the minimum requirement for his job.[26]

Expenses incurred for education required by law for various professions will also qualify for deduction.

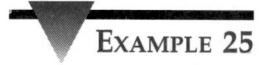

EXAMPLE 25   In order to satisfy the State Board of Public Accountancy rules for maintaining her CPA license, Nancy takes an auditing course sponsored by a local college. The cost of the education is deductible. ▼

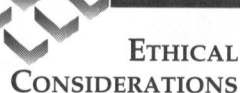

ETHICAL CONSIDERATIONS

Employer-Imposed Education Requirement

Justin, a CPA, is the owner and operator of Condor Corporation. Condor provides accounting and tax services for a number of regular businesses. These services are provided by Justin and two long-time employees, Martha and Alan. Martha and Alan have expressed a desire to attend a local college part-time and earn bachelor of accounting degrees.

When Justin hears about the college plans that Martha and Alan have made, he adopts the following resolution for Condor Corporation: "Employees performing accounting and tax services for clients must possess or be pursuing a bachelor's degree in accounting."

What is Justin trying to accomplish with the resolution? Will it work? Is this ethical behavior?

MAINTAINING OR IMPROVING EXISTING SKILLS

The "maintaining or improving existing skills" requirement in the Code has been difficult for both taxpayers and the courts to interpret. For example, a business executive is permitted to deduct the costs of obtaining an MBA on the grounds that the advanced management education is undertaken to maintain and improve existing management skills. The executive is eligible to deduct the costs of specialized, nondegree management courses that are taken for continuing education or to maintain or improve existing skills. Expenses incurred by the executive to obtain a law degree are not deductible, however, because the education constitutes training for a new trade or business. The Regulations deny a self-employed accountant a deduction for expenses relating to law school.[27]

CLASSIFICATION OF SPECIFIC ITEMS

Education expenses include books, tuition, typing, and transportation (e.g., from the office to night school) and travel (e.g., meals and lodging while away from home at summer school).

---

[26]Reg. § 1.162–5(b)(2)(iii) Example (2); *Collin J. Davidson*, 43 TCM 743, T.C.Memo. 1982–119.

[27]Reg. § 1.162–5(b)(3)(ii) Example (1).

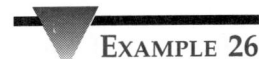

EXAMPLE 26

Bill, who holds a bachelor of education degree, is a secondary education teacher in the Los Angeles school system. The school board recently raised its minimum education requirement for new teachers from four years of college training to five. A grandfather clause allows teachers with only four years of college to continue to qualify if they show satisfactory progress toward a graduate degree. Bill enrolls at the University of California and takes three graduate courses. His unreimbursed expenses for this purpose are as follows:

Books and tuition	$2,600
Lodging while in travel status (June–August)	1,150
Meals while in travel status	800
Laundry while in travel status	220
Transportation	600

Bill has an itemized deduction as follows:

Books and tuition	$2,600
Lodging	1,150
Meals less 50% cutback (see below)	400
Laundry	220
Transportation	600
	$4,970

OTHER PROVISIONS DEALING WITH EDUCATION

The focus of this chapter is on the deduction aspects of certain items. For education, however, two important provisions involve the income aspects. One deals with the exclusion of certain scholarships from gross income.[28] The other deals with the exclusion from gross income of employer amounts provided under certain educational assistance programs.[29] Both of these provisions are discussed in Chapter 5.

ENTERTAINMENT EXPENSES

6   LEARNING OBJECTIVE
Understand how entertainment expenses are treated.

Many taxpayers attempt to deduct personal entertainment expenses as business expenses. For this reason, the tax law restricts the deductibility of entertainment expenses. The Code contains strict record-keeping requirements and provides restrictive tests for the deduction of certain types of **entertainment expenses.**

CUTBACK ADJUSTMENT

During the administration of Jimmy Carter, considerable controversy arose regarding the "three martini" business lunch. By virtue of allowing a tax deduction, should the tax law be subsidizing a practice that contained a significant element of personal pleasure? One possible remedy for the situation was to disallow any deduction for business entertainment, but this option was regarded as being too harsh. Instead the *cutback* rule was instituted. Rather than disallowing *all* of the deduction, allow only a certain percentage, and the rest of the expenditure would

---

[28]§ 117.

[29]§ 127.

be cut back. Currently, only 50 percent of meal and entertainment expenses are allowed as a deduction.[30] The limitation applies in the context of both employment and self-employment status. Although the 50 percent cutback can apply to either the employer or the employee, it will not apply twice. The cutback applies to the one who really pays (economically) for the meals or entertainment.

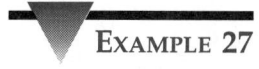

EXAMPLE 27

Jane, an employee of Pelican Corporation, entertains one of her clients. If Pelican Corporation does not reimburse Jane, she is subject to the cutback adjustment. If, however, Pelican Corporation reimburses Jane (or pays for the entertainment directly), Pelican suffers the cutback. ▼

In certain situations, however, a full 50 percent cutback seems unfair. If, for example, the hours of service are regulated (by the U.S. Department of Transportation) and away-from-home meals are frequent and necessary, the "three martini" business lunch type of abuse is unlikely. Consequently, the Taxpayer Relief Act of 1997 (TRA of 1997) eases the cutback rule for the following types of employees:

- Certain air transportation employees, such as flight crews, dispatchers, mechanics, and control tower operators.
- Interstate truck and bus drivers.
- Certain railroad employees, such as train crews and dispatchers.
- Certain merchant mariners.

Starting in 1998, the cutback is reduced by 5 percent at two-year intervals until it reaches 20 percent in year 2008 and thereafter. Thus, 80 percent of the cost of meals will eventually be allowed as a deduction.

What Is Covered.   Transportation expenses are not affected by the cutback rule—only meals and entertainment. The cutback also applies to taxes and tips relating to meals and entertainment. Cover charges, parking fees at an entertainment location, and room rental fees for a meal or cocktail party are also subject to the 50 percent rule.

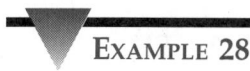

EXAMPLE 28

Joe pays a $30 cab fare to meet his client for dinner. The meal costs $120, and Joe leaves a $20 tip. His deduction is $100 [($120 + $20) × 50% + $30 cab fare]. ▼

What Is Not Covered.   The cutback rule has a number of exceptions. One exception covers the case where the full value of the meals or entertainment is included in the compensation of the employee (or independent contractor).[31]

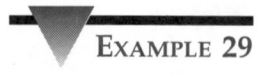

EXAMPLE 29

Myrtle wins an all-expense-paid trip to Europe for selling the most insurance for her company during the year. Her employer treats this trip as additional compensation to Myrtle. The cutback adjustment does not apply to the employer. ▼

Another exception applies to meals and entertainment in a subsidized eating facility or where the *de minimis* fringe benefit rule is met (see Chapter 5).[32]

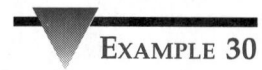

EXAMPLE 30

General Hospital has an employee cafeteria on the premises for its doctors, nurses, and other employees. The cafeteria operates at cost. The cutback rule does not apply to General Hospital. ▼

[30]§ 274(n).
[31]§§ 274(e)(2) and (9).

[32]§ 274(n)(2).

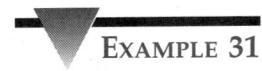

EXAMPLE 31

Canary Corporation gives a ham, a fruitcake, and a bottle of wine to each employee at year-end. Since the *de minimis* fringe benefit exclusion applies to business gifts of packaged foods and beverages, their *full* cost is deductible by Canary. ▼

A similar exception applies to employer-paid recreational activities for employees (e.g., the annual Christmas party or spring picnic).[33]

CLASSIFICATION OF EXPENSES

Entertainment expenses are categorized as follows: those *directly related* to business and those *associated with* business.[34] Directly related expenses are related to an actual business meeting or discussion. These expenses are distinguished from entertainment expenses that are incurred to promote goodwill, such as maintaining existing customer relations. To obtain a deduction for directly related entertainment, it is not necessary to show that actual benefit resulted from the expenditure as long as there was a reasonable expectation of benefit. To qualify as directly related, the expense should be incurred in a clear business setting. If there is little possibility of engaging in the active conduct of a trade or business due to the nature of the social facility, it is difficult to qualify the expenditure as directly related to business.

Expenses associated with, rather than directly related to, business entertainment must serve a specific business purpose, such as obtaining new business or continuing existing business. These expenditures qualify only if the expenses directly precede or follow a bona fide business discussion. Entertainment occurring on the same day as the business discussion meets the test.

RESTRICTIONS UPON DEDUCTIBILITY

Business Meals. Any business meal is deductible only if the following are true:[35]

- The meal is directly related to or associated with the active conduct of a trade or business.
- The expense is not lavish or extravagant under the circumstances.
- The taxpayer (or an employee) is present at the meal.

A business meal with a business associate or customer is not deductible unless business is discussed before, during, or after the meal. This requirement is not intended to disallow the deduction for a meal consumed while away from home on business.

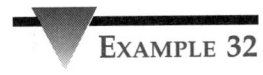

EXAMPLE 32

Lacy travels to San Francisco for a business convention. She pays for dinner with three colleagues and is not reimbursed by her employer. They do not discuss business. She can deduct 50% of the cost of her meal. However, she cannot deduct the cost of her colleagues' meals. ▼

The *clear business purpose* test requires that meals be directly related to or associated with the active conduct of a business. A meal is not deductible if it serves no business purpose.

---

[33]§ 274(e)(4).
[34]§ 274(a)(1)(A).

[35]§ 274(k).

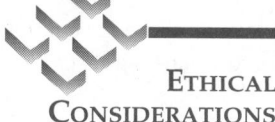

Reciprocal Entertaining

Walter (an attorney), Susan (an insurance broker), Richard (a realtor), and Nancy (a banker) are all good friends and do business with each other. Richard's accountant suggests that each might derive a substantial tax benefit if they went to lunch together as often as possible and rotated the tab. Do you believe the procedure suggested by Richard's accountant is proper? Why or why not?

The taxpayer or an employee must be present at the business meal for the meal to be deductible.[36] An independent contractor who renders significant services to the taxpayer is treated as an employee.

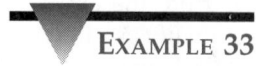

EXAMPLE 33

Lance, a party to a contract negotiation, buys dinner for other parties to the negotiation but does not attend the dinner. No deduction is allowed. ▼

Club Dues.   The Code provides: "No deduction shall be allowed . . . for amounts paid or incurred for membership in any club organized for business, pleasure, recreation, or other social purpose."[37] Although this prohibition seems quite broad, the IRS does allow a deduction for dues to clubs whose primary purpose is public service and community volunteerism (e.g., Kiwanis, Lions, Rotary).

Even though dues are not deductible, actual entertainment at a club may qualify.

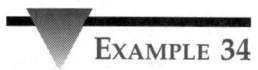

EXAMPLE 34

During the current year, Vincent spent $1,400 on business lunches at the Lakeside Country Club. The annual membership fee was $6,000, and Vincent used the facility 60% of the time for business. Presuming the lunches meet the business meal test, Vincent may claim $700 (50% × $1,400) as a deduction. None of the club dues are deductible. ▼

Ticket Purchases for Entertainment.   A deduction for the cost of a ticket for an entertainment activity is limited to the face value of the ticket.[38] This limitation is applied before the 50 percent rule. The face value of a ticket includes any tax. Under this rule, the excess payment to a scalper for a ticket is not deductible. Similarly, the fee to a ticket agency for the purchase of a ticket is not deductible.

Expenditures for the rental or use of a luxury skybox at a sports arena in excess of the face value of regular tickets are disallowed as deductions. If a luxury skybox is used for entertainment that is directly related to or associated with business, the deduction is limited to the face value of nonluxury box seats. All seats in the luxury skybox are counted, even when some seats are unoccupied.

The taxpayer may also deduct stated charges for food and beverages under the general rules for business entertainment. The deduction for skybox seats, food, and beverages is limited to 50 percent of cost.

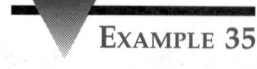

EXAMPLE 35

In the current year, Pelican Company pays $6,000 to rent a 10-seat skybox at City Stadium for three football games. Nonluxury box seats at each event range in cost from $25 to $35 a seat. In March, a Pelican representative and five clients use the skybox for the first game. The entertainment follows a bona fide business discussion, and Pelican spends $86 for food and beverages during the game. The deduction for the first sports event is as follows:

[36]§ 274(k)(1)(B).
[37]§ 274(a)(3).

[38]§ 274(l).

Food and beverages	$ 86
Deduction for seats ($35 × 10 seats)	350
Total entertainment expense	$436
50% limitation	× .50
Deduction	$218

Business Gifts.   Business gifts are deductible to the extent of $25 per donee per year.[39] An exception is made for gifts costing $4 or less (e.g., pens with the employee's or company's name on them) or promotional materials. Such items are not treated as business gifts subject to the $25 limitation. In addition, incidental costs such as engraving of jewelry and nominal charges for gift-wrapping, mailing, and delivery are not included in the cost of the gift in applying the limitation. Gifts to superiors and employers are not deductible.

Records must be maintained to substantiate business gifts.

OTHER EMPLOYEE EXPENSES

OFFICE IN THE HOME

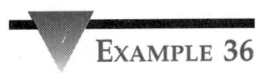

7 LEARNING OBJECTIVE
Identify other employee expenses.

Employees and self-employed individuals are not allowed a deduction for **office in the home expenses** unless a portion of the residence is used *exclusively* on a *regular basis* as either of the following:

- The principal place of business for any trade or business of the taxpayer.
- A place of business used by clients, patients, or customers.

Employees must meet an additional test: The use must be for the *convenience of the employer* rather than merely being "appropriate and helpful."[40]

The precise meaning of "principal place of business" was resolved by the U.S. Supreme Court. In a divided opinion, the Court established a *very restrictive* two-pronged test.[41] First, determine the relative importance of the activities performed at each business location (inside and outside the personal residence). Second, compare the time spent at each business location.

EXAMPLE 36

Dr. Smith is a self-employed anesthesiologist. During the year, he spends 30 to 35 hours per week administering anesthesia and postoperative care to patients in three hospitals, none of which provides him with an office. He also spends two to three hours per day in a room in his home that he uses exclusively as an office. He does not meet patients there, but he performs a variety of tasks related to his medical practice (e.g., contacting surgeons, bookkeeping, reading medical journals). None of Dr. Smith's expenses of the office in the home are deductible because the hospital procedures (administering to patients) are more important than those done at home. Also, more business time is spent outside the home than inside. ▼

---

[39]§ 274(b)(1).
[40]§ 280A(c)(1).
[41]*Comm. v. Soliman*, 93–1 USTC ¶50,014, 71 AFTR2d 93–463, 113 S.Ct. 701 (USSC, 1993) *rev'g.* 91–1 USTC ¶50,291, 67 AFTR2d 91–1112, 935 F.2d 52 (CA–4, 1991) and 94 T.C. 20 (1990).

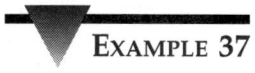

EXAMPLE 37

Lori is a salesperson. Her only office is a room in her home that she uses regularly and exclusively to set up appointments, store product samples, and write up orders and other reports for the companies whose products she sells. Lori makes most of her sales to customers by telephone or mail from her home office. She spends an average of 30 hours a week working at home and 12 hours a week visiting prospective customers to deliver products and occasionally take orders. Under these circumstances, Lori qualifies for the office in the home deduction. Visiting customers is less important to the business than the activities conducted in Lori's office.[42] ▼

Apparently, Congress was not satisfied with the U.S. Supreme Court's interpretation of the meaning of "principal place of business." In TRA of 1997, the Code was amended to provide that an office in the home qualifies as a principal place of business if both of the following are true:

- The office is used by the taxpayer to conduct administrative or management activities of a trade or business.
- There is no other fixed location of the trade or business where the taxpayer conducts these activities.

Unfortunately, the amendment is not effective until taxable years beginning after December 31, 1998. Once in place, however, the new rule will negate the result reached in Example 36.

The exclusive use requirement means that a specific part of the home must be used *solely* for business purposes. A deduction, if permitted, requires an allocation of total expenses of operating the home between business and personal use based on floor space or number of rooms.

Even if the taxpayer meets the above requirements, the allowable home office expenses cannot exceed the gross income from the business less all other business expenses attributable to the activity. Furthermore, the home office expenses that are allowed as itemized deductions anyway (e.g., mortgage interest and real estate taxes) must be deducted first. All home office expenses of an employee are miscellaneous itemized deductions, except those (such as interest and taxes) that qualify as other personal itemized deductions. Home office expenses of a self-employed individual are trade or business expenses and are deductible *for* AGI.

Any disallowed home office expenses are *carried forward* and used in future years subject to the same limitations.

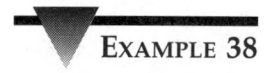

EXAMPLE 38

Rick is a certified public accountant employed by a regional CPA firm as a tax manager. He operates a separate business in which he refinishes furniture in his home. For this business, he uses two rooms in the basement of his home exclusively and regularly. The floor space of the two rooms constitutes 10% of the floor space of his residence. Gross income from the business totals $8,000. Expenses of the business (other than home office expenses) are $6,500. Rick incurs the following home office expenses:

Real property taxes on residence	$ 4,000
Interest expense on residence	7,500
Operating expenses of residence	2,000
Depreciation on residence (based on 10% business use)	250

Rick's deductions are determined as follows:

---

[42]Notice 93–12, 1993–1 C.B. 298 amplified by Rev.Rul. 94–24,1994–1 C.B. 87.

Business income		$ 8,000
Less: Other business expenses		(6,500)
		$ 1,500
Less: Allocable taxes ($4,000 × 10%)	$400	
Allocable interest ($7,500 × 10%)	750	(1,150)
		$ 350
Allocable operating expenses of the residence ($2,000 × 10%)		(200)
		$ 150
Allocable depreciation ($250, limited to remaining income)		(150)
		$ –0–

Rick has a carryover of $100 (the unused excess depreciation). Because he is self-employed, the allocable taxes and interest ($1,150), the other deductible office expenses ($200 + $150), and $6,500 of other business expenses are deductible *for* AGI. ▼

Form 8829 (Expenses for Business Use of Your Home) is available from the IRS for computation of the office in the home deduction.

The home office limitation cannot be circumvented by leasing part of one's home to an employer, using it as a home office, and deducting the expenses as a rental expense under § 212.

MISCELLANEOUS EMPLOYEE EXPENSES

Deductible miscellaneous employee expenses include special clothing and its upkeep, union dues, and professional expenses. Also deductible are professional dues, professional meetings, and employment agency fees for seeking employment in the same trade or business, whether or not a new job is secured.

To be deductible, *special clothing* must be both specifically required as a condition of employment and not adaptable for regular wear. For example, a police officer's uniform is not suitable for off-duty activities. An exception is clothing used to the extent that it takes the place of regular clothing (e.g., military uniforms).

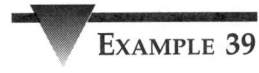

EXAMPLE 39

Captain Roberts is on active duty in the U.S. Army. The cost of his regular uniforms is not deductible since such clothing is suitable for regular wear. Captain Roberts, however, spends over $1,100 purchasing "dress blues." Under military regulations, dress uniforms can only be worn during ceremonial functions (e.g., official events, parades). The $1,100 cost, to the extent it exceeds any clothing allowance, qualifies as a deduction. ▼

The current position of the IRS is that expenses incurred in *seeking employment* are deductible if the taxpayer is seeking employment in the same trade or business. The deduction is allowed whether or not the attempts to secure employment are successful. An unemployed taxpayer can take a deduction providing there has been no substantial lack of continuity between the last job and the search for a new one. No deduction is allowed for persons seeking their first job or seeking employment in a new trade or business.

The basic cost of one *telephone* in the home is not deductible, even if used for business. Any long-distance or toll charges relating to business are deductible.

SOME NBA REFEREES MAY PAY A PRICE FOR A TAXABLE (BUT NOT REPORTED) PAY RAISE

Several NBA referees are the focus of an IRS investigation into a scheme involving millions of dollars in phony travel expenses.

The NBA says it merely reimbursed the referees for travel based on their receipts. But some of the referees say the NBA knowingly paid higher travel reimbursements as a substitute for better pay.

The scheme apparently worked this way: Referees purchased first-class tickets and submitted photocopies of them to the NBA for reimbursement. They then exchanged the tickets for coach seats and pocketed the difference. Needless to say, the referees did not report the difference as income.

As of Fall 1997, at least four referees have been indicted by Federal grand juries for income tax fraud with three pleading guilty. Further indictments are expected.

CONTRIBUTIONS TO INDIVIDUAL RETIREMENT ACCOUNTS

An important and popular deduction *for* AGI is the amount contributed to an Individual Retirement Account (IRA). This amount may be as great as $2,000 per year for an individual (or $4,000 for spousal IRAs). IRAs are covered in detail in Chapter 19.

CLASSIFICATION OF EMPLOYEE EXPENSES

8   LEARNING OBJECTIVE
Appreciate the difference between accountable and nonaccountable employee plans.

The classification of employee expenses depends on whether they are reimbursed by the employer under an accountable plan. If so, then they are not reported by the employee at all. In effect, therefore, this result is equivalent to treating the expenses as deductions *for* AGI.[43] If the expenses are reimbursed under a nonaccountable plan or are not reimbursed at all, then they are classified as deductions *from* AGI and can only be claimed if the employee-taxpayer itemizes. An exception is made for moving expenses and the employment-related expenses of a qualified performing artist.[44] Here, deduction *for* AGI classification is allowed.

For classification purposes, therefore, the difference between accountable and nonaccountable plans is significant.

ACCOUNTABLE PLANS

In General.   An **accountable plan** requires the employee to satisfy these two requirements:

- Adequately account for (substantiate) the expenses. An employee renders an *adequate accounting* by submitting a record, with receipts and other substantiation, to the employer.[45]

---

[43]§ 62(a)(2).
[44]As defined in § 62(b).

[45]Reg. § 1.162–17(b)(4).

- Return any excess reimbursement or allowance. An "excess reimbursement or allowance" is any amount that the employee does not adequately account for as an ordinary and necessary business expense.

Substantiation.   The law provides that no deduction is allowed for any travel, entertainment, business gift, or listed property (automobiles, computers) expenditure unless properly substantiated by adequate records. The records should contain the following information:[46]

- The amount of the expense.
- The time and place of travel or entertainment (or date of gift).
- The business purpose of the expense.
- The business relationship of the taxpayer to the person entertained (or receiving the gift).

This means the taxpayer must maintain an account book or diary in which the above information is recorded at the time of the expenditure. Documentary evidence, such as itemized receipts, is required to support any expenditure for lodging while traveling away from home and for any other expenditure of $75 or more. If a taxpayer fails to keep adequate records, each expense must be established by a written or oral statement of the exact details of the expense and by other corroborating evidence.[47]

EXAMPLE 40

Bertha has travel expenses substantiated only by canceled checks. The checks establish the date, place, and amount of the expenditure. Because neither the business relationship nor the business purpose is established, the deduction is disallowed.[48] ▼

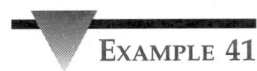
EXAMPLE 41

Dwight has travel and entertainment expenses substantiated by a diary showing the time, place, and amount of the expenditure. His oral testimony provides the business relationship and business purpose. However, since he has no receipts, any expenditures of $75 or more are disallowed.[49] ▼

Deemed Substantiation.   In lieu of reimbursing actual expenses for travel away from home, many employers reduce their paperwork by adopting a policy of reimbursing employees with a *per diem* allowance, a flat dollar amount per day of business travel. Of the substantiation requirements listed above, the *amount* of the expense is proved, or *deemed substantiated*, by using such a per diem allowance or reimbursement procedure. The amount of expenses that is deemed substantiated is equal to the lesser of the per diem allowance or the amount of the Federal per diem rate.

The regular Federal per diem rate is the highest amount that the Federal government will pay to its employees for lodging and meals[50] while in travel status away from home in a particular area. The rates are different for different locations.[51]

The use of the standard Federal per diem for meals constitutes an adequate accounting. Employees and self-employed persons can use the standard meal allowance instead of deducting the actual cost of daily meals, even if not reimbursed. There is no standard lodging allowance, however.

---

[46]§ 274(d).

[47]Reg. § 1.274–5T(c)(3).

[48] *William T. Whitaker*, 56 TCM 47, T.C.Memo. 1988–418.

[49]*W. David Tyler*, 43 TCM 927, T.C.Memo. 1982–160.

[50]The meals per diem rate also covers incidental expenses, including laundry and cleaning of clothing and tips for waiters. Taxi fares and telephone calls are not included.

[51]Each current edition of *Per Diem Rates* (IRS Publication 1542) contains the list and amounts for that year.

Only the amount of the expense is considered substantiated under the deemed substantiated method. The other substantiation requirements must be provided: place, date, business purpose of the expense, and the business relationship of the parties involved.

NONACCOUNTABLE PLANS

A **nonaccountable plan** is one in which an adequate accounting or return of excess amounts, or both, is not required. All reimbursements of expenses are reported in full as wages on the employee's Form W–2. Any allowable expenses are deductible in the same manner as are unreimbursed expenses.

Unreimbursed Employee Expenses.   Unreimbursed employee expenses are treated in a straightforward manner. Meals and entertainment expenses are subject to the 50 percent limit. Total unreimbursed employee business expenses are usually reported as miscellaneous itemized deductions subject to the 2 percent-of-AGI floor (see below). If the employee could have received, but did not seek, reimbursement for whatever reason, none of the employment-related expenses are deductible.

Failure to Comply with Accountable Plan Requirements.   An employer may have an accountable plan and require employees to return excess reimbursements or allowances, but an employee may fail to follow the rules of the plan. In that case, the expenses and reimbursements are subject to nonaccountable plan treatment.

REPORTING PROCEDURES

The reporting requirements range from no reporting at all (accountable plans when all requirements are met) to the use of some or all of the following forms: Form W–2 (Wage and Tax Statement), Form 2106 (Employee Business Expenses) or Form 2106–EZ (Unreimbursed Employee Business Expenses), and Schedule A (Itemized Deductions) for nonaccountable plans and unreimbursed employee expenses.

Reimbursed employee expenses that are adequately accounted for under an accountable plan are deductible *for* AGI on Form 2106. Allowed excess expenses, expenses reimbursed under a nonaccountable plan, and unreimbursed expenses are deductible *from* AGI on Schedule A, subject to the 2 percent-of-AGI floor.

When a reimbursement under an accountable plan is paid in separate amounts relating to designated expenses such as meals or entertainment, no problem arises. The reimbursements and expenses are reported as such on the appropriate forms. If the reimbursement is made in a single amount, an allocation must be made to determine the appropriate portion of the reimbursement that applies to meals and entertainment and to other employee expenses.

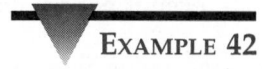

EXAMPLE 42

Elizabeth, who is employed by Green Company, had AGI of $42,000. During the year, she incurred $2,000 of transportation and lodging expense and $1,000 of meals and entertainment expense, all fully substantiated. Elizabeth received $1,800 reimbursement under an accountable plan. The reimbursement rate that applies to meals and entertainment is 33.33% ($1,000 meals and entertainment expense/$3,000 total expenses). Thus, $600 ($1,800 × 33.33%) of the reimbursement applies to meals and entertainment, and $1,200 ($1,800 − $600) applies to transportation and lodging. Elizabeth's itemized deduction consists of the $800 ($2,000 total − $1,200 reimbursement) of unreimbursed transportation and lodging expenses and $400 ($1,000 − $600) of unreimbursed meal and entertainment expenses as follows:

Transportation and lodging	$ 800
Meals and entertainment ($400 × 50%)	200
Total (reported on Form 2106)	$1,000
Less: 2% of $42,000 AGI (see limitation discussed below)	(840)
Deduction (reported on Schedule A)	$ 160

In summary, Elizabeth reports $3,000 of expenses and the $1,800 reimbursement on Form 2106 and $160 as a miscellaneous itemized deduction on Schedule A. ▼

LIMITATIONS ON ITEMIZED DEDUCTIONS

9 ▼ **LEARNING OBJECTIVE**
Work with the limitations on miscellaneous itemized deductions.

Many itemized deductions, such as medical expenses and charitable contributions, are subject to limitations expressed as a percentage of AGI. These limitations may be expressed as floors or ceilings. These limitations are discussed in Chapter 10.

MISCELLANEOUS ITEMIZED DEDUCTIONS SUBJECT TO THE 2 PERCENT FLOOR

Certain miscellaneous itemized deductions, including most *unreimbursed employee business expenses*, are aggregated and then reduced by 2 percent of AGI.[52] Expenses subject to the 2 percent floor include the following:

- All § 212 expenses, except expenses of producing rent and royalty income (refer to Chapter 6).
- All unreimbursed employee expenses (after the 50 percent reduction, if applicable) except moving.
- Professional dues and subscriptions.
- Union dues and work uniforms.
- Employment-related education expenses.
- Malpractice insurance premiums.
- Expenses of job hunting (including employment agency fees and resumé-writing expenses).
- Home office expenses of an employee or outside salesperson.
- Legal, accounting, and tax return preparation fees.
- Hobby expenses (up to hobby income).
- Investment expenses, including investment counsel fees, subscriptions, and safe deposit box rental.
- Custodial fees relating to income-producing property or an IRA or a Keogh plan.
- Any fees paid to collect interest or dividends.
- Appraisal fees establishing a casualty loss or charitable contribution.

MISCELLANEOUS ITEMIZED DEDUCTIONS NOT SUBJECT TO THE 2 PERCENT FLOOR

Certain miscellaneous itemized deductions, including the following, are not subject to the 2 percent floor:

---

[52]§ 67.

- Impairment-related work expenses of handicapped individuals.
- Gambling losses to the extent of gambling winnings.
- Certain terminated annuity payments.

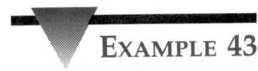

EXAMPLE 43

Ted, who has AGI of $20,000, has the following miscellaneous itemized deductions:

Gambling losses (to extent of gains)	$1,200
Tax return preparation fees	300
Unreimbursed employee transportation	200
Professional dues and subscriptions	260
Safe deposit box rental	30

Ted's itemized deductions are as follows:

Deduction not subject to 2% floor (gambling losses)		$1,200
Deductions subject to 2% floor ($300 + $200 + $260 + $30)	$ 790	
Less 2% of AGI	(400)	390
Total miscellaneous itemized deductions		$1,590

If instead Ted's AGI is $40,000, the floor is $800 (2% of $40,000), and he cannot deduct any expenses subject to the 2% floor. ▼

10 **LEARNING OBJECTIVE**
Develop tax planning ideas related to employee business expenses.

SELF-EMPLOYED INDIVIDUALS

Some taxpayers have the flexibility to be classified as either employees or self-employed individuals. Examples include real estate agents and direct sellers. These taxpayers should carefully consider all factors and not automatically assume that self-employed status is preferable.

It is advantageous to deduct one's business expenses *for* AGI and avoid the 2 percent floor. However, a self-employed individual may have higher expenses, such as local gross receipts taxes, license fees, franchise fees, personal property taxes, and occupation taxes. In addition, the record-keeping and filing requirements can be quite burdensome.

One of the most expensive considerations is the Social Security tax versus the self-employment tax. For an employee in 1998, for example, the Social Security tax applies at a rate of 6.2 percent on a base amount of wages of $68,400, and the Medicare tax applies at a rate of 1.45 percent with no limit on the base amount. For self-employed persons, the rate, but not the base amount, for each tax doubles. Even though a deduction *for* AGI is allowed for one-half of the self-employment tax paid, an employee and a self-employed individual are not in the same tax position on equal amounts of earnings. The self-employment tax is explained in Chapter 13. For the applicability of these taxes to employees, see Chapter 1.

After analyzing all these factors, a taxpayer may decide that employee status is preferable to self-employed status.

SHIFTING DEDUCTIONS BETWEEN EMPLOYER AND EMPLOYEE

An employee can avoid the 2 percent floor for employee business expenses. Typically, an employee incurs travel and entertainment expenses in the course of employment. The employer gets the deduction if it reimburses the employee, and

TAX IN THE NEWS

MOVING EXPENSE REIMBURSEMENT DEPENDS ON WHO YOU ARE

With young hires and lower management transferees, most employers tend to be moderate (or even frugal) in paying for employee moving expenses. In the case of a choice CEO with great potential, however, the amount involved can turn from moderate to lavish.

Consider, for example, the $777,311 PepsiCo, Inc., paid its CEO as a relocation allowance for moving from Texas to New York. Or, the $1.1 million Bankers Trust New York paid to move its CEO to New York from Washington, D.C.

Compensation experts say it is no longer extraordinary for a new CEO's moving costs and temporary housing to exceed $500,000. "When you really want to recruit a great CEO, you're willing to gobble up this kind of expense," concurs a recruiting consultant. Moreover, rich relocation packages are seen as a way to pump up CEO pay without ballooning the highly visible salary and bonus lines in a proxy statement.

SOURCE: Adapted from Lublin and White, "More Companies Relocate CEOs in Style," *Wall Street Journal*, April 7, 1997, pp. B1 and B6.

the employee gets the deduction *for* AGI. An adequate accounting must be made, and excess reimbursements cannot be kept by the employee.

TRANSPORTATION AND TRAVEL EXPENSES

Adequate detailed records of all transportation and travel expenses should be kept. Since the regular mileage allowance is 32.5 cents per mile, a new, expensive automobile used primarily for business may generate a higher expense based on actual cost. The election to expense part of the cost of the automobile under § 179 (although normally not a wise choice), MACRS depreciation, insurance, repairs and maintenance, automobile club dues, and other related costs may result in automobile expenses greater than the automatic mileage allowance.

If a taxpayer wishes to sightsee or vacation on a business trip, it would be beneficial to schedule business on both a Friday and a Monday to turn the weekend into business days for allocation purposes. It is especially crucial to schedule appropriate business days when foreign travel is involved.

MOVING EXPENSES

Persons who retire and move to a new location incur personal nondeductible moving expenses. If the retired person accepts a full-time job in the new location before moving, the moving expenses are deductible.

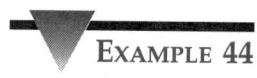

EXAMPLE 44

At the time of his retirement from the national office of a major accounting firm, Gordon had an annual salary of $220,000. He moves from New York City to Seattle to retire. To qualify for the moving expense deduction, Gordon accepts a full-time teaching position at a Seattle junior college at an annual salary of $15,000. If Gordon satisfies the 39-week test, his moving expenses are deductible. The disparity between the two salaries (previous and current) is of no consequence. ▼

EDUCATION EXPENSES

Education expenses are treated as nondeductible personal items unless the individual is employed or is engaged in a trade or business. A temporary leave of absence for further education is one way to reasonably assure that the taxpayer is still qualified, even if a full-time student. An individual was permitted to deduct education expenses even though he resigned from his job, returned to school full-time for two years, and accepted another job in the same field upon graduation. The Court held that the student had merely suspended active participation in his field.[53]

If the time out of the field is too long, educational expense deductions will be disallowed. For example, a teacher who left the field for four years to raise her child and curtailed her employment searches and writing activities was denied a deduction. She was not actively engaged in the trade or business of being an educator.[54]

To secure the deduction, an individual should arrange his or her work situation to preserve employee or business status.

ENTERTAINMENT EXPENSES

Proper documentation of expenditures is essential because of the strict record-keeping requirements and the restrictive tests that must be met. For example, documentation that consists solely of credit card receipts and canceled checks may be inadequate to substantiate the business purpose and business relationship.[55] Taxpayers should maintain detailed records of amounts, time, place, business purpose, and business relationships. A credit card receipt details the place, date, and amount of the expense. A notation made on the receipt of the names of the person(s) attending, the business relationship, and the topic of discussion should constitute proper documentation.

Associated with or goodwill entertainment is not deductible unless a business discussion is conducted immediately before or after the entertainment. Furthermore, a business purpose must exist for the entertainment. Taxpayers should arrange for a business discussion before or after such entertainment. They must provide documentation of the business purpose, such as obtaining new business from a prospective customer.

Unreimbursed meals and entertainment are subject to the 50 percent cutback rule in addition to the 2 percent floor. Consequently, the procedure of negotiating a salary reduction, as discussed below under Unreimbursed Employee Business Expenses, is even more valuable to the taxpayer.

UNREIMBURSED EMPLOYEE BUSINESS EXPENSES

The 2 percent floor for unreimbursed employee business expenses offers a tax planning opportunity for married couples. If one spouse has high miscellaneous expenses subject to the floor, it may be beneficial for the couple to file separate returns. If they file jointly, the 2 percent floor is based on the incomes of both. Filing separately lowers the reduction to 2 percent of only one spouse's income.

Other provisions of the law should be considered, however. For example, filing separately could cost a couple losses of up to $25,000 from self-managed rental units under the passive activity loss rules (discussed in Chapter 11).

---

[53]*Stephen G. Sherman*, 36 TCM 1191, T.C.Memo. 1977–301.

[54]*Brian C. Mulherin*, 42 TCM 834, T.C.Memo. 1981–454; *George A. Baist*, 56 TCM 778, T.C.Memo. 1988–554.

[55]*Kenneth W. Guenther*, 54 TCM 382, T.C.Memo. 1987–440.

Another possibility is to negotiate a salary reduction with one's employer in exchange for the 100 percent reimbursement of employee expenses. The employee is better off because the 2 percent floor does not apply. The employer is better off because certain expense reimbursements are not subject to Social Security and other payroll taxes.

KEY TERMS

Accountable plan, 9–22

Automatic mileage method, 9–6

Education expenses, 9–13

Entertainment expenses, 9–15

Independent contractor, 9–2

Moving expenses, 9–11

Nonaccountable plan, 9–24

Office in the home expenses, 9–19

Statutory employees, 9–4

Transportation expenses, 9–5

Travel expenses, 9–7

PROBLEM MATERIALS

DISCUSSION QUESTIONS

1. Why might a business prefer to classify a worker as an independent contractor (i.e., self-employed) rather than as an employee?

2. What difference does it make if an individual's expenses are classified as employment-related expenses or as expenses from self-employment?

3. Can a person be both employed and self-employed during the same year? Explain.

4. Joanne is a well-known freelance columnist who works at home. Most of her income comes from this source, but she also receives some income from speaking engagements (both local and out-of-town). Also, she teaches a class in creative writing at a local university. Suggest some of the deductible work-related expenses Joanne might have.

5. Byron is a salesperson with a rather extensive sales territory. He just purchased a new car that will be used in his job. He plans to use the actual operating cost method for the first few years and then switch to the automatic mileage method. What are some of the hurdles Byron may face in carrying out these plans?

6. Distinguish between transportation expenses and travel expenses.

7. Hollis is a key player for the Miami Sharks. During the football season, Hollis lives in a rented apartment near Shark Stadium. For the rest of the year, he stays with his parents in Springfield, Missouri. In the off-season, Hollis is a public relations vice president of a Springfield bank. Presuming no reimbursement, discuss the employment-related expenses Hollis should be able to deduct.

8. Jim works in St. Louis. On Tuesday morning he flies to San Francisco for a business meeting. After the meeting, Jim has lunch by himself and then flies back to St. Louis that same evening. Is the cost of Jim's lunch deductible? Why or why not?

9. Refer to the facts set forth in Example 12 (page 9–8 of the text). What are some of the things Bill might do to avoid the potential tax disaster he faces?

10. Dr. Fuerst, a practicing orthodontist in Buffalo, travels to New York City to attend a two-day convention on experimental orthodontia procedures. Mr. Fuerst accompanies his wife since he prepares their tax return and knows how to properly prepare the required substantiation for the trip. Comment on the deductibility of the trip.

11. Under what circumstances, if any, can travel expenses qualify for the education deduction?

12. Josephine took a combined business and pleasure trip to Europe. She traveled to London from New York on Friday, vacationed on Saturday and Sunday, conducted business on Monday, got snowed in at the airport on Tuesday, traveled to Paris on Wednesday, relaxed on Thursday (a legal holiday), conducted business on Friday, went sightseeing on Saturday and Sunday, picked up business samples and papers on Monday, and flew back to New York on Tuesday. What portion of her airfare can she deduct?

13. Zane is an air-traffic director for Los Angeles International Airport. Since his daily commuting distance of 120 miles (60 miles each way) is exhausting, he sells his residence and moves to Santa Monica. The new home requires a commute of only 6 miles. Are Zane's moving expenses deductible? Why or why not?

14. During 1997, Kelsey incurs qualified moving expenses in changing jobs. By April 1998 when Kelsey files her 1997 income tax return, she has not yet satisfied the 39-week time test.
    a. What are Kelsey's options regarding the handling of the moving expenses?
    b. Suppose Kelsey never meets the time test. Can the moving expenses still be deductible? Explain.

15. What difference does it make whether a taxpayer is improving existing skills or acquiring new ones for the purpose of the education deduction? On what general tax principle is the justification for this rule based?

16. Nancy, a self-employed tax accountant, enrolls in the evening program of a local law school. Although she has no intention of practicing as an attorney, Nancy feels that a legal education would improve the quality of her present work. Comment on the deductibility of Nancy's law school expenses.

17. In each of the following situations, indicate whether there is a cutback adjustment and, if so, to whom it applies (i.e., employer or employee).
    a. The employer expects certain employees to entertain their key customers. The employer does not reimburse the employees for these costs.
    b. Same as (a) except that the employees are reimbursed for these costs.
    c. Each year the employer awards its top salesperson an expense-paid trip to the Cayman Islands.
    d. The employer has a cafeteria for its employees where meals are furnished at cost.
    e. The employer sponsors an annual Fourth of July picnic for its employees.
    f. Every Christmas, the employer gives each employee a turkey.

18. What was the original justification for the cutback adjustment? Has its application been particularly detrimental to certain types of taxpayers? Explain.

19. Discuss the requirements for the deductibility of business meals.

20. Currently, which club dues are deductible? Not deductible?

21. Sandra pays annual dues to belong to the Wichita Country Club. In addition to social and leisure activities, she also utilizes the facilities for business lunches. Presuming adequate substantiation, are any of Sandra's expenses involving the club deductible? Explain.

22. Gull Corporation has purchased several skyboxes at the Superdome for the home games of the New Orleans Saints. It plans to use these facilities to entertain key customers. Discuss the tax treatment of the costs that will be incurred.

23. To what extent may a taxpayer take a deduction for business gifts to a business associate? To an employee? To a superior?

24. Lieutenant Hebert is on active duty with the U.S. Army. To what extent, if any, is the cost of her uniforms deductible?

25. Trent, a resident of Florida, attends Vanderbilt University. After graduation, he moves to New Orleans where he begins a job search. Shortly thereafter, he accepts

a position with a local radio station as an announcer. Trent's college degree is in management. Presuming no reimbursement, what employment-related expenses might Trent be eligible to deduct?

26. What constitutes an adequate accounting to an employer?

27. What tax return reporting procedures must be followed by an employee under the following circumstances?
    a. Expenses and reimbursements are equal under an accountable plan.
    b. Reimbursements at the appropriate Federal per diem rate exceed expenses, and an adequate accounting is made to the employer.
    c. Expenses exceed reimbursements under a nonaccountable plan.

28. Kim has just graduated from college and is interviewing for a position in marketing. Crane Corporation has offered her a job as a sales representative that will require extensive travel and entertainment but provide valuable experience. Under the offer, she has two options: a salary of $48,000 and she absorbs all expenses; a salary of $35,000 and Crane reimburses for all expenses. Crane assures Kim that the $13,000 difference in the two options will be adequate to cover the expenses incurred. What issues should have an impact on Kim's choice?

29. Jeff has been practicing as a physician in Boston. Shortly, he plans to sell his practice to his partners and retire in Taos, New Mexico. Besides the sale of his practice, what should be some of Jeff's concerns?

30. Martha is an associate with a law firm in New York City. Although she already has a J.D. degree, she feels a master of laws from New York University would improve her promotion potential. She can earn the degree on a part-time basis, but Martha is inclined to shorten her career interruption as much as possible. What should be some of Martha's concerns?

PROBLEMS

31. To support his family, Horace holds two jobs during 1998. The relevant distances are as follows:

	Miles
Residence to main job	40
Main job to second job	30
Second job to residence	45

During the 260 days he worked, Horace drove the family car from his residence to the main job. After eight hours, Horace then drove to the second job and worked for four hours. On his way back to the residence, he stopped for dinner. He paid $390 for parking at the second job and $1,100 for dinners. What, if any, is Horace's deduction for the year?

32. Alec has two jobs in 1998. He drives 40 miles to his first job. The distance from the first job to the second is 32 miles. During 1998, Alec worked 200 days at both jobs. On 150 days, he drove from the first job to the second job. On the remaining 50 days, he drove home (40 miles) and then to the second job (42 miles). Presuming the automatic mileage method is used, how much qualifies as a deduction?

33. In 1995, Heidi bought a new automobile for $32,000. The car is used 80% for business. *Total* miles driven are as follows: 11,000 in 1995, 18,000 in 1996, 12,000 in 1997, and 14,000 in 1998. If Heidi uses the automatic mileage method, what is her basis in the car as of January 1, 1999?

34. Louis took a business trip from Chicago to Seattle. He spent two days in travel, conducted business for eight days, and visited friends for five days. He incurred the following expenses:

Airfare	$ 950
Lodging	2,400
Meals	1,200
Entertainment of clients	800

Louis received no reimbursements. What amount can he deduct?

35. Macy is in charge of sales for the Georgia region of a national insurance company and is home-based in Atlanta. The untimely death of the Alabama sales director has created serious transitional problems for Macy's employer. Consequently, Macy spends several consecutive months handling the Alabama business. During this period, Macy flies to Birmingham on Sunday night and returns home to Atlanta on Friday evening. The cost of spending the weekend in Birmingham would have been $310, while the cost of coming home is $320.

    a. Presuming no reimbursement, how much, if any, may Macy deduct for the week-end trips?

    b. Would the answer to part (a) change if the cost of coming home is $200 (not $320)?

36. Chad is a self-employed computer consultant. During the year, he attended a two-day conference on the latest developments in computer technology. His expenses for the conference are as follows:

Airfare	$420
Hotel room	330
Meals	160
Registration fee and course materials	280

How much may Chad deduct for the conference? How is the deduction classified?

37. Odette is a professor of European history at a major midwestern university. In connection with a research paper she is to present at a history symposium, Odette travels to Vienna. While there, she examines archives dealing with the Hapsburg dynasty. During her three-week stay, she goes sightseeing only during nonbusiness hours (e.g., weekends and evenings). Odette's expenses, all carefully documented, are as follows:

Airfare	$1,400
Meals	1,800
Lodging	3,200
Transportation (taxis, airport limos)	210

Presuming no reimbursement, how much, if any, may Odette deduct for the trip?

38. Monica travels from her office in Boston to Lisbon, Portugal, on business. Her absence of 13 days was spent as follows:

Thursday	Depart for and arrive at Lisbon
Friday	Business transacted
Saturday and Sunday	Vacationing
Monday through Friday	Business transacted
Saturday and Sunday	Vacationing
Monday	Business transacted
Tuesday	Depart Lisbon and return to office in Boston

    a. For tax purposes, how many days has Monica spent on business?

    b. What difference does it make?

    c. Could Monica have spent more time than she did vacationing on the trip without loss of existing tax benefits? Explain.

39. Cole is both a CPA and an attorney. For several years, he has practiced law as an employee of a large law firm in Dallas. In 1998, Cole decides to quit his job and move to El Paso, Texas. Four months after arriving in El Paso, Cole establishes a private practice as a CPA. Expenses in moving from Dallas to El Paso are as follows:

Cost of moving household effects	$5,100
Meals	120
Lodging	240

Mileage on two personal autos involved in the move is 1,400.
a. How much, if any, can be deducted?
b. How is the deduction, if any, classified?

40. To satisfy a newly imposed school board requirement, Troy spends part of the summer at a college pursuing a master of education degree. Troy, a high school math teacher, spent the following amounts:

Books and tuition	$2,600
Lodging while in travel status	1,800
Meals while in travel status	1,200
Laundry while in travel status	250
Transportation	600

Much to Troy's surprise, after the summer he is promoted to be associate principal of his school.
a. How much of these amounts may Troy deduct?
b. How is the deduction classified?

41. After graduating from college with a degree in general business, Shari accepted employment with a bank. Currently, she works in the bank's loan department. During the year, Shari enrolled in an evening MBA program at a local university. In this connection, her expenses are as follows:

Books and tuition	$2,300
Transportation	180
Meals (before or after classes)	310

Shari also takes a correspondence course (cost of $190) entitled "How to Generate Customer Confidence."

Presuming no reimbursement, what amount of these expenses may Shari deduct?

42. Dudley is a self-employed landscape architect. Since the business is quite competitive, Dudley is compelled to entertain extensively. During 1998, he incurred expenses for business meals as follows:

Taxi fares	$ 380
Meals	4,100
Tips	720
Cover charges	600

Presuming adequate substantiation, what is Dudley's deduction?

43. Swan Corporation spends $25,000 to purchase a 15-seat skybox for eight professional football games. Regular seats at these games normally sell for $40 each. At one game, an employee of Swan entertained 10 clients; Swan furnished food and beverages for the event at a cost of $242. The game was preceded by a bona fide business discussion, and all expenses are adequately substantiated.

a. How much may Swan Corporation deduct for this event?

b. Would the answer change if the employee took 14 clients (rather than 10) to the game, and all seats were occupied? Explain.

44. During the current year, Kevin, the assistant manager of a truck leasing firm, made gifts that cost the following amounts:

To Darlene (Kevin's secretary) for Christmas ($2 was for gift wrapping)	$32
To George (Kevin's boss) on his birthday	31
To Susan (a key client) for Christmas	20
To John (a key client) for Christmas	28

Kevin also gave Darlene a box of candy (cost of $18) on her birthday. Presuming Kevin has adequate substantiation and is not reimbursed, how much can he deduct?

45. Ruth is a professor who consults on the side. She uses one-fifth of her home exclusively for her consulting business, and clients regularly meet her there. Ruth is single and under age 65. Her AGI (before considering consulting income) is $50,000. Other relevant data follow:

Income from consulting business	$5,000
Consulting expenses other than home office	2,400
Total costs relating to home	
Interest and taxes	6,000
Utilities	2,000
Maintenance and repairs	600
Depreciation (business part only)	1,500

Calculate Ruth's AGI for 1998.

46. Paige incurred the following expenses related to her employment as a chief executive officer:

Lodging while away from home	$2,800
Meals while away from home	1,200
Entertainment while away from home	2,000
Dues, subscriptions, and books	1,000
Transportation expenses	4,000

Her AGI was $100,000, and she received $6,600 under her employer's accountable plan. What are Paige's deductions *for* and *from* AGI?

47. Kenneth received $4,400 in reimbursements under an accountable plan after he had made an adequate accounting to his employer. His expenses were as follows:

Transportation expenses	$3,200
Meals	1,400
Lodging and incidentals	2,300
Dues and subscriptions	100
Entertainment	1,000

How much can Kenneth deduct *for* and *from* AGI? Assume he had AGI of $50,000 and no other miscellaneous itemized deductions.

48. Thelma, who is age 42 and single, earned a salary of $60,000. She had other income consisting of interest of $2,000, dividends of $1,600, and long-term capital gains of $4,000. Thelma incurred the following expenses during the year:

Transportation	$2,300
Meals	1,600
Dues and subscriptions	800
Entertainment of clients	300
Total	$5,000

Thelma received reimbursements of $3,000 under an accountable plan. Calculate her AGI and itemized employee business expenses.

49. Kyle and Sharon are married, have no dependents, and are full-time employees. Both work for employers who do not reimburse for job-related costs but expect the employee to absorb the expenses. Kyle and Sharon's expenses for 1998 are as follows:

Kyle's union dues	$ 610
Kyle's safety items (e.g., work shoes, glasses, gloves)	340
Kyle's lab clothing	405
Laundry of Kyle's lab clothing	120
Sharon's business lunches with clients	1,340
Sharon's professional dues and journals	610
Sharon's taxi fares to and from work (when personal car was being repaired)	160
Other itemized deductions (e.g., interest on home mortgage, property taxes, charitable contributions)	10,200

If Kyle and Sharon file a joint return and have AGI of $72,000, what is their taxable income?

CUMULATIVE PROBLEMS

50. Debra Bond, age 42 and single, is the personnel manager of the northwest regional office of Olympia Insurance Company. Her Social Security number is 432–60–1000. Debra lives in her own home at 524 Wilcrest Drive, Seattle, WA 98122. Lisa Wall, Debra's 20-year-old niece, lives with her and is a full-time student at a local college. Except for a $3,600 nontaxable scholarship Lisa receives for tuition, Debra provides all of her niece's support. Lisa's Social Security number is 444–11–5555.

Olympia Insurance Company does not reimburse its employees for employment-related expenses. Instead, it estimates the expected expenses of each class of employees and sets their base salary accordingly. During 1998, Debra had the following employment-related expenses:

- Mileage of 5,350 on personal auto (includes 2,200 miles for commuting and 900 for other personal use). Parking and toll charges (not related to commuting or other personal use) are $190.

- Business lunches for potential hires are $1,424. Taxi fares of $132 are not included in this amount.

- Debra attended a three-day seminar on improving managerial skills by using a team approach. The sessions were held at a convention center in Portland, Oregon. Debra's expenses are summarized below.

Transportation	$210
Registration	750
Meals	290
Hotel	375

- Dues to professional organizations of $205 and subscriptions to professional journals of $310.

In 1998, Debra earned wages of $61,200 (not including any bonus). Usually, Olympia Insurance Company follows a policy of issuing a bonus to its employees. The bonus for any one year is determined and paid in January of the following year. Debra's bonus for 1997 (received in January 1998) was $5,900, while her bonus for 1998 (received in January 1999) was $6,100. Debra's employer withheld Federal income taxes of $10,000 and the appropriate amount of FICA.

In 1998, Debra had a certificate of deposit with Bank of the Northwest that earned $1,400 in interest, and she received cash dividends of $1,150 from Mauve, Inc. stock she owns. She also received a check for $120 from Silver Insurance Company as an adjustment on the homeowners insurance premium she paid in 1997. The carrier had mistakenly overcharged Debra by $120.

Expenditures incurred by Debra in 1998 include the following:

Interest on home mortgage	$6,900
Property taxes on personal residence	2,600
Charitable contributions	1,450
Political contribution to reelect representative to Congress	200

Compute Debra's Federal income tax payable or refund due for 1998. Suggested software (if available): *TurboTax*.

51. George M. and Martha J. Jordan have no dependents and are both under age 65. George is a statutory employee of Consolidated Jobbers (business code is 2634), and his Social Security number is 582–99–4444. Martha is an executive with General Corporation, and her Social Security number is 241–88–6642. The Jordans live at 321 Oak Street, Lincoln, NV 89553. They both want to contribute to the Presidential Election Campaign Fund.

In 1997, George earned $49,000 in commissions. His employer withholds FICA but not Federal income taxes. George paid $10,000 in estimated taxes. Martha earned $62,000, from which $8,500 was withheld for Federal income taxes and the appropriate amount was withheld for FICA taxes. Neither George nor Martha received any expense reimbursements.

George uses his two-year-old car (purchased on January 3, 1995) on sales calls and keeps a log of all miles driven. In 1997, he drove 36,000 miles, 24,554 of them for business. He made several out-of-state sales trips, incurring transportation costs of $1,600, meals of $800, and lodging costs of $750. During the year, he also spent $1,400 taking customers to lunch.

Martha incurred the following expenses related to her work: taxi fares of $125, business lunches of $615, and a yearly commuter train ticket of $800. During the year, Martha received $1,200 in interest from the employees' credit union, $100,000 life insurance proceeds upon the death of her mother in December, and $500 in dividends from General Motors. She contributed $2,000 to her Individual Retirement Account. Neither George nor Martha is covered by an employee retirement plan. Martha gave a gift valued at $500 to the president of her firm upon his promotion to that position.

The Jordans had additional expenditures as follows:

Charitable contributions (cash)	$1,200
Medical and dental expenses	1,400
Real property taxes	1,200
Home mortgage interest	9,381
Tax return preparation fee	150

Part 1—Tax Computation
Compute the Jordans' Federal income tax payable or refund due, assuming they file a joint income tax return, for 1997. If they have overpaid, they want the amount refunded. You will need Form 1040, and Schedules A, B, and C. Suggested software (if available): *TurboTax*.

Part 2—Tax Planning

Martha and George ask your help in deciding what to do with the $100,000 of life insurance proceeds Martha received in 1997. They are considering two conservative investment alternatives:

- Invest in 8% long-term U.S. bonds.

- Invest in 6.5% municipal bonds.

a. Calculate the best alternative for next year. Assume that Martha and George will have the same income and deductions in 1998, except for the income from the investment they choose. In computing the tax, use the tax rate schedules for 1998.
b. What other factors should the Jordans take into account?
c. Write a memo to the Jordans, explaining their alternatives.

Suggested software (if available): *TurboTax.*

RESEARCH PROBLEMS

*Note: Use the **RIA OnPoint System 4 Student Version** CD-ROM, which is available to accompany this text, in preparing solutions to the Research Problems. Alternatively, tax research materials found in a standard tax library can be used.*

Research Problem 1.   Richard Harding is the sheriff of Howard County, Indiana. In addition to the usual law enforcement duties, the sheriff has the responsibility of maintaining the detention facility (i.e., county jail). Further, he must furnish meals for all prisoners in accordance with certain nutritional standards prescribed by the state. Although the sheriff must absorb the cost of the meals, the county provides a personal allowance.

During 1995, Sheriff Harding received a salary of $35,000 (as reported on a Form W–2 issued by Howard County). He spent $90,000 on prisoner meals and received meal allowances of $110,000. On his 1995 income tax return, he reported the salary as employee income, but listed the allowances and meals on a Schedule C. Thus, he treated himself as self-employed by claiming the cost of the meals as a deduction *for* AGI.

Upon audit, the IRS determined that the Schedule C treatment was improper. Harding was not in a separate trade or business of providing meals, but was merely carrying out his employment-related duties. The costs of the meals are employee business expenses deductible only as miscellaneous itemized deductions on Schedule A. As such, they are subject to the 2%-of-AGI floor.

Is Sheriff Harding or the IRS correct? Why?

Partial list of research aids:
Reg. § 1.61–3(a).
Max Sobel Wholesale Liquors, 69 T.C. 477 (1977).
John D. Beatty, 106 T.C. 268 (1996).

Research Problem 2.   Tom Roberts, a chemical engineer, is a long-time employee of Teal Chemical Corporation. Tom's specialty is the design and construction of special-purpose chemical processing plants. Teal has decided to expand its presence in France and plans to transfer Tom to Paris on a three-year assignment. The planned foreign assignment will take Tom to age 65, Teal's normal retirement age.

Tom has been advised regarding the major income tax ramifications of working abroad. He has not, however, been told about the treatment of moving expenses. Since Teal Corporation pays its employees a substantial foreign service salary increment, it does not reimburse for moving expenses. In connection with the move, Tom plans to sell his residence and place most of his furniture in storage. Probabilities are good that the sale of the residence will result in a loss.

a. Write a letter to Tom regarding the income tax treatment of his moving expenses. Tom's address is 1389 Wilson Drive, Trent, NJ 08102. Be sure to include in the discussion the move from France back to the United States.
b. Prepare a memo for your firm's client files.

Research Problem 3. Rick Beam has been an independent sales representative for various textile manufacturers for many years. His products consist of soft goods, such as tablecloths, curtains, and drapes. Rick's customers are clothing store chains, department stores, and smaller specialty stores. The employees of these companies who are responsible for purchasing merchandise are known as buyers. These companies generally prohibit their buyers from accepting gifts from manufacturers' sales representatives.

Each year Rick gives cash gifts (never more than $25) to most of the buyers who are his customers. Generally, he cashes a large check in November and gives the money personally to the buyers around Christmas. Rick says, "This is one of the ways that I maintain my relationship with my buyers." He maintains adequate substantiation of all the gifts.

Rick's deductions for these gifts have been disallowed by the IRS, based on Code § 162(c)(2). Rick is confused and comes to you, a CPA, for advice.

a. Write a letter to Rick concerning his tax position on this issue. Rick's address is 948 Octavia Street, New Orleans, LA 70113.

b. Prepare a memo for your files supporting the advice you have given.

Research Problem 4. Lyle has been a schoolteacher since he earned his bachelor of education degree 10 years ago. In 1996, the governing board of his school district passed a resolution requiring all teachers to begin pursuing an advanced degree in education. Because of this new requirement, Lyle spent the summer of 1997 taking graduate courses in education at a major university. For the summer activity, Lyle *estimates* his expenses to be:

Books	$ 220
Tuition	3,200
Room and board	1,800
Transportation	1,500

Lyle kept no receipts and made no record of these expenses. When he files his income tax return for 1997, Lyle claims all of these expenses on Schedule C of Form 1040. In the event Lyle is audited by the IRS, comment on his vulnerability.

Partial list of research aids:
§§ 274(d), 6001, and 6662(b)(1).
Cohan v. Comm., 2 USTC ¶489, 8 AFTR 10552, 39 F.2d 540 (CA–2, 1930).
William F. Sanford, 50 T.C. 823 (1968).

Use the tax resources of the Internet to address the following questions. Do not restrict your search to the World Wide Web, but include a review of newsgroups and general reference materials, practitioner sites and resources, primary sources of the tax law, chat rooms and discussion groups, and other opportunities.

Research Problem 5. In the last few years, the IRS has been diligent in applying existing rules to classify self-employed individuals as employees of those who engage their services. What are the current criteria that the IRS utilizes in resolving the employee versus independent contractor issue? Were any changes in these criteria proposed during the formulation of TRA of 1997? In this regard, what eventually happened?

Research Problem 6. Find a newsgroup frequented by individuals who are likely to perform some work in a home office. Post a message to the newsgroup informing its members of a recent judicial or administrative development in applying the rules of § 280A.

Research Problem 7. Determine whether your city qualifies for the "high-cost" travel per diem allowances provided by the IRS.

TEAM PROJECT: ARTHUR ANDERSEN TAX CHALLENGE CASES

For more information on the Arthur Andersen Tax Challenge Cases, refer to Chapter 1, page 1–37.

Information related to tax issues and problems that are discussed in this chapter may be found in the

Day and Ball case on pages 1, 18, and 21
Fence case on pages 39, 41, 57, and 59

Read and analyze the case you have been assigned and *identify* any issues and problems that are related to material covered in this chapter. If the information provided in the case is complete, prepare answers for this part of the case at this time. If you need information that is contained in the later parts of the case, write a memo summarizing the questions or problems so you can prepare a complete answer at a later date.

DEDUCTIONS AND LOSSES: CERTAIN ITEMIZED DEDUCTIONS

LEARNING OBJECTIVES

After completing Chapter 10, you should be able to:

1. Distinguish between deductible and nondeductible personal expenses.

2. Define medical expenses and compute the medical expense deduction.

3. Contrast deductible taxes and nondeductible fees, licenses, etc.

4. Understand the Federal tax treatment of state and local income taxes.

5. Distinguish between deductible and nondeductible interest and apply the appropriate limitations to deductible interest.

6. Understand charitable contributions and their related measurement problems and percentage limitations.

7. List the business and personal expenditures that are deductible either as miscellaneous itemized deductions or as other itemized deductions.

8. Recognize the limitation on certain itemized deductions applicable to high-income taxpayers.

9. Identify tax planning procedures that can maximize the benefit of itemized deductions.

GENERAL CLASSIFICATION OF EXPENSES

1 LEARNING OBJECTIVE
Distinguish between deductible and nondeductible personal expenses.

As a general rule, the deduction of personal expenditures is disallowed by § 262 of the Code. However, Congress has chosen to allow certain personal expenditures to be deducted as itemized deductions. Personal expenditures that are deductible as itemized deductions include medical expenses, certain taxes, mortgage interest, investment interest, and charitable contributions. These expenditures and other personal expenditures that are allowed as itemized deductions are covered in this chapter. Any personal expenditures not specifically allowed as itemized deductions by the tax law are nondeductible.

Allowable itemized deductions are deductible *from* AGI in arriving at taxable income if the taxpayer elects to itemize. The election to itemize is appropriate when total itemized deductions exceed the standard deduction based on the taxpayer's filing status (refer to Chapter 3).[1]

MEDICAL EXPENSES

GENERAL REQUIREMENTS

2 LEARNING OBJECTIVE
Define medical expenses and compute the medical expense deduction.

Medical expenses paid for the care of the taxpayer, spouse, and dependents are allowed as an itemized deduction to the extent the expenses are not reimbursed. The **medical expense** deduction is limited to the amount by which such expenses *exceed* 7.5 percent of the taxpayer's AGI.

---

[1]The total standard deduction is the sum of the basic standard deduction and the additional standard deduction (refer to Chapter 3).

Chapter 3 also describes the situations in which a taxpayer is not eligible for the standard deduction.

TAX IN THE NEWS

AVERAGE ITEMIZED DEDUCTIONS

Are your itemized deductions close to average for your income level? Actually, if you're a typical taxpayer, you take the standard deduction instead of itemizing. Approximately 70 percent of individual taxpayers take the standard deduction each year.

The IRS recently released statistics on the approximately 30 percent of individual taxpayers who did itemize in 1995—a year that saw itemized deductions rise nearly 10 percent over 1994. Statistics for the most popular deductions are listed in the following table. The table omits medical expenses because few taxpayers (approximately 5 percent) have medical expenses in excess of the 7.5 percent floor. Similarly, casualty losses (subject to a 10 percent floor) and miscellaneous itemized deductions (subject to a 2 percent floor) are omitted. For comparison, the standard deduction in 1995 was $3,900 for single taxpayers, $6,550 for married taxpayers filing jointly, and $5,750 for heads of household.

AGI	Taxes	Contributions	Interest	Total
$ 15,000–29,999	$ 2,270	$ 1,338	$ 5,442	$ 9,050
30,000–49,999	3,112	1,465	5,715	10,292
50,000–74,999	4,429	1,768	6,587	12,784
75,000–99,999	6,171	2,286	8,063	16,520
100,000–199,999	9,758	3,433	11,107	24,298
200,000+	36,076	16,882	25,046	78,004

These statistics reveal some interesting aspects of the U.S. lifestyle. For one thing, taxpayers at all income levels—even those with AGI of more than $200,000—owe money. For another, as AGI increases, the percentage given to charity decreases. Those with AGI of $15,000 to $29,999 contribute 5.88 percent of their median income; least generous are taxpayers with AGI of $100,000 to $199,999, who contribute only 2.29 percent of their median income.

Finally, consider what taxpayers have left after meeting the expenses reflected in the table. A single taxpayer with income of $22,500, for example, would have only $13,450 left after paying typical itemized deductions for that income level ($22,500 – $9,050 itemized deductions). After paying $1,646 of this amount as Federal income taxes, the taxpayer would have $11,804 left for other expenses.

SOURCE: Information from "Tax Report: Itemized Deductions Surged on 1995 Returns," *Wall Street Journal*, July 16, 1997, p. A1.

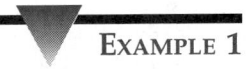

EXAMPLE 1

During the year, Iris had medical expenses of $4,800, of which $1,000 was reimbursed by her insurance company. If her AGI for the year is $40,000, the itemized deduction for medical expenses is limited to $800 [$4,800 – $1,000 = $3,800 – (7.5% × $40,000)]. ▼

MEDICAL EXPENSES DEFINED

The term *medical care* includes expenditures incurred for the "diagnosis, cure, mitigation, treatment, or prevention of disease, or for the purpose of affecting any

▼ **EXHIBIT 10–1**
Examples of Deductible and
Nondeductible Medical
Expenses

Deductible	Nondeductible
Medical (including dental, mental, and hospital) care	Funeral, burial, or cremation expenses
Prescription drugs	Nonprescription drugs (except insulin)
Special equipment	Bottled water
Wheelchairs	Toiletries, cosmetics
Crutches	Diaper service, maternity clothes
Artificial limbs	Programs for the *general* improvement of health
Eyeglasses (including contact lenses)	Weight reduction
Hearing aids	Health spas
Transportation for medical care	Stop-smoking clinic
Medical and hospital insurance premiums	Social activities (e.g., dancing and swimming lessons)
Cost of alcohol and drug rehabilitation	Unnecessary cosmetic surgery

structure or function of the body."[2] A *partial* list of deductible and nondeductible medical items appears in Exhibit 10–1.

A medical expense does not have to relate to a particular ailment to be deductible. Since the definition of medical care is broad enough to cover preventive measures, the cost of periodic physical and dental exams qualifies even for a taxpayer in good health.

Amounts paid for unnecessary *cosmetic surgery* are not deductible medical expenses. However, if cosmetic surgery is deemed necessary, it is deductible as a medical expense. Cosmetic surgery is necessary when it ameliorates (1) a deformity arising from a congenital abnormality, (2) a personal injury, or (3) a disfiguring disease.

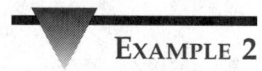

EXAMPLE 2   Art, a calendar year taxpayer, paid $11,000 to a plastic surgeon for a face lift. Art, age 75, merely wanted to improve his appearance. The $11,000 does not qualify as a medical expense since the surgery was unnecessary. ▼

EXAMPLE 3   As a result of a serious automobile accident, Marge's face is disfigured. The cost of restorative cosmetic surgery is deductible as a medical expense. ▼

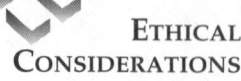

ETHICAL
CONSIDERATIONS

Necessary or Unnecessary Cosmetic Surgery?

Steven, age 37, had his nose broken in a high school football game 20 years ago. As a result, his nose is slightly crooked. In addition, he thinks his nose is too long. In March, he scheduled an appointment with Dr. Keane to discuss surgery to improve his appearance, primarily to shorten his nose. Dr. Keane presented him with computer simulations showing several different possibilities for the size and shape of his nose. Steven selected a nose that was much shorter and completely straight.

_____

[2]§ 213(d)(1)(A).

Steven called his CPA to ask if the cost of the surgery would be deductible. His CPA told him that unnecessary cosmetic surgery is not deductible, but hinted that most doctors can come up with a medical reason that would make such surgery deductible.

Steven discussed the tax issue with Dr. Keane on his next visit, and the doctor indicated that the surgery would be necessary to repair Steven's deviated septum, which was caused by his football injury. Dr. Keane said that he would be willing to write a letter for Steven's files, stating that the surgery was medically necessary. Is Steven justified in taking a deduction for the cosmetic surgery?

The cost of care in a *nursing home or home for the aged*, including meals and lodging, can be included in deductible medical expenses if the primary reason for being in the home is to get medical care. If the primary reason for being there is personal, any costs for medical or nursing care can be included in deductible medical expenses, but the cost of meals and lodging must be excluded.[3]

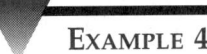

EXAMPLE 4

Norman has a chronic heart ailment. His family decides to place Norman in a nursing home equipped to provide medical and nursing care facilities. Total nursing home expenses amount to $15,000 per year. Of this amount, $4,500 is directly attributable to medical and nursing care. Since Norman is in need of significant medical and nursing care and is placed in the facility primarily for this purpose, all $15,000 of the nursing home costs are deductible (subject to the 7.5% floor). ▼

Tuition expenses of a dependent at a special school may be deductible as a medical expense. The cost of medical care can include the expenses of a special school for a mentally or physically handicapped individual. The deduction is allowed if a principal reason for sending the individual to the school is the school's special resources for alleviating the infirmities. In this case, the cost of meals and lodging, in addition to the tuition, is a proper medical expense deduction.[4]

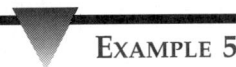

EXAMPLE 5

Jason's daughter Marcia attended public school through the seventh grade. Because Marcia was a poor student, she was examined by a psychiatrist who diagnosed an organic problem that created a learning disability. Upon the recommendation of the psychiatrist, Marcia is enrolled in a private school so that she can receive individual attention. The school has no special program for students with learning disabilities and does not provide special medical treatment. The expense related to Marcia's attendance is not deductible as a medical expense. The cost of any psychiatric care, however, qualifies as a medical expense. ▼

Example 5 shows that the recommendation of a physician does not automatically make the expenditure deductible.

CAPITAL EXPENDITURES FOR MEDICAL PURPOSES

Some examples of *capital expenditures* for medical purposes are swimming pools if the taxpayer does not have access to a neighborhood pool and air conditioners if they do not become permanent improvements (e.g., window units).[5] Other examples

---

[3]Reg. § 1.213–1(e)(1)(v).
[4]*Donald R. Pfeifer*, 37 TCM 816, T.C.Memo. 1978–189. Also see Rev.Rul. 78–340, 1978–2 C.B. 124.

[5]Rev.Rul. 55–261, 1955–1 C.B. 307, modified by Rev.Rul. 68–212, 1968–1 C.B. 91.

include dust elimination systems,[6] elevators,[7] and a room built to house an iron lung. These expenditures are medical in nature if they are incurred as a medical necessity upon the advice of a physician, the facility is used primarily by the patient alone, and the expense is reasonable.

Capital expenditures normally are adjustments to basis and are not deductible. However, both a capital expenditure for a permanent improvement and expenditures made for the operation or maintenance of the improvement may qualify as medical expenses. If a capital expenditure qualifies as a medical expense, the allowable cost is deductible in the year incurred. Although depreciation is required for most other capital expenditures, it is not required for capital expenditures for medical purposes.

A capital improvement that ordinarily would not have a medical purpose qualifies as a medical expense if it is directly related to prescribed medical care and is deductible to the extent that the expenditure *exceeds* the increase in value of the related property. Appraisal costs related to capital improvements are also deductible, but not as medical expenses. These costs are expenses incurred in the determination of the taxpayer's tax liability.[8]

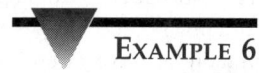

EXAMPLE 6

Fred is afflicted with heart disease. His physician advises him to install an elevator in his residence so he will not be required to climb the stairs. The cost of installing the elevator is $3,000, and the increase in the value of the residence is determined to be only $1,700. Therefore, $1,300 ($3,000 − $1,700) is deductible as a medical expense. Additional utility costs to operate the elevator and maintenance costs are deductible as medical expenses as long as the medical reason for the capital expenditure continues to exist. ▼

The full cost of certain home-related capital expenditures incurred to enable a *physically handicapped* individual to live independently and productively qualifies as a medical expense. Qualifying costs include expenditures for constructing entrance and exit ramps to the residence, widening hallways and doorways to accommodate wheelchairs, installing support bars and railings in bathrooms and other rooms, and adjusting electrical outlets and fixtures.[9] These expenditures are subject to the 7.5 percent floor only, and the increase in the home's value is deemed to be zero.

MEDICAL EXPENSES INCURRED FOR SPOUSE AND DEPENDENTS

In computing the medical expense deduction, a taxpayer may include medical expenses for a spouse and for a person who was a dependent at the time the expenses were paid or incurred. Of the five requirements that normally apply in determining dependency status,[10] neither the gross income nor the joint return test applies in determining dependency status for medical expense deduction purposes.

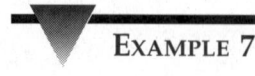

EXAMPLE 7

Ernie (age 22) is married and a full-time student at a university. During the year, Ernie incurred medical expenses that were paid by Matilda (Ernie's mother). She provided more than half of Ernie's support for the year. Even if Ernie files a joint return with his wife, Matilda may claim the medical expenses she paid for him. Matilda would combine Ernie's expenses with her own before applying the 7.5% floor. ▼

---

[6]*F. S. Delp*, 30 T.C. 1230 (1958).

[7]*Riach v. Frank*, 62–1 USTC ¶9419, 9 AFTR2d 1263, 302 F.2d 374 (CA–9, 1962).

[8]§ 212(3).

[9]For a complete list of the items that qualify, see Rev.Rul. 87–106, 1987–2 C.B. 67.

[10]Refer to Chapter 3 for discussion of these requirements.

For *divorced persons* with children, a special rule applies to the noncustodial parent. The noncustodial parent may claim any medical expenses he or she pays even though the custodial parent claims the children as dependents. This rule applies if the dependency exemptions could have been shifted to the noncustodial parent by the custodial parent's waiver (refer to Chapter 3).

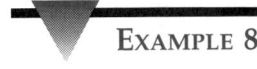

EXAMPLE 8

Irv and Joan are divorced in 1997, and Joan is awarded custody of their child, Keith. During 1998, Irv makes the following payments to Joan: $3,600 for child support and $2,500 for Keith's medical bills. Together, Irv and Joan provide more than half of Keith's support. Even though Joan claims Keith as a dependent, Irv can combine the $2,500 of medical expenses that he pays for Keith with his own. ▼

TRANSPORTATION, MEAL, AND LODGING EXPENSES FOR MEDICAL TREATMENT

Payments for transportation to and from a point of treatment for medical care are deductible as medical expenses (subject to the 7.5 percent floor). Transportation expenses for medical care include bus, taxi, train, or plane fare, charges for ambulance service, and out-of-pocket expenses for the use of an automobile. A mileage allowance of ten cents per mile[11] may be used instead of actual out-of-pocket automobile expenses. Whether the taxpayer chooses to claim out-of-pocket automobile expenses or the ten cents per mile automatic mileage option, related parking fees and tolls can also be deducted. The cost of meals while en route to obtain medical care is not deductible.

A deduction is also allowed for the transportation expenses of a parent who must accompany a child who is receiving medical care or for a nurse or other person giving assistance to a person who is traveling to get medical care and cannot travel alone.

A deduction is allowed for lodging while away from home for medical expenses if the following requirements are met:[12]

- The lodging is primarily for and essential to medical care.
- Medical care is provided by a doctor in a licensed hospital or a similar medical facility (e.g., a clinic).
- The lodging is not lavish or extravagant under the circumstances.
- There is no significant element of personal pleasure, recreation, or vacation in the travel away from home.

The deduction for lodging expenses included as medical expenses cannot exceed $50 *per* night for *each* person. The deduction is allowed not only for the patient but also for a person who must travel with the patient (e.g., a parent traveling with a child who is receiving medical care).

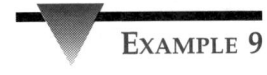

EXAMPLE 9

Herman, a resident of Winchester, Kentucky, is advised by his family physician that Martha, Herman's dependent and disabled mother, needs specialized treatment for her heart condition. Consequently, Herman and Martha fly to Cleveland, Ohio, where Martha receives the therapy at a heart clinic on an out-patient basis. Expenses in connection with the trip are as follows:

Round trip airfare ($250 each)	$500
Lodging in Cleveland for two nights ($60 each per night)	240

---

[11]This amount is adjusted periodically.   [12]§ 213(d)(2).

Herman's medical expense deduction for transportation is $500, and his medical expense deduction for lodging is $200 ($50 per night per person). Because Martha is disabled, it is assumed that his accompanying her is justified. ▼

No deduction is allowed for the cost of meals unless they are part of the medical care and are furnished at a medical facility. When allowable, such meals are not subject to the 50 percent limit.

AMOUNTS PAID FOR MEDICAL INSURANCE PREMIUMS

Medical insurance premiums are included with other medical expenses subject to the 7.5 percent floor. Premiums paid by the taxpayer under a group plan or an individual plan are included as medical expenses. If an employer pays all or part of the taxpayer's medical insurance premiums, the amount paid by the employer is not included in gross income by the employee. Likewise, the premium is not included in the employee's medical expenses.

If a taxpayer is *self-employed,* 45 percent[13] of insurance premiums paid for medical coverage in 1998 is deductible as a *business* expense (*for* AGI). Any excess can be treated as a *medical* expense. The deduction *for* AGI is allowed for premiums paid on behalf of the taxpayer, the taxpayer's spouse, and dependents of the taxpayer. The deduction is not allowed to any taxpayer who is eligible to participate in a subsidized health plan maintained by any employer of the taxpayer or of the taxpayer's spouse. Premiums paid for medical insurance coverage of *employees* are deductible as business expenses.

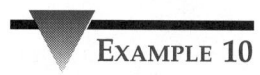

EXAMPLE 10

Ellen, a sole proprietor of a restaurant, has two dependent children. During 1998, she paid health insurance premiums of $1,800 for her own coverage and $1,000 for coverage of her two children. Ellen can deduct $1,260 ($2,800 × 45%) as a business deduction (for AGI) in computing net income from her business. She can include the remaining $1,540 ($2,800 − $1,260) as a medical expense (subject to the 7.5% floor) in computing itemized deductions. ▼

YEAR OF DEDUCTION

Regardless of a taxpayer's method of accounting, medical expenses are deductible only in the year *paid.* In effect, this places all individual taxpayers on a cash basis as far as the medical expense deduction is concerned. One exception, however, is allowed for deceased taxpayers. If the medical expenses are paid within one year from the day following the day of death, they can be treated as being paid at the time they were *incurred.* Thus, such expenses may be reported on the final income tax return of the decedent or on earlier returns if incurred before the year of death.

No current deduction is allowed for payment of medical care to be rendered in the future unless the taxpayer is under an obligation to make the payment.[14] Whether an obligation to make the payment exists depends upon the policy of the physician or the institution furnishing the medical care.

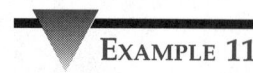

EXAMPLE 11

Upon the recommendation of his regular dentist, in late December 1998 Gary consults Dr. Smith, a prosthodontist, who specializes in crown and bridge work. Dr. Smith tells Gary that he can do the restorative work for $12,000. To cover his lab bill, however, Dr. Smith requires that 40% of this amount be prepaid. Accordingly, Gary pays $4,800 in December

---

[13]§ 162(l). The rate will be 45% in tax years 1998 and 1999, 50% in 2000 and 2001, 60% in 2002, 80% in 2003 through 2005, 90% for 2006, and 100% in 2007 and thereafter. The rate was 40% in 1997.

[14]*Robert S. Basset,* 26 T.C. 619 (1956).

1998. The balance of $7,200 is paid when the work is completed in July 1999. Under these circumstances, the qualifying medical expenses are $4,800 for 1998 and $7,200 in 1999. The result would be the same even if Gary prepaid the full $12,000 in 1998. ▼

REIMBURSEMENTS

If medical expenses are reimbursed in the same year as paid, no problem arises. The reimbursement merely reduces the amount that would otherwise qualify for the medical expense deduction. But what happens if the reimbursement occurs in a later year than the expenditure? In computing casualty losses, any reasonable prospect of recovery must be considered (refer to Chapter 7). For medical expenses, however, any expected reimbursement is disregarded in measuring the amount of the deduction. Instead, the reimbursement is accounted for separately in the year in which it occurs.

Under the *tax benefit rule*, a taxpayer who receives an insurance reimbursement for medical expenses deducted in a previous year might have to include the reimbursement in gross income in the year of receipt. However, a taxpayer who did not itemize deductions in the year the expenses were paid did not receive a tax benefit and is *not* required to include a reimbursement in gross income.

The tax benefit rule applies to reimbursements if the taxpayer itemized deductions in the previous year. In this case, the taxpayer may be required to report some or all of the medical expense reimbursement in income in the year the reimbursement is received. Under the tax benefit rule, the taxpayer must include the reimbursement in income up to the amount of the deductions that decreased taxable income in the earlier year.

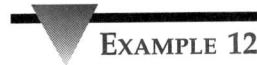

EXAMPLE 12

Homer had AGI of $20,000 for 1998. He was injured in a car accident and paid $1,300 for hospital expenses and $700 for doctor bills. Homer also incurred medical expenses of $600 for his dependent child. In 1999, Homer was reimbursed $650 by his insurance company for the medical expenses attributable to the car accident. His deduction for medical expenses in 1998 is computed as follows:

Hospitalization	$ 1,300
Bills for doctor's services	700
Medical expenses for dependent	600
Total	$ 2,600
Less: 7.5% of $20,000	(1,500)
Medical expense deduction (assuming Homer itemizes his deductions)	$ 1,100

Assume that Homer would have elected to itemize his deductions even if he had no medical expenses in 1998. If the reimbursement for medical care had occurred in 1998, the medical expense deduction would have been only $450 [$2,600 (total medical expenses) − $650 (reimbursement) − $1,500 (floor)], and Homer would have paid more income tax.

Since the reimbursement was made in a subsequent year, Homer would include $650 in gross income for 1999. If Homer had not itemized in 1998, he would not include the $650 reimbursement in 1999 gross income because he would have received no tax benefit in 1998. ▼

MEDICAL SAVINGS ACCOUNTS

Certain employees and self-employed taxpayers may deduct contributions to Medical Savings Accounts (MSAs). MSAs, which may be used in connection with *high-deductible* health insurance, can be used to accumulate funds for the payment of health care expenses. Individuals who contribute to MSAs may deduct the contributions as deductions *for* AGI. Individuals whose employers contribute to MSAs may exclude the contributions from gross income. Earnings on MSAs are not included in the gross income of the current year. MSA distributions that are used to pay for amounts not covered by a high-deductible plan are not subject to tax. However, distributions used for purposes other than the payment of medical expenses are taxable and are subject to an additional 15 percent penalty if made before age 65, death, or disability.

MSAs can be established by employers with 50 or fewer employees, self-employed individuals, and individuals without insurance coverage. High-deductible policies are those with deductibles between $1,500 and $2,250 for individuals (between $3,000 and $4,500 for families). The deduction is limited to 65 percent of the policy deductible for individuals (75 percent for families). MSAs are available on a four-year pilot basis, and eligibility is limited to 750,000 MSAs. After the four-year pilot period is over, Congress will decide whether to retain the MSA provisions and extend eligibility.

TAXES

3 LEARNING OBJECTIVE
Contrast deductible taxes and nondeductible fees, licenses, etc.

A deduction is allowed for certain state and local taxes paid or accrued by a taxpayer.[15] The deduction was created to relieve the burden of multiple taxes upon the same source of revenue.

DEDUCTIBILITY AS A TAX

A distinction must be made between a tax and a fee, since fees are not deductible unless incurred as an ordinary and necessary business expense or as an expense in the production of income. The IRS has defined a tax as follows:

> A tax is an enforced contribution exacted pursuant to legislative authority in the exercise of taxing power, and imposed and collected for the purpose of raising revenue to be used for public or governmental purposes, and not as payment for some special privilege granted or service rendered. Taxes are, therefore, distinguished from various other contributions and charges imposed for particular purposes under particular powers or functions of the government. In view of such distinctions, the question whether a particular contribution or charge is to be regarded as a tax depends upon its real nature.[16]

Accordingly, fees for dog licenses, automobile inspection, automobile titles and registration, hunting and fishing licenses, bridge and highway tolls, drivers' licenses, parking meter deposits, postage, etc., are not deductible if personal in nature. These items, however, could be deductible if incurred as a business expense or for the production of income. Deductible and nondeductible taxes are summarized in Exhibit 10–2.[17]

PROPERTY TAXES

State, local, and foreign taxes on real property are generally deductible only by the person upon whom the tax is imposed. Deductible personal property

---

[15] § 164.
[16] Rev.Rul. 57–345, 1957–2 C.B. 132, and Rev.Rul. 70–622, 1970–2 C.B. 41.

[17] Most deductible taxes are listed in § 164, while the nondeductible items are included in § 275.

▼ **EXHIBIT 10–2**
Deductible and Nondeductible
Taxes

Deductible	Nondeductible
State, local, and foreign real property taxes	Federal income taxes
	FICA taxes imposed on employees
State and local personal property taxes	Employer FICA taxes paid on domestic household workers
State, local, and foreign income taxes	Estate, inheritance, and gift taxes
	General sales taxes
The environmental tax	Federal, state, and local excise taxes (e.g., gasoline, tobacco, spirits)
	Foreign income taxes if the taxpayer chooses the foreign tax credit option
	Taxes on real property to the extent such taxes are to be apportioned and treated as imposed on another taxpayer

taxes must be *ad valorem* (assessed in relation to the value of the property). Therefore, a motor vehicle tax based on weight, model, year, and horsepower is not an ad valorem tax. However, a tax based on value and other criteria may qualify in part.

EXAMPLE 13

A state imposes a motor vehicle registration tax on 4% of the value of the vehicle plus 40 cents per hundredweight. Belle, a resident of the state, owns a car having a value of $4,000 and weighing 3,000 pounds. Belle pays an annual registration fee of $172. Of this amount, $160 (4% of $4,000) is deductible as a personal property tax. The remaining $12, based on the weight of the car, is not deductible. ▼

Assessments for Local Benefits.   As a general rule, real property taxes do not include taxes assessed for local benefits since such assessments tend to increase the value of the property (e.g., special assessments for streets, sidewalks, curbing, and other similar improvements). A taxpayer was denied a deduction for the cost of a new sidewalk (relative to a personal residence), even though the construction was required by the city and the sidewalk may have provided an incidental benefit to the public welfare.[18] Such assessments are added to the adjusted basis of the taxpayer's property.

Apportionment of Real Property Taxes between Seller and Purchaser.
Real estate taxes for the entire year are apportioned between the buyer and seller on the basis of the number of days the property was held by each during the real property tax year. This apportionment is required whether the tax is paid by the buyer or the seller or is prorated according to the purchase agreement. It is the apportionment that determines who is entitled to deduct the real estate taxes in the year of sale. In making the apportionment, the assessment date and the lien date are disregarded. The date of sale counts as a day the property is owned by the buyer.

---

[18]*Erie H. Rose,* 31 TCM 142, T.C. Memo. 1972–39; Reg. § 1.164–4(a).

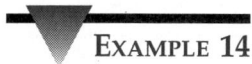

EXAMPLE 14

A county's real property tax year runs from April 1 to March 31. Susan, the owner on April 1, 1998, of real property located in the county, sells the real property to Bob on June 30, 1998. Bob owns the real property from June 30, 1998, through March 31, 1999. The tax for the real property tax year April 1, 1998, through March 31, 1999, is $730. The portion of the real property tax treated as imposed upon Susan, the seller, is $180 [(90/365) × $730, April 1 through June 29, 1998], and $550 [(275/365) × $730, June 30, 1998, through March 31, 1999] of the tax is treated as imposed upon Bob, the purchaser. ▼

If the actual real estate taxes are not prorated between the buyer and seller as part of the purchase agreement, adjustments are required. The adjustments are necessary to determine the amount realized by the seller and the adjusted basis of the property to the buyer. If the buyer pays the entire amount of the tax, he or she has, in effect, paid the seller's portion of the real estate tax and has therefore paid more for the property than the actual purchase price. Thus, the amount of real estate tax that is apportioned to the seller (for Federal income tax purposes) and paid by the buyer is added to the buyer's adjusted basis. The seller must increase the amount realized on the sale by the same amount.

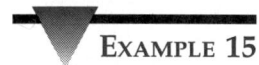

EXAMPLE 15

Seth sells real estate on October 3, 1998, for $50,000. The buyer, Wilma, pays the real estate taxes of $1,095 for the 1998 calendar year, which is the real estate property tax year. Of the real estate taxes, $825 (for 275 days) is apportioned to and is deductible by the seller, Seth, and $270 (for 90 days) of the taxes is deductible by Wilma. The buyer has, in effect, paid Seth's real estate taxes of $825 and has therefore paid $50,825 for the property. Wilma's basis is increased to $50,825, and the amount realized by Seth from the sale is increased to $50,825. ▼

The opposite result occurs if the seller (rather than the buyer) pays the real estate taxes. In this case, the seller reduces the amount realized from the sale by the amount that has been apportioned to the buyer. The buyer is required to reduce his or her adjusted basis by a corresponding amount.

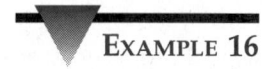

EXAMPLE 16

Ruth sells real estate to Butch for $50,000 on October 3, 1998. While Ruth held the property, she paid the real estate taxes of $1,095 for the calendar year, which is the real estate property tax year. Although Ruth paid the entire $1,095 of real estate taxes, $270 of that amount is apportioned to Butch and is therefore deductible by him. The effect is that the buyer, Butch, has paid only $49,730 for the property. The amount realized by Ruth, the seller, is reduced by $270, and Butch reduces his basis in the property to $49,730. ▼

STATE AND LOCAL INCOME TAXES

4 **LEARNING OBJECTIVE**
Understand the Federal tax treatment of state and local income taxes.

The position of the IRS is that state and local income taxes imposed upon an individual are deductible only as itemized deductions, even if the taxpayer's sole source of income is from a business, rents, or royalties.

Cash basis taxpayers are entitled to deduct state income taxes withheld by the employer in the year the taxes are withheld. In addition, estimated state income tax payments are deductible in the year the payment is made by cash basis taxpayers even if the payments relate to a prior or subsequent year.[19] If the taxpayer overpays state income taxes because of excessive withholdings or estimated tax payments, the refund received is included in gross income of the following year to the extent that the deduction reduced the tax liability in the prior year.

---

[19]Rev.Rul. 71–190, 1971–1 C.B. 70. See also Rev.Rul. 82–208, 1982–2 C.B. 58, where a deduction is not allowed when the taxpayer cannot, in good faith, reasonably determine that there is additional state income tax liability.

EXAMPLE 17

Leona, a cash basis, unmarried taxpayer, had $800 of state income tax withheld during 1998. Additionally in 1998, Leona paid $100 that was due when she filed her 1997 state income tax return and made estimated payments of $300 on her 1998 state income tax. When Leona files her 1998 Federal income tax return in April 1999, she elects to itemize deductions, which amount to $5,500, including the $1,200 of state income tax payments and withholdings, all of which reduce her tax liability.

As a result of overpaying her 1998 state income tax, Leona receives a refund of $200 early in 1999. She will include this amount in her 1999 gross income in computing her Federal income tax. It does not matter whether Leona received a check from the state for $200 or applied the $200 toward her 1999 state income tax. ▼

INTEREST

5 **LEARNING OBJECTIVE**
Distinguish between deductible and nondeductible interest and apply the appropriate limitations to deductible interest.

A deduction for interest has been allowed since the income tax law was enacted in 1913. Despite its long history of congressional acceptance, the interest deduction has been one of the most controversial areas in the tax law. The controversy centered around the propriety of allowing the deduction of interest charges for the purchase of consumer goods and services and interest on borrowings used to acquire investments (investment interest). Personal (consumer) interest is not deductible. This includes credit card interest, interest on car loans, and any other interest that is not investment interest, home mortgage interest, or business interest. **Investment interest** and **qualified residence** (home mortgage) **interest** continue to be deductible, subject to limits discussed on the following pages.

ALLOWED AND DISALLOWED ITEMS

The Supreme Court has defined *interest* as compensation for the use or forbearance of money.[20] The general rule permits a deduction for interest paid or accrued within the taxable year on indebtedness.[21]

Investment Interest. Taxpayers frequently borrow funds that they use to acquire investment assets. When the interest expense is large relative to the income from the investments, substantial tax benefits could result. Congress has therefore

---

[20]*Old Colony Railroad Co. v. Comm.*, 3 USTC ¶880, 10 AFTR 786, 52 S.Ct. 211 (USSC, 1932).

[21]§ 163(a).

limited the deductibility of interest on funds borrowed for the purpose of purchasing or continuing to hold investment property. Investment interest expense is *now* limited to net investment income for the year.[22]

Investment income is gross income from interest, dividends, annuities, and royalties not derived in the ordinary course of a trade or business. Income from a passive activity and income from a real estate activity in which the taxpayer actively participates are not included in investment income (see Chapter 11).

Net capital gain attributable to the disposition of property producing the types of income just enumerated or from property held for investment purposes is *not* included in investment income unless the taxpayer elects to do so.

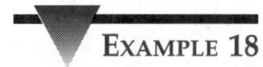

EXAMPLE 18

Terry incurred $13,000 of interest expense related to her investments during the year. Her investment income included $4,000 of interest, $2,000 of dividends, and a $5,000 net capital gain on the sale of securities. Her investment income for purposes of computing the investment income limitation is $6,000 ($4,000 interest + $2,000 dividends). ▼

Taxpayers may *elect* to include the capital gains as investment income, but only if they agree to reduce capital gains qualifying for the alternative tax computation for net capital gain (see Chapter 16) by an equivalent amount.

Net investment income is the excess of investment income over investment expenses. Investment expenses are those deductible expenses directly connected with the production of investment income. Investment expenses *do not* include interest expense. When investment expenses fall into the category of miscellaneous itemized deductions that are subject to the 2 percent-of-AGI floor, some may not enter into the calculation of net investment income because of the floor.

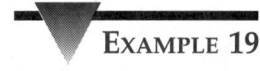

EXAMPLE 19

Gina has AGI of $80,000, which includes dividends and interest income of $18,000. Besides investment interest expense, she paid $3,000 of city ad valorem property tax on stocks and bonds and had the following miscellaneous itemized expenses:

Safe deposit box rental (to hold investment securities)	$ 120
Investment counsel fee	1,200
Unreimbursed business travel	850
Uniforms	600

Before Gina can determine her investment expenses for purposes of calculating net investment income, those miscellaneous expenses that are not investment expenses are disallowed before any investment expenses are disallowed under the 2%-of-AGI floor. This is accomplished by selecting the *lesser* of the following:

1. The amount of investment expenses included in the total of miscellaneous itemized deductions subject to the 2%-of-AGI floor.
2. The amount of miscellaneous expenses deductible after the 2%-of-AGI rule is applied.

The amount under item 1 is $1,320 [$120 (safe deposit box rental) + $1,200 (investment counsel fee)]. The item 2 amount is $1,170 [$2,770 (total of miscellaneous expenses) − $1,600 (2% of $80,000 AGI)].

Then, Gina's investment expenses are calculated as follows:

Deductible miscellaneous deductions investment expense (the lesser of item 1 or item 2)	$1,170
Plus: Ad valorem tax on investment property	3,000
Total investment expenses	$4,170

---

[22]§ 63(d).

Gina's net investment income is $13,830 ($18,000 investment income – $4,170 investment expenses). ▼

After net investment income is determined, deductible investment interest expense can be calculated.

EXAMPLE 20   Adam is a single person employed by a law firm. His investment activities for the year are as follows:

Net investment income	$30,000
Investment interest expense	44,000

Adam's investment interest deduction is $30,000. ▼

The amount of investment interest disallowed is carried over to future years. In Example 20, therefore, the amount that is carried over to the following year is $14,000 ($44,000 investment interest expense – $30,000 allowed). No limit is placed on the length of the carryover period. The investment interest expense deduction is determined by completing Form 4952 (see Appendix B).

Qualified Residence Interest.   *Qualified residence interest* is interest paid or accrued during the taxable year on indebtedness (subject to limitations) *secured* by any property that is a qualified residence of the taxpayer. Qualified residence interest falls into two categories: (1) interest on acquisition indebtedness and (2) interest on home equity loans. Before discussing each of these categories, however, the term qualified residence must be defined.

A *qualified residence* includes the taxpayer's principal residence and one other residence of the taxpayer or spouse. The *principal residence* is one that meets the requirement for nonrecognition of gain upon sale under § 121 (see Chapter 15). The *one other residence*, or second residence, refers to one that is used as a residence if not rented or, if rented, meets the requirements for a personal residence under the rental of vacation home rules (refer to Chapter 6). A taxpayer who has more than one second residence can make the selection each year of which one is the qualified second residence. A residence includes, in addition to a house in the ordinary sense, cooperative apartments, condominiums, and mobile homes and boats that have living quarters (sleeping accommodations and toilet and cooking facilities).

Although in most cases interest paid on a home mortgage would be fully deductible, there are limitations.[23] Interest paid or accrued during the tax year on aggregate **acquisition indebtedness** of $1 million or less ($500,000 for married persons filing separate returns) is deductible as qualified residence interest. Acquisition indebtedness refers to amounts incurred in acquiring, constructing, or substantially improving a qualified residence of the taxpayer.

Qualified residence interest also includes interest on **home equity loans.** These loans utilize the personal residence of the taxpayer as security. Because the funds from home equity loans can be used for personal purposes (e.g., auto purchases, medical expenses), what would otherwise have been nondeductible consumer interest becomes deductible qualified residence interest.

However, interest is deductible only on the portion of a home equity loan that does not exceed the *lesser of*:

---

[23]§ 163(h)(3).

- The fair market value of the residence, reduced by the acquisition indebtedness, *or*
- $100,000 ($50,000 for married persons filing separate returns).

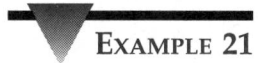

EXAMPLE 21

Larry owns a personal residence with a fair market value of $150,000 and an outstanding first mortgage of $120,000. Therefore, his equity in his home is $30,000 ($150,000 − $120,000). Larry issues a lien on the residence and in return borrows $15,000 to purchase a new family automobile. All interest on the $135,000 of debt is treated as qualified residence interest. ▼

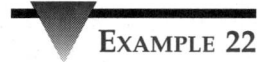

EXAMPLE 22

Leon and Pearl, married taxpayers, took out a mortgage on their home for $200,000 in 1983. In March of the current year, when the home had a fair market value of $400,000 and they owed $195,000 on the mortgage, Leon and Pearl took out a home equity loan for $120,000. They used the funds to purchase a boat to be used for recreational purposes. The boat, which does not have living quarters, does not qualify as a personal residence. On a joint return, Leon and Pearl can deduct all of the interest on the first mortgage since it is acquisition indebtedness. Of the $120,000 home equity loan, only the interest on the first $100,000 is deductible. The interest on the remaining $20,000 is not deductible because it exceeds the statutory ceiling of $100,000. ▼

Interest Paid for Services.   Mortgage loan companies commonly charge a fee for finding, placing, or processing a mortgage loan. Such fees are often called **points** and are expressed as a percentage of the loan amount. Borrowers often have to pay points to obtain the necessary financing. To qualify as deductible interest, the points must be considered compensation to a lender solely for the use or forbearance of money. The points cannot be a form of service charge or payment for specific services if they are to qualify as deductible interest.[24]

Points must be capitalized and are amortized and deductible ratably over the life of the loan. A special exception permits the purchaser of a personal residence to deduct qualifying points in the year of payment.[25] The exception also covers points paid to obtain funds for home improvements.

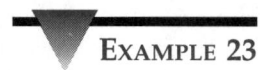

EXAMPLE 23

During 1998, Thelma purchased a new residence for $130,000 and paid points of $2,600 to obtain mortgage financing. At Thelma's election, the $2,600 can be claimed as an interest deduction for tax year 1998. ▼

Points paid to *refinance* an existing home mortgage cannot be immediately expensed, but must be capitalized and amortized as interest expense over the life of the new loan.[26]

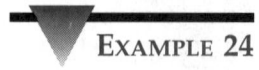

EXAMPLE 24

Sandra purchased her residence four years ago, obtaining a 30-year mortgage at an annual interest rate of 12%. In the current year, Sandra refinances the mortgage in order to reduce the interest rate to 9%. To obtain the refinancing, she had to pay points of $2,600. The $2,600 paid comes under the usual rule applicable to points. The $2,600 must be capitalized and amortized over the life of the mortgage. ▼

The rules governing the deductibility of points *paid by a seller* to help a buyer finance the purchase of the residence were changed in 1994.[27] Under prior rules, such points were not deductible by the buyer, but were treated by the seller as a reduction of the selling price of the property.

---

[24]Rev.Rul. 67–297, 1967–2 C.B. 87.
[25]§ 461(g)(2).

[26]Rev.Rul. 87–22, 1987–1 C.B. 146.
[27]Rev.Proc. 94–27, 1994–1 C.B. 613.

The IRS changed its position on this issue, retroactive to tax years beginning after December 31, 1990. In effect, points paid by the seller are treated as an adjustment to the price of the residence, and the buyer is treated as having used cash to pay the points that were paid by the seller. A buyer may deduct seller-paid points in the tax year in which they are paid if several conditions are met. Refer to Revenue Procedure 94–27 for a complete list of these conditions (see footnote 27 for citation).

Prepayment Penalty. When a mortgage or loan is paid off in full in a lump sum before its term (early), the lending institution may require an additional payment of a certain percentage applied to the unpaid amount at the time of prepayment. This is known as a prepayment penalty and is considered to be interest (e.g., personal, qualified residence, investment) in the year paid. The general rules for deductibility of interest also apply to prepayment penalties.

Interest Paid to Related Parties. Nothing prevents the deduction of interest paid to a related party as long as the payment actually took place and the interest meets the requirements for deductibility. Recall from Chapter 6 that a special rule for related taxpayers applies when the debtor uses the accrual basis and the related creditor is on the cash basis. If this rule is applicable, interest that has been accrued but not paid at the end of the debtor's tax year is not deductible until payment is made and the income is reportable by the cash basis recipient.

Tax-Exempt Securities. The tax law provides that no deduction is allowed for interest on debt incurred to purchase or carry tax-exempt securities.[28] A major problem for the courts has been to determine what is meant by the words *to purchase or carry*. Refer to Chapter 6 for a detailed discussion of these issues.

RESTRICTIONS ON DEDUCTIBILITY AND TIMING CONSIDERATIONS

Taxpayer's Obligation. Allowed interest is deductible if the related debt represents a bona fide obligation for which the taxpayer is liable.[29] Thus, a taxpayer may not deduct interest paid on behalf of another individual. For interest to be deductible, both the debtor and creditor must intend for the loan to be repaid. Intent of the parties can be especially crucial between related parties such as a shareholder and a closely held corporation. A shareholder may not deduct interest paid by the corporation on his or her behalf.[30] Likewise, a husband may not deduct interest paid on his wife's property if he files a separate return, except in the case of qualified residence interest. If both husband and wife consent in writing, either the husband or the wife may deduct the allowed interest on the principal residence and one other residence.

Time of Deduction. Generally, interest must be paid to secure a deduction unless the taxpayer uses the accrual method of accounting. Under the accrual method, interest is deductible ratably over the life of the loan.

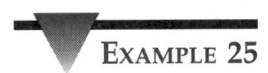

EXAMPLE 25   On November 1, 1998, Ramon borrows $1,000 to purchase appliances for a rental house. The loan is payable in 90 days at 12% interest. On the due date in January 1999, Ramon pays the $1,000 note and interest amounting to $30. Ramon can deduct the accrued portion

---

[28]§ 265(a)(2).
[29]*Arcade Realty Co.*, 35 T.C. 256 (1960).

[30]*Continental Trust Co.*, 7 B.T.A. 539 (1927).

▼

CONCEPT SUMMARY 10–1

Deductibility of Personal, Investment, and Mortgage Interest

Type	Deductible	Comments
Personal (consumer) interest	No	Includes any interest that is not home mortgage interest, investment interest, or business interest. Examples include car loans, credit cards, etc.
Investment interest (*not* related to rental or royalty property)	Yes	Itemized deduction; limited to net investment income for the year; disallowed interest can be carried over to future years.
Investment interest (related to rental or royalty property)	Yes	Deduction *for* AGI; limited to net investment income for the year; disallowed interest can be carried over to future years.
Qualified residence interest on acquisition indebtedness	Yes	Deductible as an itemized deduction; limited to indebtedness of $1 million.
Qualified residence interest on home equity indebtedness	Yes	Deductible as an itemized deduction; limited to indebtedness equal to lesser of $100,000 or FMV of residence minus acquisition indebtedness.

(⅔ × $30 = $20) of the interest in 1998 only if he is an accrual basis taxpayer. Otherwise, the entire amount of interest ($30) is deductible in 1999. ▼

Prepaid Interest.   Accrual method reporting is imposed on cash basis taxpayers for interest prepayments that extend beyond the end of the taxable year.[31] Such payments must be allocated to the tax years to which the interest payments relate. These provisions are intended to prevent cash basis taxpayers from *manufacturing* tax deductions before the end of the year by prepaying interest.

CLASSIFICATION OF INTEREST EXPENSE

Whether interest is deductible *for* AGI or as an itemized deduction *(from)* depends on whether the indebtedness has a business, investment, or personal purpose. If the indebtedness is incurred in relation to a business (other than performing services as an employee) or for the production of rent or royalty income, the interest is deductible *for* AGI. If the indebtedness is incurred for personal use, such as qualified residence interest, any deduction allowed is reported on Schedule A of Form 1040 if the taxpayer elects to itemize. If the taxpayer is an employee who incurs debt in relation to his or her employment, the interest is considered to be personal, or consumer, interest. Business expenses appear on Schedule C of Form 1040, and expenses related to rents or royalties are reported on Schedule E.

If a taxpayer deposits money in a certificate of deposit (CD) that has a term of one year or less and the interest cannot be withdrawn without penalty, the full amount of the interest must still be included in income, even though part of the interest is forfeited due to an early withdrawal. However, the taxpayer will be allowed a deduction *for* AGI as to the forfeited amount.

---

[31]§ 461(g)(1).

CHARITABLE CONTRIBUTIONS

6 **LEARNING OBJECTIVE**
Understand charitable
contributions and their related
measurement problems and
percentage limitations.

Individuals and corporations are allowed to deduct contributions made to qualified *domestic* organizations.[32] Contributions to qualified charitable organizations serve certain social welfare needs and thus relieve the government of the cost of providing these needed services to the community.

The **charitable contribution** provisions are among the most complex in the tax law. To determine the amount deductible as a charitable contribution, several important questions must be answered:

- What constitutes a charitable contribution?
- Was the contribution made to a qualified organization?
- When is the contribution deductible?
- What record-keeping and reporting requirements apply to charitable contributions?
- How is the value of donated property determined?
- What special rules apply to contributions of property that has increased in value?
- What percentage limitations apply to the charitable contribution deduction?

These questions are addressed in the sections that follow.

CRITERIA FOR A GIFT

A *charitable contribution* is defined as a gift made to a qualified organization.[33] The major elements needed to qualify a contribution as a gift are a donative intent, the absence of consideration, and acceptance by the donee. Consequently, the taxpayer has the burden of establishing that the transfer was made from motives of *disinterested generosity* as established by the courts.[34] This test is quite subjective and has led to problems of interpretation (refer to the discussion of gifts in Chapter 5).

Benefit Received Rule. When a donor derives a tangible benefit from a contribution, he or she cannot deduct the value of the benefit.

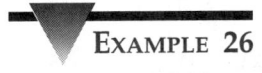
EXAMPLE 26

Ralph purchases a ticket at $100 for a special performance of the local symphony (a qualified charity). If the price of a ticket to a symphony concert is normally $35, Ralph is allowed only $65 as a charitable contribution. ▼

An exception to this benefit rule provides for the deduction of an automatic percentage of the amount paid for the right to purchase athletic tickets from colleges and universities.[35] Under this exception, 80 percent of the amount paid to or for the benefit of the institution qualifies as a charitable contribution deduction.

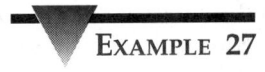
EXAMPLE 27

Janet donates $500 to State University's athletic department. The payment guarantees that she will have preferred seating on the 50-yard line. Subsequently, Janet buys four $35 game tickets. Under the exception to the benefit rule, she is allowed a $400 (80% of $500) charitable contribution deduction for the taxable year.

---

[32]§ 170.
[33]§ 170(c).
[34]*Comm. v. Duberstein*, 60–2 USTC ¶9515, 5 AFTR2d 1626, 80 S.Ct. 1190 (USSC, 1960).

[35]§ 170(l).

If, however, Janet's $500 donation includes four $35 tickets, that portion [$140 ($35 × 4)] and the remaining portion of $360 ($500 − $140) are treated as separate amounts. Thus, Janet is allowed a charitable contribution deduction of $288 (80% of $360). ▼

Contribution of Services. No deduction is allowed for a contribution of one's services to a qualified charitable organization. However, unreimbursed expenses related to the services rendered may be deductible. For example, the cost of a uniform (without general utility) that is required to be worn while performing services may be deductible, as are certain out-of-pocket transportation costs incurred for the benefit of the charity. In lieu of these out-of-pocket costs for an automobile, a standard mileage rate of 14 cents per mile is allowed for tax years beginning after December 31, 1997.[36] Deductions are permitted for transportation, reasonable expenses for lodging, and the cost of meals while away from home incurred in performing the donated services. The travel may not involve a significant element of personal pleasure, recreation, or vacation.[37]

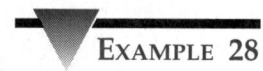

EXAMPLE 28

Grace, a delegate representing her church in Miami, Florida, travels to a two-day national meeting in Denver, Colorado, in February. After the meeting, Grace spends two weeks at a nearby ski resort. Under these circumstances, none of the transportation, meals, or lodging is deductible since the travel involved a significant element of personal pleasure, recreation, or vacation. ▼

Nondeductible Items. In addition to the benefit received rule and the restrictions placed on contribution of services, the following items may *not* be deducted as charitable contributions:

- Dues, fees, or bills paid to country clubs, lodges, fraternal orders, or similar groups.
- Cost of raffle, bingo, or lottery tickets.
- Cost of tuition.
- Value of blood given to a blood bank.
- Donations to homeowners associations.
- Gifts to individuals.
- Rental value of property used by a qualified charity.

QUALIFIED ORGANIZATIONS

To be deductible, a contribution must be made to one of the following organizations:[38]

- A state or possession of the United States or any subdivisions thereof.
- A corporation, trust, or community chest, fund, or foundation that is situated in the United States and is organized and operated exclusively for religious, charitable, scientific, literary, or educational purposes or for the prevention of cruelty to children or animals.
- A veterans' organization.
- A fraternal organization operating under the lodge system.
- A cemetery company.

---

[36]§ 170(i). The rate was 12 cents per mile for tax year 1997.   [38]§ 170(c).
[37]§ 170(j).

The IRS publishes a list of organizations that have applied for and received tax-exempt status under § 501 of the Code.[39] This publication is updated frequently and may be helpful in determining if a gift has been made to a qualifying charitable organization.

Because gifts made to needy individuals are not deductible, a deduction will not be permitted if a gift is received by a donee in an individual capacity rather than as a representative of a qualifying organization.

ETHICAL CONSIDERATIONS

An Indirect Route to a Contribution Deduction

In July, a devastating tornado touched down in the city of Feldston, causing over $1 million in damage. Arethia's church, a qualified charitable organization, initiated a fund-raising drive to help Feldston citizens whose homes had been damaged. Arethia donated $40,000 to the church and suggested to the pastor that $25,000 of her contribution should be given to her sister, Keisha, whose home had suffered extensive damage. The pastor appointed a committee to award funds to needy citizens. The committee solicited applications from the community and awarded Keisha $18,000. Is Arethia justified in deducting $40,000 as a charitable contribution?

TIME OF DEDUCTION

A charitable contribution generally is deducted in the year the payment is made. This rule applies to both cash and accrual basis individuals. A contribution is ordinarily deemed to have been made on the delivery of the property to the donee. For example, if a gift of securities (properly endorsed) is made to a qualified charitable organization, the gift is considered complete on the day of delivery or mailing. However, if the donor delivers the certificate to his or her bank or broker or to the issuing corporation, the gift is considered complete on the date the stock is transferred on the books of the corporation.

A contribution made by check is considered delivered on the date of mailing. Thus, a check mailed on December 31, 1998, is deductible on the taxpayer's 1998 tax return. If the contribution is charged on a bank credit card, the date the charge is made determines the year of deduction.

RECORD-KEEPING AND VALUATION REQUIREMENTS

Record-Keeping Requirements.   No deduction is allowed for contributions of $250 or more unless the taxpayer obtains *written substantiation* of the contribution from the charitable organization. The substantiation must specify the amount of cash and a description (but not value) of any property other than cash contributed. The substantiation must be obtained before the earlier of (1) the due date (including extensions) of the return for the year the contribution is claimed or (2) the date such return is filed.[40]

---

[39]Although this *Cumulative List of Organizations*, IRS Publication 78 (available by purchase from the Superintendent of Documents, U.S. Government Printing Office, Washington, DC 20402), may be helpful, qualified organizations are not required to be listed. Not all organizations that qualify are listed in this publication. The list is also available on the Web at http://www.irs.ustreas.gov.

[40]§ 170(f)(8).

Additional information is required if the value of the donated property is over $500 but not over $5,000. Also, the taxpayer must file Section A of Form 8283 (Noncash Charitable Contributions) for such contributions.

For noncash contributions with a claimed value in excess of $5,000 ($10,000 in the case of nonpublicly traded stock), the taxpayer must obtain a qualified appraisal and must file Section B of Form 8283. This schedule must show a summary of the appraisal and must be attached to the taxpayer's return. Failure to comply with these reporting rules may result in disallowance of the charitable contribution deduction. Additionally, significant overvaluation exposes the taxpayer to rather stringent penalties.

Valuation Requirements.   Property donated to a charity is generally valued at fair market value at the time the gift is made. The Code and Regulations give very little guidance on the measurement of the fair market value except to say, "The fair market value is the price at which the property would change hands between a willing buyer and a willing seller, neither being under any compulsion to buy or sell and both having reasonable knowledge of relevant facts."

Generally, charitable organizations do not attest to the fair market value of the donated property. Nevertheless, the taxpayer must maintain reliable written evidence of the following information concerning the donation:

• The fair market value of the property and how that value was determined.
• The amount of the reduction in the value of the property (if required) for certain appreciated property and how that reduction was determined.
• Terms of any agreement with the charitable organization dealing with the use of the property and potential sale or other disposition of the property by the organization.
• A signed copy of the appraisal if the value of the property was determined by appraisal. Only for a contribution of art with an aggregate value of $20,000 or more must the appraisal be attached to the taxpayer's return.

LIMITATIONS ON CHARITABLE CONTRIBUTION DEDUCTION

In General.   The potential charitable contribution deduction is the total of all donations, both money and property, that qualify for the deduction. After this determination is made, the actual amount of the charitable contribution deduction that is allowed for individuals for the tax year is limited as follows:

• If the qualifying contributions for the year total 20 percent or less of AGI, they are fully deductible.
• If the qualifying contributions are more than 20 percent of AGI, the deductible amount may be limited to either 20 percent, 30 percent, or 50 percent of AGI, depending on the type of property given and the type of organization to which the donation is made.
• In any case, the maximum charitable contribution deduction may not exceed 50 percent of AGI for the tax year.

To understand the complex rules for computing the amount of a charitable contribution, it is necessary to understand the distinction between capital gain property and ordinary income property. In addition, it is necessary to understand when the 50 percent, 30 percent, and 20 percent limitations apply. If a taxpayer's contributions for the year exceed the applicable percentage limitations, the excess contributions may be carried forward and deducted during a five-year carryover period. These topics are discussed in the sections that follow.

Ordinary Income Property. **Ordinary income property** is any property that, if sold, will result in the recognition of ordinary income. The term includes inventory for sale in the taxpayer's trade or business, a work of art created by the donor, and a manuscript prepared by the donor. It also includes, *for purposes of the charitable contribution calculation*, a capital asset held by the donor for less than the required holding period for long-term capital gain treatment (for charitable contribution purposes, long term is a period longer than one year). To the extent that disposition of property results in the recognition of ordinary income due to the recapture of depreciation, it is ordinary income property.[41]

If ordinary income property is contributed, the deduction is equal to the fair market value of the property less the amount of ordinary income that would have been reported if the property were sold. In most instances, the deduction is limited to the adjusted basis of the property to the donor.

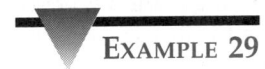

EXAMPLE 29

Tim owned stock in White Corporation that he donated to a university on May 1, 1998. Tim had purchased the stock for $2,500 on March 3, 1998, and the stock had a value of $3,600 when he made the donation. Since he had not held the property long enough to meet the long-term capital gain requirement, Tim would have recognized a short-term capital gain of $1,100 if he had sold the property. Since short-term capital gain property is treated as ordinary income property for charitable contribution purposes, Tim's charitable contribution deduction is limited to the property's adjusted basis of $2,500 ($3,600 − $1,100 = $2,500). ▼

In Example 29, suppose the stock had a fair market value of $2,300 (rather than $3,600) when it was donated to charity. Because the fair market value now is less than the adjusted basis, the charitable contribution deduction is $2,300.

Capital Gain Property. **Capital gain property** is any property that would have resulted in the recognition of long-term capital gain or § 1231 gain if the property had been sold by the donor.[42] As a general rule, the deduction for a contribution of capital gain property is equal to the fair market value of the property.

Two major exceptions disallow the deductibility of the appreciation on long-term capital gain property. One exception concerns certain private foundations. Private foundations are organizations that traditionally do not receive their funding from the general public (e.g., the Ford Foundation). Generally, foundations fall into two categories: operating and nonoperating. A private *operating* foundation is one that spends substantially all of its income in the active conduct of the charitable undertaking for which it was established. Other private foundations are *nonoperating* foundations. However, if a private nonoperating foundation distributes the contributions it receives according to special rules within two and one-half months following the year of the contribution, the organization is treated the same as public charities and private operating foundations. Often, only the private foundation knows its status (operating or nonoperating) for sure, and the status can change from year to year.

If capital gain property is contributed to a private nonoperating foundation, the taxpayer must reduce the contribution by the long-term capital gain that would

---

[41]For a more complete discussion of the difference between ordinary income and capital gain property, see Chapter 16.

[42]For charitable contribution purposes, the term "long term" includes both the mid-term and long-term holding periods. See General Scheme of Taxation in Chapter 16.

have been recognized if the property had been sold at its fair market value. The effect of this provision is to limit the deduction to the property's adjusted basis.[43]

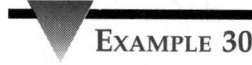

EXAMPLE 30

Walter purchases land for $800 on January 1, 1975, and donates it to a private nonoperating foundation on June 21, 1998, when it is worth $2,000. Walter's charitable contribution is $800 ($2,000 − $1,200), the land's basis. ▼

If, in Example 30, Walter had donated the land to either a public charity or a private operating foundation, his charitable contribution would be $2,000, the fair market value of the land.

A second exception applying to capital gain property relates to *tangible personalty*. Tangible personalty is all property that is not realty (land and buildings) and does not include intangible property such as stock or securities. If tangible personalty is contributed to a public charity such as a museum, church, or university, the charitable deduction may have to be reduced. The amount of the reduction is the long-term capital gain that would have been recognized if the property had been sold for its fair market value. The reduction is required *if* the property is put to an unrelated use. The term *unrelated use* means a use that is unrelated to the exempt purpose or function of the charitable organization.

A taxpayer in this instance must establish that the property is not in fact being put to an unrelated use by the donee. The taxpayer must also establish that at the time of the contribution it was reasonable to anticipate that the property would not be put to an unrelated use. For a contribution of personalty to a museum, if the work of art is the kind of art normally retained by the museum, it is reasonable for a donor to anticipate that the work of art will not be put to an unrelated use. This is the case even if the object is later sold or exchanged by the museum.[44]

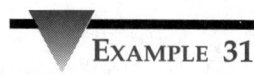

EXAMPLE 31

Myrtle contributes a Picasso painting, for which she paid $20,000, to a local museum. She had owned the painting for four years. It had a value of $30,000 at the time of the donation. The museum displayed the painting for two years and subsequently sold it for $50,000. The charitable contribution is $30,000. It is not reduced by the unrealized appreciation since the painting was put to a related use even though it was later sold by the museum. ▼

Fifty Percent Ceiling.   Contributions made to public charities may not exceed 50 percent of an individual's AGI for the year. Excess contributions may be carried over to the next five years. The 50 percent ceiling on contributions applies to the following types of public charities:

- A church or a convention or association of churches.
- An educational organization that maintains a regular faculty and curriculum.
- A hospital or medical school.
- An organization supported by the government that holds property or investments for the benefit of a college or university.
- A Federal, state, or local governmental unit.
- An organization normally receiving a substantial part of its support from the public or a governmental unit.

---

[43]For a limited period, taxpayers who donate *qualified appreciated stock* to private nonoperating foundations may deduct the fair market value of the stock. Qualified appreciated stock is stock for which market quotations are readily available on an established securities market. This provision applies to stock contributed from July 1, 1996, through May 31, 1998.

[44]Reg. § 1.170A–4(b)(3)(ii)(b).

In the remaining discussion of charitable contributions, public charities and private foundations (both operating and nonoperating) that qualify for the 50 percent ceiling will be referred to as *50 percent organizations*.

The 50 percent ceiling also applies to contributions to the following organizations:

- All private operating foundations.
- Certain private nonoperating foundations that distribute the contributions they receive to public charities and private operating foundations within two and one-half months following the year they receive the contribution.
- Certain private nonoperating foundations in which the contributions are pooled in a common fund and the income and principal sum are paid to public charities.

Thirty Percent Ceiling. A 30 percent ceiling applies to contributions of cash and ordinary income property to private nonoperating foundations that are not 50 percent organizations. The 30 percent ceiling also applies to contributions of appreciated capital gain property to 50 percent organizations unless the taxpayer makes a special election (see below).

In the event the contributions for any one tax year involve both 50 percent and 30 percent property, the allowable deduction comes first from the 50 percent property.

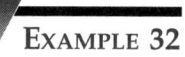

EXAMPLE 32

During the year, Lisa made the following donations to her church: cash of $2,000 and unimproved land worth $30,000. Lisa had purchased the land four years ago for $22,000 and held it as an investment. Therefore, it is long-term capital gain property. Lisa's AGI for the year is $50,000. Disregarding percentage limitations, Lisa's potential deduction is $32,000 [$2,000 (cash) + $30,000 (fair market value of land)].

In applying the percentage limitations, however, the *current* deduction for the land is limited to $15,000 [30% (limitation applicable to long-term capital gain property) × $50,000 (AGI)]. Thus, the total deduction is $17,000 ($2,000 cash + $15,000 land). Note that the total deduction does not exceed $25,000, which is 50% of Lisa's AGI. ▼

Under a special election, a taxpayer may choose to forgo a deduction of the appreciation on capital gain property. Referred to as the *reduced deduction election*, this enables the taxpayer to move from the 30 percent limitation to the 50 percent limitation.

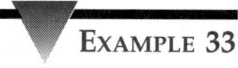

EXAMPLE 33

Assume the same facts as in Example 32, except that Lisa makes the reduced deduction election. Now the deduction becomes $24,000 [$2,000 (cash) + $22,000 (basis in land)] because both donations fall under the 50% limitation. Thus, by making the election, Lisa has increased her charitable contribution deduction by $7,000 [$24,000 – $17,000 (Example 32)]. ▼

Although the reduced deduction election appears attractive, it should be considered carefully. The election sacrifices a deduction for the appreciation on long-term capital gain property that might eventually be allowed. Note that in Example 32, the potential deduction was $32,000, yet in Example 33 only $24,000 is allowed. The reason the potential deduction is decreased by $8,000 ($32,000 – $24,000) is that no carryover is allowed for the amount sacrificed by the election.

CONCEPT SUMMARY 10–2

Determining the Deduction for Contributions of Appreciated Property by Individuals

If the Type of Property Contributed Is:	And the Property Is Contributed to:	The Contribution Is Measured by:	But the Deduction Is Limited to:
1. Capital gain property	A 50% organization	Fair market value of the property	30% of AGI
2. Ordinary income property	A 50% organization	The basis of the property*	50% of AGI
3. Capital gain property (and the property is tangible personal property put to an unrelated use by the donee)	A 50% organization	The basis of the property*	50% of AGI
4. Capital gain property (and the reduced deduction is elected)	A 50% organization	The basis of the property	50% of AGI
5. Capital gain property	A private nonoperating foundation that is not a 50% organization	The basis of the property*	The lesser of: 1. 20% of AGI 2. 50% of AGI minus other contributions to 50% organizations

*If the fair market value of the property is less than the adjusted basis (i.e., the property has declined in value instead of appreciating), the fair market value is used.

Twenty Percent Ceiling.   A 20 percent ceiling applies to contributions of appreciated long-term capital gain property to private nonoperating foundations that are not 50 percent organizations.

Contribution Carryovers.   Contributions that exceed the percentage limitations for the current year can be carried over for five years. In the carryover process, such contributions do not lose their identity for limitation purposes. Thus, if the contribution originally involved 30 percent property, the carryover will continue to be classified as 30 percent property in the carryover year.

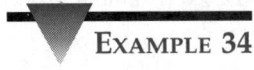

EXAMPLE 34   Assume the same facts as in Example 32. Because only $15,000 of the $30,000 value of the land was deducted in the current year, the balance of $15,000 may be carried over to the following year. But the carryover will still be treated as long-term capital gain property and is subject to the 30%-of-AGI limitation. ▼

In applying the percentage limitations, current charitable contributions must be claimed first before any carryovers can be considered. If carryovers involve more than one year, they are utilized in a first-in, first-out order.

MISCELLANEOUS ITEMIZED DEDUCTIONS

7 LEARNING OBJECTIVE
List the business and personal expenditures that are deductible either as miscellaneous itemized deductions or as other itemized deductions.

No deduction is allowed for personal, living, or family expenses.[45] However, a taxpayer may incur a number of expenditures related to employment. If an employee or outside salesperson incurs unreimbursed business expenses or expenses that are reimbursed under a nonaccountable plan, including travel and transportation, the expenses are deductible as **miscellaneous itemized deductions.**[46] Certain other expenses also fall into the special category of miscellaneous itemized deductions. Some are deductible only if, in total, they exceed 2 percent of the taxpayer's AGI. These miscellaneous itemized deductions include (but are not limited to) the following:

- Professional dues to membership organizations.
- Uniforms or other clothing that cannot be used for normal wear.
- Fees incurred for the preparation of one's tax return or fees incurred for tax litigation before the IRS or the courts.
- Job-hunting costs.
- Fee paid for a safe deposit box used to store papers and documents relating to taxable income-producing investments.
- Investment expenses that are deductible under § 212 as discussed in Chapter 6.
- Appraisal fees to determine the amount of a casualty loss or the fair market value of donated property.
- Hobby losses up to the amount of hobby income (see Chapter 6).
- Unreimbursed employee expenses (see Chapter 9).

Certain employee business expenses that are reimbursed are not itemized deductions, but are deducted *for* AGI. Employee business expenses are discussed in depth in Chapter 9.

OTHER MISCELLANEOUS DEDUCTIONS

Certain expenses and losses do not fall into any category of itemized deductions already discussed but are nonetheless deductible. The following expenses and losses are deductible on line 27 of Schedule A as Other Miscellaneous Deductions.

- Gambling losses up to the amount of gambling winnings.
- Impairment-related work expenses of a handicapped person.
- Federal estate tax on income in respect of a decedent.
- Deduction for repayment of amounts under a claim of right if more than $3,000 (discussed in Chapter 18).
- The unrecovered investment in an annuity contract when the annuity ceases by reason of death, discussed in Chapter 4.

Unlike the expenses and losses discussed previously under Miscellaneous Itemized Deductions, the above expenses and losses are not subject to the 2 percent-of-AGI floor.

---

[45]§ 262.
[46]Actors and performing artists who meet certain requirements are not subject to this rule.

Comprehensive Example of Schedule A

Harry and Jean Brown, married filing jointly, had the following transactions for the current year:

• Medicines that required a prescription	$ 430
• Doctor and dentist bills paid and not reimbursed	2,120
• Medical insurance premium payments	1,200
• Contact lenses	175
• Transportation for medical purposes (380 miles × 10 cents/mile + $5.00 parking)	43
• State income tax withheld	620
• Real estate taxes	1,580
• Interest paid on qualified residence mortgage	2,840
• Charitable contributions in cash	860
• Transportation in performing charitable services (800 miles × 14 cents/mile + $7.00 parking and tolls)	119
• Unreimbursed employee expenses (from a Form 2106)	870
• Tax return preparation	150
• Safe deposit box (used for keeping investment documents and tax records)	170

The Browns' AGI is $40,000. Their completed 1997 Schedule A on the following page reports itemized deductions totaling $7,377.

Overall Limitation on Certain Itemized Deductions

8 ▼ **Learning Objective**
Recognize the limitation on certain itemized deductions applicable to high-income taxpayers.

Congress has enacted several provisions limiting tax benefits for high-income taxpayers. These limitations include the exemption phase-out (refer to Chapter 3) and a phase-out of itemized deductions. The phase-out of itemized deductions (also referred to as a cutback adjustment) applies to taxpayers whose AGI exceeds $124,500 ($62,250 for married taxpayers filing separately).[47] The limitation applies to the following frequently encountered itemized deductions:[48]

• Taxes.
• Home mortgage interest, including points.
• Charitable contributions.
• Unreimbursed employee expenses subject to the 2 percent-of-AGI floor.
• All other expenses subject to the 2 percent-of-AGI floor.

The following deductions are *not* subject to the limitation on itemized deductions:

• Medical and dental expenses.

---

[47]For 1997, the limitation applied if AGI exceeded $121,200 ($60,600 for married taxpayers filing separately).
[48]Other deductions subject to the limitation include Federal estate tax on income in respect of a decedent, certain amortizable bond premiums, the deduction for repayment of certain amounts, certain unrecovered investments in an annuity, and impairment-related work expenses.

SCHEDULES A&B	**Schedule A—Itemized Deductions**				OMB No. 1545-0074	
(Form 1040)	(Schedule B is on back)				**1997**	
Department of the Treasury Internal Revenue Service (99)	▶ Attach to Form 1040. ▶ See Instructions for Schedules A and B (Form 1040).				Attachment Sequence No. **07**	

Name(s) shown on Form 1040: *Harry and Jean Brown* Your social security number: 371 30 3987

Medical and Dental Expenses

Caution: Do not include expenses reimbursed or paid by others.
1 Medical and dental expenses (see page A-1) — 3,968
2 Enter amount from Form 1040, line 33. | 2 | 40,000 |
3 Multiply line 2 above by 7.5% (.075) — 3,000
4 Subtract line 3 from line 1. If line 3 is more than line 1, enter -0- — **4** 968

Taxes You Paid (See page A-2.)
5 State and local income taxes — 620
6 Real estate taxes (see page A-2) — 1,580
7 Personal property taxes
8 Other taxes. List type and amount ▶
9 Add lines 5 through 8 — **9** 2,200

Interest You Paid (See page A-2.) Note: Personal interest is not deductible.
10 Home mortgage interest and points reported to you on Form 1098 — 2,840
11 Home mortgage interest not reported to you on Form 1098. If paid to the person from whom you bought the home, see page A-3 and show that person's name, identifying no., and address ▶
12 Points not reported to you on Form 1098. See page A-3 for special rules
13 Investment interest. Attach Form 4952 if required. (See page A-3.)
14 Add lines 10 through 13 — **14** 2,840

Gifts to Charity If you made a gift and got a benefit for it, see page A-3.
15 Gifts by cash or check. If you made any gift of $250 or more, see page A-3 — 860
16 Other than by cash or check. If any gift of $250 or more, see page A-3. You **MUST** attach Form 8283 if over $500 — 119
17 Carryover from prior year
18 Add lines 15 through 17 — **18** 979

Casualty and Theft Losses
19 Casualty or theft loss(es). Attach Form 4684. (See page A-4.) — **19**

Job Expenses and Most Other Miscellaneous Deductions (See page A-5 for expenses to deduct here.)
20 Unreimbursed employee expenses—job travel, union dues, job education, etc. You **MUST** attach Form 2106 or 2106-EZ if required. (See page A-4.) ▶ *Form 2106 $870* — 870
21 Tax preparation fees — 150
22 Other expenses—investment, safe deposit box, etc. List type and amount ▶ *Safe deposit box $170* — 170
23 Add lines 20 through 22 — 1,190
24 Enter amount from Form 1040, line 33. | 24 | 40,000 |
25 Multiply line 24 above by 2% (.02) — 800
26 Subtract line 25 from line 23. If line 25 is more than line 23, enter -0- — **26** 390

Other Miscellaneous Deductions
27 Other—from list on page A-5. List type and amount ▶ — **27**

Total Itemized Deductions
28 Is Form 1040, line 33, over $121,200 (over $60,600 if married filing separately)?
NO. Your deduction is not limited. Add the amounts in the far right column for lines 4 through 27. Also, enter on Form 1040, line 35, the **larger** of this amount or your standard deduction. ▶ **28** 7,377
YES. Your deduction may be limited. See page A-5 for the amount to enter.

For Paperwork Reduction Act Notice, see Form 1040 instructions. Cat. No. 11330X Schedule A (Form 1040) 1997

- Investment interest expense.
- Nonbusiness casualty and theft losses.
- Gambling losses.

Taxpayers subject to the limitation must reduce itemized deductions by the lesser of:

- 3 percent of the amount by which AGI exceeds $124,500 ($62,250 if married filing separately).
- 80 percent of itemized deductions that are affected by the limit.

The overall limitation is applied after applying all other limitations to itemized deductions that are affected by the overall limitation. Other limitations apply to charitable contributions, certain meals and entertainment expenses, and certain miscellaneous itemized deductions.

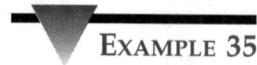

EXAMPLE 35

Herman, who is single, had AGI of $200,000 for 1998. He incurred the following expenses and losses during the year:

Medical expenses before 7.5%-of-AGI limitation	$16,000
State and local income taxes	3,200
Real estate taxes	2,800
Home mortgage interest	7,200
Charitable contributions	2,000
Casualty loss before 10% limitation (after $100 floor)	21,500
Unreimbursed employee expenses subject to 2%-of-AGI limitation	4,300
Gambling losses (Herman had $3,000 gambling income)	7,000

Herman's itemized deductions *before* the overall limitation are computed as follows:

Medical expenses [$16,000 − (7.5% × $200,000)]	$ 1,000
State and local income taxes	3,200
Real estate taxes	2,800
Home mortgage interest	7,200
Charitable contributions	2,000
Casualty loss [$21,500 − (10% × $200,000)]	1,500
Unreimbursed employee expenses ($4,300 − (2% × $200,000)]	300
Gambling losses ($7,000 loss limited to $3,000 of gambling income)	3,000
Total itemized deductions before overall limitation	$21,000

Herman's itemized deductions subject to the overall limitation are as follows:

State and local income taxes	$ 3,200
Real estate taxes	2,800
Home mortgage interest	7,200
Charitable contributions	2,000
Unreimbursed employee expenses	300
Total	$15,500

Herman must reduce this amount by the smaller of the following:

- 3% ($200,000 AGI − $124,500) $ 2,265
- 80% of itemized deductions subject to limitation ($15,500 × .80)   12,400

FEW TAXPAYERS ARE AFFECTED BY THE THREE PERCENT FLOOR

The IRS *Statistics of Income Bulletin* for 1994 (the latest year available) shows that few taxpayers have to be concerned about the 3 percent floor for itemized deductions. In 1994, the AGI threshold for application of this limitation was $111,800 ($55,900 for married taxpayers filing separately). The IRS statistics for 1994 show that taxpayers with AGI of $91,226 or more ranked in the top 5 percent. Obviously, fewer than 5 percent of all taxpayers were subject to the 3 percent floor in 1994.

Therefore, the amount of the reduction is $2,265, and Herman has $18,735 of deductible itemized deductions, computed as follows:

Deductible itemized deductions subject to overall limitation ($15,500 − $2,265)	$13,235
Itemized deductions not subject to overall limitation:	
Medical expenses	1,000
Casualty loss	1,500
Gambling losses	3,000
Deductible itemized deductions	$18,735

TAX PLANNING CONSIDERATIONS

9 LEARNING OBJECTIVE
Identify tax planning procedures that can maximize the benefit of itemized deductions.

EFFECTIVE UTILIZATION OF ITEMIZED DEDUCTIONS

Since an individual may use the standard deduction in one year and itemize deductions in another year, it is frequently possible to obtain maximum benefit by shifting itemized deductions from one year to another. For example, if a taxpayer's itemized deductions and the standard deduction are approximately the same for each year of a two-year period, the taxpayer should use the standard deduction in one year and shift itemized deductions (to the extent permitted by law) to the other year. The individual could, for example, prepay a church pledge for a particular year to shift the deduction to the current year or avoid paying end-of-the-year medical expenses to shift the deduction to the following year.

UTILIZATION OF MEDICAL DEDUCTIONS

When a taxpayer anticipates that medical expenses will approximate the percentage floor, much might be done to generate a deductible excess. Any of the following procedures can help build a deduction by the end of the year:

- Incur the obligation for needed dental work or have needed work carried out.[49] Orthodontic treatment, for example, may have been recommended for a member of the taxpayer's family.
- Have elective remedial surgery that may have been postponed from prior years (e.g., tonsillectomies, vasectomies, correction of hernias, hysterectomies).

[49]Prepayment of medical expenses does not generate a current deduction unless the taxpayer is under an obligation to make the payment.

• Incur the obligation for capital improvements to the taxpayer's personal residence recommended by a physician (e.g., an air filtration system to alleviate a respiratory disorder).

As an aid to taxpayers who may experience temporary cash-flow problems at the end of the year, the use of bank credit cards is deemed to be payment for purposes of timing the deductibility of charitable and medical expenses.

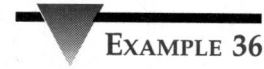
EXAMPLE 36

On December 13, 1998, Marge (a calendar year taxpayer) purchases two pairs of prescription contact lenses and one pair of prescribed orthopedic shoes for a total of $305. These purchases are separately charged to Marge's credit card. On January 6, 1999, Marge receives her statement containing these charges and makes payment shortly thereafter. The purchases are deductible as medical expenses in the year charged (1998) and not in the year the account is settled (1999). ▼

Recognizing which expenditures qualify for the medical deduction also may be crucial to exceeding the percentage limitations.

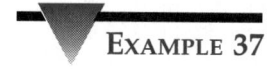
EXAMPLE 37

Mortimer employs Lana (an unrelated party) to care for his incapacitated and dependent mother. Lana is not a trained nurse but spends approximately one-half of the time performing nursing duties (e.g., administering injections and providing physical therapy) and the rest of the time doing household chores. An allocable portion of Lana's wages that Mortimer pays (including the employer's portion of FICA taxes) qualifies as a medical expense. ▼

TIMING THE PAYMENT OF DEDUCTIBLE TAXES

It is sometimes possible to defer or accelerate the payment of certain deductible taxes, such as state income tax, real property tax, and personal property tax. For instance, the final installment of estimated state income tax is generally due after the end of a given tax year. Accelerating the payment of the final installment could result in larger itemized deductions for the current year.

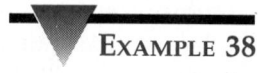
EXAMPLE 38

Jenny, who is single, expects to have itemized deductions of $3,900 in 1998 and $2,500 in 1999. She plans to pay $900 as the final installment on her 1998 estimated state income tax, which is due on January 15, 1999. If Jenny does not pay the final installment until 1999, she will not itemize in either 1998 or 1999. However, if she pays the final installment in December 1998, her itemized deductions will be $4,800 ($3,900 + $900) in 1999, and she will benefit from itemizing. ▼

PROTECTING THE INTEREST DEDUCTION

Although the deductibility of prepaid interest by a cash basis taxpayer has been severely restricted, a notable exception allows a deduction for points paid by the buyer to obtain financing for the purchase or improvement of a principal residence in the year of payment. However, such points must actually be paid by the taxpayer obtaining the loan and must represent a charge for the use of money. It has been held that points paid from the mortgage proceeds do not satisfy the payment requirement.[50] Also, the portion of the points attributable to service charges does not represent deductible interest.[51] Taxpayers financing

---

[50]*Alan A. Rubnitz*, 67 T.C. 621 (1977). Seller-paid points may also be deductible by the buyer under the provisions of Rev.Proc. 94–27, cited in footnote 27.

[51]*Donald L. Wilkerson*, 70 T.C. 240 (1978).

home purchases or improvements usually should direct their planning toward avoiding these two hurdles to immediate deductibility.

In rare instances, a taxpayer may find it desirable to forgo the immediate expensing of points in the year paid. Instead, it could prove beneficial to capitalize the points and write them off as interest expense over the life of the mortgage.

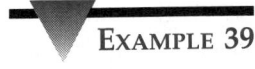
EXAMPLE 39

Gerald purchases a home on December 15, 1998, for $95,000 with $30,000 cash and a 15-year mortgage of $65,000 financed by the Greater Metropolis National Bank. Gerald pays two points in addition to interest allocated to the period from December 15 until December 31, 1998, at an annual rate of 10%. Since Gerald does not have enough itemized deductions to exceed the standard deduction for 1998, he should elect to capitalize the interest expense by amortizing the points over 15 years. In this instance, Gerald would deduct $86.67 for 1999, as part of his qualified residence interest expense [$1,300 (two points) divided by 15 years], if he elects to itemize that year. ▼

Because personal (consumer) interest is not deductible, taxpayers should consider making use of home equity loans. Recall that these loans utilize the personal residence of the taxpayer as security. Since the tracing rules do not apply to home equity loans, the funds from these loans can be used for personal purposes (e.g., auto loans, education). By making use of home equity loans, therefore, what would have been nondeductible consumer interest becomes deductible qualified residence interest.

ASSURING THE CHARITABLE CONTRIBUTION DEDUCTION

For a charitable contribution deduction to be available, the recipient must be a qualified charitable organization. Sometimes the mechanics of how the contribution is carried out can determine whether or not a deduction results.

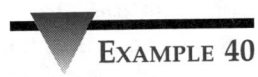
EXAMPLE 40

Fumiko wants to donate $5,000 to her church's mission in Kobe, Japan. In this regard, she considers three alternatives:

1. Send the money directly to the mission.
2. Give the money to her church with the understanding that it is to be passed on to the mission.
3. Give the money directly to the missionary in charge of the mission who is currently in the United States on a fund-raising trip.

If Fumiko wants to obtain a deduction for the contribution, she should choose alternative 2. A direct donation to the mission (alternative 1) is not deductible because the mission is a foreign charity. A direct gift to the missionary (alternative 3) does not comply since an individual cannot be a qualified charity for income tax purposes.[52] ▼

When making noncash donations, the type of property chosen can have decided implications in determining the amount, if any, of the deduction.

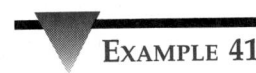
EXAMPLE 41

Sam wants to give $60,000 in value to his church in some form other than cash. In this connection, he considers four alternatives:

1. Stock held for two years as an investment with a basis of $100,000 and a fair market value of $60,000.
2. Stock held for five years as an investment with a basis of $10,000 and a fair market value of $60,000.

---

[52]*Thomas E. Lesslie*, 36 TCM 495, T.C.Memo. 1977–111.

3. The rent-free use for a year of a building that normally leases for $5,000 a month.
4. A valuable stamp collection held as an investment and owned for 10 years with a basis of $10,000 and a fair market value of $60,000. The church plans to sell the collection if and when it is donated.

Alternative 1 is ill-advised as the subject of the gift. Even though Sam would obtain a deduction of $60,000, he would forgo the potential loss of $40,000 that would be recognized if the property were sold.[53] Alternative 2 makes good sense since the deduction still is $60,000 and none of the $50,000 of appreciation that has occurred must be recognized as income. Alternative 3 yields no deduction at all and is not a wise choice. Alternative 4 involves tangible personalty that the recipient does not plan to use. As a result, the amount of the deduction is limited to $10,000, the stamp collection's basis.[54] ▼

For property transfers (particularly real estate), the ceiling limitations on the amount of the deduction allowed in any one year (50 percent, 30 percent, or 20 percent of AGI, as the case may be) could be a factor to take into account. With proper planning, donations can be controlled to stay within the limitations and therefore avoid the need for a carryover of unused charitable contributions.

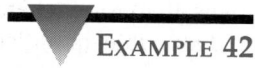

EXAMPLE 42

Andrew wants to donate a tract of unimproved land held as an investment to the University of Maryland (a qualified charitable organization). The land has been held for six years and has a current fair market value of $300,000 and a basis to Andrew of $50,000. Andrew's AGI for the current year is estimated to be $200,000, and he expects much the same for the next few years. In the current year, he deeds (transfers) an undivided one-fifth interest in the real estate to the university. ▼

What has Andrew in Example 42 accomplished for income tax purposes? In the current year, he will be allowed a charitable contribution deduction of $60,000 (⅕ × $300,000), which will be within the applicable limitation of AGI (30% × $200,000). Presuming no other charitable contributions for the year, Andrew has avoided the possibility of a carryover. In future years, Andrew can arrange donations of undivided interests in the real estate to stay within the bounds of the percentage limitations. The only difficulty with this approach is the need to revalue the real estate each year before the donation, since the amount of the deduction is based on the fair market value of the interest contributed at the time of the contribution.

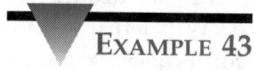

EXAMPLE 43

Tiffany dies in October 1998. In completing her final income tax return for 1998, Tiffany's executor determines the following information: AGI of $104,000 and a donation by Tiffany to her church of stock worth $60,000. Tiffany had purchased the stock two years ago for $50,000 and held it as an investment. Tiffany's executor makes the reduced deduction election and, as a consequence, claims a charitable contribution deduction of $50,000. With the election, the potential charitable contribution deduction of $50,000 ($60,000 – $10,000) is less than the 50% ceiling of $52,000 ($104,000 × 50%). If the executor had not made the election, the potential charitable contribution deduction of $60,000 would have been reduced by the 30% ceiling to $31,200 ($104,000 × 30%). No carryover of the $28,800 ($60,000 – $31,200) would have been available. ▼

---

[53]*LaVar M. Withers*, 69 T.C. 900 (1978).
[54]No reduction of appreciation is necessary in alternative 2 since stock is intangible property and not tangible personalty.

KEY TERMS

Acquisition indebtedness, 10–15

Capital gain property, 10–23

Charitable contribution, 10–19

Home equity loans, 10–15

Investment income, 10–14

Investment interest, 10–13

Medical expense, 10–2

Miscellaneous itemized deductions, 10–27

Net investment income, 10–14

Ordinary income property, 10–23

Points, 10–16

Qualified residence interest, 10–13

PROBLEM MATERIALS

DISCUSSION QUESTIONS

1. Dan, a self-employed individual taxpayer, prepared his own income tax return for the past year and asked you to check it over for accuracy. Your review indicates that Dan failed to claim certain business entertainment expenses.
   a. Will the correction of this omission affect the amount of medical expenses Dan can deduct? Explain.
   b. Would it matter if Dan were employed rather than self-employed?

2. Pat incurred the following expenses during the year: $450 for an annual physical exam, $80 for a dental checkup, $600 for a weight reduction program, $1,800 for alcohol rehabilitation, and $200 for a stop-smoking clinic. Which of these expenses qualify for the medical deduction? Explain.

3. Juanita, your client, had an accident while competing in a bicycle race. She sustained facial injuries that required cosmetic surgery. While having the surgery done to restore her appearance, she has additional surgery done to reshape her nose, which was not injured in the accident. Under what circumstances, if any, will the cost of Juanita's cosmetic surgery qualify as a deductible medical expense?

4. Don, who lives in a small town in North Dakota, has a back problem that requires regular exercise. He is unable to get outdoor exercise during the cold North Dakota winters. His doctor has recommended that Don go to Arizona and play golf and hike during the winter. He takes his doctor's advice and incurs expenses for transportation, meals, lodging, greens fees, and hiking equipment while in Arizona. Discuss the deductibility of those costs and any limits that will apply to the deduction.

5. Andres was injured in an automobile accident and is confined to a wheelchair. Because he lives alone, he must have extensive modifications made to various rooms in his home, including the kitchen, bathrooms, and hallways. Do the capital expenditures incurred to modify his home constitute a valid medical expense? If so, how much of the expense is deductible?

6. Betty, a sole proprietor of an antique shop, has two dependent children. During the year, she paid health insurance premiums of $1,600 for her own coverage and $2,400 for coverage of her children. How will these premium payments affect Betty's taxable income computation?

7. Rebecca took her daughter, Susan, from Chicago to Rochester, Minnesota, for surgery at the Mayo Clinic. She incurred expenses for gasoline, highway tolls, and meals while traveling. Rebecca stayed in a motel near the clinic for six days while Susan was hospitalized. Discuss the extent to which transportation, meals, and lodging costs incurred by Susan and Rebecca are deductible as medical expenses (ignore the 7.5% floor).

8. Erin incurred medical expenses in 1998 and received a reimbursement from her insurance company in 1999. Under what circumstances must Erin report all or part of the reimbursement in gross income for 1999? Under what circumstances may she exclude the reimbursement from gross income for 1999?

9. By December 1, Ethel had medical expenses of $5,300, of which $1,200 was reimbursed by her insurance company. She expects her AGI for the year to be $60,000 and her other itemized deductions to be $5,600. Can you suggest any tax planning ideas that will enable Ethel to increase her medical expense deduction for the year?

10. A local opthalmologist's advertising campaign included a certificate for a free radial keratotomy for the lucky winner of a drawing. Ahmad held the winning ticket, which was drawn in December 1997. Ahmad had no vision problems and was uncertain what he should do with the prize. In February 1998, Ahmad's daughter, who lives with his former wife, was diagnosed with a vision problem that could be treated either with prescription glasses or a radial keratotomy. The divorce decree requires that Ahmad pay for all medical expenses incurred for his daughter. Identify the relevant tax issues for Ahmad.

11. Julie acquired a personal residence in an older neighborhood that had no sidewalks. The city council passed an ordinance requiring all homeowners to reimburse the city for the cost of installing sidewalks in front of their homes. What is the appropriate tax treatment for the amount Julie is assessed for the sidewalk?

12. Donald owns a principal residence in Chicago, a vacation lodge in New Mexico, and a yacht (with living quarters) on Lake Michigan. All three properties have mortgages on which Donald pays interest. Discuss any limitations that apply to Donald's mortgage interest deduction, and suggest any strategy Donald should consider to maximize his deduction.

13. Ed borrows $20,000 and purchases an automobile. Jack borrows $20,000 to purchase a diamond engagement ring for his fiancée. Ed qualifies for an interest deduction on the amount he borrowed, but Jack does not. Can you offer any explanation for the difference?

14. Jerry purchased a personal residence from Kim. In order to sell the residence, Kim agreed to pay $3,000 in points related to Jerry's mortgage. Discuss the deductibility of the points.

15. Ellen borrows $50,000 from her parents for a down payment on a condominium. She paid interest of $4,200 in 1996, $0 in 1997, and $11,000 in 1998. The IRS disallows the deduction. Can you offer any explanation for the disallowance?

16. The city of Ogden was devastated by a tornado in April 1997, leaving many families in need of food, clothing, shelter, and other necessities. Betty contributed $500 to a family whose home was completely destroyed by the tornado. Jack contributed $700 to the family's church, which gave the money to the family. Discuss the deductibility of these contributions.

17. Sara purchased a ticket to a fund-raising banquet and dance for the Cincinnati Symphony, a public charity. The ticket cost $300, and the normal cost of such an event is $60. How much can Sara deduct as a charitable contribution?

18. Joe, who is in the 39.6% tax bracket in 1998, expects to retire in 1999 and be in the 28% tax bracket. He plans to donate $50,000 to his church. Because he will not have the cash available until 1999, Joe donates land (long-term capital gain property) with a basis of $10,000 and fair market value of $50,000 to the church in December 1998. He reacquires the land for $50,000 in February 1999. Discuss Joe's tax objectives and all tax issues related to his actions.

19. Zina decided to have a garage sale to get rid of a number of items that she no longer needed, including books, old stereo equipment, clothing, bicycles, and furniture. She scheduled the sale for Friday and Saturday, but was forced to close at noon Friday because of a torrential downpour. She had collected $500 for the items she sold before closing. The heavy rains continued through the weekend, and Zina was unable to

continue the sale. She had not enjoyed dealing with the people who came to the sale on Friday morning, so she donated the remaining items to several local organizations. Zina has asked your advice on how she should treat these events on her tax return. List some of the tax issues you would discuss with her.

20. Paula contributed Orange Corporation common stock to the United Way. In addition, she contributed tables and chairs from her proprietorship's inventory to the high school in her city. Should Paula's charitable contribution deduction for these contributions be determined by the basis or fair market value of the contributed items?

21. During the year, Sam donated four suits to Goodwill. He had purchased the suits three years ago at a cost of $1,600 and worn them as personal attire. Because the suits are long-term capital assets, Sam plans to deduct $1,600 on his income tax return. Comment on Sam's understanding of the tax law governing charitable contributions.

22. The Skins Game, which involves four of the top golfers on the PGA Tour, is held each year on the weekend after Thanksgiving. Total prize money amounts to $510,000, and the leading money winner also receives an automobile as a prize. The announcers point out that 10% of the money won by each player goes to charity. In addition, on some holes, the winner of the hole receives the keys to an automobile, which goes to the player's favorite charity. Identify the relevant tax issues for the players. Consider the following possibilities with respect to the car won by the leading money winner: (1) he might keep the car for his own use and sell his present car; (2) he might sell the new car; (3) he might give the car to a friend or relative; (4) he might donate the car to charity; or (5) he might give the car to his caddy.

23. Henry is a television evangelist. In August 1997, the IRS ruled that his organization was no longer a qualified charitable organization because of violations of the tax law. Miguel donated $10,000 to Henry's organization in September 1997. At the time, he did not know that Henry's organization had been disqualified as a charitable organization. In 1998, Henry was jailed for mail fraud. Miguel has filed a civil suit demanding return of the $10,000 plus $100,000 in damages. Identify the relevant tax issues for Miguel.

PROBLEMS

24. Ed and Laura are married and together have AGI of $60,000 in 1998. They have no dependents and file a joint return. During the year, they paid $1,600 for medical insurance, $6,000 in doctor bills and hospital expenses, and $900 for prescribed medicine and drugs.
    a. In December 1998, Ed and Laura received an insurance reimbursement of $1,200 for hospitalization expenses. Determine the deduction allowable for medical expenses paid during the year.
    b. Assume instead that Ed and Laura received the $1,200 insurance reimbursement in February 1999. Determine the deduction allowable for medical expenses incurred in 1998.
    c. Assume again that Ed and Laura received the $1,200 insurance reimbursement in February 1999. Discuss whether the reimbursement will be included in their gross income for 1999.

25. Frank, a widower, had a serious stroke and is no longer capable of caring for himself. He has three sons, all of whom live in different states. Because they are unable to care for Frank in their homes, his sons have placed him in a nursing home equipped to provide medical and nursing care facilities. Total nursing home expenses amount to $45,000 per year. Of this amount, $18,000 is directly attributable to medical and nursing care. Frank's Social Security benefits are used to pay for $12,000 of the nursing home charges. He has no other income. His sons plan to split the remaining medical expenses equally.
    a. What portion of the nursing home charges is potentially deductible as a medical expense?
    b. Can you provide Frank's sons with a tax planning idea for maximizing the deduction for his medical expenses?

26. Ibrahim developed a severe allergy condition, and his physician advised him to install a special air conditioning, heating, and filtration system in his home. The cost of installing the system was $7,200, and the increase in the value of the residence was determined to be $2,300. Ibrahim's AGI for the year was $40,000.
    a. How much of the expenditure can Ibrahim deduct as a medical expense?
    b. Assume the same facts as in (a), except that Ibrahim was paralyzed in a skiing accident and the expenditures were incurred to build entrance and exit ramps and widen the hallways in his home to accommodate his wheelchair. How much of the expenditure can Ibrahim deduct as a medical expense?

27. For calendar year 1998, Julie was a self-employed real estate broker with no employees. She had $80,000 net profit from real estate transactions and paid $5,000 in medical insurance premiums on a policy covering 1998. How much of these premiums may Julie deduct as a deduction *for* AGI and how much may she deduct as an itemized deduction?

28. During the current year, Sara incurred and paid the following expenses for Seth (her son), Emma (her mother), and herself:

Surgery for Seth	$3,800
Trout Valley Academy charges for Seth:	
Tuition	8,000
Room, board, and other expenses	7,600
Psychiatric treatment	6,500
Doctor bills for Emma	2,900
Prescription drugs for Sara, Seth, and Emma	1,100
Insulin for Emma	1,080
Nonprescription drugs for Sara, Seth, and Emma	700
Charges at Riverview Nursing Home for Emma:	
Medical care	6,800
Lodging	7,200
Meals	3,500

Seth qualifies as Sara's dependent, and Emma would also qualify except that she receives $6,100 of taxable retirement benefits from her former employer. Seth's psychiatrist recommended Trout Valley Academy because of its small class sizes and specialized psychiatric treatment program that is needed to treat Seth's illness. Emma is a paraplegic and diabetic, and Riverview offers the type of care that she requires.

Upon the recommendation of a physician, Sara has an air filtration system installed in her personal residence. She suffers from severe allergies. In connection with this equipment, Sara incurs and pays the following amounts during the year:

Filtration system and cost of installation	$6,400
Increase in utility bills due to the system	750
Cost of certified appraisal	320

The system has an estimated useful life of 10 years. The appraisal was to determine the value of Sara's residence with and without the system. The appraisal states that the system increased the value of Sara's residence by $1,200. Ignoring the 7.5% floor, what is the total of Sara's expenses that qualifies for the medical expense deduction?

29. In May, Rebecca's daughter, Susan, sustained a serious injury that made it impossible for her to continue living alone. Susan, who is a novelist, moved back into Rebecca's home after the accident. Susan has begun writing a new novel based on her recent experiences. To accommodate Susan, Rebecca incurred significant remodeling expenses (widening hallways, building a separate bedroom and bathroom, making kitchen appliances accessible to Susan). In addition, Rebecca had an indoor swimming pool constructed so Susan could do rehabilitation exercises prescribed by her physician.

In September, Susan underwent major reconstructive surgery in Denver. The surgery was performed by Dr. Rama Patel, who specializes in treating injuries of the type sustained by Susan. Rebecca drove Susan from Champaign, Illinois, to Denver, a total of 1,100 miles, in Susan's specially equipped van. They left Champaign on Tuesday morning and arrived in Denver on Thursday afternoon. Rebecca incurred expenses for gasoline, highway tolls, meals, and lodging while traveling to Denver. Rebecca stayed in a motel near the clinic for eight days while Susan was hospitalized. Identify the relevant tax issues based on this information and prepare a list of questions that you would need to ask Rebecca and Susan in order to advise them as to the resolution of any issues you have identified.

30. In Meigs County, the real property tax year is the calendar year. The real property tax becomes a personal liability of the owner of real property on January 1 in the current real property tax year, 1998. The tax is payable on June 1, 1998. On May 31, 1998, Geraldo sells his house to Janet for $220,000. On June 1, 1998, Janet pays the entire real estate tax of $8,760 for the year ending December 31, 1998.
    a. How much of the property taxes may Geraldo deduct?
    b. How much of the property taxes may Janet deduct?

31. Assume the same facts as in Problem 30.
    a. What is Janet's basis for the residence?
    b. How much did Geraldo realize from the sale of the residence?

32. Andrea, who uses the cash method of accounting, lives in a state that imposes an income tax. In April 1998, she files her state income tax return for 1997 and pays an additional $1,000 in state income taxes. During 1998, her withholdings for state income tax purposes amount to $7,400, and she pays estimated state income tax of $700. In April 1999, she files her state income tax return for 1998 claiming a refund of $1,800. Andrea receives the refund in August 1999.
    a. Assuming Andrea itemizes deductions in 1998, how much may she claim as a deduction for state income taxes on her Federal return for calendar year 1998 (filed in April 1999)?
    b. Assuming Andrea itemized deductions in 1998, how will the refund of $1,800 that she received in 1999 be treated for Federal income tax purposes?
    c. Assume Andrea itemizes deductions in 1998 and elects to have the $1,800 refund applied toward her 1999 state income tax liability. How will the $1,800 be treated for Federal income tax purposes?
    d. Assuming Andrea did not itemize deductions in 1998, how will the refund of $1,800 received in 1999 be treated for Federal income tax purposes?

33. Irina incurred $39,000 of interest expense related to her investments in 1998. Her investment income included $10,000 of interest, $6,000 of dividends, and a $15,000 net capital gain on the sale of securities.
    a. What is the maximum amount that Irina can treat as investment income for the year?
    b. What other tax factors should Irina consider in deciding whether to elect to include the net capital gain in her investment income?

34. In 1998, Myrna has $8,000 of investment income and the following miscellaneous itemized deductions:

Unreimbursed employee business expenses (meals included at 50%)	$1,400
Tax return preparation fee	440
Investment expenses	500

    For purposes of the investment interest expense limitation, what is the total of Myrna's net investment income in each of the following independent situations:
    a. AGI of $20,000.
    b. AGI of $60,000.
    c. AGI of $110,000.

35. Sid and Sara, married taxpayers, took out a mortgage on their home for $100,000 in 1988. In March of the current year, when the home had a fair market value of $200,000 and they owed $85,000 on the mortgage, Sid and Sara took out a home equity loan for

$110,000. They used the funds to purchase an airplane to be used for recreational purposes. What is the maximum amount on which they can deduct home equity interest?

36. Cindy purchased her residence five years ago, obtaining a 20-year mortgage at an annual interest rate of 11%. On January 2, 1998, Cindy refinanced with a 15-year mortgage in order to reduce the interest rate to 7.25%. To obtain the refinancing, she was required to pay points of $3,500. How much, if any, of the $3,500 points can Cindy deduct in 1998?

37. Erin donates $1,000 to State University's athletic department. The payment guarantees that Erin will have preferred seating on the 50-yard line.
    a. Assume Erin subsequently buys four $50 game tickets. How much can she deduct as a charitable contribution to the university's athletic department?
    b. Assume that Erin's $1,000 donation includes four $50 tickets. How much can she deduct as a charitable contribution to the university's athletic department?

38. Diana owned stock in Hippo Corporation with a basis of $7,500. She donated the stock to a qualified charitable organization on June 1, 1998.
    a. What is the amount of Diana's deduction, assuming that she had purchased the stock on February 3, 1998, and the stock had a fair market value of $9,600 when she made the donation?
    b. Assume the same facts as in (a), except that Diana had purchased the stock on June 3, 1995.
    c. Assume the same facts as in (a), except that the stock had a fair market value of $6,900 (rather than $9,600) when Diana donated it to the charity.

39. Darby contributed a painting to an art museum in 1998. She had owned the painting for 20 years, and it had a value of $120,000 at the time of the donation. The museum displayed the painting in its impressionist gallery.
    a. Assume that Darby's AGI is $230,000 and her basis for the painting is $80,000. Would you recommend that she make the reduced deduction election?
    b. Assume that Darby's AGI is $230,000 and her basis for the painting is $115,000. Would you recommend that she make the reduced deduction election?

40. During the year, Al made the following contributions to his church:

Cash	$20,000
Stock in Thrush Corporation (a publicly traded corporation)	30,000

The stock in Thrush Corporation was acquired as an investment three years ago at a cost of $10,000. Al's AGI is $70,000.
    a. What is Al's charitable contribution deduction?
    b. How are excess amounts, if any, treated?

41. Steven, who had AGI of $180,000 in 1998, contributed stock in Azure Corporation (a publicly traded corporation) to State University, a qualified charitable organization. The stock was worth $105,000, and Steven had acquired it as an investment two years ago at a cost of $84,000.
    a. What is the total amount that Steven can deduct as a charitable contribution, assuming he carries over any disallowed contribution from 1998 to future years?
    b. What is the maximum amount that Steven can deduct as a charitable contribution in 1998?
    c. What factors should Steven consider in deciding how to treat the contribution for Federal income tax purposes?
    d. Assume Steven dies in December 1998. What advice would you give the executor of his estate with regard to possible elections that can be made relative to the contribution?

42. On December 30, 1998, Roberta purchased four tickets to a charity ball sponsored by the city of San Diego for the benefit of underprivileged children. Each ticket cost $200 and had a fair market value of $35. On the same day as the purchase, Roberta gave the tickets to the minister of her church for personal use by his family. At the time of the gift of the tickets, Roberta pledged $4,000 to the building fund of her church. The pledge was satisfied by check dated December 31, 1998, but not mailed until January 3, 1999.

a. Presuming Roberta is a cash basis and calendar year taxpayer, how much can she deduct as a charitable contribution for 1998?

b. Would the amount of the deduction be any different if Roberta is an accrual basis taxpayer? Explain.

43. In December each year, Alice Young contributes 10% of her gross income to the United Way (a 50% organization). Alice, who is in the 36% marginal tax bracket, is considering the following alternatives as charitable contributions in December 1998:

	Fair Market Value
(1) Cash donation	$21,000
(2) Unimproved land held for six years ($3,000 basis)	21,000
(3) Blue Corporation stock held for eight months ($3,000 basis)	21,000
(4) Gold Corporation stock held for two years ($26,000 basis)	21,000

Alice has asked you to help her decide which of the potential contributions listed above will be most advantageous taxwise. Evaluate the four alternatives and write a letter to Alice to communicate your advice to her. Her address is 2622 Bayshore Drive, Berkeley, CA 94709.

44. Manuel and Rosa Garcia, both age 45, are married and have no dependents. They have asked you to advise them whether they should file jointly or separately in 1998. They present you with the following information:

	Manuel	Rosa	Joint
Salary	$40,000		
Business net income		$100,000	
Interest income	400	1,200	$2,200
Deductions *for* AGI	2,000	13,000	
Medical expenses	9,500	600	
State income tax	800	2,000	
Real estate tax			3,400
Mortgage interest			5,200
Unreimbursed employee expenses	1,100		

If they file separately, Manuel and Rosa will split the real estate tax and mortgage interest deductions equally. Write Manuel and Rosa a letter in which you make and explain a recommendation on filing status for 1998. Manuel and Rosa reside at 5904 Stevens Avenue, Durham, NC 27707.

45. For calendar year 1998, Joe and Sandra file a joint return reflecting AGI of $180,000. Their itemized deductions are as follows:

Medical expenses	$15,000
Casualty loss (not covered by insurance)	21,000
Interest on home mortgage	11,000
Property taxes on home	12,000
Charitable contributions	13,000
State income tax	17,000

After all necessary adjustments are made, what is the amount of itemized deductions Joe and Sandra may claim?

46. Chris, who is single, had AGI of $220,000 during 1998. He incurred the following expenses and losses during the year:

Medical expenses before 7.5%-of-AGI limitation	$19,000
State and local income taxes	4,100
Real estate taxes	2,200
Home mortgage interest	5,600
Charitable contributions	3,500
Casualty loss before 10% limitation (after $100 floor)	25,000
Unreimbursed employee expenses subject to 2%-of-AGI limitation	5,700
Gambling losses (Chris had $4,200 of gambling income)	8,000

Compute Chris's itemized deductions before and after the overall limitation.

47. Barry and Emily are married, have no dependents, and file a joint return for 1998. Information for the year includes the following:

AGI	$252,500
State and local income taxes	6,000
Real estate taxes	7,800
Home mortgage interest	7,100
Charitable contributions	8,500
Gambling losses (gambling income of $4,500 was included in AGI)	7,000

   a. Compute allowable itemized deductions for 1998 for Barry and Emily.
   b. Compute taxable income for Barry and Emily for 1998.

48. Andy, who is single, had AGI of $180,000 for 1998. He incurred the following expenses and losses during the year:

Medical expenses before 7.5%-of-AGI limitation	$15,000
State and local income taxes	2,600
Real estate taxes	3,400
Home mortgage interest	6,600
Charitable contribution	3,500
Casualty loss before 10% limitation (after $100 floor)	20,600
Unreimbursed employee expenses subject to 2%-of-AGI limitation	4,100
Gambling losses (Andy had $3,500 of gambling income)	7,000

Calculate Andy's allowable itemized deductions for the year.

CUMULATIVE PROBLEMS

49. Alice and Bruce Byrd are married taxpayers, ages 47 and 45, who file a joint return. Their Social Security numbers are 034–48–4382 and 016–50–9556, respectively. They live at 473 Revere Avenue, Ames, MA 01850. Alice is the office manager for a dental clinic and earns an annual salary of $46,000. Bruce is the manager of a fast-food outlet owned and operated by Plymouth Corporation. His annual salary is $37,000.

   The Byrds have two children, Cynthia (age 23 and S.S. no. 017–44–9126) and John (age 22 and S.S. no. 017–27–4148), who live with them. Both children are full-time students at a nearby college. Alice's mother, Myrtle Jones (age 74 and S.S. no. 016–15–8266), also lives with them. Her sole source of income is from Social Security benefits, which she deposits in a savings account.

   During 1997, the Byrds furnished one-third of the total support of Bruce's widower father, Sam Byrd (age 70 and S.S. no. 034–82–8583). Sam lives alone and receives the rest of his support from Bruce's sister and brother (one-third each). They have signed a multiple support agreement allowing Bruce to claim Sam as a dependent for 1997. Sam died in November, and Bruce received life insurance proceeds of $270,000 on December 28.

   The Byrds had the following expenses relating to their personal residence during 1997:

Property taxes	$2,400
Interest on home mortgage	6,900
Repairs to roof	2,000
Utilities	3,200
Fire and theft insurance	1,300

Medical expenses for 1997 include:

Medical insurance premiums	$4,800
Doctor bill for Sam incurred in 1996 and not paid until 1997	2,600
Operation for Sam	4,900

The operation for Sam represents the one-third Bruce contributed toward his father's support.

Other relevant information follows:

- Alice and Bruce had $2,600 ($1,400 for Alice and $1,200 for Bruce) withheld from their salaries for state income taxes. When they filed their 1996 state return in 1997, they paid additional tax of $480.

- During 1997, Alice and Bruce attended a dinner dance sponsored by the Ames Police Disability Association (a qualified charitable organization). The Byrds paid $100 for the tickets. Cost of comparable entertainment would normally be $40. The Byrds contributed $1,700 to their church and gave used clothing (cost of $800 and fair market value of $200) to the Salvation Army. All donations are supported by receipts.

- In 1997, the Byrds received interest income of $1,950 from a savings account they maintained.

- Alice's employer requires that all employees wear uniforms to work. During 1997, Alice spent $440 on new uniforms and $112 on laundry charges. Bruce paid $120 for an annual subscription to the *Journal of Franchise Management*. Neither Alice's nor Bruce's employers reimburse for employee expenses.

- Alice and Bruce had $6,800 ($3,700 for Alice and $3,100 for Bruce) of Federal income tax withheld in 1997 and paid no estimated Federal income tax. Neither Alice nor Bruce wishes to designate $3 to the Presidential Election Campaign Fund.

Part 1—Tax Computation
Compute net tax payable or refund due for Alice and Bruce Byrd for 1997. If they have overpaid, the amount is to be refunded. If you use tax forms for your computations, you will need Form 1040 and Schedules A and B. Suggested software (if available): *TurboTax*.

Part 2—Tax Planning
Alice and Bruce are planning some significant changes for 1998. They have provided you with the following information and asked you to project their taxable income and tax liability for 1998.

Myrtle became seriously ill in December 1997 and is no longer able to care for herself. As a result, Alice plans to take a one-year leave of absence from work during 1998 to care for her. The Byrds will use $70,000 of the life insurance proceeds they received as a result of Sam's death and pay off their mortgage in early January 1998. They will invest the remaining $200,000 in short-term certificates of deposit (CDs) and use the interest for living expenses during 1998. They expect to earn total interest of $13,500 on the CDs. Bruce has been awarded a 5% raise for 1998, and withholdings on his salary will increase accordingly.

The Byrds will not incur any additional costs related to Sam's medical problem. Alice will not work at all during 1998, so none of her job-related expenses or withholdings will continue. The Byrds do not expect to owe additional state income tax when they file their 1997 return, but they do expect their charitable contributions and medical insurance premiums to continue at the 1997 level. Assume all other income and deduction items will continue at the same level in 1998 unless you have information that indicates otherwise.

50. Paul and Donna Decker are married taxpayers, ages 44 and 42, who file a joint return for 1998. The Deckers live at 1121 College Avenue, Carmel, IN 46032. Paul is an assistant manager at Carmel Motor Inn, and Donna is a teacher at Carmel Elementary School. They present you with W–2 forms that reflect the following information:

	Paul	**Donna**
Salary	$37,000	$41,000
Federal tax withheld	6,992	5,900
State income tax withheld	700	760
FICA (Social Security) withheld	2,831	3,137
Social Security numbers	222–11–4567	333–11–9872

Donna is the custodial parent of two children from a previous marriage who reside with the Deckers through the school year. The children, Larry and Jane Parker, reside with their father, Bob, during the summer. Relevant information for the children follows:

	Larry	**Jane**
Age	11	9
Social Security numbers	305–11–4567	303–11–9872
Months spent with Deckers	9	9

Under the divorce decree, Bob pays child support of $150 per month per child during the nine months the children live with the Deckers. Bob says he spends $200 per month per child during the three summer months they reside with him. Donna and Paul can document that they provide $1,800 support per child per year. The divorce decree is silent as to which parent can claim the exemption for the children.

In August, Paul and Donna added a suite to their home to provide more comfortable accommodations for Hannah Snyder (263–33–4738), Donna's mother, who had moved in with them in February 1997 after the death of Donna's father. Not wanting to borrow money for this addition, Paul sold 300 shares of Acme Corporation stock for $50 per share on May 3, 1998, and used the proceeds of $15,000 to cover construction costs. The Deckers had purchased the stock on April 29, 1995, for $22 per share. They received dividends of $550 on the jointly owned stock a month before the sale.

Hannah, who is 66 years old, received $7,200 in Social Security benefits during the year, of which she gave the Deckers $1,700 to use toward household expenses and deposited the remainder in her personal savings account. The Deckers determine that they have spent $1,500 of their own money for food, clothing, medical expenses, and other items for Hannah. They do not know what the rental value of Hannah's suite would be, but they estimate it would be at least $300 per month.

Interest paid during the year included the following:

Home mortgage interest (paid to Carmel Federal Savings & Loan)	$4,890
Interest on an automobile loan (paid to Carmel National Bank)	920
Interest on Citibank Visa card	855

In July, Paul hit a submerged rock while boating. Fortunately, he was thrown from the boat, landed in deep water, and was uninjured. However, the boat, which was uninsured, was destroyed. Paul had paid $18,000 for the boat in June 1997, and its value was appraised at $14,500 on the date of the accident.

The Deckers paid doctor and hospital bills of $4,100 and were reimbursed $1,600 by their insurance company. They spent $780 for prescription drugs and medicines and

$1,440 for premiums on their health insurance policy. They have filed additional claims of $700 with their insurance company and have been told they will receive payment for that amount in January 1999. Included in the amounts paid for doctor and hospital bills were payments of $360 for Hannah and $750 for the children.

Additional information of potential tax consequence follows:

Real estate taxes paid	$1,900
Cash contributions to church	800
Appraised value of books donated to public library	450
Paul's unreimbursed employee expenses to attend hotel management convention:	
Airfare	340
Hotel	130
Meals	95
Registration fee	100
Refund of state income tax for 1997 (the Deckers itemized on their 1997 return)	910

Compute net tax payable or refund due for the Deckers for 1998. If they have overpaid, the amount is to be credited toward their taxes for 1999. Suggested software (if available): *TurboTax*.

RESEARCH PROBLEMS

*Note: Use the **RIA OnPoint System 4 Student Version CD-ROM**, which is available to accompany this text, in preparing solutions to the Research Problems. Alternatively, tax research materials found in a standard tax library can be used.*

Research Problem 1. Jane suffers from a degenerative spinal disorder. Her physician recommended the installation of a swimming pool at her residence for her use to prevent the onset of permanent paralysis. Jane's residence had a market value of approximately $500,000 before the swimming pool was installed. The swimming pool was built, and an appraiser estimated that the value of Jane's home increased by $98,000 because of the addition.

The pool cost $194,000, and Jane claimed a medical deduction of $96,000 on her tax return. Upon audit of the return, the IRS determined that an adequate pool should have cost $70,000 and would increase the property value by only $31,000. Thus, the IRS claims that Jane should be entitled to a deduction of only $39,000.
a. Is there any ceiling limitation on the amount deductible as a medical expense?
b. Can capital expenditures be deducted as medical expenses?
c. What is the significance of a "minimum adequate facility"? Should aesthetic or architectural qualities be considered in this determination?

Research Problem 2. Tom and Mary Smith, whose son was found murdered in a parking lot, offered a $100,000 reward for the city police to use to obtain information leading to the arrest and conviction of the murderer. As a result of the reward, a person who had overheard the murderer telling a friend about the crime reported the conversation to the police. The murderer was arrested and convicted, and the Smiths contributed the money to the police department. Can the Smiths treat this payment as a charitable contribution?

Research Problem 3. In January, Ron, a fireman, was injured in the line of duty as a result of interference by a homeowner. He incurred medical expenses of $6,500 related to his injuries. Ron sued the homeowner and was awarded damages of $26,500 in December. The court indicated that $6,500 of the award was for payment of Ron's medical expenses and $20,000 was for punitive damages. Ron has prepared his return for the year and has asked you to review it. You notice that Ron has not reported any part of the award as income and has included the medical expense in computing his itemized deductions. Write a brief summary of the advice you should give Ron.

Research Problem 4.   Tamika, a shareholder in a corporation with stores in five states, donated stock with a basis of $10,000 to a qualified charitable organization in 1995. Although the stock of the corporation was not traded on a public stock exchange, many shares had been sold over the last three years. Based on the average selling price for the stock in 1995, Tamika deducted $95,000 on her 1995 tax return. Tamika received a notice from the IRS that the $95,000 deduction had been reduced to $10,000 because she had not obtained a qualified appraisal or attached a summary of an appraisal to her tax return. Tamika has asked you to advise her on this matter. Write a letter containing your conclusions to Ms. Tamika Claussen, 2422 Arthur Court, San Bruno, CA 94066.

Partial list of research aids:
Reg.§ 1.170A–13(c)(2).

Use the tax resources of the Internet to address the following question. Do not restrict your search to the World Wide Web, but include a review of newsgroups and general reference materials, practitioner sites and resources, primary sources of the tax law, chat rooms and discussion groups, and other opportunities.

Research Problem 5.   Look over the Web pages of several large charities. Print some of the most effective materials by which such organizations solicit charitable contributions over the Internet. Concentrate especially on the solicitation of gifts of appreciated securities and on the use of private foundations as the recipients of large charitable gifts.

TEAM PROJECT: ARTHUR ANDERSEN TAX CHALLENGE CASES

For more information on the Arthur Andersen Tax Challenge Cases, refer to Chapter 1, page 1–37.

Information related to tax issues and problems that are discussed in this chapter may be found in the

Day and Ball case on pages 3, 4, 5, 7, 11, 12, 25–28, and 33
Fence case on pages 40, 41, 51–55, 58, 62, and 66

Read and analyze the case you have been assigned and *identify* any issues and problems that are related to material covered in this chapter. If the information provided in the case is complete, prepare answers for this part of the case at this time. If you need information that is contained in the later parts of the case, write a memo summarizing the questions or problems so you can prepare a complete answer at a later date.

PASSIVE ACTIVITY LOSSES

LEARNING OBJECTIVES

After completing Chapter 11, you should be able to:

1. Discuss tax shelters and the reasons for at-risk and passive loss limitations.

2. Explain the at-risk limitation.

3. Describe how the passive loss rules limit deductions for losses, and identify the taxpayers subject to these restrictions.

4. Discuss the definition of passive activities and the rules for identifying an activity.

5. Analyze and apply the tests for material participation.

6. Understand the nature of rental activities under the passive loss rules.

7. Recognize the relationship between the at-risk and passive activity limitations.

8. Discuss the special treatment available to real estate activities.

9. Determine the proper tax treatment upon the disposition of a passive activity.

10. Suggest tax planning strategies to minimize the effect of the passive loss limitations.

THE TAX SHELTER PROBLEM

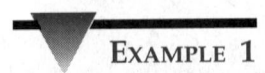

1   LEARNING OBJECTIVE
Discuss tax shelters and the
reasons for at-risk and passive
loss limitations.

Before Congress enacted legislation to reduce or eliminate their effectiveness, **tax shelters** were popular investments for tax avoidance purposes because they could generate deductions and other benefits that could be used to offset income from other sources. Because of the tax avoidance potential of many tax shelters, they were attractive to wealthy taxpayers in high income tax brackets. Many tax shelters merely provided an opportunity for "investors" to buy deductions and credits in ventures that were not expected to generate a profit, even in the long run.

Although it may seem odd that a taxpayer would intentionally invest in an activity that was designed to produce losses, there is a logical explanation. The typical tax shelter operated as a partnership and relied heavily on nonrecourse financing.[1] Accelerated depreciation and interest expense deductions generated large losses in the early years of the activity. At the very least, the tax shelter deductions deferred the recognition of any net income from the venture until the activity was sold. In the best of situations, the investor could realize additional tax savings by offsetting other income (e.g., salary, interest, and dividends) with deductions flowing from the tax shelter. Ultimately, the sale of the investment would result in capital gain. The following examples illustrate what was possible *before* Congress enacted legislation to curb tax shelter abuses.

EXAMPLE 1

Bob, who earned a salary of $300,000 as a business executive and dividend income of $15,000, invested $20,000 for a 10% interest in a cattle-breeding tax shelter. Through the use of $800,000 of nonrecourse financing and available cash of $200,000, the partnership acquired a herd of an exotic breed of cattle costing $1 million. Depreciation, interest, and other deductions related to the activity resulted in a loss of $400,000, of which Bob's share was $40,000. Bob was allowed to deduct the $40,000 loss, even though he had invested and stood to lose only $20,000 if the investment turned sour. The net effect of the $40,000 deduction from the partnership was that a portion of Bob's salary and dividend income was "sheltered," and as a result, he was required to calculate his tax liability on only $275,000 of income [$315,000 (salary and dividends) – $40,000 (deduction)]

---

[1]Nonrecourse debt is an obligation for which the borrower is not personally liable. An example of nonrecourse debt is a liability on real estate acquired by a partnership without the partnership or any of the partners assuming any liability for the mortgage. The acquired property generally is pledged as collateral for the loan.

rather than $315,000. If this deduction were available under current law and if Bob was in the 39.6% income tax bracket, this deduction would generate a tax savings of $15,840 ($40,000 × 39.6%) in the first year alone! ▼

A review of Example 1 shows that the taxpayer took a *two-for-one* write-off ($40,000 deduction, $20,000 investment). In the heyday of tax shelters, promoters often promised *multiple* write-offs for the investor.

The first major provision aimed at tax shelters was the **at-risk limitation.** Its objective is to limit a taxpayer's deductions to the amount at risk, that is, the amount the taxpayer stands to lose if the investment turns out to be a financial disaster.

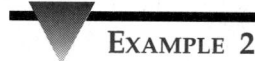

EXAMPLE 2

Returning to the facts of Example 1, under the current at-risk rules Bob would be allowed to deduct $20,000 (i.e., the amount that he could lose if the business failed). This deduction would reduce his other income and as a result, Bob would have to report only $295,000 of income ($315,000 − $20,000). The remaining nondeductible $20,000 loss and any future losses flowing from the partnership would be suspended under the at-risk rules and would be deductible in the future only as his at-risk amount increased. ▼

The second major attack on tax shelters came with the passage of the passive activity loss rules. These rules were intended to halt an investor's ability to benefit from the mismatching of an entity's expenses and income that often occurs in the early years of the business. Congress observed that despite the at-risk limitations, investors could still deduct losses flowing from an entity and thereby defer their tax liability on other income. In effect, passive activity rules have, to a great degree, made the term *tax shelter* obsolete. Now such ventures where investors are not involved in the day-to-day operations of the business are generally referred to as passive investments, or *passive activities*, rather than tax shelters.

The **passive loss** rules require the taxpayer to segregate all income and losses into three categories: active, passive, and portfolio. In general, the passive loss limits disallow the deduction of passive losses against active or portfolio income, even when the taxpayer is at risk to the extent of the loss. Normally, passive losses can only offset passive income.

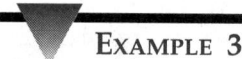

EXAMPLE 3

Returning to the facts of Example 1, the passive activity loss rules further restrict Bob's ability to claim the $20,000 tax deduction shown in Example 2. Because Bob is a passive investor and does not materially participate in any meaningful way in the activities of the cattle-breeding operation, the $20,000 loss allowed under the at-risk rules is disallowed under the passive loss rules. The passive loss is disallowed because Bob does not generate any passive income that could absorb his passive loss. Further, his salary (active income) and dividends (portfolio income) cannot be used to absorb any of the passive loss. Consequently, Bob's current-year taxable income must reflect his nonpassive income of $315,000, and he receives no current benefit from his share of the partnership loss. However, all is not lost because Bob's share of the entity's loss is *suspended;* it is carried forward and can be deducted in the future when he has passive income or sells his interest in the activity. ▼

This chapter explores the nature of the at-risk limits and passive activity loss rules and their impact on investors. An interesting consequence of these rules is that now investors evaluating potential investments must consider mainly the economics of the venture instead of the tax benefits or tax avoidance possibilities that an investment may generate.

THE IMPACT OF RECENT TAX LEGISLATION ON INVESTMENT CHOICES

With the recent reduction in the income tax rates on capital transactions, real estate investments are relatively more attractive than under earlier law. Gains on the sale of capital assets held for more than 18 months are taxed to individuals at no more than 20 percent. Persons contemplating investing in real estate, however, may be better off with stock and securities, which are subject to the same beneficial capital gain rates as real estate, but avoid the difficulties of dealing with the at-risk and passive loss rules. Sorting out the tax differences between the investment choices is not simple, as the tax rate is not the only or most important factor. In arriving at a decision, an investor would need to weigh other factors such as the following:

- Some people don't want the hassle of collecting rents and managing property. Others like the idea of owning physical assets that they can control. Stock investors, unfortunately, are essentially at the mercy of the people who manage the corporation.
- A real estate investor has more leverage than a stockholder. Real estate can be purchased with only a down payment, and the property appreciates while the rental receipts are used to pay off the loan.
- Property owners usually can count on a steady stream of rent income that can be offset for tax purposes by depreciation deductions.

SOURCE: Information from *USA Today*, August 15, 1997, p. 4B.

AT-RISK LIMITS

2   **LEARNING OBJECTIVE**
Explain the at-risk limitation.

The at-risk provisions limit the deductibility of losses from business and income-producing activities. These provisions, which apply to individuals and closely held corporations, are designed to prevent taxpayers from deducting losses in excess of their actual economic investment in an activity. In the case of an S corporation or a partnership, the at-risk limits apply at the owner level. Under the at-risk rules, a taxpayer's deductible loss from an activity for any taxable year is limited to the amount the taxpayer has at risk at the end of the taxable year (the amount the taxpayer could actually lose in the activity).

While the amount at risk generally vacillates over time, the initial amount considered at risk consists of the following:[2]

- The amount of cash and the adjusted basis of property contributed to the activity by the taxpayer.
- Amounts borrowed for use in the activity for which the taxpayer is personally liable or has pledged as security property not used in the activity.

This amount generally is increased each year by the taxpayer's share of income and is decreased by the taxpayer's share of losses and withdrawals from the activity. In addition, because general partners are jointly and severally liable for recourse

---

[2]§ 465(b)(1).

debts of the partnership, their at-risk amounts are increased when the partnership increases its debt and are decreased when the partnership reduces its debt. However, a taxpayer generally is not considered at risk with respect to borrowed amounts if either of the following is true:

- The taxpayer is not personally liable for repayment of the debt (e.g., nonrecourse debt).
- The lender has an interest (other than as a creditor) in the activity.

An important exception provides that in the case of an activity involving the holding of real property, a taxpayer is considered at risk for his or her share of any *qualified nonrecourse financing* that is secured by real property used in the activity.[3]

Subject to the passive activity rules discussed later in the chapter, a taxpayer may deduct a loss as long as the at-risk amount is positive. However, once the at-risk amount is exhausted, any remaining loss cannot be deducted until a later year. Any losses disallowed for any given taxable year by the at-risk rules may be deducted in the first succeeding year in which the rules do not prevent the deduction—that is, when and to the extent of a positive at-risk amount.

EXAMPLE 4   In 1998, Sue invests $40,000 in an oil partnership that, by the use of nonrecourse loans, spends $60,000 on deductible intangible drilling costs applicable to her interest. Assume Sue's interest in the partnership is subject to the at-risk limits but is not subject to the passive loss limits. Since Sue has only $40,000 of capital at risk, she cannot deduct more than $40,000 against her other income and must reduce her at-risk amount to zero ($40,000 at-risk amount − $40,000 loss deducted). The nondeductible loss of $20,000 ($60,000 loss generated − $40,000 loss allowed) can be carried over to 1999. ▼

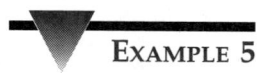

EXAMPLE 5   In 1999, Sue has taxable income of $15,000 from the oil partnership and invests an additional $10,000 in the venture. Her at-risk amount is now $25,000 ($0 beginning balance + $15,000 taxable income + $10,000 additional investment). This enables Sue to deduct the carryover loss and requires her to reduce her at-risk amount to $5,000 ($25,000 at-risk amount − $20,000 carryover loss allowed). ▼

An additional complicating factor is that previously allowed losses must be recaptured to the extent the at-risk amount is reduced below zero.[4] That is, previous losses that were allowed must be offset by the recognition of enough income to bring the at-risk amount up to zero. This rule applies in such situations as when the amount at risk is reduced below zero by distributions to the taxpayer or when the status of indebtedness changes from recourse to nonrecourse.

PASSIVE LOSS LIMITS

CLASSIFICATION AND IMPACT OF PASSIVE INCOME AND LOSSES

3   **LEARNING OBJECTIVE**
Describe how the passive loss rules limit deductions for losses, and identify the taxpayers subject to these restrictions.

Classification.   The passive loss rules require income and losses to be classified into one of three categories: active, passive, or portfolio. **Active income** includes, but is not limited to, the following:

- Wages, salary, commissions, bonuses, and other payments for services rendered by the taxpayer.
- Profit from a trade or business in which the taxpayer is a material participant.

---

[3]§ 465(b)(6).   [4]§ 465(e).

Calculation of At-Risk Amount

Increases to a taxpayer's at-risk amount:

- Cash and the adjusted basis of property contributed to the activity.
- Amounts borrowed for use in the activity for which the taxpayer is personally liable or has pledged as security property not used in the activity.
- Taxpayer's share of amounts borrowed for use in the activity that are qualified nonrecourse financing.
- Taxpayer's share of the activity's income.

Decreases to a taxpayer's at-risk amount:

- Withdrawals from the activity.
- Taxpayer's share of the activity's loss.
- Taxpayer's share of any reductions of debt for which recourse against the taxpayer exists or reductions of qualified nonrecourse debt.

- Gain on the sale or other disposition of assets used in an active trade or business.
- Income from intangible property if the taxpayer's personal efforts significantly contributed to the creation of the property.

Portfolio income includes, but is not limited to, the following:

- Interest, dividends, annuities, and royalties not derived in the ordinary course of a trade or business.
- Gain or loss from the disposition of property that produces portfolio income or is held for investment purposes.

Section 469 provides that income or loss from the following activities is treated as *passive:*

- Any trade or business or income-producing activity in which the taxpayer does not materially participate.
- Subject to certain exceptions, all rental activities, whether the taxpayer materially participates or not.

Although the Code defines rental activities as passive activities, several exceptions allow losses from certain real estate rental activities to be offset against nonpassive (active or portfolio) income. The exceptions are discussed under Special Passive Activity Rules for Real Estate Activities later in the chapter.

General Impact. Deductions or expenses generated by passive activities can be deducted only to the extent of income from all of the taxpayer's passive activities. Any excess may not be used to offset income from active sources or portfolio income. Instead, any unused passive losses are suspended and carried forward to future years to offset passive income generated in those years. Otherwise, suspended losses may be used only when a taxpayer disposes of his or her entire interest in an activity. In that event, all current and suspended losses related to the activity may offset active and portfolio income.

ALL THAT GLITTERS IN TAX REFORM IS NOT GOLD

The topic of major tax reform is arising more frequently as our tax laws have become more complex. Inevitably, various proposals for a "flat tax" are touted as panaceas to these complexity problems. In such discussions, both supporters and opponents of the flat tax may present theoretical, practical, and political arguments, but often the implications of any particular plan are difficult to understand. For example, investors in financial instruments producing interest, dividend, and capital gain income could benefit under some flat tax proposals because they exclude such income from taxation. Individuals who invest in real estate may not be as fortunate, however.

Under certain proposals, the taxpayer could claim a deduction for the full cost of a building and land in the year of purchase, rather than having to capitalize these assets and depreciate only the building over a prolonged period of time. If the entity holding the property is a partnership or S corporation, the deduction would flow through to the entity's owners. The result would be a huge loss at the owner level. For real estate investors, however, the losses may not be deductible in the current year due to the passive activity loss rules. The losses would generate no current benefit unless the investor had a like amount of passive income. Under a flat tax regime, the appeal of real estate investments relative to financial investments could decline.

EXAMPLE 6

Kim, a physician, earns $150,000 from her full-time practice. She also receives $10,000 in dividends and interest from various portfolio investments, and her share of a passive loss from a tax shelter not limited by the at-risk rules is $60,000. Because the loss is a passive loss, it is not deductible against her other income. The loss is suspended and is carried over to the future. If Kim has passive income from this investment or from other passive investments in the future, she can offset the suspended loss against that passive income. If she does not have passive income to offset this suspended loss in the future, she will be allowed to offset the loss against other types of income when she eventually disposes of the passive activity. ▼

Impact of Suspended Losses.   When a taxpayer disposes of his or her entire interest in a passive activity, the actual economic gain or loss from the investment, including any suspended losses, can finally be determined. As a result, under the passive loss rules, upon a fully taxable disposition, any overall loss realized from the activity by the taxpayer is recognized and can be offset against any income.

A fully taxable disposition generally involves a sale of the property to a third party at arm's length and thus, presumably, for a price equal to the property's fair market value. Gain recognized upon a transfer of an interest in a passive activity generally is treated as passive and is first offset by the suspended losses from that activity.

EXAMPLE 7

Rex sells an apartment building, a passive activity, with an adjusted basis of $100,000 for $180,000. In addition, he has suspended losses of $60,000 associated with the building. His total gain, $80,000, and his taxable gain, $20,000, are calculated as follows:

Net sales price	$ 180,000
Less: Adjusted basis	(100,000)
Total gain	$ 80,000
Less: Suspended losses	(60,000)
Taxable gain (passive)	$ 20,000

If current and suspended losses of the passive activity exceed the gain realized or if the sale results in a realized loss, the amount of

- any loss from the activity for the tax year (including losses suspended in the activity disposed of)

in excess of

- net income or gain for the tax year from all passive activities (without regard to the activity disposed of)

is treated as a loss that is not from a passive activity. In computing the loss from the activity for the year of disposition, any gain or loss recognized is included.

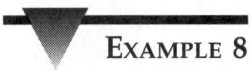

EXAMPLE 8   Dean sells an apartment building with an adjusted basis of $100,000 for $150,000. In addition, he has current and suspended losses of $60,000 associated with the building and has no other passive activities. His total gain, $50,000, and his deductible loss, $10,000, are calculated as follows:

Net sales price	$ 150,000
Less: Adjusted basis	(100,000)
Total gain	$ 50,000
Less: Suspended losses	(60,000)
Deductible loss	($ 10,000)

The $10,000 deductible loss is offset against Dean's active income and portfolio income. ▼

Carryovers of Suspended Losses.   In the above examples, it was assumed that the taxpayer had an interest in only one passive activity, and as a result, the suspended loss was related exclusively to the activity that was disposed of. Taxpayers often own interests in more than one activity, however, and in that case, any suspended losses must be allocated among the activities in which the taxpayer has an interest. The allocation to an activity is made by multiplying the disallowed passive activity loss from all activities by the following fraction:

$$\frac{\text{Loss from activity}}{\text{Sum of losses for taxable year from all activities having losses}}$$

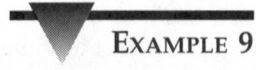

EXAMPLE 9   Diego has investments in three passive activities with the following income and losses for 1997:

Activity A	($ 30,000)
Activity B	(20,000)
Activity C	25,000
Net passive loss	($ 25,000)
Net passive loss allocated to:	
Activity A ($25,000 × $30,000/$50,000)	($ 15,000)
Activity B ($25,000 × $20,000/$50,000)	(10,000)
Total suspended losses	($ 25,000)

▼

Suspended losses are carried over indefinitely and are offset in the future against any passive income from the activities to which they relate.[5]

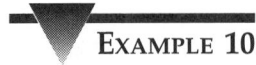
EXAMPLE 10

Assume the same facts as in Example 9 and that Activity A produces $10,000 of income in 1998. Of the suspended loss of $15,000 from 1997 for Activity A, $10,000 is offset against the income from this activity. If Diego sells Activity A in early 1999, then the remaining $5,000 suspended loss is used in determining his taxable gain or loss. ▼

Passive Credits.   Credits arising from passive activities are limited in much the same way as passive losses. Passive credits can be utilized only against regular tax attributable to passive income,[6] which is calculated by comparing the tax on all income (including passive income) with the tax on income excluding passive income.

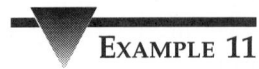
EXAMPLE 11

Sam owes $50,000 of tax, disregarding net passive income, and $80,000 of tax, considering both net passive and other taxable income (disregarding the credits in both cases). The amount of tax attributable to the passive income is $30,000.

Tax due (before credits) including net passive income	$ 80,000
Less: Tax due (before credits) without including net passive income	(50,000)
Tax attributable to passive income	$ 30,000

▼

Sam in the preceding example can claim a maximum of $30,000 of passive activity credits; the excess credits are carried over. These passive activity credits (such as the low-income housing credit and rehabilitation credit) can only be used against the *regular* tax attributable to passive income. If a taxpayer has a net loss from passive activities during a given year, no credits can be used. Likewise, if a taxpayer has net passive income but the alternative minimum tax applies to that year, no passive activity credits can be used. (The alternative minimum tax is discussed in Chapter 12.)

Carryovers of Passive Credits.   Tax credits attributable to passive activities can be carried forward indefinitely much like suspended passive losses. Unlike passive losses, however, passive credits are lost forever when the activity is disposed of in a taxable transaction where loss is recognized. Credits are allowed on dispositions only when there is sufficient tax on passive income to absorb them.

EXAMPLE 12

Alicia sells a passive activity for a gain of $10,000. The activity had suspended losses of $40,000 and suspended credits of $15,000. The $10,000 gain is offset by $10,000 of the suspended losses, and the remaining $30,000 of suspended losses is deductible against Alicia's active and portfolio income. The suspended credits are lost forever because the sale of the activity did not generate any tax. This is true even if Alicia has positive taxable income or is subject to the alternative minimum tax. ▼

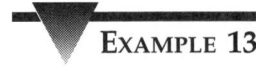
EXAMPLE 13

If Alicia in Example 12 had realized a $100,000 gain on the sale of the passive activity, the suspended credits could have been used to the extent of regular tax attributable to the net passive income.

Gain on sale	$ 100,000
Less: Suspended losses	(40,000)
Taxable gain	$ 60,000

[5] § 469(b).   [6] § 469(d)(2).

If the tax attributable to the taxable gain of $60,000 is $15,000 or more, the entire $15,000 of suspended credits can be used. If the tax attributable to the gain is less than $15,000, the excess of the suspended credits over the tax attributable to the gain is lost forever. ▼

When a taxpayer has adequate regular tax liability from passive activities to trigger the use of suspended credits, the credits lose their character as passive credits. They are reclassified as regular tax credits and made subject to the same limits as other credits (discussed in Chapter 13).

TAXPAYERS SUBJECT TO THE PASSIVE LOSS RULES

The passive loss rules apply to individuals, estates, trusts, personal service corporations, and closely held C corporations.[7] Passive income or loss from investments in S corporations or partnerships (see Chapter 20) flows through to the owners, and the passive loss rules are applied at the owner level.

Personal Service Corporations. Application of the passive loss limitations to **personal service corporations** is intended to prevent taxpayers from sheltering personal service income by creating personal service corporations and acquiring passive activities at the corporate level.

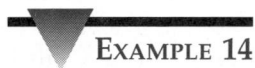

EXAMPLE 14

Five tax accountants, who earn a total of $1 million a year in their individual practices, form a personal service corporation. Shortly after its formation, the corporation invests in a passive activity that produces a $200,000 loss during the year. Because the passive loss rules apply to personal service corporations, the corporation may not deduct the $200,000 loss against the $1 million of active income. ▼

Determination of whether a corporation is a *personal service corporation* is based on rather broad definitions. A personal service corporation is a corporation that meets *both* of the following conditions:

- The principal activity is the performance of personal services.
- Such services are substantially performed by employee-owners.

Generally, personal service corporations include those in the fields of health, law, engineering, architecture, accounting, actuarial science, performing arts, and consulting.[8] A corporation is treated as a personal service corporation if more than 10 percent of the stock (by value) is held by employee-owners.[9] A shareholder is treated as an employee-owner if he or she is an employee or shareholder on *any day* during the testing period.[10] For these purposes, shareholder status and employee status do not even have to occur on the same day.

Closely Held C Corporations. Application of the passive loss rules to closely held (non-personal service) corporations is also intended to prevent individuals from incorporating to avoid the passive loss limitations. A corporation is classified as a **closely held corporation** if at any time during the taxable year, more than 50 percent of the value of its outstanding stock is owned, directly or indirectly, by or for not more than five individuals. Closely held C corporations (other than personal service corporations) may offset passive losses against *active* income, but not against portfolio income.

---

[7]§ 469(a).
[8]§ 448(d)(2).

[9]§ 469(j)(2).
[10]§ 269A(b)(2).

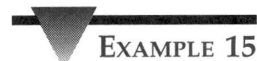
EXAMPLE 15

Silver Corporation, a closely held (non-personal service) C corporation, has $500,000 of passive losses from a rental activity, $400,000 of active income, and $100,000 of portfolio income. The corporation may offset $400,000 of the $500,000 passive loss against the $400,000 of active business income, but may not offset the remainder against the $100,000 of portfolio income. Thus, $100,000 of the passive loss is suspended ($500,000 passive loss − $400,000 offset against active income). ▼

Application of the passive loss limitations to closely held corporations prevents taxpayers from transferring their portfolio investments to such corporations in order to offset passive losses against portfolio income.

PASSIVE ACTIVITIES DEFINED

4 **LEARNING OBJECTIVE**
Discuss the definition of passive activities and the rules for identifying an activity.

Section 469 specifies that the following types of activities are to be treated as passive:

- Any trade or business or income-producing activity in which the taxpayer does not materially participate.
- Subject to certain exceptions, all rental activities.

To understand the meaning of the term *passive activity* and the impact of the rules, one must address the following issues, each of which is the subject of statutory or administrative guidance:

- What constitutes an activity?
- What is meant by material participation?
- When is an activity a rental activity?

Even though guidance is available to help the taxpayer deal with these issues, their resolution is anything but simple.

Identification of an Activity. Identifying what constitutes an activity is a necessary first step in applying the passive loss limitations. Taxpayers who are involved in complex business operations need to be able to determine whether a given segment of their overall business operations constitutes a separate activity or is to be treated as part of a single activity. Proper treatment is necessary in order to determine whether income or loss from an activity is active or passive:

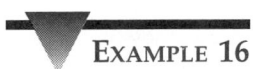
EXAMPLE 16

Ben owns a business with two separate departments. Department A generates net income of $120,000, and Department B generates a net loss of $95,000. Ben participates for 700 hours in the operations of Department A and for 100 hours in Department B. If Ben is allowed to treat the departments as components of a single activity, he can offset the $95,000 loss from Department B against the $120,000 income from Department A. ▼

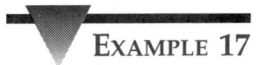
EXAMPLE 17

Assume the same facts as in the previous example. If Ben is required to treat each department as a separate activity, the tax result is not as favorable. Because he is a material participant in Department A (having devoted 700 hours to it), the $120,000 profit is active income. However, he is not considered a material participant in Department B (100 hours), and the $95,000 loss is a passive loss. Therefore, Ben cannot offset the $95,000 passive loss from Department B against the $120,000 of active income from Department A. (A complete discussion of the material participation rules follows.) ▼

Recall that on the disposition of a passive activity, a taxpayer is allowed to offset suspended losses from the activity against other types of income. Therefore, identifying what constitutes an activity is of crucial importance for this purpose too.

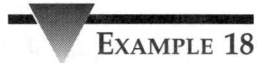

EXAMPLE 18

Linda owns a business with two departments. Department A has a net loss of $125,000 in the current year, and Department B has a $70,000 net loss. She disposes of Department B at the end of the year. Assuming Linda is allowed to treat the two departments as separate passive activities, she can offset the passive loss from Department B against other types of income in the following order: gain from disposition of the passive activity, other passive income, and nonpassive income. This treatment leaves her with a suspended loss of $125,000 from Department A. If Departments A and B are treated as components of the same activity, however, on the disposal of Department B, its $70,000 net loss would be suspended along with the other $125,000 of suspended loss of the activity. ▼

The current rules used to delineate what constitutes an activity for purposes of the passive loss limitations are provided in Regulations.[11] These guidelines state that, in general, a taxpayer can treat one or more trade or business activities or rental activities as a single activity if those activities form an *appropriate economic unit* for measuring gain or loss. To determine what ventures form an appropriate economic unit, all of the relevant facts and circumstances must be considered. Taxpayers may use any reasonable method in applying the facts and circumstances. However, the following five factors are given the greatest weight in determining whether activities constitute an appropriate economic unit. It is not necessary to meet all of these conditions in order to treat multiple activities as a single activity.

- Similarities and differences in the types of business conducted in the various trade or business or rental activities.
- The extent of common control over the various activities.
- The extent of common ownership of the activities.
- The geographical location of the different units.
- Interdependencies among the activities.

The following examples, adapted from the Regulations, illustrate the application of the general rules for grouping activities.[12]

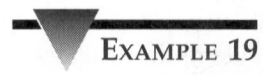

EXAMPLE 19

George owns a men's clothing store and a video game parlor in Chicago. He also owns a men's clothing store and a video game parlor in Milwaukee. Reasonable methods of applying the facts and circumstances test may result in any of the following groupings:

- All four activities may be grouped into a single activity.
- The clothing stores may be grouped into an activity, and the video game parlors may be grouped into a separate activity.
- The Chicago activities may be grouped into an activity, and the Milwaukee activities may be grouped into a separate activity.
- Each of the four activities may be treated as a separate activity. ▼

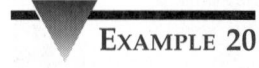

EXAMPLE 20

Sharon is a partner in a business that sells snack items to drugstores. She also is a partner in a partnership that owns and operates a warehouse. Both partnerships, which are under common control, are located in the same industrial park. The predominant part of the warehouse business is warehousing items for the snack business, and it is the only warehousing business in which Sharon is involved. Sharon should treat the snack business and the warehousing business as a single activity. ▼

Regrouping of Activities.   Taxpayers should carefully consider all tax factors in deciding how to group their activities. Once activities have been grouped, they cannot be regrouped unless the original grouping was clearly inappropriate or

---

[11]Reg. § 1.469–4.   [12]Reg. § 1.469–4(c)(3).

there has been a material change in the facts and circumstances. If a regrouping is necessary for either of these reasons, the taxpayer is required to disclose to the IRS all information relevant to the regrouping.

The Regulations also grant the IRS the right to regroup activities when both of the following conditions exist:[13]

- The taxpayer's grouping fails to reflect one or more appropriate economic units.
- One of the primary purposes of the taxpayer's grouping is to avoid the passive loss limitations.

The following example, adapted from the Regulations, illustrates a situation where the IRS would exercise its prerogative to regroup a taxpayer's activities.

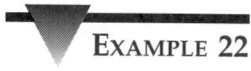

EXAMPLE 21 Baker, Edwards, Andrews, Clark, and Henson are physicians who operate their own separate practices. Each of the physicians owns interests in activities that generate passive losses, so they devise a plan to set up an entity that will generate passive income. They form the BEACH Partnership to acquire and operate X-ray equipment, and each receives a limited partnership interest. They select an unrelated person to operate the X-ray business as a general partner, and none of the limited partners participates in the activity. Substantially all of the services provided by BEACH are provided to the physicians who own limited partnership interests, and fees are set at a level that assures a profit for BEACH. Each physician treats his medical practice and his interest in the partnership as separate activities and offsets losses from passive investments against the passive income from the partnership. The IRS would interpret the physicians' separate groupings as attempts to avoid the passive loss limitations and would regroup each medical practice and the services performed by the partnership as an appropriate economic unit. ▼

Special Grouping Rules for Rental Activities. Two rules deal specifically with the grouping of rental activities. These provisions are designed to prevent taxpayers from grouping rental activities, which are generally passive, with other businesses in a way that would result in a tax advantage.

First, a rental activity may be grouped with a trade or business activity only if one activity is insubstantial in relation to the other. That is, the rental activity must be insubstantial in relation to the trade or business activity, or the trade or business activity must be insubstantial in relation to the rental activity. The Regulations provide no clear guidelines as to the meaning of insubstantial.[14]

EXAMPLE 22 Schemers, a firm of CPAs, owns a building in downtown Washington, D.C., in which they conduct their practice of public accounting. The firm also rents space on the street level of the building to several retail establishments. Of the total revenue generated by the firm, 95% is associated with the practice of public accounting, and 5% is related to the rental operation. It is likely that the rental activity would be considered insubstantial relative to the accounting practice and the two ventures could be grouped as one nonrental activity. This grouping could be advantageous to the firm, particularly if the rental operation generates a loss! ▼

Second, taxpayers generally may not treat an activity involving the rental of real property and an activity involving the rental of personal property as a single activity.

---

[13]Reg. § 1.469–4(f).

[14]Reg. § 1.469–4(d).

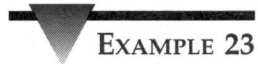

5   LEARNING OBJECTIVE
Analyze and apply the tests for material participation.

Material Participation. If an individual taxpayer materially participates in a nonrental trade or business activity, any loss from that activity is treated as an active loss that can be offset against active or portfolio income. If a taxpayer does not materially participate, however, the loss is treated as a passive loss, which can only be offset against passive income. Therefore, controlling whether a particular activity is treated as active or passive is an important part of the tax strategy of a taxpayer who owns an interest in one or more businesses. Consider the following examples.

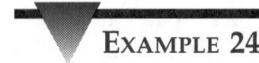

EXAMPLE 23

Dewayne, a corporate executive, earns a salary of $200,000 per year. In addition, he owns a separate business in which he participates. The business produces a loss of $100,000 during the year. If Dewayne materially participates in the business, the $100,000 loss is an active loss that may be offset against his active income from his corporate employer. If he does not materially participate, the loss is passive and is suspended. Dewayne may use the suspended loss in the future only when he has passive income or disposes of the activity. ▼

EXAMPLE 24

Kay, an attorney, earns $250,000 a year in her law practice. She owns interests in two activities, A and B, in which she participates. Activity A, in which she does *not* materially participate, produces a loss of $50,000. Kay has not yet met the material participation standard for Activity B, which produces income of $80,000. However, she can meet the material participation standard if she spends an additional 50 hours in Activity B during the year. Should Kay attempt to meet the material participation standard for Activity B? If she continues working in Activity B and becomes a material participant, the $80,000 of income from the activity is *active*, and the $50,000 passive loss from Activity A must be suspended. A more favorable tax strategy is for Kay to *not meet* the material participation standard for Activity B, thus making the income from that activity passive. This enables her to offset the $50,000 passive loss from Activity A against the passive income from Activity B. ▼

It is possible to devise numerous scenarios in which the taxpayer could control the tax outcome by increasing or decreasing his or her participation in different activities. Examples 23 and 24 demonstrate some of the possibilities. The conclusion reached in most analyses of this type is that taxpayers will benefit by having profitable activities classified as passive, so that any passive losses can be used to offset passive income. If the activity produces a loss, however, the taxpayer will benefit if it is classified as active so the loss is not subject to the passive loss limitations.

As discussed above, a nonrental trade or business in which a taxpayer owns an interest must be treated as a passive activity unless the taxpayer materially participates. As the Staff of the Joint Committee on Taxation explained, a material participant is one who has "a significant nontax economic profit motive" for taking on activities and selects them for their economic value. In contrast, a passive investor mainly seeks a return from a capital investment (including a possible reduction in taxes) as a supplement to an ongoing source of livelihood.[15] Even if the concept or the implication of being a material participant is clear, the precise meaning of the term **material participation** can be vague. As enacted, § 469 requires a taxpayer to participate on a *regular, continuous, and substantial* basis in order to be a material participant. In many situations, however, it is difficult or impossible to gain any assurance that this nebulous standard is met.

---

[15]*General Explanation of the Tax Reform Act of 1986 ("Blue Book"),* prepared by The Staff of the Joint Committee on Taxation, May 4, 1987, H.R. 3838, 99th Cong., p. 212.

In response to this dilemma, Temporary Regulations[16] provide seven tests that are intended to help taxpayers cope with these issues. Material participation is achieved by meeting any one of the tests. These tests can be divided into three categories:

- Tests based on current participation.
- Tests based on prior participation.
- Test based on facts and circumstances.

Tests Based on Current Participation. The first four tests are quantitative tests that require measurement, in hours, of the taxpayer's participation in the activity during the year.

1. *Does the individual participate in the activity for more than 500 hours during the year?*

The purpose of the 500-hour requirement is to restrict deductions from the types of trade or business activities Congress intended to treat as passive activities. The 500-hour standard for material participation was adopted for the following reasons:[17]

- Few investors in traditional tax shelters devote more than 500 hours a year to such an investment.
- The IRS believes that income from an activity in which the taxpayer participates for more than 500 hours a year should not be treated as passive.

2. *Does the individual's participation in the activity for the taxable year constitute substantially all of the participation in the activity of all individuals (including nonowner employees) for the year?*

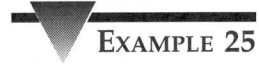
EXAMPLE 25

Ned, a physician, operates a separate business in which he participates for 80 hours during the year. He is the only participant and has no employees in the separate business. Ned meets the material participation standard of Test 2. If he had employees, it would be difficult to apply Test 2, because the Temporary Regulations do not define the term *substantially all.* ▼

3. *Does the individual participate in the activity for more than 100 hours during the year, and is the individual's participation in the activity for the year not less than the participation of any other individual (including nonowner employees) for the year?*

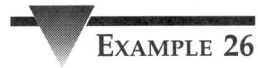
EXAMPLE 26

Adam, a college professor, owns a separate business in which he participates 110 hours during the year. He has an employee who works 90 hours during the year. Adam meets the material participation standard under Test 3, but probably does not meet it under Test 2 because his participation is only 55% of the total participation. It is unlikely that 55% would meet the *substantially all* requirement of Test 2. ▼

Tests 2 and 3 are included because the IRS recognizes that the operation of some activities does not require more than 500 hours of participation during the year.

---

[16]Temp. and Prop.Reg. § 1.469–5T(a). The Temporary Regulations are also Proposed Regulations. Temporary Regulations have the same effect as final Regulations. Refer to Chapter 2 for a discussion of the different categories of Regulations.

[17]T.D. 8175, 1988–1 C.B. 191.

4. *Is the activity a significant participation activity for the taxable year, and does the individual's aggregate participation in all significant participation activities during the year exceed 500 hours?*

A **significant participation activity** is a trade or business in which the individual's participation exceeds 100 hours during the year. This test treats taxpayers as material participants if their aggregate participation in several significant participation activities exceeds 500 hours. Test 4 thus accords the same treatment to an individual who devotes an aggregate of more than 500 hours to several significant participation activities as to an individual who devotes more than 500 hours to a single activity.

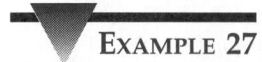
EXAMPLE 27

Mike owns five different businesses. He participated in each activity during the year as follows:

Activity	Hours of Participation
A	110
B	140
C	120
D	150
E	100

Activities A, B, C, and D are significant participation activities, and Mike's aggregate participation in those activities is 520 hours. Therefore, Activities A, B, C, and D are not treated as passive activities. Activity E is not a significant participation activity (not more than 100 hours), so it is not included in applying the 500-hour test. Activity E is treated as a passive activity, unless Mike meets one of the other material participation tests for that activity. ▼

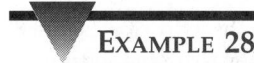
EXAMPLE 28

Assume the same facts as in the previous example, except that Activity A does not exist. All of the activities are now treated as passive. Activity E is not counted in applying the more-than-500-hour test, so Mike's aggregate participation in significant participation activities is 410 hours (140 in Activity B + 120 in Activity C + 150 in Activity D). He could meet the significant participation test for Activity E by participating for one more hour in the activity. This would cause Activities B, C, D, and E to be treated as nonpassive activities. However, before deciding whether to participate for at least one more hour in Activity E, Mike should assess how the participation would affect his overall tax liability. ▼

Tests Based on Prior Participation.   Tests 5 and 6 are based on material participation in prior years. Under these tests, a taxpayer who is no longer a participant in an activity can continue to be *classified* as a material participant. The IRS takes the position that material participation in a trade or business for a long period of time is likely to indicate that the activity represents the individual's principal livelihood, rather than a passive investment. Consequently, withdrawal from the activity, or reduction of participation to the point where it is not material, does not change the classification of the activity from active to passive.

5. *Did the individual materially participate in the activity for any 5 taxable years (whether consecutive or not) during the 10 taxable years that immediately precede the taxable year?*

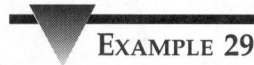
EXAMPLE 29

Dawn, who owns a 50% interest in a restaurant, was a material participant in the operations of the restaurant from 1992 through 1996. She retired at the end of 1996 and is no longer involved in the restaurant except as an investor. Dawn will be treated as a material participant in the restaurant in 1997. Even if she does not become involved in the restaurant as a material participant again, she will continue to be treated as a material participant in 1998, 1999, 2000, and 2001. In 2002 and later years, Dawn's share of income or loss from the restaurant will be classified as passive unless she materially participates in those years. ▼

6. *Is the activity a personal service activity, and did the individual materially participate in the activity for any three preceding taxable years (whether consecutive or not)?*

As indicated above, the material participation standards differ for personal service activities and other businesses. An individual who was a material participant in a personal service activity for *any three years* prior to the taxable year continues to be treated as a material participant after withdrawal from the activity.

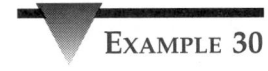

EXAMPLE 30

Evan, a CPA, retires from the EFG Partnership after working full-time in the partnership for 30 years. As a retired partner, he will continue to receive a share of the profits of the firm for the next 10 years, even though he will not participate in the firm's operations. Evan also owns an interest in a passive activity that produces a loss for the year. He continues to be treated as a material participant in the EFG Partnership, and his income from the partnership is active income. Therefore, he is not allowed to offset the loss from his passive investment against the income from the EFG Partnership. ▼

Facts and Circumstances Test. Test 7 is a facts and circumstances test to determine whether the taxpayer has materially participated.

7. *Based on all the facts and circumstances, did the individual participate in the activity on a regular, continuous, and substantial basis during the year?*

The Temporary Regulations do not define what constitutes regular, continuous, and substantial participation except to say that the taxpayer's activities will *not* be considered material participation under Test 7 in the following three circumstances:[18]

- The taxpayer satisfies the participation standards (whether or not a *material participant*) of any Code section other than § 469.
- The taxpayer manages the activity, unless
  - no other person receives compensation for management services, and
  - no individual spends more hours during the tax year managing the activity than does the taxpayer.
- The taxpayer participates in the activity for 100 hours or less during the tax year.

A part of the Temporary Regulations has been reserved for further development of this test. Presumably, additional guidelines will be issued in the future. For the time being, taxpayers should rely on Tests 1 through 6 in determining whether the material participation standards have been met.

Participation Defined. Participation generally includes any work done by an individual in an activity that he or she owns. Participation does not include work if it is of a type not customarily done by owners *and* if one of its principal purposes is to avoid the disallowance of passive losses or credits. Also, work done in an individual's capacity as an investor (e.g., reviewing financial reports in a non-managerial capacity) is not counted in applying the material participation tests. However, participation by an owner's spouse counts as participation by the owner.[19]

---

[18]Temp. and Prop.Reg. § 1.469–5T(b)(2).

[19]Temp. and Prop.Reg. § 1.469–5T(f)(3).

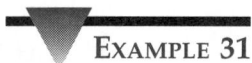

EXAMPLE 31

Tom, who is a partner in a CPA firm, owns a computer store that has operated at a loss during the year. In order to offset this loss against the income from his CPA practice, Tom would like to avoid having the computer business classified as a passive activity. Through December 15, he has worked 400 hours in the business in management and selling activities. During the last two weeks of December, he works 80 hours in management and selling activities and 30 hours doing janitorial chores. Also during the last two weeks in December, Tom's wife participates 40 hours as a salesperson. She has worked as a salesperson in the computer store in prior years, but has not done so during the current year. If any of Tom's work is of a type not customarily done by owners *and* if one of its principal purposes is to avoid the disallowance of passive losses or credits, it is not counted in applying the material participation tests. It is likely that Tom's 480 hours of participation in management and selling activities will count as participation, but the 30 hours spent doing janitorial chores will not. However, the 40 hours of participation by his wife will count, and Tom will qualify as a material participant under the more-than-500-hour rule (480 + 40 = 520). ▼

Limited Partners. A *limited* partner is one whose liability to third-party creditors of the partnership is limited to the amount the partner has invested in the partnership. Such a partnership must have at least one *general* partner, who is fully liable in an individual capacity for the debts of the partnership to third parties. Generally, a *limited partner* is not considered a material participant unless he or she qualifies under Test 1, 5, or 6 in the above list. However, a *general partner* may qualify as a material participant by meeting any of the seven tests. If an unlimited, or general, partner also owns a limited interest in the same limited partnership, all interests are treated as a general interest.[20]

ETHICAL CONSIDERATIONS

A Lovers' Triangle and the Passive Loss Rules

The troubled marriage of John and Eleanor finally reached an impasse, and they mutually agreed to divorce. Shortly after the divorce was finalized, John married Kristen. The three have known each other for years from working together to harvest the grapes of a vineyard owned by John. Prior to the divorce, each had worked 200 hours in the vineyard in the current year. Because the investment generates a loss for the current year, John wants to classify it as an active rather than a passive loss. In order for the loss to be classified as active, the participation of John and his wife together must exceed 500 hours. John claims that meeting that threshold is no problem. He worked 200 hours and Eleanor, who was his wife when the work was done, worked 200 hours. Kristen, who files a joint return with John, worked 200 hours. "Besides," says John, "there is nothing in the law that says I can't do this." John feels it is proper to aggregate Eleanor's and Kristen's participation with his own. This makes the loss deductible in full. As John's tax return preparer, how do you react?

6 **LEARNING OBJECTIVE**
Understand the nature of rental activities under the passive loss rules.

Rental Activities Defined. As discussed previously, § 469 specifies that, subject to certain exceptions, all rental activities are to be treated as passive activities.[21] A **rental activity** is defined as any activity where payments are received principally for the use of tangible (real or personal) property.[22] Importantly, an activity that

---

[20]Temp. and Prop.Reg. § 1.469–5T(e)(3)(ii).
[21]§ 469(c)(2).

[22]§ 469(j)(8).

is classified as a rental activity is subject to the passive activity loss rules, even if the taxpayer involved is a material participant.

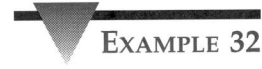

EXAMPLE 32   Sarah owns an apartment building and spends an average of 60 hours a week in its operation. Assuming that the apartment building operation is classified as a rental activity, it is automatically subject to the passive activity rules, even though Sarah spends more than 500 hours a year in its operation. ▼

As suggested, Temporary Regulations provide that in certain situations activities involving rentals of real and personal property are *not* to be *treated* as rental activities.[23]

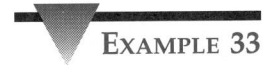

EXAMPLE 33   Dan owns a videocassette rental business. Because the average period of customer use is seven days or less, Dan's videocassette business is not treated as a rental activity. ▼

The fact that Dan's videocassette business in the previous example is not treated as a rental activity does not necessarily mean that it is classified as a nonpassive activity. Instead, the videocassette business is treated as a trade or business activity subject to the material participation standards. If Dan is a material participant, the business is treated as active. If he is not a material participant, it is treated as a passive activity.

Therefore, activities covered by any of the following six exceptions provided by the Temporary Regulations are not *automatically* treated as passive activities because they would not be classified as rental activities. Instead, the activities are subject to the material participation tests.

1.   *The average period of customer use of the property is seven days or less.*

Under this exception, activities involving the short-term use of tangible property such as automobiles, videocassettes, tuxedos, tools, and other such property are not treated as rental activities. The provision also applies to short-term rentals of hotel or motel rooms.

This exception is based on the presumption that a person who rents property for seven days or less is generally required to provide *significant services* to the customer. Providing such services supports a conclusion that the person is engaged in a service business rather than a rental business.

2.   *The average period of customer use of the property is 30 days or less, and the owner of the property provides significant personal services.*

For longer-term rentals, the presumption that significant services are provided is not automatic, as it is in the case of the seven-day exception. Instead, the taxpayer must be able to *prove* that significant personal services are rendered in connection with the activity. Relevant facts and circumstances include the frequency with which such services are provided, the type and amount of labor required to perform the services, and the value of the services relative to the amount charged for the use of the property. Significant personal services include only services provided by *individuals*.[24]

3.   *The owner of the property provides extraordinary personal services. The average period of customer use is of no consequence in applying this test.*

---

[23]Temp. and Prop.Reg. § 1.469–1T(e)(3)(ii).   [24]Temp. and Prop.Reg. § 1.469–1T(e)(3)(iv).

Extraordinary personal services are services provided by individuals where the customers' use of the property is incidental to their receipt of the services. For example, a patient's use of a hospital bed is incidental to his or her receipt of medical services. Another example is the use of a boarding school's dormitory, which is incidental to the scholastic services received.

4. *The rental of the property is treated as incidental to a nonrental activity of the taxpayer.*

Rentals of real property incidental to a nonrental activity are not considered a passive activity. The Temporary Regulations provide that the following rentals are not passive activities:[25]

- *Property held primarily for investment.* This occurs where the principal purpose for holding the property is the expectation of gain from the appreciation of the property and the gross rent income is less than 2 percent of the lesser of (1) the unadjusted basis or (2) the fair market value of the property.

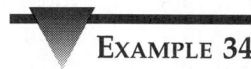

EXAMPLE 34   Ramon invests in vacant land for the purpose of realizing a profit on its appreciation. He leases the land during the period it is held. The land's unadjusted basis is $250,000, and the fair market value is $350,000. The lease payments are $4,000 per year. Because gross rent income is less than 2% of $250,000, the activity is not a rental activity. ▼

- *Property used in a trade or business.* This occurs where the property is owned by a taxpayer who is an owner of the trade or business using the rental property. The property must also have been used in the trade or business during the year or during at least two of the five preceding taxable years. The 2 percent test above also applies in this situation.

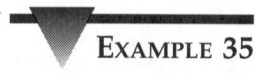

EXAMPLE 35   A farmer owns land with an unadjusted basis of $250,000 and a fair market value of $350,000. He used it for farming purposes in 1996 and 1997. In 1998, he leased the land to another farmer for $4,000. The activity is not a rental activity. ▼

- *Property held for sale to customers.* If property is held for sale to customers and rented during the year, the rental of the property is not a rental activity. If, for instance, an automobile dealer rents automobiles held for sale to customers to persons who are having their own cars repaired, the activity is not a rental activity.
- *Lodging rented for the convenience of an employer.* If an employer provides lodging for an employee incidental to the employee's performance of services in the employer's trade or business, no rental activity exists.
- A partner who rents property to a partnership that is used in the partnership's trade or business does not have a rental activity.

These rules were written to prevent taxpayers from converting active or portfolio income into a passive activity for the purpose of offsetting other passive losses.

5. *The taxpayer customarily makes the property available during defined business hours for nonexclusive use by various customers.*

---

[25]Temp. and Prop.Regs. §§ 1.469–1T(e)(3)(vi)(B) through (E).

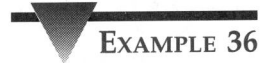

EXAMPLE 36

Pat is the owner-operator of a public golf course. Some customers pay daily greens fees each time they use the course, while others purchase weekly, monthly, or annual passes. The golf course is open every day from sunrise to sunset, except on certain holidays and on days when the course is closed due to inclement weather conditions. Pat is not engaged in a rental activity, regardless of the average period customers use the course. ▼

6. *The property is provided for use in an activity conducted by a partnership, S corporation, or joint venture in which the taxpayer owns an interest.*

EXAMPLE 37

Joe, a partner in the Skyview Partnership, contributes the use of a building to the partnership. The partnership has net income of $30,000 during the year, of which Joe's share is $10,000. Unless the partnership is engaged in a rental activity, none of Joe's income from the partnership is income from a rental activity. ▼

INTERACTION OF THE AT-RISK AND PASSIVE ACTIVITY LIMITS

7 ▼ **LEARNING OBJECTIVE**
Recognize the relationship between the at-risk and passive activity limitations.

The determination of whether a loss is suspended under the passive loss rules is made after application of the at-risk rules, as well as other provisions relating to the measurement of taxable income. A loss that is not allowed for the year because the taxpayer is not at risk with respect to it is suspended under the at-risk provision and not under the passive loss rules. Further, a taxpayer's basis is reduced by deductions (e.g., depreciation) even if the deductions are not currently usable because of the passive loss rules.

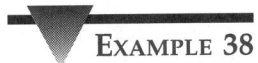

EXAMPLE 38

Jack's adjusted basis in a passive activity is $10,000 at the beginning of 1997. His loss from the activity in 1997 is $4,000. Since Jack had no passive activity income, the $4,000 cannot be deducted. At year-end, Jack has an adjusted basis and an at-risk amount of $6,000 in the activity and a suspended passive loss of $4,000. ▼

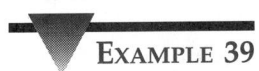

EXAMPLE 39

Jack in Example 38 had a loss of $9,000 in the activity in 1998. Since the $9,000 exceeds his at-risk amount ($6,000) by $3,000, that $3,000 loss is disallowed by the at-risk rules. If Jack has no passive activity income, the remaining $6,000 is suspended under the passive activity rules. At year-end, he has a $3,000 loss suspended under the at-risk rules, $10,000 of suspended passive losses, and an adjusted basis and an at-risk amount in the activity of zero. ▼

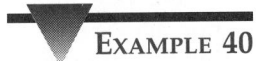

EXAMPLE 40

Jack in Example 39 realized $1,000 of passive income in 1999. Because the $1,000 increases his at-risk amount, $1,000 of the $3,000 unused loss can be reclassified as a passive loss. If he has no other passive income, the $1,000 income is offset by $1,000 of suspended passive losses. At the end of 1999, Jack has no taxable passive income, $2,000 ($3,000 − $1,000) of unused losses under the at-risk rules, $10,000 of (reclassified) suspended passive losses ($10,000 + $1,000 of reclassified unused at-risk losses − $1,000 of passive losses offset against passive income), and an adjusted basis and an at-risk amount in the activity of zero. ▼

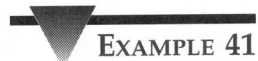

EXAMPLE 41

In 2000, Jack had no gain or loss from the activity in Example 40. He contributed $5,000 more to the passive activity. Because the $5,000 increases his at-risk amount, the $2,000 of losses suspended under the at-risk rules is reclassified as passive. Jack gets no passive loss deduction in 2000. At year-end, he has no suspended losses under the at-risk rules, $12,000 of suspended passive losses ($10,000 + $2,000 of reclassified suspended at-risk losses), and an adjusted basis and an at-risk amount of $3,000 ($5,000 additional investment − $2,000 of reclassified losses). ▼

8 ▼   **LEARNING OBJECTIVE**
Discuss the special treatment
available to real estate activities.

SPECIAL PASSIVE ACTIVITY RULES FOR REAL ESTATE ACTIVITIES

The passive loss limits contain two exceptions related to real estate activities. These exceptions allow all or part of real estate rental losses to be offset against active or portfolio income, even though the activity is a passive activity.

Material Participation in a Real Property Trade or Business.   Losses from real estate rental activities are *not* treated as passive losses for certain real estate professionals.[26] To qualify for nonpassive treatment, a taxpayer must satisfy both of the following requirements:

- More than half of the personal services that the taxpayer performs in trades or businesses are performed in real property trades or businesses in which the taxpayer materially participates.
- The taxpayer performs more than 750 hours of services in these real property trades or businesses as a material participant.

Taxpayers who do not satisfy the above requirements must continue to treat losses from real estate rental activities as passive losses.

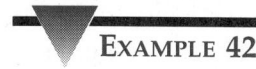

EXAMPLE 42

During the current year, Della performed personal service activities as follows: 900 hours as a personal financial planner, 550 hours in a real estate development and leasing business, and 600 hours in real estate rental activities. Any loss Della incurred in either real estate activity will *not* be subject to the passive loss rules, since more than 50% of her personal services were devoted to real property trades or businesses, and her material participation in those real estate activities exceeded 750 hours. Thus, any loss from the real estate rental activity could offset active and portfolio sources of income. ▼

As discussed earlier, a spouse's work is taken into consideration in satisfying the material participation requirement. However, the hours worked by a spouse are *not* taken into account when ascertaining whether a taxpayer has worked for more than 750 hours in real property trades or businesses during a year.[27] Services performed by an employee are not treated as being related to a real estate trade or business unless the employee performing the services owns more than a 5 percent interest in the employer. Additionally, a closely held C corporation may also qualify for the passive loss relief if more than 50 percent of its gross receipts for the year are derived from real property trades or businesses in which it materially participates.

Real Estate Rental Activities.   The second exception is more significant in that it is not restricted to real estate professionals. This exception allows individuals to deduct up to $25,000 of losses on real estate rental activities against active and portfolio income.[28] The potential annual $25,000 deduction is reduced by 50 percent of the taxpayer's AGI in excess of $100,000. Thus, the entire deduction is phased out at $150,000 of AGI. If married individuals file separately, the $25,000 deduction is reduced to zero unless they lived apart for the entire year. If they lived apart for the entire year, the loss amount is $12,500 each, and the phase-out begins at $50,000. AGI for purposes of the phase-out is calculated without regard to IRA deductions, Social Security benefits, and net losses from passive activities.

To qualify for the $25,000 exception, a taxpayer must meet the following requirements:[29]

---

[26]§ 469(c)(7).
[27]§ 469(c)(7)(B) and Reg. § 1.469–9.

[28]§ 469(i).
[29]§ 469(i)(6).

- Actively participate in the real estate rental activity.
- Own 10 percent or more (in value) of all interests in the activity during the entire taxable year (or shorter period during which the taxpayer held an interest in the activity).

The difference between *active participation* and *material participation* is that the former can be satisfied without regular, continuous, and substantial involvement in operations as long as the taxpayer participates in making management decisions in a significant and bona fide sense. In this context, relevant management decisions include such decisions as approving new tenants, deciding on rental terms, and approving capital or repair expenditures.

The $25,000 allowance is available after all active participation rental losses and gains are netted and applied to other passive income. If a taxpayer has a real estate rental loss in excess of the amount that can be deducted under the real estate rental exception, that excess is treated as a passive loss.

 EXAMPLE 43

Brad, who has $90,000 of AGI before considering rental activities, has $85,000 of losses from a real estate rental activity in which he actively participates. He also actively participates in another real estate rental activity from which he has $25,000 of income. He has other passive income of $36,000. The net rental loss of $60,000 is absorbed by the $36,000 of passive income, leaving $24,000 that can be deducted against other income. ▼

The $25,000 offset allowance is an aggregate of both deductions and credits in deduction equivalents. The deduction equivalent of a passive activity credit is the amount of deductions that reduces the tax liability for the taxable year by an amount equal to the credit.[30] A taxpayer with $5,000 of credits and a tax bracket of 28 percent would have a deduction equivalent of $17,857 ($5,000 ÷ 28%).

If the total deduction and deduction equivalent exceed $25,000, the taxpayer must allocate on a pro rata basis, first among the losses (including real estate rental activity losses suspended in prior years) and then to credits in the following order:

---

[30]§ 469(j)(5).

(1) credits other than rehabilitation and low-income housing credits, (2) rehabilitation credits, and (3) low-income housing credits.

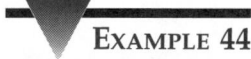

EXAMPLE 44   Kevin is an active participant in a real estate rental activity that produces $8,000 of income, $26,000 of deductions, and $1,500 of credits. Kevin, who is in the 28% tax bracket, may deduct the net passive loss of $18,000 ($8,000 − $26,000). After deducting the loss, he has an available deduction equivalent of $7,000 ($25,000 − $18,000 passive loss). Therefore, the maximum amount of credits that he may claim is $1,960 ($7,000 × 28%). Since the actual credits are less than this amount, Kevin may claim the entire $1,500 credit. ▼

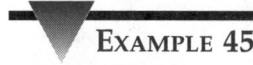

EXAMPLE 45   Kelly, who is in the 28% tax bracket, is an active participant in three separate real estate rental activities. The relevant tax results for each activity are as follows:

- Activity A: $20,000 of losses.
- Activity B: $10,000 of losses.
- Activity C: $4,200 of credits.

Kelly's deduction equivalent from the credits is $15,000 ($4,200 ÷ 28%). Therefore, the total passive deductions and deduction equivalents are $45,000 ($20,000 + $10,000 + $15,000), which exceeds the maximum allowable amount of $25,000. Consequently, Kelly must allocate pro rata first from among losses and then from among credits. Deductions from losses are limited as follows:

- Activity A {$25,000 × [$20,000 ÷ ($20,000 + $10,000)]} = $16,667.
- Activity B {$25,000 × [$10,000 ÷ ($20,000 + $10,000)]} = $8,333.

Since the amount of passive deductions exceeds the $25,000 maximum, the deduction balance of $5,000 and passive credits of $4,200 must be carried forward. Kelly's suspended losses and credits by activity are as follows:

| | Total | Activity | | |
		A	B	C
Allocated losses	$ 30,000	$ 20,000	$ 10,000	$ –0–
Allocated credits	4,200	–0–	–0–	4,200
Utilized losses	(25,000)	(16,667)	(8,333)	–0–
Suspended losses	5,000	3,333	1,667	–0–
Suspended credits	4,200	–0–	–0–	4,200

▼

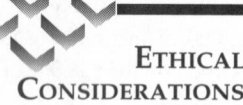

ETHICAL CONSIDERATIONS

Applying the Rules on Rental Real Estate

Adam, a management consultant, owns an apartment complex that produces a profit of $60,000 in the current year. He earns $120,000 in his consulting business and has a $40,000 loss on a passive activity (not real estate). Adam works 800 hours at the apartment complex during the year, but characterizes the $60,000 profit as passive income so that he can utilize the $40,000 passive loss. He claims that he is doing nothing wrong because the law is designed only to protect the loss deduction of real estate professionals and is not applicable to profits.

Further, Adam thinks that he is justified in classifying the profit as passive because of the nature of the work he performs during the time he devotes to managing the apartments. Adam feels certain that of the 800 hours, between 300 and 400 hours were spent coaching and supporting about 20 underprivileged children living in the apartment complex as part of a year-round sports program. Adam says that his involvement not only benefits the children, but will make the apartment complex a more desirable place to live. Consequently, his coaching work benefits him economically in the long run. He sees the hours devoted to the sports program as an integral part of his job in managing the apartment complex, but feels that they should not count in determining whether the activity is passive. Adam asks you to prepare his return. What actions should you take?

DISPOSITIONS OF PASSIVE INTERESTS

9 LEARNING OBJECTIVE
Determine the proper tax treatment upon the disposition of a passive activity.

Recall from an earlier discussion that if a taxpayer disposes of an entire interest in a passive activity, any suspended losses (and in certain cases, suspended credits) may be utilized when calculating the final economic gain or loss on the investment. In addition, if a loss ultimately results, that loss can be offset against other types of income. However, the consequences may differ if the activity is disposed of in a transaction that is other than a fully taxable transaction. The following discusses the treatment of suspended passive losses in other types of dispositions.

Disposition of a Passive Activity at Death. A transfer of a taxpayer's interest in an activity by reason of the taxpayer's death results in suspended losses being allowed (to the decedent) to the extent they exceed the amount, if any, of the step-up in basis allowed.[31] Suspended losses are lost to the extent of the amount of the basis increase. The losses allowed generally are reported on the final return of the deceased taxpayer.

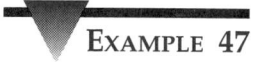
EXAMPLE 46

A taxpayer dies with passive activity property having an adjusted basis of $40,000, suspended losses of $10,000, and a fair market value at the date of the decedent's death of $75,000. The increase (i.e., step-up) in basis (see Chapter 14) is $35,000 (fair market value at date of death in excess of adjusted basis). None of the $10,000 suspended loss is deductible by either the decedent or the beneficiary. The suspended losses ($10,000) are lost because they do not exceed the step-up in basis ($35,000). ▼

EXAMPLE 47

A taxpayer dies with passive activity property having an adjusted basis of $40,000, suspended losses of $10,000, and a fair market value at the date of the decedent's death of $47,000. Since the step-up in basis is only $7,000 ($47,000 − $40,000), the suspended losses allowed are limited to $3,000 ($10,000 suspended loss at time of death − $7,000 increase in basis). The $3,000 loss available to the decedent is reported on the decedent's final income tax return. ▼

Disposition of a Passive Activity by Gift. In a disposition of a taxpayer's interest in a passive activity by gift, the suspended losses are added to the basis of the property.[32]

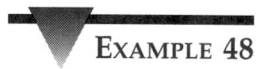
EXAMPLE 48

A taxpayer makes a gift of passive activity property having an adjusted basis of $40,000, suspended losses of $10,000, and a fair market value at the date of the gift of $100,000. The taxpayer cannot deduct the suspended losses in the year of the disposition. However, the suspended losses transfer with the property and are added to the adjusted basis of the property. ▼

---

[31]§ 469(g)(2).

[32]§ 469(j)(6).

Installment Sale of a Passive Activity.   An installment sale of a taxpayer's entire interest in a passive activity triggers the recognition of the suspended losses.[33] The losses are allowed in each year of the installment obligation in the ratio that the gain recognized in each year bears to the total gain on the sale.

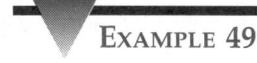

EXAMPLE 49

Stan sold his entire interest in a passive activity for $100,000. His adjusted basis in the property was $60,000. If he uses the installment method, his gross profit ratio is 40% ($40,000/$100,000). If Stan received a $20,000 down payment, he would recognize a gain of $8,000 (40% of $20,000). If the activity had a suspended loss of $25,000, Stan would deduct $5,000 [($8,000 ÷ $40,000) × $25,000] of the suspended loss in the first year. ▼

Passive Activity Changes to Active.   If a formerly passive activity becomes an active one, suspended losses are allowed to the extent of income from the now active business.[34] If any of the suspended loss remains, it continues to be treated as a loss from a passive activity. The excess suspended loss can be deducted from passive income or carried over to the next tax year and deducted to the extent of income from the now active business in the succeeding year(s). The activity must continue to be the same activity.

Nontaxable Exchange of a Passive Activity.   In a nontaxable exchange of a passive investment, the taxpayer keeps the suspended losses, which generally become deductible when the acquired property is sold. If the activity of the old and new property are the same, suspended losses can be used.

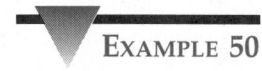

EXAMPLE 50

A taxpayer exchanged a duplex for a limited partnership interest in a § 721 nonrecognition transaction (see Chapter 20 for details). The suspended losses from the duplex are not deductible until the limited partnership interest is sold. Two separate activities exist: a real estate rental activity and a limited partnership activity. If the taxpayer had continued to own the duplex and the duplex had future taxable income, the suspended losses would have become deductible before the time of disposition. ▼

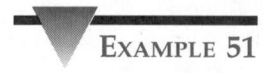

EXAMPLE 51

In a § 1031 nontaxable exchange (see Chapter 15 for details), a taxpayer exchanged a duplex for an apartment building. The suspended losses from the duplex are deductible against future taxable income of the apartment building. The same activity exists. ▼

TAX PLANNING CONSIDERATIONS

UTILIZING PASSIVE LOSSES

Taxpayers who have passive activity losses (PALs) should adopt a strategy of generating passive activity income that can be sheltered by existing passive losses. One approach is to buy an interest in a passive activity that is generating income (referred to as passive income generators, or PIGs). Then the PAL can offset income from the PIG. From a tax perspective, it would be foolish to buy a loss-generating passive activity (PAL) unless one has other passive income (PIG) to shelter or the activity is rental real estate that can qualify for the $25,000 exception or the exception available to real estate professionals.

10   **LEARNING OBJECTIVE**
Suggest tax planning strategies to minimize the effect of the passive loss limitations.

A taxpayer with existing passive losses might consider buying rental property. If a large down payment is made and the straight-line method of MACRS (discussed in Chapter 8) is elected, a positive net income could be realized. The income would be sheltered by other passive losses, and depreciation expense would be spread out evenly and preserved for future years. Future gain realized

---

[33]§ 469(g)(3).   [34]§ 469(f).

CONCEPT SUMMARY 11–2

Passive Activity Loss Rules: General Concepts

What is the fundamental passive activity rule?	Passive activity losses may be deducted only against passive activity income and gains. Losses not allowed are suspended and used in future years.
Who is subject to the passive activity rules?	Individuals. Estates. Trusts. Personal service corporations. Closely held C corporations.
What is a passive activity?	Trade or business or income-producing activity in which the taxpayer does not materially participate during the year, or rental activities, subject to certain exceptions, regardless of the taxpayer's level of participation.
What is an activity?	One or more trade or business or rental activities that comprise an appropriate economic unit.
How is an appropriate economic unit determined?	Based on a reasonable application of the relevant facts and circumstances.
What is material participation?	In general, the taxpayer participates in a regular, continuous, and substantial basis. More specifically, when the taxpayer meets the conditions of one of the seven tests provided in the Regulations.
What is a rental activity?	In general, an activity where payments are received for the use of tangible property. More specifically, a rental activity that does *not* meet one of the six exceptions provided in the Regulations. Special rules apply to rental real estate.

upon the sale of the rental property could be sheltered by existing suspended passive losses.

Taxpayers with passive losses should consider all other trades or businesses in which they have an interest. If they show that they do not materially participate in the activity, the activity becomes a passive activity. Any income generated could be sheltered by existing passive losses and suspended losses. Family partnerships in which certain members do not materially participate would qualify. The silent partner in any general partnership engaged in a trade or business would also qualify.

As the chapter has shown, the passive loss rules can have a dramatic effect on a taxpayer's ability to claim passive losses currently. However, several steps can be taken to mitigate their impact:

- Replace passive activity debt with home equity indebtedness.
- Carefully select the year in which a passive activity is to be disposed of at a gain, as it can be to the taxpayer's advantage to wait until sufficient passive losses have been generated to completely offset the gain recognized on the asset's disposition.
- Keep accurate records of all sources of income and losses, particularly any suspended passive losses and credits and the activities to which they relate, so that their potential tax benefit will not be lost.

Finally, because of the restrictive nature of the passive activity loss rules, it may be advantageous for a taxpayer to use a vacation home enough to convert it to a second residence. This would enable all of the qualified interest and real estate taxes to be deducted without limitation. However, this strategy would lead to the loss of other deductions, such as repairs, maintenance, and insurance.

KEY TERMS

Active income, 11–5

At-risk limitation, 11–3

Closely held corporation, 11–10

Extraordinary personal services, 11–20

Material participation, 11–14

Passive loss, 11–3

Personal service corporation, 11–10

Portfolio income, 11–6

Rental activity, 11–18

Significant participation activity, 11–16

Tax shelters, 11–2

PROBLEM MATERIALS

DISCUSSION QUESTIONS

1. Describe the general purpose and effect of the two major provisions discussed in this chapter: the at-risk rules and the passive activity loss rules.

2. Alice invested $50,000 for a 25% interest in a partnership in which she is not a material participant. The partnership borrowed $100,000 from a bank and used the proceeds to acquire a building. What is Alice's at-risk amount if the $100,000 was borrowed on a recourse loan?

3. List some events that increase and decrease an investor's at-risk amount. What are some strategies that a taxpayer can employ to increase the at-risk amount in order to claim a higher deduction for losses?

4. Roy invested $15,000 in a cattle-feeding operation that used nonrecourse notes to purchase $150,000 in feed, which was fed to the cattle and expensed. His share of the expense was $27,000. How much can Roy deduct?

5. Explain the meaning of the terms *active income, portfolio income,* and *passive income.*

6. Manuel owns an interest in an activity that produces a $100,000 loss during the year. Would he generally prefer to have the activity classified as active or passive? Discuss.

7. Kim owns an interest in an activity that produces $100,000 of income during the year. Would Kim prefer to have the activity classified as active or passive? Discuss.

8. Felicia owns a passive activity that she acquired several years ago. She has incurred losses on the activity since its acquisition. This is the only passive activity she has ever owned. How will these passive losses affect Felicia's taxable income when she disposes of the activity?

9. On the taxable disposition of a passive activity, what happens to the suspended losses? The suspended credits?

10. Discuss whether the passive loss rules apply to the following: individuals, closely held C corporations, S corporations, partnerships, and personal service corporations.

11. Gray Corporation has $100,000 of active income and a $55,000 passive loss for the year. Under what circumstances is the corporation prohibited from deducting the loss? Under what circumstances is the corporation allowed to deduct the loss?

12. What factors are given the greatest weight in determining whether activities constitute an appropriate economic unit?

13. Discuss what constitutes a passive activity.

14. Under what circumstances may the IRS regroup activities in a different way than the taxpayer has grouped them? Give an example of a situation to which the regrouping rule would be applied.

15. What is the significance of the term *material participation*? Why is the extent of a taxpayer's participation in an activity important in determining whether a loss from the activity is deductible or nondeductible?

16. Why did the IRS adopt the more-than-500-hour standard for material participation?

17. Keith, a physician, operates a separate business that he acquired nine years ago. During the current year, he participates for 90 hours in the business, which incurs a loss of $20,000. Under what circumstances will the loss be deductible as an active loss?

18. Rene retired from public accounting after a long and successful career of 45 years. As part of her retirement package, she continues to share in the profits and losses of the firm, albeit at a lower rate than when she was working full-time. Because Rene wants to stay busy during her retirement years, she has invested and works in a local hardware business, operated as a partnership. Unfortunately, the business has recently gone through a slump and has not been generating profits. Identify relevant tax issues for Rene.

19. Some types of work are counted in applying the material participation standards, and some types are not counted. Discuss and give examples of each type.

20. During the current year, Alan is determined to make better use of the tax losses that tend to flow from the various businesses that he owns. He is particularly sensitive to the limitations that the passive loss rules place on the deductibility of losses because of the disaster that occurred last year: his accountant informed him that he would not be able to claim any of the losses on his income tax return because of his lack of material participation. He has even suggested to his wife that she may have to put in some time at the businesses if his goals are to be accomplished. Identify the tax issues that Alan faces.

21. What are *significant personal services*, and what role do they play in determining whether a rental activity is treated as a passive activity?

22. What are *extraordinary personal services*, and what is their importance in determining whether a rental activity is treated as a passive activity?

23. How is passive activity defined in the Code, and what aspects of the definition have been clarified by final or Temporary Regulations?

24. Laura owns an apartment building and a videocassette rental business. She participates for more than 500 hours in the operations of each activity. Are the businesses active or passive?

25. Hilda incurred a loss of $60,000 on a real estate rental activity during the current year. Under what circumstances can Hilda treat the entire loss as nonpassive?

26. In the current year, George and Susie White, both successful CPAs, made a cash investment for a limited partnership interest in a California avocado grove. In addition to the cash generated from the investors, the grove's management borrowed a substantial sum to purchase assets necessary for its operation. The Whites' investment adviser told them that their share of the tax loss in the first year alone would be in excess of their initial cash investment, followed by several more years of losses. They feel confident that their interest in the avocado grove is a sound investment. Identify the tax issues facing the Whites.

27. Rick, a full-time real estate professional, earns $5,000 for development services rendered to an S corporation that owns and manages apartment units. He also owns an interest in the entity. His share of the S corporation's losses for the year totals $5,000. Identify the issues that are relevant in determining how the items of income and loss are treated for tax purposes.

28. Matt owns a small apartment building that generated a loss during the year. Under what circumstances can Matt deduct a loss from the rental activity, and what limitations apply?

29. In connection with passive activities, what is a *deduction equivalent*? How is a deduction equivalent computed?

30. What are the differences between material participation and active participation under the passive loss rules?

 31. Betty and Steve received a substantial windfall due to a recent inheritance. Because they have always loved spending time at the beach, they plan to devote some of the newly available cash to a beach-related investment. Their analysis identifies two possibilities that seem to be logical given their particular situation. They could purchase a beach cottage and use it for both personal and rental purposes; or they could pool their money with Steve's brother and purchase several cottages, one of which would be held strictly for personal use, while the others would be held solely for rental use. Identify the tax issues facing Betty and Steve.

PROBLEMS

32. In 1997, Fred invested $50,000 in a partnership. Fred's interest is not considered to be a passive activity. In 1997, his share of the partnership loss was $35,000 and in 1998, his share of the loss is $25,000. How much can Fred deduct in 1997 and 1998?

 33. In the current year, Bill Parker (54 Oak Drive, St. Paul, MN 55162) is considering making an investment of $60,000 in Best Choice Partnership. The prospectus provided by Bill's broker indicates that the partnership investment is not a passive activity and that Bill's share of the entity's loss in the current year will likely be $40,000, while his share of the partnership loss next year will probably be $25,000. Write a letter to Bill in which you indicate how the losses would be treated for tax purposes in the current and next years.

 34. Carmen wishes to invest $25,000 in a relatively safe venture and has discovered two alternatives that would produce the following reportable income and loss over the next three years:

Year	Alternative 1 Income (Loss)	Alternative 2 Income (Loss)
1	($15,000)	($30,000)
2	(15,000)	20,000
3	45,000	25,000

She is interested in the after-tax effects of these alternatives over a three-year horizon. Assume that Carmen's investment portfolio produces sufficient passive income to offset any potential passive loss that may arise from these alternatives, that her cost of capital is 8% (the present value factors are 0.92593, 0.85734, and 0.79383), that she is in the 28% tax bracket, that each investment alternative possesses equal growth potential, and that each alternative exposes her to comparable financial risk. In addition, assume that in the loss years for each alternative, there is no cash flow from or to the investment (i.e., the loss is due to depreciation), while in those years when the income is positive, cash flows to Carmen equal the amount of the income. Based on these facts, compute the present value of these two investment alternatives and determine which option Carmen should choose.

35. Tina acquired passive Activity A in January 1993 and Activity B in September 1994. Until 1997, Activity A was profitable. Activity A produced a loss of $200,000 in 1997 and a loss of $100,000 in 1998. Tina has passive income from Activity B of $20,000 in 1997 and $40,000 in 1998. After offsetting passive income, how much of the net losses may she deduct?

36. In 1993, Kay acquired an interest in a partnership in which she is not a material participant. The partnership was profitable until 1997. Kay's basis in her partnership interest at the beginning of 1997 was $40,000. In 1997, Kay's share of the partnership loss was $35,000. In 1998, her share of the partnership income was $15,000. How much can Kay deduct in 1997 and 1998?

37. Bob, an attorney, earns $200,000 from his law practice in the current year. He receives $45,000 in dividends and interest during the year. In addition, he incurs a loss of $50,000 from an investment in a passive activity acquired three years ago. What is Bob's net income for the current year after considering the passive investment?

38. Sarah has $100,000 that she wishes to invest, and she is considering the following two options:

   • Option A—Investment in Bluebird Equity Mutual fund, which would be expected to produce dividends of $8,000 per year.

   • Option B—Investment in Redbird Limited Partnership (buys, sells, and operates avocado groves). Sarah's share of the partnership's income and loss over the next three years is expected to be:

Year	Income (Loss)
1	($ 8,000)
2	(2,000)
3	34,000

   Sarah is interested in the after-tax effects of these alternatives over a three-year horizon. Assume that Sarah's investment portfolio produces no passive income, that her cost of capital is 8% (the present value factors are 0.92593, 0.85734, and 0.79383), that she is in the 31% tax bracket, that each investment alternative possesses equal growth potential, and that each alternative exposes her to comparable financial risk. Based on these facts, compute the present value of these two investment alternatives and determine which option Sarah should choose.

39. Hazel has two investments in nonrental passive activities. Activity A, which was acquired seven years ago, was profitable until the current year. Activity B was acquired this year. Currently, Hazel's share of the loss from Activity A is $10,000, and her share of the loss from Activity B is $6,000. What is the total of Hazel's suspended losses from these activities as of the end of the current year?

40. Leanne has investments in four passive activity partnerships purchased several years ago. Last year, the income and losses were as follows:

Activity	Income (Loss)
A	$ 60,000
B	(30,000)
C	(30,000)
D	(40,000)

   In the current year, she sold her interest in Activity D for a $20,000 gain. Activity D, which had been profitable until last year, had a current loss of $1,000. How will the sale of Activity D affect Leanne's taxable income in the current year?

41. Leon sells his interest in a passive activity for $100,000 during the year. Determine the tax effect based on each of the following sets of independent facts:
   a. His adjusted basis in this investment is $35,000. Losses from prior years that were not deductible due to the passive loss restrictions total $40,000.

b. His adjusted basis in this investment is $75,000. Losses from prior years that were not deductible due to the passive loss restrictions total $40,000.

c. His adjusted basis in this investment is $75,000. Losses from prior years that were not deductible due to the passive loss restrictions total $40,000. In addition, suspended credits total $10,000.

42. Brown Corporation, a personal service corporation, earns active income of $500,000 in the current year. The corporation receives $60,000 in dividends during the year. In addition, Brown incurs a loss of $80,000 from an investment in a passive activity acquired three years ago. What is Brown's income for the current year after considering the passive investment?

43. White, Inc., earns $400,000 from operations in the current year. White also receives $36,000 in dividends and interest on various portfolio investments. During the year, White pays $150,000 to acquire a 20% interest in a passive activity that produces a $200,000 loss.

a. How will these facts affect White's taxable income, assuming the corporation is a personal service corporation?

b. How will these facts affect White's taxable income, assuming the corporation is a closely held, non-personal service corporation?

44. Green Corporation, a closely held, non-personal service corporation, earns active income of $50,000 in the current year. Green receives $60,000 in dividends during the year. In addition, Green incurs a loss of $80,000 from an investment in a passive activity acquired last year. What is Green's net income for the current year after considering the passive investment?

45. Eleanor owns interests in a hardware store, bowling alley, and grocery store. Several full-time employees work at each of the enterprises. As of the end of November of the current year, Eleanor has worked 150 hours in the hardware store, 250 hours at the bowling alley, and 80 hours at the grocery store. In reviewing her financial records, you learn that she has no passive investments that are generating income and that she expects these three ventures collectively to produce a loss. What recommendation would you offer Eleanor as she plans her activities for the remainder of the year?

46. Ann acquired an activity four years ago. The loss from the activity is $50,000 in the current year. She has AGI of $140,000 before considering the loss from the activity. The activity is a service station, and Ann is a material participant. What is her AGI after considering this activity?

47. Lee acquired a 20% interest in the ABC Partnership for $60,000 in 1993. The partnership was profitable until 1998, and Lee's amount at risk in the partnership interest was $120,000 at the end of 1997. ABC incurs a loss of $400,000 in 1998 and reports income of $200,000 in 1999. Assuming Lee is not a material participant in ABC, how much of his loss from ABC Partnership is deductible in 1998 and 1999, respectively?

48. Ken has a $40,000 loss from an investment in a partnership in which he does not participate. He paid $30,000 for his interest in the partnership. How much of the loss is disallowed by the at-risk rules? How much is disallowed by the passive loss rules?

49. Last year, Fran invested $40,000 for an interest in a partnership in which she is a material participant. Her share of the partnership's loss for the year was $50,000. In the current year, Fran's share of the partnership's income is $30,000. What is the effect on her taxable income for the current year?

50. Soong, a physician, earns $200,000 from his practice. He also receives $18,000 in dividends and interest on various portfolio investments. During the year, he pays $45,000 to acquire a 20% interest in a partnership that produces a $300,000 loss.

a. Compute Soong's AGI assuming he does not participate in the operations of the partnership.

b. Compute Soong's AGI assuming he is a material participant in the operations of the partnership.

51. Sam invested $150,000 in a passive activity five years ago. On January 1, 1997, his amount at risk in the activity was $30,000. His shares of the income and losses in the activity were as follows:

Year	Income (Loss)
1997	($40,000)
1998	(30,000)
1999	50,000

How much can Sam deduct in 1997 and 1998? What is his taxable income from the activity in 1999? Keep in mind the at-risk rules as well as the passive loss rules.

52. Joe Cook (125 Hill Street, Charleston, WV 25311) acquired an activity four years ago. The loss from the activity is $50,000 in the current year. He has AGI of $140,000 before considering the loss from the activity. The activity is an apartment building in an exclusive part of the city, and Joe is an active participant. Write a letter to Joe in which you explain what his AGI is after the loss is considered.

53. Beth acquired an activity four years ago. The loss from the activity is $50,000 in the current year. She has AGI of $140,000 before considering the loss from the activity. The activity is an apartment building, and Beth is not an active participant. What is her AGI after considering the activity?

54. During the current year, Donald works 1,200 hours as a computer consultant, 600 hours in a real estate development business, and 500 hours in real estate rental activities. He earns $60,000 as a computer consultant, but loses $18,000 in the development business and $26,000 in the real estate rental business. How should Donald treat the losses on his current Federal income tax return?

55. During the current year, Roger performs the following personal services in three separate activities: 800 hours as a CPA in his tax practice, 400 hours in a real estate development business (i.e., not a material participant), and 600 hours in an apartment leasing operation. He expects that losses will be realized from the two real estate ventures while his tax practice will show a profit. Roger files a joint return with his wife whose salary is $200,000. What is the character of the income and losses generated by these activities?

56. Hal and Wanda are married with no dependents and live together in Ohio, which is not a community property state. Since Wanda has large medical expenses, they seek your advice about filing separately to save taxes. Their income and expenses for 1998 are as follows:

Hal's salary	$ 30,000
Wanda's salary	50,000
Dividends and interest (joint)	1,800
Rental loss from actively managed apartments (joint)	(20,000)
Wanda's unreimbursed medical expenses	6,500
All other itemized deductions:*	
Hal	8,000
Wanda	2,000

*None subject to limitations.

Determine whether Hal and Wanda should file jointly or separately for 1998.

57. Lucy and Leon have owned a beach cottage on the New Jersey shore for several years and have always used it as a family retreat. When they acquired the property, they had no intentions of renting it, but because their family circumstances have changed, they are considering using the cottage for only two weeks a year and renting it for the remainder of the year. Their AGI is currently approximately $80,000 per year, and they are in the 33% tax bracket (combined Federal and state). Their financial records indicate

that interest and real estate taxes have totaled $8,000 per year, and Lucy and Leon expect these expenditures to continue at this level into the foreseeable future. In addition, if they rent the property, their *incremental* revenue and expenses are projected to be:

Rent income	$ 20,000
Rental commissions	(3,000)
Maintenance expenses	(12,000)
Depreciation expense	(10,000)
	($ 5,000)

If they do convert the cottage to rental property, they insist that they will be actively involved in key rental and maintenance decisions. Given the tax effects of converting the property to rental use, would the cash flow resulting from renting the property be enough to meet the $12,000 annual mortgage payment? This is an important factor in Lucy and Leon's decision.

58. During the current year, Gene performs services as follows: 1,800 hours as a CPA in his tax practice and 50 hours in an apartment leasing operation in which he has a 15% interest. Because of his oversight duties, Gene is considered to be an active participant. He expects that his share of the loss realized from the apartment leasing operation will be $30,000 while his tax practice will show a profit of approximately $80,000. Gene is single and has no other income besides that stated above. Discuss the character of the income and losses generated by these activities.

59. Ella has $105,000 of losses from a real estate rental activity in which she actively participates. She has other rental income of $25,000 and other passive income of $32,000. How much rental loss can Ella deduct against active and portfolio income (ignoring the at-risk rules)? Does she have any suspended losses to carry over?

60. Faye dies owning an interest in a passive activity property with an adjusted basis of $160,000, suspended losses of $16,000, and a fair market value of $170,000. What can be deducted on her final income tax return?

61. In the current year, Leon gives an interest in a passive activity to his daughter, Lucy. The value of the interest at the date of the gift is $25,000. The adjusted basis of the property to Leon is $13,000. During the time that Leon owned the investment, losses that were not deductible due to the passive loss limitations totaled $3,000. What treatment is given to the suspended passive activity losses?

62. Tonya sells a passive activity in the current year for $150,000. Her adjusted basis in the activity is $50,000, and she uses the installment method of reporting the gain. The activity has suspended losses of $12,000. Tonya receives $60,000 in the year of sale. What is her gain? How much of the suspended losses can she deduct?

RESEARCH PROBLEMS

*Note: Use the **RIA OnPoint System 4 Student Version CD-ROM**, which is available to accompany this text, in preparing solutions to the Research Problems. Alternatively, tax research materials found in a standard tax library can be used.*

Research Problem 1.   Having become relatively affluent due to their success as respected dentists, George and Julie Sharp decide to invest $100,000 of their excess cash in a nearby resort community. Their investment gives them ownership rights in a cottage that normally will be rented out to vacationers for six-day periods by Paradise Resorts, Inc. Though the Sharps are legally the sole owners of the cottage, they are required to allow Paradise Resorts to market their cottage's availability and maintain the unit. George and Julie are permitted to use the cottage rent-free every year for no more than 14 days.

During the first year, Paradise Resorts reports that the Sharps' loss from the property is $25,000. During that period, the Sharps have accumulated documentation showing that they have spent 300 hours of their time on the following activities:

preparing an annual budget for their cottage investment, marketing Paradise Resorts in conversations with their friends and at their country club, attending the annual business meeting of Paradise Resorts with the other cottage owners, and receiving and depositing net revenues received from rental of their cottage.

As the Sharps' tax adviser, how would you recommend that they report their loss from this investment on their tax return? Write a memo to the tax files to document your recommendation.

Research Problem 2.   Bill owns an interest in a small engine repair shop in which he works 425 hours during the year. He has four full-time employees at the repair shop. Bill also owns an apartment building to which he devotes 1,300 hours during the year. He has no employees for the apartment activity. Are these activities active or passive? In your response, consider the impact of the significant participation activity rules.

Research Problem 3.   Over the years, Bill Johnson (30 Brookfield Drive, Hampton, VA 23666) has taken great pride in his ability to spot exceptional rental real estate investments, particularly in terms of their appreciation potential. As a result, he has accumulated several properties. In the early years of his investment activities, he was able to devote only a limited amount of time to these ventures. In the current year, he retires from his full-time job and is able to devote most of his time to the management and operation of the rental activities. Bill summarizes the relevant tax attributes of each of the properties as follows:

Property	Suspended Passive Losses	Expected Current Year's Income (Loss)
A	None	$ 25,000
B	($20,000)	15,000
C	(40,000)	(15,000)

Bill is astute enough to know that he is a qualifying real estate professional for the current year and materially participates in all three properties within the meaning of § 469(c)(7). However, he is uncertain whether he should treat the properties as three separate activities or aggregate them and treat them as one activity.

Write a letter to Bill to assist him in making the decision. Because of Bill's expertise in the tax law, feel free to use technical language in your letter.

Partial list of research aids:
Reg. § 1.469–9(e).

Use the tax resources of the Internet to address the following questions. Do not restrict your search to the World Wide Web, but include a review of newsgroups and general reference materials, practitioner sites and resources, primary sources of the tax law, chat rooms and discussion groups, and other opportunities.

Research Problem 4.   Scan the materials offered in several newsgroups frequented by tax consultants. In what context are "tax shelters" still discussed by these professionals? Do these advisers adequately take into account the rules of §§ 465 and 469? Post a message to one of these newsgroups explaining the interaction of these two sections in a paragraph or two.

Research Problem 5.   Download and print a copy of Form 8582 and its instructions. Use these materials to complete the requirements of Problem 52.

TEAM PROJECT: ARTHUR ANDERSEN TAX CHALLENGE CASES

For more information on the Arthur Andersen Tax Challenge Cases, refer to Chapter 1, page 1–37.

Information related to tax issues and problems that are discussed in this chapter may be found in the

Day and Ball case on pages: None
Fence case on pages: 40, 50, 64, 65, 67, and 68

Read and analyze the case you have been assigned and *identify* any issues and problems that are related to material covered in this chapter. If the information provided in the case is complete, prepare answers for this part of the case at this time. If you need information that is contained in the later parts of the case, write a memo summarizing the questions or problems so you can prepare a complete answer at a later date.

IV

Special Tax Computation Methods, Payment Procedures, and Tax Credits

Part IV presents several topics that relate to the theme of tax liability determination. The taxpayer must calculate the tax liability in accordance with the basic tax formula and also in accordance with the tax formula for the alternative minimum tax (AMT). The basic tax formula was presented in Part I, and the AMT formula is covered in Part IV. Tax credits reduce the amount of the calculated tax liability. The specific procedures for the timing of the payment of the tax liability are also discussed.

12

ALTERNATIVE MINIMUM TAX

LEARNING OBJECTIVES

After completing Chapter 12, you should be able to:

1. Explain the rationale for the alternative minimum tax (AMT).

2. Understand the formula for computing the AMT for individuals.

3. Identify the adjustments made in calculating the AMT.

4. Identify the tax preferences that are included in calculating the AMT.

5. Apply the formula for computing the AMT and illustrate Form 6251.

6. Describe the role of the AMT credit in the alternative minimum tax structure.

7. Understand the basic features of the corporate AMT.

8. Identify tax planning opportunities to minimize the AMT.

▼ **1** LEARNING OBJECTIVE
Explain the rationale for the alternative minimum tax (AMT).

Bob and Carol are unmarried individuals who work for the same employer and have the same amount of gross income and the same amount of deductions. Bob's tax return is prepared by Adam, and Carol's tax return is prepared by Eve. While discussing their tax liability one day at lunch, Carol is dismayed to learn that she paid $15,000 more in Federal income taxes than Bob did for the tax year. Carol meets with Eve that evening. Eve reviews Carol's tax return and assures her that her tax liability was properly calculated.

The above events raise a number of interesting questions for Bob and Carol that can be answered after completing this chapter. Why didn't Bob and Carol have the same tax liability? Were both tax returns properly prepared? Should Carol consider replacing her tax return preparer Eve with Adam? Is it possible and/or desirable for Carol to file an amended return? Should Bob do anything?

The tax law contains many incentives that are intended to influence the economic and social behavior of taxpayers (refer to Chapter 1). Some taxpayers have been able to take advantage of enough of these incentives to avoid or minimize any liability for Federal income tax. Although these taxpayers were reducing taxes legally, Congress became concerned about the inequity that results when taxpayers with substantial economic incomes can avoid paying any income tax. The **alternative minimum tax (AMT)** was enacted as a backup to the regular income tax. The rationale for the AMT was expressed as follows:

> [T]he minimum tax should serve one overriding objective: to ensure that no taxpayer with substantial economic income can avoid significant tax liability by using exclusions, deductions, and credits. Although these provisions may provide incentives for worthy goals, they become counterproductive when taxpayers are allowed to use them to avoid virtually all tax liability. The ability of high-income taxpayers to pay little or no tax undermines respect for the entire tax system and, thus, for the incentive provisions themselves. In addition, even aside from public perceptions ... it is inherently unfair for high-income taxpayers to pay little or no tax due to their ability to utilize tax preferences.[1]

---

[1]*General Explanation of the Tax Reform Act of 1986 ("Blue Book"),* prepared by The Staff of the Joint Committee on Taxation, May 4, 1987, H.R. 3838, 99th Cong., pp. 432–433.

The individual AMT is discussed in the first part of this chapter. The corporate AMT is similar to the individual AMT, but differs in several important ways. Details of the corporate AMT are presented in the last part of the chapter.

INDIVIDUAL ALTERNATIVE MINIMUM TAX

AMT FORMULA FOR ALTERNATIVE MINIMUM TAXABLE INCOME (AMTI)

2 ▼ LEARNING OBJECTIVE
Understand the formula for computing the AMT for individuals.

The AMT is separate from, but parallel to, the regular income tax system.[2] Most income and expense items are treated the same way for both regular income tax and AMT purposes. For example, a taxpayer's salary is included in computing taxable income and is also included in alternative minimum taxable income (AMTI). Alimony paid is allowed as a deduction *for* AGI for both regular income tax and AMT purposes. Certain itemized deductions, such as charitable contributions and gambling losses, are allowed for both regular income tax and AMT purposes.

On the other hand, some income and expense items are treated differently for regular income tax and AMT purposes. For example, interest income on bonds issued by state, county, or local governments is *excluded* in computing taxable income. However, interest on such bonds is *included* in computing AMTI if the bonds are private activity bonds. The deduction for personal and dependency exemptions is *allowed* for regular income tax purposes, but is *disallowed* for AMT purposes.

In other cases, certain items are considered in both the regular income tax and AMT computations, but the amounts are different. For example, the completed contract method can be used to report income from some long-term contracts for regular income tax purposes, but the percentage of completion method is required for AMT purposes. Thus, the amount of income included in taxable income will differ from the amount included in AMTI. Depreciation is allowed as a deduction for both regular income tax and AMT purposes, but the *amount* of the regular income tax deduction may be different from the amount of the AMT deduction. Medical expenses are deductible in calculating both taxable income and AMTI, but the floor on the deduction is different.

The parallel but separate nature of the AMT means that AMTI will differ from taxable income. It is possible to compute AMTI by direct application of the AMT provisions, using the following formula:

> Gross income computed by applying the AMT rules
>
> **Minus:** Deductions computed by applying the AMT rules
>
> **Equals:** AMTI before tax preferences
>
> **Plus:** Tax preferences
>
> **Equals:** Alternative minimum taxable income

While the direct approach for computing AMTI appears quite logical, both the tax law and the tax forms provide a very different approach. Both of these use taxable income (for Form 6251, taxable income *before* the deduction for personal exemptions and dependency deductions) as the starting point for computing AMTI, as shown in Figure 12–1. This indirect approach for computing AMTI is analogous to the indirect approach used in calculating a net operating loss.

---

[2]§ 55.

▼ **FIGURE 12–1**
Alternative Minimum Taxable
Income (AMTI) Formula

Taxable income

Plus: Positive AMT adjustments

Minus: Negative AMT adjustments

Equals: Taxable income after AMT adjustments

Plus: Tax preferences

Equals: Alternative minimum taxable income

The purpose of the AMT formula is to *reconcile* taxable income to AMTI. This reconciliation is similar to a bank reconciliation, which reconciles a checkbook balance to a bank balance by considering differences between the depositor's records and the bank's records. The reconciliation of taxable income to AMTI is accomplished by entering reconciling items to account for differences between regular income tax provisions and AMT provisions. These reconciling items are referred to as **AMT adjustments** or **tax preferences.** *Adjustments* can be either positive or negative, as shown in the formula in Figure 12–1. Tax preferences are always positive.

Adjustments.   Most adjustments relate to *timing differences* that arise because of *separate* regular income tax and AMT treatments. Adjustments that are caused by timing differences will eventually *reverse*; that is, positive adjustments will be offset by negative adjustments in the future, and vice versa.[3]

For example, **circulation expenditures** can give rise to a timing difference that requires an AMT adjustment. For regular income tax purposes, circulation expenditures can be deducted in the year incurred. For AMT purposes, however, circulation expenditures must be deducted over a three-year period. This difference

TAX IN THE NEWS

MAKING OUR TAX SYSTEM MORE FRIENDLY

When the National Commission on Restructuring the IRS heard testimony on the current tax system, a frequent complaint was the complexity of the system. Representative of such testimony was that of Michael E. Mares, head of the tax executive committee of the American Institute of CPAs. According to Mares, needless complexity is undermining the system. Although a truly simple system may be impossible, a simpler system is an achievable goal.

Contributing to the complexity is the AMT. Opponents argue that it is a remarkably complex system. Though the AMT was intended to assure that most wealthy taxpayers pay at least some Federal income taxes, its impact is growing and extending beyond the wealthy. In addition, many taxpayers not subject to the AMT must deal with its complexity in ascertaining that it does not apply to them.

SOURCE: Adapted from Tom Herman, "Tax Complexity Draws Growing Fire, Even from Experts," *Wall Street Journal*, November 13, 1996, p. A1.

[3]§ 56.

in treatment will be used to illustrate the role of adjustments in the formula for computing AMTI.

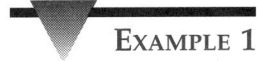

EXAMPLE 1

Bob had taxable income of $100,000 in 1997. In computing taxable income, he deducted $30,000 of circulation expenditures incurred in 1997. Bob's allowable deduction for AMT purposes was only $10,000. Therefore, an AMT adjustment was required in 1997 as follows:

Taxable income		$ 100,000
+AMT adjustment:		
Circulation expenditures deducted for regular income tax purposes	$ 30,000	
Circulation expenditures allowed for AMT purposes	(10,000)	
Positive adjustment		20,000
=AMTI before tax preferences		$ 120,000
+Tax preferences		–0–
AMTI		$ 120,000

Analysis of this computation shows that the allowable AMT deduction is $20,000 less than the allowable regular income tax deduction. Therefore, AMTI is $20,000 greater than taxable income. This is accomplished by entering a positive AMT adjustment of $20,000. ▼

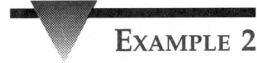

EXAMPLE 2

Assume that Bob from Example 1 has taxable income of $95,000 in 1998. He is allowed to deduct $10,000 of circulation expenditures for AMT purposes, but is not allowed a deduction for regular income tax purposes because all $30,000 was deducted in 1997. Therefore, a *negative* AMT adjustment is required.

Taxable income		$ 95,000
–AMT adjustment:		
Circulation expenditures deducted for regular income tax purposes	$ –0–	
Circulation expenditures allowed for AMT purposes	(10,000)	
Negative adjustment		(10,000)
=AMTI before tax preferences		$ 85,000
+Tax preferences		–0–
AMTI		$ 85,000

Analysis of this computation shows that the allowable AMT deduction is $10,000 more than the allowable regular income tax deduction. Therefore, AMTI is $10,000 less than taxable income. This is accomplished by entering a negative AMT adjustment of $10,000. ▼

As noted previously, timing differences eventually reverse. Therefore, total positive adjustments will be offset by total negative adjustments with respect to a particular item.

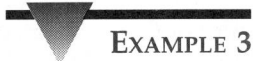

EXAMPLE 3

Refer to Examples 1 and 2. The difference in regular income tax and AMT treatments of circulation expenditures will result in AMT adjustments over a three-year period.

Year	Income Tax Deduction	AMT Deduction	AMT Adjustment
1997	$30,000	$10,000	+$20,000
1998	–0–	10,000	–10,000
1999	–0–	10,000	–10,000
Total	$30,000	$30,000	$ –0–

As the last column illustrates, if positive and negative AMT adjustments with respect to a particular item are caused by a timing difference, they will eventually net to zero. ▼

The adjustments for circulation expenditures and other items are discussed in detail under AMT Adjustments.

Although most adjustments relate to timing differences, there are exceptions. See the subsequent discussion of such items under Itemized Deductions. Adjustments that do not relate to timing differences result in a permanent difference between taxable income and AMTI.

Tax Preferences.   Some deductions and exclusions allowed to taxpayers for regular income tax purposes provide extraordinary tax savings. Congress has chosen to single out these items, which are referred to as tax preferences.[4] The AMT is designed to take back all or part of the tax benefits derived through the use of preferences in the computation of taxable income for regular income tax purposes. This is why taxable income, which is the starting point in computing AMTI, is increased by tax preference items. The effect of adding these preference items is to disallow for *AMT purposes* those preferences that were allowed in the regular income tax computation. Tax preferences include the following items, which are discussed in detail under AMT Preferences:

- Percentage depletion in excess of the property's adjusted basis.
- Excess intangible drilling costs reduced by 65 percent of the net income from oil, gas, and geothermal properties.
- Interest on certain private activity bonds.
- Excess of accelerated over straight-line depreciation on real property placed in service before 1987.
- Excess of accelerated over straight-line depreciation on *leased* personal property placed in service before 1987.
- Excess of amortization allowance over depreciation on pre-1987 certified pollution control facilities.
- Forty-two percent of the exclusion from gross income associated with gains on the sale of certain small business stock.

AMT FORMULA: OTHER COMPONENTS

To convert AMTI to AMT, other formula components including the exemption, rates, credit, and regular tax liability must be considered. The impact of each of these components is depicted in the AMT formula in Figure 12–2.

The relationship between the regular tax liability and the tentative AMT is key to the AMT formula. If the regular tax liability exceeds tentative AMT, then the AMT is zero. If the tentative AMT exceeds the regular tax liability, the amount of the excess is the AMT. In essence, the taxpayer will pay whichever tax liability is greater—that calculated using the regular income tax rules or that calculated using the AMT rules. However, both the tax law and Form 6251 adopt this excess approach with the taxpayer paying the regular tax liability plus any AMT.

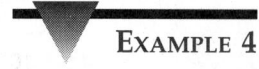

EXAMPLE 4   Anna, an unmarried individual, has regular taxable income of $100,000. She has positive adjustments of $40,000 and tax preferences of $25,000. Calculate her AMT for 1998. Anna's regular tax liability is $25,863. Her AMT is calculated as follows:

Taxable income (TI)	$100,000
Plus: Adjustments	40,000
Equals: TI after AMT adjustments	$140,000
Plus: Tax preferences	25,000
Equals: AMTI	$165,000
Minus: AMT exemption ($33,750 − $13,125)	(20,625)*
Equals: AMT base	$144,375
Times: AMT rate	× 26%
Equals: Tentative AMT	$ 37,538
Minus: Regular tax liability	(25,863)
Equals: AMT	$ 11,675

*Discussed below under Exemption Amount.

Anna will pay the IRS a total of $37,538, consisting of her regular tax liability of $25,863 plus her AMT of $11,675. ▼

Exemption Amount.   The exemption amount can be thought of as a materiality provision. As such, it enables a taxpayer with a small amount of positive adjustments and tax preferences to avoid being subject to the burden of the AMT.

The *initial* exemption amount is $45,000 for married taxpayers filing joint returns, $33,750 for single taxpayers, and $22,500 for married taxpayers filing separate returns.[5] However, the exemption is *phased out* at a rate of 25 cents on the dollar when AMTI exceeds these levels:

- $112,500 for single taxpayers.
- $150,000 for married taxpayers filing jointly.
- $75,000 for married taxpayers filing separately.

The phase-out of the exemption amount is an application of the wherewithal to pay concept. As a taxpayer's income level increases, so does his or her ability to pay income taxes.

▼ **FIGURE 12–2**
Alternative Minimum Tax
Formula

Regular taxable income
Plus or minus: Adjustments
Equals: Taxable income after AMT adjustments
Plus: Tax preferences
Equals: Alternative minimum taxable income
Minus: Exemption
Equals: Alternative minimum tax base
Times: 26% or 28% rate
Equals: Tentative minimum tax before foreign tax credit
Minus: Alternative minimum tax foreign tax credit
Equals: Tentative minimum tax
Minus: Regular tax liability*
Equals: Alternative minimum tax (if amount is positive)

*This is the regular tax liability for the year reduced by any allowable foreign tax credit.

[5]§ 55(d).

TAX IN THE NEWS

THE AMT AND INFLATION

The AMT contains exemption amounts for the different taxpayer filing statuses. When the taxpayer's income reaches a certain amount, the exemption is subject to phase-out.

Neither the AMT exemption nor the AMT rates are subject to indexing. Currently, only about 600,000 (0.5 percent) individual income tax returns must pay the AMT. Kenneth Kies, chief of staff of Congress's Joint Tax Committee, estimates that by 2006, the absence of indexing and the increase in AMT rates contained in the Revenue Reconciliation Act of 1993 (RRA of 1993) will cause about 6.2 million (4.5 percent) individual income tax returns to be subject to the AMT.

Several proposals were made to include an indexing provision for the AMT in the Taxpayer Relief Act of 1997 (TRA of 1997), but none of them was included in the AMT legislation that was enacted.

SOURCE: Adapted from Tom Herman, "Chances Improve for Important Changes in the Alternative Minimum Tax," *Wall Street Journal*, May 21, 1997, p. A1.

The following example explains the calculation of the phase-out of the AMT exemption.

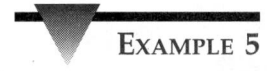

EXAMPLE 5

Hugh, who is single, has AMTI of $192,500 for the year. His $33,750 initial exemption amount is reduced by $20,000 [($192,500 − $112,500) × 25% phase-out rate]. Hugh's AMT exemption is $13,750 ($33,750 exemption − $20,000 reduction). ▼

The following table shows the beginning and end of the AMT exemption phase-out range for each filing status.

Status	Exemption	Phase-out Begins at	Phase-out Ends at
Married, joint	$45,000	$150,000	$330,000
Single or head of household	33,750	112,500	247,500
Married, separate	22,500	75,000	165,000

AMT Rate Schedule. A graduated, two-tier AMT rate schedule applies to noncorporate taxpayers. A 26 percent rate applies to the first $175,000 of the AMT base ($87,500 for married, filing separately), and a 28 percent rate applies to the AMT base in excess of $175,000 ($87,500 for married, filing separately).[6] The Taxpayer Relief Act of 1997 (TRA of 1997) provides that the net capital gain included in the AMT base is taxed at the favorable alternative tax rates for capital gains (20 percent or 10 percent) rather than at the AMT statutory rates. This provision applies to gains occurring after May 6, 1997, in tax years ending after May 6, 1997. See the discussion of the alternative tax on capital gains in Chapter 16.

Regular Tax Liability. The AMT is equal to the tentative minimum tax minus the *regular tax liability*. In most cases, the regular tax liability is equal to the amount of tax from the Tax Table or Tax Rate Schedules decreased by any foreign tax credit

---

[6]§ 55(b)(1).

allowable for regular income tax purposes. Only the foreign tax credit is allowed as a reduction of the tentative minimum tax. Therefore, taxpayers who pay AMT lose the benefit of all other nonrefundable credits. Furthermore, the foreign tax credit cannot offset more than 90 percent of the tentative minimum tax.

In an AMT year, the taxpayer's total tax liability is equal to the tentative minimum tax (refer to Figure 12–2). The tentative minimum tax consists of two potential components: the regular tax liability and the AMT. The disallowance of credits does not affect a taxpayer's total liability in an AMT year. However, it does decrease the amount of the AMT and, as a consequence, reduces the minimum tax credit (discussed subsequently) available to be carried forward. Thus, for AMT purposes, the government denies all the credits (except the foreign tax credit) that apply in computing the regular income tax liability.

It is also possible that taxpayers who have adjustments and preferences but *do not pay* AMT will lose the benefit of some or all of their nonrefundable credits. This result occurs because a taxpayer may claim nonrefundable credits only to the extent that his or her regular tax liability exceeds the tentative minimum tax.[7]

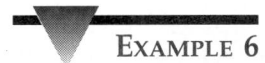

EXAMPLE 6

Vern has total nonrefundable credits of $10,000, regular tax liability of $33,000, and tentative minimum tax of $25,000. He can claim only $8,000 of the nonrefundable credits in the current year ($33,000 − $8,000 = $25,000). The disallowed $2,000 credit is lost unless a carryover provision applies. ▼

ETHICAL CONSIDERATIONS

Minimizing the Tax Liability

Billy, a single individual, projects his taxable income for 1998 to be approximately $300,000. He also has positive adjustments and tax preferences of $200,000. Billy anticipates taxable income for 1999 to be about the same with no adjustments or tax preferences for AMT purposes. He is evaluating several proposed transactions that would have the effect of reducing his 1998 tax liability.

One such transaction involves an office building for which he is currently negotiating a lease. The starting date for the lease will be July 1, 1998. The annual rent is going to be around $20,000 with an 18-month prepayment clause. Though Billy favors a five-year lease, a real estate agent has suggested that he lease the office building for an 18-month period with a 42-month renewal option. The real estate agent indicates that there are tax advantages (i.e., Billy can deduct the $30,000 of rent paid at the inception of the lease) as well as business reasons for structuring the transaction this way.

Billy takes the agent's advice and calculates his projected tax liability for 1998 with the 18-month lease with the renewal option and with the five-year lease. Based on his calculations, his regular income tax liability and AMT under each option would be as follows:

	18-Month Lease	5-Year Lease
Regular income tax liability	$ 85,658	$ 93,273
AMT	42,442	40,427
Total	$128,100	$133,700

[7]§ 26(a).

Is it appropriate for Billy to avoid taxes in this manner? Is it wise? Would you be willing to prepare and sign Billy's tax return showing the lease transaction as proposed by the real estate agent?

AMT ADJUSTMENTS

3 ▼ **LEARNING OBJECTIVE**
Identify the adjustments made in calculating the AMT.

Direction of Adjustments.
It is necessary to determine not only the amount of an adjustment, but also whether the adjustment is positive or negative. Careful study of Example 3 reveals the following pattern with regard to *deductions:*

- If the deduction allowed for regular income tax purposes exceeds the deduction allowed for AMT purposes, the difference is a positive adjustment.
- If the deduction allowed for AMT purposes exceeds the deduction allowed for regular income tax purposes, the difference is a negative adjustment.

Conversely, the direction of an adjustment attributable to an *income* item can be determined as follows:

- If the income reported for regular income tax purposes exceeds the income reported for AMT purposes, the difference is a negative adjustment.
- If the income reported for AMT purposes exceeds the income reported for regular income tax purposes, the difference is a positive adjustment.

Circulation Expenditures.
For regular income tax purposes, circulation expenditures, other than those the taxpayer elects to charge to a capital account, may be expensed in the year incurred.[8] These expenditures include expenses incurred to establish, maintain, or increase the circulation of a newspaper, magazine, or other periodical.

Circulation expenditures are not deductible in the year incurred for AMT purposes. In computing AMTI, these expenditures must be capitalized and amortized ratably over the three-year period beginning with the year in which the expenditures were made.[9]

The AMT adjustment for circulation expenditures is the amount expensed for regular income tax purposes minus the amount that can be amortized for AMT purposes. The adjustment can be either positive or negative (refer to Examples 1, 2, and 3). A taxpayer can avoid the AMT adjustments for circulation expenditures by electing to write off the expenditures over a three-year period for regular income tax purposes.[10]

Depreciation of Post-1986 Real Property.
For real property placed in service after 1986 (MACRS property), AMT depreciation is computed under the alternative depreciation system (ADS), which uses the straight-line method over a 40-year life. The depreciation lives for regular tax purposes are 27.5 years for residential rental property and 39 years for all other real property.[11] The difference between AMT depreciation and regular income tax depreciation is treated as an adjustment in computing the AMT. The differences will be positive during the regular income tax life of the asset because the cost is written off over a shorter period for regular income tax purposes. For example, during the 27.5-year income tax life of residential real property, the regular income tax depreciation

---

[8]§ 173(a).
[9]§ 56(b)(2)(A)(i).
[10]§ 59(e)(2)(A).

[11]The 39-year life generally applies to nonresidential real property placed in service on or after May 13, 1993.

will exceed the AMT depreciation because AMT depreciation is computed over a 40-year period.

Table 8–7 is used to compute regular income tax depreciation on real property placed in service after 1986. For AMT purposes, depreciation on real property placed in service after 1986 is computed under the ADS (refer to Table 8–12).

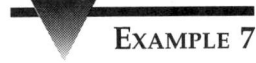

EXAMPLE 7

In January 1998, Sara placed in service a residential building that cost $100,000. Depreciation for 1998 for regular income tax purposes is $3,485 ($100,000 cost × 3.485% from Table 8–7). For AMT purposes, depreciation is $2,396 ($100,000 cost × 2.396% from Table 8–12). In computing AMTI for 1998, Sara has a positive adjustment of $1,089 ($3,485 regular income tax depreciation – $2,396 AMT depreciation). ▼

After real property has been held for the entire depreciation period for regular income tax purposes, the asset will be fully depreciated. However, the depreciation period under the ADS is 41 years due to application of the half-year convention, so depreciation will continue for AMT purposes. This causes negative adjustments after the property has been fully depreciated for regular income tax purposes.

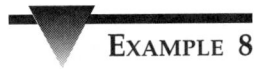

EXAMPLE 8

Assume the same facts as in the previous example, and compute the AMT adjustment for 2026 (the twenty-ninth year of the asset's life). Regular income tax depreciation is zero (refer to Table 8–7). AMT depreciation is $2,500 ($100,000 cost × 2.500% from Table 8–12). Therefore, Sara has a negative AMT adjustment of $2,500 ($0 regular income tax depreciation – $2,500 AMT depreciation). ▼

After real property is fully depreciated for both regular income tax and AMT purposes, the positive and negative adjustments that have been made for AMT purposes will net to zero.

TRA of 1997 eliminated the AMT adjustment for real property by providing that the MACRS recovery periods used in calculating the regular income tax apply in calculating the AMT. Note, however, that this AMT recovery period conformity provision applies only to property placed in service after December 31, 1998. Thus, the adjustment continues to apply for real property placed in service before January 1, 1999.

Depreciation of Post-1986 Personal Property. For most personal property placed in service after 1986 (MACRS property), the modified ACRS (MACRS) deduction for regular income tax purposes is based on the 200 percent declining-balance method with a switch to straight-line when that method produces a larger depreciation deduction for the asset. Refer to Table 8–2 for computing regular income tax depreciation.

For AMT purposes, the taxpayer must use the ADS. This method is based on the 150 percent declining-balance method with a similar switch to straight-line for all personal property.[12] Refer to Table 8–10 for percentages to be used in computing AMT depreciation.

All personal property placed in service after 1986 may be taken into consideration in computing one net adjustment. Using this netting process, the AMT adjustment for a tax year is the difference between the total MACRS depreciation for all personal property computed for regular income tax purposes and the total ADS depreciation computed for AMT purposes. When the total of MACRS deductions

---

[12]§ 56(a)(1).

exceeds the total of ADS deductions, the amount of the adjustment is positive. When the total of ADS deductions exceeds the total of MACRS deductions, the adjustment for AMTI is negative.

The MACRS deduction for personal property is larger than the ADS deduction in the early years of an asset's life. However, the ADS deduction is larger in the later years. This is so because ADS lives (based on class life) are longer than MACRS lives (based on recovery period).[13] Over the ADS life of the asset, the same amount of depreciation is deducted for both regular income tax and AMT purposes. In the same manner as other timing adjustments, the AMT adjustments for depreciation will net to zero over the ADS life of the asset.

The taxpayer may elect to use the ADS for regular income tax purposes. If this election is made, no AMT adjustment is required because the depreciation deduction is the same for regular income tax and for the AMT. The election eliminates the burden of maintaining two sets of tax depreciation records.

TRA of 1997 either reduces or eliminates the AMT adjustment for the depreciation of personal property. Prior to the effective date of this provision, the difference between regular income tax depreciation and AMT depreciation was caused by longer recovery periods for the AMT (class life versus MACRS recovery periods) and more accelerated depreciation methods for the regular income tax (200 percent declining balance rather than 150 percent declining balance). TRA of 1997 provides that the MACRS recovery periods are to be used in calculating AMT depreciation. Thus, if the taxpayer elects to use the 150 percent declining-balance method for regular income tax purposes, there are no AMT adjustments. Conversely, if the taxpayer uses the 200 percent declining-balance method for regular income tax purposes, there is an AMT adjustment for depreciation. Note, however, that this AMT recovery period conformity provision applies only to property placed in service after December 31, 1998. Thus, the adjustment continues to apply for personal property placed in service before January 1, 1999.

Pollution Control Facilities.   For regular income tax purposes, the cost of certified pollution control facilities may be amortized over a period of 60 months. For AMT purposes, the cost of these facilities placed in service after 1986 must be depreciated under the ADS over the appropriate class life, determined as explained above for depreciation of post-1986 property.[14] The required adjustment for AMTI is equal to the difference between the amortization deduction allowed for regular income tax purposes and the depreciation deduction computed under the ADS. The adjustment may be positive or negative.

TRA of 1997 reduces the AMT adjustment for pollution control facilities for property placed in service after December 31, 1998. This reduction is achieved by providing conformity in the recovery periods used for regular income tax purposes and AMT purposes (MACRS recovery periods).

Expenditures Requiring 10-Year Write-off for AMT Purposes.   Certain expenditures that may be deducted in the year incurred for regular income tax purposes must be written off over a 10-year period for AMT purposes. These rules apply to (1) mining exploration and development costs and (2) research and experimental expenditures.

---

[13]Class lives and recovery periods are established for all assets in Rev.Proc. 87–56, 1987–2 C.B. 674.

[14]§ 56(a)(5).

In computing taxable income, taxpayers are allowed to deduct certain mining exploration and development expenditures. The deduction is allowed for expenditures paid or incurred during the taxable year for exploration (ascertaining the existence, location, extent, or quality of a deposit or mineral) and for development of a mine or other natural deposit, other than an oil or gas well.[15] Mining development expenditures are expenses paid or incurred after the existence of ores and minerals in commercially marketable quantities has been disclosed.

For AMT purposes, however, mining exploration and development costs must be capitalized and amortized ratably over a 10-year period.[16] The AMT adjustment for mining exploration and development costs that are expensed is equal to the amount expensed minus the allowable expense if the costs had been capitalized and amortized ratably over a 10-year period. This provision does not apply to costs relating to an oil or gas well.

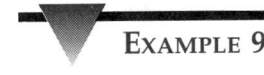

EXAMPLE 9

In 1998, Eve incurs $150,000 of mining exploration expenditures and deducts this amount for regular income tax purposes. For AMT purposes, these mining exploration expenditures must be amortized over a 10-year period. Eve must make a positive adjustment for AMTI of $135,000 ($150,000 allowed for regular income tax – $15,000 for AMT) for 1998, the first year. In each of the next nine years for AMT purposes, Eve is required to make a negative adjustment of $15,000 ($0 allowed for regular income tax – $15,000 for AMT). ▼

To avoid the AMT adjustments for mining exploration and development costs, a taxpayer may elect to write off the expenditures over a 10-year period for regular income tax purposes.[17]

Similar rules apply to computation of the adjustment for research and experimental expenditures.

Use of Completed Contract Method of Accounting. For a long-term contract, taxpayers are required to use the percentage of completion method for AMT purposes.[18] However, in limited circumstances, taxpayers can use the completed contract method for regular income tax purposes.[19] Thus, a taxpayer recognizes a different amount of income for regular income tax purposes than for AMT purposes. The resulting AMT adjustment is equal to the difference between income reported under the percentage of completion method and the amount reported using the completed contract method. The adjustment can be either positive or negative, depending on the amount of income recognized under the different methods.

A taxpayer can avoid an AMT adjustment on long-term contracts by using the percentage of completion method for regular income tax purposes rather than the completed contract method.

Incentive Stock Options. **Incentive stock options (ISOs)** are granted by employers to help attract new personnel and retain those already employed. At the time an ISO is granted, the employer corporation sets an option price for the corporate stock. If the value of the stock increases during the option period, the employee can obtain stock at a favorable price by exercising the option. Employees are generally restricted as to when they can dispose of stock acquired under an ISO (e.g., a certain length of employment may be required). Therefore, the stock may not be freely transferable until some specified period has passed. See Chapter 19 for details regarding ISOs.

---

[15]§§ 617(a) and 616(a).
[16]§ 56(a)(2).
[17]§§ 59(e)(2)(D) and (E).

[18]§ 56(a)(3).
[19]See Chapter 18 for a detailed discussion of the completed contract and percentage of completion methods of accounting.

The exercise of an ISO does not increase regular taxable income.[20] However, for AMT purposes, the excess of the fair market value of the stock over the exercise price (the *spread*) is treated as an adjustment in the first taxable year in which the rights in the stock are freely transferable or are not subject to a substantial risk of forfeiture.[21]

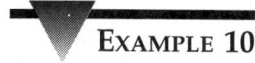

EXAMPLE 10

In 1996, Manuel exercised an ISO that had been granted by his employer, Gold Corporation. Manuel acquired 1,000 shares of Gold stock for the option price of $20 per share. The stock became freely transferable in 1998. The fair market value of the stock at the date of exercise was $50 per share. For AMT purposes, Manuel has a positive adjustment of $30,000 ($50,000 fair market value – $20,000 option price) for 1998. The transaction does not affect regular taxable income in 1996 or 1998. ▼

No adjustment is required if the taxpayer exercises the option and disposes of the stock in the same tax year because the bargain element gain is reported for both regular income tax and AMT purposes in the same tax year.

The regular income tax basis of stock acquired through exercise of ISOs is different from the AMT basis. The regular income tax basis of the stock is equal to its cost, whereas the AMT basis is equal to the fair market value on the date the options are exercised. Consequently, the gain or loss upon disposition of the stock is different for regular income tax purposes and AMT purposes.

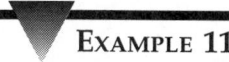

EXAMPLE 11

Assume the same facts as in the previous example and that Manuel sells the stock for $60,000 in 2000. His gain for regular income tax purposes is $40,000 ($60,000 amount realized – $20,000 regular income tax basis). For AMT purposes, the gain is $10,000 ($60,000 amount realized – $50,000 AMT basis). Therefore, Manuel has a $30,000 negative adjustment in computing AMT in 2000 ($40,000 regular income tax gain – $10,000 AMT gain). Note that the $30,000 negative adjustment upon disposition in 2000 offsets the $30,000 positive adjustment when the stock became freely transferable in 1998. ▼

Adjusted Gain or Loss.   When property is sold during the year or a casualty occurs to business or income-producing property, gain or loss reported for regular income tax may be different than gain or loss determined for the AMT. This difference occurs because the adjusted basis of the property for AMT purposes must reflect any current and prior AMT adjustments for the following:[22]

- Depreciation.
- Circulation expenditures.
- Research and experimental expenditures.
- Mining exploration and development costs.
- Amortization of certified pollution control facilities.

A negative gain or loss adjustment is required if:

- the gain for AMT purposes is less than the gain for regular income tax purposes;
- the loss for AMT purposes is more than the loss for regular income tax purposes; or
- a loss is computed for AMT purposes and a gain is computed for regular income tax purposes.

Otherwise, the AMT gain or loss adjustment is positive.

---

[20]§ 421(a).
[21]§ 56(b)(3).

[22]§ 56(a)(7).

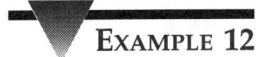

EXAMPLE 12

In January 1998, Kate paid $100,000 for a duplex acquired for rental purposes. Regular income tax depreciation in 1998 was $3,485 ($100,000 cost × 3.485% from Table 8–7). AMT depreciation was $2,396 ($100,000 cost × 2.396% from Table 8–12). For AMT purposes, Kate made a positive adjustment of $1,089 ($3,485 regular income tax depreciation − $2,396 AMT depreciation). ▼

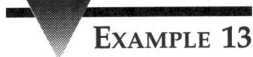

EXAMPLE 13

Kate sold the duplex on December 20, 1999, for $105,000. Regular income tax depreciation for 1999 is $3,485 [($100,000 cost × 3.636% from Table 8–7) × (11.5/12)]. AMT depreciation for 1999 is $2,396 [($100,000 cost × 2.500% from Table 8–12) × (11.5/12)]. Kate's positive AMT adjustment for 1999 is $1,089 ($3,485 regular income tax depreciation − $2,396 AMT depreciation). ▼

Because depreciation on the duplex differs for regular income tax and AMT purposes, the adjusted basis is different for regular income tax and AMT purposes. Consequently, the gain or loss on disposition of the duplex is different for regular income tax and AMT purposes.

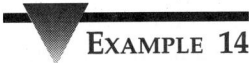

EXAMPLE 14

The adjusted basis of Kate's duplex for regular income tax purposes is $93,030 ($100,000 cost − $3,485 depreciation for 1998 − $3,485 depreciation for 1999). For AMT purposes, the adjusted basis is $95,208 ($100,000 cost − $2,396 depreciation for 1998 − $2,396 depreciation for 1999). The regular income tax gain is $11,970 ($105,000 amount realized − $93,030 regular income tax basis). The AMT gain is $9,792 ($105,000 amount realized − $95,208 AMT basis). Because the regular income tax and AMT gain on the sale of the duplex differ, Kate must make a negative AMT adjustment of $2,178 ($11,970 regular income tax gain − $9,792 AMT gain). Note that this negative adjustment offsets the $2,178 total of the two positive adjustments for depreciation ($1,089 in 1998 + $1,089 in 1999). ▼

Passive Activity Losses. Losses on passive activities are not deductible in computing either the regular income tax or the AMT. This does not, however, eliminate the possibility of adjustments attributable to passive activities.

The rules for computing taxable income differ from the rules for computing AMTI. It follows, then, that the rules for computing a loss for regular income tax purposes differ from the AMT rules for computing a loss. Therefore, any *passive loss* computed for regular income tax purposes may differ from the passive loss computed for AMT purposes.[23]

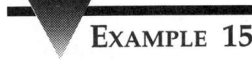

EXAMPLE 15

Soong acquired two passive activities in 1998. He received net passive income of $10,000 from Activity A and had no AMT adjustments or preferences in connection with the activity. Activity B had gross income of $27,000 and operating expenses (not affected by AMT adjustments or preferences) of $19,000. Soong claimed MACRS depreciation of $20,000 for Activity B; depreciation under the ADS would have been $15,000. In addition, Soong deducted $10,000 of percentage depletion in excess of basis. The following comparison illustrates the differences in the computation of the passive loss for regular income tax and AMT purposes for Activity B.

[23]See Chapter 11.

	Regular Income Tax	**AMT**
Gross income	$ 27,000	$ 27,000
Deductions:		
Operating expenses	($ 19,000)	($ 19,000)
Depreciation	(20,000)	(15,000)
Depletion	(10,000)	–0–
Total deductions	($ 49,000)	($ 34,000)
Passive loss	($ 22,000)	($ 7,000)

Because the adjustment for depreciation ($5,000) applies and the preference for depletion ($10,000) is not taken into account in computing AMTI, the regular income tax passive activity loss of $22,000 for Activity B is reduced by these amounts, resulting in a passive activity loss of $7,000 for AMT purposes. ▼

For regular income tax purposes, Soong would offset the $10,000 of net passive income from Activity A with $10,000 of the passive loss from Activity B. For AMT purposes, he would offset the $10,000 of net passive income from Activity A with the $7,000 passive activity loss allowed from Activity B, resulting in passive activity income of $3,000. Thus, in computing AMTI, Soong makes a positive passive loss adjustment of $3,000 [$10,000 (passive activity loss allowed for regular income tax) − $7,000 (passive activity loss allowed for the AMT)]. To avoid duplication, the AMT adjustment for depreciation and the preference for depletion are *not* reported separately. They are accounted for in determining the AMT passive loss adjustment.

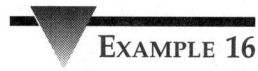

EXAMPLE 16   Assume the same facts as in the previous example. For regular income tax purposes, Soong has a suspended passive loss of $12,000 [$22,000 (amount of loss) − $10,000 (used in 1998)]. This suspended passive loss can offset passive income in the future or can offset active or portfolio income when Soong disposes of the loss activity (refer to Chapter 11). For AMT purposes, Soong's suspended passive loss is $0 [$7,000 (amount of loss) − $7,000 (amount used in 1998)]. ▼

Alternative Tax Net Operating Loss Deduction.   In computing taxable income, taxpayers are allowed to deduct net operating loss (NOL) carryovers and carrybacks (refer to Chapter 7). The regular income tax NOL must be modified, however, in computing AMTI. The starting point in computing the **alternative tax NOL deduction (ATNOLD)** is the NOL computed for regular income tax purposes. The regular income tax NOL is then modified for AMT adjustments and tax preferences with the result being the ATNOLD. Thus, preferences and adjustment items that have benefited the taxpayer in computing the regular income tax NOL are added back, thereby reducing or eliminating the ATNOLD.[24]

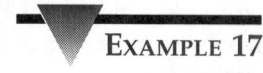

EXAMPLE 17   In 1998, Adam incurred an NOL of $100,000. Adam had no AMT adjustments, but his deductions included tax preferences of $18,000. His ATNOLD carryback to 1996 is $82,000 ($100,000 regular income tax NOL − $18,000 tax preferences deducted in computing the NOL). ▼

In Example 17, if the adjustment was not made to the regular income tax NOL, the $18,000 in tax preference items deducted in 1998 would have the effect of

---

[24]§ 56(a)(4).

reducing AMTI in the year (or years) the 1998 NOL is utilized. This would weaken the entire concept of the AMT.

A ceiling exists on the amount of the ATNOLD that can be deducted in the carryback or carryforward year. The deduction is limited to 90 percent of AMTI (before the ATNOLD) for the carryback or carryforward year.

EXAMPLE 18

Assume the same facts as in the previous example. Adam's AMTI (before the ATNOLD) in 1996 is $90,000. Therefore, of the $82,000 ATNOLD carried back to 1996 from 1998, only $81,000 ($90,000 × 90%) can be used in recalculating the 1996 AMT. The unused $1,000 of 1998 ATNOLD is now carried to 1997 for use in recalculating the 1997 AMT. ▼

A taxpayer who has an ATNOLD that is carried back or over to another year must use the ATNOLD against AMTI in the carryback or carryforward year even if the regular income tax, rather than the AMT, applies.

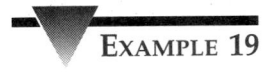

EXAMPLE 19

Matt's ATNOLD for 1999 (carried over from 1998) is $10,000. AMTI before considering the ATNOLD is $25,000. If Matt's regular income tax exceeds the AMT, the AMT does not apply. Nevertheless, Matt's ATNOLD of $10,000 is "used up" in 1999 and is not available for carryover to a later year. ▼

For regular income tax purposes, the NOL can be carried back 2 years and forward 20 years. However, the taxpayer may elect to forgo the 2-year carryback. These rules generally apply to the ATNOLD as well, except that the election to forgo the 2-year carryback is available for the ATNOLD only if the taxpayer elected it for the regular income tax NOL.

Itemized Deductions. Most of the itemized deductions that are allowed for regular income tax purposes are allowed for AMT purposes. Itemized deductions that are allowed for AMT purposes include the following:

- Casualty losses.
- Gambling losses.
- Charitable contributions.
- Medical expenses in excess of 10 percent of AGI.
- Estate tax on income in respect of a decedent.
- Qualified interest.

Taxes (state, local, foreign income, and property taxes) and miscellaneous itemized deductions that are subject to the 2 percent-of-AGI floor are not allowed in computing AMT.[25] A positive AMT adjustment in the total amount of the regular income tax deduction for each is required.

If the taxpayer's gross income includes the recovery of any tax deducted as an itemized deduction for regular income tax purposes, a negative AMT adjustment in the amount of the recovery is allowed for AMTI purposes.[26] For example, state, local, and foreign income taxes can be deducted for regular income tax purposes, but cannot be deducted in computing AMTI. Because of this, any refund of such taxes from a prior year is not included in AMTI. Therefore, in calculating AMTI, the taxpayer must make a negative adjustment for an income tax refund that has been included in computing regular taxable income. Under the tax benefit rule, a tax refund is included in regular taxable income to the extent that the taxpayer obtained a tax benefit by deducting the tax in a prior year.

---

[25]§ 56(b)(1)(A).

[26]§ 56(b)(1)(D).

Cutback Adjustment. The 3 percent cutback adjustment that applies to regular income tax itemized deductions of certain high-income taxpayers (refer to Chapter 10) does not apply in computing AMT.[27] The effect of the 3 percent cutback adjustment is to disallow a portion of the taxpayer's itemized deductions for regular income tax purposes. Because this cutback adjustment does not apply for AMT purposes, taxable income, which is the starting point for computing AMTI, must be reduced by the amount of the disallowed deductions. Although this reduction has the same effect on AMTI as a negative adjustment, it is not shown on Form 6251 as such. Instead, it is shown on a separate line (line 18) as a subtraction from taxable income.

Medical Expenses. The rules for determining the AMT deductions for medical expenses are sufficiently complex to require further explanation. For regular income tax purposes, medical expenses are deductible to the extent they exceed 7.5 percent of AGI. However, for AMT purposes, medical expenses are deductible only to the extent they exceed 10 percent of AGI.[28]

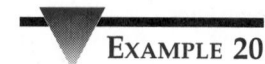

EXAMPLE 20

Joann incurred medical expenses of $16,000 in 1998. She had AGI of $100,000 for the year. Her AMT adjustment for medical expenses is computed as follows:

	Regular Income Tax	AMT
Medical expenses incurred	$ 16,000	$ 16,000
Less reduction:		
$100,000 AGI × 7.5%	(7,500)	
$100,000 AGI × 10%		(10,000)
Medical expense deduction	$ 8,500	$ 6,000

Joann's AMT adjustment for medical expenses is $2,500 ($8,500 regular income tax deduction − $6,000 AMT deduction). ▼

Interest in General. The AMT itemized deduction allowed for interest expense includes only qualified housing interest and investment interest to the extent of net investment income that is included in the determination of AMTI.[29] Any interest that is deducted in calculating the regular income tax that is not permitted in calculating the AMT is treated as a positive adjustment.

In computing regular taxable income, taxpayers who itemize can deduct the following types of interest (refer to Chapter 10):

- Qualified residence interest.
- Investment interest, subject to the investment interest limitations (discussed under Investment Interest below).
- Qualified interest on student loans.

Housing Interest. Under current regular income tax rules, taxpayers who itemize can deduct *qualified residence interest* on up to two residences. The deduction is limited to interest on acquisition indebtedness up to $1 million and home equity indebtedness up to $100,000. Acquisition indebtedness is debt that is incurred in acquiring, constructing, or substantially improving a qualified residence of the

---

[27]§ 56(b)(1)(F).
[28]§ 56(b)(1)(B).

[29]§ 56(b)(1)(C).

taxpayer and is secured by the residence. Home equity indebtedness is indebtedness secured by a qualified residence of the taxpayer, but does not include acquisition indebtedness.

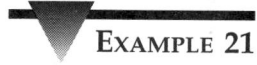

EXAMPLE 21

Gail, who used the proceeds of a mortgage to acquire a personal residence, paid mortgage interest of $112,000 in 1998. Of this amount, $14,000 is attributable to acquisition indebtedness in excess of $1 million. For regular income tax purposes, Gail may deduct mortgage interest of $98,000 ($112,000 total – $14,000 disallowed). ▼

The mortgage interest deduction for AMT purposes is limited to *qualified housing interest*, rather than *qualified residence interest*. Qualified housing interest includes only interest incurred to acquire, construct, or substantially improve the taxpayer's principal residence and such interest on one other qualified dwelling used for personal purposes. A home equity loan qualifies only if it meets the definition of qualified housing interest, which frequently is not the case. When additional mortgage interest is incurred (e.g., a mortgage refinancing), interest paid is deductible as qualified housing interest for AMT purposes only if:

- The proceeds are used to acquire or substantially improve a qualified residence.
- Interest on the prior loan was qualified housing interest.
- The amount of the loan was not increased.

A positive AMT adjustment is required in the amount of the difference between qualified *residence* interest allowed as an itemized deduction for regular income tax purposes and qualified *housing* interest allowed in the determination of AMTI.

Investment Interest.   Investment interest is deductible for regular income tax purposes and for AMT purposes to the extent of qualified net investment income.

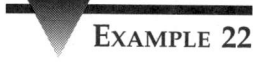

EXAMPLE 22

For the year, Dan had net investment income of $16,000 before deducting investment interest. He incurred investment interest expense of $30,000 during the year. His investment interest deduction is $16,000. ▼

Even though investment interest is deductible for both regular income tax and AMT purposes, an adjustment is required if the amount of investment interest deductible for regular income tax purposes differs from the amount deductible for AMT purposes. For example, an adjustment will arise if proceeds from a home equity loan are used to purchase investments. Interest on a home equity loan is deductible as qualified residence interest for regular income tax purposes, but is not deductible for AMT purposes unless the proceeds are used to acquire or substantially improve a qualified residence. For AMT purposes, however, interest on a home equity loan is deductible as investment interest expense if proceeds from the loan are used for investment purposes.

To determine the AMT adjustment for investment interest expense, it is necessary to compute the investment interest deduction for both regular income tax and AMT purposes. This computation is illustrated in the following example.

EXAMPLE 23

Tom had $20,000 interest income from corporate bonds and $5,000 dividends from preferred stock. He reported the following amounts of investment income for regular income tax and AMT purposes:

	Regular Income Tax	AMT
Corporate bond interest	$20,000	$20,000
Preferred stock dividends	5,000	5,000
Net investment income	$25,000	$25,000

Tom incurred investment interest expense of $10,000 related to the corporate bonds. He also incurred $4,000 interest on a home equity loan and used the proceeds of the loan to purchase preferred stock. For regular income tax purposes, this $4,000 is deductible as qualified residence interest. His *investment* interest expense for regular income tax and AMT purposes is computed below:

	Regular Income Tax	AMT
To carry corporate bonds	$10,000	$10,000
On home equity loan to carry preferred stock	–0–	4,000
Total investment interest expense	$10,000	$14,000

Investment interest expense is deductible to the extent of net investment income. Because the amount deductible for regular income tax purposes ($10,000) differs from the amount deductible for AMT purposes ($14,000), an AMT adjustment is required. The adjustment is computed as follows:

AMT deduction for investment interest expense	$ 14,000
Regular income tax deduction for investment interest expense	(10,000)
Negative AMT adjustment	$ 4,000

As discussed subsequently under AMT Preferences, the interest on private activity bonds is a tax preference for AMT purposes. Such interest can also affect the calculation of the AMT investment interest deduction in that it is included in the calculation of net investment income.

Other Adjustments.   The standard deduction is not allowed as a deduction in computing AMTI.[30] Although a person who does not itemize is rarely subject to the AMT, it is possible. In such a case, the taxpayer is required to enter a positive adjustment for the standard deduction in computing the AMT.

The personal and dependency exemption amount deducted for regular income tax purposes is not allowed in computing AMT.[31] Therefore, taxpayers must enter a positive AMT adjustment for the personal and dependency exemption amount claimed in computing the regular income tax. A separate exemption (see Exemption Amount) is allowed for AMT purposes. To allow both the regular income tax exemption amount and the AMT exemption amount would result in extra benefits for taxpayers.

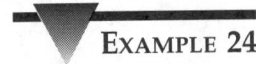

EXAMPLE 24   Eli, who is single, has no dependents and does not itemize deductions. He earned a salary of $106,950 in 1998. Based on this information, Eli's taxable income for 1998 is $100,000 ($106,950 – $4,250 standard deduction – $2,700 exemption). ▼

---

[30]§ 56(b)(1)(E).   [31]§ 56(b)(1)(E).

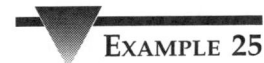

EXAMPLE 25 Assume the same facts as in Example 24. In addition, assume Eli's tax preferences for the year totaled $150,000. Eli's AMTI is $256,950 ($100,000 taxable income + $4,250 adjustment for standard deduction + $2,700 adjustment for exemption + $150,000 tax preferences). ▼

AMT PREFERENCES

4 ☐ LEARNING OBJECTIVE
Identify the tax preferences that are included in calculating the AMT.

Percentage Depletion. Congress originally enacted the percentage depletion rules to provide taxpayers with incentives to invest in the development of specified natural resources. Percentage depletion is computed by multiplying a rate specified in the Code times the gross income from the property (refer to Chapter 8). The percentage rate is based on the type of mineral involved. The basis of the property is reduced by the amount of depletion taken until the basis reaches zero. However, once the basis of the property reaches zero, taxpayers are allowed to continue taking percentage depletion deductions. Thus, over the life of the property, depletion deductions may greatly exceed the cost of the property.

The percentage depletion preference is equal to the excess of the regular income tax deduction for percentage depletion over the adjusted basis of the property at the end of the taxable year.[32] Basis is determined without regard to the depletion deduction for the taxable year. This preference item is figured separately for each piece of property for which the taxpayer is claiming depletion.

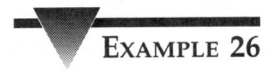

EXAMPLE 26 Kim owns a mineral property that qualifies for a 22% depletion rate. The basis of the property at the beginning of the year is $10,000. Gross income from the property for the year is $100,000. For regular income tax purposes, Kim's percentage depletion deduction (assume it is not limited by taxable income from the property) is $22,000. For AMT purposes, Kim has a tax preference of $12,000 ($22,000 − $10,000). ▼

Intangible Drilling Costs. In computing the regular income tax, taxpayers are allowed to deduct certain intangible drilling and development costs in the year incurred, although such costs are normally capital in nature (refer to Chapter 8). The deduction is allowed for costs incurred in connection with oil and gas wells and geothermal wells.

For AMT purposes, excess intangible drilling costs (IDC) for the year are treated as a preference.[33] The preference for excess IDC is computed as follows:

IDC expensed in the year incurred

Minus: Deduction if IDC were capitalized and amortized over 10 years

Equals: Excess of IDC expense over amortization

Minus: 65% of net oil and gas and geothermal income

Equals: Tax preference item

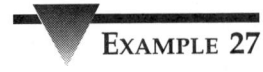

EXAMPLE 27 Ben, who incurred IDC of $50,000 during the year, elected to expense that amount. His net oil and gas income for the year was $60,000. Ben's tax preference for IDC is $6,000 [($50,000 IDC − $5,000 amortization) − (65% × $60,000 income)]. ▼

A taxpayer can avoid the preference for IDC by electing to write off the expenditures over a 10-year period for regular income tax purposes.

---

[32]§ 57(a)(1). Note that the preference label does not apply to percentage depletion on oil and gas wells for independent producers and royalty owners as defined in § 613A(c).

[33]§ 57(a)(2).

Interest on Private Activity Bonds.   Income from private activity bonds is not included in taxable income, and expenses related to carrying such bonds are not deductible for regular income tax purposes. However, interest on private activity bonds is included as a preference in computing AMTI. Therefore, expenses incurred in carrying the bonds are offset against the interest income in computing the tax preference.[34]

The Code contains a lengthy, complex definition of private activity bonds.[35] In general, **private activity bonds** are bonds issued by states or municipalities with more than 10 percent of the proceeds being used for private business use. For example, a bond issued by a city whose proceeds are used to construct a factory that is leased to a private business at a favorable rate is a private activity bond.

Depreciation.   For real property and leased personal property placed in service before 1987, there is an AMT preference for the excess of accelerated depreciation over straight-line depreciation.[36] However, examination of the cost recovery tables for pre-1987 real property (refer to Chapter 8) reveals that from the eighth year on, accelerated depreciation will not exceed straight-line depreciation. Consequently, taxpayers no longer have preferences attributable to pre-1987 real property.

Accelerated depreciation on pre-1987 leased personal property was computed using specified ACRS percentages (refer to Table 8–1, Chapter 8). AMT depreciation was based on the straight-line method, which was computed using the half-year convention, no salvage value, and a longer recovery period.[37] As a result, in the early years of the life of the asset, the cost recovery allowance used in computing the regular income tax was greater than the straight-line depreciation deduction allowed in computing AMT. The excess depreciation was treated as a tax preference item. For all leased personal property placed in service before 1987 (3-year, 5-year, and 10-year), except for 15-year public utility property, the cost recovery period has expired. Since there is no excess depreciation, there is no tax preference for AMT purposes.

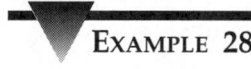

EXAMPLE 28

Paul acquired personal property on January 1, 1986, at a cost of $30,000. The property, which was placed in service as leased personal property on January 1, was 10-year ACRS property. Paul's 1986 depreciation deduction for regular income tax purposes was $2,400 ($30,000 cost × 8% rate from Table 8–1). For AMT purposes, the asset was depreciated over the AMT life of 15 years using the straight-line method with the half-year convention. Thus, AMT depreciation for 1986 was $1,000 [($30,000 ÷ 15) × ½ year convention]. Paul's tax preference for 1986 was $1,400 ($2,400 − $1,000). ACRS depreciation for 1998 is $0 ($30,000 × 0% ACRS rate), and straight-line depreciation is $2,000 ($30,000 ÷ 15). Thus, Paul's tax preference for 1998 is $0 since there is no excess depreciation. ▼

The preference item for excess depreciation on leased personal property is figured separately for each piece of property. No preference is reported in the year the taxpayer disposes of the property.

---

[34]§ 57(a)(5).
[35]§ 141.
[36]§ 57(a)(6).

[37]The specified lives for AMT purposes are 5 years for 3-year property, 8 years for 5-year property, 15 years for 10-year property, and 22 years for 15-year property.

Fifty Percent Exclusion for Certain Small Business Stock.

Fifty percent of the gain on the sale of certain small business stock is excludible from gross income for regular income tax purposes. Forty-two percent of the excluded amount is a tax preference for AMT purposes.[38]

5 LEARNING OBJECTIVE
Apply the formula for computing the AMT and illustrate Form 6251.

ILLUSTRATION OF THE AMT COMPUTATION

The computation of the AMT is illustrated in the following example.

EXAMPLE 29

Hans Sims, who is single, had taxable income for 1998 as follows:

Salary		$ 92,000
Interest		8,000
Adjusted gross income		$ 100,000
Less itemized deductions:		
Medical expenses ($17,500 – 7.5% of $100,000 AGI)[a]	$ 10,000	
State income taxes	4,000	
Interest[b]		
Home mortgage (for qualified housing)	20,000*	
Investment interest	3,300*	
Contributions (cash)	5,000*	
Casualty losses ($14,000 – 10% of $100,000 AGI)	4,000*	(46,300)
		$ 53,700
Less exemption		(2,700)
Taxable income		$ 51,000

[a]Total medical expenses were $17,500, reduced by 7.5% of AGI, resulting in an itemized deduction of $10,000. However, for AMT purposes, the reduction is 10%, which leaves an AMT itemized deduction of $7,500 ($17,500 – 10% of $100,000 AGI). Therefore, an adjustment of $2,500 ($10,000 – $7,500) is required for medical expenses disallowed for AMT purposes.

[b]In this illustration, all interest is deductible in computing AMTI. Qualified housing interest is deductible. Investment interest ($3,300) is deductible to the extent of net investment income included in the minimum tax base. For this purpose, the $8,000 of interest income is treated as net investment income.

Deductions marked by an asterisk are allowed as *alternative minimum tax itemized deductions,* and AMT adjustments are required for the other itemized deductions. Thus, adjustments are required for state income taxes and for medical expenses to the extent the medical expenses deductible for regular income tax purposes are not deductible in computing AMT (see note (a) above). In addition to the items that affected taxable income, Hans had $35,000 interest on private activity bonds (an exclusion tax preference). AMTI is computed as follows:

---

[38]§ 57(a)(7). Prior to the effective date of TRA of 1997 for this provision (tax years ending after May 6, 1997), the preference was 50% of the excluded amount.

Taxable income	$ 51,000
Plus: Adjustments	
State income taxes	4,000
Medical expenses (see note (a) above)	2,500
Personal exemption	2,700
Plus: Tax preference (interest on private activity bonds)	35,000
Equals: AMTI	$ 95,200
Minus: AMT exemption	(33,750)
Equals: Minimum tax base	$ 61,450
Times: AMT rate	× 26%
Equals: Tentative AMT	$ 15,977
Minus: Regular income tax on taxable income	(10,985)
Equals: AMT	$ 4,992

The solution to Example 29 is also presented on Form 6251. Though this example is for 1998, 1997 tax forms are used because the 1998 tax forms were not available at the time of this writing.

Note that the $2,700 personal exemption amount is a positive adjustment in the Example 29 solution, but does not appear as an adjustment in Form 6251. This difference occurs because line 16 of Form 6251 includes the amount from line 36 of Form 1040. Line 36 of Form 1040 is taxable income before the deduction for personal and dependency exemptions.

ETHICAL CONSIDERATIONS

Effect of the Absence of Inflation Adjustments

Many areas of the regular income tax (e.g., rates, standard deductions, personal and dependency exemptions) are indexed annually for the effect of inflation. The alternative minimum tax system, the AMT, is not subject to indexing.

The AMT is defined as the excess of the tentative AMT over the regular income tax liability. Thus, the AMT calculation results in an AMT tax liability only if there is such an excess. Due to the absence of indexing for the AMT, this AMT tax liability can increase even though no other changes occur in the taxpayer's tax position.

Suppose that for 1997 a taxpayer's regular income tax liability is $110,000 and the tentative AMT is $120,000. The AMT is therefore $10,000. For 1998 all of the taxpayer's tax information is identical to that for 1997. Because of indexing, however, the regular income tax liability is only $107,000. Therefore, the AMT for 1998 is $13,000 ($120,000 – $107,000).

Evaluate the propriety of only the regular income tax being subject to indexing.

AMT CREDIT

6 ⯆ LEARNING OBJECTIVE
Describe the role of the AMT credit in the alternative minimum tax structure.

As discussed previously, timing differences give rise to adjustments to the minimum tax base. In later years, the timing differences reverse, as was illustrated in several of the preceding examples. To provide equity for the taxpayer when timing differences reverse, the regular income tax liability may be reduced by a tax credit for prior years' minimum tax liability attributable to timing differences. The **alternative**

Form **6251**

Department of the Treasury
Internal Revenue Service (99)

Alternative Minimum Tax—Individuals

▶ See separate instructions.

▶ Attach to Form 1040 or Form 1040NR.

OMB No. 1545-0227

1997

Attachment
Sequence No. **32**

Name(s) shown on Form 1040   *Hans Sims*   Your social security number

Part I   Adjustments and Preferences

1	If you itemized deductions on Schedule A (Form 1040), go to line 2. Otherwise, enter your standard deduction from Form 1040, line 35, here and go to line 6	1	
2	Medical and dental. Enter the smaller of Schedule A (Form 1040), line 4 **or** 2½% of Form 1040, line 33	2	*2,500*
3	Taxes. Enter the amount from Schedule A (Form 1040), line 9	3	*4,000*
4	Certain interest on a home mortgage not used to buy, build, or improve your home	4	
5	Miscellaneous itemized deductions. Enter the amount from Schedule A (Form 1040), line 26	5	
6	Refund of taxes. Enter any tax refund from Form 1040, line 10 or line 21	6 (	)
7	Investment interest. Enter difference between regular tax and AMT deduction	7	
8	Post-1986 depreciation. Enter difference between regular tax and AMT depreciation	8	
9	Adjusted gain or loss. Enter difference between AMT and regular tax gain or loss	9	
10	Incentive stock options. Enter excess of AMT income over regular tax income	10	
11	Passive activities. Enter difference between AMT and regular tax income or loss	11	
12	Beneficiaries of estates and trusts. Enter the amount from Schedule K-1 (Form 1041), line 9	12	
13	Tax-exempt interest from private activity bonds issued after 8/7/86	13	*35,000*

14   Other. Enter the amount, if any, for each item below and enter the total on line 14.

a Charitable contributions	**h** Loss limitations		
b Circulation expenditures	**i** Mining costs		
c Depletion	**j** Patron's adjustment		
d Depreciation (pre-1987)	**k** Pollution control facilities		
e Installment sales	**l** Research and experimental		
f Intangible drilling costs	**m** Tax shelter farm activities		
g Long-term contracts	**n** Related adjustments	14	

15	**Total Adjustments and Preferences.** Combine lines 1 through 14 ▶	15	*41,500*

Part II   Alternative Minimum Taxable Income

16	Enter the amount from **Form 1040, line 36.** If less than zero, enter as a (loss) ▶	16	*53,700*
17	Net operating loss deduction, if any, from Form 1040, line 21. Enter as a positive amount	17	
18	If Form 1040, line 33, is over $121,200 (over $60,600 if married filing separately), and you itemized deductions, enter the amount, if any, from line 9 of the worksheet for Schedule A (Form 1040), line 28	18 (	)
19	Combine lines 15 through 18 ▶	19	*95,200*
20	Alternative tax net operating loss deduction. See page 5 of the instructions	20	
21	**Alternative Minimum Taxable Income.** Subtract line 20 from line 19. (If married filing separately and line 21 is more than $165,000, see page 5 of the instructions.) ▶	21	*95,200*

Part III   Exemption Amount and Alternative Minimum Tax

22   **Exemption Amount.** (If this form is for a child under age 14, see page 6 of the instructions.)

IF your filing status is . . .	AND line 21 is not over . . .	THEN enter on line 22 . . .		
Single or head of household	$112,500	$33,750		
Married filing jointly or qualifying widow(er)	150,000	45,000	22	*33,750*
Married filing separately	75,000	22,500		

If line 21 is **over** the amount shown above for your filing status, see page 6 of the instructions.

23	Subtract line 22 from line 21. If zero or less, enter -0- here and on lines 26 and 28 ▶	23	*61,450*
24	If you completed Schedule D (Form 1040), and had an amount on line 25 or line 27 (as refigured for the AMT, if necessary), go to Part IV of Form 6251 to figure line 24. **All others:** If line 23 is $175,000 or less ($87,500 or less if married filing separately), multiply line 23 by 26% (.26). Otherwise, multiply line 23 by 28% (.28) and subtract $3,500 ($1,750 if married filing separately) from the result ▶	24	*15,977*
25	Alternative minimum tax foreign tax credit. See page 7 of the instructions	25	
26	Tentative minimum tax. Subtract line 25 from line 24 ▶	26	*15,977*
27	Enter your tax from Form 1040, line 39 (minus any tax from Form 4972 and any foreign tax credit from Form 1040, line 43)	27	*10,985*
28	**Alternative Minimum Tax.** (If this form is for a child under age 14, see page 7 of the instructions.) Subtract line 27 from line 26. If zero or less, enter -0-. Enter here and on Form 1040, line 48 ▶	28	*4,992*

For Paperwork Reduction Act Notice, see separate instructions.   Cat. No. 13600G   Form **6251** (1997)

minimum tax credit may be carried over indefinitely. Therefore, there is no need to keep track of when the minimum tax credit arose.[39]

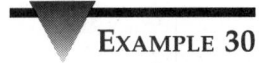

EXAMPLE 30

Assume the same facts as in Example 3. Also assume that in 1997, Bob paid AMT as a result of the $20,000 positive adjustment arising from the circulation expenditures. In 1998, $10,000 of the timing difference reverses, resulting in regular taxable income that is $10,000 greater than AMTI. Because Bob has already paid AMT as a result of the write-off of circulation expenditures, he is allowed an AMT credit in 1998. The AMT credit can offset Bob's regular income tax liability in 1998 to the extent that his regular income tax liability exceeds his tentative AMT. ▼

The AMT credit is applicable only for the AMT that results from timing differences. It is not available in connection with **AMT exclusions,** which represent permanent differences rather than timing differences between the regular income tax liability and the AMT. These AMT exclusions include the following:

- The standard deduction.
- Personal exemptions.
- Medical expenses, to the extent deductible for regular income tax purposes but not deductible in computing AMT.
- Other itemized deductions not allowable for AMT purposes, including miscellaneous itemized deductions, taxes, and interest expense.
- Excess percentage depletion.
- Tax-exempt interest on specified private activity bonds.

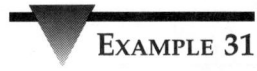

EXAMPLE 31

Don, who is single, has zero taxable income for 1998. He also has positive timing adjustments of $300,000 and AMT exclusions of $100,000. His AMT base is $400,000 because his AMT exemption is phased out completely due to the level of AMTI. Don's tentative AMT is $108,500 [($175,000 × 26% AMT rate) + ($225,000 × 28% AMT rate)]. ▼

To determine the amount of AMT credit to carry over, the AMT must be recomputed reflecting only the AMT exclusions and the AMT exemption amount.

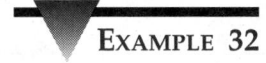

EXAMPLE 32

Assume the same facts as in the previous example. If there had been no positive timing adjustments for the year, Don's tentative AMT would have been $17,225 [($100,000 AMT exclusions – $33,750 exemption) × 26% AMT rate]. Don may carry over an AMT credit of $91,275 ($108,500 AMT – $17,225 related to AMT exclusions) to 1999 and subsequent years. ▼

CORPORATE ALTERNATIVE MINIMUM TAX

7 ▼   **LEARNING OBJECTIVE**
Understand the basic features of the corporate AMT.

The AMT applicable to corporations is similar to that applicable to noncorporate taxpayers. However, there are several important differences:

- The corporate AMT rate is 20 percent versus a top rate of 28 percent for noncorporate taxpayers.[40]
- The AMT exemption for corporations is $40,000 reduced by 25 percent of the amount by which AMTI exceeds $150,000.[41]

---

[39]§ 53.
[40]§ 55(b)(1)(B).

[41]§§ 55(d)(2) and (3).

Concept Summary 12–1

AMT Adjustments and Preferences for Individuals

Adjustments	Positive	Negative	Both*
Circulation expenditures			X
Depreciation of post-1986 real property			X
Depreciation of post-1986 personal property			X
Pollution control facilities			X
Mining exploration and development costs			X
Research and experimental expenditures			X
Completed contract method			X
Incentive stock options	X**		
Adjusted gain or loss			X
Passive activity losses			X
Alternative tax NOLD			X
Itemized deductions:			
Medical expenses	X		
State income tax	X		
Property tax on realty	X		
Property tax on personalty	X		
Miscellaneous itemized deductions	X		
Tax benefit rule for state income tax refund		X	
Cutback adjustment		X	
Qualified interest on student loans	X		
Qualified residence interest that is not qualified housing interest	X		
Qualified residence interest that is AMT investment interest	X	X	
Private activity bond interest that is AMT investment interest		X	
Standard deduction	X		
Personal exemptions and dependency deductions	X		

Preferences			
Percentage depletion in excess of adjusted basis	X		
Intangible drilling costs	X		
Private activity bond interest income	X		
Depreciation on pre-1987 leased personal property	X		
§ 1202 exclusion for certain small business stock	X		

*Timing differences.

**While the adjustment is a positive adjustment, the AMT basis for the stock is increased by the amount of the positive adjustment.

- Tax preferences applicable to noncorporate taxpayers are also applicable to corporate taxpayers, but some adjustments differ (see below).

Although there are computational differences, the corporate AMT and the noncorporate AMT have the identical objective: to force taxpayers who are more

▼ **FIGURE 12–3**
AMT Formula for Corporations

Taxable income

Plus: Income tax NOL deduction

Plus or minus: AMT adjustments

Plus: Tax preferences

Equals: AMTI before ATNOLD

Minus: ATNOLD (limited to 90% of AMTI before ATNOLD)

Equals: AMTI

Minus: Exemption

Equals: AMT base

Times: 20% rate

Equals: Tentative minimum tax before AMT foreign tax credit

Minus: AMT foreign tax credit (limited to 90% of AMT before AMT foreign tax credit)

Equals: Tentative minimum tax

Minus: Regular tax liability before credits minus regular foreign tax credit

Equals: AMT if positive

profitable than their taxable income reflects to pay additional tax. The formula for determining the corporate AMT appears in Figure 12–3.

REPEAL OF AMT FOR SMALL CORPORATIONS

TRA of 1997 has repealed the AMT for small corporations for tax years beginning after December 31, 1997. For this purpose, a corporation is classified as a small corporation if it had average annual gross receipts of less than $5 million for the three-year period beginning after December 1994. A corporation will continue to be classified as a small corporation if its average annual gross receipts for the three-year period preceding the current tax year do not exceed $7.5 million.

AMT ADJUSTMENTS

Adjustments Applicable to Individuals and Corporations.   The following adjustments that were discussed in connection with the individual AMT also apply to the corporate AMT:

- Excess of MACRS over ADS depreciation on real and personal property placed in service after 1986.
- Pollution control facilities placed in service after 1986 (AMT requires ADS depreciation over the asset's ADR life; 60-month amortization is allowed for regular income tax purposes).
- Mining and exploration expenditures (AMT requires amortization over 10 years versus immediate expensing allowed for regular income tax purposes).
- Income on long-term contracts (AMT requires percentage of completion method; completed contract method is allowed in limited circumstances for regular income tax purposes).
- Dispositions of assets (if gain or loss for AMT purposes differs from gain or loss for regular income tax purposes).
- Allowable ATNOLD (which cannot exceed 90 percent of AMTI before deduction for ATNOLD).

TAX IN THE NEWS

SOME WITH A TAX HEADACHE RECEIVE A PAINKILLER

Some small business owners should feel better as a result of TRA of 1997 because small corporations are now exempt from the AMT. About three million corporations will qualify under this provision (i.e., about 95 percent of incorporated businesses). The Treasury Department estimates that this exemption will save these businesses about $762 million in taxes over the next 10 years. Perhaps equally beneficial, the repeal of the AMT for qualifying small corporations reduces the compliance costs of determining the amount of the AMT.

SOURCE: Adapted from Elizabeth MacDonald, "An Alternative Minimum Tax Headache Gets a Painkiller from the New Tax Law," *Wall Street Journal*, August 8, 1997, p. B1.

Adjustments Applicable Only to Corporations. Three AMT adjustments are applicable only to corporations:[42]

- The adjusted current earnings (ACE) adjustment.
- The Merchant Marine capital construction fund adjustment.
- The adjustment for special deductions allowed to Blue Cross/Blue Shield organizations.

The latter two adjustments apply to specific types of corporations and are not discussed in the chapter. On the other hand, the **ACE adjustment** generally applies to all corporations[43] and has a significant impact on both tax and financial accounting.

Corporations are subject to an AMT adjustment equal to 75 percent of the excess of ACE over AMTI before the ACE adjustment.[44] Historically, the government has not required conformity between tax accounting and financial accounting. For many years, the only *direct* conformity requirement was that a corporation that used the LIFO method for tax accounting also had to use LIFO for financial accounting.[45] Through the ACE adjustment, Congress is *indirectly* imposing a conformity requirement on corporations. While a corporation may still choose to use different methods for tax and financial accounting purposes, it may no longer be able to do so without incurring AMT as a result of the ACE adjustment. Thus, a corporation may incur AMT not only because of specifically targeted adjustments and preferences, but also as a result of any methods that cause ACE to exceed AMTI before the ACE adjustment.

The ACE adjustment can be either a positive or a negative amount. AMTI is increased by 75 percent of the excess of ACE over unadjusted AMTI. Or AMTI is reduced by 75 percent of the excess of unadjusted AMTI over ACE. The negative adjustment is limited to the aggregate of the positive adjustments under ACE for prior years, reduced by the previously claimed negative adjustments. See Concept Summary 12–2. Thus, the ordering of the timing differences is crucial because any lost negative adjustment is permanent. Unadjusted AMTI is AMTI without the ACE adjustment or the ATNOLD.[46]

---

[42]§ 56(c).
[43]The ACE adjustment does not apply to S corporations. § 56(g)(6).
[44]§ 56(g).

[45]§ 472(c).
[46]§§56(g)(1) and (2).

CONCEPT SUMMARY 12–2

Determining the ACE Adjustment*

```
                    ┌──────────────────────────┐
                    │  Calculate Taxable Income │
                    └──────────────────────────┘
                                 │
           ┌─────────────────────────────────────────┐
           │ Calculate AMTI by adjusting Taxable     │
           │ Income as required by § 56 and § 58     │
           │ and increasing Taxable Income by § 57   │
           │ tax preference items                    │
           └─────────────────────────────────────────┘
                                 │
           ┌─────────────────────────────────────────┐
           │ Calculate Adjusted Current Earnings     │
           │ by adjusting AMTI as required (many     │
           │ of the adjustments based on earnings    │
           │ and profits adjustments)                │
           └─────────────────────────────────────────┘
                                 │
                          ◇ Is Adjusted Current
                            Earnings AMTI
          Yes ─────────────  greater than pre-  ───────────── No
           │                  adjustment                       │
           │                     AMTI?                          │
           │                                                    │
┌──────────────────────────────┐          ┌──────────────────────────────┐
│ Increase AMTI by 75% of the  │          │ Decrease AMTI by 75% of the  │
│ excess of Adjusted Current    │          │ excess of AMTI (pre-         │
│ Earnings over AMTI            │          │ adjustment) over Adjusted    │
│ (pre-adjustment)              │          │ Current Earnings to extent   │
│                               │          │ of net previous increases    │
└──────────────────────────────┘          └──────────────────────────────┘
```

*Adapted from "Corporate Alternative Minimum Tax: The Impact of Current Earnings Adjustment on Oil and Gas Companies" by Gallun and Zachry, which appeared in the September 1989 issue of the *Oil and Gas Tax Quarterly*, published and copyrighted 1989 by Matthew Bender & Co., and appears here with their permission.

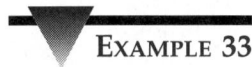

EXAMPLE 33

A calendar year corporation has the following data:

	1997	1998	1999
Pre-adjusted AMTI	$3,000	$3,000	$3,100
Adjusted current earnings	4,000	3,000	2,000

In 1997, because ACE exceeds unadjusted AMTI by $1,000, $750 (75% × $1,000) is included as a positive adjustment to AMTI. No adjustment is necessary for 1998. As unadjusted AMTI exceeds ACE by $1,100 in 1999, there is a potential negative adjustment to AMTI of $825 ($1,100 × 75%). Since the total increases to AMTI for prior years equal $750 and there are no previously claimed negative adjustments, only $750 of the potential negative adjustment reduces AMTI for 1999. Further, $75 of the negative amount is lost forever. ▼

ACE should not be confused with current earnings and profits. Although many items are treated in the same manner, certain variations exist. For example, Federal income taxes, deductible in computing earnings and profits, are not deductible in determining ACE.

The starting point for computing ACE is AMTI, which is defined as regular taxable income after AMT adjustments (other than the ATNOLD and ACE adjustments) and tax preferences. The resulting figure is adjusted for several items in order to arrive at ACE.

TAX PREFERENCES

AMTI includes designated tax preference items. In some cases, this has the effect of subjecting nontaxable income to the AMT. Tax preference items that apply to individuals also apply to corporations.

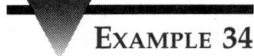

EXAMPLE 34

The following information applies to Brown Corporation (a calendar year taxpayer) for 1998:

Taxable income	$200,000
Mining exploration costs	50,000
Percentage depletion claimed (the property has a zero adjusted basis)	70,000
Interest on City of Elmira (Michigan) private activity bonds	30,000

Brown Corporation's AMTI for 1998 is determined as follows:

Taxable income		$200,000
Adjustments:		
Excess mining exploration costs [$50,000 (amount expensed) − $5,000 (amount allowed over a 10-year amortization period)]		45,000
Tax preferences:		
Excess depletion	$70,000	
Interest on private activity bonds	30,000	100,000
AMTI		$345,000

EXEMPTION

The tentative AMT is 20 percent of AMTI that exceeds the corporation's exemption amount. The exemption amount for a corporation is $40,000 reduced by 25 percent of the amount by which AMTI exceeds $150,000.

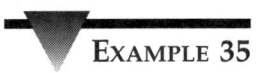

EXAMPLE 35

Blue Corporation has AMTI of $180,000. The exemption amount is reduced by $7,500 [25% × ($180,000 − $150,000)], and the amount remaining is $32,500 ($40,000 − $7,500). Thus, Blue Corporation's AMT base (refer to Figure 12–3) is $147,500 ($180,000 − $32,500). ▼

Note that the exemption phases out entirely when AMTI reaches $310,000.

OTHER ASPECTS OF THE AMT

Foreign tax credits can be applied against only 90 percent of tentative AMT liability. The 90 percent limit does not apply to certain corporations meeting specified requirements.

All of a corporation's AMT is available for carryover as a minimum tax credit. This is so regardless of whether the adjustments and preferences originate from timing differences or AMT exclusions.

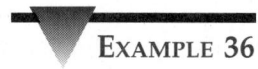

EXAMPLE 36

In Example 34, the AMTI exceeds $310,000, so no exemption is allowed. The tentative minimum tax is $69,000 (20% of $345,000). The regular income tax liability is $61,250, and the AMT liability is $7,750 ($69,000 − $61,250). The amount of the minimum tax credit carryover is $7,750, which is all of the current year's AMT. ▼

TAX PLANNING CONSIDERATIONS

8 LEARNING OBJECTIVE
Identify tax planning opportunities to minimize the AMT.

RESPONDING TO BOB AND CAROL

The chapter began with a set of circumstances involving Bob and Carol that raised a number of interesting questions. By now, the student should have arrived at a logical reason for the difference in Bob and Carol's tax liabilities and expect the following to happen to Bob.

Bob contacts Adam, his tax return preparer, and explains in an excited voice that he has received a bill from the IRS for $15,000 plus interest associated with the underpayment of his tax liability. Adam has Bob fax him a copy of the IRS deficiency notice. He checks Bob's tax file and then calls Bob to explain that Bob does owe the IRS the $15,000 plus interest. Somehow Bob's tax return was prepared without including a Form 6251 (the alternative minimum tax). Adam suggests that Bob stop by his office later that afternoon to discuss the disposition of the matter further.

AVOIDING PREFERENCES AND ADJUSTMENTS

Several strategies and elections are available to help taxpayers avoid having preferences and adjustments.

- A taxpayer who is in danger of incurring AMT liability should not invest in tax-exempt private activity bonds unless doing so makes good investment sense. Any AMT triggered by interest on private activity bonds reduces the yield on an investment in the bonds. Other tax-exempt bonds or taxable corporate bonds might yield a better after-tax return.
- A taxpayer may elect to expense certain costs in the year incurred or to capitalize and amortize the costs over some specified period. The decision should be based on the present discounted value of after-tax cash flows under the available alternatives. Costs subject to elective treatment include circulation expenditures, mining exploration and development costs, and research and experimental expenditures.

CONTROLLING THE TIMING OF PREFERENCES AND ADJUSTMENTS

The AMT exemption often keeps items of tax preference from being subject to the AMT. To use the AMT exemption effectively, taxpayers should avoid bunching preferences and positive adjustments in any one year. To avoid this bunching, taxpayers should attempt to control the timing of such items when possible.

TAKING ADVANTAGE OF THE AMT/REGULAR TAX RATE DIFFERENTIAL

A taxpayer who cannot avoid triggering the AMT in a given year can usually save taxes by taking advantage of the rate differential between the AMT and the regular income tax.

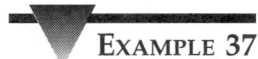

EXAMPLE 37

Peter, a real estate dealer who expects to be in the 31% tax bracket in 1999, is subject to the AMT in 1998. He is considering the sale of a parcel of land (inventory) at a gain of $100,000. If he sells the land in 1999, he will have to pay tax of $31,000 ($100,000 gain × 31% regular income tax rate). However, if he sells the land in 1998, he will pay tax of $26,000 ($100,000 gain × 26% AMT rate). Thus, accelerating the sale into 1998 will save Peter $5,000 in tax. ▼

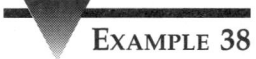

EXAMPLE 38

Cora, who expects to be in the 39.6% tax bracket in 1999, is subject to the AMT in 1998. She is going to contribute $10,000 in cash to her alma mater, State University. If Cora makes the contribution in 1999, she will save tax of $3,960 ($10,000 contribution × 39.6% regular income tax rate). However, if she makes the contribution in 1998, she will save tax of $2,600 ($10,000 contribution × 26% AMT rate). Thus, deferring the contribution until 1999 will save Cora $1,360 in tax. ▼

This deferral/acceleration strategy should be considered for any income or expenses where the taxpayer can control the timing. This strategy applies to corporations as well as to individuals.

KEY TERMS

ACE adjustment, 12–29

Alternative minimum tax (AMT), 12–2

Alternative minimum tax credit, 12–24

Alternative tax NOL deduction (ATNOLD), 12–16

AMT adjustments, 12–4

AMT exclusions, 12–26

Circulation expenditures, 12–4

Incentive stock options (ISOs), 12–13

Private activity bonds, 12–22

Tax preferences, 12–4

PROBLEM MATERIALS

DISCUSSION QUESTIONS

1. Since there is a regular income tax, why is there a need for an AMT?

2. Distinguish between the direct method of calculating the AMT and the indirect method.

3. What is the difference between AMT adjustments and tax preferences?

4. Identify which of the following are tax preferences:
   a. Forty-two percent exclusion associated with gains on the sale of certain small business stock.
   b. Exclusion on the receipt of property by gift.
   c. Exclusion associated with payment of premiums by the employer on group term life insurance for coverage not in excess of $50,000.
   d. Percentage depletion in excess of the property's adjusted basis.
   e. Tax-exempt interest on certain private activity bonds.

5. Identify which of the following are tax preferences:
   a. Exclusion on the receipt of property by inheritance.
   b. Exclusion to employee on the employer's contribution to the employee's pension plan.
   c. Excess of deduction for circulation expenditures for regular income tax purposes over the deduction for AMT purposes.

     d. Excess of amortization allowance over depreciation on pre-1987 certified pollution control facilities.

     e. Excess of accelerated over straight-line depreciation on real property placed in service before 1987.

6. Describe the tax formula for the AMT.

7. If the regular income tax liability exceeds the tentative AMT, there is no AMT liability, and the total income tax liability is equal to the regular income tax liability. Evaluate the correctness of this statement.

8. For the exemption amount, indicate the following:
     a. Purpose for the exemption.
     b. Amount of the exemption.
     c. Reason for the phase-out of the exemption.

9. What are the AMT rates for an individual taxpayer? To what levels of income do the rates apply?

10. How do nonrefundable tax credits affect the calculation of the AMT?

11. How can an individual taxpayer avoid having an AMT adjustment for circulation expenditures?

12. Tom, who owns and operates a sole proprietorship, acquired machinery and placed it in service in February 1998. If Tom has to pay AMT in 1998, will he be required to make an AMT adjustment for depreciation on the machinery? Explain.

13. Rick, who is single, incurs mining exploration and development costs associated with his energy company. He would expense the costs in the current year in order to reduce his regular income tax, but is aware that this would create a positive adjustment for AMT purposes. His AGI is large enough to reduce the AMT exemption amount to zero. Therefore, he is considering electing to amortize the mining exploration and development costs over 10 years to avoid having to pay any AMT. Advise Rick.

14. Janice owns a construction company and uses the completed contract method for all of her contracts. April owns a construction company and uses the percentage of completion method for all of her construction contracts. Why does Janice have to be concerned with the AMT associated with her construction company whereas April does not?

15. If the stock received under an incentive stock option (ISO) is sold in the year of exercise, there is no AMT adjustment. If the stock is sold in a later year, there will be an AMT adjustment. Evaluate the validity of these statements.

16. Lucy acquired a machine for $30,000 for use in her business two years ago and depreciated it using an accelerated method under MACRS. When she sold the machine at a gain this year, should her recognized gain for regular income tax purposes be the same as her recognized gain for AMT purposes?

17. Carol is going to be subject to the AMT in 1998. She owns an investment building and is considering disposing of it and investing in other realty. Based on an appraisal of the building's value, the realized gain would be $20,000. Ed has offered to purchase the building from Carol with the closing date being December 29, 1998. Ed wants to close the transaction in 1998 because certain beneficial tax consequences will result only if the transaction is closed prior to the beginning of 1999. Abby has offered to purchase the building with the closing date being January 2, 1999. The building has a $25,000 greater AMT adjusted basis. For regular income tax purposes, Carol expects to be in the 28% tax bracket. What are the relevant tax issues that Carol faces in making her decision?

18. Passive activity losses are not deductible in computing either taxable income or AMTI. Explain why an adjustment for passive activity losses may be required for AMT purposes.

19. What effect do adjustments and preferences have on the calculation of the ATNOLD?

20. The following itemized deductions are allowed for regular income tax purposes: medical expenses, state and local income taxes, real estate taxes, personal property taxes, home mortgage interest, investment interest, charitable contributions of cash, charitable contributions of long-term capital gain property, casualty losses, unreimbursed employee business expenses, and gambling losses. Which of these itemized deductions can result in an AMT adjustment?

21. Matt, who is single, has always elected to itemize deductions rather than take the standard deduction. In prior years, his itemized deductions always exceeded the standard deduction by a substantial amount. As a result of paying off the mortgage on his residence, he projects that his itemized deductions for 1998 will exceed the standard deduction by only $500. Matt anticipates that the amount of his itemized deductions will remain about the same in the foreseeable future. Matt's AGI is $150,000. He is investing the amount of his former mortgage payment each month in tax-exempt bonds. A friend recommends that Matt buy a beach house in order to increase his itemized deductions. What are the relevant tax issues for Matt?

22. Wally's 3% cutback adjustment for regular income tax purposes reduces his itemized deductions from $25,000 to $21,000. What effect will this have in calculating Wally's AMTI?

23. Could computation of the AMT ever require an adjustment for the standard deduction or personal and dependency exemptions? Explain.

24. Alvin owns a mineral deposit that qualifies for the 15% percentage depletion rate. Under what circumstances will the depletion deduction for regular income tax purposes and AMT purposes not be the same?

25. Ira received a gift of $100,000 from his Aunt Lillian. He is going to invest the proceeds in either taxable bonds earning interest at an 8% rate or tax-exempt bonds earning interest at a 6% rate. What are the relevant tax issues for Ira?

26. What is the purpose of the AMT credit? Briefly describe how the credit is computed.

27. What requirements must be satisfied for a corporation to be exempt from the AMT?

28. Some observers believe the ACE adjustment causes corporations to change some of the methods they use for financial accounting and tax accounting purposes. Comment.

29. What is the ACE adjustment, and does it apply to both the individual taxpayer and the corporate taxpayer?

30. Is it ever advisable for a taxpayer to defer deductions from an AMT year into a non-AMT year where the regular income tax applies? Explain and give an example of how such a deferral might be accomplished.

PROBLEMS

31. Use the following data to calculate Rachel's AMT base:

Taxable income	$130,000
Positive AMT adjustments	50,000
Negative AMT adjustments	20,000
AMT preferences	25,000

Rachel is not married.

32. Arthur East, an unmarried individual who is age 66, has taxable income of $100,000. He has AMT positive adjustments of $70,000 and tax preferences of $45,000.
    a. What is Arthur's AMT?
    b. What is the total amount of Arthur's tax liability?
    c. Draft a letter to Arthur explaining why he must pay more than the regular income tax liability. Arthur's address is 100 Colonel's Way, Conway, SC 29526.

33. Calculate the AMT for the following cases. The taxpayer has regular taxable income of $500,000 and does not have any credits.

Filing Status	Tentative AMT	
	Case 1	Case 2
Single	$190,000	$175,000
Married, filing jointly	190,000	175,000

34. Calculate the exemption amount for the following cases for a single taxpayer, a married taxpayer filing jointly, and a married taxpayer filing separately.

Case	AMTI
1	$100,000
2	200,000
3	400,000

35. Leona has nonrefundable credits of $30,000 for 1998. Her regular income tax liability before credits is $42,000, and her tentative AMT is $25,000.
    a. What is the amount of Leona's AMT?
    b. What is the amount of Leona's regular income tax liability after credits?

36. Angela, who is single, incurs circulation expenditures of $123,000 during 1998. She is in the process of deciding whether to expense the $123,000 or to capitalize it and elect to deduct it over a three-year period. Angela already knows that she will be subject to the AMT for 1998 at the 28% rate. Angela is in the 31% bracket for regular income tax purposes this year and expects to remain in that bracket in the future. Advise Angela on whether she should elect the three-year write-off rather than expensing the $123,000 in 1998.

37. Vito owns and operates a news agency (as a sole proprietorship). During 1998, he incurred expenses of $60,000 to increase circulation of newspapers and magazines that his agency distributes. For regular income tax purposes, he elected to expense the $60,000 in 1998. In addition, he incurred $30,000 in circulation expenditures in 1999 and again elected expense treatment. What AMT adjustments will be required in 1998 and 1999 as a result of the circulation expenditures?

38. Lance is a landlord who owns two apartment buildings. He acquired Longwood Acres on February 21, 1986, for $300,000, with $90,000 of the cost allocated to the land. He acquired Colony Square on March 5, 1994, for $800,000, and $175,000 of the cost was allocated to land. Neither apartment complex is low-income housing. Lance elected to write off the cost of each building as fast as possible. What is the effect of depreciation (cost recovery) on Lance's AMTI for 1998?

39. In March 1998, Helen Carlon acquired equipment for her business at a cost of $250,000. The equipment is 5-year class property for regular income tax purposes and 9.5-year class property for AMT purposes.
    a. If Helen depreciates the equipment using the method that will produce the greatest deduction for 1998, what is the amount of the AMT adjustment?
    b. How can Helen reduce the AMT adjustment to $0? What circumstances would motivate her to do so?
    c. Draft a letter to Helen regarding the choice of depreciation methods. Helen's address is 500 Monticello Avenue, Glendale, AZ 85306.

40. In 1998, Gary incurred $180,000 of mining and exploration expenditures. He elects to deduct the expenditures as quickly as the tax law allows for regular income tax purposes.
    a. How will Gary's treatment of mining and exploration expenditures affect his regular income tax and AMT computations for 1998?

b. How can Gary avoid having AMT adjustments related to the mining and exploration expenditures?

c. What factors should Gary consider in deciding whether to deduct the expenditures in the year incurred?

41. Josepi's construction company builds personal residences that qualify for the use of the completed contract method. During the three-year period 1998–2000, Josepi recognized the following income on his two construction contracts:

Year	Contract 1	Contract 2
1998	$600,000*	$ –0–
1999	–0–	–0–
2000	–0–	700,000**

*Construction completed in 1998.
**Construction completed in 2000.

If Josepi had used the percentage of completion method, he would have recognized the following income:

Year	Contract 1	Contract 2
1998	$40,000	$175,000
1999	–0–	225,000
2000	–0–	300,000

Calculate the amount of the AMT adjustment for 1998, 1999, and 2000.

42. Burt, the CFO of Amber, Inc., is granted stock options in 1998 that qualify as incentive stock options (ISOs). In 2003, the rights in the stock become freely transferable and not subject to a substantial risk of forfeiture. Burt exercises the stock options in 2002 when the option price is $70,000 and the fair market value of the stock is $100,000. He sells the stock in 2006 for $150,000. What are the regular income tax consequences and the AMT consequences for Burt in:
    a. 1998?
    b. 2002?
    c. 2003?
    d. 2006?

43. In 1998, Lori exercised an incentive stock option that had been granted by her employer, Black Corporation. Lori acquired 100 shares of Black stock for the option price of $175 per share. The rights in the stock become freely transferable and not subject to a substantial risk of forfeiture in 1998. The fair market value of the stock at the date of exercise was $210 per share. Lori sells the stock for $320 per share in 1998. What is the amount of her AMT adjustment in 1998, and what is her recognized gain on the sale for regular income tax purposes and AMT purposes?

44. Bobby sells an apartment building for $500,000. His adjusted basis is $300,000 for regular income tax purposes and $330,000 for AMT purposes.
    a. Calculate Bobby's gain for regular income tax purposes.
    b. Calculate Bobby's gain for AMT purposes.
    c. Calculate Bobby's AMT adjustment, if any.

45. Freda acquired a passive activity in 1998. Gross income from operations of the activity was $150,000. Operating expenses, not including depreciation, were $135,000. Regular income tax depreciation of $37,500 was computed under MACRS. AMT depreciation, computed under ADS, was $24,000. Compute Freda's passive loss deduction and passive loss suspended for regular income tax purposes and for AMT purposes.

46. Wally and Gloria incur and pay medical expenses in excess of insurance reimbursements during the year as follows:

For Wally	$8,000
For Gloria (spouse)	3,000
For Chuck (son)	1,000
For Carter (Gloria's father)	9,000

    Wally and Gloria's AGI is $200,000. They file a joint return. Chuck and Carter are Wally and Gloria's dependents.
    a. What is Wally and Gloria's medical expense deduction for regular income tax purposes?
    b. What is Wally and Gloria's medical expense deduction for AMT purposes?
    c. What is the amount of the AMT adjustment for medical expenses?

47. Wolfgang had the following itemized deductions for 1998:

Medical expenses [$5,000 − (7.5% × $50,000)]	$ 1,250
State income taxes	3,000
Charitable contributions	5,000
Home mortgage interest on his personal residence	6,000
Casualty loss	1,500
Miscellaneous itemized deductions [$3,500 − 2%($50,000)]	2,500
	$19,250

    a. Calculate Wolfgang's itemized deductions for AMT purposes.
    b. What is the amount of the AMT adjustment?

48. Tom, who is single, owns a personal residence in the city. He also owns a cabin near a ski resort in the mountains. He uses the cabin as a vacation home. In February 1998, he borrowed $60,000 on a home equity loan and used the proceeds to pay off credit card obligations and other debt. During 1998, he paid the following amounts of interest:

On his personal residence	$12,000
On the cabin	4,800
On the home equity loan	5,000
On credit card obligations	1,200

    What amount, if any, must Tom recognize as an AMT adjustment in 1998?

49. Gail pays investment interest of $45,000. She has interest income of $12,000 on taxable bonds, $6,000 on tax-exempt bonds that are private activity bonds, and $5,000 on tax-exempt bonds that are not private activity bonds. Her other investment expenses are $3,000, none of which relates to the tax-exempt bonds.
    a. What is Gail's deduction for investment interest for regular income tax purposes?
    b. What is the amount of her investment interest carryover for regular income tax purposes?
    c. What is the amount of the adjustment for AMT purposes?

50. Bill, who is single with no dependents, had AGI of $100,000 in 1998. His AGI included net investment income of $15,000 and gambling income of $1,100. Bill incurred the following expenses during the year, all of which resulted in itemized deductions for income tax purposes:

Medical expenses (before 7.5%-of-AGI floor)	$11,000
State income taxes	3,200
Personal property tax	2,000
Real estate tax	8,400
Interest on personal residence	12,200
Interest on vacation home (never rented to others)	3,800
Interest on home equity loan (proceeds were used to buy a new automobile)	2,700
Investment interest expense	3,300
Charitable contribution	5,000
Casualty loss (after $100 floor, before 10%-of-AGI floor)	13,000
Unreimbursed employee expenses (before 2%-of-AGI floor)	2,400
Gambling losses	900

What is the amount of Bill's AMT adjustment for itemized deductions in 1998, and is it positive or negative?

51. Peggy, who is single and has no dependents, had taxable income of $148,000 and tax preferences of $57,500 in 1998. She did not itemize deductions for regular income tax purposes. Compute Peggy's AMT exemption and AMTI for 1998.

52. Hector owns a silver mine that he purchased several years ago for $800,000. His adjusted basis at the beginning of the year is $300,000. For the year, he deducts depletion of $450,000 (greater of cost depletion of $230,000 or percentage depletion of $450,000) for regular income tax purposes.
    a. Calculate Hector's AMT adjustment.
    b. Calculate Hector's adjusted basis for regular income tax purposes.
    c. Calculate Hector's adjusted basis for AMT purposes.

53. Amos incurred and expensed intangible drilling costs (IDC) of $70,000. His net oil and gas income was $60,000. What is the amount of Amos's tax preference item for IDC?

54. Jack, who is single with no dependents and does not itemize, provides you with the following information for 1998:

Short-term capital loss	$ 5,000
Long-term capital gain	25,000
Municipal bond interest received on private activity bonds acquired in 1990	9,000
Dividends from General Motors	1,500
Excess of FMV over cost of incentive stock options (the rights became freely transferable and not subject to a substantial risk of forfeiture in 1998)	35,000

What is the total amount of Jack's tax preference items and AMT adjustments for 1998?

55. Jason receives $10,000 of interest on bonds issued by the State of Iowa that are appropriately classified as private activity bonds. Related carrying costs are $1,000.
    a. Determine the effect on Jason's regular taxable income.
    b. Determine the effect on AMTI.
    c. Calculate the amount of Jason's AMT adjustment.

56. Rosa and Steve, who are married, had taxable income of $150,000 for 1998. They had positive AMT adjustments of $40,000, negative AMT adjustments of $10,000, and tax preference items of $67,500.
    a. Compute their AMTI.
    b. Compute their tentative minimum tax.

57. Tara, who is single, has no dependents and does not itemize. She has the following items relative to her tax return for 1998:

Bargain element from the exercise of an incentive stock option (no restrictions apply to the stock)	$ 45,000
Accelerated depreciation on leased equipment acquired before 1987 (straight-line depreciation would have yielded $26,000)	41,000
Percentage depletion in excess of property's adjusted basis	50,000
Taxable income for regular income tax purposes	121,000

    a. Determine Tara's AMT adjustments and preferences for 1998.
    b. Calculate the AMT (if any) for 1998.

58. Lynn is single and has no dependents. Based on the financial information presented below, compute Lynn's AMT for 1998.

Income:	
Salary	$33,000
Taxable interest on corporate bonds	1,800
Dividend income	1,900
Business income	64,000
Expenditures:	
Medical expenses	12,000
State income taxes	6,000
Real estate taxes	8,500
Mortgage (qualified housing) interest	9,200
Investment interest	5,500
Cash contributions to various charities	2,900

Additional information:
    a. The $64,000 business income is from Acme Office Supplies Company, a sole proprietorship Lynn owns and operates. Acme claimed MACRS depreciation of $3,175 on real property used in the business. ADS depreciation on the property would have been $2,500.
    b. Lynn received interest of $30,000 on City of Columbus private activity bonds.

59. Bonnie, who is single, had taxable income of $0 in 1998. She has positive timing adjustments of $200,000 and AMT exclusion items of $100,000 for the year. What is the amount of Bonnie's AMT credit for carryover to 1999?

60. Aqua, Inc., a calendar year corporation, has the following gross receipts and taxable income for 1994–1998:

Year	Gross Receipts	Taxable Income
1994	$11,000,000	$3,000,000
1995	4,800,000	900,000
1996	5,300,000	1,500,000
1997	4,600,000	700,000
1998	8,500,000	1,900,000

    a. Is Aqua subject to the AMT for 1998?
    b. Is Aqua subject to the AMT for 1999?

61. Gray Corporation (a calendar year corporation) reports the following information for the years listed below:

	1997	1998	1999
Unadjusted AMTI	$3,000	$2,000	$5,000
Adjusted current earnings	4,000	3,000	2,000

Compute the ACE adjustment for each year.

62. In each of the following independent situations, determine the tentative AMT:

	AMTI (Before the Exemption Amount)
Quincy Corporation	$150,000
Redland Corporation	160,000
Tanzen Corporation	320,000

63. Amber, Inc., has taxable income of $200,000. During the year, Amber paid dividends of $30,000. The corporation had $20,000 of positive AMT adjustments and $25,000 of tax preferences.
    a. Calculate Amber's regular income tax liability.
    b. Calculate Amber's AMTI and AMT.

CUMULATIVE PROBLEMS

64. Ron T. Freeman, age 38, is divorced and has no dependents. He pays alimony of $24,000 per year to his former wife, Kate. Kate's husband was killed in a hunting accident in 1998. At the time of the accident, their baby was only six weeks old. Ron decided to invest $5,000 each year in a mutual fund in Kate's baby's name to be used as a college fund. He made the initial $5,000 investment in 1998. Ron's Social Security number is 444–11–2222, and Kate's is 555–67–2222. Ron's address is 201 Front Street, Missoula, MT 59812. He is independently wealthy as a result of having inherited sizable holdings in real estate and corporate stocks and bonds. Ron is a minister at First Methodist Church, but he accepts no salary from the church. However, he does reside in the church's parsonage free of charge. The rental value of the parsonage is $600 a month. The church also provides him a cash grocery allowance of $150 a week. Examination of Ron's financial records provides the following information for 1998:
    a. On January 16, 1998, Ron sold 2,000 shares of stock for a gain of $30,000. The stock was acquired four years ago.
    b. He received $40,000 of interest on private activity bonds.
    c. He received gross rent income of $145,000 from an apartment complex he owns and manages.
    d. Expenses related to the apartment complex, which he acquired in 1983, were $190,000.
    e. Ron's dividend and interest income (on a savings account) totaled $26,000.
    f. On October 9, 1996, Ron exercised his rights under Egret Corporation's incentive stock option plan. For an option price of $20,000, he acquired stock worth $55,000. The stock became freely transferable in 1998.
    g. Ron had the following potential itemized deductions *from* AGI:

       • $3,000 fair market value of stock contributed to Methodist Church (basis of stock was $2,000). He owned the stock for five years.

       • $2,000 interest on consumer purchases.

       • $2,900 state and local taxes.

       • $7,000 medical expenses (before 7.5% floor) for himself and $4,000 of hospital expenses associated with Kate's deceased husband.

       • $100 for a safe deposit box that is used to store investments and related legal documents.

       • $10,000 of losses associated with playing the state lottery. Ron had no winnings during 1998. Any net winnings would be contributed to the church.

    Compute Ron's tax liability, including AMT if applicable, before prepayments or credits, for 1998. Suggested software (if available): *TurboTax*.

65. Robert M. and Jane R. Armstrong live at 1802 College Avenue, Carmel, IN 46302. They are married and file a joint return for 1997. The Armstrongs have two dependent children, Ellen J. and Sean M., who are 10-year-old twins. Ellen's Social Security number is 333–42–3368, and Sean's is 333–42–3369. Robert pays child support of $3,000 for Amy, his 17-year-old daughter from his previous marriage. Amy's Social Security number is 111–22–4300. According to the divorce decree, Margaret, Robert's former wife, has legal custody of Amy. Margaret provides the balance of Amy's support (about $7,000).

Robert (224–36–9987) is a factory foreman, and Jane (443–56–3421) is a computer systems analyst. The Armstrongs' W-2 forms for 1997 reflect the following information:

	Robert	Jane
Salary (Indiana Foundry, Inc.)	$56,000	
Salary (Carmel Computer Associates)		$80,000
Federal income tax withheld	7,170	15,200
Social Security wages	56,000	65,400
Social Security withheld	3,472	4,055
Medicare wages	56,000	80,000
Medicare tax withheld	812	1,160
State wages	56,000	80,000
State income tax withheld	1,650	2,400

In addition to their salaries, the Armstrongs had the following income items in 1997:

Interest income (Carmel Sanitation District Bonds)	$14,800
Interest income (Carmel National Bank)	2,100
Dividend income (Able Computer Corporation)	2,900
Gambling income	3,000

Jane inherited $200,000 from her grandfather in January and invested the money in the Carmel Sanitation District Bonds, which are private activity bonds.

The Armstrongs incurred the following expenses during 1997:

Medical expenses (doctor and hospital bills)	$16,725
Real property tax on personal residence	4,200
Mortgage interest on personal residence (reported on Form 1098)	5,000
Investment interest expense	1,900
Contributions to Salvation Army	18,000
Gambling losses	3,750

On March 1, Robert and Jane contributed Ace stock to the Carmel Salvation Army, a public charity. They had acquired the stock on February 9, 1979, for $1,500. The stock was listed on the New York Stock Exchange at a value of $18,000 on the date of the contribution.

Robert received a gift of 25 acres of land from his Uncle Ted on May 15. The appraised value of the land at the date of the gift was $63,000, and Uncle Ted's adjusted basis was $10,000. Uncle Ted was not required to pay any gift tax.

Use Forms 1040, 4952, 6251, and 8283 and Schedules A and B to compute the tax liability (including AMT) for Robert and Jane Armstrong for 1997. Suggested software (if available): *TurboTax*. Write a letter to the Armstrongs indicating whether they have a refund or balance due for 1997, and suggest possible tax planning strategies for 1998.

RESEARCH PROBLEMS

*Note: Use the **RIA OnPoint System 4 Student Version CD-ROM**, which is available to accompany this text, in preparing solutions to the Research Problems. Alternatively, tax research materials found in a standard tax library can be used.*

Research Problem 1. Tony Bost is a full-time gambler whose only source of income is money that he wins from his gambling activities. The IRS contends that Tony's gambling losses should be treated as itemized deductions for purposes of computing the AMT. Tony argues that the gambling losses should be treated as trade or business expenses. Write a letter to Tony that contains your advice on the classification of the gambling losses. Also prepare a memo for the tax files. Tony's address is 200 Cole Lane, Wichita Falls, TX 76308.

Research Problem 2. Carol owns two warehouses that were placed in service before 1987. Accelerated depreciation for 1998 on Warehouse A was $12,000, and straight-line depreciation would have been $8,000. On Warehouse B, accelerated depreciation was $6,000, and straight-line depreciation would have been $7,500. What is the amount of Carol's tax preference for excess depreciation in 1998?

Research Problem 3. Stuart is a journalist for a metropolitan newspaper. He has a degree in journalism from a major midwestern university.

For the past 10 years, Stuart has prepared his own income tax return. He finds doing so to be challenging and stimulating and believes that he pays lower taxes than he would if he hired a tax return preparer.

His 1997 return is audited. Although it included an AMT form (Form 6251), Stuart had not prepared it properly. Data from his Form 1040 were transferred to the wrong line in several places. In other cases, positive adjustments were not included because Stuart had failed to calculate them (e.g., did not recalculate itemized deductions for AMT purposes and did not have a positive adjustment for the personal exemption). Based on the IRS's calculation, a deficiency of $3,000 was assessed. Stuart's response to the IRS is that Form 6251 is ambiguous and misleading and, therefore, he should not be liable for the AMT. Evaluate Stuart's argument.

Partial list of research aids:
William M. Christine, 66 TCM 1025, T.C.Memo. 1993–473.

Research Problem 4. On his 1997 Federal income tax return, Walter deducted state income taxes of $8,000 for amounts withheld and estimated tax payments made in 1997. When he filed his 1997 state income tax return in April 1998, he discovered that he had overpaid his state income taxes by $1,500. Rather than having the $1,500 refunded to him, he treated it as a 1998 estimated tax payment. The year 1997 was not an AMT year for Walter.

In preparing his 1998 Federal income tax return, Walter is confused about how he should treat the $1,500 in calculating his Federal income tax liability. He knows that under the § 111 tax benefit rule, he should include the $1,500 in gross income in calculating his regular taxable income. However, since he is going to be subject to the AMT, he is uncertain as to how he should treat the $1,500 in calculating AMT. He thinks that the amount could be treated as a negative adjustment in converting taxable income to AMTI if 1997 had been an AMT year. Since it was not, Walter is unsure of the treatment.

Advise Walter on the appropriate treatment of the $1,500 in calculating his 1998 Federal income tax liability.

Use the tax resources of the Internet to address the following questions. Do not restrict your search to the World Wide Web, but include a review of newsgroups and general reference materials, practitioner sites and resources, primary sources of the tax law, chat rooms and discussion groups, and other opportunities.

Research Problem 5. Locate an outstanding proposal to modify the structure or scope of the AMT for individuals. Describe the proposal, the entity making the proposal, and potential motivations for submitting the modification to Congress.

Research Problem 6.   Go to one of the tax newsgroups and post a short note on one of the following items relative to individuals who are subject to the AMT.
   a. Interest deductions on vacation homes.
   b. Charitable contributions of appreciated securities.
   c. Tax preparation fees.

TEAM PROJECT: ARTHUR ANDERSEN TAX CHALLENGE CASES

For more information on the Arthur Andersen Tax Challenge Cases, refer to Chapter 1, page 1–37.

Information related to tax issues and problems that are discussed in this chapter may be found in the

Day and Ball case on pages: None
Fence case on pages 44, 56, and 64

Read and analyze the case you have been assigned and *identify* any issues and problems that are related to material covered in this chapter. If the information provided in the case is complete, prepare answers for this part of the case at this time. If you need information that is contained in the later parts of the case, write a memo summarizing the questions or problems so you can prepare a complete answer at a later date.

Tax Credits and Payment Procedures

LEARNING OBJECTIVES

After completing Chapter 13, you should be able to:

1. Explain how tax credits are used as a tool of Federal tax policy.

2. Distinguish between refundable and nonrefundable credits and understand the order in which they can be used by taxpayers.

3. Describe various business-related tax credits.

4. Describe several other tax credits that are available primarily to individual taxpayers.

5. Understand the tax withholding and payment procedures applicable to employers.

6. Understand the payment procedures applicable to self-employed persons.

7. Identify tax planning opportunities related to tax credits and payment procedures.

As explained in Chapter 1, Federal tax law often serves other purposes besides merely raising revenue for the government. Evidence of equity, social, and economic considerations, among others, is found throughout the tax law. These considerations also bear heavily in the area of **tax credits.** Consider the following examples:

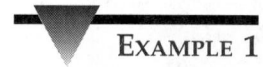

EXAMPLE 1

Paul and Peggy, husband and wife, are both employed outside the home. Their combined salaries are $50,000. However, after paying for child care expenses of $2,000 on behalf of their daughter, Polly, the net economic benefit from both spouses working is $48,000. The child care expenses are, in a sense, business related since they would not have been incurred if both spouses did not work outside the home. If no tax benefits are associated with the child care expenditures, $50,000 is subject to tax.

Another couple, Alicia and Diego, also have a child, John. Diego stays at home to care for John (the value of those services is $2,000) while Alicia earns a $48,000 salary. Because the value of Diego's services rendered is not subject to tax, only Alicia's earnings of $48,000 are subject to tax. ▼

The credit for child and dependent care expenses mitigates the inequity felt by working taxpayers who must pay for child care services in order to work outside the home.

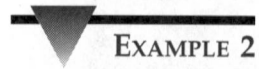

EXAMPLE 2

Olaf is a retired taxpayer who received $10,000 of Social Security benefits as his only source of income in 1998. His Social Security benefits are excluded from gross income. Therefore, Olaf's income tax is $0. In 1998, Olga, a single taxpayer 66 years of age, has, as her sole source of income, $10,000 from a pension plan funded by her former employer. Assuming Olga has no itemized deductions or deductions *for* AGI, her income tax for 1998 (before credits) is $300, based on the following computation:

Pension plan benefits	$ 10,000
Less: Basic standard deduction	(4,250)
Additional standard deduction	(1,050)
Personal exemption	(2,700)
Taxable income	$ 2,000
Income tax (at 15%)	$ 300

▼

The tax credit for elderly or disabled taxpayers was enacted to mitigate this inequity.

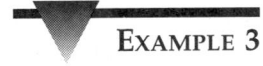

EXAMPLE 3

Jane is a single parent who depends on the government's "safety net" for survival—she receives Aid for Dependent Children in the amount of $10,000 per year. However, she very much wishes to work. Jane has located a job that will pay $10,500 per year and has found an individual to care for her child at no cost. But, with the $803.25 ($10,500 × 7.65%) payroll deduction for Social Security and Medicare taxes, the economic benefit from working is less than remaining reliant on the government ($9,696.75 as compared to $10,000). ▼

To help offset the effect of Social Security and Medicare taxes on wages of the working poor and to provide an incentive to work, the earned income credit is used to increase the after-tax earnings of qualified individuals. In addition, the earned income credit helps offset the regressive nature of certain taxes, such as the Social Security and Medicare taxes, which impose a relatively larger burden on low-income taxpayers than on more affluent taxpayers.

These three tax credits and many of the other important tax credits available to individuals and other types of taxpayers are a major focus of this chapter. The chapter begins by discussing important tax policy considerations relevant to tax credits. Tax credits are categorized as being either refundable or nonrefundable. The distinction between refundable and nonrefundable credits is important because it may affect the taxpayer's ability to enjoy a tax benefit from a particular credit.

Next an overview of the priority of tax credits is presented. The credit portion of the chapter continues with a discussion of the credits available to businesses and to individual taxpayers and the ways in which credits enter into the calculation of the tax liability.

The Federal tax system has long been based on the pay-as-you-go concept. That is, taxpayers or their employers are required to make regular deposits with the Federal government during the year as payment toward the tax liability that will be determined at the end of the tax year. These deposits are in effect refundable credits. The chapter concludes with a discussion of procedures used in calculating tax deposits, special problems encountered by self-employed persons when estimating their tax payments, and penalties imposed on underpayments.

TAX POLICY CONSIDERATIONS

1 LEARNING OBJECTIVE
Explain how tax credits are used as a tool of Federal tax policy.

Congress has generally used tax credits to achieve social or economic objectives or to promote equity among different types of taxpayers. For example, the disabled access credit was enacted to accomplish a social objective: to encourage taxpayers to renovate older buildings so they would be in compliance with the Americans with Disabilities Act. This Act requires businesses and institutions to make their facilities more accessible to persons with various types of disabilities. As another example, the foreign tax credit, which has been a part of the law for decades, has as its purpose the economic and equity objectives of mitigating the burden of multiple taxation on a single stream of income.

A tax credit should not be confused with an income tax deduction. Certain expenditures of individuals (e.g., business expenses) are permitted as deductions from gross income in arriving at adjusted gross income (AGI). Additionally, individuals are allowed to deduct certain nonbusiness and investment-related expenses *from* AGI. While the tax benefit received from a tax deduction depends on the tax rate, a tax credit is not affected by the tax rate of the taxpayer.

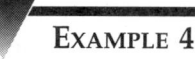

EXAMPLE 4

Assume Congress wishes to encourage a certain type of expenditure. One way to accomplish this objective is to allow a tax credit of 25% for such expenditures. Another way is to allow an itemized deduction for the expenditures. Assume Abby's tax rate is 15%, while Bill's tax rate is 39.6%. In addition, assume that Carmen does not incur enough qualifying expenditures to itemize deductions. The following tax benefits are available to each taxpayer for a $1,000 expenditure:

	Abby	**Bill**	**Carmen**
Tax benefit if a 25% credit is allowed	$250	$250	$250
Tax benefit if an itemized deduction is allowed	150	396	–0–

As these results indicate, tax credits provide benefits on a more equitable basis than do tax deductions. Equally apparent is that the deduction approach in this case benefits only taxpayers who itemize deductions, while the credit approach benefits all taxpayers who make the specified expenditure. ▼

For many years, Congress has used the tax credit provisions of the Code liberally in implementing tax policy. Although budget constraints and economic considerations often have dictated the repeal of some credits, other credits, such as those applicable to expenses incurred for child and dependent care, have been kept to respond to important social policy considerations. Still other credits, such as the one available to low-income workers, have been retained based on economic and equity considerations. Finally, as the myriad of tax proposals so frequently pending before Congress makes clear, the use of tax credits as a tax policy tool continues to evolve as economic and political circumstances change.

▼ **EXHIBIT 13–1**
Partial Listing of Refundable and
Nonrefundable Credits

Refundable Credits

Taxes withheld on wages
Earned income credit

Nonrefundable Credits

Credit for child and dependent care expenses
Credit for the elderly or disabled
Adoption expenses credit
Child tax credit
Education tax credits
Foreign tax credit
General business credit, which is the sum of the
following:

- Tax credit for rehabilitation expenditures
- Business energy credits
- Work opportunity tax credit*
- Welfare-to-work credit**
- Research activities credit***
- Low-income housing credit
- Disabled access credit

---

*Not available for employees hired after June 30, 1998.
**Not available for employees hired after April 30, 1999.
***Scheduled to expire after June 30, 1998.

OVERVIEW AND PRIORITY OF CREDITS

REFUNDABLE VERSUS NONREFUNDABLE CREDITS

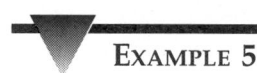 **LEARNING OBJECTIVE**
Distinguish between refundable
and nonrefundable credits and
understand the order in which
they can be used by taxpayers.

As illustrated in Exhibit 13–1, certain credits are refundable while others are non-refundable. **Refundable credits** are paid to the taxpayer even if the amount of the credit (or credits) exceeds the taxpayer's tax liability.

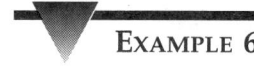 **EXAMPLE 5**

Ted, who is single, had taxable income of $21,000 in 1998. His income tax from the 1998 Tax Rate Schedule is $3,150. During 1998, Ted's employer withheld income tax of $3,500. Ted is entitled to a refund of $350 because the credit for tax withheld on wages is a refundable credit. ▼

Nonrefundable credits are not paid if they exceed the taxpayer's tax liability.

EXAMPLE 6

Tina is single, age 67, and retired. Her taxable income for 1998 is $1,320, and the tax on this amount is $198. Tina's tax credit for the elderly is $225. This credit can be used to reduce her net tax liability to zero, but it will not result in a refund, even though the credit ($225) exceeds Tina's tax liability ($198). This result occurs because the tax credit for the elderly is a nonrefundable credit. ▼

Some nonrefundable credits, such as the foreign tax credit, are subject to carry-over provisions if they exceed the amount allowable as a credit in a given year. Other nonrefundable credits, such as the tax credit for the elderly (refer to Example

6), are not subject to carryover provisions and are lost if they exceed the limitations. Because some credits are subject to carryover provisions while others are not, the order in which credits are offset against the tax liability is important. The Code provides that nonrefundable credits are to be offset against a taxpayer's income tax liability in the order shown in Exhibit 13–1.

GENERAL BUSINESS CREDIT

As shown in Exhibit 13–1, the **general business credit** is comprised of a number of other credits, each of which is computed separately under its own set of rules. The general business credit combines these credits into one amount to limit the amount of business credits that can be used to offset a taxpayer's income tax liability. The idea behind combining the credits is to prevent a taxpayer from completely avoiding an income tax liability in any one year by offsetting it with business credits that would otherwise be available.

Two special rules apply to the general business credit. First, any unused credit must be carried back 1 year, then forward 20 years. Second, for any tax year, the general business credit is limited to the taxpayer's *net income tax* reduced by the greater of:[1]

- The *tentative minimum tax*.
- 25 percent of *net regular tax liability* that exceeds $25,000.[2]

In order to understand the general business credit limitation, several terms need defining:

- *Net income tax* is the sum of the regular tax liability and the alternative minimum tax reduced by certain nonrefundable tax credits.
- *Tentative minimum tax* for this purpose is reduced by the foreign tax credit allowed.
- *Regular tax liability* is determined from the appropriate tax table or tax rate schedule, based on taxable income. However, the regular tax liability does not include certain taxes (e.g., alternative minimum tax).
- *Net regular tax liability* is the regular tax liability reduced by certain nonrefundable credits (e.g., credit for child and dependent care expenses, foreign tax credit).

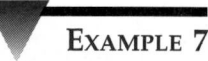
EXAMPLE 7

Floyd's general business credit for the current year is $70,000. His net income tax is $150,000, tentative minimum tax is $130,000, and net regular tax liability is $150,000. He has no other tax credits. Floyd's general business credit allowed for the tax year is computed as follows:

Net income tax	$ 150,000
Less: The greater of	
• $130,000 (tentative minimum tax)	
• $31,250 [25% × ($150,000 – $25,000)]	(130,000)
Amount of general business credit allowed for tax year	$ 20,000

Floyd then has $50,000 ($70,000 – $20,000) of unused general business credits that may be carried back or forward as discussed below. ▼

---

[1] § 38(c).
[2] This amount is $12,500 for married taxpayers filing separately unless one of the spouses is not entitled to the general business credit.

TREATMENT OF UNUSED GENERAL BUSINESS CREDITS

Effective for tax years beginning after December 31, 1997, unused general business credits are initially carried back one year and are applied to reduce the tax liability during that year. Thus, the taxpayer may receive a tax refund as a result of the carryback. Any remaining unused credits are then carried forward 20 years.[3] For unused general business credits arising in tax years beginning before January 1, 1998, the carryback period is 3 years and the carryforward period is 15 years.

A FIFO method is applied to the carryovers, carrybacks, and utilization of credits earned during a particular year. The oldest credits are used first in determining the amount of the general business credit. The FIFO method minimizes the potential for loss of a general business credit benefit due to the expiration of credit carryovers, since the earliest years are used before the current credit for the taxable year.

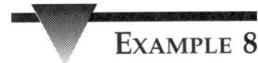

EXAMPLE 8

This example illustrates the use of general business credit carryovers.

General business credit carryovers		
1995	$ 4,000	
1996	6,000	
1997	2,000	
Total carryovers	$ 12,000	
1998 general business credit		$ 40,000
Total credit allowed in 1998 (based on tax liability)	$ 50,000	
Less: Utilization of carryovers		
1995	(4,000)	
1996	(6,000)	
1997	(2,000)	
Remaining credit allowed	$ 38,000	
Applied against		
1998 general business credit		(38,000)
1998 unused amount carried forward to 1999		$ 2,000

SPECIFIC BUSINESS-RELATED TAX CREDIT PROVISIONS

3 **LEARNING OBJECTIVE**
Describe various business-related tax credits.

Each component of the general business credit is determined separately under its own set of rules. The components are explained here in the order listed in Exhibit 13–1.

TAX CREDIT FOR REHABILITATION EXPENDITURES

Taxpayers are allowed a tax credit for expenditures incurred to rehabilitate industrial and commercial buildings and certified historic structures. The **rehabilitation expenditures credit** is intended to discourage businesses from moving from older, economically distressed areas (e.g., inner city) to newer locations and to encourage the preservation of historic structures. The current operating features of this credit follow:[4]

---

[3]§ 39(a)(1).   [4]§ 47.

Rate of the Credit for Rehabilitation Expenses	Nature of the Property
10%	Nonresidential buildings and residential rental property, other than certified historic structures, originally placed in service before 1936
20%	Nonresidential and residential certified historic structures

When taking the credit, the basis of a rehabilitated building must be reduced by the full rehabilitation credit allowed.[5]

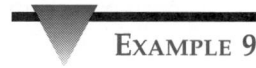
EXAMPLE 9

Juan spent $60,000 to rehabilitate a building (adjusted basis of $40,000) that had originally been placed in service in 1932. He is allowed a credit of $6,000 (10% × $60,000) for rehabilitation expenditures. Juan then increases the basis of the building by $54,000 [$60,000 (rehabilitation expenditures) – $6,000 (credit allowed)]. If the building were a historic structure, the credit allowed would be $12,000 (20% × $60,000), and the building's depreciable basis would increase by $48,000 [$60,000 (rehabilitation expenditures) – $12,000 (credit allowed)]. ▼

To qualify for the credit, buildings must be substantially rehabilitated. A building has been *substantially rehabilitated* if qualified rehabilitation expenditures exceed the greater of:

- The adjusted basis of the property before the rehabilitation expenditures, or
- $5,000.

Qualified rehabilitation expenditures do not include the cost of acquiring a building, the cost of facilities related to a building (such as a parking lot), and the cost of enlarging an existing building. Stringent rules apply concerning the retention of internal and external walls.

Recapture of Tax Credit for Rehabilitation Expenditures. The rehabilitation credit taken must be recaptured if the rehabilitated property is disposed of prematurely or if it ceases to be qualifying property. The **rehabilitation expenditures credit recapture** is based on a holding period requirement of five years and is added to the taxpayer's regular tax liability in the recapture year. In addition, the recapture amount is *added* to the adjusted basis of the rehabilitation expenditures for purposes of determining the amount of gain or loss realized on the property's disposition.

The portion of the credit recaptured is a specified percentage of the credit that was taken by the taxpayer. This percentage is based on the period the property was held by the taxpayer, as shown in Table 13–1.

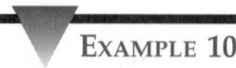
EXAMPLE 10

On March 15, 1995, Rashad placed in service $30,000 of rehabilitation expenditures on a building qualifying for the 10% credit. A credit of $3,000 ($30,000 × 10%) was allowed, and the basis of the building was increased by $27,000 ($30,000 – $3,000). The building was sold on December 15, 1998. Rashad must recapture a portion of the rehabilitation credit based on the schedule in Table 13–1. Because he held the rehabilitated property for more than three years but less than four, 40% of the credit, or $1,200, must be added to his 1998 tax liability. Also, the adjusted basis of the rehabilitation expenditures is increased by the $1,200 recapture amount. ▼

▼ **TABLE 13–1**
Recapture Calculation for
Rehabilitation Expenditures
Credit

If the Property Is Held for	The Recapture Percentage Is
Less than 1 year	100
One year or more but less than 2 years	80
Two years or more but less than 3 years	60
Three years or more but less than 4 years	40
Four years or more but less than 5 years	20
Five years or more	0

BUSINESS ENERGY CREDITS

For many years, **business energy credits** have been allowed to encourage the conservation of natural resources and the development of alternative energy sources (to oil and natural gas). Over the years, some of these credits have expired while new ones have been added. The most important business energy credits that remain are the 10 percent credits for solar energy property and geothermal property.

WORK OPPORTUNITY TAX CREDIT

The **work opportunity tax credit** was enacted to encourage employers to hire individuals from one or more of a number of targeted and economically disadvantaged groups who start work before June 30, 1998. Examples of such targeted persons include qualified ex-felons, high-risk youths, food stamp recipients, veterans, summer youth employees, and persons receiving certain welfare benefits.[6]

Computation of the Work Opportunity Tax Credit: General. The credit generally is equal to 40 percent of the first $6,000 of wages (per eligible employee) for the first 12 months of employment. Thus, the credit is not available for any wages paid to an employee after the first year of employment. If the employee's first year overlaps two of the employer's tax years, however, the employer may take the credit over two tax years. If the credit is elected, the employer's tax deduction for wages is reduced by the amount of the credit. For an employer to qualify for the 40 percent credit, the employee must (1) be certified by a designated local agency as being a member of one of the targeted groups and (2) have completed at least 400 hours of service to the employer. If an employee meets the first condition but not the second, the credit rate is reduced to 25 percent provided the employee has completed a minimum of 120 hours of service to the employer.

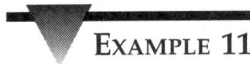

EXAMPLE 11

In January 1998, Green Company hires four individuals who are certified to be members of a qualifying targeted group. Each employee is paid wages of $8,000 during the year. Green Company's work opportunity credit is $9,600 [($6,000 × 40%) × 4 employees]. If the tax credit is taken, Green must reduce its deduction for wages paid by $9,600. No credit is available for wages paid to these employees after their first year of employment. ▼

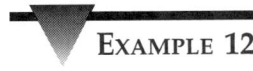

EXAMPLE 12

On June 1, 1998, Maria, a calendar year taxpayer, hired Joe, a member of a targeted group, and obtained the required certification. During the last seven months of 1998, Joe is paid $3,500 for more than 400 hours of work. Maria is allowed a credit of $1,400 ($3,500 × 40%) for 1998. Joe continues to work for Maria in 1999 and is paid $7,000 through May 31, 1999. Because up to $6,000 of first-year wages are eligible for the credit, Maria is allowed a 40% credit on $2,500 [$6,000 − $3,500 (wages paid in 1998)] of wages paid in 1999, or $1,000

---

[6]§ 51.

($2,500 × 40%). None of Joe's wages paid after May 31, the end of the first year of employment, is eligible for the credit. Likewise, under current law, no credit is allowed for wages paid to persons newly hired after June 30, 1998. ▼

Computation of the Work Opportunity Tax Credit: Qualified Summer Youth Employees. The credit for qualified summer youth employees is allowed on wages for services during any 90-day period between May 1 and September 15. The maximum wages eligible for the credit are $3,000 per summer youth employee. The credit rate is the same as that under the general provision for the work opportunity tax credit. If the employee continues employment after the 90-day period as a member of another targeted group, the amount of the wages eligible for the general work opportunity tax credit as a member of the new target group is reduced by the wages paid to the employee as a qualified summer youth employee.

A *qualified summer youth employee* must be age 16 or 17 on the hiring date. An additional requirement for qualifying is that the individual's principal place of abode must be within an empowerment zone or an enterprise community.

WELFARE-TO-WORK CREDIT

Beginning in 1998, a **welfare-to-work credit**[7] is available to employers hiring individuals who have been long-term recipients of family assistance welfare benefits. In general, long-term recipients are those individuals who are certified by a designated local agency as being a member of a family receiving assistance under a public aid program for at least an 18-month period ending on the hiring date. Unlike the work opportunity credit, which applies only to first-year wages paid to qualified individuals, the welfare-to-work credit is available for qualified wages paid in the first two years of employment. If an employee's first and second work years overlap two or more of the employer's tax years, the employer may take the credit during the applicable tax years. If the welfare-to-work credit is taken, the employer's tax deduction for wages is reduced by the amount of the credit.

An employer is prohibited from taking both the work opportunity credit and the welfare-to-work credit for wages paid to a qualified employee in a given tax year. The welfare-to-work credit is not available for employees hired after April 30, 1999.

Maximum Credit. The credit is equal to 35 percent of the first $10,000 of qualified wages paid to an employee in the first year of employment, plus 50 percent of the first $10,000 of qualified wages paid in the second year of employment, resulting in a maximum credit per qualified employee of $8,500 [$3,500 (year 1) + $5,000 (year 2)]. The credit rate is higher for second-year wages to encourage employers to retain qualified individuals, thereby promoting the overall welfare-to-work goal.

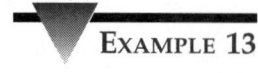
EXAMPLE 13

In April 1998, Blue Company hired three individuals who are certified as long-term family assistance recipients. Each employee is paid $12,000 during 1998. Two of the three individuals continue to work for Blue Company in 1999, earning $9,000 each during the year. No additional qualified employees are hired in 1999. Blue Company's welfare-to-work credit is $10,500 [(35% × $10,000) × 3 employees] for 1998 and $9,000 [(50% × $9,000) × 2 employees] for 1999. ▼

---

[7]§ 51A.

RESEARCH ACTIVITIES CREDIT

To encourage research and experimentation, usually described as research and development (R & D), a credit is allowed for certain qualifying expenditures paid or incurred from July 1, 1996 through June 30, 1998. The **research activities credit** is the *sum* of two components: an incremental research activities credit and a basic research credit.[8]

Incremental Research Activities Credit. The incremental research activities credit applies at a 20 percent rate to the *excess* of qualified research expenses for the taxable year (the credit year) over the base amount.

In general, *research expenditures* qualify if the research relates to discovering technological information that is intended for use in the development of a new or improved business component of the taxpayer. Such expenses qualify fully if the research is performed in-house (by the taxpayer or employees). If the research is conducted by persons outside the taxpayer's business (under contract), only 65 percent of the amount paid qualifies for the credit.[9]

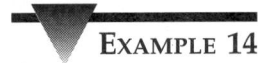
EXAMPLE 14

George incurs the following research expenditures for the tax year.

In-house wages, supplies, computer time	$50,000
Paid to Cutting Edge Scientific Foundation for research	30,000

George's qualified research expenditures are $69,500 [$50,000 + ($30,000 × 65%)]. ▼

Beyond the general guidelines described above, the Code does not give specific examples of qualifying research. However, the credit is *not* allowed for research that falls into certain categories, including the following:[10]

- Research conducted after the beginning of commercial production of the business component.
- Surveys and studies such as market research, testing, and routine data collection.
- Research conducted *outside* the United States.
- Research in the social sciences, arts, or humanities.

Determining the *base amount* involves a relatively complex series of computations. In addition, when the research credit is available for less than a full tax year, as is the case under current law, the base amount is adjusted further. A discussion of these computations is beyond the scope of this presentation.

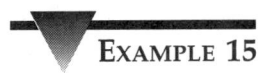
EXAMPLE 15

Jack, a calendar year taxpayer, incurs qualifying research expenditures of $200,000 during 1998. Assuming the base amount is $100,000, the incremental research activities credit is $20,000 [($200,000 − $100,000) × 20%]. ▼

Qualified research and experimentation expenditures are not only eligible for the 20 percent credit, but can also be *expensed* in the year incurred.[11] In this regard, a taxpayer has two choices:[12]

---

[8]§ 41.
[9]§ 41(b)(3)(A). In the case of payments to a qualified research consortium, 75% of the amount paid qualifies for the credit.
[10]§ 41(d).

[11]§ 174. Also refer to the discussion of rules for deducting research and experimental expenditures in Chapter 7.
[12]§ 280C(c).

- Use the full credit and reduce the expense deduction for research expenses by 100 percent of the credit.
- Retain the full expense deduction and reduce the credit by the product of 100 percent of the credit times the maximum corporate tax rate.

As an alternative to the expense deduction, the taxpayer may *capitalize* the research expenses and *amortize* them over 60 months or more. In this case, the amount capitalized and subject to amortization is reduced by the full amount of the credit *only* if the credit exceeds the amount allowable as a deduction.

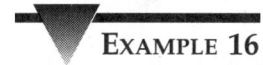
EXAMPLE 16

Assume the same facts as in Example 15, which shows that the potential incremental research activities credit is $20,000. The expense that the taxpayer can deduct and the credit amount are as follows:

	Credit Amount	Deduction Amount
• Full credit and reduced deduction		
$20,000 – $0	$20,000	
$200,000 – $20,000		$180,000
• Reduced credit and full deduction		
$20,000 – [(1.00 × $20,000) × .35]	13,000	
$200,000 – $0		200,000
• Full credit and capitalize and elect to amortize costs over 60 months		
$20,000 – $0	20,000	
($200,000/60) × 12		40,000

Basic Research Credit.   Corporations (other than S corporations or personal service corporations) are allowed an additional 20 percent credit for basic research payments from July 1, 1996 through June 30, 1998, in *excess* of a base amount. This credit is not available to individual taxpayers. *Basic research payments* are defined as amounts paid in cash to a qualified basic research organization, such as a college or university or a tax-exempt organization operated primarily to conduct scientific research.

Basic research is defined generally as any original investigation for the advancement of scientific knowledge not having a specific commercial objective. The definition excludes basic research conducted outside the United States and basic research in the social sciences, arts, or humanities. This reflects the intent of Congress to encourage high-tech research in the United States.

The calculation of this additional credit for basic research expenditures is complex and is based on expenditures in excess of a specially defined base amount.[13] The portion of the basic research expenditures not in excess of the base amount is treated as a part of the qualifying expenditures for purposes of the regular credit for incremental research activities.

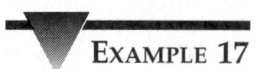
EXAMPLE 17

Orange Corporation, a qualifying corporation, pays $75,000 to a university for basic research. Assume that Orange's base amount for the basic research credit is $50,000. The basic research activities credit allowed is $5,000 [($75,000 – $50,000) × 20%]. The $50,000 of basic research expenditures that equal the base amount are treated as research expenses for purposes of the regular incremental research activities credit. ▼

---

[13]§ 41(e).

13–13

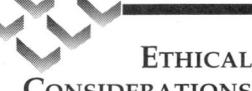

ETHICAL
CONSIDERATIONS

When Does "Research" Qualify as R & D?

The research activities credit is designed to encourage taxpayers to engage in research relating to the discovery of technological information that is intended for use in the development of a new or improved business component of the taxpayer.

You are employed as a staff accountant for a privately held corporation that manufactures medical equipment. During the current year, the corporation purchases new communication software and related document-management systems with the goal of enhancing employee efficiency and productivity. To familiarize employees with these new systems, an outside firm is hired to conduct numerous software training seminars during the first six months the new systems are in place. Substantial costs are incurred in connection with these training seminars. Not surprisingly, various inefficiencies are also encountered until the employees have had sufficient training and time to use the new systems.

The corporation's new president, ever mindful of the company's profitability and tax position, urges you to claim the research activities credit with respect to the software training costs. The president justifies this position on the grounds that the employees were "researching" the new software and its use. How do you respond?

LOW-INCOME HOUSING CREDIT

To encourage building owners to make affordable housing available for low-income individuals, Congress has made a credit available to owners of qualified low-income housing projects.[14]

More than any other, the **low-income housing credit** is influenced by nontax factors. For example, certification of the property by the appropriate state or local agency authorized to provide low-income housing credits is required. These credits are issued based on a nationwide allocation.

The amount of the credit is based on the qualified basis of the property. The qualified basis depends on the number of units rented to low-income tenants. Tenants are low-income tenants if their income does not exceed a specified percentage of the area median gross income. The amount of the credit is determined by multiplying the qualified basis by the applicable percentage; the credit is allowed over a 10-year period if the property continues to meet the required conditions.

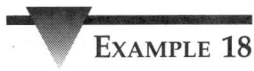

EXAMPLE 18

Sarah spends $100,000 to build a qualified low-income housing project completed January 1, 1998. The entire project is rented to low-income families. The credit rate for property placed in service during January 1998 is 8.41%.[15] Sarah may claim a credit of $8,410 ($100,000 × 8.41%) in 1998 and in each of the following nine years. Generally, first-year credits are prorated based on the date the project is placed in service. A full year's credit is taken in each of the next nine years, and any remaining first-year credit is claimed in the eleventh year. ▼

Recapture of a portion of the credit may be required if the number of units set aside for low-income tenants falls below a minimum threshold, if the taxpayer disposes of the property or the interest in it, or if the taxpayer's amount at risk decreases.

---

[14]§ 42.
[15]Rev.Rul. 98–4, I.R.B. No. 2, 18. The rate is subject to adjustment every month by the IRS.

DISABLED ACCESS CREDIT

The **disabled access credit** is designed to encourage small businesses to make their businesses more accessible to disabled individuals. The credit is available for any eligible access expenditures paid or incurred by an eligible small business. The credit is calculated at the rate of 50 percent of the eligible expenditures that exceed $250 but do not exceed $10,250. Thus, the maximum amount for the credit is $5,000 ($10,000 × 50%).[16]

An *eligible small business* is one that during the previous year either had gross receipts of $1 million or less or had no more than 30 full-time employees. An eligible business can include a sole proprietorship, partnership, regular corporation, or S corporation.

Eligible access expenditures are generally any reasonable and necessary amounts that are paid or incurred to make certain changes to facilities. These changes must involve the removal of architectural, communication, physical, or transportation barriers that would otherwise make a business inaccessible to disabled and handicapped individuals. Examples of qualifying projects include installing ramps, widening doorways, and adding raised markings on elevator control buttons. However, eligible expenditures do *not* include amounts that are paid or incurred in connection with any facility that has been placed into service after the enactment (November 5, 1990) of the provision.

To the extent a disabled access credit is available, no deduction or credit is allowed under any other provision of the tax law. The adjusted basis for depreciation is reduced by the amount of the credit.

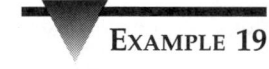

EXAMPLE 19

This year Red, Inc., an eligible business, made $11,000 of capital improvements to business realty that had been placed in service in June 1990. The expenditures were intended to make Red's business more accessible to the disabled and were considered eligible expenditures for purposes of the disabled access credit. The amount of the credit is $5,000 [($10,250 − $250) × 50%]. Although $11,000 of eligible expenditures were incurred, only the excess of $10,250 over $250 qualifies for the credit. Further, the depreciable basis of the capital improvement is $6,000 because the basis must be reduced by the amount of the credit [$11,000 (cost) − $5,000 (amount of the credit)]. ▼

OTHER TAX CREDITS

EARNED INCOME CREDIT

4   **LEARNING OBJECTIVE**
Describe several other tax credits that are available primarily to individual taxpayers.

The **earned income credit,** which has been a part of the law for many years, consistently has been justified as a means of providing tax equity to the working poor. More recently, the credit has also been designed to help offset regressive taxes that are a part of our tax system, such as the gasoline and Social Security taxes. In addition, the credit has been intended to encourage economically disadvantaged individuals to become contributing members of the workforce.[17]

In 1998, the earned income credit is determined by multiplying a maximum amount of earned income by the appropriate credit percentage (see Table 13–2). Generally, earned income includes employee compensation and net earnings from self-employment but excludes items such as interest, dividends, pension benefits, and alimony. If a taxpayer has children, the credit percentage used in the calculation depends on the number of qualifying children. Thus, in 1998, the maximum earned

---

[16]§ 44.   [17]§ 32.

▼ **TABLE 13–2**

Earned Income Credit and
Phase-out Percentages

Tax Year	Number of Qualifying Children	Maximum Earned Income	Credit Percentage	Phase-out Begins	Phase-out Percentage	Phase-out Ends
1998	One child	$6,680	34.00	$12,260	15.98	$26,473
	Two or more children	9,390	40.00	12,260	21.06	30,095
	No qualifying children	4,460	7.65	5,570	7.65	10,030
1997	One child	6,500	34.00	11,930	15.98	25,760
	Two or more children	9,140	40.00	11,930	21.06	29,290
	No qualifying children	4,340	7.65	5,430	7.65	9,770

income credit for a taxpayer with one qualifying child is $2,271 ($6,680 × 34%) and $3,756 ($9,390 × 40%) for a taxpayer with two or more qualifying children. However, the maximum earned income credit is phased out completely if the taxpayer's earned income or AGI exceeds certain thresholds as shown in Table 13–2.[18] To the extent that the greater of earned income or AGI exceeds $12,260 in 1998, the difference, multiplied by the appropriate phase-out percentage, is subtracted from the maximum earned income credit.

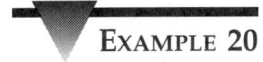

EXAMPLE 20

In 1998, Grace, who otherwise qualifies for the earned income credit, receives wages of $14,000 and has no other income. She has one qualifying child. Grace's earned income credit is $2,271 ($6,680 × 34%) reduced by $278 [($14,000 – $12,260) × 15.98%]. Thus, Grace's earned income credit is $1,993. If Grace has two or more qualifying children, the calculation would produce a credit of $3,756 ($9,390 × 40%) reduced by $366 [($14,000 – $12,260) × 21.06%]. Thus, Grace's earned income credit would be $3,390. ▼

Earned Income Credit Table.   It is not necessary to compute the credit as was done in Example 20. As part of the tax simplification process, the IRS issues an Earned Income Credit Table for the determination of the appropriate amount of the earned income credit. This table and a worksheet are included in the instructions to both Form 1040 and Form 1040A.

Eligibility Requirements.   *Eligibility* for the credit may depend not only on the taxpayer meeting the earned income and AGI thresholds, but also on whether he or she has a qualifying child. A *qualifying child* must meet the following tests:

- *Relationship test.* The individual must be a son, daughter, descendant of the taxpayer's son or daughter, stepson, stepdaughter, or an eligible foster child of the taxpayer. A legally adopted child of the taxpayer is considered the same as a child by blood.
- *Residency test.* The qualifying child must share the taxpayer's principal place of abode, which must be located within the United States, for more than one-half of the tax year of the taxpayer. Temporary absences (e.g., due to illness or education) are disregarded for purposes of this test. For foster children, however, the child must share the taxpayer's home for the entire year.

---

[18]§ 32(a)(2)(B). AGI is modified for the purpose of this calculation. See § 32(c)(5).

- *Age test.* The child must not have reached the age of 19 (24 in the case of a full-time student) as of the end of the tax year. In addition, a child who is permanently and totally disabled at any time during the year is considered to meet the age test.

In addition to being available for taxpayers with qualifying children, the earned income credit is also available to certain *workers without children*. However, this provision is available only to taxpayers aged 25 through 64 who cannot be claimed as a dependent on another taxpayer's return. As shown in Table 13–2, the credit for 1998 is calculated on a maximum earned income of $4,460 times 7.65 percent and reduced by 7.65 percent of earned income over $5,570. This credit is phased out completely at $10,030.

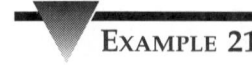

EXAMPLE 21

Walt, who is single, 28 years of age, and is not claimed as a dependent on anyone else's return, earns $6,500 during 1998. Even though he does not have any qualifying children, he qualifies for the earned income credit. His credit is $341 ($4,460 × 7.65%) reduced by $71 [($6,500 − $5,570) × 7.65%]. Thus, Walt's earned income credit is $270. If, instead, Walt's earned income is $4,900, his earned income credit is $341. In this situation, there is no phase-out of the maximum credit because his earned income is not in excess of $5,570. ▼

Advance Payment.   The earned income credit is a form of negative income tax (a refundable credit for taxpayers who do not have a tax liability). An eligible individual may elect to receive advance payments of the earned income credit from his or her employer (rather than receiving the credit from the IRS upon filing the tax return). The amount that can be received in advance is limited to 60 percent of the credit that is available to a taxpayer with only one qualifying child. If this election is made, the taxpayer must file a certificate of eligibility (Form W–5) with his or her employer and *must* file a tax return for the year the income is earned.

TAX CREDIT FOR ELDERLY OR DISABLED TAXPAYERS

The credit for the elderly was originally enacted in 1954 as the retirement income credit to provide tax relief on retirement income for individuals who were not receiving substantial benefits from tax-free Social Security payments.[19]

Currently, the **tax credit for the elderly or disabled** applies to the following:

- Taxpayers age 65 or older.
- Taxpayers under age 65 who are retired with a permanent and total disability and who have disability income from a public or private employer on account of the disability.

The *maximum* allowable credit is $1,125 (15% × $7,500 of qualifying income), but the credit will be less for a taxpayer who receives Social Security benefits or has AGI exceeding specified amounts. Under these circumstances, the base used in the credit computation is reduced. Many taxpayers receive Social Security benefits or have AGI high enough to reduce the base for the credit to zero.

The eligibility requirements and the tax computation are somewhat complicated. Consequently, an individual may elect to have the IRS compute his or her tax and the amount of the tax credit.

---

[19]§ 22. This credit is not subject to indexation.

"EARNED INCOME CREDIT" OR "EASY INCOME FOR CHEATS"?

The earned income credit was designed to mitigate the effects of the regressive tax system on low-income taxpayers and to encourage individuals to seek work rather than welfare. Recently, however, the benefits the credit provides are being underused and abused.

To be considered a success, the earned income credit would have to be used by those persons it is intended to help. For example, workers who have a qualifying child and income below a certain amount are allowed to receive advance payment of the credit. However, less than 1 percent of qualifying Americans take advantage of this advance payment opportunity. Some commentators contend that the provisions, which have been changed more than 10 times since 1976, have become overly complex, difficult to comply with, and almost unusable by the low-income workers the credit is intended to aid. Estimates show that 14 percent of persons qualifying for the credit fail to claim it.

On the other hand, others who don't qualify have found the lure of the credit too good to pass up. In a recent IRS study, one-half of the electronically filed returns that claimed the earned income credit contained errors suspected to be intentional. In fact, some of the tax fraud schemes involving the credit have been initiated by persons in prison. One IRS investigation uncovered a scam operating out of the Maine Correctional Center. A dozen current and former inmates were indicted for improperly seeking refunds for earned income credit claims. Another taxpayer convicted of cheating the government by improperly using the credit testified before Congress that the earned income tax credit could stand for "easy income for cheats!" In an attempt to curb such abuses, Congress recently enacted several compliance provisions aimed at denying the credit to persons who negligently or fraudulently claimed the earned income credit in prior years.

▼ **TABLE 13–3**
Base Amounts for Tax Credit for Elderly or Disabled Taxpayers

Status	Base Amount
Single, head of household, or surviving spouse	$5,000
Married, joint return, only one spouse qualified	5,000
Married, joint return, both spouses qualified	7,500
Married, separate returns, spouses live apart the entire year	3,750 each

The credit generally is based on an initial amount (referred to as the *base amount*) and the filing status of the taxpayer in accordance with Table 13–3. To qualify for the credit, married taxpayers who live together must file a joint return. For taxpayers under age 65 who are retired on permanent and total disability, the base amounts could be less than those shown in Table 13–3 because these amounts are limited to taxable disability income.

This initial base amount is *reduced* by (1) Social Security, Railroad Retirement, and certain excluded pension benefits and (2) one-half of the taxpayer's AGI in excess of a threshold amount, which is a function of the taxpayer's filing status. The credit may be calculated using the procedure presented in the following template:

Base amount ($3,750, $5,000, or $7,500—see Table 13–3)	
Less: Qualifying nontaxable benefits	_____
One-half of excess of AGI over: $7,500 for single, head of household, or surviving spouse taxpayers $10,000 for married taxpayers $5,000 for married taxpayers filing separately	
Total reductions	_____
Balance subject to credit	══════
Multiply balance subject to credit by 15%—this is the tax credit allowed	══════

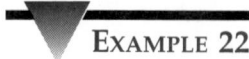

EXAMPLE 22   Paul and Peggy, husband and wife, are both over age 65 and received Social Security benefits of $2,400 in the current year. On a joint return, they reported AGI of $14,000.

Base amount ($3,750, $5,000, or $7,500—see Table 13–3)		$ 7,500
Less: Qualifying nontaxable benefits	$ 2,400	
One-half of excess of AGI over: $7,500 for single, head of household, or surviving spouse taxpayers $10,000 for married taxpayers $5,000 for married taxpayers filing separately	2,000	
Total reductions		(4,400)
Balance subject to credit		$ 3,100
Multiply balance subject to credit by 15%—this is the tax credit allowed		$ 465

Schedule R of Form 1040 (see Appendix B) is used to calculate and report the credit.

FOREIGN TAX CREDIT

Both individual taxpayers and corporations may claim a tax credit for foreign income tax paid on income earned and subject to tax in another country or a U.S. possession.[20] As an alternative, a taxpayer may claim a deduction instead of a credit.[21] In most instances, the **foreign tax credit (FTC)** is advantageous since it provides a direct offset against the tax liability.

The purpose of the FTC is to mitigate double taxation since income earned in a foreign country is subject to both U.S. and foreign taxes. However, the ceiling limitation formula may result in some form of double taxation or taxation at rates in excess of U.S. rates when the foreign tax rates are higher than the U.S. rates. This is a distinct possibility because U.S. tax rates are lower than those of many foreign countries.

Other special tax treatments applicable to taxpayers working outside the United States include the foreign earned income exclusion (refer to Chapter 5) and

---

[20]Section 27 provides for the credit, but the qualifications and calculation procedure for the credit are contained in §§ 901–908.   [21]§ 164.

limitations on deducting expenses of employees working outside the United States (refer to Chapter 9). Recall from the earlier discussion that a taxpayer may not take advantage of *both* the FTC and the foreign earned income exclusion.

Computation. Taxpayers are required to compute the FTC based upon an overall limitation.[22] The FTC allowed is the *lesser* of the foreign taxes imposed or the *overall limitation* determined according to the following formula:

$$\frac{\text{Foreign-source taxable income}}{\text{Worldwide taxable income}} \times \begin{array}{c} \text{U.S. tax} \\ \text{before FTC} \end{array}$$

For individual taxpayers, worldwide taxable income in the overall limitation formula is determined *before* personal and dependency exemptions are deducted.

EXAMPLE 23

In 1998, Carlos, a calendar year taxpayer, has $10,000 of income from Country Y, which imposes a 15% tax, and $20,000 from Country Z, which imposes a 50% tax. He has taxable income of $59,200 from within the United States, is married filing a joint return, and claims two dependency exemptions. Thus, although Carlos's taxable income for purposes of determining U.S. tax is $89,200, taxable income amounts used in the limitation formula are not reduced by personal and dependency exemptions. Thus, for this purpose, taxable income is $100,000 [$89,200 + (4 × $2,700)]. Assume that Carlos's U.S. tax before the credit is $19,471. Overall limitation:

$$\frac{\text{Foreign-source taxable income}}{\text{Worldwide taxable income}} = \frac{\$30,000}{\$100,000} \times \$19,471 = \$5,841$$

In this case, $5,841 is allowed as the FTC because this amount is less than the $11,500 of foreign taxes imposed [$1,500 (Country Y) + $10,000 (Country Z)]. ▼

Thus, the overall limitation may result in some of the foreign income being subjected to double taxation. Unused FTCs [e.g., the $5,659 ($11,500 − $5,841) from Example 23] can be carried back two years and forward five years.[23]

Only foreign income taxes, war profits taxes, and excess profits taxes (or taxes paid in lieu of such taxes) qualify for the credit. In determining whether or not a tax is an income tax, U.S. criteria are applied. Thus, value added taxes (VAT), severance taxes, property taxes, and sales taxes do not qualify because they are not regarded as taxes on income. Such taxes may be deductible, however.

ADOPTION EXPENSES CREDIT

Beginning in 1997, qualifying adoption expenses paid or incurred by a taxpayer may give rise to the **adoption expenses credit**.[24] The provision is intended to assist taxpayers who incur nonrecurring costs directly associated with the adoption process, such as adoption fees, attorney fees, court costs, social service review costs, and transportation costs.

Up to $5,000 of costs incurred to adopt an eligible child qualify for the credit.[25] An eligible child is one who is:

- under 18 years of age at the time of the adoption or
- physically or mentally incapable of taking care of himself or herself.

---

[22]§ 904.

[23]§ 904(c) and Reg. § 1.904–2(g), Example 1.

[24]§ 23.

[25]§ 23(b)(1). The maximum amount of qualifying expenses increases to $6,000 for a "child with special needs." See § 23(d)(3).

A taxpayer may claim the credit in the year qualifying expenses were paid or incurred if the expenses were paid or incurred *during or after* the year in which the adoption was finalized. For qualifying expenses paid or incurred in a tax year *prior* to the year when the adoption was finalized, the credit must be claimed in the year the adoption was finalized. A married couple must file a joint return.

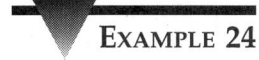

EXAMPLE 24

In late 1998, Sam and Martha pay $2,500 in legal fees, adoption fees, and other expenses directly related to the adoption of an infant daughter, Susan. In 1999, they pay an additional $1,000, and in 2000, the year in which the adoption becomes final, they pay $3,000. Sam and Martha are eligible for a $5,000 credit in 2000. ▼

The amount of the credit that is otherwise available is phased out for taxpayers whose AGI (modified for this purpose) exceeds $75,000, and the credit is completely eliminated when the AGI reaches $115,000. The resulting credit is calculated by reducing the allowable credit (determined without this reduction) by the allowable credit multiplied by the ratio of the excess of the taxpayer's AGI over $75,000 to $40,000.

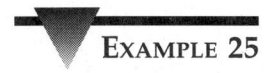

EXAMPLE 25

Assume the same facts as in the previous example, except that Sam and Martha's AGI is $100,000 in each of the relevant years. As a result, their available credit in 2000 is reduced from $5,000 to $1,875 {$5,000 − [$5,000($25,000/$40,000)]}. ▼

The credit is nonrefundable and is available to taxpayers only in a year in which this credit and the other nonrefundable credits do not exceed the taxpayer's tax liability. However, any unused adoption expenses credit may be carried over for up to five years, being utilized on a first-in, first-out basis.

CHILD TAX CREDIT

For the first time, beginning in 1998, individual taxpayers are permitted to take a tax credit based solely on the *number* of their dependent children under age 17. This **child tax credit**[26] is one of several "family-friendly" provisions enacted as part of the Taxpayer Relief Act of 1997 (TRA of 1997). To be eligible for the credit, the child must be under age 17, a U.S. citizen, and claimed as a dependent on the taxpayer's return.

Maximum Credit and Phase-outs.   The maximum credit available is $400 per child beginning in 1998, rising to $500 per child in 1999 and years thereafter. The available credit is phased out for higher-income taxpayers beginning when AGI[27] reaches $110,000 for joint filers ($55,000 for married taxpayers filing separately) and $75,000 for single taxpayers. The credit is phased out by $50 for each $1,000 (or part thereof) of AGI above the threshold amounts. Since the maximum credit amount available to taxpayers depends on the number of qualifying children, the income level at which the credit is phased out completely also depends on the number of children qualifying for the credit.

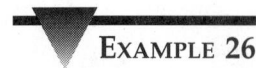

EXAMPLE 26

Juanita and Alberto are married and file a joint tax return claiming their two children, ages six and eight, as dependents. Their AGI for 1998 is $122,400. Juanita and Alberto's available child tax credit for 1998 is $150, computed as their maximum credit of $800 ($400 × 2 children) reduced by a $650 phase-out. Since Juanita and Alberto's AGI is in excess of the $110,000 threshold, the maximum credit must be reduced by $50 for every $1,000 (or part thereof)

---

[26]§ 24.

[27]AGI is modified for purposes of this calculation. See § 24(b)(1).

above the threshold amount {$50 × [($122,400 − $110,000)/$1,000]}. Thus, the credit reduction equals $650 [$50 × 13 (rounded from 12.4)]. Therefore, Juanita and Alberto's child tax credit is $150 for 1998. ▼

CREDIT FOR CHILD AND DEPENDENT CARE EXPENSES

A credit is allowed to taxpayers who incur employment-related expenses for child or dependent care.[28] The **credit for child and dependent care expenses** is a specified percentage of expenses incurred to enable the taxpayer to work or to seek employment. Expenses on which the credit for child and dependent care expenses is based are subject to limitations.

Eligibility.   To be eligible for the credit, an individual must maintain a household for either of the following:

- A dependent under age 13.
- A dependent or spouse who is physically or mentally incapacitated.

Generally, married taxpayers must file a joint return to obtain the credit. The credit may also be claimed by the custodial parent for a nondependent child under age 13 if the noncustodial parent is allowed to claim the child as a dependent under a pre-1985 divorce agreement or under a waiver in the case of a post-1984 agreement.

Eligible Employment-Related Expenses.   Eligible expenses include amounts paid for household services and care of a qualifying individual that are incurred to enable the taxpayer to be employed. Child and dependent care expenses include expenses incurred in the home, such as payments for a housekeeper. Out-of-the-home expenses incurred for the care of a dependent under the age of 13 also qualify for the credit. In addition, out-of-the-home expenses incurred for an older dependent or spouse who is physically or mentally incapacitated qualify for the credit if that person regularly spends at least eight hours each day in the taxpayer's household. This makes the credit available to taxpayers who keep handicapped older children and elderly relatives in the home instead of institutionalizing them. Out-of-the-home expenses incurred for services provided by a dependent care center will qualify only if the center complies with all applicable laws and regulations of a state or unit of local government.

Child care payments to a relative are eligible for the credit unless the relative is a dependent of the taxpayer or the taxpayer's spouse or is a child (under age 19) of the taxpayer.

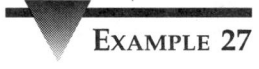

EXAMPLE 27   Wilma is an employed mother of an eight-year-old child. She pays her mother, Rita, $1,500 per year to care for the child after school. Wilma does not claim Rita as a dependent. Wilma pays her daughter Eleanor, age 17, $900 for the child's care during the summer. Of these amounts, only the $1,500 paid to Rita qualifies as employment-related child care expenses. ▼

Earned Income Ceiling.   The total for qualifying employment-related expenses is limited to an individual's earned income. For married taxpayers, this limitation applies to the spouse with the *lesser* amount of earned income. Special rules are provided for taxpayers with nonworking spouses who are disabled or are full-time students. If a nonworking spouse is physically or mentally disabled or is a full-time student, he or she is *deemed* to have earned income for purposes of this limitation.

---

[28]§ 21.

The deemed amount is $200 per month if there is one qualifying individual in the household or $400 per month if there are two or more qualifying individuals in the household. In the case of a student-spouse, the student's income is *deemed* to be earned only for the months that the student is enrolled on a full-time basis at an educational institution.

Calculation of the Credit.   In general, the credit is equal to a percentage of *unreimbursed* employment-related expenses up to $2,400 for one qualifying individual and $4,800 for two or more individuals. The credit rate varies between 20 percent and 30 percent, depending on the taxpayer's AGI. The following chart shows the applicable percentage for taxpayers as AGI increases:

Adjusted Gross Income		Applicable Rate of Credit
Over	**But Not Over**	
$ 0	$10,000	30%
10,000	12,000	29%
12,000	14,000	28%
14,000	16,000	27%
16,000	18,000	26%
18,000	20,000	25%
20,000	22,000	24%
22,000	24,000	23%
24,000	26,000	22%
26,000	28,000	21%
28,000	No limit	20%

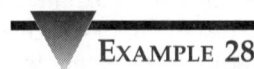

EXAMPLE 28

Nancy, who has two children under age 13, worked full-time while her spouse, Ron, was attending college for 10 months during the year. Nancy earned $21,000 and incurred $5,000 of child care expenses. Ron is *deemed* to be fully employed and to have earned $400 for each of the 10 months (or a total of $4,000). Since Nancy and Ron have AGI of $21,000, they are allowed a credit rate of 24%. Nancy and Ron are limited to $4,000 in qualified child care expenses (the lesser of $4,800 or $4,000). Therefore, they are entitled to a tax credit of $960 (24% × $4,000) for the year. ▼

Dependent Care Assistance Program.   Recall from Chapter 5 that a taxpayer is allowed an exclusion from gross income for a limited amount reimbursed for child or dependent care expenses. However, the taxpayer is not allowed both an exclusion from gross income and a child and dependent care credit on the same amount. The $2,400 and $4,800 ceilings for allowable child and dependent care expenses are reduced dollar for dollar by the amount of reimbursement.[29]

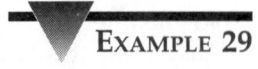

EXAMPLE 29

Assume the same facts as in Example 28, except that of the $5,000 paid for child care, Nancy was reimbursed $2,500 by her employer under a qualified dependent care assistance program. Under the employer's plan, the reimbursement reduces Nancy's taxable wages. Thus, Nancy and Ron have AGI of $18,500 ($21,000 – $2,500). The maximum amount of child care expenses for two or more dependents of $4,800 is reduced by the $2,500 reimbursement, resulting in a tax credit of $575 [25% × ($4,800 – $2,500)]. ▼

[29]§ 21(c).

Reporting Requirements. The credit is claimed by completing and filing Form 2441, Credit for Child and Dependent Care Expenses (see Appendix B).

EDUCATION TAX CREDITS

Beginning in 1998, two new credits, the **HOPE scholarship credit** and **lifetime learning credit,**[30] are available to help qualifying low- and middle-income individuals defray the cost of higher education. The credits, both of which are nonrefundable, are available for qualifying tuition and related expenses incurred by students pursuing undergraduate or graduate degrees or vocational training. Room, board, and book costs are ineligible for the credits.

Maximum Credit. The HOPE scholarship credit permits a maximum credit of $1,500 per year (100 percent of first $1,000 of tuition expenses plus 50 percent of the next $1,000 of tuition expenses) for the *first two years* of postsecondary education. The lifetime learning credit permits a maximum credit of 20 percent of tuition expenses (up to $5,000 per year) incurred after June 30, 1998, and in a year in which the HOPE scholarship credit is not claimed with respect to a given student's tuition and related expenses. The lifetime learning credit is intended for individuals who are beyond the first two years of postsecondary education. Beginning in 2003, the lifetime learning credit will be available on the first $10,000 of qualifying costs incurred per year.

Eligible Individuals. Both education credits are available for qualified tuition and related expenses incurred by a taxpayer, taxpayer's spouse, or taxpayer's dependent. The HOPE scholarship credit is available per eligible student, while the lifetime learning credit is calculated per taxpayer. To be eligible for the HOPE credit, students must take at least one-half the full-time course load for at least one academic term at a qualifying educational institution. No comparable requirement exists for the lifetime learning credit. Therefore, taxpayers who are seeking new job skills or maintaining existing skills through graduate training or continuing education are eligible for the lifetime learning credit. Taxpayers who are married must file joint returns in order to claim either education credit.

Timing of Expenses. Qualifying tuition expenses must be *paid* during the tax year for education furnished by a qualifying institution during an academic year *beginning* during the tax year in question. If tuition expenses are paid during the tax year for an academic period beginning during the first three months of the following tax year, the expenses may be claimed during the payment year for purposes of the credit computation. This aspect of the credit computation permits taxpayers to prepay tuition expenses in order to maximize the available education credit. As a related item, qualifying tuition expenses paid with student loans are eligible for the education credits during the tax year when the costs are incurred and paid, not the tax year in which the loan is repaid.

Income Limitations. Both education credits are subject to income limitations and are combined for purposes of the limitation calculation. The allowable credit amount is phased out, beginning when the taxpayer's AGI[31] reaches $40,000 ($80,000 for married taxpayers filing jointly). The credits are completely eliminated when AGI reaches $50,000 ($100,000 for married filing jointly). The calculated credit amount is reduced by the extent to which AGI exceeds $40,000 ($80,000 for married

---

[30]§ 25A.

[31]AGI is modified for purposes of this calculation. See § 25A(d)(3).

filing jointly) as a percentage of the $10,000 ($20,000 for married filing jointly) phase-out range.

Restrictions on Double Tax Benefit. Taxpayers are prohibited from receiving a double tax benefit associated with qualifying educational expenses. Therefore, taxpayers who claim an education credit may not deduct the expenses, nor may they claim the credit for amounts that are otherwise excluded from income (e.g., scholarships and employer-paid educational assistance).

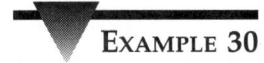

EXAMPLE 30

Dean and Audry are married, file a joint tax return, have modified AGI under $80,000, and have two children. During fall 1998, Raymond is beginning his freshman year at State University, and Kelsey is beginning her senior year. Both Raymond and Kelsey are full-time students and may be claimed as dependents on their parents' tax return. Raymond's qualifying tuition expenses and fees total $4,600 for the academic year ($2,300 per semester) while Kelsey's qualifying expenses total $5,200 for the academic year ($2,600 per semester). Dean and Audry pay the tuition and related expenses in full at the beginning of each semester. For 1998, Dean and Audry may claim a $1,500 HOPE scholarship credit [(100% × $1,000) + (50% × $1,000)] relating to Raymond's expenses and a $520 lifetime learning credit (20% × $2,600) relating to Kelsey's expenses. Kelsey's tuition expenses are ineligible for the HOPE credit because she is beyond the first two years of postsecondary education. Finally, Dean and Audry could have increased their available lifetime learning credit for 1998 by prepaying some of Kelsey's tuition expenses. ▼

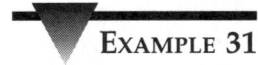

EXAMPLE 31

Assume the same facts as in Example 30, except that Dean and Audry's AGI for 1998 is $92,000. Dean and Audry are eligible to claim $808 in total education credits for 1998. Their available credits totaling $2,020 ($1,500 HOPE credit + $520 lifetime learning credit) must be reduced because their AGI exceeds the $80,000 limit for married taxpayers. The percentage reduction is computed as the amount by which AGI exceeds the limit, expressed as a percentage of the phase-out range, or [($92,000 − $80,000)/$20,000)], resulting in a 60% reduction. Therefore, the maximum available credit for 1998 is $808 ($2,020 × 40% allowable portion). ▼

PAYMENT PROCEDURES

5   **LEARNING OBJECTIVE**
Understand the tax withholding and payment procedures applicable to employers.

The tax law contains elaborate rules that require the prepayment of various Federal taxes. Consistent with the pay-as-you-go approach to the collection of taxes, these rules carry penalties for lack of compliance.[32] Prepayment procedures fall into two major categories: those applicable to employers and those applicable to self-employed persons. For employers, both payroll taxes (FICA and FUTA) and income taxes may be involved. With self-employed taxpayers, the focus is on the income tax and the self-employment tax.

PROCEDURES APPLICABLE TO EMPLOYERS

Employment taxes include FICA (Federal Insurance Contributions Act) and FUTA (Federal Unemployment Tax Act). The employer usually is responsible for withholding the employee's share of FICA (commonly referred to as Social Security tax) and appropriate amounts for income taxes. In addition, the employer must

---

[32]See, for example, § 3403 (employer liable for any taxes withheld and not paid over to the IRS), § 6656 (up to 15% penalty on amounts withheld and not paid over), and § 6654 (penalty for failure by an individual to pay estimated income taxes).

PAYING FOR COLLEGE—UNDERSTANDING THE TAX LAW MAY BE HALF THE BATTLE

Taxpayers with college-bound children are the beneficiaries of several new tax breaks courtesy of the Taxpayer Relief Act of 1997. Although these new provisions will cut the cost of a college education, many people will likely need help from their friendly neighborhood tax adviser to understand the law and take advantage of these new provisions.

In particular, the 1997 tax bill created five new ways to help pay for college. Beginning in 1998, parents can contribute $500 per year to an education individual retirement account for any child under age 18. No tax is due on the account earnings as long as the money is used for education expenses. Taxpayers will also be able to make penalty-free withdrawals from two other IRAs—a regular IRA or the new Roth IRA. The tax bill also expanded prepaid tuition plans to cover room and board costs in addition to tuition expenses and reinstated the deductibility of interest on student loans. Beginning in 1998, taxpayers can take an "above-the-line" deduction for up to $1,000 in student-loan interest, with the deduction rising to $2,500 in 2001.

Probably, the most significant tax breaks in the 1997 bill were the creation of two new education credits—the HOPE scholarship credit and the lifetime learning credit. The HOPE scholarship credit permits a maximum credit of $1,500 per year for the first two years of college tuition expenses. The lifetime learning credit can be used in subsequent years to save up to $1,000 per year in taxes if tuition expenses equal at least $5,000.

Although these tax law changes seem appealing, consider some of the intricacies involved in their use. To begin with, many of the benefits are phased out for higher-income taxpayers. For married taxpayers filing a joint return, the ability to contribute to an education IRA starts phasing out at $150,000, the student-loan interest deduction starts disappearing at $60,000, and the education credits begin phasing out at $80,000. Unfortunately, the complexity doesn't stop there.

Many of the new provisions are mutually exclusive to prevent taxpayers from receiving a double benefit. For example, taxpayers are prevented from contributing to both an education IRA and a state-sponsored prepaid tuition plan in the same year. Likewise, if money is withdrawn from an education IRA to pay for college, the taxpayer is prohibited from taking either education credit with respect to those expenditures. The new education credits can also create problems for taxpayers with Series EE savings bonds. If a taxpayer cashes in the bonds to pay for college and elects to exclude the bond interest from income, the credits are also unavailable.

Perhaps most subtle of all is the impact of the new education credits on a student's ability to receive financial aid. If the credits are used, the family's disposable income will rise, potentially reducing the amount of financial aid available in future years.

In sum, given the changes made by the 1997 bill, understanding the tax law may indeed be half the battle when paying for college.

SOURCE: Adapted from Jonathan Clements, "Tax Law Leads to Confusion about How to Pay for College," *Wall Street Journal*, August 26, 1997, p. C1.

match the FICA portion withheld and fully absorb the cost of FUTA. The sum of the employment taxes and the income tax withholdings must be paid to the IRS at specified intervals.

CONCEPT SUMMARY 13–1

Tax Credits

Credit	Computation	Comments
Tax withheld on wages (§ 31)	Amount is reported to employee on W–2 form.	Refundable credit.
Earned income (§ 32)	Amount is determined by reference to Earned Income Credit Table published by IRS. Computations of underlying amounts in Earned Income Credit Table are illustrated in Example 20.	Refundable credit. A form of negative income tax to assist low-income taxpayers. Earned income and AGI must be less than certain threshold amounts. Generally, one or more qualifying children must reside with the taxpayer.
Child and dependent care (§ 21)	Rate ranges from 20% to 30% depending on AGI. Maximum base for credit is $2,400 for one qualifying individual, $4,800 for two or more.	Nonrefundable personal credit. No carryback or carryforward. Benefits taxpayers who incur employment-related child or dependent care expenses in order to work or seek employment. Eligible dependents include children under age 13 or dependent (any age) or spouse who is physically or mentally incapacitated.
Elderly or disabled (§ 22)	15% of sum of base amount minus reductions for (a) Social Security and other nontaxable benefits and (b) excess AGI. Base amount is fixed by law (e.g., $5,000 for a single taxpayer).	Nonrefundable personal credit. No carryback or carryforward. Provides relief for taxpayers not receiving substantial tax-free retirement benefits.
Adoption expenses (§ 23)	Up to $5,000 of costs incurred to adopt an eligible child qualify for the credit. Taxpayer claims the credit in the year qualified expenses were paid or incurred if expenses were paid during or after year in which adoption was finalized. For expenses paid or incurred in a year prior to when adoption was finalized, credit must be claimed in year adoption was finalized.	Nonrefundable credit. Unused credit may be carried forward 5 years. Purpose is to assist taxpayers who incur nonrecurring costs associated with the adoption process.
Child (§ 24)	Credit is based on *number* of qualifying dependent children under age 17. Maximum credit is $400 per child in 1998 ($500 per child in 1999 and thereafter). Credit is phased out for higher-income taxpayers.	Nonrefundable credit. Purpose is to provide tax relief for low- to moderate-income families with children.
Education (§ 25A)	HOPE scholarship credit is available for qualifying tuition expenses of students in first two years of post-secondary education. Maximum credit is $1,500 per year per eligible student. Credit is phased out for higher-income taxpayers.	Nonrefundable credit. Credit is designed to help defray costs of first two years of higher education for low- to middle-income families.
	Lifetime learning credit permits a maximum credit of 20% of qualifying tuition expenses (up to $5,000 per year) for costs incurred after June 30, 1998, provided HOPE scholarship is not claimed with respect to those expenses. Credit is calculated per taxpayer, not per student, and is phased out for higher-income taxpayers.	Nonrefundable credit. Credit is designed to help defray costs of higher education beyond first two years, and for costs incurred in maintaining or improving existing job skills, for low- to middle-income taxpayers.

CONCEPT SUMMARY 13–1

Tax Credits—Continued

Credit	Computation	Comments
Foreign tax (§ 27)	Foreign income/total worldwide taxable income × U.S. tax = overall limitation. Lesser of foreign taxes imposed or overall limitation.	Nonrefundable credit. Unused credits may be carried back two years and forward five years. Purpose is to prevent double taxation of foreign income.
General business (§ 38)	May not exceed net income tax minus the greater of tentative minimum tax or 25% of net regular tax liability that exceeds $25,000.	Nonrefundable credit. Components include tax credit for rehabilitation expenditures, business energy credits, work opportunity tax credit, welfare-to-work credit, research activities credit, low-income housing credit, and disabled access credit. Unused credit may be carried back 1 year and forward 20 years. FIFO method applies to carryovers, carrybacks, and credits earned during current year.
Investment (§ 46)	Qualifying investment times energy percentage or rehabilitation percentage, depending on type of property. Part of general business credit and subject to its limitations.	Nonrefundable credit. Part of general business credit and therefore subject to same carryback, carryover, and FIFO rules. Energy percentage is 10%. Regular rehabilitation rate is 10%; rate for certified historic structures is 20%.
Research activities (§ 41)	Incremental credit is 20% of excess of computation year expenditures minus the base amount. Basic research credit is allowed to certain corporations for 20% of cash payments to qualified organizations that exceed a specially calculated base amount. To qualify for the credit, research expenditures must be made from July 1, 1996 through June 30, 1998.	Nonrefundable credit. Part of general business credit and therefore subject to same carryback, carryover, and FIFO rules. Purpose is to encourage high-tech research in the United States.
Low-income housing (§ 42)	Appropriate rate times eligible basis (portion of project attributable to low-income units).	Nonrefundable credit. Part of general business credit and therefore subject to same carryback, carryover, and FIFO rules. Credit is available each year for 10 years. Recapture may apply. Purpose is to encourage construction of housing for low-income individuals.
Disabled access (§ 44)	Credit is 50% of eligible access expenditures that exceed $250, but do not exceed $10,250. Maximum credit is $5,000.	Nonrefundable credit. Part of general business credit and therefore subject to same carryback, carryover, and FIFO rules. Available only to eligible small businesses. Purpose is to encourage small businesses to become more accessible to disabled individuals.

CONCEPT SUMMARY 13–1

Tax Credits—Continued

Credit	Computation	Comments
Work opportunity (§ 51)	Credit is limited to 40% of the first $6,000 of wages paid to each eligible employee. The employee must begin work before June 30, 1998.	Nonrefundable credit. Part of the general business credit and therefore subject to the same carryback, carryover, and FIFO rules. Purpose is to encourage employment of individuals in specified groups.
Welfare-to-work (§ 51A)	Credit is limited to 35% of first $10,000 of wages paid to eligible employee in first year of employment, plus 50% of first $10,000 of wages paid to eligible employee in second year of employment.	Nonrefundable credit. Part of general business credit and therefore subject to same carryback, carryover, and FIFO rules. Purpose is to encourage employment of long-term recipients of family assistance welfare benefits.

The key to employer compliance in this area involves the resolution of the following points:

- Ascertaining which employees and wages are covered by employment taxes and are subject to withholding for income taxes.
- Arriving at the amount to be paid and/or withheld.
- Reporting and paying employment taxes and income taxes withheld to the IRS on a timely basis through the use of proper forms.

Coverage Requirements.   Circular E, Employer's Tax Guide (Publication 15) and Employer's Supplemental Tax Guide (Publication 15–A), issued by the IRS, contain a discussion or listing of which employees and which wages require withholdings for income taxes and employment taxes. Excerpts from these publications appear in Exhibit 13–2. In working with Exhibit 13–2, consider the following observations:

- The designation "Exempt" in the income tax withholding column does not mean that the amount paid is nontaxable to the employee. It merely relieves the employer from having to withhold.

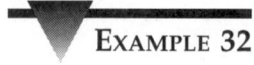

EXAMPLE 32   Lee works for Yellow Corporation and has the type of job where tips are not common but do occur. If Lee's total tips amount to less than $20 per month, Yellow Corporation need not withhold Federal income taxes on the tips. Nevertheless, Lee must include the tips in his gross income. ▼

- In some cases, income tax withholding is not required but is voluntary. This is designated "Exempt (withhold if both employer and employee voluntarily agree)."

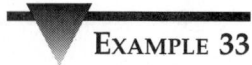

EXAMPLE 33   Pat is employed as a gardener by a wealthy family. In the past, he has encountered difficulty in managing his finances so as to be in a position to pay the income tax due every April 15. To ease the cash-flow problem that develops in April, Pat asks his employer to withhold income taxes from his wages. ▼

▼ **EXHIBIT 13–2**
Withholding Classifications

Special Classes of Employment and Special Types of Payments	Treatment under Different Employment Taxes		
	Income Tax Withholding	Social Security and Medicare	Federal Unemployment
Family employees:			
a. Child employed by parent (or by partnership consisting only of parents) in a trade or business.	Withhold	Exempt until age 18	Exempt until age 21
b. Spouse employed by spouse.	Withhold	Taxable if in course of spouse's business	Exempt
c. Parent employed by a child.	Withhold	Taxable if in course of the child's business.	Exempt
Household employees (domestic service in private homes; farmers, see Circular A).	Exempt (withhold if both employer and employee voluntarily agree).	Taxable if paid $1,000 or more in cash in 1998. Exempt if performed by an individual under age 18 during any portion of the calendar year and is not the principal occupation of the employee.	Taxable if employer paid cash wages of $1,000 or more (for all household employees) in any quarter in the current or preceding calendar year.
Interns working in hospitals.	Withhold	Taxable	Exempt
Meals and lodging.	a. Meals—Subject to withholding and taxable unless furnished for employer's convenience and on the employer's premises. b. Lodging—Subject to withholding and taxable unless furnished on employer's premises, for the employer's convenience, and as a condition of employment.		
Ministers of churches performing duties as such.*	Exempt (withhold if both the minister and the church voluntarily agree).	Exempt (withhold if both the church and the minister voluntarily agree)	Exempt
Moving expense reimbursement:			
a. Qualified expenses.	Exempt, unless you have knowledge that the employee deducted the expenses in a prior year.		
b. Nonqualified expenses.	Withhold	Taxable	Taxable
Newspaper carriers under age 18.	Exempt (withhold if both employer and employee voluntarily agree).	Exempt	Exempt
Severance or dismissal pay.	Withhold	Taxable	Taxable
Tips, if less than $20 in a month.	Exempt	Exempt	Exempt
Workers' compensation.	Exempt	Exempt	Exempt

*In the typical case, ministers are considered to be self-employed rather than employees of the church.

- The Social Security and Medicare (FICA) column refers to the employer's share. The same is true of the Federal Unemployment (FUTA) column since the employee does not contribute to this tax.

▼ **TABLE 13–4**
FICA Rates and Base

	Social Security Tax				Medicare Tax				
	Percent	×	Base Amount	+	Percent	×	Base Amount	=	Maximum Tax
1990	6.20%	×	$51,300	+	1.45%	×	$ 51,300	=	$3,924.45
1991	6.20%	×	53,400	+	1.45%	×	125,000	=	5,123.30
1992	6.20%	×	55,500	+	1.45%	×	130,200	=	5,328.90
1993	6.20%	×	57,600	+	1.45%	×	135,000	=	5,528.70
1994	6.20%	×	60,600	+	1.45%	×	Unlimited	=	Unlimited
1995	6.20%	×	61,200	+	1.45%	×	Unlimited	=	Unlimited
1996	6.20%	×	62,700	+	1.45%	×	Unlimited	=	Unlimited
1997	6.20%	×	65,400	+	1.45%	×	Unlimited	=	Unlimited
1998	6.20%	×	68,400	+	1.45%	×	Unlimited	=	Unlimited
1999 on	6.20%	×	*	+	1.45%	×	Unlimited	=	Unlimited

*Not yet determined.

Amount of FICA Taxes.   The FICA tax is comprised of two components: Social Security tax (old age, survivors, and disability insurance) *and* Medicare tax (hospital insurance). The tax rates and wage base under FICA have increased both frequently and substantially over the years. There appears to be every reason to predict that the rates and/or base amount will continue to rise in the future. As Table 13–4 shows, the top base amount differs for the Medicare portion (now unlimited) and for the Social Security portion. Also note that Table 13–4 represents the employee's share of the tax. The employer must match the employee's portion.

Withholdings from employees must continue until the maximum base amount is reached. In 1998, for example, FICA withholding ceases for the Social Security portion (6.2 percent) once the employee has earned wages subject to FICA in the amount of $68,400. For the Medicare portion (1.45 percent), however, the employer is required to withhold on all wages without limit. This contrasts with years prior to 1994 when a maximum base existed for the Medicare portion also.

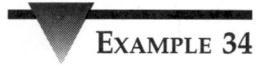

EXAMPLE 34   In 1998, Keshia earned a salary of $140,000 from her employer. Therefore, FICA taxes withheld from her salary are $4,241 ($68,400 × 6.2%) plus $2,030 ($140,000 × 1.45%) for a total of $6,271. In addition to paying the amount withheld from Keshia's salary to the government, her employer will also have to pay $6,271. ▼

In at least two situations, it is possible for an employee to have paid excess FICA taxes.

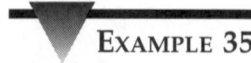

EXAMPLE 35   During 1998, Kevin changed employers in the middle of the year and earned $40,000 (all of which was subject to FICA) from each job. As a result, each employer withheld $3,060 [(6.2% × $40,000) + (1.45% × $40,000)] for a total of $6,120. Although each employer acted properly, Kevin's total FICA tax liability for the year is only $5,401 [(6.2% × $68,400) + (1.45% × $80,000)]. Thus, Kevin has overpaid his share of FICA taxes by $719 [$6,120 (amount paid) – $5,401 (amount of correct liability)]. He should claim this amount as a tax credit when filing his income tax return for 1998. The tax credit will reduce any income tax Kevin might owe or, possibly, generate a tax refund. ▼

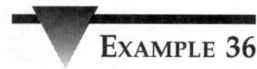

EXAMPLE 36   During 1998, Lori earned $60,000 from her regular job and $20,000 from a part-time job (all of which was subject to FICA). As a result, one employer withheld $4,590 [(6.2% × $60,000) + (1.45% × $60,000)] while the other employer withheld $1,530 [(6.2% × $20,000) + (1.45% × $20,000)] for a total of $6,120. Lori's total FICA tax liability for the year is

only $5,401 [(6.2% × $68,400) + (1.45% × $80,000)]. Thus, Lori has overpaid her share of FICA taxes by $719 [$6,120 (amount paid) – $5,401 (amount of correct liability)]. She should claim this amount as a tax credit when filing her income tax return for 1998. ▼

In Examples 35 and 36, the employee was subject to overwithholding. In both cases, however, the employee was able to obtain a credit for the excess withheld. The same result does not materialize for the portion paid by the employer. Since this amount is not refundable, in some situations employers may pay more FICA taxes than the covered employees.

The mere fact that a husband and wife are both employed does not, by itself, result in overwithholding of FICA taxes.

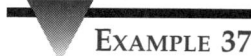

EXAMPLE 37

During 1998, Jim and Betty (husband and wife) are both employed, and each earns wages subject to FICA of $40,000. Accordingly, each has $3,060 FICA withheld [(6.2% × $40,000) + (1.45% × $40,000)] for a total of $6,120. Since neither spouse paid FICA tax on wages in excess of $68,400 (Social Security tax) [see Table 13–4], there is no overwithholding. ▼

A spouse employed by another spouse is subject to FICA. However, children under the age of 18 who are employed in a parent's trade or business are exempted.

ETHICAL CONSIDERATIONS

Being Paid Once Every Two Years

Sally is a CPA and the sole shareholder of her small public accounting practice, which has grown over the years. Sally has reached the point where she is financially comfortable with significant short-term and long-term savings balances. Because her practice involves a substantial amount of tax work, it is to her advantage to keep alert for possible tax savings strategies that she may be able to employ, either for her clients or for herself. One recent idea she has discovered involves manipulating the time at which her salary is paid in order to minimize the FICA taxes incurred by her corporation and herself.

In recent years, she has paid herself an annual salary of approximately $100,000 and the corresponding employer and employee portions of the FICA tax have been $11,382 (using the 1998 rates, the employer and employee portions of the FICA tax on $100,000 are calculated as [($68,400 × 6.2%) × 2 + ($100,000 × 1.45%) × 2]. Thus, over a two-year period, the FICA tax would aggregate to $22,764 ($11,382 × 2), based on an annual salary of $100,000 and without any changes in the FICA calculation. Alternatively, if Sally's corporation were to pay her a $200,000 salary *every other year*, the total FICA cost during the same two-year period would be $14,282 (using the 1998 rates, the employer and employee portions of the FICA tax on $200,000 are calculated as [($68,400 × 6.2%) × 2 + ($200,000 × 1.45%) × 2]. Therefore, if Sally were to implement this plan, her FICA tax savings would be $8,482 ($22,764 – $14,282). What are the ethical implications of Sally's plan?

Amount of Income Tax Withholding.   Arriving at the amount to be withheld for income tax purposes is not so simple. It involves three basic steps:[33]

---

[33]The withholding provisions are contained in §§ 3401 and 3402. These Sections will not be referenced specifically in the discussion that follows.

- Have the employee complete Form W–4, Employee's Withholding Allowance Certificate.
- Determine the employee's payroll period.
- Compute the amount to be withheld, usually using either the wage-bracket tables or the percentage method.

Form W–4 reflects the employee's marital status and **withholding allowances.** Generally, it need not be filed with the IRS and is retained by the employer as part of the payroll records.

The employer need not verify the number of exemptions claimed. Any misinformation in the form will be attributed to the employee. However, if the employer has reason to believe that the employee made a false statement, the IRS District Director should be notified. In the meantime, the Form W–4 should be honored. Employees are subject to both civil and criminal penalties for filing false withholding statements.

On the current Form W–4, an employee may claim *withholding allowances* for the following: personal exemptions for self and spouse (unless either is claimed as a dependent of another person) and dependency exemptions. One *special withholding allowance* may be claimed if the employee is single and has only one job, if the employee is married and has only one job and the spouse is not employed, or if wages from a second job or a spouse's wages (or both) are $1,000 or less. An additional allowance is available if the employee expects to file using the head-of-household status or if the employee expects to claim a credit for child and dependent care expenses on qualifying expenditures of at least $1,500. An employee who plans to itemize deductions or claim adjustments to income (e.g., alimony, deductible IRA contributions) should use the worksheet provided on Form W–4 to determine the correct number of additional allowances.

To avoid having too little tax withheld, some employees may find it necessary to reduce their withholding allowances. This might be the case for an employee who has more than one job or who has other sources of income that are not subject to adequate withholding. Likewise, a married employee who has a working spouse or more than one job might wish to claim fewer allowances.

If both spouses of a married couple are employed, they may allocate their total allowances between themselves as they see fit. The same allocation procedure is required if a taxpayer has more than one job. In no event should the same allowance be claimed more than once at the same time. It is permissible to declare *fewer* allowances than the taxpayer is entitled to in order to increase the amount of withholding. Doing so, however, does not affect the number of exemptions allowable on the employee's income tax return. An employee is also permitted to have the employer withhold a certain dollar amount in addition to the required amount. This additional dollar amount can be arbitrary or calculated in accordance with a worksheet and tables on Form W–4.

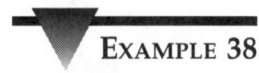

EXAMPLE 38

Carl, who earns $15,000, is married to Carol, who earns $25,000. They have three dependent children and will claim the standard deduction. Together they should be entitled to five allowances [2 (for personal exemptions) + 3 (for dependency exemptions)]. The special withholding allowance is not available since both spouses earn more than $1,000. If Carl is the spouse first employed and his Form W–4 reflects five allowances, Carol's Form W–4 should report none. They could, however, reallocate their allowances between them as long as the total claimed does not exceed five. ▼

The period of service for which an employee is paid is known as the *payroll period.* Daily, weekly, biweekly, semimonthly, and monthly periods are the most common arrangements. If an employee has no regular payroll period, he or she is considered to be paid on a daily basis.

Once the allowances are known (as reflected on Form W–4) and the payroll period determined, the amount to be withheld for Federal income taxes can be computed. The computation usually is made by using the wage-bracket tables or the percentage method.

Wage-bracket tables are available for daily, weekly, biweekly, semimonthly, and monthly payroll periods for single (including heads of household) and married taxpayers. An extract of the tables dealing with married persons on a monthly payroll period is reproduced in Table 13–5. The data in Table 13–5 are for the period after December 31, 1997. Example 39 illustrates the use of withholding tables.

EXAMPLE 39

Tom is married and has three dependent children and no additional allowances for itemized deductions, adjustments to income, or credit for child and dependent care expenses. In his job with Pink Corporation, he earns $2,770 in May 1998. Assuming Tom's wife is not employed and all available allowances are claimed on Form W–4, Pink should withhold $134 a month from his wages. This amount is taken from the six allowances column in the $2,760–$2,800 wage bracket. The six allowances result from personal exemptions (two) plus the special withholding allowance (one) plus dependency exemptions (three). ▼

Although the wage-bracket table requires few, if any, calculations, the percentage method is equally acceptable. Its use may be necessary for payroll periods where no wage-bracket tables are available (quarterly, semiannual, and annual payroll periods) and where wages paid exceed the amount allowed for use of the wage-bracket tables. The percentage method is particularly useful when payroll computations are computerized. This method, however, requires the use of a conversion chart based on one withholding allowance. That is, the amount of one allowance is equal to the exemption amount divided by the number of payroll periods in a year. For example, the amount of one allowance for a taxpayer who is paid weekly is $51.92 ($2,700/52 payroll periods)—see Table 13–6.

To use the percentage method, proceed as follows:

Step 1. Multiply the amount of one allowance (as specified in the conversion chart in Table 13–6) by the employee's total allowances (taken from Form W–4).

Step 2. Subtract the product reached in step 1 from the employee's wages. The remainder is called "amount of wages."

Step 3. Using the result derived in step 2, compute the income tax withholding under the proper percentage-method table.

The table used in applying the percentage method for those with monthly payroll periods is reproduced in Table 13–7. An illustration of the percentage method follows.

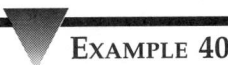

EXAMPLE 40

Assume the same facts as in Example 39, except that Tom's income tax withholding is determined using the percentage method.

Step 1. $225 (amount of one allowance for a monthly payroll period) × 6 (total allowances) = $1,350.

Step 2. $2,770 (monthly salary) – $1,350 (step 1) = $1,420 (amount of wages).

Step 3. Referring to Table 13–7: 15% × $882 (excess of step 2 amount over $538) = $132.30. ▼

Note that the wage-bracket tables yield an amount for income tax withholding of $134 (refer to Example 39) while the percentage method results in $132.30 (refer to Example 40). The difference occurs because the wage-bracket table amounts are derived by computing the withholding on the median wage within each bracket.

Reporting and Payment Procedures.   Proper handling of employment taxes and income tax withholdings requires considerable compliance effort on the part of the employer. Among the Federal forms that have to be filed are the following:

Form Designation	Title
SS–4	Application for Employer Identification Number
W–2	Wage and Tax Statement
W–3	Transmittal of Wage and Tax Statements
940 or 940 EZ	Employer's Annual Federal Unemployment (FUTA) Tax Return
941	Employer's Quarterly Federal Tax Return

Form SS–4 is the starting point since it provides the employer with an identification number that must be used on all of the other forms filed with the IRS and the Social Security Administration. The number issued consists of nine digits and is hyphenated between the second and third digits (e.g., 72–1987316).

Form W–2 furnishes essential information to employees concerning wages paid, FICA, and income tax withholdings. Copies of Form W–2 are distributed to several parties for various purposes: to enable the employee to complete his or her income tax return, to inform the Social Security Administration of the amount of FICA wages earned by the employee, and to serve as a permanent record for the employer and employee of the payroll information contained on the form. Form W–2 must be furnished to an employee not later than January 31 of the following year. If an employee leaves a place of employment before the end of the year, Form W–2 can be given to him or her at any time after employment ends but no later than the following January 31. However, if the terminated employee asks for Form W–2, it must be given to him or her within 30 days after the request or the final wage payment, whichever is later.

Form W–3 must accompany the copies of Forms W–2 filed by the employer with the Social Security Administration. Its basic purpose is to summarize and reconcile the amounts withheld for FICA and income taxes from *all* employees.

Form 940 (or Form 940 EZ) constitutes the employer's annual accounting for FUTA purposes. Generally, it must be filed on or before January 31 of the following year and must be accompanied by the payment of any undeposited FUTA due the Federal government.

Regardless of whether or not deposits[34] are required, most employers must settle their employment taxes every quarter. To do this, Form 941 must be filed on or before the last day of the month following the end of each calendar quarter.

Backup Withholding.   Some types of payments made to individuals by banks or businesses are subject to backup withholding under certain conditions. Backup withholding is designed to ensure that income tax is collected on interest and other payments reported on a Form 1099. If backup withholding applies, the payer must withhold 31 percent of the gross amount. Backup withholding applies when the

---

[34]Deposit requirements are specified in each current issue of Circular E, *Employer's Tax Guide*, IRS Publication 15. Under current rules, most employers must make deposits on a monthly or semiweekly basis.

▼ **TABLE 13–5**
Withholding Table

MARRIED Persons—MONTHLY Payroll Period

(For Wages Paid in 1998)

If the wages are—		And the number of withholding allowances claimed is—										
At least	But less than	0	1	2	3	4	5	6	7	8	9	10
		The amount of income tax to be withheld is—										
$0	$540	0	0	0	0	0	0	0	0	0	0	0
540	560	2	0	0	0	0	0	0	0	0	0	0
560	580	5	0	0	0	0	0	0	0	0	0	0
580	600	8	0	0	0	0	0	0	0	0	0	0
600	640	12	0	0	0	0	0	0	0	0	0	0
640	680	18	0	0	0	0	0	0	0	0	0	0
680	720	24	0	0	0	0	0	0	0	0	0	0
720	760	30	0	0	0	0	0	0	0	0	0	0
760	800	36	3	0	0	0	0	0	0	0	0	0
800	840	42	9	0	0	0	0	0	0	0	0	0
840	880	48	15	0	0	0	0	0	0	0	0	0
880	920	54	21	0	0	0	0	0	0	0	0	0
920	960	60	27	0	0	0	0	0	0	0	0	0
960	1,000	66	33	0	0	0	0	0	0	0	0	0
1,000	1,040	72	39	5	0	0	0	0	0	0	0	0
1,040	1,080	78	45	11	0	0	0	0	0	0	0	0
1,080	1,120	84	51	17	0	0	0	0	0	0	0	0
1,120	1,160	90	57	23	0	0	0	0	0	0	0	0
1,160	1,200	96	63	29	0	0	0	0	0	0	0	0
1,200	1,240	102	69	35	1	0	0	0	0	0	0	0
1,240	1,280	108	75	41	7	0	0	0	0	0	0	0
1,280	1,320	114	81	47	13	0	0	0	0	0	0	0
1,320	1,360	120	87	53	19	0	0	0	0	0	0	0
1,360	1,400	126	93	59	25	0	0	0	0	0	0	0
1,400	1,440	132	99	65	31	0	0	0	0	0	0	0
1,440	1,480	138	105	71	37	3	0	0	0	0	0	0
1,480	1,520	144	111	77	43	9	0	0	0	0	0	0
1,520	1,560	150	117	83	49	15	0	0	0	0	0	0
1,560	1,600	156	123	89	55	21	0	0	0	0	0	0
1,600	1,640	162	129	95	61	27	0	0	0	0	0	0
1,640	1,680	168	135	101	67	33	0	0	0	0	0	0
1,680	1,720	174	141	107	73	39	6	0	0	0	0	0
1,720	1,760	180	147	113	79	45	12	0	0	0	0	0
1,760	1,800	186	153	119	85	51	18	0	0	0	0	0
1,800	1,840	192	159	125	91	57	24	0	0	0	0	0
1,840	1,880	198	165	131	97	63	30	0	0	0	0	0
1,880	1,920	204	171	137	103	69	36	2	0	0	0	0
1,920	1,960	210	177	143	109	75	42	8	0	0	0	0
1,960	2,000	216	183	149	115	81	48	14	0	0	0	0
2,000	2,040	222	189	155	121	87	54	20	0	0	0	0
2,040	2,080	228	195	161	127	93	60	26	0	0	0	0
2,080	2,120	234	201	167	133	99	66	32	0	0	0	0
2,120	2,160	240	207	173	139	105	72	38	4	0	0	0
2,160	2,200	246	213	179	145	111	78	44	10	0	0	0
2,200	2,240	252	219	185	151	117	84	50	16	0	0	0
2,240	2,280	258	225	191	157	123	90	56	22	0	0	0
2,280	2,320	264	231	197	163	129	96	62	28	0	0	0
2,320	2,360	270	237	203	169	135	102	68	34	0	0	0
2,360	2,400	276	243	209	175	141	108	74	40	6	0	0
2,400	2,440	282	249	215	181	147	114	80	46	12	0	0
2,440	2,480	288	255	221	187	153	120	86	52	18	0	0
2,480	2,520	294	261	227	193	159	126	92	58	24	0	0
2,520	2,560	300	267	233	199	165	132	98	64	30	0	0
2,560	2,600	306	273	239	205	171	138	104	70	36	3	0
2,600	2,640	312	279	245	211	177	144	110	76	42	9	0
2,640	2,680	318	285	251	217	183	150	116	82	48	15	0
2,680	2,720	324	291	257	223	189	156	122	88	54	21	0
2,720	2,760	330	297	263	229	195	162	128	94	60	27	0
2,760	2,800	336	303	269	235	201	168	134	100	66	33	0
2,800	2,840	342	309	275	241	207	174	140	106	72	39	5
2,840	2,880	348	315	281	247	213	180	146	112	78	45	11
2,880	2,920	354	321	287	253	219	186	152	118	84	51	17
2,920	2,960	360	327	293	259	225	192	158	124	90	57	23
2,960	3,000	366	333	299	265	231	198	164	130	96	63	29
3,000	3,040	372	339	305	271	237	204	170	136	102	69	35
3,040	3,080	378	345	311	277	243	210	176	142	108	75	41
3,080	3,120	384	351	317	283	249	216	182	148	114	81	47
3,120	3,160	390	357	323	289	255	222	188	154	120	87	53
3,160	3,200	396	363	329	295	261	228	194	160	126	93	59
3,200	3,240	402	369	335	301	267	234	200	166	132	99	65

▼ **TABLE 13–6**
Conversion Chart for 1998

Payroll Period	Amount of One Allowance
Daily	$ 10.38
Weekly	51.92
Biweekly	103.84
Semimonthly	112.50
Monthly	225.00
Quarterly	675.00
Semiannual	1,350.00
Annual	2,700.00

▼ **TABLE 13–7**
Table for Percentage Method of Withholding*

TABLE 4—MONTHLY Payroll Period

(a) SINGLE person (including head of household)—

If the amount of wages (after subtracting withholding allowances) is: The amount of income tax to withhold is:

Not over $221 . . . . $0

Over—	But not over—		of excess over—
$221	—$2,242	. . 15%	—$221
$2,242	—$4,788	. . $303.15 plus 28%	—$2,242
$4,788	—$10,804	. . $1,016.03 plus 31%	—$4,788
$10,804	—$23,333	. . $2,880.99 plus 36%	—$10,804
$23,333	. . . . .	. $7,391.43 plus 39.6%	—$23,333

(b) MARRIED person—

If the amount of wages (after subtracting withholding allowances) is: The amount of income tax to withhold is:

Not over $538 . . . . $0

Over—	But not over—		of excess over—
$538	—$3,896	. . 15%	—$538
$3,896	—$8,038	. . $503.70 plus 28%	—$3,896
$8,038	—$13,363	. . $1,663.46 plus 31%	—$8,038
$13,363	—$23,571	. . $3,314.21 plus 36%	—$13,363
$23,571	. . . . .	. $6,989.09 plus 39.6%	—$23,571

*This table is for wages paid in 1998.

taxpayer does not give the business or bank his or her identification number in the required manner and in certain other situations.[35]

PROCEDURES APPLICABLE TO SELF-EMPLOYED PERSONS

6 ▼ **LEARNING OBJECTIVE**
Understand the payment procedures applicable to self-employed persons.

Although the following discussion largely centers on self-employed taxpayers, some of the procedures may be applicable to employed persons. In many cases, for example, employed persons may be required to pay estimated tax if they have income other than wages that is not subject to withholding. An employee may conduct a second trade or business in a self-employment capacity. Depending on the circumstances, the second job may require the payment of a self-employment tax. In addition, taxpayers whose income consists primarily of rentals, dividends, or interest (this list is not all-inclusive) may be required to pay estimated tax.

Estimated Tax for Individuals.   **Estimated tax** is the amount of tax (including alternative minimum tax and self-employment tax) an individual expects to owe for the year after subtracting tax credits and income tax withheld. Any individual who has estimated tax for the year of $1,000 or more *and* whose withholding does not equal or exceed the required annual payment (discussed below) must make quarterly payments.[36] Otherwise, a penalty may be assessed. No quarterly payments are required (and no penalty will apply on an underpayment) if the taxpayer's

---

[35]§ 3406(a).   [36]§ 6654(c)(1).

estimated tax is under $1000. No penalty will apply if the taxpayer had no tax liability for the preceding tax year *and* the preceding tax year was a taxable year of 12 months *and* the taxpayer was a citizen or resident for the entire preceding tax year. In this regard, having no tax liability is not the same as having no additional tax to pay.

The required annual payment must first be computed. This is the *smaller* of the following amounts:

- Ninety percent of the tax shown on the current year's return.
- One hundred percent of the tax shown on the preceding year's return (the return must cover the full 12 months of the preceding year). For tax years beginning in 1999, the 100 percent requirement is increased to 105 percent if the AGI on the preceding year's return exceeds $150,000 ($75,000 if married filing separately).

In general, one-fourth of this required annual payment is due on April 15, June 15, and September 15 of the tax year and January 15 of the following year.

An equal part of withholding is deemed paid on each due date. Thus, the quarterly installment of the required annual payment reduced by the applicable withholding is the estimated tax to be paid. Payments are to be accompanied by the payment voucher for the appropriate date from Form 1040–ES.

Married taxpayers may make joint estimated tax payments even though a joint income tax return is not subsequently filed. In such event, the estimated tax payments may be applied against the separate return liability of the spouses as they see fit. If a husband and wife cannot agree on a division of the estimated tax payments, the Regulations provide that the payments are to be allocated in proportion to the tax liability on the separate returns.

Penalty on Underpayments. A nondeductible penalty is imposed on the amount of underpayment of estimated tax. The rate for this penalty is the same as the rate for underpayments of tax and is adjusted quarterly to reflect changes in the average prime rate.

An *underpayment* occurs when any installment (the sum of estimated tax paid and income tax withheld) is less than 25 percent of the required annual payment. The penalty is applied to the amount of the underpayment for the period of the underpayment.[37]

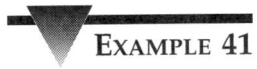

EXAMPLE 41

Marta made the following payments of estimated tax for 1998 and had no income tax withheld:

April 15, 1998	$1,400
June 15, 1998	2,300
September 15, 1998	1,500
January 15, 1999	1,800

Marta's actual tax for 1998 is $8,000, and her tax in 1997 was $10,000. Therefore, each installment should have been at least $1,800 [($8,000 × 90%) × 25%]. Of the payment on June 15, $400 will be credited to the unpaid balance of the first quarterly installment due on April 15,[38] thereby effectively stopping the underpayment penalty for the first quarterly period. Of the remaining $1,900 payment on June 15, $100 is credited to the September 15

---

[37]§ 6654(b)(2).

[38]Payments are credited to unpaid installments in the order in which the installments are required to be paid. § 6654(b)(3).

payment, resulting in this third quarterly payment being $200 short. Then $200 of the January 15 payment is credited to the September 15 shortfall, ending the period of underpayment for that portion due. The January 15, 1999, installment is now underpaid by $200, and a penalty will apply from January 15, 1999, to April 15, 1999 (unless paid sooner). Marta's underpayments for the periods of underpayment are as follows:

1st installment due:	$400 from April 15–June 15
2nd installment due:	Paid in full
3rd installment due:	$200 from September 15, 1998–January 15, 1999
4th installment due:	$200 from January 15–April 15, 1999

If a possible underpayment of estimated tax is indicated, Form 2210 (see Appendix B) should be filed to compute the penalty due or to justify that no penalty applies.

Self-Employment Tax. The tax on self-employment income is levied to provide Social Security and Medicare benefits (old age, survivors, and disability insurance and hospital insurance) for self-employed individuals. Individuals with net earnings of $400 or more from self-employment are subject to the **self-employment tax.**[39] For 1998, the self-employment tax is 15.3 percent on self-employment income up to $68,400 and 2.9 percent on self-employment income in excess of $68,400. In other words, for 1998 the self-employment tax is 12.4 percent of self-employment earnings up to $68,400 (for the Social Security portion) *plus* 2.9 percent of the total amount of self-employment earnings (for the Medicare portion)—see Table 13–8.

Currently, self-employed taxpayers are allowed a deduction from net earnings from self-employment, at one-half of the self-employment rate, for purposes of determining self-employment tax[40] *and* an income tax deduction for one-half the amount of self-employment tax paid.[41]

Determining the amount of self-employment tax to be paid for 1998 involves completing the steps in Figure 13–1. The result of step 3 or 4 is the amount of self-employment tax to be paid. For *income tax purposes*, the amount to be reported is net earnings from self-employment before the deduction for one-half of the self-employment tax. Then the taxpayer is allowed a deduction *for AGI* of one-half of the self-employment tax.

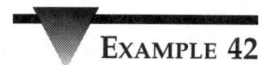
EXAMPLE 42

Using the format in Figure 13–1, the self-employment tax is determined for two taxpayers with net earnings from self-employment for 1998 as follows: Ned, $55,000 and Terry, $80,000.

▼ **TABLE 13–8**
Self-Employment Tax: Social Security and Medicare Portions

Year		Tax Rate	Ceiling Amount
1998	Social Security portion	12.4%	$68,400
	Medicare portion	2.9%	Unlimited
	Aggregate rate	15.3%	
1997	Social Security portion	12.4%	$65,400
	Medicare portion	2.9%	Unlimited
	Aggregate rate	15.3%	

[39]§ 6017.
[40]§ 1402(a)(12).

[41]§ 164(f).

▼ **FIGURE 13–1**
1998 Self-Employment Tax Worksheet

1. Net earnings from self-employment. _____

2. Multiply line 1 by 92.35%. _____

3. If the amount on line 2 is $68,400 or less, multiply the line 2 amount by 15.3%. This is the self-employment tax. _____

4. If the amount on line 2 is more than $68,400, multiply the excess of line 2 over $68,400 by 2.9% and add $10,465.20. This is the self-employment tax. _____

▼ **FIGURE 13–2**
1997 Self-Employment Tax Worksheet

1. Net earnings from self-employment. _____

2. Multiply line 1 by 92.35%. _____

3. If the amount on line 2 is $65,400 or less, multiply the line 2 amount by 15.3%. This is the self-employment tax. _____

4. If the amount on line 2 is more than $65,400, multiply the excess of line 2 over $65,400 by 2.9% and add $10,006.20. This is the self-employment tax. _____

Ned's Self-Employment Tax Worksheet

1. Net earnings from self-employment. $ 55,000.00

2. Multiply line 1 by 92.35%. $ 50,792.50

3. If the amount on line 2 is $68,400 or less, multiply the line 2 amount by 15.3%. This is the self-employment tax. $ 7,771.25

4. If the amount on line 2 is more than $68,400, multiply the excess over $68,400 by 2.9% and add $10,465.20. This is the self-employment tax. _____

Terry's Self-Employment Tax Worksheet

1. Net earnings from self-employment. $ 80,000.00

2. Multiply line 1 by 92.35%. $ 73,880.00

3. If the amount on line 2 is $68,400 or less, multiply the line 2 amount by 15.3%. This is the self-employment tax. _____

4. If the amount on line 2 is more than $68,400, multiply the excess over $68,400 by 2.9% and add $10,465.20. This is the self-employment tax. $ 10,624.12

For income tax purposes, Ned has net earnings from self-employment of $55,000 and a deduction *for* AGI of $3,885.63 (one-half of $7,771.25). Terry has net earnings from self-employment of $80,000 and a deduction *for* AGI of $5,312.06 (one-half of $10,624.12). Both taxpayers benefit from the deduction for one-half of the self-employment tax paid. ▼

For 1997, the self-employment tax computations are similar to those for 1998. The only difference is that the tax base was lower for 1997 than it is for 1998 (see Table 13–8 and Figure 13–2).

If an individual also receives wages subject to FICA tax, the ceiling amount of the Social Security portion on which the self-employment tax is computed is reduced. Thus, self-employment tax may be reduced if a self-employed individual also receives FICA wages in excess of the ceiling amount.

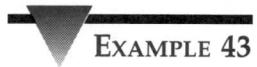

EXAMPLE 43

In 1998, Kelly had $45,000 of net earnings from the conduct of a bookkeeping service (trade or business activity). She also received wages as an employee amounting to $30,000 during the year. The amount of Kelly's self-employment income subject to the Social Security portion (12.4%) is $38,400 ($68,400 − $30,000), producing a tax of $4,761.60 ($38,400 × 12.4%). All of Kelly's net self-employment earnings are subject to the Medicare portion of the self-employment tax of 2.9%. Therefore, the self-employment tax on this portion is $1,205.18 ($41,558 × 2.9%).

	Social Security Portion
Ceiling amount	$ 68,400
Less: FICA wages	(30,000)
Net ceiling	$ 38,400
Net self-employment income ($45,000 × 92.35%)	$ 41,558
Lesser of net ceiling or net self-employment income	$ 38,400

Net earnings from self-employment include gross income from a trade or business less allowable trade or business deductions, the distributive share of any partnership income or loss derived from a trade or business activity, and net income from the rendering of personal services as an independent contractor. Gain or loss from the disposition of property (including involuntary conversions) is excluded from the computation of self-employment income unless the property involved is inventory.

TAX PLANNING CONSIDERATIONS

7 **LEARNING OBJECTIVE**
Identify tax planning opportunities related to tax credits and payment procedures.

FOREIGN TAX CREDIT

A U.S. citizen or resident working abroad (commonly referred to as an *expatriate*) may elect to take either a foreign tax credit or the foreign earned income exclusion. In cases where the income tax of a foreign country is higher than the U.S. income tax, the credit choice usually is preferable. If the reverse is true, electing the foreign earned income exclusion probably reduces the overall tax burden.

Unfortunately, the choice between the credit and the earned income exclusion is not without some limitations. The election of the foreign earned income exclusion, once made, can be revoked for a later year. However, once revoked, the earned income exclusion will not be available for a period of five years unless the IRS consents to an earlier date. This will create a dilemma for expatriates whose job assignments over several years shift between low- and high-bracket countries.

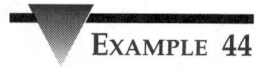

EXAMPLE 44

In 1997, Ira, a calendar year taxpayer, is sent by his employer to Saudi Arabia (a low-tax country). For 1997, therefore, Ira elects the foreign earned income exclusion. In 1998, Ira's employer transfers him to France (a high-tax country). Accordingly, he revokes the foreign earned income exclusion election for 1998 and chooses instead to use the foreign tax credit. If Ira is transferred back to Saudi Arabia (or any other low-tax country) within five years, he may not utilize the foreign earned income exclusion. ▼

CREDIT FOR CHILD AND DEPENDENT CARE EXPENSES

A taxpayer may incur employment-related expenses that also qualify as medical expenses (e.g., a nurse is hired to provide in-the-home care for an ill and incapacitated dependent parent). Such expenses may be either deducted as medical expenses (subject to the 7.5 percent limitation) or utilized in determining the credit for child and dependent care expenses. If the credit for child and dependent care expenses is chosen and the employment-related expenses exceed the limitation ($2,400, $4,800, or earned income, as the case may be), the excess may be considered a medical expense. If, however, the taxpayer chooses to deduct qualified employment-related expenses as medical expenses, any portion that is not deductible because of the 7.5 percent limitation may not be used in computing the credit for child and dependent care expenses.

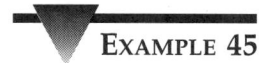

EXAMPLE 45

Alicia, a single taxpayer, has the following tax position for the current tax year.

Adjusted gross income		$30,000
Potential itemized deductions *from* AGI—		
Other than medical expenses	$3,500	
Medical expenses	6,000	$ 9,500

All of Alicia's medical expenses were incurred to provide nursing care for her disabled father while she was working. The father lives with Alicia and qualifies as her dependent. ▼

What should Alicia do in this situation? One approach would be to use $2,400 of the nursing care expenses to obtain the maximum credit for child and dependent care expenses allowed of $480 (20% × $2,400). The balance of these expenses should be claimed as medical expenses. After a reduction of 7.5 percent of AGI, this would produce a medical expense deduction of $1,350 [$3,600 (remaining medical expenses) − (7.5% × $30,000)].

Another approach would be to claim the full $6,000 as a medical expense and forgo the credit for child and dependent care expenses. After the 7.5 percent adjustment of $2,250 (7.5% × $30,000), a deduction of $3,750 remains.

The choice, then, is between a credit of $480 plus a deduction of $1,350 or a credit of $0 plus a deduction of $3,750. Which is better, of course, depends on the relative tax savings involved.

One of the traditional goals of *family tax planning* is to minimize the total tax burden within the family unit. With proper planning and implementation, the credit for child and dependent care expenses can be used to help achieve this goal. For example, payments to certain relatives for the care of qualifying dependents and children qualify for the credit if the care provider is *not* a dependent of the taxpayer or the taxpayer's spouse or is *not* a child (under age 19) of the taxpayer. Thus, if the care provider is in a lower tax bracket than the taxpayer, the following benefits result:

- Income is shifted to a lower-bracket family member.
- The taxpayer qualifies for the credit for child and dependent care expenses.

In addition, the goal of minimizing the family income tax liability can be enhanced in some other situations, but only if the credit's limitations are recognized and avoided. For example, tax savings may still be enjoyed even if the qualifying expenditures incurred by a cash basis taxpayer have already reached the annual ceiling ($2,400 or $4,800). To the extent that any additional payments can be shifted into future tax years, the benefit from the credit may be preserved on these excess expenditures.

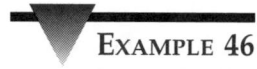

EXAMPLE 46

Andre, a calendar year and cash basis taxpayer, has spent $2,400 by December 1 on qualifying child care expenditures for his dependent 11-year-old son. The $200 that is due the care provider for child care services rendered in December does not generate a tax credit benefit if the amount is paid in the current year because the $2,400 ceiling has been reached. However, if the payment can be delayed until the next year, the total credit over the two-year period for which Andre is eligible may be increased. ▼

A similar shifting of expenditures to a subsequent year may be wise if the potential credit otherwise generated would exceed the tax liability available to absorb the credit.

ADJUSTMENTS TO INCREASE WITHHOLDING

The penalty for underpayment of estimated tax by individuals is computed for each quarter of the tax year. A taxpayer can play *catch-up* to a certain extent. Each quarterly payment is credited to the unpaid portion of any previous required installment. Thus, the penalty stops on that portion of the underpayment for the previous quarter. Since income tax withheld is assumed to have been paid evenly throughout the year and is allocated equally among the four installments in computing any penalty, a taxpayer who would otherwise be subject to a penalty for underpayment should increase withholdings late in the year. This can be done by changing the number of allowances claimed on Form W–4 or by special arrangement with the employer to increase the amount withheld.

A similar way to avoid (or reduce) a penalty for underpayment is to have the employer continue Social Security withholding beyond the base amount.

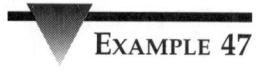

EXAMPLE 47

Rose, a calendar year taxpayer, earns $75,000 from her job. In late August 1998, she realizes that she will be subject to a penalty for underpayment of estimated tax due to income from outside sources. Consequently, she instructs her employer to continue FICA withholdings for the rest of 1998. If this is done, an extra $6,600 [$75,000 (annual salary) − $68,400 (base amount of the Social Security portion for 1998)] will be subject to the 6.2% Social Security portion of the FICA tax [7.65% (total FICA rate) − 1.45% (Medicare portion of the FICA rate)]. Thus, Rose generates an additional $409 (6.2% × $6,600) that will be deemed withheld ratably during 1998. ▼

ADJUSTMENTS TO AVOID OVERWITHHOLDING

Publication 505, Tax Withholding and Estimated Tax, contains worksheets that taxpayers may use to take advantage of special provisions for avoiding overwithholding. Extra exemptions for withholding purposes are allowed if the taxpayer has unusually large itemized deductions, deductions *for* AGI, or tax credits. Net losses from Schedules C, D, E, and F may be considered in computing the number of extra withholding exemptions. Net operating loss carryovers may also be considered in the computation. A taxpayer who is entitled to extra withholding exemptions for any of these reasons should file a new Form W–4, Employee's Withholding Allowance Certificate, with his or her employer.

KEY TERMS

Adoption expenses credit, 13–19

Business energy credits, 13–9

Child tax credit, 13–20

Credit for child and dependent care expenses, 13–21

Disabled access credit, 13–14

Earned income credit, 13–14

Employment taxes, 13–24

Estimated tax, 13–36

Foreign tax credit (FTC), 13–18

General business credit, 13–6

HOPE scholarship credit, 13–23

Lifetime learning credit, 13–23

Low-income housing credit, 13–13

Nonrefundable credits, 13–5

Refundable credits, 13–5

Rehabilitation expenditures credit, 13–7

Rehabilitation expenditures credit recapture, 13–8

Research activities credit, 13–11

Self-employment tax, 13–38

Tax credits, 13–2

Tax credit for the elderly or disabled, 13–16

Welfare-to-work credit, 13–10

Withholding allowances, 13–32

Work opportunity tax credit, 13–9

PROBLEM MATERIALS

DISCUSSION QUESTIONS

1. Would an individual taxpayer receive greater benefit from deducting an expenditure or from taking a credit equal to 25% of the expenditure?

2. What is a refundable credit? Give examples. What is a nonrefundable credit? Give examples.

3. Discuss the order in which credits are offset against the tax liability. Why is the order in which credits are utilized important?

4. Discuss the treatment of unused general business credits.

5. John graduated from college several years ago with high hopes and expectations of enjoying a very successful business career. Almost as soon as he completed his final exams, he borrowed over $250,000 from a local bank (the loan was guaranteed by his parents) in order to make several "hot" investments. The investments, as expected, spun off huge tax losses and tax credits in their early years. More recently, however, John has begun to have doubts as to the wisdom of these investments as they have not begun to generate profits as promised. As a result, he is contemplating selling the investments, at yet another loss. Because his investments have not as yet produced any profits to support his lifestyle, he has been forced to live at home with his parents. Identify the relevant tax issues.

6. Clint is a self-employed engineering consultant. He is contemplating purchasing an old building for renovation. After the work is completed, Clint plans to rent out two-thirds of the floor space to businesses and live and work in the remaining portion. Identify the relevant tax issues for Clint.

7. If property on which the tax credit for rehabilitation expenditures was claimed is prematurely disposed of or ceases to be qualified property, how is the tax liability affected in the year of the disposition or disqualification?

8. Discuss the purpose of the work opportunity tax credit. Who receives the tax benefits from the credit? Give examples of the types of individuals who, if hired, give rise to the credit.

9. Explain the purpose and calculation procedure of the welfare-to-work credit.

10. Explain the alternatives a taxpayer has in claiming the deduction and credit for research and experimentation expenditures incurred.

11. Explain the purpose of the disabled access credit and describe the general characteristics of its computation.

12. What three tests must be met for a child to be considered a qualifying child for purposes of the earned income credit? Describe.

13. Briefly discuss the requirements that must be satisfied for a taxpayer to qualify for the earned income tax credit.

14. Individuals who receive substantial Social Security benefits are usually not eligible for the tax credit for the elderly or disabled because these benefits effectively eliminate the base upon which the credit is computed. Explain.

15. What purpose is served by the overall limitation to the foreign tax credit?

16. In general, when would an individual taxpayer find it more beneficial to take advantage of the foreign earned income exclusion rather than the foreign tax credit in computing his or her income tax liability?

17. Sally was recently called into the partner's office and offered a one-year assignment in her public accounting firm's Prague office. Realizing Sally will face incremental expenses while in Prague, such as for foreign income taxes and rent, the firm will try to make her "whole" from a financial perspective by increasing her salary to help offset the expenses she will incur while living overseas. If Sally takes the assignment, she will likely rent her personal residence and sell several major tangible assets such as her personal automobile. Identify the relevant tax issues.

18. Discuss, in general, the calculation of the adoption expenses credit.

19. Distinguish between the child tax credit and the credit for child and dependent care expenses.

20. Pete is not concerned about the credit for child and dependent care expenses because his AGI is considerably in excess of $20,000. Is Pete under a misconception regarding the tax law? Explain.

21. Polly and her spouse, Leo, file a joint return and expect to report AGI of $45,000 in the current year. Polly's employer offers a child and dependent care reimbursement plan that allows up to $2,500 of qualifying expenses to be reimbursed in exchange for a $2,500 reduction in the employee's salary. Because Polly and Leo have one minor child requiring child care that costs $2,500 each year, she is wondering if she should sign up for the program instead of taking advantage of the credit for child and dependent care expenses. Assuming Polly and Leo are in the 28% tax bracket, analyze the effect of the two alternatives. How would your answer differ if Polly and Leo's AGI was $20,000 instead of $45,000?

22. Camilla, a college freshman, was pleased to read of recent tax law changes permitting education tax credits. However, she is confused as to the applicability of the different credits. Briefly explain (1) who is eligible and (2) what the maximum credit amount is for the HOPE scholarship credit and the lifetime learning credit.

23. Discuss the rationale underlying the enactment of the following tax credits:
    a. Tax credit for rehabilitation expenditures.
    b. Low-income housing credit.
    c. Research activities credit.
    d. Earned income credit.

    e. Foreign tax credit.
    f. Business energy credits.

24. Sam and Martha have two preschool-age children. On several occasions during the current year, Sam and Martha took out-of-town trips due to Sam's business. While Sam and Martha were out of town, a 14-year-old neighbor cared for the children during the day; at night, they stayed with their grandparents. Sam and Martha had a neighborhood teenager mow their lawn, but only once, because of the damage he did to Martha's flower garden. On a later out-of-town trip, they hired a professional lawn service to mow the lawn. Identify the relevant tax issues.

25. Elaborate rules exist that require employers to prepay various types of Federal taxes. Summarize the major issues that an employer must resolve if it is to comply with the requirements.

26. At a social function you attended in early July of 1998, you overhear a guest, the CEO of a corporation, remark, "Thank goodness this is the end of FICA for a while!" Interpret this remark.

27. Keith, a sole proprietor, owns and operates a grocery store. Keith's wife and his 17-year-old son work in the business and are paid wages. Will the wife and son be subject to FICA? Explain.

28. Although Vicki is entitled to four allowances, she claimed just one on her Form W–4.
    a. Why would Vicki claim fewer allowances than she is entitled to?
    b. Is this procedure permissible?
    c. Will this affect the number of personal and dependency exemptions Vicki can claim on her Federal income tax return?

29. Describe the exposure (i.e., wage base and tax rate) that a self-employed individual has to the self-employment tax for 1998.

30. You read that self-employed taxpayers get a double deduction for one-half of the self-employment tax, not only as a deduction in computing the self-employment tax but also as a deduction *for* AGI. Is this true? Explain.

PROBLEMS

31. Carol has a tentative general business credit of $110,000 for 1998. Her net regular tax liability before the general business credit is $125,000, and her tentative minimum tax is $100,000. Compute Carol's allowable general business credit for the year.

32. Tan Corporation has the following general business credit carryovers:

1994	$10,000
1995	30,000
1996	10,000
1997	40,000
Total carryovers	$90,000

    If the general business credit generated by activities during 1998 equals $90,000 and the total credit allowed during the current year is $160,000 (based on tax liability), what amounts of the current general business credit and carryovers are utilized against the 1998 income tax liability? What is the amount of unused credit carried forward to 1999?

33. In January 1996, William purchased and placed into service a pre-1936 building that houses retail businesses. The cost was $200,000, of which $25,000 applied to the land. In modernizing the facility, William incurred $250,000 of renovation costs of the type that qualify for the rehabilitation credit. These improvements were placed into service in October 1998.
    a. Compute William's rehabilitation tax credit for 1998.
    b. Calculate the cost recovery deductions for the building and the renovation costs for 1998.

34. Red Company hires six individuals on January 15, 1998, qualifying Red for the work opportunity tax credit. Three of these individuals receive wages of $7,000 each during 1998 with each working more than 400 hours during the year. The other three receive wages of $4,000 each in 1998 with each working 300 hours during the year.
    a. Calculate the amount of Red's work opportunity tax credit for 1998.
    b. Assume Red pays total wages of $120,000 to its employees during the year. How much of this amount is deductible in 1998 if the work opportunity tax credit is taken?

35. In March 1998, Wren Corporation hired three individuals, Trent, Bernice, and Benita, all of whom are certified as long-term family assistance recipients. Each employee is paid $11,000 during 1998. Only Bernice continued to work for Wren in 1999, earning $13,500. In February 1999, Wren hired Cassie, who was also certified as a long-term family assistance recipient. During 1999, Cassie earned $12,000. Wren does not claim the work opportunity credit with respect to any of the employees hired in 1998 or 1999.
    a. Compute Wren Corporation's welfare-to-work credit for 1998 and 1999.
    b. Assume Wren Corporation pays total wages of $325,000 to its employees during 1998 and $342,000 during 1999. How much may Wren claim as a wage deduction for 1998 and 1999 if the welfare-to-work credit is claimed in both years?

36. Matt, a calendar year taxpayer, informs you that during the year he incurs expenditures of $30,000 that qualify for the incremental research activities credit. In addition, it is determined that his base amount for the year is $22,800.
    a. Determine Matt's incremental research activities credit for the year.
    b. Matt is in the 28% tax bracket. Determine which approach to the research expenditures and the research activities credit (other than capitalization and subsequent amortization) would provide the greater tax benefit to Matt.

37. Ahmed Zinna (16 Southside Drive, Charlotte, NC 28204), one of your clients, owns two retail establishments in downtown Charlotte, North Carolina, and has come to you seeking advice concerning the tax consequences of complying with the Americans with Disabilities Act. He understands that he needs to install various features at his stores (e.g., ramps, doorways, and restrooms that are handicapped accessible) to make them more accessible to disabled individuals. He inquires whether any tax credits will be available to help offset the cost of the necessary changes. He estimates the cost of the planned changes to his facilities as follows:

Location	Projected Cost
Oak Street	$20,000
Maple Avenue	9,000

He reminds you that the Oak Street store was constructed in 1995 while the Maple Avenue store is in a building that was constructed in 1902. Ahmed operates his business as a sole proprietorship and has approximately eight employees at each location. Write a letter to Ahmed in which you summarize your conclusions concerning the tax consequences of his proposed capital improvements.

38. Which of the following individuals qualify for the earned income credit for 1999?
    a. Eduardo is single, 19 years of age, and has no dependents. His income consists of $8,000 of wages.
    b. Kate maintains a household for a dependent 12-year-old son and is eligible for head-of-household tax rates. Her income consists of $10,500 of salary and $300 of taxable interest.
    c. Keith and Susan are married and file a joint return. Keith and Susan have no dependents. Their combined income consists of $18,500 of salary and $100 of taxable interest. Adjusted gross income is $18,600.
    d. George is a 26-year-old single taxpayer. He has no dependents and generates earnings of $9,000.

39. Vern, a widower, lives in an apartment with his three minor children (ages 3, 4, and 5) whom he supports. Vern earned $19,500 during 1998. He contributed $500 to a deductible IRA and uses the standard deduction. Calculate the amount, if any, of Vern's earned income credit.

40. Joyce, a widow, lives in an apartment with her two minor children (ages 8 and 10) whom she supports. Joyce earns $28,000 during 1998. She uses the standard deduction.
    a. Calculate the amount, if any, of Joyce's earned income credit.
    b. During the year, Joyce is offered a new job that has greater future potential than her current job. If she accepts the job offer, her earnings for the year would be $31,000; however, she will not qualify for the earned income credit. Using after-tax cash-flow calculations, determine whether Joyce should accept the new job offer.

41. Joe, age 68, and Emily, age 69, are married retirees who receive the following income and retirement benefits during the current year:

Fully taxable pension from Joe's former employer	$ 5,000
Dividends and interest	8,000
Social Security benefits	1,750
Total	$14,750

Assume Joe and Emily file a joint return, have no deductions *for* AGI, and do not itemize. Are they eligible for the tax credit for the elderly? If so, calculate the amount of the credit assuming their tax liability (before credits) is $150.

42. Kim, a U.S. citizen and resident, owns and operates a novelty goods business. During 1998, Kim has taxable income of $100,000, made up as follows: $50,000 from foreign sources and $50,000 from U.S. sources. In calculating taxable income, the standard deduction is used. The income from foreign sources is subject to foreign income taxes of $26,000. For 1998, Kim files a joint return claiming his three children as dependents.
    a. Assuming Kim chooses to claim the foreign taxes as an income tax credit, what is his income tax liability for 1998?
    b. Recently, Kim has become disenchanted with the location of his business and is considering moving his foreign operation to a different country. Based on his research, if he moves his business to his country of choice, all relevant revenues and costs would remain approximately the same except that the income taxes payable to that country would be only $10,000. Given that all of the foreign income taxes paid are available to offset the U.S. tax liability (whether he operates in a high-tax or a low-tax foreign jurisdiction), what impact will this have on his decision regarding the potential move?

43. Purple Corporation is an international wholesaler headquartered in the United States. Of its worldwide taxable income of $3 billion, $1.25 billion is foreign-sourced. Before any credits, Purple's U.S. income tax liability is $1.05 billion. If income taxes paid to foreign countries totaled $600 million, what is Purple's U.S. income tax liability after benefiting from the foreign tax credit?

44. Ann and Bill had been on the list of a local adoption agency for several years seeking to adopt a child. Finally, in 1998, good news came their way and an adoption seemed imminent. They paid qualified adoption expenses of $2,000 in 1998 and $4,000 in 1999. Assume the adoption becomes final in 1999. Ann and Bill always file a joint income tax return.
    a. Determine the amount of the adoption expenses credit available to Ann and Bill assuming their combined annual income is $50,000. What year(s) will they benefit from the credit?
    b. Assuming Ann and Bill's modified AGI in 1998 and 1999 is $100,000, calculate the amount of the adoption expense credit.

45. Durell and Earline are married, file a joint return, and claim dependency exemptions for their two children, ages 5 years and 6 months. They also claim Earline's son from

a previous marriage, age 18, as a dependent. Durell and Earline's combined AGI for 1998 is $56,000.

a. Compute Durell and Earline's child tax credit for 1998.

b. Assume the same facts, except that Durell and Earline's combined AGI for 1998 is $119,000. Compute their child tax credit for 1998.

46. Jim and Jill are husband and wife and have two dependent children under the age of 13. They both are gainfully employed and during the current year earned salaries as follows: $12,000 (Jim) and $4,500 (Jill). To care for their children while they work, they pay Megan (Jim's mother) $5,600. Megan does not qualify as a dependent of Jim and Jill. Assuming Jim and Jill file a joint return, what, if any, is their credit for child and dependent care expenses?

47. Kevin and Jane are husband and wife and have one dependent child, age 9. Kevin is a full-time student for all of the current year, while Jane earns $20,000 as a nurse's aid. In order to provide care for their child while Kevin attends classes and Jane works, they pay Sara (Jane's 17-year-old sister) $2,100. Sara is not a dependent of Kevin and Jane. Assuming Kevin and Jane file a joint return, what, if any, is their credit for child and dependent care expenses?

48. Colin has requested information concerning the availability of the HOPE scholarship credit and lifetime learning credit. Colin has two college-age children, Eliza, a freshman at State University, and Rhett, a senior at Out-of-State University. Both Eliza and Rhett are full-time students. Eliza's expenses for the 1998–1999 academic year are as follows: $4,500 for tuition ($2,250 per semester), $800 for books and supplies, and $3,000 for room and board. Rhett's expenses for the 1998–1999 academic year are as follows: $8,000 for tuition ($4,000 per semester), $900 for books and supplies, and $3,500 for room and board. Tuition and the applicable room and board costs are paid at the beginning of each semester. Colin is married, files a joint tax return, claims both children as dependents, and has a combined AGI with his wife of $95,000 for 1998.

a. Determine Colin's available education tax credit for 1998.

b. What tax planning alternative would you suggest to Colin to increase his education tax credit for 1998?

49. Bernadette, a long-time client of yours, is an architect and president of the local Rotary chapter. To keep up-to-date with the latest developments in her profession, she attends continuing education seminars offered by the national association of architects. During 1998, Bernadette spent $2,000 on course tuition to attend such seminars. She also spent another $400 on architecture books during the year. Bernadette's son is a senior majoring in engineering at the University of the Midwest. During the 1998–1999 academic year, Bernadette's son incurred the following expenses: $4,200 for tuition ($2,100 per semester) and $750 for books and supplies. Bernadette has the option of paying her son's tuition in advance or in installments throughout the academic year. Bernadette's son, whom she claims as a dependent, lives at home while attending school full-time. Bernadette is married, files a joint return, and has a combined AGI with her husband of $88,000.

a. Calculate Bernadette's education tax credit for 1998 assuming her son's tuition expenses are paid in a manner to maximize the available credit in 1998.

b. In her capacity as a president of the local Rotary chapter, Bernadette has asked you to make a 30–45 minute speech outlining the different ways the tax law helps defray (1) the cost of higher education and (2) the cost of continuing education once someone is in the workforce. Prepare an outline of possible topics for presentation. A tentative title for your presentation is "How the Tax Law Can Help Pay for College and Continuing Professional Education."

50. In each of the following independent situations, determine the amount of FICA that should be withheld from the employee's 1998 salary by the employer:

a. Harry earns a $40,000 salary, files a joint return, and claims four withholding allowances.

b. Hazel earns a $80,000 salary, files a joint return, and claims four withholding allowances.

c. Tracy earns a $160,000 salary, files a joint return, and claims four withholding allowances.

d. Alicia's 17-year-old son, Carlos, earns $5,000 at the family business.

51. During 1998, Greg Cruz (1401 Orangedale Road, Troy, MI 48084) worked for Maple Corporation and Gray Company. He earned $60,000 at Maple Corporation where he was a full-time employee. Greg also worked part-time for Gray Company for wages of $30,000.

   a. Did Greg experience an overwithholding of FICA taxes? Write a letter to Greg and a memo for the tax files in which you explain your conclusion.

   b. Did Maple Corporation and Gray Company overpay the employer's portion of FICA? Explain.

52. In each of the following independent situations, determine the maximum withholding allowances permitted Eli (an employee) on Form W–4:

   a. Eli is single with no dependents.

   b. Eli is married to a nonemployed spouse, and they have no dependents.

   c. Eli is married to Vera, an employed spouse, and they have three dependent children. On the Form W–4 that she filed with the employer, Vera claimed zero allowances.

   d. Assume the same facts as in (c), except that Eli and Vera fully support Eli's mother, who lives with them. The mother (age 70 and blind) qualifies as their dependent. (Refer to Chapter 3.)

   e. Eli is single with no dependents but works for two employers, one on a full-time basis and the other on a part-time basis. The Form W–4 filed with the first employer (the full-time job) reflects two withholding exemptions. The wages from each job exceed $1,000.

   f. Assume the same facts as in (e), except that Eli is married to a nonemployed spouse.

53. Norm is married to a nonemployed spouse and has four dependents. He is employed by Beige Corporation and is paid a monthly salary of $2,620 ($31,440 per year). Using these facts, determine the amount to be withheld by Beige Corporation for Federal income tax purposes under the wage-bracket tables and under the percentage method for 1998.

54. Samantha, being self-employed, is required to make estimated payments of her tax liability for the year. Her tax liability for 1997 was $15,000. For 1998, Samantha ultimately determines that her income tax liability is $18,000. During the year, however, she made the following payments, totaling $13,000:

April 15, 1998	$ 4,500
June 15, 1998	2,800
September 15, 1998	4,100
January 15, 1999	1,600
	$13,000

Because she prepaid so little of her ultimate income tax liability, she now realizes that she may be subject to the penalty for underpayment of estimated tax. Determine Samantha's exposure to the penalty for underpayment of estimated tax.

55. During 1998, Helen, the owner of a store, had the following income and expenses:

Gross profit on sales	$63,000
Income from part-time job (subject to FICA)	24,000
Business expenses (related to store)	15,000
Fire loss on store building	1,200
Dividend income	200
Long-term capital gain on the sale of a stock investment	2,000

Using the format illustrated in the text, compute Helen's self-employment tax and allowable income tax deduction for the self-employment tax paid.

56. In 1998, Fran has self-employed earnings of $150,000. Using the format illustrated in the text, compute Fran's self-employment tax liability and the allowable income tax deduction for the self-employment tax paid.

CUMULATIVE PROBLEMS

57. Wade and Jane London are married and file a joint return. His Social Security number is 222–33–1111 and her Social Security number is 111–22–5555. They reside at 100 Olive Lane, Covington, LA 70400. They have two dependent children, Sean and Debra, ages 12 and 16, respectively. Wade is a self-employed businessman (sole proprietor of an unincorporated business), and Jane is a corporate executive. Wade has the following income and expenses from his business:

Gross income	$280,000
Business expenses	166,000

Records related to Jane's employment provide the following information:

Salary	$130,000
Unreimbursed travel expenses (including $200 of meals)	1,000
Unreimbursed entertainment expenses	600

Other pertinent information relating to 1998 follows:

Proceeds from sale of stock acquired on July 15, 1998 (cost of $10,000) and sold on August 1	$ 8,000
Proceeds from sale of stock acquired on September 18, 1995 (cost of $6,000) and sold on October 5	4,800
Wages paid to full-time domestic worker for housekeeping and child supervision	10,000
Dividends ($6,000) and interest ($2,000) received	8,000
Total itemized deductions (not including any potential deductions above)	26,900
Federal income tax withheld	29,000
Estimated payments on Federal income tax	43,000

Part 1—Tax Computation
Compute the net tax payable or refund due for Wade and Jane London for 1998. Suggested software (if available): *TurboTax*.

Part 2—Tax Planning
Provide tax planning suggestions to Wade and Jane concerning how they might reduce their tax liability for 1999.

58. Beth R. Jordan lives at 2322 Skyview Road, Mesa, AZ 85202. She is a tax accountant with Mesa Manufacturing Company. She also writes computer software programs for tax practitioners and has a part-time tax practice. Beth, age 35, is single and has no dependents. Her Social Security number is 111–35–2222. She wants to contribute $3 to the Presidential Election Campaign Fund.

During 1997, Beth earned a salary of $50,000 from her employer. She received interest of $290 from Home Federal Savings and Loan and $335 from Home State Bank. She received dividends of $500 from Gray Corporation, $400 from Blue Corporation, and $300 from Orange Corporation.

Beth received a $1,200 income tax refund from the state of Arizona on May 12, 1997. On her 1996 Federal income tax return, she reported total itemized deductions of $6,700, which included $2,000 of state income tax withheld by her employer.

Fees earned from her part-time tax practice in 1997 totaled $3,800. She paid $400 to have the tax returns processed by a computerized tax return service.

On February 1, 1997, Beth bought 500 shares of Gray Corporation common stock for $17.60 a share. On July 16, Beth sold the stock for $15 a share.

Beth bought a used sports utility vehicle for $3,000 on June 5, 1997. She purchased the vehicle from her brother-in-law, who was unemployed and was in need of cash. On November 2, 1997, she sold the vehicle to a friend for $3,400.

On January 2, 1997, Beth acquired 100 shares of Blue Corporation common stock for $30 a share. She sold the stock on December 19, 1997, for $75 a share.

During 1997, Beth received royalties of $14,000 on a software program she had written. Beth incurred the following expenditures in connection with her software-writing activities:

Cost of personal computer (100% business use)	$7,000
Cost of printer (100% business use)	2,000
Furniture	3,000
Supplies	650
Fee paid to computer consultant	3,500

Beth elected to expense the maximum portion of the cost of the computer, printer, and furniture allowed under the provisions of § 179. This equipment and furniture were placed in service on January 15, 1997.

Although her employer suggested that Beth attend a convention on current developments in corporate taxation, Beth was not reimbursed for the travel expenses of $1,420 she incurred in attending the convention. The $1,420 included $200 for the cost of meals.

During 1997, Beth paid $300 for prescription medicines and $2,875 in doctor bills, hospital bills, and medical insurance premiums. Her employer withheld state income tax of $1,954. Beth paid real property taxes of $1,766 on her home. Interest on her home mortgage was $3,845, and interest to credit-card companies was $320. Beth contributed $20 each week to her church and $10 each week to the United Way. Professional dues and subscriptions totaled $350.

Beth's employer withheld Federal income taxes of $9,500 during 1997. Beth paid estimated taxes of $1,600. What is the amount of Beth's net tax payable or refund due for 1997? If Beth has a tax refund due, she wants to have it credited toward her 1998 income tax. If you use tax forms for your solution, you will need Forms 1040, 2106, and 4562 and Schedules A, B, C, D, and SE. Suggested software (if available): *TurboTax*.

RESEARCH PROBLEMS

Note: Use the **RIA OnPoint System 4 Student Version CD-ROM,** *which is available to accompany this text, in preparing solutions to the Research Problems. Alternatively, tax research materials found in a standard tax library can be used.*

Research Problem 1. A friend of yours, George Daley, who works full-time as an electrical engineer at the Johnson Space Center in Houston, Texas, approaches you about the tax implications of a decision that is on his mind. He explains that earlier in the year he inherited a working farm in Alabama from his father and now must decide whether to keep the farm going. George feels that giving up his secure, rewarding job in Houston to become an Alabama farmer is not in his best interests. Attempting to be a weekend farmer is also out of the question. The farm has been in his family for generations, and for sentimental reasons, George is hesitant to sell it. George has contacted a local farmer whom the family has known for years and has asked if he would be interested in sharecropping the land (i.e., George and the farmer would share the profits from the farming operation conducted by the local farmer). They have tentatively negotiated a satisfactory arrangement, particularly given George's inability to visit the farm regularly and his strong desire to keep the farm going and in his family. However, George is concerned that any income generated under such an arrangement would be subject to the self-employment tax in addition to the Federal income tax. George has decided that if he has to pay the self-employment tax, he will look at other options and will not pursue the sharecropping arrangement. What will George decide?

Partial list of research aids:
§§ 1401, 1402(a)(1).
Reg. § 1.1402(a)–(4)(b).

Research Problem 2.   Sandy and John Via (12 Maple Avenue, Albany, NY 12205) are married, file a joint Federal income tax return, and have a 12-year-old son and a 10-year-old daughter. Sandy is currently in the U.S. Air Force and has been stationed in Germany for the entire year. John and their children have remained in the United States where John picks up work only on an irregular basis. In working on their Federal income tax return for 1997, John wonders if they qualify for the earned income credit. Sandy's income consists of salary of $18,000 (taxable) and food and lodging provided by the Air Force, valued at $7,000 (not taxable), while John's earnings for the current year total $5,000. John approaches you and asks your advice. Write a letter to Sandy and John that contains your conclusion and prepare a memo for the tax files.

Research Problem 3.   Isabella, a lover of early twentieth-century American history and architecture, discovers a 1920s house in a downtown district of Atlanta during a recent visit. She decides not only to purchase and renovate this particular home, but also to move the structure to her hometown of Little Rock, Arkansas, so her community can enjoy its architectural features. Also, being aware of the availability of the tax credit for rehabilitation expenditures incurred on old structures, she wants to maximize her use of the provision once the renovation work begins in Arkansas. Comment on whether the renovation expenditures incurred will qualify for the tax credit for rehabilitation expenditures.

Research Problem 4.   Oriole Corporation is a large wholesaler of office products. To remain competitive in a fiercely competitive industry, Oriole has automated and computerized many of its business operations. Specifically, the corporation has developed several new software programs to (1) maintain files of customer histories, (2) create a paperless invoicing system, (3) develop a computer-to-computer order entry system, and (4) monitor inventory levels more closely. Oriole estimates that it spent more than $1 million to develop and test the new software programs that are used throughout the business. To date, Oriole has not sold the software programs to the public but is contemplating doing so. Oriole Corporation has claimed a research and experimentation deduction for the costs associated with developing the software programs. The corporation also wants to claim the research activities credit relating to the software development. Can Oriole Corporation do so?

Use the tax resources of the Internet to address the following questions. Do not restrict your search to the World Wide Web, but include a review of newsgroups and general reference materials, practitioner sites and resources, primary sources of the tax law, chat rooms and discussion groups, and other opportunities.

Research Problem 5.   Find several news reports concerning the government's effort to extend the use of the earned income credit to more of the taxpayers who qualify for it. Which agencies in your area are involved in this effort?

Research Problem 6.   The foreign tax credit is especially valuable when a U.S. individual works in a country whose income tax rates exceed those of the United States. List five countries whose tax rates on individuals exceed those of the United States, and five where the corresponding U.S. rates are higher.

Research Problem 7.   Download a copy of Form W–4 and complete the accompanying worksheet. File the worksheet with your employer if you discover that you currently are being under- or overwithheld.

TEAM PROJECT: ARTHUR ANDERSEN TAX CHALLENGE CASES

For more information on the Arthur Andersen Tax Challenge Cases, refer to Chapter 1, page 1–37.

Information related to tax issues and problems that are discussed in this chapter may be found in the

Day and Ball case on pages 2, 4, 5, 7, 11–13, 15, 29, 31, 32, and 36
Fence case on pages 44, 55, 58, 59, and 61

Read and analyze the case you have been assigned and *identify* any issues and problems that are related to material covered in this chapter. If the information provided in the case is complete, prepare answers for this part of the case at this time. If you need information that is contained in the later parts of the case, write a memo summarizing the questions or problems so you can prepare a complete answer at a later date.

V

PROPERTY TRANSACTIONS

Part V presents the tax treatment of sales, exchanges, and other dispositions of property. Included are the determination of the realized gain or loss, recognized gain or loss, and the classification of the recognized gain or loss as capital or ordinary. The topic of basis is evaluated both in terms of its effect on the calculation of the gain or loss and in terms of the determination of the basis of any contemporaneous or related subsequent acquisitions of property.

PROPERTY TRANSACTIONS: DETERMINATION OF GAIN OR LOSS AND BASIS CONSIDERATIONS

LEARNING OBJECTIVES

After completing Chapter 14, you should be able to:

1. Understand the computation of realized gain or loss on property dispositions.

2. Distinguish between realized and recognized gain or loss.

3. Apply the recovery of capital doctrine.

4. Explain how basis is determined for various methods of asset acquisition.

5. Describe various loss disallowance provisions.

6. Identify tax planning opportunities related to selected property transactions.

OUTLINE

This chapter and the following three chapters are concerned with the income tax consequences of property transactions (the sale or other disposition of property). The following questions are considered with respect to the sale or other disposition of property:

- Is there a realized gain or loss?
- If so, is the gain or loss recognized?
- If the gain or loss is recognized, is it ordinary or capital?
- What is the basis of any replacement property that is acquired?

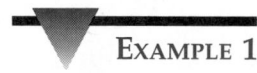

EXAMPLE 1

Alice owns a house that she received from her mother seven months ago. Her mother's cost for the house was $75,000. Alice is considering selling the house to her favorite nephew, Dan, for $75,000. Alice anticipates she will have no gain or loss on the transaction. She comes to you for advice.

As Alice's tax adviser, you need answers to the following questions:

- You are aware that Alice's mother died around the time Alice indicates she received the house from her mother. Did Alice receive the house by gift prior to her mother's death? If so, what was the mother's adjusted basis? If instead Alice inherited the house from her mother, what was the fair market value of the house on the date of her mother's death?
- Was the house Alice's principal residence during the period she owned it and was it her principal residence prior to receiving it from her mother?
- How long did Alice's mother own the house?
- What is the fair market value of the house?
- Does Alice intend for the transaction with Dan to be a sale or part sale and part gift?
- What does Alice intend to do with the sale proceeds?

Once you have the answers to these questions, you can advise Alice on the tax consequences of the proposed transaction. ▼

Chapters 14 and 15 discuss the determination of realized and recognized gain or loss and the basis of property. Chapters 16 and 17 cover the classification of the recognized gain or loss as ordinary or capital.

DETERMINATION OF GAIN OR LOSS

REALIZED GAIN OR LOSS

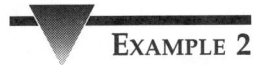 **LEARNING OBJECTIVE**
Understand the computation of realized gain or loss on property dispositions.

Realized gain or loss is measured by the difference between the amount realized from the sale or other disposition of property and the property's adjusted basis on the date of disposition. If the amount realized exceeds the property's adjusted basis, the result is a **realized gain.** Conversely, if the property's adjusted basis exceeds the amount realized, the result is a **realized loss.**[1]

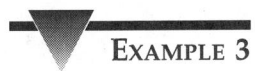 **EXAMPLE 2**

Tab sells Swan Corporation stock with an adjusted basis of $3,000 for $5,000. Tab's realized gain is $2,000. If Tab had sold the stock for $2,000, he would have had a $1,000 realized loss. ▼

Sale or Other Disposition. The term *sale or other disposition* is defined broadly in the tax law and includes virtually any disposition of property. Thus, transactions such as trade-ins, casualties, condemnations, thefts, and bond retirements are treated as dispositions of property. The most common disposition of property is through a sale or exchange. The key factor in determining whether a disposition has taken place usually is whether an identifiable event has occurred[2] as opposed to a mere fluctuation in the value of the property.[3]

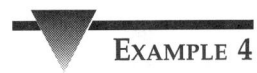 **EXAMPLE 3**

Lori owns Tan Corporation stock that cost $3,000. The stock has appreciated in value by $2,000 since Lori purchased it. Lori has no realized gain since mere fluctuation in value is not a disposition or identifiable event for tax purposes. Nor would Lori have a realized loss had the stock declined in value by $2,000. ▼

Amount Realized. The **amount realized** from a sale or other disposition of property is the sum of any money received plus the fair market value of other property received. The amount realized also includes any real property taxes treated as imposed on the seller that are actually paid by the buyer.[4] The reason for including these taxes in the amount realized is that by paying the taxes, the purchaser is, in effect, paying an additional amount to the seller of the property.

The amount realized also includes any liability on the property disposed of, such as a mortgage debt, if the buyer assumes the mortgage or the property is sold subject to the mortgage.[5] The amount of the liability is included in the amount realized even if the debt is nonrecourse and the amount of the debt is greater than the fair market value of the mortgaged property.[6]

EXAMPLE 4

Barry sells property on which there is a mortgage of $20,000 to Cole for $50,000 cash. Barry's amount realized from the sale is $70,000 if Cole assumes the mortgage or takes the property subject to the mortgage. ▼

---

[1]§ 1001(a) and Reg. § 1.1001–1(a).
[2]Reg. § 1.1001–1(c)(1).
[3]*Lynch v. Turrish*, 1 USTC ¶18, 3 AFTR 2986, 38 S.Ct. 537 (USSC, 1918).
[4]§ 1001(b) and Reg. § 1.1001–1(b). Refer to Chapter 10 for a discussion of this subject.
[5]*Crane v. Comm.*, 47–1 USTC ¶9217, 35 AFTR 776, 67 S.Ct. 1047 (USSC, 1947). Although a legal distinction exists between the direct assumption of a mortgage and taking property subject to a mort-

gage, the tax consequences in calculating the amount realized are the same.
[6]*Comm. v. Tufts*, 83–1 USTC ¶9328, 51 AFTR2d 83–1132, 103 S.Ct. 1826 (USSC, 1983).

TAX IN THE NEWS

WHAT IS THE AMOUNT REALIZED?

Determining the "amount realized" may be difficult, but usually can be done. The statutory definition is as follows: the sum of any money received plus the fair market value of property received. In a foreclosure sale, the amount realized includes the indebtedness discharged as the result of the foreclosure. In a real-world situation, however, the facts may not be nearly as clear as they are in a textbook situation.

In a recent case [*Wicker v. Comm.* 95–1 USTC ¶50,182, 75 AFTR2d 95–1701 (CA–8, 1995)], the Court of Appeals affirmed a Tax Court decision regarding the inability to calculate the "amount realized." In the case, both the IRS and the taxpayer could be viewed as losers or as winners, depending on one's perspective. The taxpayer had claimed a loss on his return associated with the foreclosure of mortgaged properties (i.e., the creditor accepted the mortgaged properties in exchange for the mortgage, with the properties being sold at a foreclosure sale). The IRS's position was that the foreclosure transaction produced a gain.

Because there was no evidence as to whether the loan was recourse or nonrecourse or the amount of the proceeds from the foreclosure sale, the Court concluded that the amount realized from the foreclosure could not be determined. Without a determination of the amount realized, it was not possible to ascertain if the foreclosure resulted in a gain or loss.

The **fair market value** of property received in a sale or other disposition has been defined by the courts as the price at which property will change hands between a willing seller and a willing buyer when neither is compelled to sell or buy.[7] Fair market value is determined by considering the relevant factors in each case.[8] An expert appraiser is often required to evaluate these factors in arriving at fair market value. When the fair market value of the property received cannot be determined, the value of the property surrendered may be used.[9]

In calculating the amount realized, selling expenses such as advertising, commissions, and legal fees relating to the disposition are deducted. The amount realized is the net amount received directly or indirectly by the taxpayer from the disposition of property in the form of cash or anything else of value.

Adjusted Basis.   The **adjusted basis** of property disposed of is the property's original basis adjusted to the date of disposition.[10] Original basis is the cost or other basis of the property on the date the property is acquired by the taxpayer. *Capital additions* increase and *recoveries of capital* decrease the original basis so that on the date of disposition the adjusted basis reflects the unrecovered cost or other basis of the property.[11] Adjusted basis is determined as follows:

---

[7]*Comm. v. Marshman*, 60–2 USTC ¶9484, 5 AFTR2d 1528, 279 F.2d 27 (CA–6, 1960).

[8]*O'Malley v. Ames*, 52–1 USTC ¶9361, 42 AFTR 19, 197 F.2d 256 (CA–8, 1952).

[9]*U.S. v. Davis*, 62–2 USTC ¶9509, 9 AFTR2d 1625, 82 S.Ct. 1190 (USSC, 1962).

[10]§ 1011(a) and Reg. § 1.1011–1.

[11]§ 1016(a) and Reg. § 1.1016–1.

Cost (or other adjusted basis) on date of acquisition

+ Capital additions

− Capital recoveries

= Adjusted basis on date of disposition

Capital Additions.   Capital additions include the cost of capital improvements and betterments made to the property by the taxpayer. These expenditures are distinguishable from expenditures for the ordinary repair and maintenance of the property that are neither capitalized nor added to the original basis (refer to Chapter 6). The latter expenditures are deductible in the current taxable year if they are related to business or income-producing property. Amounts representing real property taxes treated as imposed on the seller but paid or assumed by the buyer are part of the cost of the property.[12] Any liability on property that is assumed by the buyer is also included in the buyer's original basis of the property. The same rule applies if property is acquired subject to a liability. Amortization of the discount on bonds increases the adjusted basis of the bonds.[13]

Capital Recoveries.   The following are examples of capital recoveries:

1. *Depreciation and cost recovery allowances.* The original basis of depreciable property is reduced by the annual depreciation charges (or cost recovery allowances) while the property is held by the taxpayer. The amount of depreciation that is subtracted from the original basis is the greater of the *allowed* or *allowable* depreciation on an annual basis.[14] In most circumstances, the allowed and allowable depreciation amounts are the same (refer to Chapter 8).
2. *Casualties and thefts.* A casualty or theft may result in the reduction of the adjusted basis of property.[15] The adjusted basis is reduced by the amount of the deductible loss. In addition, the adjusted basis is reduced by the amount of insurance proceeds received. However, the receipt of insurance proceeds may result in a recognized gain rather than a deductible loss. The gain increases the adjusted basis of the property.[16]

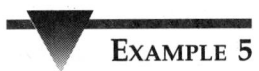 **EXAMPLE 5**   An insured truck used in a trade or business is destroyed in an accident. The adjusted basis is $8,000, and the fair market value is $6,500. Insurance proceeds of $6,500 are received. The amount of the casualty loss is $1,500 ($6,500 insurance proceeds − $8,000 adjusted basis). The adjusted basis is reduced by the $1,500 casualty loss and the $6,500 of insurance proceeds received. ▼

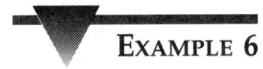 **EXAMPLE 6**   An insured truck used in a trade or business is destroyed in an accident. The adjusted basis is $6,500, and the fair market value is $8,000. Insurance proceeds of $8,000 are received. The amount of the casualty gain is $1,500 ($8,000 insurance proceeds − $6,500 adjusted basis). The adjusted basis is increased by the $1,500 casualty gain and is reduced by the $8,000 of insurance proceeds received ($6,500 basis before casualty + $1,500 casualty gain − $8,000 insurance proceeds = $0 basis). ▼

---

[12]Reg. §§ 1.1001–1(b)(2) and 1.1012–1(b). Refer to Chapter 10 for a discussion of this subject.

[13]See Chapter 16 for a discussion of bond discount and the related amortization.

[14]§ 1016(a)(2) and Reg. § 1.1016–3(a)(1)(i).

[15]Refer to Chapter 7 for the discussion of casualties and thefts.

[16]Reg. § 1.1016–6(a).

3. *Certain corporate distributions.* A corporate distribution to a shareholder that is not taxable is treated as a return of capital, and it reduces the basis of the shareholder's stock in the corporation.[17] For example, if a corporation makes a cash distribution to its shareholders and has no earnings and profits, the distributions are treated as a return of capital. Once the basis of the stock is reduced to zero, the amount of any subsequent distributions is a capital gain if the stock is a capital asset. These rules are illustrated in Example 20 of Chapter 20.

ETHICAL CONSIDERATIONS

Reporting of a Distribution: Dividend versus Return of Capital

Rebecca purchased 100 shares of stock in Bluebird, Inc., on December 24, 1998, for $50,000. In January 1999, Rebecca receives a Form 1099 for 1998 from the corporation indicating that she should report dividend income of $2,000 on her tax return. While she did receive a check from Bluebird on January 4, 1999 (postmarked December 31), she believes that it is a return of capital. Therefore, she reduces her adjusted basis for the stock to $48,000 and reports no dividend income for 1998. Her justification is that the corporation reported a loss in its fourth quarter financial statements. Evaluate Rebecca's reporting of the $2,000 distribution.

---

4. *Amortizable bond premium.* The basis in a bond purchased at a premium is reduced by the amortizable portion of the bond premium.[18] Investors in taxable bonds may *elect* to amortize the bond premium, but the premium on tax-exempt bonds *must be* amortized.[19] The amount of the amortized premium on taxable bonds is permitted as an interest deduction. Therefore, the election produces the opportunity for an annual interest deduction to offset ordinary income in exchange for a larger capital gain or smaller capital loss on the disposition of the bond. No such interest deduction is permitted for tax-exempt bonds.

The amortization deduction is allowed for taxable bonds because the premium is viewed as a cost of earning the taxable interest from the bonds. The reason the basis of taxable bonds is reduced is that the amortization deduction is a recovery of the cost or basis of the bonds. The basis of tax-exempt bonds is reduced even though the amortization is not allowed as a deduction. No amortization deduction is permitted on tax-exempt bonds since the interest income is exempt from tax and the amortization of the bond premium merely represents an adjustment of the effective amount of such income.

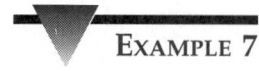

EXAMPLE 7

Antonio purchases Eagle Corporation taxable bonds with a face value of $100,000 for $110,000, thus paying a premium of $10,000. The annual interest rate is 7%, and the bonds mature 10 years from the date of purchase. The annual interest income is $7,000

---

[17]§ 1016(a)(4) and Reg. § 1.1016–5(a).

[18]§ 1016(a)(5) and Reg. § 1.1016–5(b). The accounting treatment of bond premium amortization is the same as for tax purposes. The amortization results in a decrease in the bond investment account.

[19]§ 171(c).

CONCEPT SUMMARY 14–1

Recognized Gain or Loss

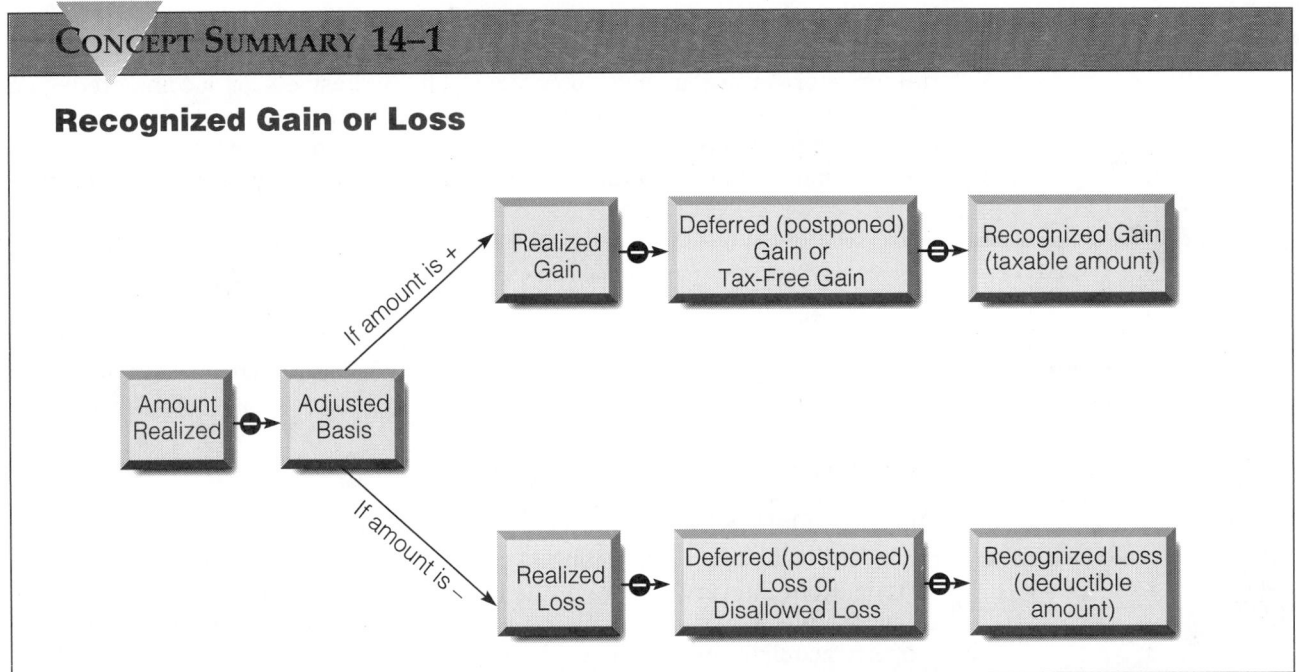

(7% × $100,000). If Antonio elects to amortize the bond premium, the $10,000 premium is deducted over the 10-year period. Antonio's basis for the bonds is reduced each year by the amount of the amortization deduction. Note that if the bonds were tax-exempt, amortization of the bond premium and the basis adjustment would be mandatory. However, no deduction would be allowed for the amortization. ▼

2 **LEARNING OBJECTIVE**
Distinguish between realized and recognized gain or loss.

RECOGNIZED GAIN OR LOSS

Recognized gain is the amount of the realized gain included in the taxpayer's gross income.[20] A **recognized loss,** on the other hand, is the amount of a realized loss that is deductible for tax purposes.[21] As a general rule, the entire amount of a realized gain or loss is recognized.[22]

Concept Summary 14–1 summarizes the realized gain or loss and recognized gain or loss concepts.

NONRECOGNITION OF GAIN OR LOSS

In certain cases, a realized gain or loss is not recognized upon the sale or other disposition of property. One of the exceptions to the recognition of gain or loss involves nontaxable exchanges, which are covered in Chapter 15. Additional exceptions include losses realized upon the sale, exchange, or condemnation of personal use assets (as opposed to business or income-producing property) and gains realized upon the sale of a residence (see Chapter 15). In addition, realized losses from the sale or exchange of business or income-producing property between certain related parties are not recognized.[23]

[20]§ 61(a)(3) and Reg. § 1.61–6(a).
[21]§ 165(a) and Reg. § 1.165–1(a).
[22]§ 1001(c) and Reg. § 1.1002–1(a).
[23]§ 267(a)(1).

Sale, Exchange, or Condemnation of Personal Use Assets.   A realized loss from the sale, exchange, or condemnation of personal use assets (e.g., a personal residence or an automobile not used at all for business or income-producing purposes) is not recognized for tax purposes. An exception exists for casualty or theft losses from personal use assets (see Chapter 7). In contrast, any gain realized from the sale or other disposition of personal use assets is, generally, fully taxable.

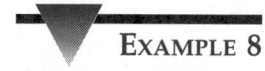

EXAMPLE 8

Freda sells an automobile, which is held exclusively for personal use, for $6,000. The adjusted basis of the automobile is $5,000. Freda has a realized and recognized gain of $1,000. ▼

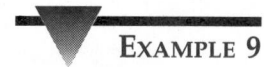

EXAMPLE 9

Freda sells the automobile in Example 8 for $4,000. She has a realized loss of $1,000, but the loss is not recognized. ▼

RECOVERY OF CAPITAL DOCTRINE

3   **LEARNING OBJECTIVE**
Apply the recovery of capital doctrine.

Doctrine Defined.   The **recovery of capital doctrine** is very significant and pervades all the tax rules relating to property transactions. The doctrine derives its roots from the very essence of the income tax—a tax on income. Therefore, as a general rule, a taxpayer is entitled to recover the cost or other original basis of property acquired and is not taxed on that amount.

The cost or other original basis of depreciable property is recovered through annual depreciation deductions. The basis is reduced as the cost is recovered over the period the property is held. Therefore, when property is sold or otherwise disposed of, it is the adjusted basis (unrecovered cost or other basis) that is compared to the amount realized from the disposition to determine realized gain or loss.

Relationship of the Recovery of Capital Doctrine to the Concepts of Realization and Recognition.   If a sale or other disposition results in a realized gain, the taxpayer has recovered more than the adjusted basis of the property. Conversely, if a sale or other disposition results in a realized loss, the taxpayer has recovered less than the adjusted basis.

The general rules for the relationship between the recovery of capital doctrine and the realized and recognized gain and loss concepts are summarized as follows:

Rule 1. A realized gain that is *never recognized* results in the *permanent recovery* of more than the taxpayer's cost or other basis for tax purposes. For example, all or a portion of the realized gain on the sale of a personal residence can be excluded from gross income under § 121.

Rule 2. A realized gain on which *recognition is postponed* results in the *temporary recovery* of more than the taxpayer's cost or other basis for tax purposes. For example, an exchange of like-kind property under § 1031 and an involuntary conversion under § 1033 are both eligible for postponement treatment.

Rule 3. A realized loss that is *never recognized* results in the *permanent recovery* of less than the taxpayer's cost or other basis for tax purposes. For example, a loss on the sale of an automobile held for personal use is not deductible.

Rule 4. A realized loss on which *recognition is postponed* results in the *temporary recovery* of less than the taxpayer's cost or other basis for tax purposes. For example, the realized loss on the exchange of like-kind property under § 1031 is postponed.

These rules are illustrated in discussions to follow in this and the next chapter.

BASIS CONSIDERATIONS

DETERMINATION OF COST BASIS

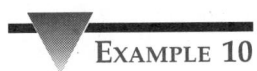

4 **LEARNING OBJECTIVE**
Explain how basis is determined for various methods of asset acquisition.

The basis of property is generally the property's cost. Cost is the amount paid for the property in cash or other property.[24] This general rule follows logically from the recovery of capital doctrine; that is, the cost or other basis of property is to be recovered tax-free by the taxpayer.

A *bargain purchase* of property is an exception to the general rule for determining basis. A bargain purchase may result when an employer transfers property to an employee at less than the property's fair market value (as compensation for services) or when a corporation transfers property to a shareholder at less than the property's fair market value (a dividend). The basis of property acquired in a bargain purchase is the property's fair market value.[25] If the basis of the property were not increased by the bargain amount, the taxpayer would be taxed on this amount again at disposition.

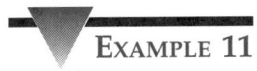

EXAMPLE 10

Wade buys a machine from his employer for $10,000 on December 30. The fair market value of the machine is $15,000. Wade must include the $5,000 difference between cost and the fair market value of the machine in gross income for the taxable year. The bargain element represents additional compensation to Wade. His basis for the machine is $15,000, the machine's fair market value. ▼

Identification Problems.   Cost identification problems are frequently encountered in securities transactions. For example, the Regulations require that the taxpayer adequately identify the particular stock that has been sold.[26] A problem arises when the taxpayer has purchased separate lots of stock on different dates or at different prices and cannot adequately identify the lot from which a particular sale takes place. In this case, the stock is presumed to come from the first lot or lots purchased (a FIFO presumption).[27] When securities are left in the custody of a broker, it may be necessary to provide specific instructions and receive written confirmation as to which securities are being sold.

EXAMPLE 11

Polly purchases 100 shares of Olive Corporation stock on July 1, 1996, for $5,000 ($50 a share) and another 100 shares of Olive stock on July 1, 1997, for $6,000 ($60 a share). She sells 50 shares of the stock on January 2, 1998. The cost of the stock sold, assuming Polly cannot adequately identify the shares, is $50 a share, or $2,500. This is the cost Polly will compare to the amount realized in determining the gain or loss from the sale. ▼

Allocation Problems.   When a taxpayer acquires *multiple assets in a lump-sum purchase*, the total cost must be allocated among the individual assets.[28] Allocation is necessary because some of the assets acquired may be depreciable (e.g., buildings) and others not (e.g., land). In addition, only a portion of the assets acquired may be sold, or some of the assets may be capital or § 1231 assets that receive special tax treatment upon subsequent sale or other disposition. The lump-sum cost is allocated on the basis of the fair market values of the individual assets acquired.

---

[24]§ 1012 and Reg. § 1.1012–1(a).
[25]Reg. §§ 1.61–2(d)(2)(i) and 1.301–1(j).
[26]Reg. § 1.1012–1(c)(1).

[27]*Kluger Associates, Inc.,* 69 T.C. 925 (1978).
[28]Reg. § 1.61–6(a).

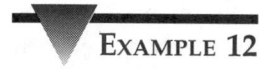

EXAMPLE 12

Harry purchases a building and land for $800,000. Because of the depressed nature of the industry in which the seller was operating, Harry was able to negotiate a very favorable purchase price. Appraisals of the individual assets indicate that the fair market value of the building is $600,000 and that of the land is $400,000. Harry's basis for the building is $480,000 [($600,000/$1,000,000) × $800,000], and his basis for the land is $320,000 [($400,000/$1,000,000) × $800,000]. ▼

If a business is purchased and **goodwill** is involved, a special allocation rule applies. Initially, the purchase price is assigned to the assets, excluding goodwill, to the extent of their total fair market value. This assigned amount is allocated among the assets on the basis of the fair market value of the individual assets acquired. Goodwill is then assigned the residual amount of the purchase price. The resultant allocation is applicable to both the buyer and the seller.[29]

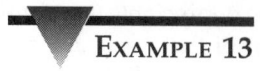

EXAMPLE 13

Rocky sells his business to Paul. They agree that the values of the individual assets are as follows:

Inventory	$ 50,000
Building	500,000
Land	200,000
Goodwill	150,000

[29]§ 1060.

After negotiations, Rocky and Paul agree on a sales price of $1 million. Applying the residual method with respect to goodwill results in the following allocation of the $1 million purchase price:

Inventory	$ 50,000
Building	500,000
Land	200,000
Goodwill	250,000

The residual method requires that all of the excess of the purchase price over the fair market value of the assets ($1,000,000 – $900,000 = $100,000) be allocated to goodwill. Without this requirement, the purchaser could allocate the excess pro rata to all of the assets, including goodwill, based on their respective fair market values. This would have resulted in only $166,667 [$150,000 + ($150,000 ÷ $900,000 × $100,000)] being assigned to goodwill. ▼

In the case of *nontaxable stock dividends*, the allocation depends upon whether the dividend is a common stock dividend on common stock or a preferred stock dividend on common stock. If the dividend is common on common, the cost of the original common shares is allocated to the total shares owned after the dividend.[30]

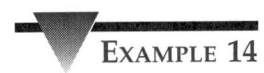

EXAMPLE 14

Susan owns 100 shares of Sparrow Corporation common stock for which she paid $1,100. She receives a 10% common stock dividend, giving her a new total of 110 shares. Before the stock dividend, Susan's basis was $11 per share ($1,100 ÷ 100 shares). The basis of each share after the stock dividend is $10 ($1,100 ÷ 110 shares). ▼

If the dividend is preferred stock on common, the cost of the original common shares is allocated between the common and preferred shares on the basis of their relative fair market values on the date of distribution.[31]

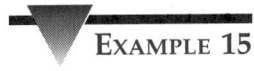

EXAMPLE 15

Fran owns 100 shares of Cardinal Corporation common stock for which she paid $1,000. She receives a stock dividend of 50 shares of preferred stock on her common stock. The fair market values on the date of distribution of the preferred stock dividend are $30 a share for common stock and $40 a share for preferred stock. Thus, the total fair market value is $3,000 ($30 × 100) for common stock and $2,000 ($40 × 50) for preferred stock. The basis of Fran's common stock after the dividend is $600, or $6 a share [($3,000/$5,000) × $1,000], and the basis of the preferred stock is $400, or $8 a share [($2,000/$5,000) × $1,000]. ▼

In the case of *nontaxable stock rights*, the basis of the rights is zero unless the taxpayer elects or is required to allocate a portion of the cost of the stock to the rights. If the fair market value of the rights is 15 percent or more of the fair market value of the stock, the taxpayer is required to allocate. If the value of the rights is less than 15 percent of the fair market value of the stock, the taxpayer may elect to allocate.[32] The result is that either the rights will have no basis or the cost of the stock on which the rights are received will be allocated between the stock and rights on the basis of their relative fair market values.

---

[30]§§ 305(a) and 307(a). The holding period of the new shares includes the holding period of the old shares. § 1223(5) and Reg. § 1.1223–1(e). See Chapter 16 for a discussion of the importance of the holding period.

[31]Reg. § 1.307–1(a).
[32]§ 307(b).

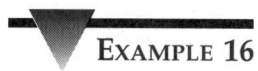

EXAMPLE 16

Donald receives nontaxable stock rights with a fair market value of $1,000. The fair market value of the stock on which the rights were received is $8,000 (cost $10,000). Donald does not elect to allocate. The basis of the rights is zero. If he exercises the rights, the basis of the new stock is the exercise (subscription) price. ▼

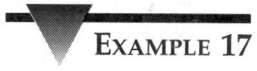

EXAMPLE 17

Assume the same facts as in Example 16, except the fair market value of the rights is $3,000. Donald must allocate because the value of the rights is 15% or more of the value of the stock ($3,000/$8,000 = 37.5%). The basis of the rights is $2,727 [($3,000/$11,000) × $10,000], and the basis of the stock is $7,273 [($8,000/$11,000) × $10,000]. If Donald exercises the rights, the basis of the new stock is the exercise (subscription) price plus the basis of the rights. If he sells the rights, he recognizes gain or loss to the extent of the difference between the amount realized and the basis of the rights. This allocation rule applies only when the rights are exercised or sold. Therefore, if the rights are allowed to lapse (expire), they have no basis, and the basis of the original stock is the stock's cost, $10,000. ▼

The holding period of nontaxable stock rights includes the holding period of the stock on which the rights were distributed. However, if the rights are exercised, the holding period of the newly acquired stock begins with the date the rights are exercised.[33] The significance of the holding period for capital assets is discussed in Chapter 16.

GIFT BASIS

When a taxpayer receives property as a gift, there is no cost to the recipient. Thus, under the cost basis provision, the donee's basis would be zero. However, this would violate the statutory intent that gifts are not subject to the income tax. With a zero basis, a sale by the donee would result in all of the amount realized being treated as realized gain. Therefore, a basis is assigned to the property received depending on the following:[34]

- The date of the gift.
- The basis of the property to the donor.
- The amount of the gift tax paid.
- The fair market value of the property.

Gift Basis Rules if No Gift Tax Is Paid.   Property received by gift can be referred to as *dual basis* property; that is, the basis for gain and the basis for loss might not be the same amount. The present basis rules for gifts of property are as follows:

- If the donee subsequently disposes of gift property in a transaction that results in a gain, the basis to the donee is the same as the donor's adjusted basis.[35] The donee's basis in this case is referred to as the *gain basis*. Therefore, a *realized gain* results if the amount realized from the disposition exceeds the donee's gain basis.

---

[33] § 1223(5) and Reg. §§ 1.1223–1(e) and (f).
[34] § 102(a).
[35] § 1015(a) and Reg. § 1.1015–1(a)(1). See Reg. § 1.1015–1(a)(3) for cases in which the facts necessary to determine the donor's adjusted

basis are unknown. Refer to Example 24 for the effect of depreciation deductions by the donee.

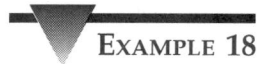

EXAMPLE 18

Melissa purchased stock in 1997 for $10,000. She gave the stock to her son, Joe, in 1998, when the fair market value was $15,000. Assume no gift tax is paid on the transfer and Joe subsequently sells the property for $15,000. Joe's basis is $10,000, and he has a realized gain of $5,000. ▼

- If the donee subsequently disposes of gift property in a transaction that results in a loss, the basis to the donee is the *lower* of the donor's adjusted basis or fair market value on the date of the gift. The donee's basis in this case is referred to as the *loss basis*. Therefore, a *realized loss* results if the amount realized from the disposition is less than the donee's loss basis.

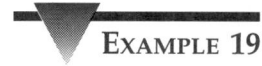

EXAMPLE 19

Burt purchased stock in 1997 for $10,000. He gave the stock to his son, Cliff, in 1998, when the fair market value was $7,000. Assume no gift tax is paid on the transfer. Cliff later sells the stock for $6,000. Cliff's basis is $7,000 (fair market value is less than donor's adjusted basis of $10,000), and the realized loss from the sale is $1,000 ($6,000 amount realized – $7,000 basis). ▼

The amount of the loss basis will *differ* from the amount of the gain basis only if at the date of the gift the adjusted basis of the property exceeds the property's fair market value. Note that the loss basis rule prevents the donee from receiving a tax benefit from the decline in value while the donor held the property. Therefore, in Example 19, Cliff has a loss of only $1,000 rather than a loss of $4,000. The $3,000 difference represents the decline in value while Burt held the property. Ironically, however, the gain basis rule may eventually result in the donee's being subject to income tax on the appreciation that occurred while the donor held the property, as illustrated in Example 18.

If the amount realized from sale or other disposition is *between* the basis for loss and the basis for gain, no gain or loss is realized.

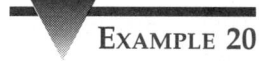

EXAMPLE 20

Assume the same facts as in Example 19, except that Cliff sold the stock for $8,000. The application of the gain basis rule produces a loss of $2,000 ($8,000 – $10,000). The application of the loss basis rule produces a gain of $1,000 ($8,000 – $7,000). Therefore, Cliff recognizes neither a gain nor a loss because the amount realized is between the gain basis and the loss basis. ▼

Adjustment for Gift Tax.   If gift taxes are paid by the donor, the donee's gain basis may exceed the adjusted basis of the property to the donor. This occurs only if the fair market value of the property at the date of the gift is greater than the donor's adjusted basis (the property has appreciated in value). The portion of the gift tax paid that is related to the appreciation is added to the donor's basis in calculating the donee's gain basis for the property. In this circumstance, the following formula is used for calculating the donee's gain basis:[36]

$$\text{Donee's gain basis} = \text{Donor's adjusted basis} + \left(\frac{\text{Unrealized appreciation}}{\text{Fair market value at date of gift}} \times \text{Gift tax paid} \right)$$

---

[36]§ 1015(d)(6).

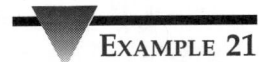

EXAMPLE 21

Bonnie made a gift of stock to Peggy in 1998, when the fair market value of the stock was $40,000. Bonnie had purchased the stock in 1982 for $10,000. Because the unrealized appreciation is $30,000 ($40,000 fair market value – $10,000 adjusted basis) and the fair market value is $40,000, three-fourths ($30,000/$40,000) of the gift tax paid is added to the basis of the property. If Bonnie paid gift tax of $4,000, Peggy's basis in the property is $13,000 [$10,000 + $3,000 (¾ of the $4,000 gift tax)]. ▼

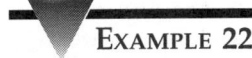

EXAMPLE 22

Don made a gift of stock to Matt in 1998, when the fair market value of the stock was $40,000. Gift tax of $4,000 was paid by Don, who had purchased the stock in 1982 for $45,000. Because there is no unrealized appreciation at the date of the gift, none of the gift tax paid is added to Don's basis in calculating Matt's gain basis. Therefore, Matt's gain basis is $45,000. ▼

For *gifts made before 1977*, the full amount of the gift tax paid is added to the donor's basis. However, the ceiling on this total is the fair market value of the property at the date of the gift. Thus, in Example 21, if the gift had been made before 1977, the basis of the property would be $14,000 ($10,000 + $4,000). In Example 22, the gain basis would still be $45,000 ($45,000 + $0).

Holding Period. The **holding period** for property acquired by gift begins on the date the donor acquired the property if the gain basis rule applies.[37] The holding period starts on the date of the gift if the loss basis rule applies.[38] The significance of the holding period for capital assets is discussed in Chapter 16.

The following example summarizes the basis and holding period rules for gift property:

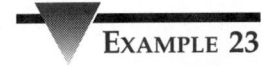

EXAMPLE 23

Jill acquires 100 shares of Wren Corporation stock on December 30, 1982, for $40,000. On January 3, 1998, when the stock has a fair market value of $38,000, Jill gives it to Dennis and pays gift tax of $4,000. The basis is not increased by a portion of the gift tax paid because the property has not appreciated in value at the time of the gift. Therefore, Dennis's gain basis is $40,000. Dennis's basis for determining loss is $38,000 (fair market value) because the fair market value on the date of the gift is less than the donor's adjusted basis.

- If Dennis sells the stock for $45,000, he has a recognized gain of $5,000. The holding period for determining whether the capital gain is short term, mid-term, or long term begins on December 30, 1982, the date Jill acquired the property.
- If Dennis sells the stock for $36,000, he has a recognized loss of $2,000. The holding period for determining whether the capital loss is short term, mid-term, or long term begins on January 3, 1998, the date of the gift.
- If Dennis sells the property for $39,000, there is no gain or loss since the amount realized is less than the gain basis of $40,000 and more than the loss basis of $38,000. ▼

Basis for Depreciation. The basis for depreciation on depreciable gift property is the donee's gain basis.[39] This rule is applicable even if the donee later sells the property at a loss and uses the loss basis rule in calculating the amount of the realized loss.

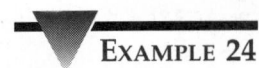

EXAMPLE 24

Vito gave a machine to Tina in 1998, when the adjusted basis was $32,000 (cost of $40,000 – accumulated depreciation of $8,000) and the fair market value was $26,000. No gift tax was paid. Tina's gain basis at the date of the gift is $32,000, and her loss

[37]§ 1223(2) and Reg. § 1.1223–1(b).
[38]Rev.Rul. 59–86, 1959–1 C.B. 209.

[39]§ 1011 and Reg. §§ 1.1011–1 and 1.167(g)–1.

basis is $26,000. During 1998, Tina deducts depreciation (cost recovery) of $10,240 ($32,000 × 32%). Therefore, at the end of 1998, Tina's gain basis and loss basis are calculated as follows:

	Gain Basis	Loss Basis
Donor's basis or fair market value	$ 32,000	$ 26,000
Depreciation	(10,240)	(10,240)
	$ 21,760	$ 15,760

PROPERTY ACQUIRED FROM A DECEDENT

General Rules. The basis of property acquired from a decedent is generally the property's fair market value at the date of death (referred to as the *primary valuation amount*).[40] The property's basis is the fair market value six months after the date of death if the executor or administrator of the estate *elects* the alternate valuation date for estate tax purposes. This amount is referred to as the *alternate valuation amount*.

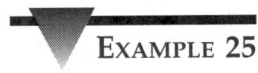 **EXAMPLE 25**

Linda and various other family members inherited property from Linda's father, who died in 1998. At the date of death, her father's adjusted basis for the property Linda inherited was $35,000. The property's fair market value at date of death was $50,000. The alternate valuation date was not elected. Linda's basis for income tax purposes is $50,000. This is commonly referred to as a *stepped-up basis*. ▼

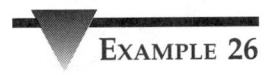 **EXAMPLE 26**

Assume the same facts as in Example 25, except the property's fair market value at date of death was $20,000. Linda's basis for income tax purposes is $20,000. This is commonly referred to as a *stepped-down basis*. ▼

If an estate tax return does not have to be filed because the estate is below the threshold amount for being subject to the estate tax, the alternate valuation date and amount are not available. Even if an estate tax return is filed and the executor elects the alternate valuation date, the six months after death date is available only for property that the executor has not distributed before this date. Any property distributed or otherwise disposed of by the executor during this six-month period will have an adjusted basis to the beneficiary equal to the fair market value on the date of distribution or other disposition.[41]

The alternate valuation date can be *elected only* if the election results in both the value of the gross estate and the estate tax liability being reduced below the amounts they would have been if the primary valuation date had been used. This provision prevents the alternate valuation election from being used to increase the basis of the property to the beneficiary for income tax purposes without simultaneously increasing the estate tax liability (because of estate tax deductions or credits).[42]

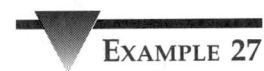 **EXAMPLE 27**

Nancy inherited all the property of her father, who died in 1998. Her father's adjusted basis for the property at date of death was $35,000. The property's fair market value was $750,000 at date of death and $760,000 six months after death. The alternate valuation date cannot

---

[40]§ 1014(a).
[41]§ 2032(a)(1) and Rev.Rul. 56–60, 1956–1 C.B. 443.

[42]§ 2032(c).

be elected because the value of the gross estate has increased during the six-month period. Nancy's basis for income tax purposes is $750,000. ▼

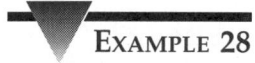

EXAMPLE 28

Assume the same facts as in Example 27, except the property's fair market value six months after death was $745,000. If the executor elects the alternate valuation date, Nancy's basis for income tax purposes is $745,000. ▼

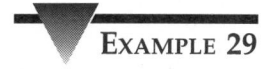

EXAMPLE 29

Assume the same facts as in the previous example, except the property is distributed four months after the date of the decedent's death. At the distribution date, the property's fair market value is $747,500. Since the executor elected the alternate valuation date, Nancy's basis for income tax purposes is $747,500. ▼

For inherited property, both unrealized appreciation and decline in value are taken into consideration in determining the basis of the property for income tax purposes. Contrast this with the carryover basis rules for property received by gift.

Deathbed Gifts.   The Code contains a provision designed to eliminate a tax avoidance technique referred to as *deathbed gifts*. If the time period between the date of the gift of appreciated property and the date of the donee's death is not longer than one year, the usual basis rule (stepped-up basis) for inherited property may not apply. The adjusted basis of such property inherited by the donor or his or her spouse from the donee shall be the same as the decedent's adjusted basis for the property rather than the fair market value at the date of death or the alternate valuation date.[43]

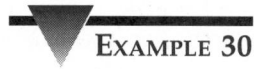

EXAMPLE 30

Ned gives stock to his uncle, Vern, in 1998. Ned's basis for the stock is $1,000, and the fair market value is $9,000. No gift tax is paid. Eight months later, Ned inherits the stock from Vern. At the date of Vern's death, the fair market value of the stock is $12,000. Ned's adjusted basis for the stock is $1,000. ▼

ETHICAL CONSIDERATIONS

Helping a Friend Increase Basis

Holly owns stock with an adjusted basis of $2,500 and a fair market value of $9,500. Holly expects the stock to continue to appreciate. Alice, Holly's best friend, has recently been operated on for cancer. Alice's physicians have told her that her life expectancy is between six months and one and a half years.

One day at lunch, the two friends were discussing their tax situations (both feel they pay too much), when Alice mentioned that she had read a newspaper article about a tax planning opportunity that might be suitable for Holly. Holly would make a gift of the appreciated stock to Alice. In her will, Alice would bequeath the stock to Holly. Since Alice is confident that she will live longer than a year, the basis of the stock to Holly would be the fair market value on the date of Alice's death. Alice would "feel good" because she had helped Holly "beat the tax system."

You are Holly's tax adviser. How will you respond to Alice's proposal to Holly?

---

[43]§ 1014(e).

Survivor's Share of Property.   Both the decedent's share and the survivor's share of *community property* have a basis equal to fair market value on the date of the decedent's death.[44] This result applies to the decedent's share of the community property because the property flows to the surviving spouse from the estate (fair market value basis for inherited property). Likewise, the surviving spouse's share of the community property is deemed to be acquired by bequest, devise, or inheritance from the decedent. Therefore, it also has a basis equal to fair market value.

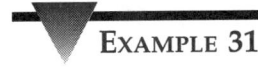

EXAMPLE 31   Floyd and Vera reside in a community property state. They own community property (200 shares of Crow stock) that was acquired in 1974 for $100,000. Assume that Floyd dies in 1998, when the securities are valued at $300,000. One-half of the Crow stock is included in Floyd's estate. If Vera inherits Floyd's share of the community property, the basis for determining gain or loss is $300,000, determined as follows:

Vera's one-half of the community property (stepped up from $50,000 to $150,000 due to Floyd's death)	$150,000
Floyd's one-half of the community property (stepped up from $50,000 to $150,000 due to inclusion in his gross estate)	150,000
Vera's new basis	$300,000

In a *common law* state, only one-half of jointly held property of spouses (tenants by the entirety or joint tenants with rights of survivorship) is includible in the estate.[45] In such a case, no adjustment of the basis is permitted for the excluded property interest (the surviving spouse's share).

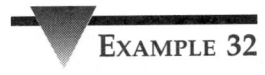

EXAMPLE 32   Assume the same facts as in the previous example, except that the property is jointly held by Floyd and Vera who reside in a common law state. Also assume that Floyd purchased the property and made a gift of one-half of the property when the stock was acquired, with no gift tax being paid. Only one-half of the Crow stock is included in Floyd's estate. Vera's basis for determining gain or loss in the excluded half is not adjusted upward for the increase in value to date of death. Therefore, Vera's basis is $200,000, determined as follows:

Vera's one-half of the jointly held property (carryover basis of $50,000)	$ 50,000
Floyd's one-half of the jointly held property (stepped up from $50,000 to $150,000 due to inclusion in his gross estate)	150,000
Vera's new basis	$200,000

Holding Period of Property Acquired from a Decedent.   The holding period of property acquired from a decedent is *deemed to be long term* (held for the required long-term holding period). This provision applies regardless of whether the property is disposed of at a gain or a loss.[46]

DISALLOWED LOSSES

5   **LEARNING OBJECTIVE**
Describe various loss disallowance provisions.

Related Taxpayers.   Section 267 provides that realized losses from sales or exchanges of property, directly or indirectly, between certain related parties are not recognized. This loss disallowance provision applies to several types of related-party transactions. The most common involve (1) members of a family and

---

[44]§ 1014(b)(6). See the listing of community property states in Chapter 4.

[45]§ 2040(b).
[46]§ 1223(11).

(2) transactions between an individual and a corporation in which the individual owns, directly or indirectly, more than 50 percent in value of the corporation's outstanding stock. Section 707 provides a similar loss disallowance provision if the related parties are a partner and a partnership in which the partner owns, directly or indirectly, more than 50 percent of the capital interests or profits interests in the partnership. The rules governing the relationships covered by § 267 were discussed in Chapter 6. See Chapter 15 for the discussion of the special rules under § 1041 for property transfers between spouses or incident to divorce.

If income-producing or business property is transferred to a related taxpayer and a loss is disallowed, the basis of the property to the recipient is the property's cost to the transferee. However, if a subsequent sale or other disposition of the property by the original transferee results in a realized gain, the amount of gain is reduced by the loss that was previously disallowed.[47] This *right of offset* is not applicable if the original sale involved the sale of a personal use asset (e.g., the sale of a personal residence between related taxpayers). Likewise, this right of offset is available only to the original transferee (the related-party buyer).

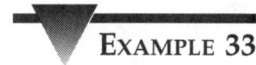

EXAMPLE 33

Pedro sells business property with an adjusted basis of $50,000 to his daughter, Josefina, for its fair market value of $40,000.

- Pedro's realized loss of $10,000 is not recognized.
- How much gain will Josefina recognize if she sells the property for $52,000? Josefina recognizes a $2,000 gain. Her realized gain is $12,000 ($52,000 less her basis of $40,000), but she can offset Pedro's $10,000 loss against the gain.
- How much gain will Josefina recognize if she sells the property for $48,000? Josefina recognizes no gain or loss. Her realized gain is $8,000 ($48,000 less her basis of $40,000), but she can offset $8,000 of Pedro's $10,000 loss against the gain. Note that Pedro's loss can only offset Josefina's gain. It cannot create a loss for Josefina.
- How much loss will Josefina recognize if she sells the property for $38,000? Josefina recognizes a $2,000 loss, the same as her realized loss ($38,000 less $40,000 basis). Pedro's loss does not increase Josefina's loss. His loss can be offset only against a gain. Since Josefina has no realized gain, Pedro's loss cannot be used and is never recognized. This example assumes that the property is business or income producing to Josefina. If not, her $2,000 loss is personal and is not recognized. ▼

The loss disallowance rules are designed to achieve two objectives. First, the rules prevent a taxpayer from directly transferring an unrealized loss to a related taxpayer in a higher tax bracket who could receive a greater tax benefit from the recognition of the loss. Second, the rules eliminate a substantial administrative burden on the Internal Revenue Service as to the appropriateness of the selling price (fair market value or not). The loss disallowance rules are applicable even where the selling price is equal to fair market value and can be validated (e.g., listed stocks).

The holding period of the buyer for the property is not affected by the holding period of the seller. That is, the buyer's *holding period* includes only the period of time he or she has held the property.[48]

Wash Sales.   Section 1091 stipulates that in certain cases, a realized loss on the sale or exchange of stock or securities is not recognized. Specifically, if a taxpayer sells or exchanges stock or securities and within 30 days before *or* after the date of the sale or exchange acquires substantially identical stock or securities, any loss

---

[47]§ 267(d) and Reg. § 1.267(d)–1(a).   [48]§§ 267(d) and 1223(2) and Reg. § 1.267(d)–1(c)(3).

Year-End Tax Planning and Property Transactions

As the end of the year approaches, taxpayers should evaluate their investment assets as a way to minimize Federal income tax liability. Underperforming investments whose disposition would produce a loss can be sold before year-end to offset recognized gains.

One procedure that will not work is to sell a security where there is a realized loss before the end of the year to offset recognized gains and then repurchase the same security shortly after the beginning of the year. Section 1091 classifies such a sale and repurchase as a "wash sale" and disallows the recognition of loss on the sale. From a planning perspective, § 1091 disallowance treatment can be avoided by not repurchasing the security within 30 days before or after the sales date. Thus, a little planning can produce much better tax results.

SOURCE: Adapted from Tom Herman, "Late Moves to Pare Taxes: Now's the Time," *Wall Street Journal*, December 4, 1996, p. C1.

realized from the sale or exchange is not recognized because the transaction is a **wash sale.**[49] The term *acquire* means acquire by purchase or in a taxable exchange and includes an option to purchase substantially identical securities. *Substantially identical* means the same in all important particulars. Corporate bonds and preferred stock are normally not considered substantially identical to the corporation's common stock. However, if the bonds and preferred stock are convertible into common stock, they may be considered substantially identical under certain circumstances.[50] Attempts to avoid the application of the wash sales rules by having a related taxpayer repurchase the securities have been unsuccessful.[51] The wash sales provisions do *not* apply to gains.

Recognition of the loss is disallowed because the taxpayer is considered to be in substantially the same economic position after the sale and repurchase as before the sale and repurchase. This disallowance rule does not apply to taxpayers engaged in the business of buying and selling securities.[52] Investors, however, are not allowed to create losses through wash sales to offset income for tax purposes.

Realized loss that is not recognized is added to the *basis* of the substantially identical stock or securities whose acquisition resulted in the nonrecognition of loss.[53] In other words, the basis of the replacement stock or securities is increased by the amount of the unrecognized loss. If the loss were not added to the basis of the newly acquired stock or securities, the taxpayer would never recover the entire basis of the old stock or securities.

The basis of the new stock or securities includes the unrecovered portion of the basis of the formerly held stock or securities. Therefore, the *holding period* of the new stock or securities begins on the date of acquisition of the old stock or securities.[54]

---

[49]§ 1091(a) and Reg. §§ 1.1091–1(a) and (f).
[50]Rev.Rul. 56–406, 1956–2 C.B. 523.
[51]*McWilliams v. Comm.*, 47–1 USTC ¶9289, 35 AFTR 1184, 67 S.Ct. 1477 (USSC, 1947).

[52]Reg. § 1.1091–1(a).
[53]§ 1091(d) and Reg. § 1.1091–2(a).
[54]§ 1223(4) and Reg. § 1.1223–1(d).

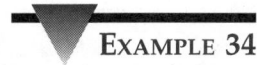

EXAMPLE 34

Bhaskar owns 100 shares of Green Corporation stock (adjusted basis of $20,000), 50 shares of which he sells for $8,000. Ten days later, he purchases 50 shares of the same stock for $7,000. Bhaskar's realized loss of $2,000 ($8,000 amount realized – $10,000 adjusted basis of 50 shares) is not recognized because it resulted from a wash sale. Bhaskar's basis in the newly acquired stock is $9,000 ($7,000 purchase price + $2,000 unrecognized loss from the wash sale). ▼

The taxpayer may acquire less than the number of shares sold in a wash sale. In this case, the loss from the sale is prorated between recognized and unrecognized loss on the basis of the ratio of the number of shares acquired to the number of shares sold.[55]

CONVERSION OF PROPERTY FROM PERSONAL USE TO BUSINESS OR INCOME-PRODUCING USE

As discussed previously, losses from the sale of personal use assets are not recognized for tax purposes, but losses from the sale of business and income-producing assets are deductible. Can a taxpayer convert a personal use asset that has declined in value to business (or income-producing) use and then sell the asset to recognize a business (or income-producing) loss? The tax law prevents this by specifying that the *original basis for loss* on personal use assets converted to business or income-producing use is the *lower* of the property's adjusted basis or fair market value on the date of conversion.[56] The *gain basis* for converted property is the property's adjusted basis on the date of conversion. The tax law is not concerned with gains on converted property because gains are recognized regardless of whether property is business, income producing, or personal use.

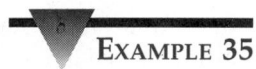

EXAMPLE 35

Diane's personal residence has an adjusted basis of $75,000 and a fair market value of $60,000. Diane converts the personal residence to rental property. Her basis for loss is $60,000 (lower of $75,000 adjusted basis and fair market value of $60,000). The $15,000 decline in value is a personal loss and can never be recognized for tax purposes. Diane's basis for gain is $75,000. ▼

The basis for loss is also the *basis for depreciating* the converted property.[57] This is an exception to the general rule that provides that the basis for depreciation is the gain basis (e.g., property received by gift). This exception prevents the taxpayer from recovering a personal loss indirectly through depreciation of the higher original basis. After the property is converted, both its basis for loss and its basis for gain are adjusted for depreciation deductions from the date of conversion to the date of disposition. These rules apply only if a conversion from personal to business or income-producing use has actually occurred.

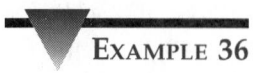

EXAMPLE 36

At a time when his personal residence (adjusted basis of $40,000) is worth $50,000, Keith converts one-half of it to rental use. Assume the property is not MACRS recovery property. At this point, the estimated useful life of the residence is 20 years, and there is no estimated salvage value. After renting the converted portion for five years, Keith sells the property for $44,000. All amounts relate only to the building; the land has been accounted for sepa-

---

[55]§ 1091(b) and Reg. § 1.1091–1(c).
[56]Reg. § 1.165–9(b)(2).

[57]Reg. § 1.167(g)–1.

rately. Keith has a $2,000 realized gain from the sale of the personal use portion of the residence and a $7,000 realized gain from the sale of the rental portion. These gains are computed as follows:

	Personal Use	Rental
Original basis for gain and loss—adjusted basis on date of conversion (fair market value is greater than the adjusted basis)	$20,000	$20,000
Depreciation—five years	None	5,000
Adjusted basis—date of sale	$20,000	$15,000
Amount realized	22,000	22,000
Realized gain	$ 2,000	$ 7,000

As discussed in Chapter 15, Keith may be able to exclude the $2,000 realized gain from the sale of the personal use portion of the residence under § 121. The $7,000 gain from the rental portion is recognized.

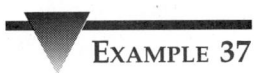

EXAMPLE 37

Assume the same facts as in the previous example, except that the fair market value on the date of conversion is $30,000 and the sales proceeds are $16,000. Keith has a $12,000 realized loss from the sale of the personal use portion of the residence and a $3,250 realized loss from the sale of the rental portion. These losses are computed as follows:

	Personal Use	Rental
Original basis for loss—fair market value on date of conversion (fair market value is less than the adjusted basis)	*	$15,000
Depreciation—five years	None	3,750
Adjusted basis—date of sale	$ 20,000	$11,250
Amount realized	8,000	8,000
Realized loss	$(12,000)	$ (3,250)

*Not applicable.

The $12,000 loss from the sale of the personal use portion of the residence is not recognized. The $3,250 loss from the rental portion is recognized. ▼

ADDITIONAL COMPLEXITIES IN DETERMINING REALIZED GAIN OR LOSS

Amount Realized. The calculation of the amount realized may appear to be one of the least complex areas associated with property transactions. However, because numerous positive and negative adjustments may be required, the calculation of this amount can be complex and confusing. In addition, the determination of the fair market value of the items received by the taxpayer can be difficult. The following example provides insight into various items that can have an impact on the amount realized.

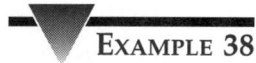

EXAMPLE 38

Ridge sells an office building and the associated land on October 1, 1998. Under the terms of the sales contract, Ridge is to receive $600,000 in cash. The purchaser is to assume Ridge's mortgage of $300,000 on the property. To enable the purchaser to obtain adequate financing to pay the $600,000, Ridge is to pay the $15,000 in points charged by the lender. The broker's commission on the sale is $45,000. The purchaser agrees to pay the $12,000 in property taxes for the entire year. The amount realized by Ridge is calculated as follows:

Selling price		
Cash	$600,000	
Mortgage assumed by purchaser	300,000	
Seller's property taxes paid by purchaser ($12,000 × 9/12)	9,000	$ 909,000
Less		
Broker's commission	$ 45,000	
Points paid by seller	15,000	(60,000)
Amount realized		$ 849,000

Adjusted Basis. Three types of items tend to complicate the determination of adjusted basis. First, the applicable tax provisions for calculating the adjusted basis are dependent on how the property was acquired (e.g., purchase, taxable exchange, nontaxable exchange, gift, inheritance). Second, if the asset is subject to depreciation, cost recovery, amortization, or depletion, adjustments must be made to the basis during the time period the asset is held by the taxpayer. Upon disposition of the asset, the taxpayer's records for both of these items may be deficient. For example, the donee does not know the amount of the donor's basis or the amount of gift tax paid by the donor, or the taxpayer does not know how much depreciation he or she has deducted. Third, the complex positive and negative adjustments encountered in calculating the amount realized are also involved in calculating the adjusted basis.

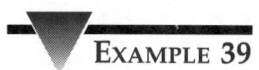

EXAMPLE 39

Jane purchased a personal residence in 1991. The purchase price and the related closing costs were as follows:

Purchase price	$ 125,000
Recording costs	140
Title fees and title insurance	815
Survey costs	115
Attorney's fees	750
Appraisal fee	60

Other relevant tax information for the house during the time Jane owned it is as follows:

- Constructed a swimming pool for medical reasons. The cost was $10,000, of which $3,000 was deducted as a medical expense.
- Added a solar heating system. The cost was $15,000.
- Deducted home office expenses of $6,000. Of this amount, $3,200 was for depreciation.

The adjusted basis for the house is calculated as follows:

Purchase price	$ 125,000
Recording costs	140
Title fees and title insurance	815
Survey costs	115
Attorney's fees	750
Appraisal fee	60
Swimming pool ($10,000 – $3,000)	7,000
Solar heating system	15,000
	$ 148,880
Less: Depreciation deducted on home office	(3,200)
Adjusted basis	$ 145,680

▼

SUMMARY OF BASIS ADJUSTMENTS

Some of the more common items that either increase or decrease the basis of an asset appear in Concept Summary 14–2.

In discussing the topic of basis, a number of specific techniques for determining basis have been presented. Although the various techniques are responsive to and mandated by transactions occurring in the marketplace, they do possess enough common characteristics to be categorized as follows:

- The basis of the asset may be determined by reference to the asset's cost.
- The basis of the asset may be determined by reference to the basis of another asset.
- The basis of the asset may be determined by reference to the asset's fair market value.
- The basis of the asset may be determined by reference to the basis of the asset to another taxpayer.

TAX PLANNING CONSIDERATIONS

6 **LEARNING OBJECTIVE**
Identify tax planning opportunities related to selected property transactions.

TAX CONSEQUENCES OF ALICE'S PROPOSED TRANSACTION

In Example 1 earlier in the chapter, Alice's tax adviser asked a number of questions in order to advise her on a proposed transaction. Alice provided the following answers:

- Alice inherited the house from her mother. The fair market value of the house at the date of her mother's death, based on the estate tax return, was $200,000. Based on an appraisal, the house is worth $230,000. Alice's mother lived in the house for 48 years. According to the mother's attorney, her adjusted basis for the house was $75,000.
- As a child, Alice lived in the house for 10 years. She has not lived there during the 35 years she has been married.
- The house has been vacant during the seven months that Alice has owned it. She has been trying to decide whether she should sell it for its fair market value or sell it to her nephew for $75,000. Alice has suggested a $75,000 price for the sale to Dan because she believes this is the amount at which she will have no gain or loss.
- Alice intends to invest the $75,000 in stock.

You advise Alice that her adjusted basis for the house is the $200,000 fair market value on the date of her mother's death. If Alice sells the house for $230,000 (assuming no selling expenses), she would have a recognized gain of $30,000

($230,000 amount realized – $200,000 adjusted basis). The house is a capital asset, and her holding period is long term since she inherited the house. Thus, the gain would be classified as a long-term capital gain. If, instead, Alice sells the house to her nephew for $75,000, she will have a part sale and part gift. The realized gain on the sale of $9,783 is recognized.

Amount realized	$ 75,000
Less: Adjusted basis	(65,217)*
Realized gain	$ 9,783
Recognized gain	$ 9,783

*[($75,000/$230,000) × $200,000] = $65,217.

The gain is classified as a long-term capital gain. Alice is then deemed to have made a gift to Dan of $155,000 ($230,000 – $75,000).

With this information, Alice can make an informed selection between the two options.

COST IDENTIFICATION AND DOCUMENTATION CONSIDERATIONS

When multiple assets are acquired in a single transaction, the contract price must be allocated for several reasons. First, some of the assets may be depreciable while others are not. From the different viewpoints of the buyer and the seller, this may produce a tax conflict that needs to be resolved. That is, the seller prefers a high allocation for nondepreciable assets, whereas the purchaser prefers a high allocation for depreciable assets (see Chapters 16 and 17). Second, the seller needs to know the amount realized on the sale of the capital assets and the ordinary income assets so that the recognized gains and losses can be classified as capital or ordinary. For example, an allocation to goodwill or to a covenant not to compete (see Chapters 8, 16, and 17) produces different tax consequences to the seller. Third, the buyer needs the adjusted basis of each asset to calculate the realized gain or loss on a subsequent sale or other disposition of each asset.

SELECTION OF PROPERTY FOR MAKING GIFTS

A donor can achieve several tax advantages by making gifts of appreciated property. Income tax on the unrealized gain that would have occurred had the donor sold the property is avoided by the donor. A portion of this amount can be permanently avoided because the donee's adjusted basis is increased by part or all of any gift tax paid by the donor. Even without this increase in basis, the income tax liability on the sale of the property by the donee can be less than the income tax liability that would have resulted from the donor's sale of the property, if the donee is in a lower tax bracket than the donor. In addition, any subsequent appreciation during the time the property is held by the lower tax bracket donee results in a tax savings on the sale or other disposition of the property. Such gifts of appreciated property can be an effective tool in family tax planning.

Taxpayers should generally not make gifts of depreciated property (property that, if sold, would produce a realized loss) because the donor does not receive an income tax deduction for the unrealized loss element. In addition, the donee receives no benefit from this unrealized loss upon the subsequent sale of the property because of the loss basis rule. The loss basis rule provides that the donee's basis is the lower of the donor's basis or fair market value at the date of the gift. If the donor anticipates that the donee will sell the property upon receiving it, the donor

CONCEPT SUMMARY 14–2

Adjustments to Basis

Item	Effect	Refer to Chapter	Explanation
Amortization of bond discount.	Increase	16	Amortization is mandatory for certain taxable bonds and elective for tax-exempt bonds.
Amortization of bond premium.	Decrease	14	Amortization is mandatory for tax-exempt bonds and elective for taxable bonds.
Amortization of covenant not to compete.	Decrease	16	Covenant must be for a definite and limited time period. The amortization period is a statutory period of 15 years.
Amortization of intangibles.	Decrease	8	Even goodwill is now subject to amortization.
Assessment for local benefits.	Increase	10	To the extent not deductible as taxes (e.g., assessment for streets and sidewalks that increase the value of the property versus one for maintenance or repair or for meeting interest charges).
Bad debts.	Decrease	7	Only the specific charge-off method is permitted.
Capital additions.	Increase	14	Certain items, at the taxpayer's election, can be capitalized or deducted (e.g., selected medical expenses).
Casualty.	Decrease	7	For a casualty loss, the amount of the adjustment is the summation of the deductible loss and the insurance proceeds received. For a casualty gain, the amount of the adjustment is the insurance proceeds received reduced by the recognized gain.
Condemnation.	Decrease	15	See casualty explanation.
Cost recovery.	Decrease	8	§ 168 is applicable to tangible assets placed in service after 1980 whose useful life is expressed in terms of years.
Depletion.	Decrease	8	Use the greater of cost or percentage depletion. Percentage depletion can still be deducted when the basis is zero.
Depreciation.	Decrease	8	§ 167 is applicable to tangible assets placed in service before 1981 and to tangible assets not depreciated in terms of years.
Easement.	Decrease	14	If the taxpayer does not retain any use of the land, all of the basis is allocable to the easement transaction. However, if only part of the land is affected by the easement, only part of the basis is allocable to the easement transaction.
Improvements by lessee to lessor's property.	Increase	5	Adjustment occurs only if the lessor is required to include the fair market value of the improvements in gross income under § 109.
Imputed interest.	Decrease	18	Amount deducted is not part of the cost of the asset.
Inventory: lower of cost or market.	Decrease	18	Not available if the LIFO method is used.
Limited expensing under § 179.	Decrease	8	Occurs only if the taxpayer elects § 179 treatment.

Item	Effect	Refer to Chapter	Explanation
Medical capital expenditure permitted as a medical expense.	Decrease	10	Adjustment is the amount of the deduction (the effect on basis is to increase it by the amount of the capital expenditure net of the deduction).
Real estate taxes: apportionment between the buyer and seller.	Increase or decrease	10	To the extent the buyer pays the seller's pro rata share, the buyer's basis is increased. To the extent the seller pays the buyer's pro rata share, the buyer's basis is decreased.
Rebate from manufacturer.	Decrease		Since the rebate is treated as an adjustment to the purchase price, it is not included in the buyer's gross income.
Stock dividend.	Decrease	5	Adjustment occurs only if the stock dividend is nontaxable. While the basis per share decreases, the total stock basis does not change.
Stock rights.	Decrease	14	Adjustment to stock basis occurs only for nontaxable stock rights and only if the fair market value of the rights is at least 15% of the fair market value of the stock or, if less than 15%, the taxpayer elects to allocate the basis between the stock and the rights.
Theft.	Decrease	7	See casualty explanation.

should sell the property and take the loss deduction, assuming the loss is deductible. The donor can then give the proceeds from the sale to the donee.

SELECTION OF PROPERTY FOR MAKING BEQUESTS

A decedent's will should generally make bequests of appreciated property. Doing so enables both the decedent and the heir to avoid income tax on the unrealized gain because the recipient takes the fair market value as his or her basis.

Taxpayers generally should not make bequests of depreciated property (property that, if sold, would produce a realized loss) because the decedent does not receive an income tax deduction for the unrealized loss element. In addition, the heir will receive no benefit from this unrealized loss upon the subsequent sale of the property.

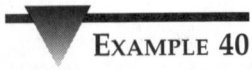

EXAMPLE 40

On the date of her death, Marta owned land held for investment purposes. The land had an adjusted basis of $600,000 and a fair market value of $100,000. If Marta had sold the property before her death, the recognized loss would have been $500,000. If Roger inherits the property and later sells it for $60,000, the recognized loss is $40,000 (the decline in value since Marta's death). In addition, regardless of the period of time Roger holds the property, the holding period is long term (see Chapter 16). ▼

From an income tax perspective, it is preferable to transfer appreciated property as a bequest rather than as a gift. This results because inherited property receives a step-up in basis, whereas property received by gift has a carryover basis to the donee. However, in making this decision, the estate tax consequences of the bequest should also be weighed against the gift tax consequences of the gift.

DISALLOWED LOSSES

Section 267 Disallowed Losses.
Taxpayers should be aware of the desirability of avoiding transactions that activate the loss disallowance provisions for related parties. This is so even in light of the provision that permits the related-party buyer to offset his or her realized gain by the related-party seller's disallowed loss. Even with this offset, several inequities exist. First, the tax benefit associated with the disallowed loss ultimately is realized by the wrong party (the related-party buyer rather than the related-party seller). Second, the tax benefit of this offset to the related-party buyer does not occur until the buyer disposes of the property. Therefore, the longer the time period between the purchase and disposition of the property by the related-party buyer, the less the economic benefit. Third, if the property does not appreciate to at least its adjusted basis to the related-party seller during the time period the related-party buyer holds it, part or all of the disallowed loss is permanently lost. Fourth, since the right of offset is available only to the original transferee (the related-party buyer), all of the disallowed loss is permanently lost if the original transferee subsequently transfers the property by gift or bequest.

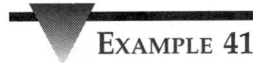

EXAMPLE 41

Tim sells property with an adjusted basis of $35,000 to Wes, his brother, for $25,000, the fair market value of the property. The $10,000 realized loss to Tim is disallowed by § 267. If Wes subsequently sells the property to an unrelated party for $37,000, he has a recognized gain of $2,000 (realized gain of $12,000 reduced by disallowed loss of $10,000). Therefore, from the perspective of the family unit, the original $10,000 realized loss ultimately is recognized. However, if Wes sells the property for $29,000, he has a recognized gain of $0 (realized gain of $4,000 reduced by disallowed loss of $4,000 necessary to offset the realized gain). From the perspective of the family unit, $6,000 of the realized loss of $10,000 is permanently wasted ($10,000 realized loss – $4,000 offset permitted). ▼

Wash Sales.
The wash sales provisions can be avoided if the security is replaced within the statutory time period with a similar rather than a substantially identical security. For example, the sale of Bethlehem Steel common stock and a purchase of Inland Steel common stock is not treated as a wash sale. Such a procedure can enable the taxpayer to use an unrealized capital loss to offset a recognized capital gain. The taxpayer can sell the security before the end of the taxable year, offset the recognized capital loss against the capital gain, and invest the sales proceeds in a similar security.

Because the wash sales provisions do not apply to gains, it may be desirable to engage in a wash sale before the end of the taxable year. This recognized capital gain may be used to offset capital losses or capital loss carryovers from prior years. Since the basis of the replacement stock or securities will be the purchase price, the taxpayer in effect has exchanged a capital gain for an increased basis for the stock or securities.

KEY TERMS

Adjusted basis, 14–4	Holding period, 14–14	Recognized loss, 14–7
Amount realized, 14–3	Realized gain, 14–3	Recovery of capital doctrine, 14–8
Fair market value, 14–4	Realized loss, 14–3	
Goodwill, 14–10	Recognized gain, 14–7	Wash sale, 14–19

PROBLEM MATERIALS

DISCUSSION QUESTIONS

1. Upon the sale or other disposition of property, what four questions should be considered for income tax purposes?

2. Define each of the following terms:
   a. Amount realized.
   b. Realized gain.
   c. Realized loss.

3. Which of the following would be treated as a "sale or other disposition"?
   a. Sale for cash.
   b. Sale on credit.
   c. Exchange.
   d. Involuntary conversion.
   e. Bond retirement.

4. Ivan invests in land and Grace invests in taxable bonds. The land appreciates by $5,000 each year, and the bonds earn interest of $5,000 each year. After holding the land and bonds for five years, Ivan and Grace sell them. There is a $25,000 realized gain on the sale of the land and no realized gain or loss on the sale of the bonds. Are the tax consequences to Ivan and Grace the same for each of the five years? Explain.

5. Carol and Dave each purchase 100 shares of stock of Burgundy, Inc., a publicly owned corporation, in July for $10,000 each. Carol sells her stock on December 31 for $14,000. Since Burgundy's stock is listed on a national exchange, Dave is able to ascertain that his shares are worth $14,000 on December 31. Does the tax law treat the appreciation in value of the stock differently for Carol and Dave? Explain.

6. If a taxpayer sells property for cash, the amount realized consists of the net proceeds from the sale. For each of the following, indicate the effect on the amount realized:
   a. The property is sold on credit.
   b. A mortgage on the property is assumed by the buyer.
   c. The buyer acquires the property subject to a mortgage of the seller.
   d. The seller pays real property taxes that are treated as imposed on the purchaser.
   e. Stock that has a basis to the purchaser of $6,000 and a fair market value of $10,000 is received by the seller as part of the consideration.

7. If the buyer pays real property taxes that are treated as imposed on the seller, what are the effects on the seller's amount realized and the buyer's adjusted basis for the property? If the seller pays real property taxes that are treated as imposed on the buyer, what are the effects on the seller's amount realized and the buyer's adjusted basis for the property?

8. Tom is negotiating to buy some land. Under the first option, Tom will give Sandra $70,000 and assume her mortgage on the land for $30,000. Under the second option, Tom will give Sandra $100,000, and she will immediately pay off the mortgage. Tom would like for his basis for the land to be as high as possible. Given this objective, which option should Tom select?

9. Edith purchases land from Gail. Edith gives Gail $40,000 in cash and agrees to pay Gail an additional $80,000 one year later plus interest at 8%.
   a. What is Edith's adjusted basis for the land at the date purchased?
   b. What is Edith's adjusted basis for the land one year later?

10. The taxpayer owns land and a building with an adjusted basis of $75,000 and a fair market value of $240,000. The property is subject to a mortgage of $360,000. Since the taxpayer is in arrears on the mortgage payments, the creditor is willing to accept the property in return for canceling the amount of the mortgage.
    a. How can the adjusted basis of the property be less than the amount of the mortgage?
    b. If the creditor's offer is accepted, what are the effects on the amount realized, the adjusted basis, and the realized gain or loss?
    c. Does it matter in (b) if the mortgage is recourse or nonrecourse?

11. Discuss the relationship between the adjusted basis and capital additions and between the adjusted basis and capital recoveries.

12. On August 16, 1998, Todd acquires land and a building for $300,000 to use in his sole proprietorship. Of the purchase price, $200,000 is allocated to the building, and $100,000 is allocated to the land. Cost recovery of $1,926 is deducted in 1998 for the building.
    a. What is the adjusted basis for the land and the building at the acquisition date?
    b. What is the adjusted basis for the land and the building at the end of 1998?

13. Abby owns stock in Orange Corporation and Blue Corporation. She receives a $1,000 distribution from both corporations. The instructions from Orange state that the $1,000 is a dividend. The instructions from Blue state that the $1,000 is not a dividend. What could cause the instructions to differ as to the tax consequences?

14. A taxpayer who acquires a taxable bond at a premium may elect to amortize the premium, whereas a taxpayer who acquires a tax-exempt bond at a premium must amortize the premium. Why would a taxpayer make the amortization election for taxable bonds? What effect does the mandatory amortization of tax-exempt bonds have on taxable income?

15. Kara owns two assets that she is considering selling. One has appreciated in value by $3,000, and the other has declined in value by $3,000. Both assets are held for personal use. Kara believes that she should sell both assets in the same taxable year so that the loss of $3,000 can offset the gain of $3,000. Advise Kara regarding the tax consequences.

16. Ron sold a sailboat for a $5,000 loss in the current year because he was diagnosed as having skin cancer. His spouse wants him to sell his Harley Davidson motorcycle because her brother broke his leg while riding his motorcycle. Since Ron no longer has anyone to ride with, he is seriously considering accepting his wife's advice. Because the motorcycle is a classic, Ron has received two offers. Each offer would result in a $5,000 gain. Joe would like to purchase the motorcycle before Christmas, and Jeff would like to purchase it after New Year's. Identify the relevant tax issues Ron faces in making his decision.

17. Lee owns a life insurance policy that will pay $100,000 to Rita, his spouse, on his death. At the date of Lee's death, he had paid total premiums on the policy of $65,000. In accordance with § 101(a)(1), Rita excludes the $100,000 of insurance proceeds. Discuss the relationship, if any, between the § 101 exclusion and the recovery of capital doctrine.

18. For a bargain purchase, why is the adjusted basis of the property to the buyer equal to the fair market value of the property rather than the purchase price?

19. When a business is purchased and goodwill is involved, why is the adjusted basis of the goodwill determined using the residual method rather than the amount assigned to the goodwill in the purchase contract?

20. Distinguish between the process for determining the basis of stock received as a nontaxable stock dividend when the stock dividend is a common stock dividend on common stock and the process when the stock dividend is a preferred stock dividend on common stock.

21. Explain how a donee can sell investment property received by gift and recognize neither gain nor loss even though the selling price differs from the donee's adjusted basis for the investment property.

22. Simon, who is retired, owns Teal, Inc., stock that has declined in value since he purchased it. He has decided to give the stock to his nephew, Fred, who is a high school teacher, or to sell the stock and give the proceeds to Fred. Because nearly all of his wealth is invested in tax-exempt bonds, Simon is in the 15% tax bracket. Fred will use the cash or the proceeds from his sale of the stock to make the down payment on the purchase of a house. Based on a recent conversation, Simon is aware that Fred is in the 28% bracket. Identify the tax issues relevant to Simon in deciding whether to give the stock or the sale proceeds to Fred.

23. Different basis rules apply for property received by gift and that received by inheritance. Under what circumstance will the basis be the same?

24. Agnes has been diagnosed with a terminal disease. Her nephew, Stan, will graduate from college in May. She has stock worth $50,000 that she intends to give him as a graduation present. Since she may not be alive then, Agnes is considering giving the stock to him now (i.e., four months prior to graduation). If Agnes should die before making the gift, her will stipulates that Stan will receive the stock. Identify the relevant tax issues that Agnes should consider in making her decision.

25. Gary makes a gift of an appreciated building to Carmen. She dies three months later, and Gary inherits the building from her. During the period that Carmen held the building, she deducted depreciation and made a capital expenditure. What effect might these items have on Gary's basis for the inherited building?

26. Immediately before his death in 1998, Kirby sells securities (adjusted basis of $100,000) for their fair market value of $20,000. The sale was not to a related party. The securities were community property, and Kirby is survived by his wife, Zina, who inherits all of his property.
    a. Did Kirby act wisely? Why or why not?
    b. Suppose the figures are reversed (sale for $100,000 of property with an adjusted basis of $20,000). Would the sale be wise? Why or why not?

27. How can an investor avoid the loss disallowance provision for wash sales of stock or securities?

28. Losses on the disposition of property used in a trade or business or held for investment are recognized whereas losses on the disposition of personal use property are disallowed. Is it possible to avoid this disallowance by reclassifying the personal use loss as a business or an investment loss through converting the personal use property to either trade or business property or investment property prior to the disposition?

PROBLEMS

29. Anne sold her home for $260,000 in 1998. Selling expenses were $15,000. She had purchased it in 1990 for $190,000. During the period of ownership, Anne had:

    • Deducted $50,500 office-in-home expenses, which included $14,500 in depreciation. (Refer to Chapter 9.)

    • Deducted a casualty loss of residential trees destroyed by a hurricane. The total loss was $19,000 (after the $100 floor and the 10%-of-AGI floor), and Anne's insurance company reimbursed her for $13,500. (Refer to Chapter 7.)

    • Paid street paving assessment of $7,000 and added sidewalks for $11,000.

    • Installed an elevator for medical reasons. The total cost was $20,000, and Anne deducted $12,000 as medical expenses. (Refer to Chapter 10.)

    • Received $7,500 from a utility company for an easement to install underground utility lines across the property.

    What is Anne's realized gain?

30. Kareem bought a rental house at the beginning of 1993 for $80,000, of which $10,000 is allocated to the land and $70,000 to the building. Early in 1995, he had a tennis court built in the backyard at a cost of $5,000. Kareem has deducted $32,200 for depreciation on the house and $1,300 for depreciation on the court. At the beginning of 1998, he sells the house and tennis court for $125,000 cash.
    a. What is Kareem's realized gain or loss?
    b. If an original mortgage of $20,000 is still outstanding and the buyer assumes the mortgage in addition to the cash payment, what is Kareem's realized gain or loss?
    c. If the buyer takes the property subject to the mortgage, what is Kareem's realized gain or loss?

31. Norm is negotiating the sale of a tract of his land to Pat. Use the following classification scheme to classify each of the items contained in the proposed sales contract:

Legend

DARN = Decreases amount realized by Norm

IARN = Increases amount realized by Norm

DABN = Decreases adjusted basis to Norm

IABN = Increases adjusted basis to Norm

DABP = Decreases adjusted basis to Pat

IABP = Increases adjusted basis to Pat

---

   a. Norm is to receive cash of $50,000.
   b. Norm is to receive Pat's note payable for $25,000, payable in three years.
   c. Pat assumes Norm's mortgage of $5,000 on the land.
   d. Pat agrees to pay the realtor's sales commission of $8,000.
   e. Pat agrees to pay the property taxes on the land for the entire year. If each party paid his or her respective share, Norm's share would be $1,000, and Pat's share would be $3,000.
   f. Pat pays legal fees of $500.
   g. Norm pays legal fees of $750.

32. Gayla owns a building (adjusted basis of $366,500 on January 1, 1998) that she rents to Len who operates a restaurant in the building. The municipal health department closed the restaurant for two months during 1998 because of health code violations. Under MACRS, the cost recovery deduction for 1998 would be $12,000. However, Gayla deducted cost recovery only for the 10 months the restaurant was open since she waived the rent income during the two-month period the restaurant was closed.
   a. What is the amount of the cost recovery deduction that Gayla should report on her 1998 income tax return?
   b. Calculate the adjusted basis of the building at the end of 1998.

33. Mitch's automobile, which is used exclusively in his business, is stolen. The adjusted basis is $30,000, and the fair market value is $33,000. Mitch's AGI is $50,000.
   a. If Mitch receives insurance proceeds of $33,000, what effect do the theft and the receipt of the insurance proceeds have on the adjusted basis of the automobile?
   b. If the automobile is not insured, what effect do the theft and the absence of insurance have on the adjusted basis of the automobile?

34. Aaron owns stock in Dove Corporation. His adjusted basis for the stock is $57,000. During the year, he receives a distribution from the corporation of $51,000 that is labeled a return of capital (i.e., Dove has no earnings and profits).
   a. Determine the tax consequences to Aaron.
   b. Assume instead that the amount of the distribution is $60,000. Determine the tax consequences to Aaron.
   c. Assume instead in (a) that the $51,000 distribution is labeled a taxable dividend (i.e., Dove has earnings and profits of at least $51,000).

35. Chee purchases Tan, Inc., bonds for $110,000 on January 2, 1998. The face value of the bonds is $100,000, the maturity date is December 31, 2002, and the annual interest rate is 8%. Chee will amortize the premium only if he is required to do so. Chee sells the bonds on July 1, 2000, for $109,000.
   a. Determine the interest income Chee should report for 1998.
   b. Calculate Chee's recognized gain or loss on the sale of the bonds in 2000.

36. Which of the following would definitely result in a recognized gain or loss?
   a. Kay sells her lakeside cabin (not her personal residence), which has an adjusted basis of $100,000, for $150,000.
   b. Adam sells his personal residence, which has an adjusted basis of $150,000, for $100,000.

c. Carl's personal residence is on the site of a proposed airport and is condemned by the city. Carl receives $55,000 for the house, which has an adjusted basis of $65,000.

d. Olga's land is worth $40,000 at the end of the year. Olga had purchased the land six months earlier for $25,000.

e. Vera's personal use vehicle is stolen. Her adjusted basis is $22,000. She receives a check from the insurance company for $23,000. Vera has decided that in the future she will use mass transit rather than owning an automobile.

f. Jerry sells used clothing, adjusted basis of $500, to a thrift store for $50.

37. Hubert's personal residence is condemned as part of an urban renewal project. His adjusted basis for the residence is $200,000. He receives condemnation proceeds of $180,000 and invests the proceeds in stock.

a. Calculate Hubert's realized and recognized gain or loss.

b. If the condemnation proceeds are $225,000, what are Hubert's realized and recognized gain or loss?

c. What are Hubert's realized and recognized gain or loss in (a) if the house was rental property?

38. Walt Barnes is a real estate agent for Governor's Farms, a residential real estate development. Because of his outstanding sales performance, Walt is permitted to buy a lot that normally would sell for $125,000 for $100,000. Walt is the only real estate agent for Governor's Farms who is permitted to do so.

a. Does Walt have gross income from the transaction?

b. What is Walt's adjusted basis for the land?

c. Write a letter to Walt informing him of the tax consequences of his acquisition of the lot. His address is 100 Tower Road, San Diego, CA 92182.

39. Karen makes the following purchases and sales of stock:

Transaction	Date	Number of Shares	Company	Price per Share
Purchase	1–1–96	300	MDG	$ 75
Purchase	6–1–96	150	GRU	300
Purchase	11–1–96	60	MDG	70
Sale	12–3–96	180	MDG	70
Purchase	3–1–97	120	GRU	375
Sale	8–1–97	90	GRU	330
Sale	1–1–98	150	MDG	90
Sale	2–1–98	75	GRU	500

Assuming that Karen is unable to identify the particular lots that are sold with the original purchase, what is the realized gain or loss on each type of stock as of:

a. 7–1–96.

b. 12–31–96.

c. 12–31–97.

d. 7–1–98.

40. Frank purchases 100 shares of Bluebird Corporation stock on June 3, 1998, for $150,000. On August 25, 1998, Frank purchases an additional 50 shares of Bluebird stock for $60,000. According to market quotations, Bluebird stock is selling for $1,100 per share on December 31, 1998. Frank sells 60 shares of Bluebird stock on March 1, 1999, for $51,000.

a. What is the adjusted basis of Frank's Bluebird stock on December 31, 1998?

b. What is Frank's recognized gain or loss from the sale of Bluebird stock on March 1, 1999, assuming the shares sold are from the shares purchased on June 3, 1998?

c. What is Frank's recognized gain or loss from the sale of Bluebird stock on March 1, 1999, assuming Frank cannot adequately identify the shares sold?

41. Randy Morgan purchases Agnes's sole proprietorship for $900,000. The assets of the business are as follows:

Asset	Agnes's Adjusted Basis	FMV
Accounts receivable	$ 70,000	$ 70,000
Inventory	90,000	100,000
Equipment	150,000	160,000
Furniture and fixtures	95,000	130,000
Building	190,000	250,000
Land	25,000	75,000

Randy and Agnes agree that $50,000 of the purchase price is for Agnes's five-year covenant not to compete.
   a. Calculate Agnes's realized and recognized gain.
   b. Determine Randy's basis for each of the assets.
   c. Write a letter to Randy informing him of the tax consequences of the purchase. His address is 300 Riverside Drive, Cincinnati, OH 45207.

42. Diane owns 1,000 shares of Robin, Inc., common stock with an adjusted basis of $100,000. During the year she receives the following distributions associated with the stock:

   • $3,000 taxable cash dividend.

   • 2% stock dividend in the form of 20 shares of preferred stock. The fair market value of the common stock was $110,000, and the fair market value of the preferred stock was $2,000.

   • 5% stock dividend in the form of 50 shares of common stock. The fair market value of the 1,000 shares of common stock was $115,000.

   Determine the tax consequences to Diane.

43. Shontelle owns 1,000 shares of Gray Corporation stock with a basis of $15,000 and a fair market value of $20,000. She receives nontaxable stock rights to purchase additional shares. The rights have a fair market value of $2,000.
   a. What is the basis of the stock and the basis of the stock rights?
   b. What is the holding period for the stock rights?
   c. What is the recognized gain or loss if the stock rights are sold for $2,000?
   d. What is the recognized gain or loss if the stock rights are allowed to lapse?

44. Rick received various gifts over the years. He has decided to dispose of the following assets that he received as gifts:
   a. In 1949, he received land worth $25,000. The donor's adjusted basis was $30,000. Rick sells the land for $87,000 in 1998.
   b. In 1955, he received stock in Gold Company. The donor's adjusted basis was $10,000. The fair market value on the date of the gift was $28,000. Rick sells the stock for $40,000 in 1998.
   c. In 1961, he received land worth $12,000. The donor's adjusted basis was $25,000. Rick sells the land for $8,000 in 1998.
   d. In 1994, he received stock worth $30,000. The donor's adjusted basis was $45,000. Rick sells the stock in 1998 for $39,000.

   What is the realized gain or loss from each of the preceding transactions? Assume in each of the gift transactions that no gift tax was paid.

45. Beth received a car from Sam as a gift. Sam paid $18,000 for the car. He had used it for business purposes and had deducted $8,000 for depreciation up to the time he gave the car to Beth. The fair market value of the car is $6,000.
   a. Assuming Beth uses the car for business purposes, what is her basis for depreciation?

b. If the estimated useful life is two years (from the date of the gift), what is her depreciation deduction for each year? Assume Beth elects the straight-line method.

c. If Beth sells the car for $900 one year after receiving it, what is her gain or loss?

d. If Beth sells the car for $6,000 one year after receiving it, what is her gain or loss?

46. In 1998, Ron receives a gift of property that has a fair market value of $100,000 on the date of the gift. The donor's adjusted basis for the property was $32,000. Assume the donor paid gift tax of $20,000 on the gift.

a. What is Ron's basis for gain and loss and for depreciation?

b. If Ron had received the gift of property in 1975, what would his basis be for gain and loss and for depreciation?

47. On September 18, 1998, Jerry received land and a building from his Uncle Ted as a gift. Uncle Ted's adjusted basis and the fair market value at the date of the gift were as follows:

Asset	Adjusted Basis	FMV
Land	$100,000	$200,000
Building	80,000	100,000

Uncle Ted paid gift tax of $45,000.

a. Determine Jerry's adjusted basis for the land and building.

b. Assume instead that the FMV of the land was $90,000 and the FMV of the building was $60,000. Determine Jerry's adjusted basis for the land and building.

48. Ira Cook is planning to make a charitable contribution of Crystal, Inc., stock worth $20,000 to the Boy Scouts. The stock Ira is considering contributing has an adjusted basis of $15,000. A friend has suggested that Ira sell the stock and contribute the $20,000 in proceeds rather than contribute the stock.

a. Should Ira follow the friend's advice? Why?

b. Assume the fair market value is only $13,000. In this case, should Ira follow the friend's advice? Why?

c. Rather than make a charitable contribution to the Boy Scouts, Ira is going to make a gift to Nancy, his niece. Advise Ira regarding (a) and (b).

d. Write a letter to Ira regarding whether in (a) he should sell the stock and contribute the cash or contribute the stock. He has informed you that he purchased the stock six years ago. Ira's address is 500 Ireland Avenue, De Kalb, IL 60115.

49. Dena inherits property from Mary, her mother. Mary's adjusted basis for the property is $100,000, and the fair market value is $725,000. Six months after Mary's death, the fair market value is $740,000. Dena is the sole beneficiary of Mary's estate.

a. Can the executor of Mary's estate elect the alternate valuation date?

b. What is Dena's basis for the property?

50. Earl's estate includes, among other assets, the following available for distribution to Robert, one of Earl's beneficiaries:

Asset	Earl's Adjusted Basis	FMV at Date of Death	FMV at Alternate Valuation Date
Cash	$10,000	$ 10,000	$ 10,000
Stock	40,000	125,000	60,000
Apartment building	60,000	300,000	325,000
Land	75,000	100,000	110,000

The fair market value of the stock six months after Earl's death was $60,000. However, believing that the stock would continue to decline in value, the executor of the estate distributed the stock to Robert one month after Earl's death. Robert immediately sold the stock for $85,000.

   a. Determine Robert's basis for the assets if the primary valuation date and amount apply.
   b. Determine Robert's basis for the assets if the executor elects the alternate valuation date and amount.

51. Emily makes a gift of 100 shares of appreciated stock to her uncle, George, on January 5, 1998. The basis of the stock is $3,150, and the fair market value is $5,250. George dies on October 8, 1998. During the period that George held the stock, he received a 5% nontaxable stock dividend. Under the provisions of George's will, Emily inherits 100 shares of the stock. The value of the stock for Federal estate tax purposes is $55 per share.
   a. What is the basis of the inherited stock to Emily?
   b. What is the basis of the inherited stock to Emily if she had given the stock to George on January 5, 1997?

52. Larry and Grace live in Arizona, a community property state. They own land (community property) that has an adjusted basis to them of $150,000. When Grace dies, Larry inherits her share of the land. At the date of Grace's death, the fair market value of the land is $200,000. Six months after Grace's death, the land is worth $220,000.
   a. What is Larry's basis for the land?
   b. What would Larry's basis for the land be if he and Grace lived in Kansas, a common law state, and Larry inherited Grace's share?

53. Sheila sells land to Elane, her sister, for $40,000. Six months later Elane gives the land to Jacob, her son. No gift taxes are paid. At the date of the gift, the land is worth $42,000. Jacob sells the land one month later for $43,000.
   a. Assuming Sheila's adjusted basis for the land is $25,000, what are Sheila and Jacob's recognized gain or loss on their respective sales?
   b. Assuming Sheila's adjusted basis for the land is $50,000, what are Sheila and Jacob's recognized gain or loss on their respective sales?

54. Ted owns a 60% capital and profits interest in TS Partnership, which sells property to Ted for $65,000. The partnership's adjusted basis for the property is $90,000.
   a. Calculate the realized and recognized loss to the partnership.
   b. Calculate the basis of the property to Ted.
   c. If Ted subsequently sells the property for $87,000, calculate his realized and recognized gain or loss.
   d. If Ted gives the property to his daughter, Donna, who subsequently sells it for $87,000, calculate Donna's realized and recognized gain or loss. Assume no gift tax is paid on the gift and the fair market value on the date of the gift is $80,000.
   e. Determine the tax consequences in (a) through (d) if Ted is a shareholder and TS is a corporation.

55. Susan owns 100 shares of Drake, Inc., stock with an adjusted basis of $50,000. On December 12, 1998, she sells the 100 shares for their fair market value of $45,000. On January 4, 1999, she purchases 125 shares of Drake stock for $57,500.
   a. What is Susan's realized and recognized gain or loss on the sale of the 100 shares sold on December 12, 1998?
   b. What is Susan's adjusted basis for the 125 shares purchased on January 4, 1999?
   c. How would your answers in (a) and (b) change if Susan purchased only 75 shares for $34,500 on January 4, 1999?
   d. How would your answers in (a) and (b) change if Susan purchased 125 shares on January 15, 1999, instead of January 4, 1999?

56. Kramer sells 150 shares of Lavender, Inc., stock on December 28, 1998, for $75,000. On January 10, 1999, he purchases 100 shares of Lavender, Inc., stock for $80,000.
   a. Assuming Kramer's adjusted basis for the stock sold is $60,000, what is his recognized gain or loss, and what is his basis for the new shares?
   b. Assuming Kramer's adjusted basis for the stock sold is $90,000, what is his recognized gain or loss, and what is his basis for the new shares?
   c. Advise Kramer on how he can avoid any negative tax consequences encountered in (b).

57. James retires from a public accounting firm to enter private practice. He had bought a home two years earlier for $40,000. Upon opening his business, he converts one-fourth of his home into an office. The fair market value of the home on the date of conversion (January 1, 1993) is $75,000. The adjusted basis is $56,000 (ignore land). James lives and works in the home for six years (after converting it to business use) and sells it at the end of the sixth year. He deducted $2,630 of cost recovery using the statutory percentage method.
   a. How much gain or loss is recognized if James sells the property for $44,000?
   b. If he sells the property for $70,000?

58. Surendra's personal residence originally cost $180,000 (ignore land). After living in the house for five years, he converts it to rental property. At the date of conversion, the fair market value of the house is $150,000.
   a. Calculate Surendra's basis for loss for the rental property.
   b. Calculate Surendra's basis for depreciation for the rental property.
   c. Calculate Surendra's basis for gain for the rental property.

59. Hun, age 93, has accumulated substantial assets during his life. Among his many assets are the following, which he is considering giving to Koji, his grandson.

Asset	Adjusted Basis	Fair Market Value
Red Corporation stock	$ 50,000	$700,000
Silver Corporation stock	70,000	71,000
Emerald Corporation stock	200,000	50,000

Hun has been in ill health for the past five years. His physician has informed him that he probably will not live for more than six months. Advise Hun which of the stocks should be transferred as gifts and which as bequests.

CUMULATIVE PROBLEMS

60. John Custer, age 35, is single. His Social Security number is 443–11–2222, and he resides at 150 Highway 51, Tangipahoa, LA 70443.

   John has a five-year-old child, Kendra, who lives with her mother, Katy. John pays alimony of $15,000 per year to Katy and child support of $12,000. The $12,000 of child support covers 70% of Katy's costs of rearing Kendra. Kendra's Social Security number is 432–60–1000, and Katy's is 444–00–1234.

   John's mother, Sally, lived with him until her death in early September 1998. He incurred and paid medical expenses for her of $9,000 and other support payments of $4,000. Sally's only sources of income were $3,000 of interest income on certificates of deposit and $2,400 of Social Security benefits, which she spent on her medical expenses and helping to maintain John's household. Sally's Social Security number was 400–10–2000.

   John is employed by the Highway Department of the State of Louisiana in an executive position. His salary is $80,000. The appropriate amounts of Social Security and Medicare taxes were withheld. In addition, $16,000 was withheld for Federal income taxes, and $2,500 was withheld for state income taxes.

   Upon the death of his Aunt Josie in December 1997, John, her only recognized heir, inherited the following assets:

Asset	Josie's Adjusted Basis	FMV at Date of Death
Car	$ 22,000	$ 14,000
Land—300 acres	150,000	600,000
IBM stock	50,000	125,000
Cash	33,000	33,000

Six months prior to her death, Josie gave John a beachhouse. Her adjusted basis for the beachhouse was $200,000, and the fair market value was $250,000. She paid a gift tax of $18,000.

During the year, John had the following transactions:

• On February 1, 1998, he sold for $40,000 Exxon stock that he inherited from his father four years ago. His father's adjusted basis was $20,000, and the fair market value at the date of the father's death was $35,000.

• The car John inherited from Josie was destroyed in a wreck on October 1, 1998. He had loaned the car to Katy to use for a two-week period while the engine in her car was being replaced. Fortunately, neither Katy nor Kendra was injured. John received insurance proceeds of $12,000, the fair market value of the car on October 1.

• On October 30, 1998, John gambled away the $33,000 he inherited on a riverboat casino in Biloxi. He had hoped this activity would help with the bouts of depression he had been suffering since Sally's death.

• On December 28, John sold the 300 acres of land to his brother, James, for its fair market value of $575,000. James planned on using the land for his dairy farm.

Other sources of income for John were as follows:

Dividend income	$20,000
Interest income:	
Guaranty Bank	11,000
City of Kentwood water bonds	12,000
Award from State of Louisiana for outstanding suggestion for highway beautification	6,000

Potential itemized deductions for John, in addition to items already mentioned, were:

Property taxes paid on his residence	$7,000
Property taxes paid on personalty	2,000
Estimated Federal income taxes paid	2,300
Estimated state income taxes paid	2,500
Charitable contributions	6,000
Mortgage interest on his residence	5,500
Orthodontic expenses for Kendra	3,000
Psychiatric expenses for John	2,000

Part 1—Tax Computation
Compute John's net tax payable or refund due for 1998. Suggested software (if available): *TurboTax*.

Part 2—Tax Planning
Assume that rather than selling the land to James, John is considering leasing it to him for $30,000 annually with the lease beginning on October 1, 1998. James would prepay the lease payments through December 31, 1998. Thereafter, he would make monthly lease payments at the beginning of each month. What effect would this have on John's 1998 tax liability? What potential problem might John encounter? Write a letter to John in which you advise him of the tax consequences of leasing versus selling. Also, prepare a memo for the tax files.

 61. Lori Ann (age 27) and Albert Welch (age 28) are married and file a joint return. They have one child, Margaret (age 3). Lori Ann's Social Security number is 366–55–2222, Albert's is 555–66–4300, and Margaret's is 555–77–7333. They reside at 400 Aspen Drive, Williamsburg, VA 23185.

Lori Ann is employed as an accountant at the College of William and Mary at an annual salary of $48,000. Albert is an executive with Historic Williamsburg and receives a salary of $40,000 annually. The appropriate amounts for FICA taxes were withheld. For Federal income taxes, $10,250 was withheld by Lori Ann's employer, and $7,000 was withheld by Albert's employer. For state income tax purposes, $1,800 was withheld by Lori Ann's employer, and $1,600 was withheld by Albert's employer.

Items of potential tax significance include the following:

- Albert received $1,900 of interest income on certificates of deposit and $900 of interest income on bonds issued by the City of Norfolk.

- Lori Ann received dividend income of $2,750 on Green, Inc., stock. She received the stock as a gift from her Aunt Jane on January 10, 1997, when it was worth $9,500. Aunt Jane's adjusted basis was $2,000 and she had owned the stock for two months.

- On May 10, 1997, Albert sold land for $24,000 that he had inherited from his father in December 1993. His father's adjusted basis for the land was $12,000, and the fair market value on the date of the father's death was $26,000. Albert sold the land to his sister, Marge.

- On August 5, 1997, Lori Ann sold the Green, Inc., stock for $25,000.

- Lori Ann and Albert received rent income of $1,500 for their mountain getaway, which they rented for one week in December. During the year, they spent 80 days at their mountain home. Expenses associated with the mountain home for the year were as follows:

Property taxes	$1,500
Mortgage interest	1,200
Repairs, maintenance, and insurance	1,400
Utilities	600

They purchased the house in January 1994 for $100,000 with $20,000 being allocable to land.

- Potential itemized deductions, in addition to items already mentioned, were:

Charitable contributions	$1,600
Mortgage interest on residence	3,600
Real property taxes	1,700
Personal property taxes	300
State and local sales taxes	3,000
Medical expenses (less reimbursements)	350

- Albert receives a bonus of $5,000 in January 1998 associated with the outstanding performance of his unit in 1997.

- Lori Ann and Albert made estimated tax payments of $4,000.

Compute their net tax payable or refund due for 1997. If you use tax forms for your computations, you will need Form 1040 and Schedules A, B, and D. Suggested software (if available): *TurboTax*.

RESEARCH PROBLEMS

*Note: Use the **RIA OnPoint System 4 Student Version CD-ROM**, which is available to accompany this text, in preparing solutions to the Research Problems. Alternatively, tax research materials found in a standard tax library can be used.*

Research Problem 1.   Amy sold land to Chuck two years ago for $200,000. Her adjusted basis for the land was $150,000. The consideration received for the land was $125,000 in cash and a debt instrument for $75,000. At the time of the sale, Amy reported a recognized gain of $50,000 ($200,000 amount realized − $150,000 adjusted basis).

In accordance with the sales agreement, Chuck pledged stock (Stock A) worth $75,000 as collateral for the note. The land was not pledged because Chuck was going to contribute it to a real estate partnership in which he would receive a 10% interest. Under the terms of the sales agreement, if the value of the stock declined below the principal amount of the note by at least $5,000, substitute collateral would be required. Because the value of the stock has declined, Chuck is required to substitute Stock B for Stock A. The value of Stock B exceeds the value of Stock A by $5,000.

Does Amy have a recognized gain or loss from the substitution?

Research Problem 2.   Terry owns real estate with an adjusted basis of $600,000 and a fair market value of $1,100,000. The amount of the nonrecourse mortgage on the property is $2,500,000. Because of substantial past and projected future losses associated with the real estate development (occupancy rate of only 37% after three years), Terry deeds the property to the creditor.
   a. What are the tax consequences to Terry?
   b. Assume the data are the same, except the fair market value of the property is $2,525,000. Therefore, when Terry deeds the property to the creditor, she also receives $25,000 from the creditor. What are the tax consequences to Terry?

Partial list of research aids:
Rev.Rul. 76–111, 1976–1 C.B. 214.
Crane v. Comm., 47 USTC ¶9217, 35 AFTR 776, 67 S.Ct. 1047 (USSC, 1947).

Research Problem 3.   Olaf gives stock worth $400,000 to Hazel. Olaf's adjusted basis in the stock is $50,000. The gift taxes due are $118,400. As a condition for receiving the gift of stock, Hazel agrees to pay the gift tax. The stock is transferred to Hazel on February 5, 1998.
   a. What are the income tax consequences to Olaf?
   b. What are the income tax consequences to Olaf if the gift was made on February 5, 1981?

Research Problem 4.   As the result of a large inheritance from her grandmother, Beverly has a substantial investment portfolio. The securities are held in street name by her brokerage firm. Beverly's broker, Max, has standing oral instructions from her on sales transactions to sell the shares with the highest cost basis.

In October 1996, Beverly phoned Max and instructed him to sell 6,000 shares of Color, Inc. Her portfolio has 15,000 shares of Color, Inc., which were purchased in several transactions over a three-year period. At the end of each month, the brokerage firm provides Beverly with a monthly statement that includes sales transactions. It does not identify the specific certificates transferred.

In filing her 1996 income tax return, Beverly used the specific identification method to calculate the $90,000 gain on the sale of the Color shares. Now her 1996 return is being audited. The Revenue Agent has taken the position that under Reg. § 1.1012–1(c) Beverly should have used the FIFO method to report the sale of the Color shares. This would result in a recognized gain of $160,000. According to his interpretation of the Regulations, Beverly may not use the specific identification method and must use the FIFO method because the broker did not provide written confirmation of Beverly's sales instructions as required by the Regulations.

Beverly has come to you for tax advice.

Research Problem 5.   Ruth Ames died on January 10, 1998. In filing the estate tax return, her executor, Melvin Sims, elects the primary valuation date and amount (fair market value on date of death). On March 12, 1998, Melvin invests $30,000 of cash that Ruth had in her money market account in acquiring 1,000 shares of Orange, Inc. ($30 per share). On January 10, 1998, Orange was selling for $29 per share. The stock is distributed to a beneficiary, Annette Rust, on June 1, 1998, when it is selling for $33 per share. Melvin would like for you to inform him at what amount the Orange shares should appear on the estate tax return and of Annette's adjusted basis for the stock. Write a letter to Melvin in which you respond to his inquiry and prepare a memo for the tax files. His address is 100 Center Lane, Salem, VA 24153.

Use the tax resources of the Internet to address the following questions. Do not restrict your search to the World Wide Web, but include a review of newsgroups and general reference materials, practitioner sites and resources, primary sources of the tax law, chat rooms and discussion groups, and other opportunities.

Research Problem 6. The "step up in basis at death" rule of § 1014 is seen by many as an expensive tax loophole enjoyed by the wealthy.

a. Find the latest estimates of the revenue loss to the Treasury that is attributable to this rule.

b. How does Canada tax law determine the basis of property acquired from a decedent?

c. Send an e-mail message to a member of the House Ways and Means Committee expressing a preference for the preservation of the current § 1014 rule or a modification to it.

TEAM PROJECT: ARTHUR ANDERSEN TAX CHALLENGE CASES

For more information on the Arthur Andersen Tax Challenge Cases, refer to Chapter 1, page 1–37.

Information related to tax issues and problems that are discussed in this chapter may be found in the

Day and Ball case on page 5
Fence case on pages 40, 47, 53, 56, and 59

Read and analyze the case you have been assigned and *identify* any issues and problems that are related to material covered in this chapter. If the information provided in the case is complete, prepare answers for this part of the case at this time. If you need information that is contained in the later parts of the case, write a memo summarizing the questions or problems so you can prepare a complete answer at a later date.

PROPERTY TRANSACTIONS: NONTAXABLE EXCHANGES

LEARNING OBJECTIVES

After completing Chapter 15, you should be able to:

1. Understand the rationale for nonrecognition (postponement) of gain or loss in certain property transactions.

2. Apply the nonrecognition provisions and basis determination rules for like-kind exchanges.

3. Explain the nonrecognition provisions available on the involuntary conversion of property.

4. Describe the provision for the permanent exclusion of gain on the sale of a personal residence.

5. Identify other nonrecognition provisions contained in the Code.

6. Identify tax planning opportunities related to the nonrecognition provisions discussed in the chapter.

GENERAL CONCEPT OF A NONTAXABLE EXCHANGE

1 **LEARNING OBJECTIVE**
Understand the rationale for nonrecognition (postponement) of gain or loss in certain property transactions.

A taxpayer who is going to replace a productive asset (e.g., machinery) used in a trade or business may structure the transactions as a sale of the old asset and the purchase of a new asset. Using this approach, any realized gain or loss on the asset sale is recognized. The basis of the new asset is its cost. Conversely, the taxpayer may be able to trade the old asset for the new asset. This exchange of assets may produce beneficial tax consequences by qualifying for nontaxable exchange treatment.

The tax law recognizes that nontaxable exchanges result in a change in the *form* but not in the *substance* of the taxpayer's relative economic position. The replacement property received in the exchange is viewed as substantially a continuation of the old investment.[1] Additional justification for nontaxable exchange treatment is that this type of transaction does not provide the taxpayer with the wherewithal to pay the tax on any realized gain.

The nonrecognition provisions for nontaxable exchanges do not apply to realized losses from the sale or exchange of personal use assets. Such losses are not recognized (are disallowed) because they are personal in nature and not because of any nonrecognition provision.

---

[1]Reg. § 1.1002–1(c).

In a **nontaxable exchange,** realized gains or losses are not recognized. However, the nonrecognition is usually temporary. The recognition of gain or loss is *postponed* (deferred) until the property received in the nontaxable exchange is subsequently disposed of in a taxable transaction. This is accomplished by assigning a carryover basis to the replacement property.

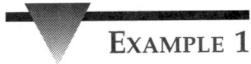

EXAMPLE 1

Debra exchanges property with an adjusted basis of $10,000 and a fair market value of $12,000 for property with a fair market value of $12,000. The transaction qualifies for nontaxable exchange treatment. Debra has a realized gain of $2,000 ($12,000 amount realized − $10,000 adjusted basis). Her recognized gain is $0. Her basis in the replacement property is a carryover basis of $10,000. Assume the replacement property is nondepreciable. If Debra subsequently sells the replacement property for $12,000, her realized and recognized gain will be the $2,000 gain that was postponed (deferred) in the nontaxable transaction. If the replacement property is depreciable, the carryover basis of $10,000 is used in calculating depreciation. ▼

In some nontaxable exchanges, only part of the property involved in the transaction qualifies for nonrecognition treatment. If the taxpayer receives cash or other nonqualifying property, part or all of the realized gain from the exchange is recognized. In these instances, gain is recognized because the taxpayer has changed or improved his or her relative economic position and has the wherewithal to pay income tax to the extent of cash or other property received.

It is important to distinguish between a nontaxable disposition, as the term is used in the statute, and a tax-free transaction. First, a direct exchange is not required in all circumstances (e.g., replacement of involuntarily converted property). Second, as previously mentioned, the term *nontaxable* refers to postponement of recognition via a carryover basis. In a *tax-free* transaction, the nonrecognition is permanent (e.g., see the discussion later in the chapter of the § 121 exclusion of realized gain on the sale of a personal residence). Therefore, the basis of any property acquired in a tax-free transaction does not depend on the basis of the property disposed of by the taxpayer.

LIKE–KIND EXCHANGES—§ 1031

2 **LEARNING OBJECTIVE**
Apply the nonrecognition provisions and basis determination rules for like-kind exchanges.

Section 1031 provides for nontaxable exchange treatment if the following requirements are satisfied:[2]

- The form of the transaction is an exchange.
- Both the property transferred and the property received are held either for productive use in a trade or business or for investment.
- The property is like-kind property.

Like-kind exchanges include business for business, business for investment, investment for business, or investment for investment property. Property held for personal use, inventory, and partnership interests (both limited and general) do not qualify under the like-kind exchange provisions. Securities, even though held for investment, do not qualify for like-kind exchange treatment.

[2]§ 1031(a) and Reg. § 1.1031(a)–1(a).

The nonrecognition provision for like-kind exchanges is *mandatory* rather than elective. A taxpayer who wants to recognize a realized gain or loss will have to structure the transaction in a form that does not satisfy the statutory requirements for a like-kind exchange. This topic is discussed further under Tax Planning Considerations.

LIKE-KIND PROPERTY

"The words 'like-kind' refer to the nature or character of the property and not to its grade or quality. One kind or class of property may not . . . be exchanged for property of a different kind or class."[3]

Although the term *like-kind* is intended to be interpreted very broadly, three categories of exchanges are not included. First, livestock of different sexes do not qualify as like-kind property. Second, real estate can be exchanged only for other real estate, and personalty can be exchanged only for other personalty. For example, the exchange of a machine (personalty) for an office building (realty) is not a like-kind exchange. *Real estate* (or realty) includes principally rental buildings, office and store buildings, manufacturing plants, warehouses, and land. It is immaterial whether real estate is improved or unimproved. Thus, unimproved land can be exchanged for an apartment house. Personalty includes principally machines, equipment, trucks, automobiles, furniture, and fixtures. Third, real property located in the United States exchanged for foreign real property (and vice versa) does not qualify as like-kind property.

EXAMPLE 2

Wade made the following exchanges during the taxable year:

a. Inventory for a machine used in business.
b. Land held for investment for a building used in business.
c. Stock held for investment for equipment used in business.
d. A business truck for a business truck.
e. An automobile used for personal transportation for an automobile used in business.
f. Livestock for livestock of a different sex.
g. Land held for investment in New York for land held for investment in London.

Exchanges (b), investment real property for business real property, and (d), business personalty for business personalty, qualify as exchanges of like-kind property. Exchanges (a), inventory; (c), stock; (e), personal use automobile (not held for business or investment purposes); (f), livestock of different sexes; and (g), U.S. and foreign real estate do not qualify. ▼

A special provision applies for personal property with respect to the location of its use. Personal property used predominantly within the United States and personal property used predominantly outside the United States are not like-kind property. The location of use for the personal property given up is its location during the two-year period ending on the date of disposition of the property. The location of use for the personal property received is its location during the two-year period beginning on the date of the acquisition.

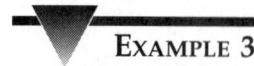
EXAMPLE 3

In October 1997, Walter exchanges a machine used in his factory in Denver for a machine that qualifies as like-kind property. In January 1998, the factory, including the machine, is moved to Berlin. As of January 1998, the exchange is not an exchange of like-kind property. The predominant use of the original machine was in the United States, whereas the predominant use of the new machine is foreign. ▼

---

[3]Reg. § 1.1031(a)–1(b).

Another special provision applies if the taxpayers involved in the exchange are *related parties* under § 267(b). To qualify for like-kind exchange treatment, the taxpayer and the related party must not dispose of the like-kind property received in the exchange within the two-year period following the date of the exchange. If such an early disposition does occur, the postponed gain is recognized as of the date of the early disposition. Dispositions due to death, involuntary conversions, and certain non-tax avoidance transactions are not treated as early dispositions.

Regulations dealing with § 1031 like-kind exchange treatment provide that if the exchange transaction involves multiple assets of a business (e.g., a television station for another television station), the determination of whether the assets qualify as like-kind property will not be made at the business level.[4] Instead, the underlying assets must be evaluated.

The Regulations also provide for greater specificity in determining whether depreciable tangible personal property is of a like kind or class. Such property held for productive use in a business is of a like class only if the exchanged property is within the same *general business asset class* (as specified by the IRS in Revenue Procedure 87–57 or as subsequently modified) or the same *product class* (as specified by the Department of Commerce). Property included in a general business asset class is evaluated under this system rather than under the product class system.

The following are examples of general business asset classes:

- Office furniture, fixtures, and equipment.
- Information systems (computers and peripheral equipment).
- Airplanes.
- Automobiles and taxis.
- Buses.
- Light general-purpose trucks.
- Heavy general-purpose trucks.

These Regulations have made it more difficult for depreciable tangible personal property to qualify for § 1031 like-kind exchange treatment. For example, the exchange of office equipment for a computer does not qualify as an exchange of like-kind property. Even though both assets are depreciable tangible personal property, they are not like-kind property because they are in different general business asset classes.

EXCHANGE REQUIREMENT

The transaction must actually involve a direct exchange of property to qualify as a like-kind exchange. The sale of old property and the purchase of new property, even though like kind, is generally not an exchange. However, if the two transactions are mutually dependent, the IRS may treat them as a like-kind exchange. For example, if the taxpayer sells an old business machine to a dealer and purchases a new one from the same dealer, like-kind exchange treatment could result.[5]

The taxpayer may want to avoid nontaxable exchange treatment. Recognition of gain gives the taxpayer a higher basis for depreciation (see Example 31). To the extent that such gains would, if recognized, either receive favorable capital gain treatment or be passive activity income that could offset passive activity losses, it may be preferable to avoid the nonrecognition provisions through an indirect exchange transaction. For example, a taxpayer may sell property to one individual and subsequently purchase similar property from another individual. The taxpayer

---

[4]Reg. § 1.1031(j)–1.

[5]Rev.Rul. 61–119, 1961–1 C.B. 395.

may also want to avoid nontaxable exchange treatment so that a realized loss can be recognized.

BOOT

If the taxpayer in a like-kind exchange gives or receives some property that is not like-kind property, recognition may occur. Property that is not like-kind property, including cash, is referred to as **boot.** Although the term *boot* does not appear in the Code, tax practitioners commonly use it rather than saying "property that is not like-kind property."

The *receipt* of boot will trigger recognition of gain if there is realized gain. The amount of the recognized gain is the *lesser* of the boot received or the realized gain (realized gain serves as the ceiling on recognition).

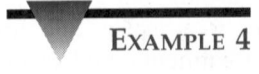

EXAMPLE 4

Emily and Fran exchange machinery, and the exchange qualifies as like-kind under § 1031. Since Emily's machinery (adjusted basis of $20,000) is worth $24,000 and Fran's machine has a fair market value of $19,000, Fran also gives Emily cash of $5,000. Emily's recognized gain is $4,000, the lesser of the realized gain ($24,000 amount realized − $20,000 adjusted basis = $4,000) or the fair market value of the boot received ($5,000). ▼

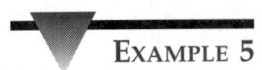

EXAMPLE 5

Assume the same facts as in the previous example, except that Fran's machine is worth $21,000 (not $19,000). Under these circumstances, Fran gives Emily cash of $3,000 to make up the difference. Emily's recognized gain is $3,000, the lesser of the realized gain ($24,000 amount realized − $20,000 adjusted basis = $4,000) or the fair market value of the boot received ($3,000). ▼

The receipt of boot does not result in recognition if there is realized loss.

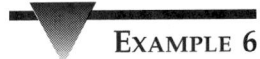

EXAMPLE 6   Assume the same facts as in Example 4, except that the adjusted basis of Emily's machine is $30,000. Emily's realized loss is $6,000 ($24,000 amount realized – $30,000 adjusted basis = $6,000 realized loss). The receipt of the boot of $5,000 does not trigger recognition. Therefore, the recognized loss is $0. ▼

The *giving* of boot usually does not trigger recognition. If the boot given is cash, any realized gain or loss is not recognized.

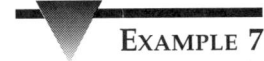

EXAMPLE 7   Fred and Gary exchange equipment in a like-kind exchange. Fred receives equipment with a fair market value of $25,000 and transfers equipment worth $21,000 (adjusted basis of $15,000) and cash of $4,000. Fred's realized gain is $6,000 ($25,000 amount realized – $15,000 adjusted basis – $4,000 cash). However, none of the realized gain is recognized. ▼

If, however, the boot given is appreciated or depreciated property, gain or loss is recognized to the extent of the differential between the adjusted basis and the fair market value of the boot. For this purpose, *appreciated or depreciated property* is defined as property whose adjusted basis is not equal to the fair market value.

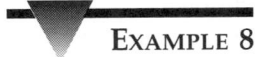

EXAMPLE 8   Assume the same facts as in the previous example, except that Fred transfers equipment worth $10,000 (adjusted basis of $12,000) and boot worth $15,000 (adjusted basis of $9,000). Fred's realized gain appears to be $4,000 ($25,000 amount realized – $21,000 adjusted basis). Since realization previously has served as a ceiling on recognition, it appears that the recognized gain is $4,000 (lower of realized gain of $4,000 or amount of appreciation on boot of $6,000). However, the recognized gain actually is $6,000 (full amount of the appreciation on the boot). In effect, Fred must calculate the like-kind and boot parts of the transaction separately. That is, the realized loss of $2,000 on the like-kind property is not recognized ($10,000 fair market value – $12,000 adjusted basis), and the $6,000 realized gain on the boot is recognized ($15,000 fair market value – $9,000 adjusted basis). ▼

BASIS AND HOLDING PERIOD OF PROPERTY RECEIVED

If an exchange does not qualify as nontaxable under § 1031, gain or loss is recognized, and the basis of property received in the exchange is the property's fair market value. If the exchange qualifies for nonrecognition, the basis of property received must be adjusted to reflect any postponed (deferred) gain or loss. The *basis of like-kind property* received in the exchange is the property's fair market value less postponed gain or plus postponed loss. If the exchange partially qualifies for nonrecognition (if recognition is associated with boot), the basis of like-kind property received in the exchange is the property's fair market value less postponed gain or plus postponed loss. The *basis* of any *boot* received is the boot's fair market value.

If there is a postponed loss, nonrecognition creates a situation in which the taxpayer has recovered *less* than the cost or other basis of the property exchanged in an amount equal to the unrecognized loss. If there is a postponed gain, the taxpayer has recovered *more* than the cost or other basis of the property exchanged in an amount equal to the unrecognized gain.

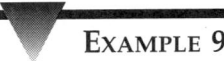

EXAMPLE 9   Jaime exchanges a building (used in his business) with an adjusted basis of $30,000 and fair market value of $38,000 for land with a fair market value of $38,000. The land is to be held as an investment. The exchange qualifies as like kind (an exchange of business real property for investment real property). Thus, the basis of the land is $30,000 (the land's fair market value of $38,000 less the $8,000 postponed gain on the building). If the land is later sold for its fair market value of $38,000, the $8,000 postponed gain is recognized. ▼

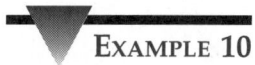

EXAMPLE 10

Assume the same facts as in the previous example, except that the building has an adjusted basis of $48,000 and fair market value of only $38,000. The basis in the newly acquired land is $48,000 (fair market value of $38,000 plus the $10,000 postponed loss on the building). If the land is later sold for its fair market value of $38,000, the $10,000 postponed loss is recognized. ▼

The Code provides an alternative approach for determining the basis of like-kind property received:

> Adjusted basis of like-kind property surrendered
> + Adjusted basis of boot given
> + Gain recognized
> − Fair market value of boot received
> − Loss recognized
> = *Basis of like-kind property received*

This approach is logical in terms of the recovery of capital doctrine. That is, the unrecovered cost or other basis is increased by additional cost (boot given) or decreased by cost recovered (boot received). Any gain recognized is included in the basis of the new property. The taxpayer has been taxed on this amount and is now entitled to recover it tax-free. Any loss recognized is deducted from the basis of the new property. The taxpayer has received a tax benefit on that amount.

The holding period of the property surrendered in the exchange carries over and *tacks on* to the holding period of the like-kind property received.[6] The logic of this rule is derived from the basic concept of the new property as a continuation of the old investment. The boot received has a new holding period (from the date of exchange) rather than a carryover holding period.

Depreciation recapture potential carries over to the property received in a like-kind exchange.[7] See Chapter 17 for a discussion of this topic.

The following comprehensive example illustrates the like-kind exchange rules.

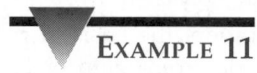

EXAMPLE 11

Vicki exchanged the following old machines for new machines in five independent like-kind exchanges:

Exchange	Adjusted Basis of Old Machine	Fair Market Value of New Machine	Adjusted Basis of Boot Given	Fair Market Value of Boot Received
1	$4,000	$9,000	$ –0–	$ –0–
2	4,000	9,000	3,000	–0–
3	4,000	9,000	6,000	–0–
4	4,000	9,000	–0–	3,000
5	4,000	3,500	–0–	300

Vicki's realized and recognized gains and losses and the basis of each of the like-kind properties received are as follows:

---

[6]§ 1223(1) and Reg. § 1.1223–1(a). For this carryover holding period rule to apply to like-kind exchanges after March 1, 1954, the like-kind property surrendered must have been either a capital asset or § 1231

property. See Chapters 16 and 17 for the discussion of capital assets and § 1231 property.
[7]Reg. §§ 1.1245–2(a)(4) and 1.1250–2(d)(1).

	Realized Gain (Loss)	Recognized Gain (Loss)	New Basis Calculation									
Exchange			Old Adj. Basis	+	Boot Given	+	Gain Recognized	–	Boot Received	=	New Basis
1	$ 5,000	$ –(0)–	$4,000	+	$ –0–	+	$ –0–	–	$ –0–	=	$ 4,000*
2	2,000	–(0)–	4,000	+	3,000	+	–0–	–	–0–	=	7,000*
3	(1,000)	–(0)–	4,000	+	6,000	+	–0–	–	–0–	=	10,000**
4	8,000	3,000	4,000	+	–0–	+	3,000	–	3,000	=	4,000*
5	(200)	–(0)–	4,000	+	–0–	+	–0–	–	300	=	3,700**

*Basis may be determined in gain situations under the alternative method by subtracting the gain not recognized from the fair market value of the new property:
$9,000 – $5,000 = $4,000 for exchange 1.
$9,000 – $2,000 = $7,000 for exchange 2.
$9,000 – $5,000 = $4,000 for exchange 4.
**In loss situations, basis may be determined by adding the loss not recognized to the fair market value of the new property:
$9,000 + $1,000 = $10,000 for exchange 3.
$3,500 + $200 = $3,700 for exchange 5.
The basis of the boot received is the boot's fair market value. ▼

If the taxpayer either assumes a liability or takes property subject to a liability, the amount of the liability is treated as boot given. For the taxpayer whose liability is assumed or whose property is taken subject to the liability, the amount of the liability is treated as boot received. Example 12 illustrates the effect of such a liability. In addition, the example illustrates the tax consequences for both parties involved in the like-kind exchange.

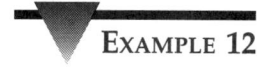

EXAMPLE 12

Jane and Leo exchange real estate investments. Jane gives up property with an adjusted basis of $250,000 (fair market value $400,000) that is subject to a mortgage of $75,000 (assumed by Leo). In return for this property, Jane receives property with a fair market value of $300,000 (adjusted basis $200,000) and cash of $25,000.

- Jane's realized gain is $150,000. She gave up property with an adjusted basis of $250,000. Jane received $400,000 from the exchange ($300,000 fair market value of like-kind property plus $100,000 boot received). The boot received consists of the $25,000 cash received from Leo and Jane's mortgage of $75,000 that Leo assumes.
- Jane's recognized gain is $100,000. The realized gain of $150,000 is recognized to the extent of boot received.
- Jane's basis in the real estate received from Leo is $250,000. This basis can be computed by subtracting the postponed gain ($50,000) from the fair market value of the real estate received ($300,000). It can also be computed by adding the recognized gain ($100,000) to the adjusted basis of the real estate given up ($250,000) and subtracting the boot received ($100,000).
- Leo's realized gain is $100,000. Leo gave up property with an adjusted basis of $200,000 plus boot of $100,000 ($75,000 mortgage assumed + $25,000 cash) or a total of $300,000. Leo received $400,000 from the exchange (fair market value of like-kind property received).
- Leo has no recognized gain because he did not receive any boot. The entire realized gain of $100,000 is postponed.
- Leo's basis in the real estate received from Jane is $300,000. This basis can be computed by subtracting the postponed gain ($100,000) from the fair market value of the real estate received ($400,000). It can also be computed by adding the boot given ($75,000 mortgage assumed by Leo + $25,000 cash) to the adjusted basis of the real estate given up ($200,000).[8] ▼

---

[8]Example (2) of Reg. § 1.1031(d)–2 illustrates a special situation where both the buyer and the seller transfer liabilities that are assumed or property is acquired subject to a liability by the other party.

INVOLUNTARY CONVERSIONS—§ 1033

3 ▼ **LEARNING OBJECTIVE**
Explain the nonrecognition provisions available on the involuntary conversion of property.

Section 1033 provides that a taxpayer who suffers an involuntary conversion of property may postpone recognition of *gain* realized from the conversion. The objective of this provision is to provide relief to the taxpayer who has suffered hardship and does not have the wherewithal to pay the tax on any gain realized from the conversion. Postponement of realized gain is permitted to the extent that the taxpayer *reinvests* the amount realized from the conversion in replacement property. The rules for nonrecognition of gain are as follows:

- If the amount reinvested in replacement property *equals or exceeds* the amount realized, realized gain is *not recognized*.
- If the amount reinvested in replacement property is *less than* the amount realized, realized gain *is recognized* to the extent of the deficiency.

If a *loss* occurs on an involuntary conversion, § 1033 does not modify the normal rules for loss recognition. That is, if a realized loss would otherwise be recognized, § 1033 does not change the result.

INVOLUNTARY CONVERSION DEFINED

An **involuntary conversion** results from the destruction (complete or partial), theft, seizure, requisition or condemnation, or the sale or exchange under threat or imminence of requisition or condemnation of the taxpayer's property.[9] To prove the existence of a threat or imminence of condemnation, the taxpayer must obtain confirmation that there has been a decision to acquire the property for public use. In addition, the taxpayer must have reasonable grounds to believe the property will be taken.[10] The property does not have to be sold to the authority threatening to condemn it to qualify for § 1033 postponement. If the taxpayer satisfies the confirmation and reasonable grounds requirements, he or she can sell the property to another party.[11] Likewise, the sale of property to a condemning authority by a taxpayer who acquired the property from its former owner with the knowledge

---

[9]§ 1033(a) and Reg. §§ 1.1033(a)–1(a) and –2(a).
[10]Rev.Rul. 63–221, 1963–2 C.B. 332, and *Joseph P. Balistrieri*, 38 TCM 526, T.C.Memo. 1979–115.

[11]Rev.Rul. 81–180, 1981–2 C.B. 161.

that the property was under threat of condemnation also qualifies as an involuntary conversion under § 1033.[12] A voluntary act, such as a taxpayer destroying his or her own property by arson, is not an involuntary conversion.[13]

COMPUTING THE AMOUNT REALIZED

The amount realized from the condemnation of property usually includes only the amount received as compensation for the property.[14] Any amount received that is designated as severance damages by both the government and the taxpayer is not included in the amount realized. *Severance awards* usually occur when only a portion of the entire property is condemned (e.g., a strip of land is taken to build a highway). Severance damages are awarded because the value of the taxpayer's remaining property has declined as a result of the condemnation. Such damages reduce the basis of the property. However, if either of the following requirements is satisfied, the nonrecognition provision of § 1033 applies to the severance damages.

- Severance damages are used to restore the usability of the remaining property.
- The usefulness of the remaining property is destroyed by the condemnation, and the property is sold and replaced at a cost equal to or exceeding the sum of the condemnation award, severance damages, and sales proceeds.

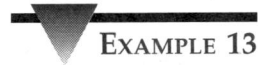

EXAMPLE 13   The government condemns a portion of Ron's farmland to build part of an interstate highway. Because the highway denies his cattle access to a pond and some grazing land, Ron receives severance damages in addition to the condemnation proceeds for the land taken. Ron must reduce the basis of the property by the amount of the severance damages. If the amount of the severance damages received exceeds the adjusted basis, Ron recognizes gain. ▼

EXAMPLE 14   Assume the same facts as in the previous example, except that Ron used the proceeds from the condemnation and the severance damages to build another pond and to clear woodland for grazing. Therefore, all the proceeds are eligible for § 1033 treatment. Thus, there is no possibility of gain recognition as the result of the amount of the severance damages received exceeding the adjusted basis. ▼

REPLACEMENT PROPERTY

The requirements for replacement property generally are more restrictive than those for like-kind property under § 1031. The basic requirement is that the replacement property be similar or related in service or use to the involuntarily converted property.[15]

Different interpretations of the phrase *similar or related in service or use* apply depending on whether the involuntarily converted property is held by an *owner-user* or by an *owner-investor* (e.g., lessor). A taxpayer who uses the property in his or her trade or business is subject to a more restrictive test in terms of acquiring replacement property. For an owner-user, the *functional use test* applies, and for an owner-investor, the *taxpayer use test* applies.

Taxpayer Use Test.   The taxpayer use test for owner-investors provides the taxpayer with more flexibility in terms of what qualifies as replacement property than does the functional use test for owner-users. Essentially, the properties must

---

[12]Rev.Rul. 81–181, 1981–2 C.B. 162.
[13]Rev.Rul. 82–74, 1982–1 C.B. 110.

[14]*Pioneer Real Estate Co.*, 47 B.T.A. 886 (1942), *acq.* 1943 C.B. 18.
[15]§ 1033(a) and Reg. § 1.1033(a)–1.

CONCEPT SUMMARY 15–1

Replacement Property Tests

Type of Property and User	Like-Kind Test	Taxpayer Use Test	Functional Use Test
Land used by a manufacturing company is condemned by a local government authority.	X		
Apartment and land held by an investor are sold due to the threat or imminence of condemnation.	X		
An investor's rented shopping mall is destroyed by fire; the mall may be replaced by other rental properties (e.g., an apartment building).		X	
A manufacturing plant is destroyed by fire; replacement property must consist of another manufacturing plant that is functionally the same as the property converted.			X
Personal residence of taxpayer is condemned by a local government authority; replacement property must consist of another personal residence.			X

be used by the taxpayer (the owner-investor) in similar endeavors. For example, rental property held by an owner-investor qualifies if replaced by other rental property, regardless of the type of rental property involved. The test is met when an investor replaces a manufacturing plant with a wholesale grocery warehouse if both properties are held for the production of rent income.[16] The replacement of a rental residence with a personal residence does not meet the test.[17]

Functional Use Test.   Under this test, the taxpayer's use of the replacement property and of the involuntarily converted property must be the same. Replacing a manufacturing plant with a wholesale grocery warehouse, whether rented or not, does not meet this test. As indicated above, the IRS applies the taxpayer use test to owner-investors. However, the functional use test still applies to owner-users (e.g., a manufacturer whose manufacturing plant is destroyed by fire is required to replace the plant with another facility of similar functional use). Replacing a rental residence with a personal residence does not meet this test.

Special Rules.   Under one set of circumstances, the broader replacement rules for like-kind exchanges are substituted for the narrow replacement rules normally used for involuntary conversions. This beneficial provision applies if business real property or investment real property is condemned. Therefore, the taxpayer has substantially more flexibility in selecting replacement property. For example, improved real property can be replaced with unimproved real property.

The rules concerning the nature of replacement property are illustrated in Concept Summary 15–1.

---

[16]*Loco Realty Co. v. Comm.*, 62–2 USTC ¶9657, 10 AFTR2d 5359, 306 F.2d 207 (CA–8, 1962).

[17]Rev.Rul. 70–466, 1970–2 C.B. 165.

TIME LIMITATION ON REPLACEMENT

The taxpayer normally has a two-year period after the close of the taxable year in which any gain is realized from the involuntary conversion to replace the property (*the latest date*).[18] This rule affords as much as three years from the date of realization of gain to replace the property if the realization of gain took place on the first day of the taxable year.[19] If the involuntary conversion involved the condemnation of real property used in a trade or business or held for investment, a three-year period is substituted for the normal two-year period. In this case, the taxpayer can actually have as much as four years from the date of realization of gain to replace the property.

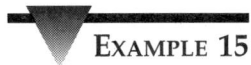

EXAMPLE 15

Megan's warehouse is destroyed by fire on December 16, 1997. The adjusted basis is $325,000. Megan receives $400,000 from the insurance company on January 10, 1998. She is a calendar year taxpayer. The latest date for replacement is December 31, 2000 (the end of the taxable year in which realized gain occurred plus two years). The critical date is not the date the involuntary conversion occurred, but rather the date of gain realization. ▼

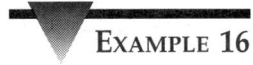

EXAMPLE 16

Assume the same facts as in the previous example, except that Megan's warehouse is condemned. The latest date for replacement is December 31, 2001 (the end of the taxable year in which realized gain occurred plus three years). ▼

The *earliest date* for replacement typically is the date the involuntary conversion occurs. However, if the property is condemned, it is possible to replace the condemned property before this date. In this case, the earliest date is the date of the threat or imminence of requisition or condemnation of the property. The purpose of this provision is to enable the taxpayer to make an orderly replacement of the condemned property.

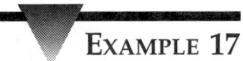

EXAMPLE 17

Assume the same facts as in Example 16. Megan can replace the warehouse before December 16, 1997 (the condemnation date). The earliest date for replacement is the date of the threat or imminence of requisition or condemnation of the warehouse. ▼

ETHICAL CONSIDERATIONS

Postponing Realized Gain from an Involuntary Conversion

Peggy, age 63 and in frail health, owns a furniture store in Petersburg. Because of competition from two large furniture retailers who opened stores in the Petersburg area during the past three years, Peggy's furniture store has been unprofitable.

Due to this lack of profitability as well as her advancing age, Peggy would like to retire. Unfortunately, she has been unable to locate a purchaser for her store. Her prayers seem to be answered when a tornado destroys her building and its contents. Fortunately, no one is injured or killed by the tornado.

Peggy anticipates that she can live on the insurance proceeds of $800,000 for the rest of her life. However, her realized gain on the involuntary conversion would produce a combined state and Federal tax liability of approximately $175,000. In order to forgo paying

---

[18]§§ 1033(a)(2)(B) and (g)(4) and Reg. § 1.1033(a)–2(c)(3).
[19]The taxpayer can apply for an extension of this time period anytime before its expiration [Reg. § 1.1033(a)–2(c)(3)]. Also, the period for

filing the application for extension can be extended if the taxpayer shows reasonable cause.

this amount associated with her 1998 income tax returns, Peggy elects postponement treatment under § 1033, indicating that she intends to replace the involuntarily converted property with similar property even though she does not intend to do so. Her justification, based on her participation in a 12-step program, is that she lives "one day at a time."

Evaluate Peggy's election of § 1033 postponement under these circumstances.

NONRECOGNITION OF GAIN

Nonrecognition of gain can be either mandatory or elective, depending upon whether the conversion is direct (into replacement property) or into money (indirect).

Direct Conversion.   If the conversion is directly into replacement property rather than into money, nonrecognition of realized gain is *mandatory*. In this case, the basis of the replacement property is the same as the adjusted basis of the converted property. Direct conversion is rare in practice and usually involves condemnations. The following example illustrates the application of the rules for direct conversions.

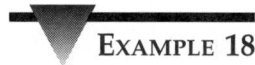

EXAMPLE 18

Lupe's property with an adjusted basis of $20,000 is condemned by the state. Lupe receives property with a fair market value of $50,000 as compensation for the property taken. Since the nonrecognition of realized gain is mandatory for direct conversions, Lupe's realized gain of $30,000 is not recognized, and the basis of the replacement property is $20,000 (adjusted basis of the condemned property). ▼

Conversion into Money.   If the conversion is into money, at the election of the taxpayer, the realized gain is recognized only to the extent the amount realized from the involuntary conversion exceeds the cost of the qualifying replacement property.[20] This is the usual case, and nonrecognition (postponement) is *elective*. If the election is not made, the realized gain is recognized.

The basis of the replacement property is the property's cost less postponed (deferred) gain.[21] If the election to postpone gain is made, the holding period of the replacement property includes the holding period of the converted property.

Section 1033 applies *only to gains* and *not to losses*. Losses from involuntary conversions are recognized if the property is held for business or income-producing purposes. Personal casualty losses are recognized, but condemnation losses related to personal use assets (e.g., a personal residence) are neither recognized nor postponed.

Examples 19 and 20 illustrate the application of the involuntary conversion provisions.

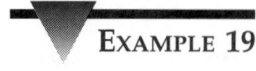

EXAMPLE 19

Walt's building (used in his trade or business), with an adjusted basis of $50,000, is destroyed by fire in 1998. Walt is a calendar year taxpayer. In 1998, he receives an insurance reimbursement of $100,000 for the loss. Walt invests $80,000 in a new building.

- Walt has until December 31, 2000, to make the new investment and qualify for the nonrecognition election.

---

[20]§ 1033(a)(2)(A) and Reg. § 1.1033(a)–2(c)(1).   [21]§ 1033(b).

- Walt's realized gain is $50,000 ($100,000 insurance proceeds received − $50,000 adjusted basis of old building).
- Assuming the replacement property qualifies as similar or related in service or use, Walt's recognized gain is $20,000. He reinvested $20,000 less than the insurance proceeds received ($100,000 proceeds − $80,000 reinvested). Therefore, his realized gain is recognized to that extent.
- Walt's basis in the new building is $50,000. This is the building's cost of $80,000 less the postponed gain of $30,000 (realized gain of $50,000 − recognized gain of $20,000).
- The computation of realization, recognition, and basis would apply even if Walt was a real estate dealer and the building destroyed by fire was part of his inventory. Unlike § 1031, § 1033 generally does not exclude inventory. ▼

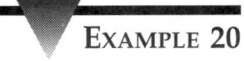

EXAMPLE 20

Assume the same facts as in the previous example, except that Walt receives only $45,000 (instead of $100,000) of insurance proceeds. He has a realized and recognized loss of $5,000. The basis of the new building is the building's cost of $80,000. If the destroyed building was held for personal use, the recognized loss is subject to the following additional limitations.[22] The loss of $5,000 is limited to the decline in fair market value of the property, and the amount of the loss is reduced first by $100 and then by 10% of adjusted gross income (refer to Chapter 7). ▼

INVOLUNTARY CONVERSION OF A PERSONAL RESIDENCE

The tax consequences of the involuntary conversion of a personal residence depend upon whether the conversion is a casualty or condemnation and whether a realized loss or gain results.

Loss Situations. If the conversion is a condemnation, the realized loss is not recognized. Loss from the condemnation of a personal use asset is never recognized. If the conversion is a casualty (a loss from fire, storm, etc.), the loss is recognized subject to the personal casualty loss limitations (refer to Chapter 7).

Gain Situations. If the conversion is a casualty, theft, or condemnation, the gain may be postponed under § 1033 or excluded under § 121. That is, the taxpayer may treat the involuntary conversion as a sale under the exclusion of gain rules relating to the sale of a personal residence under § 121 (presented subsequently).

REPORTING CONSIDERATIONS

Involuntary conversions from casualty and theft are reported first on Form 4684, Casualties and Thefts. Casualty and theft losses on personal use property for the individual taxpayer are carried from Form 4684 to Schedule A of Form 1040. For other casualty and theft items, the Form 4684 amounts are generally reported on Form 4797, Sales of Business Property, unless Form 4797 is not required. In the latter case, the amounts are reported directly on the tax return involved.

Except for personal use property, recognized gains and losses from involuntary conversions other than by casualty and theft are reported on Form 4797. As stated previously, if the property involved in the involuntary conversion (other than by casualty and theft) is personal use property, any realized loss is not recognized. Any realized gain is treated as gain on a voluntary sale.

[22]§ 165(c)(3) and Reg. § 1.165–7.

TAX IN THE NEWS

WHAT GOES DOWN MAY GO UP

Many of us are either not investors or not good investors. Nevertheless, most of us view our home as an asset that we can eventually sell for a higher price than we paid.

Yet what does one do if the home does not turn out to be a good investment? In some areas of the country, housing prices still have not regained their former levels. So, if taxpayers sell, they have a realized loss that is disallowed for tax purposes. To make matters worse, the disallowed loss cannot be added to the basis of the replacement residence.

In this situation, what can the taxpayer who buys a new residence do? Among the options are the following:

- Convert the old residence to rental property until its price increases.
- If the new residence is in the same area as the old residence and is more suitable for renting, convert it to rental property until the price of the old residence increases.
- Sell the house, deduct the loss, and hope your tax return is not audited.
- Sell the house knowing that the loss cannot be deducted on your tax return.

The first two options require careful planning in order to avoid certain tax pitfalls (e.g., satisfying the two-year ownership and use requirement within the five-year window). They also are based on the assumption that the real estate market for housing in the particular area will rebound. The third option should be avoided. With the fourth option, the taxpayer's ego suffers because this is an admission that he or she is not a good investor.

SOURCE: Adapted from Scott R. Schmedel, "Housing and the Tax Man: When Selling at a Loss, the Consequences Are Tricky," *Wall Street Journal*, February 28, 1997, p. C1.

SALE OF A RESIDENCE—§ 121

4 **LEARNING OBJECTIVE**
Describe the provision for the permanent exclusion of gain on the sale of a personal residence.

A taxpayer's **personal residence** is a personal use asset. Therefore, a realized loss from the sale of a personal residence is not recognized.[23]

A realized gain from the sale of a personal residence is subject to taxation. Limited relief from recognition of gain is provided in the form of the **§ 121 exclusion.** Under this provision, a taxpayer can exclude up to $250,000 of realized gain on the sale.[24]

REQUIREMENTS FOR EXCLUSION TREATMENT

At the date of the sale, the residence must have been *owned* and *used* by the taxpayer as the principal residence for at least two years during the five-year period ending on the date of the sale.[25]

---

[23]§ 165(c).
[24]§ 121(b).

[25]§ 121(a).

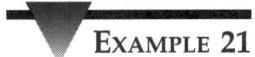

EXAMPLE 21

Alice sells her principal residence on September 18, 1998. She had purchased it on July 5, 1996, and lived in it since then. The sale of Alice's residence qualifies for the § 121 exclusion. ▼

The five-year window enables the taxpayer to qualify for the § 121 exclusion even though the property is not his or her principal residence at the date of the sale.

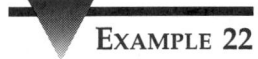

EXAMPLE 22

Benjamin sells his principal residence on August 16, 1998. He had purchased it on April 1, 1990, and lived in it until July 1, 1997, when he converted it to rental property. Even though the property is rental property on August 16, 1998, rather than Benjamin's principal residence, the sale qualifies for the § 121 exclusion. During the five-year period from August 16, 1993, to August 16, 1998, Benjamin owned and used the property as his principal residence for at least two years. ▼

Taxpayers might be tempted to make liberal use of the § 121 exclusion as a means of speculating when the price of residential housing is rising. Without any time restriction on its use, § 121 would permit the exclusion of realized gain on multiple sales of principal residences. The Code curbs this approach by denying the application of the § 121 exclusion to sales occurring within two years of its last use.[26]

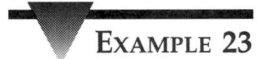

EXAMPLE 23

After Seth sells his principal residence (the first residence) in June 1997 for $150,000 (realized gain of $60,000), he buys and sells the following (all of which qualify as principal residences):

	Date of Purchase	Date of Sale	Amount Involved
Second residence	July 1997		$160,000
Second residence		April 1998	180,000
Third residence	May 1998		200,000

Because multiple sales have taken place within a period of two years, § 121 does not apply to the sale of the second residence. Thus, the realized gain of $20,000 [$180,000 (selling price) – $160,000 (purchase price)] must be recognized. ▼

The two-year ownership and use requirement and the "only once every two years" provision could create a hardship for taxpayers in certain situations that are beyond their control. Thus, under the following special circumstances, the requirements are waived:[27]

- Change in place of employment.
- Health.
- To the extent provided in the Regulations, other unforeseen circumstances.

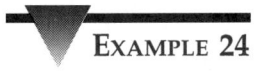

EXAMPLE 24

Assume the same facts as in the previous example, except that in March 1998, Seth's employer transfers him to a job in another state. Thus, the sale of the second residence and the purchase of the third residence were due to the relocation of employment. Consequently, the § 121 exclusion is partially available on the sale of the second residence. ▼

The full amount of the § 121 exclusion is not available under this relief provision, however.[28] See the discussion under Relief Provision later in this chapter for the amount of the exclusion.

---

[26]§ 121(b)(3).
[27]§ 121(c).

[28]§ 121(c)(1).

CALCULATION OF THE AMOUNT OF THE EXCLUSION

General Provisions.   The amount of the available § 121 exclusion on the sale of a principal residence is $250,000.[29] If the realized gain does not exceed $250,000, there is no recognized gain.

Realized gain is calculated in the normal manner. The *amount realized* is the selling price less the selling expenses, which include items such as the cost of advertising the property for sale, real estate broker commissions, legal fees in connection with the sale, and loan placement fees paid by the taxpayer as a condition of arranging financing for the buyer. Repairs and maintenance made by the seller to aid in selling the property are treated neither as selling expenses nor as adjustments to the taxpayer's adjusted basis for the residence.

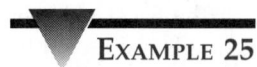

EXAMPLE 25

Mandy, who is single, sells her personal residence (adjusted basis of $130,000) for $290,000. She has owned and lived in the residence for three years. Her selling expenses are $18,000. Three weeks prior to the sale, Mandy paid a carpenter and a painter $1,000 to make some repairs and paint the two bathrooms. Her recognized gain is calculated as follows:

Amount realized ($290,000 – $18,000)	$ 272,000
Adjusted basis	(130,000)
Realized gain	$ 142,000
§ 121 exclusion	(142,000)
Recognized gain	$ –0–

Since the available § 121 exclusion of $250,000 exceeds Mandy's realized gain of $142,000, her recognized gain is $0. ▼

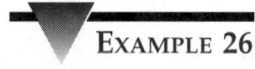

EXAMPLE 26

Assume the same facts as in the previous example, except that the selling price is $490,000.

Amount realized ($490,000 – $18,000)	$ 472,000
Adjusted basis	(130,000)
Realized gain	$ 342,000
§ 121 exclusion	(250,000)
Recognized gain	$ 92,000

Since the realized gain of $342,000 exceeds the § 121 exclusion amount of $250,000, Mandy's recognized gain is $92,000 ($342,000 – $250,000). ▼

Effect on Married Couples.   If a married couple files a joint return, the $250,000 amount is increased to $500,000 if the following requirements are satisfied:[30]

- Either spouse meets the at-least-two-years *ownership* requirement.
- Both spouses meet the at-least-two-years *use* requirement.
- Neither spouse is ineligible for the § 121 exclusion on the sale of the current principal residence because of the sale of another principal residence within the prior two years.

[29]§ 121(b)(1).   [30]§ 121(b)(2).

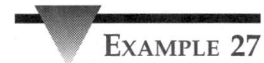
EXAMPLE 27

Margaret sells her personal residence (adjusted basis of $150,000) for $650,000. She has owned and lived in the residence for six years. Her selling expenses are $40,000. Margaret is married to Ted, and they file a joint return. Ted has lived in the residence since they were married two and one-half years ago.

Amount realized ($650,000 – $40,000)	$ 610,000
Adjusted basis	(150,000)
Realized gain	$ 460,000
§ 121 exclusion	(460,000)
Recognized gain	$ –0–

Since the realized gain of $460,000 is less than the available § 121 exclusion amount of $500,000, no gain is recognized. ▼

If the taxpayer and spouse each own a qualified principal residence, they can separately qualify for the $250,000 exclusion on the sale of their own residence even if they file a joint return.[31]

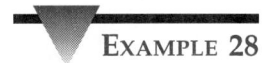
EXAMPLE 28

Anne and Samuel are married on August 1, 1998. They each own a residence that is eligible for the § 121 exclusion. Anne sells her residence on September 7, 1998, and Samuel sells his residence on October 9, 1998. Relevant data on the sales are as follows:

	Anne	Samuel
Selling price	$320,000	$425,000
Selling expenses	20,000	25,000
Adjusted basis	190,000	110,000

Anne and Samuel intend to rent a condo in Florida or Arizona and to travel. The recognized gain of each is calculated as follows:

	Anne	Samuel
Amount realized	$ 300,000	$ 400,000
Adjusted basis	(190,000)	(110,000)
Realized gain	$ 110,000	$ 290,000
§ 121 exclusion	(110,000)	(250,000)
Recognized gain	$ –0–	$ 40,000

Anne has no recognized gain because the available $250,000 exclusion amount exceeds her realized gain of $110,000. Samuel's recognized gain is $40,000 as his realized gain of $290,000 exceeds the $250,000 exclusion amount. The recognized gains calculated above result regardless of whether Anne and Samuel file a joint return or separate returns. ▼

Relief Provision. As discussed earlier in Requirements for Exclusion Treatment, partial § 121 exclusion treatment may be available when all the statutory requirements are not satisfied. Under the relief provision, the realized gain (limited to the § 121 exclusion amount) is multiplied by a fraction, the numerator of which is the number of qualifying months and the denominator of which is 24 months. The resulting amount is the excluded gain.[32]

---

[31]§ 121(b)(1).   [32]§ 121(c)(1).

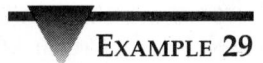

EXAMPLE 29

Rich and Audrey live in Chicago and sell their personal residence on October 1, 1997. The realized gain of $225,000 is excluded under § 121. They purchase another personal residence for $300,000 on October 2, 1997. Audrey's employer transfers her to the Denver office in August 1998. Rich and Audrey sell their Chicago residence on August 2, 1998, and purchase a residence in Denver shortly thereafter. The realized gain on the sale is $120,000.

The $225,000 gain on the first Chicago residence is excluded under § 121. The sale of the second Chicago residence is within the two-year window of the prior sale, but because it resulted from a change in employment, Rich and Audrey can qualify for partial § 121 exclusion treatment as follows:

Realized gain	$120,000
§ 121 exclusion: $\frac{10 \text{ months}}{24 \text{ months}} \times \$120,000 = \$50,000$	(50,000)
Recognized gain	$ 70,000

▼

Basis of New Residence.   As § 121 is an exclusion provision rather than a postponement of gain provision, the basis of a new residence is its cost.[33]

PRINCIPAL RESIDENCE

To be eligible for the § 121 exclusion, the residence must have been owned and used by the taxpayer as the principal residence at least two years during the five-year window (subject to partial exclusion treatment under the relief provision). Whether property is the taxpayer's principal residence "... depends upon all of the facts and circumstances in each case."[34]

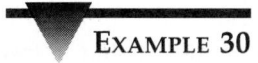

EXAMPLE 30

Mitch graduates from college and moves to Boston, where he is employed. He decides to rent an apartment in Boston because of its proximity to his place of employment. He purchases a beach condo in the Cape Cod area that he occupies most weekends. Mitch does not intend to live at the beach condo except on weekends. The apartment in Boston is his principal residence. ▼

A residence does not have to be a house. For example, a houseboat or a house trailer can qualify.[35]

OTHER NONRECOGNITION PROVISIONS

5 **LEARNING OBJECTIVE**
Identify other nonrecognition provisions contained in the Code.

The typical taxpayer experiences the sale of a personal residence or an involuntary conversion more frequently than the other types of nontaxable exchanges. Several additional nonrecognition provisions that are not as common are treated briefly in the remainder of this chapter.

EXCHANGE OF STOCK FOR PROPERTY—§ 1032

Under § 1032, a corporation does not recognize gain or loss on the receipt of money or other property in exchange for its stock (including treasury stock). In other words, a corporation does not recognize gain or loss when it deals in its own stock. This provision is consistent with the accounting treatment of such transactions.

---

[33]§ 1012.
[34]Reg. § 1.1034–1(c)(3).

[35]Reg. § 1.1034–1(c)(3)(i).

CERTAIN EXCHANGES OF INSURANCE POLICIES—§ 1035

Under this provision, no gain or loss is recognized from the exchange of certain insurance contracts or policies. The rules relating to exchanges not solely in kind and the basis of the property acquired are the same as under § 1031. Exchanges qualifying for nonrecognition include the following:

- The exchange of life insurance contracts.
- The exchange of a life insurance contract for an endowment or annuity contract.
- The exchange of an endowment contract for another endowment contract that provides for regular payments beginning at a date not later than the date payments would have begun under the contract exchanged.
- The exchange of an endowment contract for an annuity contract.
- The exchange of annuity contracts.

EXCHANGE OF STOCK FOR STOCK OF THE SAME CORPORATION—§ 1036

A shareholder does not recognize gain or loss on the exchange of common stock solely for common stock in the same corporation or from the exchange of preferred stock for preferred stock in the same corporation. Exchanges between individual shareholders as well as between a shareholder and the corporation are included. The rules relating to exchanges not solely in kind and the basis of the property acquired are the same as under § 1031. For example, a nonrecognition exchange occurs when common stock with different rights, such as voting for nonvoting, is exchanged. A shareholder usually recognizes gain or loss from the exchange of common for preferred or preferred for common even though the stock exchanged is in the same corporation.

CERTAIN REACQUISITIONS OF REAL PROPERTY—§ 1038

Under this provision, no loss is recognized from the repossession of real property sold on an installment basis. Gain is recognized to a limited extent.

TRANSFERS OF PROPERTY BETWEEN SPOUSES OR INCIDENT TO DIVORCE—§ 1041

Section 1041 provides that transfers of property *between spouses or former spouses incident to divorce* are nontaxable transactions. Therefore, the basis to the recipient is a carryover basis. To be treated as incident to the divorce, the transfer must be related to the cessation of marriage or occur within one year after the date on which the marriage ceases.

Section 1041 also provides for nontaxable exchange treatment on property transfers *between spouses during marriage*. The basis to the recipient spouse is a carryover basis.

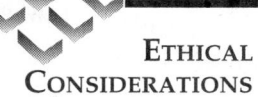

ETHICAL CONSIDERATIONS

Incident to Divorce or Not?

Randy and Judy are divorced in late 1997 after being married for 10 years. Several years ago they purchased a beach lot for $80,000. They planned to construct a beach house where they "could get away from it all" on weekends and holidays.

Eleven months after the divorce, Randy transfers his interest in the beach lot to Judy for $60,000 (i.e., 50 percent of the fair market value of $120,000). Since Randy is in a lower tax bracket than Judy (15 percent for Randy and 36 percent for Judy), they treat the sales transaction as not incident to the divorce. Randy recognizes a gain of $20,000 ($60,000 – $40,000), and Judy's adjusted basis is $100,000 ($40,000 + $60,000).

Evaluate Randy and Judy's treatment of the sales transaction.

ROLLOVERS INTO SPECIALIZED SMALL BUSINESS INVESTMENT COMPANIES—§ 1044

A postponement opportunity is available for some sellers of publicly traded securities. If the amount realized is reinvested in the common stock or partnership interest of a specialized small business investment company (SSBIC), the realized gain is not recognized. Any amount not reinvested will trigger the recognition of the realized gain on the sale to the extent of the deficiency. The taxpayer must reinvest the proceeds within 60 days of the date of sale in order to qualify. In calculating the basis of the SSBIC stock, the amount of the purchase price is reduced by the amount of the postponed gain.

Statutory ceilings are imposed on the amount of realized gain that can be postponed for any taxable year as follows:

- Individual taxpayer: Lesser of:
  - $50,000 ($25,000 for married filing separately).
  - $500,000 ($250,000 for married filing separately) reduced by the amount of such nonrecognized gain in prior taxable years.
- Corporate taxpayer: Lesser of:
  - $250,000.
  - $1,000,000 reduced by the amount of such nonrecognized gain in prior taxable years.

Investors *ineligible* for this postponement treatment include partnerships, S corporations, estates, and trusts.

ROLLOVER OF GAIN FROM QUALIFIED SMALL BUSINESS STOCK INTO ANOTHER QUALIFIED SMALL BUSINESS STOCK—§ 1045

Realized gain from the sale of qualified small business stock held for more than six months may be postponed if the taxpayer acquires other qualified small business stock within 60 days. Any amount not reinvested will trigger the recognition of the realized gain on the sale to the extent of the deficiency. In calculating the basis of the acquired qualified small business stock, the amount of the purchase price is reduced by the amount of the postponed gain.

Qualified small business stock is stock of a qualified small business that is acquired by the taxpayer at its original issue in exchange for money or other property (excluding stock) or as compensation for services. A qualified small business is a domestic corporation that satisfies the following requirements:

- The aggregate gross assets prior to the issuance of the small business stock do not exceed $50 million.
- The aggregate gross assets immediately after the issuance of the small business stock do not exceed $50 million.

TAX PLANNING
CONSIDERATIONS

6 LEARNING OBJECTIVE
Identify tax planning
opportunities related to the
nonrecognition provisions
discussed in the chapter.

LIKE-KIND EXCHANGES

Since application of the like-kind exchange provisions is mandatory rather than elective, in certain instances it may be preferable to avoid qualifying for § 1031 nonrecognition. If the like-kind exchange provisions do not apply, the end result may be the recognition of capital gain in exchange for a higher basis in the newly acquired asset. Also, the immediate recognition of gain may be preferable in certain situations. Examples where immediate recognition is beneficial include the following:

- Taxpayer has unused net operating loss carryovers.
- Taxpayer has unused general business credit carryovers.
- Taxpayer has suspended or current passive activity losses.
- Taxpayer expects his or her effective tax rate to increase in the future.

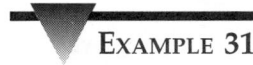
EXAMPLE 31

Alicia disposes of a machine (used in her business) with an adjusted basis of $3,000 for $4,000. She also acquires a new business machine for $9,000. If § 1031 applies, the $1,000 realized gain is not recognized, and the basis of the new machine is reduced by $1,000 (from $9,000 to $8,000). If § 1031 does not apply, a $1,000 gain is recognized and may receive favorable capital gain treatment to the extent that the gain is not recognized as ordinary income due to the depreciation recapture provisions (see Chapter 17). In addition, the basis for depreciation on the new machine is $9,000 rather than $8,000 since there is no unrecognized gain. ▼

The application of § 1031 nonrecognition treatment should also be avoided when the adjusted basis of the property being disposed of exceeds the fair market value.

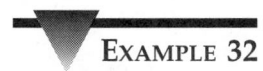
EXAMPLE 32

Assume the same facts as in the previous example, except that the fair market value of the machine is $2,500. If § 1031 applies, the $500 realized loss is not recognized. To recognize the loss, Alicia should sell the old machine and purchase the new one. The purchase and sale transactions should be with different taxpayers. ▼

On the other hand, the like-kind exchange procedure can be utilized to control the amount of recognized gain.

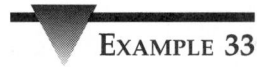
EXAMPLE 33

Rex has property with an adjusted basis of $40,000 and a fair market value of $100,000. Sandra wants to buy Rex's property, but Rex wants to limit the amount of recognized gain on the proposed transaction. Sandra acquires other like-kind property (from an outside party) for $80,000. She then exchanges this property and $20,000 cash for Rex's property. Rex has a realized gain of $60,000 ($100,000 amount realized – $40,000 adjusted basis). His recognized gain is only $20,000, the lower of the $20,000 boot received or the $60,000 realized gain. Rex's basis for the like-kind property is $40,000 ($40,000 adjusted basis + $20,000 gain recognized – $20,000 boot received). If Rex had sold the property to Sandra for its fair market value of $100,000, the result would have been a $60,000 recognized gain ($100,000 amount realized – $40,000 adjusted basis) to him. It is permissible for Rex to identify the like-kind property that he wants Sandra to purchase.[36] ▼

---

[36]*Franklin B. Biggs*, 69 T.C. 905 (1978); Rev.Rul. 57–244, 1957–1 C.B. 247; Rev.Rul. 73–476, 1973–2 C.B. 300; *Starker v. U.S.*, 79–2 USTC ¶9541, 44 AFTR2d 79–5525, 602 F.2d 1341 (CA–9, 1979); and *Baird Publishing Co.*, 39 T.C. 608 (1962).

INVOLUNTARY CONVERSIONS

In certain cases, a taxpayer may prefer to recognize gain from an involuntary conversion. Keep in mind that § 1033, unlike § 1031 (dealing with like-kind exchanges), generally is an elective provision.

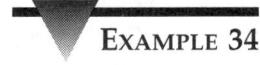

EXAMPLE 34

Ahmad has a $40,000 realized gain from the involuntary conversion of an office building. He reinvests the entire proceeds of $450,000 in a new office building. He does not elect to postpone gain under § 1033, however, because of an expiring net operating loss carryover that is offset against the gain. Therefore, none of the realized gain of $40,000 is postponed. By not electing § 1033 postponement, Ahmad's basis in the replacement property is the property's cost of $450,000 rather than $410,000 ($450,000 reduced by the $40,000 realized gain). ▼

SALE OF A PRINCIPAL RESIDENCE

Election.   The § 121 exclusion automatically applies if the taxpayer is eligible. That is, the taxpayer does not have to make an election. However, if § 121 exclusion treatment is not wanted on an otherwise eligible sale, the taxpayer may elect to avoid the § 121 exclusion.[37]

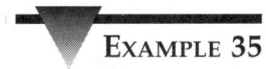

EXAMPLE 35

George owns two personal residences that satisfy the two-year ownership and use test with respect to the five-year window. The Elm Street residence has appreciated by $25,000, and the Maple Street residence has appreciated by $230,000. He intends to sell both of them and move into rental property. He sells the Elm Street residence in December 1998 and expects to sell the Maple Street residence early next year.

Unless George elects not to apply the § 121 exclusion to the sale of the Elm Street residence, he will exclude the $25,000 realized gain on that residence in 1998. In 1999, however, he will have a recognized gain of $230,000 on the sale of the Maple Street residence.

By making the election, George will report a recognized gain of $25,000 on the sale of the Elm Street residence in 1998. But by using the § 121 exclusion in 1999, he will eliminate the recognized gain of $230,000 on the sale of the Maple Street residence. ▼

Negative Effect of Renting or Using as a Home Office.   The residence does not have to be the taxpayer's principal residence at the date of sale. During part of the five-year window, it could have been rental property (e.g., either a vacation home or entirely rental property). In addition, the taxpayer may have used part of the principal residence as a qualifying office in the home.

In either the rental or the home office setting, the taxpayer will have deducted depreciation. Any realized gain on the sale that is attributable to depreciation is not eligible for the § 121 exclusion.[38]

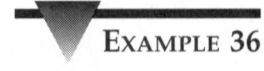

EXAMPLE 36

On December 5, 1998, Amanda sells her principal residence, which qualifies for the § 121 exclusion. Her realized gain is $190,000. From January through November 1998, she rented the residence to a college student. For this period, she deducted MACRS cost recovery of $7,000. Without the depreciation provision, Amanda could exclude the $190,000 realized gain. However, the depreciation taken requires her to recognize $7,000 of the realized gain. ▼

Qualification for § 121 Exclusion.   The key requirement is for the taxpayer to have *owned* and *used* the property as a principal residence for at least two years

---

[37]§ 121(f).   [38]§ 121(d)(6).

during the five-year window. As taxpayers advance in age, they quite frequently make decisions such as the following:

- Sell the principal residence and buy a smaller residence or rent the principal residence.
- Sell vacation homes they own.
- Sell homes they are holding as rental property.

There could be substantial appreciation on each of the above. Clearly, the sale of the principal residence is eligible for the § 121 exclusion. Less clear, however, is that proper planning may make it possible to qualify for the exclusion as to the vacation home or the rental property. Although this strategy may require taxpayers to be flexible about where they live, it can result in substantial tax savings.

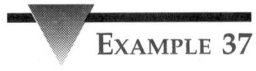

EXAMPLE 37

Thelma and David are approaching retirement. They have substantial appreciation on their principal residence and on a house they own at the beach (about two hours away). After retirement, they plan to move to Florida. They have owned and lived in the principal residence for 28 years and have owned the beach house for 9 years. If they sell their principal residence, it qualifies for the § 121 exclusion. At retirement, they could move into their beach house for two years and make it eligible for the exclusion. If the beach house were not so far away, they could sell the principal residence now and move into the beach house to start the running of the two-year use period. Note that any realized gain on the beach house attributable to depreciation is not eligible for the § 121 exclusion. ▼

Record Keeping. The taxpayer is required to report the details of the sale of the residence on the tax return (Form 2119, Sale of Your Home) for the taxable year in which the gain is realized. This is the case even if the entire amount of the gain is excluded under § 121. Most, if not all, of the data required should be available on the closing statement associated with the sale.

The taxpayer needs to maintain records on the adjusted basis of the residence including the original cost, any capital improvements, and any deductions that decrease basis (e.g., depreciation on a home office or rental use).

Chapter 15 has covered certain situations in which realized gains or losses are not recognized (nontaxable exchanges). Chapters 16 and 17 are concerned with the *classification* of recognized gains and losses. That is, if a gain or loss is recognized, is it an ordinary or capital gain or loss? Chapter 16 discusses the tax consequences of capital gains and losses.

KEY TERMS

Boot, 15–6	Like-kind exchange, 15–3	Personal residence, 15–16
Involuntary conversion, 15–10	Nontaxable exchange, 15–3	Section 121 exclusion, 15–16

PROBLEM MATERIALS

DISCUSSION QUESTIONS

1. What is the justification for nontaxable exchange treatment?

2. Distinguish between a loss that is not recognized on a nontaxable exchange and a loss that is not recognized on the sale or exchange of a personal use asset.

3. What are the three requirements that must be satisfied for a transaction to qualify for nontaxable exchange treatment under § 1031?

4. Can the exchange of personal use property for property held for productive use in a trade or business qualify for like-kind exchange treatment?

5. Amos owns a lathe that he uses in his trade or business. The adjusted basis is $40,000. Although the lathe is only two years old, Amos needs to replace it due to advances in technology. He exchanges the lathe and $20,000 in cash for a new lathe worth $50,000. May Amos elect not to treat the transaction as a like-kind exchange so that the realized loss of $10,000 can be recognized?

6. Which of the following qualify as like-kind exchanges under § 1031?
   a. Improved for unimproved real estate.
   b. Vending machine (used in business) for inventory.
   c. Rental house for personal residence.
   d. Business equipment for securities.
   e. Warehouse for office building (both used for business).
   f. Truck for computer (both used in business).
   g. Rental house for land (both held for investment).
   h. Ten shares of stock in Blue Corporation for 10 shares of stock in Red Corporation.
   i. Office furniture for office equipment (both used in business).
   j. General partnership interest in Green Partnership for general partnership interest in Brown Partnership.

7. Melissa owns a residential lot held for investment in Spring Creek that has appreciated substantially in value. She is considering exchanging the lot with her father for a residential lot in McComb that she also will hold for investment. Identify the relevant tax issues for Melissa.

8. Ross would like to dispose of some land that he acquired five years ago because he believes that it will not continue to appreciate. Its value has increased by $50,000 during the five-year period. He also intends to sell stock that has declined in value by $50,000 during the eight-month period he has owned it. Ross has four offers to acquire the stock and land:

Buyer number 1:	Exchange land.
Buyer number 2:	Purchase land for cash.
Buyer number 3:	Exchange stock.
Buyer number 4:	Purchase stock for cash.

   Identify the tax issues relevant to Ross in disposing of this land and stock.

9. What is boot, and how does it affect the recognition of gain or loss on a like-kind exchange when received by the taxpayer? How is the recognition of gain or loss affected when boot is given?

10. The receipt of boot in a § 1031 exchange triggers the recognition of realized gain. The gain recognition will affect the basis of the property received by the taxpayer.
   a. Discuss the relationship between the realized gain and the boot received if the boot received is greater than the realized gain.
   b. Discuss the relationship between the realized gain and the boot received if the boot received is less than the realized gain.
   c. What effect does the recognition of gain have on the basis of the like-kind property received? Of the boot received?

11. In connection with like-kind exchanges, discuss each of the following:
   a. Realized gain.
   b. Realized loss.
   c. Recognized gain.
   d. Recognized loss.
   e. Postponed gain.
   f. Postponed loss.

g. Basis of like-kind property received.

h. Basis of boot received.

12. Aaron exchanges a machine used in his business for another machine and stock of Teal, Inc. Explain why the machine has a carryover holding period and the stock has a new (date of exchange) holding period.

13. Mortgaged real estate may be received in a like-kind exchange. If the taxpayer assumes the mortgage, what effect does the mortgage have on the recognition of realized gain? On the basis of the real estate received?

14. A taxpayer's appreciated property is involuntarily converted. She receives insurance proceeds equal to the fair market value of the property. What is the minimum amount the taxpayer must reinvest in qualifying property to defer recognition of realized gain?

15. Beth's retail store building is destroyed by a tornado. She receives insurance proceeds of $200,000, which is the appraised value of the building prior to its destruction. Her adjusted basis in the building is $225,000. What is the maximum amount that Beth can reinvest in another retail store building and still recognize the $25,000 loss?

16. Ed receives severance damages from the state government for a public road built across his property. Under what circumstances can the § 1033 involuntary conversion provision apply to prevent the recognition of gain?

17. Julia owns a shopping mall that she leases to tenants. The shopping mall is destroyed by a tornado. Is the functional use test or the taxpayer use test applied in terms of appropriate replacement property? Explain the differences between the two tests.

18. Rebecca, a calendar year taxpayer, owns an office building that she uses in her business. The building is involuntarily converted on June 15, 1998. On October 5, 1998, Rebecca receives proceeds large enough to produce a realized gain. What is the latest date she can replace the building if the form of the conversion is:

a. A flood?

b. A condemnation?

c. A tornado?

19. What is the earliest date that a taxpayer can replace involuntarily converted property if the form of the conversion is:

a. A casualty?

b. A theft?

c. A condemnation?

20. Bob is notified by the city public housing authority on October 5, 1998, that his apartment building is going to be condemned as part of an urban renewal project. On October 12, 1998, Carol offers to buy the building from Bob. Bob sells the building to Carol on October 30, 1998. Condemnation occurs on February 1, 1999, and Carol receives the condemnation proceeds from the city. Assume both Bob and Carol are calendar year taxpayers.

a. What is the earliest date that Bob can dispose of the building and qualify for § 1033 postponement treatment?

b. Does the sale to Carol qualify as a § 1033 involuntary conversion?

c. What is the latest date that Carol can acquire qualifying replacement property and qualify for postponement of the realized gain?

d. What type of property will be qualifying replacement property?

21. A warehouse owned by Martha and used in her business (i.e., to store inventory) is being condemned by the city to provide a right of way for a highway. The warehouse has appreciated by $100,000 based on Martha's estimate of fair market value. In the negotiations, the city is offering $40,000 less than what Martha believes the property is worth. Alan, a real estate broker, has offered to purchase Martha's property for $25,000 more than the city's offer. Martha plans to invest the proceeds she will receive in an office building that she will lease to various tenants. Identify the relevant tax issues for Martha.

22. Samantha, who is age 39, would like to quit her job, sell her house, buy a sailboat, and sail the seven seas. The projected realized loss on the sale of her personal residence is $50,000. Is it possible for Samantha to recognize the loss or to elect to defer the loss?

23. What requirements must be satisfied to qualify for the § 121 exclusion on the sale of a principal residence?

24. Are there any limitations on the frequency with which the § 121 exclusion on the sale of a principal residence can be used?

25. Sandy owns a personal residence that she has lived in since its acquisition. It has appreciated by $90,000 during this period. Now, however, the school board has redrawn the boundaries for the school districts, and her son will have to transfer to a different high school for his senior year. Sandy is considering selling her residence and buying another one that will enable her son to remain in the same high school. Without this reason, she would not sell the house. Identify the relevant tax issues for Sandy.

26. Define each of the following associated with the sale of a residence:
    a. Amount realized.
    b. Selling expenses.
    c. Realized gain.
    d. Recognized gain.
    e. § 121 excluded gain.
    f. Basis of new residence.

27. What is the maximum amount of the § 121 exclusion for an unmarried taxpayer? For a married couple?

28. Mort owns a beach house and a cabin in the mountains. He stays in each during different parts of the year. Mort also rents a townhouse in the city where he is employed. If Mort sells both the beach house and the cabin at a gain, how does he decide which of these properties is his principal residence?

PROBLEMS

29. Kay owns undeveloped land with an adjusted basis of $180,000. She exchanges it for other undeveloped land worth $250,000.
    a. What are Kay's realized and recognized gain or loss?
    b. What is Kay's basis in the undeveloped land she receives?

30. Kareem owns an automobile that he uses exclusively in his business. The adjusted basis is $19,000, and the fair market value is $16,000. Kareem exchanges the car for a car that he will use exclusively in his business.
    a. What are Kareem's realized and recognized gain or loss?
    b. What is his basis in the new car?
    c. What are the tax consequences to Kareem in (a) and (b) if he used the old car and will use the new car exclusively for personal purposes?

31. Tex Wall owns undeveloped land that he is holding for investment. His adjusted basis is $175,000. On October 7, 1998, he exchanges the land with his 23-year-old daughter, Paige, for other undeveloped land that he will hold for investment. The appraised value of Paige's land is $250,000.
    a. Calculate Tex's realized and recognized gain or loss from the exchange with Paige and on a subsequent sale of the land by Tex to Baxter, a real estate broker, for $300,000 on February 15, 1999.
    b. Calculate Tex's realized and recognized gain or loss on the exchange with Paige if Tex does not sell the land received from Paige, but Paige sells the land received from Tex on February 15, 1999. Calculate Tex's basis for the land on October 7, 1998, and on February 15, 1999.
    c. Write a letter to Tex advising him on how he could avoid any recognition of gain associated with the October 7, 1998, exchange prior to his actual sale of the land. His address is The Corral, El Paso, TX 79968.

32. Bonnie owns a personal computer that she uses exclusively in her business. The adjusted basis is $5,000. Bonnie transfers the personal computer and cash of $7,000 to Don for a laser printer worth $16,000 that she will use in her business.
    a. Calculate Bonnie's recognized gain or loss on the exchange.
    b. Calculate Bonnie's basis for the printer.

33. Chee exchanges a light-duty truck used exclusively in his business for a light-duty truck that will be used in his business. The adjusted basis for the old truck is $12,000, and the fair market value of the old truck is $10,000.
    a. Calculate Chee's recognized gain or loss on the exchange.
    b. Calculate Chee's basis for the truck he receives.
    c. How could Chee structure the transaction to produce better tax consequences?

34. Cary owns undeveloped land with an adjusted basis of $110,000. He exchanges it for an office building (fair market value of $120,000) and $40,000 in cash. He will use the building in his business.
    a. What is Cary's realized gain or loss?
    b. His recognized gain or loss?
    c. His basis in the office building?

35. Olga owns a machine that she uses in her business. The adjusted basis is $60,000, and the fair market value is $95,000. She exchanges it for another machine worth $70,000. Olga also receives stock worth $25,000.
    a. Calculate Olga's realized and recognized gain or loss on the exchange.
    b. Calculate Olga's basis for the new machine.
    c. Calculate Olga's basis for the stock she received.

36. Ed owns investment land with an adjusted basis of $35,000. Polly has offered to purchase the land from Ed for $175,000 for use in a real estate development. The amount offered by Polly is $10,000 in excess of what Ed perceives as the fair market value of the land. Ed would like to dispose of the land to Polly but does not want to incur the tax liability that would result. He identifies an office building with a fair market value of $175,000 that he would like to acquire. Polly purchases the office building and then exchanges the office building for Ed's land.
    a. Calculate Ed's realized and recognized gain on the exchange and his basis for the office building.
    b. Calculate Polly's realized and recognized gain on the exchange and her basis in the land.

37. What is the basis of the new property in each of the following exchanges?
    a. Apartment building held for investment (adjusted basis $150,000) for office building to be held for investment (fair market value $200,000).
    b. Land and building used as a barber shop (adjusted basis $30,000) for land and building used as a grocery store (fair market value $350,000).
    c. Office building (adjusted basis $30,000) for bulldozer (fair market value $42,000), both held for business use.
    d. IBM common stock (adjusted basis $14,000) for Exxon common stock (fair market value $18,000).
    e. Rental house (adjusted basis $90,000) for mountain cabin to be held for personal use (fair market value $115,000).

38. Norm owns Machine A, which he uses in his business. The adjusted basis of Machine A is $12,000, and the fair market value is $18,000. Norm is considering two options for the disposal of Machine A. Under the first option, Norm will transfer Machine A and $3,000 cash to Joan, a dealer, in exchange for Machine B, which has a fair market value of $21,000. Under the second option, Norm will sell Machine A for $18,000 to Tim, who is a dealer. Norm will then purchase Machine B from Joan for $21,000. Machine A and Machine B qualify as like-kind property.
    a. Calculate Norm's recognized gain or loss and the basis for Machine B under the first option.

b. Calculate Norm's recognized gain or loss and the basis for Machine B under the second option.

c. Advise Norm on which option he should select.

39. Gus exchanges real estate held for investment plus stock for real estate to be held for investment. The stock transferred has an adjusted basis of $15,000 and a fair market value of $10,000. The real estate transferred has an adjusted basis of $15,000 and a fair market value of $45,000. The real estate acquired has a fair market value of $55,000.

a. What is Gus's realized gain or loss?

b. His recognized gain or loss?

c. The basis of the newly acquired real estate?

40. Agnes exchanges a warehouse and the related land with Damon for an office building and the related land. Agnes's adjusted basis for her warehouse and land is $420,000. The fair market value of Damon's office building and land is $410,000. Agnes's property has a $90,000 mortgage that Damon assumes.

a. Calculate Agnes's realized and recognized gain or loss.

b. Calculate Agnes's adjusted basis for the office building and land received.

c. As an alternative, Damon has proposed that rather than assuming the mortgage, he will transfer cash of $90,000 to Agnes. Agnes would use the cash to pay off the mortgage. Advise Agnes on whether this alternative would be beneficial to her from a tax perspective.

41. Determine the realized, recognized, and postponed gain or loss and the new basis for each of the following like-kind exchanges:

	Adjusted Basis of Old Asset	Boot Given	Fair Market Value of New Asset	Boot Received
a.	$ 7,000	$ –0–	$12,000	$4,000
b.	14,000	2,000	15,000	–0–
c.	3,000	7,000	8,000	500
d.	22,000	–0–	32,000	–0–
e.	10,000	–0–	11,000	1,000
f.	10,000	–0–	8,000	–0–

42. Shontelle owns an apartment house that has an adjusted basis of $1,100,000 but is subject to a mortgage of $250,000. She transfers the apartment house to Dave and receives from him $125,000 in cash and an office building with a fair market value of $1,125,000 at the time of the exchange. Dave assumes the $250,000 mortgage on the apartment house.

a. What is Shontelle's realized gain or loss?

b. Her recognized gain or loss?

c. The basis of the newly acquired office building?

43. Carmen's office building, which has an adjusted basis of $200,000, is destroyed by a tornado. Since Carmen's business has excess office space, she decides not to replace the office building, but instead to contribute the proceeds to the working capital of her business.

a. If the insurance proceeds are $225,000, what is Carmen's recognized gain or loss?

b. If the insurance proceeds are $180,000, what is Carmen's recognized gain or loss?

44. Albert owns 100 acres of land on which he grows spruce Christmas trees. His adjusted basis for the land is $100,000. He receives condemnation proceeds of $10,000 when the city's new beltway takes 5 acres along the eastern boundary of his property. He also receives a severance award of $6,000 associated with the possible harmful effects of exhaust fumes on his Christmas trees. Albert invests the $16,000 in a growth mutual fund.

a. Determine the tax consequences to Albert of the condemnation proceeds.

b. Determine the tax consequences to Albert of the severance award.

45. For each of the following involuntary conversions, indicate whether the property acquired qualifies as replacement property:
    a. Frank owns a shopping mall that is destroyed by a tornado. The space in the mall was rented to various tenants. Frank uses the insurance proceeds to build a shopping mall in a neighboring community where no property has been damaged by tornadoes.
    b. Ivan owns a warehouse that he uses in his business. The warehouse is destroyed by fire. Due to economic conditions in the area, Ivan decides not to rebuild the warehouse. Instead, he uses the insurance proceeds to build a warehouse to be used in his business in another state.
    c. Ridge's personal residence is condemned as part of a local government project to widen the highway from two lanes to four lanes. He uses the condemnation proceeds to purchase another personal residence.
    d. Juanita owns a building that she uses in her retail business. The building is destroyed by a hurricane. Due to an economic downturn in the area caused by the closing of a military base, she decides to rent space for her retail outlet rather than to replace the building. She uses the insurance proceeds to buy a four-unit apartment building in another city. A realtor in that city will handle the rental of the apartments for her.
    e. Susan and Rick's personal residence is destroyed by a tornado. Since they would like to travel, they decide not to acquire a replacement residence. Instead, they invest the insurance proceeds in a duplex that they rent to tenants.

46. The building that houses LaToya's designer clothing store is destroyed in a mud slide associated with a flood on June 27, 1998. LaToya had anticipated the flood and moved her inventory, furniture, and fixtures to a warehouse outside the floodplain on June 20, 1998. Her adjusted basis for the building is $150,000, and she receives insurance proceeds of $160,000 on July 15, 1998. LaToya intends to purchase another building for her store, but would like to have time to locate one in a safer location. Her taxable year ends on June 30.
    a. What are the earliest and latest dates that LaToya can make a qualified replacement?
    b. Assuming LaToya makes a qualified replacement costing $160,000, what are her realized gain, recognized gain, and basis for the replacement property?
    c. What are the earliest and latest dates that LaToya can make a qualified replacement if the form of the involuntary conversion is a condemnation by a governmental authority? She was officially notified of the pending condemnation on June 1, 1998.

47. Lynn's office building, which is used in her business, is destroyed by a hurricane in September 1998. The adjusted basis is $210,000. Lynn receives insurance proceeds of $390,000 in October 1998.
    a. Calculate Lynn's realized gain or loss, recognized gain or loss, and basis for the replacement property if she acquires an office building for $390,000 in October 1998.
    b. Calculate Lynn's realized gain or loss, recognized gain or loss, and basis for the replacement property if she acquires an office building for $350,000 in October 1998.
    c. Calculate Lynn's realized gain or loss and recognized gain or loss if she does not acquire replacement property.

48. Carlos's warehouse, which has an adjusted basis of $325,000 and a fair market value of $490,000, is condemned by an agency of the Federal government to make way for a highway interchange. The initial condemnation offer is $450,000. After substantial negotiations, the agency agrees to transfer to Carlos a surplus warehouse that he believes is worth $490,000.
    a. What are the recognized gain or loss and the basis of the replacement warehouse if Carlos's objective is to recognize as much gain as possible?
    b. Advise Carlos regarding what he needs to do by what date in order to achieve his objective.

49. What are the *maximum* postponed gain or loss and the basis for the replacement property for the following involuntary conversions?

Property	Type of Conversion	Amount Realized	Adjusted Basis	Amount Reinvested
a. Drugstore (business)	Casualty	$160,000	$130,000	$110,000
b. Apartments (investment)	Condemned	100,000	125,000	175,000
c. Grocery store (business)	Casualty	400,000	300,000	450,000
d. Residence (personal)	Casualty	16,000	18,000	17,000
e. Vacant lot (investment)	Condemned	240,000	160,000	220,000
f. Residence (personal)	Casualty	20,000	18,000	19,000
g. Residence (personal)	Condemned	18,000	20,000	26,000
h. Apartments (investment)	Condemned	150,000	100,000	200,000

50. Rental property owned by Freda, a calendar year taxpayer, is destroyed by a tornado on January 1, 1998. Freda had originally paid $150,000 for the property, of which $125,000 was allocated to the building and $25,000 was allocated to the land. During the time Freda owned the property, MACRS deductions of $46,250 were taken. MACRS deductions of $57,500 would have been taken, except that Freda chose to forgo deductions of $11,250 one year when her tax return showed a net operating loss. Freda receives insurance proceeds of $60,000 in November 1998. As a result of continuing negotiations with the insurance company, Freda receives additional proceeds of $35,000 in August 1999.
    a. What is Freda's adjusted basis for the property?
    b. What is Freda's realized gain or loss on the involuntary conversion in 1998? In 1999?
    c. What is the latest date that Freda can replace the involuntarily converted property to qualify for § 1033 postponement?
    d. What is the latest date that Freda can replace the involuntarily converted property to qualify for § 1033 postponement if the form of the involuntary conversion is a condemnation?

51. On May 1, 1998, Kay sells her principal residence for $225,000. Kay had purchased the residence on January 2, 1997, for $180,000. During 1996, she had lived in it as a tenant under a lease with an option to buy clause. On May 2, 1998, Kay purchases a new residence for $200,000.
    a. What is Kay's recognized gain? Her basis for the new residence?
    b. Assume instead that Kay purchased her original residence on January 2, 1996, rather than on January 2, 1997. What is Kay's recognized gain? Her basis for the new residence?
    c. What could you recommend to Kay to minimize her recognized gain in (a)?

52. Tina has owned and occupied her personal residence for three years, and it has an adjusted basis of $150,000. In April 1998, she sells the residence for $310,000 (selling expenses are $20,000). On the same day as the sale, Tina purchases another house for $350,000. Because of noisy neighbors, she sells the new house after just nine months. The selling price is $385,000 (selling expenses are $18,000).
    a. What is Tina's recognized gain on the sale of the first residence?
    b. What is Tina's basis for her second residence?
    c. What is Tina's recognized gain on the sale of the second residence?
    d. Assume instead that the sale of the second residence was due to Tina's job transfer to another state. What is her recognized gain on the sale of the second residence?

53. Milton, who is single, listed his personal residence with a realtor on March 3, 1998, at a listed price of $250,000. He rejected several offers in the $200,000 range during the summer. Finally, on August 16, 1998, he and the purchaser signed a contract to sell for $245,000. The sale (i.e., closing) took place on September 7, 1998. The closing statement showed the following disbursements being made:

Realtor's commission	$ 14,000
Appraisal fee	500
Exterminator's certificate	300
Recording fees	400
Mortgage to First Bank	180,000
Cash to seller	49,800

Milton's adjusted basis for the house is $150,000. He had owned and occupied the house for eight years. On October 1, Milton purchases another residence for $210,000.
  a. Calculate Milton's recognized gain on the sale.
  b. What is Milton's adjusted basis for the new residence?
  c. Assume instead that the selling price is $735,000. What is Milton's recognized gain? His adjusted basis for the new residence?

54. What are the realized, recognized, and excluded gain or loss and the new basis in each of the following cases?
  a. Susan sells her residence for $390,000. The adjusted basis was $55,000. The selling expenses were $15,000. Repair expenses incurred to get the house ready to sell were $3,000. She did not reinvest in a new residence.
  b. Rocky sells his residence for $270,000. The adjusted basis was $120,000. The selling expenses were $9,000. Repair expenses incurred to get the house ready to sell were $6,000. Rocky reinvested $260,000 in a new residence.
  c. Veneia sells her residence for $465,000. The adjusted basis was $35,000. The selling expenses were $17,000. Repair expenses incurred to get the house ready to sell were $2,000. She reinvested $400,000 in a new residence.
  d. Barry sells his residence for $70,000. The adjusted basis was $65,000. The selling expenses were $6,000. He reinvested $80,000 in a new residence.
  e. Carl sells his residence for $100,000 in cash, and his mortgage is assumed by the buyer. The adjusted basis was $80,000; the mortgage, $50,000. The selling expenses were $4,000. Repair expenses incurred to get the house ready to sell were $2,000. He reinvested $120,000 in a new residence.

55. Pedro, age 57, is the sole owner of his principal residence. He has owned and occupied it for 10 years. Maria, his spouse, has also lived there for 10 years. He sells the house for a realized gain of $240,000. Pedro does not intend to acquire a replacement residence.
  a. Can Pedro use the § 121 exclusion if he and Maria file a joint return? If so, what are the available amount of the exclusion and the recognized gain?
  b. Can Pedro use the § 121 exclusion if he files a separate return? If so, what are the available amount of the exclusion and the recognized gain?
  c. Assume instead that the realized gain is $340,000 and a joint return is filed.
  d. Assume instead that the realized gain is $340,000 and separate returns are filed.

56. Meg and Walt are going to be married in three months. Meg has owned and lived in her home for 42 years, and Walt has owned and occupied his home for 35 years. They both have listed their homes for sale. They anticipate the sales results will be as follows:

	Meg	Walt
Selling price	$450,000	$190,000
Selling expenses	40,000	19,000
Adjusted basis	75,000	60,000

They intend to purchase a residence in an extended care facility for $400,000. They have come to you for advice regarding the following:
  a. What is their recognized gain if they marry before they sell their residences?
  b. What is their recognized gain if they marry after they sell their residences?

    c. Does it matter whether the new residence is jointly owned or owned only by Meg as Walt would prefer to invest his sales proceeds in the stock market?

    d. Should Meg and Walt delay their marriage if they have not yet sold their residences?

57. Nell, Nina, and Nora Sanders, who are sisters, sell their principal residence in which they have lived for the past 20 years. The youngest of the sisters is age 58. The selling price is $750,000, selling expenses and legal fees are $75,000, and the adjusted basis is $60,000 (the fair market value of the residence when inherited from their parents 20 years ago). Since the sisters are going to live in rental housing, they do not plan to acquire another residence. Nell has contacted you on behalf of the three sisters regarding the tax consequences of the sale.

    a. Write a letter to Nell advising her of the tax consequences and how taxes can be minimized. Nell's address is 100 Oak Avenue, Billings, MT 59101.

    b. Prepare a memo for the tax files.

58. Jeff and Jill are divorced on August 1, 1998. According to the terms of the divorce decree, Jeff's ownership interest in the house is to be transferred to Jill in exchange for the release from marital rights. Before the divorce, the house was separately owned by Jeff. The adjusted basis and the fair market value at the date of the transfer are $175,000 and $200,000, respectively.

    a. Does the transfer of the house produce recognized gain to either Jeff or Jill?

    b. What is the basis of the house to Jill?

    c. If the same transfer was made by Jeff to Jill for $200,000 and was not associated with a divorce, would either Jeff or Jill have recognized gain?

59. Sam, age 63, owns a residence in which he has lived for 20 years. The residence is destroyed by fire on August 8, 1998. The adjusted basis is $170,000, and the fair market value is $350,000. Sam receives insurance proceeds of $350,000 for the residence. He is trying to decide whether to purchase a comparable house. He anticipates that he will retire in two years and will move to a warmer climate where he will rent in case he decides to live in different places.

    a. Advise Sam of the tax consequences of replacing versus not replacing the residence.

    b. Which do you recommend to him?

CUMULATIVE PROBLEMS

60. Tammy Walker, age 37, is a self-employed accountant. Tammy's Social Security number is 333–40–1111. Her address is 101 Glass Road, Richmond, VA 23236. Her income and expenses associated with her accounting practice for 1998 are as follows:

Revenues (cash receipts during 1998)	$224,000
Expenses	
Salaries	$ 95,000
Office supplies	2,100
Postage	1,500
Depreciation of equipment	23,000
Telephone	800
	$122,400

Since Tammy is a cash method taxpayer, she does not record her receivables as revenue until she receives cash payment. At the beginning of 1998, her accounts receivable were $22,000, and the balance had decreased to $9,000 by the end of the year. The balance on December 31, 1998, would have been $15,000, except that an account for $6,000 had become uncollectible in November.

    Tammy used one room in her 10-room house as the office for her accounting practice (400 square feet out of a total square footage of 4,000). She paid the following expenses related to the house during 1998:

Utilities	$4,000
Insurance	800
Property taxes	4,000
Repairs	1,400

Tammy had purchased the house on September 1, 1997, for $200,000. She sold her previous house on August 15, 1997, for $105,000. Her selling expenses had been $9,000, and repair expenses related to the sale were $1,100. Tammy and her former husband, Lou, had purchased the house in 1993 for $80,000. Tammy had received Lou's 50% ownership interest as part of their divorce settlement in August 1996. Tammy had not used any part of the former residence as a home office.

Tammy has one child, Thomas, age 17. Thomas lives with his father during the summer and with Tammy for the rest of the year. Tammy can document that she spent $8,000 during 1998 for the child's support. The father normally provides about $2,000 per year, but this year he gave the child a new car for Christmas. The cost of the car was $18,000. The divorce decree is silent regarding the dependency exemption for the child.

Under the terms of the divorce decree, Tammy is to receive alimony of $900 per month. The payments will terminate at Tammy's death or if she should remarry.

Tammy provides part of the support of her mother, age 67. The total support for 1998 for her mother was as follows:

Social Security benefits	$5,300
From Tammy	1,700
From Bob, Tammy's brother	1,200
From Susan, Tammy's sister	1,800

Bob and Susan have both indicated their willingness to sign a multiple support waiver form if it will benefit Tammy.

Tammy's deductible itemized deductions during 1998, excluding any itemized deductions related to the house, were $13,000. She made estimated tax payments of $31,000.

Part 1—Tax Computation
Compute Tammy's lowest net tax payable or refund due for 1998. Suggested software (if available): *TurboTax.*

Part 2—Tax Planning
Tammy and her former husband have been discussing the $900 alimony he pays her each month. Due to a health problem of his new wife, he does not feel that he can afford to continue to pay the $900 each month. He is in the 15% tax bracket. If Tammy will agree to decrease the amount by 25%, he will agree that the amount paid is not alimony for tax purposes. Assume that the other data used in calculating Tammy's taxable income for 1998 will apply for her 1999 tax return. Write a letter to Tammy that contains your advice on whether she should agree to her former husband's proposal. Also prepare a memo for the tax files. Suggested software (if available): *TurboTax.*

61. Arnold Young, age 39, is single. He lives at 1507 Iris Lane, Tucson, AZ 85721. His Social Security number is 999–55–2000. Arnold does not wish to have $3 go to the Presidential Election Campaign Fund.

Arnold was divorced in 1993 after 15 years of marriage. He pays alimony of $36,000 a year to his former spouse, Carol. Carol's Social Security number is 999–33–3000. Arnold's son, Tom, who is age 13, resides with Carol. Arnold pays child support of $6,000 per year.

Arnold owns a sole proprietorship that is on the accrual method of accounting. His revenues and expenses for 1997 are as follows:

Sales revenue	$688,000
Cost of goods sold	430,000
Salary expense	90,000
Rent expense	24,000
Utilities	12,000
Telephone	3,000
Advertising	4,000
Bad debts	6,000
Depreciation	15,000
Insurance	7,000
Accounting and legal fees	4,000
Supplies	1,000

Other income received by Arnold includes the following:

Dividend income:	
Swan, Inc.	$8,000
Wren, Inc.	3,000
Interest income:	
First Bank	5,000
Second Bank	1,000
Lottery winnings (tickets purchased cost $700)	6,000

During the year, Arnold and his sole proprietorship had the following property transactions:

a. Sold Blue, Inc., stock for $27,000 on March 12, 1997. He had purchased the stock on September 5, 1994, for $30,000.

b. Received an inheritance of $50,000 from his Uncle Steve. Arnold used the $50,000 to purchase Green, Inc., stock on May 15, 1997.

c. Received Orange, Inc., stock worth $7,500 as a gift from his Aunt Jane on June 17, 1997. Her adjusted basis for the stock was $5,000. No gift taxes were paid on the transfer. Aunt Jane had purchased the stock on April 1, 1991. Arnold sold the stock on July 1, 1997, for $8,000.

d. On July 15, 1997, Arnold sold one-half of the Green, Inc., stock for $29,000.

e. Arnold is notified on August 1, 1997, that Yellow, Inc., stock he purchased from a colleague on September 1, 1996, for $20,000 is worthless. While he perceived the investment was risky, he did not anticipate that the corporation would declare bankruptcy.

f. On August 15, 1997, Arnold received a parcel of land in Phoenix worth $160,000 in exchange for a parcel of land he owned in Tucson. Since the Tucson parcel was worth $200,000, he also received $40,000 cash. Arnold's adjusted basis for the Tucson parcel was $190,000. He originally purchased it on September 18, 1994.

g. Sold the condominium in which he had been living for the past 10 years on December 1, 1997. He and Carol had purchased the condominium as joint owners for $120,000. Arnold had received Carol's ownership interest as part of the divorce proceedings. The fair market value at that time was $150,000. The sales price is $250,000, selling expenses are $15,000, and repair expenses related to the sale are $5,000. Although he has not yet purchased a replacement residence, negotiations are under way and are likely to be concluded during the first half of 1998. Arnold estimates that the purchase price will be about $235,000.

Arnold's itemized deductions are as follows:

Medical expenses (before the 7.5% floor)	$ 7,000
Property taxes on residence	5,000
State income taxes	6,000
Charitable contributions	10,000
Mortgage interest on residence	8,500

During the year, Arnold makes estimated Federal income tax payments of $20,000.

Compute Arnold's lowest net tax payable or refund due for 1997, assuming he makes any available elections that will reduce the tax. If you use tax forms for your computations, you will need Forms 1040, 2119, and 8824, and Schedules A, B, C, D, and SE. Suggested software (if available): *TurboTax*.

RESEARCH PROBLEMS

*Note: Use the **RIA OnPoint System 4 Student Version CD-ROM,** which is available to accompany this text, in preparing solutions to the Research Problems. Alternatively, tax research materials found in a standard tax library can be used.*

Research Problem 1.   Penelope and Stuart have been married for nine years. For the past six years, they have lived in the house Penelope owns at 100 Oriena Avenue. In July 1997, Stuart purchases the house from Penelope for $350,000. Her adjusted basis for the house is $130,000. No closing costs are incurred.

Penelope and Stuart continue to live in the house until February 1998 when Stuart sells it for $390,000. Selling expenses are $12,000. Penelope and Stuart file separate returns in 1998. Determine if Stuart is eligible for the § 121 exclusion and, if so, the amount of the exclusion. Also determine his recognized gain.

Partial list of research aids:
§ 121(d)(3)(A).

Research Problem 2.   You are the new general manager of the Cleveland Indians, Inc. In order for the Indians to become a more serious contender to win the World Series, you believe that player changes are necessary. In particular, you believe that you need to improve your pitching staff. Discussions are in progress with the general manager of the Seattle Mariners. He has offered to trade Randy Johnson (an all-star pitcher) and $5 million to the Indians in exchange for Marquis Grissom (an outfielder) and David Justice (an all-star outfielder). You have countered by expressing interest in receiving Johnson and Edgar Martinez (an all-star third baseman) rather than cash. You believe that if you are going to give up the speed provided by Grissom and the power of Justice, you need more than a starting pitcher in return. In addition, you vaguely remember from your MBA days that a player trade with no cash involved will provide better tax results. Before you finalize a trade, you need to know the tax consequences. Obtain a written opinion from your CPA on the way you should structure the trade. The mailing address is Jacobs Field, Cleveland, OH 44118.

Research Problem 3.   Greenside Construction, Inc., is in the road construction business. Greenside exchanges a grader used in its road construction business and $20,000 in cash for a scraper to be used in its road construction business. The adjusted basis of the grader is $50,000, and the fair market value of the scraper is $85,000. What are the tax consequences to Greenside of the exchange transaction?

Research Problem 4.   Tex, a calendar year taxpayer, owns a dairy farm in Louisiana. He normally milks 100 cows per day and sells about 10% of his dairy cows per year. He replaces those sold with cows he has bred and raised. Due to a severe drought in 1998, he abandons his normal practice of sale and replacement and reduces the size of his herd by 25%. The sales proceeds associated with the herd reduction are $60,000, and the adjusted basis for the cows sold is $12,000. In the future, Tex plans to gradually increase the size of his herd back to 100. If Tex's objective is to minimize gain recognition, calculate his recognized gain on the sale.

Use the tax resources of the Internet to address the following questions. Do not restrict your search to the World Wide Web, but include a review of newsgroups and general reference materials, practitioner sites and resources, primary sources of the tax law, chat rooms and discussion groups, and other opportunities.

Research Problem 5.   The Taxpayer Relief Act of 1997 enacted a new § 121 exclusion on the sale of a personal residence. The taxpayer can elect not to have this exclusion apply. Obtain planning ideas from at least two sites for when to make this election.

Research Problem 6.   A number of public policy think tanks, taxpayer unions, and other private interest groups have proposed changes to the tax rules that apply to like-kind exchanges of realty. Summarize several of these proposals, including your assessment of the motivations underlying the suggested changes.

TEAM PROJECT: ARTHUR ANDERSEN TAX CHALLENGE CASES

For more information on the Arthur Andersen Tax Challenge Cases, refer to Chapter 1, page 1–37.

Information related to tax issues and problems that are discussed in this chapter may be found in the

Day and Ball case on page 5
Fence case on pages 41, 51, 53, and 69

Read and analyze the case you have been assigned and *identify* any issues and problems that are related to material covered in this chapter. If the information provided in the case is complete, prepare answers for this part of the case at this time. If you need information that is contained in the later parts of the case, write a memo summarizing the questions or problems so you can prepare a complete answer at a later date.

16

PROPERTY TRANSACTIONS: CAPITAL GAINS AND LOSSES

LEARNING OBJECTIVES

After completing Chapter 16, you should be able to:

1. Understand the rationale for separate reporting of capital gains and losses.

2. Distinguish capital assets from ordinary assets.

3. Understand the relevance of a sale or exchange to classification as a capital gain or loss and apply the special rules for the capital gain or loss treatment of the retirement of corporate obligations, options, patents, franchises, and lease cancellation payments.

4. Determine whether the holding period for a capital asset is long term, mid-term, or short term.

5. Describe the beneficial tax treatment for capital gains and the detrimental tax treatment for capital losses for noncorporate taxpayers.

6. Describe the tax treatment for capital gains and the detrimental tax treatment for capital losses for corporate taxpayers.

7. Identify tax planning opportunities arising from the sale or exchange of capital assets.

GENERAL CONSIDERATIONS

RATIONALE FOR SEPARATE REPORTING OF CAPITAL GAINS AND LOSSES

1 **LEARNING OBJECTIVE**
Understand the rationale for separate reporting of capital gains and losses.

Fourteen years ago, a taxpayer purchased 100 shares of IBM stock for $17 a share. This year the taxpayer sells the shares for $97 a share. Should the $80 per share gain receive any special tax treatment? The $80 gain has built up over 14 years, so it may not be fair to tax it the same as income that was all earned this year.

What if the stock had been purchased for $97 per share and sold for $17 a share? Should the loss be fully deductible? The tax law has an intricate approach to answering these investment activity-related questions.

As you study this chapter, keep in mind that how investment-related gains and losses are taxed can dramatically affect whether taxpayers make investments and which investments are made. Except for a brief discussion in Chapter 3, earlier chapters dwelt on how to determine the amount of gain or loss from a property disposition, but did not discuss the classification of gains and losses. This chapter will focus on that topic.

The tax law requires **capital gains** and **capital losses** to be separated from other types of gains and losses. There are two reasons for this treatment. First, long-term capital gains may be taxed at a lower rate than ordinary gains. An *alternative tax computation* is used to determine the tax when taxable income includes net long-term capital gain. Capital gains and losses must therefore be matched with one another to see if a net long-term capital gain exists. The alternative tax computation is discussed later in the chapter under Tax Treatment of Capital Gains and Losses of Noncorporate Taxpayers.

The second reason the Code requires separate reporting of gains and losses and a determination of their tax character is that a net capital loss is only deductible up to $3,000 per year. Excess loss over the annual limit carries over and may be

CAMPAIGNING ON CAPITAL GAINS TAX CUTS

In the 1996 presidential election campaign, both candidates proposed changes in the taxation of capital gains. Candidate Bob Dole proposed reducing the tax rate on capital gains from a maximum of 28 percent to a maximum of 15 percent. President Bill Clinton did not propose any change in the capital gains rate, but wanted to exclude all capital gains from the sale of a principal residence.

The Taxpayer Relief Act of 1997 (TRA of 1997) reduced the maximum capital gains rate to as low as 10 percent in some circumstances and generally made up to $250,000 ($500,000 for a married couple) of capital gains from the sale of a principal residence excludible from gross income.

deductible in a future tax year. Capital gains and losses must be matched with one another to see if a net capital loss exists.

For these reasons, capital gains and losses must be distinguished from other types of gains and losses. Most of this chapter and the next chapter describe the intricate rules for determining what type of gains and losses the taxpayer has.

As a result of the need to distinguish and separately match capital gains and losses, the individual tax forms include very extensive reporting requirements for capital gains and losses. This chapter explains the principles underlying the forms. The forms are illustrated with examples at the end of the chapter.

GENERAL SCHEME OF TAXATION

Recognized gains and losses must be properly classified. Proper classification depends upon three characteristics:

- The tax status of the property.
- The manner of the property's disposition.
- The holding period of the property.

The three possible tax statuses are capital asset, § 1231 asset, or ordinary asset. Property disposition may be by sale, exchange, casualty, theft, or condemnation.

There are three holding periods: short term, mid-term, and long term. The short-term holding period is one year or less. The mid-term holding period is more than one year, but less than or equal to 18 months. The long-term holding period is more than 18 months. For most purposes, however, both the long-term and the mid-term holding period are categorized as "long-term." Hence, in this chapter, when the phrases "long-term capital gain," "long-term capital loss," and "long term" are used, *both* the mid-term and the long-term holding period are being referred to unless otherwise specified. When the *alternative tax on net capital gain* is discussed later in this chapter, the difference in the tax on mid-term and long-term capital gains will be illustrated (this is the case where the distinction between mid-term and long term is relevant).

The major focus of this chapter is capital gains and losses. Capital gains and losses usually result from the disposition of a capital asset. The most common disposition is a sale of the asset. Capital gains and losses can also result from the disposition of § 1231 assets, which is discussed in Chapter 17.

CAPITAL ASSETS

DEFINITION OF A CAPITAL ASSET

2 ▼ **LEARNING OBJECTIVE**
Distinguish capital assets from
ordinary assets.

Personal use assets and investment assets are the most common capital assets owned by individual taxpayers. Personal use assets usually include items such as clothing, recreation equipment, a residence, and automobiles. Investment assets usually include corporate stocks and bonds, government bonds, and vacant land. Remember, however, that losses from the sale or exchange of personal use assets are not recognized. Therefore, the classification of such losses as capital losses can be ignored.

Due to the historical preferential treatment of capital gains, taxpayers have preferred that gains be capital gains rather than ordinary gains. As a result, a great many statutes, cases, and rulings have accumulated in the attempt to define what is and what is not a capital asset.

Capital assets are not directly defined in the Code. Instead, § 1221 defines what is *not* a capital asset. A **capital asset** is property held by the taxpayer (whether or not it is connected with the taxpayer's business) that is *not* any of the following:

- Inventory or property held primarily for sale to customers in the ordinary course of a business. The Supreme Court, in *Malat v. Riddell*, defined *primarily* as meaning *of first importance* or *principally*.[1]
- Accounts and notes receivable acquired from the sale of inventory or acquired for services rendered in the ordinary course of business.
- Depreciable property or real estate used in a business.
- Certain copyrights; literary, musical, or artistic compositions; or letters, memoranda, or similar property held by (1) a taxpayer whose efforts created the property; (2) in the case of a letter, memorandum, or similar property, a taxpayer for whom it was produced; or (3) a taxpayer in whose hands the basis of the property is determined, for purposes of determining gain from a sale or exchange, in whole or in part by reference to the basis of such property in the hands of a taxpayer described in (1) or (2).
- U.S. government publications that are (1) received by a taxpayer from the U.S. government other than by purchase at the price at which they are offered for sale to the public or (2) held by a taxpayer whose basis, for purposes of determining gain from a sale or exchange, is determined by reference to a taxpayer described in (1).

The Code defines what is not a capital asset. From the preceding list, it is apparent that inventory, accounts and notes receivable, and most fixed assets of a business are not capital assets. The following discussion provides further detail on each part of the capital asset definition.

Inventory.   What constitutes inventory is determined by the taxpayer's business.

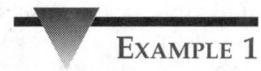
EXAMPLE 1

Green Company buys and sells used cars. Its cars are inventory. Its gains from the sale of the cars are ordinary income. ▼

---

[1]66–1 USTC ¶9317, 17 AFTR2d 604, 86 S.Ct. 1030 (USSC, 1966).

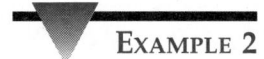

EXAMPLE 2

Soong sells her personal use automobile at a $500 gain. The automobile is a personal use asset and, therefore, a capital asset. The gain is a capital gain. ▼

Accounts and Notes Receivable.   Collection of an accrual basis account receivable usually does not result in a gain or loss because the amount collected equals the receivable's basis. The sale of an account or note receivable may generate a gain or loss, and the gain or loss is ordinary because the receivable is not a capital asset. The sale of an accrual basis receivable may result in a gain or loss because it will probably be sold for more or less than its basis. A cash basis account receivable has no basis. Sale of such a receivable generates a gain. Collection of a cash basis receivable generates ordinary income rather than a gain. A gain usually requires a sale of the receivable. See the discussion of Sale or Exchange later in this chapter.

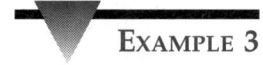

EXAMPLE 3

Oriole Company has accounts receivable of $100,000. Because it needs working capital, it sells the receivables for $83,000 to a financial institution. If Oriole is an accrual basis taxpayer, it has a $17,000 ordinary loss. Revenue of $100,000 would have been recorded and a $100,000 basis would have been established when the receivable was created. If Oriole is a cash basis taxpayer, it has $83,000 of ordinary income because it would not have recorded any revenue earlier; thus, the receivable has no tax basis. ▼

Business Fixed Assets.   Depreciable personal property and real estate (both depreciable and nondepreciable) used by a business are not capital assets. Thus, *business fixed assets* are generally not capital assets.

The Code has a very complex set of rules pertaining to such property. One of these rules is discussed under Real Property Subdivided for Sale in this chapter; the remainder of the rules are discussed in Chapter 17. Although business fixed assets are not capital assets, a long-term capital gain can sometimes result from their sale. Chapter 17 discusses the potential capital gain treatment for business fixed assets under § 1231.

Copyrights and Creative Works.   Generally, the person whose efforts led to the copyright or creative work has an ordinary asset, not a capital asset. *Creative works* include the works of authors, composers, and artists. Also, the person for whom a letter, memorandum, or other similar property was created has an ordinary asset. Finally, a person receiving a copyright, creative work, letter, memorandum, or similar property by gift from the creator or the person for whom the work was created has an ordinary asset.

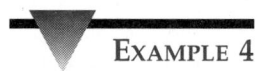

EXAMPLE 4

Wanda is a part-time music composer. A music publisher purchases one of her songs for $5,000. Wanda has a $5,000 ordinary gain from the sale of an ordinary asset. ▼

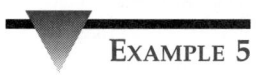

EXAMPLE 5

Ed received a letter from the President of the United States in 1962. In the current year, Ed sells the letter to a collector for $300. Ed has a $300 ordinary gain from the sale of an ordinary asset (because the letter was created for Ed). ▼

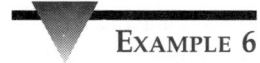

EXAMPLE 6

Isabella gives a song she composed to her son. The son sells the song to a music publisher for $5,000. The son has a $5,000 ordinary gain from the sale of an ordinary asset. If the son inherits the song from Isabella, his basis for the song is its fair market value at Isabella's death. The song is a capital asset because the son's basis is not related to Isabella's basis for the song. ▼

(Patents are subject to special statutory rules discussed later in the chapter.)

U.S. Government Publications.   U.S. government publications received from the U.S. government (or its agencies) for a reduced price are not capital assets. This prevents a taxpayer from later donating the publications to charity and claiming a charitable contribution equal to the fair market value of the publications. A charitable contribution of a capital asset generally yields a deduction equal to the fair market value. A charitable contribution of an ordinary asset generally yields a deduction equal to less than the fair market value. If such property is received by gift from the original purchaser, the property is not a capital asset to the donee. (For a more comprehensive explanation of charitable contributions of property, refer to Chapter 10.)

EFFECT OF JUDICIAL ACTION

Court decisions play an important role in the definition of capital assets. Because the Code only lists categories of what are *not* capital assets, judicial interpretation is sometimes required to determine whether a specific item fits into one of those categories. The Supreme Court follows a literal interpretation of the categories. For instance, corporate stock is not mentioned in § 1221. Thus, corporate stock is *usually* a capital asset. However, what if corporate stock is purchased for resale to customers? Then it is *inventory* and not a capital asset because inventory is one of the categories in § 1221. (See the discussion of Dealers in Securities below.)

A Supreme Court decision was required to distinguish between capital asset and non-capital asset status when a taxpayer who did not normally acquire stock for resale to customers acquired stock with the intention of resale.[2] The Court decided that since the stock was not acquired primarily for sale to customers (the taxpayer did not sell the stock to its regular customers), the stock was a capital asset.

Often the crux of the capital asset determination hinges on whether the asset is held for investment purposes (capital asset) or business purposes (ordinary asset). The taxpayer's *use* of the property often provides objective evidence.

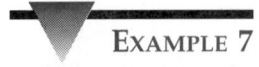

EXAMPLE 7

David's business buys an expensive painting. If the painting is used to decorate David's office and is not of investment quality, the painting is depreciable and, therefore, not a capital asset. If David's business is buying and selling paintings, the painting is inventory and, therefore, an ordinary asset. If the painting is of investment quality and the business purchased it for investment, the painting is a capital asset, even though it serves a decorative

---

[2]*Arkansas Best v. Comm.,* 88–1 USTC ¶9210, 61 AFTR2d 88–655, 108 S.Ct. 971 (USSC, 1988).

purpose in David's office. *Investment quality* generally means that the painting is expected to appreciate in value. ▼

Because of the uncertainty associated with capital asset status, Congress has enacted several Code Sections to clarify the definition. These statutory expansions of the capital asset definition are discussed in the following section.

STATUTORY EXPANSIONS

Congress has often expanded the § 1221 general definition of what is *not* a capital asset.

Dealers in Securities.   As a general rule, securities (stocks, bonds, and other financial instruments) held by a dealer are considered to be inventory and are not, therefore, subject to capital gain or loss treatment. A *dealer in securities* is a merchant (e.g., a brokerage firm) that regularly engages in the purchase and resale of securities to customers. The dealer must identify any securities being held for investment. Generally, if a dealer clearly identifies certain securities as held for investment purposes by the close of business on the acquisition date, gain from the securities' sale will be capital gain. However, the gain will not be capital gain if the dealer ceases to hold the securities for investment prior to the sale. Losses are capital losses if at any time the securities have been clearly identified by the dealer as held for investment.[3]

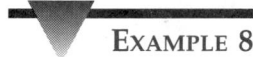

EXAMPLE 8

Tracy is a securities dealer. She purchases 100 shares of Swan stock. If Tracy takes no further action, the stock is inventory and an ordinary asset. If she designates in her records that the stock is held for investment, the stock is a capital asset. Tracy must designate the investment purpose by the close of business on the acquisition date. If Tracy maintains her investment purpose and later sells the stock, the gain or loss is capital gain or loss. If Tracy redesignates the stock as held for resale (inventory) and then sells it, any gain is ordinary, but any loss is capital loss. Stock designated as held for investment and then sold at a loss always yields a capital loss. ▼

ETHICAL CONSIDERATIONS

Capital Asset Status for Stock Held by Securities Dealers

A securities dealer purchases stock for her own account at 10:00 A.M. At the close of business that day, the stock has dropped slightly in price, so the dealer does not designate it as held for investment. By 10:30 A.M. the next morning, however, the value of the stock has risen substantially above the dealer's purchase price. Using her knowledge of computer programming, the dealer could manipulate the firm's computer records so that the stock will appear to have been designated as held for investment at the end of the previous day. She is absolutely certain that neither the firm nor the IRS will ever discover what she has done. Comment on the securities dealer's potential behavior and the motivation for it.

---

[3]§§ 1236(a) and (b) and Reg. § 1.1236–1(a).

Real Property Subdivided for Sale. Substantial real property development activities may result in the owner being considered a dealer for tax purposes. Income from the sale of real estate property lots is treated as the sale of inventory (ordinary income) if the owner is considered to be a dealer. However, § 1237 allows real estate investors capital gain treatment if they engage *only* in *limited* development activities. To be eligible for § 1237 treatment, the following requirements must be met:

- The taxpayer may not be a corporation.
- The taxpayer may not be a real estate dealer.
- No substantial improvements may be made to the lots sold. *Substantial* generally means more than a 10 percent increase in the value of a lot. Shopping centers and other commercial or residential buildings are considered substantial, while filling, draining, leveling, and clearing operations are not.
- The taxpayer must have held the lots sold for at least 5 years, except for inherited property. The substantial improvements test is less stringent if the property is held at least 10 years.

If the preceding requirements are met, all gain is capital gain until the tax year in which the *sixth* lot is sold. Sales of contiguous lots to a single buyer in the same transaction count as the sale of one lot. Beginning with the tax year the *sixth* lot is sold, some of the gain may be ordinary income. Five percent of the revenue from lot sales is potential ordinary income. That potential ordinary income is offset by any selling expenses from the lot sales. Practically, sales commissions often are at least 5 percent of the sales price, so none of the gain is treated as ordinary income.

Section 1237 does not apply to losses. A loss from the sale of subdivided real property is an ordinary loss unless the property qualifies as a capital asset under § 1221. The following example illustrates the application of § 1237.

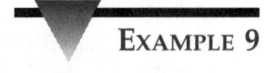

EXAMPLE 9

Jack owns a large tract of land and subdivides it for sale. Assume Jack meets all the requirements of § 1237 and during the tax year sells the first 10 lots to 10 different buyers for $10,000 each. Jack's basis in each lot sold is $3,000, and he incurs total selling expenses of $4,000 on the sales. Jack's gain is computed as follows:

Selling price (10 × $10,000)		$100,000	
Basis (10 × $3,000)		(30,000)	
Excess over basis		$ 70,000	
Five percent of selling price	$5,000		
Selling expenses	(4,000)		
Amount of ordinary income			$ 1,000
Five percent of selling price	$5,000		
Excess of expenses over 5% of selling price	–0–	(5,000)	
Capital gain			65,000
Total gain ($70,000 – $4,000 selling expenses)			$66,000

Lump-Sum Distributions. A *lump-sum distribution* is generally a distribution of an employee's entire qualified pension or profit sharing plan balance within one tax year. The distribution must result from the employee's (1) death, (2) reaching age 59½, or (3) separation from service with an employer. TRA of 1986 repealed a provision that allowed a portion of a lump-sum distribution to be treated as capital gain. However, partial capital gain treatment may still be available because transition rules allow certain taxpayers to continue using prior law. See Chapter 19 for a further discussion of lump-sum distributions.

Nonbusiness Bad Debts.   A loan not made in the ordinary course of business is classified as a nonbusiness receivable. In the year the receivable becomes completely worthless, it is a *nonbusiness bad debt*, and the bad debt is treated as a short-term capital loss. Even if the receivable was outstanding for more than one year, the loss is still a short-term capital loss. Chapter 7 discusses nonbusiness bad debts more thoroughly.

SALE OR EXCHANGE

3   **LEARNING OBJECTIVE**
Understand the relevance of a sale or exchange to classification as a capital gain or loss and apply the special rules for the capital gain or loss treatment of the retirement of corporate obligations, options, patents, franchises, and lease cancellation payments.

Recognition of capital gain or loss usually requires a sale or exchange of a capital asset. The Code uses the term **sale or exchange,** but does not define it. Generally, a property sale involves the receipt of money by the seller and/or the assumption by the purchaser of the seller's liabilities. An exchange involves the transfer of property for other property. Thus, an involuntary conversion (casualty, theft, or condemnation) is not a sale or exchange. In several situations, the determination of whether a sale or exchange has taken place has been clarified by the enactment of Code Sections that specifically provide for sale or exchange treatment.

Recognized gains or losses from the cancellation, lapse, expiration, or any other termination of a right or obligation with respect to personal property (other than stock) that is or would be a capital asset in the hands of the taxpayer are capital gains or losses.[4] See the discussion under Options later in the chapter for more details.

WORTHLESS SECURITIES AND § 1244 STOCK

Occasionally, securities such as stock and, especially, bonds may become worthless due to the insolvency of their issuer. If such a security is a capital asset, the loss is deemed to have occurred as the result of a sale or exchange on the *last day* of the tax year.[5] This last-day rule may have the effect of converting what otherwise would have been a short-term capital loss into a long-term capital loss. See Treatment of Capital Losses later in this chapter.

Section 1244 allows an ordinary deduction on disposition of stock at a loss. The stock must be that of a small business company, and the ordinary deduction is limited to $50,000 ($100,000 for married individuals filing jointly) per year. For a more detailed discussion, refer to Chapter 7.

SPECIAL RULE—RETIREMENT OF CORPORATE OBLIGATIONS

A debt obligation (e.g., a bond or note payable) may have a tax basis in excess of or less than its redemption value because it may have been acquired at a premium or discount. Consequently, the collection of the redemption value may result in a loss or gain. Generally, the collection of a debt obligation is *treated* as a sale or exchange.[6] Therefore, any loss or gain can be a capital loss or capital gain because a sale or exchange has taken place. However, if the debt obligation was issued by

---

[4]§ 1234A.
[5]§ 165(g)(1).

[6]§ 1271.

a human being prior to June 9, 1997, and/or purchased by the taxpayer prior to June 9, 1997, the collection of the debt obligation is not a sale or exchange.

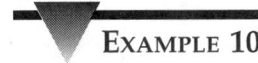

EXAMPLE 10

Fran acquires $1,000 of Osprey Corporation bonds for $980 in the open market. If the bonds are held to maturity, the $20 difference between Fran's collection of the $1,000 redemption value and her cost of $980 is treated as capital gain. If the obligation had been issued to Fran by an individual prior to June 9, 1997, her $20 gain would be ordinary, since she did not sell or exchange the debt. ▼

Original Issue Discount.   The benefit of the sale or exchange exception that allows a capital gain from the collection of certain obligations is reduced when the obligation has original issue discount. **Original issue discount (OID)** arises when the issue price of a debt obligation is less than the maturity value of the obligation. OID must generally be amortized over the life of the debt obligation using the effective interest method. The OID amortization increases the basis of the bond. Most new publicly traded bond issues do not carry OID since the stated interest rate is set to make the market price on issue the same as the bond's face amount. In addition, even if the issue price is less than the face amount, the difference is not considered to be OID if the difference is less than one-fourth of 1 percent of the redemption price at maturity multiplied by the number of years to maturity.[7]

In the case where OID does exist, it may or may not have to be amortized, depending upon the date the obligation was issued. When OID is amortized, the amount of gain upon collection, sale, or exchange of the obligation is correspondingly reduced. The obligations covered by the OID amortization rules and the method of amortization are presented in §§ 1272–1275. Similar rules for other obligations can be found in §§ 1276–1288.

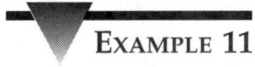

EXAMPLE 11

Jerry purchases $10,000 of newly issued White Corporation bonds for $6,000. The bonds have OID of $4,000. Jerry must amortize the discount over the life of the bonds. The OID amortization *increases* his interest income. (The bonds were selling at a discount because the market rate of interest was greater than the bonds' interest rate.) After Jerry has amortized $1,800 of OID, he sells the bonds for $8,000. Jerry has a capital gain of $200 [$8,000 − ($6,000 cost + $1,800 OID amortization)]. The OID amortization rules prevent him from converting ordinary interest income into capital gain. Without the OID amortization, Jerry would have capital gain of $2,000 ($8,000 − $6,000 cost). ▼

OPTIONS

Frequently, a potential buyer of property wants some time to make the purchase decision, but wants to control the sale and/or the sale price in the meantime. **Options** are used to achieve these objectives. The potential purchaser (grantee) pays the property owner (grantor) for an option on the property. The grantee then becomes the option holder. The option usually sets a price at which the grantee can buy the property and expires after a specified period of time.

Sale of an Option.   A grantee may sell or exchange the option rather than exercising it or letting it expire. Generally, the grantee's sale or exchange of the option results in capital gain or loss if the option property is (or would be) a capital asset to the grantee.[8]

---

[7]§ 1273(a)(3).

[8]§ 1234(a) and Reg. § 1.1234–1(a)(1). Stock options are discussed in Chapter 19.

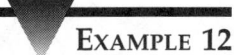

EXAMPLE 12

Rosa wants to buy some vacant land for investment purposes. She cannot afford the full purchase price. Instead, she convinces the landowner (grantor) to sell her the right to purchase the land for $100,000 anytime in the next two years. Rosa (grantee) pays $3,000 to obtain this option to buy the land. The option is a capital asset for Rosa because if she actually purchased the land, the land would be a capital asset. Three months after purchasing the option, Rosa sells it for $7,000. She has a $4,000 ($7,000 – $3,000) short-term capital gain on this sale since she held the option for one year or less. ▼

Failure to Exercise Options.   If an option holder (grantee) fails to exercise the option, the lapse of the option is considered a sale or exchange on the option expiration date. Thus, the loss is a capital loss if the property subject to the option is (or would be) a capital asset in the hands of the grantee.

The grantor of an option on *stocks, securities, commodities, or commodity futures* receives short-term capital gain treatment upon the expiration of the option. Options on property other than stocks, securities, commodities, or commodity futures result in ordinary income to the grantor when the option expires. For example, an individual investor who owns certain stock (a capital asset) may sell a call option, entitling the buyer of the option to acquire the stock at a specified price higher than the value at the date the option is granted. The writer of the call receives a premium (e.g., 10 percent) for writing the option. If the price of the stock does not increase during the option period, the option will expire unexercised. Upon the expiration of the option, the grantor must recognize short-term capital gain. These provisions do not apply to options held for sale to customers (the inventory of a securities dealer).

Exercise of Options by Grantee.   If the option is exercised, the amount paid for the option is added to the optioned property's selling price. This increases the gain (or reduces the loss) to the grantor resulting from the sale of the property. The grantor's gain or loss is capital or ordinary depending on the tax status of the property. The grantee adds the cost of the option to the basis of the property purchased.

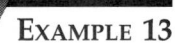

EXAMPLE 13

On September 1, 1990, Wes purchases 100 shares of Eagle Company stock for $5,000. On April 1, 1998, he writes a call option on the stock, giving the grantee the right to buy the stock for $6,000 during the following six-month period. Wes (the grantor) receives a call premium of $500 for writing the call.

- If the call is exercised by the grantee on August 1, 1998, Wes has $1,500 ($6,000 + $500 – $5,000) of long-term capital gain from the sale of the stock. The grantee has a $6,500 ($500 option premium + $6,000 purchase price) basis for the stock.
- Assume that Wes decides to sell his stock prior to exercise for $6,000 and enters into a closing transaction by purchasing a call on 100 shares of Eagle Company stock for $5,000. Since the Eagle stock is selling for $6,000, Wes must pay a call premium of $1,000. He recognizes a $500 short-term capital loss [$1,000 (call premium paid) – $500 (call premium received)] on the closing transaction. On the actual sale of the Eagle stock, Wes has a long-term capital gain of $1,000 [$6,000 (selling price) – $5,000 (cost)]. The grantee is not affected by Wes's closing transaction. The original option is still in existence, and the grantee's tax consequences will depend on what action the grantee takes—exercising the option, letting the option expire, or selling the option.
- Assume that the original option expired unexercised. Wes has a $500 short-term capital gain equal to the call premium received for writing the option. This gain is not recognized until the option expires. The grantee has a loss from expiration of the option. The nature of the loss will depend upon whether the option was a capital asset or an ordinary asset. ▼

Options

| Event | Effect on | |
	Grantor	Grantee
Option is granted.	Receives value and has a contract obligation (a liability).	Pays value and has a contract right (an asset).
Option expires.	Has a short-term capital gain if the option property is stocks, securities, commodities, or commodity futures. Otherwise, gain is ordinary income.	Has a loss (capital loss if option property would have been a capital asset for the grantee).
Option is exercised.	Amount received for option increases proceeds from sale of the option property.	Amount paid for option becomes part of the basis of the option property purchased.
Option is sold or exchanged by grantee.	Result depends upon whether option later expires or is exercised (see above).	Could have gain or loss (capital gain or loss if option property would have been a capital asset for the grantee).

Concept Summary 16–1 summarizes the rules for options.

PATENTS

Transfer of a **patent** is treated as the sale or exchange of a long-term capital asset when all substantial rights to the patent (or an undivided interest that includes all such rights) are transferred by a holder.[9] The transferor/holder may receive payment in virtually any form. Lump-sum or periodic payments are most common. The amount of the payments may also be contingent on the transferee/purchaser's productivity, use, or disposition of the patent. If the transfer meets these requirements, any gain or loss is *automatically a long-term* capital gain or loss from property held more than 18 months. Whether the asset was a capital asset for the transferor, whether a sale or exchange occurred, and how long the transferor held the patent are not relevant.

This special long-term capital gain or loss treatment for patents is intended to encourage technological progress. Ironically, authors, composers, and artists are not eligible for capital gain treatment when their creations are transferred. Books, songs, and artists' works may be copyrighted, but copyrights and the assets they represent are not capital assets. Thus, the disposition of those assets by their creators usually results in ordinary gain or loss. The following example illustrates the special treatment for patents.

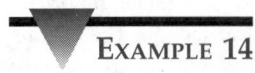

EXAMPLE 14

Diana, a druggist, invents a pill-counting machine, which she patents. In consideration of a lump-sum payment of $200,000 plus $10 per machine sold, Diana assigns the patent to Drug Products, Inc. Assuming Diana has transferred all substantial rights, the question of whether the transfer is a sale or exchange of a capital asset is not relevant. Diana automatically has a long-term capital gain from both the lump-sum payment and the $10 per machine royalty to the extent these proceeds exceed her basis for the patent. ▼

[9]§ 1235.

Substantial Rights. To receive favorable capital gain treatment, all *substantial rights* to the patent (or an undivided interest in it) must be transferred. All substantial rights to a patent means all rights (whether or not then held by the grantor) that are valuable at the time the patent rights (or an undivided interest in the patent) are transferred. All substantial rights have not been transferred when the transfer is limited geographically within the issuing country or when the transfer is for a period less than the remaining life of the patent. The circumstances of the entire transaction, rather than merely the language used in the transfer instrument, are to be considered in deciding whether all substantial rights have been transferred.[10]

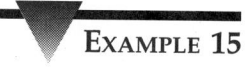

EXAMPLE 15   Assume Diana, the druggist in Example 14, only licensed Drug Products, Inc., to manufacture and sell the invention in Michigan. She retained the right to license the machine elsewhere in the United States. Diana has retained a substantial right and is not eligible for automatic long-term capital gain treatment. ▼

Holder Defined. The *holder* of a patent must be an *individual* and is usually the invention's creator. A holder may also be an individual who purchases the patent rights from the creator before the patented invention is reduced to practice. However, the creator's employer and certain parties related to the creator do not qualify as holders. Thus, in the common situation where an employer has all rights to an employee's inventions, the employer is not eligible for long-term capital gain treatment. More than likely, the employer will have an ordinary asset because the patent was developed as part of its business.

FRANCHISES, TRADEMARKS, AND TRADE NAMES

A mode of operation, a widely recognized brand name (trade name), and a widely known business symbol (trademark) are all valuable assets. These assets may be licensed (commonly known as franchising) by their owner for use by other businesses. Many fast-food restaurants (such as McDonald's and Taco Bell) are franchises. The franchisee usually pays the owner (franchisor) an initial fee plus a contingent fee. The contingent fee is often based upon the franchisee's sales volume.

For Federal income tax purposes, a **franchise** is an agreement that gives the franchisee the right to distribute, sell, or provide goods, services, or facilities within a specified area.[11] A franchise transfer includes the grant of a franchise, a transfer by one franchisee to another person, or the renewal of a franchise.

A franchise transfer is generally not a sale or exchange of a capital asset. Section 1253 provides that a transfer of a franchise, trademark, or trade name is not a transfer of a capital asset when the transferor retains any significant power, right, or continuing interest in the property transferred.

Significant Power, Right, or Continuing Interest. *Significant powers, rights, or continuing interests* include control over assignment, quality of products and services, sale or advertising of other products or services, and the right to require that substantially all supplies and equipment be purchased from the transferor. Also included are the right to terminate the franchise at will and the right to substantial contingent payments. Most modern franchising operations involve some or all of these powers, rights, or continuing interests.

In the unusual case where no significant power, right, or continuing interest is retained by the transferor, a sale or exchange may occur, and capital gain or loss

---

[10]Reg. § 1.1235–2(b)(1).   [11]§ 1253(b)(1).

treatment may be available. For capital gain or loss treatment to be available, the asset transferred must qualify as a capital asset.

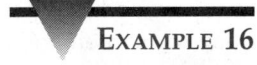

EXAMPLE 16

Orange, Inc., a franchisee, sells the franchise to a third party. Payments to Orange are not contingent, and all significant powers, rights, and continuing interests are transferred. The gain (payments – adjusted basis) on the sale is a capital gain to Orange. ▼

Noncontingent Payments.   When the transferor retains a significant power, right, or continuing interest, the transferee's noncontingent payments to the trans-feror are ordinary income to the transferor. The franchisee capitalizes the payments and amortizes them over 15 years. The amortization is subject to recapture under § 1245.[12]

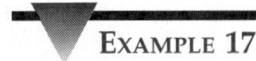

EXAMPLE 17

Grey Company signs a 10-year franchise agreement with DOH Donuts. Grey (the franchisee) makes payments of $3,000 per year for the first 8 years of the franchise agreement—a total of $24,000. Grey cannot deduct $3,000 per year as the payments are made. Instead, Grey may amortize the $24,000 total over 15 years. Thus, Grey may deduct $1,600 per year for each of the 15 years of the amortization period. The same result would occur if Grey made a $24,000 lump-sum payment at the beginning of the franchise period. Assuming DOH Donuts (the franchisor) retains significant powers, rights, or a continuing interest, it will have ordinary income when it receives the payments from Grey. ▼

Contingent Payments.   Whether or not the transferor retains a significant power, right, or continuing interest, contingent franchise payments are ordinary income for the franchisor and an ordinary deduction for the franchisee. For this purpose, a payment qualifies as a contingent payment only if the following require-ments are met:

- The contingent amounts are part of a series of payments that are paid at least annually throughout the term of the transfer agreement.
- The payments are substantially equal in amount or are payable under a fixed formula.

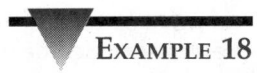

EXAMPLE 18

TAK, a spicy chicken franchisor, transfers an eight-year franchise to Otis. TAK retains a significant power, right, or continuing interest. Otis, the franchisee, agrees to pay TAK 15% of sales. This contingent payment is ordinary income to TAK and a business deduction for Otis as the payments are made. ▼

Sports Franchises.   Professional sports franchises (e.g., the Detroit Tigers) are not covered by § 1253.[13] However, § 1056 restricts the allocation of sports franchise acquisition costs to player contracts. Player contracts are usually one of the major assets acquired with a sports franchise. These contracts last only for the time stated in the contract. Therefore, owners of sports franchises would like to allocate franchise acquisition costs disproportionately to the contracts so that the acquisition costs will be amortizable over the contracts' lives. Section 1056 prevents this by generally limiting the amount that can be allocated to player contracts to no more than 50 percent of the franchise acquisition cost. In addition, the seller of the sports franchise has ordinary income under § 1245 for the portion of the gain allocable to the disposition of player contracts.[14]

Concept Summary 16–2 summarizes the rules for franchises.

---

[12]See Chapter 17 for a discussion of the recapture provisions.
[13]§ 1253(e).

[14]See Chapter 17 for a discussion of the recapture provisions.

CONCEPT SUMMARY 16–2

Franchises

Event	Effect on	
	Franchisor	**Franchisee**
Franchisor Retains Significant Powers and Rights		
Noncontingent payment	Ordinary income.	Capitalized and amortized over 15 years as an ordinary deduction; if franchise is sold, amortization is subject to recapture under § 1245.
Contingent payment	Ordinary income.	Ordinary deduction.
Franchisor Does *Not* Retain Significant Powers and Rights		
Noncontingent payment	Ordinary income if franchise rights are an ordinary asset; capital gain if franchise rights are a capital asset (unlikely).	Capitalized and amortized over 15 years as an ordinary deduction; if the franchise is sold, amortization is subject to recapture under § 1245.
Contingent payment	Ordinary income.	Ordinary deduction.

LEASE CANCELLATION PAYMENTS

The tax treatment of payments received for canceling a lease depends on whether the recipient is the **lessor** or the **lessee** and whether the lease is a capital asset or not.

Lessee Treatment.   Lease cancellation payments received by a lessee are treated as an exchange.[15] Thus, these payments are capital gains if the lease is a capital asset. Generally, a lessee's lease is a capital asset if the property (either personalty or realty) is used for the lessee's personal use (e.g., his or her residence). A lessee's lease is an ordinary asset if the property is used in the lessee's trade or business.[16]

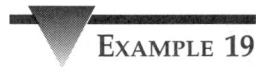

EXAMPLE 19   Mark owns an apartment building that he is going to convert into an office building. Vicki is one of the apartment tenants and receives $1,000 from Mark to cancel the lease. Vicki has a capital gain of $1,000 (which is long term or short term depending upon how long she has held the lease). Mark has an ordinary deduction of $1,000. ▼

Lessor Treatment.   Payments received by a lessor for a lease cancellation are always ordinary income because they are considered to be in lieu of rental payments.[17]

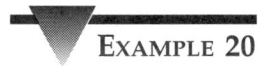

EXAMPLE 20   Floyd owns an apartment building near a university campus. Hui-Fen is one of the tenants. Hui-Fen is graduating early and offers Floyd $800 to cancel the apartment lease. Floyd accepts the offer. Floyd has ordinary income of $800. Hui-Fen has a nondeductible payment since the apartment was personal use property. ▼

---

[15]§ 1241 and Reg. § 1.1241–1(a).
[16]Reg. § 1.1221–1(b).

[17]*Hort v. Comm.*, 41–1 USTC ¶9354, 25 AFTR 1207, 61 S.Ct. 757 (USSC, 1941).

HOLDING PERIOD

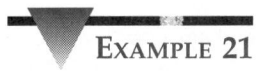

4 LEARNING OBJECTIVE
Determine whether the holding period for a capital asset is long term, mid-term, or short term.

Property must be held more than one year to qualify for long-term capital gain or loss treatment.[18] Property not held for the required long-term period results in short-term capital gain or loss. To compute the **holding period,** start counting on the day after the property was acquired and include the day of disposition.

EXAMPLE 21

Marge purchases a capital asset on January 15, 1997, and sells it on January 16, 1998. Marge's holding period is more than one year. If Marge had sold the asset on January 15, 1998, the holding period would have been exactly one year, and the gain or loss would have been short term. ▼

To be held for more than one year, a capital asset acquired on the last day of any month must not be disposed of until on or after the first day of the thirteenth succeeding month.[19]

EXAMPLE 22

Leo purchases a capital asset on February 28, 1997. If Leo sells the asset on February 28, 1998, the holding period is one year, and Leo will have a short-term capital gain or loss. If Leo sells the asset on March 1, 1998, the holding period is more than one year, and he will have a long-term capital gain or loss. ▼

REVIEW OF SPECIAL HOLDING PERIOD RULES

There are several special holding period rules.[20] The application of these rules depends on the type of asset and how it was acquired.

Nontaxable Exchanges. The holding period of property received in a like-kind exchange includes the holding period of the former asset if the property that has been exchanged is a capital asset or a § 1231 asset. In certain nontaxable transactions involving a substituted basis, the holding period of the former property is *tacked on* to the holding period of the newly acquired property.

EXAMPLE 23

Vern exchanges a business truck for another truck in a like-kind exchange. The holding period of the exchanged truck tacks on to the holding period of the new truck. ▼

Certain Nontaxable Transactions Involving a Carryover of Another Taxpayer's Basis. A former owner's holding period is tacked on to the present owner's holding period if the transaction is nontaxable and the former owner's basis carries over to the present owner.

EXAMPLE 24

Kareem acquires 100 shares of Robin Corporation stock for $1,000 on December 31, 1989. He transfers the shares by gift to Megan on December 31, 1997, when the stock is worth $2,000. Kareem's basis of $1,000 becomes the basis for determining gain or loss on a subsequent sale by Megan. Megan's holding period begins with the date the stock was acquired by Kareem. ▼

EXAMPLE 25

Assume the same facts as in Example 24, except that the fair market value of the shares is only $800 on the date of the gift. The holding period begins on the date of the gift if Megan sells the stock for a loss. The value of the shares at the date of the gift is used in the

---

[18]§ 1222.
[19]Rev.Rul. 66–7, 1966–1 C.B. 188.

[20]§ 1223.

determination of her basis for loss. If she sells the shares for $500 on April 1, 1998, Megan has a $300 recognized capital loss, and the holding period is from December 31, 1997, to April 1, 1998 (thus, the loss is short term). ▼

Certain Disallowed Loss Transactions. Under several Code provisions, realized losses are disallowed. When a loss is disallowed, there is no carryover of holding period. Losses can be disallowed under § 267 (sale or exchange between related taxpayers) and § 262 (sale or exchange of personal use assets) as well as other Code Sections. Taxpayers who acquire property in a disallowed loss transaction will have a new holding period begin and will have a basis equal to the purchase price.

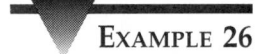

Janet sells her personal automobile at a loss. She may not deduct the loss because it arises from the sale of personal use property. Janet purchases a replacement automobile for more than the selling price of her former automobile. Janet has a basis equal to the cost of the replacement automobile, and her holding period begins when she acquires the replacement automobile. ▼

Inherited Property. The holding period for inherited property is treated as being *more than 18 months* and thus is long term, no matter how long the property is actually held by the heir. The holding period of the decedent or the decedent's estate is not relevant for the heir's holding period.

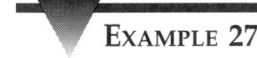

Shonda inherits Blue Company stock from her father. She receives the stock on April 1, 1998, and sells it on November 1, 1998. Even though the stock was not held more than one year by Shonda, she receives long-term capital gain or loss treatment on the sale. ▼

SPECIAL RULES FOR SHORT SALES

General. The Code provides special rules for determining the holding period of property sold short.[21] A **short sale** occurs when a taxpayer sells borrowed property and repays the lender with substantially identical property either held on the date of the sale or purchased after the sale. Short sales usually involve corporate stock. The seller's objective is to make a profit in anticipation of a decline in the stock's price. If the price declines, the seller in a short sale recognizes a profit equal to the difference between the sales price of the borrowed stock and the price paid for the replacement stock.

A *short sale against the box* occurs when the stock is borrowed from a broker by a seller who already owns the same stock. The box is the safe deposit box where stock owners routinely used to keep stock certificates. Although today stockbrokers generally keep stock certificates for their customers, the terminology short sale against the box is still used.

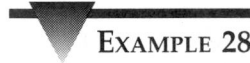

Chris does not own any shares of Brown Corporation. However, Chris sells 30 shares of Brown. The shares are borrowed from Chris's broker and must be replaced within 45 days. Chris has a short sale because he was short the shares he sold. He will *close* the short sale by purchasing Brown shares and delivering them to his broker. If the original 30 shares were sold for $10,000 and Chris later purchases 30 shares for $8,000, he has a gain of $2,000. Chris's hunch that the price of Brown stock would decline was correct. Chris was able to profit from selling high and buying low. If Chris had to purchase Brown shares for $13,000 to close the short sale, he would have a loss of $3,000. In this case, Chris has sold low and

[21]§ 1233.

New Rules for Short Sales Against the Box

"Short sales against the box" have been controversial because they allow gain to be deferred until the short sale is closed. Many wealthy taxpayers use this technique at the end of a tax year to defer gains until the next tax year. Several times during recent years, the IRS has encouraged Congress to outlaw short sales against the box. The IRS contended that only very rich taxpayers use this technique and that, therefore, it is a "tax shelter" for the wealthy.

The Taxpayer Relief Act of 1997 (TRA of 1997) included new § 1259, which, although it did not outlaw short sales against the box, removed some of their tax advantage.

bought high—not the result he wanted! Chris would be making a short sale against the box if he borrowed shares from his broker to sell and then closed the short sale by delivering other Brown shares he owned at the time he made the short sale. ▼

A short sale gain or loss is a capital gain or loss to the extent that the short sale property constitutes a capital asset of the taxpayer. The gain or loss is not recognized until the short sale is closed. Generally, the holding period of the short sale property is determined by how long the property used to close the short sale was held. However, if *substantially identical property* (e.g., other shares of the same stock) is held by the taxpayer, the short-term or long-term character of the short sale gain or loss may be affected:

- If substantially identical property has *not* been held for the long-term holding period on the short sale date, the short sale *gain or loss* is short term.
- If substantially identical property has *been* held for the long-term holding period on the short sale date, the short sale *gain* is long term if the substantially identical property is used to close the short sale and short term if it is not used to close the short sale.
- If substantially identical property has *been* held for the long-term holding period on the short sale date, the short sale *loss* is long term whether or not the substantially identical property is used to close the short sale.
- If substantially identical property is acquired *after* the short sale date and on or before the closing date, the short sale *gain or loss* is short term.

Concept Summary 16–3 summarizes the short sale rules. These rules are intended to prevent the conversion of short-term capital gains into long-term capital gains and long-term capital losses into short-term capital losses.

Disposition Rules for Short Sales against the Box.   In a short sale against the box, the taxpayer either owns securities that are substantially identical to the securities sold short at the short sale date or acquires such securities before the closing date. TRA of 1997 contains provisions designed to remove some of the taxpayer's flexibility as to when the short sale gain must be reported (a constructive sale approach). If the taxpayer has not closed the short sale by delivering the short sale securities to the broker *before* January 31 of the year following the short sale, the short sale is deemed to have been closed on the *earlier* of two events:

- On the short sale date if the taxpayer owned substantially identical securities at that time.

CONCEPT SUMMARY 16–3

Short Sales of Securities

Has the taxpayer held substantially identical securities for the required long-term holding period at the date of the short sale?

Yes

No

To the extent of the number of shares sold short, any loss arising from the closing of the short sale is long-term loss regardless of the holding period of the securities used to close the short sale.
If the securities held for the required long-term holding period are used to close the short sale, any gain is long term.

Any gain or loss from the close of the short sale is short term.

And

And

For the number of shares sold short, the holding period of substantially identical securities not held long term at the short sale date or acquired after the short sale date and before the closing date begins with the earlier of the date of sale of those securities or the closing date of the short sale. This holding period rule applies in the order of the acquisition dates of the substantially identical property.

- On the date during the year of the short sale that the taxpayer acquired substantially identical securities.[22]

The basis of the shares in the deemed transfer of shares is used to compute the gain or loss on the short sale. Later, when shares are *actually* transferred to the broker to close the short sale, there may be a gain or loss because the shares transferred will have a basis equal to the short sale date price and the value at the *actual* short sale closing date may be different from the short sale date price.

Illustrations. The following examples illustrate the treatment of short sales and short sales against the box.

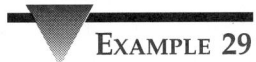

EXAMPLE 29

On January 4, 1998, Donald purchases five shares of Osprey Corporation common stock for $100. On April 14, 1998, he engages in a short sale of five shares of the same stock for $150.

---
[22]§ 1259.

On August 15, Donald closes the short sale by repaying the borrowed stock with the five shares purchased on January 4. Donald has a $50 short-term capital gain from the short sale because he had not held substantially identical shares for the long-term holding period on the short sale date. ▼

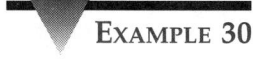

EXAMPLE 30

Assume the same facts as in the previous example, except that Donald closes the short sale on January 28, 1999, by repaying the borrowed stock with five shares purchased on January 27, 1999, for $200. The stock used to close the short sale was not the property purchased on January 4, 1998, but since Donald held short-term property at the April 14, 1998, short sale date, the gain or loss from closing the short sale is short term. Donald has a $50 short-term capital loss ($200 cost of stock purchased January 27, 1999, and a short sale selling price of $150). ▼

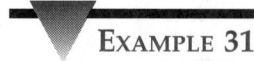

EXAMPLE 31

Assume the same facts as in Example 30. On January 31, 1999, Donald sells for $200 the stock purchased January 4, 1998. Donald's holding period for that stock begins January 28, 1999, because the holding period portion of the short sale rules applies to the substantially identical property in order of acquisition. Donald has a short-term capital gain of $100 ($100 cost of stock purchased January 4, 1998, and a selling price of $200). ▼

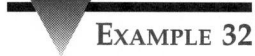

EXAMPLE 32

On January 18, 1997, Rita purchases 200 shares of Owl Corporation stock for $1,000. On November 11, 1998, she sells short for $1,300 200 shares of Owl Corporation stock that she borrows from her broker. On February 10, 1999, Rita closes the short sale by delivering the 200 shares of Owl Corporation stock that she had acquired in 1997. On that date, Owl Corporation stock had a market price of $3 per share. Since Rita owned substantially identical stock on the date of the short sale and did not close the short sale before January 31, 1999, she is *deemed* to have closed the short sale on November 11, 1998 (the date of the short sale). On her 1998 tax return, she reports a $300 long-term capital gain ($1,300 short sale price − $1,000 basis). On February 10, 1999, Rita has a $700 short-term capital loss [$600 short sale closing date price (200 shares × $3 per share) − $1,300 basis] because the holding period of the shares used to close the short sale commences with the date of the short sale. ▼

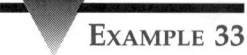

EXAMPLE 33

Assume the same facts as in Example 32, except that Rita did not own any Owl Corporation stock on the short sale date and acquired the 200 shares of Owl Corporation stock for $1,000 on December 12, 1998 (after the November 11, 1998 short sale date). The *deemed* closing of the short sale is December 12, 1998, because Rita held substantially identical shares at the end of 1998 and did not close the short sale before January 31, 1999. Her 1998 short sale gain is a *short-term* gain of $300 ($1,300 short sale price − $1,000 basis), and she still has a short-term capital loss of $700 on February 10, 1999. ▼

TAX TREATMENT OF CAPITAL GAINS AND LOSSES OF NONCORPORATE TAXPAYERS

5 **LEARNING OBJECTIVE**
Describe the beneficial tax treatment for capital gains and the detrimental tax treatment for capital losses for noncorporate taxpayers.

All taxpayers net their capital gains and losses. Short-term gains and losses (if any) are netted against one another, and long-term gains and losses (if any) are netted against one another. The results will be net short-term gain or loss and net long-term gain or loss. If these two net positions are of opposite sign (one is a gain and one is a loss), they are netted against one another.

Six possibilities exist for the result after all possible netting has been completed. Three of these final results are gains, and three are losses. One possible result is a net long-term capital gain (NLTCG). Net long-term capital gains of noncorporate taxpayers are subject to beneficial treatment. A second possibility is a net short-term capital gain (NSTCG). Third, the netting may result in both NLTCG and NSTCG.

The NLTCG portion of these results is eligible for an alternative tax calculation. As many as four different tax rates may be used in the calculation—10, 20, 25, and 28 percent. The tax savings from the alternative tax calculation range from a low of 5 percentage points (15 percent regular tax rate – 10 percent alternative tax rate) to a high of 19.6 percentage points (39.6 percent regular tax rate – 20 percent alternative tax rate). The alternative tax computation is discussed later in the chapter under Alternative Tax on Net Capital Gain.

The last three results of the capital gain and loss netting process are losses. Thus, a fourth possibility is a net long-term capital loss (NLTCL). A fifth result is a net short-term capital loss (NSTCL). Finally, a sixth possibility includes both an NLTCL and an NSTCL. Neither NLTCLs nor NSTCLs are treated as ordinary losses. Treatment as an ordinary loss generally is preferable to capital loss treatment since ordinary losses are deductible in full while the deductibility of capital losses is subject to certain limitations. An individual taxpayer may deduct a maximum of $3,000 of net capital losses for a taxable year.[23]

CAPITAL GAIN AND LOSS NETTING PROCESS

Holding Periods for Capital Gain and Loss Netting Purposes. As mentioned earlier in this chapter, there are two types of long-term capital gain and loss—mid-term and long term. Thus, there are three holding periods for purposes of the capital gain and loss netting process:

- *Short term*—Assets held 12 months or less.
- *Mid-term*—Assets held more than 12 months and less than or equal to 18 months; *collectibles* held more than 12 months.
- *Long term*—Assets held more than 18 months.

Net short-term capital gain is not eligible for any special tax rate. It is taxed at the same rate as the taxpayer's other taxable income. *Net mid-term capital gain* is eligible for an alternative tax rate of 28 percent if that rate is lower than the regular tax rate on such income. *Net long-term capital gain* is generally eligible for one or more of *three* alternative tax rates: 10 percent, 20 percent, and 25 percent.[24] For simplicity, the net **mid-term capital gain** is referred to as the *28% gain*. The net long-term capital gain components are referred to as the *10%/20% gain* and the *25% gain*. The *25% gain* is technically called the **unrecaptured § 1250 gain** and is related to gain from disposition of § 1231 assets. Gains and losses from disposition of § 1231 assets are discussed in Chapter 17. In this chapter, the discussion will focus only on how the *25% gain* is taxed and not on how it is determined.

When the combination of mid-term and long-term capital gain exceeds net short-term capital loss, a **net capital gain (NCG)** exists. Net capital gain qualifies for beneficial alternative tax treatment (see the coverage later in the chapter).[25]

Because of the three holding periods, there are three types of capital gain or loss. Thus, an *ordering procedure* is required to net them against each other.

Step 1. Group all gains and losses into short term, mid-term (including collectibles), 25% long term, and 10%/20% long term.

Step 2. Net the gains and losses within each group to obtain net short-term, mid-term, 25% long-term, and 10%/20% long-term gain or loss.

[23]§ 1211(b).

[24]In addition, an 8% or 18% rate can apply for capital assets purchased after 2000 and held for more than 5 years.

[25]§ 1222(11).

Step 3. Offset the net mid-term and net long-term (25% long-term gain first) amounts if they are of opposite sign. Add them if they have the same sign.

Step 4. Offset the result of step 3 with the net short-term gain or loss from step 2 if they are of opposite sign. The netting rules offset net capital losses against the *highest taxed gain first*. Consequently, if there is a net short-term capital loss, it first offsets any net mid-term gain, any remaining loss offsets 25% long-term *gain*, and then any remaining loss offsets *10%/20% gain*.

If the result of step 4 is *only* a short-term capital gain, the taxpayer is not eligible for a reduced tax rate. If the result of step 4 is a loss, the taxpayer may be eligible for a *capital loss deduction* (discussed later in this chapter). If there was no offsetting in step 4 because the short-term and step 3 results were both gains *or* if the result of the offsetting is either a mid-term and/or a long-term gain, a net capital gain exists, and the taxpayer may be eligible for a reduced tax rate. The net capital gain may consist of *10%/20% gain, 25% gain,* and/or *28% gain.*

The four steps outlined above can have as many as 14 unique final results. See Concept Summary 16–5 later in the chapter for a partial list and the tax effect of each result. The following series of examples illustrates the capital gain and loss netting process.

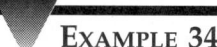

EXAMPLE 34

This example shows how a net short-term capital gain may result from the netting process.

			Long Term		
Step	**Short Term**	**Mid-Term**	**25% Gain**	**10%/20%**	**Comment**
1	$13,000	$ 12,000		$ 3,000	
	(2,000)	(20,000)			
2	$11,000	($ 8,000)		$ 3,000	
3		8,000	→	(8,000)	Netted because of
		$ –0–		($ 5,000)	opposite sign.
4	(5,000)	←	←	5,000	
	$ 6,000			$ –0–	The net short-term capital gain is taxed as ordinary income.

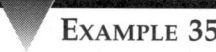

EXAMPLE 35

This example shows how a net mid-term capital gain may result from the netting process.

			Long Term		
Step	**Short Term**	**Mid-Term**	**25% Gain**	**10%/20%**	**Comment**
1	$ 3,000	$ 15,000	$ 4,000	$ 3,000	
	(5,000)	(7,000)		(8,000)	
2	($ 2,000)	$ 8,000	$ 4,000	($ 5,000)	
3		(5,000)	←	5,000	Net 10%/20% loss is netted against 28% gain first.
		$ 3,000		$ –0–	
4	2,000	→ (2,000)			STCL is netted against 28% gain first.
	$ –0–	$ 1,000	$ 4,000		
		Net 28% gain	Net 25% gain		

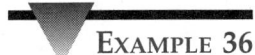
EXAMPLE 36

This example shows how a net long-term capital loss may result from the netting process.

Step	Short Term	Mid-Term	Long Term 25% Gain	10%/20%	Comment
1	$ 3,000	$ 1,000		$ 3,000 (8,000)	
2	$ 3,000	$ 1,000		($ 5,000)	
3		(1,000) $ –0–	→	1,000 ($ 4,000)	Netted because of opposite sign.
4	(3,000) $ –0–	→	→	3,000 ($ 1,000)	The net short-term gain is netted against the net long-term loss, and the remaining loss is eligible for the capital loss deduction.

Use of Capital Loss Carryovers.   A short-term capital loss carryover to the current year retains its character as short term and is combined with the short-term items of the current year. A mid-term and/or long-term net capital loss carries over as a mid-term capital loss and is combined with the current-year mid-term items.

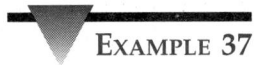
EXAMPLE 37

In 1998, Abigail has a $4,000 short-term capital gain, a $36,000 mid-term capital gain, and a $13,000 long-term capital gain. She also has a $3,000 short-term capital loss carryover and a $2,000 long-term capital loss carryover from 1997. This produces a $1,000 short-term capital gain ($4,000 − $3,000), a $34,000 mid-term capital gain ($36,000 − $2,000), and a $13,000 long-term capital gain for 1998. ▼

Definition of Collectibles.   Collectibles held more than 12 months are classified as mid-term capital assets. Even if the collectibles are held more than 18 months, they are not eligible for the 10%/20% alternative tax.

For capital gain or loss purposes, **collectibles** include:[26]

- Any work of art.
- Any rug or antique.
- Any metal or gem.
- Any stamp.
- Any alcoholic beverage.
- Most coins.

ALTERNATIVE TAX ON NET CAPITAL GAIN

Section 1 contains the statutory provisions that enable the *net capital gain* to be taxed at special rates (10, 20, 25, and 28 percent). This calculation is referred to as the **alternative tax** on net capital gain.[27] The alternative tax applies only if taxable income includes some mid-term and/or long-term capital gain (there is net capital gain). Taxable income includes *all* of the net capital gain unless taxable income is less than the net capital gain. In addition, the net capital gain is taxed *last*, after other taxable income (including any short-term capital gain).

[26]§ 408(m).   [27]§1(h).

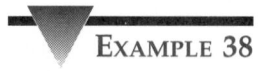

EXAMPLE 38

Joan, an unmarried taxpayer, has 1998 taxable income of $78,000, including a $12,000 net capital gain. The last $12,000 of her $78,000 taxable income is the layer related to the net capital gain. The first $66,000 ($78,000 – $12,000) of her taxable income is not subject to any special tax rate, so it is taxed using the regular tax rates. ▼

Since the net capital gain may be made up of various *rate layers*, it is important to know in what order those layers will be taxed. For *each* of the layers, the taxpayer compares the regular tax rate on that layer of income and the alternative tax rate on that portion of the capital gain. The layers are taxed in the following order: *25% gain*, *28% gain*, the 10 percent portion of the *10%/20% gain*, and then the 20 percent portion of the *10%/20% gain*. As a result of this layering, a taxpayer will benefit from the 10 percent alternative tax rate only when the total of other taxable income plus the 25 percent and 28 percent capital gain layers does not put the taxpayer above the 15 percent regular tax bracket.

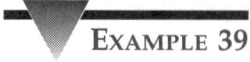

EXAMPLE 39

Assume that Joan's $12,000 net capital gain in Example 38 is made up of $10,000 *28% gain* and $2,000 *10%/20% gain*. Examination of the 1998 tax rates reveals that $66,000 of taxable income for a single individual puts Joan at a marginal tax rate of 31%. Consequently, she will use the alternative tax on both the $10,000 gain and the $2,000 gain. Her alternative tax liability for 1998 is $18,523 [$15,323 (tax on $66,000 of taxable income) + $2,800 ($10,000 × .28) + $400 ($2,000 × .20)]. Since the combination of her $66,000 other taxable income and her 28% gain put her above the 15% regular tax bracket, none of the $2,000 *10%/20% gain* is taxed at 10%. Her regular tax liability for 1998 on $78,000 would be $19,043. Thus, Joan saves $520 ($19,043 – $18,523) by using the alternative tax computation. ▼

CONCEPT SUMMARY 16–4

Income Layers for Alternative Tax on Capital Gain Computation

Compute tax on: Ordinary taxable income (including net short-term capital gain) using the regular tax rates.

Compute tax on: Each of the layers below using the *lower* of the alternative tax rate or the regular tax rate for that layer (or portion of a layer) of taxable income.

+   25% gain (unrecaptured § 1250 gain) portion of taxable income

+   28% mid-term capital gain

+   10% capital gain (portion of 10%/20% capital gain that is taxed at 10%; available only if ordinary taxable income plus 25% and 28% capital gain layers do not put taxpayer above the 15% bracket; 10% rate is no longer available once income including the portion of the gain taxed at 10% puts taxpayer out of the 15% rate bracket)

+   20% capital gain (remaining portion of 10%/20% capital gain)

=   Alternative tax on taxable income

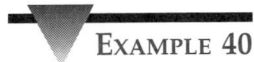

EXAMPLE 40

Assume the same facts as in Example 39 except that Joan's taxable income is $23,000. Of this amount, $12,000 is net capital gain, and $11,000 is other taxable income. Her tax liability using the alternative tax computation is $3,350 [$1,650 ($11,000 other taxable income × .15) + $1,500 ($10,000 × .15) + $200 ($2,000 × .10)]. Since her marginal rate after the other taxable income of $11,000 is taxed is still 15%, she uses the 15% regular rate rather than the 28% alternative rate on the $10,000 mid-term capital gain. At that point, $21,000 of the $23,000 taxable income has been taxed, but Joan is still in the 15% regular rate bracket. Consequently, she gets a 10% rate on her *10%/20% gain until the total of that gain plus the earlier taxed gains puts her above the 15% regular rate bracket.* Her total taxable income including the last $2,000 of gain still leaves her in the 15% regular rate bracket, so all of the $2,000 *10%/20% gain* is taxed at 10%. Joan's regular tax liability on $23,000 would be $3,450. Thus, she saves $100 ($3,450 – $3,350) by using the alternative tax computation. ▼

The alternative tax computation allows the taxpayer to receive the *lower of* the regular tax or the alternative tax on *each layer* of net capital gain or *portion of each layer* of net capital gain.

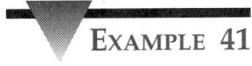

EXAMPLE 41

Assume the same facts as in Example 39, except that Joan's taxable income is $28,000. Of this amount, $12,000 is net capital gain, and $16,000 is other taxable income. Her tax liability using the alternative tax computation is $4,385 [$2,400 ($16,000 other taxable income × 15%) + $1,403 ($9,350 × .15) + $182 ($650 × .28) + $400 ($2,000 × .20)]. Since her marginal rate after the other taxable income of $16,000 is taxed is still 15%, she uses the 15% regular rate rather than the 28% on $9,350 ($25,350 – $16,000) of the $10,000 mid-term capital gain. At that point, $25,350 of the $28,000 taxable income has been taxed, and Joan is at the end of the 15% regular rate bracket. Consequently, she gets a 20% rate on her *10%/20% gain.* Joan's regular tax liability on $28,000 would be $4,545. Thus, she saves $160 ($4,545 – $4,385) by using the alternative tax computation. ▼

Concept Summary 16–4 summarizes the alternative tax computation.

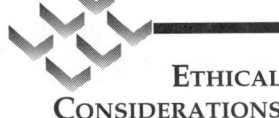

ETHICAL CONSIDERATIONS

Failure to Report a Taxable Capital Gain

Jennifer and Fred have been married for three years. Because they worked in different cities 200 miles apart, they each maintained a separate principal residence until six months ago, when Jennifer moved to Fred's house and took a job nearby. She had not owned a house in the city where she had been living. Fred had owned and lived in his house for 10 years. He made a gift of a 50 percent interest in the house to Jennifer when she moved in.

This year they sell the house and have a $350,000 gain. At the closing for the sale of the house, the title transfer agent gave Jennifer and Fred a form to sign indicating that they were eligible to exclude up to $500,000 gain on the sale since they jointly owned the home being sold. Jennifer and Fred signed the form, and as a consequence, the IRS received no notification that the sale had occurred. Jennifer thinks they should report $100,000 of capital gain (the excess over the $250,000 limit on the exclusion of gain for a single person), because she lived in the house for only six months. Fred thinks that reporting the gain would only lead to more problems because the IRS does not even know about the sale. What do you advise?

TREATMENT OF CAPITAL LOSSES

Computation of Net Capital Loss.   A **net capital loss (NCL)** results if capital losses exceed capital gains for the year. An NCL may be all long term, all short term, or part long and part short term.[28] As used here, *long term* means mid-term net capital loss and/or long-term net capital loss. The characterization of an NCL as long or short term is important in determining the capital loss deduction (discussed later in this chapter).

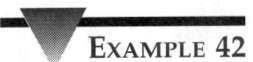

EXAMPLE 42

Three different individual taxpayers have the following capital gains and losses during the year:

Taxpayer	LTCG	LTCL	STCG	STCL	Result of Netting	Description of Result
Robert	$1,000	($2,800)	$1,000	($ 500)	($1,300)	NLTCL
Carlos	1,000	(500)	1,000	(2,800)	(1,300)	NSTCL
Troy	400	(1,200)	500	(1,200)	(1,500)	NLTCL ($800)
						NSTCL ($700)

Robert's NCL of $1,300 is all long term. Carlos's NCL of $1,300 is all short term. Troy's NCL is $1,500, $800 of which is long term and $700 of which is short term. ▼

Treatment of Net Capital Loss.   An NCL is deductible from gross income to the extent of $3,000 per tax year.[29] Capital losses exceeding the loss deduction limits carry forward indefinitely. Thus, although there may or may not be beneficial

---

[28]Section 1222(10) defines a net capital loss as the net loss after the capital loss deduction. However, that definition confuses the discussion of net capital loss. Therefore, net capital loss is used here to mean the result after netting capital gains and losses and before considering the capital loss deduction. The capital loss de-

duction is discussed under Treatment of Net Capital Loss in this chapter.

[29]§ 1211(b)(1). Married persons filing separate returns are limited to a $1,500 deduction per tax year.

treatment for capital gains, there is *unfavorable* treatment for capital losses in terms of the $3,000 annual limitation on deducting NCL against ordinary income. If the NCL includes both long-term and short-term capital loss, the short-term capital loss is counted first toward the $3,000 annual limitation.

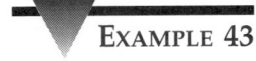

EXAMPLE 43

Burt has an NCL of $5,500, of which $2,000 is STCL and $3,500 is LTCL. Burt has a capital loss deduction of $3,000 ($2,000 of STCL and $1,000 of LTCL). He has an LTCL carryforward of $2,500 ($3,500 − $1,000). ▼

Carryovers. Taxpayers are allowed to carry over unused capital losses indefinitely. The short-term capital loss (STCL) retains its character as STCL, but the long-term capital loss (LTCL), whether it is made up of mid-term capital loss (MTCL) and/or LTCL, becomes MTCL in the year to which it is carried.

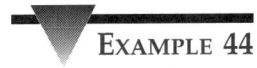

EXAMPLE 44

In 1998, Mark incurred $1,000 of STCL and $11,000 of LTCL. In 1999, Mark has a $400 LTCG.

- Mark's NCL for 1998 is $12,000. Mark deducts $3,000 ($1,000 STCL and $2,000 LTCL). He has $9,000 of MTCL carried forward to 1999.
- Mark combines the $9,000 MTCL carryforward with the $400 LTCG for 1999. He has an $8,600 NMTCL for 1999. Mark deducts $3,000 of MTCL in 1999 and carries forward $5,600 of MTCL to 2000. ▼

When a taxpayer has both a capital loss deduction and negative taxable income, a special computation of the capital loss carryover is required.[30] Specifically, the capital loss carryover is the NCL minus the lesser of:

- The capital loss deduction claimed on the return.
- The negative taxable income increased by the capital loss deduction claimed on the return and the personal and dependency exemption deduction.

Without this provision, some of the tax benefit of the capital loss deduction would be wasted when the deduction drives taxable income below zero.

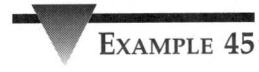

EXAMPLE 45

In 1998, Joanne has a $13,000 NCL (all long term), a $2,700 personal exemption deduction, and $4,000 negative taxable income. The negative taxable income includes a $3,000 capital loss deduction. The capital loss carryover to 1999 is $11,300 computed as follows:

- The $4,000 negative taxable income is treated as a negative number, but the capital loss deduction and personal exemption deduction are treated as positive numbers.
- The normal ceiling on the capital loss deduction is $3,000.
- However, if the $3,000 capital loss deduction and the $2,700 exemption deduction are added back to the $4,000 negative taxable income, only $1,700 of the $3,000 capital loss deduction is needed to make taxable income equal to zero.
- Therefore, this special computation results in only $1,700 of the $13,000 NCL being consumed. The MTCL carryforward is $11,300 ($13,000 − $1,700). ▼

Concept Summary 16–5 summarizes the rules for noncorporate taxpayers' treatment of capital gains and losses.

REPORTING PROCEDURES

The following discusses only 1997 tax forms because the 1998 tax forms were not available at the time of this writing.

---

[30]§ 1212(b).

CONCEPT SUMMARY 16–5

Some Possible Final Results of the Capital Gain and Loss Netting Process

Result	Maximum Tax Rate	Comments
Net short-term capital loss	—	Eligible for capital loss deduction ($3,000 maximum per year).
Net long-term capital loss (includes MTCL and/or LTCL)	—	Eligible for capital loss deduction ($3,000 maximum per year).
Net short-term capital loss *and* net long-term capital loss (includes MTCL and/or LTCL)	—	Eligible for capital loss deduction ($3,000 maximum per year). Short-term capital losses are counted first toward the deduction.
Net short-term capital gain	15–39.6%	Taxed as ordinary income.
Net long-term capital gain without 25% unrecaptured § 1250 gain	20%	Some or all of 20% gain may be taxed at 10% if other taxable income does not put taxpayer out of 15% rate bracket.
Net long-term capital gain with 25% unrecaptured § 1250 gain	20% generally; but 25% on unrecaptured § 1250 gain	Some or all of 20% gain may be taxed at 10% if other taxable income (including 25% gain) does not put taxpayer out of the 15% rate bracket; unrecaptured § 1250 gain is taxed at 25%.
Net mid-term capital gain	28%	This gain is eligible for the alternative tax calculation at a 28% rate.
Net long-term capital gain (without 25% unrecaptured § 1250 gain) *and* net mid-term capital gain	28% on net MTCG; 10%/20% on net LTCG	The portion of taxable income taxed below 28% is absorbed first by ordinary taxable income and then by 28% MTCG.
Net long-term capital gain (with 25% unrecaptured § 1250 gain) *and* net mid-term capital gain	28% on net MTCG; 25% on unrecaptured § 1250 gain; 10%/20% on remainder of net LTCG (if any)	The portion of taxable income taxed below 28% is absorbed first by ordinary taxable income and then by 28% MTCG and 25% gain; then 10%/20% eligible gain is taxed.
Net long-term capital gain (without 25% unrecaptured § 1250 gain) *and* net mid-term capital gain *and* net short-term capital gain	Ordinary tax rate on net STCG; 28% on net MTCG; 10%/20% on net LTCG	The portion of taxable income taxed below 28% is absorbed first by ordinary taxable income (including the net STCG), and then by 28% MTCG.
Net long-term capital gain (with 25% unrecaptured § 1250 gain) *and* net mid-term capital gain *and* net short-term capital gain	Ordinary tax rate on net STCG; 28% on net MTCG; 25% on unrecaptured § 1250 gain; 10%/20% on remainder of net LTCG	The portion of taxable income taxed below 28% is absorbed first by ordinary taxable income (including the net STCG) and then by 28% MTCG and 25% gain; then 10%/20% gain is taxed.

Capital gains and losses are reported on Schedule D of the 1997 Form 1040 (reproduced on pages 16–30 and 16–31). Part I of Schedule D is used to report short-term capital gains and losses. Part II of Schedule D is used to report mid-term and long-term capital gains and losses. Part III summarizes the results of Parts I and II. Part IV is the alternative tax on net capital gain. Although the form reaches the same answer as the approach to the alternative tax computation discussed in this text, this is not readily apparent from an examination of the form. Part IV lists the capital gain layers as 10 percent, 20 percent,

25 percent, and 28 percent, but actually taxes them in the same order detailed in Concept Summary 16–4. Nowhere in Part II of Schedule D is the *25% gain* mentioned, but it would be part of the gain reported on line 11, which is transferred from Form 4797. The *25% gain* appears for the first time in Schedule D as a separate number on line 25 in Part IV. Another confusing aspect of the form is that *28% gains and losses* are reported in both column f *and* column g of Part II.

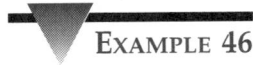

EXAMPLE 46

During 1997, Joan Rapson (Social Security number 467–37–8383) had the following sales of capital assets. (A 1997 example and form are used because the 1998 form was not available). In addition, she has other taxable income of $11,000.

Description	Acquired On	Date Sold	Sales Price	Tax Basis	Gain or Loss	Character
100 shares Blue stock	1/21/97	11/11/97	$11,000	$17,000	($ 6,000)	STCL
50 shares Green stock	9/12/96	10/12/97	36,000	20,000	16,000	MTCG
100 shares Purple stock	3/14/95	10/12/97	14,000	12,000	2,000	LTCG

Note that Joan's tax position is the same as that of Joan in Example 40. Joan has a $10,000 NMTCG ($16,000 MTCG – $6,000 STCL) and a $2,000 LTCG. Her net capital gain is $12,000 ($10,000 MTCG + $2,000 LTCG). Her $23,000 taxable income includes $11,000 of other taxable income. This example is filled in on the Schedule D on the next page. Joan's total stock sales were reported to her on Form 1099–B by her stockbroker. ▼

TAX TREATMENT OF CAPITAL GAINS AND LOSSES OF CORPORATE TAXPAYERS

6 LEARNING OBJECTIVE
Describe the tax treatment for capital gains and the detrimental tax treatment for capital losses for corporate taxpayers.

The treatment of a corporation's net capital gain or loss differs from the rules for individuals. Briefly, the differences are as follows:

- There is an NCG alternative tax rate of 35 percent.[31] However, since the maximum corporate tax rate is 35 percent, the alternative tax is not beneficial.
- Capital losses offset only capital gains. No deduction of capital losses is permitted against ordinary taxable income (whereas a $3,000 deduction is allowed to individuals).[32]
- There is a three-year carryback and a five-year carryover period for net capital losses.[33] Corporate carryovers and carrybacks are always treated as short term, regardless of their original nature.
- There are no mid-term capital gains and losses. There are only long-term capital gains and losses for capital assets held more than 12 months.

EXAMPLE 47

Sparrow Corporation has a $15,000 NLTCL for the current year and $57,000 of ordinary taxable income. Sparrow may not offset the $15,000 NLTCL against its ordinary income by taking a capital loss deduction. The $15,000 NLTCL becomes a $15,000 STCL for carryback

---

[31]§ 1201.
[32]§ 1211(a).

[33]§ 1212(a)(1).

SCHEDULE D
(Form 1040)
Department of the Treasury
Internal Revenue Service   (99)

Capital Gains and Losses

▶ Attach to Form 1040.   ▶ See Instructions for Schedule D (Form 1040).

▶ Use Schedule D-1 for more space to list transactions for lines 1 and 8.

OMB No. 1545-0074

1997

Attachment
Sequence No. **12**

Name(s) shown on Form 1040

Joan Rapson

Your social security number

467 : 37 : 8383

Part I	Short-Term Capital Gains and Losses---Assets Held One Year or Less					
(a) Description of property (Example: 100 sh. XYZ Co.)	**(b)** Date acquired (Mo., day, yr.)	**(c)** Date sold (Mo., day, yr.)	**(d)** Sales price (see page D-3)	**(e)** Cost or other basis (see page D-4)	**(f)** GAIN or (LOSS) FOR ENTIRE YEAR. Subtract (e) from (d)	
1 *100 shares Blue stock*	*1/21/97*	*11/11/97*	*11,000*	*17,000*	(*6,000*)	

2 Enter your short-term totals, if any, from Schedule D-1, line 2 . . . .   **2**

3 **Total short-term sales price amounts.** Add column (d) of lines 1 and 2 . . .   **3** *11,000*

4 Short-term gain from Forms 2119 and 6252, and short-term gain or (loss) from Forms 4684, 6781, and 8824 . . . .   **4**

5 Net short-term gain or (loss) from partnerships, S corporations, estates, and trusts from Schedule(s) K-1 . . . .   **5**

6 Short-term capital loss carryover. Enter the amount, if any, from line 9 of your 1996 Capital Loss Carryover Worksheet . . . .   **6** ( )

7 **Net short-term capital gain or (loss).** Combine lines 1 through 6 in column (f) . . . . ▶   **7** (*6,000*)

Part II	Long-Term Capital Gains and Losses---Assets Held More Than One Year					
(a) Description of property (Example: 100 sh. XYZ Co.)	**(b)** Date acquired (Mo., day, yr.)	**(c)** Date sold (Mo., day, yr.)	**(d)** Sales price (see page D-3)	**(e)** Cost or other basis (see page D-4)	**(f)** GAIN or (LOSS) FOR ENTIRE YEAR. Subtract (e) from (d)	**(g)** 28% RATE GAIN * or (LOSS) (see instr. below)
8 *50 shares Green stock*	*9/12/96*	*10/12/97*	*36,000*	*20,000*	*16,000*	*16,000*
100 shares Purple stock	*3/14/95*	*10/12/97*	*14,000*	*12,000*	*2,000*	

9 Enter your long-term totals, if any, from Schedule D-1, line 9 . . . .   **9**

10 **Total long-term sales price amounts.** Add column (d) of lines 8 and 9 . . .   **10** *50,000*

11 Gain from Form 4797, Part I; long-term gain from Forms 2119, 2439, and 6252; and long-term gain or (loss) from Forms 4684, 6781, and 8824 . .   **11**

12 Net long-term gain or (loss) from partnerships, S corporations, estates, and trusts from Schedule(s) K-1. . . . . . .   **12**

13 Capital gain distributions **13**

14 Long-term capital loss carryover. Enter in both columns (f) and (g) the amount, if any, from line 14 of your 1996 Capital Loss Carryover Worksheet . . .   **14** ( ) ( )

15 Combine lines 8 through 14 in column (g) **15** *16,000*

16 **Net long-term capital gain or (loss).** Combine lines 8 through 14 in column (f). ▶   **16** *18,000*

***28% Rate Gain or Loss** includes all gains and losses in Part II, column (f) from sales, exchanges, or conversions (including installment payments received) **either:** • **Before** May 7, 1997, **or**
• **After** July 28, 1997, for assets held more than 1 year but **not** more than 18 months.
It also includes **ALL** "collectibles gains and losses" (as defined on page D-4).

For Paperwork Reduction Act Notice, see Form 1040 instructions.   Cat. No. 11338H   Schedule D (Form 1040) 1997

Part III Summary of Parts I and II

17 Combine lines 7 and 16. If a loss, go to line 18. If a gain, enter the gain on Form 1040, line 13 | **17** | *12,000*

Next: Complete Form 1040 through line 38. Then, go to **Part IV** to figure your tax if:
   Both lines 16 and 17 are gains, **and**
   Form 1040, line 38, is more than zero.

18 If line 17 is a loss, enter here and as a (loss) on Form 1040, line 13, the **smaller** of these losses:
   The loss on line 17; **or**
   ($3,000) or, if married filing separately, ($1,500) . . . . | **18** ( )

Next: Complete Form 1040 through line 36. Then, complete the **Capital Loss Carryover Worksheet** on page D-4 if:
   The loss on line 17 exceeds the loss on line 18, **or**
   Form 1040, line 36, is a loss.

Part IV Tax Computation Using Maximum Capital Gains Rates

19	Enter your taxable income from Form 1040, line 38		*23,000*
20	Enter the **smaller** of line 16 or line 17	**20** *12,000*	
21	If you are filing Form 4952, enter the amount from Form 4952, line 4e	**21**	
22	Subtract line 21 from line 20. If zero or less, enter -0-	**22** *12,000*	
23	Combine lines 7 and 15. If zero or less, enter -0-	**23** *10,000*	
24	Enter the **smaller** of line 15 or line 23, but not less than zero	**24** *10,000*	
25	Enter your unrecaptured section 1250 gain, if any (see page D-4)	**25** *0*	
26	Add lines 24 and 25	**26** *10,000*	
27	Subtract line 26 from line 22. If zero or less, enter -0-		*2,000*
28	Subtract line 27 from line 19. If zero or less, enter -0-		*21,000*
29	Enter the **smaller** of line 19 or $41,200 ($24,650 if single; $20,600 if married filing separately; $33,050 if head of household)		*23,000*
30	Enter the **smaller** of line 28 or line 29		*21,000*
31	Subtract line 22 from line 19. If zero or less, enter -0-		*11,000*
32	Enter the **larger** of line 30 or line 31		*21,000*
33	Figure the tax on the amount on line 32. Use the Tax Table or Tax Rate Schedules, whichever applies		*3,150*
34	Enter the amount from line 29		*23,000*
35	Enter the amount from line 28		*21,000*
36	Subtract line 35 from line 34. If zero or less, enter -0-		*2,000*
37	Multiply line 36 by 10% (.10)		*200*
38	Enter the **smaller** of line 19 or line 27		*2,000*
39	Enter the amount from line 36		*2,000*
40	Subtract line 39 from line 38. If zero or less, enter -0-		*0*
41	Multiply line 40 by 20% (.20)		*0*
42	Enter the **smaller** of line 22 or line 25		*0*
43	Add lines 22 and 32	**43** *33,000*	
44	Enter the amount from line 19	**44** *23,000*	
45	Subtract line 44 from line 43. If zero or less, enter -0-		*10,000*
46	Subtract line 45 from line 42. If zero or less, enter -0-		*0*
47	Multiply line 46 by 25% (.25)		*0*
48	Enter the amount from line 19		*23,000*
49	Add lines 32, 36, 40, and 46		*23,000*
50	Subtract line 49 from line 48		*0*
51	Multiply line 50 by 28% (.28)		*0*
52	Add lines 33, 37, 41, 47, and 51		*3,350*
53	Figure the tax on the amount on line 19. Use the Tax Table or Tax Rate Schedules, whichever applies		*3,450*
54	**Tax.** Enter the **smaller** of line 52 or line 53 here and on Form 1040, line 39		*3,350*

and carryover purposes. This amount may be offset by capital gains in the three-year carryback period or, if not absorbed there, offset by capital gains in the five-year carry-forward period. ▼

The rules applicable to corporations are discussed in greater detail in Chapter 20.

TAX PLANNING CONSIDERATIONS

7 **LEARNING OBJECTIVE**
Identify tax planning opportunities arising from the sale or exchange of capital assets.

IMPORTANCE OF CAPITAL ASSET STATUS

Why is capital asset status important? Capital asset status enables the taxpayer to be eligible for the alternative tax on net capital gain. For a taxpayer in the 28, 31, 36, or 39.6 percent regular tax bracket, a 20 percent rate is available on capital assets held longer than 18 months, and a 28 percent rate is available for capital assets held longer than 12 months. For a taxpayer in the 15 percent regular tax bracket, a 10 percent rate is available on capital assets held longer than 18 months. Thus, individuals who can receive income in the form of long-term capital gains have an advantage over taxpayers who cannot receive income in this form.

Capital asset status is also important because capital gains must be offset by capital losses. If a net capital loss results, the maximum deduction is $3,000 per year.

Consequently, capital gains and losses must be segregated from other types of gains and losses and must be reported separately on Schedule D of Form 1040.

PLANNING FOR CAPITAL ASSET STATUS

It is important to keep in mind that capital asset status often is a question of objective evidence. Thus, property that is not a capital asset to one party may qualify as a capital asset to another party.

EXAMPLE 48

Diane, a real estate dealer, transfers by gift a tract of land to Jeff, her son. The land was recorded as part of Diane's inventory (it was held for resale) and was therefore not a capital asset to her. Jeff, however, treats the land as an investment. The land is a capital asset in Jeff's hands, and any later taxable disposition of the property by him will yield a capital gain or loss. ▼

If proper planning is carried out, even a dealer may obtain long-term capital gain treatment on the sale of the type of property normally held for resale.

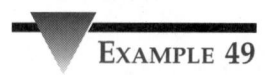
EXAMPLE 49

Jim, a real estate dealer, segregates tract A from the real estate he regularly holds for resale and designates the property as being held for investment purposes. The property is not advertised for sale and is disposed of several years later. The negotiations for the subsequent sale were initiated by the purchaser and not by Jim. Under these circumstances, it would appear that any gain or loss from the sale of tract A should be a capital gain or loss.[34] ▼

When a business is being sold, one of the major decisions usually concerns whether a portion of the sales price is for goodwill. For the seller, goodwill generally represents the disposition of a capital asset. Goodwill has no basis and represents a residual portion of the selling price that cannot be allocated reasonably to the known assets. The amount of goodwill thus represents capital gain.

---

[34]*Toledo, Peoria & Western Railroad Co.*, 35 TCM 1663, T.C.Memo. 1976–366.

From a legal perspective, the buyer may prefer that the residual portion of the purchase price be allocated to a covenant not to compete (a promise that the seller will not compete against the buyer by conducting a business similar to the one that the buyer has purchased). Both purchased goodwill and a covenant not to compete are § 197 intangibles. Thus, both must be capitalized and can be amortized over a 15-year statutory period.

To the seller, a covenant produces ordinary income. Thus, the seller would prefer that the residual portion of the selling price be allocated to goodwill—a capital asset. If the buyer does not need the legal protection provided by a covenant, the buyer is neutral regarding whether the residual amount be allocated to a covenant or to goodwill. Since the seller would receive a tax advantage from labeling the residual amount as goodwill, the buyer should factor this into the negotiation of the purchase price.

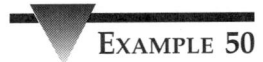

EXAMPLE 50

Marcia is buying Jack's dry cleaning proprietorship. An appraisal of the assets indicates that a reasonable purchase price would exceed the value of the known assets by $30,000. If the purchase contract does not specify the nature of the $30,000, the amount will be for goodwill, and Jack will have a long-term capital gain of $30,000. Marcia will have a 15-year amortizable $30,000 asset. If Marcia is paying the extra $30,000 to prevent Jack from conducting another dry cleaning business in the area (a covenant not to compete), Jack will have $30,000 of ordinary income. Marcia will have a $30,000 deduction over the statutory 15-year amortization period rather than over the actual life of the covenant (e.g., 5 years). ▼

EFFECT OF CAPITAL ASSET STATUS IN TRANSACTIONS OTHER THAN SALES

The nature of an asset (capital or ordinary) is important in determining the tax consequences that result when a sale or exchange occurs. It may, however, be just as significant in circumstances other than a taxable sale or exchange. When a capital asset is disposed of, the result is not always a capital gain or loss. Rather, in general, the disposition must be a sale or exchange. Collection of a debt instrument having a basis less than the face value results in a capital gain if the debt instrument is a capital asset. The collection is a sale or exchange. Sale of the debt shortly before the due date for collection will produce a capital gain.[35] If selling the debt in such circumstances could produce a capital gain but collecting could not, the consistency of what constitutes a capital gain or loss would be frustrated. Another illustration of the sale or exchange principle involves a donation of certain appreciated property to a qualified charity. Recall that in certain circumstances, the measure of the charitable contribution is fair market value when the property, if sold, would have yielded a long-term capital gain (refer to Chapter 10 and the discussion of § 170(e)).

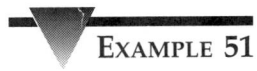

EXAMPLE 51

Sharon wants to donate a tract of unimproved land (basis of $40,000 and fair market value of $200,000) held for the required long-term holding period to State University (a qualified charitable organization). However, Sharon currently is under audit by the IRS for capital gains she reported on certain real estate transactions during an earlier tax year. Although Sharon is not a licensed real estate broker, the IRS agent conducting the audit is contending that she has achieved dealer status by virtue of the number and frequency of the real estate transactions she has conducted. Under these circumstances, Sharon would be well-advised to postpone the donation to State University until her status is clarified. If she has achieved dealer status, the unimproved land may be inventory (refer to Example 49 for another possible result), and Sharon's charitable contribution deduction would be limited to $40,000.

---

[35]§ 1271(b).

If not, and if the land is held as an investment, Sharon's deduction is $200,000 (the fair market value of the property). ▼

STOCK SALES

The following rules apply in determining the date of a stock sale:

- The date the sale is executed is the date of the sale. The execution date is the date the broker completes the transaction on the stock exchange.
- The settlement date is the date the cash or other property is paid to the seller of the stock. This date is *not* relevant in determining the date of sale.

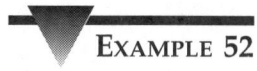
EXAMPLE 52

Lupe, a cash basis taxpayer, sells stock that results in a gain. The sale was executed on December 30, 1997. The settlement date is January 2, 1998. The date of sale is December 30, 1997 (the execution date). The holding period for the stock sold ends with the execution date. ▼

MAXIMIZING BENEFITS

Ordinary losses generally are preferable to capital losses because of the limitations imposed on the deductibility of net capital losses and the requirement that capital losses be used to offset capital gains. The taxpayer may be able to convert what would otherwise have been capital loss to ordinary loss. For example, business (but not nonbusiness) bad debts, losses from the sale or exchange of small business investment company stock, and losses from the sale or exchange of small business company stock all result in ordinary losses.[36]

Although capital losses can be carried over indefinitely, *indefinite* becomes definite when a taxpayer dies. Any loss carryovers not used by the taxpayer are permanently lost. That is, no tax benefit can be derived from the carryovers subsequent to death.[37] Therefore, the potential benefit of carrying over capital losses diminishes when dealing with older taxpayers.

It is usually beneficial to spread gains over more than one taxable year. In some cases, this can be accomplished through the installment sales method of accounting.

YEAR-END PLANNING

The following general rules can be applied for timing the recognition of capital gains and losses near the end of a taxable year:

- If the taxpayer already has recognized more than $3,000 of capital loss, sell assets to generate capital gain equal to the excess of the capital loss over $3,000.

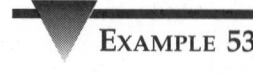
EXAMPLE 53

Kevin has already incurred a $7,000 STCL. Kevin should generate $4,000 of capital gain. The gain will offset $4,000 of the loss. The remaining loss of $3,000 can be deducted against ordinary income. ▼

- If the taxpayer already has recognized capital gain, sell assets to generate capital loss equal to the capital gain. The gain will not be taxed, and the loss will be fully *deductible* against the gain.

---

[36]§§ 166(d), 1242, and 1244. Refer to the discussion in Chapter 7.   [37]Rev.Rul. 74–175, 1974–1 C.B. 52.

• Generally, if the taxpayer has a choice between recognizing short-term capital gain, mid-term capital gain, or long-term capital gain, long-term capital gain should be recognized because it has the lowest tax rate.

KEY TERMS

Alternative tax, 16–23

Capital asset, 16–4

Capital gains, 16–2

Capital losses, 16–2

Collectibles, 16–23

Franchise, 16–13

Holding period, 16–16

Lessee, 16–15

Lessor, 16–15

Mid-term capital gain, 16–21

Net capital gain (NCG), 16–21

Net capital loss (NCL), 16–26

Options, 16–10

Original issue discount (OID), 16–10

Patent, 16–12

Sale or exchange, 16–9

Short sale, 16–17

Unrecaptured § 1250 gain, 16–21

PROBLEM MATERIALS

DISCUSSION QUESTIONS

1. Upon what three characteristics does proper classification of recognized gains and losses depend?

2. Can the sale of personal use assets generally result in capital losses?

3. What broad class of assets is excluded from the capital asset category for tax purposes, but is labeled a capital asset in accounting textbooks for the capital asset budgeting decision?

4. Todd owns the following assets. Which of them are capital assets?
   a. Ten shares of Standard Motors common stock.
   b. A copyright on a song Todd wrote.
   c. A U.S. government savings bond.
   d. A note Todd received when he loaned $100 to a friend.
   e. A very rare copy of "Your Federal Income Tax" (a U.S. government publication that Todd purchased many years ago from the U.S. Government Printing Office).
   f. Todd's personal use automobile.
   g. A letter Todd received from a former U.S. President. Todd received the letter because he had complained to the President about the President's foreign policy.

5. Why doesn't the collection of an accrual basis account receivable usually result in a gain or loss?

6. Joanne purchases song copyrights from composers. What tax issues does Joanne face in determining whether the copyrights are capital assets for her?

7. Why do court decisions play an important role in the definition of capital assets?

8. In what circumstances may real estate held for resale receive capital gain treatment?

9. Jonathan lent $2,000 to a friend who became unemployed unexpectedly. Shortly thereafter, the friend took a new job in another state. After very diligent efforts to locate the friend, Jonathan was unable to find him, and payment of the loan is now 14 months overdue. Assuming the loan is fully noncollectible, what tax issues does Jonathan face?

10. Recognition of capital gain or loss usually requires a sale or exchange of a capital asset. Define "sale" and "exchange."

11. A corporate bond is worthless due to a bankruptcy on May 10. At what date does the tax loss occur? (Assume the bond was held by an individual for investment purposes.)

12. Why does the Code require amortization of original issue discount? What is the effect of this amortization on the interest income of the taxpayer owning the bond? On the adjusted basis?

13. David purchased a one-year option on 40 acres of farmland for $25,000. David's plans for the property did not work out, so he let the option expire unexercised. What tax issues does David face in determining how to treat the $25,000?

14. If a grantee of an option exercises the option, do the grantor's proceeds from the sale of the option property increase? Why?

15. When does the transfer of a patent result in long-term capital gain? Short-term capital gain? Ordinary income?

16. What is a franchise? In practice, does the transfer of a franchise usually result in capital gain or loss treatment? Why or why not?

17. How does § 1056 restrict the allocation of sports franchise acquisition costs to player contracts?

18. For a lease cancellation to be treated as an exchange, does the lease have to be a capital asset? Why or why not?

19. A capital asset is purchased on the last day of the month. What is the first day that the holder may dispose of the asset and receive long-term treatment?

20. When is the former owner's holding period tacked on to the current owner's holding period?

21. Helen exchanges a computer used in her business for another computer that she will use in her business. The transaction qualifies as a like-kind exchange. Helen had held the computer given up in the exchange for four years. The computers are § 1231 assets. What is the holding period of the computer received in the exchange on the day of its acquisition?

22. Juan purchased corporate stock for $10,000 on April 10, 1996. On July 14, 1998, when the stock was worth $7,000, he gave it to his son, Miguel. What has to happen to the value of the property while Miguel holds it if Miguel is to tack Juan's holding period on to his own holding period?

23. John inherits stock on July 17, 1998. John's father had purchased the stock on April 10, 1997, for $12,000. The stock was worth $15,000 when the father died on December 20, 1997. The stock was worth $18,000 when John received it on July 17, 1998. When does John's holding period for the stock begin?

24. Define a short sale. Why does a seller enter into a short sale?

25. After all possible capital gain and loss netting is complete, what are the outcomes that include a net capital gain?

26. After all possible capital gain and loss netting is complete, what are the outcomes that include a net capital loss?

27. Sue has taxable income of $44,000 including $40,000 of net capital gain. Sue is single, and all of the net capital gain is *10%/20% gain*. What factors will determine whether all of Sue's net capital gain is taxed at 10%?

28. Near the end of 1998, Byron realizes that he has a net short-term capital loss of $13,000 for the year. Byron has taxable income (not including the loss) of $123,000 and is single. He owns numerous stocks that could be sold for a mid-term or long-term capital gain. What should he do before the end of 1998?

29. When a noncorporate taxpayer has both a capital loss deduction and negative taxable income, why is a special computation of the capital loss carryover required?

30. Differentiate between the capital loss carryover rules for unused capital losses of individuals and corporations.

PROBLEMS

31. Nancy had three property transactions during the year. She sold a vacation home used for personal purposes at a $21,000 loss. The home had been held for five years and had never been rented. Nancy also sold an antique clock for $3,500 that she had inherited from her grandmother. The clock was valued in Nancy's grandmother's estate at $2,000. Nancy owned the clock for only four months. Nancy sold these assets to finance her full-time occupation as a songwriter. Near the end of the year, Nancy sold one of the songs she had written two years earlier. She received cash of $38,000 and a royalty interest in revenues derived from the merchandising of the song. Nancy had no tax basis for the song. Nancy had no other income and $18,000 in deductible songwriting expenses. Assuming the year is 1998, what is Nancy's adjusted gross income?

32. Revez owns an antique shop. He buys property from estates, often at much less than the retail value of the property. Recently, Revez sold for $4,000 an antique desk for which he had paid $125. Revez had held the desk in his shop for 25 months before selling it. Revez would like the gain on the sale of the desk to be a long-term capital gain. How can he achieve that objective?

33. Gary makes a gift to Barbara of the copyright on his song, "I Love the Spartans." The song has a basis of $20,000 to Gary. Gary had owned the copyright for two years. The copyright has a fair market value of $25,000 at the date of the gift. Three years after receiving the copyright, Barbara sells it to Jim for $30,000.
    a. What is Barbara's recognized gain on the sale?
    b. What is the nature of Barbara's gain?

34. Brenda Reynolds is a dealer in securities. She has spotted a fast-rising company and would like to buy and hold its stock for investment. The stock is currently selling for $45 per share, and Brenda thinks it will climb to $93 a share within two years. Brenda's co-workers have told her that there is "no way" she can get long-term capital gain treatment when she purchases stock because she is a securities dealer. Brenda has asked you to calculate her potential gain and tell her whether her co-workers are right. Draft a letter to Brenda responding to her request. Her address is 200 Morningside Drive, Hattiesburg, MS 39406.

35. Gordon has owned a large tract of land for 15 years and subdivides it for sale. Assume Gordon meets all the requirements of § 1237. During the first year of sales, Gordon sells 20 lots for $20,000 each. His selling expenses are 7% of the sales price of each lot. Gordon has a basis of $11,000 in each lot. Compute Gordon's total gain from the sale of these lots and indicate the nature of the gain.

36. Sue has had a bad year with her investments. She lent a friend $3,700; the friend did not repay the loan when it was due, and then declared bankruptcy. The loan is totally uncollectible. Sue also was notified by her broker that the Willow corporate bonds she owned became worthless on October 13, 1998. She had purchased the bonds for $10,000 on November 10, 1997. Sue also had a $20,000 loss on the disposition of § 1244 corporate stock that she purchased several years ago. Sue is single.
    a. What are the nature and amount of Sue's losses?
    b. What is Sue's AGI for 1998 assuming she has $65,000 of ordinary gross income from sources other than those discussed above?
    c. What are the nature and amount of Sue's loss carryforwards?

37. Fred purchases $100,000 of newly issued Gold Corporation bonds for $54,000. The bonds have original issue discount of $46,000. After Fred has held the bonds for two years and has amortized $14,000 of the original issue discount, he sells the bonds for $98,000. What is Fred's adjusted basis for the bonds when he sells them, and what are the amount and nature of the gain from the disposition of the bonds?

38. Samantha is in the business of buying song copyrights from struggling songwriters, holding those copyrights, and then reselling the songs to major record companies and singers. Samantha has a four-month option to purchase a song copyright. She paid $2,000 for this option. A famous singer has heard the song and is willing to buy the option from Samantha for $10,000. Samantha thinks the song may be worth $35,000 in six months. If Samantha exercises the option, she will have to pay $20,000 for the song. Assuming Samantha is in the 36% tax bracket, which of these alternatives will give her a better after-tax cash flow?

39. Marta is looking for vacant land to buy. She would hold the land as an investment. For $10,000, she is granted an 11-month option on January 1, 1998, to buy 10 acres of vacant land for $300,000. The owner (who is holding the land for investment) paid $12,000 for the land several years ago.
    a. Does the landowner have gross income when $10,000 is received for granting the option?
    b. Does Marta have an asset when the option is granted?
    c. If the option lapses, does the landowner have a recognized gain? If so, what type of gain? Does Marta have a recognized loss? If so, what type of loss?
    d. If the option is exercised and an additional $300,000 is paid for the land, how much recognized gain does the seller have? What type of gain? What is Marta's tax basis for the property?

40. Frank owns a patent on a part that Teal Corporation wishes to use as a component in a product it manufactures. Frank had purchased the patent from the inventor before the inventor reduced the patent to practice. Frank had intended to use the patented part in his business, but found that it was not suitable. Teal is willing to pay Frank $5,000 per month plus 1% of the manufactured cost of the part. How should Frank construct the contract with Teal so that the $5,000 per month and 1% of manufactured cost are long-term capital gain?

41. Freys, Inc., sells a 12-year franchise to Reynaldo. The franchise contains many restrictions on how Reynaldo may operate his store. For instance, Reynaldo cannot use less than Grade 10 Idaho potatoes, must fry the potatoes at a constant 410 degrees, dress store personnel in Freys-approved uniforms, and have a Freys sign that meets detailed specifications on size, color, and construction. When the franchise contract is signed, Reynaldo makes a noncontingent $40,000 payment to Freys. During the same year, Reynaldo pays Freys $25,000—14% of Reynaldo's sales. How does Freys treat each of these payments? How does Reynaldo treat each of the payments?

42. Irene lives in an apartment near her college campus. Her lease runs out in July 1999, but her landlord could sell the building if he can convince all the tenants to cancel their leases and move out by the end of 1998. The landlord has offered Irene $1,000 to cancel her lease. Irene's lease began on August 1, 1998. What tax factors should Irene consider in deciding whether to take the landlord's offer?

43. On August 10, 1998, Peter received 100 shares of Brown Corporation stock as a gift from his father, John. On that date, the stock was worth $18 per share. John had paid $23 per share for the stock on July 11, 1987. On December 20, 1998, Peter sold all of the shares for $16 per share. What are the amount and the nature of Peter's gain or loss from disposition of the Brown shares?

44. Dennis sells short 100 shares of ARC stock at $20 per share on January 15, 1998. He buys 200 shares of ARC stock on April 1, 1998, at $25 per share. On May 2, 1998, he closes the short sale by delivering 100 of the shares purchased on April 1.
    a. What are the amount and nature of Dennis's loss upon closing the short sale?
    b. When does the holding period for the remaining 100 shares begin?
    c. If Dennis sells (at $27 per share) the remaining 100 shares on January 20, 1999, what will be the nature of his gain or loss?

45. Elaine Case (single with no dependents) has the following transactions in 1998:

Adjusted gross income (exclusive of capital gains and losses)	$240,000
Long-term capital gain	12,000
Mid-term capital loss	(5,000)
Short-term capital gain	19,000
Short-term capital loss	(23,000)

What is Elaine's net capital gain or loss? Draft a letter to Elaine describing how the net capital gain or loss will be treated on her tax return. Assume Elaine's income from other sources puts her in the 36% bracket. Elaine's address is 300 Ireland Avenue, Shepherdstown, WV 25443.

46. In 1998, Betty (head of household with three dependents) had an $18,000 loss from the sale of a personal residence. She also purchased from an individual inventor for $8,000 (and resold in two months for $7,000) a patent on a rubber bonding process. The patent had not yet been reduced to practice. Betty purchased the patent as an investment. Additionally, she had the following capital gains and losses from stock transactions:

Long-term capital loss	($ 3,000)
Mid-term capital loss carryover from 1997	(12,000)
Short-term capital gain	21,000
Short-term capital loss	(6,000)

What is Betty's net capital gain or loss? Draft a letter to Betty explaining the tax treatment of the sale of her personal residence. Assume Betty's income from other sources puts her in the 36% bracket. Betty's address is 1120 West Street, Ashland, OR 97520.

47. For 1998, Nikko has *negative* taxable income of $6,000. In computing his taxable income, Nikko claimed a $3,000 short-term capital loss deduction, the standard deduction, one personal exemption, and two dependency exemptions. Nikko is 67 years old and had a net short-term capital loss for the year of $15,200. How much of Nikko's $15,200 of capital loss carries over to 1999?

48. For 1998, Ahmad completes the following stock transactions:

	Date Acquired	Cost	Date Sold	Selling Price
1,000 shares ABC	1/6/98	$4,000	8/2/98	$12,000
200 shares DEF	7/1/82	8,800	9/18/98	19,400
3,500 shares GHI	5/2/98	7,000	11/2/98	8,900
5,000 shares JKL	7/15/97	9,700	12/15/98	5,000

a. What is Ahmad's includible gain or deductible loss resulting from these stock sales?
b. Assuming Ahmad's taxable income from sources other than those detailed above is $13,200, what is Ahmad's tax liability?

49. Consuela, a head of household with two dependents, has the following 1998 transactions:

Adjusted gross income (exclusive of capital gains and losses)	$125,250
Long-term capital loss	(5,000)
Mid-term capital gain *just 21% because of*	20,000
Short-term capital loss carryover	(2,000)

a. What is Consuela's net capital gain or loss?
b. What is Consuela's taxable income assuming she does not itemize?
c. What is Consuela's tax on taxable income?

50. Gold, Inc., has determined its 1998 taxable income as $45,000 before considering the results of its capital gain or loss transactions. Gold has a short-term capital loss of $4,000, a long-term capital loss of $18,000, and a short-term capital gain of $19,000. What is Gold's 1998 taxable income, and what (if any) are the amount and nature of its capital loss carryover?

51. Doria is going to purchase a sole proprietorship that June has owned for five years. They have agreed on a price for all the assets except goodwill and June's covenant not to compete against Doria. June is willing to give Doria a two-year covenant not to compete for only $1 of compensation, but would like $25,000 for the business goodwill. Doria would like to pay June $25,000 for the covenant not to compete and only $1 for the business goodwill. June is in the 36% tax bracket, and Doria is in the 31% tax bracket. Which of these approaches is better for June? For Doria?

CUMULATIVE PROBLEMS

52. Nikki Hassad is a graduate student at State University. She is single and has no dependents. During 1998, she had $5,500 wages from a full-time job she held until returning to school in August. Nikki received a $3,000 scholarship from State University and used all of the scholarship money to pay for tuition and fees. In June 1998, she won $135,000 with an instant lottery ticket and immediately invested in various stocks. The following table summarizes her stock transactions for 1998:

	Date Acquired	Cost	Date Sold	Selling Price
150 shares Clay	7/2/98	$5,000	12/11/98	$6,200
100 shares Gold	7/2/98	5,000	11/6/98	3,300
120 shares Iron	7/2/98	3,100	10/8/98	8,000
25 shares Sand	7/2/98	1,900		
100 shares Uranium	6/16/91	2,000	12/11/98	9,600

Nikki does not have many itemized deductions, so she will take the standard deduction. Her Social Security number is 393–86–4502, and she lives at 518 Marigold Lane, Okemos, MI 48864. She had $600 of Federal income tax withheld on her wages and $37,000 of Federal income tax withheld on her lottery winnings. She also made Federal estimated income tax payments of $3,500.

Compute Nikki's lowest legal tax liability for 1998. Suggested software (if available): *TurboTax.*

Draft a brief letter to Nikki describing (1) how long she must hold the Sand stock for it to become "long term," (2) what the 1999 tax consequences would be if she sold that stock for a $4,000 long-term capital gain, and (3) what would happen if she was eligible for the alternative tax on net capital gain. Also, prepare a memo for Nikki's tax file.

53. Sue Lowe lives at 1310 Meadow Lane, Lima, OH 23412 and her Social Security number is 312–55–8000. Sue is single and has a 10-year-old son, Kania. His Social Security number is 480–01–9030. Kania lives with Sue and she fully supports him. During 1997, Sue spent $2,700 on qualifying support for Kania at the Happy Daze Child Care Center, 18 Oak Lane, Lima, OH 23410. The center's identifying number is 38–6933367.

Sue owns the Lowe Enterprises sole proprietorship (38–1234567) which is located at 456 Hill Street, Lima, OH 23401. Her 1997 Form 1040 Schedule C for Lowe Enterprises shows net income of $30,000. Sue personally purchases health insurance on herself and Kania. The premiums are $3,000 per year.

Sue has an extensive stock portfolio and has prepared the following analysis:

Stock	Number of Shares	Date Purchased	Date Sold	Per Share Cost	Per Share Selling Price	Per Share Dividends
Blue	10	10/18/96	10/11/97	$80	$72	$3
Green	30	10/11/92	10/11/97	33	47	1
Purple	15	3/10/96	3/02/97	62	33	2
Yellow	100	4/11/89	8/02/97	18	46	1
Gold	35	7/12/96	10/11/97	7	12	0
White	100	10/11/96		82		1
Tan	20	4/02/96		15		0
Beige	17	4/11/89		11		0
Amber	75	3/10/94		43		2

Note: The per share cost includes commissions, and the per share selling price is net of commissions. Also, the per share dividends are the actual dividends received in 1997.

Sue had $800 of interest income from State of Ohio bonds and $600 of interest income on her Lima Savings Bank account. She also received $5,000 of alimony payments.

Sue itemizes her deductions and had the following items, which may be relevant to her return:

Item	Amount	Comment
Unreimbursed medical expenses for Sue and Kania (all for visits to doctors)	$1,786	Does not include health insurance premiums.
State income taxes paid	1,830	
Real property taxes on personal residence	3,230	
Interest paid on loans used to purchase stock held for investment	830	
Interest paid on home mortgage (Form 1098)	8,137	The loan is secured by the residence and was incurred when the home was purchased.
Charitable contributions	940	Cash paid to Sue's church.

Sue made a $6,000 Federal estimated income tax payment, does not wish any of her taxes to finance Presidential elections, has no foreign bank accounts or trusts, and wishes any refund to be applied against her 1998 taxes.

Compute Sue's net tax payable or refund due for 1997. If you use tax forms for your computations, you will need Form 1040 and Schedules A, B, C, D, and SE and Forms 2441 and 4952. Suggested software (if available): *TurboTax*.

RESEARCH PROBLEMS

*Note: Use the **RIA OnPoint System 4 Student Version CD-ROM**, which is available to accompany this text, in preparing solutions to the Research Problems. Alternatively, tax research materials found in a standard tax library can be used.*

Research Problem 1. Ali owns 100 shares of Brown Corporation stock. He purchased the stock at five different times and at five different prices per share as indicated:

Share Block	Number of Shares	Per Share Price	Purchase Date
A	10	$60	10/10/93
B	20	20	8/11/94
C	15	15	10/24/94
D	35	30	4/23/96
E	20	25	7/28/96

On April 28, 1998, Ali will sell 40 shares of Brown stock for $40 per share. All of Ali's shares are held by his stockbroker. The broker's records track when the shares were purchased. May Ali designate the shares he sells and, if so, which shares should he sell? Assume Ali wants to maximize his gain because he has a capital loss carryforward.

Research Problem 2.   Clean Corporation runs a chain of dry cleaners. Borax is used heavily in Clean's dry cleaning process and has been in short supply several times in the past. Clean Corporation buys a controlling interest in Dig Corporation—a borax mining concern. Clean's sole reason for purchasing the Dig stock is to assure Clean of a continuous supply of borax if another shortage develops. Although borax must be refined before it is usable for dry cleaning purposes, a well-established commodities market exists for trading unrefined borax for refined borax. After owning the Dig stock for several years, Clean sells the stock at a loss because Dig is in difficult financial straits. Clean no longer needs to own Dig because Clean has obtained an alternative source of borax. What is the nature of Clean's loss on the disposition of the Dig Corporation stock? Write a letter to the controller, Salvio Guitterez, that contains your advice and prepare a memo for the tax files. The mailing address of Clean Corporation is 4455 Whitman Way, San Mateo, CA 44589.

Research Problem 3.   Oak Corporation, a manufacturing company, hired several executives during 1998. The executives had homes in other cities when Oak hired them. If the executives were unable to sell those homes, they would be unable to buy replacement homes in Oak's area. Consequently, if the executives were unable to sell their homes within 30 days of listing them for sale, Oak bought the homes from the executives for 10% less than the list price. Oak immediately put the homes it purchased up for sale. Each home Oak purchased was sold at a loss. By the end of 1998, Oak did not own any homes, but had suffered a loss totaling $125,000. Oak is uncertain how to report the sale of the homes. Oak has a $32,000 short-term capital gain from stock investment transactions during 1998. What is the nature of the $125,000 loss on the sale of the homes? What is Oak's net capital gain or loss for 1998?

Partial list of research aids:
Rev.Rul. 82–204, 1982–2 CB 192.
Azar Nut Co., 91–1 USTC ¶50,257, 67 AFTR2d 91–987, 931 F.2d 314 (CA–5, 1991).

Research Problem 4.   In 1997, John has a $4,000 long-term capital loss after reduction by the $3,000 capital loss deduction. He wants to be sure that the $4,000 loss carries forward as a *mid-term* capital loss. Find the Code Section that grants this treatment.

Use the tax resources of the Internet to address the following questions. Do not restrict your search to the World Wide Web, but include a review of newsgroups and general reference materials, practitioner sites and resources, primary sources of the tax law, chat rooms and discussion groups, and other opportunities.

Research Problem 5.   Go to a newsgroup frequented by inventors and patent consultants. Answer one of the queries there relative to the tax effects of buying and selling patents, receiving royalties on patents, or otherwise investing in new technology.

Research Problem 6.   Download the text of one of the landmark Supreme Court cases defining capital asset status.

TEAM PROJECT: ARTHUR ANDERSEN TAX CHALLENGE CASES

For more information on the Arthur Andersen Tax Challenge Cases, refer to Chapter 1, page 1–37.

Information related to tax issues and problems that are discussed in this chapter may be found in the

Day and Ball case on pages 19 and 22
Fence case on pages 39, 40, 50, and 56

Read and analyze the case you have been assigned and *identify* any issues and problems that are related to material covered in this chapter. If the information provided in the case is complete, prepare answers for this part of the case at this time. If you need information that is contained in the later parts of the case, write a memo summarizing the questions or problems so you can prepare a complete answer at a later date.

17

PROPERTY TRANSACTIONS: SECTION 1231 AND RECAPTURE PROVISIONS

LEARNING OBJECTIVES

After completing Chapter 17, you should be able to:

1. Understand the rationale for and the nature and treatment of gains and losses from the disposition of business assets.

2. Distinguish § 1231 assets from ordinary assets and capital assets and calculate the § 1231 gain or loss.

3. Determine when § 1245 recapture applies and how it is computed.

4. Determine when § 1250 recapture applies and how it is computed.

5. Understand considerations common to §§ 1245 and 1250.

6. Apply the special recapture provisions for related parties and IDC and be aware of the special recapture provision for corporations.

7. Describe and apply the reporting procedures for §§ 1231, 1245, and 1250.

8. Identify tax planning opportunities associated with §§ 1231, 1245, and 1250.

Generic Motors Corporation sold machinery, office furniture, and unneeded production plants for $100 million last year. The corporation's disposition of these assets resulted in $60 million of gains and $13 million of losses. How are these gains and losses treated for tax purposes? Do any special tax rules apply? Could any of the gains and losses receive capital gain or loss treatment? This chapter answers these questions by explaining how to *classify* gains and losses from the disposition of assets that are used in the business rather than held for resale. Chapter 8 discussed how to *depreciate* such assets. Chapters 14 and 15 discussed how to determine the *adjusted basis* and the *amount* of gain or loss from their disposition.

A long-term capital gain was defined in Chapter 16 as the recognized gain from the sale or exchange of a capital asset held for the required long-term holding period.[1] As discussed in Chapter 16, there actually are two "long-term" categories—(1) mid-term and (2) long term. Mid-term capital assets are capital assets held more than 12 months but not more than 18 months and collectibles held more than 12 months. Long-term capital assets are capital assets held more than 18 months. Unless otherwise indicated, the discussion in this chapter will refer to both mid-term and long-term assets as long term. Only if the tax treatment of the mid-term and the long-term categories differs will a distinction be made.

This chapter is concerned with classification under § 1231, which applies to the sale or exchange of business properties and to certain involuntary conversions. The business properties are not capital assets because they are depreciable and/or are real property used in business or for the production of income. Section 1221(2) provides that such assets are not capital assets. Nonetheless, these business properties may be held for long periods of time and may be sold at a gain. Congress decided many years ago that such assets deserved *limited* capital gain–type treatment. Unfortunately, this limited capital gain–type treatment is very complex and difficult to understand.

Because the limited capital gain–type treatment sometimes gives too much tax advantage if assets are eligible for depreciation (or cost recovery), certain recapture

---

[1]§ 1222(3). To be eligible for any beneficial tax treatment, the holding period must be more than one year.

A DEFINITION FOR UNRECAPTURED § 1250 GAIN

The Taxpayer Relief Act of 1997 (TRA of 1997) significantly changed the taxation of long-term capital gains for individuals. Long-term capital gains may now be taxed at 10, 20, 25, or 28 percent depending on the circumstances of the taxpayer. Only a very careful reading of the legislation reveals that § 1231 assets were also involved in the change because § 1231 gains may be taxed as capital gains. On July 28, 1997, the congressional committee shaping the final legislation unexpectedly and with little forethought created the capital gain category that is taxed at 25 percent. This gain is called the "unrecaptured § 1250 gain." Congress failed to specifically define this gain and left it to the IRS to define it in the tax forms and the instructions to those forms. The unrecaptured § 1250 gain is initially a § 1231 gain. Determining *which* of the § 1231 gain is this 25% gain is quite complex, but also very important. Many real estate sales involve § 1231 gain that is ultimately reported as capital gain. Whether that gain is taxed at 10, 20, 25 or 28 percent can make a difference of millions of dollars in tax.

rules may remove the capital gain treatment when depreciation is taken. Thus, this chapter also covers the recapture provisions that tax as ordinary income certain gains that might otherwise qualify for long-term capital gain treatment.

SECTION 1231 ASSETS

RELATIONSHIP TO CAPITAL ASSETS

1 **LEARNING OBJECTIVE**
Understand the rationale for and the nature and treatment of gains and losses from the disposition of business assets.

Depreciable property and real property used in business are not capital assets.[2] Thus, the recognized gains from the disposition of such property (principally machinery, equipment, buildings, and land) would appear to be ordinary income rather than capital gain. Due to § 1231, however, *net gain* from the disposition of such property is sometimes *treated* as *long-term capital gain*. A long-term holding period requirement must be met; the disposition must generally be from a sale, exchange, or involuntary conversion; and certain recapture provisions must be satisfied for this result to occur. Section 1231 may also apply to involuntary conversions of capital assets. Since an involuntary conversion is not a sale or exchange, such a disposition would not normally result in a capital gain.

If the disposition of depreciable property and real property used in business results in a *net loss*, § 1231 *treats* the *loss* as an *ordinary loss* rather than as a capital loss. Ordinary losses are fully deductible *for* adjusted gross income (AGI). Capital losses are offset by capital gains, and, if any loss remains, the loss is deductible to the extent of $3,000 per year for individuals and currently is not deductible at all by regular corporations. It seems, therefore, that § 1231 provides the *best* of both potential results: net gain may be treated as long-term capital gain, and net loss is treated as ordinary loss.

---

[2]§ 1221(2).

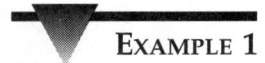

EXAMPLE 1

Roberto sells business land and building at a $5,000 gain and business equipment at a $3,000 loss. Both properties were held for the long-term holding period. Roberto's net gain is $2,000, and that net gain may (depending on various recapture rules discussed later in this chapter) be treated as a long-term capital gain under § 1231. ▼

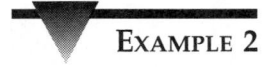

EXAMPLE 2

Samantha sells business equipment at a $10,000 loss and business land at a $2,000 gain. Both properties were held for the long-term holding period. Samantha's net loss is $8,000, and that net loss is an ordinary loss. ▼

The rules regarding § 1231 treatment do *not* apply to *all* business property. Important in this regard are the holding period requirements and the fact that the property must be either depreciable property or real estate used in business. Nor is § 1231 necessarily limited to business property. Transactions involving certain capital assets may fall into the § 1231 category. Thus, § 1231 singles out only some types of business property.

As discussed in Chapter 16, long-term capital gains receive beneficial tax treatment. Section 1231 requires netting of **§ 1231 gains and losses.** If the result is a gain, it may be treated as a long-term capital gain. The net gain is added to the "real" long-term capital gains (if any) and netted with capital losses (if any). Thus, the net § 1231 gain may eventually be eligible for beneficial capital gain treatment or help avoid the unfavorable net capital loss result. The § 1231 gain and loss netting may result in a loss. In this case, the loss is an ordinary loss and is deductible *for* AGI. Finally, § 1231 assets are treated the same as capital assets for purposes of the appreciated property charitable contribution provisions (refer to Chapter 10).

JUSTIFICATION FOR FAVORABLE TAX TREATMENT

The favorable capital gain/ordinary loss treatment sanctioned by § 1231 can be explained by examining several historical developments. Before 1938, business property had been included in the definition of capital assets. Thus, if such property was sold for a loss (not an unlikely possibility during the depression years), a capital loss resulted. If, however, the property was depreciable and could be retained for its estimated useful life, much (if not all) of its costs could be recovered in the form of depreciation. Because the allowance for depreciation was fully deductible whereas capital losses were not, the tax law favored those who did not dispose of an asset. Congress recognized this inequity when it removed business property from the capital asset classification. During the period 1938–1942, therefore, all such gains and losses were ordinary gains and losses.

With the advent of World War II, two developments in particular forced Congress to reexamine the situation regarding business assets. First, the sale of business assets at a gain was discouraged because the gain would be ordinary income. Gains were common because the war effort had inflated prices. Second, taxpayers who did not want to sell their assets often were required to because the government acquired them through condemnation. Often, as a result of the condemnation awards, taxpayers who were forced to part with their property experienced large gains and were deprived of the benefits of future depreciation deductions. Of course, the condemnations constituted involuntary conversions, so taxpayers could defer the gain by timely reinvestment in property that was "similar or related in service or use." But where was such property to be found in view of wartime restrictions and other governmental condemnations? The end result did not seem equitable: a large ordinary gain due to government action and no possibility of deferral due to government restrictions.

In recognition of these conditions, in 1942, Congress eased the tax bite on the disposition of some business property by allowing preferential capital gain treatment. Thus, the present scheme of § 1231 and the dichotomy of capital gain/ordinary loss treatment evolved from a combination of economic considerations existing in 1938 and 1942.

PROPERTY INCLUDED

2 **LEARNING OBJECTIVE**
Distinguish § 1231 assets from ordinary assets and capital assets and calculate the § 1231 gain or loss.

Section 1231 property includes the following:

- Depreciable or real property used in business or for the production of income (principally machinery and equipment, buildings, and land).
- Timber, coal, or domestic iron ore to which § 631 applies.
- Livestock held for draft, breeding, dairy, or sporting purposes.
- Unharvested crops on land used in business.
- Certain *purchased* intangible assets (such as patents and goodwill) that are eligible for amortization.

PROPERTY EXCLUDED

Section 1231 property does *not* include the following:

- Property not held for the long-term holding period. Since the benefit of § 1231 is long-term capital gain treatment, the holding period must correspond to the more-than-one-year holding period that applies to capital assets. Livestock must be held at least 12 months (24 months in some cases). Unharvested crops do not have to be held for the required long-term holding period, but the land must be held for the long-term holding period.
- Property where casualty losses exceed casualty gains for the taxable year. If a taxpayer has a net casualty loss, the individual casualty gains and losses are treated as ordinary gains and losses.
- Inventory and property held primarily for sale to customers.
- Copyrights; literary, musical, or artistic compositions, etc.; and certain U.S. government publications.
- Accounts receivable and notes receivable arising in the ordinary course of the trade or business.

SPECIAL RULES FOR CERTAIN § 1231 ASSETS

A rather diverse group of assets is included under § 1231. The following discussion summarizes the special rules for some of those assets.

Timber. A taxpayer can *elect* to treat the cutting of timber held for sale or for use in business as a sale or exchange.[3] If the taxpayer makes this election, the transaction qualifies under § 1231. The taxpayer must have owned the timber or a contract to cut it on the first day of the year and for the long-term holding period before the date the cutting takes place. The recognized § 1231 gain or loss is determined at the time the timber is cut and is equal to the difference between the timber's fair market value as of the first day of the taxable year and the adjusted basis for depletion. If a taxpayer sells the timber for more or less than the fair

---

[3]§ 631(a) and Reg. § 1.631–1.

CONCEPT SUMMARY 17–1

Section 1231 Netting Procedure

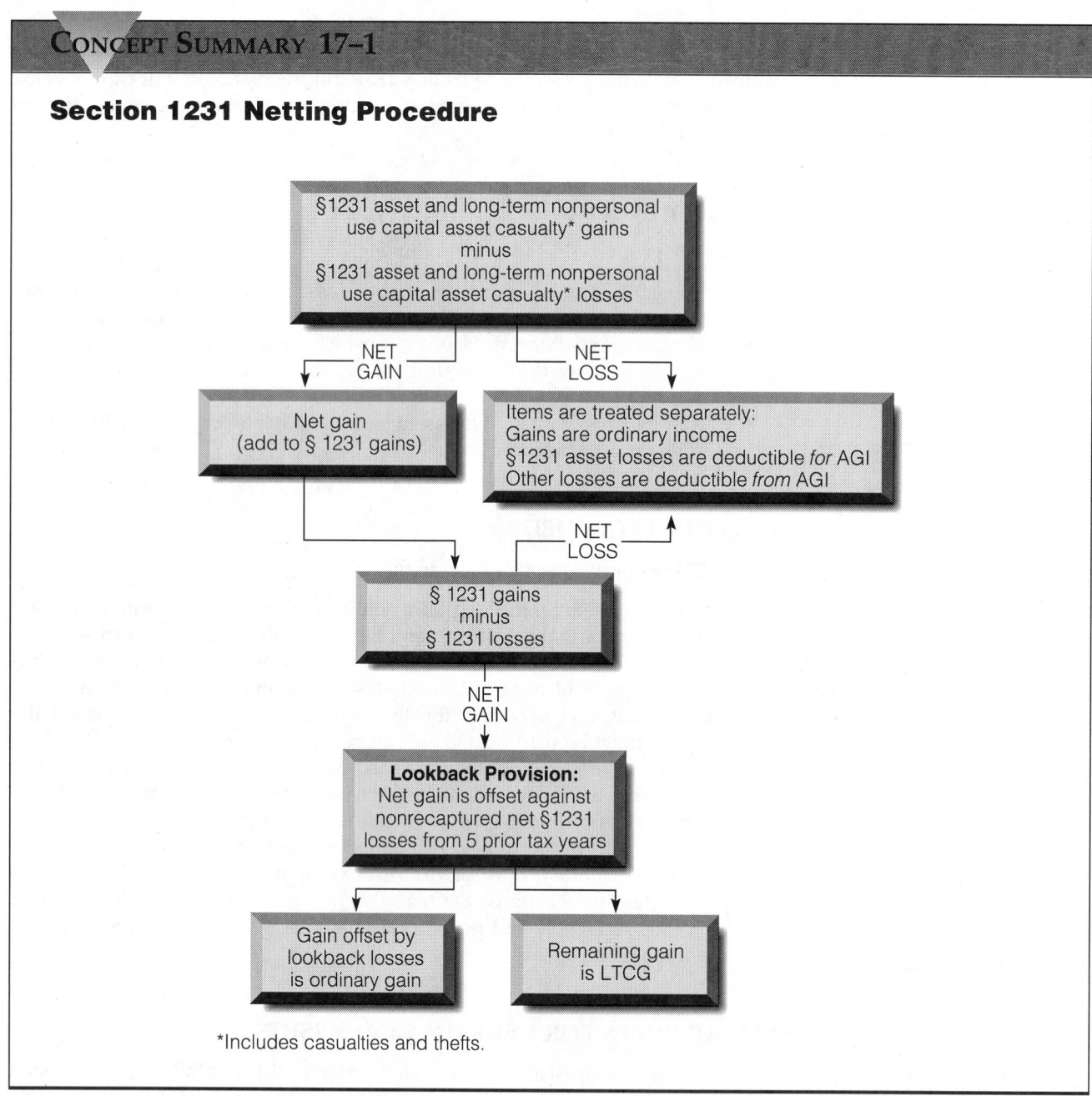

*Includes casualties and thefts.

market value as of the first day of the taxable year in which it is cut, the difference is ordinary income or loss.

This provision was enacted to provide preferential treatment relative to the natural growth value of timber, which takes a relatively long time to mature. Congress believed this favorable treatment would encourage reforestation of timber lands. If a taxpayer disposes of timber held for the long-term holding period, either by sale or under a royalty contract (where the taxpayer retains an economic interest in the property), the disposal is treated as a sale of the timber. Therefore, any gain or loss qualifies under § 1231.

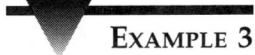

EXAMPLE 3

Several years ago, Tom purchased a tract of land with a substantial stand of trees on it. The land cost $40,000, and the timber cost $100,000. On the first day of 1998, the timber was appraised at $250,000. In August 1998, Tom cut the timber and sold it for $265,000. Tom elects to treat the cutting as a sale or exchange under § 1231. He has a $150,000 § 1231 gain ($250,000 − $100,000) and a $15,000 ordinary gain ($265,000 − $250,000).

What if the timber had been sold for $235,000? Tom would still have a $150,000 § 1231 gain, but would also have a $15,000 ordinary loss. The price for computation of § 1231 gain is the price at the beginning of the year. Any difference between that price and the sales price is ordinary gain or loss. Here, since the price declined by $15,000, Tom has an ordinary loss in that amount. ▼

Livestock.   Cattle and horses must be held 24 months or more and other livestock must be held 12 months or more to qualify under § 1231.[4] The primary reason for enacting this provision was the considerable amount of litigation over the character of livestock (whether livestock was held primarily for sale to customers [ordinary income] or for use in a trade or business [§ 1231 property]). Poultry is not livestock for purposes of § 1231.

ETHICAL
CONSIDERATIONS

Determining How Long an Asset Has Been Held

George, a dairy farmer sells a milk cow for $12,000. Normally, George does not sell his cows, but he received an offer he could not refuse for this "super milker." George is not sure exactly when the cow was born, but he does know that it is the calf of another cow he owns. Consequently, he has a zero tax basis for the cow that was sold. George owns 500 cows.

When George's tax adviser points out that the cow must have been held 24 months to be eligible for § 1231 treatment, George gets very upset. The tax adviser knows that George's records are a mess. George thinks the cow was born "within the last 27 months." After the tax adviser explains the tax benefits of the sale qualifying for § 1231 treatment, George decides the cow was more than 24 months old.

Section 1231 Assets Disposed of by Casualty or Theft.   When § 1231 assets are disposed of by casualty or theft, a special netting rule is applied. For simplicity, the term *casualty* is used to mean both casualty and theft dispositions. First, the casualty gains and losses from § 1231 assets *and* the casualty gains and losses from **long-term nonpersonal use capital assets** are determined. A nonpersonal use capital asset might be an investment painting or a baseball card collection held by a nondealer in baseball cards.

Next, the § 1231 asset casualty gains and losses and the nonpersonal use capital asset casualty gains and losses are netted together (see Concept Summary 17–1). If the result is a *net loss*, the § 1231 casualty gains and the nonpersonal use capital asset casualty gains are treated as ordinary gains, the § 1231 casualty losses are deductible *for* AGI, and the nonpersonal use capital asset casualty losses are deductible *from* AGI subject to the 2 percent-of-AGI limitation.

---

[4]Note that the holding period is "12 months or more" and not "more than 12 months."

If the result of the netting is a *net gain*, the net gain is treated as a § 1231 gain. Thus, a § 1231 asset disposed of by casualty may or may not get § 1231 treatment, depending on whether the netting process results in a gain or a loss. Also, a nonpersonal use capital asset disposed of by casualty may get § 1231 treatment or ordinary treatment, but will not get capital gain or loss treatment!

Personal use property casualty gains and losses are not subject to the § 1231 rules. If the result of netting these gains and losses is a gain, the net gain is a capital gain. If the netting results in a loss, the net loss is a deduction *from* AGI to the extent it exceeds 10 percent of AGI.

Casualties, thefts, and condemnations are *involuntary conversions*. Involuntary conversion gains may be deferred if conversion proceeds are reinvested; involuntary conversion losses are recognized currently (refer to Chapter 15) regardless of whether the conversion proceeds are reinvested. Thus, the special netting process discussed above for casualties and thefts would not include gains that are not currently recognizable because the insurance proceeds are reinvested.

The special netting process for casualties and thefts also does not include condemnation gains and losses. Consequently, a § 1231 asset disposed of by condemnation will receive § 1231 treatment. This variation between recognized casualty and condemnation gains and losses sheds considerable light on what § 1231 is all about. Section 1231 has no effect on whether or not *realized* gain or loss is recognized. Instead, § 1231 merely dictates how such *recognized* gain or loss is *classified* (ordinary, capital, or § 1231) under certain conditions.

Personal use property condemnation gains and losses are not subject to the § 1231 rules. The gains are capital gains (because personal use property is a capital asset), and the losses are nondeductible because they arise from the disposition of personal use property.

GENERAL PROCEDURE FOR § 1231 COMPUTATION

The tax treatment of § 1231 gains and losses depends on the results of a rather complex *netting* procedure. The steps in this netting procedure are as follows.

Step 1: Casualty Netting.   Net all recognized long-term gains and losses from casualties of § 1231 assets and nonpersonal use capital assets. Casualty gains result when insurance proceeds exceed the adjusted basis of the property. This casualty netting is beneficial because if there is a net gain, the gain may receive long-term capital gain treatment. If there is a net loss, it receives ordinary loss treatment.

a. If the casualty gains exceed the casualty losses, add the excess to the other § 1231 gains for the taxable year.

b. If the casualty losses exceed the casualty gains, exclude all casualty losses and gains from further § 1231 computation. If this is the case, all casualty gains are ordinary income. Section 1231 asset casualty losses are deductible *for* AGI. Other casualty losses are deductible *from* AGI.

Step 2: § 1231 Netting.   After adding any net casualty gain from Step 1a to the other § 1231 gains and losses (including recognized § 1231 asset condemnation gains and losses), net all § 1231 gains and losses.

a. If the gains exceed the losses, the net gain is offset by the "lookback" nonrecaptured § 1231 losses (see below) from the five prior tax years. To the extent of this offset, the net § 1231 gain is classified as ordinary gain. Any remaining gain is long-term capital gain.

b. If the losses exceed the gains, all gains are ordinary income. Section 1231 asset losses are deductible *for* AGI. Other casualty losses are deductible *from* AGI.

Step 3: § 1231 Lookback Provision.   The net § 1231 gain from Step 2a is offset by the nonrecaptured net § 1231 losses for the five preceding taxable years. For 1998, the lookback years are 1993, 1994, 1995, 1996, and 1997. To the extent of the nonrecaptured net § 1231 loss, the current-year net § 1231 gain is ordinary income. The *nonrecaptured* net § 1231 losses are those that have not already been used to offset net § 1231 gains. Only the net § 1231 gain exceeding this net § 1231 loss carryforward is given long-term capital gain treatment. Concept Summary 17–1 summarizes the § 1231 computational procedure. Examples 6 and 7 illustrate the **§ 1231 lookback** provision.

Examples 4 through 7 illustrate the application of the § 1231 computation procedure.

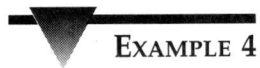

EXAMPLE 4

During 1998, Ross had $125,000 of AGI before considering the following recognized gains and losses:

Capital Gains and Losses	
Long-term capital gain	$3,000
Long-term capital loss	(400)
Short-term capital gain	1,000
Short-term capital loss	(200)

Casualties	
Theft of diamond ring (owned four months)	($800)*
Fire damage to personal residence (owned 10 years)	(400)*
Gain from insurance recovery on fire loss to business building (owned two years)	200

§ 1231 Gains and Losses from Depreciable Business Assets Held Long Term	
Asset A	$ 300
Asset B	1,100
Asset C	(500)

Gains and Losses from Sale of Depreciable Business Assets Held Short Term

Asset D	$ 200
Asset E	(300)

*As adjusted for the $100 floor on personal casualty losses.

Ross had no net § 1231 losses in tax years before 1998.

Disregarding the recapture of depreciation (discussed later in the chapter), Ross's gains and losses receive the following tax treatment:

- The diamond ring and the residence are personal use assets. Therefore, these casualties are not § 1231 transactions. The $800 (ring) plus $400 (residence) losses are potentially deductible *from* AGI. However, the total loss of $1,200 does not exceed 10% of AGI. Thus, only the business building (a § 1231 asset) casualty gain remains. The netting of the § 1231 asset and nonpersonal use capital asset casualty gains and losses contains only one item—the $200 gain from the business building. Consequently, there is a net gain and that gain is treated as a § 1231 gain (added to the § 1231 gains).
- The gains from § 1231 transactions (Assets A, B, and C and the § 1231 asset casualty gain) exceed the losses by $1,100 ($1,600 – $500). This excess is a long-term capital gain and is added to Ross's other long-term capital gains.
- Ross's net long-term capital gain is $3,700 ($3,000 + $1,100 from § 1231 transactions – $400 long-term capital loss). Ross's net short-term capital gain is $800 ($1,000 – $200). The result is capital gain net income of $4,500. The $3,700 net long-term capital gain portion is eligible for beneficial capital gain treatment, and the $800 net short-term capital gain is subject to tax as ordinary income.[5]
- Ross treats the gain and loss from Assets D and E (depreciable business assets held for less than the long-term holding period) as ordinary gain and loss.

Results of the Gains and Losses on Ross's Tax Computation

NLTCG	$ 3,700
NSTCG	800
Ordinary gain from sale of Asset D	200
Ordinary loss from sale of Asset E	(300)
AGI from other sources	125,000
AGI	$129,400

- Ross will have personal use property casualty losses of $1,200 [$800 (diamond ring) + $400 (personal residence)]. A personal use property casualty loss is deductible only to the extent it exceeds 10% of AGI. Thus, none of the $1,200 is deductible ($129,400 × 10% = $12,940). ▼

EXAMPLE 5   Assume the same facts as in Example 4, except the loss from Asset C was $1,700 instead of $500.

- The treatment of the casualty losses is the same as in Example 4.
- The losses from § 1231 transactions now exceed the gains by $100 ($1,700 – $1,600). As a result, the gains from Assets A and B and the § 1231 asset casualty gain are ordinary income, and the loss from Asset C is a deduction *for* AGI (a business loss).

---

[5]Ross's taxable income (unless the itemized deductions and the personal exemption and dependency deductions are extremely large) will put him in at least the 31% bracket. Thus, the alternative tax computation will yield a lower tax. See Example 39 in Chapter 16.

The same result can be achieved by simply treating the $100 net loss as a deduction *for* AGI.

• Capital gain net income is $3,400 ($2,600 long-term + $800 short-term). The $2,600 net long-term capital gain portion is eligible for beneficial capital gain treatment, and the $800 net short-term capital gain is subject to tax as ordinary income.

Results of the Gains and Losses on Ross's Tax Computation

NLTCG	$ 2,600
NSTCG	800
Net ordinary loss on Assets A, B, and C and § 1231 casualty gain	(100)
Ordinary gain from sale of Asset D	200
Ordinary loss from sale of Asset E	(300)
AGI from other sources	125,000
AGI	$128,200

• None of the personal use property casualty losses will be deductible since $1,200 does not exceed 10% of $128,200. ▼

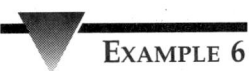
EXAMPLE 6

Assume the same facts as in Example 4, except that Ross has a $700 nonrecaptured net § 1231 loss from 1997.

• The treatment of the casualty losses is the same as in Example 4.
• The 1998 net § 1231 gain of $1,100 is treated as ordinary income to the extent of the 1997 nonrecaptured § 1231 loss of $700. The remaining $400 net § 1231 gain is a long-term capital gain and is added to Ross's other long-term capital gains.
• Ross's net long-term capital gain is $3,000 ($3,000 + $400 from § 1231 transactions − $400 long-term capital loss). Ross's net short-term capital gain is still $800 ($1,000 − $200). The result is capital gain net income of $3,800. The $3,000 net long-term capital gain portion is eligible for beneficial capital gain treatment, and the $800 net short-term capital gain is subject to tax as ordinary income.

Results of the Gains and Losses on Ross's Tax Computation

NLTCG	$ 3,000
NSTCG	800
Ordinary gain from recapture of § 1231 losses	700
Ordinary gain from sale of Asset D	200
Ordinary loss from sale of Asset E	(300)
AGI from other sources	125,000
AGI	$129,400

• None of the personal use property casualty losses will be deductible since $1,200 does not exceed 10% of $129,400. ▼

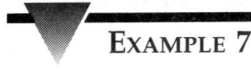
EXAMPLE 7

Assume the same facts as in Example 4, except that Ross had a net § 1231 loss of $2,700 in 1996 and a net § 1231 gain of $300 in 1997.

• The treatment of the casualty losses is the same as in Example 4.
• The 1996 net § 1231 loss of $2,700 will have carried over to 1997 and been offset against the 1997 net § 1231 gain of $300. Thus, the $300 gain will have been classified as ordinary income, and $2,400 of nonrecaptured 1996 net § 1231 loss will carry over

to 1998. The 1998 net § 1231 gain of $1,100 will be offset against this loss, resulting in $1,100 of ordinary income. The nonrecaptured net § 1231 loss of $1,300 ($2,400 – $1,100) carries over to 1999.

- Capital gain net income is $3,400 ($2,600 net long-term capital gain + $800 net short-term capital gain). The $2,600 net long-term capital gain portion is eligible for beneficial capital gain treatment, and the $800 net short-term capital gain is subject to tax as ordinary income.

Results of the Gains and Losses on Ross's Tax Computation	
NLTCG	$ 2,600
NSTCG	800
Ordinary gain from recapture of § 1231 losses	1,100
Ordinary gain from sale of Asset D	200
Ordinary loss from sale of Asset E	(300)
AGI from other sources	125,000
AGI	$129,400

- None of the personal use property casualty losses will be deductible since $1,200 does not exceed 10% of $129,400. ▼

SECTION 1245 RECAPTURE

3 **LEARNING OBJECTIVE**
Determine when § 1245 recapture applies and how it is computed.

Now that the basic rules of § 1231 have been introduced, it is time to add some complications. The Code contains two major *recapture* provisions—§§ 1245 and 1250. These provisions cause *gain* to be treated *initially* as ordinary gain. Thus, what may appear to be a § 1231 gain is ordinary gain instead. These recapture provisions may also cause a gain in a nonpersonal use casualty to be *initially* ordinary gain rather than casualty gain. Classifying gains (and losses) properly initially is important because improper initial classification may lead to incorrect mixing and matching of gains and losses. This section discusses the § 1245 recapture rules, and the next section discusses the § 1250 recapture rules.

ETHICAL CONSIDERATIONS

"Lost" Depreciation Recapture Potential

Macklin, the owner of a sole proprietorship, has used a drafting table in his business and fully depreciated its $3,700 cost. He bought a new drafting table for the business and took the old drafting table home for use as a workbench. Purchasing a similar workbench for use at home would have cost Macklin $450. Macklin does not report anything about the conversion of the old drafting table on his tax return.

Section 1245 requires taxpayers to treat all gain as ordinary gain unless the property is disposed of for more than was paid for it. This result is accomplished by requiring that all gain be treated as ordinary gain to the extent of the depreciation taken on the property disposed of. Section 1231 gain results only when the property is disposed of for more than its original cost. The excess of the sales price over the original cost is § 1231 gain. Section 1245 applies primarily to non-real estate property such as machinery, trucks, and office furniture. Section 1245 does not apply if property is disposed of at a loss. Generally, the loss will be a § 1231 loss unless the form of the disposition is a casualty.

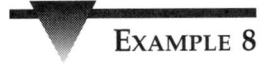
EXAMPLE 8

Alice purchased a $100,000 business machine and deducted $70,000 depreciation before selling it for $80,000. If it were not for § 1245, the $50,000 gain would be § 1231 gain ($80,000 amount realized − $30,000 adjusted basis). Section 1245 prevents this potentially favorable result by treating as ordinary income (not as § 1231 gain) any gain to the extent of depreciation taken. In this example, the entire $50,000 gain would be ordinary income. If Alice had sold the machine for $120,000, she would have a gain of $90,000 ($120,000 amount realized − $30,000 adjusted basis). The § 1245 gain would be $70,000 (equal to the depreciation taken), and the § 1231 gain would be $20,000 (equal to the excess of the sales price over the original cost). ▼

Section 1245 recapture provides, in general, that the portion of recognized gain from the sale or other disposition of § 1245 property that represents depreciation (including § 167 depreciation, § 168 cost recovery, § 179 immediate expensing, and § 197 amortization) is *recaptured* as ordinary income. Thus, in Example 8, $50,000 of the $70,000 depreciation taken is recaptured as ordinary income when the business machine is sold for $80,000. Only $50,000 is recaptured rather than $70,000 because Alice is only required to recognize § 1245 recapture ordinary gain equal to the lower of the depreciation taken or the gain recognized.

The method of depreciation (e.g., accelerated or straight-line) does not matter. All depreciation taken is potentially subject to recapture. Thus, § 1245 recapture is often referred to as *full recapture*. Any remaining gain after subtracting the amount recaptured as ordinary income will usually be § 1231 gain. The remaining gain would be casualty gain if it were disposed of in a casualty event. If the business machine in Example 8 had been disposed of by casualty and the $80,000 received had been an insurance recovery, Alice would still have a gain of $50,000, and the gain would still be recaptured by § 1245 as ordinary gain. The § 1245 recapture rules apply before there is any casualty gain. Since all the $50,000 gain is recaptured, no casualty gain arises from the casualty.

Although § 1245 applies primarily to non-real estate property, it does apply to certain real estate. Nonresidential real estate acquired after 1980 and before 1987 and for which accelerated depreciation (the statutory percentage method of the accelerated cost recovery system) is used is subject to the § 1245 recapture rules. Such property includes 15-year, 18-year, and 19-year nonresidential real estate.

The following examples illustrate the general application of § 1245.

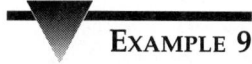

EXAMPLE 9

On January 1, 1998, Gary sold for $13,000 a machine acquired several years ago for $12,000. He had taken $10,000 of depreciation on the machine.

- The recognized gain from the sale is $11,000. This is the amount realized of $13,000 less the adjusted basis of $2,000 ($12,000 cost – $10,000 depreciation taken).
- Depreciation taken is $10,000. Therefore, since § 1245 recapture gain is the lower of depreciation taken or gain recognized, $10,000 of the $11,000 recognized gain is ordinary income, and the remaining $1,000 gain is § 1231 gain.
- The § 1231 gain of $1,000 is also equal to the excess of the sales price over the original cost of the property ($13,000 – $12,000 = $1,000 § 1231 gain). ▼

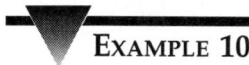

EXAMPLE 10

Assume the same facts as in the previous example, except the asset is sold for $9,000 instead of $13,000.

- The recognized gain from the sale is $7,000. This is the amount realized of $9,000 less the adjusted basis of $2,000.
- Depreciation taken is $10,000. Therefore, since the $10,000 depreciation taken exceeds the recognized gain of $7,000, the entire $7,000 recognized gain is ordinary income.
- The § 1231 gain is zero. There is no § 1231 gain because the selling price ($9,000) does not exceed the original purchase price ($12,000). ▼

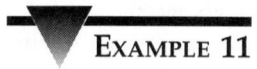

EXAMPLE 11

Assume the same facts as in Example 9, except the asset is sold for $1,500 instead of $13,000.

- The recognized loss from the sale is $500. This is the amount realized of $1,500 less the adjusted basis of $2,000.
- Since there is a loss, there is no depreciation recapture. All of the loss is § 1231 loss. ▼

If § 1245 property is disposed of in a transaction other than a sale, exchange, or involuntary conversion, the maximum amount recaptured is the excess of the property's fair market value over its adjusted basis. See the discussion under Considerations Common to §§ 1245 and 1250 later in the chapter.

SECTION 1245 PROPERTY

Generally, **§ 1245 property** includes all depreciable personal property (e.g., machinery and equipment), including livestock. Buildings and their structural components generally are not § 1245 property. The following property is *also* subject to § 1245 treatment:

- Amortizable personal property such as goodwill, patents, copyrights, and leaseholds of § 1245 property. Professional baseball and football player contracts are § 1245 property.
- Amortization of reforestation expenditures.
- Expensing of costs to remove architectural and transportation barriers that restrict the handicapped and/or elderly.

- Section 179 immediate expensing of depreciable tangible personal property costs.
- Elevators and escalators acquired before January 1, 1987.
- Certain depreciable tangible real property (other than buildings and their structural components) employed as an integral part of certain activities such as manufacturing and production. For example, a natural gas storage tank where the gas is used in the manufacturing process is § 1245 property.
- Pollution control facilities, railroad grading and tunnel bores, on-the-job training, and child care facilities on which amortization is taken.
- Single-purpose agricultural and horticultural structures and petroleum storage facilities (e.g., a greenhouse or silo).
- As noted above, 15-year, 18-year, and 19-year nonresidential real estate for which accelerated cost recovery is used is subject to the § 1245 recapture rules, although it is technically not § 1245 property. Such property would have been placed in service after 1980 and before 1987.

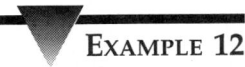

EXAMPLE 12   James acquired nonresidential real property on January 1, 1986, for $100,000. He used the statutory percentage method to compute the ACRS cost recovery. He sells the asset on January 15, 1998, for $120,000. The amount and nature of James's gain are computed as follows:

Amount realized		$120,000
Adjusted basis		
Cost	$100,000	
Less cost recovery: 1986–1997	(70,400)	
1998	(175)	
January 15, 1998, adjusted basis		(29,425)
Gain realized and recognized		$ 90,575

The gain of $90,575 is treated as ordinary income to the extent of *all* depreciation taken because the property is 19-year nonresidential real estate for which accelerated depreciation was used. Thus, James reports ordinary income of $70,575 ($70,400 + $175) and § 1231 gain of $20,000 ($90,575 – $70,575). ▼

OBSERVATIONS ON § 1245

- In most instances, the total depreciation taken will exceed the recognized gain. Therefore, the disposition of § 1245 property usually results in ordinary income rather than § 1231 gain. Thus, generally, no § 1231 gain will occur unless the § 1245 property is disposed of for more than its original cost. Refer to Examples 9 and 10.
- Recapture applies to the total amount of depreciation allowed or allowable regardless of the depreciation method used.
- Recapture applies regardless of the holding period of the property. Of course, the entire recognized gain would be ordinary income if the property were held for less than the long-term holding period because § 1231 would not apply.
- Section 1245 does not apply to losses, which receive § 1231 treatment.
- Gains from the disposition of § 1245 assets may also be treated as passive activity gains (see Chapter 11).

SECTION 1250 RECAPTURE

4 ▼ LEARNING OBJECTIVE
Determine when § 1250 recapture applies and how it is computed.

Generally, **§ 1250 property** is depreciable real property (principally buildings and their structural components) that is not subject to § 1245.[6] Intangible real property, such as leaseholds of § 1250 property, is also included.

Section 1250 recapture is substantially less punitive than § 1245 recapture since only the amount of additional depreciation is subject to recapture. To have additional depreciation, accelerated depreciation must have been taken on the asset. Straight-line depreciation (except for property held one year or less) is not recaptured. Since real property placed in service after 1986 can only be depreciated using the straight-line method, there will be *no § 1250 depreciation recapture* on such property.

Section 1250 was enacted in 1964 for depreciable real property and has been revised many times. If straight-line depreciation is taken on the property, § 1250 does not apply. Nor does § 1250 apply if the real property is sold at a loss. The loss will generally be a § 1231 loss unless the property is disposed of by casualty.

Section 1250 as originally enacted required recapture of a percentage of the additional depreciation deducted by the taxpayer. **Additional depreciation** is the excess of accelerated depreciation actually deducted over depreciation that would have been deductible if the straight-line method had been used. Since only the additional depreciation is subject to recapture, § 1250 recapture is often referred to as *partial recapture*.

Post-1969 additional depreciation on nonresidential real property is subject to 100 percent recapture (see Example 13). Post-1969 additional depreciation on residential real property may be subject to less than 100 percent recapture (see Example 14).

If § 1250 property is disposed of in a transaction other than a sale, exchange, or involuntary conversion, the maximum amount recaptured is the excess of the property's fair market value over the adjusted basis. For example, if a corporation distributes property to its shareholders as a dividend, the property will have been disposed of at a gain if the fair market value is greater than the adjusted basis. The maximum amount of § 1250 recapture will be the amount of the gain.

The following discussion describes the computational steps prescribed in § 1250 and reflected on Form 4797 (Sales of Business Property).

COMPUTING RECAPTURE ON NONRESIDENTIAL REAL PROPERTY

For § 1250 property other than residential rental property, the potential recapture is equal to the amount of additional depreciation taken since December 31, 1969. This nonresidential real property includes buildings such as offices, warehouses, factories, and stores. (The definition of and rules for residential rental housing are discussed later in the chapter.) The lower of the potential § 1250 recapture amount or the recognized gain is ordinary income. The following general rules apply:

- Post-1969 additional depreciation is depreciation taken in excess of straight-line after December 31, 1969.
- If the property is held for one year or less (usually not the case), all depreciation taken, even under the straight-line method, is additional depreciation.

---

[6]As previously discussed, in one limited circumstance, § 1245 does apply to nonresidential real estate. If the nonresidential real estate was placed in service after 1980 and before 1987 and accelerated depreciation was used, the § 1245 recapture rules rather than the § 1250 recapture rules apply.

The following procedure is used to compute recapture on nonresidential real property under § 1250:

- Determine the recognized gain from the sale or other disposition of the property.
- Determine post-1969 additional depreciation.
- The lower of the recognized gain or the post-1969 additional depreciation is ordinary income.
- If any recognized gain remains (total recognized gain less recapture), it is § 1231 gain. However, it would be casualty gain if the disposition was by casualty.

The following example shows the application of the § 1250 computational procedure.

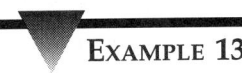

EXAMPLE 13

On January 3, 1980, Larry acquired a new building at a cost of $200,000 for use in his business. The building had an estimated useful life of 50 years and no estimated salvage value. Depreciation has been taken under the 150% declining-balance method through December 31, 1997. Pertinent information with respect to depreciation taken follows:

Year	Undepreciated Balance (Beginning of the Year)	Current Depreciation Provision	Straight-Line Depreciation	Additional Depreciation
1980–1996	$200,000	$80,835	$68,000	$12,835
1997	119,165	3,575	4,000	(425)
Total 1980–1997		$84,410	$72,000	$12,410

On January 2, 1998, Larry sold the building for $180,000. Compute the amount of his § 1250 ordinary income and § 1231 gain.

- Larry's recognized gain from the sale is $64,410. This is the difference between the $180,000 amount realized and the $115,590 adjusted basis ($200,000 cost − $84,410 depreciation taken).
- Post-1969 additional depreciation is $12,410.
- The amount of post-1969 ordinary income is $12,410. Since the post-1969 additional depreciation of $12,410 is less than the recognized gain of $64,410, the entire gain is not recaptured.
- The remaining $52,000 ($64,410 − $12,410) gain is § 1231 gain. ▼

COMPUTING RECAPTURE ON RESIDENTIAL RENTAL HOUSING

Section 1250 recapture applies to the sale or other disposition of residential rental housing. Property qualifies as *residential rental housing* only if at least 80 percent of gross rent income is rent income from dwelling units.[7] The rules are the same as for other § 1250 property, except that only the post-1975 additional depreciation may be recaptured. The post-1969 through 1975 recapture percentage is 100 percent

---

[7]§ 168(e)(2)(A). Note that there may be residential, nonrental housing (e.g., a bunkhouse on a cattle ranch). Such property is commonly regarded as "nonresidential real estate." The rules for such property were discussed in the previous section.

less one percentage point for each full month the property is held over 100 months.[8] Therefore, the additional depreciation for periods after 1975 is initially applied against the recognized gain, and such amounts may be recaptured in full as ordinary income. If any of the recognized gain is not absorbed by the recapture rules pertaining to the post-1975 period, the remaining gain is § 1231 gain.

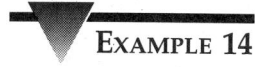

EXAMPLE 14

Assume the same facts as in the previous example, except the building is residential rental housing.

- Post-1975 ordinary income is $12,410 (post-1975 additional depreciation of $12,410).
- The remaining $52,000 ($64,410 – $12,410) gain is § 1231 gain. ▼

Under § 1250, when straight-line depreciation is used, there is no § 1250 recapture potential unless the property is disposed of in the first year of use. Before 1987, accelerated depreciation on real estate generally was available. For real property placed in service after 1986, however, only straight-line depreciation is allowed. Therefore, the § 1250 recapture rules do not apply to such property unless the property is disposed of in the first year of use.

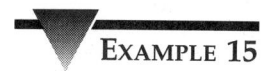

EXAMPLE 15

Sanjay acquires a residential rental building on January 1, 1997, for $300,000. He receives an offer of $450,000 for the building in 1998 and sells it on December 23, 1998.

- Sanjay takes $20,909 {($300,000 × .03485) + [$300,000 × .03636 × (11.5/12)] = $20,909} of total depreciation for 1997 and 1998, and the adjusted basis of the property is $279,091 ($300,000 – $20,909).
- Sanjay's recognized gain is $170,909 ($450,000 – $279,091).
- All of the gain is § 1231 gain. ▼

SECTION 1250 RECAPTURE SITUATIONS

The § 1250 recapture rules apply to the following property for which accelerated depreciation was used:

- Residential rental real estate acquired before 1987.
- Nonresidential real estate acquired before 1981.
- Real property used predominantly outside the United States.
- Certain government-financed or low-income housing.[9]

Concept Summary 17–2 compares and contrasts the § 1245 and § 1250 depreciation recapture rules.

UNRECAPTURED § 1250 GAIN (REAL ESTATE 25% GAIN)

This section will explain what gain is eligible for the 25 percent tax rate on **unrecaptured § 1250 gain.** This gain is used in the alternative tax computation for net capital gain discussed in Chapter 16. Unrecaptured § 1250 gain (25% gain) is some or all of the § 1231 gain that is treated as long-term capital gain and relates to a sale of depreciable real estate.

---

[8]§§ 1250(a)(1) and (2) and Reg. § 1.1250–1(d)(1)(i)(c). Since the post-1969 through 1975 recapture percentage is 100% less one percentage point for each full month the property is held over 100 months, this approach now yields a zero percentage no matter when the property was acquired in the 1969–1975 period. For instance, if a building was acquired on January 3, 1975, and sold on January 3, 1998, it would have been held 276 months. The recapture percentage is zero because 100% – (276% – 100%) is less than zero.
[9]Described in § 1250(a)(1)(B).

Comparison of § 1245 and § 1250 Depreciation Recapture

	§ 1245	§ 1250
Property affected	All depreciable personal property, but also nonresidential real property acquired after December 31, 1980, and before January 1, 1987, for which accelerated cost recovery was used. Also includes miscellaneous items such as § 179 expense and § 197 amortization of intangibles such as goodwill, patents, and copyrights.	Residential rental real property acquired after December 31, 1980, and before January 1, 1987, on which accelerated cost recovery was taken. Nonresidential real property acquired after December 31, 1969, and before January 1, 1976, on which accelerated depreciation was taken. Residential real and nonresidential real property acquired after December 31, 1975, and before January 1, 1981, on which accelerated depreciation was taken.
Depreciation recaptured	Potentially all depreciation taken. If the selling price is greater than or equal to the original cost, all depreciation is recaptured. If the selling price is between the adjusted basis and the original cost, only some depreciation is recaptured.	Additional depreciation (the excess of accelerated cost recovery over straight-line cost recovery or the excess of accelerated depreciation over straight-line depreciation).
Limit on recapture	Lower of depreciation taken or gain recognized.	Lower of additional depreciation or gain recognized.
Treatment of gain exceeding recapture gain	Usually § 1231 gain.	Usually § 1231 gain.
Treatment of loss	No depreciation recapture; loss is usually § 1231 loss.	No depreciation recapture; loss is usually § 1231 loss.

The maximum amount of this 25% gain is the depreciation taken on real property sold at a recognized gain. That maximum amount is reduced in one or more of the following ways:

- The recognized gain from disposition is less than the depreciation taken. The 25% gain is reduced to the recognized gain amount. Refer to Example 13. The depreciation taken was $84,410, but the recognized gain was only $64,410. Consequently, *all* of the recognized gain is potential 25% § 1231 gain.
- There is § 1250 depreciation recapture because the property is residential real estate acquired in 1981–1986 on which accelerated depreciation was taken. The § 1250 recapture reduces the 25% gain. Refer to Example 13 again. Of the $64,410 recognized gain, $12,410 was recaptured by § 1250 as ordinary income, leaving $52,000 of the potential 25% § 1231 gain.
- There is § 1245 depreciation recapture because the property is nonresidential real estate acquired in 1981–1986 on which accelerated depreciation was taken. No 25% § 1231 gain will be left because § 1245 will recapture all of the depreciation or the recognized gain, whichever is less. Refer to Example 12. Depreciation of $70,575 was taken, but all of it was recaptured as ordinary income by § 1245. Thus, there is no remaining potential 25% § 1231 gain. The entire $20,000 § 1231 gain in Example 12 is potential 10%/20% gain.

- § 1231 loss from disposition of other § 1231 assets held long term reduces the gain from real estate.
- § 1231 lookback losses convert some or all of the potential 25% § 1231 gain to ordinary income. According to the IRS, § 1231 lookback losses first absorb 28% § 1231 gain, then 25% § 1231 gain, and then 10%/20% § 1231 gain.

Prior to the enactment of TRA of 1997, gain surviving the § 1231 netting process could receive long-term capital gain treatment and potentially be taxed at a maximum rate of 28 percent. Now real estate gain surviving the § 1231 netting process can receive long-term capital gain treatment and potentially be taxed at a maximum rate of 28, 25, or 10/20 percent.

If the § 1231 gain arises from real property held mid-term (more than 12 months but not more than 18 months), there is no potential 25% gain. If the disposition occurs after July 28, 1997, the 25% gain can only arise from assets held for more than 18 months.

Net § 1231 Gain Limitation.   The amount of unrecaptured § 1250 gain may not exceed the net § 1231 gain that is eligible to be treated as long-term capital gain. The unrecaptured § 1250 gain is the *lesser of* the unrecaptured § 1250 gain or the net § 1231 gain that is treated as capital gain. Thus, if there is a net § 1231 gain, but it is all recaptured by the five-year § 1231 lookback loss provision, there is no surviving § 1231 gain or unrecaptured § 1250 gain. Refer to Example 6. There was $200 of § 1231 gain from the building fire that would also be potential 25% gain if at least $200 of depreciation was taken. The net § 1231 gain was $1,100 including the $200 building gain. Assume all the § 1231 assets were held more than 18 months. The $700 of § 1231 lookback losses would *first* absorb the $200 building gain, so the $400 of § 1231 gain that is treated as long-term capital gain includes no 25% gain.

Section 1250 Property for Purposes of the Unrecaptured § 1250 Gain.   TRA of 1997 did not change the definition of § 1250 property. Such property includes any real property (other than § 1245 property) that is or has been depreciable. Land is *not* § 1250 property because it is not depreciable.

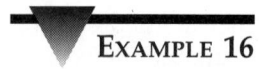

EXAMPLE 16

Bill is a single taxpayer with taxable income of $84,000 comprised of:

- $64,000 ordinary taxable income,
- $3,000 short-term capital loss,
- $15,000 long-term capital gain from sale of stock, and
- $8,000 § 1231 gain that is all unrecaptured § 1250 gain (the actual unrecaptured gain was $11,000, but net § 1231 gain is only $8,000).

Bill's net capital gain is $20,000 ($15,000 long-term capital gain + $8,000 unrecaptured § 1250 gain/net § 1231 gain − $3,000 short-term capital loss). The $3,000 short term capital loss is offset against the $8,000 unrecaptured § 1250 gain, reducing that gain to $5,000 (see the discussion in Chapter 16 concerning netting of capital losses). Bill's adjusted net capital gain is $15,000 ($20,000 net capital gain − $5,000 unrecaptured § 1250 gain). Bill's total tax (using the alternative tax calculation discussed in Chapter 16) is $18,953 [$14,703 (tax on ordinary taxable income) + $1,250 ($5,000 unrecaptured § 1250 gain × 25%) + $3,000 ($15,000 adjusted net capital gain × 20%)]. ▼

CONSIDERATIONS COMMON TO §§ 1245 AND 1250

EXCEPTIONS

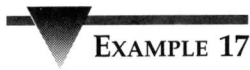

5 **LEARNING OBJECTIVE**
Understand considerations common to §§ 1245 and 1250.

Recapture under §§ 1245 and 1250 does not apply to the following transactions.

Gifts. The recapture potential carries over to the donee.[10]

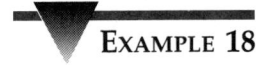

EXAMPLE 17

Wade gives his daughter, Helen, § 1245 property with an adjusted basis of $1,000. The amount of recapture potential is $700. Helen uses the property in her business and claims further depreciation of $100 before selling it for $1,900. Helen's recognized gain is $1,000 ($1,900 amount realized − $900 adjusted basis), of which $800 is recaptured as ordinary income ($100 depreciation taken by Helen + $700 recapture potential carried over from Wade). The remaining gain of $200 is § 1231 gain. Even if Helen used the property for personal purposes, the $700 recapture potential would still be carried over. ▼

Death. Although not a very attractive tax planning approach, death eliminates all recapture potential.[11] In other words, any recapture potential does not carry over from a decedent to an estate or heir.

EXAMPLE 18

Assume the same facts as in Example 17, except Helen receives the property as a result of Wade's death. The $700 recapture potential from Wade is extinguished. Helen has a basis for the property equal to the property's fair market value (assume $1,700) at Wade's death. She will have a $300 gain when the property is sold because the selling price ($1,900) exceeds the property's adjusted basis of $1,600 ($1,700 original basis to Helen − $1,000 depreciation) by $300. Because of § 1245, $100 is ordinary income. The remaining gain of $200 is § 1231 gain. ▼

Charitable Transfers. The recapture potential reduces the amount of the charitable contribution deduction under § 170.[12]

EXAMPLE 19

Kanisha donates to her church § 1245 property with a fair market value of $10,000 and an adjusted basis of $7,000. Assume that the amount of recapture potential is $2,000 (the amount of recapture that would occur if the property were sold). Her charitable contribution deduction (subject to the limitations discussed in Chapter 10) is $8,000 ($10,000 fair market value − $2,000 recapture potential). ▼

Certain Nontaxable Transactions. These are transactions in which the transferor's adjusted basis of property carries over to the transferee.[13] The recapture potential also carries over to the transferee.[14] Included in this category are transfers of property pursuant to the following:

- Nontaxable incorporations under § 351.
- Certain liquidations of subsidiary companies under § 332.
- Nontaxable contributions to a partnership under § 721.
- Nontaxable reorganizations.

---

[10]§§ 1245(b)(1) and 1250(d)(1) and Reg. §§ 1.1245–4(a)(1) and 1.1250–3(a)(1).

[11]§§ 1245(b)(2) and 1250(d)(2).

[12]§ 170(e)(1)(A) and Reg. § 1.170A–4(b)(1). In certain circumstances, § 1231 gain also reduces the amount of the charitable contribution. See § 170(e)(1)(B).

[13]§§ 1245(b)(3) and 1250(d)(3) and Reg. §§ 1.1245–4(c) and 1.1250–3(c).

[14]Reg. §§ 1.1245–2(a)(4) and –2(c)(2) and 1.1250–2(d)(1) and (3) and –3(c)(3).

Gain may be recognized in these transactions if boot is received. If gain is recognized, it is treated as ordinary income to the extent of the recapture potential or recognized gain, whichever is lower.[15]

Like-Kind Exchanges (§ 1031) and Involuntary Conversions (§ 1033). Realized gain will be recognized to the extent of boot received under § 1031. Realized gain also will be recognized to the extent the proceeds from an involuntary conversion are not reinvested in similar property under § 1033. Such recognized gain is subject to recapture as ordinary income under §§ 1245 and 1250. The remaining recapture potential, if any, carries over to the property received in the exchange. Realized losses are not recognized in like-kind exchanges, but are recognized in involuntary conversions (see Chapter 15).

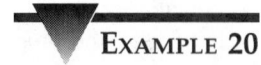

EXAMPLE 20

Anita exchanges § 1245 property with an adjusted basis of $300 for § 1245 property with a fair market value of $6,000. The exchange qualifies as a like-kind exchange under § 1031. Anita also receives $1,000 cash (boot). Her realized gain is $6,700 ($7,000 amount realized – $300 adjusted basis of property). Assuming the recapture potential is $7,500, Anita recognizes § 1245 gain of $1,000 because she received boot of $1,000. The remaining recapture potential of $6,500 carries over to the like-kind property received. ▼

OTHER APPLICATIONS

Sections 1245 and 1250 apply notwithstanding any other provisions in the Code.[16] That is, the recapture rules under these Sections *override* all other Sections. Special applications include installment sales and property dividends.

Installment Sales. Recapture gain is recognized in the year of the sale regardless of whether gain is otherwise recognized under the installment method.[17] All gain is ordinary income until the recapture potential is fully absorbed. Nonrecapture (§ 1231) gain is recognized under the installment method as cash is received.

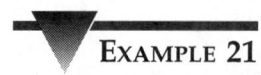

EXAMPLE 21

Seth sells § 1245 property for $20,000, to be paid in 10 annual installments of $2,000 each plus interest at 10%. Seth realizes a $6,000 gain from the sale, of which $4,000 is attributable to depreciation taken. If Seth uses the installment method, he recognizes the entire $4,000 of recapture gain as ordinary income in the year of the sale. The $2,000 of nonrecapture (§ 1231) gain will be recognized at the rate of $200 per year for 10 years. ▼

Gain is also recognized on installment sales in the year of sale in an amount equal to the § 179 (immediate expensing) deductions taken with respect to the property sold.

Property Dividends. A corporation generally recognizes gain if it distributes appreciated property as a dividend. Recapture under §§ 1245 and 1250 applies to the extent of the lower of the recapture potential or the excess of the property's fair market value over the adjusted basis.[18]

---

[15]§§ 1245(b)(3) and 1250(d)(3) and Reg. §§ 1.1245–4(c) and 1.1250–3(c). Some of these special corporate problems are discussed in Chapter 20. Partnership contributions are also discussed in Chapter 20.

[16]§§ 1245(d) and 1250(i).

[17]§ 453(i). The installment method of reporting gains on the sale of property is discussed in Chapter 18.

[18]§ 311(b) and Reg. §§ 1.1245–1(c) and –6(b) and 1.1250–1(a)(4), –1(b)(4), and –1(c)(2).

CONCEPT SUMMARY 17–3

Depreciation Recapture and § 1231 Netting Procedure

```
┌─────────────────┐                    ┌────────────────────────┐          ┌──────────────────┐
│ §1231 asset and │                    │ §1231 asset and long-term │        │ §1231 asset and  │
│ long-term       │   Remaining Gain   │ nonpersonal use capital │          │ long-term        │
│ nonpersonal     │ ─────────────────▶ │ asset casualty* gains   │ ◀────── │ nonpersonal      │
│ use capital asset│                   │ minus                   │          │ use capital asset│
│ casualty gains  │                    │ §1231 asset and long-term │        │ casualty losses  │
└─────────────────┘                    │ nonpersonal use capital │          └──────────────────┘
        │                               │ asset casualty* losses  │
   Depreciation                         └────────────────────────┘
   Recapture                              NET GAIN      NET LOSS
        ▼                                    │             │
┌─────────────────┐          ┌────────────────────────┐   ┌──────────────────────────────────┐
│ Ordinary        │          │ Net gain               │   │ Items are treated separately:      │
│ income          │          │ (add to § 1231 gains)  │   │ Gains are ordinary income          │
└─────────────────┘          └────────────────────────┘   │ §1231 asset losses are deductible  │
        ▲                               │                  │   for AGI                          │
   Depreciation                    NET GAIN    NET LOSS    │ Other losses are deductible from   │
   Recapture                            │         │        │   AGI                              │
        │                               │         │        └──────────────────────────────────┘
┌─────────────────┐   Remaining Gain ┌────────────────────────┐          ┌──────────────────┐
│ § 1231 assets   │ ───────────────▶ │ § 1231 gains           │ ◀─────── │ § 1231 assets    │
│ sold at a gain  │                  │ minus                  │          │ sold at a loss   │
└─────────────────┘                  │ § 1231 losses          │          └──────────────────┘
                                      └────────────────────────┘
                                            NET GAIN
                                               │
                                               ▼
                                      ┌────────────────────────┐
                                      │ Lookback Provision:     │
                                      │ Net gain is offset against │
                                      │ nonrecaptured net § 1231 │
                                      │ losses from 5 prior tax years │
                                      └────────────────────────┘
                                         │                  │
                              ┌──────────────────┐  ┌──────────────────┐
                              │ Gain offset by   │  │ Remaining gain   │
                              │ lookback losses  │  │ is LTCG          │
                              │ is ordinary gain │  └──────────────────┘
                              └──────────────────┘
```

*Includes casualties and thefts.

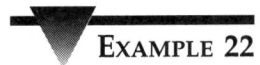

EXAMPLE 22

Emerald Corporation distributes § 1245 property as a dividend to its shareholders. The amount of the recapture potential is $300, and the excess of the property's fair market value over the adjusted basis is $800. Emerald recognizes $300 of ordinary income and $500 of § 1231 gain. ▼

Concept Summary 17–3 integrates the depreciation recapture rules with the § 1231 netting process. It is an expanded version of Concept Summary 17–1.

SPECIAL RECAPTURE PROVISIONS

SPECIAL RECAPTURE FOR CORPORATIONS

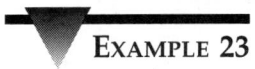

6   **LEARNING OBJECTIVE**
Apply the special recapture provisions for related parties and IDC and be aware of the special recapture provision for corporations.

Corporations selling depreciable real estate may have ordinary income in addition to that required by § 1250.[19] See the discussion of this topic in Chapter 20.

GAIN FROM SALE OF DEPRECIABLE PROPERTY BETWEEN CERTAIN RELATED PARTIES

When the sale or exchange of property, which in the hands of the *transferee* is depreciable property (principally machinery, equipment, and buildings, but not land), is between certain related parties, any gain recognized is ordinary income.[20] This provision applies to both direct and indirect sales or exchanges. A **related party** is defined as an individual and his or her controlled corporation or partnership or a taxpayer and any trust in which the taxpayer (or the taxpayer's spouse) is a beneficiary.

EXAMPLE 23

Isabella sells a personal use automobile (therefore nondepreciable) to her controlled corporation. The automobile, which was purchased two years ago, originally cost $5,000 and is sold for $7,000. The automobile is to be used in the corporation's business. If the related-party provision did not exist, Isabella would realize a $2,000 long-term capital gain. The income tax consequences would be favorable because Isabella's controlled corporation is entitled to depreciate the automobile based upon the purchase price of $7,000. Under the related-party provision, Isabella's $2,000 gain is ordinary income. ▼

INTANGIBLE DRILLING COSTS

Taxpayers may elect to either *expense or capitalize* intangible drilling and development costs for oil, gas, or geothermal properties.[21] **Intangible drilling and development costs (IDC)** include operator (one who holds a working or operating interest in any tract or parcel of land) expenditures for wages, fuel, repairs, hauling, and supplies. These expenditures must be incident to and necessary for the drilling of wells and preparation of wells for production. In most instances, taxpayers elect to expense IDC to maximize tax deductions during drilling.

Intangible drilling and development costs are subject to § 1254 recapture when the property is disposed of. The gain on the disposition of the property is subject to recapture as ordinary income.

REPORTING PROCEDURES

7   **LEARNING OBJECTIVE**
Describe and apply the reporting procedures for §§ 1231, 1245, and 1250.

Noncapital gains and losses are reported on Form 4797, Sales of Business Property. Before filling out Form 4797, however, Form 4684, Casualties and Thefts, Part B, must be completed to determine whether or not any casualties will enter into the § 1231 computation procedure. Recall that gains from § 1231 asset casualties may be recaptured by § 1245 or § 1250. These gains will not appear on Form 4684. The § 1231 gains and nonpersonal use long-term capital gains are netted against § 1231

---

[19]§ 291(a)(1).
[20]§ 1239.

[21]§ 263(c).

losses and nonpersonal use long-term capital losses on Form 4684 to determine if there is a net gain to transfer to Form 4797, Part I.

Because the 1998 tax forms were unavailable at this writing, 1997 tax forms are used in the remainder of the discussion.

Form 4797 is divided into four parts, summarized as follows:

Part	Function
I	To report regular § 1231 gains and losses (including recognized gains and losses from certain involuntary conversions [condemnations]).
II	To report ordinary gains and losses.
III	To determine the portion of the gain that is subject to recapture (e.g., §§ 1245 and 1250 gain).
IV	Computation of recapture amounts under §§ 179 and 280F when business use of depreciable property drops to 50% or less.

Generally, the best approach to completing Form 4797 is to start with Part III. Once the recapture amount has been determined, it is transferred to Part II. The balance of any gain remaining after the recapture has been accounted for is transferred from Part III to Part I. Also transferred to Part I is any net gain from certain casualties and thefts as reported on Form 4684, Part B (refer to above and Chapter 15). If the netting process in Form 4797, Part I, results in a gain, it is reduced by the nonrecaptured net § 1231 losses from prior years (line 8 of Part I). Any remaining gain is shifted to Schedule D, Capital Gains and Losses, of Form 1040. If the netting process in Part I of Form 4797 results in a loss, it goes to Part II to be treated as an ordinary loss.

The changes in the alternative tax on net capital gain for individuals, estates, and trusts affect the reporting of gains and losses from the disposition of business and rental assets. S corporations, partnerships, individuals, estates, and trusts that use Form 4797 must provide information sufficient to determine what portion of the gain surviving Form 4797, Part I (the gain that goes to Schedule D) is 28% gain, 25% gain, or 10%/20% gain.

The process explained below is based upon an analysis of Form 1040, Schedule D, and Form 4797 and their instructions. One key point to remember is that all the gains and losses that end up being treated as ordinary gains and losses (and, therefore, end up in Part II of Form 4797) are not eligible for any of the special tax rates for net capital gain. Another key point is that the gain that goes from Part I of Form 4797 to Schedule D will go to line 11 of Schedule D (long-term capital gains and losses). The entire gain from Form 4797 goes in column 11(f), but only the 28% gain portion of the gain from Form 4797 goes in column 11(g).

The 25% gain (if any) from Form 4797 is part of the Schedule D, line 11(f) gain. *Nothing on the face of Form 4797 or Schedule D identifies this gain.* Only when the alternative tax on net capital gain is computed in Part IV of Schedule D is the 25% gain portion of the Form 4797 net gain specifically mentioned on line 25.

Also remember that § 1231 assets are assets held more than 12 months. Therefore, no gain or loss is reportable on Form 4797, Part I, unless that holding period requirement is satisfied.

The 1997 Form 4797 has an additional column (column h) in Part I. The purpose of column (h) is to capture the portion of net § 1231 gain that is 28% gain.

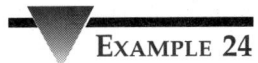

EXAMPLE 24

For 1997, Troy Williams, a single taxpayer (Social Security number 467–85–3036), had taxable income of $133,000 *including* the following recognized gains and losses (a 1997 example has been used since 1998 forms were unavailable):

Sale of Depreciable Business Assets Held Long Term

Asset A (Note 1)	$36,500
Asset B (Note 2)	29,976
Asset C (Note 3)	(880)

Sale of Depreciable Business Assets Held Short Term

Asset D (Note 4)	($ 600)

Capital Assets

Long-term gain (Note 5)	$ 3,000
Short-term loss (Note 6)	(200)

Note 1. Asset A was acquired on June 23, 1994, for $50,000. It was five-year MACRS property, and four years' cost recovery allowances totaled $38,480. The property was sold for $48,020 on August 31, 1997.

Note 2. Asset B was purchased on May 10, 1986, for $37,000. It was 19-year ACRS property. Using the statutory percentage method, cost recovery totaled $23,976. The property was sold for $43,000 on November 10, 1997. The building was residential rental property, and straight-line cost recovery for the period of ownership would have totaled $20,831.

Note 3. Asset C was purchased on December 9, 1994, for $16,000. It was five-year MACRS property, and four years' cost recovery totaled $12,314. The property was sold for $2,806 on December 30, 1997.

Note 4. Asset D was purchased for $7,000 on July 27, 1997. It was five-year MACRS property but proved unsuitable to Troy's business. Troy sold it for $6,400 on November 3, 1997.

Note 5. The LTCG resulted from the sale of 100 shares of Orange Corporation stock purchased for $10,000 on April 5, 1986. The shares were sold on October 21, 1997, for $13,223. Expenses of sale were $223.

Note 6. The STCL resulted from the sale of 50 shares of Blue Corporation stock purchased for $350 on March 14, 1997. The shares were sold for $170 on August 20, 1997. Expenses of sale were $20.

The sale of assets A and B at a gain results in the recapture of cost recovery deductions. That recapture is shown in Part III of Form 4797. Some of the gain from the sale of asset B exceeds the recapture amount and is carried from line 32 to Part I, line 6, of Form 4797. On line 2, the loss from asset C appears. Part I is where the § 1231 netting process takes place. Assume Troy Williams has no nonrecaptured net § 1231 losses from prior years. The net gain on line 7 is transferred to Schedule D, line 11. In Part II of Form 4797, the ordinary gains are accumulated. On line 13, the recapture from line 31 (Part III) is shown. On line 10, the loss from asset D is shown. The net gain on line 18 is ordinary income and is transferred to Form 1040, line 14.

Schedule D, Part I, line 1, reports the short-term capital loss from the Blue Corporation stock. Part II of Schedule D has the net § 1231 gain transferred from Form 4797 on line 11 and the Orange Corporation gain on line 8. The net capital gain is determined on line 17, Part III. The capital gain is then carried to line 13 of Form 1040.

Schedule D, Part IV, line 25, shows an unrecaptured § 1250 gain of $19,751. This gain results from the $23,976 depreciation on Asset B (less than recognized gain of $29,976) less the $3,145 § 1250 depreciation recapture and less the $880 § 1231 loss on Asset C, for a net amount of $19,951. The $25,951 net § 1231 gain transferred from line 7 of Form 4797 to Schedule D, line 11, is made up of this $19,951 unrecaptured § 1250 gain (25% gain) and

$6,000 of 10%/20% gain. Since there is a $200 net short-term capital loss and no net mid-term capital gain, the short-term loss *first* offsets the 25% gain, reducing it to $19,751. ▼

The 1997 tax forms solution for Example 24 appear on the following pages.

 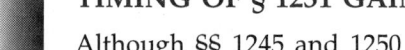

TAX PLANNING CONSIDERATIONS

8 LEARNING OBJECTIVE
Identify tax planning opportunities associated with §§ 1231, 1245, and 1250.

TIMING OF § 1231 GAIN

Although §§ 1245 and 1250 recapture much of the gain from the disposition of business property, sometimes § 1231 gain is still substantial. For instance, land held as a business asset will generate either § 1231 gain or § 1231 loss. If the taxpayer already has a capital loss for the year, the sale of land at a gain should be postponed so that the net § 1231 gain is not netted against the capital loss. The capital loss deduction will therefore be maximized for the current tax year, and the capital loss carryforward (if any) may be offset against the gain when the land is sold. If the taxpayer already has a § 1231 loss, § 1231 gains might be postponed to maximize the ordinary loss deduction this year. However, the carryforward of nonrecaptured § 1231 losses will make the § 1231 gain next year an ordinary gain.

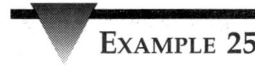
EXAMPLE 25

Mark has a $2,000 net STCL for 1998. He could sell business land held 27 months for a $3,000 § 1231 gain. He will have no other capital gains and losses or § 1231 gains and losses in 1998 or 1999. He has no nonrecaptured § 1231 losses from prior years. Mark is in the 28% tax bracket in 1998 and 1999. If he sells the land in 1998, he will have a $1,000 net LTCG ($3,000 § 1231 gain – $2,000 STCL) and will pay a tax of $200 ($1,000 × 20%). If Mark sells the land in 1999, he will have a 1998 tax savings of $560 ($2,000 capital loss deduction × 28% tax rate on ordinary income). In 1999, he will pay tax of $600 ($3,000 × 20%). By postponing the sale for a year, Mark will have the use of $760 ($560 + $200). ▼

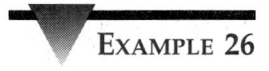
EXAMPLE 26

Beth has a $15,000 § 1231 loss in 1998. She could sell business equipment held 30 months for a $20,000 § 1231 gain and a $12,000 § 1245 gain. Beth is in the 28% tax bracket in 1998 and 1999. She has no nonrecaptured § 1231 losses from prior years. If she sells the equipment in 1998, she will have a $5,000 net § 1231 gain and $12,000 of ordinary gain. Her tax would be $4,360 [($5,000 § 1231 gain × 20%) + ($12,000 ordinary gain × 28%)].

If Beth postpones the equipment sale until 1999, she would have a 1998 ordinary loss of $15,000 and tax savings of $4,200 ($15,000 × 28%). In 1999, she would have $5,000 of § 1231 gain (the 1998 § 1231 loss carries over and recaptures $15,000 of the 1999 § 1231 gain as ordinary income) and $27,000 of ordinary gain. Her tax would be $8,560 [($5,000 § 1231 gain × 20%) + ($27,000 ordinary gain × 28%)]. By postponing the equipment sale, Beth has the use of $8,560 ($4,200 + $4,360). ▼

TIMING OF RECAPTURE

Since recapture is usually not triggered until the property is sold or disposed of, it may be possible to plan for recapture in low-bracket or loss years. If a taxpayer has net operating loss carryovers that are about to expire, the recognition of ordinary income from recapture may be advisable to absorb the loss carryovers.

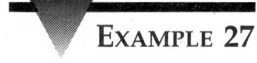
EXAMPLE 27

Ahmad has a $15,000 net operating loss carryover that will expire this year. He owns a machine that he plans to sell in the early part of next year. The expected gain of $17,000 from the sale of the machine will be recaptured as ordinary income under § 1245. Ahmad sells the machine before the end of this year and offsets $15,000 of the ordinary income against the net operating loss carryover. ▼

Form **4797**		**Sales of Business Property**	OMB No. 1545-0184

Form **4797**

Department of the Treasury
Internal Revenue Service (99)

Sales of Business Property
(Also Involuntary Conversions and Recapture Amounts
Under Sections 179 and 280F(b)(2))
► Attach to your tax return.   ► See separate instructions.

OMB No. 1545-0184

19**97**

Attachment
Sequence No. **27**

Name(s) shown on return	Identifying number
Troy Williams	*467-85-3036*

1 Enter here the gross proceeds from the sale or exchange of real estate reported to you for 1997 on Form(s) 1099-S (or a substitute statement) that you will be including on line 2, 10, or 20 . . . . | **1** | *43,000*

Part I Sales or Exchanges of Property Used in a Trade or Business and Involuntary Conversions From Other Than Casualty or Theft—Property Held More Than 1 Year

	(a) Description of property	(b) Date acquired (mo., day, yr.)	(c) Date sold (mo., day, yr.)	(d) Gross sales price	(e) Depreciation allowed or allowable since acquisition	(f) Cost or other basis, plus improvements and expense of sale	(g) GAIN or (LOSS) for entire year. Subtract (f) from the sum of (d) and (e)	(h) 28% RATE GAIN or (LOSS) * (see instr. below)
2	*Asset C*	*12/9/94*	*12/30/97*	*2,806*	*12,314*	*16,000*	(*880*)	

3 Gain, if any, from Form 4684, line 39	**3**		
4 Section 1231 gain from installment sales from Form 6252, line 26 or 37	**4**		
5 Section 1231 gain or (loss) from like-kind exchanges from Form 8824	**5**		
6 Gain, if any, from line 32, from other than casualty or theft	**6**	*26,831*	
7 Combine lines 2 through 6 in columns (g) and (h). Enter gain or (loss) here, and on the appropriate line as follows:	**7**	*25,951*	

Partnerships—Enter the gain or (loss) on Form 1065, Schedule K, lines 6a and 6b. Skip lines 8, 9, 11, and 12 below.

S corporations—Report the gain or (loss) following the instructions for Form 1120S, Schedule K, lines 5 and 6. Skip lines 8, 9, 11, and 12 below, unless line 7, column (g) is a gain and the S corporation is subject to the capital gains tax.

All others—If line 7, column (g) is zero or a loss, enter that amount on line 11 below and skip lines 8 and 9. If line 7, column (g) is a gain and you did not have any prior year section 1231 losses, or they were recaptured in an earlier year, enter the gain or (loss) in each column as a long-term capital gain or (loss) on Schedule D and skip lines 8, 9, and 12 below.

8 Nonrecaptured net section 1231 losses from prior years (see instructions) . . . . | **8** |

9 Subtract line 8 from line 7. If zero or less, enter -0-. Also enter on the appropriate line as follows (see instructions): | **9** |

S corporations—Enter only the gain in column (g) on Schedule D (Form 1120S), line 14, and skip lines 11 and 12 below.

All others—If line 9, column (g) is zero, enter the gain from line 7, column (g) on line 12 below. If line 9, column (g) is more than zero, enter the amount from line 8, column (g) on line 12 below, and enter the gain or (loss) in each column of line 9 as a long-term capital gain or (loss) on Schedule D.

* Corporations (other than S corporations) should not complete column (h). Partnerships and S corporations must complete column (h). All others must complete column (h) only if line 7, column (g), is a gain. 28% rate gain or loss includes all gains and losses in column (g) from sales, exchanges, or conversions (including installment payments received) **either (a) before** 5/7/97 **or (b) after** 7/28/97 for assets held more than 1 year but not more than 18 months.

Part II Ordinary Gains and Losses

10 Ordinary gains and losses not included on lines 11 through 17 (include property held 1 year or less):

	(a)	(b)	(c)	(d)	(e)	(f)	(g)	
	Asset D	*7/27/97*	*11/3/97*	*6,400*	*0*	*7,000*	(*600*)	

11 Loss, if any, from line 7, column (g)	**11**		
12 Gain, if any, from line 7, column (g) or amount from line 8, column (g) if applicable	**12**		
13 Gain, if any, from line 31	**13**	*39,645*	
14 Net gain or (loss) from Form 4684, lines 31 and 38a	**14**		
15 Ordinary gain from installment sales from Form 6252, line 25 or 36	**15**		
16 Ordinary gain or (loss) from like-kind exchanges from Form 8824	**16**		
17 Recapture of section 179 expense deduction for partners and S corporation shareholders from property dispositions by partnerships and S corporations (see instructions)	**17**		
18 Combine lines 10 through 17 in column (g). Enter gain or (loss) here, and on the appropriate line as follows:	**18**	*39,045*	

a For all except individual returns: Enter the gain or (loss) from line 18 on the return being filed.

b For individual returns:

(1) If the loss on line 11 includes a loss from Form 4684, line 35, column (b)(ii), enter that part of the loss here and on line 22 of Schedule A (Form 1040). Identify as from "Form 4797, line 18b(1)." See instructions . . . . | **18b(1)** |

(2) Redetermine the gain or (loss) on line 18, excluding the loss, if any, on line 18b(1). Enter here and on Form 1040, line 14 . . . . | **18b(2)** | *39,045* |

For Paperwork Reduction Act Notice, see separate instructions.   Cat. No. 13086I   Form **4797** (1997)

Form 4797 (1997) Page **2**

Part III Gain From Disposition of Property Under Sections 1245, 1250, 1252, 1254, and 1255

19	(a) Description of section 1245, 1250, 1252, 1254, or 1255 property:	(b) Date acquired (mo., day, yr.)	(c) Date sold (mo., day, yr.)
A	Asset A	6/23/94	8/31/97
B	Asset B	5/10/86	11/10/97
C			
D			

	These columns relate to the properties on lines 19A through 19D. ►		Property A	Property B	Property C	Property D
20	Gross sales price (**Note:** See line 1 before completing.)	20	48,020	43,000		
21	Cost or other basis plus expense of sale	21	50,000	37,000		
22	Depreciation (or depletion) allowed or allowable	22	38,480	23,976		
23	Adjusted basis. Subtract line 22 from line 21	23	11,520	13,024		
24	Total gain. Subtract line 23 from line 20	24	36,500	29,976		
25	**If section 1245 property:**					
a	Depreciation allowed or allowable from line 22	25a	38,480			
b	Enter the **smaller** of line 24 or 25a	25b	36,500			
26	**If section 1250 property:** If straight line depreciation was used, enter -0- on line 26g, except for a corporation subject to section 291.					
a	Additional depreciation after 1975 (see instructions)	26a		3,145		
b	Applicable percentage multiplied by the **smaller** of line 24 or line 26a (see instructions)	26b		3,145		
c	Subtract line 26a from line 24. If residential rental property or line 24 is not more than line 26a, skip lines 26d and 26e	26c		26,831		
d	Additional depreciation after 1969 and before 1976	26d		0		
e	Enter the **smaller** of line 26c or 26d	26e		0		
f	Section 291 amount (corporations only)	26f		0		
g	Add lines 26b, 26e, and 26f	26g		3,145		
27	**If section 1252 property:** Skip this section if you did not dispose of farmland or if this form is being completed for a partnership.					
a	Soil, water, and land clearing expenses	27a				
b	Line 27a multiplied by applicable percentage (see instructions)	27b				
c	Enter the **smaller** of line 24 or 27b	27c				
28	**If section 1254 property:**					
a	Intangible drilling and development costs, expenditures for development of mines and other natural deposits, and mining exploration costs (see instructions)	28a				
b	Enter the **smaller** of line 24 or 28a	28b				
29	**If section 1255 property:**					
a	Applicable percentage of payments excluded from income under section 126 (see instructions)	29a				
b	Enter the **smaller** of line 24 or 29a (see instructions)	29b				

Summary of Part III Gains. Complete property columns A through D through line 29b before going to line 30.

30	Total gains for all properties. Add property columns A through D, line 24	30	66,476
31	Add property columns A through D, lines 25b, 26g, 27c, 28b, and 29b. Enter here and on line 13	31	39,645
32	Subtract line 31 from line 30. Enter the portion from casualty or theft on Form 4684, line 33. Enter the portion from other than casualty or theft on Form 4797, line 6, column (g), and if applicable, column (h)	32	26,831

Part IV Recapture Amounts Under Sections 179 and 280F(b)(2) When Business Use Drops to 50% or Less See instructions.

			(a) Section 179	(b) Section 280F(b)(2)
33	Section 179 expense deduction or depreciation allowable in prior years	33		
34	Recomputed depreciation. See instructions	34		
35	Recapture amount. Subtract line 34 from line 33. See the instructions for where to report	35		

| SCHEDULE D (Form 1040) Department of the Treasury Internal Revenue Service (99) | Capital Gains and Losses ► Attach to Form 1040.   ► See Instructions for Schedule D (Form 1040). ► Use Schedule D-1 for more space to list transactions for lines 1 and 8. | OMB No. 1545-0074 1997 Attachment Sequence No. **12** |

Name(s) shown on Form 1040

Troy Williams

Your social security number 467 : 85 : 3036

Part I   **Short-Term Capital Gains and Losses—Assets Held One Year or Less**

(a) Description of property (Example: 100 sh. XYZ Co.)	(b) Date acquired (Mo., day, yr.)	(c) Date sold (Mo., day, yr.)	(d) Sales price (see page D-3)	(e) Cost or other basis (see page D-4)	(f) GAIN or (LOSS) FOR ENTIRE YEAR. Subtract (e) from (d)	
1 *Blue Corp.* *(50 shares)*	*3/14/97*	*8/20/97*	*170*	*370*	(*200*)	

2 Enter your short-term totals, if any, from Schedule D-1, line 2	**2**					
3 **Total short-term sales price amounts.** Add column (d) of lines 1 and 2 . . .	**3**	*170*				
4 Short-term gain from Forms 2119 and 6252, and short-term gain or (loss) from Forms 4684, 6781, and 8824	**4**					
5 Net short-term gain or (loss) from partnerships, S corporations, estates, and trusts from Schedule(s) K-1 . . .	**5**					
6 Short-term capital loss carryover. Enter the amount, if any, from line 9 of your 1996 Capital Loss Carryover Worksheet . . .	**6** (	)				
7 **Net short-term capital gain or (loss).** Combine lines 1 through 6 in column (f). . . . . ►	**7** (	*200*)				

Part II   **Long-Term Capital Gains and Losses—Assets Held More Than One Year**

(a) Description of property (Example: 100 sh. XYZ Co.)	(b) Date acquired (Mo., day, yr.)	(c) Date sold (Mo., day, yr.)	(d) Sales price (see page D-3)	(e) Cost or other basis (see page D-4)	(f) GAIN or (LOSS) FOR ENTIRE YEAR. Subtract (e) from (d)	(g) 28% RATE GAIN or (LOSS) * (see instr. below)
8 *Orange Corp.* *(100 shares)*	*4/5/86*	*10/21/97*	*13,223*	*10,223*	*3,000*	

9 Enter your long-term totals, if any, from Schedule D-1, line 9	**9**					
10 **Total long-term sales price amounts.** Add column (d) of lines 8 and 9 . . .	**10**	*13,223*				
11 Gain from Form 4797, Part I; long-term gain from Forms 2119, 2439, and 6252; and long-term gain or (loss) from Forms 4684, 6781, and 8824 . .	**11**	*25,951*				
12 Net long-term gain or (loss) from partnerships, S corporations, estates, and trusts from Schedule(s) K-1.	**12**					
13 Capital gain distributions	**13**					
14 Long-term capital loss carryover. Enter in both columns (f) and (g) the amount, if any, from line 14 of your 1996 Capital Loss Carryover Worksheet . . .	**14** (	) (	)			
15 Combine lines 8 through 14 in column (g)	**15**					
16 **Net long-term capital gain or (loss).** Combine lines 8 through 14 in column (f). . . . . ►	**16**	*28,951*				

*28% Rate Gain or Loss includes all gains and losses in Part II, column (f) from sales, exchanges, or conversions (including installment payments received) **either:** ● **Before** May 7, 1997, **or**

● **After** July 28, 1997, for assets held more than 1 year but **not** more than 18 months.

It also includes **ALL** "collectibles gains and losses" (as defined on page D-4).

For Paperwork Reduction Act Notice, see Form 1040 instructions.   Cat. No. 11338H   **Schedule D (Form 1040) 1997**

Schedule D (Form 1040) 1997   Page **2**

Part III	**Summary of Parts I and II**

17	Combine lines 7 and 16. If a loss, go to line 18. If a gain, enter the gain on Form 1040, line 13	**17**	28,751

Next: Complete Form 1040 through line 38. Then, go to **Part IV** to figure your tax if:
- Both lines 16 and 17 are gains, **and**
- Form 1040, line 38, is more than zero.

18	If line 17 is a loss, enter here and as a (loss) on Form 1040, line 13, the **smaller** of these losses:		
	• The loss on line 17; **or**		
	• ($3,000) or, if married filing separately, ($1,500)	**18**	( )

Next: Complete Form 1040 through line 36. Then, complete the **Capital Loss Carryover Worksheet** on page D-4 if:
- The loss on line 17 exceeds the loss on line 18, **or**
- Form 1040, line 36, is a loss.

Part IV	**Tax Computation Using Maximum Capital Gains Rates**

19	Enter your taxable income from Form 1040, line 38	**19**	133,000
20	Enter the **smaller** of line 16 or line 17	**20** 28,751	
21	If you are filing Form 4952, enter the amount from Form 4952, line 4e	**21**	
22	Subtract line 21 from line 20. If zero or less, enter -0-	**22** 28,751	
23	Combine lines 7 and 15. If zero or less, enter -0-	**23** 0	
24	Enter the **smaller** of line 15 or line 23, but not less than zero . . .	**24** 0	
25	Enter your unrecaptured section 1250 gain, if any (see page D-4) .	**25** 19,751	
26	Add lines 24 and 25	**26** 19,751	
27	Subtract line 26 from line 22. If zero or less, enter -0-	**27**	9,000
28	Subtract line 27 from line 19. If zero or less, enter -0-	**28**	124,000
29	Enter the **smaller** of line 19 or $41,200 ($24,650 if single; $20,600 if married filing separately; $33,050 if head of household)	**29**	24,650
30	Enter the **smaller** of line 28 or line 29	**30**	24,650
31	Subtract line 22 from line 19. If zero or less, enter -0-	**31**	104,249
32	Enter the **larger** of line 30 or line 31	**32**	104,249
33	Figure the tax on the amount on line 32. Use the Tax Table or Tax Rate Schedules, whichever applies . . . . ▶	**33**	27,320
34	Enter the amount from line 29	**34**	24,650
35	Enter the amount from line 28	**35**	124,000
36	Subtract line 35 from line 34. If zero or less, enter -0-	**36**	0
37	Multiply line 36 by 10% (.10) . . . . ▶	**37**	0
38	Enter the **smaller** of line 19 or line 27	**38**	9,000
39	Enter the amount from line 36	**39**	0
40	Subtract line 39 from line 38. If zero or less, enter -0-	**40**	9,000
41	Multiply line 40 by 20% (.20) . . . . ▶	**41**	1,800
42	Enter the **smaller** of line 22 or line 25	**42**	19,751
43	Add lines 22 and 32	**43** 133,000	
44	Enter the amount from line 19	**44** 133,000	
45	Subtract line 44 from line 43. If zero or less, enter -0-	**45**	0
46	Subtract line 45 from line 42. If zero or less, enter -0-	**46**	19,751
47	Multiply line 46 by 25% (.25) . . . . ▶	**47**	4,938
48	Enter the amount from line 19	**48**	133,000
49	Add lines 32, 36, 40, and 46	**49**	133,000
50	Subtract line 49 from line 48	**50**	0
51	Multiply line 50 by 28% (.28) . . . . ▶	**51**	0
52	Add lines 33, 37, 41, 47, and 51	**52**	34,058
53	Figure the tax on the amount on line 19. Use the Tax Table or Tax Rate Schedules, whichever applies	**53**	36,651
54	**Tax.** Enter the **smaller** of line 52 or line 53 here and on Form 1040, line 39 . . . . ▶	**54**	34,058

POSTPONING AND SHIFTING RECAPTURE

It is also possible to postpone recapture or to shift the burden of recapture to others. For example, recapture is avoided upon the disposition of a § 1231 asset if the taxpayer replaces the property by entering into a like-kind exchange. In this instance, recapture potential is merely carried over to the newly acquired property (refer to Example 20).

Recapture can be shifted to others through the gratuitous transfer of § 1245 or § 1250 property to family members. A subsequent sale of such property by the donee will trigger recapture to the donee rather than the donor (refer to Example 17). This procedure would be advisable only if the donee is in a lower income tax bracket than the donor.

AVOIDING RECAPTURE

The immediate expensing election (§ 179) is subject to § 1245 recapture. If the election is not made, the § 1245 recapture potential will accumulate more slowly (refer to Chapter 8). Since using the immediate expense deduction complicates depreciation and book accounting for the affected asset, not taking the deduction may make sense even though the time value of money might indicate it should be taken.

KEY TERMS

Additional depreciation, 17–16	Section 1231 gains and losses, 17–4	Section 1245 recapture, 17–13
Intangible drilling and development costs (IDC), 17–24	Section 1231 lookback, 17–9	Section 1250 property, 17–16
Long-term nonpersonal use capital assets, 17–7	Section 1231 property, 17–5	Section 1250 recapture, 17–16
Related party, 17–24	Section 1245 property, 17–14	Unrecaptured § 1250 gain, 17–18

PROBLEM MATERIALS

DISCUSSION QUESTIONS

1. If there is a net loss from § 1231 asset transactions, what is the character of the loss and how is it deducted?

2. What three requirements must be met for *net gain* from the disposition of § 1231 property to be treated as long-term capital gain?

3. What two developments near the start of World War II caused Congress to reexamine the tax treatment of business assets?

4. Is it possible to recognize both a gain and a loss on the sale of timber in one taxable year? How?

5. Ahmad is a farmer who is thinking about raising ostriches. Ostrich meat is very high in protein, low in calories, and low in fat. Ahmad would like to know what tax issues he would face if he decides to raise ostriches in addition to the cattle he is currently raising.

6. Aretha's 100% business use 1996 automobile was destroyed when a tree fell on it. She had a loss of $4,000 after her insurance recovery. She also sold some business land held 10 years for a gain of $3,000. What factors would influence how the automobile loss interacts with the land gain?

7. Sally lives in an area that was hit hard by a hurricane. She has correctly determined that she has a $15,000 business property long-term casualty loss and a $11,000 business property long-term casualty gain. What tax issues must Sally deal with?

8. How are personal use property condemnation gains and losses treated?

9. What treatment does a personal use property condemnation loss receive?

10. Phil has nearly completed the tax return for a new client. The client has a net § 1231 gain. Phil had not done tax returns for the client in previous years and does not have the client's returns for prior years. What tax issues do these circumstances present for Phil?

11. Some of Max's business equipment that had been held long term was stolen in a burglary. The property had been purchased for $80,000, and the insurance company paid Max $33,000. What tax issues do these circumstances present for Max?

12. A business machine held for three years is disposed of at a gain. The cost of the machine was greater than the selling price. What is the nature of the gain?

13. If a farmer buys a pig and uses MACRS, are the cost recovery deductions subject to § 1245 recapture if the pig is sold at a gain?

14. How could a taxpayer avoid having any depreciation recapture on the disposition of depreciable business equipment held more than 12 months?

15. A business machine held for several years is sold at a gain. Part of the gain is § 1245 gain, and part is § 1231 gain. There is no other § 1231 gain or loss this year, but there is a nonrecaptured § 1231 lookback loss that exceeds the current-year § 1231 gain. Describe the treatment of the gain from the disposition of the machine.

16. Differentiate between the types of property covered by §§ 1245 and 1250.

17. In 1985, a warehouse was acquired and depreciated using accelerated depreciation. In 1998, the warehouse is sold for less than was originally paid for it. What is the nature of the gain?

18. Why does § 1250 generally not apply to real estate acquired after 1986?

19. Examine Example 13 in this chapter. Why is the amount in the "additional depreciation" column negative for 1997?

20. Residential rental real estate is acquired and disposed of in 1998. There is a small gain on the disposition of the property. The gain is less than the depreciation taken on the property. What is the nature of that gain?

21. What is the definition of residential rental housing?

22. Abigail sells one § 1231 asset during the year at a gain of $45,000. The asset was depreciable real estate she had held for seven years. She wants to know what her maximum unrecaptured § 1250 gain might be.

23. Death eliminates all recapture potential. Do you agree? Why or why not?

24. What provisions of the Internal Revenue Code do the §§ 1245 and 1250 recapture rules override?

25. May an installment sale trigger § 1245 recapture even though no gain would otherwise be currently recognizable?

26. May corporations transferring real estate have depreciation recapture in addition to § 1250 recapture?

27. In general, how does the related-party ordinary income provision differ from §§ 1245 and 1250?

28. What three tax forms may be required to properly report the gains and losses discussed in Chapter 17?

29. Where in the tax forms is the §§ 1245 and 1250 depreciation recapture shown?

30. What line in the tax forms for reporting property transactions involving the sale of depreciable real estate first specifically identifies the unrecaptured § 1250 gain?

PROBLEMS

31. Sue-Jen purchased a contract to cut timber on a 100-acre tract of land in South Dakota in March 1996 for $20,000. On January 1, 1997, the timber had a fair market value of $50,000. Because of careless cutting in November 1997, when the fair market value was $55,000, the wood was sold on January 30, 1998, for $49,000.
    a. What gain (loss) was realized in 1996, 1997, and 1998? What gain (loss) was recognized in 1996, 1997, and 1998?
    b. What was the nature of the gains (losses) in (a)? What assumption must be made?
    c. Does the answer change if the timber was sold in December 1997? Why?
    d. If the timber was worth only $18,000 on January 1, 1997, was cut in November when worth $21,000, and was sold in December for $19,000, how would the answers to (a) and (b) change?

32. Bob owns a farming sole proprietorship. During the year, Bob sold a milk cow that he had owned for 13 months and a workhorse that he had owned for 56 months. The cow had an adjusted basis of $800 and was sold for $1,050. The horse had an adjusted basis of $350 and was sold for $1,000. Bob also has a $200 long-term capital loss from the sale of corporate stock. He has $55,000 of other AGI (not associated with the items above) for the year. He has $2,000 nonrecaptured § 1231 losses from the previous five years. What is the nature of the gains or losses from the disposition of the farm animals, and what is Bob's AGI for the year?

33. A painting that Kwan Lee held for investment was destroyed in a flood. The painting was insured, and Kwan had a $10,000 gain from this casualty. He also had a $7,000 loss from an uninsured antique vase that was destroyed by the flood. The vase was also held for investment. Kwan had no other property transactions during the year and has no nonrecaptured § 1231 losses from prior years. Both the painting and the vase had been held more than 18 months when the flood occurred. Compute Kwan's net gain or loss and identify how it would be treated. Also, write a letter to Kwan explaining the nature of the gain or loss. Kwan's address is 2367 Meridian Road, Hannibal Point, MO 34901.

34. Vicki has the following net § 1231 results for each of the years shown. What would be the nature of the net gains in 1997 and 1998?

Tax Year	Net § 1231 Loss	Net § 1231 Gain
1993	$16,000	
1994	13,000	
1995	22,000	
1996		$10,000
1997		20,000
1998		29,000

35. Yoshida owns two parcels of business land (§ 1231 assets). One parcel can be sold at a loss of $30,000, and the other parcel can be sold at a gain of $40,000. Yoshida has no nonrecaptured § 1231 losses from prior years. The parcels could be sold at any time because potential purchasers are abundant. Yoshida has a $25,000 short-term capital

loss carryover from a prior tax year and no capital assets that could be sold to generate long-term capital gains. Both the land parcels have been held more than 18 months. What should Yoshida do based upon these facts? (Assume tax rates are constant and ignore the present value of future cash flow.)

36. Gray Industries (a sole proprietorship) sold three § 1231 assets during 1998. Data on these property dispositions are as follows:

Asset	Cost	Acquired	Depreciation	Sold for	Sold on
Rack	$100,000	10/10/94	$60,000	$55,000	10/10/98
Forklift	35,000	10/16/95	23,000	5,000	10/10/98
Bin	87,000	03/12/97	34,000	60,000	10/10/98

a. Determine the amount and the character of the recognized gain or loss from the disposition of each asset.
b. Assuming Gray has no nonrecaptured net § 1231 losses from prior years, how much of the 1998 recognized gains are treated as capital gains?

37. Green Industries (a sole proprietorship) sold three § 1231 assets during 1998. Data on these property dispositions are as follows:

Asset	Cost	Acquired	Depreciation	Sold for	Sold on
Rack	$100,000	10/10/94	$60,000	$155,000	10/10/98
Forklift	35,000	10/16/95	23,000	5,000	10/10/98
Bin	87,000	03/12/97	34,000	60,000	10/10/98

a. Determine the amount and the character of the recognized gain or loss from the disposition of each asset.
b. Assuming Green has $5,000 nonrecaptured net § 1231 losses from the five prior years, how much of the 1998 recognized gains are treated as capital gains?

38. Magenta Industries (a sole proprietorship) sold three § 1231 assets during the year. Data on these property dispositions are as follows:

Asset	Cost	Acquired	Depreciation	Sold for	Sold on
Rack	$110,000	10/10/95	$60,000	$55,000	10/10/98
Forklift	45,000	10/16/94	23,000	5,000	10/10/98
Bin	97,000	03/12/97	34,000	60,000	10/10/98

a. Determine the amount and the character of the recognized gain or loss from the disposition of each asset.
b. Assuming Magenta has $2,000 nonrecaptured net § 1231 losses from prior years, how much of the 1998 recognized gains are treated as capital gains?

39. On December 1, 1996, Gray Manufacturing Company (a corporation) purchased another company's assets, including a patent. The patent was used in Gray's manufacturing operations; $40,500 was allocated to the patent, and it was amortized at the rate of $225 per month. On June 30, 1998, Gray sold the patent for $60,000. Nineteen months of amortization had been taken on the patent. What are the amount and nature of the gain Gray recognizes on the disposition of the patent? Write a letter to Gray discussing the treatment of the gain. Gray's address is 6734 Grover Street, Back Bay Harbor, ME 23890. The letter should be addressed to Siddim Sadatha, Controller.

40. On June 1, 1994, Sparrow Enterprises (not a corporation) acquired a retail store for $400,000. The store was 39-year real property, and the straight-line cost recovery method was used. The store was sold on June 21, 1998, for $370,000.

a. Compute the cost recovery and adjusted basis for the store using Table 8–7 from Chapter 8.
b. What are the amount and nature of Sparrow's gain or loss from disposition of the store? What amount, if any, of the gain is unrecaptured § 1250 gain?

41. On January 1, 1986, Esteban acquired a $600,000 residential building for use in his rental activity. He took $450,000 of cost recovery on the building before disposing of it for $800,000 on January 1, 1998. For the period Esteban held the building, straight-line cost recovery would have been $400,000. What are the amount and nature of Esteban's gain from the disposition of the property? What amount, if any, of the gain is unrecaptured § 1250 gain?

42. Dave is the sole proprietor of a trampoline shop. During 1998, the following transactions occurred:

• Unimproved land adjacent to the store was condemned by the city on February 1. The condemnation proceeds were $25,000. The land, acquired in 1982, had an allocable basis of $40,000. Dave has additional parking across the street and plans to use the condemnation proceeds to build his inventory.

• A truck used to deliver trampolines was sold on January 2 for $3,500. The truck was purchased on January 2, 1994, for $6,000. On the date of sale, the adjusted basis was $2,509.

• Dave sold an antique rowing machine at an auction. Net proceeds were $3,900. The rowing machine was purchased as used equipment 17 years ago for $5,200 and is fully depreciated.

• Dave sold an apartment building for $200,000 on September 1. The rental property was purchased on September 1, 1995, for $150,000 and was being depreciated over a 27.5-year life using the straight-line method. At the date of sale, the adjusted basis was $124,783.

• Dave's personal yacht was stolen September 5. The yacht had been purchased in August at a cost of $25,000. The fair market value immediately preceding the theft was $20,000. Dave was insured for 50% of the original cost, and he received $12,500 on December 1.

• Dave sold a Buick on May 1 for $9,600. The vehicle had been used exclusively for personal purposes. It was purchased on September 1, 1994, for $20,800.

• An adding machine used by Dave's bookkeeper was sold on June 1. Net proceeds of the sale were $135. The machine was purchased on June 2, 1994, for $350. It was being depreciated over a five-year life employing the straight-line method. The adjusted basis on the date of sale was $95.

• Dave's trampoline stretching machine (owned two years) was stolen on May 5, but the business's insurance company will not pay any of the machine's value because Dave failed to pay the insurance premium. The machine had a fair market value of $8,000 and an adjusted basis of $6,000 at the time of theft.

• Dave had AGI of $4,000 from sources other than those described above.

• Dave has no nonrecaptured § 1231 lookback losses.

a. For each transaction, what are the amount and nature of recognized gain or loss?
b. What is Dave's 1998 AGI?

43. On January 1, 1986, Cora Hassant acquired depreciable real property for $100,000. She used accelerated depreciation to compute the asset's cost recovery. The asset was sold for $89,000 on January 3, 1998, when its adjusted basis was $38,000. Straight-line cost recovery for the period of time the asset was held would have been $52,700.
a. What are the amount and nature of the gain if the real property was residential?
b. What are the amount and nature of the gain if the real property was nonresidential?

c. Cora is curious about how the recapture rules differ for residential rental real estate acquired in 1986 and for residential rental real estate acquired in 1987 and thereafter. Write a letter to Cora explaining the differences. Her address is 2345 Westridge Street #23, Homer, MT 67342.

44. Joanne is in the 39.6% tax bracket and owns depreciable business equipment that she purchased several years ago for $135,000. She has taken $100,000 of depreciation on the equipment, and it is worth $85,000. Joanne's niece, Susan, is starting a new business and is short of cash. Susan has asked Joanne to gift the equipment to her so that Susan can use it in her business. Joanne no longer needs the equipment. Identify the alternatives available to Joanne if she wishes to help Susan and the tax effects of those alternatives. (Assume all alternatives involve the business equipment in one way or another, and ignore the gift tax.)

45. Gregor owns business equipment with a $55,000 adjusted basis. He paid $100,000 for the equipment, and it is currently worth $73,000. Gregor dies suddenly, and his son Adrian inherits the property. What is Adrian's basis for the property, and what happens to the § 1245 depreciation recapture potential?

46. Burt transferred forklifts used in his factory with recapture potential of $6,500 to a dealer in exchange for new forklifts worth $8,000 and $1,500 of marketable securities. The transaction qualified as a § 1031 like-kind exchange. Burt had an adjusted basis of $16,000 in the equipment.
    a. What are Burt's realized and recognized gain or loss?
    b. What is the nature of the recognized gain or loss?
    c. How would your answer to (a) or (b) change if no marketable securities were involved?

47. Cathy sells § 1245 property for $35,000, to be paid in 10 annual installments of $3,500 each plus interest at 8%. Cathy realizes a $12,000 gain from the sale, of which $12,000 is attributable to depreciation taken. Cathy would like to use the installment method to recognize the gain on the sale. May she do so?

48. Ray owns an unimproved parking lot that was used in his parking lot business for 10 years. A real estate developer purchases the lot from Ray for a total of $300,000. Ray receives $50,000 in 1998 and will receive $50,000 (plus 10% interest) each year for the next five years. Ray has a $120,000 adjusted basis for the lot. What are the nature and amount of the gain recognized in 1998?

49. Orange Corporation sells depreciable equipment for $59,000 to its sole shareholder, Jane. Orange had a $45,000 adjusted basis for the equipment and had originally paid $85,000 for it. Jane will use the equipment in her sole proprietorship business. The $59,000 sale price is the property's fair market value at the time of the sale. What are the consequences of this sale for Orange? For Jane?

50. Elsie, a sole proprietor, sold business land for a gain of $42,000. She held the land for 14 months. Refer to the sample Form 4797 in the text. Where on Form 4797 should this transaction be entered?

51. Refer to the sample Form 4797 and Form 1040 Schedule D in the text. Ernest has the following items on these forms:

Item	Form 4797		Schedule D
Property A (§ 1245 property)	Line 22	$86,000	
	Line 24	96,000	
Property B (§ 1250 property)	Line 24	34,000	
	Line 26a	32,000	
Property C			Line 8(f) ($3,000)

Ernest has no nonrecaptured § 1231 losses from prior years. All the assets were held more than 18 months. What is Ernest's entry on line 11 of Schedule D?

52. Jay sold three items of business equipment for a total of $300,000. None of the equipment was appraised to determine its value. Jay's cost and adjusted basis for the assets are as follows:

Asset	Cost	Adjusted Basis
Skidder	$230,000	$ 40,000
Driller	120,000	60,000
Platform	620,000	–0–
Total	$970,000	$100,000

Jay has been unable to establish the fair market values of the three assets. All he can determine is that combined they were worth $300,000 to the buyer in this arm's length transaction. How should Jay allocate the sales price and figure the gain or loss on the sale of the three assets?

CUMULATIVE PROBLEMS

53. Glen and Diane Okumura are married, file a joint return, and live at 39 Kaloa Street, Honolulu, Hawaii 56790. Glen's Social Security number is 777–88–2000 and Diane's is 888–77–1000. The Okumuras have two dependent children, Amy (age 15) and John (age 9). Glen works for the Hawaii Public Works Department, and Diane owns and materially participates in a retail dress shop. The Okumuras had the following transactions during 1998:
   a. Glen earned $197,000 in wages and had Federal income tax withholding of $9,000.
   b. Diane had a $18,000 profit from the dress shop. Diane made Federal estimated income tax payments of $1,000.
   c. The Okumuras sold a small apartment building for $68,000 on November 15, 1998. The building was acquired in October 1992 for $300,000; cost recovery was $86,820.
   d. Diane sold a delivery truck used in her business. The truck cost $35,000, $21,700 of cost recovery had been taken, and it was sold for $18,000.
   e. The Okumuras received $13,000 in dividends on various domestic corporation stocks that they own.
   f. The Okumuras sold stock for a $15,000 long-term capital gain and other stock at a $6,000 short-term capital loss.
   g. The Okumuras had the following itemized deductions: $11,000 unreimbursed medical expenses; $10,500 personal use real property taxes; $7,000 qualified residence interest; $1,500 of Glen's unreimbursed employee business expenses; $535 of investment-related expenses; and $6,300 of state income taxes paid.

Compute the Okumuras' 1998 net tax payable or refund due. (Ignore self-employment tax.) Suggested software (if available): *TurboTax*. Also write a letter to the Okumuras describing how the sale of the apartment building affects their return.

54. Felix Montoya (Social Security number 390–88–3912) owns Montoya Enterprises, a computer retail sole proprietorship. Felix lives at 112 Green Road, Encidio, CA 45678. The store is located at 3456 Purple Road, Encidio, CA 45679. The following summary reflects the store's results of operations for 1997:

Item	Amount
Sales	$1,875,000
Sales returns and allowances	(5,000)
Beginning inventory (FIFO)	187,000
Purchases	573,000
Ending inventory (FIFO)	129,000
Expenses:	
Advertising	18,000
Employee wages	233,000
Employer FICA	23,000
Depreciation	25,000
Charitable contributions	3,000
Utilities	12,000
Store property taxes	17,000
Lodging and transportation expenses while away from home overnight on store business (no meals)	3,000
Meals and entertainment expense in connection with store business	2,000
Store insurance	15,000
Interest on store mortgage	35,000
Professional service fees	4,000

Other information is as follows:

- In connection with the business, the following information may be relevant: The principal business code is 3747, and the employer ID number is 382345678. The business uses the accrual method of accounting. Felix materially participated in the business, which was started in 1988. The lower of cost or market was used to cost inventory; no store labor was added to inventory; and there was no change from prior years in the method of determining inventories. No vehicles were used in connection with the business.

- Montoya Enterprises has no fringe benefits for its employees. However, Felix paid $5,600 in health insurance premiums for coverage on himself.

- On December 8, 1997, Montoya Enterprises sold office equipment used in its business for $33,000. The equipment had been purchased for $83,000 on January 20, 1994, and $62,000 of depreciation (including 1997) had been taken on it.

- On December 9, 1997, Montoya Enterprises sold for $80,000 a storage building it had used to store excess inventory. The building cost $80,000 on June 10, 1989, and $12,000 of straight-line depreciation (including 1997) had been taken on it.

- Felix has $3,000 (total) of nonrecaptured net § 1231 losses from the prior five years.

- Felix is age 38, single, and has no dependents. He does not wish to contribute to the Presidential Election Campaign Fund. Felix made $150,000 of timely Federal estimated income tax payments. During 1997, he made $67,000 of timely state estimated income tax payments. He wants any Federal tax refund to be applied to his 1998 estimated tax.

- Felix made deductible alimony payments of $350,000 during the year. His former spouse's Social Security number is 309–67–2345.

- Felix had $45,000 of interest income from the Diversified Corporate Bond Fund. He also received a $13,000 mid-term capital gain distribution from the Green High Growth Stock Fund. Felix does not have an interest in any foreign bank accounts or trusts.

- Felix had the following itemized deductions (all with proper documentation):

Unreimbursed medical expenses	$ 3,000
Real estate taxes on his home	45,000
Home mortgage interest	67,000
Charitable contributions	56,000

Compute Felix Montoya's net tax payable or refund due for 1997. If you use tax forms for your computations, you will need Form 1040 and Schedules A, B, C, D, and SE and Form 4797. Suggested software (if available): *TurboTax*.

RESEARCH PROBLEMS

*Note: Use the **RIA OnPoint System 4 Student Version CD-ROM**, which is available to accompany this text, in preparing solutions to the Research Problems. Alternatively, tax research materials found in a standard tax library can be used.*

Research Problem 1.   Sidney owns a professional football franchise. He has received an offer of $80 million for the franchise, all the football equipment, the rights to concession receipts, the rights to a stadium lease, and the rights to all the player contracts he owns. Most of the players have been with the team for quite a long time and have contracts that were signed several years ago. The contracts have been substantially depreciated. Sidney is concerned about potential § 1245 recapture when the contracts are sold. He has heard about "previously unrecaptured depreciation with respect to initial contracts" and would like to know more about it. Find a definition for that phrase and write an explanation of it.

Research Problem 2.   Green Manufacturing purchases a propane storage tank and support system for $3,000,000. The system is placed outside Green's plant. The propane is drawn from the tank through a hose and valve system into the burners underneath Green's chemical vats. After $1,800,000 of depreciation has been taken on the system, it is sold for $2,300,000. What is the nature and amount of Green's gain or loss from the disposition of the system?

Partial list of research aids:
§§ 1221, 1231, 1245, 1250.

Research Problem 3.   Amata is both a real estate developer and the owner and manager of rental real estate. Amata is retiring and is going to sell both the land he is holding for future development and the rental properties he owns. Straight-line depreciation was used to depreciate the rental real estate. The rental properties will be sold at a substantial loss, and the development property will be sold at a substantial gain. What is the nature of these gains and losses?

Research Problem 4.   Brown Corporation, a software development company, was formed in 1995 and has always been an S corporation. In 1998, due to rapid growth, it sold its office building for a $70,000 gain and bought a larger building. How does § 291 affect the character of this gain?

Use the tax resources of the Internet to address the following questions. Do not restrict your search to the World Wide Web, but include a review of newsgroups and general reference materials, practitioner sites and resources, primary sources of the tax law, chat rooms and discussion groups, and other opportunities.

Research Problem 5.   Summarize tax planning strategies that are presented on the Internet by tax advisers looking for clients relative to each of the following topics.
   a. An asset replacement strategy for companies in capital-intensive industries.
   b. A tax minimization strategy for farmers with significant annual asset turnover.

Research Problem 6.   How did proposals to change capital and § 1231 asset definitions play into the campaign promises made by politicians running in the last election? Look at several campaign web sites to identify trends in such tax proposals.

Research Problem 7. Find an article that provides tax advice to owners of small businesses who want to deduct their costs for home office equipment. Send an e-mail message to the author of the article, providing him or her with a computational example that could be incorporated in the next revision of the article.

TEAM PROJECT: ARTHUR ANDERSEN TAX CHALLENGE CASES

For more information on the Arthur Andersen Tax Challenge Cases, refer to Chapter 1, page 1–37.

Information related to tax issues and problems that are discussed in this chapter may be found in the

Day and Ball case on pages: None
Fence case on pages: None

Read and analyze the case you have been assigned and *identify* any issues and problems that are related to material covered in this chapter. If the information provided in the case is complete, prepare answers for this part of the case at this time. If you need information that is contained in the later parts of the case, write a memo summarizing the questions or problems so you can prepare a complete answer at a later date.

VI

ACCOUNTING PERIODS, ACCOUNTING METHODS, AND DEFERRED COMPENSATION

Part VI provides a more comprehensive examination of the accounting periods and accounting methods that were introduced in Part II. A discussion of special accounting methods is also included. Part VI concludes with an analysis of the tax consequences of deferred compensation transactions.

ACCOUNTING PERIODS AND METHODS

LEARNING OBJECTIVES

After completing Chapter 18, you should be able to:

1. Understand the relevance of the accounting period concept, the different types of accounting periods, and the limitations on their use.

2. Apply the cash method, accrual method, and hybrid method of accounting.

3. Utilize the procedure for changing accounting methods.

4. Determine when the installment method of accounting can be utilized and apply the related calculation techniques.

5. Understand the alternative methods of accounting for long-term contracts (the completed contract method and the percentage of completion method) including the limitations on the use of the completed contract method.

6. Know when accounting for inventories must occur, recognize the types of costs that must be included in inventories, and apply the LIFO method.

7. Identify tax planning opportunities related to accounting periods and accounting methods.

Tax practitioners must deal with the issue of *when* particular items of income and expense are recognized as well as the basic issue of *whether* the items are includible in taxable income. Earlier chapters discussed the types of income subject to tax (gross income and exclusions) and allowable deductions (the *whether* issue).[1] This chapter focuses on the related issue of the periods in which income and deductions are reported (the *when* issue). Generally, a taxpayer's income and deductions must be assigned to particular 12-month periods—calendar years or fiscal years.

TAX IN THE NEWS

ACCELERATION OF INCOME

In 1993, the *Wall Street Journal* and various other print and broadcast news sources reported that Hillary Rodham Clinton had the opportunity to receive compensation income in 1992 or 1993. She chose to accelerate the income into 1992. This appears to be at variance with the normal tax planning mode of deferring the reporting of income and accelerating the reporting of deductions.

One possible explanation for reporting the income in 1992 rather than in 1993 is that the family's taxable income was expected to be greater in 1993 than in 1992. However, while the President earns substantially more as President of the United States than as the Governor of Arkansas, the First Lady earns substantially less than she did as a partner in an Arkansas law firm.

Another possible explanation is the expectation that the Revenue Reconciliation Act of 1993 with its retroactive increase in tax rates would be passed by Congress. In any event, the First Lady followed sound tax advice in accelerating the income into 1992.

---

[1]See Chapters 4, 5, and 6.

Income and deductions are placed within particular years through the use of tax accounting methods. The basic accounting methods are the cash method, accrual method, and hybrid method. Other special purpose methods, such as the installment method and the methods used for long-term construction contracts, are available for specific circumstances or types of transactions.

Over the long run, the accounting period used by a taxpayer will not affect the aggregate amount of reported taxable income. However, taxable income for any particular year may vary significantly due to the use of a particular reporting period. Also, through the choice of accounting methods or accounting periods, it is possible to postpone the recognition of taxable income and to enjoy the benefits from deferring the related tax. This chapter discusses the taxpayer's alternatives for accounting periods and accounting methods.

ACCOUNTING PERIODS

IN GENERAL

1 **LEARNING OBJECTIVE**
Understand the relevance of the accounting period concept, the different types of accounting periods, and the limitations on their use.

A taxpayer who keeps adequate books and records may be permitted to elect a **fiscal year,** a 12-month period ending on the *last day* of a month other than December, for the **accounting period.** Otherwise, a *calendar year* must be used.[2] Frequently, corporations can satisfy the record-keeping requirements and elect to use a fiscal year.[3] Often the fiscal year conforms to a natural business year (e.g., a summer resort's fiscal year may end on September 30, after the close of the season). Individuals seldom use a fiscal year because they do not maintain the necessary books and records and because complications can arise as a result of changes in the tax law (e.g., often the transition rules and effective dates differ for fiscal year taxpayers).

Generally, a taxable year may not exceed 12 calendar months. However, if certain requirements are met, a taxpayer may elect to use an annual period that varies from 52 to 53 weeks.[4] In that case, the year-end must be on the same day of the week (e.g., the Tuesday falling closest to October 31 or the last Tuesday in October). The day of the week selected for ending the year will depend upon business considerations. For example, a retail business that is not open on Sundays may end its tax year on a Sunday so that it can take an inventory without interrupting business operations.

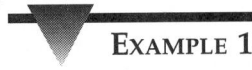

EXAMPLE 1

Wade is in the business of selling farm supplies. His natural business year terminates at the end of October with the completion of harvesting. At the end of the fiscal year, Wade must take an inventory, which is most easily accomplished on a Tuesday. Therefore, Wade could adopt a 52–53 week tax year ending on the Tuesday closest to October 31. If Wade selects this method, the year-end date may fall in the following month if that Tuesday is closer to October 31. The tax year ending in 1998 will contain 53 weeks beginning on Wednesday, October 29, 1997, and ending on Tuesday, November 3, 1998. The tax year ending in 1999 will have 52 weeks beginning on Wednesday, November 4, 1998, and ending on Tuesday, November 2, 1999. ▼

---

[2]§ 441(c) and Reg. § 1.441–1(b)(1)(ii).
[3]Reg. § 1.441–1(e)(2).

[4]§ 441(f).

SPECIFIC PROVISIONS FOR PARTNERSHIPS, S CORPORATIONS, AND PERSONAL SERVICE CORPORATIONS

Partnerships and S Corporations.   When a partner's tax year and the partnership's tax year differ, the partner will enjoy a deferral of income. This results because the partner reports his or her share of the partnership's income and deductions for the partnership's tax year ending within or with the partner's tax year.[5] For example, if the tax year of the partnership ends on January 31, a calendar year partner will not report partnership profits for the first 11 months of the partnership tax year until the following year. Therefore, partnerships are subject to special tax year requirements.

In general, the partnership tax year must be the same as the tax year of the majority interest partners. The **majority interest partners** are the partners who own a greater-than-50 percent interest in the partnership capital and profits. If the majority owners do not have the same tax year, the partnership must adopt the same tax year as its principal partners. A **principal partner** is a partner with a 5 percent or more interest in the partnership capital or profits.[6]

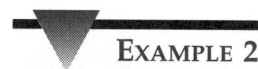

EXAMPLE 2

The RST Partnership is owned equally by Rose Corporation, Silver Corporation, and Tom. The partners have the following tax years.

Partner's Tax Year Ending	
Rose	June 30
Silver	June 30
Tom	December 31

The partnership's tax year must end on June 30. If Silver Corporation's as well as Tom's year ended on December 31, the partnership would be required to adopt a calendar year. ▼

If the principal partners do not all have the same tax year and no majority of partners have the same tax year, the partnership must use a year that results in the *least aggregate deferral* of income.[7] Under the **least aggregate deferral method,** the different tax years of the principal partners are tested to determine which produces the least aggregate deferral. This is calculated by first multiplying the combined percentages of the principal partners with the same tax year by the months of deferral for the test year. Once this is done for each set of principal partners with the same tax year, the resulting products are summed to produce the aggregate deferral. After calculating the aggregate deferral for each of the test years, the test year with the smallest summation (the least aggregate deferral) is the tax year for the partnership.

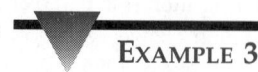

EXAMPLE 3

The DE Partnership is owned equally by Diane and Emily. Diane's fiscal year ends on March 31, and Emily's fiscal year ends on August 31. The partnership must use the partner's fiscal year that will result in the least aggregate deferral of income. Therefore, the fiscal years ending March 31 and August 31 must both be tested.

---

[5]Reg. § 1.706–1(a).
[6]§§ 706(b)(1)(B) and 706(b)(3).

[7]Temp.Reg. § 1.706–1T(a)(2).

Test for Fiscal Year Ending March 31				
Partner	**Year Ends**	**Profit %**	**Months of Deferral**	**Product**
Diane	3–31	50	0	0
Emily	8–31	50	5	2.5
Aggregate deferral months				2.5

Thus, with a year ending March 31, Emily would be able to defer her half of the income for five months. That is, Emily's share of the partnership income for the fiscal year ending March 31, 1999, would not be included in her income until August 31, 1999.

Test for Fiscal Year Ending August 31				
Partner	**Year Ends**	**Profit %**	**Months of Deferral**	**Product**
Diane	3–31	50	7	3.5
Emily	8–31	50	0	0
Aggregate deferral months				3.5

Thus, with a year ending August 31, Diane would be able to defer her half of the income for seven months. That is, Diane's share of the partnership income for the fiscal year ending August 31, 1999, would not be included in her income until March 31, 2000.

The year ending March 31 must be used because it results in the least aggregate deferral of income. ▼

Generally, S corporations must adopt a calendar year.[8] However, partnerships and S corporations may *elect* an otherwise *impermissible year* under any of the following conditions:

- A business purpose for the year can be demonstrated.[9]
- The partnership's or S corporation's year results in a deferral of not more than three months' income, and the entity agrees to make required tax payments.[10]
- The entity retains the same year as was used for the fiscal year ending in 1987, provided the entity agrees to make required tax payments.

Business Purpose. The only business purpose for a fiscal year that the IRS has acknowledged is the need to conform the tax year to the natural business year of a business.[11] Generally, only seasonal businesses have a natural business year. For example, the natural business year for a department store may end on January 31, after Christmas returns have been processed and clearance sales have been completed.

Required Tax Payments. Under the required payments system, tax payments are due from a fiscal year partnership or S corporation by April 15 of each tax year.[12] The amount due is computed by applying the highest individual tax rate plus 1 percent to an estimate of the deferral period income. The deferral period runs from the close of the fiscal year to the end of the calendar year. Estimated

[8]§§ 1378(a) and (b).
[9]§§ 706(b)(1)(C) and 1378(b)(2).
[10]§ 444.

[11]Rev.Rul. 87–57, 1987–2 C.B. 117.
[12]§§ 444(c) and 7519. No payment is required if the calculated amount is $500 or less.

income for this period is based on the average monthly earnings for the previous fiscal year. The amount due is reduced by the amount of required tax payments for the previous year.[13]

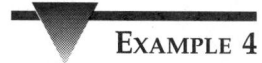

EXAMPLE 4   Brown, Inc., an S corporation, elected a fiscal year ending September 30. Bob is the only shareholder. For the fiscal year ending September 30, 1998, Brown earned $100,000. The required tax payment for the previous year was $5,000. The corporation must pay $5,150 by April 15, 1999, calculated as follows:

$$(\$100,000 \times \tfrac{3}{12} \times 40.6\%*) - \$5,000 = \$5,150$$

*Maximum § 1 rate of 39.6% + 1%.

**ETHICAL
CONSIDERATIONS**

Required Tax Years

Before 1987, partnerships could generally use a fiscal year ending September 30, and S corporations could use any fiscal year. With this latitude, accountants often recommended that their partnership and S corporation clients not use a calendar year. This enabled the accountants to spread their work throughout the year and created a tax deferral for the clients.

Members of the accounting profession argued vociferously against the calendar year requirement that was included in the Tax Reform Act of 1986. The choice Congress had to make was whether some groups should be allowed to benefit (i.e., the accountants and their clients) at the expense of the rest of the general public. Of course, the accounting profession viewed the choices differently: Should some groups be burdened (i.e., the accounting profession) for little benefit to the remaining taxpayers?

The compromise reached was the required payments scheme, whereby the burden was lifted from the accounting profession without the clients enjoying tax deferrals. Was this an acceptable compromise?

Personal Service Corporations.   A **personal service corporation (PSC)** is a corporation whose shareholder-employees provide personal services (e.g., medical, dental, legal, accounting, engineering, actuarial, consulting, or performing arts). Generally, a PSC must use a calendar year.[14] However, a PSC can *elect* a fiscal year under any of the following conditions:

- A business purpose for the year can be demonstrated.
- The PSC year results in a deferral of not more than three months' income, the corporation pays the shareholder-employee's salary during the portion of the calendar year after the close of the fiscal year, and the salary for that period is at least proportionate to the shareholder-employee's salary received for the preceding fiscal year.[15]
- The PSC retains the same year it used for the fiscal year ending in 1987, provided it satisfies the latter two requirements in the preceding option.

---

[13]§ 7519(b).
[14]§ 441(i).

[15]§§ 444 and 280H.

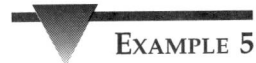

EXAMPLE 5

Nancy's corporation paid Nancy a salary of $120,000 during its fiscal year ending September 30, 1998. The corporation cannot satisfy the business purpose test for a fiscal year. The corporation can continue to use its fiscal year without any negative tax effects, provided Nancy receives at least $30,000 [(3 months/12 months) × $120,000] as salary during the period October 1 through December 31, 1998. ▼

If the salary test is not satisfied, the PSC can retain the fiscal year, but the corporation's deduction for salary for the fiscal year is limited to the following:

A + A(F/N)

Where A = Amount paid after the close of the fiscal year

F = Number of months in fiscal year minus number of months from the end of the fiscal year to the end of the ongoing calendar year

N = Number of months from the end of the fiscal year to the end of the ongoing calendar year

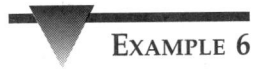

EXAMPLE 6

Assume the corporation in the previous example paid Nancy $10,000 of salary during the period October 1 through December 31, 1998. The deduction for Nancy's salary for the corporation's fiscal year ending September 30, 1999, is thus limited to $40,000 calculated as follows:

$$\$10,000 + \left[\$10,000 \left(\frac{12 - 3}{3} \right) \right] = \$10,000 + \$30,000 = \$40,000$$

▼

MAKING THE ELECTION

A taxpayer elects to use a calendar or fiscal year by the timely filing of his or her initial tax return. For all subsequent years, the taxpayer must use this same period unless approval for change is obtained from the IRS.[16]

CHANGES IN THE ACCOUNTING PERIOD

A taxpayer must obtain consent from the IRS before changing the tax year.[17] This power to approve or not to approve a change is significant in that it permits the IRS to issue authoritative administrative guidelines that must be met by taxpayers who wish to change their accounting period. An application for permission to change tax years must be made on Form 1128, Application for Change in Accounting Period. The application must be filed on or before the fifteenth day of the second calendar month following the close of the short period that results from the change in accounting period.[18]

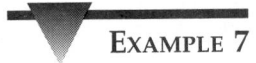

EXAMPLE 7

Beginning in 1998, Gold Corporation, a calendar year taxpayer, would like to switch to a fiscal year ending March 31. The corporation must file Form 1128 by May 15, 1998. ▼

IRS Requirements. The IRS will not grant permission for the change unless the taxpayer can establish a substantial business purpose for the request. One substantial business purpose is to change to a tax year that coincides with the *natural business year* (the completion of an annual business cycle). The IRS applies

---

[16]Reg. §§ 1.441–1(b)(3) and 1.441–1(b)(4).

[17]§ 442. Under certain conditions, corporations are allowed to change tax years without obtaining IRS approval. See Reg. § 1.442–1(c)(1).

[18]Reg. § 1.442–1(b)(1). In Example 7, the first period after the change in accounting period (January 1, 1998 through March 31, 1998) is less than a 12-month period and is referred to as a *short period*.

an objective gross receipts test to determine if the entity has a natural business year. At least 25 percent of the entity's gross receipts for the 12-month period must be realized in the final 2 months of the 12-month period for three consecutive years.[19]

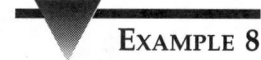

EXAMPLE 8

A Virginia Beach motel had gross receipts as follows:

	1996	**1997**	**1998**
July–August receipts	$ 300,000	$250,000	$ 325,000
September 1–August 31 receipts	1,000,000	900,000	1,250,000
Receipts for 2 months divided by receipts for 12 months	30.0%	27.8%	26.0%

Since it satisfies the natural business year test, the motel will be allowed to use a fiscal year ending August 31. ▼

The IRS usually establishes certain conditions that the taxpayer must accept if the approval for change is to be granted. In particular, if the taxpayer has a net operating loss for the short period, the IRS may require that the loss be carried forward and allocated equally over the 6 following years.[20] As you may recall (refer to Chapter 7), net operating losses are ordinarily carried back for 2 years and forward for 20 years.

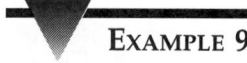

EXAMPLE 9

Parrot Corporation changed from a calendar year to a fiscal year ending September 30. The short-period return for the nine months ending September 30, 1998, reflected a $60,000 net operating loss. The corporation had taxable income for 1996 and 1997. As a condition for granting approval, the IRS requires Parrot to allocate the $60,000 loss over the next six years, rather than carrying the loss back to the two preceding years (the usual order for applying a net operating loss). Thus, Parrot Corporation will reduce its taxable income by $10,000 each year ending September 30, 1999, through September 30, 2004. ▼

TAXABLE PERIODS OF LESS THAN ONE YEAR

A **short taxable year** (or **short period**) is a period of less than 12 calendar months. A taxpayer may have a short year for (1) the first income tax return, (2) the final income tax return, or (3) a change in the tax year. If the short period results from a change in the taxpayer's annual accounting period, the taxable income for the period must be annualized. Due to the progressive tax rate structure, taxpayers could reap benefits from a short-period return if some adjustments were not required. Thus, the taxpayer is required to do the following:

1. Annualize the short-period income.

$$\text{Annualized income} = \text{Short-period income} \times \frac{12}{\begin{array}{c}\text{Number of months}\\ \text{in the short period}\end{array}}$$

2. Compute the tax on the annualized income.

---

[19]Rev.Proc. 87–32, 1987–1 C.B. 131, and Rev.Rul. 87–57, 1987–2 C.B. 117.   [20]Rev.Proc. 85–16, 1985–1 C.B. 517.

3. Convert the tax on the annualized income to a short-period tax.

$$\text{Short-period tax} = \text{Tax on annualized income} \times \frac{\text{Number of months in the short period}}{12}$$

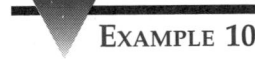

EXAMPLE 10

Gray Corporation obtained permission to change from a calendar year to a fiscal year ending September 30, beginning in 1998. For the short period January 1 through September 30, 1998, the corporation's taxable income was $48,000. The relevant tax rates and the resultant short-period tax are as follows:

Amount of Taxable Income	Tax Rates
$1–$50,000	15% of taxable income
$50,001–$75,000	$7,500 plus 25% of taxable income in excess of $50,000

Calculation of Short-Period Tax

Annualized income
    ($48,000 × $\frac{12}{9}$) = $64,000
Tax on annualized income
    $7,500 + .25($64,000 − $50,000) =
    $7,500 + $3,500 = $11,000
Short-period tax = ($11,000 × $\frac{9}{12}$) = $8,250
Annualizing the income increased the tax by $1,050:

Tax with annualizing	$ 8,250
Tax without annualizing (.15 × $48,000)	(7,200)
	$ 1,050

Rather than annualize the short-period income, the taxpayer can (1) elect to calculate the tax for a 12-month period beginning on the first day of the short period and (2) convert the tax in (1) to a short-period tax as follows:[21]

$$\frac{\text{Taxable income for short period}}{\text{Taxable income for the 12-month period}} \times \begin{array}{c}\text{Tax on the 12 months of} \\ \text{income}\end{array}$$

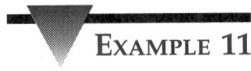

EXAMPLE 11

Assume Gray Corporation's taxable income for the calendar year 1998 was $60,000. The tax on the full 12 months of income would have been $10,000 [$7,500 + .25($60,000 − $50,000)]. The short-period tax would be $8,000 [($48,000/$60,000) × $10,000]. Thus, if the corporation utilized this option, the tax for the short period would be $8,000 (rather than $8,250, as calculated in Example 10). ▼

For individuals, annualizing requires some special adjustments:[22]

- Deductions must be itemized for the short period (the standard deduction is not allowed).
- Personal and dependency exemptions must be prorated.

Fortunately, individuals rarely change tax years.

---

[21]§ 443(b)(1).

[22]§ 443(b)(2) and Reg. § 1.443–1(a)(2).

MITIGATION OF THE ANNUAL ACCOUNTING PERIOD CONCEPT

Several provisions in the Code are designed to give the taxpayer relief from the seemingly harsh results that may be produced by the combined effects of an arbitrary accounting period and a progressive rate structure. For example, under the net operating loss carryback and carryover rules, a loss in one year can be carried back and offset against taxable income for the preceding 2 years. Unused net operating losses are then carried over for 20 years.[23] In addition, the Code provides special relief provisions for casualty losses pursuant to a disaster and for the reporting of insurance proceeds from destruction of crops.[24]

Restoration of Amounts Received under a Claim of Right.   The court-made **claim of right doctrine** applies when the taxpayer receives property as income and treats it as his or her own but a dispute arises over the taxpayer's rights to the income.[25] According to the doctrine, the taxpayer must include the amount as income in the year of receipt. The rationale for the doctrine is that the Federal government cannot await the resolution of all disputes before exacting a tax. As a corollary to the doctrine, if the taxpayer is later required to repay the funds, generally a deduction is allowed in the year of repayment.[26]

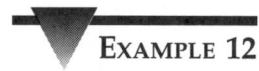

EXAMPLE 12

In 1998, Pedro received a $5,000 bonus computed as a percentage of profits. In 1999, Pedro's employer determined that the 1998 profits had been incorrectly computed, and Pedro had to refund the $5,000 in 1999. Pedro was required to include the $5,000 in his 1998 income, but he can claim a $5,000 deduction in 1999. ▼

In Example 12 the transactions were a wash; that is, the income and deduction were the same ($5,000). Suppose, however, Pedro was in the 36 percent tax bracket in 1998 but in the 15 percent bracket in 1999. Without some relief provision, the mistake would be costly to Pedro. He paid $1,800 tax in 1998 (.36 × $5,000), but the deduction reduced his tax liability in 1999 by only $750 (.15 × $5,000). The Code does provide the needed relief in such cases. Under § 1341, when income that has been taxed under the claim of right doctrine must later be repaid, in effect, the taxpayer gets to apply to the deduction the tax rate of the year that will produce the greatest tax benefit. Thus, in Example 12, the repayment in 1999 would reduce Pedro's 1999 tax liability by the greater 1998 rate (.36) applied to the $5,000. However, relief is provided only in cases where the tax is significantly different; that is, when the deduction for the amount previously included in income exceeds $3,000.

ACCOUNTING METHODS

2   **LEARNING OBJECTIVE**
Apply the cash method, accrual method, and hybrid method of accounting.

PERMISSIBLE METHODS

Section 446 requires the taxpayer to compute taxable income using the method of accounting regularly employed in keeping his or her books, provided the method clearly reflects income. The Code recognizes the following as generally permissible **accounting methods:**

---

[23]§ 172. Refer to Chapter 7.
[24]§§ 165(i) and 451(d). Refer to Chapter 7.
[25]*North American Consolidated Oil Co. v. Burnet*, 3 USTC ¶943, 11 AFTR 16, 52 S.Ct. 613 (USSC, 1932).

[26]*U.S. v. Lewis*, 51–1 USTC ¶9211, 40 AFTR 258, 71 S.Ct. 522 (USSC, 1951).

- The cash receipts and disbursements method.
- The accrual method.
- A hybrid method (a combination of cash and accrual).

The Regulations refer to these alternatives as *overall methods* and add that the term *method of accounting* includes not only the overall method of accounting of the taxpayer but also the accounting treatment of any item.[27]

Generally, any of the three methods of accounting may be used if the method is consistently employed and clearly reflects income. However, the taxpayer is required to use the accrual method for sales and costs of goods sold if inventories are an income-producing factor to the business.[28] Other situations in which the accrual method is required are discussed later. Special methods are also permitted for installment sales, long-term construction contracts, and farmers.

A taxpayer who has more than one trade or business may use a different method of accounting for each trade or business activity.[29] Furthermore, a different method of accounting may be used to determine income from a trade or business than is used to compute nonbusiness items of income and deductions.[30]

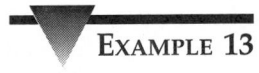

EXAMPLE 13

Linda operates a grocery store and owns stock and bonds. The sales and cost of goods sold from the grocery store must be computed by the accrual method because inventories are material. However, Linda can report her dividends and interest under the cash method. ▼

The Code grants the IRS broad powers to determine whether the taxpayer's accounting method *clearly reflects income*. Thus, if the method employed does not clearly reflect income, the IRS has the power to prescribe the method to be used by the taxpayer.[31]

CASH RECEIPTS AND DISBURSEMENTS METHOD—CASH BASIS

Most individuals and many businesses use the cash basis to report income and deductions. The popularity of this method can largely be attributed to its simplicity and flexibility.

Under the **cash method,** income is not recognized until the taxpayer actually receives, or constructively receives, cash or its equivalent. Cash is constructively received if it is available to the taxpayer.[32] Deductions are generally permitted in the year of payment. Thus, year-end accounts receivable, accounts payable, and accrued income and deductions are not included in the determination of taxable income.

In many cases, a taxpayer using the cash method can choose the year in which a deduction is claimed simply by postponing or accelerating the payment of expenses. For fixed assets, however, the cash basis taxpayer claims deductions through depreciation or amortization, the same as an accrual basis taxpayer does. In addition, prepaid expenses must be capitalized and amortized if the life of the asset extends substantially beyond the end of the tax year.[33] Most courts have applied the one-year rule (**one-year rule for prepaid expenses**) to determine whether capitalization and amortization are required. According to this rule, capitalization is

---

[27]Reg. § 1.446–1(a)(1).
[28]Reg. § 1.446–1(a)(4)(i).
[29]§ 446(d).
[30]Reg. § 1.446–1(c)(1)(iv)(b).

[31]§ 446(b).
[32]Reg. § 1.451–1(a). Refer to Chapter 4 for a discussion of constructive receipt.
[33]Reg. § 1.461–1(a)(1).

TAX IN THE NEWS

TAXPAYER AWARDED ATTORNEY FEES IN THE IRS'S FAILED ATTEMPT TO IMPOSE THE ACCRUAL METHOD

In a 1997 Tax Court case, the IRS contended that a corporation that provided nursing services was required to use the accrual method of accounting. The corporation generally paid its employees before the customer paid for the nursing services. At the end of the year, the company had almost $250,000 in accounts receivable that were not included in its cash basis income although all of the related employee expense had been deducted. The IRS argued that the accrual method was required because of the mismatching of revenues and expenses that occurred under the taxpayer's method of accounting. Furthermore, argued the IRS, the substantial difference in taxable income as computed by the cash and accrual methods was evidence that the cash method did not clearly reflect income.

The Tax Court concluded that the cash method had been consistently applied, that the taxpayer was not deliberately prepaying expenses nor deferring income, and that the mismatching was the usual result of applying the cash method of accounting. Furthermore, Congress is well aware that the cash method results in some mismatching but has specifically authorized its use. In short, the Tax Court concluded that the IRS had subjected the taxpayer to a lot of expense when the IRS's position was not substantially supported by the law. Therefore, the IRS was required to pay the taxpayer's attorney fees.

SOURCE: *Laura E. Austin*, T.C.Memo. 1997–157: 73 TCM 2470.

---

required only if the asset has a life that extends beyond the tax year following the year of payment.[34]

Restrictions on Use of the Cash Method.   Using the cash method to measure income from a merchandising or manufacturing operation would often yield a distorted picture of the results of operations. Income for the period would largely be a function of when payments were made for goods or materials. Thus, the Regulations prohibit the use of the cash method (and require the accrual method) to measure sales and cost of goods sold if inventories are material to the business.[35]

The prohibition on the use of the cash method if inventories are material and the rules regarding prepaid expenses (discussed above) are intended to assure that annual income is clearly reflected. However, certain taxpayers may not use the cash method of accounting for Federal income tax purposes regardless of whether inventories are material. The accrual basis must be used to report the income earned by (1) a corporation (other than an S corporation), (2) a partnership with a corporate partner, and (3) a tax shelter.[36] This accrual basis requirement has three exceptions:[37]

---

[34]*Zaninovich v. Comm.*, 80–1 USTC ¶9342, 45 AFTR2d 80–1442, 616 F.2d 429 (CA–9, 1980), *rev'g* 69 T.C. 605 (1978). Refer to Chapter 6 for further discussion of the one-year rule.
[35]Reg. § 1.446–1(a)(4)(i).

[36]§ 448(a). For this purpose, the hybrid method of accounting is considered the same as the cash method.
[37]§ 448(b).

- A farming business.
- A qualified personal service corporation (e.g., a corporation performing services in health, law, engineering, architecture, accounting, actuarial science, performing arts, or consulting).
- An entity that is not a tax shelter whose average annual gross receipts for the most recent three-year period are $5 million or less.

Farming.   Although inventories are material to farming operations, the IRS long ago created an exception to the general rule that allows farmers to use the cash method of accounting.[38] The purpose of the exception is to relieve the small farmer from the bookkeeping burden of accrual accounting. However, tax shelter promoters recognized, for example, that by deducting the costs of a crop in one tax year and harvesting the crop in a later year, income could be deferred from tax. Thus, §§ 447 and 464 were enacted to prevent certain farming corporations and limited partnerships (farming syndicates) from using the cash method.[39]

Farmers who are allowed to use the cash method of accounting must nevertheless capitalize their costs of raising trees when the preproduction period is longer than two years.[40] Thus, a cash basis apple farmer must capitalize the cost of raising trees until the trees produce in merchantable quantities. Cash basis farmers can elect not to capitalize these costs, but if the election is made, the alternative depreciation system (refer to Chapter 8) must be used for all farming property.

Generally, the cost of purchasing an animal must be capitalized. However, the cash basis farmer's cost of raising the animal can be expensed.[41]

ACCRUAL METHOD

All Events Test for Income.   Under the **accrual method,** an item is generally included in gross income for the year in which it is earned, regardless of when the income is collected. An item of income is earned when (1) all the events have occurred to fix the taxpayer's right to receive the income and (2) the amount of income (the amount the taxpayer has a right to receive) can be determined with reasonable accuracy.[42]

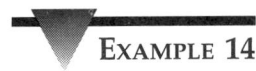

EXAMPLE 14

Andre, a calendar year taxpayer who uses the accrual basis of accounting, was to receive a bonus equal to 6% of Blue Corporation's net income for its fiscal year ending each June 30. For the fiscal year ending June 30, 1998, Blue Corporation had net income of $240,000, and for the six months ending December 31, 1998, the corporation's net income was $150,000. Andre will report $14,400 (.06 × $240,000) for 1998 because his right to the amount became fixed when Blue Corporation's year closed. However, Andre would not accrue income based on the corporation's profits for the last six months of 1998 since his right to the income does not accrue until the close of the corporation's tax year. ▼

In a situation where the accrual basis taxpayer's right to income is being contested and the income has not yet been collected, generally no income is recognized until the dispute has been settled.[43] Before the settlement, "all of the events have not occurred that fix the right to receive the income."

---

[38]Reg. § 1.471–6(a).
[39]Section 447(c) contains counterexceptions that allow certain closely held corporations to use the cash method. See also § 464(c).
[40]§ 263A(d).
[41]Reg. § 1.162–12(a).

[42]Reg. § 1.451–1(a). Refer to Chapter 4 for further discussion of the accrual basis.
[43]*Burnet v. Sanford & Brooks Co.*, 2 USTC ¶636, 9 AFTR 603, 51 S.Ct. 150 (USSC, 1931).

All Events and Economic Performance Tests for Deductions.   An **all events test** applies to accrual basis deductions. A deduction cannot be claimed until (1) all the events have occurred to create the taxpayer's liability and (2) the amount of the liability can be determined with reasonable accuracy.[44] Once these requirements are satisfied, the deduction will be permitted only if economic performance has occurred.[45]

The **economic performance test** addresses situations in which the taxpayer has either of the following obligations:

1. To pay for services or property to be provided in the future.
2. To provide services or property (other than money) in the future.

When services or property are to be provided to the taxpayer in the future (situation 1), economic performance occurs when the property or services are actually provided by the other party.

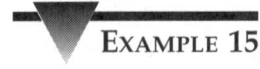

EXAMPLE 15
An accrual basis calendar year taxpayer, JAB, Inc., promoted a boxing match held in the company's arena on December 31, 1998. CLN, Inc., had contracted to clean the arena for $5,000, but did not actually perform the work until January 1, 1999. JAB, Inc., did not pay the $5,000 until 2000. Although financial accounting would require JAB, Inc., to accrue the $5,000 cleaning expense in 1998 to match the revenues from the fight, the economic performance test was not satisfied until 1999, when CLN, Inc., performed the service. Thus, JAB, Inc., must deduct the expense in 1999. ▼

If the taxpayer is obligated to provide property or services (situation 2), economic performance occurs (and thus the deduction is allowed) in the year the taxpayer provides the property or services.

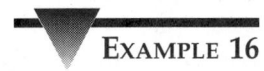

EXAMPLE 16
Copper Corporation, an accrual basis taxpayer, is in the strip mining business. According to the contract with the landowner, the company must reclaim the land. The estimated cost of reclaiming land mined in 1998 was $500,000, but the land was not actually reclaimed until 2000. The all events test was satisfied in 1998. The obligation existed, and the amount of the liability could be determined with reasonable accuracy. However, the economic performance test was not satisfied until 2000. Therefore, the deduction is not allowed until 2000.[46] ▼

The economic performance test is waived, and thus year-end accruals can be deducted, if all the following conditions (*recurring item exception*) are met:

- The obligation exists and the amount of the liability can be reasonably estimated.
- Economic performance occurs within a reasonable period (but not later than 8½ months after the close of the taxable year).
- The item is recurring in nature and is treated consistently by the taxpayer.
- Either the accrued item is not material, or accruing it results in a better matching of revenues and expenses.

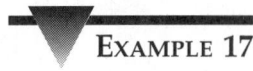

EXAMPLE 17
Green Corporation often sells goods that are on hand but cannot be shipped for another week. Thus, the sales account usually includes revenues for some items that have not been shipped at year-end. Green Corporation is obligated to pay shipping costs. Although the

---

[44]§ 461(h)(4).
[45]§ 461(h).

[46]See § 468 for an elective method for reporting reclamation costs.

company's obligation for shipping costs can be determined with reasonable accuracy, economic performance is not satisfied until Green (or its agent) actually delivers the goods. However, accruing shipping costs on sold items will better match expenses with revenues for the period. Therefore, the company should be allowed to accrue the shipping costs on items sold but not shipped at year-end. ▼

The economic performance test as set forth in the Code does not address all possible accrued expenses. That is, in some cases, the taxpayer incurs cost even though no property or services were received. In these instances, according to Regulations, economic performance generally is not satisfied until the liability is paid. The following liabilities are cases in which payment is generally the only means of satisfying economic performance:[47]

1. Workers' compensation.
2. Torts.
3. Breach of contract.
4. Violation of law.
5. Rebates and refunds.
6. Awards, prizes, and jackpots.
7. Insurance, warranty, and service contracts.[48]
8. Taxes.

EXAMPLE 18   Yellow Corporation sold defective merchandise that injured a customer. Yellow admitted liability in 1998, but did not pay the claim until January 1999. The customer's tort claim cannot be deducted until it is paid. ▼

However, items (5) through (8) above are eligible for the aforementioned recurring item exception.

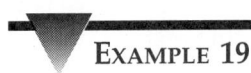

EXAMPLE 19   Pelican Corporation filed its 1998 state income tax return in March 1999. At the time the return was filed, Pelican was required to pay an additional $5,000. The state taxes are eligible for the recurring item exception. Thus, the $5,000 of state income taxes can be deducted on the corporation's 1998 Federal tax return. The deduction is allowed because all the events had occurred to fix the liability as of the end of 1998, the payment was made within 8½ months after the end of the tax year, the item is recurring in nature, and allowing the deduction in 1998 produces a good matching of revenues and expenses. ▼

Reserves.   Generally, the all events and economic performance tests will prevent the use of reserves (e.g., for product warranty expense) frequently used in financial accounting to match expenses with revenues. However, small banks are allowed to use a bad debt reserve.[49] Furthermore, an accrual basis taxpayer in a service business is permitted to not accrue revenue that appears uncollectible based on experience. In effect, this approach indirectly allows a reserve.[50]

HYBRID METHOD

A **hybrid method** of accounting involves the use of more than one method. For example, a taxpayer who uses the accrual basis to report sales and cost of goods

---

[47]Reg. §§ 1.461–4(g)(2)–(6) and 1.461–5(c).

[48]This item applies to contracts the taxpayer enters into for his or her own protection, rather than the taxpayer's liability as insurer, warrantor, or service provider.

[49]§ 585.

[50]§ 448(d)(5).

sold but uses the cash basis to report other items of income and expense is employing a hybrid method. The Code permits the use of a hybrid method provided the taxpayer's income is clearly reflected.[51] A taxpayer who uses the accrual method for business expenses must also use the accrual method for business income (a cash method may not be used for income items if the taxpayer's expenses are accounted for under the accrual method).

It may be preferable for a business that is required to report sales and cost of goods sold on the accrual method to report other items of income and expense under the cash method. The cash method permits greater flexibility in the timing of income and expense recognition.

CHANGE OF METHOD

3 **LEARNING OBJECTIVE**
Utilize the procedure for changing accounting methods.

The taxpayer, in effect, makes an election to use a particular accounting method when an initial tax return is filed using that method. If a subsequent change in method is desired, the taxpayer must obtain the permission of the IRS. The request for change is made on Form 3115, Application for Change in Accounting Method. Generally, the form must be filed within the taxable year of the desired change.[52]

As previously mentioned, the term *accounting method* encompasses not only the overall accounting method used by the taxpayer (the cash or accrual method) but also the treatment of any material item of income or deduction.[53] Thus, a change in the method of deducting property taxes from a cash basis to an accrual basis that results in a deduction for taxes in a different year constitutes a change in an accounting method. Another example of accounting method change is a change involving the method or basis used in the valuation of inventories. However, a change in treatment resulting from a change in underlying facts does not constitute a change in the taxpayer's method of accounting.[54] For example, a change in employment contracts so that an employee accrues one day of vacation pay for each month of service rather than 12 days of vacation pay for a full year of service is a change in the underlying facts and is therefore not an accounting method change.

Correction of an Error.   A change in accounting method should be distinguished from the *correction of an error*. The taxpayer can correct an error (by filing amended returns) without permission, and the IRS can simply adjust the taxpayer's liability if an error is discovered on audit of the return. Some examples of errors are incorrect postings, errors in the calculation of tax liability or tax credits, deductions of business expense items that are actually personal, and omissions of income and deductions.[55] Unless the taxpayer or the IRS corrects the error within the statute of limitations, the taxpayer's total lifetime taxable income will be overstated or understated by the amount of the error.

Change from an Incorrect Method.   An *incorrect accounting method* is the consistent (year-after-year) use of an incorrect rule to report an item of income or expense. The incorrect accounting method generally will not affect the taxpayer's total lifetime income (unlike the error). That is, an incorrect method has a self-balancing mechanism. For example, deducting freight on inventory in the year the goods are purchased, rather than when the inventory is sold,

---

[51]§ 446(c).
[52]Rev.Proc. 97–27, I.R.B. No. 21, 10.
[53]Reg. § 1.446–1(a)(1).

[54]Reg. § 1.446–1(e)(2)(ii).
[55]Reg. § 1.446–1(e)(2)(ii)(b).

is an incorrect accounting method. The total cost of goods sold over the life of the business is not affected, but the year-to-year income is incorrect.[56]

If a taxpayer is employing an incorrect method of accounting, permission must be obtained from the IRS to change to a correct method. An incorrect method is not treated as a mechanical error that can be corrected by merely filing an amended tax return.

The tax return preparer as well as the taxpayer will be subject to penalties if the tax return is prepared using an incorrect method of accounting and permission for a change to a correct method has not been requested.[57]

Net Adjustments Due to Change in Accounting Method. In the year of a change in accounting method, some items of income and expense may have to be adjusted to prevent the change from distorting taxable income.

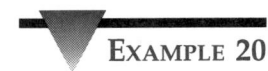

EXAMPLE 20

In 1998, White Corporation, with consent from the IRS, switched from the cash to the accrual basis for reporting sales and cost of goods sold. The corporation's accrual basis gross profit for the year was computed as follows:

Sales		$100,000
Beginning inventory	$ 15,000	
Purchases	60,000	
Less: Ending inventory	(10,000)	
Cost of goods sold		(65,000)
Gross profit		$ 35,000

At the end of the previous year, White Corporation had accounts receivable of $25,000 and accounts payable for merchandise of $34,000. The accounts receivable from the previous year in the amount of $25,000 were never included in gross income since White was on the cash basis and did not recognize the uncollected receivables. In the current year, the $25,000 was not included in the accrual basis sales since the sales were made in a prior year. Therefore, a $25,000 adjustment to income is required to prevent the receivables from being omitted from income.

The corollary of the failure to recognize a prior year's receivables is the failure to recognize a prior year's accounts payable. The beginning of the year's accounts payable was not included in the current or prior year's purchases. Thus, a deduction for the $34,000 was not taken in either year and is therefore included as an adjustment to income for the period of change.

An adjustment is also required to reflect the $15,000 beginning inventory that White deducted (due to the use of a cash method of accounting) in the previous year. In this instance, the cost of goods sold during the year of change was increased by the beginning inventory and resulted in a double deduction.

The net adjustment due to the change in accounting method is computed as follows:

Beginning inventory (deducted in prior and current year)	$ 15,000
Beginning accounts receivable (omitted from income)	25,000
Beginning accounts payable (omitted from deductions)	(34,000)
Net increase in taxable income	$ 6,000

▼

---

[56]But see *Korn Industries v. U.S.*, 76–1 USTC ¶9354, 37 AFTR2d 76–1228, 532 F.2d 1352 (Ct.Cls., 1976).

[57]§ 446(f). See *West's Federal Taxation: Corporations, Partnerships, Estates, and Trusts*, Chapter 16.

Disposition of the Net Adjustment.   Generally, if the IRS *requires* the taxpayer to change an accounting method, the net adjustment is added to or subtracted from the income for the year of the change. In cases of positive (an increase in income) adjustments in excess of $3,000, the taxpayer is allowed to calculate the tax by spreading the adjustment over one or more previous years.[58]

To encourage taxpayers to *voluntarily* change from incorrect methods and to facilitate changes from one correct method to another, the IRS generally allows the taxpayer to spread the adjustment into future years. One-fourth of the adjustment is applied to the year of the change, and one-fourth of the adjustment is applied to each of the next three taxable years.[59]

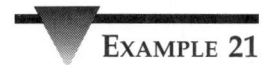

EXAMPLE 21

White Corporation in Example 20 voluntarily changed from an incorrect method (the cash basis was incorrect because inventories were material to the business) to a correct method. The company must add $1,500 (¼ × $6,000 positive adjustment) to its 1998, 1999, 2000, and 2001 income. ▼

SPECIAL ACCOUNTING METHODS

Generally, accrual basis taxpayers recognize income when goods are sold and shipped to the customer. Cash basis taxpayers generally recognize income from a sale on the collection of cash from the customer. The tax law provides special accounting methods for certain installment sales and long-term contracts. These special methods were enacted, in part, to assure that the tax will be due when the taxpayer is best able to pay the tax.

4 LEARNING OBJECTIVE
Determine when the installment method of accounting can be utilized and apply the related calculation techniques.

INSTALLMENT METHOD

Under the general rule for computing the gain or loss from the sale of property, the taxpayer recognizes the entire amount of gain or loss upon the sale or other disposition of the property.

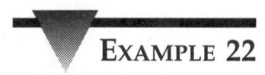

EXAMPLE 22

Mark sells property to Fran for $10,000 cash plus Fran's note (fair market value and face amount of $90,000). Mark's basis for the property was $15,000. Gain or loss is computed under either the cash or accrual basis as follows:

Amount realized	
Cash down payment	$ 10,000
Note receivable	90,000
	$100,000
Basis in the property	(15,000)
Realized gain	$ 85,000

▼

In Example 22, the general rule for recognizing gain or loss requires Mark to pay a substantial amount of tax on the gain in the year of sale even though he received only $10,000 cash. Congress enacted the installment sales provisions to prevent this sort of hardship by allowing the taxpayer to spread the gain from installment sales over the collection period. The installment method is a very important planning tool because of the tax deferral possibilities.

---

[58]§ 481(b).   [59]Rev.Proc. 97–27, I.R.B. No. 21, 10.

ART GALLERY WAS NOT A DEALER WHILE ITS PRINCIPAL EMPLOYEE WAS IN JAIL

After four trips to the courthouse, Andrew Crispo Gallery, Inc., was allowed to use the installment method to report gains from the sales of paintings seized by creditors. Generally, a dealer in personal property cannot use the installment method to report gains from the sale of inventory. In *Andrew Crispo Gallery, Inc. v. Comm.*, 96–1 USTC ¶50,313, 77 AFTR2d 96–2517, 86 F.3d 42 (CA–2, 1996), however, the character of the property changed while the owner of the gallery, who was also its principal salesperson, was in prison for tax fraud. The property was seized and sold to satisfy creditors 21 months after the gallery had been closed. In the first trial, the Tax Court held the property was inventory because it was purchased for resale. In the second trip to the courthouse, the appellate court held that the character of the property had to be determined at the time it was sold (not when it was acquired), and remanded the case to the Tax Court. But the Tax Court reached the same result the third time the gallery was in court on tax matters. Finally, the appellate court held that the paintings were not inventory because they were not held for sale to customers in the ordinary course of business.

Installment sales treatment was especially beneficial to the gallery because if the profits from the sales could be deferred, the company could increase its net operating loss carryback. This would generate additional cash to pay creditors.

Eligibility and Calculations. The **installment method** applies to *gains* (but not losses) from the sale of property where the seller will receive at least one payment *after* the year of sale. For many years, practically all gains from the sale of property were eligible for the installment method. However, over the years, the Code has been amended to *deny* the use of the installment method for the following:[60]

- Gains on property held for sale in the ordinary course of business.
- Depreciation recapture under § 1245 or § 1250.
- Gains on stocks or securities traded on an established market.

As an exception to the first item, the installment method may be used to report gains from sales of the following:[61]

- Time-share units (e.g., the right to use real property for two weeks each year).
- Residential lots (if the seller is not to make any improvements).
- Any property used or produced in the trade or business of farming.

The Nonelective Aspect. Regardless of the taxpayer's method of accounting, as a general rule, eligible sales *must* be reported by the installment method.[62] A special election is required to report the gain by any other method of accounting (see the discussion in a subsequent section of this chapter).

Computing the Gain for the Period. The gain reported on each sale is computed by the following formula:

---

[60]§§ 453(b), (i), and (l).
[61]§ 453(l)(2).

[62]§ 453(a).

$$\frac{\text{Total gain}}{\text{Contract price}} \times \text{Payments received} = \text{Recognized gain}$$

The taxpayer must compute each variable as follows:

1. *Total gain* is the selling price reduced by selling expenses and the adjusted basis of the property. The selling price is the total consideration received by the seller, including notes receivable from the buyer and the seller's liabilities assumed by the buyer.
2. *Contract price* is the selling price less the seller's liabilities that are assumed by the buyer. Generally, the contract price is the amount, other than interest, the seller will receive from the purchaser.
3. *Payments received* are the collections on the contract price received in the tax year. This generally is equal to the cash received less the interest income collected for the period. If the buyer pays any of the seller's expenses, the seller regards the amount paid as a payment received.

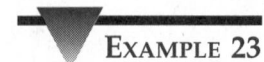

EXAMPLE 23

The seller is not a dealer, and the facts are as follows:

Sales price		
Cash down payment	$ 1,000	
Seller's mortgage assumed	3,000	
Notes payable to the seller	13,000	$ 17,000
Selling expenses		(500)
Seller's basis		(10,000)
Total gain		$ 6,500

The contract price is $14,000 ($17,000 − $3,000). Assuming the $1,000 is the only payment in the year of sale, the recognized gain in that year is computed as follows:

$$\frac{\$6,500 \text{ (total gain)}}{\$14,000 \text{ (contract price)}} \times \$1,000 = \$464 \quad \begin{array}{l}\text{(gain recognized} \\ \text{in year of sale)}\end{array}$$

▼

If the sum of the seller's basis and selling expenses is less than the liabilities assumed by the buyer, the difference must be added to the contract price and to the payments (treated as *deemed payments*) received in the year of sale.[63] This adjustment to the contract price is required so that the ratio of total gain to contract price will not be greater than one. The adjustment also accelerates the reporting of income from the deemed payments.

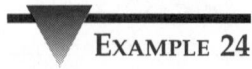

EXAMPLE 24

Assume the same facts as in Example 23, except that the seller's basis in the property is only $2,000. The total gain, therefore, is $14,500 [$17,000 − ($2,000 + $500)]. Payments in the year of sale are $1,500 and are calculated as follows:

Down payment	$1,000
Excess of mortgage assumed over seller's basis and expenses ($3,000 − $2,000 − $500)	500
	$1,500

---

[63]Temp.Reg. § 15a.453-1(b)(2)(iii).

The contract price is $14,500 [$17,000 (selling price) – $3,000 (seller's mortgage assumed) + $500 (excess of mortgage assumed over seller's basis and selling expenses)]. The gain recognized in the year of sale is computed as follows:

$$\frac{\$14,500 \text{ (total gain)}}{\$14,500 \text{ (contract price)}} \times \$1,500 = \$1,500$$

In subsequent years, all amounts the seller collects on the note principal ($13,000) will be recognized gain ($13,000 × 100%). ▼

As previously discussed, gains attributable to ordinary income recapture under §§ 1245 and 1250 are *ineligible* for installment reporting. Therefore, the § 1245 or § 1250 gain realized must be recognized in the year of sale, and the installment sale gain is the remaining gain.

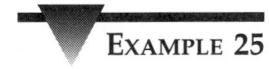

EXAMPLE 25

Olaf sold an apartment building for $50,000 cash and a $75,000 note due in two years. Olaf's basis in the property was $25,000, and he recaptured $40,000 ordinary income under § 1250.

Olaf's realized gain is $100,000 ($125,000 – $25,000), and the $40,000 recapture must be recognized in the year of sale. Of the $60,000 remaining § 1231 gain, $24,000 must be recognized in the year of sale:

$$\frac{\text{§ 1231 gain}}{\text{Contract price}} \times \text{Payments received} = \frac{\$125,000 - \$25,000 - \$40,000}{\$125,000} \times \$50,000$$

$$= \frac{\$60,000}{\$125,000} \times \$50,000 = \$24,000$$

The remaining realized gain of $36,000 ($60,000 – $24,000) will be recognized as the $75,000 note is collected. ▼

Imputed Interest. If a deferred payment contract for the sale of property with a selling price greater than $3,000 does not contain a reasonable interest rate, a reasonable rate is imputed.[64] The imputing of interest effectively restates the selling price of the property to equal the sum of the payments at the date of the sale and the discounted present value of the future payments. The difference between the present value of a future payment and the payment's face amount is taxed as interest income, as discussed in the following paragraphs. Thus, the **imputed interest** rules prevent sellers of capital assets from increasing the selling price to reflect the equivalent of unstated interest on deferred payments and thereby converting ordinary (interest) income into long-term capital gains. In addition, the imputed interest rules are important because they affect the timing of income recognition.

Generally, if the contract does not charge at least the Federal rate, interest will be imputed at the Federal rate. The Federal rate is the interest rate the Federal government pays on new borrowing and is published monthly by the IRS.[65]

As a general rule, the buyer and seller must account for interest on the accrual basis with semiannual compounding.[66] Requiring the use of the accrual basis assures that the seller's interest income and the buyer's interest expense are reported in the same tax year. Under pre-1984 law, the cash basis seller did not report interest income until it was actually collected, but an accrual basis buyer could deduct the interest as it accrued. The following example illustrates the calculation and amortization of imputed interest.

---

[64]§§ 483 and 1274.
[65]§ 1274(d)(1). There are three Federal rates: short-term (not over three years), mid-term (over three years but not over nine years), and long-term (over nine years).

[66]§§ 1274(a), 1273(a), and 1272(a).

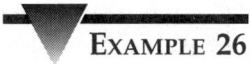

EXAMPLE 26

Peggy, a cash basis taxpayer, sold land on January 1, 1998, for $200,000 cash and $6 million due on December 31, 1999, with 5% interest payable December 31, 1998, and December 31, 1999. At the time of the sale, the Federal rate was 8% (compounded semiannually). Because Peggy did not charge at least the Federal rate, interest will be imputed at 8% (compounded semiannually).

Date	Payment	Present Value (at 8%) on 1/1/1998	Imputed Interest
12/31/1998	$ 300,000	$ 277,500	$ 22,500
12/31/1999	6,300,000	5,386,500	913,500
	$6,600,000	$5,664,000	$936,000

Thus, the selling price will be restated to $5,864,000 ($200,000 + $5,664,000) rather than $6,200,000 ($200,000 + $6,000,000), and Peggy will recognize interest income in accordance with the following amortization schedule:

	Beginning Balance	Interest Income (at 8%)*	Received	Ending Balance
1998	$5,664,000	$462,182	$ 300,000	$5,826,182
1999	5,826,182	473,818	6,300,000	–0–

*Compounded semiannually.

Congress has created several exceptions regarding the rate at which interest is imputed and the method of accounting for the interest income and expense. The general rules and exceptions are summarized in Concept Summary 18–1.

Related-Party Sales of Nondepreciable Property.   If the Code did not contain special rules, a taxpayer could make an installment sale of property to a related party (e.g., a family member) who would obtain a basis in the property equal to the purchase price (the fair market value of the property). Then, the purchasing family member could immediately sell the property to an unrelated party for cash with no recognized gain or loss (the amount realized would equal the basis). The related-party purchaser would not pay the installment note to the selling family member until a later year or years. The net result would be that the family has the cash, but no taxable gain is recognized until the intrafamily transfer of the cash (the purchasing family member makes payments on the installment note).

Under special rules designed to combat the scheme described above, the proceeds from the subsequent sale (the second sale) by the purchasing family member are treated as though they were used to pay the installment note due the selling family member (the first sale). As a result, the recognition of gain from the original sale between the related parties is accelerated.[67]

However, even with these special rules, Congress did not eliminate the benefits of all related-party installment sales.

---

[67]§ 453(e).

Interest on Installment Sales

	Imputed Interest Rate
General rule	Federal rate
Exceptions:	
• Principal amount not over $2.8 million.[1]	Lesser of Federal rate or 9%
• Sale of land (with a calendar year ceiling of $500,000) between family members (the seller's spouse, brothers, sisters, ancestors, or lineal descendants).[2]	Lesser of Federal rate or 6%

	Method of Accounting for Interest	
	Seller's Interest Income	Buyer's Interest Expense
General rule[3]	Accrual	Accrual
Exceptions:		
• Total payments under the contract are $250,000 or less.[4]	Taxpayer's overall method	Taxpayer's overall method
• Sale of a farm (sales price of $1 million or less).[5]	Taxpayer's overall method	Taxpayer's overall method
• Sale of a principal residence.[6]	Taxpayer's overall method	Taxpayer's overall method
• Sale for a note with a principal amount of not over $2 million, the seller is on the cash basis, the property sold is not inventory, and the buyer agrees to report expense by the cash method.[7]	Cash	Cash

[1]§ 1274A. This amount is adjusted annually for inflation. For 1998, the amount is $3,823,100.
[2]§§ 1274(c)(3)(F) and 483(e).
[3]§§ 1274(a) and 1272(a)(3).
[4]§§ 1274(c)(3)(C) and 483.
[5]§§ 1274(c)(3)(A) and 483.
[6]§§ 1274(c)(3)(B) and 483.
[7]§ 1274A(c). This amount is adjusted annually for inflation. For 1998, the amount is $2,730,800.

- Related parties include the first seller's brothers, sisters, ancestors, lineal descendants, controlled corporations, and partnerships, trusts, and estates in which the seller has an interest.[68]
- There is no acceleration if the second disposition occurs more than two years after the first sale.[69]

Thus, if the taxpayer can sell the property to an unrelated party (not a related party) or patient family member, the intrafamily installment sale is still a powerful tax planning tool. Other exceptions also can be applied in some circumstances.[70]

---

[68]§ 453(f)(1), cross-referencing §§ 267(b) and 318(a). Although spouses are related parties, the exemption of gain between spouses (§ 1041) makes the second-disposition rules inapplicable when the first sale was between spouses.

[69]§ 453(e)(2). But see § 453(e)(2)(B) for extensions of the two-year period.
[70]See §§ 453(e)(6) and (7).

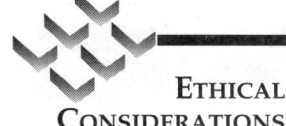

ETHICAL CONSIDERATIONS

A Related-Party Installment Sale Has Unexpected Results

Amos has been in the farming business for over 40 years. Since he is nearing retirement age—although he will never retire—he would like to slow down. He decides to sell 300 acres of his land to his 26-year-old son, Chuck, for $465,000 so Chuck can go into the farming business. Amos's basis for the land is $50,000. Since Chuck does not have much equity and Amos would like to keep the financing of the land in the family, the sales contract calls for a $15,000 down payment and annual payments of $30,000 for 15 years plus interest at 8 percent. Amos anticipates Chuck's profit from the farm will be adequate to cover these payments and provide Chuck with a decent living.

Chuck makes the payment for the first year. Unfortunately, he then gets involved with some young people from a nearby city and develops a drug problem. To finance his drug dependency, 14 months after acquiring the farm, he sells it for $500,000 cash to a real estate developer who intends to build 1,000 tract houses on the land.

When Amos learns of this, he is furious. He disowns Chuck and vows never to speak to him again.

Now Amos's CPA tells him that he has another problem. The sale of the land by Chuck should be treated as if Chuck had paid Amos the remaining balance on the installment sale. The CPA explains to Amos that this result occurs because his original sale to Chuck was a related-party transaction. Amos finds this ridiculous and says he no longer has a son.

Who is correct, Amos or the CPA? Evaluate the equity of the related-party provision.

Related-Party Sales of Depreciable Property.   The installment method cannot be used to report a gain on the sale of depreciable property to a controlled entity. The purpose of this rule is to prevent the seller from deferring gain (until collections are received) while the related purchaser is enjoying a stepped-up basis for depreciation purposes.[71]

The prohibition on the use of the installment method applies to sales between the taxpayer and a partnership or corporation in which the taxpayer holds a more-than-50 percent interest. Constructive ownership rules are used in applying the ownership test (e.g., the taxpayer is considered to own stock owned by a spouse and certain other family members).[72] However, if the taxpayer can establish that tax avoidance was not a principal purpose of the transaction, the installment method can be used to report the gain.

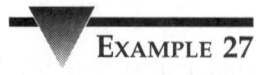

EXAMPLE 27

Alan purchased an apartment building from his controlled corporation, Emerald Corporation. Alan was short of cash at the time of the purchase (December 1998), but was to collect a large cash payment in January 1999. The agreement required Alan to pay the entire arm's length price in January 1999. Alan had good business reasons for acquiring the building. Emerald Corporation should be able to convince the IRS that tax avoidance was not a principal purpose for the installment sale because the tax benefits are not overwhelming. The corporation will report all of the gain in the year following the year of sale, and the building must be expensed over 27.5 years (the cost recovery period). ▼

---

[71]§ 453(g).   [72]§§ 1239(b) and (c).

DISPOSITION OF INSTALLMENT OBLIGATIONS

Generally, a taxpayer must recognize the deferred profit from an installment sale when the obligation is transferred to another party or otherwise relinquished. The rationale for accelerating the gain is that the deferral should continue for no longer than the taxpayer owns the installment obligation.[73]

The gift or cancellation of an installment note is treated as a taxable disposition by the donor. The amount realized from the cancellation is the face amount of the note if the parties (obligor and obligee) are related to each other.[74]

▼ **EXAMPLE 28**   Liz cancels a note issued by Tina (Liz's daughter) that arose in connection with the sale of property. At the time of the cancellation, the note had a basis to Liz of $10,000, a face amount of $25,000, and a fair market value of $20,000. Presuming the initial sale by Liz qualified as an installment sale, the cancellation results in gain of $15,000 ($25,000 − $10,000) to Liz. ▼

Certain exceptions to the recognition of gain provisions are provided for transfers of installment obligations pursuant to tax-free incorporations under § 351, contributions of capital to a partnership, certain corporate liquidations, transfers due to the taxpayer's death, and transfers between spouses or incident to divorce.[75] In such instances, the deferred profit is merely shifted to the transferee, who is responsible for the payment of tax on the subsequent collections of the installment obligations.

INTEREST ON DEFERRED TAXES

With the installment method, the seller earns interest on the receivable. The receivable includes the deferred gain. Thus, one could argue that the seller is earning interest on the deferred taxes. Some commentators reason that the government is, in effect, making interest-free loans to taxpayers who report gains by the installment method. Following the argument that the amount of the deferred taxes is a loan, the taxpayer is required to pay interest on the deferred taxes in some situations.[76]

The taxpayer is required to pay interest on the deferred taxes only if *both* of the following requirements are met:

- The installment obligation arises from the sale of property (other than farming property) for more than $150,000.
- Such installment obligations outstanding at the close of the tax year exceed $5 million.

Interest on the deferred taxes is payable only for the portion of the taxes that relates to the installment obligations in *excess* of $5 million. The interest is calculated using the underpayment rate in § 6621.

ELECTING OUT OF THE INSTALLMENT METHOD

A taxpayer can *elect not to use* the installment method. The election is made by reporting on a timely filed return the gain computed by the taxpayer's usual method of accounting (cash or accrual).[77] However, the Regulations provide that the amount realized by a cash basis taxpayer cannot be less than the value of the property sold. This rule differs from the usual cash basis accounting rules (discussed earlier),[78]

---

[73]§ 453B(a).
[74]§ 453B(f)(2).
[75]§§ 453B(c), (d), and (g). See Chapter 20 for a discussion of some of these subjects.

[76]§ 453A.
[77]§ 453(d) and Temp.Reg. § 15a.453–1(d). See also Rev.Rul. 82–227, 1982–2 C.B. 89.
[78]Refer to Chapter 4, Example 5.

which measure the amount realized in terms of the fair market value of the property received. The net effect of the Regulations is to allow the cash basis taxpayer to report his or her gain as an accrual basis taxpayer. The election is frequently applied to year-end sales by taxpayers who expect to be in a higher tax bracket in the following year.

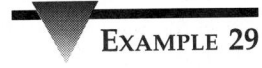

EXAMPLE 29

On December 31, 1998, Kurt sold land to Jodie for $20,000 (fair market value). The cash was to be paid on January 4, 1999. Kurt is a cash basis taxpayer, and his basis in the land is $8,000. Kurt has a large casualty loss and very little other income in 1998. Thus, his marginal tax rate in 1998 is 15%. He expects his rate to increase to 36% in 1999.

 The transaction constitutes an installment sale because a payment will be received in a tax year after the tax year of disposition. Jodie's promise to pay Kurt is an installment obligation, and under the Regulations, the value of the installment obligation is equal to the value of the property sold ($20,000). If Kurt elects out of the installment method, he would shift $12,000 of gain ($20,000 − $8,000) from the expected higher rate in 1999 to the 15% rate in 1998. The expected tax savings based on the rate differentials may exceed the benefit of the tax deferral available with the installment method. ▼

Revocation of the Election.   Permission of the IRS is required to revoke an election not to use the installment method.[79] The stickiness of the election is an added peril.

LONG-TERM CONTRACTS

5 ▼ **LEARNING OBJECTIVE**
Understand the alternative methods of accounting for long-term contracts (the completed contract method and the percentage of completion method) including the limitations on the use of the completed contract method.

A **long-term contract** is a building, installation, construction, or manufacturing contract that is entered into but not completed within the same tax year. However, a *manufacturing* contract is long term *only* if the contract is to manufacture (1) a unique item not normally carried in finished goods inventory or (2) items that normally require more than 12 calendar months to complete.[80] An item is *unique* if it is designed to meet the customer's particular needs and is not suitable for use by others. A contract to perform services (e.g., auditing or legal services) is not considered a contract for this purpose and thus cannot qualify as a long-term contract.

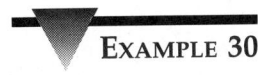

EXAMPLE 30

Rocky, a calendar year taxpayer, entered into two contracts during the year. One contract was to construct a building foundation. Work was to begin in October 1998 and was to be completed by June 1999. The contract is long term because it will not be entered into and completed in the same tax year. The fact that the contract requires less than 12 calendar months to complete is not relevant because the contract is not for manufacturing. The second contract was for architectural services to be performed over two years. These services will not qualify for long-term contract treatment because the taxpayer will not build, install, construct, or manufacture a product. ▼

 Generally, the taxpayer must accumulate all of the direct and indirect costs incurred under a contract. This means the production costs must be accumulated and allocated to individual contracts. Furthermore, mixed services costs, costs that benefit contracts as well as the general administrative operations of the business, must be allocated to production. Exhibit 18–1 lists the types of costs that must be accumulated and allocated to contracts. The taxpayer must develop reasonable bases for cost allocations.[81]

---

[79]§ 453(d)(3) and Temp.Reg. § 15a.453–1(d)(4).
[80]§ 460(f) and Reg. § 1.451–3(b).

[81]Reg. §§ 1.263A–1T(b)(3)(iii)(A)(1) and 1.451–3(d)(9).

▼ **EXHIBIT 18–1**
Contract Costs, Mixed Services
Costs, and Current Expense
Items for Contracts

	Contracts Eligible for the Completed Contract Method	Other Contracts
Contract costs:		
Direct materials (a part of the finished product).	Capital	Capital
Indirect materials (consumed in production but not in the finished product, e.g., grease and oil for equipment).	Capital	Capital
Storage, handling, and insurance on materials.	Expense	Capital
Direct labor (worked on the product).	Capital	Capital
Indirect labor (worked in the production process but not directly on the product, e.g., a construction supervisor).	Capital	Capital
Fringe benefits for direct and indirect labor (e.g., vacation, sick pay, unemployment, and other insurance).	Capital	Capital
Pension costs for direct and indirect labor:		
• Current cost.	Expense	Capital
• Past service costs.	Expense	Capital
Depreciation on production facilities:		
• For financial statements.	Capital	Capital
• Tax depreciation in excess of financial statements.	Expense	Capital
Depreciation on idle facilities.	Expense	Expense
Property taxes, insurance, rent, and maintenance on production facilities.	Capital	Capital
Bidding expenses—successful.	Expense	Capital
Bidding expenses—unsuccessful.	Expense	Expense
Interest to finance real estate construction.	Capital	Capital
Interest to finance personal property:		
• Production period of one year or less.	Expense	Expense
• Production period exceeds one year and costs exceed $1 million.	Capital	Capital
• Production period exceeds two years.	Capital	Capital
Mixed services costs:		
• Personnel operations.	Expense	Allocate
• Data processing.	Expense	Allocate
• Purchasing.	Expense	Allocate
Selling, general, and administrative expenses (including an allocated share of mixed services)	Expense	Expense
Losses	Expense	Expense

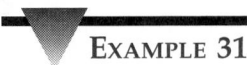

EXAMPLE 31 Falcon, Inc., uses detailed cost accumulation records to assign labor and materials to its contracts in progress. The total cost of fringe benefits is allocated to a contract on the following basis:

$$\frac{\text{Labor on the contract}}{\text{Total salaries and labor}} \times \text{Total cost of fringe benefits}$$

Similarly, storage and handling costs for materials are allocated to contracts on the following basis:

$$\frac{\text{Contract materials}}{\text{Materials purchases}} \times \text{Storage and handling costs}$$

The cost of the personnel operations, a mixed services cost, is allocated between production and general administration based on the number of employees in each function. The personnel cost allocated to production is allocated to individual contracts on the basis of the formula used to allocate fringe benefits. ▼

The accumulated costs are deducted when the revenue from the contract is recognized. Generally, two methods of accounting are used in varying circumstances to determine when the revenue from a contract is recognized:[82]

- The completed contract method.
- The percentage of completion method.

The *completed contract method may be used* for (1) home construction contracts (contracts in which at least 80 percent of the estimated costs are for dwelling units in buildings with four or fewer units) and (2) certain other real estate construction contracts. Other real estate contracts can qualify for the completed contract method if the following requirements are satisfied:

- The contract is expected to be completed within the two-year period beginning on the commencement date of the contract.
- The contract is performed by a taxpayer whose average annual gross receipts for the three taxable years preceding the taxable year in which the contract is entered into do not exceed $10 million.

All other contractors must use the percentage of completion method.

Completed Contract Method.   Under the **completed contract method**, no revenue from the contract is recognized until the contract is completed and accepted. However, a taxpayer may not delay completion of a contract for the principal purpose of deferring tax.[83]

In some instances, the original contract price may be disputed, or the buyer may want additional work to be done on a long-term contract. If the disputed amount is substantial (it is not possible to determine whether a profit or loss will ultimately be realized on the contract), the Regulations provide that no amount of income or loss is recognized until the dispute is resolved. In all other cases, the profit or loss (reduced by the amount in dispute) is recognized in the current period on completion of the contract. However, additional work may need to be performed with respect to the disputed contract. In this case, the difference between the amount in dispute and the actual cost of the additional work is recognized in the year the work is completed rather than in the year in which the dispute is resolved.[84]

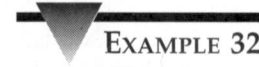

EXAMPLE 32

Ted, a calendar year taxpayer utilizing the completed contract method of accounting, constructed a building for Brad under a long-term contract. The gross contract price was $500,000. Ted finished construction in 1998 at a cost of $475,000. When Brad examined the building, he insisted that the building be repainted or the contract price be reduced. The estimated cost of repainting is $10,000. Since under the terms of the contract, Ted is assured of a profit of at least $15,000 ($500,000 − $475,000 − $10,000) even if the dispute is ultimately resolved in Brad's favor, Ted must include $490,000 ($500,000 − $10,000) in gross income and is allowed deductions of $475,000 for 1998.

---

[82]§ 460.
[83]Reg. § 1.451–3(b)(2).

[84]Reg. § 1.451–3(d)(2)(ii)–(vii), Example (2).

In 1999, Ted and Brad resolve the dispute, and Ted repaints certain portions of the building at a cost of $6,000. Ted must include $10,000 in 1999 gross income and may deduct the $6,000 expense in that year. ▼

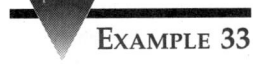

EXAMPLE 33

Assume the same facts as in the previous example, except the estimated cost of repainting the building is $50,000. Since the resolution of the dispute completely in Brad's favor would mean a net loss on the contract for Ted ($500,000 − $475,000 − $50,000 = $25,000 loss), Ted does not recognize any income or loss until the year the dispute is resolved. ▼

Frequently, a contractor receives payment at various stages of completion. For example, when the contract is 50 percent complete, the contractor may receive 50 percent of the contract price less a retainage. The taxation of these payments is generally governed by Regulation § 1.451–5 "advance payments for goods and long-term contracts" (discussed in Chapter 4). Generally, contractors are permitted to defer the advance payments until the payments are recognized as income under the taxpayer's method of accounting.

Percentage of Completion Method. The percentage of completion method must be used to account for long-term contracts unless the taxpayer qualifies for one of the two exceptions that permit the completed contract method to be used (home construction contracts and certain other real estate construction contracts).[85] Under the **percentage of completion method,** a portion of the gross contract price is included in income during each period as the work progresses. The revenue accrued each period (except for the final period) is computed as follows:[86]

$$\frac{C}{T} \times P$$

Where C = Contract costs incurred during the period
T = Estimated total cost of the contract
P = Contract price

All of the costs allocated to the contract during the period are deductible from the accrued revenue.[87] The revenue reported in the final period is simply the unreported revenue from the contract. Because T in this formula is an estimate that frequently differs from total actual costs, which are not known until the contract has been completed, the profit on a contract for a particular period may be overstated or understated.

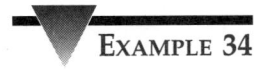

EXAMPLE 34

Tan, Inc., entered into a contract that was to take two years to complete, with an estimated cost of $2,250,000. The contract price was $3,000,000. Costs of the contract for 1998, the first year, totaled $1,350,000. The gross profit reported by the percentage of completion method for 1998 was $450,000 [($1,350,000/$2,250,000 × $3,000,000) − $1,350,000]. The contract was completed at the end of 1999 at a total cost of $2,700,000. In retrospect, 1998 profit should have been $150,000 [($1,350,000/$2,700,000 × $3,000,000) − $1,350,000]. Thus, taxes were overpaid for 1998. ▼

A *de minimis* rule enables the contractor to delay the recognition of income for a particular contract under the percentage of completion method. If less than 10 percent of the estimated contract costs have been incurred by the end of the taxable

---

[85]Certain residential construction contracts that do not qualify for the completed contract method may nevertheless use that method to account for 30% of the profit from the contract, with the remaining 70% reported by the percentage of completion method.

[86]§ 460(b)(1)(A).
[87]Reg. § 1.451–3(c)(3).

year, the taxpayer can elect to defer the recognition of income and the related costs until the taxable year in which cumulative contract costs are at least 10 percent of the estimated contract costs.[88]

Lookback Provisions.   In the year a contract is completed, a *lookback* provision requires the recalculation of annual profits reported on the contract under the percentage of completion method. Interest is paid to the taxpayer if taxes were overpaid, and interest is payable by the taxpayer if there was an underpayment.[89] For a corporate taxpayer, the lookback interest paid by the taxpayer is deductible, but for an individual taxpayer, it is nondeductible personal interest associated with a tax liability.

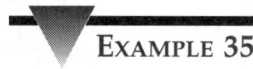

EXAMPLE 35

Assume Tan, Inc., in Example 34, was in the 35% tax bracket in both years and the relevant interest rate was 10%. For 1998, the company paid excess taxes of $105,000 [($450,000 – $150,000) × .35]. When the contract is completed at the end of 1999, Tan, Inc., should receive interest of $10,500 for one year on the tax overpayment ($105,000 × .10). ▼

INVENTORIES

6   **LEARNING OBJECTIVE**
Know when accounting for inventories must occur, recognize the types of costs that must be included in inventories, and apply the LIFO method.

Generally, tax accounting and financial accounting for inventories are much the same:

- The use of inventories is necessary to clearly reflect the income of any business engaged in the production and sale or purchase and sale of goods.[90]
- The inventories should include all finished goods, goods in process, and raw materials and supplies that will become part of the product (including containers).
- Inventory rules must give effect to the *best* accounting practice of a particular trade or business, and the taxpayer's method should be consistently followed from year to year.
- All items included in inventory should be valued at either (1) cost or (2) the lower of cost or market value.

The following are *not* acceptable methods or practices in valuing inventories:

- A deduction for a reserve for anticipated price changes.
- The use of a constant price or nominal value for a so-called normal quantity of materials or goods in stock (e.g., the base stock method).
- The inclusion in inventory of stock in transit to which title is not vested in the taxpayer.
- The direct costing approach (excluding fixed indirect production costs from inventory).
- The prime costing approach (excluding all indirect production costs from inventory).

The reason for the similarities between tax and financial accounting for inventories is that § 471 sets forth what appears to be a two-prong test. Under this provision "inventories shall be taken ... on such basis ... as conforming as nearly as may be to the *best accounting practice* in the trade or business and as most *clearly reflecting the income*." The best accounting practice is synonymous

---

[88]§ 460(b)(5).

[89]§§ 460(b)(2) and (b)(6). The taxpayer can elect to not apply the lookback method in situations where the cumulative taxable income

as of the close of each prior year is within 10% of the correct income for each prior year.

[90]§ 471(a) and Reg. §§ 1.471–1 and –2.

with generally accepted accounting principles (hereafter referred to as GAAP). However, the IRS determines whether an inventory method clearly reflects income.

In *Thor Power Tool Co. v. Comm.*, there was a conflict between the two tests.[91] The taxpayer's method of valuing obsolete parts was in conformity with GAAP. The IRS, however, successfully argued that the clear reflection of income test was not satisfied because the taxpayer's procedures for valuing its inventories were contrary to the Regulations. Under the taxpayer's method, inventories for parts in excess of estimated future sales were written off (expensed), although the parts were kept on hand and their asking prices were not reduced. [Under Regulation § 1.471–4(b), inventories cannot be written down unless the selling prices also are reduced.] The taxpayer contended that conformity to GAAP creates a presumption that the method clearly reflects income. The Supreme Court disagreed, concluding that the clear reflection of income test was *paramount*. Moreover, it is the opinion of the IRS that controls in determining whether the method of inventory clearly reflects income. Thus, the best accounting practice test was rendered practically meaningless. It follows that the taxpayer's method of inventory must strictly conform to the Regulations regardless of what GAAP may require.

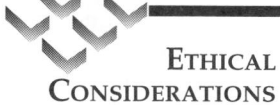

ETHICAL CONSIDERATIONS

Competitive Pressures to Play Dumb

You do not observe the taking of the physical inventory of your client. However, while reviewing other information relevant to the tax return, you discover that your client has rented a storage building that contains inventory items that were not included in the physical inventory sheets that you reviewed. Your relationship with your client is already strained because you told him that many of his entertainment expenses are nondeductible personal items. At the time, the client commented that he knows accountants who would claim the deduction "and they don't charge any more than you do." Does the situation call for selective perception?

DETERMINING INVENTORY COST

For merchandise purchased, cost is the invoice price less trade discounts plus freight and other handling charges.[92] Cash discounts approximating a fair interest rate can be deducted or capitalized at the taxpayer's option, providing the method used is consistently applied.

Uniform Capitalization.   Section 263A provides that for inventory and property produced by the taxpayer, "... (A) the direct cost of such property, and (B) such property's share of those indirect costs (including taxes) part or all of which are allocable to such property" must be capitalized. The Committee Reports observe that Congress is attempting to achieve a set of capitalization rules that will apply to all types of businesses: contractors, manufacturers, farmers, wholesalers, and retailers.[93] Congress has labeled the system the **uniform capitalization rules,** and practitioners refer to the rules as a *super-full absorption costing system.*

---

[91]79–1 USTC ¶9139, 43 AFTR2d 79–362, 99 S.Ct. 773 (USSC, 1979).
[92]Reg. § 1.471–3(b).

[93]H. Rep. 99–841, 99th Cong., 2nd Sess., 1986, pp. 302–309. See also Reg. § 1.263A–1(a).

To value inventory under the uniform capitalization rules, a *producer* must apply the following steps:

- Classify all costs into three categories: (1) production, (2) general administrative expense, and (3) mixed services.
- Allocate mixed services costs to production and general administrative expenses.[94]
- Allocate the production costs between the cost of goods sold and the ending inventory.

Exhibit 18–1 (see the "Other Contracts" column) lists typical items that are included in the three classes of costs. The mixed services costs should be allocated to production on a rational basis. For example, the costs of operating the personnel department may be allocated between production and general administration based on the number of applications processed or the number of employees. In lieu of allocating each mixed services cost, the taxpayer can elect a *simplified method* whereby the total of all mixed services costs is allocated to production as follows:[95]

$$MSP = \frac{TP}{TC} \times TMS$$

Where MSP = Mixed services costs allocated to production
  TP = Total production costs, other than interest and mixed services
  TC = Total costs, other than interest, state, local or foreign income taxes, and mixed services costs
 TMS = Total mixed services costs

The usual cost accounting techniques (e.g., average cost per equivalent unit) can be used to allocate the costs between the cost of goods sold and the ending inventory.

Alternatively, the producer can elect to allocate mixed services costs to production on the basis of labor charges only (production labor as a percentage of total labor costs).

The costs included in the inventory of *wholesalers and retailers* are comparable to those of the producer. However, many of these costs are captured in the price these taxpayers pay for the goods. The following additional costs must be capitalized by these taxpayers:

- All storage costs for wholesalers.
- Offsite storage costs for retailers.
- Purchasing costs (e.g., buyers' wages or salaries).
- Handling, processing, assembly, and repackaging.
- The portion of mixed services costs allocable to these functions.

Mixed services costs must be allocated to offsite storage, purchasing, and packaging on the basis of direct labor costs of these departments as a percentage of total payroll. Thus, the storage, purchasing, and packaging costs allocated to ending inventory include some mixed services costs.

The uniform capitalization rules may result in some costs being capitalized for tax purposes but not for financial accounting purposes. For example, a wholesaler's or a manufacturer's storage costs are generally expensed for financial reporting purposes, but are capitalized for tax purposes. Also, the taxpayer may capitalize

---

[94]Producers with mixed services costs of less than $200,000 for the year are not required to allocate mixed services costs if the simplified method is used to allocate their production costs. Reg. § 1.263A–1(b)(12).

[95]Reg. § 1.263A–1(h)(5).

straight-line depreciation of production equipment for financial accounting purposes, but the total tax depreciation must be capitalized under uniform capitalization.

Lower of Cost or Market.   Except for those taxpayers who use the LIFO method, inventories may be valued at the **lower of cost or market (replacement cost).**[96] Taxpayers using LIFO must value inventory at cost. However, the write-down of damaged or shopworn merchandise and goods that are otherwise unsalable at normal prices is not considered to be an application of the lower of cost or market method. Such items should be valued at bona fide selling price less direct cost of disposal.[97]

In the case of excess inventories (as in *Thor Power Tool Co.,* discussed above), the goods can be written down only to the taxpayer's offering price. If the offering price on the goods is not reduced, the goods must be valued at cost.

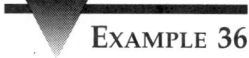
EXAMPLE 36

The Cardinal Publishing Company invested $50,000 in printing 10,000 copies of a book. Although only 7,000 copies were sold in the first 3 years and none in the next 5 years, management is convinced that the book will become a classic in 20 years. Cardinal leaves the price the same as it was when the book was first distributed ($15 per copy). The remaining 3,000 books must be valued at cost ($15,000). Note that the tax law provides an incentive for the taxpayer to destroy or abandon its excess inventory and obtain an immediate deduction rather than wait for the event of future sales. ▼

In applying the lower of cost or market method, *each* item included in the inventory must be valued at the lower of its cost or market value.[98]

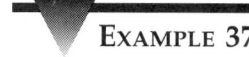
EXAMPLE 37

The taxpayer's ending inventory is valued as follows:

Item	Cost	Market	Lower of Cost or Market
A	$5,000	$ 4,000	$4,000
B	3,000	2,000	2,000
C	1,500	6,000	1,500
	$9,500	$12,000	$7,500

Under the lower of cost or market method, the taxpayer's inventory is valued at $7,500 rather than $9,500. ▼

Inventory Shrinkage.   The difference between the inventory per physical count and according to the company's records is referred to as *inventory shrinkage.* Inventory shrinkage is the result of accidents, theft, and errors in recording. Many companies take physical inventories at times other than the last day of the tax year and adjust their inventory per books to agree with the physical count. The inventory of the last day of the tax year, which is used to compute cost of goods sold, is based on the perpetual records. Such companies often adjust the ending inventory for the estimated shrinkage that has occurred between the date of the physical inventory and the last day of the tax year. The adjustment is often based on the historical relationship between inventory shrinkage and sales. The Taxpayer Relief Act of 1997 (TRA of 1997) permits

---

[96]Reg. § 1.472–4.
[97]Reg. § 1.471–2(c).

[98]Reg. § 1.471–4(c).

this shrinkage adjustment and resolves a long-running controversy between taxpayers and the IRS.[99]

Determining Cost—Specific Identification, FIFO, and LIFO.   In some cases, it is feasible to determine the cost of the particular item sold. For example, an automobile dealer can easily determine the specific cost of each automobile that has been sold. However, in most businesses it is necessary to resort to a flow of goods assumption such as *first in, first out (FIFO)*, *last in, first out (LIFO)*, or an *average cost* method. A taxpayer may use any of these methods, provided the method selected is consistently applied from year to year.

During a period of rising prices, LIFO will generally produce a lower ending inventory valuation and will result in a greater cost of goods sold than would be obtained under the FIFO method. The following example illustrates how LIFO and FIFO affect the computation of the cost of goods sold.

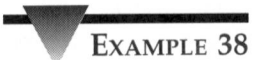

EXAMPLE 38

On January 1, 1998, the taxpayer opened a retail store to sell refrigerators. At least 10 refrigerators must be carried in inventory to satisfy customer demands. The initial investment in the 10 refrigerators is $5,000. During the year, 10 refrigerators were sold at $750 each and were replaced at a cost of $6,000 ($600 each). Gross profit under the LIFO and FIFO methods is computed as follows:

	FIFO		LIFO	
Sales (10 × $750)		$ 7,500		$ 7,500
Beginning inventory	$ 5,000		$ 5,000	
Purchases	6,000		6,000	
	$11,000		$11,000	
Ending inventory				
10 × $600	(6,000)			
10 × $500			(5,000)	
Cost of goods sold		(5,000)		(6,000)
Gross profit		$ 2,500		$ 1,500

Dollar-Value LIFO.   In the previous example, the taxpayer was buying and selling a single product, a particular model of a refrigerator. The taxpayer employed the specific goods LIFO technique. Under the specific goods approach, if the identical items are not on hand at the end of the period, the LIFO inventory is depleted, and all of the deferred profit must be recaptured. Thus, taxpayers who frequently change the items carried in inventory would realize little benefit from LIFO. However, the dollar-value LIFO technique avoids the LIFO depletion problem associated with the specific goods technique.

Under **dollar-value LIFO,** each inventory item is assigned to a pool. A *pool* is a collection of similar items and is treated as a separate inventory. Determining whether items are similar involves considerable judgment. In general, however, the taxpayer would prefer broad pools so that when a particular item is sold out, it can be replaced by increases in other items in the same pool. Generally, all products manufactured at a particular plant can be treated as a pool.[100] A department store may have a separate pool for each department. An automobile dealer may

---

[99]§ 471(b).

[100]See, generally, Reg. § 1.472–8.

have separate pools for new cars, lightweight trucks, heavy-duty trucks, and car and truck parts.

At the end of the period, the ending inventory must be valued at the current year prices and then at the LIFO base period (the year LIFO was adopted). The ratio of the ending inventory at current prices to the ending inventory at base period prices is the *LIFO index*. If the total current inventory at base period prices is greater than the base period inventory at base period prices, a LIFO layer must be added. The LIFO index is applied to the LIFO layer to convert it to current prices.

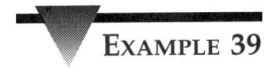

EXAMPLE 39

Black Company adopted LIFO effective January 1, 1998. The base LIFO inventory (from December 31, 1997) was $1,000,000. On December 31, 1998, the inventory was $1,320,000 at end-of-1998 prices and $1,200,000 at end-of-1997 (the base period) prices. Thus, Black added a 1998 layer of $200,000 ($1,200,000 − $1,000,000) at base period prices. The layer must be converted to 1998 prices as follows:

$$\text{LIFO index} = \$1,320,000/\$1,200,000 = 1.10$$

$$\text{1998 layer} \times \text{LIFO index} = \$200,000 \times 1.10 = \$220,000$$

Therefore, the 1998 ending inventory is $1,000,000 + $220,000 = $1,220,000.

The inventory on December 31, 1999, is $1,325,000 using 1999 prices and $1,250,000 using base period prices. Thus, the LIFO index for 1999 is $1,325,000/$1,250,000 = 1.06. The LIFO inventory is $1,273,000, computed as follows:

BLACK COMPANY
LIFO Inventory
December 31, 1999

	Base Period Cost	LIFO Index	LIFO Layers
Base inventory	$1,000,000	1.00	$1,000,000
1998 layer	200,000	1.10	220,000
1999 layer	50,000	1.06	53,000
	$1,250,000		$1,273,000

THE LIFO ELECTION

A taxpayer may adopt LIFO by merely using the method in the tax return for the year of the change and by attaching Form 970 (Application to Use LIFO Inventory Method) to the tax return. Thus, a taxpayer does not have to request approval for the change. Once the election is made, it cannot be revoked. However, a prospective change from LIFO to any other inventory method can be made only if the consent of the IRS is obtained.[101]

The beginning inventory valuation for the first year LIFO is used is computed by the costing method employed in the preceding year. Thus, the beginning LIFO inventory is generally the same as the closing inventory for the preceding year. However, since lower of cost or market cannot be used in conjunction with LIFO, previous write-downs to market for items included in the beginning inventory must be restored to income. The amount the inventories are written up is an

---

[101]Reg. §§ 1.472–3(a) and 1.472–5 and Rev.Proc. 84–74, 1984–2 C.B. 736 at 742.

adjustment due to a change in accounting method.[102] However, the usual rules for disposition of the adjustments under Revenue Procedure 97–27 are not applicable.[103] The taxpayer is allowed to spread the adjustment ratably over the year of the change and the two succeeding years.

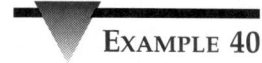

EXAMPLE 40

In 1997, Paul used the lower of cost or market FIFO inventory method. The FIFO cost of his ending inventory was $30,000, and the market value of the inventory was $24,000. Therefore, the ending inventory for 1997 was $24,000. Paul switched to LIFO in 1998 and was required to write up the beginning inventory to $30,000. Paul must add $2,000 ($6,000 ÷ 3) to his income for each of the years 1998, 1999 and 2000. ▼

Congress added this provision to the Code to overrule the previous IRS policy of requiring the taxpayer to include the entire adjustment in income for the year preceding the change to LIFO.[104]

Once the LIFO election is made for tax purposes, the taxpayer's financial reports to owners and creditors must also be prepared on the basis of LIFO.[105] The *conformity* of financial reports to tax reporting is specifically required by the Code and is strictly enforced by the IRS. However, the Regulations permit the taxpayer to make a footnote disclosure of the net income computed by another method of inventory valuation (e.g., FIFO).[106]

TAX PLANNING CONSIDERATIONS

7 **LEARNING OBJECTIVE**
Identify tax planning opportunities related to accounting periods and accounting methods.

TAXABLE YEAR

Under the general rules for tax years, partnerships and S corporations frequently will be required to use a calendar year. However, if the partnership or S corporation can demonstrate a business purpose for a fiscal year, the IRS will allow the entity to use the requested year. The advantage to a fiscal year is that the calendar year partners and S corporation shareholders may be able to defer from tax the income earned from the close of the fiscal year until the end of the calendar year. Tax advisers for these entities should apply the IRS's gross receipts test described in Revenue Procedure 87–32 to determine if permission for the fiscal year will be granted.

CASH METHOD OF ACCOUNTING

The cash method of accounting gives the taxpayer considerable control over the recognition of expenses and some control over the recognition of income. This method can be used by proprietorships, partnerships, and small corporations (gross receipts of $5 million or less) that provide services (inventories are not material to the service business). Farmers (except certain farming corporations) can also use the cash method.

INSTALLMENT METHOD

Unlike the cash and accrual methods, the installment method often results in an interest-free loan (of deferred taxes) from the government. The installment method is not available for the sale of inventory. Nevertheless, the installment method is

---

[102]Reg. § 1.472–2(c). In Rev.Rul. 76–282, 1976–2 C.B. 137, the IRS required the restoration of write-downs for damaged and shopworn goods when the taxpayer switched to LIFO.
[103]I.R.B. No. 21, 10.

[104]§ 472(d), overruling the IRS position cited in Footnote 102.
[105]§ 472(c).
[106]Reg. § 1.472–2(e).

an important tax planning technique and should be considered when a sale of eligible property is being planned. That is, if the taxpayer can benefit from deferring the tax, the terms of sale can be arranged so that the installment method rules apply. If, on the other hand, the taxpayer expects to be in a higher tax bracket when the payments will be received, he or she can elect to not use the installment method.

Related Parties. Intrafamily installment sales can still be a useful family tax planning tool. If the related party holds the property more than two years, a subsequent sale will not accelerate the gain from the first disposition. Patience and forethought are rewarded.

The 6 percent limitation on imputed interest on sales of land between family members enables the seller to convert ordinary income into capital gain or make what is, in effect, a nontaxable gift. If the selling price is raised to adjust for the low interest rate charges on an installment sale, the seller has more capital gain but less ordinary income than would be realized from a sale to an unrelated party. If the selling price is not raised and the specified interest of 6 percent is charged, the seller enables the relative to have the use of the property without having to pay for its full market value. As an additional benefit, the bargain sale is not a taxable gift.

Disposition of Installment Obligations. A disposition of an installment obligation is also a serious matter. Gifts of the obligations will accelerate income to the seller. The list of taxable and nontaxable dispositions of installment obligations should not be trusted to memory. In each instance where transfers of installment obligations are contemplated, the practitioner should conduct research to be sure he or she knows the consequences.

COMPLETED CONTRACT METHOD

Generally, large contractors must use the percentage of completion method of accounting for reporting the income from long-term contracts. Under the percentage of completion method, the taxpayer must recognize profit in each period costs are incurred. Profit is reported in proportion to the cost incurred for the period as a proportion of the total contract cost. However, small contractors (average annual gross receipts do not exceed $10 million) working on contracts that are completed within a two-year period can elect to use the completed contract method and defer profit until the year in which the contract is completed.

INVENTORIES

Lower of Cost or Market. Generally, under tax accounting rules, a deduction cannot be taken for a loss before the loss is realized. Inventories with a replacement cost below their original cost are the major exception to this rule. The rationale for the lower of cost or market method is that when the replacement cost of the goods has decreased, the taxpayer's selling price must likewise be reduced. Under the lower of cost or market method, the taxpayer is allowed to anticipate a reduction in the expected selling price of the goods by taking a deduction in the period the replacement cost decreases, rather than waiting until the goods are actually sold. Thus, the lower of cost or market method is a tax deferral technique.

LIFO. While the lower of cost or market method defers tax when replacement costs are declining, LIFO defers tax when prices are rising. However, when some goods are increasing in value while others are decreasing, the taxpayer cannot use the lower of cost or market method for the goods declining in value and LIFO for the goods whose replacement costs are rising. That is, LIFO cannot be used in conjunction with the lower of cost or market method. Assuming that prices generally are rising, the taxpayer generally should elect LIFO. The only major disadvantage to LIFO is the financial-tax conformity requirement. However, even this disadvantage can be overcome through footnote disclosure of earnings as computed under FIFO.

KEY TERMS

Accounting methods, 18–10

Accounting period, 18–3

Accrual method, 18–13

All events test, 18–14

Cash method, 18–11

Claim of right doctrine, 18–10

Completed contract method, 18–28

Dollar-value LIFO, 18–34

Economic performance test, 18–14

Fiscal year, 18–3

Hybrid method, 18–15

Imputed interest, 18–21

Installment method, 18–19

Least aggregate deferral method, 18–4

Long-term contract, 18–26

Lower of cost or market (replacement cost), 18–33

Majority interest partners, 18–4

One-year rule for prepaid expenses, 18–11

Percentage of completion method, 18–29

Personal service corporation (PSC), 18–6

Principal partner, 18–4

Short taxable year (short period), 18–8

Uniform capitalization rules, 18–31

PROBLEM MATERIALS

DISCUSSION QUESTIONS

1. Why would a department store often use a tax year ending the last day of January or February instead of December 31?

2. Megan recently began conducting an office supply business as a corporation. Vito began conducting his law practice through a corporation. Neither corporation has made an S election. What tax year alternatives are available to Megan's business that are not available to Vito's business?

3. How does a partnership establish a business purpose for a tax year that differs from its partners' tax years?

4. Dan, a calendar year taxpayer, recently became a licensed orthopedic surgeon. He has incorporated his practice. Dan's brother suggested that the corporation's tax year should end on September 30 and thus avoid the end-of-the-calendar-year rush. What complications could result from the corporation filing its return on the basis of a fiscal year ending September 30?

5. Amber Corporation began business on October 1 and reports its income on the basis of a calendar year. Jeff, who operated a sole proprietorship, died on September 30. Copper Corporation has reported its income according to the calendar year for the past 10 years, but is changing to a fiscal year ending September 30. Which of these taxpayers is (are) required to annualize their income for the current tax year?

6. Freda is a cash basis taxpayer. In 1998, she overcharged a customer $5,000. In 1999, Freda discovered the overcharge and refunded $5,000 to the customer. In 1998, she paid $3,000 on her estimated state income taxes. In 1999, she filed her state tax return and

received a $1,000 refund of her 1998 taxes paid. Freda was in the 36% marginal tax bracket in 1998 and in the 15% marginal tax bracket in 1999. Is Freda treated fairly under the system of an annual accounting period?

7. Albert is a <u>cash basis</u> taxpayer and reports his income on a calendar year. Recently, Albert became a partner in a company that imports flowers. If the partnership uses the accrual method of accounting, must Albert change to the accrual method?

8. The Cardinal Insurance Agency is a newly formed corporation, and its gross receipts will probably never exceed $2 million in a year. Generally, it takes approximately two months to collect accounts receivable. Accounts payable generally equal expenses for one month. Cardinal does not expect accounts payable and accounts receivable to increase significantly. It prepares monthly financial statements using the accrual method of accounting. Given that the accounts receivable and accounts payable will not significantly change, would Cardinal derive any benefit from filing its tax return using the cash method of accounting?

9. Earl, a certified public accountant, recently obtained a new client. The client is a retail grocery store that has used the cash method to report its income since it began doing business. Will Earl incur any liability if he prepares the tax return in accordance with the cash method and does not advise the client of the necessity of seeking the IRS's permission to change to the accrual method?

10. In December 1998, a cash basis taxpayer paid January through June 1999 management fees in connection with his rental properties. The fees were $4,000 per month. Compute the 1998 expense under the following assumptions:
    a. The fees were paid by an individual who derived substantially all of his income from the properties.
    b. The fees were paid by a tax-shelter partnership.

11. Osprey Corporation, an accrual basis taxpayer, had taxable income for 1998. However, Osprey's accountant was ill, and the taxable income for 1998 was not computed until July 1999. The state income tax return for 1998 was filed on August 13, 1999, and $3,000 in state income taxes were paid at that time. Can the 1998 state income taxes be deducted in calculating the corporation's 1998 Federal taxable income?

12. Compare the cash basis and accrual basis of accounting as applied to the following:
    a. Fixed assets.
    b. Prepaid rent income.
    c. Prepaid interest expense.
    d. A note received for services performed if the market value and face amount of the note differ.

13. Salmon Corporation and Betty have formed a partnership to rent real estate and operate a grocery store. Salmon uses the accrual method of accounting, and the company's tax year ends March 31. Betty is a cash basis, calendar year taxpayer. What are the tax accounting issues that the partnership must address?

14. In financial accounting, reserves (or allowances) are frequently used. For example, reserves are created for bad debts and product warranties. Why are reserves generally not allowed for <u>tax purposes</u>?

15. What difference does it make whether the taxpayer or the IRS initiates the change in accounting method?

16. Generally, what incentives are provided to encourage a taxpayer to change voluntarily from an incorrect method of accounting?

17. Irene has made Sara an offer on the purchase of a capital asset. Irene will pay (1) $200,000 cash or (2) $50,000 cash and a 9% installment note for $150,000 guaranteed by City Bank of New York. If Sara sells for $200,000 cash, she will invest the after-tax proceeds in certificates of deposit yielding 9% interest. Sara's cost of the asset is $25,000. Why would Sara prefer the installment sale?

18. How does the buyer's assumption of the seller's liabilities in an installment sale affect the following?
   a. Selling price.
   b. Contract price.
   c. Buyer's payments in the year of sale.

19. Sally sold an apartment building to Leroy for a stated selling price of $100,000. She received $20,000 cash and a note for $80,000 due in two years, bearing interest at the rate of 4%. At the time of the sale, the applicable Federal rate was 8%. What effects will the imputed interest rules have on the selling price and the amount of interest that Sally will report?

20. On June 1, 1996, Father sold land to Son for $100,000. Father reported the gain by the installment method, with the gain to be spread over five years. In May 1998, Son received an offer of $150,000 for the land, to be paid over three years. What would be the tax consequences of Son's sale? How could the tax consequences be improved?

21. In 1998, Bhaskar sold a building to his 100% controlled corporation. The entire purchase price is to be paid in 1999. When should Bhaskar report the gain on the sale of the building?

22. Sal sold real estate on the installment method to Renee. Three years later, when the balance on the installment obligation is $300,000, Renee is considering selling the property to Chuck, her spouse. Renee has asked Sal whether he would be willing to allow Chuck to assume Renee's note payable to Sal. Alternatively, Renee would attempt to find a buyer with sufficient cash to retire the note. Assuming that Chuck is a good credit risk, what would be the tax implications of Sal substituting Chuck for Renee on the note?

23. If the taxpayer is required to pay interest on the taxes deferred through the use of the installment method, what is the advantage of reporting gain by the installment method?

24. Juan, a cash basis taxpayer, sold land in December 1998. At the time of the sale, Juan received $10,000 cash and a note for $90,000 due in 90 days. Juan expects to be in a much higher tax bracket in 1999. Should Juan report the sale in 1998 or 1999?

25. What is the advantage of using the completed contract method as compared to the percentage of completion method?

26. What is the purpose of the lookback rules applicable to long-term contracts reported by the percentage of completion method?

27. What are the implications of overestimating the costs of a contract whose income is reported by the percentage of completion method?

28. The Eagle Corporation builds yachts. All vessels are practically identical and sell for more than $2 million. Production does not begin until the company has a contract to sell the vessel. The company has recently changed its production techniques to reduce the time for producing a yacht from 15 months to 9 months. What are the accounting method implications of the change?

29. The taxpayer has consistently treated manufacturing employees' vacation pay as an expense in the year the employee is paid. A representative of the IRS insists that the vacation pay must be added to production costs. What difference does it make?

30. Brown, Inc., a wholesaler and retailer of building materials, accounted for storage costs as a current expense. What tax accounting issues are raised by Brown's error?

31. During a period of rising prices, is the LIFO or FIFO cost determination method more likely to produce a smaller profit?   ⌐ when price are going down

32. Egret, Inc., uses the LIFO method for tax purposes. However, Egret is about to make a public offering of its stock and would like to communicate to potential investors the company's income as computed by the FIFO inventory method. How can this be done without violating the LIFO conformity provisions?

33. Can an estimate of inventory shrinkage be used in calculating the ending inventory to be used in determining cost of goods sold?

PROBLEMS

34. Red, White, and Blue are unrelated corporations engaged in real estate development. The three corporations formed a joint venture (treated as a partnership) to develop a tract of land. Assuming the venture does not have a natural business year, what tax year must the joint venture adopt under the following circumstances?

		Tax Year Ending	Interest in Joint Venture
a.	Red	Sept. 30	60%
	Blue	March 31	20%
	White	May 31	20%
b.	Red	Sept. 30	30%
	White	June 30	40%
	Blue	January 31	30%

35. The Cardinal Wholesale Company is an S corporation that began business on March 1, 1998. Robert, a calendar year taxpayer, owns 100% of the Cardinal stock. He has $400,000 taxable income from other sources each year. Robert will work approximately 30 hours a week for the corporation. Cardinal sells swimming pool supplies, and its natural business year ends in September. Approximately 80% of Cardinal's gross receipts occur in June through September.
   a. What tax year should Cardinal elect, assuming that Robert anticipates the company will produce a net profit for all years?
   b. What tax year should Cardinal elect, assuming it will lose $10,000 a month for the first 12 months and an average of $5,000 a month for the next 12 months? In the third year, the corporation will earn taxable income.

36. Zack conducted his professional practice through Zack, Inc. The corporation uses a fiscal year ending September 30 even though the business purpose test for a fiscal year cannot be satisfied. For the year ending September 30, 1998, the corporation paid Zack a salary of $180,000, and during the period January through September 1998, the corporation paid him a salary of $150,000.
   a. How much salary should Zack receive during the period October 1 through December 31, 1998?
   b. Assume Zack received only $30,000 salary during the period October 1 through December 31, 1998. What would be the consequences to Zack, Inc.?

37. Brown Maintenance Corporation has consistently used a fiscal year ending September 30 and generally earns $100,000 per year. Brown's business is seasonal, and the company earns approximately three-fourths of its annual profits during the quarter beginning October 1 and ending December 31. Assume the applicable corporate tax rates are 15% on taxable income of $50,000 or less, 25% on taxable income over $50,000 but not over $75,000, 34% on taxable income over $75,000 but not over $100,000, and 39% on taxable income in excess of $100,000 through $335,000. Brown changes to a calendar year.
   a. Compute Brown's tax liability on taxable income of $75,000 earned during the short period October 1 through December 31.
   b. Why could changing to the calendar year prove costly to Brown?

38. Carlos is a branch manager of the White Laundry. Each December he receives a bonus equal to 5% of the branch profits for the previous 12 months. In December 1998, Carlos received a $15,000 bonus. He included the bonus in his gross income, and his taxable income was $35,000. Carlos is single and itemized deductions in 1998. In 1999, the employer concluded that Carlos's 1998 bonus was overstated by $5,000, and Carlos was required to refund that amount. Carlos refunded the $5,000, but was so angry with the

employer that he quit his job. The next day Carlos received a $2,000 refund of 1998 state income taxes. Carlos did not work the remainder of the year, and his taxable income in 1999, before considering the above, was $14,000.

   a. How does the $5,000 payment by Carlos affect his tax liability for 1998?

   b. How does the $5,000 payment by Carlos affect his tax liability for 1999?

   c. How does the refund of state income taxes affect Carlos's tax liability for 1999?

39. Gold, Inc., is an accrual basis taxpayer. In 1998, an employee accidentally spilled hazardous chemicals on leased property. The chemicals destroyed trees on neighboring property, resulting in $30,000 damages. In 1998, the owner of the property sued Gold, Inc., for the $30,000. Gold's attorney feels that it is liable and the only issue is whether the neighbor will also seek punitive damages that could be as much as three times the actual damages. In addition, as a result of the spill, Gold was in violation of its lease and was therefore required to pay the landlord $15,000. However, the amount due for the lease violation was not payable until the termination of the lease in 2001. None of these costs were covered by insurance. Jeff Stuart, the president of Gold, Inc., is generally familiar with the accrual basis tax accounting rules and is concerned about when the company will be allowed to deduct the amounts the company is required to pay as a result of this environmental disaster. Write Mr. Stuart a letter explaining these issues. Gold's address is 200 Elm Avenue, San Jose, CA 95192.

40. Compute the taxpayer's income or deductions for 1998 using (1) the cash basis and (2) the accrual basis for each of the following:

   a. In 1998, the taxpayer purchased new equipment for $100,000. The taxpayer paid $25,000 in cash and gave a $75,000 interest-bearing note for the balance. The equipment has a MACRS life of five years, the mid-year convention applies, and the § 179 election was not made.

   b. In December 1998, the taxpayer collected $10,000 for January rents. In January 1999, the taxpayer collected $2,000 for December 1998 rents.

   c. In December 1998, the taxpayer paid office equipment insurance premiums of $30,000 for January–June 1999.

41. Which of the following businesses must use the accrual method of accounting?

   a. A corporation with annual gross receipts of $12 million from equipment rentals.

   b. A partnership (not a tax shelter) engaged in farming and with annual gross receipts of $8 million.

   c. A corporation that acts as an insurance agent, with annual gross receipts of $1 million.

   d. A manufacturer with annual gross receipts of $600,000.

   e. A retailer with annual gross receipts of $250,000.

42. Pink Company calculated its accrual basis income for its first year of operations. Net income before tax was $30,000. For tax purposes, the company would like to elect the method that will minimize its taxable income for the year. Compute Pink's minimum taxable income, given the following information at the end of the first year:

Inventory	$47,000
Accounts receivable	25,000
Office supplies	2,700
Prepaid insurance (6 months)	1,200
Accounts payable (merchandise)	16,000

43. The Beige Products Manufacturing Company offers a $50 rebate to purchasers of its new appliances. The customer purchases the appliance from a dealer and then must apply to Beige Products for the rebate. The rebate opportunity expires 90 days after the date of sale. According to Beige's accounting records, 50,000 products subject to rebate were sold during 1998. As of the end of 1998, 44,000 rebate requests had been received, and 43,000 had been paid. In January 1999, Beige received an additional 5,000 requests for rebates from the 1998 sales. All unpaid requests were paid in January. No additional rebate requests were received by the company before the expiration date. Beige has had the program in effect for several years. Write a letter to Gerald Fine,

Beige's president, explaining the tax consequences of the rebate program. The company's address is 905 Mason Drive, Floyd, VA 24030.

44. In 1998, the taxpayer changed from the cash to the accrual basis of accounting for sales, cost of goods sold, and accrued expenses. Taxable income for 1998 computed under the cash method was $45,000. Relevant account balances are as follows:

	Beginning of the Year	End of the Year
Accounts receivable	$ 6,000	$13,000
Accounts payable	–0–	–0–
Accrued expenses	4,000	6,000
Inventory	10,000	9,000

   a. Compute the accrual basis taxable income for 1998 and the adjustment due to the change in accounting method.
   b. Assuming the change was voluntary, how will the adjustment due to the change be treated?

45. Crow Finance Company experiences bad debts of about 3% of its outstanding loans. At the end of the year, the company had outstanding receivables of $28 million. This balance included $3 million of accrued interest receivable. Crow's loan loss reserve for the year was computed as follows:

Balance, January 1, 1998	$800,000
Accounts written off as uncollectible	
Loans made in 1998	(25,000)
Loans made in prior years	(15,000)
Collections on loans previously written off	12,000
Adjustment to required balance	68,000
Balance, December 31, 1998	$840,000

   a. Determine the effects of the above on Crow's taxable income for 1998.
   b. Assume that Crow has used the reserve method to compute its taxable income for the 10 years the company has been in existence. In 1998, you begin preparing Crow's tax return. What should be done with regard to the reserve?

46. Jeffrey Robin, the president of Robin Furniture Corporation (average annual gross receipts of $4 million), has prepared the company's financial statements and income tax return for the past 25 years. However, in July 1999, after Jeffrey had filed the 1998 return, he hired you to prepare the 1999 corporate tax return because he has not studied taxes for over 20 years and suspects that the rules may have changed. Based upon an initial examination of his trial balance and some account analyses, you have determined that the following items may require adjustments:

   • The company uses the LIFO inventory method, as valued at cost. At the end of 1998, the company has written off $25,000 for inventory items that were still on hand but probably were not marketable (because the products are obsolete). No such write-off had been taken in prior years.

   • The company expenses all freight on merchandise when the goods are received. The expensed freight allocable to the beginning inventory for 1999 was $12,000.

   • The company accrues salaries and commissions, but expenses payroll taxes in the year paid. Because of large 1998 year-end bonuses that were not paid until the beginning of 1999, the company had $24,000 in accrued payroll taxes at the beginning of 1999.

   • The company uses the accrual method and has a reserve for bad debts equal to 3% of accounts receivable, which is an accurate percentage. The balance in the account at the beginning of the year is $15,000.

Write a letter to Mr. Robin explaining the adjustments that will be required and how the changes will be implemented. The address of Robin Furniture Corporation is 1000 East Maryland, Evansville, IL 47722.

47. Floyd, a cash basis taxpayer, has agreed to sell land to Beige, Inc., a well-established and highly profitable company. Beige is willing to (1) pay $100,000 cash or (2) pay $25,000 cash and the balance ($75,000) plus interest at 10% (the Federal rate) in two years. Floyd is in the 35% marginal tax bracket (combined Federal and state) for all years and believes he can reinvest the sales proceeds and earn a 12% before-tax rate of return.
   a. Should Floyd accept the deferred payments option if his basis in the land is $10,000?
   b. Do you think your results would change if Floyd's basis in the land is $90,000?

48. Sandra, a cash method taxpayer, sells investment land on October 1, 1998, to Alfred subject to the following terms:

Selling price	$100,000
Selling expenses	2,000
Adjusted basis	18,000
Down payment	10,000
Three installment payments of	21,000
Seller's mortgage assumed by buyer	27,000

Each of the payments plus related interest is due on October 1 of 1999, 2000, and 2001, respectively. The market interest rate of 10% applies. Determine the tax consequences to Sandra in 1998, 1999, 2000, and 2001.

49. Kay, who is not a dealer, sold an apartment house to Polly during the current year (1998). The closing statement for the sale is as follows:

Total selling price		$100,000
Add: Polly's share of property taxes (6 months) paid by Kay		2,500
Less: Kay's 11% mortgage assumed by Polly	$55,000	
Polly's refundable binder ("earnest money") paid in 1997	1,000	
Polly's 11% installment note given to Kay	30,000	
Kay's real estate commissions and attorney's fees	7,500	(93,500)
Cash paid to Kay at closing		$ 9,000
Cash due from Polly = $9,000 + $7,500 expenses		$ 16,500

During 1998, Kay collected $4,000 in principal on the installment note and $2,000 interest. Kay's basis in the property was $70,000 [$85,000 − $15,000 (depreciation)], and there was $9,000 in potential depreciation recapture under § 1250. The Federal rate is 9%.
   a. Compute the following:
      1. Total gain.
      2. Contract price.
      3. Payments received in the year of sale.
      4. Recognized gain in the year of sale and the character of such gain.

   (*Hint:* Think carefully about the manner in which the property taxes are handled before you begin your computations.)
   b. Same as (a)(2) and (3), except Kay's basis in the property was $45,000.

50. On June 30, 1998, Kelly sold property for $250,000 cash on the date of sale and a $750,000 note due on September 30, 1999. No interest was stated in the contract. The present value of the note (using 13.2%, which was the Federal rate) was $640,000. Kelly's basis in the property was $400,000, and $40,000 of the gain was depreciation recapture under § 1245. Expenses of the sale totaled $10,000, and Kelly was not a dealer in the property sold.
   a. Compute Kelly's gain to be reported in 1998.
   b. Compute Kelly's interest income for 1999.

51. On July 1, 1997, a cash basis taxpayer sold land for $800,000 due on the date of the sale and $6 million principal and $741,600 interest (6%) due on June 30, 1999. The seller's basis in the land was $1 million. The Federal short-term rate was 8%, compounded semiannually.
    a. Compute the seller's interest income and gain in 1997, 1998, and 1999.
    b. Same as (a), except that the amount due in two years was $2 million principal and $508,800 interest and the purchaser will use the cash method to account for interest.

52. On December 30, 1998, Father sold land to Son for $10,000 cash and a 7% installment note with a face amount of $190,000. In 1999, after paying $30,000 on the principal of the note, Son sold the land. In 2000, Son paid Father $25,000 on the note principal. Father's basis in the land was $50,000. Assuming Son sold the land for $250,000, compute Father's taxable gain in 1999.

53. George sold land to an unrelated party in 1997. His basis in the land was $40,000, and the selling price was $100,000—$25,000 payable at closing and $25,000 (plus 10% interest) due January 1, 1998, 1999, and 2000. What would be the tax consequences of the following? [Treat each part independently and assume (1) George did not elect out of the installment method and (2) the installment obligations have values equal to their face amounts.]
    a. In 1998, George gave to his daughter the right to collect all future payments on the installment obligations.
    b. In 1998, after collecting the payment due on January 1, George transferred the installment obligation to his 100%–controlled corporation in exchange for additional shares of stock.
    c. On December 31, 1998, George received the payment due on January 1, 1999. On December 15, 1999, George died, and the remaining installment obligation was transferred to his estate. The estate collected the amount due on January 1, 2000.

54. The Dove Construction Company reports its income by the completed contract method. At the end of 1998, the company completed a contract to construct a building at a total cost of $980,000. The contract price was $1,200,000. However, the customer refused to accept the work and would not pay anything on the contract because he claimed the roof did not meet specifications. Dove's engineers estimated it would cost $140,000 to bring the roof up to the customer's standards. In 1999, the dispute was settled in the customer's favor; the roof was improved at a cost of $170,000, and the customer accepted the building and paid the $1,200,000.
    a. What would be the effects of the above on Dove's taxable income for 1998 and 1999?
    b. Same as (a), except Dove had $1,100,000 accumulated cost under the contract at the end of 1998.

 55. Rust Company is a real estate construction company with average annual gross receipts of $4 million. Rust uses the completed contract method, and the contracts require 18 months to complete.
    a. Which of the following costs would be allocated to construction in progress by Rust?
        1. The payroll taxes on direct labor.
        2. The current services pension costs for employees whose wages are included in direct labor.
        3. Accelerated depreciation on equipment used on contracts.
        4. Sales tax on materials assigned to contracts.
        5. The past service costs for employees whose wages are included in direct labor.
        6. Bidding expenses for contracts awarded.
    b. Assume that Rust generally builds commercial buildings under contracts with the owners and reports the income by the completed contract method. The company is considering building a series of similar stores for a retail chain. The gross profit margin would be a low percentage, but the company's gross receipts would triple. Write a letter to your client, Rust Company, explaining the tax accounting implications of entering into these contracts. Rust's mailing address is P.O. Box 1000, Harrisonburg, VA 22807.

56. Indicate the accounting method that should be used to compute the income from the following contracts:

    a. A contract to build six jet aircraft.
    b. A contract to build a new home. The contractor's average annual gross receipts are $15 million.
    c. A contract to manufacture 3,000 pairs of boots for a large retail chain. The manufacturer has several contracts to produce the same boot for other retailers.
    d. A contract to pave a parking lot. The contractor's average annual gross receipts are $2 million.

57. Ostrich Company makes gasoline storage tanks. Everything produced is under contract (that is, the company does not produce until it gets a contract for a product). Ostrich makes three basic models. However, the tanks must be adapted to each individual customer's location and needs (e.g., the location of the valves, the quality of the materials and insulation). Discuss the following issues relative to Ostrich's operations:

    a. An examining IRS agent contends that each of the company's contracts is to produce a "unique product." What difference does it make whether the product is unique or a "shelf item"?
    b. Producing one of the tanks takes over one year from start to completion, and the total cost is in excess of $1 million. What costs must be capitalized for this contract that are not subject to capitalization for a contract with a shorter duration and lower cost?
    c. What must Ostrich do with the costs of bidding on contracts?
    d. Ostrich frequently makes several cost estimates for a contract, using various estimates of materials costs. These costs fluctuate almost daily. Assuming Ostrich must use the percentage of completion method to report the income from the contract, what will be the consequence if the company uses the highest estimate of a contract's cost and the actual cost is closer to the lowest estimated cost?

58. Swallow Company is a large real estate construction company that reports its income by the percentage of completion method. In 1999, the company completed a contract at a total cost of $1,960,000. The contract price was $2,400,000. At the end of 1998, the year the contract was begun, Swallow estimated the total cost of the contract would be $2,100,000, and total accumulated costs on the contract at the end of 1998 were $1,400,000. The relevant tax rate is 34%, and the relevant Federal interest rate is 7%. Assume that all returns were filed and taxes were paid on March 15 following the close of the calendar tax year.

    a. Compute the gross profit on the contract for 1998 and 1999.
    b. Compute the lookback interest due with the 1999 return.
    c. Before bidding on a contract, Swallow generally makes three estimates of total contract costs: (1) optimistic, (2) pessimistic, and (3) most likely (based on a blending of optimistic and pessimistic assumptions). The company has asked you to write a letter explaining which of these estimates should be used for percentage of completion purposes. In writing your letter, you should consider the fact that Swallow is incorporated and has made an S corporation election; therefore, the income and deductions flow through to the shareholders who are all individuals in the 36% marginal tax bracket. The relevant Federal interest rate is 8%. Swallow's mailing address is 400 Front Avenue, Ashland, OR 97520.

59. In 1998, Quail Construction Company began two contracts that were completed in 1999:

    • Contract #1. The company reported $300,000 cost and $150,000 profit on the contract. In 1999, the company completed the contract, incurring additional cost of $200,000 and reporting an additional $50,000 profit on the contract.

    • Contract #2. The company reported $500,000 cost and $100,000 profit on the contract. In 1999, the company incurred an additional $200,000 to complete the contract. The contract price was $650,000.

Quail is a large real estate contractor and reports its profits by the percentage of completion method. The company's marginal tax rate in all relevant years was 34%, and the relevant Federal interest rate was 7%.

a. Compute the lookback interest payable or receivable by Quail.

b. Write a letter to Amos Brown, the president of Quail Construction Company, explaining to him the consequences of the company's errors in estimating contract costs. Quail's mailing address is 200 Country Road, Orono, ME 04469.

60. Bluebird Company, a furniture retailer, is adding a new line of merchandise. In the current year, the company purchased merchandise with an invoice price of $700,000, less a 2% discount for early payment. Freight and handling charges totaled $60,000. The company had to lease additional storage space in a warehouse three blocks from the store. The lease on the storage space was $30,000 for the year. A buyer was added to handle the new line of merchandise, and her salary was $35,000 for the year. Also, as a result of the increase in inventory of goods on hand, the company's insurance increased by $5,000. The invoice cost of the goods on hand at the end of the year was $105,000. Compute the company's ending inventory under the FIFO method.

61. Lavender Manufacturing Company began business in the current year. The company uses the simplified method to allocate mixed services costs to production. The company's costs and expenses for the year were as follows:

Direct labor	$1,750,000
Direct materials	2,000,000
Factory supervision	250,000
Personnel department	100,000
Computer operations	50,000
General administration	150,000
Marketing	100,000
Interest	25,000
	$4,425,000

a. Determine Lavender's total production costs for the year.

b. What suggestions can you offer regarding the allocation of the company's mixed services costs?

62. Copper Corporation is a calendar year taxpayer and uses the LIFO inventory method. In November a fire destroyed 25% of the company's raw materials inventory. The LIFO value of the company's inventory was $800,000, and its current replacement cost is $1,000,000. The company could continue operations until January without replacing the destroyed goods. Alternatively, it could acquire the replacement goods by the end of December. The latter option would increase storage costs. What would be the tax implications of this decision?

63. In 1998, Gail changed from the use of the lower of cost or market FIFO method to the LIFO method. The ending inventory for 1997 was computed as follows:

Item	FIFO Cost	Replacement Cost	Lower of Cost or Market
A	$10,500	$11,000	$10,500
B	25,000	23,000	23,000
			$33,500

a. What is the correct beginning inventory in 1998 under the LIFO method?

b. What immediate tax consequences (if any) would result from the switch to LIFO?

64. Amber Company has used the dollar-value LIFO technique for the past three years. The company has only one inventory pool. Its beginning inventory for the current year was computed as follows:

	Base Period Cost	**LIFO Index**	**LIFO Layer**
Base inventory	$1,250,000	1.0	$1,250,000
Year 1 layer	450,000	1.15	517,500
Year 2 layer	100,000	1.05	105,000
	$1,800,000		$1,872,500

The ending inventory is $1,955,000 at current period prices and $1,700,000 at base period prices. Determine the company's LIFO inventory value as of the end of the current year.

65. Your client, Bob Young, is negotiating a sale of investment real estate for $12 million. Bob believes that the buyer would pay cash of $8 million and a note for $4 million, or $3 million cash and a note for $9 million. The notes will pay interest at slightly above the market rate. Bob realizes that the second option involves more risks of collection, but he is willing to accept that risk if the tax benefits of the installment sale are substantial. Write a letter to Bob advising him of the tax consequences of choosing the lower down payment and larger note option, assuming he has no other installment receivables. Bob's address is 200 Jerdone, Gettysburg, PA 17325.

RESEARCH PROBLEMS

*Note: Use the **RIA OnPoint System 4 Student Version CD-ROM**, which is available to accompany this text, in preparing solutions to the Research Problems. Alternatively, tax research materials found in a standard tax library can be used.*

Research Problem 1. White Electric Company generates electricity that it sells to residential, commercial, and industrial customers. The company uses coal to generate the electricity and accounts for the cost of the coal on a LIFO basis. That is, the coal on hand at the end of the year is deemed to be from the earliest purchases. This LIFO assumption is generally consistent with how the coal is actually used because newly purchased coal is placed on top of the coal on hand at the time of the delivery. The IRS agent contends that LIFO cannot be used to account for the coal because it is a supply rather than inventory. You concede that the coal is not inventory; however, you contend that because the LIFO assumption accurately depicts the cost of the coal used, the method used clearly reflects income, and therefore the IRS cannot change the method. Help your client resolve this issue with the IRS agent.

Research Problem 2. The Salmon Computer Company manufactures, sells, and services a computer specially designed for the oil refining business. Practically all customers who purchase the computer also purchase a service contract. Salmon charges a monthly rate for the service and guarantees that the company's service personnel will be on the customer's premises within two hours of notice. Generally, when a computer requires parts, the service person takes the customer's part out of the computer and installs a new or reworked part. The removed part is then reworked for use on another service call. To provide the fast service, Salmon must maintain a stock of parts on hand, which it calls "rotable parts." This pool of rotable parts is constantly replenished as broken parts taken from customers are reworked. The IRS agent contends that the parts are inventory. Salmon has accounted for the pool of parts as a fixed asset, taken a deduction for depreciation, and expensed the cost of reworking the parts. Advise Salmon as to the correct tax classification for these parts.

Research Problem 3. Rex Custer has incorporated his insurance agency. Rex is the only shareholder, and he handles all of the company's cash receipts and disbursements. In 1998, Rex did not take any salary from the corporation because he had substantial income from other sources. The corporation earned $50,000 for the year, and the corporate tax rate was far lower than Rex's personal tax rate. The IRS contends that Rex constructively received the $50,000 because he had the power to withdraw the funds from the corporation and did not take the money out of the corporation (as salary) solely to avoid his higher marginal tax rate. Is the IRS correct in its application of the constructive receipt doctrine?

Partial list of research aids:
William A. Carahan, 67 TCM 2689, T.C.Memo. 94–163 (1994).

Research Problem 4. You recently contracted to perform tax services for a new funeral home. In preparing the initial tax return, you must decide whether the funeral home can use the cash method of accounting. When discussing this issue with the manager, the manager points out that the company is actually a service business and that the only materials involved are caskets, which average only 15% of the price of a funeral. Is the funeral home required to use the accrual method of accounting?

Research Problem 5. In 1998, your client, Clear Corporation, changed from the cash to the accrual method of accounting for its radio station. The company had a positive § 481 adjustment of $2,400,000 as a result of the change and began amortizing the adjustment in 1998. In 1999, Clear received an offer to purchase the assets of the radio station business (this would be considered a sale of a trade or business under § 1060). If the offer is accepted, Clear plans to purchase a satellite television business. Clear has asked you to explain the consequences of the sale of the radio station on the amortization of the § 481 adjustment.

Use the tax resources of the Internet to address the following questions. Do not restrict your search to the World Wide Web, but include a review of newsgroups and general reference materials, practitioner sites and resources, primary sources of the tax law, chat rooms and discussion groups, and other opportunities.

Research Problem 6. Find a solicitation for a purchase of electronic equipment or furniture advertised as "no payment" or "no interest due" until next year. Analyze the language of the solicitation in light of applicable Federal income tax law.

Research Problem 7. Send an e-mail message to the site of a tax adviser suggesting a planning technique related to the LIFO election. Ask the administrator of the site to relate a field experience with respect to inventory management.

TEAM PROJECT: ARTHUR ANDERSEN TAX CHALLENGE CASES

For more information on the Arthur Andersen Tax Challenge Cases, refer to Chapter 1, page 1–37.

Information related to tax issues and problems that are discussed in this chapter may be found in the

Day and Ball case on pages 20 and 22
Fence case on pages: None

Read and analyze the case you have been assigned and *identify* any issues and problems that are related to material covered in this chapter. If the information provided in the case is complete, prepare answers for this part of the case at this time. If you need information that is contained in the later parts of the case, write a memo summarizing the questions or problems so you can prepare a complete answer at a later date.

DEFERRED COMPENSATION

LEARNING OBJECTIVES

After completing Chapter 19, you should be able to:

1. Distinguish between qualified (defined contribution and defined benefit) and nonqualified compensation arrangements.

2. Identify the qualification requirements for qualified plans.

3. Discuss the tax consequences of qualified plans.

4. Calculate the limitations on contributions to and benefits from qualified plans.

5. Understand the qualified plan (Keogh plan) available to a self-employed person.

6. Describe the benefits of the different types of Individual Retirement Accounts (IRAs).

7. Understand the rationale for nonqualified deferred compensation plans and the related tax treatment.

8. Explain the value of restricted property plans.

9. Differentiate the tax treatment of qualified and nonqualified stock options.

10. Identify tax planning opportunities available with deferred compensation.

Compensation is important in any type of organization. For example, the average player salary in the National Basketball Association is approximately $1.9 million. At the top, Michael Jordan has a one-year contract for $30.14 million. His teammate Dennis Rodman receives a $4 million per year base salary. Meanwhile, some other productive players such as Dominique Wilkins with the San Antonio Spurs and the Toronto Raptors' Walt Williams receive the minimum salary of $247,500. For comparison, a new second lieutenant in the U.S. Army receives approximately $24,000, and an entry-level accountant earns approximately $35,000.

The correlation between salary and performance in the NBA is not always precise. Michael Jordan makes 15 times more than the league's average, but cannot produce more than 15 times the stats of the average player. Kevin Garnett, a 6-foot 11-inch forward with the Minnesota Timberwolves, has the richest contract at $126 million over six years. In his first two seasons, he has yet to average 20 points and 10 rebounds.

The high salaries for sports stars motivated the mayor of Chicago, Richard J. Daley, to suggest that the city of Chicago should tax the salaries of the Chicago Cubs and White Sox players directly, rather than impose an entertainment tax on tickets sold at the Chicago baseball parks. Obviously, such a tax would punish the players, rather than the ticket holders.

If you have not yet chosen a profession, consider becoming a major league baseball player. The average salary in 1997 was $1.3 million, up from $329,000 in 1984. In 1997, the New York Yankees had the highest paid team in major league baseball with a payroll of $66.8 million, followed by Baltimore at $63.0 million, Cleveland at $58.5 million, Flordia at $53.5 million, and Atlanta at $52.0 million.

In August 1997, Greg Maddux signed a five-year, $57.5 million contract extension with the Atlanta Braves. With a 25-game season and 100 pitches per game, Maddux will get about $4,600 per pitch, whether he throws a ball, strike, or wild pitch or hits a batter. Maddux's pitching teammate John Smoltz, with a 15–12 pitching record in 1997, has a four-year, $7.75 million annual salary, or about $2,900 per pitch. The San Francisco Giants' Barry Bonds receives a salary of $11.45 million per year, followed by the White Sox's Albert Belle at $11 million. Compare these individual salaries with Oakland's total payroll of $12.9 million, the lowest in the major leagues. Does Oakland ever have a shot at the World Series?

At the same time, consider the tax consequences. A professional athlete's lifetime sports income is compressed into about 10 years. Yet income averaging is not allowed for Federal income tax purposes. As a result, the athlete will lose a larger portion of lifetime earned income in the form of taxes than someone with a comparable amount of earned income over a typical worklife cycle. The athlete does, however, have a method available for reducing the Federal income tax liability in the form of deferred compensation.

This chapter discusses the various types of deferred compensation arrangements available to employees and self-employed individuals. With **deferred compensation,** an employee receives compensation for services in a later period than that in which the services were performed—quite often during retirement years. The tax law encourages employers to offer deferred compensation plans to their employees to supplement the Federal Social Security retirement system.

Qualified deferred compensation plans receive particularly favorable tax treatment. The amounts that may be deferred under these plans are limited, so they might not be perfect for Michael Jordan or Greg Maddux. For employers and more traditional employees, however, they provide tax advantages that are exceedingly helpful. For example, contributors to qualified pension, profit sharing, or stock bonus plans receive three major tax advantages:

- Contributions are immediately deductible by the employer.
- Employees are not taxed until these funds are made available to them.
- Income earned by the plan trust, which has received the contributions, is not subject to tax until made available to the employees.

A variety of deferred compensation arrangements are being offered to employees, including the following:

- Qualified profit sharing plans.
- Qualified pension plans.
- Employee stock ownership plans.
- Cash or deferred arrangement plans.
- SIMPLE IRA.
- Tax-deferred annuities.
- Incentive stock option plans.
- Nonqualified deferred compensation plans.
- Restricted property plans.
- Cafeteria benefit plans.

In a 1997 survey, KPMG Peat Marwick found that 96 percent of employers with 200 or more employees offered some kind of retirement plan, up from 89 percent in 1994. For the first time, more employees were offered a § 401(k) plan (a defined contribution plan) than a defined benefit plan. Yet defined benefit plans cover 61 percent of employees. The KPMG survey also found employers are increasing the retirement financial education they offer employees, with more than half reporting they provide education. Defined benefit and defined contribution plans are defined in the following section.

In addition to the various types of deferred compensation, employees may receive other valuable fringe benefits, some of which may be tax-free. Examples of such benefits include group term life insurance, medical reimbursement plans,

COMPENSATION AND PERFORMANCE

An interesting measure of performance for a major league baseball team is its "cost per win" for the regular season. The answer for some teams may be surprising. For the final four in 1997, the cost per win was as follows:

Atlanta	$574,257
Florida	597,826
Baltimore	642,857
Cleveland	697,674

Based on the above, Cleveland and Florida should have been in the World Series (they were). Likewise, Cleveland should have won the World Series (they came close).

Some big spenders per win did not make it to the Series. The biggest spender per win was St. Louis (73 wins) at $712,328. The low spender per win was Pittsburgh (79 wins) at $202,531.

SOURCE: Adapted from Steve McKee, "Can a Baseball Team Buy Its Way to the World Series? A Score Card," *Wall Street Journal*, October 17, 1997, p. B1.

company-supplied automobiles, education expense reimbursement plans, and group legal services.[1]

QUALIFIED PENSION, PROFIT SHARING, AND STOCK BONUS PLANS

1 LEARNING OBJECTIVE
Distinguish between qualified (defined contribution and defined benefit) and nonqualified compensation arrangements.

To ensure that retired people will not be dependent solely on government programs, the Federal government encourages private pension and profit sharing plans. Therefore, the Federal tax law provides substantial tax benefits for plans that meet certain requirements (qualified plans). The major requirement for qualification is that a plan not discriminate in favor of highly compensated employees.

TYPES OF PLANS

The tax law defines three types of qualified plans: pension, profit sharing, and stock bonus plans.

Pension Plans. A **pension plan** is a deferred compensation arrangement that provides for systematic payments of definitely determinable retirement benefits to employees who meet the requirements set forth in the plan. Benefits are generally measured by and based on such factors as years of service and employee compensation. Employer contributions under a qualified pension plan must *not* depend on

---

[1]Refer to the discussions in Chapters 4 and 5.

profits. In addition, they must be sufficient to provide definitely determinable benefits on some actuarial basis (except for a defined contribution pension plan).

There are basically two types of qualified pension plans: defined benefit plans and defined contribution plans.

A **defined benefit plan** includes a formula that defines the benefits employees are to receive.[2] Under such a plan, an employer must make annual contributions based upon actuarial computations that will be sufficient to pay the required retirement benefits. If a plan document permits, employees may make contributions to the pension fund. A separate account is not maintained for each participant. A defined benefit plan provides some sense of security for employees since the benefits may be expressed in fixed dollar amounts.

A **defined contribution pension plan** (or money purchase plan) defines the amount the employer is required to contribute (e.g., a flat dollar amount, an amount based on a special formula, or an amount equal to a certain percentage of compensation). A separate account must be maintained for each participant. Benefits are based solely on (1) the amount contributed and (2) income from the fund that accrues to the participant's account.[3] Consequently, actuarial calculations are not required to determine the employer's annual contribution. Upon retirement, an employee's pension amount depends on the value of his or her account. Although it is not mandatory, a plan may require or permit employee contributions to the pension fund.

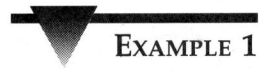

EXAMPLE 1

The qualified pension plan of Rose Company calls for both the employer and the employee to contribute annually to the pension trust an amount equal to 5% of the employee's compensation. Since the employer's rate of contribution is fixed, this pension plan is a defined contribution plan. If the plan called for contributions sufficient to provide retirement benefits equal to 30% of the employee's average salary for the last five years of employment, it would be a defined benefit plan. ▼

Concept Summary 19–1 compares and contrasts a defined benefit plan and a defined contribution plan.

Profit Sharing Plans. A **profit sharing plan** is a deferred compensation arrangement established and maintained by an employer to provide for employee participation in the company's profits. Contributions are paid from the employer's current or accumulated profits to a trustee and are commingled in a single trust fund. Thus, an employer does not have to have a profit for the current year to make a contribution (the contribution can be from accumulated profits).

In a profit sharing plan, a separate account is maintained for each participant. The plan must provide a definite, predetermined formula for allocating the contributions made to the trustee among the participants. Likewise, it must include a definite, predetermined formula for distributing the accumulated funds after a fixed number of years, on the attainment of a stated age, or on the occurrence of certain events such as illness, layoff, or retirement. A company is not required to contribute a definite, predetermined amount to the plan, although substantial and recurring contributions must be made to meet the permanency requirement. Forfeitures arising under this plan do not have to be used to reduce the employer's contribution. Instead, forfeitures may be used to increase the individual accounts of the remaining participants as long as these increases do not result in prohibited

---

[2]§ 414(j).   [3]§ 414(i).

CONCEPT SUMMARY 19–1

Defined Benefit Plan and Defined Contribution Plan Compared

Defined Benefit Plan	Defined Contribution Plan
Includes a pension plan.	Includes profit sharing, stock bonus, money purchase, target benefit, qualified cash or deferred compensation, employee stock ownership plans, and some pension plans.
Determinable benefits based upon years of service and average compensation. Benefits calculated by a formula.	An account for each participant. Ultimate benefits depend upon contributions and investment performance.
Maximum annual *benefits* payable may not exceed the smaller of (1) $130,000 (in 1998)* or (2) 100% of the participant's average earnings in the three highest years of employment.	Maximum annual *contribution* to an account may not exceed the smaller of (1) $30,000* or (2) 25% of the participant's compensation (15% for a profit sharing plan).
Forfeitures must reduce subsequent funding costs and cannot increase the benefits any participant can receive under the plan.	Forfeitures may be allocated to the accounts of remaining participants.
Subject to minimum funding requirement in order to avoid penalties.	Exempt from funding requirements.
Greater administrative and actuarial costs and greater reporting requirements.	Costs and reporting requirements less burdensome.
Subject to plan termination insurance.	Not subject to plan termination insurance.
More favorable to employees who are older when plan is adopted since it is possible to fund higher benefits over a shorter period.	More favorable to younger employees since, over a longer period, higher benefits may result.

*This amount is subject to indexing annually in $5,000 increments.

discrimination.[4] Since a profit sharing plan does not necessarily emphasize retirement income, benefits to employees may normally be distributed through lump-sum payouts.

Stock Bonus Plans. A **stock bonus plan** is another form of deferred compensation. In this case, an employer establishes and maintains the plan in order to contribute shares of its stock. The contributions need not be dependent on the employer's profits. A stock bonus plan is subject to the same requirements as a profit sharing plan for purposes of allocating and distributing the stock among the employees.[5] Any benefits of the plan are distributable in the form of stock of the employer company, except that distributable fractional shares may be paid in cash.

Employee Stock Ownership Plans. An **employee stock ownership plan (ESOP)** is a stock bonus trust that qualifies as a tax-exempt employee trust under § 401(a). Technically, an ESOP is a defined contribution plan that is either a qualified stock bonus plan or a stock bonus and a money purchase plan, each of which is qualified under § 401(a). An ESOP must invest primarily in qualifying employer securities.[6]

---

[4]Reg. §§ 1.401–1(b) and 1.401–4(a)(1)(iii).
[5]Reg. § 1.401–1(b)(1)(iii).

[6]§ 4975(e)(7).

Since the corporation can contribute stock rather than cash, there is no cash-flow drain. If stock is contributed, no cash outlay is required, and the corporation receives a tax deduction equal to the fair market value of the stock. Under § 1032, the employer-corporation does not recognize a gain or loss on the contributed stock. The corporation may deduct dividends paid in cash (or dividends used to repay certain ESOP loans) on shares held by an ESOP. The tax savings accruing under the plan may have a favorable impact on the company's working capital. An ESOP also provides flexibility, since contributions may vary from year to year and, in fact, may be omitted in any one year.[7]

A company can fund the ESOP with unissued stock or by acquiring outstanding shares of stock from its shareholders, who receive capital gain treatment upon the sale of their stock. Owners of small, closely held corporations may elect nonrecognition treatment for any gain realized on the sale of securities to an ESOP where qualified replacement property is purchased during a 15-month period.[8] This 15-month period begins 3 months before the date of the sale and ends 12 months after that date. Nonrecognition treatment is permitted only if the seller has held the securities for at least three years prior to the sale to the ESOP.

Employees are not taxed until they receive a distribution of stock or cash from the trust. Distributions to employees may be made entirely in cash or partly in cash and partly in employer securities. A participant must have the right to demand the entire distribution in the form of employer securities.[9]

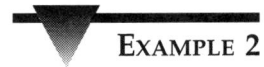

EXAMPLE 2

Gray Company establishes an ESOP for its employees and contributes unissued stock to the ESOP trust. The company receives a deduction for the contribution, and there is no cash-flow drain. The employees are not subject to tax until a subsequent stock or cash distribution from the trust. ▼

EXAMPLE 3

The ESOP of Gray Company borrows $100,000 from City Bank in January 1998. The loan is secured by the stock interest and is guaranteed by the company. The ESOP buys stock for the trust from a shareholder of Gray Company for $100,000. The shareholder has owned the stock for four years. The shares are then allocated among the employees' retirement accounts. The shareholder obtains capital gain treatment on the sale or can elect nonrecognition treatment if qualified replacement securities are purchased during a 15-month period. Gray Company makes deductible cash contributions to the ESOP, which, in turn, pays off the loan. ▼

QUALIFICATION REQUIREMENTS

2 ▼ **LEARNING OBJECTIVE**
Identify the qualification requirements for qualified plans.

To be *qualified*, and thereby to receive favorable tax treatment, a plan must satisfy the following requirements:

- Exclusive benefit requirement.
- Nondiscrimination requirements.
- Participation and coverage requirements.
- Vesting requirements.
- Distribution requirements.

These qualification rules are highly technical and numerous. Thus, an employer should submit a retirement plan to the IRS for a determination letter regarding the qualified status of the plan and trust. A favorable determination letter may be

---

[7]Reg. § 1.401–1(b)(2).   [9]§ 409(h)(1).
[8]Qualified replacement property is defined in § 1042(c)(4).

expected within 6 to 12 months, indicating that the plan meets the qualification requirements and that the trust is tax-exempt. However, the continued qualification of the plan depends upon its actual operations. Therefore, the operations of the plan should be reviewed periodically.

Exclusive Benefit Requirement.   A pension, profit sharing, or stock bonus trust must be created by an employer for the exclusive benefit of employees or their beneficiaries. Under a prudent person concept, the IRS specifies four investment conditions for meeting the *exclusive benefit* requirement:[10]

- The cost of the investment must not exceed the fair market value at the time of purchase.
- A fair return commensurate with prevailing rates must be provided.
- Sufficient liquidity must be maintained to permit distributions in accordance with the terms of the qualified plan.
- The safeguards and diversity that a prudent investor would adhere to must be present.

Nondiscrimination Requirements.   The contributions and benefits under a plan must *not discriminate* in favor of highly compensated employees. A plan is not considered discriminatory merely because contributions and benefits are proportional to compensation.[11] For example, a pension plan that provides for the allocation of employer contributions based upon a flat 3 percent of each employee's compensation would not be discriminatory even though highly paid employees receive greater benefits.

Qualified plans may be *integrated* with Social Security (employer FICA contributions for covered employees may be taken into account) to avoid giving lower-level employees proportionately greater benefits or contributions. Integrated plans may not reduce a participant's benefits or contributions to less than one-half of what they would have been without integration.

Participation and Coverage Requirements.   A qualified plan must provide, at a minimum, that all employees in the covered group who are 21 years of age are eligible to participate after completing one year of service. A year of service is generally defined as the completion of 1,000 hours of service within a measuring period of 12 consecutive months. As an alternative, where the plan provides that 100 percent of an employee's accrued benefits will be vested upon entering the plan, the employee's participation may be postponed until the later of age 21 or two years from the date of employment.[12] Once the age and service requirements are met, an employee must begin participating no later than the *earlier* of the following:

- The first day of the first plan year beginning after the date upon which the requirements were satisfied.
- Six months after the date on which the requirements were satisfied.[13]

EXAMPLE 4

Coffee Corporation has a calendar year retirement plan covering its employees. The corporation adopts the most restrictive eligibility rules permitted. Wilma, age 21, is hired on January 31, 1997, and meets the service requirement over the next 12 months (completes at least 1,000 hours by January 31, 1998). Wilma must be included in this plan no later than July 31, 1998, because the 6-month limitation would be applicable. If the company had adopted

---

[10]§ 401(a); Rev.Rul. 65–178, 1965–2 C.B. 94, and Rev.Rul. 73–380, 1973–2 C.B. 124.
[11]§§ 401(a)(4) and (5).

[12]§§ 410(a)(1)(A) and (B).
[13]§ 410(a)(4).

the two-year participation rule, Wilma must be included in the plan no later than July 31, 1999. ▼

Since a qualified plan must be primarily for the benefit of employees and be nondiscriminatory, the plan has to cover a reasonable percentage of the company employees. A plan will be qualified only if it satisfies one of the following tests:[14]

- The plan benefits at least 70 percent of all non-highly compensated employees (the *percentage test*).
- The plan benefits a percentage of non-highly compensated employees equal to at least 70 percent of the percentage of highly compensated employees benefiting under the plan (the *ratio test*).
- The plan meets the *average benefits test*, which is described below.

If a company has no highly compensated employees, the retirement plan will automatically satisfy the coverage rules.

To satisfy the *average benefits test*, the plan must benefit any employees who qualify under a classification set up by the employer and found by the Secretary of the Treasury not to be discriminatory in favor of highly compensated employees (the classification test). In addition, the average benefit percentage for non-highly compensated employees must be at least 70 percent of the average benefit percentage for highly compensated employees. The *average benefit percentage* means, with respect to any group of employees, the average of the benefit percentages calculated separately for each employee in the group. The term *benefit percentage* means the employer-provided contributions (including forfeitures) or benefits of an employee under all qualified plans of the employer, expressed as a percentage of that employee's compensation.

An employee is a **highly compensated employee** if, at any time during the year or the preceding year, the employee satisfies *either* of the following:[15]

- Was a 5 percent owner of the company.
- Received more than $80,000 (in 1998) in annual compensation from the employer *and* was a member of the top-paid group of the employer.[16] The top-paid group clause is applicable only if the employer elects to have it apply. An employee whose compensation is in the top 20 percent of the employees is a member of the top-paid group.

An additional *minimum participation test* must also be met. A plan must cover at least 40 percent of all employees or, if fewer, at least 50 employees on one representative day of the plan year. In determining all employees, nonresident aliens, certain union members, and employees not fulfilling the minimum age or years-of-service requirement of the plan may be excluded.[17]

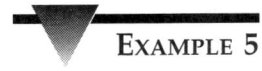

EXAMPLE 5

Rust Corporation's retirement plan meets the 70% test (the percentage test) because 70% of all non-highly compensated employees are benefited. The company has 100 employees, but only 38 of these employees are covered by the plan. Therefore, this retirement plan does not meet the minimum participation requirement. ▼

Vesting Requirements. The purpose of the **vesting requirements** is to protect an employee who has worked a reasonable period of time for an employer from losing employer contributions because of being fired or changing jobs. An employee's right to accrued benefits derived from his or her own contributions

---

[14]§ 410(b).
[15]§§ 401(a)(4) and 414(q).

[16]The $80,000 amount is to be indexed annually.
[17]§§ 401(a)(26) and 410(b)(3) and (4).

▼ **TABLE 19–1**
Three-to-Seven-Year Vesting

Years of Service	Nonforfeitable Percentage
3	20%
4	40%
5	60%
6	80%
7 or more	100%

must be nonforfeitable from the date of contribution. The accrued benefits derived from employer contributions must be nonforfeitable in accordance with one of *two alternative minimum vesting schedules.*

To satisfy the *first alternative,* a participant must have a nonforfeitable right to 100 percent of his or her accrued benefits derived from employer contributions upon completion of not more than five years of service (five-year or cliff vesting). The *second alternative* is satisfied if a participant has a nonforfeitable right at least equal to a percentage of the accrued benefits derived from employer contributions as depicted in Table 19–1 (graded vesting). Of the two alternatives, cliff vesting minimizes administration expenses for a company and provides more vesting for a long-term employee. Neither vesting schedule applies to top-heavy plans (discussed later in the chapter).

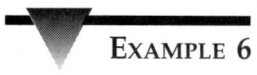

EXAMPLE 6

Mitch has six years of service completed as of February 2, 1998, his employment anniversary date. If his defined benefit plan has a five-year (cliff) vesting schedule, 100% of Mitch's accrued benefits are vested. If, however, the plan uses the graded vesting rule, Mitch's nonforfeitable percentage is 80%. ▼

Distribution Requirements.   Uniform *minimum distribution rules* exist for all qualified defined benefit and defined contribution plans, traditional Individual Retirement Accounts (IRAs) and annuities, unfunded deferred compensation plans of state and local governments and tax-exempt employers, and tax-sheltered custodial accounts and annuities. Distributions to a participant must begin by April 1 of the calendar year *following the later* of (1) the calendar year in which the employee attains age 70½ or (2) the calendar year in which the employee retires. Thus, an employee can delay receiving distributions until retirement. However, distributions to a 5 percent owner or a traditional IRA holder must begin no later than April 1 of the calendar year *following* the year in which the 5 percent owner or the IRA holder reaches age 70½.[18] A holder of a Roth IRA does *not* have to take a distribution by April 1 of the calendar year following the calendar year in which the holder attains age 70½.

Minimum annual distributions must be made over the life of the participant or the lives of the participant and a designated individual beneficiary. The amount of the required minimum distribution for a particular year is determined by dividing the account balance as of December 31 of the prior year by the applicable life expectancy. The life expectancy of the owner and his or her beneficiary is based upon the expected return multiples in the Regulations, using ages attained within the calendar year the participant reaches age 70½.[19]

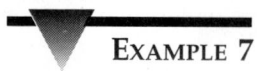

EXAMPLE 7

Beth reaches age 70½ in 1998, and she will also be age 71 in 1998. Her retirement account has a balance of $120,000 on December 31, 1997. If Beth is retired, a 5% owner, or the holder

---

[18]§ 401(a)(9).

[19]Reg. § 1.72–9. Refer to Chapter 4.

of a traditional IRA, she must withdraw $7,843 for the 1998 calendar year, assuming her multiple is 15.3 ($120,000 ÷ 15.3). This distribution need not be made until April 1, 1999, but a second distribution must be made by December 31, 1999. ▼

Failure to make a minimum required distribution to a particular participant results in a *50 percent nondeductible excise tax* on the excess in any taxable year of the amount that should have been distributed over the amount that actually was distributed. The tax is imposed on the individual required to take the distribution (the payee).[20] The Secretary of the Treasury is authorized to waive the tax for a given taxpayer year if the taxpayer is able to establish that the shortfall is due to reasonable error and that reasonable steps are being taken to remedy the shortfall.

If a taxpayer receives an *early distribution* from a qualified retirement plan, a 10 percent additional tax is levied on the full amount of any distribution includible in gross income.[21] For this purpose, the term qualified retirement plan includes a qualified defined benefit plan or defined contribution plan, a tax-sheltered annuity or custodial account, or a traditional IRA. The following distributions, however, are *not* treated as early distributions:

- Distributions made on or after the date the employee attains age 59½.
- Distributions made to a beneficiary (or the estate of an employee) on or after the death of the employee.
- Distributions attributable to the employee's being disabled.
- Distributions made as part of a scheduled series of substantially equal periodic payments (made not less frequently than annually) for the life of the participant (or the joint lives of the participant and the participant's beneficiary).
- Distributions made to an employee after separation from service because of early retirement under the plan after attaining age 55. This exception to early distribution treatment does not apply to a traditional IRA.
- Distributions used to pay medical expenses to the extent that the expenses are deductible under § 213 (determined regardless of whether or not the taxpayer itemizes deductions).
- IRA distributions that are used to pay qualified higher education expenses of the taxpayer, the spouse, or any child or grandchild of the taxpayer or the taxpayer's spouse.
- IRA distributions up to $10,000 that are used to pay expenses incurred by qualified first-time home buyers.

TAX CONSEQUENCES TO THE EMPLOYEE AND EMPLOYER

3 ⬤ LEARNING OBJECTIVE
Discuss the tax consequences of qualified plans.

In General. Although employer contributions to qualified plans are generally deductible immediately (subject to contribution and deductibility rules), these amounts are not subject to taxation until distributed to employees.[22] If benefits are paid with respect to an employee (to a creditor of the employee, a child of the employee, etc.), the benefits paid are treated as if paid to the employee. When benefits are distributed to employees, or paid with respect to an employee, the employer does not receive another deduction.

The tax benefit to the employee amounts to a substantial tax deferral and may be viewed as an interest-free loan from the government to the trust fund. Another

[20] § 4974(a).
[21] § 72(t). See Ltr.Rul. 8837071.

[22] § 402(a)(1).

advantage of a qualified plan is that any income earned by the trust is not taxable to the trust.[23] Employees, in effect, are taxed on such earnings when they receive the retirement benefits.

The taxation of amounts received by employees in periodic or installment payments is generally subject to the annuity rules in § 72 (refer to Chapter 4). In most situations, employee contributions have been subject to tax previously and are therefore included in the employee's *investment in the contract.* Two other alternative options are available for benefit distributions. A taxpayer may (1) receive the distribution in a lump-sum payment or (2) roll over the benefits into an IRA or another qualified employer retirement plan.

Lump-Sum Distributions from Qualified Plans. A **lump-sum distribution** occurs when an employee receives his or her entire payout from a qualified plan in a single payment rather than receiving the amount in installments. The annuity rules do not apply to a lump-sum distribution. All such payments are taxed in one year. Since lump-sum payments have been accumulated over a number of years, bunching retirement benefits into one taxable year may impose a high tax burden because of progressive rates. To overcome this bunching effect, for many years the tax law has provided favorable treatment for certain lump-sum distributions. Major changes were made in the lump-sum distribution rules by TRA of 1986. Transitional provisions allow a participant who reached age 50 before January 1, 1986 (born before 1936) to elect the pre-1987 rules on a limited basis.

Under the *pre-1987 rules,* the taxable amount is allocated between a capital gain portion and an ordinary income portion (which may be subject to a special 10-year averaging treatment).[24] That portion attributable to the employee's service before 1974 qualifies for capital gain treatment. That portion attributable to the employee's service after 1973 is included as ordinary income when received and may be taxed under the 10-year averaging provision. An employee must be a plan participant for at least five years to take advantage of the 10-year averaging option.

An employee may *elect* to forgo the capital gain treatment and treat all of the distribution as ordinary income subject to the 10-year forward averaging provision.[25] In some instances, ordinary income treatment is preferable to long-term capital gain treatment because of the favorable averaging technique.

Special preferential 10-year averaging treatment of qualified lump-sum distributions can be used only once during a recipient's lifetime. In the case of a small lump-sum distribution, a recipient may prefer to pay ordinary income tax on the amount and save the averaging election for a possible larger lump-sum distribution in the future.

To determine the tax on a lump-sum distribution, it is necessary to compute the taxable portion of the distribution by subtracting employee contributions and the net unrealized appreciation in the value of any distributed securities of the employer corporation.[26] The taxable amount is then reduced by a minimum distribution allowance to arrive at the amount that is eligible for the 10-year income averaging provisions.[27] The following portion of the lump-sum distribution is treated as a long-term capital gain:

---

[23]§ 501(a).

[24]§ 402(e)(1)(C) of the IRC of 1954.

[25]§ 402(e)(4)(L).

[26]Section 402(e)(4)(J) provides that before any distribution a taxpayer may elect not to have this subtraction associated with employer securities apply.

[27]Section 402(e)(1)(D) defines the *minimum distribution allowance* as the smaller of $10,000 or one-half of the total taxable amount of the lump-sum distribution, reduced by 20% of the amount, if any, by which such total taxable amount exceeds $20,000. Thus, for lump-sum distributions of $70,000 or more, there will be no minimum distribution allowance.

$$\text{Taxable amount} \times \frac{\text{Years of service before 1974}}{\text{Total years of service}}$$
(computed without being reduced by the minimum distribution allowance)

The applicable capital gain rate is 20 percent.

After 1986, subject to the transition rule for recipients born before 1936 mentioned earlier, the 10-year forward averaging rule for lump-sum distributions is replaced by a 5-year forward averaging rule.[28] Only one lump-sum distribution received after age 59½ is eligible for the averaging treatment. Furthermore, capital gain treatment for lump-sum distributions (associated with participation before 1974) is repealed.

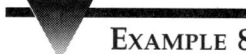

EXAMPLE 8

Esteban, age 65 and married, retires at the end of 1998 and receives a lump-sum distribution of $100,000 from his company's profit sharing plan. This plan includes $5,000 of his own contributions and $10,000 of unrealized appreciation on his employer's common stock. Esteban was a participant in the plan for 30 years. Since Esteban attained age 50 before January 1, 1986, he is eligible to elect the pre-1987 10-year forward averaging technique (using 1986 rates and the **zero bracket amount**). Refer to the computation model in Concept Summary 19–2.

Taxable portion of the lump-sum distribution		$85,000
Less: Minimum distribution allowance (½ of the taxable amount up to $20,000)	$ 10,000	
Less: 20% of the taxable amount in excess of $20,000: 20% × ($85,000 − $20,000)	(13,000)	
Minimum distribution allowance		–0–
Taxable amount		$85,000
Computation of tax under 10-year averaging: Long-term capital gain portion: $85,000 \times \frac{5 \text{ (service before 1974)}}{30 \text{ (total service years)}} = \$14,167 \times .20 =$		$ 2,833
Ordinary income portion: 10 times the tax on $9,563[29] [$\frac{1}{10}$ ($85,000 − $14,167) + $2,480]		9,640
Tax on lump-sum distribution		$12,473

Thus, Esteban's capital gain on the distribution is $14,167 and is subject to a 20% capital gain rate. Here Esteban may wish to elect to treat the entire distribution as ordinary income using the 10-year forward averaging approach rather than taxing the capital gain portion at the 20% capital gain rate. The tax liability of $11,905 would be less than the previously calculated tax liability of $12,473. The capital gain on the unrealized appreciation in the employer's common stock is not taxable until Esteban sells the stock. In essence, the cost basis of the securities to the trust becomes the tax basis to the employee.[30] If Esteban keeps the securities until he dies, there may be some income tax savings on this gain to the extent his estate or heirs obtain a step-up in basis. ▼

---

[28]§ 402(e)(1). The 5-year averaging for lump-sum distributions is repealed for tax years beginning after December 31, 1999. The grandfathered 10-year averaging and capital gains provisions for participants who attained age 50 by January 1, 1986, are retained.

[29]In making the tax computation, it is necessary to use the 1986 Tax Rate Schedule for single taxpayers and to add $2,480 (the zero bracket amount) to the taxable income. Thus, the tax was

computed on $9,563, which is $7,083 ($\frac{1}{10}$ of $70,833) plus $2,480. Note that the tax rates provided in the instructions for Form 4972 (Tax on Lump-Sum Distributions) have already been adjusted for the zero bracket amount (i.e., it is not necessary to add the zero bracket amount in making the calculation.)

[30]§ 402(e)(4)(J).

CONCEPT SUMMARY 19–2

Model for Lump-Sum Distribution Computation

1. Start with the total lump-sum distribution and deduct any employee contributions and unrealized appreciation in employer securities.
2. Divide the result into the capital gain portion and the ordinary income portion.*
3. Multiply the capital gain portion by the capital gain rate of 20%.
4. Reduce the ordinary income portion by the minimum distribution allowance.
5. Divide the ordinary income portion into 5 or 10 equal portions, whichever is appropriate.
6. Compute the tax on the result in step 5 using the 1986 or current rate schedules (whichever is appropriate) for single taxpayers.
7. Multiply the resulting tax by 5 or 10, whichever is appropriate.
8. Add the results in steps 3 and 7.

*In certain circumstances, none of the taxable amount of the distribution will be eligible for capital gain treatment. In other circumstances, the taxpayer may choose to treat none of the taxable amount as capital gain even though part could qualify.

If Esteban (in Example 8) uses the 5-year forward averaging provision instead, the following results are produced:

Taxable amount	$85,000
Computation of tax under 5-year averaging:	
Long-term capital gain portion:	
$85,000 \times \dfrac{5 \text{ (service before 1974)}}{30 \text{ (total service years)}} = \$14,167 \times .20 =$	$ 2,833
Ordinary income portion:	
5 times the tax on $14,167[31] [⅕ ($85,000 − $14,167)]	10,625
Tax on lump-sum distribution	$13,458

Thus, Esteban's capital gain on the distribution is $14,167 (the same as in the 10-year averaging calculation). The capital gain is subject to a 20 percent capital gain rate.[32] Once again the taxpayer may wish to elect to treat the entire distribution as ordinary income using the 5-year forward averaging approach rather than taxing the capital gain portion at the 20 percent capital gain rate. The tax liability of $12,750 would be less than the previously calculated tax liability of $13,458. Since the ordinary income tax under 10-year forward averaging is less than the ordinary income tax under 5-year forward averaging, it appears that Esteban's best alternative is to use the 10-year forward averaging provision and treat the capital gain as ordinary income.

Rollover Treatment. A taxpayer who receives a distribution can avoid current taxation by rolling the distribution into another qualified employer retirement plan or into an IRA.[33] The taxation of the distribution is deferred until distributions are made from the recipient qualified employer retirement plan or IRA. The rollover can be *direct* with the balance in the account going directly from a qualified employer retirement plan to another qualified employer retirement plan or an IRA. The

---

[31]In making the tax computation, it is necessary to use the 1998 Tax Rate Schedule for single taxpayers.

[32]Note that since Esteban qualifies under the transition rules (attained age 50 before January 1, 1986), he is eligible to elect capital gain treatment in conjunction with 5-year forward averaging.

[33]§ 402(c).

rollover can be *indirect* with the proceeds going to the taxpayer who has 60 days to transfer the proceeds into another qualified employer retirement plan or an IRA. A benefit of the direct rollover is that it is not subject to the 20 percent withholding applicable to indirect rollovers.[34]

LIMITATIONS ON CONTRIBUTIONS TO AND BENEFITS FROM QUALIFIED PLANS

4 LEARNING OBJECTIVE
Calculate the limitations on contributions to and benefits from qualified plans.

In General. The limitations on contributions to and benefits from qualified plans appearing in § 415 must be written into a qualified plan. The plan terminates if these limits are exceeded. Section 404 sets the limits on deductibility applicable to the employer. The limit on the amount deductible under § 404 may have an impact on the amount the employer is willing to contribute. In fact, a defined benefit plan or defined contribution plan is not allowed a deduction for the amount that exceeds the § 415 limitations.[35]

Defined Contribution Plans. Under a *defined contribution plan* (money purchase pension, profit sharing, or stock bonus plan), the annual addition to an employee's account cannot exceed the smaller of $30,000 or 25 percent of the employee's compensation.[36] The $30,000 amount is to be indexed (in $5,000 increments).[37]

Defined Benefit Plans. Under a *defined benefit plan*, the annual benefit payable to an employee is limited to the smaller of $130,000 (in 1998)[38] or 100 percent of the employee's average compensation for the highest three years of employment. This benefit limit is subject to a $10,000 *de minimis* floor. The $130,000 limitation is reduced actuarially if the benefits begin before the Social Security normal retirement age (currently age 65) and is increased actuarially if the benefits begin after the Social Security normal retirement age. The dollar limit on annual benefits ($130,000) is reduced by one-tenth for each year of *participation* under 10 years by the employee. Furthermore, the 100 percent of compensation limitation and the $10,000 *de minimis* floor are reduced proportionately for a participant who has less than 10 years of *service* with the employer.[39]

EXAMPLE 9

Adam's average compensation for the highest three years of employment is $87,000. The defined benefit plan would not qualify if the plan provides for benefits in excess of the smaller of (1) $87,000 or (2) $130,000 for Adam in 1998 (assuming retirement age of 65). ▼

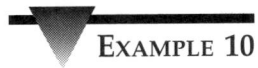

EXAMPLE 10

Peggy has participated for four years in a defined benefit plan and has six years of service with her employer. Her average compensation for the three highest years is $60,000. Her four years of participation reduce her dollar limitation to $52,000 ($130,000 × ⁴/₁₀). Her six years of service reduce her 100% of compensation limitation to 60%. Therefore, her limit on annual benefits is $36,000 ($60,000 × 60%). ▼

For collectively bargained plans with at least 100 participants, the annual dollar limitation is the greater of $68,212 or one-half of the $130,000 monetary limit.

The amount of compensation that may be taken into account under any plan is limited to $160,000 (in 1998).[40] Thus, the benefits highly compensated individuals

---

[34]§ 3405(c).
[35]§ 404(j).
[36]§§ 415(c) and (d).
[37]§415(d)(4).

[38]This amount is indexed annually.
[39]§ 415(b).
[40]§§ 401(a)(17) and 404(l). This amount is to be indexed annually.

receive may be smaller as a percentage of their pay than those received by non-highly compensated employees.

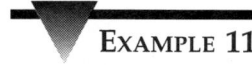

EXAMPLE 11

Swan Corporation has a defined contribution plan with a 10% contribution formula. An employee earning less than $160,000 in 1998 would not be affected by this includible compensation limitation. However, an employee earning $320,000 in 1998 would have only 5% of compensation allocated to his or her account because of the $160,000 limit on includible compensation. ▼

The maximum deduction a corporation is permitted for contributions to pension plans may be determined by either of two methods. First, an aggregate cost method allows an actuarially determined deduction based on a level amount, or a level percentage, of compensation over the remaining future service of covered participants. Second, the employer is permitted to deduct the so-called normal cost plus no more than 10 percent of the past service costs. The *normal cost* represents the estimated contribution required associated with work performed by employees in the current year. *Past service costs* are costs relating to the inception of the plan and costs that result from changes in the retirement plan.

The employer's contribution is deductible in the tax year such amounts are paid to the pension trust. However, both cash and accrual basis employers may defer the payment of contributions with respect to any tax year until the date fixed for filing the taxpayer's Federal income tax return for that year (including extensions).[41] In effect, the corporation is allowed a deduction to the extent it is compelled to make such contributions to satisfy the funding requirement. If an amount in excess of the allowable amount is contributed in any tax year, the excess may be carried forward and deducted in succeeding tax years (to the extent the carryover plus the succeeding year's contribution does not exceed the deductible limitation for that year).[42]

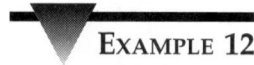

EXAMPLE 12

During 1998, Green Corporation contributes $17,500 to its qualified pension plan. Normal cost for this year is $7,200, and the amount necessary to pay retirement benefits on behalf of employee services before 1998 is $82,000 (past service costs). The corporation's maximum deduction would be $15,400. This amount consists of the $7,200 normal cost plus 10% ($8,200) of the past service costs. The corporation would have a $2,100 [$17,500 (contribution) − $15,400 (deduction)] contribution carryover. ▼

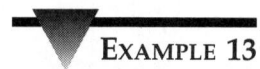

EXAMPLE 13

Assume in the previous example that Green Corporation has normal cost of $7,200 in 1999 and contributes $10,000 to the pension trust. The corporation's maximum deduction would be $15,400. Green Corporation may deduct $12,100, composed of this year's contribution ($10,000) plus the $2,100 contribution carryover. ▼

A 10 percent excise tax is imposed on nondeductible contributions. The tax is levied on the employer making the contribution. The tax applies to nondeductible contributions for the current year and any nondeductible contributions for the preceding year that have not been eliminated by the end of the current year (as a carryover or by being returned to the employer in the current year).[43]

Profit Sharing and Stock Bonus Plan Limitations.   The maximum deduction permitted to an employer each year for contributions to profit sharing and stock bonus plans is 15 percent of the compensation paid or accrued with respect to

---

[41]§§ 404(a)(1) and (6).
[42]§ 404(a)(1)(D).

[43]§ 4972.

plan participants. The maximum amount of compensation that may be taken into account under a plan for an employee is $160,000 (in 1998). Any nondeductible excess, a so-called contribution carryover, may be carried forward indefinitely and deducted in subsequent years. The maximum deduction in any succeeding year is 15 percent of all compensation paid or accrued during that taxable year. An employer can circumvent the 15 percent limitation by establishing a money purchase pension plan as a supplement to the profit sharing or stock bonus plan. When there are two or more plans, a maximum deduction of 25 percent of the compensation paid is allowable.[44]

ETHICAL CONSIDERATIONS

Personal Benefit versus Employees' Benefit

As an owner of a small business, Brotherhood, Inc., you are interested when your insurance adviser tells you about a new age-weighted and cross-tested profit sharing plan that satisfies the nondiscrimination requirements of Code § 401(a)(4). He points out that currently only $160,000 of your $250,000 salary is used to calculate your 15 percent annual contribution (e.g., limited to $24,000). Under the new plan, your limit will be 25 percent, up to $30,000.

By changing to this age-weighted and cross-tested plan, you can keep much of the annual contributions you currently make to the business retirement plan for your employees. You will be able to exclude many lower-paid employees and reduce the annual contributions made to the plan on behalf of rank-and-file employees.

Should you agree to this tax shelter, which blends rules for retirement savings plans with rules applicable to pension plans? Most of the affected employees are your friends, and you play softball with them on your company's team.

TOP-HEAVY PLANS

A special set of rules is imposed upon so-called top-heavy plans to discourage retirement plans from conferring disproportionate benefits upon key employees. Top-heaviness is determined on an annual basis.

In general, a **top-heavy plan** allocates more than 60 percent of the cumulative benefits to key employees; a plan may also be part of a top-heavy plan. *Key employees* are employees who fit into at least one of the following categories:

- Officers. However, for purposes of this definition, only the smaller of (1) 50 officers or (2) three employees or 10 percent of all employees (whichever is greater) may be considered officers. Officers paid $45,000 or less per year are not included.
- The 10 employees owning the largest interest in the employer (using the constructive ownership rules of § 318). For purposes of this provision, a key employee does not include an employee whose annual compensation from the employer is $30,000 or less.
- A greater-than-5 percent owner of the employer.
- A greater-than-1 percent owner of the employer with annual compensation in excess of $150,000.[45]

---

[44]§§ 404(a)(3)(A) and (a)(7).

[45]§ 416(i)(1).

▼ **TABLE 19–2**
Top-Heavy Graded Vesting

Years of Service	Vested Percentage
2	20%
3	40%
4	60%
5	80%
6 or more	100%

Employees receiving no compensation for five years are disregarded in testing for top-heavy status.

A top-heavy plan must provide for greater portability for participants who are non-key employees. An employee's right to the accrued benefits derived from employer contributions must become nonforfeitable under either of two vesting schedules. Under the first schedule, an employee who has at least three years of service with the employer must have a nonforfeitable right to 100 percent of his or her accrued benefits derived from employer contributions. Under the second schedule, a six-year graded vesting schedule must be met (see Table 19–2).[46]

To prevent an employer from avoiding the top-heavy rules by establishing a one-person corporate shell, § 269A allows the IRS to allocate any income or deductions between a personal service corporation and its employee-owner. An employee-owner is any employee who owns more than 10 percent of the outstanding stock of the personal service corporation on any day during the tax year.

§ 401(k) PLANS

General.   A **§ 401(k) plan** allows participants to elect either to receive up to $10,000 (in 1998)[47] in cash (taxed currently) or to have a contribution made on their behalf to a profit sharing or stock bonus plan. The plan may also be in the form of a salary-reduction agreement between an eligible participant and an employer under which a contribution will be made only if the participant elects to reduce his or her compensation or to forgo an increase in compensation.

Any pretax amount elected by the employee as a plan contribution is not includible in gross income and is 100 percent vested. Any employer contributions are tax deferred, as are earnings on contributions in the plan.

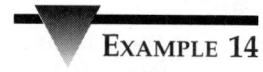

EXAMPLE 14

Sam participates in a § 401(k) plan of his employer. The plan permits the participants to choose between a full salary or a reduced salary where the reduction becomes a before-tax contribution to a retirement plan. Sam elects to contribute 10% of his annual compensation of $30,000 to the plan. Income taxes are paid on only $27,000. No income taxes are paid on the $3,000—or on any earnings—until it is distributed from the plan to Sam. The main benefit of a § 401(k) plan is that Sam can shift a portion of his income to a later taxable year. ▼

The maximum employee annual elective contribution to a § 401(k) plan is $10,000 (in 1998), but that amount is reduced dollar for dollar by other salary-reduction contributions to tax-sheltered annuities and simplified employee pension plans. Elective contributions in excess of the maximum limitation are taxable in the year of deferral. These amounts may be distributed from the plan tax-free before April 15 of the following year. Excess amounts not timely distributed will

---

[46]§ 416(b).

[47]This amount is indexed annually. For 1997, the amount was $9,500.

be taxable in the year of distribution, even though they were included in income in the year of deferral. Annual elective contributions are also limited by complicated nondiscrimination requirements and the defined contribution plan limitations.

A 10 percent excise tax is imposed on the employer for excess contributions not withdrawn from the plan within 2½ months after the close of the plan year. The plan will lose its qualified status if these excess contributions (and any related income) are not withdrawn by the end of the plan year following the plan year in which the excess contributions were made.[48]

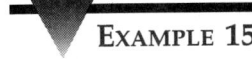

EXAMPLE 15

Carmen, an employee of a manufacturing corporation, defers $12,000 in a § 401(k) plan in 1998. The $2,000 excess over the $10,000 limit, along with the appropriate earnings, must be returned to Carmen by April 15, 1999. This $2,000 excess amount plus related income is taxable to her in 1998 and will be taxed again upon distribution (if made after April 15, 1999). There will be a 10% tax on Carmen's employer on any excess contributions not returned within 2½ months after the close of the plan year. ▼

ETHICAL CONSIDERATIONS

Everything Including the Kitchen Sink

Many § 401(k) and profit sharing plans have some strange assets stuffed away in them: bags of old coins, antique violins, parking lots, antique automobiles, and real estate. The reason is that § 401(k) plans and profit sharing plans are exempt from some pension plan rules, including diversification requirements. So these plans can invest most or all of the money in employer-related real estate or securities, whereas pension plans are limited to only 10 percent in such assets. In addition, these plans are not insured by the Labor Department's Pension Benefit Guaranty Corporation.

For example, Color Tile, Inc., a Texas floor-covering chain, had a § 401(k) plan that invested heavily in Color Tile's own stores and then leased the stores back to the company. Color Tile moved into Chapter 11 bankruptcy in 1996, and some stores stopped paying rent. Many workers were laid off, but they were not allowed to take their money out of their § 401(k) accounts. In another example, British Rail earned a 13.1 percent return per year over the 22-year life of the massive artwork collection inside its pension fund. The fund acquired more than 2,400 pieces over seven years.

Many companies have large holdings of their own stock in their retirement plans. Among these companies are WalMart Stores, Cooper Tire and Rubber, Hanson Industries, Nalco Chemicals, Banc One, and McDonald's.

Should companies invest a large percentage of § 401(k) plan money in company stores and their own stock?

SIMPLE Plans.   Employers with 100 or fewer employees who do not maintain another qualified retirement plan may establish a *savings incentive match plan for employees* (SIMPLE plan).[49] The plan can be in the form of a § 401(k) plan or an IRA. The SIMPLE plan is not subject to the nondiscrimination and top-heavy rules that are normally applicable to § 401(k) plans.

All employees who received at least $5,000 in compensation from the employer during any two preceding years and who reasonably expect to receive at least $5,000 in compensation during the current year must be eligible to participate in

---

[48]§ 4979(a).   [49]§ 408(p).

the plan. The decision to participate is up to the employee. A self-employed individual may also participate in the plan.

The contributions made by the employee (a salary reduction approach) must be expressed as a percentage of compensation rather than as a fixed dollar amount. The plan must not permit the elective employee contribution for the year to exceed $6,000 (in 1998). Generally, the employer must either match elective employee contributions up to 3 percent of the employee's compensation or provide nonmatching contributions of 2 percent of compensation for each eligible employee. Thus, the maximum amount that may be contributed to the plan for 1998 is $10,800 [$6,000 employee contributions + $4,800 ($160,000 compensation ceiling × 3%) employer match].

No other contributions may be made to the plan other than the employee elective contribution and the required employer matching contribution (or nonmatching contribution under the 2 percent rule). All contributions are fully vested. An employer is required to make contributions to a SIMPLE § 401(k) plan once it is established, whereas an employer's contributions to a traditional § 401(k) plan are optional.

An employer's deduction for contributions to a SIMPLE § 401(k) plan is limited to the greater of 15 percent of the compensation paid or accrued or the amount that the employer is required to contribute to the plan. Thus, an employer may deduct contributions to a SIMPLE § 401(k) plan in excess of 15 percent of the $160,000 salary cap. A traditional § 401(k) plan is limited to 15 percent of the total compensation of plan participants for the year.

An employer is allowed a deduction for matching contributions only if the contributions are made by the due date (including extensions) for the employer's tax return. Contributions to a SIMPLE plan are excludible from the employee's gross income, and the SIMPLE plan is tax-exempt.

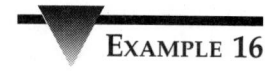

EXAMPLE 16

The Mauve Company has a SIMPLE plan for its employees under which it provides nonmatching contributions of 2% of compensation for each eligible employee. The maximum amount that can be added to each participant's account in 1998 is $9,200, composed of the $6,000 employee salary reduction plus an employer contribution of $3,200 ($160,000 × 2%). ▼

Distributions from a SIMPLE plan are taxed under the IRA rules. Tax-free rollovers can be made from one SIMPLE account to another. A SIMPLE account can be rolled over to an IRA tax-free after a two-year period has expired since the individual first participated in the plan. Withdrawals of contributions during the two-year period beginning on the date an employee first participates in the SIMPLE plan are subject to a 25 percent early withdrawal tax rather than the 10 percent early withdrawal tax that otherwise would apply.

RETIREMENT PLANS FOR SELF-EMPLOYED INDIVIDUALS

5 **LEARNING OBJECTIVE**
Understand the qualified plan (Keogh plan) available to a self-employed person.

Self-employed individuals (e.g., partners and sole proprietors) and their employees are eligible to receive qualified retirement benefits under the SIMPLE plans described above or under what are known as **H.R. 10 (Keogh) plans.** Because of contribution limitations and other restrictions, self-employed plans previously were less attractive than corporate plans. Contributions and benefits of a self-employed person now are subject to the general corporate provisions, putting self-employed persons on a parity with corporate employees. Consequently, Keogh plans can provide a self-employed person with an adequate retirement base.

A variety of funding vehicles can be used for Keogh investments, such as mutual funds, annuities, real estate shares, certificates of deposit, debt instruments, commodities, securities, and personal properties. Investment in most collectibles is not allowed in a self-directed plan. When an individual decides to make all investment decisions, a self-directed retirement plan is established. However, the individual may prefer to invest the funds with a financial institution such as a broker, a bank, or a savings and loan institution.

COVERAGE REQUIREMENTS

Generally, the corporate coverage rules apply to Keogh plans. Thus, the percentage, ratio, and average benefits tests previously discussed also apply to self-employed plans. In addition, the more restrictive top-heavy plan rules apply to Keogh plans.[50] An individual covered under a qualified corporate plan as an employee may also establish a Keogh plan for earnings from self-employment.

CONTRIBUTION LIMITATIONS

A self-employed individual may annually contribute the smaller of $30,000 or 25 percent of earned income to a *defined contribution* Keogh plan.[51] However, if the defined contribution plan is a profit sharing plan, a 15 percent deduction limit applies. Under a *defined benefit* Keogh plan, the annual benefit payable to an employee is limited to the smaller of $130,000 (in 1998) or 100 percent of the employee's average compensation for the three highest years of employment.[52] An employee includes a self-employed person. More restrictive rules apply to a top-heavy plan.

Earned income refers to net earnings from self-employment as defined in § 1402(a).[53] Net earnings from self-employment means the gross income derived by an individual from any trade or business carried on by that individual, less appropriate deductions, plus the distributive share of income or loss from a partnership.[54] Earned income is reduced by contributions to a Keogh plan on the individual's behalf and by 50 percent of any self-employment tax.[55]

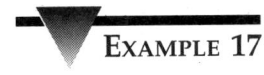 **EXAMPLE 17** | Pat, a partner, has earned income of $130,000 in 1998 (after the deduction for one-half of self-employment tax, but before any Keogh contribution). The maximum contribution Pat may make to a defined contribution Keogh plan is $26,000, calculated from the following formula: $130,000 − .25X = X$, where X is earned income reduced by Pat's Keogh contribution. Solving this equation, $X = \$104,000$; thus, the contribution limit is $.25 \times \$104,000 = \$26,000$. To achieve the maximum contribution of $30,000, Pat would have to earn at least $150,000. In essence, a self-employed individual can contribute 20% of *gross* earned income. (Pat could contribute only 13.043% of self-employment gross earned income if this were a profit sharing plan.) ▼

Many Keogh plans will be considered top-heavy plans (refer to the previous discussion). For nondiscrimination purposes, the 25 percent limitation on the employee contribution is computed on the first $160,000 (in 1998) of earned income.

---

[50] § 401(d).
[51] § 415(c)(1).
[52] § 415(b)(1). This amount is indexed annually.

[53] § 401(c)(2).
[54] § 1402(a).
[55] §§ 401(c)(2)(A)(v) and 164(f).

▼ **TABLE 19–3**
Phase-Out of IRA Deduction of
an Active Participant in 1998

AGI Filing Status	Phase-Out Begins*	Phase-Out Ends
Single and head of household	$30,000	$40,000
Married, filing joint return	50,000	60,000
Married, filing separate return	–0–	10,000

*The starting point for the phase-out is increased each year through 2007 for married filing
 jointly and through 2005 for other filing statuses.

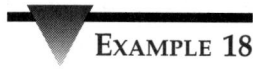

EXAMPLE 18

Terry, a self-employed accountant, has a money purchase plan with a contribution rate of 15% of compensation. Terry's earned income after the deduction for one-half of self-employment tax, but before the retirement contribution is $250,000. Terry's contribution would be limited to $20,870 ($160,000 − .15X = X), since X = $139,130 and .15 × $139,130 = $20,870. ▼

Although a Keogh plan must be established before the end of the year in question, contributions may be made up to the normal filing date for that year.

INDIVIDUAL RETIREMENT ACCOUNTS (IRAs)

GENERAL RULES

6 LEARNING OBJECTIVE
Describe the benefits of the
different types of Individual
Retirement Accounts (IRAs).

Employees not covered by another qualified plan can establish their own tax-deductible **Individual Retirement Accounts (IRAs).** The contribution ceiling is the smaller of $2,000 (or $4,000 for spousal IRAs) or 100 percent of compensation.[56] If the taxpayer is an active participant in another qualified plan, the traditional IRA deduction limitation is phased out *proportionately* between certain adjusted gross income (AGI) ranges, as shown in Table 19–3.[57]

AGI is calculated taking into account any § 469 passive losses and § 86 taxable Social Security benefits and ignoring any § 911 foreign income exclusion, § 135 savings bonds interest exclusion, and the IRA deduction. There is a $200 floor on the IRA deduction limitation for individuals whose AGI is not above the phase-out range.

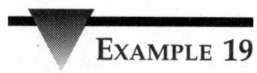

EXAMPLE 19

Dan, who is single, has compensation income of $37,000 in 1998. He is an active participant in his employer's qualified retirement plan. Dan contributes $600 to an IRA. The deductible amount is reduced from $2,000 by $1,400 because of the phase-out mechanism:

$$\frac{\$7,000}{\$10,000} \times \$2,000 = \$1,400 \text{ reduction}$$

▼

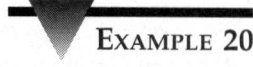

EXAMPLE 20

Ben, an unmarried individual, is an active participant in his employer's qualified retirement plan. With AGI of $39,500, he would normally have an IRA deduction limit of $100 {$2,000 − [($39,500 − $30,000)/$10,000 × $2,000]}. However, because of the special floor provision, Ben is allowed a $200 IRA deduction. ▼

An individual is not considered an active participant in a qualified plan merely because the individual's spouse is an active participant in such a plan for any part

---

[56]§§ 219(b)(1) and (c)(2).   [57]§ 219(g).

of a plan year. Thus, most homemakers may take a full $2,000 deduction regardless of the participation status of their spouse, unless the couple has AGI above $150,000. If their AGI is above $150,000, the phase-out of the deduction begins at $150,000 and ends at $160,000 (phase-out over the $10,000 range.)[58]

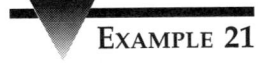

EXAMPLE 21

Nell is covered by a qualified employer retirement plan at work. Her husband, Nick, is not an active participant in a qualified plan. If Nell and Nick's combined AGI is $135,000, Nell cannot make a deductible IRA contribution because she exceeds the income threshold for an active participant. However, since Nick is not an active participant, and their combined AGI does not exceed $150,000, he can make a deductible contribution of $2,000 to an IRA. ▼

To the extent that an individual is ineligible to make a deductible contribution to an IRA, *nondeductible contributions* can be made to separate accounts.[59] The nondeductible contributions are subject to the same dollar limits as deductible contributions ($2,000 of earned income, $4,000 for a spousal IRA). Income in the account accumulates tax-free until distributed. Only the account earnings are taxed upon distribution because the account basis equals the contributions made by the taxpayer. A taxpayer may elect to treat deductible IRA contributions as nondeductible. If an individual has no taxable income for the year after taking into account other deductions, the election would be beneficial. The election is made on the individual's tax return for the taxable year to which the designation relates.

Roth IRAs.   Beginning in 1998, TRA of 1997 authorizes a new type of IRA called a Roth IRA. Contributions to a Roth IRA are nondeductible. Qualified distributions from a Roth IRA are tax-free.[60]

A taxpayer can make tax-free withdrawals from a Roth IRA after a five-year holding period if any of the following requirements is satisfied:

- The distribution is made on or after the date on which the participant attains age 59½.
- The distribution is made to a beneficiary (or the participant's estate) on or after the participant's death.
- The participant becomes disabled.
- The distribution is used to pay for qualified first-time home buyer's expenses.

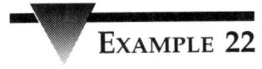

EXAMPLE 22

Edith establishes a Roth IRA at age 42 and contributes $2,000 per year for 20 years. The account is now worth $96,400, consisting of $40,000 of nondeductible contributions and $56,400 in accumulated earnings that have not been taxed. Edith may withdraw the $96,400 tax-free from the Roth IRA because she is over age 59½ and has met the five-year holding period requirement. ▼

If the taxpayer receives a distribution from a Roth IRA and does not satisfy the aforementioned requirements, the distribution may be taxable. If the distribution represents a return of capital, it is not taxable. Conversely, if the distribution represents a payout of earnings, it is taxable. Under the ordering rules for Roth IRA distributions, distributions are treated as first made from contributions (return of capital).

---

[58]§ 219(g)(7). However, a special rule in § 219(g)(4) allows a married person filing a separate return to avoid the phase-out rules even though the spouse is an active participant. The individual must live apart from the spouse at all times during the taxable year and must not be an active participant in another qualified plan.

[59]§ 408(o).
[60]§ 408A.

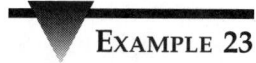

EXAMPLE 23

Assume the same facts as in Example 22, except that Edith is only age 50 and receives a distribution of $35,000. Since her adjusted basis for the Roth IRA is $40,000 (contributions made), the distribution is tax-free, and her adjusted basis is reduced to $5,000 ($40,000 − $35,000). ▼

Roth IRAs are subject to income limits. The maximum annual contribution is phased out beginning at AGI of $95,000 for single taxpayers and $150,000 for married couples who file a joint return. The phase-out range is $10,000 for married filing jointly and $15,000 for single taxpayers.

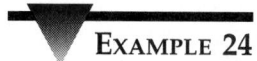

EXAMPLE 24

Bev, who is single, would like to contribute $2,000 to her Roth IRA. However, her AGI is $105,000, so her contribution is limited to $667 ($2,000 − $1,333) calculated as follows:

$$\frac{\$10,000}{\$15,000} \times \$2,000 = \$1,333 \text{ reduction}$$

▼

Education IRAs. Beginning in 1998, a distribution from an IRA to pay for qualified higher education expenses receives favorable tax treatment.[61] Qualified higher education expenses include tuition, fees, books, supplies, and related equipment. Room and board qualify if the student's course load is at least one-half of the full-time course load. If the education IRA is used to pay the qualified higher education expenses of the designated beneficiary, the withdrawals are tax-free. To the extent the distributions during a tax year exceed qualified higher education expenses, part of the excess is treated as a return of capital (the contributions), and part is treated as a distribution of earnings. The distribution is presumed to be pro rata from each category. The exclusion for the distribution of earnings part is calculated as follows:

$$\frac{\text{Qualified higher education expenses}}{\text{Total distributions}} \times \text{Earnings} = \text{Exclusion}$$

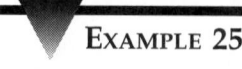

EXAMPLE 25

Meg receives a $2,500 distribution from her education IRA. She uses $2,000 to pay for qualified higher education expenses. On the date of the distribution, Meg's IRA account balance is $10,000, $6,000 of which represents her contributions. Since 60% ($6,000/$10,000) of her account balance represents her contributions, $1,500 ($2,500 × 60%) of the distribution is a return of capital, and $1,000 ($2,500 × 40%) is a distribution of earnings. The excludible amount of the earnings is calculated as follows:

$$\frac{\$2,000}{\$2,500} \times \$1,000 = \$800$$

Meg's adjusted basis for her IRA is reduced to $4,500 ($6,000 − $1,500). ▼

The maximum amount that can be contributed annually to an education IRA for a beneficiary is $500. The contributions are not deductible. Education IRAs are subject to income limits. The maximum annual contribution is phased out beginning at $95,000 for single taxpayers and $150,000 for married couples who file a joint return. The phase-out range is $10,000 for married filing jointly and $15,000 for single taxpayers. Contributions cannot be made to an education IRA after the date on which the designated beneficiary attains age 18.

The education IRA exclusion is not available in any tax year in which the beneficiary claims the HOPE credit or the lifetime learning credit (see Chapter 13). Likewise, contributions cannot be made to a beneficiary's education IRA during

---

[61]§ 530.

▼ **CONCEPT SUMMARY 19–3**

Keogh Plan and SEP Compared

	Keogh	**SEP**
Form	Trust.	IRA.
Establishment	By end of year.	By extension due date of employer.
Type of plan	Qualified.	Qualified.
Contributions to plan	By extension due date.	By extension due date of employer.
Vesting rules	Qualified plan rules.	100% immediately.
Participants' rules	Flexible.	Stricter.
Lump-sum distributions and averaging	Yes, favorable 5-year or 10-year forward averaging.	No, ordinary income.
Deduction limitation	Varies.*	Smaller of $30,000** or 15% of earned income.
Self as trustee	Yes.	No.

*For a defined contribution pension plan, the limit is the smaller of $30,000 or 20% of self-employment income (after one-half of self-employment tax is deducted). A defined contribution profit sharing plan has a 13.043% deduction limit. A defined benefit Keogh plan's limit is the smaller of $130,000 (in 1998) or 100% of the employee's average compensation for the highest three years of employment.

**Since only $160,000 of income can be taken into consideration, the dollar limitation is effectively $24,000 ($160,000 × 15%).

any year in which contributions are made to a qualified state tuition program on behalf of the same beneficiary (see Chapter 5).

Simplified Employee Pension Plans. An employer may contribute to an IRA covering an employee an amount equal to the lesser of $30,000 or 15 percent of the employee's earned income. In such a plan, the employer must make contributions for *each* employee who has reached age 21, has performed service for the employer during the calendar year and at least three of the five preceding calendar years, and has received at least $400 (in 1998) in compensation from the employer for the year.[62] Known as **simplified employee pension (SEP) plans,** these plans are subject to many of the same restrictions applicable to qualified plans (e.g., age and period-of-service requirements, top-heavy rules, and nondiscrimination limitations). Concept Summary 19–3 compares a SEP with a Keogh plan.

The amounts contributed to a SEP by an employer on behalf of an employee and the elective deferrals of an employee under a SEP are excludible from gross income. Elective deferrals under a SEP are subject to a statutory ceiling of $10,000 (in 1998).[63] Only $160,000 (in 1998) in compensation may be taken into account in making the SEP computation. An employer is permitted to elect to use its taxable year rather than the calendar year for purposes of determining contributions to a SEP.[64]

---

[62]§§ 408(j) and (k)(2). This amount is indexed annually. For 1997, the amount also was $400.

[63]Elective deferrals by an employee were repealed by the Small Business Job Protection Act of 1996 effective after December 31, 1996. However, if the employer plan was established before January

1, 1997, contributions can continue to be made under the pre-repeal provisions.

[64]§ 404(h)(1)(A). The $10,000 and $160,000 amounts are indexed annually.

SIMPLE IRA. A SIMPLE plan can be in the form of an IRA. See the earlier discussion under SIMPLE Plans.

Spousal IRA. If both spouses work, each can individually establish an IRA. Deductible IRA contributions of up to $2,000 may be made by each spouse if the combined compensation of both spouses is at least equal to the contributed amount. Thus, if each spouse has compensation of at least $2,000, they each may contribute a maximum of $2,000. Likewise, if only one spouse is employed, they each may contribute a maximum of $2,000 if the employed spouse has compensation of at least $4,000. Finally, if both spouses are employed, but one has compensation of less than $2,000, they each may contribute a maximum of $2,000 if their combined compensation is at least $4,000.

For the spousal IRA provision to apply, a joint return must be filed.[65] The spousal IRA deduction is also proportionately reduced for active participants whose AGI exceeds the above target ranges.

EXAMPLE 26

Tony, who is married, is eligible to establish an IRA. He received $30,000 in compensation in 1998, and his spouse does not work outside the home. Tony can contribute up to $4,000 to two IRAs, to be divided in any manner between the two spouses, except that no more than $2,000 can be allocated to either spouse. ▼

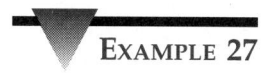

EXAMPLE 27

Assume the same facts as in the previous example, except that Tony's wife has compensation income of $1,200. Without the spousal IRA provision, Tony could contribute $2,000 to his IRA, and his spouse could contribute only $1,200 to her IRA. With the spousal IRA provision, they both can contribute $2,000 to their IRAs. ▼

Alimony is considered to be earned income for purposes of IRA contributions. Thus, a person whose only income is alimony can contribute to an IRA.

Timing of Contributions. Contributions (both deductible and nondeductible) can be made to an IRA anytime before the due date of the individual's tax return.[66] For example, an individual can establish and contribute to an IRA through April 15, 1999 (the return due date), and deduct this amount on his or her tax return for 1998. IRA contributions that are made during a tax return extension period do not satisfy the requirement of being made by the return due date. An employer can make contributions up until the time of the due date for filing the return (including extensions) and treat those amounts as a deduction for the prior year.[67] As noted earlier, a similar rule applies to Keogh plans. However, the Keogh plan must be established before the end of the tax year. Contributions to the Keogh plan may then be made anytime before the due date of the individual's tax return.

PENALTY TAXES FOR EXCESS CONTRIBUTIONS

A cumulative, nondeductible 6 percent excise penalty tax is imposed on the smaller of (1) any excess contributions or (2) the market value of the plan assets determined as of the close of the tax year. *Excess contributions* are any contributions that exceed the maximum limitation and contributions that are made during or after the tax year in which the individual reaches age 70½.[68] A taxpayer is not allowed a deduction for

---

[65]§ 219(c).
[66]§ 219(f)(3).
[67]§ 404(h)(1)(B).

[68]§§ 4973(a)(1) and (b). Contributions can be made to a Roth IRA after the tax year in which the individual reaches age 70½.

excess contributions. If the excess is corrected by contributing less than the deductible amount for a later year, a deduction then is allowable in the later year as a *makeup* deduction.

An excess contribution is taxable annually until returned to the taxpayer or reduced by the underutilization of the maximum contribution limitation in a subsequent year. The 6 percent penalty tax can be avoided if the excess amounts are returned.[69]

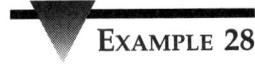

EXAMPLE 28

Nancy, age 55, establishes a traditional IRA in 1998 and contributes $2,300 in cash to the plan. She has earned income of $22,000. Nancy is allowed a $2,000 deduction *for* AGI for 1998. Assuming the market value of the plan assets is at least $300, there is a nondeductible 6% excise penalty tax of $18 ($300 × 6%). The $300 may be subject to an additional penalty tax in future years if it is not returned to Nancy or reduced by underutilization of the $2,000 maximum contribution limitation. ▼

TAXATION OF BENEFITS

A participant has a zero basis in the *deductible* contributions of a traditional IRA because the contributions were deducted.[70] Therefore, all withdrawals from a deductible IRA are taxed as ordinary income in the year of receipt. They are not eligible for the 5-year or 10-year averaging allowed for lump-sum distributions.

In addition to being included in gross income, payments from IRAs made to a participant before age 59½ are subject to a nondeductible 10 percent penalty tax on such actual, or constructive, payments.[71] However, an individual may make penalty-free withdrawals to pay for medical expenses in excess of 7.5 percent of AGI, to pay for qualified higher education expenses, and to pay for qualified, first-time home buyer expenses (up to $10,000). Note that a qualified first-time home buyer is defined as an individual (and spouse) who has not owned a principal residence in the two-year period preceding the date of acquisition of a principal residence. Further, an individual who has received unemployment compensation for at least 12 consecutive weeks may use IRA withdrawals to pay for health insurance for himself or herself, the spouse, and dependents without incurring the 10 percent penalty tax.[72]

All traditional IRAs of an individual are treated as one contract, and all distributions during a taxable year are treated as one distribution. See the earlier discussion of the special rules for distributions from Roth IRAs and traditional IRAs. If an individual who previously has made both deductible and nondeductible IRA contributions makes a withdrawal from a traditional IRA during a taxable year, the excludible amount must be calculated. The amount excludible from gross income for the taxable year is calculated by multiplying the amount withdrawn by a percentage. The percentage is calculated by dividing the individual's aggregate nondeductible IRA contributions by the aggregate balance of all of his or her traditional IRAs (including rollover IRAs and SEPs).[73]

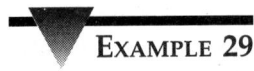

EXAMPLE 29

Carl, age 59, has a $12,000 deductible IRA and a $2,000 nondeductible traditional IRA (without any earnings). Carl withdraws $1,000 from the nondeductible IRA. The excludible portion is $143 [($2,000/$14,000) × $1,000)], and the includible portion is $857 [($12,000/$14,000) × $1,000)]. Carl must also pay a 10% penalty tax on the prorated portion considered

---

[69]§§ 408(d)(4) and 4973(b)(2).

[70]§ 408(d)(1).

[71]§ 72(t). There are limited exceptions to the penalty on early distributions.

[72]§§ 72(t)(2)(B), (D), (E), and (F). For purposes of the unemployment provision, a self-employed individual who otherwise would have been eligible for unemployment compensation will qualify.

[73]§ 408(d)(2).

withdrawn from the deductible IRA and earnings in either type of IRA. Thus, the 10% penalty tax is $85.70 (10% × $857). ▼

Rollovers: General Provisions. As introduced earlier, an IRA may be the recipient of a rollover from another qualified plan, including another IRA. Such a distribution from a qualified plan is not included in gross income if it is transferred within 60 days of receipt to an IRA or another qualified plan. For a series of distributions that constitute a lump-sum distribution, the 60-day period does not begin until the last distribution. Amounts received from IRAs may be rolled over tax-free only once in a 12-month period. If a person has more than one IRA, the one-year waiting period applies separately to each IRA.[74]

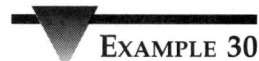

EXAMPLE 30

Nonemployer stock worth $60,000 is distributed to an employee from a qualified retirement plan. Hubert, the employee, sells the stock within 60 days for $60,000 and transfers one-half of the proceeds to a traditional IRA. Hubert will have $30,000 of ordinary income, which is not eligible for 5-year or 10-year forward averaging or for the capital gain treatment for pre-1974 contributions. One-half of the distribution, or $30,000, does escape taxation because of the rollover. ▼

A tax-free rollover for distributions from qualified plans is an alternative to the taxable 5-year or 10-year forward averaging techniques. Any rollover amount in a traditional IRA may later be rolled over into another qualified plan if the IRA consists of only the amounts from the original plan. The amount of nondeductible employee contributions included in a distribution may not be rolled over, but that amount is tax-free because the contributions were made with after-tax dollars. Partial rollovers are allowed, but the maximum amount that may be rolled over may not exceed the portion of the distribution that is otherwise includible in gross income. Rollovers are not available for required distributions under the minimum distribution rules once age 70½ is reached.

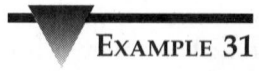

EXAMPLE 31

Jane withdraws $1,500 from her traditional IRA on May 2, 1998, but she redeposits it in the same IRA on June 28, 1998. Although the withdrawal and redeposit was a partial rollover and Jane may have used the funds for a limited time, this is a tax-free rollover.[75] ▼

A rollover is different from a direct transfer of funds from a qualified plan to an IRA or another qualified plan by a trustee or issuer. A direct transfer is not subject to the one-year waiting period and the withholding rules.[76] Further, in many states, IRA amounts are subject to claims of creditors, which is not the case for employer plans.

An employer must withhold 20 percent of any lump-sum distributions unless the transfer is a direct transfer to an IRA or another qualified plan.[77]

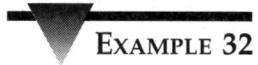

EXAMPLE 32

Kay receives a distribution from a qualified retirement plan. The amount of the distribution would have been $20,000, but Kay receives only $16,000 ($20,000 − $4,000) as a result of the 20% withholding provision. After several weeks, Kay decides to contribute $20,000 (the gross amount of the distribution) to her traditional IRA. Since she received only $16,000, she will need to contribute $4,000 from another source in order to make a $20,000 contribution. Kay will be able to claim a refund for the $4,000 that was withheld when she files her tax return for the year. ▼

---

[74]§ 408(d)(3)(B) and Prop.Reg. 1.408–4(b)(4).
[75]Ltr.Rul. 9010007.

[76]Temp.Reg. 35.3405–1.
[77]§ 3405(c).

Distributions to a traditional IRA are generally not eligible for 5- or 10-year averaging or capital gain treatment. An exception applies in the case of a *conduit IRA*, where the sole assets of a plan are rolled over into an IRA, and the assets are then rolled into a qualified plan. With a conduit IRA, the lump-sum distribution from the original plan is still eligible for the special tax treatments.

Rollovers and Conversions: Roth IRAs. A Roth IRA may be rolled over tax-free into another Roth IRA.[78]

A traditional IRA may be rolled over or converted to a Roth IRA. A conversion occurs when the taxpayer notifies the IRA trustee that the IRA is now a Roth IRA. A rollover or conversion of a traditional IRA to a Roth IRA can occur only if the following requirements are satisfied:[79]

- The participant's AGI does not exceed $100,000.
- The participant is not married filing a separate return.
- The rollover occurs within 60 days of the IRA distribution.

If a traditional IRA is rolled over or converted to a Roth IRA, the tax consequences depend on whether the traditional IRA was deductible or nondeductible. If deductible, then the basis for the IRA is zero. Thus, the entire amount of the rollover or conversion is included in gross income. If nondeductible, then the basis for the IRA is equal to the sum of the contributions. Thus, only the IRA earnings included in the rollover or conversion are included in gross income. The 10 percent penalty tax will not apply in either case.[80]

If a rollover or conversion of a traditional IRA to a Roth IRA occurs before January 1, 1999, the amount included in gross income is spread ratably over the current tax year and each of the three following tax years (e.g., for a 1998 rollover or conversion, one-fourth is included in the gross income of 1998, 1999, 2000, and 2001).[81]

▼
NONQUALIFIED DEFERRED COMPENSATION PLANS

UNDERLYING RATIONALE FOR TAX TREATMENT

▼ **LEARNING OBJECTIVE**
Understand the rationale for nonqualified deferred compensation plans and the related tax treatment.

Nonqualified deferred compensation (NQDC) plans provide a flexible way for taxpayers, particularly those in the 36 or 39.6 percent tax bracket, to defer income taxes on income payments until a possible lower tax bracket year. Where the deferred compensation is credited with annual earnings until payment, the entire deferred compensation, not the after-tax amount, is generating investment income. Also, most NQDC plans do not have to meet the discrimination, funding, coverage, and other requirements of qualified plans. In addition to these advantages for the employee, the employer may not have a current cash outflow.

The doctrine of constructive receipt is an important concept relating to the taxability of nonqualified deferred compensation.[82] In essence, if a taxpayer irrevocably earns income but may elect to receive it now or at a later date, the income is constructively received and is immediately taxed. Income is not constructively

---

[78]§ 408A(c)(3)(B).
[79]§ 408A(c)(3)(B).
[80]§ 408A(d)(3)(A)(ii).

[81]§ 408A(d)(3)(A)(iii).
[82]§ 451(a) and Reg. § 1.451–2.

CONCEPT SUMMARY 19–4

Comparison of IRAs

	Traditional		Roth IRA	Education IRA
	Deductible IRA	**Nondeductible IRA**		
Maximum contribution (per year)	$2,000*	$2,000*	$2,000*	$500
Tax-deductible contribution	Yes	No	No	No
Tax-free growth of income	Yes	Yes	Yes	Yes
Beginning of AGI phase-out for active participant (1998)	$30,000 single, $50,000 joint	N/A	$95,000 single, $150,000 joint	$95,000 single, $150,000 joint
Income tax on distributions	Yes, for entire distribution	Yes, for the earnings portion	No, if satisfy 5-year holding period**	No, if used for education expenses
50% excise tax: age 70½ minimum distributions	Yes	Yes	No	No
10% early withdrawal penalty (before age 59½)	Yes, with exceptions†	Yes, with exceptions†	Yes, with exceptions†	Yes††

*The total of deductible, nondeductible, and Roth IRA contributions may not exceed $2,000 per year.

**In addition, the distribution must satisfy one of the following: after age 59½, for qualified first-time home buyer expenses, participant is disabled, or made to a beneficiary on or after the participant's death.

†Qualified education costs and first-time home buyer (up to $10,000) avoid 10% penalty.

††On early withdrawals not used for education costs.

---

received, however, if the taxpayer's control over the amounts earned is subject to substantial limitations or restrictions.

Another important concept is the economic benefit theory. Although a taxpayer does not have a present right to income, the income will be taxable if a right in the form of a negotiable promissory note exists. Notes and other evidences of indebtedness received in payment for services constitute income to the extent of their fair market value at the time of the transfer.[83]

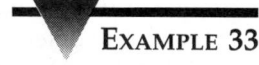 **EXAMPLE 33** Eagle Corporation and Bill, a cash basis employee, enter into an employment agreement that provides an annual salary of $120,000 to Bill. Of this amount, $100,000 is to be paid in current monthly installments, and $20,000 is to be paid in 10 annual installments beginning at Bill's retirement or death. Although Eagle Corporation maintains a separate account for Bill, that account is not funded (Bill is merely an unsecured creditor of the corporation). The $20,000 is not considered constructively received and is deferred. Compensation of $100,000 is currently taxable to Bill and deductible to Eagle. The other $20,000 will be taxable and deductible when paid in future years. ▼

TAX TREATMENT TO THE EMPLOYER AND EMPLOYEE

The tax treatment of an NQDC plan depends on whether it is *funded* or *unfunded* and whether it is *forfeitable* or *nonforfeitable*. In an unfunded NQDC plan, the employee relies upon the company's mere promise to make the compensation payment in the future. An unfunded, unsecured promise to pay, not represented

[83]Reg. § 1.61–2(d)(4).

TAX IN THE NEWS

ROTH VERSUS TRADITIONAL IRA

Taxpayers have a major decision with respect to IRA contributions: Should they benefit today or tomorrow? Under the traditional IRA, a person can enjoy a benefit today in the form of an immediate tax deduction. Anyone who is not covered by a retirement plan elsewhere can open or add to a tax-deductible IRA. Some people covered by company retirement plans can also fully fund a tax-deductible IRA if their income falls below certain levels, (e.g., AGI of $30,000 and below for a single person).

On the other hand, a Roth IRA allows a taxpayer to benefit tomorrow. A taxpayer does not get an upfront deduction, but withdrawals can be tax-free. Starting in 1998, a single person with an AGI of $95,000 and below can place up to $2,000 into a Roth IRA. The total IRA contribution per year—for both a traditional and a Roth IRA—may not exceed $2,000.

Steven Norwitz, a vice president with Baltimore's T. Rowe Price Associates, says that a "Roth IRA is almost always better." He thinks that people near retirement age whose tax bracket will drop once they quit the workforce may be better off with a tax-deductible account, but that people who are 15 or 20 years from retirement will benefit more from a Roth IRA, even if their tax bracket is lower at retirement.

SOURCE: Adapted from Jonathan Clements, "Jam Today or Jam Tomorrow? Roth IRA Will Show Many Investors It Pays to Wait," *Wall Street Journal*, September 16, 1997, p. C1.

by a negotiable note, effectively defers the recognition of income. Thus, the employee is taxed later when the compensation is actually paid or made available.[84] Similarly, the employer is allowed a deduction when the employee recognizes income.[85]

The employer can set up an escrow account to accumulate deferred payments on behalf of the employee. These funds may be invested by the escrow agent for the benefit of the employee.[86] By avoiding income recognition until the benefits from the escrow custodial account are received, the employee postpones the tax. An escrow arrangement can be appropriate for a professional athlete or entertainer whose income is earned in a few peak years.

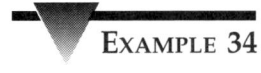

EXAMPLE 34

Ted, a professional athlete, is to receive a bonus for signing an employment contract. An NQDC plan is established to defer the income beyond Ted's peak income years. His employer transfers the bonus to an escrow agent who invests the funds in securities, etc., which may act as a hedge against inflation. The bonus is deferred for 10 years and becomes payable gradually in years 11 through 15. The bonus is taxable to Ted and deductible by his employer when Ted receives the payments in years 11 through 15. ▼

Generally, funded NQDC plans must be forfeitable to keep the compensation payments from being taxable immediately. In most instances, employees prefer to have some assurance that they will ultimately receive benefits from the NQDC (that the plan provides for nonforfeitable benefits). In such instances, the plan will

---

[84]Rev.Rul. 60–31, 1960–1 C.B. 174; Reg. § 1.451–2(a); *U.S. v. Basye*, 73–1 USTC ¶9250, 31 AFTR2d 73–802, 93 S.Ct. 1080 (USSC, 1973).

[85]§§ 404(a) and (d).

[86]Rev.Rul. 55–525, 1955–2 C.B. 543.

have to be unfunded to prevent immediate taxation to the employee. Note that most funded NQDC plans are subject to many of the provisions that apply to qualified plans.

When to Use an NQDC Arrangement.   As a general rule, NQDC plans are more appropriate for executives in a financially secure company. Because of the need for currently disposable income, such plans are usually not appropriate for young employees.

An NQDC plan can reduce an employee's overall tax payments by deferring the taxation of income to later years (possibly when the employee is in a lower tax bracket). In effect, these plans may produce a form of income averaging. Further, NQDC plans may discriminate in favor of shareholders, officers, specific highly compensated key employees, or a single individual.

Certain disadvantages should be noted. Nonqualified plans are usually required to be unfunded, which means that an employee is not assured that funds ultimately will be available to pay the benefits. Also, the employer's tax deduction is postponed until the employee is taxed on those payments.

Golden Parachute Arrangements.   Golden parachute arrangements promise monetary benefits to key employees if they lose their jobs as a result of a change in ownership of the corporation. These payments may be unreasonable or not really for services rendered. The term **golden parachute payments,** as used in the Code, means *excess severance pay.*

These excessive severance payments to employees are penalized. The Code denies a deduction to an employer who makes a payment of cash or property to an employee or independent contractor that satisfies both of the following conditions:

- The payment is contingent on a change of ownership of a corporation through a stock or asset acquisition.
- The aggregate present value of the payment equals or exceeds three times the employee's (or independent contractor's) average annual compensation.[87]

The disallowed amount is the excess of the payment over a statutory base amount (a five-year average of taxable compensation if the taxpayer was an employee for the entire five-year period). Further, a 20 percent excise tax is imposed on the recipient on the receipt of these parachute payments; the tax is withheld at the time of payment.[88]

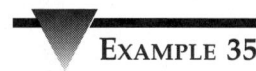

EXAMPLE 35

Irene, an executive, receives a golden parachute payment of $380,000 from her employer. Her average annual compensation for the most recent five tax years is $120,000. The corporation will be denied a deduction for $260,000 ($380,000 payment − $120,000 base amount). Irene's excise tax is $52,000 ($260,000 × 20%). ▼

Golden parachute payments do not include payments to or from qualified pension, profit sharing, stock bonus, annuity, or simplified employee pension plans. Also excluded is the amount of the payment that, in fact, represents reasonable compensation for personal services actually rendered or to be rendered. Such excluded payments are not taken into account when determining whether the threshold (the aggregate present value calculation) is exceeded.

S corporations are not subject to the golden parachute rules. Generally, corporations that do not have stock that is readily tradable on an established securities market or elsewhere are also exempt.

---

[87]§ 280G.   [88]§ 4999.

Publicly Held Companies' Compensation Limitation. For purposes of both the regular income tax and the alternative minimum tax, the deductible compensation for the top five executives of publicly traded companies is limited to $1 million for each executive. A company is publicly held if the corporation has common stock listed on a national securities exchange.[89] This $1 million deduction limitation is decreased by any nondeductible golden parachute payments made to the employee during the same year.

This deduction limitation applies when the compensation deduction would otherwise be taken. For example, in the case of a nonqualified stock option (NQSO), which is discussed later in this chapter, the deduction is normally taken in the year the NQSO is exercised, even though the option was granted with respect to services performed in a prior year.

Certain types of compensation are *not* subject to this deduction limit and are not taken into account in determining whether other compensation exceeds $1 million:

- Compensation payable on a commission basis.
- Compensation payable solely on account of the attainment of one or more performance goals when certain requirements involving the approval of outside directors and shareholders are met.
- Payments to a tax-qualified retirement plan (including salary reduction contributions).
- Amounts that are excludible from an executive's gross income (such as employer-provided health benefits and miscellaneous fringe benefits).

The most important exception is performance-based compensation. Compensation qualifies for this exception only if the following conditions are satisfied:

- The compensation is paid solely on account of the attainment of one or more performance goals.
- The performance goals are established by a compensation committee consisting solely of two or more outside directors.
- The material terms under which the compensation is to be paid (including the performance goals) are disclosed to and approved by the shareholders in a separate vote prior to payment.
- Prior to payment, the compensation committee certifies that the performance goals and any other material terms were in fact satisfied.

Compensation (other than stock options or other stock appreciation rights) is not treated as paid solely on account of the attainment of one or more performance goals unless the compensation is paid to the particular executive under a preestablished objective performance formula or standard that precludes discretion. In essence, a third party with knowledge of the relevant performance results could calculate the amount to be paid to the particular executive. A performance goal is broadly defined and includes, for example, any objective performance standard that is applied to the individual executive, a business unit (e.g., a division or a line of business), or the corporation as a whole. Performance standards could include increases in stock price, market share, sales, or earnings per share.

---

[89]§ 162(m).

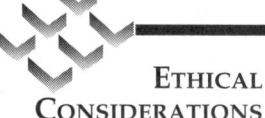

ETHICAL CONSIDERATIONS

Limiting Compensation for Executives But Not for Other Highly Paid Individuals

The top five executives of publicly traded corporations have a $1 million limit on deductible compensation. During 1995, chief executive officers in the financial services industry received the highest total compensation: median compensation of $1.5 million. Even with the limit, some CEOs received huge direct compensation. For example, the top wage earner in 1995 was Lawrence M. Coss of Green Tree Financial at $65.1 million, followed by John F. Welch, Jr., of General Electric at $22 million, Goodyear's Stanley C. Gault ($16.5 million), Compaq Computer's Eckhard Pfeiffer ($16.1 million), and Colgate-Palmolive's Reuben Mark ($15.1 million).

Yet other highly paid individuals are not subject to the $1 million compensation cap. Radio personality Paul Harvey lives comfortably on $13 million a year. A former streetcar conductor and Creole cook, Maya Angelou makes $4.3 million as a poet. Speaker Daniel Burrus pulls in $4 million, and Chef Roy Yamaquchi ($2 million) and Indian chief Skip Hayward ($1 million) also do well. Todd McFarlane, a comic book artist, makes $5 million, and Anthony Pellicano, a private investigator, makes $2 million. Sudan, a 14-year-old African lion, makes $800,000.

Similarly, many television and movie performers are receiving huge salaries (e.g., David Letterman at $14 million). Yet these entertainers and others not in the designated "top five" are not subject to the $1 million compensation cap. Some question the fairness of a policy that subjects business executives to a compensation limitation while allowing entertainers, sports stars, and others to be exempt from the limitation.

RESTRICTED PROPERTY PLANS

GENERAL PROVISIONS

8 LEARNING OBJECTIVE
Explain the value of restricted property plans.

A **restricted property plan** is an arrangement whereby an employer transfers property (e.g., stock of the employer-corporation) to an employee or other provider of services at no cost or at a bargain price. The usual purpose of a restricted stock plan is to retain the services of key employees who might otherwise leave. The employer hopes that such compensation arrangements will encourage company growth and attainment of performance objectives. Section 83 was enacted in 1969 to provide rules for the taxation of incentive compensation arrangements, which previously were governed by judicial and administrative interpretations. Although the following discussion refers to an employee as the provider of the services, the services may be performed by an independent contractor.

As a general rule, if an employee performs services and receives property (e.g., stock), the fair market value of that property in excess of any amount paid by the employee is includible in his or her gross income. The time for inclusion is the earlier of (1) the time the property is no longer subject to a substantial risk of forfeiture or (2) the time the property is transferable by the employee. The fair market value of the property is determined without regard to any restriction, except a restriction that by its terms will never lapse.[90] Since the amount of the compensation is determined at the date that the restrictions lapse or when the property is transferable, the opportunity to generate capital gain treatment on the property is denied during a period when the ordinary income element is being deferred.

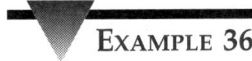

EXAMPLE 36

On October 1, 1994, Blue Corporation sold 100 shares of its stock to Ahmad, an employee, for $10 per share. At the time of the sale, the fair market value of the stock was $100 per share. Under the terms of the sale, each share of stock was nontransferable and subject to a substantial risk of forfeiture (which was not to lapse until October 1, 1998). Evidence of these restrictions was stamped on the face of the stock certificates. On October 1, 1998, the fair market value of the stock was $250 per share. Since the stock was nontransferable and was subject to a substantial risk of forfeiture, Ahmad did not include any compensation in gross income during 1994 (assuming no special election was made). Instead, Ahmad was required to include $24,000 of compensation in gross income [100 shares × ($250 – $10 per share)] during 1998. If for some reason the forfeiture had occurred (e.g., the plan required Ahmad to surrender the stock to the corporation if he voluntarily terminated his employment with the company before October 1, 1998) and Ahmad never received the stock certificates, he would have been allowed a capital loss of $1,000 (the extent of his investment). ▼

SUBSTANTIAL RISK OF FORFEITURE

A **substantial risk of forfeiture** exists if a person's rights to full enjoyment of property are conditioned upon the future performance, or the refraining from the performance, of substantial services by that individual.[91] For example, if an employee must return the property (receiving only his or her original cost, if any) should there be a failure to complete a substantial period of service (for any reason), the property is subject to a substantial risk of forfeiture. Another such situation exists when an employer can compel an employee to return the property due to a breach of a substantial covenant not to compete. Any substantial risk of forfeiture should be stated on the face of the stock certificates. Assuming that a substantial risk of forfeiture does not exist, the property received is valued at its fair market value, ignoring any restrictions, except for one instance dealing with closely held stock.

SPECIAL ELECTION AVAILABLE

An employee may elect within 30 days after the receipt of restricted property to recognize immediately as ordinary income the fair market value in excess of the amount paid for the property. Any appreciation in the value of the property after receipt is classified as capital gain instead of ordinary income. No deduction is allowed to the employee for taxes paid on the original amount included in income if the property is subsequently forfeited.[92] The employee is permitted to take a capital loss for any amounts that were actually paid for the property. Furthermore, in such a case, the employer must repay taxes saved by any compensation deduction taken in the earlier year.[93]

---

[90]§ 83(a)(1); *Miriam Sakol*, 67 T.C. 986 (1977); *T.M. Horwith*, 71 T.C. 932 (1979).

[91]§ 83(c); Regulation § 1.83–3(c)(2) includes several examples of restricted property arrangements.

[92]§ 83(b).

[93]Reg. §§ 1.83–6(c) and 2(a).

Any increase in value between the time the property is received and the time it becomes either nonforfeitable or transferable is taxed as ordinary income if the employee does not make this special election. However, if the employee elects to be taxed immediately on the difference between the cost and fair market value on the date of issue, any future appreciation is treated as capital gain. In determining whether the gain is long term or short term, the holding period starts when the employee is taxed on the ordinary income.[94]

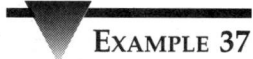

EXAMPLE 37

On July 1, 1988, Sparrow Company sold 100 shares of its preferred stock, worth $15 per share, to Diane (an employee) for $5 per share. The sale was subject to Diane's agreement to resell the preferred shares to the company for $5 per share if she terminated her employment during the following 10 years. The stock had a value of $25 per share on July 1, 1998, and Diane sold the stock for $30 per share on October 10, 1998. Diane made the special election to include the original spread (between the value of $15 in 1988 and the amount paid of $5) in income for 1988. Diane was required to recognize $1,000 of compensation income in 1988 ($15 − $5 = $10 × 100 shares), at which time her holding period in her stock began. Diane's tax basis in the stock was $1,500 ($1,000 + $500). When the preferred stock was sold in 1998, Diane recognized a $1,500 long-term capital gain ($30 × 100 shares − $1,500). ▼

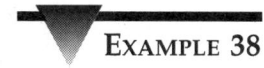

EXAMPLE 38

Assume the same facts as in Example 37, except that Diane sells the stock in 1999 (rather than 1998). She would not recognize any gain in 1998 when the substantial risk of forfeiture lapses. Instead, Diane would recognize the $1,500 long-term capital gain in 1999. ▼

This special provision is usually not elected since it results in an immediate recognition of income and adverse tax consequences result from a subsequent forfeiture. However, the special election may be attractive in the following situations:

- The bargain element is relatively small.
- Substantial appreciation is expected in the future.
- A high probability exists that the restrictions will be met.

EMPLOYER DEDUCTIONS

At the time the employee is required to include the compensation in income, the employer is allowed a tax deduction for the same amount. The employer must withhold on this amount in accordance with § 3402. In the no-election situation, the deduction is limited to the fair market value of the restricted property (without regard to the restrictions) at the time the restrictions lapse, reduced by the amount originally paid for the property by the employee.[95] When the employee elects to be taxed immediately, the corporate deduction also is accelerated and deductible in like amount. In cases of deferred income recognition, the employer can receive a very sizable deduction if the property has appreciated.

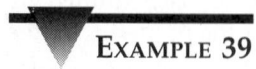

EXAMPLE 39

On March 14, 1996, Gold Corporation sold to Harry, an employee, 10 shares of Gold common stock for $100 per share. Both the corporation and Harry were calendar year taxpayers. The common stock was subject to a substantial risk of forfeiture and was nontransferable; both conditions were to lapse on March 14, 1998. At the time of the sale, the fair market value of the common stock (without considering the restrictions) was $1,000 per share. On March 14, 1998, when the fair market value of the stock was $2,000 per share, the restrictions lapsed. Harry did not make the special election. In 1998, Harry realized ordinary income of $19,000

---

[94]§ 1223(6).   [95]Reg. § 1.83–6(a).

(10 shares at $2,000 per share less the $100 per share he had paid). Likewise, Gold Corporation was allowed a $19,000 compensation deduction in 1998. ▼

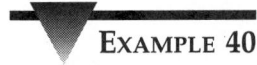

EXAMPLE 40

In the previous example, assume that Harry had made the special election. Since he was taxed on $9,000 in 1996, the corporation was allowed to deduct a like amount in 1996. No deduction would be available in 1998. ▼

STOCK OPTIONS

IN GENERAL

9 **LEARNING OBJECTIVE**
Differentiate the tax treatment of qualified and nonqualified stock options.

Various equity types of stock option programs are available for an employee's compensation package. Some authorities believe that some form of *equity kicker* is needed to attract new management, convert key officers into *partners* by giving them a share of the business, and retain the services of executives who might otherwise leave. Encouraging the managers of a business to have a proprietary interest in its successful operation should provide executives with a key motive to expand the company and improve its profits. In addition, under certain conditions, stock options may fall outside the $1 million limitation on the salaries of the top five executives of publicly traded companies.

A **stock option** gives an individual the right to purchase a stated number of shares of stock from a corporation at a certain price within a specified period of time. The optionee must be under no obligation to purchase the stock, and the option may be revocable by the corporation. The option must be in writing, and its terms must be clearly expressed.[96]

INCENTIVE STOCK OPTIONS

An equity type of stock option called an *incentive stock option (ISO)* is available. There are no tax consequences for either the issuing corporation or the recipient when the option is granted. However, the *spread* (the excess of the fair market value of the share at the date of exercise over the option price)[97] is a tax preference item to the recipient for purposes of the alternative minimum tax. The determination of fair market value is made without regard to any lapse restrictions (a restriction that will expire after a period of time). After the option is exercised and when the stock is sold, any gain from the sale is taxed as a long-term capital gain if certain holding period requirements are met. For a gain to qualify as a long-term capital gain, the employee must not dispose of the stock within two years after the option is granted or within one year after acquiring the stock.[98] If the employee meets the holding period requirements, none of these transactions generates any business deduction for the employer.[99]

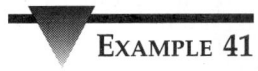

EXAMPLE 41

Wren Corporation granted an ISO for 100 shares of its stock to Rocky, an employee, on March 18, 1995. The option price was $100, and the fair market value was $100 on the date of the grant. Rocky exercised the option on April 1, 1997, when the market value of the stock was $200 per share. He sells the stock on April 6, 1998, for $300 per share. Rocky did not recognize any ordinary income on the date of the grant or the exercise date since the

[96]Reg. §§ 1.421–1(a)(1) and –7(a)(1).
[97]§§ 422(a), 421(a)(1), and 57(a)(3).

[98]§ 422(a)(1).
[99]§ 421(a)(2).

TAX IN THE NEWS

STOCK OPTIONS ARE POPULAR

Stock options are multiplying like rabbits. For example, in June 1997, Michael A. Ashcroft received $219 million of profit in Tyco International Ltd. options. Walt Disney Company Chairman Michael Eisner has received 8 million options in the past four years, equal to 1.2 percent of Disney stock. In 1997, Oprah Winfrey received 500,000 new options to purchase King World Productions, Inc., stock as part of her pay package.

For tax purposes, most companies deduct the expenses of options, thereby reducing their taxes. Some critics argue that the expenses are not real and should not be deductible.

For accounting purposes, most companies, especially in the high-tech industries, do not wish to take a hit to reported earnings. Ken Glueck, with Oracle, says that "the treatment of stock options in the earnings statement is a true conundrum." Although companies take a tax deduction, for accounting purposes the deduction is ignored.

SOURCE: Adapted from Roger Lowenstein, "Coming Clean on Company Stock Options," *Wall Street Journal*, June 26, 1997, p.C1.

---

option qualified as an ISO. Wren received no compensation deduction. Rocky has a $10,000 tax preference item on the exercise date. He has a long-term capital gain of $20,000 [($300 − $100) × 100] upon the sale of the stock in 1998, because the one-year and two-year holding periods and other requirements have been met. ▼

As a further requirement for ISO treatment, the option holder must be an employee of the issuing corporation from the date the option is granted until 3 months (12 months if disabled) before the date of exercise. The holding period and the employee-status rules just described (the one-year, two-year, and three-month requirements) are waived in the case of the death of an employee.[100]

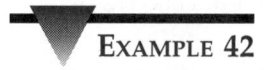

EXAMPLE 42

Assume the same facts as in the previous example, except that Rocky was not employed by Wren Corporation for six months before the date he exercised the options. Rocky must recognize ordinary income to the extent of the spread, assuming there was no substantial risk of forfeiture. Thus, Rocky recognizes $10,000 [($200 − $100) × 100] of ordinary income on the exercise date, because he was not an employee of Wren Corporation at all times during the period beginning on the grant date and ending three months before the exercise date. Wren is allowed a deduction at the same time that Rocky reports the ordinary income. ▼

If the holding period requirements are not satisfied but all other conditions are met, the tax is still deferred to the point of the sale. However, the difference between the option price and the value of the stock at the date the option was exercised is treated as ordinary income. The difference between the amount realized for the stock and the value of the stock at the date of exercise is short-term or long-term capital gain, depending on the holding period of the stock itself. The

---

[100]§§ 422(a)(2) and (c)(3). Exceptions are made for parent and subsidiary situations, corporate reorganizations, and liquidations.

Also, in certain situations involving an insolvent employee, the holding period rules are modified.

employer is allowed a deduction equal to the amount recognized by the employee as ordinary income. The employee does not have a tax preference for alternative minimum tax purposes.

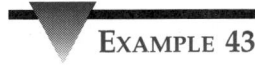
EXAMPLE 43

Assume the same facts as in Example 41, except that Rocky sells the stock on March 22, 1998, for $290 per share. Since Rocky did not hold the stock itself for at least one year, $10,000 of the gain is treated as ordinary income in 1998, and Wren Corporation is allowed a $10,000 compensation deduction in 1998. The remaining $9,000 is a short-term capital gain ($29,000 − $20,000). ▼

Qualification Requirements for Incentive Stock Option Plans. An **incentive stock option (ISO)** is an option to purchase stock of a corporation granted to an individual for any reason connected with his or her employment.[101] The option is granted by the employer-corporation or by a parent or subsidiary corporation of the employer-corporation. When exercising an option, an employee can use company stock to pay for the stock without disqualifying the ISO plan.

For an option to qualify as an ISO, the terms of the option itself must meet the following conditions:

- The option must be granted under a plan specifying the number of shares of stock to be issued and the employees or class of employees eligible to receive the options. The plan must be approved by the shareholders of the corporation within 12 months before or after the plan is adopted.
- The option must be granted within 10 years of the date the plan is adopted or of the date the plan is approved by the shareholders, whichever date is earlier.
- The option must by its terms be exercisable only within 10 years of the date it is granted.
- The option price must equal or exceed the fair market value of the stock at the time the option is granted. This requirement is deemed satisfied if there has been a good faith attempt to value the stock accurately, even if the option price is less than the stock value.
- The option by its terms must be nontransferable other than at death and must be exercisable during the employee's lifetime only by the employee.
- The employee must not, immediately before the option is granted, own stock representing more than 10 percent of the voting power or value of all classes of stock in the employer-corporation or its parent or subsidiary. (Here, the attribution rules of § 267 are applied in modified form.) However, the stock ownership limitation will be waived if the option price is at least 110 percent of the fair market value (at the time the option is granted) of the stock subject to the option and the option by its terms is not exercisable more than five years from the date it is granted.[102]

An overall limitation is imposed on the amount of ISOs that can be exercised in one year by an employee. This limit is set at $100,000 per year based on the value of the stock determined at the time the option is granted.

NONQUALIFIED STOCK OPTIONS

A **nonqualified stock option (NQSO)** does not satisfy the statutory requirements for ISOs. In addition, a stock option that otherwise would qualify as an ISO will be treated as an NQSO if the terms of the stock option provide that it is not an

---

[101]§ 422(b).

[102]§ 422(c)(5).

ISO. If the NQSO has a readily ascertainable fair market value (e.g., the option is traded on an established exchange), the value of the option must be included in the employee's income at the date of grant. Thereafter, capital gain or loss is recognized only upon the disposal of the optioned stock. The employee's basis is the amount paid for the stock plus any amount reported as ordinary income. The employer obtains a corresponding tax deduction at the same time and to the extent that ordinary income is recognized by the employee.[103]

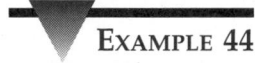

EXAMPLE 44

On February 1, 1997, Janet was granted an NQSO to purchase 100 shares of stock from her employer at $10 per share. On this date, the option was selling for $2 on an established exchange. Janet exercised the option on March 30, 1998, when the stock was worth $20 per share. On November 5, 1998, Janet sold the optioned stock for $22 per share.

- Janet must report ordinary income of $200 ($2 × 100 shares) on the date of grant (February 1, 1997), because the option has a readily ascertainable fair market value.
- Janet's adjusted basis for the stock is $1,200 ($1,000 cost + $200 recognized gain).
- Upon the sale of the stock (November 5, 1998), Janet must report a long-term capital gain of $1,000 [($22 − $12) × 100 shares].
- At the date of grant (February 1, 1997), the employer receives a tax deduction of $200, the amount of income reported by Janet. ▼

If an NQSO does not have a readily ascertainable fair market value, an employee does not recognize income at the grant date. However, as a general rule, ordinary income must then be reported in the year of exercise (the difference between the fair market value of the stock at the exercise date and the option price).[104] The amount paid by the employee for the stock plus the amount reported as ordinary income becomes the basis. Any appreciation above that basis is taxed as a long-term capital gain upon disposition (assuming the stock is held for the required long-term holding period after exercise). The corporation receives a corresponding tax deduction at the same time and to the extent that ordinary income is recognized by the employee.

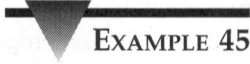

EXAMPLE 45

On February 3, 1996, Maria was granted an NQSO for 100 shares of common stock at $10 per share. On the date of the grant, there was no readily ascertainable fair market value for the option. Maria exercised the options on January 3, 1997, when the stock was selling for $15 per share. She sold one-half of the shares on April 15, 1997, and the other half on September 17, 1998. The sale price on both dates was $21 per share. Maria would not recognize any income on the grant date (February 3, 1996) but would recognize $500 ($1,500 − $1,000) of ordinary income on the exercise date (January 3, 1997). She would recognize a short-term capital gain of $300 on the sale of the first half in 1997 and a $300 long-term capital gain on the sale of the second batch of stock in 1998 [½($2,100 − $1,500)]. ▼

The major *advantages* of NQSOs can be summarized as follows:

- A tax deduction is available to the corporation without a cash outlay.
- The employee receives capital gain treatment on any appreciation in the stock starting either at the exercise date if the option does not have a readily ascertainable fair market value or at the date of grant if the option has a readily ascertainable fair market value.
- Options can be issued at more flexible terms than under ISO plans (e.g., longer exercise period and discount on exercise price).

---

[103]Reg. §§ 1.421–6(c), (d), (e), and (f); Reg. § 1.83–7.   [104]Reg. § 1.83–7(a); Reg. § 1.421–6(d).

A major *disadvantage* is that the employee must recognize ordinary income on the exercise of the option or at the date of grant without receiving cash to pay the tax.

TAX PLANNING CONSIDERATIONS

10 **LEARNING OBJECTIVE**
Identify tax planning opportunities available with deferred compensation.

DEFERRED COMPENSATION

With the higher 39.6 percent individual tax rate, taxpayers may try to lower their tax burden by participating in more deferred compensation arrangements. The $1 million annual limit on the compensation deduction for the top five executives of publicly traded companies may cause a shift into § 401(k) plans, qualified retirement plans, and especially nonqualified deferred compensation arrangements. However, the amount of compensation that can be taken into consideration for purposes of calculating contributions or benefits under a qualified pension or profit sharing plan has been reduced to $160,000. The increase to $2,000 for spousal IRAs, the SIMPLE IRA, the Roth IRA, the education IRA, and the SIMPLE § 401(k) plan should encourage more participation in retirement vehicles.

The repeal of five-year averaging after 1999 for qualified retirement plan distributions may encourage many employees to consider retiring over the next several years. The elimination of the 15 percent excise tax on excess distributions may encourage individuals to take distributions from qualified plans. The expectation that individual tax rates may increase in future years likewise encourages distributions and the receipt of cash compensation in 1998.

QUALIFIED PLANS

Qualified plans provide maximum tax benefits for employers, because the employer receives an immediate tax deduction for contributions to such plans and the income that is earned on the contributions is not taxable to the employer. The employer contributions and the trust earnings are not taxed to the employees until those funds are made available to them.

Qualified plans are most appropriate where it is desirable to provide benefits for a cross section of employees. In some closely held corporations, the primary objective is to provide benefits for the officer-shareholder group and other highly paid personnel. The nondiscrimination requirements that must be met in a qualified plan may prevent such companies from attaining these objectives. Thus, a nonqualified arrangement may be needed as a supplement to, or used in lieu of, the qualified plan.

SELF-EMPLOYED RETIREMENT PLANS

A Keogh or traditional deductible IRA participant may make a deductible contribution for a tax year up to the time prescribed for filing the individual's tax return. A Keogh plan must have been established by the end of the tax year (e.g., December 31) to obtain a current deduction for the contribution made in the subsequent year. An individual can establish an IRA after the end of the tax year and still receive a current deduction for the contribution made in the subsequent year. However, since the deductibility of contributions to IRAs has been restricted for many middle-income and upper-income taxpayers, Keogh plans are likely to become more important.

INDIVIDUAL RETIREMENT ACCOUNTS

The new Roth IRAs and education IRAs with their exclusion treatment for distributions should provide additional opportunities for the IRA participant, but also additional complexities. Should an otherwise eligible individual forgo the deduction for IRA contributions and contribute instead to IRAs providing exclusion treatment? Should a traditional IRA be rolled over into a Roth IRA even though a current tax liability results? The IRA participant will need answers to questions such as these.

COMPARISON OF § 401(k) PLAN WITH IRA

Most employees will find a § 401(k) plan more attractive than an IRA. Probably the biggest limitation of an IRA is the $2,000 maximum shelter. Under § 401(k), employees are permitted to shelter compensation up to $10,000 (in 1998).[105] The restrictions on deducting contributions to IRAs for many middle-income and upper-income taxpayers may cause many employees to utilize § 401(k) plans more frequently.

Another difference between § 401(k) plans and IRAs is the manner in which the money is treated. Money placed in an IRA may be tax deductible, whereas dollars placed in a § 401(k) plan are considered to be deferred compensation. Thus, a § 401(k) reduction may reduce profit sharing payments, group life insurance, and Social Security benefits. Concept Summary 19–5 compares a § 401(k) plan with an IRA.

NONQUALIFIED DEFERRED COMPENSATION (NQDC) PLANS

Nonqualified deferred compensation arrangements such as restricted property plans can be useful to attract executive talent or to provide substantial retirement benefits for executives. A restricted property plan may be used to retain a key employee of a closely held company when management continuity problems are anticipated. Without such employees, the untimely death or disability of one of the owners might cause a disruption of the business with an attendant loss in value for his or her heirs. Such plans may discriminate in favor of officers and other highly paid employees. The employer, however, does not receive a tax deduction until the employee is required to include the deferred compensation in income (upon the lapse of the restrictions).

The principal advantage of NQDC plans over current compensation is that the employee can defer the recognition of income to future periods when his or her income tax bracket may be lower (e.g., during retirement years). The time value benefits from the deferral of income should also be considered. However, with the trend toward increasing rates, an executive with a deferred compensation arrangement entered into in a prior year may wish to accelerate the income into 1998 since individual tax rates in future years may be even higher.

The principal disadvantage of NQDC plans could be the bunching effect that takes place on the expiration of the period of deferral. In some cases, planning can alleviate this result.

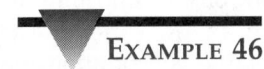

EXAMPLE 46   During 1998, Kelly, an executive, enters into an agreement to postpone a portion of her payment for current services until retirement. The deferred amount is not segregated from the company's general assets and is subject to normal business risk. The entire payment,

---

[105]This amount is indexed annually.

CONCEPT SUMMARY 19–5

Section 401(k) Plan and IRA Compared

	§ 401(k) Plan	IRA
Deduction limitation	Smaller of $10,000 (in 1998) or approximately 25% of total earnings. Limited by antidiscrimination requirements of § 401(k)(3).	$2,000 or 100% of compensation.
Distributions	Early withdrawal possible if for early retirement (55 or over) or to pay medical expenses.	10% penalty for early withdrawals, except for withdrawals to pay for certain medical expenses and health insurance, qualified education expenses, and qualified first-time home buyer expenses.
Effect on gross earnings	Gross salary reduction, which may reduce profit sharing contributions, Social Security benefits, and group life insurance.	No effect.
Employer involvement	Must keep records; monitor for compliance with antidiscrimination test.	Minimal.
Lump-sum distributions	Favorable 5-year or 10-year forward averaging.	Ordinary income.
Timing of contribution	Within 30 days of plan year-end or due date of employer's return.*	Grace period up to due date of tax return (not including extensions).
Loans from plan	Yes.	No.

*Elective contributions must be made to the plan no later than 30 days after the end of the plan year, and nonelective contributions no later than the due date of the tax return (including extensions).

not the after-tax amount, is invested in securities and variable annuity contracts. Kelly is not taxed on the payment in 1998, and the company receives no deduction in 1998. If Kelly receives the deferred payment in a lump sum when she retires, the tax rates may be higher and more progressive than in 1998. Thus, Kelly may wish to arrange for a number of payments to be made to her or a designated beneficiary over a number of years. ▼

STOCK OPTIONS

Rather than paying compensation in the form of corporate stock, a corporation may issue options to purchase stock at a specific price to an employee. Stock option plans are used more frequently by publicly traded companies than by closely held companies. This difference is due to the problems of determining the value of the stock of a company that is not publicly held.

Nonqualified stock options (NQSOs) are more flexible and less restrictive than incentive stock options (ISOs). For example, the holding period for an NQSO is not as long as that for an ISO. Further, the option price of an NQSO may be less than the fair market value of the stock at the time the option is granted. An NQSO creates an employer deduction that lowers the cost of the NQSO to the employer. The employer may pass along this tax savings to the employee in the form of a cash payment. Both the employer and the employee may be better off by combining NQSOs with additional cash payments rather than using ISOs. See Concept Summary 19–6.

CONCEPT SUMMARY 19-6

Incentive Stock Options and Nonqualified Stock Options Compared

	ISO	NQSO
Granted at any price	No	Yes
May have any duration	No	Yes
Governing Code Section	§ 422	§ 83
Spread subject to alternative minimum tax	Yes	No
Deduction to employer for spread	No	Yes
Type of gain/loss on disposal	Capital	Capital
Statutory amount ($100,000) limitation	Yes	No

The continuing reduction in capital gain rates may make stock options, particularly ISOs, an even more attractive component of the executive compensation package.

FLEXIBLE BENEFIT PLANS

Employees may be permitted to choose from a package of employer-provided fringe benefits.[106] In these so-called **cafeteria benefit plans,** some of the benefits chosen by an employee may be taxable, and some may be statutory nontaxable benefits (e.g., health and accident insurance and group term life insurance).

Employer contributions made to a flexible plan are included in an employee's gross income only to the extent that the employee actually elects the taxable benefits. Certain nondiscrimination standards with respect to coverage, eligibility for participation, contributions, and benefits must be met. Thus, such a plan must cover a fair cross section of employees. Also, a flexible plan cannot include an election to defer compensation, and a key employee is not exempt from taxation on the taxable benefits made available where more than 25 percent of the statutory nontaxable benefits are provided to key employees.

KEY TERMS

Cafeteria benefit plan, 19-44

Deferred compensation, 19-3

Defined benefit plan, 19-5

Defined contribution pension plan, 19-5

Employee stock ownership plan (ESOP), 19-6

Golden parachute payments, 19-32

Highly compensated employee, 19-9

H.R. 10 (Keogh) plan, 19-20

Incentive stock option (ISO), 19-39

Individual Retirement Account (IRA), 19-22

Lump-sum distribution, 19-12

---

[106] § 125.

Nonqualified deferred compensation (NQDC) plan, 19–29

Nonqualified stock option (NQSO), 19–39

Pension plan, 19–4

Profit sharing plan, 19–5

Restricted property plan, 19–34

Section 401(k) plan, 19–18

Simplified employee pension (SEP) plan, 19–25

Stock bonus plan, 19–6

Stock option, 19–37

Substantial risk of forfeiture, 19–35

Top-heavy plan, 19–17

Vesting requirements, 19–9

Zero bracket amount, 19–13

PROBLEM MATERIALS

DISCUSSION QUESTIONS

1. Describe the three basic types of qualified plans.

2. Compare and contrast qualified pension plans with qualified profit sharing plans.

3. Determine whether each of the following independent statements best applies to a defined contribution plan (DCP), defined benefit plan (DBP), both (B), or neither (N):
   a. Includes an employee stock ownership plan (ESOP).
   b. Forfeitures can be allocated to the remaining participants' accounts.
   c. Requires greater reporting requirements and more actuarial and administrative costs.
   d. Forfeitures can revert to the employer.
   e. More favorable to employees who are older at the time the plan is adopted.
   f. Employee forfeitures can be used to reduce future contributions by the employer.
   g. May exclude employees who begin employment within five years of normal retirement age.
   h. Annual addition to each employee's account may not exceed the smaller of $30,000 or 25% of the employee's salary.
   i. The final benefit to a participant depends upon investment performance.
   j. To avoid penalties, the amount of annual contributions must meet minimum funding requirements.

4. Indicate whether the following statements apply to a pension plan (P), a profit sharing plan (PS), both (B), or neither (N):
   a. Forfeited amounts can be used to reduce future contributions by the employer.
   b. Allocation of forfeitures may discriminate in favor of the prohibited group (highly compensated employees).
   c. Forfeitures can revert to the employer.
   d. Forfeitures can increase plan benefits by allocating the forfeitures to participants.
   e. An annual benefit of $60,000 could be payable on behalf of a participant.
   f. More favorable to employees who are older at the time the qualified plan is adopted.

5. When will the $30,000 maximum annual contribution to a defined contribution plan be indexed?

6. What are the tax and financial advantages accruing to a company that adopts an employee stock ownership plan (ESOP) for employees?

7. List the requirements that must be satisfied in order for a retirement plan to be qualified and receive favorable tax treatment.

8. Is it possible to provide greater vested benefits for highly paid employees and still meet the nondiscrimination requirements under a qualified pension plan? Explain.

9. What causes an employee to be classified as a "highly compensated employee"?

10. Once the age and service requirements are met, when must an employee begin participating in a qualified plan?

11. What is vesting, and how do vesting requirements help employees who do not remain with one employer during their working years?

12. Discuss the tax consequences of a qualified pension or profit sharing plan to the employee, the employer, and the trust.

13. Harvey Maxwell, who is age 67, is going to receive a lump-sum distribution from a qualified plan. He has asked you to provide him with a description of the alternatives available to him for taxing the lump-sum distribution. Draft a letter to Harvey in which you respond. He resides at 3000 East Glenn, Tulsa, OK 74104.

14. Which of the following would be considered a tax benefit or advantage of a qualified retirement plan?
    a. Certain lump-sum distributions may be subject to capital gain treatment.
    b. Employer contributions are deductible by the employer in the year of contribution.
    c. Employee contributions are deductible by the employee in the year of contribution.
    d. The qualified trust is tax-exempt as to all income (other than unrelated business income).
    e. In a lump-sum distribution, any capital gain tax on the portion attributable to any unrealized appreciation in the stock of the employer at the time of distribution is deferred until the time the employee disposes of the stock in a taxable transaction.
    f. Election may be made to allow a lump-sum distribution to be subject to a 5-year or 10-year forward averaging technique.

15. What ceiling limitations have been placed on employer contributions (relative to individual employees) to defined contribution and defined benefit plans?

16. What is the maximum deduction permitted to an employer each year for contributions to a profit sharing plan and a stock bonus plan?

17. Define the term *key employee* for purposes of a top-heavy plan.

18. Determine the 1998 indexed amounts for the following items:
    a. Maximum annual contribution to a defined contribution plan.
    b. Maximum annual benefits payable by a defined benefit plan.
    c. The maximum amount of the annual contribution to a cash or deferred arrangement plan.

19. Jerry Artis calls you and asks about the differences between a Roth IRA and an educational IRA. Prepare a memo for the tax files about your discussion.

20. Can a § 401(k) plan avoid the nondiscrimination tests and the top-heavy rules?

21. Can an individual make withdrawals from a deductible IRA without incurring the 10% penalty tax?

22. What tax-free alternative is available for the 5-year or 10-year forward averaging techniques for lump-sum distributions?

23. In which of the following situations is a nonqualified deferred compensation plan taxable under the constructive receipt doctrine?
    a. The contract is funded, and there is no substantial risk of forfeiture.
    b. Same as (a), except the employee must work for three years.
    c. An agreement to defer payment is entered into after compensation is earned.
    d. An agreement to defer payment is entered into before compensation is earned.
    e. In (a), the contract is not funded.

24. During his senior year in college, Mark is drafted by the Los Angeles Dodgers. When he graduates, he expects to sign a five-year contract in the range of $1.8 million per year. Mark plans to marry his girlfriend before he reports to the Dodger farm team in California. Identify the relevant tax issues facing this left-handed pitcher.

25. What is a "substantial risk of forfeiture"? Why is it necessary to impose this restriction on the transfer of restricted property?

26. Determine which of the following conditions would cause options to fall *outside* the qualification requirements for incentive stock options:
    a. The employee disposes of his stock within 15 months from the date of the granting of the options.
    b. The employee is allowed to exercise the options up to 12 years from the date the options are granted.
    c. The employee is transferred to the parent of the corporation six months before he exercises the options.
    d. The option price is 112% of the fair market value of the stock on the grant date, and the shareholder owns 15% of the stock.
    e. The option may be exercised by the employee's spouse in the event of the employee's death.

27. Would a 30-year-old corporate executive in the 39.6% tax bracket prefer an extra $20,000 bonus or the option to purchase $20,000 worth of securities for $8,000 from the employer under a nonqualified stock option plan in the current year?

28. Compare and contrast a deductible IRA and a § 401(k) plan. Do not include SIMPLE plans in your analysis.

29. Amanda is the major owner and employee of a closely held corporation. She is in the 39.6% tax bracket, living in a state with a 6% income tax rate, and has a 7.65% FICA tax rate. She needs to determine how to receive compensation from her corporation. Identify relevant tax issues facing Amanda.

30. Indicate whether each of the following items is considered a nonqualified compensation plan (N), a qualified compensation plan (Q), or both (B):
    a. Individual Retirement Account.
    b. Incentive stock option.
    c. Group term life insurance.
    d. Cafeteria plan.
    e. Pension plan.
    f. Employee stock ownership plan.
    g. Nonqualified stock option.
    h. Keogh plan.
    i. Simplified employee pension plan.

PROBLEMS

31. Red Corporation has a total of 1,000 employees, of whom 700 are non-highly compensated. The retirement plan covers 300 non-highly compensated employees and 200 highly compensated employees. Does this plan satisfy the minimum coverage test?

32. Cardinal Corporation's pension plan benefits 620 of its 1,000 highly compensated employees. How many of its 620 non-highly compensated employees must benefit to meet the ratio test for the minimum coverage requirement?

33. A retirement plan covers 72% of the non-highly compensated individuals. The plan benefits 48 of the 131 employees. Determine if the participation requirement is met.

34. Robin, Inc., uses the three-to-seven-year graded vesting approach in its retirement plan. Calculate the nonforfeitable percentage for each of the following employees based on the years of service completed:

Participant	Years of Service
Sandy	3
Rod	4
Tony	5
Heather	8

35. Tyronne, age 46, is the sole remaining participant of a money purchase pension plan. The plan is terminated, and a $200,000 taxable distribution is made to Tyronne. Calculate the amount of any early distribution penalty tax for 1998.

36. George received a distribution from a qualified plan that was entitled to capital gain treatment under § 402(a)(2). The 100 shares of the employer company stock received have a tax basis of $20 per share and a fair market value of $85 per share. George sold this stock five months after the distribution for $120 per share. Calculate the amount and character of any gain to George.

37. When Leif retires in 1998, he receives a lump-sum distribution of $50,000 from a noncontributory qualified pension plan. His active period of participation was from January 1, 1971, through December 31, 1978. Assume that Leif attained age 50 before January 1, 1986. If Leif files a joint return with his wife in 1998 and elects to use the 10-year forward averaging provision, calculate (a) his separate tax on this distribution and (b) the capital gain portion.

38. Yvonne Blair receives a $165,000 lump-sum distribution from a contributory pension plan in 1998; the distribution includes employer common stock with net unrealized appreciation of $30,000. Yvonne contributed $25,000 to the qualified plan while she was an active participant from February 10, 1973, to February 10, 1978. Yvonne attained age 50 before January 1, 1986. Yvonne wishes to know her tax consequences with respect to the lump-sum distribution. Write a letter to Yvonne that includes your calculations. Her address is 209 Barrett Street, Laramie, WY 82071.

39. Wade has been an active participant in a defined benefit plan for 21 years. During his last 5 years of employment, Wade earned $20,000, $32,000, $45,000, $50,000, and $70,000, respectively (representing his highest income years).
   a. Calculate Wade's maximum allowable benefits from this qualified plan (assume there are fewer than 100 participants).
   b. Assume that Wade's average compensation for his three high years is $140,000. Calculate Wade's maximum allowable benefits.

40. Determine the maximum annual benefits payable to an employee from a defined benefit plan in the following independent situations:
   a. Quincy, age 66, has been a participant for 13 years, and his highest average compensation for 3 years is $90,000.
   b. Wendy, age 67, has been a participant for 9 years (11 years of service), and her highest average compensation for 3 years is $90,000.
   c. Paul, age 68, has been a participant for 11 years in a collectively bargained plan with 238 participants. His highest average compensation for 3 years is $70,300.

41. The compensation paid by Orange Corporation to the plan participants of a profit sharing plan in 1998 was $33,300. During 1998, Orange Corporation contributed $10,000 to the plan.
   a. Calculate Orange Corporation's deductible amount for 1998.
   b. Calculate the amount of the contribution carryover from 1998.

42. A money purchase plan covers three employees: Samuel (annual compensation of $310,000), Mary (annual compensation of $140,000), and Larry (annual compensation of $50,000). If the contribution rate is 15%, what amount can be contributed to these employees' accounts?

43. During 1998, Keith is a key employee of a top-heavy pension plan. His salary is $290,000. Calculate Keith's maximum contribution to such a defined benefit plan.

44. In Autumn Company's defined benefit plan, $300,000 of the $410,000 of cumulative benefits are allocated to key employees. The company has contacted you asking if the plan is in danger of being labeled a top-heavy plan. Prepare a memo for the tax files that includes your analysis and conclusions.

45. Blue, Inc., uses the six-year graded vesting schedule for its top-heavy retirement plan. Calculate the nonforfeitable percentage for each of the following non-key employees based on the years of service completed:

Participant	Years of Service
Dana	2
Sally	3
Samuel	5
Janet	6

46. Miguel, a single individual, participates in a SIMPLE § 401(k) plan of his employer. The plan permits participants to contribute a percentage of their salary. Miguel elects to contribute 6% of his annual compensation of $90,000 to the plan. On what amount of his salary does Miguel pay income taxes in 1998?

47. In 1998, Susan's sole proprietorship earns $220,000 of self-employment net income (after the deduction for one-half of self-employment tax).
    a. Calculate the maximum amount that Susan can deduct for contributions to a defined contribution Keogh plan.
    b. Suppose Susan contributes more than the allowable amount to the Keogh plan. What are the consequences to her?
    c. Can Susan retire and begin receiving Keogh payments at age 55?

48. Molly is unmarried and is an active participant in a qualified deductible IRA plan. Her modified AGI is $34,000.
    a. Calculate the amount that Molly can contribute to the IRA and the amount she can deduct.
    b. Assume instead that Molly is a participant in a SIMPLE IRA and that she elects to contribute 4% of her compensation to the account, while her employer contributes 3%. What amount will be contributed for 1998? What amount will be vested?

49. Answer the following independent questions with respect to a deductible IRA and § 401(k) contributions:
    a. Govind earns a salary of $24,000 and is not an active participant in any other qualified plan. His wife has $600 of compensation income. What is the maximum total deductible contribution to their IRAs?
    b. Danos is a participant in a SIMPLE § 401(k) plan. He contributes 6% of his salary of $31,000, and his employer contributes 4%. What amount will be contributed for the year? What amount will be vested?

50. Answer the following independent questions with respect to traditional IRA contributions:
    a. Juan earns a salary of $25,000 and is not an active participant in any other qualified plan. His wife, Agnes, has no earned income. What is the maximum total deductible contribution to their IRAs? Juan wishes to contribute as much as possible to his own IRA.
    b. Abby has earned income of $23,000, and her husband has earned income of $1,900. They are not active participants in any other qualified plan. What is the maximum contribution to their IRAs?
    c. Leo's employer makes a contribution of $3,500 to Leo's simplified employee pension plan. If Leo is single, has earned income of $32,000, and has AGI of $29,000, what amount, if any, can he contribute to an IRA?

51. Kay establishes a Roth IRA at age 43 and contributes $2,000 per year to the Roth IRA account for 22 years. The account is now worth $97,000, consisting of $44,000 in contributions plus $53,000 in accumulated earnings. How much of these funds may Kay withdraw tax-free?

52. Spring, Inc., pays bonuses to its key employees each year. The specific employees to receive bonuses and the amount of bonus for each recipient are determined on

December 1 of each year. An employee eligible for a bonus may decide on or before November 15 of each year to postpone the receipt of the bonus until retirement or death. An employee electing to postpone receipt of a bonus is allowed to designate, at any time before retirement, the time and manner of the postretirement payments and to designate the persons to receive any amount payable after death. Separate accounts are not maintained for each employee. Under this compensation plan, Heather may elect to receive her $110,000 bonus in cash, or she may elect to defer the receipt of the bonus until 2002. Recommend to Heather which alternative to accept.

53. Nancy is an officer of a local bank that merges with another national bank, resulting in a change of ownership. She loses her job as a result of the merger, but she receives a cash settlement of $590,000 from her employer. Her average annual compensation for the past five tax years is $200,000.
    a. What are the tax consequences to Nancy of the $590,000 payment?
    b. Assume instead that Nancy's five-year average annual compensation was $110,000, and she receives $390,000 in the settlement. What are the tax consequences to Nancy?

54. James, an executive, receives a $600,000 payment under a golden parachute agreement. James's base amount from Silver Corporation is $140,000.
    a. What amount is not deductible to Silver Corporation under § 280G?
    b. What total tax must James pay, assuming a 39.6% tax rate?
    c. Answer (a) and (b) assuming the payment is $400,000.

55. On February 20, 1998, Tim (an executive of Hawk Corporation) purchased 100 shares of Hawk stock (selling at $20 a share) for $10. A condition of the transaction was that Tim must resell the stock to Hawk at cost if he voluntarily leaves the company within five years of receiving the stock (assume this represents a substantial risk of forfeiture).
    a. Assuming that no special election is made under § 83(b), what amount, if any, is taxable to Tim in 1998?
    b. Five years later when the stock is selling for $40 a share, Tim is still employed by Hawk. What amount of ordinary income, if any, is taxable to Tim?
    c. What amount, if any, is deductible by Hawk as compensation expense five years later?
    d. Should Tim make the § 83(b) special election in 1998? What amount would be taxable in 1998 if he makes the special election?
    e. In (d), what amount would be deductible by Hawk five years later?
    f. Under (d), assume Tim sold all the stock six years later for $65 per share. How much capital gain is included in his gross income?
    g. In (d), what loss is available to Tim if he voluntarily resigns in 2001 before the five-year period and does not sell the stock back to the corporation?
    h. In (g), in the year Tim resigns, what amount, if any, would be taxable to Hawk Corporation?

56. On July 2, 1994, Black Corporation sold 1,000 of its common shares (worth $14 per share) to Earl, an employee, for $5 per share. The sale was subject to Earl's agreement to resell the shares to the corporation for $5 per share if his employment is terminated within the following four years. The shares had a value of $24 per share on July 2, 1998. Earl sells the shares for $31 per share on September 16, 1998. No special election under § 83(b) is made.
    a. What amount, if any, will be taxed to Earl on July 2, 1994?
    b. On July 2, 1998?
    c. On September 16, 1998?
    d. What deduction, if any, will Black Corporation obtain?
    e. Assume the same facts but that Earl makes the election under § 83(b). What amount, if any, will be taxed to Earl on July 2, 1994?
    f. Will the assumption made in (e) have any effect on any deduction Black Corporation will receive? Explain.

57. Rosa exercises incentive stock options for 100 shares of Copper Corporation stock at the option price of $100 per share on May 21, 1998, when the fair market value

is $120 per share. She sells the 100 shares of common stock three and one-half years later for $140.

  a. Calculate the total long-term capital gain on this sale.

  b. Assume Rosa holds the stock seven months and sells the shares for $140 per share. Calculate any ordinary income on the sale.

  c. In (b), what amount can Copper Corporation deduct?

  d. Suppose Rosa holds the stock for two years and sells the shares for $115 per share. Calculate any capital gain on this transaction.

  e. In (a), assume the options are nonqualified options with a nonascertainable fair market value on the date of the grant. Calculate total long-term capital gain, if any, in the year of sale.

  f. In (e), assume that each option has an ascertainable fair market value of $10 on the date of the grant and no substantial risk of forfeiture exists. Calculate total long-term capital gain, if any, on the date of the sale.

58. On November 19, 1996, Rex is granted a nonqualified stock option to purchase 100 shares of Tan Company. On that date, the stock is selling for $8 per share, and the option price is $9 per share. Rex exercises the option on August 21, 1997, when the stock is selling for $10 per share. Five months later, Rex sells the shares for $11.50 per share.

  a. What amount is taxable to Rex in 1996?

  b. What amount is taxable to Rex in 1997?

  c. What amount and type of gain are taxable to Rex in 1998?

  d. What amount, if any, is deductible by Tan Company in 1997?

  e. What amount, if any, is recognized in 1998 if the stock is sold for $9.50 per share?

59. Sara Reid, the owner of a small business, is trying to decide whether to have a § 401(k) plan or a simplified employee pension plan. She is not interested in a SIMPLE § 401(k) plan. Her salary will be approximately $45,000, and she will have no employees. She asks you to provide her with information on the advantages and disadvantages of both types of plans and your recommendation. Draft a letter to Sara that contains your response. Her address is 1000 Canal Avenue, New Orleans, LA 70148.

60. Lou's employer provides a qualified cafeteria plan under which he can choose cash of $7,000 or health and accident insurance premiums worth approximately $6,000. If Lou is in the 39.6% tax bracket, advise him of his tax alternatives.

RESEARCH PROBLEMS

*Note: Use the **RIA OnPoint System 4 Student Version CD-ROM**, which is available to accompany this text, in preparing solutions to the Research Problems. Alternatively, tax research materials found in a standard tax library can be used.*

Research Problem 1. Mr. Sanjay Baker and his sister owned and operated a mail-order business in corporate form. The corporation used the homes of Mr. Baker and his sister for corporate mail-order activities (assembling, storing inventory, etc.). The corporation paid Mr. Baker and the sister rent for the use of the homes. The payments were deducted as rent and reported by the two parties on their tax returns. The IRS disallowed most of the deduction, contending that the rent was excessive. Is the excessive rent deductible as compensation? Write a letter to Mr. Baker that contains your advice and prepare a memo for the tax files. His address is 63 Rose Avenue, San Francisco, CA 94117.

Partial list of research aids:
Multnomah Operating Co., 57–2 USTC ¶9979, 52 AFTR 672, 248 F.2d 661 (CA–9, 1957).

Research Problem 2. Frank and Polly were married, but Frank died on February 25, 1998. During 1998, Frank earned $5,226 in wages, but Polly had no earned income. Neither had contributed any money to an IRA during 1998. What amount, if any, can be contributed to Frank's IRA and/or Polly's spousal IRA?

Research Problem 3. Six executives entered into elective deferred compensation agreements whereby, after rendering the necessary services, they are entitled to be paid deferred compensation plus incremental amounts designated as "interest." This "interest" is calculated by reference to a predetermined formula. On their retirement, the executives are entitled to receive the deferred compensation plus the incremental "interest" amounts. During 1998, the accrual method employer put $929,000 of deferred compensation into the deferred compensation accounts (DCAs) along with $177,500 of "interest." The DCAs were unfunded and unsecured. The employer intends to deduct the $177,500 as interest within the meaning of § 163. Is this the appropriate tax treatment?

Research Problem 4.   What is the definition of "deferred compensation"? Are stock options and stock appreciation rights classified as deferred compensation? When is nonqualified deferred compensation taken into account as wages for FICA purposes?

Research Problem 5.   What are stock appreciation rights? Outline the tax treatment.

Use the tax resources of the Internet to address the following questions. Do not restrict your search to the World Wide Web, but include a review of newsgroups and general reference materials, practitioner sites and resources, primary sources of the tax law, chat rooms and discussion groups, and other opportunities.

Research Problem 6.   Locate and download an Internet retirement calculator. Use this program to help you answer the questions in Problems 48 and 49.

Research Problem 7.   Compare and contrast several advertisements offered by brokerage firms and other financial institutions promoting the SIMPLE retirement program. Do these solicitations correctly convey the details of the tax law?

Research Problem 8.   Using newspaper and magazine articles, summarize the latest trends in the use of nonqualified deferred compensation and incentive stock options. Include in your analysis a key executive from at least one publicly traded corporation.

TEAM PROJECT: ARTHUR ANDERSEN TAX CHALLENGE CASES

For more information on the Arthur Andersen Tax Challenge Cases, refer to Chapter 1, page 1–37.

Information related to tax issues and problems that are discussed in this chapter may be found in the

Day and Ball case on pages 2, 3, 4, 5, and 30
Fence case on pages 39, 42, 48, and 56

Read and analyze the case you have been assigned and *identify* any issues and problems that are related to material covered in this chapter. If the information provided in the case is complete, prepare answers for this part of the case at this time. If you need information that is contained in the later parts of the case, write a memo summarizing the questions or problems so you can prepare a complete answer at a later date.

P · A · R · T

VII

CORPORATIONS AND PARTNERSHIPS

The primary orientation of this text is toward basic tax concepts and the individual taxpayer. Although many of these tax concepts also apply to corporations and partnerships, numerous tax concepts apply specifically to corporations or partnerships. An overview of these provisions is presented in Part VII. Comprehensive coverage of these topics appears in *West's Federal Taxation: Corporations, Partnerships, Estates, and Trusts*.

Chapter 20

Corporations and Partnerships

20

CORPORATIONS AND PARTNERSHIPS

LEARNING OBJECTIVES

After completing Chapter 20, you should be able to:

1. Identify those entities that are treated as corporations for Federal income tax purposes.

2. Contrast the income tax treatment of individuals with that applicable to corporations.

3. Recognize and calculate the tax deductions available only to corporations.

4. Determine the corporate tax liability and comply with various procedural and reporting requirements.

5. Understand the tax rules governing the formation of corporations.

6. Work with the tax rules governing the operation of corporations.

7. Recognize the tax rules governing the liquidation of corporations.

8. Appreciate the utility and effect of the Subchapter S election.

9. Understand the tax consequences of forming and operating a partnership.

10. Evaluate the advantages and disadvantages of the various forms for conducting a business.

OUTLINE

Until now this text has concentrated on the Federal income taxation of individual taxpayers. However, even the most basic business decisions require some awareness of the tax implications of other business forms.

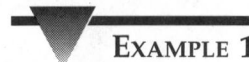

EXAMPLE 1

Gina and Tom are contemplating entering into a new business venture that will require additional capital investment by other parties. As the venture will involve financial risk, both Gina and Tom are concerned about personal liability. Further, they would prefer to avoid any income taxes at the entity level. Both Gina and Tom would like to take advantage of any losses the venture may generate during its formative period. ▼

In choosing the form for the venture, Gina and Tom will have to consider using a corporation. The corporate form limits a shareholder's liability to the amount invested in the stock. Regular corporations, however, are subject to the corporate income tax. Furthermore, losses incurred by corporations do not pass through to the shareholders. Perhaps the ideal solution would be to use the corporate form and elect to be taxed as an S corporation. The election would avoid the corporate income tax and permit the pass-through of losses while providing limited liability for the shareholders.

Although the resolution of the problem posed by Example 1 seems simple enough, it did not consider the possible use of a partnership or limited liability company. More important, the decision required *some* knowledge of corporations and the S corporation election. This chapter is intended to provide such knowledge by briefly reviewing the tax consequences of the various forms of business organization.

WHAT IS A CORPORATION?

COMPLIANCE WITH STATE LAW

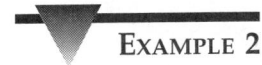

LEARNING OBJECTIVE
Identify those entities that are treated as corporations for Federal income tax purposes.

A company must comply with the specific requirements for corporate status under state law. For example, it is necessary to draft articles of incorporation and file them with the state regulatory agency, be granted a charter, and issue stock to shareholders.

Compliance with state law, although important, is not the only requirement that must be met to qualify for corporate *tax* status. For example, a corporation qualifying under state law may be disregarded as a taxable entity if it is a mere sham lacking in economic substance. The key consideration is the degree of business activity conducted at the corporate level.

EXAMPLE 2

Gene and Mike are joint owners of a tract of unimproved real estate that they wish to protect from future creditors. Gene and Mike form Falcon Corporation and transfer the land to it in return for all of the corporation's stock. The corporation merely holds title to the land and conducts no other activities. In all respects, Falcon Corporation meets the legal requirements of a corporation under applicable state law. Nevertheless, Falcon might not be recognized as a separate entity for corporate tax purposes under these facts.[1] ▼

EXAMPLE 3

Assume the same facts as in Example 2. In addition to holding title to the land, Falcon Corporation leases the property, collects rents, and pays the property taxes. Falcon probably would be treated as a corporation for Federal income tax purposes because of the scope of its activities. ▼

In some instances, the IRS has attempted to disregard (or collapse) a corporation in order to make the income taxable directly to the shareholders.[2] In other cases, the IRS has asserted that the corporation is a separate taxable entity so as to assess tax at the corporate level and to tax corporate distributions to shareholders as dividend income (double taxation).[3]

ENTITY CLASSIFICATION PRIOR TO 1997

Can an organization not qualifying as a corporation under state law still be treated as such for Federal income tax purposes? Unfortunately, the tax law defines a corporation as including "...associations, joint stock companies, and insurance companies."[4] As the Code contains no definition of an "association," the issue became the subject of frequent litigation.[5]

It was finally determined that an entity would be treated as a corporation if it had a majority of the characteristics common to corporations.[6] For this purpose, the relevant characteristics are:

- Continuity of life.
- Centralized management.
- Limited liability.
- Free transferability of interests.

---

[1]See *Paymer v. Comm.*, 45–2 USTC ¶9353, 33 AFTR 1536, 150 F.2d 334 (CA–2, 1945).

[2]*Floyd Patterson*, 25 TCM 1230, T.C.Memo. 1966–239, *aff'd.* in 68–2 USTC ¶9471, 22 AFTR2d 5810 (CA–2, 1968).

[3]*Raffety Farms Inc. v. U.S.*, 75–1 USTC ¶9271, 35 AFTR2d 75–811, 511 F.2d 1234 (CA–8, 1975).

[4]§ 7701(a)(3).

[5]See for example, *U.S. v. Kintner*, 54–2 USTC ¶9626, 46 AFTR 995, 216 F.2d 418 (CA–5, 1954).

[6]See Reg. § 301.7701–2(a) prior to repeal.

WHO IS TAXED ON A BASKETBALL STAR'S SALARY?

When he signed with the Houston Rockets, Allen Leavell agreed to be under their direction and control in carrying out all athletic activities required of him. Immediately after signing and upon the advice of his tax adviser, Allen formed the Leavell Corporation. Allen and Leavell Corporation contracted for the exclusive right to his services. Under the arrangement, all income Allen earned would belong to the corporation, and he would receive an annual salary. The amount of the salary was far less than the Rockets were paying Allen for playing point guard on the team.

During the years Allen played for the Rockets, his paychecks were turned over to the corporation, which reported those amounts on the Forms 1120 it filed. Upon audit by the IRS, Allen's pay from the Rockets was deemed taxed to him and not to Leavell Corporation.

In *Allen Leavell* [104 T.C. 140 (1995)], the Tax Court sided with the IRS. Income is taxed to whoever earns it. In this case, Allen (and not the corporation) earned the amounts paid by the Rockets. The Rockets were paying for services performed by Allen and not by his corporation.

These criteria did not resolve all of the problems that continued to arise over corporate classification. When a new type of business entity, the **limited liability company,** was developed, the IRS was deluged with inquiries about its tax status. As the limited liability company became increasingly popular with professional groups, all states enacted statutes allowing some form of this entity. The statutes invariably permitted the corporate characteristic of limited liability and, often, that of centralized management. Because continuity of life and free transferability of interests are absent, it was hoped that the entity would be classified as a partnership. This treatment would avoid the double taxation result inherent in the corporate form.

ENTITY CLASSIFICATION AFTER 1996

In late 1996, the IRS issued its so-called **check-the-box Regulations.**[7] Effective beginning in 1997, these Regulations enable taxpayers to classify a business entity for tax purposes without regard to its corporate (or noncorporate) characteristics. These new rules should simplify tax administration considerably and eliminate the type of litigation that arose with regard to association (corporation) status.

Under the new rules, entities with more than one owner can elect to be classified as either a partnership or a corporation. An entity with only one owner can elect to be classified as a corporation or a sole proprietorship. In the event of default (no election is made), entities with multiple owners will be classified as partnerships and single-person businesses as sole proprietorships.

The election is not available to entities that are actually incorporated under state law or to entities that are required to be corporations under Federal law (e.g., certain publicly traded partnerships). For purposes of these prohibitions, limited liability companies are treated as not being incorporated under state law. Consequently, they can elect either corporation or partnership status.

[7]Reg. §§ 301.7701–1 through –4, and –7.

Eligible entities make the election as to tax status by filing Form 8832 (Entity Classification Election).[8] New elections are permitted, but only after a 60-month waiting period.

Income Tax Considerations

GENERAL TAX CONSEQUENCES OF DIFFERENT FORMS OF BUSINESS ENTITIES

2 Learning Objective
Contrast the income tax treatment of individuals with that applicable to corporations.

A business operation may be conducted as a sole proprietorship, as a partnership, or in corporate form.

- Sole proprietorships are not separate taxable entities. The owner of the business reports all business transactions on his or her individual income tax return.
- Partnerships are not subject to the income tax. Under the *conduit* concept, the various tax attributes of the partnership's operations flow through to the individual partners to be reported on their personal income tax returns.
- The regular corporate form of doing business carries with it the imposition of the corporate income tax. The corporation is recognized as a separate taxpaying entity. Income is taxed to the corporation as earned and taxed again to the shareholders as dividends when distributed.
- A regular corporation may elect to be taxed as an S corporation. This special treatment is similar (although not identical) to the partnership rules. Income tax is generally avoided at the corporate level, and shareholders are taxed currently on the taxable income of the S corporation.

INDIVIDUALS AND CORPORATIONS COMPARED—AN OVERVIEW

Similarities between Corporate and Individual Tax Rules.   The gross income of a corporation is determined in much the same manner as for individuals. Both individuals and corporations are entitled to exclusions from gross income, such as interest on municipal bonds. Gains and losses from property transactions are also treated similarly. For example, whether a gain or loss is capital or ordinary depends on the nature and use of the asset rather than the type of taxpayer. Upon the sale or other taxable disposition of depreciable personalty, the recapture rules of § 1245 make no distinction between corporate and noncorporate taxpayers. In the case of the recapture of depreciation on real property (§ 1250), however, corporate taxpayers experience more severe tax consequences. As illustrated later, corporations must recognize as additional ordinary income 20 percent of the excess of the amount that would be recaptured under § 1245 over the amount recaptured under § 1250.

The business deductions of corporations parallel those available to individuals. Corporate deductions are allowed for all ordinary and necessary expenses paid or incurred in carrying on a trade or business. Corporations may also deduct interest, certain taxes, losses, bad debts, depreciation, cost recovery, charitable contributions subject to corporate limitation rules, net operating losses, research and experimental expenditures, and other less common deductions.

---

[8]Reg. § 301.7701–3(c).

Many of the tax credits available to individuals, such as the foreign tax credit, can be claimed by corporations. Not available to corporations are certain credits that are personal in nature. Examples of credits not available to corporations include the credit for child and dependent care expenses, the credit for the elderly or disabled, and the earned income credit.

Corporations usually have the same choices of accounting periods as do individuals. Like an individual, a corporation may choose a calendar year or a fiscal year for reporting purposes. Corporations do enjoy greater flexibility in the election of a tax year. For example, corporations usually can have different tax years from those of their shareholders. Also, a newly formed corporation generally has a free choice of any approved accounting period without having to obtain the consent of the IRS. As noted in Chapter 18, however, personal service corporations are subject to severe restrictions on the use of a fiscal year.

The use of the cash method of accounting is denied to large corporations (those with average annual gross receipts in excess of $5 million). Smaller corporations as well as qualified personal service corporations and other corporations engaged in the trade or business of farming have a choice between the cash or accrual method of accounting for tax purposes. Both individuals and corporations that maintain inventory for sale to customers are required to use the accrual method of accounting for determining sales and cost of goods sold.

Dissimilarities. Both noncorporate and corporate taxpayers are subject to progressive income tax rates. For individuals, the rates are 15, 28, 31, 36, and 39.6 percent. For corporations, the rates are 15, 25, 34, and 35 percent. Corporate taxpayers lose the benefits of the lower brackets (using a phase-out approach) once taxable income reaches a certain level. Noncorporate taxpayers, however, continue to enjoy the benefits of the lower brackets even though they have reached the higher taxable income levels.

Most corporate and all noncorporate taxpayers are subject to the alternative minimum tax (AMT). For AMT purposes, many adjustments and tax preference items are the same for both, but other adjustments and tax preferences apply only to corporations or only to individuals. For tax years beginning in 1998, certain small business corporations are effectively exempt from the corporate AMT. Corporate tax rates are discussed later in the chapter. The AMT is discussed at length in Chapter 12. See also the coverage in *West's Federal Taxation: Corporations, Partnerships, Estates, and Trusts.*

All allowable corporate deductions are treated as business expenses. The determination of adjusted gross income, so essential for individuals, has no relevance to corporations. Corporations need not be concerned with classifying deductions into *deduction for* and *deduction from* categories.

SPECIFIC PROVISIONS COMPARED

Corporate and individual tax rules also differ in the following areas:

- Capital gains and losses.
- Recapture of depreciation.
- Charitable contributions.
- Net operating losses.
- Special deductions for corporations.

Capital Gains and Losses. Both corporate and noncorporate taxpayers are required to aggregate gains and losses from the taxable sale or exchange of capital assets. (Refer to Chapter 16 for a description of the netting process that takes place after the aggregation has been completed.) For net mid-term and net long-term capital gains, individual taxpayers enjoy an advantage (the alternative tax). In no event will net mid-term capital gains be taxed at a rate in excess of 28 percent. In the case of net long-term capital gains, the top rate is 20 percent or, sometimes, 10 percent. In the case of corporations, all capital gains are taxed using the rates for ordinary income. Therefore, the net long-term capital gains of a corporation could be taxed at a rate of 35 percent (the highest rate applicable to corporations).

Significant differences exist in the treatment of capital losses for income tax purposes. Individuals, for example, can annually deduct up to $3,000 of net capital losses against ordinary income. Corporations are not permitted to use net capital losses to offset ordinary income. Net capital losses can be used only to offset past or future capital gains.[9] Unlike individuals, corporations are not allowed an unlimited carryover period for capital losses. Instead, they may carry back excess capital losses to the three preceding years, applying the losses initially to the earliest year. If not exhausted by the carryback, remaining unused capital losses may be carried forward for a period of five years from the year of the loss.[10]

When carried back or forward, *both* short-term capital losses and long-term capital losses are treated as short-term capital losses by corporate taxpayers. For noncorporate taxpayers, carryovers of short-term capital losses retain their identity. However, long-term and mid-term capital losses are carried over as mid-term capital losses.

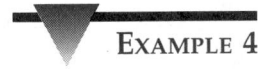

EXAMPLE 4

Hawk Corporation, a calendar year taxpayer, incurs a long-term net capital loss of $5,000 for 1998. None of the capital loss may be deducted in 1998. Hawk may, however, carry the loss back to years 1995, 1996, and 1997 (in this order) and offset any capital gains recognized in these years. If the carryback does not exhaust the loss, the loss may be carried forward to 1999, 2000, 2001, 2002, and 2003 (in this order). Such capital loss carrybacks or carryovers are treated as short-term capital losses. ▼

Recapture of Depreciation. Corporations selling depreciable real estate may have ordinary income in addition to that required by § 1250. Under § 291, the additional ordinary income element is 20 percent of the excess of the § 1245 recapture potential over the § 1250 recapture. As a result, the § 1231 gain is correspondingly decreased by the additional recapture.

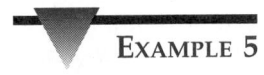

EXAMPLE 5

Condor Corporation purchases residential real property on January 3, 1984, for $300,000. Accelerated cost recovery is taken in the amount of $285,000 before the property is sold on January 5, 1998, for $350,000. Straight-line cost recovery would have been $280,000 (using a 15-year recovery period under ACRS).

First, determine the realized gain:

Sales price		$ 350,000
Less adjusted basis:		
Cost of property	$ 300,000	
Less cost recovery	(285,000)	(15,000)
Realized gain		$ 335,000

Second, determine the § 1245 recapture potential. This is the lesser of $335,000 (realized gain) or $285,000 (cost recovery claimed). Third, determine the § 1250 recapture amount:

---

[9] §§ 1211(a) and (b).   [10] § 1212(a).

Cost recovery taken	$ 285,000
Less straight-line cost recovery	(280,000)
§ 1250 ordinary income	$ 5,000

Fourth, because the taxpayer is a corporation, determine the additional § 291 amount:

§ 1245 recapture potential	$ 285,000
Less § 1250 recapture amount	(5,000)
Excess § 1245 recapture potential	$ 280,000
Apply § 291 percentage	× 20%
Additional ordinary income under § 291	$ 56,000

Condor Corporation's realized and recognized gain of $335,000 is accounted for as follows:

Ordinary income under § 1250	$ 5,000
Ordinary income under § 291	56,000
§ 1231 gain	274,000
Total recognized gain	$ 335,000

▼

Charitable Contributions.   Generally, a charitable contribution deduction is allowed only for the tax year in which the payment is made. However, an important exception is made for accrual basis corporations. The deduction may be claimed in the tax year *preceding* payment if the following conditions are satisfied:

- The contribution is authorized by the board of directors by the end of that tax year *and*
- The contribution is paid on or before the fifteenth day of the third month of the next tax year.[11]

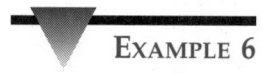
EXAMPLE 6

On December 28, 1998, the board of directors of Dove Corporation, a calendar year, accrual basis taxpayer, authorizes a $5,000 donation to a qualified charity. The donation is paid on March 14, 1999. Dove Corporation may claim the $5,000 donation as a deduction for 1998. As an alternative, Dove may claim the deduction in 1999 (the year of payment). ▼

Like individuals, corporations are not permitted an unlimited charitable contribution deduction. In any one year, a corporate taxpayer is limited to 10 percent of taxable income. For this purpose, taxable income is computed without regard to the charitable contribution deduction, any net operating loss carryback or capital loss carryback, or the dividends received deduction.[12] Any contributions in excess of the 10 percent limitation are carried forward to the five succeeding tax years. Any carryover must be added to subsequent contributions and is subject to the 10 percent limitation. In applying the limitation, the most recent contributions must be deducted first.[13]

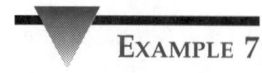
EXAMPLE 7

During 1998, Eagle Corporation (a calendar year taxpayer) had the following income and expenses:

Income from operations	$140,000
Expenses from operations	110,000
Dividends received	10,000
Charitable contributions made in 1998	5,000

---

[11]§ 170(a)(2).

[12]§ 170(b)(2).

[13]§ 170(d)(2).

For purposes of the 10% limitation only, Eagle's taxable income is $40,000 ($140,000 − $110,000 + $10,000). Consequently, the allowable charitable contribution deduction for 1998 is $4,000 (10% × $40,000). The $1,000 unused portion of the contribution is carried forward to 1999, 2000, 2001, 2002, and 2003 (in that order) until exhausted. ▼

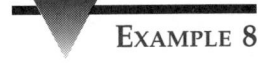

EXAMPLE 8

Assume the same facts as in Example 7. In 1999, Eagle Corporation has taxable income (after adjustments) of $50,000 and makes a charitable contribution of $4,800. The maximum deduction allowed for 1999 is $5,000 (10% × $50,000). The first $4,800 of the allowed deduction must be allocated to the 1999 contributions, and the $200 excess is carried over from 1998. The remaining $800 of the 1998 contribution is carried over to 2000, etc. ▼

As noted in Chapter 10, the deduction for charitable contributions of ordinary income property is limited to the lesser of the fair market value or the adjusted basis of the property. A special rule permits a corporation to contribute inventory (ordinary income property) to certain charitable organizations and receive a deduction equal to the adjusted basis plus one-half of the difference between the fair market value and the adjusted basis of the property.[14] In no event, however, may the deduction exceed twice the adjusted basis of the property. To qualify for this exception, the inventory must be used by the charity in its exempt purpose for the care of *children*, the *ill*, or the *needy*.

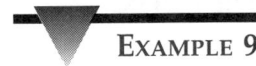

EXAMPLE 9

In the current year, Robin Company (a retail clothier) donates sweaters and overcoats to Sheltering Arms (a qualified charity caring for the homeless). The clothing is inventory and has a basis of $10,000 and a fair market value of $14,000. If Robin is a corporation, the charitable contribution that results is $12,000 [$10,000 (basis) + $2,000 (50% of the appreciation of $4,000)]. In contrast, if Robin is not a corporation, the charitable contribution is limited to $10,000 (basis). ▼

Net Operating Losses. The computation of a net operating loss (NOL) for individuals was discussed in Chapter 7. Corporations are not subject to the complex adjustments required for individuals (e.g., a corporation has no adjustments for nonbusiness deductions or capital gains and losses). Corporations are subject to fewer adjustments than individuals are because a corporation's loss more clearly approximates a true economic loss. Artificial deductions (e.g., personal and dependency exemptions) that merely generate paper losses are not permitted for corporations.

In computing the NOL of a corporation, the dividends received deduction (discussed below) can be claimed in determining the amount of the loss.[15] Generally, NOLs generated after 1997 may be carried back 2 years and forward 20 years (or taxpayers may elect to forgo the carryback period) to offset taxable income for those years.

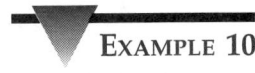

EXAMPLE 10

In 1998, Wren Corporation has gross income of $200,000 and deductions of $300,000, excluding the dividends received deduction. Wren received taxable dividends of $100,000 from Exxon stock. Wren has an NOL of $170,000, computed as follows:

Gross income (including Exxon dividends)		$ 200,000
Less: Business deductions	$300,000	
Dividends received deduction (70% × $100,000)	70,000	(370,000)
Taxable income (loss)		($ 170,000)

▼

---

[14]§ 170(e)(3).   [15]§ 172(d).

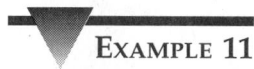

EXAMPLE 11

Assume the same facts as in Example 10 and that Wren Corporation had taxable income of $40,000 in 1996. The NOL of $170,000 is carried back to 1996 (unless Wren elects not to carry back the loss to that year). The carryover to 1997 is $130,000, computed as follows:

Taxable income for 1996	$ 40,000
Less: NOL carryback from 1998	(170,000)
Carryover of unabsorbed 1998 loss	($ 130,000)

In Example 11, the carryback to 1996 might have been ill-advised if Wren Corporation had little, if any, taxable income in 1997 and if it anticipated large amounts of taxable income in the immediate future. In that case, the *election to forgo* the carryback might generate greater tax savings. In this regard, three points should be considered. First, the time value of the tax refund that is lost by not using the carryback procedure must be considered. Second, the election to forgo an NOL carryback is irrevocable. Thus, it cannot be changed later if the future high profits do not materialize. Third, future increases or decreases in corporate income tax rates that can reasonably be anticipated should be considered.

DEDUCTIONS AVAILABLE ONLY TO CORPORATIONS

3 ▼ LEARNING OBJECTIVE
Recognize and calculate the tax deductions available only to corporations.

Dividends Received Deduction.   The purpose of the **dividends received deduction** is to prevent triple taxation. Without the deduction, income paid to a corporation in the form of a dividend would be subject to taxation for a second time (once to the distributing corporation) with no corresponding deduction to the distributing corporation. A third level of tax would be assessed on the shareholders when the recipient corporation distributed the income to its shareholders. Since the dividends received deduction may be less than 100 percent, the law provides only partial relief.

The amount of the dividends received deduction depends upon the percentage of ownership the recipient corporate shareholder holds in the corporation making the dividend distribution.[16] For dividends received or accrued, the *deduction percentage* is summarized as follows:

Percentage of Ownership by Corporate Shareholder	Deduction Percentage
Less than 20%	70%
20% or more (but less than 80%)	80%
80% or more	100%

The dividends received deduction may be limited to a percentage of the taxable income of a corporation computed without regard to the NOL deduction, the dividends received deduction, or any capital loss carryback to the current tax year. The percentage of taxable income limitation corresponds to the deduction percentage. Thus, if a corporate shareholder owns less than 20 percent of the stock in the distributing corporation, the dividends received deduction is limited to 70 percent of taxable income (as previously defined). However, this limitation does not apply if the corporation has an NOL for the current taxable year.[17]

---

[16]§ 243(a).   [17]§ 246(b).

In working with these myriad rules, the following steps need to be taken:

1. Multiply the dividends received by the deduction percentage.
2. Multiply the taxable income (as previously defined) by the deduction percentage.
3. The deduction is limited to the lesser of Step 1 or Step 2, unless subtracting the amount derived from Step 1 from taxable income (as previously defined) generates a negative number. If so, the amount derived in Step 1 should be used.

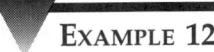

EXAMPLE 12

Crane, Osprey, and Gull Corporations, three unrelated calendar year corporations, have the following transactions for 1998:

	Crane Corporation	Osprey Corporation	Gull Corporation
Gross income from operations	$ 400,000	$ 320,000	$ 260,000
Expenses from operations	(340,000)	(340,000)	(340,000)
Dividends received from domestic corporations (less than 20% ownership)	200,000	200,000	200,000
Taxable income before the dividends received deduction	$ 260,000	$ 180,000	$ 120,000

In determining the dividends received deduction, use the step procedure just described:

	Crane Corporation	Osprey Corporation	Gull Corporation
Step 1: (70% × $200,000)	$ 140,000	$ 140,000	$ 140,000
Step 2:			
70% × $260,000 (taxable income)	$ 182,000		
70% × $180,000 (taxable income)		$ 126,000	
70% × $120,000 (taxable income)			$ 84,000
Step 3:			
Lesser of Step 1 or Step 2	$ 140,000	$ 126,000	
Generates an NOL			$ 140,000

Osprey Corporation is subject to the 70 percent of taxable income limitation. It does not qualify for the loss rule treatment, since subtracting $140,000 (Step 1) from $180,000 does not yield a loss. Gull Corporation qualifies for the loss rule treatment because subtracting $140,000 (Step 1) from $120,000 does yield a loss. In summary, each corporation has the following dividends received deduction for 1998: $140,000 for Crane, $126,000 for Osprey, and $140,000 for Gull. If a corporation already has an NOL before any dividends received deduction is claimed, the full dividends received deduction (as calculated in Step 1) is allowed.

Deduction of Organizational Expenditures.   Under § 248, a corporation may elect to amortize organizational expenses over a period of 60 months or more. If the election is not made on a timely basis, the expenditures cannot be deducted until the corporation ceases to conduct business and liquidates. The election is made in a statement attached to the corporation's return for its first taxable year. The election covers all qualifying expenses *incurred* in the corporation's first year.[18]

Organizational expenditures include the following:

- Legal services incident to organization (e.g., drafting the corporate charter, bylaws, minutes of organizational meetings, terms of original stock certificates).
- Necessary accounting services.
- Expenses of temporary directors and of organizational meetings of directors and shareholders.
- Fees paid to the state of incorporation.

Expenditures connected with issuing or selling shares of stock or other securities (e.g., commissions, professional fees, and printing costs) or with the transfer of assets to a corporation do not qualify. These expenditures are generally added to the capital account and are not subject to amortization.

4 ▼ LEARNING OBJECTIVE
Determine the corporate tax liability and comply with various procedural and reporting requirements.

DETERMINATION OF CORPORATE TAX LIABILITY

Income Tax Rates.   The rate brackets on corporations are as follows:[19]

Taxable Income	Tax Rate
Not over $50,000	15%
Over $50,000 but not over $75,000	25%
Over $75,000 but not over $100,000	34%
Over $100,000 but not over $335,000	39%*
Over $335,000 but not over $10,000,000	34%
Over $10,000,000 but not over $15,000,000	35%
Over $15,000,000 but not over $18,333,333	38%**
Over $18,333,333	35%

*Five percent of this rate represents a phase-out of the benefits of the lower tax rates on the first $75,000 of taxable income.
**Three percent of this rate represents a phase-out of the benefits of the lower tax rate (34% rather than 35%) on the first $10 million of taxable income.

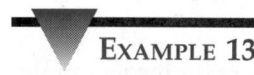

EXAMPLE 13

A calendar year corporation has taxable income of $90,000 for 1998. The income tax liability is $18,850, determined as follows: $7,500 (15% × $50,000) + $6,250 (25% × $25,000) + $5,100 (34% × $15,000). ▼

Qualified personal service corporations are taxed at a flat 35 percent rate on all taxable income. They do not enjoy the tax savings of the lower brackets. For this purpose, a *qualified* **personal service corporation** is one that is substantially employee owned and engages in one of the following activities: health, law, engineering, architecture, accounting, actuarial science, performing arts, or consulting.

Alternative Minimum Tax.   Corporations are subject to an alternative minimum tax (AMT) that is structured in the same manner as that applicable to individuals. The AMT for corporations, as for individuals, defines a more

---

[18]A cash basis taxpayer need not have paid the expenses as long as they were incurred.

[19]§ 11(b).

expansive tax base than for the regular tax. Like individuals, corporations are required to apply a minimum tax rate to the expanded base and pay the difference between the tentative AMT liability and the regular tax. Many of the adjustments and tax preference items necessary to arrive at alternative minimum taxable income (AMTI) are the same for individuals and corporations. Although the objective of the AMT is the same for individuals and for corporations, the rate and exemptions are different. As noted in Chapter 12, certain small business corporations are effectively exempt from the corporate AMT.

CORPORATE FILING REQUIREMENTS

A corporation must file a return whether it has taxable income or not.[20] A corporation that was not in existence throughout an entire annual accounting period is required to file a return for the fraction of the year during which it was in existence. In addition, the corporation must file a return even though it has ceased to do business if it has valuable claims for which it will bring suit. It is relieved of filing returns once it ceases business and dissolves.

The corporate return is filed on Form 1120 unless the corporation is a small corporation entitled to file the shorter Form 1120–A. Among the *several* requirements for filing Form 1120–A are gross receipts (or sales) of less than $500,000 and total assets of less than $500,000. Corporations making the S corporation election (discussed later in the chapter) file on Form 1120S.

The return must be filed on or before the fifteenth day of the third month following the close of the corporation's tax year. Corporations can receive an automatic extension of six months for filing the corporate return by filing Form 7004 by the due date of the return. However, the IRS may terminate an extension by mailing a 10-day notice to the taxpayer corporation.[21]

A corporation must make payments of estimated tax unless its tax liability can reasonably be expected to be less than $500.[22] For 1998, the payments must equal 100 percent of the corporation's final tax. These payments may be made in four installments due on or before the fifteenth day of the fourth, sixth, ninth, and twelfth months of the corporate taxable year. The full amount of the unpaid tax is due on the date of the return. Failure to make the required estimated tax prepayments will result in a nondeductible penalty being imposed on the corporation. The penalty can be avoided, however, if any of various exceptions apply.[23]

[20]§ 6012(a)(2).
[21]§ 6081.

[22]§ 6655(f).
[23]See § 6655 for the penalty involved and the various exceptions.

RECONCILIATION OF CORPORATE TAXABLE INCOME AND ACCOUNTING INCOME

Taxable income and accounting net income are seldom the same amount. For example, a difference may arise if the corporation uses accelerated depreciation for tax purposes and straight-line depreciation for accounting purposes.

Many items of income for accounting purposes, such as proceeds from a life insurance policy on the death of a corporate officer and interest on municipal bonds, may not be includible in calculating taxable income. Some expense items for accounting purposes, such as expenses to produce tax-exempt income, estimated warranty reserves, a net capital loss, and Federal income taxes, are not deductible for tax purposes.

Schedule M–1 on the last page of Form 1120 is used to reconcile accounting net income (net income after Federal income taxes) with taxable income (as computed on the corporate tax return before the deduction for a net operating loss and the dividends received deduction). In the left-hand column of Schedule M–1, net income per books is added to the following: the Federal income tax liability for the year, the excess of capital losses over capital gains (which cannot be deducted in the current year), income for tax purposes that is not income in the current year for accounting purposes, and expenses recorded on the books that are not deductible on the tax return. In the right-hand column, income recorded on the books that is not currently taxable or is tax-exempt and deductions for tax purposes that are not expenses for accounting purposes are totaled and subtracted from the left-hand column total to arrive at taxable income (before the net operating loss or dividends received deductions).

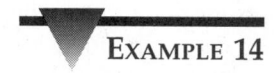

EXAMPLE 14

During 1998, Crow Corporation had the following transactions:

Net income per books (after tax)	$92,400
Taxable income	50,000
Federal income tax liability (15% × $50,000)	7,500
Interest income from tax-exempt bonds	5,000
Interest paid on loan, the proceeds of which were used to purchase the tax-exempt bonds	500
Life insurance proceeds received as a result of the death of a key employee	50,000
Premiums paid on key employee life insurance policy	2,600
Excess of capital losses over capital gains	2,000

For book and tax purposes, Crow determines depreciation under the straight-line method. Crow's Schedule M–1 for the current year follows.

Schedule M-1	Reconciliation of Income (Loss) per Books With Income per Return				
1	Net income (loss) per books	92,400	7	Income recorded on books this year not included on this return (itemize):	
2	Federal income tax	7,500		Tax-exempt interest $ 5,000	
3	Excess of capital losses over capital gains	2,000		Life insurance proceeds on key	
4	Income subject to tax not recorded on books this year (itemize):			employee $50,000	55,000
			8	Deductions on this return not charged against book income this year (itemize):	
5	Expenses recorded on books this year not deducted on this return (itemize):		a	Depreciation . . . . $	
a	Depreciation . . . . $		b	Contributions carryover $	
b	Contributions carryover $				
c	Travel and entertainment $				
	Int. on tax-exempt bonds $500,				
	Prem. on key employee ins. $2,600	3,100	9	Add lines 7 and 8	55,000
6	Add lines 1 through 5	105,000	10	Income (line 28, page 1)—line 6 less line 9	50,000

▼

Schedule M–2 reconciles unappropriated retained earnings at the beginning of the year with unappropriated retained earnings at year-end. Beginning balance plus net income per books, as entered on line 1 of Schedule M–1, less dividend distributions during the year equals ending retained earnings. Other sources of increases or decreases in retained earnings are also listed on Schedule M–2.

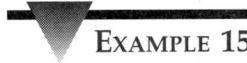

EXAMPLE 15

Assume the same facts as in Example 14. Crow Corporation's beginning balance in unappropriated retained earnings is $125,000, and Crow distributed a cash dividend of $30,000 to its shareholders during the year. Based on these further assumptions, Crow has the following Schedule M–2 for the current year.

Schedule M-2	Analysis of Unappropriated Retained Earnings per Books (Line 25, Schedule L)				
1	Balance at beginning of year	*125,000*	5	Distributions: a Cash	*30,000*
2	Net income (loss) per books	*92,400*		b Stock	
3	Other increases (itemize):			c Property	
			6	Other decreases (itemize):	
			7	Add lines 5 and 6	*30,000*
4	Add lines 1, 2, and 3	*217,400*	8	Balance at end of year (line 4 less line 7)	*187,400*

CONCEPT SUMMARY 20–1

Summary of Income Tax Consequences

	Individuals	Corporations
Computation of gross income	§ 61.	§ 61.
Computation of taxable income	§§ 62, 63(b) through (h).	§ 63(a). Concept of AGI has no relevance.
Deductions	Trade or business (§ 162); nonbusiness (§ 212); some personal and employee expenses (generally deductible as itemized deductions).	Trade or business (§ 162).
Charitable contributions	Limited in any tax year to 50% of AGI; 30% for long-term capital gain property unless election is made to reduce fair market value of gift; 20% for long-term capital gain property contributed to private nonoperating foundations.	Limited in any tax year to 10% of taxable income computed without regard to the charitable contribution deduction, net operating loss or capital loss carryback, and dividends received deduction.
	Time of deduction—year in which payment is made.	Time of deduction—year in which payment is made unless accrual basis taxpayer. Accrual basis corporation may take deduction in year preceding payment if contribution was authorized by board of directors by end of that year and contribution is paid by fifteenth day of third month of following year.

	Individuals	**Corporations**
Casualty losses	$100 floor on nonbusiness casualty and theft losses; nonbusiness casualty and theft losses deductible only to extent losses exceed 10% of AGI.	Deductible in full.
Depreciation recapture for § 1250 property	Recaptured to extent accelerated depreciation exceeds straight-line.	20% of excess of amount that would be recaptured under § 1245 over amount recaptured under § 1250 is additional ordinary income under § 291.
Net operating loss	Adjusted for nonbusiness deductions over nonbusiness income and for personal and dependency exemptions.	Generally no adjustments.
Dividend exclusion or deduction	None.	Generally 70% of dividends received.
Long-term capital gains	Taxed at a rate no higher than 20% (10% if taxpayer is in the 15% tax bracket).	Taxed using regular corporate rates.
Mid-term capital gains	Taxed at a rate no higher than 28%.	Taxed using regular corporate rates.
Capital losses	Only $3,000 of capital loss can offset ordinary income; loss is carried forward indefinitely to offset capital gains or ordinary income up to $3,000; carryovers of short-term losses remain short-term; long-term and mid-term losses carry over as mid-term.	Can offset only capital gains; carried back three years and forward five years; carrybacks and carryovers are treated as short-term losses.
Passive activity losses	Generally deductible only against income from passive activities.	For regular corporations, no limitation on deductibility. Personal service corporations and certain closely held corporations, however, are subject to same limitations as imposed on individuals. A closely held corporation is one where 5 or fewer individuals own more than 50% of the stock either directly or indirectly.
Alternative minimum tax	Applied at a graduated rate schedule of 26% and 28% to AMT base (taxable income as modified by certain adjustments plus preference items minus exemption amount); exemption allowed depending on filing status (e.g., $45,000 for married filing jointly); exemption phase-out begins when AMTI reaches a certain amount (e.g., $150,000 for married filing jointly).	Applied at a 20% rate to AMT base (taxable income as modified by certain adjustments plus preference items minus exemption amount); $40,000 exemption allowed but phase-out begins once AMTI reaches $150,000; adjustments and tax preference items similar to those applicable to individuals but also include 75% of adjusted current earnings (ACE) over AMTI. Certain small business corporations are exempt from the AMT.
Tax rates	Progressive with five rates (15%, 28%, 31%, 36%, and 39.6%).	Progressive with four rates (15%, 25%, 34%, and 35%); lower brackets phased out at higher levels.

FORMING THE CORPORATION

CAPITAL CONTRIBUTIONS

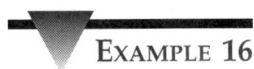

5   **LEARNING OBJECTIVE**
Understand the tax rules governing the formation of corporations.

The receipt of money or property in exchange for capital stock produces neither recognized gain nor loss to the recipient corporation.[24] Gross income of a corporation does not include shareholders' contributions of money or property to the capital of the corporation.[25] Contributions by nonshareholders are also excluded from the gross income of a corporation.[26] The basis of the property (capital transfers by nonshareholders) to the corporation is zero.

EXAMPLE 16

A city donates land worth $200,000 to Cardinal Corporation as an inducement for it to locate in the city. The receipt of the land does not represent gross income. The land's basis to the corporation is zero. ▼

Thin Capitalization.   The advantages of capitalizing a corporation with debt may be substantial. Interest on debt is deductible by the corporation, while dividend payments are not. Further, the shareholders are not taxed on loan repayments unless the payments exceed basis. If a company is capitalized solely with common stock, subsequent repayments of such capital contributions are likely to be treated as dividends to the shareholders.

In certain instances, the IRS will contend that debt is really an equity interest (**thin capitalization**) and will deny the shareholders the tax advantages of debt financing. If the debt instrument has too many features of stock, it may be treated as a form of stock, and principal and interest payments are treated as dividends.[27]

The form of the instrument will not assure debt treatment, but failure to observe certain formalities in creating the debt may lead to an assumption that the purported debt is a form of stock. The debt should be in proper legal form, bear a legitimate rate of interest, have a definite maturity date, and be repaid on a timely basis. Payments should not be contingent upon earnings. Further, the debt should not be subordinated to other liabilities, and proportionate holdings of stock and debt should be avoided or minimized.

TRANSFERS TO CONTROLLED CORPORATIONS

Without special provisions in the Code, a transfer of property to a corporation in exchange for its stock would be a sale or exchange of property and would constitute a taxable transaction to the transferor shareholder. Section 351 provides for the nonrecognition of gain or loss upon such transfers of property if the transferors are in control of the corporation immediately after the transfer. Gain or loss is merely postponed in a manner similar to a like-kind exchange.[28] The following requirements must be met to qualify under § 351:

- The transferors must be in control of the corporation immediately after the exchange. *Control* is defined as ownership of at least 80 percent of the total combined voting power of all classes of stock entitled to vote and at least 80 percent of the total number of shares of all other classes of stock.[29]

---

[24]§ 1032.
[25]§ 118.
[26]*Edwards v. Cuba Railroad Co.*, 1 USTC ¶139, 5 AFTR 5398, 45 S.Ct. 614 (USSC, 1925).

[27]Section 385 lists several factors that might be used to determine whether a debtor-creditor relationship or a shareholder-corporation relationship exists.
[28]Refer to the discussion in Chapter 15.
[29]§ 368(c).

- Realized gain (but not loss) is recognized to the extent that the transferors receive property other than stock. Such nonqualifying property is commonly referred to as *boot*.

If the requirements of § 351 are satisfied and no boot is involved, nonrecognition of gain or loss is *mandatory*.

Basis Considerations and Computation of Gain.   The nonrecognition of gain or loss is accompanied by a carryover of basis. The basis of stock received in a § 351 transfer is determined as follows:

- Start with the adjusted basis of the property transferred by the shareholder.
- Add any gain recognized by the shareholder as a result of the transfer.
- Subtract the fair market value of any boot received by the shareholder from the corporation.[30]

Shareholders who receive noncash boot have a basis in the property equal to the fair market value.

The basis of properties received by the corporation is the basis in the hands of the transferor increased by the amount of any gain recognized to the transferor shareholder.[31]

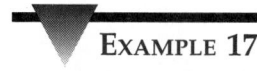

EXAMPLE 17

Ann and Lori form Bluejay Corporation. Ann transfers property with an adjusted basis of $30,000 and a fair market value of $60,000 for 50% of the stock. Lori transfers property with an adjusted basis of $40,000 and a fair market value of $60,000 for the remaining 50% of the stock. The realized gain ($30,000 for Ann and $20,000 for Lori) is not recognized on the transfer because the transfer qualifies under § 351. The basis of the stock to Ann is $30,000, and the basis of the stock to Lori is $40,000. Bluejay Corporation has a basis of $30,000 in the property transferred by Ann and a basis of $40,000 in the property transferred by Lori. ▼

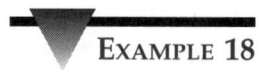

EXAMPLE 18

Mike and John form Condor Corporation with the following investments: Mike transfers property (adjusted basis of $30,000 and fair market value of $70,000), and John transfers cash of $60,000. Each receives 50 shares of the Condor stock, but Mike also receives $10,000 in cash. Assume each share of the Condor stock is worth $1,200. Mike's realized gain is $40,000, determined as follows:

Value of the Condor stock received [50 (shares) × $1,200 (value per share)]	$ 60,000
Cash received	10,000
Amount realized	$ 70,000
Less basis of property transferred	(30,000)
Realized gain	$ 40,000

Mike's recognized gain is $10,000, the lesser of the realized gain ($40,000) or the fair market value of the boot received ($10,000). Mike's basis in the Condor stock is $30,000, computed as follows:

Basis in the property transferred	$ 30,000
Plus recognized gain	10,000
	$ 40,000
Less boot received	(10,000)
Basis to Mike of the Condor stock	$ 30,000

---

[30]§ 358(a).   [31]§ 362(a).

Condor Corporation's basis in the property transferred by Mike is $40,000 [$30,000 (basis of the property to Mike) + $10,000 (gain recognized by Mike)]. John neither realizes nor recognizes gain or loss and will have a basis of $60,000 in the Condor stock. ▼

The receipt of stock for the performance of *services* always results in ordinary income to the transferor shareholder. An example might be an attorney who does not charge a fee for incorporating a business but instead receives the value equivalent in stock of the newly formed corporation. The basis of stock received for the performance of services is equal to the fair market value of the services.

OPERATING THE CORPORATION

DIVIDEND DISTRIBUTIONS

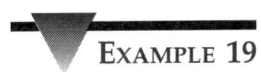

6 LEARNING OBJECTIVE
Work with the tax rules governing the operation of corporations.

Corporate distributions of cash or property to shareholders are treated as ordinary dividend income to the extent the corporation has accumulated *or* current earnings and profits (E & P).[32] In determining the source of the distribution, a dividend is deemed to have been made initially from current E & P.

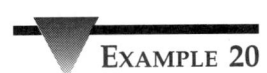

EXAMPLE 19

As of January 1, 1998, Teal Corporation has a deficit in accumulated E & P of $30,000. For tax year 1998, it has current E & P of $10,000. In 1998, the corporation distributes $5,000 to its shareholders. The $5,000 distribution is treated as a taxable dividend, since it is deemed to have been made from current E & P. This is the case even though Teal still has a deficit in its accumulated E & P at the end of 1998. ▼

If a corporate distribution is not covered by E & P (either current or past), it is treated as a return of capital (refer to the discussion of the recovery of capital doctrine in Chapter 4). This treatment allows the shareholder to apply the amount of the distribution against the basis of the stock investment and therefore represents a nontaxable return of capital. Any amount received in excess of the stock basis is classified as a capital gain (if the stock is a capital asset in the hands of the shareholder).

EXAMPLE 20

When Mallard Corporation has no E & P (either current or accumulated), it distributes cash of $30,000 to its sole shareholder, Helen. The basis of Helen's stock investment is $20,000. Based on these facts, the $30,000 distribution Helen receives is accounted for as follows:

Return of capital (nontaxable)	$20,000
Capital gain	10,000
Total amount of distribution	$30,000

After the distribution, Helen has a basis of zero in her stock investment. ▼

Concept of Earnings and Profits. The term **earnings and profits** is not defined in the Code, although § 312 does include certain transactions that affect E & P. Although E & P and the accounting concept of retained earnings have certain similarities, they differ in numerous respects. For example, although a nontaxable

[32]§ 316.

stock dividend is treated as a capitalization of retained earnings for accounting purposes, it does not decrease E & P for tax purposes. Taxable dividends do reduce E & P but cannot yield a deficit. Referring to Example 20, after the distribution, Mallard Corporation's E & P remains zero rather than being a negative amount.

Generally, *current E & P* for a taxable year is taxable income plus or minus certain adjustments (e.g., an addition is made for tax-exempt income). Federal income taxes are subtracted from taxable income in arriving at current E & P. *Accumulated E & P* is the sum of the corporation's past current E & P that has not been distributed as dividends. A detailed discussion of the concept of E & P is beyond the scope of this chapter.

Property Dividends. A distribution of property to a shareholder is measured by the fair market value of the property on the date of distribution. The shareholder's basis in the property received is also the fair market value.[33]

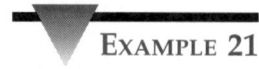

EXAMPLE 21

Drake Corporation has E & P of $60,000. It distributes land with a fair market value of $50,000 (adjusted basis of $30,000) to its sole shareholder, Art. Art has a taxable dividend of $50,000 and a basis in the land of $50,000. ▼

A corporation that distributes appreciated property to its shareholders as a dividend must recognize the amount of the appreciation as gain.[34]

EXAMPLE 22

Assume the same facts as in Example 21. Drake Corporation must recognize a gain of $20,000 on the distribution it made to Art. ▼

However, if the property distributed has a basis in excess of its fair market value, the distributing corporation cannot recognize any loss.

Constructive Dividends. Many taxpayers mistakenly assume that dividend consequences do not take place unless the distribution carries the formalities of a dividend (declaration date, record date, payment date). They further assume that dividends must be paid out to all shareholders on a pro rata basis. This may not be the case when closely held corporations are involved. Here, the key to dividend treatment depends upon whether the shareholders derive a benefit from the corporation that cannot be otherwise classified (e.g., reasonable salary). The following are examples of **constructive dividends:**

- Salaries paid to shareholder-employees that are not reasonable (refer to Example 6 in Chapter 6).
- Interest on debt owed by the corporation to shareholders that is reclassified as equity because the corporation is thinly capitalized (refer to the earlier discussion in this chapter).
- Excessive rent paid by a corporation for the use of shareholder property. The arm's length standard is used to test whether the rent is excessive (refer to Example 22 in Chapter 1).
- Advances to shareholders that are not bona fide loans.
- Interest-free (or below-market) loans to shareholders. In this situation, the dividend component is the difference between the interest provided for, if any, and that calculated using the market rate.

---

[33]§ 301.
[34]The tax consequences to a corporation of nonliquidating distributions to shareholders are covered in § 311.

• Shareholder use of corporate property for less than an arm's length rate.
• Absorption by the corporation of a shareholder's personal expenses.
• Bargain purchase of corporate property by shareholders.

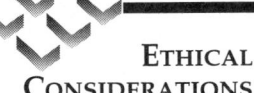

ETHICAL
CONSIDERATIONS

Who Gets the Deduction?

Alice owns all of the stock of Rose Company, a successful C corporation. During 1998, the alumni association of State University asks Alice for a donation to be used to establish a student scholarship in connection with the upcoming twentieth reunion of her class.

Alice has Rose Company issue a check to the university on her behalf in the amount of $10,000. Alice has the corporation make the contribution because it derives a greater tax benefit from the deduction than she would have.

Do you have any qualms about the approach taken by the parties? Why?

Like regular dividends, constructive dividends must be covered by E & P to carry dividend income consequences to the shareholders. As noted above, however, constructive dividends need not be available to all shareholders on a pro rata basis.

Although dividends reduce the E & P of a corporation, they are not deductible for income tax purposes. In this regard, certain constructive dividends could have subtle tax consequences for all parties concerned.

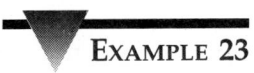

EXAMPLE 23

Grouse Corporation makes a loan to one of its shareholders, Hal. No interest is provided for, but application of the market rate would produce $20,000 of interest for the term of the loan. Presuming the loan is bona fide, the following results occur:

• Hal has dividend income of $20,000.
• Grouse Corporation has interest income of $20,000.
• Hal might obtain an interest deduction of $20,000.

Not only does Grouse Corporation have to recognize income of $20,000, but it also obtains no income tax deduction for the $20,000 constructive dividend. ▼

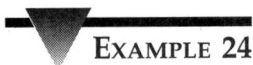

EXAMPLE 24

Assume the same facts as in Example 23, except that the loan to Hal was not bona fide. In this event, the full amount of the loan is regarded as a dividend to Hal. Therefore, the interest element is not a factor, since no bona fide loan ever existed. ▼

STOCK REDEMPTIONS

If a corporation redeems a shareholder's stock (a **stock redemption**), one of two possible outcomes occurs:

• The redemption may qualify as a sale or exchange under § 302 or § 303. In that case, capital gain or loss treatment usually applies to the qualifying shareholders.
• The redemption will be treated as a dividend under § 301, provided the distributing corporation has E & P.

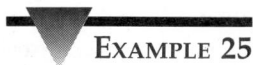

EXAMPLE 25

Reba owns 300 shares of Snipe Corporation stock as an investment. The shares have a basis to Reba of $100 each, for a total of $30,000. When the fair market value of a share is $200, Snipe redeems 200 of Reba's shares. If the redemption qualifies for sale or exchange treatment, the result is a capital gain to Reba of $20,000 [$40,000 (redemption price) – $20,000 (basis in 200 shares)]. Reba's basis in the remaining 100 shares is $10,000 [$30,000 (basis in the original shares) – $20,000 (basis in the shares redeemed)]. ▼

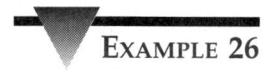

EXAMPLE 26

Assume the same facts as in Example 25, except that the redemption does not qualify for sale or exchange treatment. Presuming adequate E & P, the redemption results in $40,000 dividend income. Reba's basis in the remaining 100 shares now becomes $30,000, or $300 per share. ▼

A stock redemption qualifies as a sale or exchange if it meets any of the safe harbors of § 302 or § 303.

LIQUIDATING THE CORPORATION

7   LEARNING OBJECTIVE
Recognize the tax rules governing the liquidation of corporations.

Unlike dividend distributions or stock redemptions, where the distributing corporation continues its operations, **liquidating distributions** occur during the termination of the business. All debts are paid, and any remaining corporate assets are distributed pro rata to the shareholders in exchange for their stock. Once these distributions are completed, the corporation undergoing liquidation will cease to be a separate tax entity.

GENERAL RULE OF § 331

Under the general rule, the shareholders recognize gain or loss in a corporate liquidation. The amount of recognized gain or loss is measured by the difference between the fair market value of the assets received from the corporation and the adjusted basis of the stock surrendered. The shareholders recognize capital gain or loss if the stock is a capital asset.[35]

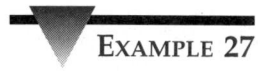

EXAMPLE 27

Pursuant to a complete liquidation, Starling Corporation distributes $100,000 in cash to Edna, one of its shareholders. If Edna's basis in the stock surrendered is $40,000, she must recognize a gain of $60,000. If Edna held the stock as an investment, the $60,000 gain is capital gain—either short term, mid-term, or long term (depending on the holding period). ▼

EXCEPTION TO THE GENERAL RULE

Section 332 is an exception to the general rule that the shareholder recognizes gain or loss on a corporate liquidation. If a parent corporation liquidates a subsidiary corporation in which it owns at least 80 percent of the voting power and value of the stock, no gain or loss is recognized by the parent company. The subsidiary must distribute all of its property in complete liquidation of all of its stock within the taxable year or within three years from the close of the tax year in which the first distribution occurred.

[35]If the stock is held as an investment, which is usually the case, gain or loss will be capital. Stock owned by a broker probably will be inventory and therefore will not constitute a capital asset. Thus, the gain or loss on this type of stock is ordinary and not capital.

BASIS DETERMINATION—§§ 334 AND 338

General Rule. Where gain or loss is recognized upon the complete liquidation of a corporation, the basis of the property received by the shareholders is the property's fair market value.[36]

Subsidiary Liquidation Basis Rules. The general rule is that the property received by the parent corporation in a complete liquidation of its subsidiary under § 332 has the same basis it had in the hands of the subsidiary (a carryover basis).[37] The parent's basis in the stock of the liquidated subsidiary disappears.

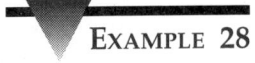

EXAMPLE 28

Swallow, the parent corporation, has a basis of $20,000 in the stock of Shrike Corporation, a subsidiary in which it owns 85% of all classes of stock. Swallow purchased the stock of Shrike Corporation 10 years ago. In the current year, Swallow liquidates Shrike Corporation and receives assets worth $50,000 with a tax basis to Shrike of $40,000. Swallow Corporation will have a basis of $40,000 in the assets, with a potential gain upon sale of $10,000. Swallow's original $20,000 basis in the Shrike stock disappears. ▼

An exception to the carryover of basis rule is provided in § 338. Under this exception, the parent company may elect to receive a basis for the assets equal to the adjusted basis of the stock of the subsidiary. In effect, the initial acquisition of the subsidiary is treated as if the parent company had acquired the assets (rather than the stock) of the subsidiary.

EFFECT OF THE LIQUIDATION ON THE CORPORATION

Having examined what happens to the shareholder upon the liquidation of a corporation, what happens at the corporate level? Here, § 336 applies to dictate the tax consequences to the corporation being liquidated.

Under § 336, the distributing corporation recognizes gain or loss upon complete liquidation. In this regard, it does not matter whether the corporation distributes the property in-kind (*as is*) to the shareholders or first sells the property and then distributes the proceeds.

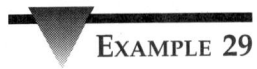

EXAMPLE 29

Pursuant to a complete liquidation, Grackle Corporation distributes the following assets to its shareholders: undeveloped land held as an investment (basis of $150,000 and fair market value of $140,000) and marketable securities (basis of $160,000 and fair market value of $200,000). Since Grackle is treated as if it had sold the property, a gain of $40,000 results from the securities, and a loss of $10,000 results from the land. ▼

ETHICAL CONSIDERATIONS

Necessity for Filing a Corporate Tax Return

For many years, Hanna has owned and operated several apartment buildings. In 1990 and upon the advice of her attorney, Hanna transferred the apartment buildings to a newly formed corporation. Her main reason for incorporating the business was to achieve limited liability.

---

[36]§ 334(a).

[37]§ 334(b)(1).

Every year since 1990, Hanna has prepared and filed a Form 1120 for the corporation. No corporate income tax has been paid because, after the deduction of various expenses (including Hanna's salary), the corporation has zero taxable income.

In 1998, Hanna decides that filing Form 1120 is a waste of time. Instead, she will report all of the financial activities of the apartment business on her own individual Form 1040.

Has Hanna acted properly or should she first liquidate the corporation?

The deductibility of losses may be restricted by the related-party rules (refer to Chapter 6) if certain conditions exist (e.g., the distributions are not pro rata).[38]

A wholly owned subsidiary corporation does not recognize gain or loss when the parent corporation uses the carryover basis option of § 334(b)(1). The reason for the special treatment is that the subsidiary's basis (and all other tax attributes) in the assets carries over to the parent corporation.

THE S ELECTION

JUSTIFICATION FOR THE ELECTION

8   **LEARNING OBJECTIVE**
Appreciate the utility and effect of the Subchapter S election.

Numerous nontax reasons exist for operating a business in the corporate form (e.g., limited liability). Consequently, the existence of income tax disadvantages (e.g., double taxation of corporate income and shareholder dividends) should not deter business people from using the corporate form. To prevent tax considerations from interfering with the exercise of sound business judgment, Congress enacted Subchapter S of the Code.

To qualify for **S corporation** status, the corporation must be a **small business corporation**.[39] This includes any corporation that has the following characteristics:

- Is a domestic corporation.
- Has no more than 75 shareholders.
- Has as its shareholders only individuals, estates, and certain trusts.
- Does not have a nonresident alien as a shareholder.
- Has only one class of stock outstanding.

These characteristics must continue to exist if an electing S corporation is to maintain S status.

Making the Election.   The election is made by filing Form 2553, and *all* shareholders must consent. For this purpose, husbands and wives are counted as a single shareholder.

To be effective for the current year, the election must be filed anytime during the preceding taxable year or on or before the fifteenth day of the third month of the current year.[40]

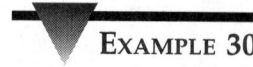

EXAMPLE 30

Heron, a calendar year taxpayer, is a regular corporation that wishes to elect S status for 1998. If the election is filed anytime from January 1, 1997, through March 15, 1998, it will be effective for 1998. ▼

---

[38]§ 336(d).
[39]§ 1361(b).

[40]§ 1362.

TAX IN THE NEWS

ONE QUESTIONABLE USE OF S CORPORATION STATUS

The suspicion exists that some taxpayers are using S corporations to cheat on FICA self-employment taxes. In partnerships, limited liability companies, and sole proprietorships, all income flowing to the partners or owners is subject to FICA taxes. In S corporations, only amounts designated as salaries are so subject. Distributions of profits are not subject to FICA taxes. Consequently, owner-employees of S corporations may attempt to reduce (or avoid) self-employment taxes by curtailing salaries and maximizing profits. In such cases, the IRS can reclassify as salaries some of the profit pass-through to properly reflect the value of the services rendered to the corporation.

The IRS has the authority to waive invalid S elections (e.g., inadvertent failure to obtain all the necessary shareholder consents to the original election) and to treat late elections as timely.

Loss of the Election. The S election may be terminated *voluntarily* (a majority of the shareholders file to revoke the election) or *involuntarily*. An involuntary termination may occur in *any* of the following ways:

- The corporation ceases to qualify as a small business corporation (e.g., the number of shareholders exceeds 75, or a partnership becomes a shareholder).
- The corporation has passive investment income (e.g., interest, dividends) in excess of 25 percent of gross receipts for a period of three consecutive years. This possibility applies only if the corporation was previously a regular corporation and has earnings and profits from that period.

If the holders of a *majority* of the shares consent to a voluntary revocation of S status, the election to revoke must be made on or before the fifteenth day of the third month of the tax year to be effective for that year.

EXAMPLE 31

The shareholders of Stork Corporation, a calendar year S corporation, elect to revoke the election on January 4, 1998. Assuming the election is duly executed and timely filed, Stork will become a regular corporation for calendar year 1998. If the election to revoke is not made until June 1998, Stork will not become a regular corporation until calendar year 1999. ▼

Suppose the shareholders in Example 31 file the election to revoke on January 4, 1998, but do not want the revocation to take place until 1999. If the election so specifies, Stork Corporation will cease to have S status as of January 1, 1999.

In the case where S status is lost because of a disqualifying act (involuntarily), the loss of the election takes effect as of the date on which the event occurs.

EXAMPLE 32

Crow Corporation has been a calendar year S corporation for several years. On August 13, 1998, one of its shareholders sells her stock to Kite Corporation. Since Crow Corporation no longer satisfies the definition of a small business corporation (it has another corporation as a shareholder), the election has been involuntarily terminated. For calendar year 1998, therefore, Crow will be an S corporation through August 12 and a regular corporation from August 13 through December 31, 1998. ▼

In the event the election is lost through a violation of the passive investment income limitation, the loss of S status starts at the beginning of the next tax year.

Barring certain exceptions, the loss of the election after 1996 places the corporation in a five-year holding period before S status can be reelected.

OPERATIONAL RULES

The S corporation is primarily a tax-reporting rather than a taxpaying entity. In this respect, the entity is taxed much like a partnership.[41] Under the conduit concept, the taxable income and losses of an S corporation flow through to the shareholders who report them on their personal income tax returns.

To ascertain the annual tax consequences to each shareholder, it is necessary to carry out two steps at the S corporation level. First, all corporate transactions that will flow through to the shareholders on an *as is* basis under the conduit approach must be set aside. Second, what remains is aggregated as the taxable income of the S corporation and is allocated to each shareholder on a per-share and per-day of stock ownership basis.[42]

Separately Stated Items.   The following are some of the items that do not lose their identity as they pass through the S corporation and are therefore picked up by each shareholder on an *as is* basis:

- Tax-exempt income.
- Long-term, mid-term, and short-term capital gains and losses.
- Section 1231 gains and losses.
- Charitable contributions.
- Foreign tax credits.
- Depletion.
- Nonbusiness income or loss under § 212.
- Intangible drilling costs.
- Investment interest, income, and expenses covered under § 163(d).
- Certain portfolio income.
- Passive activity gains, losses, and credits under § 469.
- AMT adjustments and tax preference items.

These items are separately stated because each may lead to a different tax result when combined with a particular shareholder's other transactions.

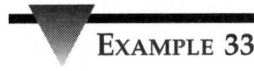

EXAMPLE 33

Arnold and Jean are equal shareholders in Lark Corporation (an S corporation). For calendar year 1998, each must account for one-half of a corporate short-term capital gain of $6,000. Arnold has no other capital asset transactions, and Jean has a short-term capital loss of $3,000 from the sale of stock in IBM Corporation. In terms of overall effect, the difference between the two taxpayers is significant. Although both must report the short-term capital gain pass-through, Jean will neutralize its inclusion in gross income by offsetting it with the $3,000 short-term capital loss from the sale of the IBM stock. For Arnold, the short-term capital gain pass-through results in a $3,000 increase in his taxable income. ▼

Taxable Income.   After the separately stated items have been removed, the balance represents the taxable income of the S corporation. In arriving at taxable income, the dividends received deduction and the net operating loss deduction

---

[41]This is not to imply that an S corporation is always free from the income tax. For example, a tax may be imposed on certain built-in gains or certain excessive passive investment income.

[42]§ 1366.

are not allowed. An S corporation does come under the regular corporate rules, however, for purposes of amortization of organizational expenditures.

Once taxable income has been determined, it passes through to each shareholder as of the last day of the S corporation's tax year.

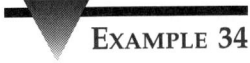

EXAMPLE 34

Harrier Corporation, a calendar year S corporation, had the following transactions during the current year:

Sales		$ 40,000
Cost of goods sold		(23,000)
Other income		
*Tax-exempt interest	$ 300	
*Long-term capital gain	500	800
Other expenses		
*Charitable contributions	$ 400	
Advertising expense	1,500	
Other operating expenses	2,000	
*Short-term capital loss	150	(4,050)
Net income per books		$ 13,750

When the items that are to be separately stated (those preceded by an asterisk [*]) and shown *as is* by each shareholder are withdrawn, Harrier has the following taxable income:

Sales		$ 40,000
Cost of goods sold		(23,000)
Other expenses		
Advertising expense	$1,500	
Other operating expenses	2,000	(3,500)
Taxable income		$ 13,500

▼

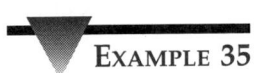

EXAMPLE 35

If Oscar owned 10% of the stock in Harrier Corporation (refer to Example 34) during all of the current year, he must account for the following:

Separately stated items	
Tax-exempt interest	$ 30
Long-term capital gain	50
Charitable contributions	40
Short-term capital loss	15
Taxable income (10% of $13,500)	1,350

Some of the separately stated items need not be reported on Oscar's individual income tax return (e.g., the tax-exempt interest). Others must be reported but may not lead to tax consequences. Oscar picks up his share of Harrier's taxable income ($1,350) as ordinary income. ▼

Treatment of Losses. As previously noted, separately stated loss items (e.g., capital losses, § 1231 losses) flow through to the shareholders on an *as is* basis. Their treatment by a shareholder depends on the shareholder's individual income tax position. If the S corporation's taxable income determination results in an operating loss, it also passes through to the shareholders. As is the case with separately stated items, the amount of the loss each shareholder receives depends on the stock ownership during the year.

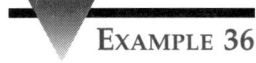

EXAMPLE 36

In 1998, Oriole Corporation (a calendar year S corporation) incurred an operating loss of $36,500. During 1998, Jason's ownership in Oriole was as follows: 20% for 200 days and 30% for 165 days. Jason's share of the loss is determined as follows:

$$[\$36,500 \times (200/365)] \times 20\% = \$4,000$$
$$[\$36,500 \times (165/365)] \times 30\% = \underline{4,950}$$

Total loss for Jason $\underline{\underline{\$8,950}}$

Presuming the basis limitation does not come into play (see the following discussion), Jason deducts $8,950 in arriving at adjusted gross income. ▼

Basis Determination.   A shareholder's *basis* in the stock of an S corporation, like that of a regular corporation, is the original investment plus additional capital contributions less return of capital distributions. At this point, however, the symmetry disappears. Generally, basis is increased by the pass-through of income items (including those separately stated) and decreased by the loss items (including those separately stated).[43]

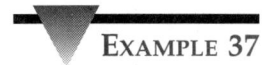

EXAMPLE 37

In 1998, Warbler Corporation is formed with an investment of $100,000, of which Janice contributed $20,000 for a 20% stock interest. A timely S election is made, and for 1998, Warbler earns taxable income of $15,000. Janice's basis in her stock investment now becomes $23,000 [$20,000 (original capital contribution) + $3,000 (the 20% share of the corporation's taxable income assigned to Janice)]. ▼

Distributions by an S corporation reduce the basis of a shareholder's stock investment. However, if the amount of the distribution exceeds basis, the excess normally receives capital gain treatment.

As previously noted, operating losses of an S corporation pass through to the shareholders and reduce the basis in their stock investment. Because the basis of the stock cannot fall below zero, an excess loss is then applied against the basis of any loans the shareholder may have made to the corporation.

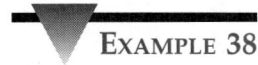

EXAMPLE 38

Flamingo Corporation, a calendar year S corporation, has an operating loss of $60,000 for 1998. Norman, a 50% shareholder, has an adjusted basis of $25,000 in his stock investment and has made loans to the corporation of $5,000. Based on these facts, Norman may take full advantage of the $30,000 loss (50% of $60,000) on his 1998 individual income tax return. Norman's basis in the stock and the loans must be reduced accordingly, and both will be zero after the pass-through. ▼

In the event the basis limitation precludes an operating loss from being absorbed, the loss can be carried forward and deducted when and if it is covered by basis.

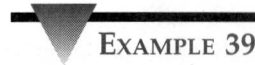

EXAMPLE 39

Assume the same facts as in Example 38, except that Norman had not made any loans to Flamingo Corporation. Further assume that Flamingo has taxable income of $15,000 in the following year (1999). Norman's tax situation for 1998 and 1999 is summarized as follows:

---

[43]§ 1367.

Ordinary loss for 1998	$25,000
Income to be reported in 1999 (50% of $15,000)	7,500
Restoration of stock basis in 1999 (50% of $15,000)	7,500
Loss allowed for 1999 ($30,000 – $25,000)	5,000
Basis in stock account after 1999 ($7,500 – $5,000)	2,500

Thus, Norman's unabsorbed loss of $5,000 from 1998 carries over to 1999 and is applied against the $7,500 of ordinary income for that year. ▼

PARTNERSHIPS

NATURE OF PARTNERSHIP TAXATION

Unlike corporations, partnerships are not considered separate taxable entities. Each member of a partnership is subject to income tax on his or her distributive share of the partnership's income, even if an actual distribution is not made. The tax return (Form 1065) required of a partnership serves only to provide information necessary in determining the character and amount of each partner's distributive share of the partnership's income and expense. Because a partnership acts as a conduit, items that pass through to the partners do not lose their identity. For example, tax-exempt income earned by a partnership is picked up by the partners as tax-exempt income. In this regard, partnerships function in much the same fashion as S corporations, which also serve as conduits.

A partnership is considered a separate taxable entity for purposes of making various elections and selecting its taxable year, method of depreciation, and accounting method. A partnership is also treated as a separate legal entity under civil law with the right to own property in its own name and to transact business free from the personal debts of its partners.

PARTNERSHIP FORMATION

Recognition of Gain or Loss. The general rule is that no gain or loss is recognized by a partnership or any of its partners on the contribution of property in exchange for a capital interest in the partnership.[44] The general rule also applies to all subsequent contributions of property.

There are certain exceptions to the nonrecognition of gain or loss rule including the following:

- If a partner transfers property to the partnership and receives money or other consideration (boot) as a result, the transaction will be treated as a sale or exchange rather than as a contribution of capital. Realized gain is recognized to the extent of the fair market value of the boot received.
- If a partnership interest is received in exchange for services rendered or to be rendered by the partner to the partnership, the fair market value of the transferred capital interest is regarded as compensation for services rendered. In such cases, the recipient of the capital interest must recognize the amount as ordinary income in the year actually or constructively received.
- If property that is subject to a liability in excess of its basis is contributed to a partnership, the contributing partner may recognize gain.

---

[44]§ 721.

Basis of a Partnership Interest.   The contributing *partner's basis* in the partnership interest received is the sum of money contributed plus the adjusted basis of any other property transferred to the partnership.[45]

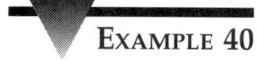
EXAMPLE 40

In return for the contribution of property (with a basis of $50,000 and a fair market value of $80,000) and cash of $10,000 to the Brown Partnership, Marcia receives a 10% capital interest worth $90,000. Although Marcia has a realized gain of $30,000 ($90,000 – $60,000) on the transfer, none of the gain is recognized. The basis of her interest in the Brown Partnership is $60,000 [$50,000 (basis of property contributed) + $10,000 (cash contribution)]. ▼

A partner's basis in the partnership interest is determined without regard to any amount reflected on the partnership's books as capital, equity, or a similar account.

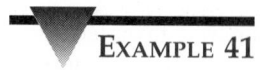
EXAMPLE 41

Marge and Clyde form the equal Blue Partnership with a cash contribution of $30,000 from Marge and a property contribution (adjusted basis of $18,000 and fair market value of $30,000) from Clyde. Although the books of the Blue Partnership may reflect a credit of $30,000 to each partner's capital account, only Marge has a tax basis of $30,000 in her partnership interest. Clyde's tax basis in his partnership interest is $18,000, the amount of his tax basis in the property contributed to the partnership. ▼

After its initial determination, the basis of a partnership interest is subject to continuous fluctuations. A partner's basis is increased by additional contributions and the sum of his or her current and prior years' distributive share of the following:

- Taxable income of the partnership, including capital gains.
- Tax-exempt income of the partnership.
- The excess of the deductions for depletion over the basis of the partnership's property subject to depletion.[46]

Similarly, the basis of a partner's interest is decreased, but not below zero, by distributions of partnership property and by the sum of the current and prior years' distributive share of the following:

- Partnership losses, including capital losses.
- Partnership expenditures that are not deductible in computing taxable income or loss and that are not capital expenditures.

Changes in the liabilities (including trade accounts payable, bank loans, etc.) of a partnership also affect the basis of a partnership interest. A partner's basis is increased by his or her assumption of partnership liabilities and by his or her pro rata share of liabilities incurred by the partnership. Likewise, the partner's basis is decreased by the amount of any personal liabilities assumed by the partnership and by the pro rata share of any decreases in the liabilities of the partnership.

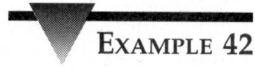
EXAMPLE 42

Tony, Martha, and Carolyn form the Orange Partnership with the following contributions: cash of $50,000 from Tony for a 50% interest in capital and profits, cash of $25,000 from Martha for a 25% interest, and property valued at $33,000 from Carolyn for a 25% interest. The property contributed by Carolyn has an adjusted basis of $15,000 and is subject to a mortgage of $8,000, which is assumed by the partnership. Carolyn's basis in her interest in the Orange Partnership is $9,000, determined as follows:

---

[45]§ 722.   [46]§ 705(a).

Adjusted basis of Carolyn's contributed property	$ 15,000
Less portion of mortgage assumed by Tony and Martha and treated as a distribution of money to Carolyn (75% of $8,000)	(6,000)
Basis of Carolyn's interest in Orange Partnership	$ 9,000

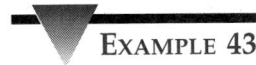

EXAMPLE 43

Assuming the same facts as in Example 42, Tony and Martha have a basis in their partnership interests of $54,000 and $27,000, respectively.

	Tony	Martha
Cash contribution	$50,000	$25,000
Plus portion of mortgage assumed and treated as an additional cash contribution:		
(50% of $8,000)	4,000	
(25% of $8,000)		2,000
Basis of interest in Orange Partnership	$54,000	$27,000

Partnership's Basis in Contributed Property. The *basis of property* contributed to a partnership by a partner is the adjusted basis of the property to the contributing partner at the time of the contribution.[47] Additionally, the holding period of the property for the partnership includes the period during which the property was held by the contributing partner. This is logical, since the partnership's basis in the property is the same basis the property had in the hands of the partner.[48]

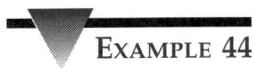

EXAMPLE 44

In 1998, Roger contributed equipment with an adjusted basis of $10,000 and fair market value of $30,000 to the Red Partnership in exchange for a one-third interest in the partnership. No gain or loss is recognized by Roger. The basis in the equipment is $10,000 to the Red Partnership. If Roger had acquired the equipment in 1986, the holding period for the Red Partnership would include the period from 1986 through 1998. ▼

PARTNERSHIP OPERATION

Measuring and Reporting Partnership Income. Although a partnership is not subject to Federal income taxation, it is required to determine its taxable income and file an income tax return for information purposes.[49] The tax return, Form 1065, is due on the fifteenth day of the fourth month following the close of the taxable year of the partnership.

In measuring and reporting partnership income, certain transactions must be segregated and reported separately on the partnership return. Items such as charitable contributions, capital gains and losses, and foreign taxes are excluded from partnership taxable income and are allocated separately to the partners.[50] These items must be segregated and allocated separately because they affect the computation of various exclusions, deductions, and credits at the individual partner level. For example, one of the partners may have made personal charitable contributions in excess of the ceiling limitations on his or her individual tax return. Therefore, partnership charitable contributions are excluded from partnership taxable income and are reported separately on the partnership return.

---

[47]§ 723.
[48]§ 1223(2).

[49]§ 6031.
[50]§ 702(a).

A second step in the measurement and reporting process is the computation of the partnership's ordinary income or loss. The taxable income of a partnership is computed in the same manner as the taxable income of an individual taxpayer. However, a partnership is not allowed the following deductions:[51]

- The deduction for personal and dependency exemptions.
- The deduction for taxes paid to foreign countries or possessions of the United States.
- The deduction for charitable contributions.
- The deduction for net operating losses.
- The additional itemized deductions allowed individuals in §§ 211 through 219.

The partnership's ordinary income or loss and each of the items requiring separate treatment are reported in the partnership's information return and allocated to the partners in accordance with their distributive shares.

Limitation on Partner's Share of Losses. A partner's deduction of the distributive share of partnership losses (including capital losses) could be limited. The limitation is the adjusted basis of the partnership interest at the end of the partnership year in which the losses were incurred.

The limitation for partnership loss deductions is similar to that applicable to losses of S corporations. Like S corporation losses, partnership losses may be carried forward by the partner and utilized against future increases in the basis of the partnership interest. Such increases might result from additional capital contributions to the partnership, from additional partnership liabilities, or from future partnership income.

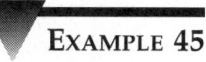

EXAMPLE 45

Florence and Donald do business as the Green Partnership, sharing profits and losses equally. All parties use the calendar year for tax purposes. As of January 1, 1998, Florence's basis in her partnership interest is $25,000. The partnership sustained an operating loss of $80,000 in 1998 and earned a profit of $70,000 in 1999. For the calendar year 1998, Florence may claim only $25,000 of her $40,000 distributive share of the partnership loss (one-half of the $80,000 loss). As a result, the basis in her partnership interest is reduced to zero as of January 1, 1999, and she must carry forward the remaining $15,000 of partnership losses. ▼

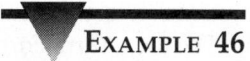

EXAMPLE 46

Assuming the same facts as in Example 45, what are the income tax consequences for Florence in 1999? Since the partnership earned a profit of $70,000 for the calendar year 1999, Florence reports income from the partnership of $20,000 ($35,000 distributive share of income for 1999 less the $15,000 loss not allowed for 1998). The adjusted basis of her partnership interest now becomes $20,000. ▼

Transactions between Partner and Partnership. A partner engaging in a transaction with the partnership is generally regarded as a nonpartner or outsider. However, the Code includes certain exceptions to prevent unwarranted tax avoidance. For instance, losses from the sale or exchange of property are disallowed if they arise in either of the following cases:

- Between a partnership and a person whose direct or indirect interest in the capital or profits of the partnership is more than 50 percent.

---

[51]§ 703(a).

- Between two partnerships in which the same persons own more than a 50 percent interest in the capital or profits.[52]

If one of the purchasers later sells the property, any gain realized will be recognized only to the extent that it exceeds the loss previously disallowed.

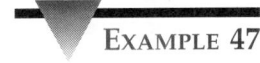
EXAMPLE 47

Pat owns a 60% interest in the capital and profits of the Rose Partnership. In the current year, Pat sells property with an adjusted basis of $50,000 to the partnership for its fair market value of $35,000. The $15,000 loss is not deductible since Pat's ownership interest is more than 50%. If the Rose Partnership later sells the property for $40,000, none of the $5,000 (sale price of $40,000 less adjusted basis to partnership of $35,000) gain will be recognized since it is offset by $5,000 of the previously disallowed loss of $15,000. The unused loss of $10,000, however, is of no tax benefit either to the partnership or to Pat. ▼

Payments made by a partnership to one of its partners for services rendered or for the use of capital, to the extent they are determined without regard to the income of the partnership, are treated by the partnership in the same manner as payments made to a person who is not a partner. Referred to as **guaranteed payments,** these are generally deductible by the partnership as a business expense.[53] The payments must be reported as ordinary income by the receiving partner. Their deductibility distinguishes guaranteed payments from a partner's distributive share of income that is not deductible by the partnership.

EXAMPLE 48

Under the terms of the Silver Partnership agreement, Kim is entitled to a fixed annual salary of $18,000 without regard to the income of the partnership. He is also to share in the profits and losses of the partnership as a one-third partner. After deducting the guaranteed payment, the partnership has $36,000 of ordinary income. Kim must include $30,000 as ordinary income on his income tax return for his tax year with or within which the partnership tax year ends ($18,000 guaranteed payment + $12,000 one-third distributive share of partnership income). ▼

Other Partnership Considerations. Complex tax provisions involving liquidating and nonliquidating distributions and the sale of a partnership interest are beyond the scope of this text and are discussed in depth in *West's Federal Taxation: Corporations, Partnerships, Estates, and Trusts.*

TAX PLANNING CONSIDERATIONS

10 LEARNING OBJECTIVE
Evaluate the advantages and disadvantages of the various forms for conducting a business.

CORPORATE VERSUS NONCORPORATE FORMS OF BUSINESS ORGANIZATION

The decision to use the corporate form in conducting a trade or business must be weighed carefully. Besides the nontax aspects of the corporate form (limited liability, continuity of life, free transferability of interests, centralized management), tax ramifications play an important role in any such decision. Close attention should be paid to the following:

1. The corporate form means the imposition of the corporate income tax. Corporate-source income will be taxed twice—once as earned by the corporation and again when distributed to the shareholders. Since dividends are not deductible, a strong incentive exists in a closely held corporation to structure corporate distributions in a deductible form. The shareholders

may bail out profits in the form of salaries, interest, or rents. These procedures lead to a multitude of problems, one of which, the reclassification of debt as equity, has been discussed. The problems of unreasonable salaries and rents were discussed in Chapter 6.

2. The applicable income tax rates also affect the choice of the form for doing business. Unfortunately, because of the wide range of possibilities involved (15 to 39.6 percent for individuals and 15 to 35 percent for corporations), this factor must be considered on a case-by-case basis. For example, the corporate form is very appealing if the anticipated taxable income falls within the 25 percent bracket while the shareholder's individual bracket is 39.6 percent. Here, the time value of the taxes saved (by not distributing dividends and postponing the effect of the double tax) could make operating a business in the corporate form advantageous.

3. Corporate-source income loses its identity as it passes through the corporation to the shareholders. Thus, items possessing preferential tax treatment (e.g., interest on municipal bonds) are not taxed as such to the shareholders.

4. As noted earlier, it may be difficult for shareholders to recover some or all of their investment in the corporation without an ordinary income result. Recall that most corporate distributions are treated as dividends to the extent of the corporation's earnings and profits. Structuring the capital of the corporation to include debt is a partial solution to this problem. Thus, the shareholder-creditor could recoup part of his or her investment through the tax-free payment of principal. Too much debt, however, may lead to the debt being reclassified as equity.

5. Corporate losses cannot be passed through to the shareholders.

6. The liquidation of a corporation may generate tax consequences to both the corporation and its shareholders.

7. The corporate form provides the shareholders with the opportunity to be treated as employees for tax purposes if they render services to the corporation. This status makes a number of attractive tax-sheltered fringe benefits available (e.g., group term life insurance). These benefits are not available to partners and sole proprietors.

REGULAR CORPORATION VERSUS S STATUS

Due to the pass-through concept, the use of S status generally avoids the income tax at the corporate level, bringing the individual income tax into play. As noted in item 2 in the previous section, the differential between the rates applicable to noncorporate and corporate taxpayers makes this a factor to be considered. The S election enables a business to operate in the corporate form, avoid the corporate income tax, and, depending on taxable income, possibly take advantage of the lower rates usually applicable to individuals. Also, losses incurred at the corporate level pass through to the shareholders, who will utilize them on their individual returns (compare with item 5).

Electing S status can present several problems. First, the election is available only to small business corporations. Consequently, many corporations will not qualify for the election. Second, S corporations are subject to the rules governing regular corporations unless otherwise specified in the Code. For example, if an S corporation carries out a stock redemption or is liquidated, the rules covering regular corporations apply. Third, some states do not recognize S status for purposes of state and local taxation. Therefore, an S corporation might be subject to a state franchise tax (refer to Chapter 1) or a state or local income tax.

USE OF AN ENTITY TO REDUCE THE FAMILY INCOME TAX BURDEN

One objective of tax planning is to keep the income from a business within the family unit but to disperse the income in such a manner as to minimize the overall tax burden. To the extent feasible, therefore, income should be shifted from higher-bracket to lower-bracket family members.

Unfortunately, the income from property (a business) cannot be shifted to another without also transferring an interest in the property. If, for example, a father wants to assign income from his sole proprietorship to his children, he must form a partnership or incorporate the business.[54] In either case, the transfer of the interest may be subject to the Federal gift tax. But any potential gift tax can be eliminated or controlled through judicious use of the annual exclusion, the election to split gifts (for married donors), and the unified tax credit (refer to the discussion of the Federal gift tax in Chapter 1).

Consequently, the first problem to be resolved becomes which form of business organization will best fit the objective of income shifting. For the partnership form, one major obstacle arises. Family partnership rules preclude the assignment of income to a family member unless capital is a material income-producing factor.[55] If not, the family member must contribute substantial or vital services. Ordinarily, capital is not a material income-producing factor if the income of the business consists principally of compensation for personal services performed by members or employees of the partnership. Conversely, capital is a material income-producing factor if the operation of the business entails a substantial investment in physical assets (e.g., inventory, plant, machinery, or equipment).

Income shifting through the use of a partnership, therefore, may be ineffectual if a personal service business is involved. In fact, it could be hopeless if the assignees are minors. The use of the corporate form usually involves no such impediment. Regardless of the nature of the business, a gift of stock carries with it the attributes of ownership. Thus, dividends paid on stock are taxed to the owner of the stock.

But what if the corporate form is utilized and the S election is made? A new hurdle arises. The Code authorizes the IRS to make adjustments in situations where shareholders are not being adequately compensated for the value of their services or capital provided to an S corporation in a family setting.[56] Thus, an S corporation suffers from the same vulnerability that exists with family partnerships.

A further factor that favors the corporate form (either a regular or an S corporation) as a device for income splitting is the ease with which it can be carried out. Presuming the entity already exists, the transfer of stock merely requires an entry in the corporation's stock ledger account. In contrast, a gift of a partnership interest probably requires an amendment to the articles of copartnership. If minors are to be the assignees (donees), a state's Uniform Gifts to Minors Act provides a useful and flexible means of holding a stock interest until the assignees become adults.[57] In the case of a partnership interest, however, a guardianship may have to be set up to achieve the same flexibility. In summary, the transfer of stock is more convenient and, since it usually avoids legal problems, can be less expensive.

Regardless of the form of organization used for the business, income shifting will not take place unless the transfer is complete.[58] If the donor continues to exercise control over the interest transferred and does not recognize and protect

---

[54]Income shifting will not work, however, if the minor is under 14 years of age. In such cases, net unearned income (refer to the discussion in Chapter 3) of the child is taxed at the parents' tax rate. § 1(g).

[55]§ 704(e).

[56]§ 1366(e).

[57]The Uniform Gifts to Minors Act is explained in Chapter 4.

[58]*Ginsberg v. Comm.,* 74–2 USTC ¶9660, 34 AFTR2d 74–5760, 502 F.2d 965 (CA–6, 1974), and *Michael F. Beirne,* 61 T.C. 268 (1973).

the ownership rights of the donee, the IRS may argue that the transfer is ineffective for tax purposes. In that case, the income from the transferred interest continues to be taxed to the donor.

KEY TERMS

Check-the-box
Regulations, 20–4

Constructive dividends,
20–20

Dividends received
deduction, 20–10

Earnings and profits,
20–19

Guaranteed payments,
20–33

Limited liability
company, 20–4

Liquidating distribution,
20–22

Organizational
expenditures, 20–12

Personal service
corporation, 20–12

S corporation, 20–24

Small business
corporation, 20–24

Stock redemption,
20–21

Thin capitalization,
20–17

PROBLEM MATERIALS

DISCUSSION QUESTIONS

1. What is the role of state law in determining whether or not an entity will be classified as a corporation for Federal income tax purposes?

2. Under what circumstances might the disregard of the corporate entity produce a favorable result for the IRS?

3. Why are limited liability companies advantageous?

4. What purpose is served by the check-the-box Regulations?

5. Can a one-person business use the check-the-box Regulations to be classified as a corporation? Explain.

6. Can a limited liability company use the check-the-box Regulations to be classified as a corporation? What if it defaults (i.e., makes no election at all)?

7. Can corporations use the cash method of accounting? Explain.

8. Are the tax brackets applied differently in any way to individuals and corporations in higher taxable income levels?

9. How does the taxation of capital gains of a corporation differ from that of individuals?

10. Contrast the corporate tax rules for deducting net capital losses with the rules for individuals. Are the corporate capital loss rules *more or less* favorable than the capital loss provisions for individuals? Why?

11. Do corporations have to recapture more depreciation than noncorporate taxpayers? Explain.

12. Is it ever possible for a corporation to deduct some (or all) of the appreciation on inventory donated to charity? Explain.

13. In computing an NOL, corporations are subject to fewer adjustments than individuals. Explain.

14. Why would a corporation elect not to carry back an NOL to a particular year?

15. What is the rationale for the dividends received deduction for corporate shareholders?

16. Mallard Corporation was formed in December 1997 and plans to use the cash basis of accounting. Mallard incurred one-half of its organizational expenses in December 1997 and one-half in January 1998. The payment of these expenses also occurred in these two months. Do you recognize any income tax problem?

17. Reportedly, some qualified personal service corporations are computing their income tax using the graduated corporate tax rates.
    a. Is this an incorrect procedure?
    b. Why might this be occurring?

18. What purpose does the Schedule M–1 reconciliation of Form 1120 serve for the taxpayer? For the IRS?

19. To encourage a corporation to open a manufacturing facility in the community, a city donates land to the corporation. Does the donation generate income to the corporation? What basis will the corporation have in the land?

20. Why is it usually advantageous to capitalize a corporation by using debt? Is it possible that the debt will be reclassified as equity? Why?

21. Several persons plan to start a business that will be conducted by a newly formed corporation. One of the organizers, however, desires to recognize gain on the appreciated property he transfers to the corporation. What do you suggest?

22. When a shareholder receives stock in a nontaxable exchange under § 351, what income tax basis will the shareholder have?

23. How do the following transactions affect the earnings and profits of a corporation?
    a. A nontaxable stock dividend issued to the shareholders.
    b. Receipt of interest on municipal bonds.
    c. Federal corporate income tax liability.

24. When is a distribution by a corporation to its shareholders treated by the shareholders as a return of capital? When can a shareholder have a capital gain on a distribution received from a corporation?

25. A corporation distributes a property dividend to its shareholders.
    a. Is any gain or loss recognized by the distributing corporation?
    b. What basis will the shareholders have in the property?

26. The stock of Loon Corporation is owned equally by a brother and two sisters: Cole, Alma, and Kara. During the year, the following transactions occur.
    a. Cole buys property from Loon Corporation.
    b. Alma rents property to Loon Corporation.
    c. Kara borrows money from Loon Corporation.
    d. Loon Corporation pays interest on bonds it sold to Cole, Alma, and Kara.

    Discuss any potential tax problems that these transactions might present.

27. What difference does it make whether a corporation's redemption of its stock qualifies as a sale or exchange?

28. What is the usual tax effect to a corporation when it liquidates?

29. How can an S corporation be utilized to reduce or avoid FICA (or self-employment) taxes on the sole shareholder?

30. Both Kimberly and Edward are shareholders in Emerald Company, an S corporation. During the current year, Emerald had losses. These losses benefited Kimberly but not Edward. How can you explain this result?

31. Compare the nonrecognition of gain or loss on contributions to a partnership with the similar provision found in corporate formation (§ 351). What are the major differences and similarities?

32. Under what circumstances does the receipt of a partnership interest result in the recognition of ordinary income? What is the effect of this on the partnership and the other partners?

33. How is a contributing partner's basis in a partnership interest determined?

34. What transactions or events will cause a partner's basis in his or her partnership interest to fluctuate continuously?

35. Describe the two-step approach used in determining partnership income. Why is the computation necessary?

36. To what extent can a partner deduct his or her distributive share of partnership losses? What happens to any unused losses?

37. What are guaranteed payments? When might such payments be used?

 38. Cecil is the sole shareholder of Stilt Corporation (an S corporation). In order to shift income to lower-bracket family members, Cecil gives 40% of the stock in Stilt to his four children. Cecil's children are all minors, and none of them works for the corporation. Do you see any potential tax problems?

PROBLEMS

39. Cardinal Corporation has net short-term capital gains of $5,000 and net long-term capital losses of $45,000 during 1998. Taxable income from other sources is $200,000. Prior years' transactions included the following:

1994	Net short-term capital gains	$20,000
1995	Net long-term capital gains	10,000
1996	Net short-term capital gains	15,000
1997	Net long-term capital gains	10,000

a. How are the capital gains and losses treated on the 1998 tax return?
b. Compute the capital loss carryback to the carryback years.
c. Compute the amount of capital loss carryover, if any, and designate the years to which the loss may be carried.

40. Starling Corporation acquired residential rental property on January 3, 1986, for $100,000. The property was depreciated using the accelerated method and a 19-year recovery period under ACRS. Depreciation in the amount of $70,575 was claimed. Straight-line depreciation for the period would have been $63,521. Starling sold the property on January 1, 1998, for $110,000. What is the gain on the sale, and how is it taxed?

41. Assume the property in Problem 40 was a commercial building and Starling Corporation used the straight-line method of depreciation with a 19-year recovery period under ACRS. What would be the gain on the sale, and how would it be taxed?

42. During 1998, Orange Corporation, a calendar year taxpayer, had the following income and expenses:

Income from operations	$300,000
Expenses from operations	180,000
Dividends from domestic corporations	20,000
NOL carryover from 1997	10,000

On May 4, 1998, Orange made a contribution to a qualified charitable organization of $15,000 in cash (not included in any of the items listed above).
a. Determine Orange's deduction for charitable contributions for 1998.
b. What happens to any portion of the contribution not deductible in 1998?

43. Warbler Company is a wholesale grocery business. During 1998, it donated canned and dried food (held as inventory) to the local Goodwill branch. The basis of the food is $15,000, and it has a fair market value of $16,500. Based on the following assumptions, what amount qualifies as a charitable contribution?
    a. Warbler Company is a sole proprietorship.
    b. Warbler Company is a regular corporation.

44. During 1998, Raven Corporation had net income from operations of $200,000. In addition, Raven received dividends in the following amounts: $10,000 from Flicker Corporation and $20,000 from Blackbird Corporation. Raven owns 14% of the stock of Flicker and 40% of the stock of Blackbird. Determine Raven Corporation's dividends received deduction for 1998.

45. In each of the following independent situations, determine the dividends received deduction. Assume that none of the corporate shareholders owns 20% or more of the stock in the corporation paying the dividends.

	Gold Corporation	Silver Corporation	Rust Corporation
Income from operations	$ 700,000	$ 800,000	$ 700,000
Expenses of operations	(600,000)	(900,000)	(740,000)
Qualifying dividends	100,000	200,000	200,000

46. In each of the following independent situations, determine the corporation's income tax liability. Assume that all corporations use a calendar year for tax purposes and that the tax year involved is 1998.

	Taxable Income
Peacock Corporation	$ 60,000
Sparrow Corporation	80,000
Robin Corporation	200,000
Nighthawk Corporation	1,000,000
Jay Corporation (a qualified personal service corporation)	40,000

47. Using the following legend, classify each statement accordingly:

Legend

I	=	Applies to the income taxation of individuals.
C	=	Applies to the income taxation of regular corporations.
B	=	Applies to the income taxation of both individuals and regular corporations.
N	=	Applies to the income taxation of neither individuals nor regular corporations.

   a. Net capital losses can be carried back.
   b. Net capital losses can be carried over indefinitely.
   c. Net capital losses can offset other income.
   d. Net long-term capital gains can be taxed at a rate in excess of 20%.
   e. A cash basis taxpayer cannot deduct charitable contributions until the year of payment.
   f. A dividends received deduction may be available.
   g. The application of § 1250 (the recapture of depreciation claimed on certain real property) may yield less ordinary income.
   h. The concept of adjusted gross income (AGI) is relevant.
   i. Percentage limitations do not restrict the amount of charitable deductions that can be claimed in any one tax year.
   j. Casualty losses are deductible in full.
   k. Tax rates are progressive.

48. Edna, Kara, and Wade form Ivory Corporation with the following investments:

	Basis	Fair Market Value	Number of Shares Issued
From Edna— Cash	$150,000	$150,000	150
From Kara— Land	150,000	180,000	135
From Wade— Services		15,000	15

In addition to stock, Kara received $45,000 in cash from the corporation. Wade received his 15 shares for performing legal and accounting services in forming the corporation. Assume each share of Ivory stock is worth $1,000.
  a. How much gain (or loss) must Kara recognize?
  b. What basis will Kara have in the stock?
  c. What basis will Ivory Corporation have in the land?
  d. How much gain, if any, must Wade recognize?
  e. What basis will Wade have in the stock?

49. Zina and Walter form the Amber Corporation with the following investments:

	Basis	Fair Market Value	Number of Shares Issued
From Zina— Cash	$200,000	$200,000	200
From Walter— Land	250,000	230,000	200

In addition to stock, Walter received $30,000 in cash. Assume each share of Amber stock is worth $1,000.
  a. How much gain (or loss) must Walter recognize?
  b. What basis will Walter have in the stock?
  c. What basis will Amber Corporation have in the land?

50. Jane, the sole shareholder of Plover Corporation, has a basis of $20,000 in her stock investment. At a time when Plover Corporation has E & P of $14,000, it distributes cash of $30,000 to Jane. What are the tax consequences to Jane of the $30,000 distribution?

51. The stock of Sandpiper Corporation is held equally by Russ and Erlyne. The shareholders would like to receive, as a dividend, value of $100,000 each. The corporation has the following assets it can spare:

Asset	Adjusted Basis to Sandpiper Corporation	Fair Market Value
Land (parcel A)	$ 60,000	$100,000
Land (parcel B)	130,000	100,000

Both assets are held as investments. Sandpiper Corporation has a capital loss carryover from the previous year of $10,000 and has accumulated E & P in excess of $1 million.
    Russ and Erlyne have come to you for advice. Suggest an attractive tax plan to carry out what the parties want. Write a letter (addressed to Sandpiper Corporation at P.O. Box 1150, St. Louis, MO 63130) describing your plan and its tax consequences.

52. In the current year, Shearwater Corporation is liquidated under the general rules of § 331. The company distributes its only asset (land with a fair market value of $100,000 and adjusted basis of $20,000) to Oscar, who holds all of the Shearwater stock as an

investment. Oscar's basis in the Shearwater stock is $60,000. Shearwater Corporation has E & P of $10,000.

a. What are the amount and character of the gain or loss recognized by Oscar upon receiving the land in exchange for the stock?

b. What is Oscar's basis in the land?

c. Is there any tax effect to Shearwater Corporation? Explain.

53. Ten years ago, Albatross Corporation purchased all of the stock of Kingbird Corporation for $100,000. In the current year, Kingbird has a basis in its assets of $300,000 and a fair market value of $400,000. Albatross liquidates Kingbird Corporation and receives all of its assets. The exception to the carryover basis rule does not apply.

a. Does Albatross Corporation recognize any gain as a result of the liquidation?

b. What is Albatross Corporation's basis for the assets it receives from Kingbird Corporation?

54. During 1998, Fuchsia (a calendar year, accrual basis S corporation) had the following transactions:

Sales	$900,000
Cost of goods sold	600,000
Depletion deduction from an investment in a gas well	12,000
Charitable contributions	9,000
Interest on City of San Diego bonds	22,000
Advertising expense	3,000
Foreign tax credit	1,200
Long-term capital gain	6,500
Employee salaries	80,000

a. Determine Fuchsia Corporation's separately stated items for 1998.

b. Determine Fuchsia Corporation's taxable income for 1998.

55. Julius Walker owns all of the stock of Mockingbird Corporation, a calendar year S corporation. For calendar year 1998, Mockingbird anticipates an operating loss of $20,000 and could, if deemed worthwhile, sell a stock investment that would generate a $3,000 long-term capital loss. Julius has an adjusted basis of $5,000 in the Mockingbird stock. He anticipates no capital asset transactions and expects to be in the 36% tax bracket in 1998.

a. Can you recommend a course of action that can save Julius taxes for 1998?

b. Write a letter to Julius explaining your recommendations. Julius's address is Box 429, Normal, AL 35762.

56. In 1998, Heron Corporation (a calendar year S corporation) had an NOL of $73,000. Otto, a calendar year individual, held stock in Heron Corporation as follows: 40% for 200 days and 60% for 165 days. Based on these facts, what is Otto's loss pass-through for 1998?

57. Sam, Bob, and Clara form the Beige Partnership on January 1, 1998. In exchange for a 30% capital interest, Sam transfers property (basis of $14,000, fair market value of $25,000) subject to a liability of $10,000. The liability is assumed by the partnership. Bob transfers property (basis of $24,000, fair market value of $15,000) for a 30% capital interest, and Clara transfers cash of $20,000 for the remaining 40% capital interest.

a. How much gain must Sam recognize on the transfer?

b. What is Sam's basis in his partnership interest?

c. How much loss may Bob recognize on the transfer?

d. What is Bob's basis in his partnership interest?

e. What is Clara's basis in her partnership interest?

f. What basis will the Beige Partnership have in the property transferred by Sam? The property transferred by Bob?

g. What would be the tax consequences to Sam if the basis of the property he contributed is only $9,000?

58. As of January 1, 1997, Victor had a basis of $26,000 in his 25% capital interest in the Gray Partnership. He and the partnership use the calendar year for tax purposes. The partnership incurred an operating loss of $120,000 for 1997 and a profit of $80,000 for 1998.
    a. How much, if any, loss may Victor recognize for 1997?
    b. How much income must Victor recognize for 1998?
    c. What basis will Victor have in his partnership interest as of January 1, 1998?
    d. What basis will Victor have in his partnership interest as of January 1, 1999?
    e. What year-end tax planning would you suggest to ensure that a partner could deduct all of his or her share of any partnership losses?

59. Sarah owns a 51% interest in the capital and profits of the Rose Partnership. In 1997, Sarah sells property (adjusted basis of $120,000) to the partnership for the property's fair market value of $109,000. In 1998, Rose Partnership sells the same property to an outsider for $112,000.
    a. What are Sarah's tax consequences on the 1997 sale?
    b. What are Rose Partnership's tax consequences on the 1998 sale?

RESEARCH PROBLEMS

Note: Use the **RIA OnPoint System 4 Student Version CD-ROM,** *which is available to accompany this text, in preparing solutions to the Research Problems. Alternatively, tax research materials found in a standard tax library can be used.*

Research Problem 1.   Rod and Eve are equal shareholders in Rust Company, a C corporation. They are also the key employees of Rust. The company is a wholesaler of costume jewelry. Because the business is very competitive, Rod and Eve must frequently entertain department store buyers.

When Rod and Eve realize that they are in a higher income tax bracket than Rust, they enact, on behalf of Rust, the following corporate resolution: "All entertainment expenses shall be the responsibility of the employee doing the entertaining and are not reimbursable."

Consequently, Rod and Eve deduct the entertainment expenses for the year on their individual income tax returns. Rust Company claims none of these expenses and does not reimburse Rod and Eve.

Have the parties acted properly? Explain.

Research Problem 2.   Leonora incorporates her retail clothing business. She transfers all her business assets (total basis of $100,000 and fair market value of $95,000) along with business liabilities of $10,000 and a personal note in the amount of $15,000 to the corporation for 100% of its stock. The note is for money borrowed from the bank six months before incorporation to finance improvements on her home. What are the tax consequences of the transfer?

Research Problem 3.   Several years ago, Mike incorporated his sole proprietorship and immediately made an election under Subchapter S. Mike lives in El Paso, Texas, and is married to Consuela, a citizen of Mexico. Since Consuela's father is ill and requires constant care, she lives with him across the border in Ciudad Juarez.

This year, the IRS audits the Forms 1120S filed by Mike's corporation and disallows its Subchapter S status. What could be the cause of the disallowance?

Research Problem 4.   Ms. Marge Bland and a number of her friends want to diversify their investment portfolios. With this in mind, they form a partnership to which they transfer appreciated securities. Each transferor receives an interest in the new partnership proportionate to the value of the securities transferred. Will the creation of the partnership be tax-free? Why or why not?
    a. Prepare a letter to Ms. Bland giving your advice. Ms. Bland's address is 349 Azalea Drive, Athens, GA 30602.
    b. Prepare a memo for your firm's client files.

APPENDIX A

Tax Rate Schedules and Tables

1997 Tax Rate Schedules

Single—Schedule X

If taxable income is: Over—	But not over—	The tax is:	of the amount over—
$0	$ 24,650	. . . . . . .15%	$0
24,650	59,750	$3,697.50 + 28%	24,650
59,750	124,650	13,525.50 + 31%	59,750
124,650	271,050	33,644.50 + 36%	124,650
271,050	. . . . . .	86,348.50 + 39.6%	271,050

Head of household—Schedule Z

If taxable income is: Over—	But not over—	The tax is:	of the amount over—
$0	$ 33,050	. . . . . . .15%	$0
33,050	85,350	$4,957.50 + 28%	33,050
85,350	138,200	19,601.50 + 31%	85,350
138,200	271,050	35,985.00 + 36%	138,200
271,050	. . . . . .	83,811.00 + 39.6%	271,050

Married filing jointly or Qualifying widow(er)—Schedule Y–1

If taxable income is: Over—	But not over—	The tax is:	of the amount over—
$0	$ 41,200	. . . . . . .15%	$0
41,200	99,600	$6,180.00 + 28%	41,200
99,600	151,750	22,532.00 + 31%	99,600
151,750	271,050	38,698.50 + 36%	151,750
271,050	. . . . . .	81,646.50 + 39.6%	271,050

Married filing separately—Schedule Y–2

If taxable income is: Over—	But not over—	The tax is:	of the amount over—
$0	$ 20,600	. . . . . . .15%	$0
20,600	49,800	$3,090.00 + 28%	20,600
49,800	75,875	11,266.00 + 31%	49,800
75,875	135,525	19,349.25 + 36%	75,875
135,525	. . . . . .	40,823.25 + 39.6%	135,525

1998 Tax Rate Schedules

Single—Schedule X

If taxable income is: Over—	But not over—	The tax is:	of the amount over—
$0	$ 25,350	. . . . . . .15%	$0
25,350	61,400	$3,802.50 + 28%	25,350
61,400	128,100	13,896.50 + 31%	61,400
128,100	278,450	34,573.50 + 36%	128,100
278,450	. . . . . .	88,699.50 + 39.6%	278,450

Head of household—Schedule Z

If taxable income is: Over—	But not over—	The tax is:	of the amount over—
$0	$ 33,950	. . . . . . .15%	$0
33,950	87,700	$5,092.50 + 28%	33,950
87,700	142,000	20,142.50 + 31%	87,700
142,000	278,450	36,975.50 + 36%	142,000
278,450	. . . . . .	86,097.50 + 39.6%	278,450

Married filing jointly or Qualifying widow(er)—Schedule Y–1

If taxable income is: Over—	But not over—	The tax is:	of the amount over—
$0	$ 42,350	. . . . . . .15%	$0
42,350	102,300	$6,352.50 + 28%	42,350
102,300	155,950	23,138.50 + 31%	102,300
155,950	278,450	39,770.00 + 36%	155,950
278,450	. . . . . .	83,870.00 + 39.6%	278,450

Married filing separately—Schedule Y–2

If taxable income is: Over—	But not over—	The tax is:	of the amount over—
$0	$ 21,175	. . . . . . .15%	$0
21,175	51,150	$3,176.25 + 28%	21,175
51,150	77,975	11,569.25 + 31%	51,150
77,975	139,225	19,885.00 + 36%	77,975
139,225	. . . . . .	41,935.00 + 39.6%	139,225

1997 Tax Table

Use if your taxable income is less than $100,000.
If $100,000 or more, use the Tax Rate Schedules.

Example. Mr. and Mrs. Brown are filing a joint return. Their taxable income on line 38 of Form 1040 is $25,300. First, they find the $25,300–25,350 income line. Next, they find the column for married filing jointly and read down the column. The amount shown where the income line and filing status column meet is $3,799. This is the tax amount they should enter on line 39 of their Form 1040.

Sample Table

At least	But less than	Single	Married filing jointly *	Married filing separately	Head of a household
			Your tax is—		
25,200	25,250	3,859	3,784	4,385	3,784
25,250	25,300	3,873	3,791	4,399	3,791
25,300	25,350	3,887	(3,799)	4,413	3,799
25,350	25,400	3,901	3,806	4,427	3,806

If line 38 (taxable income) is— At least	But less than	And you are— Single	Married filing jointly *	Married filing separately	Head of a household
		Your tax is—			
$0	$5	$0	$0	$0	$0
5	15	2	2	2	2
15	25	3	3	3	3
25	50	6	6	6	6
50	75	9	9	9	9
75	100	13	13	13	13
100	125	17	17	17	17
125	150	21	21	21	21
150	175	24	24	24	24
175	200	28	28	28	28
200	225	32	32	32	32
225	250	36	36	36	36
250	275	39	39	39	39
275	300	43	43	43	43
300	325	47	47	47	47
325	350	51	51	51	51
350	375	54	54	54	54
375	400	58	58	58	58
400	425	62	62	62	62
425	450	66	66	66	66
450	475	69	69	69	69
475	500	73	73	73	73
500	525	77	77	77	77
525	550	81	81	81	81
550	575	84	84	84	84
575	600	88	88	88	88
600	625	92	92	92	92
625	650	96	96	96	96
650	675	99	99	99	99
675	700	103	103	103	103
700	725	107	107	107	107
725	750	111	111	111	111
750	775	114	114	114	114
775	800	118	118	118	118
800	825	122	122	122	122
825	850	126	126	126	126
850	875	129	129	129	129
875	900	133	133	133	133
900	925	137	137	137	137
925	950	141	141	141	141
950	975	144	144	144	144
975	1,000	148	148	148	148
1,000					
1,000	1,025	152	152	152	152
1,025	1,050	156	156	156	156
1,050	1,075	159	159	159	159
1,075	1,100	163	163	163	163
1,100	1,125	167	167	167	167
1,125	1,150	171	171	171	171
1,150	1,175	174	174	174	174
1,175	1,200	178	178	178	178
1,200	1,225	182	182	182	182
1,225	1,250	186	186	186	186
1,250	1,275	189	189	189	189
1,275	1,300	193	193	193	193

If line 38 (taxable income) is— At least	But less than	And you are— Single	Married filing jointly *	Married filing separately	Head of a household
		Your tax is—			
1,300	1,325	197	197	197	197
1,325	1,350	201	201	201	201
1,350	1,375	204	204	204	204
1,375	1,400	208	208	208	208
1,400	1,425	212	212	212	212
1,425	1,450	216	216	216	216
1,450	1,475	219	219	219	219
1,475	1,500	223	223	223	223
1,500	1,525	227	227	227	227
1,525	1,550	231	231	231	231
1,550	1,575	234	234	234	234
1,575	1,600	238	238	238	238
1,600	1,625	242	242	242	242
1,625	1,650	246	246	246	246
1,650	1,675	249	249	249	249
1,675	1,700	253	253	253	253
1,700	1,725	257	257	257	257
1,725	1,750	261	261	261	261
1,750	1,775	264	264	264	264
1,775	1,800	268	268	268	268
1,800	1,825	272	272	272	272
1,825	1,850	276	276	276	276
1,850	1,875	279	279	279	279
1,875	1,900	283	283	283	283
1,900	1,925	287	287	287	287
1,925	1,950	291	291	291	291
1,950	1,975	294	294	294	294
1,975	2,000	298	298	298	298
2,000					
2,000	2,025	302	302	302	302
2,025	2,050	306	306	306	306
2,050	2,075	309	309	309	309
2,075	2,100	313	313	313	313
2,100	2,125	317	317	317	317
2,125	2,150	321	321	321	321
2,150	2,175	324	324	324	324
2,175	2,200	328	328	328	328
2,200	2,225	332	332	332	332
2,225	2,250	336	336	336	336
2,250	2,275	339	339	339	339
2,275	2,300	343	343	343	343
2,300	2,325	347	347	347	347
2,325	2,350	351	351	351	351
2,350	2,375	354	354	354	354
2,375	2,400	358	358	358	358
2,400	2,425	362	362	362	362
2,425	2,450	366	366	366	366
2,450	2,475	369	369	369	369
2,475	2,500	373	373	373	373
2,500	2,525	377	377	377	377
2,525	2,550	381	381	381	381
2,550	2,575	384	384	384	384
2,575	2,600	388	388	388	388
2,600	2,625	392	392	392	392
2,625	2,650	396	396	396	396
2,650	2,675	399	399	399	399
2,675	2,700	403	403	403	403

If line 38 (taxable income) is— At least	But less than	And you are— Single	Married filing jointly *	Married filing separately	Head of a household
		Your tax is—			
2,700	2,725	407	407	407	407
2,725	2,750	411	411	411	411
2,750	2,775	414	414	414	414
2,775	2,800	418	418	418	418
2,800	2,825	422	422	422	422
2,825	2,850	426	426	426	426
2,850	2,875	429	429	429	429
2,875	2,900	433	433	433	433
2,900	2,925	437	437	437	437
2,925	2,950	441	441	441	441
2,950	2,975	444	444	444	444
2,975	3,000	448	448	448	448
3,000					
3,000	3,050	454	454	454	454
3,050	3,100	461	461	461	461
3,100	3,150	469	469	469	469
3,150	3,200	476	476	476	476
3,200	3,250	484	484	484	484
3,250	3,300	491	491	491	491
3,300	3,350	499	499	499	499
3,350	3,400	506	506	506	506
3,400	3,450	514	514	514	514
3,450	3,500	521	521	521	521
3,500	3,550	529	529	529	529
3,550	3,600	536	536	536	536
3,600	3,650	544	544	544	544
3,650	3,700	551	551	551	551
3,700	3,750	559	559	559	559
3,750	3,800	566	566	566	566
3,800	3,850	574	574	574	574
3,850	3,900	581	581	581	581
3,900	3,950	589	589	589	589
3,950	4,000	596	596	596	596
4,000					
4,000	4,050	604	604	604	604
4,050	4,100	611	611	611	611
4,100	4,150	619	619	619	619
4,150	4,200	626	626	626	626
4,200	4,250	634	634	634	634
4,250	4,300	641	641	641	641
4,300	4,350	649	649	649	649
4,350	4,400	656	656	656	656
4,400	4,450	664	664	664	664
4,450	4,500	671	671	671	671
4,500	4,550	679	679	679	679
4,550	4,600	686	686	686	686
4,600	4,650	694	694	694	694
4,650	4,700	701	701	701	701
4,700	4,750	709	709	709	709
4,750	4,800	716	716	716	716
4,800	4,850	724	724	724	724
4,850	4,900	731	731	731	731
4,900	4,950	739	739	739	739
4,950	5,000	746	746	746	746

Continued on next page

* This column must also be used by a qualifying widow(er).

1997 Tax Table—*Continued*

If line 38 (taxable income) is—		And you are—			
At least	But less than	Single	Married filing jointly *	Married filing separately	Head of a household
		Your tax is—			

5,000

At least	But less than	Single	Married filing jointly *	Married filing separately	Head of household
5,000	5,050	754	754	754	754
5,050	5,100	761	761	761	761
5,100	5,150	769	769	769	769
5,150	5,200	776	776	776	776
5,200	5,250	784	784	784	784
5,250	5,300	791	791	791	791
5,300	5,350	799	799	799	799
5,350	5,400	806	806	806	806
5,400	5,450	814	814	814	814
5,450	5,500	821	821	821	821
5,500	5,550	829	829	829	829
5,550	5,600	836	836	836	836
5,600	5,650	844	844	844	844
5,650	5,700	851	851	851	851
5,700	5,750	859	859	859	859
5,750	5,800	866	866	866	866
5,800	5,850	874	874	874	874
5,850	5,900	881	881	881	881
5,900	5,950	889	889	889	889
5,950	6,000	896	896	896	896

6,000

At least	But less than	Single	Married filing jointly *	Married filing separately	Head of household
6,000	6,050	904	904	904	904
6,050	6,100	911	911	911	911
6,100	6,150	919	919	919	919
6,150	6,200	926	926	926	926
6,200	6,250	934	934	934	934
6,250	6,300	941	941	941	941
6,300	6,350	949	949	949	949
6,350	6,400	956	956	956	956
6,400	6,450	964	964	964	964
6,450	6,500	971	971	971	971
6,500	6,550	979	979	979	979
6,550	6,600	986	986	986	986
6,600	6,650	994	994	994	994
6,650	6,700	1,001	1,001	1,001	1,001
6,700	6,750	1,009	1,009	1,009	1,009
6,750	6,800	1,016	1,016	1,016	1,016
6,800	6,850	1,024	1,024	1,024	1,024
6,850	6,900	1,031	1,031	1,031	1,031
6,900	6,950	1,039	1,039	1,039	1,039
6,950	7,000	1,046	1,046	1,046	1,046

7,000

At least	But less than	Single	Married filing jointly *	Married filing separately	Head of household
7,000	7,050	1,054	1,054	1,054	1,054
7,050	7,100	1,061	1,061	1,061	1,061
7,100	7,150	1,069	1,069	1,069	1,069
7,150	7,200	1,076	1,076	1,076	1,076
7,200	7,250	1,084	1,084	1,084	1,084
7,250	7,300	1,091	1,091	1,091	1,091
7,300	7,350	1,099	1,099	1,099	1,099
7,350	7,400	1,106	1,106	1,106	1,106
7,400	7,450	1,114	1,114	1,114	1,114
7,450	7,500	1,121	1,121	1,121	1,121
7,500	7,550	1,129	1,129	1,129	1,129
7,550	7,600	1,136	1,136	1,136	1,136
7,600	7,650	1,144	1,144	1,144	1,144
7,650	7,700	1,151	1,151	1,151	1,151
7,700	7,750	1,159	1,159	1,159	1,159
7,750	7,800	1,166	1,166	1,166	1,166
7,800	7,850	1,174	1,174	1,174	1,174
7,850	7,900	1,181	1,181	1,181	1,181
7,900	7,950	1,189	1,189	1,189	1,189
7,950	8,000	1,196	1,196	1,196	1,196

8,000

At least	But less than	Single	Married filing jointly *	Married filing separately	Head of household
8,000	8,050	1,204	1,204	1,204	1,204
8,050	8,100	1,211	1,211	1,211	1,211
8,100	8,150	1,219	1,219	1,219	1,219
8,150	8,200	1,226	1,226	1,226	1,226
8,200	8,250	1,234	1,234	1,234	1,234
8,250	8,300	1,241	1,241	1,241	1,241
8,300	8,350	1,249	1,249	1,249	1,249
8,350	8,400	1,256	1,256	1,256	1,256
8,400	8,450	1,264	1,264	1,264	1,264
8,450	8,500	1,271	1,271	1,271	1,271
8,500	8,550	1,279	1,279	1,279	1,279
8,550	8,600	1,286	1,286	1,286	1,286
8,600	8,650	1,294	1,294	1,294	1,294
8,650	8,700	1,301	1,301	1,301	1,301
8,700	8,750	1,309	1,309	1,309	1,309
8,750	8,800	1,316	1,316	1,316	1,316
8,800	8,850	1,324	1,324	1,324	1,324
8,850	8,900	1,331	1,331	1,331	1,331
8,900	8,950	1,339	1,339	1,339	1,339
8,950	9,000	1,346	1,346	1,346	1,346

9,000

At least	But less than	Single	Married filing jointly *	Married filing separately	Head of household
9,000	9,050	1,354	1,354	1,354	1,354
9,050	9,100	1,361	1,361	1,361	1,361
9,100	9,150	1,369	1,369	1,369	1,369
9,150	9,200	1,376	1,376	1,376	1,376
9,200	9,250	1,384	1,384	1,384	1,384
9,250	9,300	1,391	1,391	1,391	1,391
9,300	9,350	1,399	1,399	1,399	1,399
9,350	9,400	1,406	1,406	1,406	1,406
9,400	9,450	1,414	1,414	1,414	1,414
9,450	9,500	1,421	1,421	1,421	1,421
9,500	9,550	1,429	1,429	1,429	1,429
9,550	9,600	1,436	1,436	1,436	1,436
9,600	9,650	1,444	1,444	1,444	1,444
9,650	9,700	1,451	1,451	1,451	1,451
9,700	9,750	1,459	1,459	1,459	1,459
9,750	9,800	1,466	1,466	1,466	1,466
9,800	9,850	1,474	1,474	1,474	1,474
9,850	9,900	1,481	1,481	1,481	1,481
9,900	9,950	1,489	1,489	1,489	1,489
9,950	10,000	1,496	1,496	1,496	1,496

10,000

At least	But less than	Single	Married filing jointly *	Married filing separately	Head of household
10,000	10,050	1,504	1,504	1,504	1,504
10,050	10,100	1,511	1,511	1,511	1,511
10,100	10,150	1,519	1,519	1,519	1,519
10,150	10,200	1,526	1,526	1,526	1,526
10,200	10,250	1,534	1,534	1,534	1,534
10,250	10,300	1,541	1,541	1,541	1,541
10,300	10,350	1,549	1,549	1,549	1,549
10,350	10,400	1,556	1,556	1,556	1,556
10,400	10,450	1,564	1,564	1,564	1,564
10,450	10,500	1,571	1,571	1,571	1,571
10,500	10,550	1,579	1,579	1,579	1,579
10,550	10,600	1,586	1,586	1,586	1,586
10,600	10,650	1,594	1,594	1,594	1,594
10,650	10,700	1,601	1,601	1,601	1,601
10,700	10,750	1,609	1,609	1,609	1,609
10,750	10,800	1,616	1,616	1,616	1,616
10,800	10,850	1,624	1,624	1,624	1,624
10,850	10,900	1,631	1,631	1,631	1,631
10,900	10,950	1,639	1,639	1,639	1,639
10,950	11,000	1,646	1,646	1,646	1,646

11,000

At least	But less than	Single	Married filing jointly *	Married filing separately	Head of household
11,000	11,050	1,654	1,654	1,654	1,654
11,050	11,100	1,661	1,661	1,661	1,661
11,100	11,150	1,669	1,669	1,669	1,669
11,150	11,200	1,676	1,676	1,676	1,676
11,200	11,250	1,684	1,684	1,684	1,684
11,250	11,300	1,691	1,691	1,691	1,691
11,300	11,350	1,699	1,699	1,699	1,699
11,350	11,400	1,706	1,706	1,706	1,706
11,400	11,450	1,714	1,714	1,714	1,714
11,450	11,500	1,721	1,721	1,721	1,721
11,500	11,550	1,729	1,729	1,729	1,729
11,550	11,600	1,736	1,736	1,736	1,736
11,600	11,650	1,744	1,744	1,744	1,744
11,650	11,700	1,751	1,751	1,751	1,751
11,700	11,750	1,759	1,759	1,759	1,759
11,750	11,800	1,766	1,766	1,766	1,766
11,800	11,850	1,774	1,774	1,774	1,774
11,850	11,900	1,781	1,781	1,781	1,781
11,900	11,950	1,789	1,789	1,789	1,789
11,950	12,000	1,796	1,796	1,796	1,796

12,000

At least	But less than	Single	Married filing jointly *	Married filing separately	Head of household
12,000	12,050	1,804	1,804	1,804	1,804
12,050	12,100	1,811	1,811	1,811	1,811
12,100	12,150	1,819	1,819	1,819	1,819
12,150	12,200	1,826	1,826	1,826	1,826
12,200	12,250	1,834	1,834	1,834	1,834
12,250	12,300	1,841	1,841	1,841	1,841
12,300	12,350	1,849	1,849	1,849	1,849
12,350	12,400	1,856	1,856	1,856	1,856
12,400	12,450	1,864	1,864	1,864	1,864
12,450	12,500	1,871	1,871	1,871	1,871
12,500	12,550	1,879	1,879	1,879	1,879
12,550	12,600	1,886	1,886	1,886	1,886
12,600	12,650	1,894	1,894	1,894	1,894
12,650	12,700	1,901	1,901	1,901	1,901
12,700	12,750	1,909	1,909	1,909	1,909
12,750	12,800	1,916	1,916	1,916	1,916
12,800	12,850	1,924	1,924	1,924	1,924
12,850	12,900	1,931	1,931	1,931	1,931
12,900	12,950	1,939	1,939	1,939	1,939
12,950	13,000	1,946	1,946	1,946	1,946

13,000

At least	But less than	Single	Married filing jointly *	Married filing separately	Head of household
13,000	13,050	1,954	1,954	1,954	1,954
13,050	13,100	1,961	1,961	1,961	1,961
13,100	13,150	1,969	1,969	1,969	1,969
13,150	13,200	1,976	1,976	1,976	1,976
13,200	13,250	1,984	1,984	1,984	1,984
13,250	13,300	1,991	1,991	1,991	1,991
13,300	13,350	1,999	1,999	1,999	1,999
13,350	13,400	2,006	2,006	2,006	2,006
13,400	13,450	2,014	2,014	2,014	2,014
13,450	13,500	2,021	2,021	2,021	2,021
13,500	13,550	2,029	2,029	2,029	2,029
13,550	13,600	2,036	2,036	2,036	2,036
13,600	13,650	2,044	2,044	2,044	2,044
13,650	13,700	2,051	2,051	2,051	2,051
13,700	13,750	2,059	2,059	2,059	2,059
13,750	13,800	2,066	2,066	2,066	2,066
13,800	13,850	2,074	2,074	2,074	2,074
13,850	13,900	2,081	2,081	2,081	2,081
13,900	13,950	2,089	2,089	2,089	2,089
13,950	14,000	2,096	2,096	2,096	2,096

* This column must also be used by a qualifying widow(er).

Continued on next page

1997 Tax Table—*Continued*

14,000

If line 38 (taxable income) is— At least	But less than	Single	Married filing jointly *	Married filing separately	Head of a household
				Your tax is—	
14,000	14,050	2,104	2,104	2,104	2,104
14,050	14,100	2,111	2,111	2,111	2,111
14,100	14,150	2,119	2,119	2,119	2,119
14,150	14,200	2,126	2,126	2,126	2,126
14,200	14,250	2,134	2,134	2,134	2,134
14,250	14,300	2,141	2,141	2,141	2,141
14,300	14,350	2,149	2,149	2,149	2,149
14,350	14,400	2,156	2,156	2,156	2,156
14,400	14,450	2,164	2,164	2,164	2,164
14,450	14,500	2,171	2,171	2,171	2,171
14,500	14,550	2,179	2,179	2,179	2,179
14,550	14,600	2,186	2,186	2,186	2,186
14,600	14,650	2,194	2,194	2,194	2,194
14,650	14,700	2,201	2,201	2,201	2,201
14,700	14,750	2,209	2,209	2,209	2,209
14,750	14,800	2,216	2,216	2,216	2,216
14,800	14,850	2,224	2,224	2,224	2,224
14,850	14,900	2,231	2,231	2,231	2,231
14,900	14,950	2,239	2,239	2,239	2,239
14,950	15,000	2,246	2,246	2,246	2,246

15,000

At least	But less than	Single	Married filing jointly *	Married filing separately	Head of a household
15,000	15,050	2,254	2,254	2,254	2,254
15,050	15,100	2,261	2,261	2,261	2,261
15,100	15,150	2,269	2,269	2,269	2,269
15,150	15,200	2,276	2,276	2,276	2,276
15,200	15,250	2,284	2,284	2,284	2,284
15,250	15,300	2,291	2,291	2,291	2,291
15,300	15,350	2,299	2,299	2,299	2,299
15,350	15,400	2,306	2,306	2,306	2,306
15,400	15,450	2,314	2,314	2,314	2,314
15,450	15,500	2,321	2,321	2,321	2,321
15,500	15,550	2,329	2,329	2,329	2,329
15,550	15,600	2,336	2,336	2,336	2,336
15,600	15,650	2,344	2,344	2,344	2,344
15,650	15,700	2,351	2,351	2,351	2,351
15,700	15,750	2,359	2,359	2,359	2,359
15,750	15,800	2,366	2,366	2,366	2,366
15,800	15,850	2,374	2,374	2,374	2,374
15,850	15,900	2,381	2,381	2,381	2,381
15,900	15,950	2,389	2,389	2,389	2,389
15,950	16,000	2,396	2,396	2,396	2,396

16,000

At least	But less than	Single	Married filing jointly *	Married filing separately	Head of a household
16,000	16,050	2,404	2,404	2,404	2,404
16,050	16,100	2,411	2,411	2,411	2,411
16,100	16,150	2,419	2,419	2,419	2,419
16,150	16,200	2,426	2,426	2,426	2,426
16,200	16,250	2,434	2,434	2,434	2,434
16,250	16,300	2,441	2,441	2,441	2,441
16,300	16,350	2,449	2,449	2,449	2,449
16,350	16,400	2,456	2,456	2,456	2,456
16,400	16,450	2,464	2,464	2,464	2,464
16,450	16,500	2,471	2,471	2,471	2,471
16,500	16,550	2,479	2,479	2,479	2,479
16,550	16,600	2,486	2,486	2,486	2,486
16,600	16,650	2,494	2,494	2,494	2,494
16,650	16,700	2,501	2,501	2,501	2,501
16,700	16,750	2,509	2,509	2,509	2,509
16,750	16,800	2,516	2,516	2,516	2,516
16,800	16,850	2,524	2,524	2,524	2,524
16,850	16,900	2,531	2,531	2,531	2,531
16,900	16,950	2,539	2,539	2,539	2,539
16,950	17,000	2,546	2,546	2,546	2,546

17,000

At least	But less than	Single	Married filing jointly *	Married filing separately	Head of a household
17,000	17,050	2,554	2,554	2,554	2,554
17,050	17,100	2,561	2,561	2,561	2,561
17,100	17,150	2,569	2,569	2,569	2,569
17,150	17,200	2,576	2,576	2,576	2,576
17,200	17,250	2,584	2,584	2,584	2,584
17,250	17,300	2,591	2,591	2,591	2,591
17,300	17,350	2,599	2,599	2,599	2,599
17,350	17,400	2,606	2,606	2,606	2,606
17,400	17,450	2,614	2,614	2,614	2,614
17,450	17,500	2,621	2,621	2,621	2,621
17,500	17,550	2,629	2,629	2,629	2,629
17,550	17,600	2,636	2,636	2,636	2,636
17,600	17,650	2,644	2,644	2,644	2,644
17,650	17,700	2,651	2,651	2,651	2,651
17,700	17,750	2,659	2,659	2,659	2,659
17,750	17,800	2,666	2,666	2,666	2,666
17,800	17,850	2,674	2,674	2,674	2,674
17,850	17,900	2,681	2,681	2,681	2,681
17,900	17,950	2,689	2,689	2,689	2,689
17,950	18,000	2,696	2,696	2,696	2,696

18,000

At least	But less than	Single	Married filing jointly *	Married filing separately	Head of a household
18,000	18,050	2,704	2,704	2,704	2,704
18,050	18,100	2,711	2,711	2,711	2,711
18,100	18,150	2,719	2,719	2,719	2,719
18,150	18,200	2,726	2,726	2,726	2,726
18,200	18,250	2,734	2,734	2,734	2,734
18,250	18,300	2,741	2,741	2,741	2,741
18,300	18,350	2,749	2,749	2,749	2,749
18,350	18,400	2,756	2,756	2,756	2,756
18,400	18,450	2,764	2,764	2,764	2,764
18,450	18,500	2,771	2,771	2,771	2,771
18,500	18,550	2,779	2,779	2,779	2,779
18,550	18,600	2,786	2,786	2,786	2,786
18,600	18,650	2,794	2,794	2,794	2,794
18,650	18,700	2,801	2,801	2,801	2,801
18,700	18,750	2,809	2,809	2,809	2,809
18,750	18,800	2,816	2,816	2,816	2,816
18,800	18,850	2,824	2,824	2,824	2,824
18,850	18,900	2,831	2,831	2,831	2,831
18,900	18,950	2,839	2,839	2,839	2,839
18,950	19,000	2,846	2,846	2,846	2,846

19,000

At least	But less than	Single	Married filing jointly *	Married filing separately	Head of a household
19,000	19,050	2,854	2,854	2,854	2,854
19,050	19,100	2,861	2,861	2,861	2,861
19,100	19,150	2,869	2,869	2,869	2,869
19,150	19,200	2,876	2,876	2,876	2,876
19,200	19,250	2,884	2,884	2,884	2,884
19,250	19,300	2,891	2,891	2,891	2,891
19,300	19,350	2,899	2,899	2,899	2,899
19,350	19,400	2,906	2,906	2,906	2,906
19,400	19,450	2,914	2,914	2,914	2,914
19,450	19,500	2,921	2,921	2,921	2,921
19,500	19,550	2,929	2,929	2,929	2,929
19,550	19,600	2,936	2,936	2,936	2,936
19,600	19,650	2,944	2,944	2,944	2,944
19,650	19,700	2,951	2,951	2,951	2,951
19,700	19,750	2,959	2,959	2,959	2,959
19,750	19,800	2,966	2,966	2,966	2,966
19,800	19,850	2,974	2,974	2,974	2,974
19,850	19,900	2,981	2,981	2,981	2,981
19,900	19,950	2,989	2,989	2,989	2,989
19,950	20,000	2,996	2,996	2,996	2,996

20,000

At least	But less than	Single	Married filing jointly *	Married filing separately	Head of a household
20,000	20,050	3,004	3,004	3,004	3,004
20,050	20,100	3,011	3,011	3,011	3,011
20,100	20,150	3,019	3,019	3,019	3,019
20,150	20,200	3,026	3,026	3,026	3,026
20,200	20,250	3,034	3,034	3,034	3,034
20,250	20,300	3,041	3,041	3,041	3,041
20,300	20,350	3,049	3,049	3,049	3,049
20,350	20,400	3,056	3,056	3,056	3,056
20,400	20,450	3,064	3,064	3,064	3,064
20,450	20,500	3,071	3,071	3,071	3,071
20,500	20,550	3,079	3,079	3,079	3,079
20,550	20,600	3,086	3,086	3,086	3,086
20,600	20,650	3,094	3,094	3,097	3,094
20,650	20,700	3,101	3,101	3,111	3,101
20,700	20,750	3,109	3,109	3,125	3,109
20,750	20,800	3,116	3,116	3,139	3,116
20,800	20,850	3,124	3,124	3,153	3,124
20,850	20,900	3,131	3,131	3,167	3,131
20,900	20,950	3,139	3,139	3,181	3,139
20,950	21,000	3,146	3,146	3,195	3,146

21,000

At least	But less than	Single	Married filing jointly *	Married filing separately	Head of a household
21,000	21,050	3,154	3,154	3,209	3,154
21,050	21,100	3,161	3,161	3,223	3,161
21,100	21,150	3,169	3,169	3,237	3,169
21,150	21,200	3,176	3,176	3,251	3,176
21,200	21,250	3,184	3,184	3,265	3,184
21,250	21,300	3,191	3,191	3,279	3,191
21,300	21,350	3,199	3,199	3,293	3,199
21,350	21,400	3,206	3,206	3,307	3,206
21,400	21,450	3,214	3,214	3,321	3,214
21,450	21,500	3,221	3,221	3,335	3,221
21,500	21,550	3,229	3,229	3,349	3,229
21,550	21,600	3,236	3,236	3,363	3,236
21,600	21,650	3,244	3,244	3,377	3,244
21,650	21,700	3,251	3,251	3,391	3,251
21,700	21,750	3,259	3,259	3,405	3,259
21,750	21,800	3,266	3,266	3,419	3,266
21,800	21,850	3,274	3,274	3,433	3,274
21,850	21,900	3,281	3,281	3,447	3,281
21,900	21,950	3,289	3,289	3,461	3,289
21,950	22,000	3,296	3,296	3,475	3,296

22,000

At least	But less than	Single	Married filing jointly *	Married filing separately	Head of a household
22,000	22,050	3,304	3,304	3,489	3,304
22,050	22,100	3,311	3,311	3,503	3,311
22,100	22,150	3,319	3,319	3,517	3,319
22,150	22,200	3,326	3,326	3,531	3,326
22,200	22,250	3,334	3,334	3,545	3,334
22,250	22,300	3,341	3,341	3,559	3,341
22,300	22,350	3,349	3,349	3,573	3,349
22,350	22,400	3,356	3,356	3,587	3,356
22,400	22,450	3,364	3,364	3,601	3,364
22,450	22,500	3,371	3,371	3,615	3,371
22,500	22,550	3,379	3,379	3,629	3,379
22,550	22,600	3,386	3,386	3,643	3,386
22,600	22,650	3,394	3,394	3,657	3,394
22,650	22,700	3,401	3,401	3,671	3,401
22,700	22,750	3,409	3,409	3,685	3,409
22,750	22,800	3,416	3,416	3,699	3,416
22,800	22,850	3,424	3,424	3,713	3,424
22,850	22,900	3,431	3,431	3,727	3,431
22,900	22,950	3,439	3,439	3,741	3,439
22,950	23,000	3,446	3,446	3,755	3,446

* This column must also be used by a qualifying widow(er).

Continued on next page

1997 Tax Table—Continued

If line 38 (taxable income) is—		And you are—			
At least	But less than	Single	Married filing jointly *	Married filing separately	Head of a household
		Your tax is—			
23,000					
23,000	23,050	3,454	3,454	3,769	3,454
23,050	23,100	3,461	3,461	3,783	3,461
23,100	23,150	3,469	3,469	3,797	3,469
23,150	23,200	3,476	3,476	3,811	3,476
23,200	23,250	3,484	3,484	3,825	3,484
23,250	23,300	3,491	3,491	3,839	3,491
23,300	23,350	3,499	3,499	3,853	3,499
23,350	23,400	3,506	3,506	3,867	3,506
23,400	23,450	3,514	3,514	3,881	3,514
23,450	23,500	3,521	3,521	3,895	3,521
23,500	23,550	3,529	3,529	3,909	3,529
23,550	23,600	3,536	3,536	3,923	3,536
23,600	23,650	3,544	3,544	3,937	3,544
23,650	23,700	3,551	3,551	3,951	3,551
23,700	23,750	3,559	3,559	3,965	3,559
23,750	23,800	3,566	3,566	3,979	3,566
23,800	23,850	3,574	3,574	3,993	3,574
23,850	23,900	3,581	3,581	4,007	3,581
23,900	23,950	3,589	3,589	4,021	3,589
23,950	24,000	3,596	3,596	4,035	3,596
24,000					
24,000	24,050	3,604	3,604	4,049	3,604
24,050	24,100	3,611	3,611	4,063	3,611
24,100	24,150	3,619	3,619	4,077	3,619
24,150	24,200	3,626	3,626	4,091	3,626
24,200	24,250	3,634	3,634	4,105	3,634
24,250	24,300	3,641	3,641	4,119	3,641
24,300	24,350	3,649	3,649	4,133	3,649
24,350	24,400	3,656	3,656	4,147	3,656
24,400	24,450	3,664	3,664	4,161	3,664
24,450	24,500	3,671	3,671	4,175	3,671
24,500	24,550	3,679	3,679	4,189	3,679
24,550	24,600	3,686	3,686	4,203	3,686
24,600	24,650	3,694	3,694	4,217	3,694
24,650	24,700	3,705	3,701	4,231	3,701
24,700	24,750	3,719	3,709	4,245	3,709
24,750	24,800	3,733	3,716	4,259	3,716
24,800	24,850	3,747	3,724	4,273	3,724
24,850	24,900	3,761	3,731	4,287	3,731
24,900	24,950	3,775	3,739	4,301	3,739
24,950	25,000	3,789	3,746	4,315	3,746
25,000					
25,000	25,050	3,803	3,754	4,329	3,754
25,050	25,100	3,817	3,761	4,343	3,761
25,100	25,150	3,831	3,769	4,357	3,769
25,150	25,200	3,845	3,776	4,371	3,776
25,200	25,250	3,859	3,784	4,385	3,784
25,250	25,300	3,873	3,791	4,399	3,791
25,300	25,350	3,887	3,799	4,413	3,799
25,350	25,400	3,901	3,806	4,427	3,806
25,400	25,450	3,915	3,814	4,441	3,814
25,450	25,500	3,929	3,821	4,455	3,821
25,500	25,550	3,943	3,829	4,469	3,829
25,550	25,600	3,957	3,836	4,483	3,836
25,600	25,650	3,971	3,844	4,497	3,844
25,650	25,700	3,985	3,851	4,511	3,851
25,700	25,750	3,999	3,859	4,525	3,859
25,750	25,800	4,013	3,866	4,539	3,866
25,800	25,850	4,027	3,874	4,553	3,874
25,850	25,900	4,041	3,881	4,567	3,881
25,900	25,950	4,055	3,889	4,581	3,889
25,950	26,000	4,069	3,896	4,595	3,896

If line 38 (taxable income) is—		And you are—			
At least	But less than	Single	Married filing jointly *	Married filing separately	Head of a household
		Your tax is—			
26,000					
26,000	26,050	4,083	3,904	4,609	3,904
26,050	26,100	4,097	3,911	4,623	3,911
26,100	26,150	4,111	3,919	4,637	3,919
26,150	26,200	4,125	3,926	4,651	3,926
26,200	26,250	4,139	3,934	4,665	3,934
26,250	26,300	4,153	3,941	4,679	3,941
26,300	26,350	4,167	3,949	4,693	3,949
26,350	26,400	4,181	3,956	4,707	3,956
26,400	26,450	4,195	3,964	4,721	3,964
26,450	26,500	4,209	3,971	4,735	3,971
26,500	26,550	4,223	3,979	4,749	3,979
26,550	26,600	4,237	3,986	4,763	3,986
26,600	26,650	4,251	3,994	4,777	3,994
26,650	26,700	4,265	4,001	4,791	4,001
26,700	26,750	4,279	4,009	4,805	4,009
26,750	26,800	4,293	4,016	4,819	4,016
26,800	26,850	4,307	4,024	4,833	4,024
26,850	26,900	4,321	4,031	4,847	4,031
26,900	26,950	4,335	4,039	4,861	4,039
26,950	27,000	4,349	4,046	4,875	4,046
27,000					
27,000	27,050	4,363	4,054	4,889	4,054
27,050	27,100	4,377	4,061	4,903	4,061
27,100	27,150	4,391	4,069	4,917	4,069
27,150	27,200	4,405	4,076	4,931	4,076
27,200	27,250	4,419	4,084	4,945	4,084
27,250	27,300	4,433	4,091	4,959	4,091
27,300	27,350	4,447	4,099	4,973	4,099
27,350	27,400	4,461	4,106	4,987	4,106
27,400	27,450	4,475	4,114	5,001	4,114
27,450	27,500	4,489	4,121	5,015	4,121
27,500	27,550	4,503	4,129	5,029	4,129
27,550	27,600	4,517	4,136	5,043	4,136
27,600	27,650	4,531	4,144	5,057	4,144
27,650	27,700	4,545	4,151	5,071	4,151
27,700	27,750	4,559	4,159	5,085	4,159
27,750	27,800	4,573	4,166	5,099	4,166
27,800	27,850	4,587	4,174	5,113	4,174
27,850	27,900	4,601	4,181	5,127	4,181
27,900	27,950	4,615	4,189	5,141	4,189
27,950	28,000	4,629	4,196	5,155	4,196
28,000					
28,000	28,050	4,643	4,204	5,169	4,204
28,050	28,100	4,657	4,211	5,183	4,211
28,100	28,150	4,671	4,219	5,197	4,219
28,150	28,200	4,685	4,226	5,211	4,226
28,200	28,250	4,699	4,234	5,225	4,234
28,250	28,300	4,713	4,241	5,239	4,241
28,300	28,350	4,727	4,249	5,253	4,249
28,350	28,400	4,741	4,256	5,267	4,256
28,400	28,450	4,755	4,264	5,281	4,264
28,450	28,500	4,769	4,271	5,295	4,271
28,500	28,550	4,783	4,279	5,309	4,279
28,550	28,600	4,797	4,286	5,323	4,286
28,600	28,650	4,811	4,294	5,337	4,294
28,650	28,700	4,825	4,301	5,351	4,301
28,700	28,750	4,839	4,309	5,365	4,309
28,750	28,800	4,853	4,316	5,379	4,316
28,800	28,850	4,867	4,324	5,393	4,324
28,850	28,900	4,881	4,331	5,407	4,331
28,900	28,950	4,895	4,339	5,421	4,339
28,950	29,000	4,909	4,346	5,435	4,346

If line 38 (taxable income) is—		And you are—			
At least	But less than	Single	Married filing jointly *	Married filing separately	Head of a household
		Your tax is—			
29,000					
29,000	29,050	4,923	4,354	5,449	4,354
29,050	29,100	4,937	4,361	5,463	4,361
29,100	29,150	4,951	4,369	5,477	4,369
29,150	29,200	4,965	4,376	5,491	4,376
29,200	29,250	4,979	4,384	5,505	4,384
29,250	29,300	4,993	4,391	5,519	4,391
29,300	29,350	5,007	4,399	5,533	4,399
29,350	29,400	5,021	4,406	5,547	4,406
29,400	29,450	5,035	4,414	5,561	4,414
29,450	29,500	5,049	4,421	5,575	4,421
29,500	29,550	5,063	4,429	5,589	4,429
29,550	29,600	5,077	4,436	5,603	4,436
29,600	29,650	5,091	4,444	5,617	4,444
29,650	29,700	5,105	4,451	5,631	4,451
29,700	29,750	5,119	4,459	5,645	4,459
29,750	29,800	5,133	4,466	5,659	4,466
29,800	29,850	5,147	4,474	5,673	4,474
29,850	29,900	5,161	4,481	5,687	4,481
29,900	29,950	5,175	4,489	5,701	4,489
29,950	30,000	5,189	4,496	5,715	4,496
30,000					
30,000	30,050	5,203	4,504	5,729	4,504
30,050	30,100	5,217	4,511	5,743	4,511
30,100	30,150	5,231	4,519	5,757	4,519
30,150	30,200	5,245	4,526	5,771	4,526
30,200	30,250	5,259	4,534	5,785	4,534
30,250	30,300	5,273	4,541	5,799	4,541
30,300	30,350	5,287	4,549	5,813	4,549
30,350	30,400	5,301	4,556	5,827	4,556
30,400	30,450	5,315	4,564	5,841	4,564
30,450	30,500	5,329	4,571	5,855	4,571
30,500	30,550	5,343	4,579	5,869	4,579
30,550	30,600	5,357	4,586	5,883	4,586
30,600	30,650	5,371	4,594	5,897	4,594
30,650	30,700	5,385	4,601	5,911	4,601
30,700	30,750	5,399	4,609	5,925	4,609
30,750	30,800	5,413	4,616	5,939	4,616
30,800	30,850	5,427	4,624	5,953	4,624
30,850	30,900	5,441	4,631	5,967	4,631
30,900	30,950	5,455	4,639	5,981	4,639
30,950	31,000	5,469	4,646	5,995	4,646
31,000					
31,000	31,050	5,483	4,654	6,009	4,654
31,050	31,100	5,497	4,661	6,023	4,661
31,100	31,150	5,511	4,669	6,037	4,669
31,150	31,200	5,525	4,676	6,051	4,676
31,200	31,250	5,539	4,684	6,065	4,684
31,250	31,300	5,553	4,691	6,079	4,691
31,300	31,350	5,567	4,699	6,093	4,699
31,350	31,400	5,581	4,706	6,107	4,706
31,400	31,450	5,595	4,714	6,121	4,714
31,450	31,500	5,609	4,721	6,135	4,721
31,500	31,550	5,623	4,729	6,149	4,729
31,550	31,600	5,637	4,736	6,163	4,736
31,600	31,650	5,651	4,744	6,177	4,744
31,650	31,700	5,665	4,751	6,191	4,751
31,700	31,750	5,679	4,759	6,205	4,759
31,750	31,800	5,693	4,766	6,219	4,766
31,800	31,850	5,707	4,774	6,233	4,774
31,850	31,900	5,721	4,781	6,247	4,781
31,900	31,950	5,735	4,789	6,261	4,789
31,950	32,000	5,749	4,796	6,275	4,796

* This column must also be used by a qualifying widow(er).

Continued on next page

1997 Tax Table—Continued

Footnote (*): This column must also be used by a qualifying widow(er).

32,000 – 34,000

At least	But less than	Single	Married filing jointly *	Married filing separately	Head of a household
32,000					
32,000	32,050	5,763	4,804	6,289	4,804
32,050	32,100	5,777	4,811	6,303	4,811
32,100	32,150	5,791	4,819	6,317	4,819
32,150	32,200	5,805	4,826	6,331	4,826
32,200	32,250	5,819	4,834	6,345	4,834
32,250	32,300	5,833	4,841	6,359	4,841
32,300	32,350	5,847	4,849	6,373	4,849
32,350	32,400	5,861	4,856	6,387	4,856
32,400	32,450	5,875	4,864	6,401	4,864
32,450	32,500	5,889	4,871	6,415	4,871
32,500	32,550	5,903	4,879	6,429	4,879
32,550	32,600	5,917	4,886	6,443	4,886
32,600	32,650	5,931	4,894	6,457	4,894
32,650	32,700	5,945	4,901	6,471	4,901
32,700	32,750	5,959	4,909	6,485	4,909
32,750	32,800	5,973	4,916	6,499	4,916
32,800	32,850	5,987	4,924	6,513	4,924
32,850	32,900	6,001	4,931	6,527	4,931
32,900	32,950	6,015	4,939	6,541	4,939
32,950	33,000	6,029	4,946	6,555	4,946
33,000					
33,000	33,050	6,043	4,954	6,569	4,954
33,050	33,100	6,057	4,961	6,583	4,965
33,100	33,150	6,071	4,969	6,597	4,979
33,150	33,200	6,085	4,976	6,611	4,993
33,200	33,250	6,099	4,984	6,625	5,007
33,250	33,300	6,113	4,991	6,639	5,021
33,300	33,350	6,127	4,999	6,653	5,035
33,350	33,400	6,141	5,006	6,667	5,049
33,400	33,450	6,155	5,014	6,681	5,063
33,450	33,500	6,169	5,021	6,695	5,077
33,500	33,550	6,183	5,029	6,709	5,091
33,550	33,600	6,197	5,036	6,723	5,105
33,600	33,650	6,211	5,044	6,737	5,119
33,650	33,700	6,225	5,051	6,751	5,133
33,700	33,750	6,239	5,059	6,765	5,147
33,750	33,800	6,253	5,066	6,779	5,161
33,800	33,850	6,267	5,074	6,793	5,175
33,850	33,900	6,281	5,081	6,807	5,189
33,900	33,950	6,295	5,089	6,821	5,203
33,950	34,000	6,309	5,096	6,835	5,217
34,000					
34,000	34,050	6,323	5,104	6,849	5,231
34,050	34,100	6,337	5,111	6,863	5,245
34,100	34,150	6,351	5,119	6,877	5,259
34,150	34,200	6,365	5,126	6,891	5,273
34,200	34,250	6,379	5,134	6,905	5,287
34,250	34,300	6,393	5,141	6,919	5,301
34,300	34,350	6,407	5,149	6,933	5,315
34,350	34,400	6,421	5,156	6,947	5,329
34,400	34,450	6,435	5,164	6,961	5,343
34,450	34,500	6,449	5,171	6,975	5,357
34,500	34,550	6,463	5,179	6,989	5,371
34,550	34,600	6,477	5,186	7,003	5,385
34,600	34,650	6,491	5,194	7,017	5,399
34,650	34,700	6,505	5,201	7,031	5,413
34,700	34,750	6,519	5,209	7,045	5,427
34,750	34,800	6,533	5,216	7,059	5,441
34,800	34,850	6,547	5,224	7,073	5,455
34,850	34,900	6,561	5,231	7,087	5,469
34,900	34,950	6,575	5,239	7,101	5,483
34,950	35,000	6,589	5,246	7,115	5,497

35,000 – 37,000

At least	But less than	Single	Married filing jointly *	Married filing separately	Head of a household
35,000					
35,000	35,050	6,603	5,254	7,129	5,511
35,050	35,100	6,617	5,261	7,143	5,525
35,100	35,150	6,631	5,269	7,157	5,539
35,150	35,200	6,645	5,276	7,171	5,553
35,200	35,250	6,659	5,284	7,185	5,567
35,250	35,300	6,673	5,291	7,199	5,581
35,300	35,350	6,687	5,299	7,213	5,595
35,350	35,400	6,701	5,306	7,227	5,609
35,400	35,450	6,715	5,314	7,241	5,623
35,450	35,500	6,729	5,321	7,255	5,637
35,500	35,550	6,743	5,329	7,269	5,651
35,550	35,600	6,757	5,336	7,283	5,665
35,600	35,650	6,771	5,344	7,297	5,679
35,650	35,700	6,785	5,351	7,311	5,693
35,700	35,750	6,799	5,359	7,325	5,707
35,750	35,800	6,813	5,366	7,339	5,721
35,800	35,850	6,827	5,374	7,353	5,735
35,850	35,900	6,841	5,381	7,367	5,749
35,900	35,950	6,855	5,389	7,381	5,763
35,950	36,000	6,869	5,396	7,395	5,777
36,000					
36,000	36,050	6,883	5,404	7,409	5,791
36,050	36,100	6,897	5,411	7,423	5,805
36,100	36,150	6,911	5,419	7,437	5,819
36,150	36,200	6,925	5,426	7,451	5,833
36,200	36,250	6,939	5,434	7,465	5,847
36,250	36,300	6,953	5,441	7,479	5,861
36,300	36,350	6,967	5,449	7,493	5,875
36,350	36,400	6,981	5,456	7,507	5,889
36,400	36,450	6,995	5,464	7,521	5,903
36,450	36,500	7,009	5,471	7,535	5,917
36,500	36,550	7,023	5,479	7,549	5,931
36,550	36,600	7,037	5,486	7,563	5,945
36,600	36,650	7,051	5,494	7,577	5,959
36,650	36,700	7,065	5,501	7,591	5,973
36,700	36,750	7,079	5,509	7,605	5,987
36,750	36,800	7,093	5,516	7,619	6,001
36,800	36,850	7,107	5,524	7,633	6,015
36,850	36,900	7,121	5,531	7,647	6,029
36,900	36,950	7,135	5,539	7,661	6,043
36,950	37,000	7,149	5,546	7,675	6,057
37,000					
37,000	37,050	7,163	5,554	7,689	6,071
37,050	37,100	7,177	5,561	7,703	6,085
37,100	37,150	7,191	5,569	7,717	6,099
37,150	37,200	7,205	5,576	7,731	6,113
37,200	37,250	7,219	5,584	7,745	6,127
37,250	37,300	7,233	5,591	7,759	6,141
37,300	37,350	7,247	5,599	7,773	6,155
37,350	37,400	7,261	5,606	7,787	6,169
37,400	37,450	7,275	5,614	7,801	6,183
37,450	37,500	7,289	5,621	7,815	6,197
37,500	37,550	7,303	5,629	7,829	6,211
37,550	37,600	7,317	5,636	7,843	6,225
37,600	37,650	7,331	5,644	7,857	6,239
37,650	37,700	7,345	5,651	7,871	6,253
37,700	37,750	7,359	5,659	7,885	6,267
37,750	37,800	7,373	5,666	7,899	6,281
37,800	37,850	7,387	5,674	7,913	6,295
37,850	37,900	7,401	5,681	7,927	6,309
37,900	37,950	7,415	5,689	7,941	6,323
37,950	38,000	7,429	5,696	7,955	6,337

38,000 – 40,000

At least	But less than	Single	Married filing jointly *	Married filing separately	Head of a household
38,000					
38,000	38,050	7,443	5,704	7,969	6,351
38,050	38,100	7,457	5,711	7,983	6,365
38,100	38,150	7,471	5,719	7,997	6,379
38,150	38,200	7,485	5,726	8,011	6,393
38,200	38,250	7,499	5,734	8,025	6,407
38,250	38,300	7,513	5,741	8,039	6,421
38,300	38,350	7,527	5,749	8,053	6,435
38,350	38,400	7,541	5,756	8,067	6,449
38,400	38,450	7,555	5,764	8,081	6,463
38,450	38,500	7,569	5,771	8,095	6,477
38,500	38,550	7,583	5,779	8,109	6,491
38,550	38,600	7,597	5,786	8,123	6,505
38,600	38,650	7,611	5,794	8,137	6,519
38,650	38,700	7,625	5,801	8,151	6,533
38,700	38,750	7,639	5,809	8,165	6,547
38,750	38,800	7,653	5,816	8,179	6,561
38,800	38,850	7,667	5,824	8,193	6,575
38,850	38,900	7,681	5,831	8,207	6,589
38,900	38,950	7,695	5,839	8,221	6,603
38,950	39,000	7,709	5,846	8,235	6,617
39,000					
39,000	39,050	7,723	5,854	8,249	6,631
39,050	39,100	7,737	5,861	8,263	6,645
39,100	39,150	7,751	5,869	8,277	6,659
39,150	39,200	7,765	5,876	8,291	6,673
39,200	39,250	7,779	5,884	8,305	6,687
39,250	39,300	7,793	5,891	8,319	6,701
39,300	39,350	7,807	5,899	8,333	6,715
39,350	39,400	7,821	5,906	8,347	6,729
39,400	39,450	7,835	5,914	8,361	6,743
39,450	39,500	7,849	5,921	8,375	6,757
39,500	39,550	7,863	5,929	8,389	6,771
39,550	39,600	7,877	5,936	8,403	6,785
39,600	39,650	7,891	5,944	8,417	6,799
39,650	39,700	7,905	5,951	8,431	6,813
39,700	39,750	7,919	5,959	8,445	6,827
39,750	39,800	7,933	5,966	8,459	6,841
39,800	39,850	7,947	5,974	8,473	6,855
39,850	39,900	7,961	5,981	8,487	6,869
39,900	39,950	7,975	5,989	8,501	6,883
39,950	40,000	7,989	5,996	8,515	6,897
40,000					
40,000	40,050	8,003	6,004	8,529	6,911
40,050	40,100	8,017	6,011	8,543	6,925
40,100	40,150	8,031	6,019	8,557	6,939
40,150	40,200	8,045	6,026	8,571	6,953
40,200	40,250	8,059	6,034	8,585	6,967
40,250	40,300	8,073	6,041	8,599	6,981
40,300	40,350	8,087	6,049	8,613	6,995
40,350	40,400	8,101	6,056	8,627	7,009
40,400	40,450	8,115	6,064	8,641	7,023
40,450	40,500	8,129	6,071	8,655	7,037
40,500	40,550	8,143	6,079	8,669	7,051
40,550	40,600	8,157	6,086	8,683	7,065
40,600	40,650	8,171	6,094	8,697	7,079
40,650	40,700	8,185	6,101	8,711	7,093
40,700	40,750	8,199	6,109	8,725	7,107
40,750	40,800	8,213	6,116	8,739	7,121
40,800	40,850	8,227	6,124	8,753	7,135
40,850	40,900	8,241	6,131	8,767	7,149
40,900	40,950	8,255	6,139	8,781	7,163
40,950	41,000	8,269	6,146	8,795	7,177

Continued on next page

1997 Tax Table—*Continued*

41,000 – 43,000

At least	But less than	Single	Married filing jointly *	Married filing separately	Head of a household
			Your tax is—		
41,000					
41,000	41,050	8,283	6,154	8,809	7,191
41,050	41,100	8,297	6,161	8,823	7,205
41,100	41,150	8,311	6,169	8,837	7,219
41,150	41,200	8,325	6,176	8,851	7,233
41,200	41,250	8,339	6,187	8,865	7,247
41,250	41,300	8,353	6,201	8,879	7,261
41,300	41,350	8,367	6,215	8,893	7,275
41,350	41,400	8,381	6,229	8,907	7,289
41,400	41,450	8,395	6,243	8,921	7,303
41,450	41,500	8,409	6,257	8,935	7,317
41,500	41,550	8,423	6,271	8,949	7,331
41,550	41,600	8,437	6,285	8,963	7,345
41,600	41,650	8,451	6,299	8,977	7,359
41,650	41,700	8,465	6,313	8,991	7,373
41,700	41,750	8,479	6,327	9,005	7,387
41,750	41,800	8,493	6,341	9,019	7,401
41,800	41,850	8,507	6,355	9,033	7,415
41,850	41,900	8,521	6,369	9,047	7,429
41,900	41,950	8,535	6,383	9,061	7,443
41,950	42,000	8,549	6,397	9,075	7,457
42,000					
42,000	42,050	8,563	6,411	9,089	7,471
42,050	42,100	8,577	6,425	9,103	7,485
42,100	42,150	8,591	6,439	9,117	7,499
42,150	42,200	8,605	6,453	9,131	7,513
42,200	42,250	8,619	6,467	9,145	7,527
42,250	42,300	8,633	6,481	9,159	7,541
42,300	42,350	8,647	6,495	9,173	7,555
42,350	42,400	8,661	6,509	9,187	7,569
42,400	42,450	8,675	6,523	9,201	7,583
42,450	42,500	8,689	6,537	9,215	7,597
42,500	42,550	8,703	6,551	9,229	7,611
42,550	42,600	8,717	6,565	9,243	7,625
42,600	42,650	8,731	6,579	9,257	7,639
42,650	42,700	8,745	6,593	9,271	7,653
42,700	42,750	8,759	6,607	9,285	7,667
42,750	42,800	8,773	6,621	9,299	7,681
42,800	42,850	8,787	6,635	9,313	7,695
42,850	42,900	8,801	6,649	9,327	7,709
42,900	42,950	8,815	6,663	9,341	7,723
42,950	43,000	8,829	6,677	9,355	7,737
43,000					
43,000	43,050	8,843	6,691	9,369	7,751
43,050	43,100	8,857	6,705	9,383	7,765
43,100	43,150	8,871	6,719	9,397	7,779
43,150	43,200	8,885	6,733	9,411	7,793
43,200	43,250	8,899	6,747	9,425	7,807
43,250	43,300	8,913	6,761	9,439	7,821
43,300	43,350	8,927	6,775	9,453	7,835
43,350	43,400	8,941	6,789	9,467	7,849
43,400	43,450	8,955	6,803	9,481	7,863
43,450	43,500	8,969	6,817	9,495	7,877
43,500	43,550	8,983	6,831	9,509	7,891
43,550	43,600	8,997	6,845	9,523	7,905
43,600	43,650	9,011	6,859	9,537	7,919
43,650	43,700	9,025	6,873	9,551	7,933
43,700	43,750	9,039	6,887	9,565	7,947
43,750	43,800	9,053	6,901	9,579	7,961
43,800	43,850	9,067	6,915	9,593	7,975
43,850	43,900	9,081	6,929	9,607	7,989
43,900	43,950	9,095	6,943	9,621	8,003
43,950	44,000	9,109	6,957	9,635	8,017

44,000 – 46,000

At least	But less than	Single	Married filing jointly *	Married filing separately	Head of a household
			Your tax is—		
44,000					
44,000	44,050	9,123	6,971	9,649	8,031
44,050	44,100	9,137	6,985	9,663	8,045
44,100	44,150	9,151	6,999	9,677	8,059
44,150	44,200	9,165	7,013	9,691	8,073
44,200	44,250	9,179	7,027	9,705	8,087
44,250	44,300	9,193	7,041	9,719	8,101
44,300	44,350	9,207	7,055	9,733	8,115
44,350	44,400	9,221	7,069	9,747	8,129
44,400	44,450	9,235	7,083	9,761	8,143
44,450	44,500	9,249	7,097	9,775	8,157
44,500	44,550	9,263	7,111	9,789	8,171
44,550	44,600	9,277	7,125	9,803	8,185
44,600	44,650	9,291	7,139	9,817	8,199
44,650	44,700	9,305	7,153	9,831	8,213
44,700	44,750	9,319	7,167	9,845	8,227
44,750	44,800	9,333	7,181	9,859	8,241
44,800	44,850	9,347	7,195	9,873	8,255
44,850	44,900	9,361	7,209	9,887	8,269
44,900	44,950	9,375	7,223	9,901	8,283
44,950	45,000	9,389	7,237	9,915	8,297
45,000					
45,000	45,050	9,403	7,251	9,929	8,311
45,050	45,100	9,417	7,265	9,943	8,325
45,100	45,150	9,431	7,279	9,957	8,339
45,150	45,200	9,445	7,293	9,971	8,353
45,200	45,250	9,459	7,307	9,985	8,367
45,250	45,300	9,473	7,321	9,999	8,381
45,300	45,350	9,487	7,335	10,013	8,395
45,350	45,400	9,501	7,349	10,027	8,409
45,400	45,450	9,515	7,363	10,041	8,423
45,450	45,500	9,529	7,377	10,055	8,437
45,500	45,550	9,543	7,391	10,069	8,451
45,550	45,600	9,557	7,405	10,083	8,465
45,600	45,650	9,571	7,419	10,097	8,479
45,650	45,700	9,585	7,433	10,111	8,493
45,700	45,750	9,599	7,447	10,125	8,507
45,750	45,800	9,613	7,461	10,139	8,521
45,800	45,850	9,627	7,475	10,153	8,535
45,850	45,900	9,641	7,489	10,167	8,549
45,900	45,950	9,655	7,503	10,181	8,563
45,950	46,000	9,669	7,517	10,195	8,577
46,000					
46,000	46,050	9,683	7,531	10,209	8,591
46,050	46,100	9,697	7,545	10,223	8,605
46,100	46,150	9,711	7,559	10,237	8,619
46,150	46,200	9,725	7,573	10,251	8,633
46,200	46,250	9,739	7,587	10,265	8,647
46,250	46,300	9,753	7,601	10,279	8,661
46,300	46,350	9,767	7,615	10,293	8,675
46,350	46,400	9,781	7,629	10,307	8,689
46,400	46,450	9,795	7,643	10,321	8,703
46,450	46,500	9,809	7,657	10,335	8,717
46,500	46,550	9,823	7,671	10,349	8,731
46,550	46,600	9,837	7,685	10,363	8,745
46,600	46,650	9,851	7,699	10,377	8,759
46,650	46,700	9,865	7,713	10,391	8,773
46,700	46,750	9,879	7,727	10,405	8,787
46,750	46,800	9,893	7,741	10,419	8,801
46,800	46,850	9,907	7,755	10,433	8,815
46,850	46,900	9,921	7,769	10,447	8,829
46,900	46,950	9,935	7,783	10,461	8,843
46,950	47,000	9,949	7,797	10,475	8,857

47,000 – 49,000

At least	But less than	Single	Married filing jointly *	Married filing separately	Head of a household
			Your tax is—		
47,000					
47,000	47,050	9,963	7,811	10,489	8,871
47,050	47,100	9,977	7,825	10,503	8,885
47,100	47,150	9,991	7,839	10,517	8,899
47,150	47,200	10,005	7,853	10,531	8,913
47,200	47,250	10,019	7,867	10,545	8,927
47,250	47,300	10,033	7,881	10,559	8,941
47,300	47,350	10,047	7,895	10,573	8,955
47,350	47,400	10,061	7,909	10,587	8,969
47,400	47,450	10,075	7,923	10,601	8,983
47,450	47,500	10,089	7,937	10,615	8,997
47,500	47,550	10,103	7,951	10,629	9,011
47,550	47,600	10,117	7,965	10,643	9,025
47,600	47,650	10,131	7,979	10,657	9,039
47,650	47,700	10,145	7,993	10,671	9,053
47,700	47,750	10,159	8,007	10,685	9,067
47,750	47,800	10,173	8,021	10,699	9,081
47,800	47,850	10,187	8,035	10,713	9,095
47,850	47,900	10,201	8,049	10,727	9,109
47,900	47,950	10,215	8,063	10,741	9,123
47,950	48,000	10,229	8,077	10,755	9,137
48,000					
48,000	48,050	10,243	8,091	10,769	9,151
48,050	48,100	10,257	8,105	10,783	9,165
48,100	48,150	10,271	8,119	10,797	9,179
48,150	48,200	10,285	8,133	10,811	9,193
48,200	48,250	10,299	8,147	10,825	9,207
48,250	48,300	10,313	8,161	10,839	9,221
48,300	48,350	10,327	8,175	10,853	9,235
48,350	48,400	10,341	8,189	10,867	9,249
48,400	48,450	10,355	8,203	10,881	9,263
48,450	48,500	10,369	8,217	10,895	9,277
48,500	48,550	10,383	8,231	10,909	9,291
48,550	48,600	10,397	8,245	10,923	9,305
48,600	48,650	10,411	8,259	10,937	9,319
48,650	48,700	10,425	8,273	10,951	9,333
48,700	48,750	10,439	8,287	10,965	9,347
48,750	48,800	10,453	8,301	10,979	9,361
48,800	48,850	10,467	8,315	10,993	9,375
48,850	48,900	10,481	8,329	11,007	9,389
48,900	48,950	10,495	8,343	11,021	9,403
48,950	49,000	10,509	8,357	11,035	9,417
49,000					
49,000	49,050	10,523	8,371	11,049	9,431
49,050	49,100	10,537	8,385	11,063	9,445
49,100	49,150	10,551	8,399	11,077	9,459
49,150	49,200	10,565	8,413	11,091	9,473
49,200	49,250	10,579	8,427	11,105	9,487
49,250	49,300	10,593	8,441	11,119	9,501
49,300	49,350	10,607	8,455	11,133	9,515
49,350	49,400	10,621	8,469	11,147	9,529
49,400	49,450	10,635	8,483	11,161	9,543
49,450	49,500	10,649	8,497	11,175	9,557
49,500	49,550	10,663	8,511	11,189	9,571
49,550	49,600	10,677	8,525	11,203	9,585
49,600	49,650	10,691	8,539	11,217	9,599
49,650	49,700	10,705	8,553	11,231	9,613
49,700	49,750	10,719	8,567	11,245	9,627
49,750	49,800	10,733	8,581	11,259	9,641
49,800	49,850	10,747	8,595	11,274	9,655
49,850	49,900	10,761	8,609	11,289	9,669
49,900	49,950	10,775	8,623	11,305	9,683
49,950	50,000	10,789	8,637	11,320	9,697

* This column must also be used by a qualifying widow(er).

Continued on next page

1997 Tax Table—Continued

If line 38 (taxable income) is— At least	But less than	Single	Married filing jointly *	Married filing separately	Head of a household
50,000					
50,000	50,050	10,803	8,651	11,336	9,711
50,050	50,100	10,817	8,665	11,351	9,725
50,100	50,150	10,831	8,679	11,367	9,739
50,150	50,200	10,845	8,693	11,382	9,753
50,200	50,250	10,859	8,707	11,398	9,767
50,250	50,300	10,873	8,721	11,413	9,781
50,300	50,350	10,887	8,735	11,429	9,795
50,350	50,400	10,901	8,749	11,444	9,809
50,400	50,450	10,915	8,763	11,460	9,823
50,450	50,500	10,929	8,777	11,475	9,837
50,500	50,550	10,943	8,791	11,491	9,851
50,550	50,600	10,957	8,805	11,506	9,865
50,600	50,650	10,971	8,819	11,522	9,879
50,650	50,700	10,985	8,833	11,537	9,893
50,700	50,750	10,999	8,847	11,553	9,907
50,750	50,800	11,013	8,861	11,568	9,921
50,800	50,850	11,027	8,875	11,584	9,935
50,850	50,900	11,041	8,889	11,599	9,949
50,900	50,950	11,055	8,903	11,615	9,963
50,950	51,000	11,069	8,917	11,630	9,977
51,000					
51,000	51,050	11,083	8,931	11,646	9,991
51,050	51,100	11,097	8,945	11,661	10,005
51,100	51,150	11,111	8,959	11,677	10,019
51,150	51,200	11,125	8,973	11,692	10,033
51,200	51,250	11,139	8,987	11,708	10,047
51,250	51,300	11,153	9,001	11,723	10,061
51,300	51,350	11,167	9,015	11,739	10,075
51,350	51,400	11,181	9,029	11,754	10,089
51,400	51,450	11,195	9,043	11,770	10,103
51,450	51,500	11,209	9,057	11,785	10,117
51,500	51,550	11,223	9,071	11,801	10,131
51,550	51,600	11,237	9,085	11,816	10,145
51,600	51,650	11,251	9,099	11,832	10,159
51,650	51,700	11,265	9,113	11,847	10,173
51,700	51,750	11,279	9,127	11,863	10,187
51,750	51,800	11,293	9,141	11,878	10,201
51,800	51,850	11,307	9,155	11,894	10,215
51,850	51,900	11,321	9,169	11,909	10,229
51,900	51,950	11,335	9,183	11,925	10,243
51,950	52,000	11,349	9,197	11,940	10,257
52,000					
52,000	52,050	11,363	9,211	11,956	10,271
52,050	52,100	11,377	9,225	11,971	10,285
52,100	52,150	11,391	9,239	11,987	10,299
52,150	52,200	11,405	9,253	12,002	10,313
52,200	52,250	11,419	9,267	12,018	10,327
52,250	52,300	11,433	9,281	12,033	10,341
52,300	52,350	11,447	9,295	12,049	10,355
52,350	52,400	11,461	9,309	12,064	10,369
52,400	52,450	11,475	9,323	12,080	10,383
52,450	52,500	11,489	9,337	12,095	10,397
52,500	52,550	11,503	9,351	12,111	10,411
52,550	52,600	11,517	9,365	12,126	10,425
52,600	52,650	11,531	9,379	12,142	10,439
52,650	52,700	11,545	9,393	12,157	10,453
52,700	52,750	11,559	9,407	12,173	10,467
52,750	52,800	11,573	9,421	12,188	10,481
52,800	52,850	11,587	9,435	12,204	10,495
52,850	52,900	11,601	9,449	12,219	10,509
52,900	52,950	11,615	9,463	12,235	10,523
52,950	53,000	11,629	9,477	12,250	10,537
53,000					
53,000	53,050	11,643	9,491	12,266	10,551
53,050	53,100	11,657	9,505	12,281	10,565
53,100	53,150	11,671	9,519	12,297	10,579
53,150	53,200	11,685	9,533	12,312	10,593
53,200	53,250	11,699	9,547	12,328	10,607
53,250	53,300	11,713	9,561	12,343	10,621
53,300	53,350	11,727	9,575	12,359	10,635
53,350	53,400	11,741	9,589	12,374	10,649
53,400	53,450	11,755	9,603	12,390	10,663
53,450	53,500	11,769	9,617	12,405	10,677
53,500	53,550	11,783	9,631	12,421	10,691
53,550	53,600	11,797	9,645	12,436	10,705
53,600	53,650	11,811	9,659	12,452	10,719
53,650	53,700	11,825	9,673	12,467	10,733
53,700	53,750	11,839	9,687	12,483	10,747
53,750	53,800	11,853	9,701	12,498	10,761
53,800	53,850	11,867	9,715	12,514	10,775
53,850	53,900	11,881	9,729	12,529	10,789
53,900	53,950	11,895	9,743	12,545	10,803
53,950	54,000	11,909	9,757	12,560	10,817
54,000					
54,000	54,050	11,923	9,771	12,576	10,831
54,050	54,100	11,937	9,785	12,591	10,845
54,100	54,150	11,951	9,799	12,607	10,859
54,150	54,200	11,965	9,813	12,622	10,873
54,200	54,250	11,979	9,827	12,638	10,887
54,250	54,300	11,993	9,841	12,653	10,901
54,300	54,350	12,007	9,855	12,669	10,915
54,350	54,400	12,021	9,869	12,684	10,929
54,400	54,450	12,035	9,883	12,700	10,943
54,450	54,500	12,049	9,897	12,715	10,957
54,500	54,550	12,063	9,911	12,731	10,971
54,550	54,600	12,077	9,925	12,746	10,985
54,600	54,650	12,091	9,939	12,762	10,999
54,650	54,700	12,105	9,953	12,777	11,013
54,700	54,750	12,119	9,967	12,793	11,027
54,750	54,800	12,133	9,981	12,808	11,041
54,800	54,850	12,147	9,995	12,824	11,055
54,850	54,900	12,161	10,009	12,839	11,069
54,900	54,950	12,175	10,023	12,855	11,083
54,950	55,000	12,189	10,037	12,870	11,097
55,000					
55,000	55,050	12,203	10,051	12,886	11,111
55,050	55,100	12,217	10,065	12,901	11,125
55,100	55,150	12,231	10,079	12,917	11,139
55,150	55,200	12,245	10,093	12,932	11,153
55,200	55,250	12,259	10,107	12,948	11,167
55,250	55,300	12,273	10,121	12,963	11,181
55,300	55,350	12,287	10,135	12,979	11,195
55,350	55,400	12,301	10,149	12,994	11,209
55,400	55,450	12,315	10,163	13,010	11,223
55,450	55,500	12,329	10,177	13,025	11,237
55,500	55,550	12,343	10,191	13,041	11,251
55,550	55,600	12,357	10,205	13,056	11,265
55,600	55,650	12,371	10,219	13,072	11,279
55,650	55,700	12,385	10,233	13,087	11,293
55,700	55,750	12,399	10,247	13,103	11,307
55,750	55,800	12,413	10,261	13,118	11,321
55,800	55,850	12,427	10,275	13,134	11,335
55,850	55,900	12,441	10,289	13,149	11,349
55,900	55,950	12,455	10,303	13,165	11,363
55,950	56,000	12,469	10,317	13,180	11,377
56,000					
56,000	56,050	12,483	10,331	13,196	11,391
56,050	56,100	12,497	10,345	13,211	11,405
56,100	56,150	12,511	10,359	13,227	11,419
56,150	56,200	12,525	10,373	13,242	11,433
56,200	56,250	12,539	10,387	13,258	11,447
56,250	56,300	12,553	10,401	13,273	11,461
56,300	56,350	12,567	10,415	13,289	11,475
56,350	56,400	12,581	10,429	13,304	11,489
56,400	56,450	12,595	10,443	13,320	11,503
56,450	56,500	12,609	10,457	13,335	11,517
56,500	56,550	12,623	10,471	13,351	11,531
56,550	56,600	12,637	10,485	13,366	11,545
56,600	56,650	12,651	10,499	13,382	11,559
56,650	56,700	12,665	10,513	13,397	11,573
56,700	56,750	12,679	10,527	13,413	11,587
56,750	56,800	12,693	10,541	13,428	11,601
56,800	56,850	12,707	10,555	13,444	11,615
56,850	56,900	12,721	10,569	13,459	11,629
56,900	56,950	12,735	10,583	13,475	11,643
56,950	57,000	12,749	10,597	13,490	11,657
57,000					
57,000	57,050	12,763	10,611	13,506	11,671
57,050	57,100	12,777	10,625	13,521	11,685
57,100	57,150	12,791	10,639	13,537	11,699
57,150	57,200	12,805	10,653	13,552	11,713
57,200	57,250	12,819	10,667	13,568	11,727
57,250	57,300	12,833	10,681	13,583	11,741
57,300	57,350	12,847	10,695	13,599	11,755
57,350	57,400	12,861	10,709	13,614	11,769
57,400	57,450	12,875	10,723	13,630	11,783
57,450	57,500	12,889	10,737	13,645	11,797
57,500	57,550	12,903	10,751	13,661	11,811
57,550	57,600	12,917	10,765	13,676	11,825
57,600	57,650	12,931	10,779	13,692	11,839
57,650	57,700	12,945	10,793	13,707	11,853
57,700	57,750	12,959	10,807	13,723	11,867
57,750	57,800	12,973	10,821	13,738	11,881
57,800	57,850	12,987	10,835	13,754	11,895
57,850	57,900	13,001	10,849	13,769	11,909
57,900	57,950	13,015	10,863	13,785	11,923
57,950	58,000	13,029	10,877	13,800	11,937
58,000					
58,000	58,050	13,043	10,891	13,816	11,951
58,050	58,100	13,057	10,905	13,831	11,965
58,100	58,150	13,071	10,919	13,847	11,979
58,150	58,200	13,085	10,933	13,862	11,993
58,200	58,250	13,099	10,947	13,878	12,007
58,250	58,300	13,113	10,961	13,893	12,021
58,300	58,350	13,127	10,975	13,909	12,035
58,350	58,400	13,141	10,989	13,924	12,049
58,400	58,450	13,155	11,003	13,940	12,063
58,450	58,500	13,169	11,017	13,955	12,077
58,500	58,550	13,183	11,031	13,971	12,091
58,550	58,600	13,197	11,045	13,986	12,105
58,600	58,650	13,211	11,059	14,002	12,119
58,650	58,700	13,225	11,073	14,017	12,133
58,700	58,750	13,239	11,087	14,033	12,147
58,750	58,800	13,253	11,101	14,048	12,161
58,800	58,850	13,267	11,115	14,064	12,175
58,850	58,900	13,281	11,129	14,079	12,189
58,900	58,950	13,295	11,143	14,095	12,203
58,950	59,000	13,309	11,157	14,110	12,217

* This column must also be used by a qualifying widow(er).

Continued on next page

1997 Tax Table—*Continued*

If line 38 (taxable income) is— At least	But less than	Single	Married filing jointly *	Married filing separately	Head of a household
59,000					
59,000	59,050	13,323	11,171	14,126	12,231
59,050	59,100	13,337	11,185	14,141	12,245
59,100	59,150	13,351	11,199	14,157	12,259
59,150	59,200	13,365	11,213	14,172	12,273
59,200	59,250	13,379	11,227	14,188	12,287
59,250	59,300	13,393	11,241	14,203	12,301
59,300	59,350	13,407	11,255	14,219	12,315
59,350	59,400	13,421	11,269	14,234	12,329
59,400	59,450	13,435	11,283	14,250	12,343
59,450	59,500	13,449	11,297	14,265	12,357
59,500	59,550	13,463	11,311	14,281	12,371
59,550	59,600	13,477	11,325	14,296	12,385
59,600	59,650	13,491	11,339	14,312	12,399
59,650	59,700	13,505	11,353	14,327	12,413
59,700	59,750	13,519	11,367	14,343	12,427
59,750	59,800	13,533	11,381	14,358	12,441
59,800	59,850	13,549	11,395	14,374	12,455
59,850	59,900	13,564	11,409	14,389	12,469
59,900	59,950	13,580	11,423	14,405	12,483
59,950	60,000	13,595	11,437	14,420	12,497
60,000					
60,000	60,050	13,611	11,451	14,436	12,511
60,050	60,100	13,626	11,465	14,451	12,525
60,100	60,150	13,642	11,479	14,467	12,539
60,150	60,200	13,657	11,493	14,482	12,553
60,200	60,250	13,673	11,507	14,498	12,567
60,250	60,300	13,688	11,521	14,513	12,581
60,300	60,350	13,704	11,535	14,529	12,595
60,350	60,400	13,719	11,549	14,544	12,609
60,400	60,450	13,735	11,563	14,560	12,623
60,450	60,500	13,750	11,577	14,575	12,637
60,500	60,550	13,766	11,591	14,591	12,651
60,550	60,600	13,781	11,605	14,606	12,665
60,600	60,650	13,797	11,619	14,622	12,679
60,650	60,700	13,812	11,633	14,637	12,693
60,700	60,750	13,828	11,647	14,653	12,707
60,750	60,800	13,843	11,661	14,668	12,721
60,800	60,850	13,859	11,675	14,684	12,735
60,850	60,900	13,874	11,689	14,699	12,749
60,900	60,950	13,890	11,703	14,715	12,763
60,950	61,000	13,905	11,717	14,730	12,777
61,000					
61,000	61,050	13,921	11,731	14,746	12,791
61,050	61,100	13,936	11,745	14,761	12,805
61,100	61,150	13,952	11,759	14,777	12,819
61,150	61,200	13,967	11,773	14,792	12,833
61,200	61,250	13,983	11,787	14,808	12,847
61,250	61,300	13,998	11,801	14,823	12,861
61,300	61,350	14,014	11,815	14,839	12,875
61,350	61,400	14,029	11,829	14,854	12,889
61,400	61,450	14,045	11,843	14,870	12,903
61,450	61,500	14,060	11,857	14,885	12,917
61,500	61,550	14,076	11,871	14,901	12,931
61,550	61,600	14,091	11,885	14,916	12,945
61,600	61,650	14,107	11,899	14,932	12,959
61,650	61,700	14,122	11,913	14,947	12,973
61,700	61,750	14,138	11,927	14,963	12,987
61,750	61,800	14,153	11,941	14,978	13,001
61,800	61,850	14,169	11,955	14,994	13,015
61,850	61,900	14,184	11,969	15,009	13,029
61,900	61,950	14,200	11,983	15,025	13,043
61,950	62,000	14,215	11,997	15,040	13,057

If line 38 (taxable income) is— At least	But less than	Single	Married filing jointly *	Married filing separately	Head of a household
62,000					
62,000	62,050	14,231	12,011	15,056	13,071
62,050	62,100	14,246	12,025	15,071	13,085
62,100	62,150	14,262	12,039	15,087	13,099
62,150	62,200	14,277	12,053	15,102	13,113
62,200	62,250	14,293	12,067	15,118	13,127
62,250	62,300	14,308	12,081	15,133	13,141
62,300	62,350	14,324	12,095	15,149	13,155
62,350	62,400	14,339	12,109	15,164	13,169
62,400	62,450	14,355	12,123	15,180	13,183
62,450	62,500	14,370	12,137	15,195	13,197
62,500	62,550	14,386	12,151	15,211	13,211
62,550	62,600	14,401	12,165	15,226	13,225
62,600	62,650	14,417	12,179	15,242	13,239
62,650	62,700	14,432	12,193	15,257	13,253
62,700	62,750	14,448	12,207	15,273	13,267
62,750	62,800	14,463	12,221	15,288	13,281
62,800	62,850	14,479	12,235	15,304	13,295
62,850	62,900	14,494	12,249	15,319	13,309
62,900	62,950	14,510	12,263	15,335	13,323
62,950	63,000	14,525	12,277	15,350	13,337
63,000					
63,000	63,050	14,541	12,291	15,366	13,351
63,050	63,100	14,556	12,305	15,381	13,365
63,100	63,150	14,572	12,319	15,397	13,379
63,150	63,200	14,587	12,333	15,412	13,393
63,200	63,250	14,603	12,347	15,428	13,407
63,250	63,300	14,618	12,361	15,443	13,421
63,300	63,350	14,634	12,375	15,459	13,435
63,350	63,400	14,649	12,389	15,474	13,449
63,400	63,450	14,665	12,403	15,490	13,463
63,450	63,500	14,680	12,417	15,505	13,477
63,500	63,550	14,696	12,431	15,521	13,491
63,550	63,600	14,711	12,445	15,536	13,505
63,600	63,650	14,727	12,459	15,552	13,519
63,650	63,700	14,742	12,473	15,567	13,533
63,700	63,750	14,758	12,487	15,583	13,547
63,750	63,800	14,773	12,501	15,598	13,561
63,800	63,850	14,789	12,515	15,614	13,575
63,850	63,900	14,804	12,529	15,629	13,589
63,900	63,950	14,820	12,543	15,645	13,603
63,950	64,000	14,835	12,557	15,660	13,617
64,000					
64,000	64,050	14,851	12,571	15,676	13,631
64,050	64,100	14,866	12,585	15,691	13,645
64,100	64,150	14,882	12,599	15,707	13,659
64,150	64,200	14,897	12,613	15,722	13,673
64,200	64,250	14,913	12,627	15,738	13,687
64,250	64,300	14,928	12,641	15,753	13,701
64,300	64,350	14,944	12,655	15,769	13,715
64,350	64,400	14,959	12,669	15,784	13,729
64,400	64,450	14,975	12,683	15,800	13,743
64,450	64,500	14,990	12,697	15,815	13,757
64,500	64,550	15,006	12,711	15,831	13,771
64,550	64,600	15,021	12,725	15,846	13,785
64,600	64,650	15,037	12,739	15,862	13,799
64,650	64,700	15,052	12,753	15,877	13,813
64,700	64,750	15,068	12,767	15,893	13,827
64,750	64,800	15,083	12,781	15,908	13,841
64,800	64,850	15,099	12,795	15,924	13,855
64,850	64,900	15,114	12,809	15,939	13,869
64,900	64,950	15,130	12,823	15,955	13,883
64,950	65,000	15,145	12,837	15,970	13,897

If line 38 (taxable income) is— At least	But less than	Single	Married filing jointly *	Married filing separately	Head of a household
65,000					
65,000	65,050	15,161	12,851	15,986	13,911
65,050	65,100	15,176	12,865	16,001	13,925
65,100	65,150	15,192	12,879	16,017	13,939
65,150	65,200	15,207	12,893	16,032	13,953
65,200	65,250	15,223	12,907	16,048	13,967
65,250	65,300	15,238	12,921	16,063	13,981
65,300	65,350	15,254	12,935	16,079	13,995
65,350	65,400	15,269	12,949	16,094	14,009
65,400	65,450	15,285	12,963	16,110	14,023
65,450	65,500	15,300	12,977	16,125	14,037
65,500	65,550	15,316	12,991	16,141	14,051
65,550	65,600	15,331	13,005	16,156	14,065
65,600	65,650	15,347	13,019	16,172	14,079
65,650	65,700	15,362	13,033	16,187	14,093
65,700	65,750	15,378	13,047	16,203	14,107
65,750	65,800	15,393	13,061	16,218	14,121
65,800	65,850	15,409	13,075	16,234	14,135
65,850	65,900	15,424	13,089	16,249	14,149
65,900	65,950	15,440	13,103	16,265	14,163
65,950	66,000	15,455	13,117	16,280	14,177
66,000					
66,000	66,050	15,471	13,131	16,296	14,191
66,050	66,100	15,486	13,145	16,311	14,205
66,100	66,150	15,502	13,159	16,327	14,219
66,150	66,200	15,517	13,173	16,342	14,233
66,200	66,250	15,533	13,187	16,358	14,247
66,250	66,300	15,548	13,201	16,373	14,261
66,300	66,350	15,564	13,215	16,389	14,275
66,350	66,400	15,579	13,229	16,404	14,289
66,400	66,450	15,595	13,243	16,420	14,303
66,450	66,500	15,610	13,257	16,435	14,317
66,500	66,550	15,626	13,271	16,451	14,331
66,550	66,600	15,641	13,285	16,466	14,345
66,600	66,650	15,657	13,299	16,482	14,359
66,650	66,700	15,672	13,313	16,497	14,373
66,700	66,750	15,688	13,327	16,513	14,387
66,750	66,800	15,703	13,341	16,528	14,401
66,800	66,850	15,719	13,355	16,544	14,415
66,850	66,900	15,734	13,369	16,559	14,429
66,900	66,950	15,750	13,383	16,575	14,443
66,950	67,000	15,765	13,397	16,590	14,457
67,000					
67,000	67,050	15,781	13,411	16,606	14,471
67,050	67,100	15,796	13,425	16,621	14,485
67,100	67,150	15,812	13,439	16,637	14,499
67,150	67,200	15,827	13,453	16,652	14,513
67,200	67,250	15,843	13,467	16,668	14,527
67,250	67,300	15,858	13,481	16,683	14,541
67,300	67,350	15,874	13,495	16,699	14,555
67,350	67,400	15,889	13,509	16,714	14,569
67,400	67,450	15,905	13,523	16,730	14,583
67,450	67,500	15,920	13,537	16,745	14,597
67,500	67,550	15,936	13,551	16,761	14,611
67,550	67,600	15,951	13,565	16,776	14,625
67,600	67,650	15,967	13,579	16,792	14,639
67,650	67,700	15,982	13,593	16,807	14,653
67,700	67,750	15,998	13,607	16,823	14,667
67,750	67,800	16,013	13,621	16,838	14,681
67,800	67,850	16,029	13,635	16,854	14,695
67,850	67,900	16,044	13,649	16,869	14,709
67,900	67,950	16,060	13,663	16,885	14,723
67,950	68,000	16,075	13,677	16,900	14,737

* This column must also be used by a qualifying widow(er).

Continued on next page

1997 Tax Table—Continued

If line 38 (taxable income) is—		And you are—			
At least	But less than	Single	Married filing jointly *	Married filing separately	Head of a household

Your tax is—

68,000

At least	But less than	Single	MFJ	MFS	HoH
68,000	68,050	16,091	13,691	16,916	14,751
68,050	68,100	16,106	13,705	16,931	14,765
68,100	68,150	16,122	13,719	16,947	14,779
68,150	68,200	16,137	13,733	16,962	14,793
68,200	68,250	16,153	13,747	16,978	14,807
68,250	68,300	16,168	13,761	16,993	14,821
68,300	68,350	16,184	13,775	17,009	14,835
68,350	68,400	16,199	13,789	17,024	14,849
68,400	68,450	16,215	13,803	17,040	14,863
68,450	68,500	16,230	13,817	17,055	14,877
68,500	68,550	16,246	13,831	17,071	14,891
68,550	68,600	16,261	13,845	17,086	14,905
68,600	68,650	16,277	13,859	17,102	14,919
68,650	68,700	16,292	13,873	17,117	14,933
68,700	68,750	16,308	13,887	17,133	14,947
68,750	68,800	16,323	13,901	17,148	14,961
68,800	68,850	16,339	13,915	17,164	14,975
68,850	68,900	16,354	13,929	17,179	14,989
68,900	68,950	16,370	13,943	17,195	15,003
68,950	69,000	16,385	13,957	17,210	15,017

69,000

At least	But less than	Single	MFJ	MFS	HoH
69,000	69,050	16,401	13,971	17,226	15,031
69,050	69,100	16,416	13,985	17,241	15,045
69,100	69,150	16,432	13,999	17,257	15,059
69,150	69,200	16,447	14,013	17,272	15,073
69,200	69,250	16,463	14,027	17,288	15,087
69,250	69,300	16,478	14,041	17,303	15,101
69,300	69,350	16,494	14,055	17,319	15,115
69,350	69,400	16,509	14,069	17,334	15,129
69,400	69,450	16,525	14,083	17,350	15,143
69,450	69,500	16,540	14,097	17,365	15,157
69,500	69,550	16,556	14,111	17,381	15,171
69,550	69,600	16,571	14,125	17,396	15,185
69,600	69,650	16,587	14,139	17,412	15,199
69,650	69,700	16,602	14,153	17,427	15,213
69,700	69,750	16,618	14,167	17,443	15,227
69,750	69,800	16,633	14,181	17,458	15,241
69,800	69,850	16,649	14,195	17,474	15,255
69,850	69,900	16,664	14,209	17,489	15,269
69,900	69,950	16,680	14,223	17,505	15,283
69,950	70,000	16,695	14,237	17,520	15,297

70,000

At least	But less than	Single	MFJ	MFS	HoH
70,000	70,050	16,711	14,251	17,536	15,311
70,050	70,100	16,726	14,265	17,551	15,325
70,100	70,150	16,742	14,279	17,567	15,339
70,150	70,200	16,757	14,293	17,582	15,353
70,200	70,250	16,773	14,307	17,598	15,367
70,250	70,300	16,788	14,321	17,613	15,381
70,300	70,350	16,804	14,335	17,629	15,395
70,350	70,400	16,819	14,349	17,644	15,409
70,400	70,450	16,835	14,363	17,660	15,423
70,450	70,500	16,850	14,377	17,675	15,437
70,500	70,550	16,866	14,391	17,691	15,451
70,550	70,600	16,881	14,405	17,706	15,465
70,600	70,650	16,897	14,419	17,722	15,479
70,650	70,700	16,912	14,433	17,737	15,493
70,700	70,750	16,928	14,447	17,753	15,507
70,750	70,800	16,943	14,461	17,768	15,521
70,800	70,850	16,959	14,475	17,784	15,535
70,850	70,900	16,974	14,489	17,799	15,549
70,900	70,950	16,990	14,503	17,815	15,563
70,950	71,000	17,005	14,517	17,830	15,577

71,000

At least	But less than	Single	MFJ	MFS	HoH
71,000	71,050	17,021	14,531	17,846	15,591
71,050	71,100	17,036	14,545	17,861	15,605
71,100	71,150	17,052	14,559	17,877	15,619
71,150	71,200	17,067	14,573	17,892	15,633
71,200	71,250	17,083	14,587	17,908	15,647
71,250	71,300	17,098	14,601	17,923	15,661
71,300	71,350	17,114	14,615	17,939	15,675
71,350	71,400	17,129	14,629	17,954	15,689
71,400	71,450	17,145	14,643	17,970	15,703
71,450	71,500	17,160	14,657	17,985	15,717
71,500	71,550	17,176	14,671	18,001	15,731
71,550	71,600	17,191	14,685	18,016	15,745
71,600	71,650	17,207	14,699	18,032	15,759
71,650	71,700	17,222	14,713	18,047	15,773
71,700	71,750	17,238	14,727	18,063	15,787
71,750	71,800	17,253	14,741	18,078	15,801
71,800	71,850	17,269	14,755	18,094	15,815
71,850	71,900	17,284	14,769	18,109	15,829
71,900	71,950	17,300	14,783	18,125	15,843
71,950	72,000	17,315	14,797	18,140	15,857

72,000

At least	But less than	Single	MFJ	MFS	HoH
72,000	72,050	17,331	14,811	18,156	15,871
72,050	72,100	17,346	14,825	18,171	15,885
72,100	72,150	17,362	14,839	18,187	15,899
72,150	72,200	17,377	14,853	18,202	15,913
72,200	72,250	17,393	14,867	18,218	15,927
72,250	72,300	17,408	14,881	18,233	15,941
72,300	72,350	17,424	14,895	18,249	15,955
72,350	72,400	17,439	14,909	18,264	15,969
72,400	72,450	17,455	14,923	18,280	15,983
72,450	72,500	17,470	14,937	18,295	15,997
72,500	72,550	17,486	14,951	18,311	16,011
72,550	72,600	17,501	14,965	18,326	16,025
72,600	72,650	17,517	14,979	18,342	16,039
72,650	72,700	17,532	14,993	18,357	16,053
72,700	72,750	17,548	15,007	18,373	16,067
72,750	72,800	17,563	15,021	18,388	16,081
72,800	72,850	17,579	15,035	18,404	16,095
72,850	72,900	17,594	15,049	18,419	16,109
72,900	72,950	17,610	15,063	18,435	16,123
72,950	73,000	17,625	15,077	18,450	16,137

73,000

At least	But less than	Single	MFJ	MFS	HoH
73,000	73,050	17,641	15,091	18,466	16,151
73,050	73,100	17,656	15,105	18,481	16,165
73,100	73,150	17,672	15,119	18,497	16,179
73,150	73,200	17,687	15,133	18,512	16,193
73,200	73,250	17,703	15,147	18,528	16,207
73,250	73,300	17,718	15,161	18,543	16,221
73,300	73,350	17,734	15,175	18,559	16,235
73,350	73,400	17,749	15,189	18,574	16,249
73,400	73,450	17,765	15,203	18,590	16,263
73,450	73,500	17,780	15,217	18,605	16,277
73,500	73,550	17,796	15,231	18,621	16,291
73,550	73,600	17,811	15,245	18,636	16,305
73,600	73,650	17,827	15,259	18,652	16,319
73,650	73,700	17,842	15,273	18,667	16,333
73,700	73,750	17,858	15,287	18,683	16,347
73,750	73,800	17,873	15,301	18,698	16,361
73,800	73,850	17,889	15,315	18,714	16,375
73,850	73,900	17,904	15,329	18,729	16,389
73,900	73,950	17,920	15,343	18,745	16,403
73,950	74,000	17,935	15,357	18,760	16,417

74,000

At least	But less than	Single	MFJ	MFS	HoH
74,000	74,050	17,951	15,371	18,776	16,431
74,050	74,100	17,966	15,385	18,791	16,445
74,100	74,150	17,982	15,399	18,807	16,459
74,150	74,200	17,997	15,413	18,822	16,473
74,200	74,250	18,013	15,427	18,838	16,487
74,250	74,300	18,028	15,441	18,853	16,501
74,300	74,350	18,044	15,455	18,869	16,515
74,350	74,400	18,059	15,469	18,884	16,529
74,400	74,450	18,075	15,483	18,900	16,543
74,450	74,500	18,090	15,497	18,915	16,557
74,500	74,550	18,106	15,511	18,931	16,571
74,550	74,600	18,121	15,525	18,946	16,585
74,600	74,650	18,137	15,539	18,962	16,599
74,650	74,700	18,152	15,553	18,977	16,613
74,700	74,750	18,168	15,567	18,993	16,627
74,750	74,800	18,183	15,581	19,008	16,641
74,800	74,850	18,199	15,595	19,024	16,655
74,850	74,900	18,214	15,609	19,039	16,669
74,900	74,950	18,230	15,623	19,055	16,683
74,950	75,000	18,245	15,637	19,070	16,697

75,000

At least	But less than	Single	MFJ	MFS	HoH
75,000	75,050	18,261	15,651	19,086	16,711
75,050	75,100	18,276	15,665	19,101	16,725
75,100	75,150	18,292	15,679	19,117	16,739
75,150	75,200	18,307	15,693	19,132	16,753
75,200	75,250	18,323	15,707	19,148	16,767
75,250	75,300	18,338	15,721	19,163	16,781
75,300	75,350	18,354	15,735	19,179	16,795
75,350	75,400	18,369	15,749	19,194	16,809
75,400	75,450	18,385	15,763	19,210	16,823
75,450	75,500	18,400	15,777	19,225	16,837
75,500	75,550	18,416	15,791	19,241	16,851
75,550	75,600	18,431	15,805	19,256	16,865
75,600	75,650	18,447	15,819	19,272	16,879
75,650	75,700	18,462	15,833	19,287	16,893
75,700	75,750	18,478	15,847	19,303	16,907
75,750	75,800	18,493	15,861	19,318	16,921
75,800	75,850	18,509	15,875	19,334	16,935
75,850	75,900	18,524	15,889	19,349	16,949
75,900	75,950	18,540	15,903	19,367	16,963
75,950	76,000	18,555	15,917	19,385	16,977

76,000

At least	But less than	Single	MFJ	MFS	HoH
76,000	76,050	18,571	15,931	19,403	16,991
76,050	76,100	18,586	15,945	19,421	17,005
76,100	76,150	18,602	15,959	19,439	17,019
76,150	76,200	18,617	15,973	19,457	17,033
76,200	76,250	18,633	15,987	19,475	17,047
76,250	76,300	18,648	16,001	19,493	17,061
76,300	76,350	18,664	16,015	19,511	17,075
76,350	76,400	18,679	16,029	19,529	17,089
76,400	76,450	18,695	16,043	19,547	17,103
76,450	76,500	18,710	16,057	19,565	17,117
76,500	76,550	18,726	16,071	19,583	17,131
76,550	76,600	18,741	16,085	19,601	17,145
76,600	76,650	18,757	16,099	19,619	17,159
76,650	76,700	18,772	16,113	19,637	17,173
76,700	76,750	18,788	16,127	19,655	17,187
76,750	76,800	18,803	16,141	19,673	17,201
76,800	76,850	18,819	16,155	19,691	17,215
76,850	76,900	18,834	16,169	19,709	17,229
76,900	76,950	18,850	16,183	19,727	17,243
76,950	77,000	18,865	16,197	19,745	17,257

* This column must also be used by a qualifying widow(er).

Continued on next page

1997 Tax Table—*Continued*

If line 38 (taxable income) is—		And you are—				If line 38 (taxable income) is—		And you are—				If line 38 (taxable income) is—		And you are—			
At least	But less than	Single	Married filing jointly *	Married filing separately	Head of a household	At least	But less than	Single	Married filing jointly *	Married filing separately	Head of a household	At least	But less than	Single	Married filing jointly *	Married filing separately	Head of a household
		Your tax is—						Your tax is—						Your tax is—			

77,000

At least	But less than	Single	MFJ	MFS	HoH
77,000	77,050	18,881	16,211	19,763	17,271
77,050	77,100	18,896	16,225	19,781	17,285
77,100	77,150	18,912	16,239	19,799	17,299
77,150	77,200	18,927	16,253	19,817	17,313
77,200	77,250	18,943	16,267	19,835	17,327
77,250	77,300	18,958	16,281	19,853	17,341
77,300	77,350	18,974	16,295	19,871	17,355
77,350	77,400	18,989	16,309	19,889	17,369
77,400	77,450	19,005	16,323	19,907	17,383
77,450	77,500	19,020	16,337	19,925	17,397
77,500	77,550	19,036	16,351	19,943	17,411
77,550	77,600	19,051	16,365	19,961	17,425
77,600	77,650	19,067	16,379	19,979	17,439
77,650	77,700	19,082	16,393	19,997	17,453
77,700	77,750	19,098	16,407	20,015	17,467
77,750	77,800	19,113	16,421	20,033	17,481
77,800	77,850	19,129	16,435	20,051	17,495
77,850	77,900	19,144	16,449	20,069	17,509
77,900	77,950	19,160	16,463	20,087	17,523
77,950	78,000	19,175	16,477	20,105	17,537

78,000

At least	But less than	Single	MFJ	MFS	HoH
78,000	78,050	19,191	16,491	20,123	17,551
78,050	78,100	19,206	16,505	20,141	17,565
78,100	78,150	19,222	16,519	20,159	17,579
78,150	78,200	19,237	16,533	20,177	17,593
78,200	78,250	19,253	16,547	20,195	17,607
78,250	78,300	19,268	16,561	20,213	17,621
78,300	78,350	19,284	16,575	20,231	17,635
78,350	78,400	19,299	16,589	20,249	17,649
78,400	78,450	19,315	16,603	20,267	17,663
78,450	78,500	19,330	16,617	20,285	17,677
78,500	78,550	19,346	16,631	20,303	17,691
78,550	78,600	19,361	16,645	20,321	17,705
78,600	78,650	19,377	16,659	20,339	17,719
78,650	78,700	19,392	16,673	20,357	17,733
78,700	78,750	19,408	16,687	20,375	17,747
78,750	78,800	19,423	16,701	20,393	17,761
78,800	78,850	19,439	16,715	20,411	17,775
78,850	78,900	19,454	16,729	20,429	17,789
78,900	78,950	19,470	16,743	20,447	17,803
78,950	79,000	19,485	16,757	20,465	17,817

79,000

At least	But less than	Single	MFJ	MFS	HoH
79,000	79,050	19,501	16,771	20,483	17,831
79,050	79,100	19,516	16,785	20,501	17,845
79,100	79,150	19,532	16,799	20,519	17,859
79,150	79,200	19,547	16,813	20,537	17,873
79,200	79,250	19,563	16,827	20,555	17,887
79,250	79,300	19,578	16,841	20,573	17,901
79,300	79,350	19,594	16,855	20,591	17,915
79,350	79,400	19,609	16,869	20,609	17,929
79,400	79,450	19,625	16,883	20,627	17,943
79,450	79,500	19,640	16,897	20,645	17,957
79,500	79,550	19,656	16,911	20,663	17,971
79,550	79,600	19,671	16,925	20,681	17,985
79,600	79,650	19,687	16,939	20,699	17,999
79,650	79,700	19,702	16,953	20,717	18,013
79,700	79,750	19,718	16,967	20,735	18,027
79,750	79,800	19,733	16,981	20,753	18,041
79,800	79,850	19,749	16,995	20,771	18,055
79,850	79,900	19,764	17,009	20,789	18,069
79,900	79,950	19,780	17,023	20,807	18,083
79,950	80,000	19,795	17,037	20,825	18,097

80,000

At least	But less than	Single	MFJ	MFS	HoH
80,000	80,050	19,811	17,051	20,843	18,111
80,050	80,100	19,826	17,065	20,861	18,125
80,100	80,150	19,842	17,079	20,879	18,139
80,150	80,200	19,857	17,093	20,897	18,153
80,200	80,250	19,873	17,107	20,915	18,167
80,250	80,300	19,888	17,121	20,933	18,181
80,300	80,350	19,904	17,135	20,951	18,195
80,350	80,400	19,919	17,149	20,969	18,209
80,400	80,450	19,935	17,163	20,987	18,223
80,450	80,500	19,950	17,177	21,005	18,237
80,500	80,550	19,966	17,191	21,023	18,251
80,550	80,600	19,981	17,205	21,041	18,265
80,600	80,650	19,997	17,219	21,059	18,279
80,650	80,700	20,012	17,233	21,077	18,293
80,700	80,750	20,028	17,247	21,095	18,307
80,750	80,800	20,043	17,261	21,113	18,321
80,800	80,850	20,059	17,275	21,131	18,335
80,850	80,900	20,074	17,289	21,149	18,349
80,900	80,950	20,090	17,303	21,167	18,363
80,950	81,000	20,105	17,317	21,185	18,377

81,000

At least	But less than	Single	MFJ	MFS	HoH
81,000	81,050	20,121	17,331	21,203	18,391
81,050	81,100	20,136	17,345	21,221	18,405
81,100	81,150	20,152	17,359	21,239	18,419
81,150	81,200	20,167	17,373	21,257	18,433
81,200	81,250	20,183	17,387	21,275	18,447
81,250	81,300	20,198	17,401	21,293	18,461
81,300	81,350	20,214	17,415	21,311	18,475
81,350	81,400	20,229	17,429	21,329	18,489
81,400	81,450	20,245	17,443	21,347	18,503
81,450	81,500	20,260	17,457	21,365	18,517
81,500	81,550	20,276	17,471	21,383	18,531
81,550	81,600	20,291	17,485	21,401	18,545
81,600	81,650	20,307	17,499	21,419	18,559
81,650	81,700	20,322	17,513	21,437	18,573
81,700	81,750	20,338	17,527	21,455	18,587
81,750	81,800	20,353	17,541	21,473	18,601
81,800	81,850	20,369	17,555	21,491	18,615
81,850	81,900	20,384	17,569	21,509	18,629
81,900	81,950	20,400	17,583	21,527	18,643
81,950	82,000	20,415	17,597	21,545	18,657

82,000

At least	But less than	Single	MFJ	MFS	HoH
82,000	82,050	20,431	17,611	21,563	18,671
82,050	82,100	20,446	17,625	21,581	18,685
82,100	82,150	20,462	17,639	21,599	18,699
82,150	82,200	20,477	17,653	21,617	18,713
82,200	82,250	20,493	17,667	21,635	18,727
82,250	82,300	20,508	17,681	21,653	18,741
82,300	82,350	20,524	17,695	21,671	18,755
82,350	82,400	20,539	17,709	21,689	18,769
82,400	82,450	20,555	17,723	21,707	18,783
82,450	82,500	20,570	17,737	21,725	18,797
82,500	82,550	20,586	17,751	21,743	18,811
82,550	82,600	20,601	17,765	21,761	18,825
82,600	82,650	20,617	17,779	21,779	18,839
82,650	82,700	20,632	17,793	21,797	18,853
82,700	82,750	20,648	17,807	21,815	18,867
82,750	82,800	20,663	17,821	21,833	18,881
82,800	82,850	20,679	17,835	21,851	18,895
82,850	82,900	20,694	17,849	21,869	18,909
82,900	82,950	20,710	17,863	21,887	18,923
82,950	83,000	20,725	17,877	21,905	18,937

83,000

At least	But less than	Single	MFJ	MFS	HoH
83,000	83,050	20,741	17,891	21,923	18,951
83,050	83,100	20,756	17,905	21,941	18,965
83,100	83,150	20,772	17,919	21,959	18,979
83,150	83,200	20,787	17,933	21,977	18,993
83,200	83,250	20,803	17,947	21,995	19,007
83,250	83,300	20,818	17,961	22,013	19,021
83,300	83,350	20,834	17,975	22,031	19,035
83,350	83,400	20,849	17,989	22,049	19,049
83,400	83,450	20,865	18,003	22,067	19,063
83,450	83,500	20,880	18,017	22,085	19,077
83,500	83,550	20,896	18,031	22,103	19,091
83,550	83,600	20,911	18,045	22,121	19,105
83,600	83,650	20,927	18,059	22,139	19,119
83,650	83,700	20,942	18,073	22,157	19,133
83,700	83,750	20,958	18,087	22,175	19,147
83,750	83,800	20,973	18,101	22,193	19,161
83,800	83,850	20,989	18,115	22,211	19,175
83,850	83,900	21,004	18,129	22,229	19,189
83,900	83,950	21,020	18,143	22,247	19,203
83,950	84,000	21,035	18,157	22,265	19,217

84,000

At least	But less than	Single	MFJ	MFS	HoH
84,000	84,050	21,051	18,171	22,283	19,231
84,050	84,100	21,066	18,185	22,301	19,245
84,100	84,150	21,082	18,199	22,319	19,259
84,150	84,200	21,097	18,213	22,337	19,273
84,200	84,250	21,113	18,227	22,355	19,287
84,250	84,300	21,128	18,241	22,373	19,301
84,300	84,350	21,144	18,255	22,391	19,315
84,350	84,400	21,159	18,269	22,409	19,329
84,400	84,450	21,175	18,283	22,427	19,343
84,450	84,500	21,190	18,297	22,445	19,357
84,500	84,550	21,206	18,311	22,463	19,371
84,550	84,600	21,221	18,325	22,481	19,385
84,600	84,650	21,237	18,339	22,499	19,399
84,650	84,700	21,252	18,353	22,517	19,413
84,700	84,750	21,268	18,367	22,535	19,427
84,750	84,800	21,283	18,381	22,553	19,441
84,800	84,850	21,299	18,395	22,571	19,455
84,850	84,900	21,314	18,409	22,589	19,469
84,900	84,950	21,330	18,423	22,607	19,483
84,950	85,000	21,345	18,437	22,625	19,497

85,000

At least	But less than	Single	MFJ	MFS	HoH
85,000	85,050	21,361	18,451	22,643	19,511
85,050	85,100	21,376	18,465	22,661	19,525
85,100	85,150	21,392	18,479	22,679	19,539
85,150	85,200	21,407	18,493	22,697	19,553
85,200	85,250	21,423	18,507	22,715	19,567
85,250	85,300	21,438	18,521	22,733	19,581
85,300	85,350	21,454	18,535	22,751	19,595
85,350	85,400	21,469	18,549	22,769	19,609
85,400	85,450	21,485	18,563	22,787	19,625
85,450	85,500	21,500	18,577	22,805	19,640
85,500	85,550	21,516	18,591	22,823	19,656
85,550	85,600	21,531	18,605	22,841	19,671
85,600	85,650	21,547	18,619	22,859	19,687
85,650	85,700	21,562	18,633	22,877	19,702
85,700	85,750	21,578	18,647	22,895	19,718
85,750	85,800	21,593	18,661	22,913	19,733
85,800	85,850	21,609	18,675	22,931	19,749
85,850	85,900	21,624	18,689	22,949	19,764
85,900	85,950	21,640	18,703	22,967	19,780
85,950	86,000	21,655	18,717	22,985	19,795

* This column must also be used by a qualifying widow(er).

Continued on next page

1997 Tax Table—*Continued*

If line 38 (taxable income) is— At least	But less than	Single	Married filing jointly*	Married filing separately	Head of a household
86,000					
86,000	86,050	21,671	18,731	23,003	19,811
86,050	86,100	21,686	18,745	23,021	19,826
86,100	86,150	21,702	18,759	23,039	19,842
86,150	86,200	21,717	18,773	23,057	19,857
86,200	86,250	21,733	18,787	23,075	19,873
86,250	86,300	21,748	18,801	23,093	19,888
86,300	86,350	21,764	18,815	23,111	19,904
86,350	86,400	21,779	18,829	23,129	19,919
86,400	86,450	21,795	18,843	23,147	19,935
86,450	86,500	21,810	18,857	23,165	19,950
86,500	86,550	21,826	18,871	23,183	19,966
86,550	86,600	21,841	18,885	23,201	19,981
86,600	86,650	21,857	18,899	23,219	19,997
86,650	86,700	21,872	18,913	23,237	20,012
86,700	86,750	21,888	18,927	23,255	20,028
86,750	86,800	21,903	18,941	23,273	20,043
86,800	86,850	21,919	18,955	23,291	20,059
86,850	86,900	21,934	18,969	23,309	20,074
86,900	86,950	21,950	18,983	23,327	20,090
86,950	87,000	21,965	18,997	23,345	20,105
87,000					
87,000	87,050	21,981	19,011	23,363	20,121
87,050	87,100	21,996	19,025	23,381	20,136
87,100	87,150	22,012	19,039	23,399	20,152
87,150	87,200	22,027	19,053	23,417	20,167
87,200	87,250	22,043	19,067	23,435	20,183
87,250	87,300	22,058	19,081	23,453	20,198
87,300	87,350	22,074	19,095	23,471	20,214
87,350	87,400	22,089	19,109	23,489	20,229
87,400	87,450	22,105	19,123	23,507	20,245
87,450	87,500	22,120	19,137	23,525	20,260
87,500	87,550	22,136	19,151	23,543	20,276
87,550	87,600	22,151	19,165	23,561	20,291
87,600	87,650	22,167	19,179	23,579	20,307
87,650	87,700	22,182	19,193	23,597	20,322
87,700	87,750	22,198	19,207	23,615	20,338
87,750	87,800	22,213	19,221	23,633	20,353
87,800	87,850	22,229	19,235	23,651	20,369
87,850	87,900	22,244	19,249	23,669	20,384
87,900	87,950	22,260	19,263	23,687	20,400
87,950	88,000	22,275	19,277	23,705	20,415
88,000					
88,000	88,050	22,291	19,291	23,723	20,431
88,050	88,100	22,306	19,305	23,741	20,446
88,100	88,150	22,322	19,319	23,759	20,462
88,150	88,200	22,337	19,333	23,777	20,477
88,200	88,250	22,353	19,347	23,795	20,493
88,250	88,300	22,368	19,361	23,813	20,508
88,300	88,350	22,384	19,375	23,831	20,524
88,350	88,400	22,399	19,389	23,849	20,539
88,400	88,450	22,415	19,403	23,867	20,555
88,450	88,500	22,430	19,417	23,885	20,570
88,500	88,550	22,446	19,431	23,903	20,586
88,550	88,600	22,461	19,445	23,921	20,601
88,600	88,650	22,477	19,459	23,939	20,617
88,650	88,700	22,492	19,473	23,957	20,632
88,700	88,750	22,508	19,487	23,975	20,648
88,750	88,800	22,523	19,501	23,993	20,663
88,800	88,850	22,539	19,515	24,011	20,679
88,850	88,900	22,554	19,529	24,029	20,694
88,900	88,950	22,570	19,543	24,047	20,710
88,950	89,000	22,585	19,557	24,065	20,725

If line 38 (taxable income) is— At least	But less than	Single	Married filing jointly*	Married filing separately	Head of a household
89,000					
89,000	89,050	22,601	19,571	24,083	20,741
89,050	89,100	22,616	19,585	24,101	20,756
89,100	89,150	22,632	19,599	24,119	20,772
89,150	89,200	22,647	19,613	24,137	20,787
89,200	89,250	22,663	19,627	24,155	20,803
89,250	89,300	22,678	19,641	24,173	20,818
89,300	89,350	22,694	19,655	24,191	20,834
89,350	89,400	22,709	19,669	24,209	20,849
89,400	89,450	22,725	19,683	24,227	20,865
89,450	89,500	22,740	19,697	24,245	20,880
89,500	89,550	22,756	19,711	24,263	20,896
89,550	89,600	22,771	19,725	24,281	20,911
89,600	89,650	22,787	19,739	24,299	20,927
89,650	89,700	22,802	19,753	24,317	20,942
89,700	89,750	22,818	19,767	24,335	20,958
89,750	89,800	22,833	19,781	24,353	20,973
89,800	89,850	22,849	19,795	24,371	20,989
89,850	89,900	22,864	19,809	24,389	21,004
89,900	89,950	22,880	19,823	24,407	21,020
89,950	90,000	22,895	19,837	24,425	21,035
90,000					
90,000	90,050	22,911	19,851	24,443	21,051
90,050	90,100	22,926	19,865	24,461	21,066
90,100	90,150	22,942	19,879	24,479	21,082
90,150	90,200	22,957	19,893	24,497	21,097
90,200	90,250	22,973	19,907	24,515	21,113
90,250	90,300	22,988	19,921	24,533	21,128
90,300	90,350	23,004	19,935	24,551	21,144
90,350	90,400	23,019	19,949	24,569	21,159
90,400	90,450	23,035	19,963	24,587	21,175
90,450	90,500	23,050	19,977	24,605	21,190
90,500	90,550	23,066	19,991	24,623	21,206
90,550	90,600	23,081	20,005	24,641	21,221
90,600	90,650	23,097	20,019	24,659	21,237
90,650	90,700	23,112	20,033	24,677	21,252
90,700	90,750	23,128	20,047	24,695	21,268
90,750	90,800	23,143	20,061	24,713	21,283
90,800	90,850	23,159	20,075	24,731	21,299
90,850	90,900	23,174	20,089	24,749	21,314
90,900	90,950	23,190	20,103	24,767	21,330
90,950	91,000	23,205	20,117	24,785	21,345
91,000					
91,000	91,050	23,221	20,131	24,803	21,361
91,050	91,100	23,236	20,145	24,821	21,376
91,100	91,150	23,252	20,159	24,839	21,392
91,150	91,200	23,267	20,173	24,857	21,407
91,200	91,250	23,283	20,187	24,875	21,423
91,250	91,300	23,298	20,201	24,893	21,438
91,300	91,350	23,314	20,215	24,911	21,454
91,350	91,400	23,329	20,229	24,929	21,469
91,400	91,450	23,345	20,243	24,947	21,485
91,450	91,500	23,360	20,257	24,965	21,500
91,500	91,550	23,376	20,271	24,983	21,516
91,550	91,600	23,391	20,285	25,001	21,531
91,600	91,650	23,407	20,299	25,019	21,547
91,650	91,700	23,422	20,313	25,037	21,562
91,700	91,750	23,438	20,327	25,055	21,578
91,750	91,800	23,453	20,341	25,073	21,593
91,800	91,850	23,469	20,355	25,091	21,609
91,850	91,900	23,484	20,369	25,109	21,624
91,900	91,950	23,500	20,383	25,127	21,640
91,950	92,000	23,515	20,397	25,145	21,655

If line 38 (taxable income) is— At least	But less than	Single	Married filing jointly*	Married filing separately	Head of a household
92,000					
92,000	92,050	23,531	20,411	25,163	21,671
92,050	92,100	23,546	20,425	25,181	21,686
92,100	92,150	23,562	20,439	25,199	21,702
92,150	92,200	23,577	20,453	25,217	21,717
92,200	92,250	23,593	20,467	25,235	21,733
92,250	92,300	23,608	20,481	25,253	21,748
92,300	92,350	23,624	20,495	25,271	21,764
92,350	92,400	23,639	20,509	25,289	21,779
92,400	92,450	23,655	20,523	25,307	21,795
92,450	92,500	23,670	20,537	25,325	21,810
92,500	92,550	23,686	20,551	25,343	21,826
92,550	92,600	23,701	20,565	25,361	21,841
92,600	92,650	23,717	20,579	25,379	21,857
92,650	92,700	23,732	20,593	25,397	21,872
92,700	92,750	23,748	20,607	25,415	21,888
92,750	92,800	23,763	20,621	25,433	21,903
92,800	92,850	23,779	20,635	25,451	21,919
92,850	92,900	23,794	20,649	25,469	21,934
92,900	92,950	23,810	20,663	25,487	21,950
92,950	93,000	23,825	20,677	25,505	21,965
93,000					
93,000	93,050	23,841	20,691	25,523	21,981
93,050	93,100	23,856	20,705	25,541	21,996
93,100	93,150	23,872	20,719	25,559	22,012
93,150	93,200	23,887	20,733	25,577	22,027
93,200	93,250	23,903	20,747	25,595	22,043
93,250	93,300	23,918	20,761	25,613	22,058
93,300	93,350	23,934	20,775	25,631	22,074
93,350	93,400	23,949	20,789	25,649	22,089
93,400	93,450	23,965	20,803	25,667	22,105
93,450	93,500	23,980	20,817	25,685	22,120
93,500	93,550	23,996	20,831	25,703	22,136
93,550	93,600	24,011	20,845	25,721	22,151
93,600	93,650	24,027	20,859	25,739	22,167
93,650	93,700	24,042	20,873	25,757	22,182
93,700	93,750	24,058	20,887	25,775	22,198
93,750	93,800	24,073	20,901	25,793	22,213
93,800	93,850	24,089	20,915	25,811	22,229
93,850	93,900	24,104	20,929	25,829	22,244
93,900	93,950	24,120	20,943	25,847	22,260
93,950	94,000	24,135	20,957	25,865	22,275
94,000					
94,000	94,050	24,151	20,971	25,883	22,291
94,050	94,100	24,166	20,985	25,901	22,306
94,100	94,150	24,182	20,999	25,919	22,322
94,150	94,200	24,197	21,013	25,937	22,337
94,200	94,250	24,213	21,027	25,955	22,353
94,250	94,300	24,228	21,041	25,973	22,368
94,300	94,350	24,244	21,055	25,991	22,384
94,350	94,400	24,259	21,069	26,009	22,399
94,400	94,450	24,275	21,083	26,027	22,415
94,450	94,500	24,290	21,097	26,045	22,430
94,500	94,550	24,306	21,111	26,063	22,446
94,550	94,600	24,321	21,125	26,081	22,461
94,600	94,650	24,337	21,139	26,099	22,477
94,650	94,700	24,352	21,153	26,117	22,492
94,700	94,750	24,368	21,167	26,135	22,508
94,750	94,800	24,383	21,181	26,153	22,523
94,800	94,850	24,399	21,195	26,171	22,539
94,850	94,900	24,414	21,209	26,189	22,554
94,900	94,950	24,430	21,223	26,207	22,570
94,950	95,000	24,445	21,237	26,225	22,585

* This column must also be used by a qualifying widow(er).

Continued on next page

1997 Tax Table—*Continued*

If line 38 (taxable income) is—		And you are—				If line 38 (taxable income) is—		And you are—			
At least	But less than	Single	Married filing jointly *	Married filing separately	Head of a household	At least	But less than	Single	Married filing jointly *	Married filing separately	Head of a household
		Your tax is—						Your tax is—			

95,000

95,000	95,050	24,461	21,251	26,243	22,601						
95,050	95,100	24,476	21,265	26,261	22,616						
95,100	95,150	24,492	21,279	26,279	22,632						
95,150	95,200	24,507	21,293	26,297	22,647						
95,200	95,250	24,523	21,307	26,315	22,663						
95,250	95,300	24,538	21,321	26,333	22,678						
95,300	95,350	24,554	21,335	26,351	22,694						
95,350	95,400	24,569	21,349	26,369	22,709						
95,400	95,450	24,585	21,363	26,387	22,725						
95,450	95,500	24,600	21,377	26,405	22,740						
95,500	95,550	24,616	21,391	26,423	22,756						
95,550	95,600	24,631	21,405	26,441	22,771						
95,600	95,650	24,647	21,419	26,459	22,787						
95,650	95,700	24,662	21,433	26,477	22,802						
95,700	95,750	24,678	21,447	26,495	22,818						
95,750	95,800	24,693	21,461	26,513	22,833						
95,800	95,850	24,709	21,475	26,531	22,849						
95,850	95,900	24,724	21,489	26,549	22,864						
95,900	95,950	24,740	21,503	26,567	22,880						
95,950	96,000	24,755	21,517	26,585	22,895						

96,000

96,000	96,050	24,771	21,531	26,603	22,911						
96,050	96,100	24,786	21,545	26,621	22,926						
96,100	96,150	24,802	21,559	26,639	22,942						
96,150	96,200	24,817	21,573	26,657	22,957						
96,200	96,250	24,833	21,587	26,675	22,973						
96,250	96,300	24,848	21,601	26,693	22,988						
96,300	96,350	24,864	21,615	26,711	23,004						
96,350	96,400	24,879	21,629	26,729	23,019						
96,400	96,450	24,895	21,643	26,747	23,035						
96,450	96,500	24,910	21,657	26,765	23,050						
96,500	96,550	24,926	21,671	26,783	23,066						
96,550	96,600	24,941	21,685	26,801	23,081						
96,600	96,650	24,957	21,699	26,819	23,097						
96,650	96,700	24,972	21,713	26,837	23,112						
96,700	96,750	24,988	21,727	26,855	23,128						
96,750	96,800	25,003	21,741	26,873	23,143						
96,800	96,850	25,019	21,755	26,891	23,159						
96,850	96,900	25,034	21,769	26,909	23,174						
96,900	96,950	25,050	21,783	26,927	23,190						
96,950	97,000	25,065	21,797	26,945	23,205						

97,000

97,000	97,050	25,081	21,811	26,963	23,221						
97,050	97,100	25,096	21,825	26,981	23,236						
97,100	97,150	25,112	21,839	26,999	23,252						
97,150	97,200	25,127	21,853	27,017	23,267						
97,200	97,250	25,143	21,867	27,035	23,283						
97,250	97,300	25,158	21,881	27,053	23,298						
97,300	97,350	25,174	21,895	27,071	23,314						
97,350	97,400	25,189	21,909	27,089	23,329						
97,400	97,450	25,205	21,923	27,107	23,345						
97,450	97,500	25,220	21,937	27,125	23,360						
97,500	97,550	25,236	21,951	27,143	23,376						
97,550	97,600	25,251	21,965	27,161	23,391						
97,600	97,650	25,267	21,979	27,179	23,407						
97,650	97,700	25,282	21,993	27,197	23,422						
97,700	97,750	25,298	22,007	27,215	23,438						
97,750	97,800	25,313	22,021	27,233	23,453						
97,800	97,850	25,329	22,035	27,251	23,469						
97,850	97,900	25,344	22,049	27,269	23,484						
97,900	97,950	25,360	22,063	27,287	23,500						
97,950	98,000	25,375	22,077	27,305	23,515						

98,000

At least	But less than	Single	Married filing jointly *	Married filing separately	Head of a household
98,000	98,050	25,391	22,091	27,323	23,531
98,050	98,100	25,406	22,105	27,341	23,546
98,100	98,150	25,422	22,119	27,359	23,562
98,150	98,200	25,437	22,133	27,377	23,577
98,200	98,250	25,453	22,147	27,395	23,593
98,250	98,300	25,468	22,161	27,413	23,608
98,300	98,350	25,484	22,175	27,431	23,624
98,350	98,400	25,499	22,189	27,449	23,639
98,400	98,450	25,515	22,203	27,467	23,655
98,450	98,500	25,530	22,217	27,485	23,670
98,500	98,550	25,546	22,231	27,503	23,686
98,550	98,600	25,561	22,245	27,521	23,701
98,600	98,650	25,577	22,259	27,539	23,717
98,650	98,700	25,592	22,273	27,557	23,732
98,700	98,750	25,608	22,287	27,575	23,748
98,750	98,800	25,623	22,301	27,593	23,763
98,800	98,850	25,639	22,315	27,611	23,779
98,850	98,900	25,654	22,329	27,629	23,794
98,900	98,950	25,670	22,343	27,647	23,810
98,950	99,000	25,685	22,357	27,665	23,825

99,000

At least	But less than	Single	Married filing jointly *	Married filing separately	Head of a household
99,000	99,050	25,701	22,371	27,683	23,841
99,050	99,100	25,716	22,385	27,701	23,856
99,100	99,150	25,732	22,399	27,719	23,872
99,150	99,200	25,747	22,413	27,737	23,887
99,200	99,250	25,763	22,427	27,755	23,903
99,250	99,300	25,778	22,441	27,773	23,918
99,300	99,350	25,794	22,455	27,791	23,934
99,350	99,400	25,809	22,469	27,809	23,949
99,400	99,450	25,825	22,483	27,827	23,965
99,450	99,500	25,840	22,497	27,845	23,980
99,500	99,550	25,856	22,511	27,863	23,996
99,550	99,600	25,871	22,525	27,881	24,011
99,600	99,650	25,887	22,540	27,899	24,027
99,650	99,700	25,902	22,555	27,917	24,042
99,700	99,750	25,918	22,571	27,935	24,058
99,750	99,800	25,933	22,586	27,953	24,073
99,800	99,850	25,949	22,602	27,971	24,089
99,850	99,900	25,964	22,617	27,989	24,104
99,900	99,950	25,980	22,633	28,007	24,120
99,950	100,000	25,995	22,648	28,025	24,135

$100,000 or over — use the Tax Rate Schedules on page A–2

* This column must also be used by a qualifying widow(er).

APPENDIX B
Tax Forms

Form 1040EZ

Department of the Treasury—Internal Revenue Service

Income Tax Return for Single and Joint Filers With No Dependents (99) **1997**

OMB No. 1545-0675

Use the IRS label here

Your first name and initial | Last name

If a joint return, spouse's first name and initial | Last name

Home address (number and street). If you have a P.O. box, see page 7. | Apt. no.

City, town or post office, state, and ZIP code. If you have a foreign address, see page 7.

Your social security number

Spouse's social security number

Presidential Election Campaign
(See page 7.)

Note: *Checking "Yes" will not change your tax or reduce your refund.*

Do you want $3 to go to this fund? ▶ Yes ☐ No ☐

If a joint return, does your spouse want $3 to go to this fund? ▶ Yes ☐ No ☐

Dollars | Cents

Income

Attach Copy B of Form(s) W-2 here. Enclose but do not attach any payment with your return.

1 Total wages, salaries, and tips. This should be shown in box 1 of your W-2 form(s). Attach your W-2 form(s).   1

2 Taxable interest income. If the total is over $400, you cannot use Form 1040EZ.   2

3 Unemployment compensation (see page 9).   3

4 Add lines 1, 2, and 3. This is your **adjusted gross income.** If under $9,770, see page 9 to find out if you can claim the earned income credit on line 8a.   4

Note: *You* **must** *check Yes or No.*

5 Can your parents (or someone else) claim you on their return?
Yes. Enter amount from worksheet on back. ☐
No. If **single,** enter 6,800.00. If **married,** enter 12,200.00. See back for explanation.   5

6 Subtract line 5 from line 4. If line 5 is larger than line 4, enter 0. This is your **taxable income.** ▶ 6

Payments and tax

7 Enter your Federal income tax withheld from box 2 of your W-2 form(s).   7

8a Earned income credit (see page 9).
b Nontaxable earned income: enter type and amount below.
Type ____ | $ ____   8a

9 Add lines 7 and 8a. These are your **total payments.**   9

10 Tax. Use the amount on **line 6** to find your tax in the tax table on pages 20–24 of the booklet. Then, enter the tax from the table on this line.   10

Refund

Have it directly deposited! See page 13 and fill in 11b, 11c, and 11d.

11a If line 9 is larger than line 10, subtract line 10 from line 9. This is your **refund.**   11a

b Routing number

c Type: ☐ Checking ☐ Savings   **d** Account number

Amount you owe

12 If line 10 is larger than line 9, subtract line 9 from line 10. This is the **amount you owe.** See page 13 for details on how to pay.   12

I have read this return. Under penalties of perjury, I declare that to the best of my knowledge and belief, the return is true, correct, and accurately lists all amounts and sources of income I received during the tax year.

Sign here ▶

Keep copy for your records.

Your signature | Spouse's signature if joint return

Date | Your occupation | Date | Spouse's occupation

For Official Use Only

For Privacy Act and Paperwork Reduction Act Notice, see page 18.   Cat. No. 11329W   **1997 Form 1040EZ**

1997 Form 1040EZ page 2

Use this form if
- Your filing status is single or married filing jointly.
- You do not claim any dependents.
- You had **only** wages, salaries, tips, taxable scholarship or fellowship grants, unemployment compensation, or Alaska Permanent Fund dividends, and your taxable interest income was not over $400. **But** if you earned tips, including allocated tips, that are not included in box 5 and box 7 of your W-2, you may not be able to use Form 1040EZ. See page 8.
- You did not receive any advance earned income credit payments.

- You (and your spouse if married) were under 65 on January 1, 1998, and not blind at the end of 1997.
- Your taxable income (line 6) is less than $50,000.

If you are not sure about your filing status, see page 6. If you have questions about dependents, use TeleTax topic 354 (see page 18). If you **cannot use this form,** use TeleTax topic 352 (see page 18).

Filling in your return

For tips on how to avoid common mistakes, see page 3.

Because this form is read by a machine, please print your numbers inside the boxes like this:

9 8 7 6 5 4 3 2 1 0   Do not type your numbers. Do not use dollar signs.

If you received a scholarship or fellowship grant or tax-exempt interest income, such as on municipal bonds, see the booklet before filling in the form. Also, see the booklet if you received a Form 1099-INT showing Federal income tax withheld or if Federal income tax was withheld from your unemployment compensation or Alaska Permanent Fund dividends.

Remember, you must report all wages, salaries, and tips even if you do not get a W-2 form from your employer. You must also report all your taxable interest income, including interest from banks, savings and loans, credit unions, etc., even if you do not get a Form 1099-INT.

Worksheet for dependents who checked "Yes" on line 5

Use this worksheet to figure the amount to enter on line 5 if someone can claim you (or your spouse if married) as a dependent, even if that person chooses not to do so. To find out if someone can claim you as a dependent, use TeleTax topic 354 (see page 18).

A. Enter the amount from line 1 on the front.   A. _____

B. Minimum standard deduction.   B. _____ 650.00

C. Enter the LARGER of line A or line B here.   C. _____

D. Maximum standard deduction. If single, enter 4,150.00; if married, enter 6,900.00.   D. _____

E. Enter the SMALLER of line C or line D here. This is your standard deduction.   E. _____

F. Exemption amount.
- If single, enter 0.
- If married and—
  —both you and your spouse can be claimed as dependents, enter 0.
  —only one of you can be claimed as a dependent, enter 2,650.00.   F. _____

G. Add lines E and F. Enter the total here and on line 5 on the front.   G. _____

If you checked "No" on line 5 because no one can claim you (or your spouse if married) as a dependent, enter on line 5 the amount shown below that applies to you.
- Single, enter 6,800.00. This is the total of your standard deduction (4,150.00) and your exemption (2,650.00).
- Married, enter 12,200.00. This is the total of your standard deduction (6,900.00), your exemption (2,650.00), and your spouse s exemption (2,650.00).

Mailing your return

Mail your return by **April 15, 1998.** Use the envelope that came with your booklet. If you do not have that envelope, see page 28 for the address to use.

Paid preparer s use only

See page 14.

Under penalties of perjury, I declare that I have examined this return, and to the best of my knowledge and belief, it is true, correct, and accurately lists all amounts and sources of income received during the tax year. This declaration is based on all information of which I have any knowledge.

Preparer's signature ▶	Date	Check if self-employed ☐	Preparer's SSN
Firm's name (or yours if self-employed) and address ▶		EIN	
		ZIP code	

Form
1040A (99)   **U.S. Individual Income Tax Return**   **1997**   IRS Use Only—Do not write or staple in this space.

Department of the Treasury—Internal Revenue Service

OMB No. 1545-0085

Label (See page 14.) Use the IRS label. Otherwise, please print in **ALL CAPITAL LETTERS.**

Your first name | Init. | Last name

Your social security number

If a joint return, spouse's first name | Init. | Last name

Spouse's social security number

Home address (number and street). If you have a P.O. box, see page 14. | Apt. no.

For Privacy Act and Paperwork Reduction Act Notice, see page 42.

City, town or post office. If you have a foreign address, see page 14. | State | ZIP code

Presidential Election Campaign Fund (See page 14.)

Do you want $3 to go to this fund? . . . . | Yes | No

If a joint return, does your spouse want $3 to go to this fund? . . . .

Note: *Checking "Yes" will not change your tax or reduce your refund.*

1 ☐ Single

2 ☐ Married filing joint return (even if only one had income)

3 ☐ Married filing separate return. Enter spouse's social security number above and full name here. ▶

4 ☐ Head of household (with qualifying person). (See page 15.) If the qualifying person is a child but not your dependent, enter this child's name here. ▶

5 ☐ Qualifying widow(er) with dependent child (year spouse died ▶ 19   ). (See page 16.)

6a ☐ **Yourself.** If your parent (or someone else) can claim you as a dependent on his or her tax return, **do not** check box 6a.

b ☐ **Spouse**

No. of boxes checked on 6a and 6b

c **Dependents.** If more than six dependents, see page 16.

(1) First name Last name	(2) Dependent's social security number	(3) Dependent's relationship to you	(4) No. of months lived in your home in 1997

No. of your children on 6c who:
• lived with you
• did not live with you due to divorce or separation (see page 17)
Dependents on 6c not entered above
Add numbers entered in boxes above

d Total number of exemptions claimed . . . . ▶

Dollars | Cents

7 Wages, salaries, tips, etc. Attach Form(s) W-2. | 7

8a **Taxable** interest income. Attach Schedule 1 if required. | 8a

b **Tax-exempt** interest. DO NOT include on line 8a. | 8b

9 Dividends. Attach Schedule 1 if required. | 9

10a Total IRA distributions. | 10a | 10b Taxable amount (see page 19). | 10b

11a Total pensions and annuities. | 11a | 11b Taxable amount (see page 19). | 11b

12 Unemployment compensation. | 12

13a Social security benefits. | 13a | 13b Taxable amount (see page 21). | 13b

14 Add lines 7 through 13b (far right column). This is your **total income.** ▶ | 14

15 IRA deduction (see page 21). | 15

16 Subtract line 15 from line 14. This is your **adjusted gross income.** If under $29,290 (under $9,770 if a child did not live with you), see the EIC instructions on page 27. ▶ | 16

Attach Copy B of W-2 and 1099-R here.

Cat. No. 11327A

1997 Form 1040A

1997 Form 1040A page 2

17	Enter the amount from line 16.	**17**

18a Check if: ☐ **You** were 65 or older ☐ Blind **Enter number of boxes checked ▶** 18a ☐
☐ **Spouse** was 65 or older ☐ Blind

b If you are married filing separately and your spouse itemizes deductions, see page 23 and check here . . . . ▶ 18b ☐

19 Enter the **standard deduction** for your filing status. **But** see page 24 if you checked any box on line 18a or 18b **OR** someone can claim you as a dependent.
• Single—4,150 • Married filing jointly or Qualifying widow(er)—6,900
• Head of household—6,050 • Married filing separately—3,450   **19**

20 Subtract line 19 from line 17. If line 19 is more than line 17, enter 0.   **20**

21 Multiply $2,650 by the total number of exemptions claimed on line 6d.   **21**

22 Subtract line 21 from line 20. If line 21 is more than line 20, enter 0. This is your **taxable income.** **If you want the IRS to figure your tax, see page 24.** ▶ **22**

23 Find the tax on the amount on line 22 (see page 24).   **23**

24a Credit for child and dependent care expenses. Attach Schedule 2. **24a**

b Credit for the elderly or the disabled. Attach Schedule 3. **24b**

c Adoption credit. Attach Form 8839. **24c**

d Add lines 24a, 24b, and 24c. These are your **total credits.**   **24d**

25 Subtract line 24d from line 23. If line 24d is more than line 23, enter 0.   **25**

26 Advance earned income credit payments from Form(s) W-2.   **26**

27 Household employment taxes. Attach Schedule H.   **27**

28 Add lines 25, 26, and 27. This is your **total tax.** ▶ **28**

29a Total Federal income tax withheld from Forms W-2 and 1099. **29a**

b 1997 estimated tax payments and amount applied from 1996 return. **29b**

c **Earned income credit.** Attach Schedule EIC if you have a qualifying child. **29c**

d Nontaxable earned income: amount ▶ and type ▶

e Add lines 29a, 29b, and 29c. These are your **total payments.** ▶ **29e**

30 If line 29e is more than line 28, subtract line 28 from line 29e. This is the amount you **overpaid.** **30**

31a Amount of line 30 you want **refunded to you.** If you want it directly deposited, see page 33 and fill in 31b, 31c, and 31d. **31a**

b Routing number ☐☐☐☐☐☐☐☐☐ **c** Type: ☐ Checking ☐ Savings

d Account number ☐☐☐☐☐☐☐☐☐☐☐☐☐☐☐☐☐

32 Amount of line 30 you want **applied to your 1998 estimated tax.** **32**

33 If line 28 is more than line 29e, subtract line 29e from line 28. This is the **amount you owe.** For details on how to pay, see page 34. **33**

34 Estimated tax penalty (see page 34). **34**

Sign here
Under penalties of perjury, I declare that I have examined this return and accompanying schedules and statements, and to the best of my knowledge and belief, they are true, correct, and accurately list all amounts and sources of income I received during the tax year. Declaration of preparer (other than the taxpayer) is based on all information of which the preparer has any knowledge.

Your signature   Date   Your occupation

Keep a copy of this return for your records.

Spouse's signature. If joint return, BOTH must sign.   Date   Spouse's occupation

Paid preparer's use only
Preparer's signature   Date   Check if self-employed ☐   Preparer's SSN

Firm's name (or yours if self-employed) and address   EIN

ZIP code

Schedule 1

(Form 1040A)   Department of the Treasury—Internal Revenue Service

(99)   **Interest and Dividend Income**
for Form 1040A Filers   **1997**   OMB No. 1545-0085

Name(s) shown on Form 1040A: First and initial(s)	Last	Your social security number

Part I   Interest Income   (See pages 18 and 49.)

Note: *If you received a Form 1099±INT, Form 1099±OID, or substitute statement from a brokerage firm, enter the firm's name and the total interest shown on that form.*

		Dollars	Cents
1	List name of payer. If any interest is from a seller-financed mortgage and the buyer used the property as a personal residence, see page 49 and list this interest first. Also, show that buyer's social security number and address.	1	
2	Add the amounts on line 1.	2	
3	Excludable interest on series EE U.S. savings bonds issued after 1989 from Form 8815, line 14. You **must** attach Form 8815 to Form 1040A.	3	
4	Subtract line 3 from line 2. Enter the result here and on Form 1040A, line 8a.	4	

Part II   Dividend Income   (See pages 19 and 49.)

Note: *If you received a Form 1099±DIV or substitute statement from a brokerage firm, enter the firm's name and the total dividends shown on that form.*

		Dollars	Cents
5	List name of payer	5	
6	Add the amounts on line 5. Enter the total here and on Form 1040A, line 9.	6	

For Paperwork Reduction Act Notice, see Form 1040A instructions.   Cat. No. 12075R   **1997 Schedule 1 (Form 1040A)**

Form 1040

Department of the Treasury—Internal Revenue Service

U.S. Individual Income Tax Return

1997

(99)   IRS Use Only—Do not write or staple in this space.

For the year Jan. 1–Dec. 31, 1997, or other tax year beginning _____ , 1997, ending _____ , 19 ____   OMB No. 1545-0074

Label

(See instructions on page 10.)

Use the IRS label. Otherwise, please print or type.

L A B E L   H E R E

Your first name and initial | Last name | **Your social security number**

If a joint return, spouse's first name and initial | Last name | **Spouse's social security number**

Home address (number and street). If you have a P.O. box, see page 10. | Apt. no.

City, town or post office, state, and ZIP code. If you have a foreign address, see page 10.

For help in finding line instructions, see pages 2 and 3 in the booklet.

Presidential Election Campaign (See page 10.)

Do you want $3 to go to this fund? . . . .

If a joint return, does your spouse want $3 to go to this fund? . . . .

Yes | No | **Note:** *Checking "Yes" will not change your tax or reduce your refund.*

Filing Status

Check only one box.

1 ☐ Single

2 ☐ Married filing joint return (even if only one had income)

3 ☐ Married filing separate return. Enter spouse's social security no. above and full name here. ▶ _____

4 ☐ Head of household (with qualifying person). (See page 10.) If the qualifying person is a child but not your dependent, enter this child's name here. ▶ _____

5 ☐ Qualifying widow(er) with dependent child (year spouse died ▶ 19 ___). (See page 10.)

Exemptions

If more than six dependents, see page 10.

6a ☐ **Yourself.** If your parent (or someone else) can claim you as a dependent on his or her tax return, **do not** check box 6a. . . . .

b ☐ **Spouse** . . . .

c **Dependents:**

(1) First name Last name	(2) Dependent's social security number	(3) Dependent's relationship to you	(4) No. of months lived in your home in 1997

d Total number of exemptions claimed . . . .

No. of boxes checked on 6a and 6b ____

No. of your children on 6c who:
• lived with you
• did not live with you due to divorce or separation (see page 11)

Dependents on 6c not entered above ____

Add numbers entered on lines above ▶ ☐

Income

Attach Copy B of your Forms W-2, W-2G, and 1099-R here.

If you did not get a W-2, see page 12.

Enclose but do not attach any payment. Also, please use **Form 1040-V.**

7 Wages, salaries, tips, etc. Attach Form(s) W-2 . . . . | 7 |

8a **Taxable** interest. Attach Schedule B if required . . . . | 8a |

b **Tax-exempt** interest. DO NOT include on line 8a . . . | 8b |

9 Dividends. Attach Schedule B if required . . . . | 9 |

10 Taxable refunds, credits, or offsets of state and local income taxes (see page 12) . . | 10 |

11 Alimony received . . . . | 11 |

12 Business income or (loss). Attach Schedule C or C-EZ . . . . | 12 |

13 Capital gain or (loss). Attach Schedule D . . . . | 13 |

14 Other gains or (losses). Attach Form 4797 . . . . | 14 |

15a Total IRA distributions . | 15a | b Taxable amount (see page 13) | 15b |

16a Total pensions and annuities | 16a | b Taxable amount (see page 13) | 16b |

17 Rental real estate, royalties, partnerships, S corporations, trusts, etc. Attach Schedule E | 17 |

18 Farm income or (loss). Attach Schedule F . . . . | 18 |

19 Unemployment compensation . . . . | 19 |

20a Social security benefits . | 20a | b Taxable amount (see page 14) | 20b |

21 Other income. List type and amount—see page 15 _____ | 21 |

22 Add the amounts in the far right column for lines 7 through 21. This is your **total income** ▶ | 22 |

Adjusted Gross Income

If line 32 is under $29,290 (under $9,770 if a child did not live with you), see EIC inst. on page 21.

23 IRA deduction (see page 16) . . . . | 23 |

24 Medical savings account deduction. Attach Form 8853 . | 24 |

25 Moving expenses. Attach Form 3903 or 3903-F . . . | 25 |

26 One-half of self-employment tax. Attach Schedule SE . | 26 |

27 Self-employed health insurance deduction (see page 17) | 27 |

28 Keogh and self-employed SEP and SIMPLE plans . . | 28 |

29 Penalty on early withdrawal of savings . . . . . | 29 |

30a Alimony paid b Recipient's SSN ▶ _____ | 30a |

31 Add lines 23 through 30a . . . . | 31 |

32 Subtract line 31 from line 22. This is your **adjusted gross income** . . . . . ▶ | 32 |

For Privacy Act and Paperwork Reduction Act Notice, see page 38.   Cat. No. 11320B   Form **1040** (1997)

Form 1040 (1997)   Page **2**

Tax Compu-tation	**33**	Amount from line 32 (adjusted gross income)	**33**
	34a	Check if: ☐ **You** were 65 or older, ☐ Blind; ☐ **Spouse** was 65 or older, ☐ Blind. Add the number of boxes checked above and enter the total here . . . ▶ **34a**	
	b	If you are married filing separately and your spouse itemizes deductions or you were a dual-status alien, see page 18 and check here . . . . . ▶ **34b** ☐	

	35	Enter the **larger** of your: { **Itemized deductions** from Schedule A, line 28, **OR** **Standard deduction** shown below for your filing status. **But** see page 18 if you checked any box on line 34a or 34b **or** someone can claim you as a dependent. ● Single—$4,150 ● Married filing jointly or Qualifying widow(er)—$6,900 ● Head of household—$6,050 ● Married filing separately—$3,450 }	**35**

If you want the IRS to figure your tax, see page 18.

	36	Subtract line 35 from line 33	**36**
	37	If line 33 is $90,900 or less, multiply $2,650 by the total number of exemptions claimed on line 6d. If line 33 is over $90,900, see the worksheet on page 19 for the amount to enter .	**37**
	38	**Taxable income.** Subtract line 37 from line 36. If line 37 is more than line 36, enter -0-	**38**
	39	**Tax.** See page 19. Check if any tax from **a** ☐ Form(s) 8814 **b** ☐ Form 4972 . . ▶	**39**

Credits				
	40	Credit for child and dependent care expenses. Attach Form 2441	**40**	
	41	Credit for the elderly or the disabled. Attach Schedule R .	**41**	
	42	Adoption credit. Attach Form 8839 .	**42**	
	43	Foreign tax credit. Attach Form 1116	**43**	
	44	Other. Check if from **a** ☐ Form 3800 **b** ☐ Form 8396 **c** ☐ Form 8801 **d** ☐ Form (specify) _____	**44**	
	45	Add lines 40 through 44	**45**	
	46	Subtract line 45 from line 39. If line 45 is more than line 39, enter -0- . . . . . ▶	**46**	

Other Taxes			
	47	Self-employment tax. Attach Schedule SE	**47**
	48	Alternative minimum tax. Attach Form 6251	**48**
	49	Social security and Medicare tax on tip income not reported to employer. Attach Form 4137	**49**
	50	Tax on qualified retirement plans (including IRAs) and MSAs. Attach Form 5329 if required	**50**
	51	Advance earned income credit payments from Form(s) W-2	**51**
	52	Household employment taxes. Attach Schedule H	**52**
	53	Add lines 46 through 52. This is your **total tax** . . . . ▶	**53**

Payments				
	54	Federal income tax withheld from Forms W-2 and 1099 . .	**54**	
	55	1997 estimated tax payments and amount applied from 1996 return .	**55**	
	56a	**Earned income credit.** Attach Schedule EIC if you have a qualifying child **b** Nontaxable earned income: amount ▶ [_____] and type ▶	**56a**	
Attach Forms W-2, W-2G, and 1099-R on the front.	**57**	Amount paid with Form 4868 (request for extension) . . .	**57**	
	58	Excess social security and RRTA tax withheld (see page 27)	**58**	
	59	Other payments. Check if from **a** ☐ Form 2439 **b** ☐ Form 4136	**59**	
	60	Add lines 54, 55, 56a, 57, 58, and 59. These are your **total payments** . . . . . ▶	**60**	

Refund				
	61	If line 60 is more than line 53, subtract line 53 from line 60. This is the amount you **OVERPAID**	**61**	
Have it directly deposited! See page 27 and fill in 62b, 62c, and 62d.	**62a**	Amount of line 61 you want **REFUNDED TO YOU** . . . . ▶	**62a**	
	▶ **b**	Routing number [_____] ▶ **c** Type: ☐ Checking ☐ Savings		
	▶ **d**	Account number [_____]		
	63	Amount of line 61 you want **APPLIED TO YOUR 1998 ESTIMATED TAX** ▶	**63**	

Amount You Owe			
	64	If line 53 is more than line 60, subtract line 60 from line 53. This is the **AMOUNT YOU OWE.** For details on how to pay, see page 27 . . . . ▶	**64**
	65	Estimated tax penalty. Also include on line 64	**65**	

Sign Here

Keep a copy of this return for your records.

Under penalties of perjury, I declare that I have examined this return and accompanying schedules and statements, and to the best of my knowledge and belief, they are true, correct, and complete. Declaration of preparer (other than taxpayer) is based on all information of which preparer has any knowledge.

Your signature	Date	Your occupation
Spouse's signature. If a joint return, BOTH must sign.	Date	Spouse's occupation

Paid Preparer's Use Only

Preparer's signature ▶	Date	Check if self-employed ☐	Preparer's social security no.
Firm's name (or yours if self-employed) and address ▶		EIN	
		ZIP code	

♲

SCHEDULES A&B (Form 1040) Department of the Treasury Internal Revenue Service (99)	Schedule A—Itemized Deductions (Schedule B is on back) ▶ Attach to Form 1040. ▶ See Instructions for Schedules A and B (Form 1040).	OMB No. 1545-0074 1997 Attachment Sequence No. 07

Name(s) shown on Form 1040 | Your social security number

Medical and Dental Expenses		**Caution:** *Do not include expenses reimbursed or paid by others.*	
	1	Medical and dental expenses (see page A-1)	1
	2	Enter amount from Form 1040, line 33 . 2	
	3	Multiply line 2 above by 7.5% (.075)	3
	4	Subtract line 3 from line 1. If line 3 is more than line 1, enter -0-	4
Taxes You Paid (See page A-2.)	5	State and local income taxes	5
	6	Real estate taxes (see page A-2)	6
	7	Personal property taxes	7
	8	Other taxes. List type and amount ▶ ----------------- ------------------------------------	8
	9	Add lines 5 through 8	9
Interest You Paid (See page A-2.) **Note:** Personal interest is not deductible.	10	Home mortgage interest and points reported to you on Form 1098	10
	11	Home mortgage interest not reported to you on Form 1098. If paid to the person from whom you bought the home, see page A-3 and show that person's name, identifying no., and address ▶ ------------------------------ ------------------------------------ ------------------------------------	11
	12	Points not reported to you on Form 1098. See page A-3 for special rules	12
	13	Investment interest. Attach Form 4952 if required. (See page A-3.)	13
	14	Add lines 10 through 13	14
Gifts to Charity If you made a gift and got a benefit for it, see page A-3.	15	Gifts by cash or check. If you made any gift of $250 or more, see page A-3	15
	16	Other than by cash or check. If any gift of $250 or more, see page A-3. You **MUST** attach Form 8283 if over $500	16
	17	Carryover from prior year	17
	18	Add lines 15 through 17	18
Casualty and Theft Losses	19	Casualty or theft loss(es). Attach Form 4684. (See page A-4.)	19
Job Expenses and Most Other Miscellaneous Deductions (See page A-5 for expenses to deduct here.)	20	Unreimbursed employee expenses—job travel, union dues, job education, etc. You **MUST** attach Form 2106 or 2106-EZ if required. (See page A-4.) ▶ -------------- ------------------------------------ ------------------------------------	20
	21	Tax preparation fees	21
	22	Other expenses—investment, safe deposit box, etc. List type and amount ▶ ------------------------------- ------------------------------------	22
	23	Add lines 20 through 22	23
	24	Enter amount from Form 1040, line 33. 24	
	25	Multiply line 24 above by 2% (.02)	25
	26	Subtract line 25 from line 23. If line 25 is more than line 23, enter -0-	26
Other Miscellaneous Deductions	27	Other—from list on page A-5. List type and amount ▶ ---------------- ------------------------------------	27
Total Itemized Deductions	28	Is Form 1040, line 33, over $121,200 (over $60,600 if married filing separately)? **NO.** Your deduction is not limited. Add the amounts in the far right column for lines 4 through 27. Also, enter on Form 1040, line 35, the **larger** of this amount or your standard deduction. **YES.** Your deduction may be limited. See page A-5 for the amount to enter.	▶ 28

For Paperwork Reduction Act Notice, see Form 1040 instructions.   Cat. No. 11330X   **Schedule A (Form 1040) 1997**

Schedules A&B (Form 1040) 1997   OMB No. 1545-0074   Page **2**

Name(s) shown on Form 1040. Do not enter name and social security number if shown on other side. | **Your social security number**

Schedule B—Interest and Dividend Income
Attachment Sequence No. **08**

**Part I
Interest
Income**

(See pages 12 and B-1.)

Note: *If you had over $400 in taxable interest income, you must also complete Part III.*

1 List name of payer. If any interest is from a seller-financed mortgage and the buyer used the property as a personal residence, see page B-1 and list this interest first. Also, show that buyer's social security number and address ▶

	Amount
	1

Note: If you received a Form 1099-INT, Form 1099-OID, or substitute statement from a brokerage firm, list the firm's name as the payer and enter the total interest shown on that form.

2 Add the amounts on line 1 . . . . . | 2 |
3 Excludable interest on series EE U.S. savings bonds issued after 1989 from Form 8815, line 14. You MUST attach Form 8815 to Form 1040 . . . . . . | 3 |
4 Subtract line 3 from line 2. Enter the result here and on Form 1040, line 8a ▶ | 4 |

**Part II
Dividend
Income**

(See pages 12 and B-1.)

Note: *If you had over $400 in gross dividends and/or other distributions on stock, you must also complete Part III.*

5 List name of payer. Include gross dividends and/or other distributions on stock here. Any capital gain distributions and nontaxable distributions will be deducted on lines 7 and 8 ▶

	Amount
	5

Note: If you received a Form 1099-DIV or substitute statement from a brokerage firm, list the firm's name as the payer and enter the total dividends shown on that form.

6 Add the amounts on line 5 . . . . . | 6 |
7 Capital gain distributions. Enter here and on Schedule D | 7 |
8 Nontaxable distributions. (See the inst. for Form 1040, line 9.) | 8 |
9 Add lines 7 and 8 . . . . | 9 |
10 Subtract line 9 from line 6. Enter the result here and on Form 1040, line 9 . ▶ | 10 |

**Part III
Foreign
Accounts
and
Trusts**

(See page B-2.)

You must complete this part if you **(a)** had over $400 of interest or dividends; **(b)** had a foreign account; or **(c)** received a distribution from, or were a grantor of, or a transferor to, a foreign trust. | Yes | No

11a At any time during 1997, did you have an interest in or a signature or other authority over a financial account in a foreign country, such as a bank account, securities account, or other financial account? See page B-2 for exceptions and filing requirements for Form TD F 90-22.1 . . . .
   b If "Yes," enter the name of the foreign country ▶
12 During 1997, did you receive a distribution from, or were you the grantor of, or transferor to, a foreign trust? If "Yes," you may have to file Form 3520 or 926. See page B-2 . . . . . .

For Paperwork Reduction Act Notice, see Form 1040 instructions.   **Schedule B (Form 1040) 1997**

SCHEDULE C
(Form 1040)

Department of the Treasury
Internal Revenue Service   (99)

Profit or Loss From Business
(Sole Proprietorship)

▶ Partnerships, joint ventures, etc., must file Form 1065.

▶ **Attach to Form 1040 or Form 1041.**   ▶ **See Instructions for Schedule C (Form 1040).**

OMB No. 1545-0074

1997

Attachment
Sequence No. **09**

Name of proprietor	Social security number (SSN)

A Principal business or profession, including product or service (see page C-1)

B Enter principal business code (see page C-6) ▶

C Business name. If no separate business name, leave blank.

D Employer ID number (EIN), if any

E Business address (including suite or room no.) ▶
City, town or post office, state, and ZIP code

F Accounting method: **(1)** ☐ Cash   **(2)** ☐ Accrual   **(3)** ☐ Other (specify) ▶

G Did you "materially participate" in the operation of this business during 1997? If "No," see page C-2 for limit on losses. ☐ Yes ☐ No

H If you started or acquired this business during 1997, check here ▶ ☐

Part I Income

1 Gross receipts or sales. **Caution:** *If this income was reported to you on Form W-2 and the "Statutory employee" box on that form was checked, see page C-2 and check here* ▶ ☐ | **1** |
2 Returns and allowances | **2** |
3 Subtract line 2 from line 1 | **3** |
4 Cost of goods sold (from line 42 on page 2) | **4** |
5 **Gross profit.** Subtract line 4 from line 3 | **5** |
6 Other income, including Federal and state gasoline or fuel tax credit or refund (see page C-2) | **6** |
7 **Gross income.** Add lines 5 and 6 ▶ | **7** |

Part II Expenses. Enter expenses for business use of your home **only** on line 30.

8 Advertising	**8**		19 Pension and profit-sharing plans	**19**	
9 Bad debts from sales or services (see page C-3)	**9**		20 Rent or lease (see page C-4):		
10 Car and truck expenses (see page C-3)	**10**		a Vehicles, machinery, and equipment	**20a**	
11 Commissions and fees	**11**		b Other business property	**20b**	
12 Depletion	**12**		21 Repairs and maintenance	**21**	
13 Depreciation and section 179 expense deduction (not included in Part III) (see page C-3)	**13**		22 Supplies (not included in Part III)	**22**	
			23 Taxes and licenses	**23**	
14 Employee benefit programs (other than on line 19)	**14**		24 Travel, meals, and entertainment:		
			a Travel	**24a**	
15 Insurance (other than health)	**15**		b Meals and entertainment		
16 Interest:			c Enter 50% of line 24b subject to limitations (see page C-4)		
a Mortgage (paid to banks, etc.)	**16a**		d Subtract line 24c from line 24b	**24d**	
b Other	**16b**		25 Utilities	**25**	
17 Legal and professional services	**17**		26 Wages (less employment credits)	**26**	
18 Office expense	**18**		27 Other expenses (from line 48 on page 2)	**27**	

28 **Total expenses** before expenses for business use of home. Add lines 8 through 27 in columns ▶ | **28** |

29 Tentative profit (loss). Subtract line 28 from line 7 | **29** |
30 Expenses for business use of your home. Attach **Form 8829** | **30** |
31 **Net profit or (loss).** Subtract line 30 from line 29.
  • If a profit, enter on **Form 1040, line 12,** and ALSO on **Schedule SE, line 2** (statutory employees, see page C-5). Estates and trusts, enter on Form 1041, line 3.
  • If a loss, you MUST go on to line 32. | **31** |

32 If you have a loss, check the box that describes your investment in this activity (see page C-5).
  • If you checked 32a, enter the loss on **Form 1040, line 12,** and ALSO on **Schedule SE, line 2** (statutory employees, see page C-5). Estates and trusts, enter on Form 1041, line 3.
  • If you checked 32b, you MUST attach **Form 6198.**

32a ☐ All investment is at risk.
32b ☐ Some investment is not at risk.

For Paperwork Reduction Act Notice, see Form 1040 instructions.   Cat. No. 11334P   Schedule C (Form 1040) 1997

Part III **Cost of Goods Sold** (see page C-5)

33	Method(s) used to value closing inventory:	**a** ☐ Cost **b** ☐ Lower of cost or market **c** ☐ Other (attach explanation)	

34 Was there any change in determining quantities, costs, or valuations between opening and closing inventory? If "Yes," attach explanation . . . . ☐ **Yes** ☐ **No**

35	Inventory at beginning of year. If different from last year's closing inventory, attach explanation . .	**35**	
36	Purchases less cost of items withdrawn for personal use	**36**	
37	Cost of labor. Do not include salary paid to yourself	**37**	
38	Materials and supplies	**38**	
39	Other costs	**39**	
40	Add lines 35 through 39	**40**	
41	Inventory at end of year	**41**	
42	**Cost of goods sold.** Subtract line 41 from line 40. Enter the result here and on page 1, line 4 . .	**42**	

Part IV **Information on Your Vehicle.** Complete this part **ONLY** if you are claiming car or truck expenses on line 10 and are not required to file Form 4562 for this business. See the instructions for line 13 on page C-3 to find out if you must file.

43 When did you place your vehicle in service for business purposes? (month, day, year) ▶ .... / .... / ....

44 Of the total number of miles you drove your vehicle during 1997, enter the number of miles you used your vehicle for:

a Business .... **b** Commuting .... **c** Other ....

45 Do you (or your spouse) have another vehicle available for personal use? . . . . ☐ **Yes** ☐ **No**

46 Was your vehicle available for use during off-duty hours? . . . . ☐ **Yes** ☐ **No**

47a Do you have evidence to support your deduction? . . . . ☐ **Yes** ☐ **No**

 b If "Yes," is the evidence written? . . . . ☐ **Yes** ☐ **No**

Part V **Other Expenses.** List below business expenses not included on lines 8–26 or line 30.

....		
....		
....		
....		
....		
....		
....		
....		
48 **Total other expenses.** Enter here and on page 1, line 27	**48**	

✪

SCHEDULE D (Form 1040)	Capital Gains and Losses	OMB No. 1545-0074

Department of the Treasury
Internal Revenue Service   (99)

► **Attach to Form 1040.**   ► **See Instructions for Schedule D (Form 1040).**

► **Use Schedule D-1 for more space to list transactions for lines 1 and 8.**

1997

Attachment
Sequence No. **12**

Name(s) shown on Form 1040

Your social security number

Part I   Short-Term Capital Gains and Losses—Assets Held One Year or Less

(a) Description of property (Example: 100 sh. XYZ Co.)	(b) Date acquired (Mo., day, yr.)	(c) Date sold (Mo., day, yr.)	(d) Sales price (see page D-3)	(e) Cost or other basis (see page D-4)	(f) GAIN or (LOSS) FOR ENTIRE YEAR. Subtract (e) from (d)	
1						

2 Enter your short-term totals, if any, from Schedule D-1, line 2 . . . . **2**

3 **Total short-term sales price amounts.** Add column (d) of lines 1 and 2 . . . **3**

4 Short-term gain from Forms 2119 and 6252, and short-term gain or (loss) from Forms 4684, 6781, and 8824 . . . . **4**

5 Net short-term gain or (loss) from partnerships, S corporations, estates, and trusts from Schedule(s) K-1 . . . . **5**

6 Short-term capital loss carryover. Enter the amount, if any, from line 9 of your 1996 Capital Loss Carryover Worksheet . . . . . . **6** ( )

7 **Net short-term capital gain or (loss).** Combine lines 1 through 6 in column (f). ► **7**

Part II   Long-Term Capital Gains and Losses—Assets Held More Than One Year

(a) Description of property (Example: 100 sh. XYZ Co.)	(b) Date acquired (Mo., day, yr.)	(c) Date sold (Mo., day, yr.)	(d) Sales price (see page D-3)	(e) Cost or other basis (see page D-4)	(f) GAIN or (LOSS) FOR ENTIRE YEAR. Subtract (e) from (d)	(g) 28% RATE GAIN or (LOSS) * (see instr. below)
8						

9 Enter your long-term totals, if any, from Schedule D-1, line 9 . . . . **9**

10 **Total long-term sales price amounts.** Add column (d) of lines 8 and 9 . . . **10**

11 Gain from Form 4797, Part I; long-term gain from Forms 2119, 2439, and 6252; and long-term gain or (loss) from Forms 4684, 6781, and 8824 . . **11**

12 Net long-term gain or (loss) from partnerships, S corporations, estates, and trusts from Schedule(s) K-1. . . . . **12**

13 Capital gain distributions **13**

14 Long-term capital loss carryover. Enter in both columns (f) and (g) the amount, if any, from line 14 of your 1996 Capital Loss Carryover Worksheet . . . **14** ( ) ( )

15 Combine lines 8 through 14 in column (g) **15**

16 **Net long-term capital gain or (loss).** Combine lines 8 through 14 in column (f). ► **16**

* **28% Rate Gain or Loss** includes all gains and losses in Part II, column (f) from sales, exchanges, or conversions (including installment payments received) **either:** ● **Before** May 7, 1997, **or**

● **After** July 28, 1997, for assets held more than 1 year but **not** more than 18 months.

It also includes **ALL** "collectibles gains and losses" (as defined on page D-4).

For Paperwork Reduction Act Notice, see Form 1040 instructions.   Cat. No. 11338H   **Schedule D (Form 1040) 1997**

Part III   **Summary of Parts I and II**

17   Combine lines 7 and 16. If a loss, go to line 18. If a gain, enter the gain on Form 1040, line 13   **17**

     Next: Complete Form 1040 through line 38. Then, go to **Part IV** to figure your tax if:
- Both lines 16 and 17 are gains, **and**
- Form 1040, line 38, is more than zero.

18   If line 17 is a loss, enter here and as a (loss) on Form 1040, line 13, the **smaller** of these losses:
- The loss on line 17; **or**
- ($3,000) or, if married filing separately, ($1,500) . . . .   **18**   (   )

     Next: Complete Form 1040 through line 36. Then, complete the **Capital Loss Carryover Worksheet** on page D-4 if:
- The loss on line 17 exceeds the loss on line 18, **or**
- Form 1040, line 36, is a loss.

Part IV   **Tax Computation Using Maximum Capital Gains Rates**

19	Enter your taxable income from Form 1040, line 38	**19**
20	Enter the **smaller** of line 16 or line 17	**20**
21	If you are filing Form 4952, enter the amount from Form 4952, line 4e	**21**
22	Subtract line 21 from line 20. If zero or less, enter -0-	**22**
23	Combine lines 7 and 15. If zero or less, enter -0-	**23**
24	Enter the **smaller** of line 15 or line 23, but not less than zero . . .	**24**
25	Enter your unrecaptured section 1250 gain, if any (see page D-4) . .	**25**
26	Add lines 24 and 25	**26**
27	Subtract line 26 from line 22. If zero or less, enter -0-	**27**
28	Subtract line 27 from line 19. If zero or less, enter -0-	**28**
29	Enter the **smaller** of line 19 or $41,200 ($24,650 if single; $20,600 if married filing separately; $33,050 if head of household)	**29**
30	Enter the **smaller** of line 28 or line 29	**30**
31	Subtract line 22 from line 19. If zero or less, enter -0-	**31**
32	Enter the **larger** of line 30 or line 31	**32**
33	Figure the tax on the amount on line 32. Use the Tax Table or Tax Rate Schedules, whichever applies . . . . ▶	**33**
34	Enter the amount from line 29	**34**
35	Enter the amount from line 28	**35**
36	Subtract line 35 from line 34. If zero or less, enter -0-	**36**
37	Multiply line 36 by 10% (.10) . . . . ▶	**37**
38	Enter the **smaller** of line 19 or line 27	**38**
39	Enter the amount from line 36	**39**
40	Subtract line 39 from line 38. If zero or less, enter -0-	**40**
41	Multiply line 40 by 20% (.20) . . . . ▶	**41**
42	Enter the **smaller** of line 22 or line 25	**42**
43	Add lines 22 and 32	**43**
44	Enter the amount from line 19	**44**
45	Subtract line 44 from line 43. If zero or less, enter -0-	**45**
46	Subtract line 45 from line 42. If zero or less, enter -0-	**46**
47	Multiply line 46 by 25% (.25) . . . . ▶	**47**
48	Enter the amount from line 19	**48**
49	Add lines 32, 36, 40, and 46	**49**
50	Subtract line 49 from line 48	**50**
51	Multiply line 50 by 28% (.28) . . . . ▶	**51**
52	Add lines 33, 37, 41, 47, and 51	**52**
53	Figure the tax on the amount on line 19. Use the Tax Table or Tax Rate Schedules, whichever applies	**53**
54	**Tax.** Enter the **smaller** of line 52 or line 53 here and on Form 1040, line 39 . . . . ▶	**54**

SCHEDULE E	**Supplemental Income and Loss**	OMB No. 1545-0074
(Form 1040)	(From rental real estate, royalties, partnerships, S corporations, estates, trusts, REMICs, etc.)	19**97**
Department of the Treasury Internal Revenue Service (99)	▶ **Attach to Form 1040 or Form 1041.** ▶ **See Instructions for Schedule E (Form 1040).**	Attachment Sequence No. **13**

Name(s) shown on return	Your social security number

Part I   **Income or Loss From Rental Real Estate and Royalties**   Note: *Report income and expenses from your business of renting personal property on* **Schedule C** *or* **C-EZ** *(see page E-1). Report farm rental income or loss from* **Form 4835** *on page 2, line 39.*

1 Show the kind and location of each **rental real estate property:**

A ....

B ....

C ....

2 For each rental real estate property listed on line 1, did you or your family use it during the tax year for personal purposes for more than the greater of:
- 14 days, **or**
- 10% of the total days rented at fair rental value?

(See page E-1.)

	Yes	No
A		
B		
C		

Income:		Properties			Totals (Add columns A, B, and C.)
		A	B	C	
3 Rents received					**3**
4 Royalties received	**4**				**4**
Expenses:					
5 Advertising	**5**				
6 Auto and travel (see page E-2) .	**6**				
7 Cleaning and maintenance . . .	**7**				
8 Commissions	**8**				
9 Insurance	**9**				
10 Legal and other professional fees	**10**				
11 Management fees	**11**				
12 Mortgage interest paid to banks, etc. (see page E-2)	**12**				**12**
13 Other interest	**13**				
14 Repairs	**14**				
15 Supplies	**15**				
16 Taxes	**16**				
17 Utilities	**17**				
18 Other (list) ▶	**18**				
19 Add lines 5 through 18	**19**				**19**
20 Depreciation expense or depletion (see page E-2)	**20**				**20**
21 Total expenses. Add lines 19 and 20	**21**				
22 Income or (loss) from rental real estate or royalty properties. Subtract line 21 from line 3 (rents) or line 4 (royalties). If the result is a (loss), see page E-3 to find out if you must file **Form 6198** . .	**22**				
23 Deductible rental real estate loss. **Caution:** *Your rental real estate loss on line 22 may be limited. See page E-3 to find out if you must file* **Form 8582.** *Real estate professionals must complete line 42 on page 2*	**23** (	) (	) (	)	
24 **Income.** Add positive amounts shown on line 22. **Do not** include any losses					**24**
25 **Losses.** Add royalty losses from line 22 and rental real estate losses from line 23. Enter total losses here					**25** ( )
26 Total rental real estate and royalty income or (loss). Combine lines 24 and 25. Enter the result here. If Parts II, III, IV, and line 39 on page 2 do not apply to you, also enter this amount on Form 1040, line 17. Otherwise, include this amount in the total on line 40 on page 2					**26**

For Paperwork Reduction Act Notice, see Form 1040 instructions.   Cat. No. 11344L   **Schedule E (Form 1040) 1997**

Schedule E (Form 1040) 1997 | Attachment Sequence No. **13** | Page **2**

Name(s) shown on return. Do not enter name and social security number if shown on other side. | **Your social security number**

Note: *If you report amounts from farming or fishing on Schedule E, you must enter your gross income from those activities on line 41 below. Real estate professionals must complete line 42 below.*

Part II Income or Loss From Partnerships and S Corporations
Note: *If you report a loss from an at-risk activity, you MUST check either column (e) or (f) on line 27 to describe your investment in the activity. See page E-4. If you check column (f), you must attach Form 6198.*

27	(a) Name	(b) Enter P for partnership; S for S corporation	(c) Check if foreign partnership	(d) Employer identification number	Investment At Risk?
					(e) All is at risk / (f) Some is not at risk
A					
B					
C					
D					
E					

	Passive Income and Loss		Nonpassive Income and Loss		
	(g) Passive loss allowed (attach Form 8582 if required)	(h) Passive income from Schedule K-1	(i) Nonpassive loss from Schedule K-1	(j) Section 179 expense deduction from Form 4562	(k) Nonpassive income from Schedule K-1
A					
B					
C					
D					
E					
28a Totals					
b Totals					

29	Add columns (h) and (k) of line 28a	29	
30	Add columns (g), (i), and (j) of line 28b	30 (	)
31	Total partnership and S corporation income or (loss). Combine lines 29 and 30. Enter the result here and include in the total on line 40 below	31	

Part III Income or Loss From Estates and Trusts

32	(a) Name	(b) Employer identification number
A		
B		

	Passive Income and Loss		Nonpassive Income and Loss	
	(c) Passive deduction or loss allowed (attach Form 8582 if required)	(d) Passive income from Schedule K-1	(e) Deduction or loss from Schedule K-1	(f) Other income from Schedule K-1
A				
B				
33a Totals				
b Totals				

34	Add columns (d) and (f) of line 33a	34	
35	Add columns (c) and (e) of line 33b	35 (	)
36	Total estate and trust income or (loss). Combine lines 34 and 35. Enter the result here and include in the total on line 40 below	36	

Part IV Income or Loss From Real Estate Mortgage Investment Conduits (REMICs)—Residual Holder

37	(a) Name	(b) Employer identification number	(c) Excess inclusion from Schedules Q, line 2c (see page E-5)	(d) Taxable income (net loss) from Schedules Q, line 1b	(e) Income from Schedules Q, line 3b

38	Combine columns (d) and (e) only. Enter the result here and include in the total on line 40 below	38	

Part V Summary

39	Net farm rental income or (loss) from Form 4835. Also, complete line 41 below	39	
40	TOTAL income or (loss). Combine lines 26, 31, 36, 38, and 39. Enter the result here and on Form 1040, line 17 ▶	40	
41	**Reconciliation of Farming and Fishing Income.** Enter your **gross** farming and fishing income reported on Form 4835, line 7; Schedule K-1 (Form 1065), line 15b; Schedule K-1 (Form 1120S), line 23; and Schedule K-1 (Form 1041), line 14 (see page E-5)	41	
42	**Reconciliation for Real Estate Professionals.** If you were a real estate professional (see page E-4), enter the net income or (loss) you reported anywhere on Form 1040 from all rental real estate activities in which you materially participated under the passive activity loss rules	42	

SCHEDULE EIC	Earned Income Credit	OMB No. 1545-0074
(Form 1040A or 1040)	**(Qualifying Child Information)**	**1997**
Department of the Treasury Internal Revenue Service (99)	▶ Attach to Form 1040A or 1040. ▶ See instructions on back.	Attachment Sequence No. **43**

Name(s) shown on return: First and initial(s)	Last	Your social security number

Before you begin . . .

- See the instructions for Form 1040A, lines 29c and 29d, or Form 1040, lines 56a and 56b, to find out if you can take this credit.
- If you can take the credit, fill in the Earned Income Credit Worksheet in the Form 1040A or Form 1040 instructions to figure your credit. **But if you want the IRS to figure it for you, see instructions on back.**

Then, you **must** complete and attach Schedule EIC only if you have a qualifying child (see boxes on back).

Information About Your Qualifying Child or Children

If you have more than two qualifying children, you only have to list two to get the maximum credit.

Caution: *If you do not attach Schedule EIC and fill in all the lines that apply, it will take us longer to process your return and issue your refund.*	**Child 1**		**Child 2**	
	First name	Last name	First name	Last name
1 Child's name				
2 Child's year of birth	19 ☐☐		19 ☐☐	
3 If the child was born **before 1979** AND—				
a was **under age 24** at the end of 1997 **and** a student, check the "Yes" box, **OR** . . .	☐ Yes		☐ Yes	
b was permanently and totally disabled (see back), check the "Yes" box	☐ Yes		☐ Yes	
4 Enter the child's social security number	☐☐☐ ☐☐ ☐☐☐☐		☐☐☐ ☐☐ ☐☐☐☐	
5 Child's relationship to you (for example, son, grandchild, etc.) . .				
6 Number of months child lived with you in the United States in 1997 . .	☐☐ months		☐☐ months	

TIP: Do you want the earned income credit added to your take-home pay in 1998? To see if you qualify, get **Form W-5** from your employer or by calling the IRS at 1-800-TAX-FORM (1-800-829-3676).

For Paperwork Reduction Act Notice, see Form 1040A or 1040 instructions.   Cat. No. 13339M   **Schedule EIC (Form 1040A or 1040) 1997**

Instructions

Purpose of Schedule

If you can take the earned income credit and have a qualifying child, use Schedule EIC to give information about that child. To figure the amount of your credit, use the worksheet in the instructions for Form 1040A, lines 29c and 29d, or Form 1040, lines 56a and 56b.

If you want the IRS to figure the credit for you, print "EIC" directly to the right of line 29c of Form 1040A or line 56a of Form 1040. Also, enter the amount and type of any nontaxable earned income in the spaces provided on Form 1040A, line 29d, or Form 1040, line 56b, and attach Schedule EIC to your return.

Line 1

Enter each qualifying child's name.

Line 3a

If your child was born **before 1979** but was under age 24 at the end of 1997 and a student, check the "Yes" box.

Your child was a **student** if during any 5 months of 1997 he or she—

• Was enrolled as a full-time student at a school, or

• Took a full-time, on-farm training course. The course had to be given by a school or a state, county, or local government agency.

A **school** includes technical, trade, and mechanical schools. It does not include on-the-job training courses, correspondence schools, or night schools.

Line 3b

If your child was born **before 1979** and was permanently and totally disabled during any part of 1997, check the "Yes" box.

A person is **permanently and totally disabled** if **both** of the following apply.

1. He or she cannot engage in any substantial gainful activity because of a physical or mental condition.

2. A doctor determines the condition has lasted or can be expected to last continuously for at least a year or can lead to death.

Line 4

You must enter your child's social security number (SSN) on line 4 unless he or she was born and died in 1997. If you do not enter the correct SSN, at the time we process your return, we may reduce or disallow your credit. If your child was born and died in 1997 and did not have an SSN, print "Died" on line 4 **and** attach a copy of the child's birth certificate.

If your child does not have an SSN, apply for one by filing **Form SS-5** with your local Social Security Administration office. It usually takes about 2 weeks to get a number. If your child will not have an SSN by April 15, 1998, you can get an automatic 4-month extension by filing **Form 4868** with the IRS by that date.

Line 6

Enter the number of months your child lived with you in your home in the United States during 1997. (If you were in the military on extended active duty outside the United States, your home is considered to be in the United States during that duty period.) Do not enter more than 12. Count temporary absences, such as for school, vacation, or medical care, as time lived in your home. If the child lived with you for more than half of 1997 but less than 7 months, enter "07" on line 6.

Exception. If your child, including a foster child, was born or died in 1997 and your home was the child's home for the entire time he or she was alive during 1997, enter "12" on line 6.

Qualifying Child

A **qualifying child** is a child who:

is your:		was (at the end of 1997):		who:
son daughter adopted child grandchild stepchild or foster child*	**A N D**	under age 19 or under age 24 and a full-time student or any age and permanently and totally disabled	**A N D**	lived with you in the U.S. for more than half of 1997** (or, if a foster child, for all of 1997**)

*A foster child is any child you cared for as your own child.

If the child did not live with you for the required time (for example, was born in 1997), see the **Line 6 instructions above.

If the child was married or is also a qualifying child of another person (other than your spouse if filing a joint return), special rules apply. For details, see the instructions for Form 1040A, lines 29c and 29d, or Form 1040, lines 56a and 56b. Also, the child must have an SSN (as defined in those instructions) unless he or she was born and died in 1997.

Schedule R
(Form 1040)

Department of the Treasury
Internal Revenue Service   (99)

Credit for the Elderly or the Disabled

▶ **Attach to Form 1040.**   ▶ **See separate instructions for Schedule R.**

OMB No. 1545-0074

1997

Attachment
Sequence No. **16**

Name(s) shown on Form 1040

Your social security number

You may be able to take this credit and reduce your tax if by the end of 1997:

● You were age 65 or older,   **OR** ● You were under age 65, you retired on **permanent and total** disability, and you
                                   received taxable disability income.

But you must also meet other tests. See the separate instructions for Schedule R.

TIP: In most cases, the IRS can figure the credit for you. See the instructions.

Part I   **Check the Box for Your Filing Status and Age**

If your filing status is:	And by the end of 1997:	Check only one box:
Single, Head of household, or Qualifying widow(er) with dependent child	**1** You were 65 or older **1**	☐
	2 You were under 65 and you retired on permanent and total disability . . . **2**	☐
	3 Both spouses were 65 or older **3**	☐
	4 Both spouses were under 65, but only one spouse retired on permanent and total disability **4**	☐
Married filing a joint return	**5** Both spouses were under 65, and both retired on permanent and total disability **5**	☐
	6 One spouse was 65 or older, and the other spouse was under 65 and retired on permanent and total disability **6**	☐
	7 One spouse was 65 or older, and the other spouse was under 65 and **NOT** retired on permanent and total disability **7**	☐
Married filing a separate return	**8** You were 65 or older and you lived apart from your spouse for all of 1997 . . **8**	☐
	9 You were under 65, you retired on permanent and total disability, and you lived apart from your spouse for all of 1997 . . . . **9**	☐

Did you check box 1, 3, 7, or 8?	── **Yes** ──▶ Skip Part II and complete Part III on back.
	── **No** ──▶ Complete Parts II and III.

Part II   **Statement of Permanent and Total Disability** (Complete **only** if you checked box 2, 4, 5, 6, or 9 above.)

IF: 1 You filed a physician's statement for this disability for 1983 or an earlier year, or you filed a statement for tax years
after 1983 and your physician signed line B on the statement, **AND**

   2 Due to your continued disabled condition, you were unable to engage in any substantial gainful activity in 1997,
   check this box . . . . ▶ ☐

● If you checked this box, you do not have to file another statement for 1997.
● If you **did not** check this box, have your physician complete the statement below.

Physician's Statement (See instructions on back.)

I certify that _____

Name of disabled person

was permanently and totally disabled on January 1, 1976, or January 1, 1977, **OR** was permanently and totally disabled on the
date he or she retired. If retired after 1976, enter the date retired. ▶ _____

Physician: Sign your name on **either** line A or B below.

A The disability has lasted or can be expected to
last continuously for at least a year . . . .   _____

Physician's signature   Date

B There is no reasonable probability that the
disabled condition will ever improve . . . .   _____

Physician's signature   Date

Physician's name _____   Physician's address _____

For Paperwork Reduction Act Notice, see Form 1040 instructions.   Cat. No. 11359K   **Schedule R (Form 1040) 1997**

Part III	**Figure Your Credit**

10 If you checked (in Part I):   **Enter:**

Box 1, 2, 4, or 7 . . . . $5,000 ⎫

Box 3, 5, or 6 . . . . $7,500 ⎬ **10**

Box 8 or 9 . . . . $3,750 ⎭

> **Did you check box 2, 4, 5, 6, or 9 in Part I?**
>
> **Yes** ──────▶ You **must** complete line 11.
>
> **No** ──────▶ Enter the amount from line 10 on line 12 and go to line 13.

11 If you checked:

- Box 6 in Part I, add $5,000 to the taxable disability income of the spouse who was under age 65. Enter the total. ⎫
- Box 2, 4, or 9 in Part I, enter your taxable disability income. ⎬ **11**
- Box 5 in Part I, add your taxable disability income to your spouse's taxable disability income. Enter the total. ⎭

    TIP: For more details on what to include on line 11, see the instructions.

12 If you completed line 11, enter the **smaller** of line 10 or line 11; **all others,** enter the amount from line 10 . . . . **12**

13 Enter the following pensions, annuities, or disability income that you (and your spouse if filing a joint return) received in 1997:

  a Nontaxable part of social security benefits, and

    Nontaxable part of railroad retirement benefits treated as ⎬ . . . **13a**

    social security. See instructions.

  b Nontaxable veterans' pensions, and

    Any other pension, annuity, or disability benefit that is ⎬ . . . **13b**

    excluded from income under any other provision of law. See instructions.

  c Add lines 13a and 13b. (Even though these income items are not taxable, they **must** be included here to figure your credit.) If you did not receive any of the types of nontaxable income listed on line 13a or 13b, enter -0- on line 13c **13c**

14 Enter the amount from Form 1040, line 33   **14**

15 If you checked (in Part I):   **Enter:**

Box 1 or 2 . . . . $7,500 ⎫

Box 3, 4, 5, 6, or 7 . . . . $10,000 ⎬   **15**

Box 8 or 9 . . . . $5,000 ⎭

16 Subtract line 15 from line 14. If zero or less, enter -0- **16**

17 Enter one-half of line 16 . . . .   **17**

18 Add lines 13c and 17 . . . . **18**

19 Subtract line 18 from line 12. If zero or less, **stop;** you **cannot** take the credit. Otherwise, go to line 20 . . . . **19**

20 Multiply line 19 by 15% (.15). Enter the result here and on Form 1040, line 41. **Caution:** *If you file Schedule C, C-EZ, D, E, or F (Form 1040), your credit may be limited. See the instructions for line 20 for the amount of credit you can claim* **20**

Instructions for Physician's Statement

Taxpayer

If you retired after 1976, enter the date you retired in the space provided in Part II.

Physician

A person is permanently and totally disabled if **both** of the following apply:

    1. He or she cannot engage in any substantial gainful activity because of a physical or mental condition, and

    2. A physician determines that the disability has lasted or can be expected to last continuously for at least a year or can lead to death.

SCHEDULE SE (Form 1040) Department of the Treasury Internal Revenue Service (99)	**Self-Employment Tax** ▶ See Instructions for Schedule SE (Form 1040). ▶ **Attach to Form 1040.**	OMB No. 1545-0074 19**97** Attachment Sequence No. **17**
Name of person with **self-employment** income (as shown on Form 1040)	Social security number of person with **self-employment** income ▶	

Who Must File Schedule SE

You must file Schedule SE if:

- You had net earnings from self-employment from **other than** church employee income (line 4 of Short Schedule SE or line 4c of Long Schedule SE) of $400 or more, **OR**

- You had church employee income of $108.28 or more. Income from services you performed as a minister or a member of a religious order **is not** church employee income. See page SE-1.

Note: *Even if you had a loss or a small amount of income from self-employment, it may be to your benefit to file Schedule SE and use either "optional method" in Part II of Long Schedule SE. See page SE-3.*

Exception. If your only self-employment income was from earnings as a minister, member of a religious order, or Christian Science practitioner **and** you filed Form 4361 and received IRS approval not to be taxed on those earnings, **do not** file Schedule SE. Instead, write "Exempt–Form 4361" on Form 1040, line 47.

May I Use Short Schedule SE or MUST I Use Long Schedule SE?

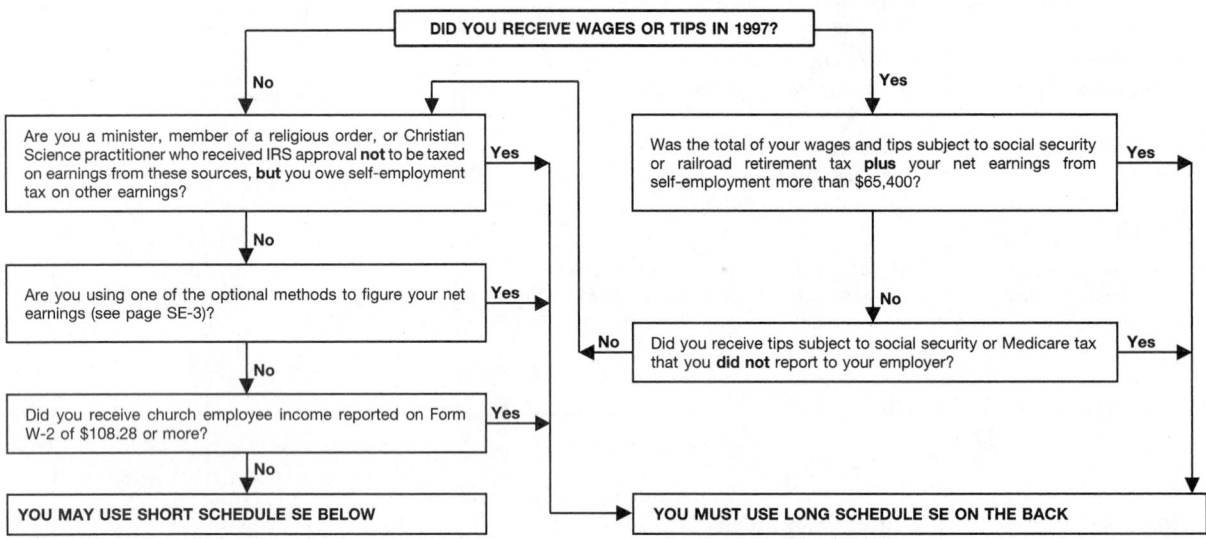

Section A—Short Schedule SE. Caution: *Read above to see if you can use Short Schedule SE.*

1	Net farm profit or (loss) from Schedule F, line 36, and farm partnerships, Schedule K-1 (Form 1065), line 15a	1	
2	Net profit or (loss) from Schedule C, line 31; Schedule C-EZ, line 3; and Schedule K-1 (Form 1065), line 15a (other than farming). Ministers and members of religious orders, see page SE-1 for amounts to report on this line. See page SE-2 for other income to report	2	
3	Combine lines 1 and 2	3	
4	**Net earnings from self-employment.** Multiply line 3 by 92.35% (.9235). If less than $400, **do not** file this schedule; you do not owe self-employment tax . . . . ▶	4	
5	Self-employment tax. If the amount on line 4 is: • $65,400 or less, multiply line 4 by 15.3% (.153). Enter the result here and on **Form 1040, line 47.** • More than $65,400, multiply line 4 by 2.9% (.029). Then, add $8,109.60 to the result. Enter the total here and on **Form 1040, line 47.**	5	
6	**Deduction for one-half of self-employment tax.** Multiply line 5 by 50% (.5). Enter the result here and on **Form 1040, line 26**	6		

For Paperwork Reduction Act Notice, see Form 1040 instructions.   Cat. No. 11358Z   **Schedule SE (Form 1040) 1997**

Schedule SE (Form 1040) 1997   Attachment Sequence No. **17**   Page **2**

Name of person with **self-employment** income (as shown on Form 1040)	Social security number of person with **self-employment** income ▶	

Section B—Long Schedule SE

Part I   Self-Employment Tax

Note: *If your only income subject to self-employment tax is* **church employee income,** *skip lines 1 through 4b. Enter -0- on line 4c and go to line 5a. Income from services you performed as a minister or a member of a religious order* **is not** *church employee income. See page SE-1.*

A   If you are a minister, member of a religious order, or Christian Science practitioner **and** you filed Form 4361, but you had $400 or more of **other** net earnings from self-employment, check here and continue with Part I . . . . . . ▶ ☐

1	Net farm profit or (loss) from Schedule F, line 36, and farm partnerships, Schedule K-1 (Form 1065), line 15a. **Note:** *Skip this line if you use the farm optional method. See page SE-3* . .	**1**		
2	Net profit or (loss) from Schedule C, line 31; Schedule C-EZ, line 3; and Schedule K-1 (Form 1065), line 15a (other than farming). Ministers and members of religious orders, see page SE-1 for amounts to report on this line. See page SE-2 for other income to report. **Note:** *Skip this line if you use the nonfarm optional method. See page SE-3.*	**2**		
3	Combine lines 1 and 2	**3**		
4a	If line 3 is more than zero, multiply line 3 by 92.35% (.9235). Otherwise, enter amount from line 3	**4a**		
b	If you elected one or both of the optional methods, enter the total of lines 15 and 17 here . .	**4b**		
c	Combine lines 4a and 4b. If less than $400, **do not** file this schedule; you do not owe self-employment tax. **Exception.** If less than $400 and you had **church employee income,** enter -0- and continue ▶	**4c**		
5a	Enter your **church employee income** from Form W-2. **Caution:** *See page SE-1 for definition of church employee income* . . . **5a**			
b	Multiply line 5a by 92.35% (.9235). If less than $100, enter -0-	**5b**		
6	**Net earnings from self-employment.** Add lines 4c and 5b	**6**		
7	Maximum amount of combined wages and self-employment earnings subject to social security tax or the 6.2% portion of the 7.65% railroad retirement (tier 1) tax for 1997	**7**	65,400	00
8a	Total social security wages and tips (total of boxes 3 and 7 on Form(s) W-2) and railroad retirement (tier 1) compensation **8a**			
b	Unreported tips subject to social security tax (from Form 4137, line 9) **8b**			
c	Add lines 8a and 8b	**8c**		
9	Subtract line 8c from line 7. If zero or less, enter -0- here and on line 10 and go to line 11 . ▶	**9**		
10	Multiply the **smaller** of line 6 or line 9 by 12.4% (.124)	**10**		
11	Multiply line 6 by 2.9% (.029)	**11**		
12	**Self-employment tax.** Add lines 10 and 11. Enter here and on **Form 1040, line 47**	**12**		
13	**Deduction for one-half of self-employment tax.** Multiply line 12 by 50% (.5). Enter the result here and on **Form 1040, line 26** **13**			

Part II   Optional Methods To Figure Net Earnings (See page SE-3.)

Farm Optional Method. You may use this method **only** if:
- Your gross farm income[1] was not more than $2,400, **or**
- Your gross farm income[1] was more than $2,400 and your net farm profits[2] were less than $1,733.

14	Maximum income for optional methods	**14**	1,600	00
15	Enter the **smaller** of: two-thirds (⅔) of gross farm income[1] (not less than zero) **or** $1,600. Also, include this amount on line 4b above	**15**		

Nonfarm Optional Method. You may use this method **only** if:
- Your net nonfarm profits[3] were less than $1,733 and also less than 72.189% of your gross nonfarm income,[4] **and**
- You had net earnings from self-employment of at least $400 in 2 of the prior 3 years.

Caution: *You may use this method no more than five times.*

16	Subtract line 15 from line 14	**16**		
17	Enter the **smaller** of: two-thirds (⅔) of gross nonfarm income[4] (not less than zero) **or** the amount on line 16. Also, include this amount on line 4b above	**17**		

[1]From Schedule F, line 11, and Schedule K-1 (Form 1065), line 15b.   [3]From Schedule C, line 31; Schedule C-EZ, line 3; and Schedule K-1 (Form 1065), line 15a.
[2]From Schedule F, line 36, and Schedule K-1 (Form 1065), line 15a.   [4]From Schedule C, line 7; Schedule C-EZ, line 1; and Schedule K-1 (Form 1065), line 15c.

Form **1040-ES**	**Estimated Tax for Individuals**	OMB No. 1545-0087
Department of the Treasury Internal Revenue Service	**This package is primarily for first-time filers of estimated tax.**	1998

Purpose of This Package

Use this package to figure and pay your estimated tax. Estimated tax is the method used to pay tax on income that is not subject to withholding (for example, earnings from self-employment, interest, dividends, rents, alimony, etc.). In addition, if you do not elect voluntary withholding, you should make estimated tax payments on unemployment compensation and the taxable part of your social security benefits. See the 1997 instructions for your tax return for more details on income that is taxable.

This package is primarily for first-time filers who are or may be subject to paying estimated tax. This package can also be used if you did not receive or have lost your preprinted 1040-ES package. The estimated tax worksheet on page 4 will help you figure the correct amount to pay. The payment vouchers in this package are for crediting your estimated tax payments to your account correctly. Use the **Record of Estimated Tax Payments** on page 6 to keep track of the payments you have made and the number and amount of your remaining payments.

After we receive your first payment voucher from this package, we will mail you a 1040-ES package with your name, address, and social security number preprinted on each payment voucher. Use the preprinted vouchers to make your **remaining** estimated tax payments for the year. This will speed processing, reduce processing costs, and reduce the chance of errors.

Do not use the vouchers in this package to notify the IRS of a **change of address.** If you have a new address, complete **Form 8822,** Change of Address, and send it to the Internal Revenue Service Center at the address shown in the Form 8822 instructions. The service center will update your record and send you new preprinted payment vouchers.

Note: *Continue to use your old preprinted payment vouchers to make payments of estimated tax until you receive the new vouchers.*

Who Must Make Estimated Tax Payments

In most cases, you must make estimated tax payments if you expect to owe at least $1,000 in tax for 1998 (after subtracting your withholding and credits) and you expect your withholding and credits to be less than the **smaller** of:

1. 90% of the tax shown on your 1998 tax return, **or**

2. The tax shown on your 1997 tax return.

However, if you did not file a 1997 tax return or that return did not cover all 12 months, item 2 above does not apply.

For this purpose, include household employment taxes when figuring the tax shown on your tax return, but **only** if **either** of the following is true:

● You will have Federal income tax withheld from wages, pensions, annuities, gambling winnings, or other income, **or**

● You would be required to make estimated tax payments to avoid a penalty even if you did not include household employment taxes when figuring your estimated tax.

Exception. You do not have to pay estimated tax if you were a U.S. citizen or resident alien for all of 1997 and you had no tax liability for the full 12-month 1997 tax year.

The estimated tax rules apply to:

● U.S. citizens and residents,

● Residents of Puerto Rico, the Virgin Islands, Guam, the Commonwealth of the Northern Mariana Islands, and American Samoa, and

● Nonresident aliens (use Form 1040-ES (NR)).

If you also receive salaries and wages, you may be able to avoid having to make estimated tax payments on your other income by asking your employer to take more tax out of your earnings. To do this, file a new **Form W-4,** Employee's Withholding Allowance Certificate, with your employer.

You can also choose to have Federal income tax withheld on certain government payments. For details, see **Form W-4V,** Voluntary Withholding Request.

Caution: *You may not make joint estimated tax payments if you or your spouse is a nonresident alien, you are separated under a decree of divorce or separate maintenance, or you and your spouse have different tax years.*

Additional Information You May Need

Most of the information you will need can be found in:

Pub. 505, Tax Withholding and Estimated Tax.

Other available information:

● **Pub. 553,** Highlights of 1997 Tax Changes.

● Instructions for the 1997 Form 1040 or 1040A.

● **What's Hot** at www.irs.ustreas.gov.

For details on how to get forms and publications, see page 4 of the instructions for Form 1040 or 1040A.

If you have tax questions, call 1-800-829-1040 for assistance.

Tax Law Changes Effective for 1998

Use your 1997 tax return as a guide in figuring your 1998 estimated tax, but be sure to consider the changes noted in this section. For more information on changes that may affect your 1998 estimated tax, see Pub. 553.

Estimated tax payments of household employment taxes. Beginning in 1998, you must **include** household employment taxes when figuring your estimated tax payments if **either** of the following applies for the year:

● You will have Federal income tax withheld from wages, pensions, annuities, gambling winnings, or other income, **or**

● You would be required to make estimated tax payments (to avoid a penalty) even if you **did not** include household employment taxes when figuring your estimated tax.

Increase in amount of tax exempt from estimated tax requirements. Beginning in 1998, the requirement to make estimated tax payments (to avoid a penalty) will not apply unless the tax you owe, after subtracting withholding and other credits, is at least $1,000.

Modification of estimated tax safe harbor for some taxpayers. For 1998, the estimated tax safe harbor that is based on the tax shown on the prior year tax return is the same for all taxpayers (except for farmers and fishermen), regardless of adjusted gross income (AGI). That safe harbor is 100% of the tax shown on the 1997 tax return.

Child tax credit. For 1998, you may be entitled to a $400 credit for each of your dependent children who is under age 17 on December 31, 1998. The credit is subject to limits based on your tax, and a phaseout, which begins when your modified AGI exceeds $75,000 ($110,000 if married filing jointly or qualifying widow(er); $55,000 if married filing separately). Above this level, the credit is reduced by $50 for each $1,000 (or fraction thereof) of modified AGI.

Credits for higher education expenses. You may be able to claim the *Hope Scholarship Credit* for tuition and related expenses you pay in 1998 for yourself, your spouse, or dependents to enroll at or attend an eligible educational institution. This credit applies only to the first 2 years of postsecondary education. The student must be enrolled in a degree, certificate, or other program leading to a recognized

Cat. No. 11340T

(Continued on page 2)

credential at an eligible educational institution and must carry at least one-half of a normal full-time work load. The maximum credit per student is $1,500 (100% of the first $1,000 of qualified tuition and related expenses, plus 50% of the next $1,000 of such expenses).

For qualified expenses paid after June 30, 1998, you may be able to claim the *Lifetime Learning Credit.* This credit does not require enrollment in a degree or other program and may be claimed for undergraduate, graduate, or professional degree expenses or for any course at an accredited institution of higher education that helps the student acquire or improve job skills. The credit is 20% of up to $5,000 of qualified tuition and related expenses (the maximum credit per tax return is $1,000).

These credits are available only for expenses paid during the tax year for an academic period beginning in that tax year and cannot be claimed for the cost of books, room and board, or similar expenses. You **cannot** claim either credit if you are married filing separately or you are claimed as a dependent on another person's 1998 tax return.

Each credit is subject to a limit based on your tax and is phased out ratably over a range that:
● Begins when your modified AGI exceeds $40,000 ($80,000 if married filing jointly or qualifying widow(er)), and
● Ends at $50,000 ($100,000 if married filing jointly or qualifying widow(er)).

Caution: *You may not claim both the Hope Scholarship Credit and the Lifetime Learning Credit on behalf of the same student in 1998. Also, you may not claim either of these credits for expenses incurred on behalf of a student in any year in which you also exclude distributions from an education IRA to pay higher education costs for that student.*

Student loan interest. You may be allowed to deduct up to $1,000 for interest due after 1997 that is paid during 1998 on a qualified higher education loan you used to pay for education expenses for yourself, your spouse, or a dependent. A loan made by a related person is not a qualified loan. The deduction is allowed in arriving at AGI (i.e., you do not have to itemize deductions to claim it). The student must have been enrolled in a degree, certificate, or other program leading to a recognized credential at an eligible educational institution and must have carried at least one-half of a normal full-time work load. The deduction is allowed only during the first 60 months in which interest payments are required.

The deduction is phased out ratably over a range that:
● Begins when your modified AGI exceeds $40,000 ($60,000 if married filing jointly or qualifying widow(er)), and
● Ends at $55,000 ($75,000 if married filing jointly or qualifying widow(er)).

You **cannot** take this deduction if you are claimed as a dependent on another person's 1998 tax return or you are married filing a separate return.

IRA deduction increased or restored for some people covered by retirement plans. The income limits for claiming an IRA deduction for 1998 have been increased if you are covered by a retirement plan. Under the new rules, the deduction is phased out ratably over a range that:
● Begins when your modified AGI exceeds $30,000 ($50,000 if married filing jointly or qualifying widow(er)), and
● Ends at $40,000 ($60,000 if married filing jointly or qualifying widow(er)).

Also, if your spouse is covered by a retirement plan but you are not, you are eligible beginning in 1998 to claim an IRA deduction (unless you are married filing a separate return). In this case, the maximum IRA deduction is phased out ratably over a range that begins at a modified AGI of $150,000 and ends at $160,000.

Distributions from IRAs to pay for qualified higher education expenses or "first-time homebuyer" expenses. Beginning with distributions made after 1997, the 10% tax on an early distribution from an IRA will not apply if you use the distribution to pay for either of the following:
● Qualified higher education expenses for academic periods beginning after 1997 for yourself, your spouse, child, grandchild, stepchild, or step-grandchild for attendance at an accredited institution of higher education.
● Certain expenses incurred to buy, build, or rebuild a "first" home that is your main home, your spouse's main home, or the main home of a child, grandchild, or ancestor of yours or your spouse's. Distributions used for this purpose are subject to a lifetime limit of $10,000. In most cases, a home is considered your "first" home if you had no present ownership in a main home during the 2-year period ending on the date you acquired your new home.

(Continued on page 3)

1998 Tax Rate Schedules

Caution: *Do not use these Tax Rate Schedules to figure your 1997 taxes. Use only to figure your 1998 estimated taxes.*

Single—Schedule X

If line 5 is: Over—	But not over—	The tax is:	of the amount over—
$0	$25,350	..........15%	$0
25,350	61,400	**$3,802.50 + 28%**	25,350
61,400	128,100	**13,896.50 + 31%**	61,400
128,100	278,450	**34,573.50 + 36%**	128,100
278,450	....	**88,699.50 + 39.6%**	278,450

Head of household—Schedule Z

If line 5 is: Over—	But not over—	The tax is:	of the amount over—
$0	$33,950	..........15%	$0
33,950	87,700	**$5,092.50 + 28%**	33,950
87,700	142,000	**20,142.50 + 31%**	87,700
142,000	278,450	**36,975.50 + 36%**	142,000
278,450	....	**86,097.50 + 39.6%**	278,450

Married filing jointly or Qualifying widow(er)—Schedule Y-1

If line 5 is: Over—	But not over—	The tax is:	of the amount over—
$0	$42,350	..........15%	$0
42,350	102,300	**$6,352.50 + 28%**	42,350
102,300	155,950	**23,138.50 + 31%**	102,300
155,950	278,450	**39,770.00 + 36%**	155,950
278,450	....	**83,870.00 + 39.6%**	278,450

Married filing separately—Schedule Y-2

If line 5 is: Over—	But not over—	The tax is:	of the amount over—
$0	$21,175	..........15%	$0
21,175	51,150	**$3,176.25 + 28%**	21,175
51,150	77,975	**11,569.25 + 31%**	51,150
77,975	139,225	**19,885.00 + 36%**	77,975
139,225	....	**41,935.00 + 39.6%**	139,225

Foreign earned income exclusion. For 1998, the maximum foreign earned income exclusion amount has been increased to $72,000.

Section 179 expense deduction increased. For 1998, the deduction to expense certain property under section 179 generally has been increased to $18,500.

Self-employed health insurance deduction increased. For 1998, the self-employed health insurance deduction is increased to 45% of health insurance expenses.

Matching contributions to 401(k) plans of self-employed individuals. Generally, matching contributions made for tax years after 1997 to 401(k) plans of self-employed persons are not treated as elective employer contributions and therefore are not subject to the $10,000 annual limit on elective contributions.

Welfare-to-work credit. Employers that pay wages to long-term family assistance recipients may qualify for the welfare-to-work credit. This new credit is based on wages paid to qualified individuals who begin work after December 31, 1997. For more details, see **Form 8861,** Welfare-to-Work Credit.

Income averaging for farmers. Starting in 1998, farmers may elect to average farm income over the 3 prior tax years. This election does not affect the computation of self-employment tax.

Standard deduction for 1998. If you do not itemize your deductions, you may take the 1998 standard deduction listed below:

Filing Status	Standard Deduction
Married filing jointly or Qualifying widow(er)	$7,100
Head of household	$6,250
Single	$4,250
Married filing separately	$3,550

However, if you can be claimed as a dependent on another person's 1998 return, your standard deduction is the greater of:

● $700, **or**
● Your earned income plus $250 (up to the standard deduction amount).

An additional amount is added to the standard deduction if:

1. You are an unmarried individual (single or head of household) and are:

65 or older or blind	$1,050
65 or older and blind	$2,100

2. You are a married individual (filing jointly or separately) or a qualifying widow(er) and are:

65 or older or blind	$850
65 or older and blind	$1,700
Both spouses 65 or older	$1,700 *
Both spouses 65 or older and blind	$3,400 *

* If married filing separately, these amounts apply only if you can claim an exemption for your spouse.

To Figure Your Estimated Tax Use:

● The **1998 Estimated Tax Worksheet** on page 4.
● The instructions on this page for the worksheet on page 4.
● The **1998 Tax Rate Schedules** on page 2.
● Your 1997 tax return and instructions as a guide to figuring your income, deductions, and credits (but be sure to consider the tax law changes noted earlier).

If you receive your income unevenly throughout the year (e.g., you operate your business on a seasonal basis), you may be able to lower or eliminate the amount of your required estimated tax payment for one or more periods by using the annualized income installment method. See Pub. 505 for details.

To amend or correct your estimated tax, see **Amending Estimated Tax Payments** on page 4.

Instructions for Worksheet on Page 4

Line 1— Use your 1997 tax return and instructions as a guide to figuring the adjusted gross income you expect in 1998 (but be sure to consider the tax law changes noted earlier). For more details on figuring your adjusted gross income, see **Expected Adjusted Gross Income** in Pub. 505. If you are self-employed, be sure to take into account the deduction for one-half of your self-employment tax.

Line 7—Additional Taxes. Enter the additional taxes from **Form 4972,** Tax on Lump-Sum Distributions, or **Form 8814,** Parents' Election To Report Child's Interest and Dividends.

Line 9—Credits. See the 1997 Form 1040, lines 40 through 45, or Form 1040A, lines 24a, 24b, and 24c, and the related instructions.

Line 11—Self-Employment Tax. If you and your spouse make joint estimated tax payments and you both have self-employment income, figure the self-employment tax for each of you separately. Enter the total on line 11. When figuring your estimate of 1998 net earnings from self-employment, be sure to use only 92.35% of your total net profit from self-employment.

Line 12—Other Taxes. Except as noted below, enter any other taxes, such as alternative minimum tax, tax on accumulation distribution of trusts, tax on a distribution from an MSA, and the tax on early distributions from **(a)** a qualified retirement plan (including your IRA), **(b)** an annuity, or **(c)** a modified endowment contract entered into after June 20, 1988.

Include household employment taxes on line 12 if **either** of the following is true:

● You will have Federal income tax withheld from wages, pensions, annuities, gambling winnings, or other income, **or**
● You would be required to make estimated tax payments (to avoid a penalty) even if you did not include household employment taxes when figuring your estimated tax.

Do not include tax on recapture of a Federal mortgage subsidy, social security and Medicare tax on unreported tip income, or uncollected employee social security and Medicare or RRTA tax on tips or group-term life insurance. These taxes are not required to be paid until your income tax return is due (not including extensions).

Payment Due Dates

You may pay all of your estimated tax by April 15, 1998, or in four equal amounts by the dates shown below:

1st payment	. . . .	April 15, 1998
2nd payment	. . . .	June 15, 1998
3rd payment	. . . .	Sept. 15, 1998
4th payment	. . . .	Jan. 15, 1999*

*You do not have to make the payment due January 15, 1999, if you file your 1998 tax return by February 1, 1999, **AND** pay the entire balance due with your return.

Note: *Payments are due by the dates indicated whether or not you are outside the United States and Puerto Rico.*

If, after March 31, 1998, you have a large change in income, deductions, additional taxes, or credits that requires you to start making estimated tax payments, you should figure the amount of your estimated tax payments by using the annualized income installment method, as explained in Pub. 505. Although your payment due dates will be the same as shown above, the payment amounts will vary based on your income, deductions, additional taxes, and credits for the months ending before each payment due date. As a result, this method may allow you to skip or lower the amount due for one or more payments. If you use the annualized income installment method, be sure to file **Form 2210,** Underpayment of Estimated Tax by Individuals, Estates, and Trusts, with your 1998 tax return, even if no penalty is owed.

(Continued on page 4)

Farmers and fishermen. If at least two-thirds of your gross income for 1997 or 1998 is from farming or fishing, you may do one of the following:
- Pay all of your estimated tax by January 15, 1999, or
- File your 1998 Form 1040 by March 1, 1999, and pay the total tax due. In this case, 1998 estimated payments are not required.

Fiscal year taxpayers. You are on a fiscal year if your 12-month tax period ends on any day except December 31. Due dates for fiscal year taxpayers are the 15th day of the 4th, 6th, and 9th months of your current fiscal year and the 1st month of the following fiscal year. If any payment date falls on a Saturday, Sunday, or legal holiday, use the next business day.

Amending Estimated Tax Payments

To change or amend your estimated payments, refigure your total estimated payments due (line 16 of the worksheet below). Then use the worksheets under **Amended estimated tax** in Chapter 2 of Pub. 505 to figure the payment due for each remaining payment period. If an estimated tax payment for a previous period is less than one-fourth of your amended estimated tax, you may owe a penalty when you file your return.

(Continued on page 5)

1998 Estimated Tax Worksheet (keep for your records)

1	Enter amount of adjusted gross income you expect in 1998 (see instructions)	**1**
2	• If you plan to itemize deductions, enter the estimated total of your itemized deductions. **Caution:** If line 1 above is over $124,500 ($62,250 if married filing separately), your deduction may be reduced. See Pub. 505 for details. • If you do not plan to itemize deductions, see **Standard Deduction for 1998** on page 3, and enter your standard deduction here.	**2**
3	Subtract line 2 from line 1	**3**
4	Exemptions. Multiply $2,700 by the number of personal exemptions. If you can be claimed as a dependent on another person's 1998 return, your personal exemption is not allowed. **Caution:** If line 1 above is over $186,800 ($155,650 if head of household; $124,500 if single; $93,400 if married filing separately), see Pub. 505 to figure the amount to enter	**4**
5	Subtract line 4 from line 3	**5**
6	**Tax.** Figure your tax on the amount on line 5 by using the 1998 Tax Rate Schedules on page 2. DO NOT use the Tax Table or the Tax Rate Schedules in the 1997 Form 1040 or Form 1040A instructions. **Caution:** If you have a net capital gain, see Pub. 505 to figure the tax.	**6**
7	Additional taxes (see instructions)	**7**
8	Add lines 6 and 7	**8**
9	Credits (see instructions). Do not include any income tax withholding on this line	**9**
10	Subtract line 9 from line 8. Enter the result, but not less than zero	**10**
11	Self-employment tax (see instructions). Estimate of 1998 net earnings from self-employment $................... ; if **$68,400 or less,** multiply the amount by 15.3%; if **more than $68,400,** multiply the amount by 2.9%, add $8,481.60 to the result, and enter the total. **Caution:** If you also have wages subject to social security tax, see Pub. 505 to figure the amount to enter . .	**11**
12	Other taxes (see instructions)	**12**
13a	Add lines 10 through 12	**13a**
b	Earned income credit and credit from **Form 4136**	**13b**
c	Subtract line 13b from line 13a. Enter the result, but not less than zero. **THIS IS YOUR TOTAL 1998 ESTIMATED TAX** . . . . ▶	**13c**
14a	Multiply line 13c by 90% (66⅔% for farmers and fishermen) . . .	**14a**
b	Enter the tax shown on your 1997 tax return.	**14b**
c	Enter the **smaller** of line 14a or 14b. **THIS IS YOUR REQUIRED ANNUAL PAYMENT TO AVOID A PENALTY** . . . . ▶	**14c**
	Caution: Generally, if you do not prepay (through income tax withholding and estimated tax payments) at least the amount on line 14c, you may owe a penalty for not paying enough estimated tax. To avoid a penalty, make sure your estimate on line 13c is as accurate as possible. Even if you pay the required annual payment, you may still owe tax when you file your return. If you prefer, you may pay the amount shown on line 13c. For more details, see Pub. 505.	
15	Income tax withheld and estimated to be withheld during 1998 (including income tax withholding on pensions, annuities, certain deferred income, etc.)	**15**
16	Subtract line 15 from line 14c. (**Note:** *If zero or less, or line 13c minus line 15 is less than $1,000, stop here. You are not required to make estimated tax payments.*)	**16**
17	If the first payment you are required to make is due April 15, 1998, enter ¼ of line 16 (minus any 1997 overpayment that you are applying to this installment) here and on your payment voucher(s)	**17**

When a Penalty Is Applied

In some cases, you may owe a penalty when you file your return. The penalty is imposed on each underpayment for the number of days it remains unpaid. A penalty may be applied if you did not pay enough estimated tax for the year, or you did not make the payments on time or in the required amount. A penalty may apply even if you have an overpayment on your tax return.

The penalty may be waived under certain conditions. See Pub. 505 for details.

How To Complete and Use the Payment Voucher

There is a separate payment voucher for each due date. The due date is shown in the upper right corner. Please be sure you use the voucher with the correct due date for each payment you make. Complete and send in the voucher **only** if you are making a payment. To complete your voucher:

● Type or print your name, address, and social security number in the space provided on the voucher. If filing a joint voucher, also enter your spouse's name and social security number. List the names and social security numbers in the same order on the joint voucher as you will on your joint return. If you and your spouse plan to file separate returns, file separate vouchers instead of a joint voucher.

● Enter on the payment line of the voucher only the amount you are sending in. When making payments of estimated tax, be sure to take into account any 1997 overpayment that you choose to credit against your 1998 tax, but do not include the overpayment amount on this line.

● Enclose your payment, making the check or money order payable to: "Internal Revenue Service" (not "IRS").

● Write your social security number and "1998 Form 1040-ES" on your check or money order.

● Do not staple or attach your payment to the voucher.

● Mail your payment voucher to the address shown on page 6 for the place where you live.

● Fill in the **Record of Estimated Tax Payments** on page 6 for your files.

If you changed your name and made estimated tax payments using your old name, attach a statement to the front of your 1998 tax return. List all of the estimated tax payments you and your spouse made for 1998, the address where you made the payments, and the name(s) and social security number(s) under which you made the payments.

Paperwork Reduction Act Notice. We ask for the information on the payment vouchers to carry out the Internal Revenue laws of the United States. You are required to give us the information. We need it to ensure that you are complying with these laws and to allow us to figure and collect the right amount of tax.

You are not required to provide the information requested on a form that is subject to the Paperwork Reduction Act unless the form displays a valid OMB control number. Books or records relating to a form or its instructions must be retained as long as their contents may become material in the administration of any Internal Revenue law. Generally, tax returns and return information are confidential, as required by Internal Revenue Code section 6103.

The time needed to complete the worksheets and prepare and file the payment vouchers will vary depending on individual circumstances. The estimated average time is: **Recordkeeping,** 1 hr., 19 min.; **Learning about the law,** 22 min.; **Preparing the worksheets and payment vouchers,** 49 min.; **Copying, assembling, and sending the payment voucher to the IRS,** 10 min. If you have comments concerning the accuracy of these time estimates or suggestions for making this package simpler, we would be happy to hear from you. You can write to the Tax Forms Committee, Western Area Distribution Center, Rancho Cordova, CA 95743-0001. **DO NOT** send the payment vouchers to this address. Instead, see **Where To File Your Payment Voucher** on page 6.

- **Tear off here** -

Form **1040-ES**
Department of the Treasury
Internal Revenue Service

1998 Payment Voucher **4**

OMB No. 1545-0087

File only if you are making a payment of estimated tax. Return this voucher with check or money order payable to the **"Internal Revenue Service."** Please write your social security number and "1998 Form 1040-ES" on your check or money order. Do not send cash. Enclose, but do not staple or attach, your payment with this voucher.

Calendar year—Due Jan. 15, 1999

Amount of payment	Please type or print	Your first name and initial	Your last name	Your social security number
		If joint payment, complete for spouse		
		Spouse's first name and initial	Spouse's last name	Spouse's social security number
$		Address (number, street, and apt. no.)		
		City, state, and ZIP code (If a foreign address, enter city, province or state, postal code, and country.)		

For Paperwork Reduction Act Notice, see instructions on page 5.

Record of Estimated Tax Payments (see page 3 for payment due dates)

Payment number	(a) Date	(b) Check or money order number	(c) Amount paid		(d) 1997 overpayment credit applied		(e) Total amount paid and credited (add (c) and (d))	
1								
2								
3								
4								
Total . . . . ▶								

Where To File Your Payment Voucher

Mail your payment voucher to the Internal Revenue Service at the address shown below for the place where you live. **Do not** mail your tax return to this address. Also, do not mail your estimated tax payments to the address shown in the Form 1040 or 1040A instructions.

Note: *For proper delivery of your estimated tax payment to a P.O. box, you must include the box number in the address. Also, note that only the U.S. Postal Service can deliver to P.O. boxes.*

If you live in: ▼	Use this address: ▼
New Jersey, New York (New York City and counties of Nassau, Rockland, Suffolk, and Westchester)	P.O. Box 162 Newark, NJ 07101-0162
New York (all other counties), Connecticut, Maine, Massachusetts, New Hampshire, Rhode Island, Vermont	P.O. Box 371999 Pittsburgh, PA 15250-7999
Delaware, District of Columbia, Maryland, Pennsylvania, Virginia	P.O. Box 8318 Philadelphia, PA 19162-8318
Florida, Georgia, South Carolina	P.O. Box 105900 Atlanta, GA 30348-5900
Indiana, Kentucky, Michigan, Ohio, West Virginia	P.O. Box 7422 Chicago, IL 60680-7422
Alabama, Arkansas, Louisiana, Mississippi, North Carolina, Tennessee	P.O. Box 1219 Charlotte, NC 28201-1219

Illinois, Iowa, Minnesota, Missouri, Wisconsin	P.O. Box 970006 St. Louis, MO 63197-0006
Kansas, New Mexico, Oklahoma, Texas	P.O. Box 970001 St. Louis, MO 63197-0001
Alaska, Arizona, California (counties of Alpine, Amador, Butte, Calaveras, Colusa, Contra Costa, Del Norte, El Dorado, Glenn, Humboldt, Lake, Lassen, Marin, Mendocino, Modoc, Napa, Nevada, Placer, Plumas, Sacramento, San Joaquin, Shasta, Sierra, Siskiyou, Solano, Sonoma, Sutter, Tehama, Trinity, Yolo, and Yuba), Colorado, Idaho, Montana, Nebraska, Nevada, North Dakota, Oregon, South Dakota, Utah, Washington, Wyoming	P.O. Box 510000 San Francisco, CA 94151-5100
California (all other counties), Hawaii	P.O. Box 54030 Los Angeles, CA 90054-0030
American Samoa	P.O. Box 8318 Philadelphia, PA 19162-8318
The Commonwealth of the Northern Mariana Islands	P.O. Box 8318 Philadelphia, PA 19162-8318
Puerto Rico (or if excluding income under section 933)	P.O. Box 8318 Philadelphia, PA 19162-8318

Guam: Nonpermanent residents	P.O. Box 8318 Philadelphia, PA 19162-8318
Permanent residents*	Department of Revenue and Taxation Government of Guam P.O. Box 23607 GMF, GU 96921

* You must prepare separate vouchers for estimated income tax and self-employment tax payments. Send the income tax vouchers to the Guam address and the self-employment tax vouchers to the address for Guam nonpermanent residents shown above.

Virgin Islands: Nonpermanent residents	P.O. Box 8318 Philadelphia, PA 19162-8318
Permanent residents*	V.I. Bureau of Internal Revenue 9601 Estate Thomas Charlotte Amalie St. Thomas, VI 00802

* You must prepare separate vouchers for estimated income tax and self-employment tax payments. Send the income tax vouchers to the Virgin Islands address and the self-employment tax vouchers to the address for Virgin Islands nonpermanent residents shown above.

All APO and FPO addresses	P.O. Box 8318 Philadelphia, PA 19162-8318
Foreign country: U.S. citizens and those filing Form 2555, Form 2555-EZ, or Form 4563	P.O. Box 8318 Philadelphia, PA 19162-8318

Form **2106**

Department of the Treasury
Internal Revenue Service (99)

Employee Business Expenses

▶ See separate instructions.

▶ Attach to Form 1040.

OMB No. 1545-0139

1997

Attachment
Sequence No. **54**

Your name	Social security number	Occupation in which you incurred expenses

Part I   Employee Business Expenses and Reimbursements

			Column A Other Than Meals and Entertainment		Column B Meals and Entertainment	
STEP 1	**Enter Your Expenses**					
1	Vehicle expense from line 22 or line 29	1				
2	Parking fees, tolls, and transportation, including train, bus, etc., that **did not** involve overnight travel or commuting to and from work . .	2				
3	Travel expense while away from home overnight, including lodging, airplane, car rental, etc. **Do not** include meals and entertainment	3				
4	Business expenses not included on lines 1 through 3. **Do not** include meals and entertainment	4				
5	Meals and entertainment expenses (see instructions)	5				
6	**Total expenses.** In Column A, add lines 1 through 4 and enter the result. In Column B, enter the amount from line 5	6				

Note: *If you were not reimbursed for any expenses in Step 1, skip line 7 and enter the amount from line 6 on line 8.*

STEP 2   Enter Reimbursements Received From Your Employer for Expenses Listed in STEP 1

7	Enter reimbursements received from your employer that were **not** reported to you in box 1 of Form W-2. Include any reimbursements reported under code "L" in box 13 of your Form W-2 (see instructions)	7				

STEP 3   Figure Expenses To Deduct on Schedule A (Form 1040)

8	Subtract line 7 from line 6	8				
	Note: *If both columns of line 8 are zero, stop here. If Column A is less than zero, report the amount as income on Form 1040, line 7.*					
9	In Column A, enter the amount from line 8. In Column B, multiply the amount on line 8 by 50% (.50). If either column is zero or less, enter -0- in that column	9				
10	Add the amounts on line 9 of both columns and enter the total here. **Also, enter the total on Schedule A (Form 1040), line 20.** (Fee-basis state or local government officials, qualified performing artists, and individuals with disabilities: See the instructions for special rules on where to enter the total.) . . . . ▶	10				

For Paperwork Reduction Act Notice, see instructions.   Cat. No. 11700N   Form **2106** (1997)

Form 2106 (1997)   Page **2**

Part II Vehicle Expenses (See instructions to find out which sections to complete.)

Section A—General Information

		(a) Vehicle 1	(b) Vehicle 2
11	Enter the date vehicle was placed in service **11**	/ /	/ /
12	Total miles vehicle was driven during 1997 . . . . **12**	miles	miles
13	Business miles included on line 12 . . . . **13**	miles	miles
14	Percent of business use. Divide line 13 by line 12 . . . . **14**	%	%
15	Average daily round trip commuting distance **15**	miles	miles
16	Commuting miles included on line 12 . . . . **16**	miles	miles
17	Other miles. Add lines 13 and 16 and subtract the total from line 12 . . **17**	miles	miles

18 Do you (or your spouse) have another vehicle available for personal purposes? . . . . ☐ Yes ☐ No

19 If your employer provided you with a vehicle, is personal use during off-duty hours permitted? ☐ Yes ☐ No ☐ Not applicable

20 Do you have evidence to support your deduction? . . . . ☐ Yes ☐ No

21 If "Yes," is the evidence written? . . . . ☐ Yes ☐ No

Section B—Standard Mileage Rate (Use this section only if you own the vehicle.)

22	Multiply line 13 by 31½¢ (.315). Enter the result here and on line 1. (Rural mail carriers, see instructions.)	**22**

Section C—Actual Expenses

			(a) Vehicle 1		(b) Vehicle 2	
23	Gasoline, oil, repairs, vehicle insurance, etc.	**23**				
24a	Vehicle rentals	**24a**				
b	Inclusion amount (see instructions)	**24b**				
c	Subtract line 24b from line 24a	**24c**				
25	Value of employer-provided vehicle (applies only if 100% of annual lease value was included on Form W-2—see instructions)	**25**				
26	Add lines 23, 24c, and 25 . .	**26**				
27	Multiply line 26 by the percentage on line 14 . . .	**27**				
28	Depreciation. Enter amount from line 38 below	**28**				
29	Add lines 27 and 28. Enter total here and on line 1.	**29**				

Section D—Depreciation of Vehicles (Use this section only if you own the vehicle.)

			(a) Vehicle 1		(b) Vehicle 2	
30	Enter cost or other basis (see instructions)	**30**				
31	Enter amount of section 179 deduction (see instructions) .	**31**				
32	Multiply line 30 by line 14 (see instructions if you elected the section 179 deduction) . . .	**32**				
33	Enter depreciation method and percentage (see instructions) .	**33**				
34	Multiply line 32 by the percentage on line 33 (see instructions) . .	**34**				
35	Add lines 31 and 34	**35**				
36	Enter the limit from the table in the line 36 instructions . . .	**36**				
37	Multiply line 36 by the percentage on line 14 . . .	**37**				
38	Enter the **smaller** of line 35 or line 37. Also, enter this amount on line 28 above	**38**				

Form **2106-EZ**

Department of the Treasury
Internal Revenue Service   (99)

Unreimbursed Employee Business Expenses

▶ **Attach to Form 1040.**

OMB No. 1545-1441

19**97**

Attachment
Sequence No. **54A**

Your name	Social security number	Occupation in which you incurred expenses

Part I   General Information

You May Use This Form ONLY if All of the Following Apply:

● You are an employee deducting expenses attributable to your job.

● You **do not** get reimbursed by your employer for any expenses (amounts your employer included in box 1 of your Form W-2 are not considered reimbursements).

● If you are claiming vehicle expense,

  a You own your vehicle, and

  b You are using the standard mileage rate for 1997 **and** also used it for the year you first placed the vehicle in service.

Part II   Figure Your Expenses

1	Vehicle expense using the standard mileage rate. Complete Part III and multiply line 8a by 31½¢ (.315)	**1**	
2	Parking fees, tolls, and transportation, including train, bus, etc., that **did not** involve overnight travel or commuting to and from work	**2**	
3	Travel expense while away from home overnight, including lodging, airplane, car rental, etc. **Do not** include meals and entertainment	**3**	
4	Business expenses not included on lines 1 through 3. **Do not** include meals and entertainment .	**4**	
5	Meals and entertainment expenses: $ _____ x 50% (.50)	**5**	
6	**Total expenses.** Add lines 1 through 5. Enter here and **on line 20 of Schedule A (Form 1040).** (Fee-basis state or local government officials, qualified performing artists, and individuals with disabilities: See the instructions for special rules on where to enter this amount.)	**6**	

Part III   Information on Your Vehicle. Complete this part **ONLY** if you are claiming vehicle expense on line 1.

7   When did you place your vehicle in service for business purposes? (month, day, year) ▶ ...... / ...... / ......

8   Of the total number of miles you drove your vehicle during 1997, enter the number of miles you used your vehicle for:

a Business ....   **b** Commuting ....   **c** Other ....

9   Do you (or your spouse) have another vehicle available for personal use? . . . .   ☐ Yes ☐ No

10   Was your vehicle available for use during off-duty hours? . . . .   ☐ Yes ☐ No

11a   Do you have evidence to support your deduction? . . . .   ☐ Yes ☐ No

  b   If "Yes," is the evidence written? . . . .   ☐ Yes ☐ No

General Instructions

Section references are to the Internal Revenue Code.

Changes To Note

● The standard mileage rate has been increased to 31½ cents for each mile of business use in 1997.

● For tax years beginning after 1986, a fee-basis state or local government official can deduct the expenses incurred for services performed in that job in figuring adjusted gross income, rather than as a miscellaneous itemized deduction subject to the 2% limit. See the line 6 instructions for more details. You should file Form 1040X to amend any prior year income tax return affected by this retroactive change. However, you generally must file Form 1040X within 3 years after the date you filed

your original return or within 2 years after the date you paid the tax, whichever is later.

Purpose of Form

You may use Form 2106-EZ instead of Form 2106 if you meet all the requirements listed in Part I of this form.

Recordkeeping

You cannot deduct expenses for travel (including meals unless you used the standard meal allowance), entertainment, gifts, or use of a car or other listed property, unless you keep records to prove the time, place, business purpose, business relationship (for entertainment and gifts), and amounts of these expenses. Generally, you must also have receipts for all lodging expenses (regardless of the amount) and any other expense of $75 or more.

For Paperwork Reduction Act Notice, see back of form.   Cat. No. 20604Q   Form **2106-EZ** (1997)

Additional Information

If you need more information about employee business expenses, you will find the following publications helpful:

Pub. 463, Travel, Entertainment, Gift, and Car Expenses

Pub. 529, Miscellaneous Deductions

Pub. 587, Business Use of Your Home (Including Use by Day-Care Providers)

Pub. 946, How To Depreciate Property

Specific Instructions

Part II—Figure Your Expenses

Line 2. See the line 8b instructions on this page for the definition of commuting.

Line 3. Enter expenses for lodging and transportation connected with overnight travel away from your tax home (defined below). You cannot deduct any expenses for travel away from your tax home for any period of temporary employment of more than 1 year. **Do not** include expenses for meals and entertainment. For more details, including limits, see Pub. 463.

Generally, your **tax home** is your main place of business or post of duty regardless of where you maintain your family home. If you do not have a regular or main place of business because of the nature of your work, then your tax home is the place where you regularly live. If you do not fit in either of these categories, you are considered an itinerant and your tax home is wherever you work. As an itinerant, you are not away from home and cannot claim a travel expense deduction. For more details on your tax home, see Pub. 463.

Line 4. Enter other job-related expenses not listed on any other line of this form. Include expenses for business gifts, education (tuition and books), home office, trade publications, etc. For details, including limits, see Pub. 463 and Pub. 529. If you are deducting home office expenses, see Pub. 587 for special instructions on how to report these expenses. If you are deducting depreciation or claiming a section 179 deduction on a cellular telephone or other similar telecommunications equipment, a home computer, etc., see **Form 4562,** Depreciation and Amortization, to figure the depreciation and section 179 deduction to enter on line 4.

Do not include expenses for meals and entertainment, taxes, or interest on line 4. Deductible taxes are entered on lines 5 through 9 of Schedule A (Form 1040). Employees cannot deduct car loan interest.

Note: If line 4 is your only entry, do not complete Form 2106-EZ unless you are:

- A fee-basis state or local government official claiming expenses in performing that job,
- A qualified performing artist claiming performing-arts-related business expenses, or
- An individual with a disability claiming impairment-related work expenses.

See the line 6 instructions for definitions. If you are not required to file Form 2106-EZ, enter your expenses directly on Schedule A (Form 1040), line 20.

Line 5. Enter your allowable meals and entertainment expense and multiply the total by 50%. Include meals while away from your tax home overnight and other business meals and entertainment. Instead of actual cost, you may be able to claim the **standard meal allowance** for your daily meals and incidental expenses while away from your tax home overnight. Under this method, you deduct a specified amount, depending on where you travel, instead of keeping records of your actual meal expenses. However, you must still keep records to prove the time, place, and business purpose of your travel. See Pub. 463 to figure your deduction using the standard meal allowance.

Line 6. If you were a **fee-basis state or local government official** (defined below), include the expenses you incurred for services performed in that job in the total on Form 1040, line 31. Write "FBO" and the amount in the space to the left of line 31. Your employee business expenses are deductible whether or not you itemize deductions. A fee-basis state or local government official is an official who is an employee of a state or political subdivision of a state and is compensated, in whole or in part, on a fee basis.

If you were a **qualified performing artist** (defined below), include your performing-arts-related expenses in the total on Form 1040, line 31. Write "QPA" and the amount in the space to the left of line 31. Your performing-arts-related business expenses are deductible whether or not you itemize deductions. The expenses are not subject to the 2% limit that applies to most other employee business expenses.

A qualified performing artist is an individual who:

1. Performed services in the performing arts as an employee for at least two employers during the tax year,

2. Received from at least two of those employers wages of $200 or more per employer,

3. Had allowable business expenses attributable to the performing arts of more than 10% of gross income from the performing arts, and

4. Had adjusted gross income of $16,000 or less before deducting expenses as a performing artist.

To be treated as a qualified performing artist, a married individual must also file a joint return, unless the individual and his or her spouse lived apart for all of 1997. On a joint return, requirements **1, 2,** and **3** must be figured separately for each spouse. However, requirement **4** applies to the combined adjusted gross income of both spouses.

If you were an **individual with a disability** and are claiming impairment-related work expenses (defined below), enter the part of the line 6 amount attributable to those expenses on Schedule A (Form 1040), line 27, instead of on Schedule A (Form 1040), line 20. Your impairment-related work expenses are not subject to the 2% limit that applies to most other employee business expenses.

Impairment-related work expenses are the allowable expenses of an individual with physical or mental disabilities for attendant care at his or her place of employment. They also include other expenses in connection with the place of employment that enable the employee to work. See Pub. 463 for more details.

Part III—Information on Your Vehicle

If you claim vehicle expense, you must provide certain information on the use of your vehicle by completing Part III. Include an attachment listing the information requested in Part III for any additional vehicles you used for business during the year.

Line 7. Date placed in service is generally the date you first start using your vehicle. However, if you first start using your vehicle for personal use and later convert it to business use, the vehicle is treated as placed in service on the date you started using it for business.

Line 8a. Do not include commuting miles on this line; commuting miles are not considered business miles. See the line 8b instructions for the definition of commuting.

Line 8b. If you do not know the total actual miles you used your vehicle for commuting during the year, figure the amount to enter on line 8b by multiplying the number of days during the year that you used your vehicle for commuting by the average daily round trip commuting distance in miles.

Generally, **commuting** is travel between your home and a work location. However, such travel is not commuting if you meet **any** of the following conditions:

1. You have at least one regular work location away from your home and you travel to a temporary work location in the same trade or business, regardless of the distance. A temporary work location is one where you perform services on an irregular or short-term basis (generally a matter of days or weeks).

2. You travel to a temporary work location outside the metropolitan area where you live and normally work.

3. Your home is your principal place of business under section 280A(c)(1)(A) (for purposes of deducting expenses for business use of your home) and you travel to another work location in the same trade or business, regardless of whether that location is regular or temporary and regardless of distance.

Paperwork Reduction Act Notice. We ask for the information on this form to carry out the Internal Revenue laws of the United States. You are required to give us the information. We need it to ensure that you are complying with these laws and to allow us to figure and collect the right amount of tax.

You are not required to provide the information requested on a form that is subject to the Paperwork Reduction Act unless the form displays a valid OMB control number. Books or records relating to a form or its instructions must be retained as long as their contents may become material in the administration of any Internal Revenue law. Generally, tax returns and return information are confidential, as required by section 6103.

The time needed to complete and file this form will vary depending on individual circumstances. The estimated average time is:

Recordkeeping	40 min.
Learning about the law or the form	5 min.
Preparing the form	28 min.
Copying, assembling, and sending the form to the IRS	20 min.

If you have comments concerning the accuracy of these time estimates or suggestions for making this form simpler, we would be happy to hear from you. See the Instructions for Form 1040.

Form 2119

Department of the Treasury
Internal Revenue Service (99)

Sale of Your Home

▶ Attach to Form 1040 for year of sale.

▶ See separate instructions.   ▶ Please print or type.

OMB No. 1545-0072

1997

Attachment
Sequence No. **20**

Your first name and initial. If a joint return, also give spouse's name and initial.	Last name	Your social security number

| **If you are filing this form by itself and not with your tax return, see instructions on page 3.** | Present address (no., street, and apt. no., rural route, or P.O. box no. if mail is not delivered to street address) | Spouse's social security number |
| | City, town or post office, state, and ZIP code | |

Part I   Gain on Sale

1	Date your former main home was sold. If sold after May 6, 1997, see page 3 . . . . . ▶	**1**	/ /
			mo. day yr.
2	Have you bought or built a new main home? . . . . ☐ Yes ☐ No		
3	If any part of either main home was ever rented out or used for business, check here ▶ ☐ and see page 3.		
4	Selling price of home. Do not include personal property items you sold with your home . .	**4**	
5	Expense of sale (see page 4)	**5**	
6	Subtract line 5 from line 4	**6**	
7	Adjusted basis of home sold (see page 4)	**7**	
8	**Gain on sale.** Subtract line 7 from line 6. **If zero or less, stop** and attach this form to your return	**8**	

   • For sales **before May 7, 1997,** you must go to Part II or Part III, whichever applies. **But** if line 2 is "No," go to line 9.

   • For sales **after May 6, 1997,** you must go to Part IV on the back to figure any exclusion. **But** if you qualify and elect to use the rules for sales before May 7, 1997, go to Part II or Part III, whichever applies.

9	If you haven't replaced your home, do you plan to do so within the **replacement period** (see page 1)? . ☐ Yes ☐ No	

   • If line 9 is "Yes," stop here, attach this form to your return, and see **Additional filing requirements** on page 1.

   • If line 9 is "No," you **must** go to Part II or Part III, whichever applies.

Part II   One-Time Exclusion of Gain for People Age 55 or Older—By completing this part, you are electing to take the one-time exclusion (see page 2). If you are not electing to take the exclusion, go to Part III now.

10	Who was age 55 or older on the date of sale? . . . . ☐ You ☐ Your spouse ☐ Both of you		
11	Did the person who was 55 or older own and use the property as his or her main home for a total of at least 3 years of the 5-year period before the sale? See page 2 for exceptions. If "No," go to Part III now . . . ☐ Yes ☐ No		
12	At the time of sale, who owned the home? . . . . ☐ You ☐ Your spouse ☐ Both of you		
13	Social security number of spouse at the time of sale if you had a different spouse from the one above. If you were not married at the time of sale, enter "None" . . . . ▶	**13**	
14	**Exclusion.** Enter the **smaller** of line 8 or $125,000 ($62,500 if married filing separate return). Then, go to line 15	**14**	

Part III   Adjusted Sales Price, Taxable Gain, and Adjusted Basis of New Home

15	If line 14 is blank, enter the amount from line 8. Otherwise, subtract line 14 from line 8 . .	**15**	

   • If line 15 is zero, stop and attach this form to your return.

   • If line 15 is more than zero and line 2 is "Yes," go to line 16 now.

   • If you are reporting this sale on the installment method, stop and see page 4.

   • All others, stop and **enter the amount from line 15 on Schedule D, line 4 or line 11.**

16	Fixing-up expenses (see page 4 for time limits)	**16**	
17	If line 14 is blank, enter amount from line 16. Otherwise, add lines 14 and 16	**17**	
18	**Adjusted sales price.** Subtract line 17 from line 6	**18**	
19a	Date you moved into new home ▶ __/__/__ **b** Cost of new home (see page 5) . .	**19b**	
20	Subtract line 19b from line 18. If zero or less, enter -0-	**20**	
21	**Taxable gain.** Enter the **smaller** of line 15 or line 20	**21**	

   • If line 21 is zero, go to line 22 and attach this form to your return.

   • If you are reporting this sale on the installment method, see the line 15 instructions and go to line 22.

   • All others, **enter the amount from line 21 on Schedule D, line 4 or line 11,** and go to line 22.

22	Postponed gain. Subtract line 21 from line 15	**22**	
23	**Adjusted basis of new home.** Subtract line 22 from line 19b	**23**	

For Paperwork Reduction Act Notice, see page 6 of instructions.   Cat. No. 11710J   Form **2119** (1997)

Form 2119 (1997)

Part IV **Exclusion and Taxable Gain for Sales After May 6, 1997**

24 Did you (or your spouse if filing a joint return) own and use the property as your main home for a total of at least 2 years of the 5-year period before the sale? See page 3 for exceptions ☐ Yes ☐ No

25 Maximum exclusion. See page 5 for the amount to enter. **25**

26 Enter the amount from line 8 . . . . **26**

27 **Exclusion.** Enter the **smaller** of line 25 or line 26. If line 26 is the smaller amount, stop and attach this form to your return. Otherwise, go to line 28 . . . . **27**

28 **Taxable gain.** Subtract line 27 from line 26 . . . . **28**

   • If you are reporting this sale on the installment method, see the line 15 instructions.

   • All others, enter the amount from line 28 on **Schedule D, line 4 or line 11.**

Sign here only if you are filing this form by itself and not with your tax return.	Under penalties of perjury, I declare that I have examined this form, including attachments, and to the best of my knowledge and belief, it is true, correct, and complete.
	Your signature Date Spouse's signature Date
	▶ _____ _____ ▶ _____ _____
	If a joint return, both must sign.

Form 2120
(Rev. January 1997)

Department of the Treasury
Internal Revenue Service

Multiple Support Declaration

▶ Attach to Form 1040 or Form 1040A of person claiming the dependent.

OMB No. 1545-0071

Attachment
Sequence No. **50**

Name of person claiming the dependent

Social security number

During the calendar year 19 ...., I paid over 10% of the support of

----
Name of person

I could have claimed this person as a dependent except that I did not pay over half of his or her support. I understand that the person named above is being claimed as a dependent on the income tax return of

----
Name

Address

I agree not to claim this person as a dependent on my Federal income tax return for any tax year that began in this calendar year.

Your signature

Your social security number

Address (number, street, apt. no.)

Date

City, state, and ZIP code

Instructions

Paperwork Reduction Act Notice

We ask for the information on this form to carry out the Internal Revenue laws of the United States. You are required to give us the information. We need it to ensure that you are complying with these laws and to allow us to figure and collect the right amount of tax.

You are not required to provide the information requested on a form that is subject to the Paperwork Reduction Act unless the form displays a valid OMB control number. Books or records relating to a form or its instructions must be retained as long as their contents may become material in the administration of any Internal Revenue law. Generally, tax returns and return information are confidential, as required by Internal Revenue Code section 6103.

The time needed to complete and file this form will vary depending on individual circumstances. The estimated average time is: **Recordkeeping,** 7 minutes; **Learning about the law or the form,** 3 minutes; **Preparing the form,** 7 minutes; and **Copying, assembling, and sending the form to the IRS,** 10 minutes.

If you have comments concerning the accuracy of these time estimates or suggestions for making this form simpler, we would be happy to hear from you. See the instructions for the tax return with which this form is filed.

Purpose of Form

When two or more persons together pay over half of another person's support, only one of them can claim the person they support as a dependent for tax purposes.

Each person who does not claim the dependent completes and signs a Form 2120 (or similar statement containing the same information required by the form) and gives the form (or statement) to the person claiming the dependent. That person attaches all the forms or statements to his or her tax return. See **How To File** on this page.

Who Can Claim the Dependent

Generally, to claim someone as a dependent, you must pay over half of that person's living expenses (support). However, even if you did not meet this support test, you might still be able to claim him or her as a dependent if **all five** of the following apply:

1. You and one or more other eligible person(s) (see below) together paid over half of another person's support.

2. You paid over 10% of the support.

3. No one alone paid over half of the person's support.

4. The other four dependency tests are met. See **Dependents** in the Form 1040 or Form 1040A instructions.

5. Each other eligible person who paid over 10% of the support agrees not to claim the dependent by completing a **Form 2120** or similar statement.

An **eligible person** is someone who could have claimed another person as a dependent except that he or she did not pay over half of that person's support.

How To File

The person claiming the dependent must attach all the completed and signed Form(s) 2120 or similar statement(s) to his or her tax return. The name and social security number of the person claiming the dependent must be at the top of each Form 2120 or similar statement.

Additional Information

See **Pub. 501,** Exemptions, Standard Deduction, and Filing Information, for details.

Cat. No. 11712F

Form **2120** (Rev. 1-97)

Form **2210** Department of the Treasury Internal Revenue Service	**Underpayment of** **Estimated Tax by Individuals, Estates, and Trusts** ▶ See separate instructions. ▶ Attach to Form 1040, 1040A, 1040NR, 1040NR-EZ, or 1041.	OMB No. 1545-0140 **1997** Attachment Sequence No. **06**

Name(s) shown on tax return	Identifying number

Note: *In most cases, you* **do not** *need to file Form 2210. The IRS will figure any penalty you owe and send you a bill. File Form 2210* **only** *if one or more boxes in Part I apply to you. If you do not need to file Form 2210, you still may use it to figure your penalty. Enter the amount from line 20 or line 32 on the penalty line of your return, but* **do not** *attach Form 2210.*

Part I **Reasons for Filing**—If 1a, b, or c below applies to you, you may be able to lower or eliminate your penalty. But you MUST check the boxes that apply and file Form 2210 with your tax return. If 1d below applies to you, check that box and file Form 2210 with your tax return.

1 Check whichever boxes apply (if none apply, see the **Note** above):

a ☐ You request a **waiver.** In certain circumstances, the IRS will waive all or part of the penalty. See **Waiver of Penalty** on page 1 of the instructions.

b ☐ You use the **annualized income installment method.** If your income varied during the year, this method may reduce the amount of one or more required installments. See page 4 of the instructions.

c ☐ You had Federal income tax withheld from wages and, for estimated tax purposes, you treat the withheld tax as paid on the dates it was actually withheld, instead of in equal amounts on the payment due dates. See the instructions for line 22 on page 3.

d ☐ Your required annual payment (line 13 below) is based on your 1996 tax and you filed or are filing a joint return for either 1996 or 1997 but not for both years.

Part II **Required Annual Payment**

2	Enter your 1997 tax after credits (see page 2 of the instructions). **Caution:** *Also see page 2 for a special rule if claiming the research credit*	**2**	
3	Other taxes (see page 2 of the instructions)	**3**	
4	Add lines 2 and 3	**4**	
5	Earned income credit	**5**	
6	Credit for Federal tax paid on fuels	**6**	
7	Add lines 5 and 6	**7**	
8	Current year tax. Subtract line 7 from line 4	**8**	
9	Multiply line 8 by 90% (.90)	**9**	
10	Withholding taxes. **Do not** include any estimated tax payments on this line (see page 2 of the instructions)	**10**	
11	Subtract line 10 from line 8. If less than $500, **stop here; do not** complete or file this form. You do not owe the penalty	**11**	
12	Enter the tax shown on your 1996 tax return (110% of that amount if the adjusted gross income shown on that return is more than $150,000, or if married filing separately for 1997, more than $75,000). **Caution:** *See page 2 of the instructions*	**12**	
13	**Required annual payment.** Enter the **smaller** of line 9 or line 12	**13**	
	Note: *If line 10 is equal to or more than line 13, stop here; you do not owe the penalty. Do not file Form 2210 unless you checked box 1d above.*		

Part III **Short Method (Caution:** *See page 2 of the instructions to find out if you can use the short method. If you checked box* **1b** *or* **c** *in Part I, skip this part and go to Part IV.)*

14	Enter the amount, if any, from line 10 above	**14**	
15	Enter the total amount, if any, of estimated tax payments you made	**15**	
16	Add lines 14 and 15	**16**	
17	**Total underpayment for year.** Subtract line 16 from line 13. If zero or less, stop here; you do not owe the penalty. Do not file Form 2210 unless you checked box 1d above	**17**	
18	Multiply line 17 by .05986	**18**	
19	● If the amount on line 17 was paid **on or after** 4/15/98, enter -0-. ● If the amount on line 17 was paid **before** 4/15/98, make the following computation to find the amount to enter on line 19. Amount on line 17 × Number of days paid before 4/15/98 × .00025	**19**	
20	**PENALTY.** Subtract line 19 from line 18. Enter the result here and on Form 1040, line 65; Form 1040A, line 34; Form 1040NR, line 65; Form 1040NR-EZ, line 26; or Form 1041, line 27 . ▶	**20**	

For Paperwork Reduction Act Notice, see page 1 of separate instructions.   Cat. No. 11744P   Form **2210** (1997)

Part IV   **Regular Method** (See page 2 of the instructions if you are filing Form 1040NR or 1040NR-EZ.)

Section A—Figure Your Underpayment

		Payment Due Dates			
		(a) 4/15/97	(b) 6/15/97	(c) 9/15/97	(d) 1/15/98
21	**Required installments.** If box 1b applies, enter the amounts from Schedule AI, line 26. Otherwise, enter ¼ of line 13, Form 2210, in each column **21**				
22	Estimated tax paid and tax withheld (see page 3 of the instructions). For column (a) only, also enter the amount from line 22 on line 26. If line 22 is equal to or more than line 21 for all payment periods, stop here; you do not owe the penalty. Do not file Form 2210 unless you checked a box in Part I **22**				
	Complete lines 23 through 29 of one column before going to the next column.				
23	Enter amount, if any, from line 29 of previous column **23**				
24	Add lines 22 and 23 . . . . **24**				
25	Add amounts on lines 27 and 28 of the previous column **25**				
26	Subtract line 25 from line 24. If zero or less, enter -0-. For column (a) only, enter the amount from line 22 . **26**				
27	If the amount on line 26 is zero, subtract line 24 from line 25. Otherwise, enter -0- **27**				
28	**Underpayment.** If line 21 is equal to or more than line 26, subtract line 26 from line 21. Then go to line 23 of next column. Otherwise, go to line 29 . ▶ **28**				
29	Overpayment. If line 26 is more than line 21, subtract line 21 from line 26. Then go to line 23 of next column **29**				

Section B—Figure the Penalty (Complete lines 30 and 31 of one column before going to the next column.)

		4/15/97	6/15/97	9/15/97	1/15/98
		Days:	*Days:*	*Days:*	*Days:*
30	Number of days FROM the date shown above line 30 TO the date the amount on line 28 was paid **or** 4/15/98, whichever is earlier **30**				
31	Underpayment on line 28 (see page 3 of the instructions) $\times \dfrac{\text{Number of days on line 30}}{365} \times .09$ ▶ **31**	$	$	$	$
32	**PENALTY.** Add the amounts in each column of line 31. Enter the total here and on Form 1040, line 65; Form 1040A, line 34; Form 1040NR, line 65; Form 1040NR-EZ, line 26; or Form 1041, line 27 . . . . ▶ **32**				$

Form 2210 (1997)   Page **3**

Schedule AI—Annualized Income Installment Method (see pages 4 and 5 of the instructions)

Estates and trusts, **do not** use the period ending dates shown to the right. Instead, use the following: 2/28/97, 4/30/97, 7/31/97, and 11/30/97.

		(a) 1/1/97–3/31/97	(b) 1/1/97–5/31/97	(c) 1/1/97–8/31/97	(d) 1/1/97–12/31/97

Part I   Annualized Income Installments   Caution: *Complete lines 20–26 of one column **before** going to the next column.*

		(a)	(b)	(c)	(d)
1	Enter your adjusted gross income for each period (see instructions). (Estates and trusts, enter your taxable income without your exemption for each period.)				
2	Annualization amounts. (Estates and trusts, see instructions.) . .	4	2.4	1.5	1
3	Annualized income. Multiply line 1 by line 2				
4	Enter your itemized deductions for the period shown in each column. If you do not itemize, enter -0- and skip to line 7. (Estates and trusts, enter -0-, skip to line 9, and enter the amount from line 3 on line 9.)				
5	Annualization amounts	4	2.4	1.5	1
6	Multiply line 4 by line 5 (see instructions if line 3 is more than $60,600)				
7	In each column, enter the full amount of your standard deduction from Form 1040, line 35, or Form 1040A, line 19 (Form 1040NR or 1040NR-EZ filers, enter -0-. **Exception:** Indian students and business apprentices, enter standard deduction from Form 1040NR, line 34 or Form 1040NR-EZ, line 10.) . . . . . ▶				
8	Enter the **larger** of line 6 or line 7. . . . . ▶				
9	Subtract line 8 from line 3				
10	In each column, multiply $2,650 by the total number of exemptions claimed (see instructions if line 3 is more than $90,900). (Estates and trusts and Form 1040NR or 1040NR-EZ filers, enter the exemption amount shown on your tax return.)				
11	Subtract line 10 from line 9				
12	Figure your tax on the amount on line 11 (see instructions) . . .				
13	Form 1040 filers only, enter your self-employment tax from line 35 below				
14	Enter other taxes for each payment period (see instructions) . .				
15	Total tax. Add lines 12, 13, and 14				
16	For each period, enter the same type of credits as allowed on Form 2210, lines 2, 5, and 6 (see instructions)				
17	Subtract line 16 from line 15. If zero or less, enter -0-				
18	Applicable percentage	22.5%	45%	67.5%	90%
19	Multiply line 17 by line 18				
20	Add the amounts in all preceding columns of line 26	▨			
21	Subtract line 20 from line 19. If zero or less, enter -0-				
22	Enter ¼ of line 13 on page 1 of Form 2210 in each column . . .				
23	Enter amount from line 25 of the preceding column of this schedule	▨			
24	Add lines 22 and 23 and enter the total				
25	Subtract line 21 from line 24. If zero or less, enter -0-				▨
26	Enter the **smaller** of line 21 or line 24 here and on Form 2210, line 21 . . . . ▶				

Part II   Annualized Self-Employment Tax

		(a)	(b)	(c)	(d)
27a	Net earnings from self-employment for the period (see instructions)				
b	Annualization amounts	4	2.4	1.5	1
c	Multiply line 27a by line 27b				
28	Social security tax limit	$65,400	$65,400	$65,400	$65,400
29	Enter actual wages subject to social security tax or the 6.2% portion of the 7.65% railroad retirement (tier 1) tax				
30	Annualization amounts	4	2.4	1.5	1
31	Multiply line 29 by line 30				
32	Subtract line 31 from line 28. If zero or less, enter -0-				
33	Multiply the smaller of line 27c or line 32 by .124				
34	Multiply line 27c by .029				
35	Add lines 33 and 34. Enter the result here and on line 13 above ▶				

Form **2441**

Department of the Treasury
Internal Revenue Service (99)

Child and Dependent Care Expenses

▶ **Attach to Form 1040.**

▶ **See separate instructions.**

OMB No. 1545-0068

1997

Attachment
Sequence No. **21**

Name(s) shown on Form 1040

Your social security number

Before you begin, you need to understand the following terms. See **Definitions** on page 1 of the instructions.

- **Dependent Care Benefits**
- **Qualifying Person(s)**
- **Qualified Expenses**
- **Earned Income**

Part I — Persons or Organizations Who Provided the Care—You **must** complete this part.
(If you need more space, use the bottom of page 2.)

1	(a) Care provider's name	(b) Address (number, street, apt. no., city, state, and ZIP code)	(c) Identifying number (SSN or EIN)	(d) Amount paid (see instructions)

| Did you receive **dependent care benefits?** | **NO** ──────▶ Complete only Part II below. |
| | **YES** ─────▶ Complete Part III on the back next. |

Caution: *If the care was provided in your home, you may owe employment taxes. See the instructions for Form 1040, line 52.*

Part II — Credit for Child and Dependent Care Expenses

2   Information about your **qualifying person(s).** If you have more than two qualifying persons, see the instructions.

(a) Qualifying person's name		(b) Qualifying person's social security number	(c) **Qualified expenses** you incurred and paid in 1997 for the person listed in column (a)
First	Last		

3	Add the amounts in column (c) of line 2. DO NOT enter more than $2,400 for one qualifying person or $4,800 for two or more persons. If you completed Part III, enter the amount from line 24	**3**	
4	Enter YOUR **earned income**	**4**	
5	If married filing a joint return, enter YOUR SPOUSE'S earned income (if student or disabled, see the instructions); **all others,** enter the amount from line 4	**5**	
6	Enter the **smallest** of line 3, 4, or 5	**6**	
7	Enter the amount from Form 1040, line 33	**7**	

8   Enter on line 8 the decimal amount shown below that applies to the amount on line 7

If line 7 is—		Decimal amount is	If line 7 is—		Decimal amount is
Over	But not over		Over	But not over	
$0—10,000		.30	$20,000—22,000		.24
10,000—12,000		.29	22,000—24,000		.23
12,000—14,000		.28	24,000—26,000		.22
14,000—16,000		.27	26,000—28,000		.21
16,000—18,000		.26	28,000—No limit		.20
18,000—20,000		.25			

8 × .

9	Multiply **line 6** by the decimal amount on line 8. Enter the result. Then, see the instructions for the amount of credit to enter on Form 1040, line 40	**9**	

For Paperwork Reduction Act Notice, see page 3 of the instructions.   Cat. No. 11862M   Form **2441** (1997)

Part III Dependent Care Benefits

10	Enter the total amount of **dependent care benefits** you received for 1997. This amount should be shown in box 10 of your W-2 form(s). DO NOT include amounts that were reported to you as wages in box 1 of Form(s) W-2	**10**			
11	Enter the amount forfeited, if any. See the instructions	**11**			
12	Subtract line 11 from line 10	**12**			

13	Enter the total amount of **qualified expenses** incurred in 1997 for the care of the **qualifying person(s)** . . .	**13**	
14	Enter the **smaller** of line 12 or 13	**14**	
15	Enter YOUR **earned income**	**15**	
16	If married filing a joint return, enter YOUR SPOUSE'S earned income (if student or disabled, see the line 5 instructions); if married filing a separate return, see the instructions for the amount to enter; **all others,** enter the amount from line 15	**16**	
17	Enter the **smallest** of line 14, 15, or 16	**17**	

18	**Excluded benefits.** Enter here the **smaller** of the following: • The amount from line 17, or • $5,000 ($2,500 if married filing a separate return **and** you were required to enter your spouse's earned income on line 16). }	**18**			
19	**Taxable benefits.** Subtract line 18 from line 12. Also, include this amount on Form 1040, line 7. On the dotted line next to line 7, write "DCB"	**19**			

To claim the child and dependent care
credit, complete lines 20–24 below.

20	Enter $2,400 ($4,800 if two or more qualifying persons)	**20**			
21	Enter the amount from line 18	**21**			
22	Subtract line 21 from line 20. If zero or less, **STOP.** You cannot take the credit. **Exception.** If you paid 1996 expenses in 1997, see the line 9 instructions	**22**			
23	Complete line 2 on the front of this form. DO NOT include in column (c) any excluded benefits shown on line 18 above. Then, add the amounts in column (c) and enter the total here	**23**			
24	Enter the **smaller** of line 22 or 23. Also, enter this amount on line 3 on the front of this form and complete lines 4–9	**24**			

Form **3800**	**General Business Credit**	OMB No. 1545–0895
Department of the Treasury Internal Revenue Service	▶ Attach to your tax return. ▶ See separate instructions.	**19 97** Attachment Sequence No. **22**

Name(s) shown on return	Identifying number

Part I   Tentative Credit

1a	Current year investment credit (Form 3468, Part I)	**1a**	
b	Current year work opportunity credit (Form 5884, Part I)	**1b**	
c	Current year welfare-to-work credit (Form 8861, Part I)	**1c**	
d	Current year credit for alcohol used as fuel (Form 6478)	**1d**	
e	Current year credit for increasing research activities (Form 6765, Part I) . .	**1e**	
f	Current year low-income housing credit (Form 8586, Part I)	**1f**	
g	Current year enhanced oil recovery credit (Form 8830, Part I)	**1g**	
h	Current year disabled access credit (Form 8826, Part I)	**1h**	
i	Current year renewable electricity production credit (Form 8835, Part I) . .	**1i**	
j	Current year Indian employment credit (Form 8845, Part I)	**1j**	
k	Current year credit for employer social security and Medicare taxes paid on certain employee tips (Form 8846, Part I)	**1k**	
l	Current year orphan drug credit (Form 8820, Part I).	**1l**	
m	Current year credit for contributions to selected community development corporations (Form 8847, Part I)	**1m**	
n	Current year trans-Alaska pipeline liability fund credit (see instructions)	**1n**	
2	**Current year general business credit.** Add lines 1a through 1n	**2**	
3	Passive activity credits included on line 2 (see instructions)	**3**	
4	Subtract line 3 from line 2	**4**	
5	Passive activity credits allowed for 1997 (see instructions)	**5**	
6	Carryforward of general business, WIN, or ESOP credit to 1997 (see instructions for the schedule to attach)	**6**	
7	Carryback of general business credit to 1997 (see instructions)	**7**	
8	**Tentative general business credit.** Add lines 4 through 7	**8**	

Part II   General Business Credit Limitation Based on Amount of Tax

9	Regular tax before credits:			
	● Individuals. Enter amount from Form 1040, line 39			
	● Corporations. Enter amount from Form 1120, Schedule J, line 3 (or Form 1120-A, Part I, line 1) . } .		**9**	
	● Other filers. Enter regular tax before credits from your return			
10a	Credit for child and dependent care expenses (Form 2441, line 9) .	**10a**		
b	Credit for the elderly or the disabled (Schedule R (Form 1040), line 20)	**10b**		
c	Mortgage interest credit (Form 8396, line 11)	**10c**		
d	Adoption credit (Form 8839, line 10)	**10d**		
e	District of Columbia first-time homebuyer credit (Form 8859) . .	**10e**		
f	Foreign tax credit (Form 1116, line 32, or Form 1118, Sch. B, line 12)	**10f**		
g	Possessions tax credit (Form 5735)	**10g**		
h	Credit for fuel from a nonconventional source	**10h**		
i	Qualified electric vehicle credit (Form 8834, line 19).	**10i**		
j	Add lines 10a through 10i		**10j**	
11	Net regular tax. Subtract line 10j from line 9		**11**	
12	Alternative minimum tax:			
	● Individuals. Enter amount from Form 6251, line 28 . . . . . . } . .			
	● Corporations. Enter amount from Form 4626, line 15 . . . . . . }		**12**	
	● Estates and trusts. Enter amount from Form 1041, Schedule I, line 42 . . }			
13	Net income tax. Add lines 11 and 12		**13**	
14	Tentative minimum tax (see instructions)	**14**		
15	If line 11 is more than $25,000, enter 25% (.25) of the excess (see instructions)	**15**		
16	Enter the greater of line 14 or line 15		**16**	
17	Subtract line 16 from line 13. If zero or less, enter -0-		**17**	
18	**General business credit allowed for current year.** Enter the **smaller** of line 8 or line 17 here and on Form 1040, line 44; Form 1120, Schedule J, line 4d; Form 1120-A, Part I, line 2a; Form 1041, Schedule G, line 2c; or the applicable line of your return. **Individuals, estates, and trusts:** See instructions if the credit for increasing research activities is claimed. **C corporations:** See instructions for Schedule A if any regular investment credit carryforward is claimed. See the instructions if the corporation has had a post-1986 "ownership change" .		**18**	

For Paperwork Reduction Act Notice, see back of form.	Cat. No. 12392F	Form **3800** (1997)

Schedule A— **Additional General Business Credit Allowed By Internal Revenue Code Section 38(c)(2) (Before Repeal by the Revenue Reconciliation Act of 1990)—Only Applicable to C Corporations**

19	Enter the portion of the credit shown on line 6 that is attributable to the regular investment credit under section 46 (before amendment by the Revenue Reconciliation Act of 1990)	**19**		
20	Tentative minimum tax (from line 14) **20**			
21	Multiply line 20 by 25% (.25)	**21**		
22	Enter the amount from line 17 . . . . **22**			
23	Enter the portion of the credit shown on line 8 that is NOT attributable to the regular investment credit under section 46 (before amendment by the Revenue Reconciliation Act of 1990) **23**			
24	Subtract line 23 from line 22 (if zero or less, enter -0-)	**24**		
25	Subtract line 24 from line 19 (if zero or less, enter -0-)	**25**		
26	For purposes of this line only, refigure the amount on line 11, Form 4626, by using zero on line 6, Form 4626, and enter the result here. **26**			
27	Multiply line 26 by 10% (.10)	**27**		
28	Net income tax (from line 13)	**28**		
29	General business credit (from line 18)	**29**		
30	Subtract line 29 from line 28	**30**		
31	Subtract line 27 from line 30	**31**		
32	Enter the smallest of line 21, line 25, or line 31	**32**		
33	Subtract line 32 from line 20	**33**		
34	Enter the greater of line 15 or line 33	**34**		
35	Subtract line 34 from line 28	**35**		
36	Enter the smaller of line 11 or line 35. Enter this amount also on line 18 instead of the amount previously figured on that line. Write "Sec. 38(c)(2)" in the margin next to your entry on line 18 .	**36**		
37	If line 35 is greater than line 36, enter the excess here and see the instructions on how to claim the additional credit	**37**		

Paperwork Reduction Act Notice. We ask for the information on this form to carry out the Internal Revenue laws of the United States. You are required to give us the information. We need it to ensure that you are complying with these laws and to allow us to figure and collect the right amount of tax.

You are not required to provide the information requested on a form that is subject to the Paperwork Reduction Act unless the form displays a valid OMB control number. Books or records relating to a form or its instructions must be retained as long as their contents may become material in the administration of any Internal Revenue law. Generally, tax returns and return information are confidential, as required by Code section 6103.

The time needed to complete and file this form will vary depending on individual circumstances. The estimated average time is:

Recordkeeping . . . .12 hr., 55 min.

Learning about the law or the form . . . . 1 hr.

Preparing and sending the form to the IRS . . 1 hr., 15 min.

If you have comments concerning the accuracy of these time estimates or suggestions for making this form simpler, we would be happy to hear from you. See the instructions for the tax return with which this form is filed.

Form **3903**

Department of the Treasury
Internal Revenue Service

Moving Expenses

▶ **Attach to Form 1040.**

OMB No. 1545-0062

1997

Attachment
Sequence No. **62**

Name(s) shown on Form 1040

Your social security number

Caution: *If you are a member of the armed forces, see the instructions before completing this form.*

1 Enter the number of miles from your **old home** to your **new workplace** . . | 1 | | miles

2 Enter the number of miles from your **old home** to your **old workplace** . . | 2 | | miles

3 Subtract line 2 from line 1. Enter the result but not less than zero . . . . | 3 | | miles

Is line 3 at least 50 miles?

Yes. Go to line 4. Also, see **Time Test** in the instructions.

No. You **cannot** deduct your moving expenses. Do not complete the rest of this form.

4 Transportation and storage of household goods and personal effects (see instructions) . . . | 4 |

5 Travel and lodging expenses of moving from your old home to your new home. **Do not** include meals (see instructions) . . . . | 5 |

6 Add lines 4 and 5 . . . . | 6 |

7 Enter the total amount your employer paid for your move (including the value of services furnished in kind) that is **not** included in the wages box (box 1) of your W-2 form. This amount should be identified with code **P** in box 13 of your W-2 form . . . . | 7 |

Is line 6 more than line 7?

Yes. Go to line 8.

No. You **cannot** deduct your moving expenses. If line 6 is less than line 7, subtract line 6 from line 7 and include the result in income on Form 1040, line 7.

8 Subtract line 7 from line 6. Enter the result here and on Form 1040, line 25. This is your **moving expense deduction** . . . . | 8 |

General Instructions

Purpose of Form

Use Form 3903 to figure your moving expense deduction if you moved to a new principal place of work (workplace) within the United States or its possessions. If you qualify to deduct expenses for more than one move, use a separate Form 3903 for each move.

For more details, see **Pub. 521,** Moving Expenses.

Note: *Use* **Form 3903-F,** *Foreign Moving Expenses, instead of this form if you are a U.S. citizen or resident alien who moved to a new principal workplace outside the United States or its possessions.*

Another Form You May Have To File

If you sold your main home in 1997, you must file **Form 2119,** Sale of Your Home, to report the sale.

Who May Deduct Moving Expenses

If you moved to a different home because of a change in job location, you may be able to deduct your moving expenses. You may be able to take the deduction whether you are self-employed or an employee. But you must meet certain tests explained next.

Distance Test

Your new principal workplace must be at least 50 miles farther from your old home than your old workplace was. For example,

if your old workplace was 3 miles from your old home, your new workplace must be at least 53 miles from that home. If you did not have an old workplace, your new workplace must be at least 50 miles from your old home. The distance between the two points is the shortest of the more commonly traveled routes between them.

Time Test

If you are an employee, you must work full time in the general area of your new workplace for at least 39 weeks during the 12 months right after you move. If you are self-employed, you must work full time in the general area of your new workplace for at least 39 weeks during the first 12 months and a total of at least 78 weeks during the 24 months right after you move.

You may deduct your moving expenses even if you have not met the time test before your return is due. You may do this

For Paperwork Reduction Act Notice, see back of form. Cat. No. 12490K Form **3903** (1997)

if you expect to meet the 39-week test by the end of 1998 or the 78-week test by the end of 1999. If you deduct your moving expenses on your 1997 return but do not meet the time test, you will have to either:

● Amend your 1997 tax return by filing **Form 1040X,** Amended U.S. Individual Income Tax Return, or

● Report the amount of your 1997 moving expense deduction that reduced your 1997 income tax as income in the year you cannot meet the test. For more details, see **Time Test** in Pub. 521.

If you do not deduct your moving expenses on your 1997 return and you later meet the time test, you may take the deduction by filing an amended return for 1997. To do this, use Form 1040X.

Exceptions to the Time Test. The time test does not have to be met if any of the following apply:

● Your job ends because of disability.

● You are transferred for your employer's benefit.

● You are laid off or discharged for a reason other than willful misconduct.

● You meet the requirements (explained later) for retirees or survivors living outside the United States.

● You are filing this form for a decedent.

Members of the Armed Forces

If you are in the armed forces, you do not have to meet the **distance and time tests** if the move is due to a permanent change of station. A permanent change of station includes a move in connection with and within 1 year of retirement or other termination of active duty.

How To Complete the Form

First, complete lines 4 through 6 using your actual expenses. **Do not** reduce your expenses by any reimbursements or allowances you received from the government in connection with the move. Also, do not include any expenses for moving services that were provided by the government. If you and your spouse and dependents are moved to or from different locations, treat the moves as a single move.

Next, enter on line 7 the total reimbursements and allowances you received from the government in connection with the expenses you claimed on lines 4 and 5. **Do not** include the value of moving services provided by the government. Then, complete line 8 if applicable.

Retirees or Survivors Living Outside the United States

If you are a retiree or survivor who moved to a home in the United States or its possessions and you meet the following requirements, you are treated as if you moved to a new workplace located in the United States. You are subject to the distance test. Use this form instead of Form 3903-F to figure your moving expense deduction.

Retirees

You may deduct moving expenses for a move to a new home in the United States when you actually retire if both your old principal workplace and your old home were outside the United States.

Survivors

You may deduct moving expenses for a move to a home in the United States if you are the spouse or dependent of a person whose principal workplace at the time of death was outside the United States. In addition, the expenses must be for a move **(1)** that begins within 6 months after the decedent's death, and **(2)** from a former home outside the United States that you lived in with the decedent at the time of death.

Reimbursements

If your employer paid for any part of your move, your employer must give you a statement showing a detailed breakdown of reimbursements or payments for moving expenses. Employers may use **Form 4782,** Employee Moving Expense Information, or their own form.

You may choose to deduct moving expenses in the year you are reimbursed by your employer, even though you paid the expenses in a different year. However, special rules apply. See **How To Report** in Pub. 521.

Specific Instructions

You may deduct the following expenses you incurred in moving your family and dependent household members. Do not deduct expenses for employees such as a maid, nanny, or nurse.

Line 4

Enter the actual cost to pack, crate, and move your household goods and personal effects. You may also include the cost to store and insure household goods and personal effects within any period of 30 days in a row after the items were moved from your old home and before they were delivered to your new home.

Line 5

Enter the costs of travel from your old home to your new home. These include transportation and lodging on the way. Include costs for the day you arrive. Although not all the members of your household have to travel together or at the same time, you may only include expenses for one trip per person.

If you use your own car(s), you may figure the expenses by using either:

● Actual out-of-pocket expenses for gas and oil, or

● Mileage at the rate of 10 cents a mile.

You may add parking fees and tolls to the amount claimed under either method. Keep records to verify your expenses.

Paperwork Reduction Act Notice. We ask for the information on this form to carry out the Internal Revenue laws of the United States. You are required to give us the information. We need it to ensure that you are complying with these laws and to allow us to figure and collect the right amount of tax.

You are not required to provide the information requested on a form that is subject to the Paperwork Reduction Act unless the form displays a valid OMB control number. Books or records relating to a form or its instructions must be retained as long as their contents may become material in the administration of any Internal Revenue law. Generally, tax returns and return information are confidential, as required by Internal Revenue Code section 6103.

The time needed to complete and file this form will vary depending on individual circumstances. The estimated average time is:

Recordkeeping	33 min.
Learning about the law or the form	7 min.
Preparing the form	13 min.
Copying, assembling, and sending the form to the IRS .	20 min.

If you have comments concerning the accuracy of these time estimates or suggestions for making this form simpler, we would be happy to hear from you. See the Instructions for Form 1040.

Form **4255** (Rev. April 1997) Department of the Treasury Internal Revenue Service	**Recapture of Investment Credit** ▶ **Attach to your income tax return.**	OMB No. 1545-0166 Attachment Sequence No. **65**

Name(s) as shown on return		Identifying number

Properties	Type of property—State whether rehabilitation, energy, reforestation, or transition property. (See the Instructions for Form 3468 for the year the investment credit property was placed in service for definitions.) If rehabilitation property, also show type of building. If energy property, show type.
A	
B	
C	
D	

Original Investment Credit

Computation Steps: (see Specific Instructions)	Properties			
	A	**B**	**C**	**D**
1 Original rate of credit				
2 Cost or other basis				
3 Original credit. Multiply line 2 by the percentage on line 1				
4 Date property was placed in service	/ /	/ /	/ /	/ /
5 Date property ceased to be qualified investment credit property	/ /	/ /	/ /	/ /
6 Number of full years between the date on line 4 and the date on line 5				

Computation of Recapture Tax

	A	B	C	D
7 Recapture percentage (see instructions)				
8 Tentative recapture tax. Multiply line 3 by the percentage on line 7.				
9 Add line 8, columns A through D				
10 Enter the recapture tax from property for which there was an increase in nonqualified nonrecourse financing (attach separate computation)				
11 Add lines 9 and 10				
12 Portion of original credit (line 3) not used to offset tax in any year, plus any carryback and carryforward of credits you now can apply to the original credit year because you have freed up tax liability in the amount of the tax recaptured. Do not enter more than line 11—see instructions				
13 Total increase in tax. Subtract line 12 from line 11. Enter here and on the appropriate line of your tax return. See section 29(b)(4) if you claim the nonconventional source fuel credit				

General Instructions

Section references are to the Internal Revenue Code unless otherwise noted.

Paperwork Reduction Act Notice

We ask for the information on this form to carry out the Internal Revenue laws of the United States. You are required to give us the information. We need it to ensure that you are complying with these laws and to allow us to figure and collect the right amount of tax.

You are not required to provide the information requested on a form that is subject to the Paperwork Reduction Act unless the form displays a valid OMB control number. Books or records relating to a form or its instructions must be retained as long as their contents may become material in the administration of any Internal Revenue law. Generally, tax returns and return information are confidential, as required by section 6103.

The time needed to complete and file this form will vary depending on individual circumstances. The estimated average time is:

Recordkeeping . . . . 6 hr., 28 min.

Learning about the law or the form . . . . 1 hr., 23 min.

Preparing, copying, assembling, and sending the form to the IRS . . . 1 hr., 33 min.

If you have comments concerning the accuracy of these time estimates or suggestions for making this form simpler, we would be happy to hear from you. You can write to the IRS at the address listed in the instructions for the tax return with which this form is filed.

Purpose of Form

Use Form 4255 to figure the increase in tax for the recapture of investment credit claimed.

Who Must Refigure the Investment Credit

Generally, you must refigure the investment credit and may have to recapture all or part of it if:

● You disposed of investment credit property before the end of 5 full years after the property was placed in service (recapture period).

● You changed the use of the property before the end of the recapture period so that it no longer qualifies as investment credit property.

● The business use of the property decreased before the end of the recapture period so that it no longer qualifies (in whole or in part) as investment credit property.

● Any building to which section 47(d) applies will no longer be a qualified rehabilitated building when placed in service.

● Any property to which section 48(a)(5) applies will no longer qualify as investment credit property when placed in service.

● Before the end of the recapture period, your proportionate interest was reduced by more than one-third in a partnership, S corporation, estate, or trust that allocated the cost or other basis of property to you for which you claimed a credit.

● You returned leased property (on which you claimed a credit) to the lessor before the end of the recapture period.

● A net increase in the amount of nonqualified nonrecourse financing occurred for any property to which section 49(a)(1) applied. For more details, see the instructions for line 10.

Exceptions to recapture.—Recapture of the investment credit does not apply to:

● A transfer because of the death of the taxpayer.

● A transfer between spouses or incident to divorce under section 1041. However, a later disposition by the transferee is subject to recapture to the same extent as if the transferor had disposed of the property at the later date.

● A transaction to which section 381(a) applies (relating to certain acquisitions of the assets of one corporation by another corporation).

● A mere change in the form of conducting a trade or business if:

1. The property is retained as investment credit property in that trade or business, AND

2. The taxpayer retains a substantial interest in that trade or business.

A mere change in the form of conducting a trade or business includes a corporation that elects to be an S corporation and a corporation whose S election is revoked or terminated.

For more details on the recapture rules, see section 50(a).

Caution: *See section 46(g)(4) (as in effect on November 4, 1990) to figure the recapture tax if you made a withdrawal from a capital construction fund set up under the Merchant Marine Act of 1936 to pay the principal of any debt incurred in connection with a vessel on which you claimed investment credit.*

Basis Adjustment on Recapture

For property subject to investment credit recapture, increase the property's basis as follows:

● For qualified rehabilitation expenditures, increase the basis by 100% of the recapture tax (or adjustment to carrybacks and carryovers).

● For energy property or qualified timber property, increase the basis by 50% of the recapture tax (or adjustment to carrybacks and carryovers).

If you are a partner or S corporation shareholder, the adjusted basis of your interest in the partnership or stock in the S corporation is adjusted to take into account the adjustment made to the basis of property held by the partnership or S corporation.

Specific Instructions

Note: *Do not figure the recapture tax on lines 1 through 9 if there is an increase in nonqualified nonrecourse financing related to certain at-risk property. Figure the recapture tax for these properties on separate schedules and enter the recapture tax on line 10. Include any unused credit for these properties on line 12.*

Partnerships, S corporations, estates, and trusts.—For a partnership, S corporation, estate, or trust that allocated any or all of the investment credit to its partners, shareholders, or beneficiaries, provide the information they need to refigure the credit. See Regulations sections 1.47-4, 1.47-5, and 1.47-6.

Partners, shareholders, and beneficiaries.—If your Schedule K-1 shows recapture of investment credit claimed in an earlier year, you will need your copy of the original Form 3468 to complete lines 1 through 6 of this Form 4255.

Lines A through D.—Describe the property for which you must refigure the credit.

Complete lines 1 through 8 for each property on which you are refiguring the credit. Use a separate column for each item. If you need more columns, use additional Forms 4255, or other schedules that include all the information shown on Form 4255. Enter the total from the separate sheets on line 9.

Line 1.—Enter the rate you used to figure the original credit from the Form 3468 that you filed.

Line 2.—Enter the cost or other basis that you used to figure the original credit.

Line 4.—Enter the month, day, and year that the property was available for service.

Line 5.—Generally, this will be the date you disposed of the property. For more details, see Regulations section 1.47-1(c).

Line 6.—Do not enter partial years. If the property was held less than 12 months, enter zero.

Line 7.—Enter the recapture percentage from the following table:

If number of full years on line 6 of Form 4255 is:	Then the recapture percentage is:
0	100
1	80
2	60
3	40
4	20
5 or more	0

Line 9.—If you have used more than one Form 4255, or separate sheets to list additional items on which you figured an increase in tax, write to the left of the entry space "Tax from attached" and the total tax from the separate sheets. Include the amount in the total for line 9.

Line 10.—For certain taxpayers, the basis or cost of property is limited to the amount the taxpayer is at risk for the property at year end. The basis or cost must be reduced by the amount of any "nonqualified nonrecourse financing" related to the property at year end. If there is an increase in nonqualified nonrecourse financing, recapture may be required. See section 49(b) for details. Attach a separate computation schedule to figure the recapture tax and enter the total tax on line 10.

Line 12.—If you did not use all the credit you originally figured, either in the year you figured it or in a carryback or carryforward year, you do not have to recapture the amount of the credit you did not use. In refiguring the credit for the original credit year, be sure to include any carryforwards from previous years, plus any carrybacks arising within the 3 tax years after the original credit year that are now allowed because the recapture and recomputation of the original credit made available some additional tax liability in that year. See Regulations section 1.47-1(d) and Rev. Rul. 72-221, 1972-1 C.B. 15, for details.

Note: *You must also take into account any applicable 35% reduction in credit under section 49(c)(2) (as in effect on November 4, 1990) when computing the amount to enter on line 12.*

Figure the unused portion on a separate sheet and enter it on this line. Do not enter more than the recapture tax on line 11.

Note: *Be sure to adjust your current unused credit to reflect any unused portion of the original credit that was entered on line 12 of this form.*

Form 4562

Department of the Treasury
Internal Revenue Service (99)

Depreciation and Amortization
(Including Information on Listed Property)

▶ See separate instructions.   ▶ Attach this form to your return.

OMB No. 1545-0172

1997

Attachment
Sequence No. **67**

Name(s) shown on return	Business or activity to which this form relates	Identifying number

Part I **Election To Expense Certain Tangible Property (Section 179)** (Note: *If you have any "listed property," complete Part V before you complete Part I.*)

1	Maximum dollar limitation. If an enterprise zone business, see page 2 of the instructions . .	**1**	$18,000
2	Total cost of section 179 property placed in service. See page 2 of the instructions	**2**	
3	Threshold cost of section 179 property before reduction in limitation	**3**	$200,000
4	Reduction in limitation. Subtract line 3 from line 2. If zero or less, enter -0-	**4**	
5	Dollar limitation for tax year. Subtract line 4 from line 1. If zero or less, enter -0-. If married filing separately, see page 2 of the instructions	**5**	

(a) Description of property	(b) Cost (business use only)	(c) Elected cost
6		

7	Listed property. Enter amount from line 27	**7**	
8	Total elected cost of section 179 property. Add amounts in column (c), lines 6 and 7 . . .	**8**	
9	Tentative deduction. Enter the smaller of line 5 or line 8	**9**	
10	Carryover of disallowed deduction from 1996. See page 3 of the instructions	**10**	
11	Business income limitation. Enter the smaller of business income (not less than zero) or line 5 (see instructions)	**11**	
12	Section 179 expense deduction. Add lines 9 and 10, but do not enter more than line 11 . .	**12**	
13	Carryover of disallowed deduction to 1998. Add lines 9 and 10, less line 12 ▶	**13**	

Note: *Do not use Part II or Part III below for listed property (automobiles, certain other vehicles, cellular telephones, certain computers, or property used for entertainment, recreation, or amusement). Instead, use Part V for listed property.*

Part II **MACRS Depreciation For Assets Placed in Service ONLY During Your 1997 Tax Year (Do Not Include Listed Property.)**

Section A—General Asset Account Election

14	If you are making the election under section 168(i)(4) to group any assets placed in service during the tax year into one or more general asset accounts, check this box. See page 3 of the instructions . . . . ▶	☐

Section B—General Depreciation System (GDS) (See page 3 of the instructions.)

(a) Classification of property	(b) Month and year placed in service	(c) Basis for depreciation (business/investment use only—see instructions)	(d) Recovery period	(e) Convention	(f) Method	(g) Depreciation deduction
15a 3-year property						
b 5-year property						
c 7-year property						
d 10-year property						
e 15-year property						
f 20-year property						
g 25-year property			25 yrs.		S/L	
h Residential rental property			27.5 yrs.	MM	S/L	
			27.5 yrs.	MM	S/L	
i Nonresidential real property			39 yrs.	MM	S/L	
				MM	S/L	

Section C—Alternative Depreciation System (ADS) (See page 6 of the instructions.)

(a)			(d)	(e)	(f)	(g)
16a Class life					S/L	
b 12-year			12 yrs.		S/L	
c 40-year			40 yrs.	MM	S/L	

Part III **Other Depreciation (Do Not Include Listed Property.)** (See page 6 of the instructions.)

17	GDS and ADS deductions for assets placed in service in tax years beginning before 1997	**17**	
18	Property subject to section 168(f)(1) election	**18**	
19	ACRS and other depreciation	**19**	

Part IV **Summary** (See page 7 of the instructions.)

20	Listed property. Enter amount from line 26	**20**	
21	**Total.** Add deductions on line 12, lines 15 and 16 in column (g), and lines 17 through 20. Enter here and on the appropriate lines of your return. Partnerships and S corporations—see instructions . .	**21**	
22	For assets shown above and placed in service during the current year, enter the portion of the basis attributable to section 263A costs	**22**	

For Paperwork Reduction Act Notice, see the separate instructions.   Cat. No. 12906N   Form **4562** (1997)

Form 4562 (1997)

Page **2**

Part V — Listed Property—Automobiles, Certain Other Vehicles, Cellular Telephones, Certain Computers, and Property Used for Entertainment, Recreation, or Amusement

Note: *For any vehicle for which you are using the standard mileage rate or deducting lease expense, complete **only** 23a, 23b, columns (a) through (c) of Section A, all of Section B, and Section C if applicable.*

Section A—Depreciation and Other Information (**Caution:** *See page 8 of the instructions for limits for passenger automobiles.*)

23a Do you have evidence to support the business/investment use claimed? ☐ **Yes** ☐ **No**   **23b** If "Yes," is the evidence written? ☐ **Yes** ☐ **No**

(a) Type of property (list vehicles first)	(b) Date placed in service	(c) Business/ investment use percentage	(d) Cost or other basis	(e) Basis for depreciation (business/investment use only)	(f) Recovery period	(g) Method/ Convention	(h) Depreciation deduction	(i) Elected section 179 cost
24 Property used more than 50% in a qualified business use (See page 7 of the instructions.):								
		%						
		%						
		%						
25 Property used 50% or less in a qualified business use (See page 7 of the instructions.):								
		%			S/L –			
		%			S/L –			
		%			S/L –			

26 Add amounts in column (h). Enter the total here and on line 20, page 1 . . . . . . **26**

27 Add amounts in column (i). Enter the total here and on line 7, page 1 . . . . **27**

Section B—Information on Use of Vehicles

Complete this section for vehicles used by a sole proprietor, partner, or other "more than 5% owner," or related person.

If you provided vehicles to your employees, first answer the questions in Section C to see if you meet an exception to completing this section for those vehicles.

		(a) Vehicle 1	(b) Vehicle 2	(c) Vehicle 3	(d) Vehicle 4	(e) Vehicle 5	(f) Vehicle 6
28	Total business/investment miles driven during the year (DO NOT include commuting miles)						
29	Total commuting miles driven during the year						
30	Total other personal (noncommuting) miles driven						
31	Total miles driven during the year. Add lines 28 through 30.						

		Yes	No	Yes	No	Yes	No	Yes	No	Yes	No	Yes	No
32	Was the vehicle available for personal use during off-duty hours?												
33	Was the vehicle used primarily by a more than 5% owner or related person?												
34	Is another vehicle available for personal use?												

Section C—Questions for Employers Who Provide Vehicles for Use by Their Employees

*Answer these questions to determine if you meet an exception to completing Section B for vehicles used by employees who **are not** more than 5% owners or related persons.*

		Yes	No
35	Do you maintain a written policy statement that prohibits all personal use of vehicles, including commuting, by your employees?		
36	Do you maintain a written policy statement that prohibits personal use of vehicles, except commuting, by your employees? See page 9 of the instructions for vehicles used by corporate officers, directors, or 1% or more owners		
37	Do you treat all use of vehicles by employees as personal use?		
38	Do you provide more than five vehicles to your employees, obtain information from your employees about the use of the vehicles, and retain the information received?		
39	Do you meet the requirements concerning qualified automobile demonstration use? See page 9 of the instructions . .		

Note: *If your answer to 35, 36, 37, 38, or 39 is "Yes," you need not complete Section B for the covered vehicles.*

Part VI — Amortization

(a) Description of costs	(b) Date amortization begins	(c) Amortizable amount	(d) Code section	(e) Amortization period or percentage	(f) Amortization for this year
40 Amortization of costs that begins during your 1997 tax year:					

41 Amortization of costs that began before 1997 . . . . **41**

42 **Total.** Enter here and on "Other Deductions" or "Other Expenses" line of your return . . . **42**

✿

Form 4684

Department of the Treasury
Internal Revenue Service

Casualties and Thefts

▶ See separate instructions.
▶ Attach to your tax return.
▶ Use a separate Form 4684 for each different casualty or theft.

OMB No. 1545-0177

1997

Attachment
Sequence No. **26**

Name(s) shown on tax return

Identifying number

SECTION A—Personal Use Property (Use this section to report casualties and thefts of property **not** used in a trade or business or for income-producing purposes.)

1 Description of properties (show type, location, and date acquired for each):

Property **A** ....

Property **B** ....

Property **C** ....

Property **D** ....

		Properties (Use a separate column for each property lost or damaged from one casualty or theft.)			
		A	**B**	**C**	**D**
2 Cost or other basis of each property	**2**				
3 Insurance or other reimbursement (whether or not you filed a claim). See instructions **Note:** *If line 2 is **more than** line 3, skip line 4.*	**3**				
4 Gain from casualty or theft. If line 3 is **more than** line 2, enter the difference here and skip lines 5 through 9 for that column. See instructions if line 3 includes insurance or other reimbursement you did not claim, or you received payment for your loss in a later tax year	**4**				
5 Fair market value **before** casualty or theft	**5**				
6 Fair market value **after** casualty or theft	**6**				
7 Subtract line 6 from line 5	**7**				
8 Enter the **smaller** of line 2 or line 7	**8**				
9 Subtract line 3 from line 8. If zero or less, enter -0-	**9**				

10 Casualty or theft loss. Add the amounts on line 9. Enter the total **10**

11 Enter the amount from line 10 or $100, whichever is **smaller** **11**

12 Subtract line 11 from line 10 . . . . **12**

Caution: *Use only one Form 4684 for lines 13 through 18.*

13 Add the amounts on line 12 of all Forms 4684 . . . . **13**

14 Combine the amounts from line 4 of all Forms 4684 . . . . **14**

15 • If line 14 is **more than** line 13, enter the difference here and on Schedule D. Do not complete the rest of this section (see instructions).
• If line 14 is **less than** line 13, enter -0- here and continue with the form. **15**
• If line 14 is **equal to** line 13, enter -0- here. Do not complete the rest of this section.

16 If line 14 is **less than** line 13, enter the difference **16**

17 Enter 10% of your adjusted gross income (Form 1040, line 33). Estates and trusts, see instructions **17**

18 Subtract line 17 from line 16. If zero or less, enter -0-. Also enter result on Schedule A (Form 1040), line 19. Estates and trusts, enter on the "Other deductions" line of your tax return **18**

For Paperwork Reduction Act Notice, see page 4 of separate instructions.   Cat. No. 12997O   Form **4684** (1997)

Form 4684 (1997)   Attachment Sequence No. **26**   Page **2**

Name(s) shown on tax return. Do not enter name and identifying number if shown on other side.	Identifying number

SECTION B—Business and Income-Producing Property (Use this section to report casualties and thefts of property used in a trade or business or for income-producing purposes.)

Part I   Casualty or Theft Gain or Loss (Use a separate Part I for each casualty or theft.)

19 Description of properties (show type, location, and date acquired for each):

Property **A** ....

Property **B** ....

Property **C** ....

Property **D** ....

Properties (Use a separate column for each property lost or damaged from one casualty or theft.)

		A	B	C	D
20	Cost or adjusted basis of each property				
21	Insurance or other reimbursement (whether or not you filed a claim). See the instructions for line 3 . **Note:** *If line 20 is more than line 21, skip line 22.*				
22	Gain from casualty or theft. If line 21 is **more than** line 20, enter the difference here and on line 29 or line 34, column (c), except as provided in the instructions for line 33. Also, skip lines 23 through 27 for that column. See the instructions for line 4 if line 21 includes insurance or other reimbursement you did not claim, or you received payment for your loss in a later tax year				
23	Fair market value **before** casualty or theft . . .				
24	Fair market value **after** casualty or theft				
25	Subtract line 24 from line 23				
26	Enter the **smaller** of line 20 or line 25				
	Note: *If the property was totally destroyed by casualty or lost from theft, enter on line 26 the amount from line 20.*				
27	Subtract line 21 from line 26. If zero or less, enter -0-				
28	Casualty or theft loss. Add the amounts on line 27. Enter the total here and on line 29 **or** line 34 (see instructions).	**28**			

Part II   Summary of Gains and Losses (from separate Parts I)

(a) Identify casualty or theft	(b) Losses from casualties or thefts		(c) Gains from casualties or thefts includible in income
	(i) Trade, business, rental or royalty property	(ii) Income-producing property	

Casualty or Theft of Property Held One Year or Less

	(a)	(b)(i)	(b)(ii)	(c)
29		( )	( )	
		( )	( )	
30	Totals. Add the amounts on line 29 . . . . **30**	( )	( )	

31 Combine line 30, columns (b)(i) and (c). Enter the net gain or (loss) here and on Form 4797, line 14. If Form 4797 is not otherwise required, see instructions **31**

32 Enter the amount from line 30, column (b)(ii) here and on Schedule A (Form 1040), line 22. Partnerships, S corporations, estates and trusts, see instructions **32**

Casualty or Theft of Property Held More Than One Year

	(a)	(b)(i)	(b)(ii)	(c)
33	Casualty or theft gains from Form 4797, line 32			**33**
34		( )	( )	
		( )	( )	
35	Total losses. Add amounts on line 34, columns (b)(i) and (b)(ii) . . . **35**	( )	( )	
36	Total gains. Add lines 33 and 34, column (c)			**36**
37	Add amounts on line 35, columns (b)(i) and (b)(ii)			**37**

38 If the loss on line 37 is **more than** the gain on line 36:

a Combine line 35, column (b)(i) and line 36, and enter the net gain or (loss) here. Partnerships and S corporations see the note below. All others enter this amount on Form 4797, line 14. If Form 4797 is not otherwise required, see instructions **38a**

b Enter the amount from line 35, column (b)(ii) here. Partnerships and S corporations see the note below. Individuals enter this amount on Schedule A (Form 1040), line 22. Estates and trusts, enter on the "Other deductions" line of your tax return **38b**

39 If the loss on line 37 is **equal to** or **less than** the gain on line 36, combine these lines and enter here. Partnerships, see the note below. All others, enter this amount on Form 4797, line 3, column (g) and the net 28% rate gain or (loss), if applicable, in column (h) **39**

Note: *Partnerships, enter the amount from line 38a, 38b, or line 39 on Form 1065, Schedule K, line 7. S corporations, enter the amount from line 38a or 38b on Form 1120S, Schedule K, line 6.*

Form **4797**

Department of the Treasury
Internal Revenue Service (99)

Sales of Business Property
(Also Involuntary Conversions and Recapture Amounts
Under Sections 179 and 280F(b)(2))
▶ Attach to your tax return.   ▶ See separate instructions.

OMB No. 1545-0184

1997

Attachment
Sequence No. **27**

Name(s) shown on return

Identifying number

1   Enter here the gross proceeds from the sale or exchange of real estate reported to you for 1997 on Form(s) 1099-S (or a substitute statement) that you will be including on line 2, 10, or 20 . . . . | **1** |

Part I   Sales or Exchanges of Property Used in a Trade or Business and Involuntary Conversions From Other Than Casualty or Theft—Property Held More Than 1 Year

(a) Description of property	(b) Date acquired (mo., day, yr.)	(c) Date sold (mo., day, yr.)	(d) Gross sales price	(e) Depreciation allowed or allowable since acquisition	(f) Cost or other basis, plus improvements and expense of sale	(g) GAIN or (LOSS) for entire year. Subtract (f) from the sum of (d) and (e)	(h) 28% RATE GAIN or (LOSS) * (see instr. below)
2							

3   Gain, if any, from Form 4684, line 39 . . . . | **3** |
4   Section 1231 gain from installment sales from Form 6252, line 26 or 37 . . . . . . | **4** |
5   Section 1231 gain or (loss) from like-kind exchanges from Form 8824 . . . . | **5** |
6   Gain, if any, from line 32, from other than casualty or theft . . . . | **6** |
7   Combine lines 2 through 6 in columns (g) and (h). Enter gain or (loss) here, and on the appropriate line as follows: | **7** |

Partnerships—Enter the gain or (loss) on Form 1065, Schedule K, lines 6a and 6b. Skip lines 8, 9, 11, and 12 below.

S corporations—Report the gain or (loss) following the instructions for Form 1120S, Schedule K, lines 5 and 6. Skip lines 8, 9, 11, and 12 below, unless line 7, column (g) is a gain and the S corporation is subject to the capital gains tax.

All others—If line 7, column (g) is zero or a loss, enter that amount on line 11 below and skip lines 8 and 9. If line 7, column (g) is a gain and you did not have any prior year section 1231 losses, or they were recaptured in an earlier year, enter the gain or (loss) in each column as a long-term capital gain or (loss) on Schedule D and skip lines 8, 9, and 12 below.

8   Nonrecaptured net section 1231 losses from prior years (see instructions) . . . . . . | **8** |
9   Subtract line 8 from line 7. If zero or less, enter -0-. Also enter on the appropriate line as follows (see instructions): | **9** |

S corporations—Enter only the gain in column (g) on Schedule D (Form 1120S), line 14, and skip lines 11 and 12 below.

All others—If line 9, column (g) is zero, enter the gain from line 7, column (g) on line 12 below. If line 9, column (g) is more than zero, enter the amount from line 8, column (g) on line 12 below, and enter the gain or (loss) in each column of line 9 as a long-term capital gain or (loss) on Schedule D.

*   Corporations (other than S corporations) should not complete column (h). Partnerships and S corporations must complete column (h). All others must complete column (h) only if line 7, column (g), is a gain. 28% rate gain or loss includes all gains and losses in column (g) from sales, exchanges, or conversions (including installment payments received) **either (a) before 5/7/97 or (b) after 7/28/97** for assets held more than 1 year but not more than 18 months.

Part II   Ordinary Gains and Losses

10 Ordinary gains and losses not included on lines 11 through 17 (include property held 1 year or less):

11 Loss, if any, from line 7, column (g) . . . . | **11** |
12 Gain, if any, from line 7, column (g) or amount from line 8, column (g) if applicable . . . . | **12** |
13 Gain, if any, from line 31 . . . . | **13** |
14 Net gain or (loss) from Form 4684, lines 31 and 38a . . . . | **14** |
15 Ordinary gain from installment sales from Form 6252, line 25 or 36 . . . . | **15** |
16 Ordinary gain or (loss) from like-kind exchanges from Form 8824 . . . . . . | **16** |
17 Recapture of section 179 expense deduction for partners and S corporation shareholders from property dispositions by partnerships and S corporations (see instructions) . . . . . | **17** |
18 Combine lines 10 through 17 in column (g). Enter gain or (loss) here, and on the appropriate line as follows: | **18** |
  a For all except individual returns: Enter the gain or (loss) from line 18 on the return being filed.
  b For individual returns:
    (1) If the loss on line 11 includes a loss from Form 4684, line 35, column (b)(ii), enter that part of the loss here and on line 22 of Schedule A (Form 1040). Identify as from "Form 4797, line 18b(1)." See instructions . . . . | **18b(1)** |
    (2) Redetermine the gain or (loss) on line 18, excluding the loss, if any, on line 18b(1). Enter here and on Form 1040, line 14 . . . . | **18b(2)** |

For Paperwork Reduction Act Notice, see separate instructions.   Cat. No. 13086I   Form **4797** (1997)

Part III   Gain From Disposition of Property Under Sections 1245, 1250, 1252, 1254, and 1255

19	(a) Description of section 1245, 1250, 1252, 1254, or 1255 property:	(b) Date acquired (mo., day, yr.)	(c) Date sold (mo., day, yr.)
A			
B			
C			
D			

	These columns relate to the properties on lines 19A through 19D. ▶		Property A	Property B	Property C	Property D
20	Gross sales price (**Note:** *See line 1 before completing.*)	20				
21	Cost or other basis plus expense of sale	21				
22	Depreciation (or depletion) allowed or allowable	22				
23	Adjusted basis. Subtract line 22 from line 21	23				
24	Total gain. Subtract line 23 from line 20	24				
25	**If section 1245 property:**					
a	Depreciation allowed or allowable from line 22	25a				
b	Enter the **smaller** of line 24 or 25a	25b				
26	**If section 1250 property:** If straight line depreciation was used, enter -0- on line 26g, except for a corporation subject to section 291.					
a	Additional depreciation after 1975 (see instructions)	26a				
b	Applicable percentage multiplied by the **smaller** of line 24 or line 26a (see instructions)	26b				
c	Subtract line 26a from line 24. If residential rental property or line 24 is not more than line 26a, skip lines 26d and 26e	26c				
d	Additional depreciation after 1969 and before 1976	26d				
e	Enter the **smaller** of line 26c or 26d	26e				
f	Section 291 amount (corporations only)	26f				
g	Add lines 26b, 26e, and 26f	26g				
27	**If section 1252 property:** Skip this section if you did not dispose of farmland or if this form is being completed for a partnership.					
a	Soil, water, and land clearing expenses	27a				
b	Line 27a multiplied by applicable percentage (see instructions)	27b				
c	Enter the **smaller** of line 24 or 27b	27c				
28	**If section 1254 property:**					
a	Intangible drilling and development costs, expenditures for development of mines and other natural deposits, and mining exploration costs (see instructions)	28a				
b	Enter the **smaller** of line 24 or 28a	28b				
29	**If section 1255 property:**					
a	Applicable percentage of payments excluded from income under section 126 (see instructions)	29a				
b	Enter the **smaller** of line 24 or 29a (see instructions)	29b				

Summary of Part III Gains. Complete property columns A through D through line 29b before going to line 30.

30	Total gains for all properties. Add property columns A through D, line 24	30	
31	Add property columns A through D, lines 25b, 26g, 27c, 28b, and 29b. Enter here and on line 13	31	
32	Subtract line 31 from line 30. Enter the portion from casualty or theft on Form 4684, line 33. Enter the portion from other than casualty or theft on Form 4797, line 6, column (g), and if applicable, column (h)	32	

Part IV   Recapture Amounts Under Sections 179 and 280F(b)(2) When Business Use Drops to 50% or Less   See instructions.

			(a) Section 179	(b) Section 280F(b)(2)
33	Section 179 expense deduction or depreciation allowable in prior years	33		
34	Recomputed depreciation. See instructions	34		
35	Recapture amount. Subtract line 34 from line 33. See the instructions for where to report	35		

Form **4868**	**Application for Automatic Extension of Time To File U.S. Individual Income Tax Return**	OMB No. 1545-0188
Department of the Treasury Internal Revenue Service		19**97**

General Instructions

Purpose of Form

Use Form 4868 to apply for 4 more months to file **Form 1040EZ, Form 1040A,** or **Form 1040.**

To get the extra time you **MUST:**

● Properly estimate your 1997 tax liability using the information available to you,

● Enter your tax liability on line 9 of Form 4868, **AND**

● File Form 4868 by the regular due date of your return.

You are not required to send a payment of the tax you estimate as due. However, see **Interest** and **Late Payment Penalty** on page 3. Any remittance you send with your application for extension will be treated as a payment of tax.

You do not have to explain why you are asking for the extension. We will contact you only if your request is denied.

Do not file Form 4868 if you want the IRS to figure your tax or you are under a court order to file your return by the regular due date.

If you need an additional extension, see **If You Need Additional Time** on this page.

Note: *An extension of time to file your 1997* **calendar year** *income tax return also extends the time to file a gift or generation-skipping transfer (GST) tax return* **(Form 709 or 709-A)** *for 1997.*

Out of the Country

If you already had 2 extra months to file because you were a U.S. citizen or resident and were out of the country, use this form to obtain an additional 2 months to file. Write "Taxpayer Abroad" across the top of Form 4868. "Out of the country" means either **(a)** you live outside the United States and Puerto Rico **and** your main place of work is outside the United States and Puerto Rico, **or (b)** you are in military or naval service outside the United States and Puerto Rico.

When To File Form 4868

File Form 4868 by April 15, 1998. Fiscal year taxpayers, file Form 4868 by the regular due date of the return.

If you had 2 extra months to file your return because you were out of the country, file Form 4868 by June 15, 1998, for a 1997 calendar year return.

How To Send In Your Payment

● When sending a payment with Form 4868, use the addresses in the middle column under **Where To File** on page 2.

● Make your check or money order payable to "Internal Revenue Service" (not "IRS"). Do not send cash.

● Write your social security number, daytime phone number, and "1997 Form 4868"on the front of your check or money order.

● Do not staple or attach your payment to the form.

If You Need Additional Time

If the automatic 4-month extension (until August 17, 1998, for most calendar year taxpayers) does not give you enough time, you can ask for additional time later. But you will have to give a good reason, and it must be approved by the IRS. To ask for the additional time, you must **either:**

1. File **Form 2688,** Application for Additional Extension of Time To File U.S. Individual Income Tax Return, or

2. Explain your reason in a letter. Mail it to the address in the right column under **Where To File** on page 2.

File Form 4868 **before** you file Form 2688 or write a letter asking for more time. Only in cases of undue hardship will the IRS approve your request for an additional extension without receiving Form 4868 first. Ask early for this extra time. Then, you can still file your return on time if your request is not approved.

For Paperwork Reduction Act Notice, see page 4.   Cat. No. 13141W   Form **4868** (1997)

▼ DETACH HERE ▼

Form **4868**	**Application for Automatic Extension of Time To File U.S. Individual Income Tax Return**	OMB No. 1545-0188
Department of the Treasury Internal Revenue Service	For calendar year 1997, or other tax year beginning ,1997, ending ,19 .	19**97**

Part I Identification	**Part II** Individual Taxes
1 Your name(s) (see instructions)	**4** Total tax liability for 1997 . . . . $ _____
	5 Total 1997 payments . . . . . . _____
Address (see instructions)	**6** **Balance.** Subtract 5 from 4 . . . . . _____
City, town or post office, state, and ZIP code	**Part III** **Gift/GST Tax**—If you are not filing a gift or GST tax return, go to Part IV now. See the instructions.
2 Your social security number **3** Spouse's social security no.	**7** Your gift or GST tax payment. . . $ _____
	8 **Your spouse's** gift/GST tax payment . _____
This form also extends the time for filing a gift or generation-skipping transfer (GST) tax return if you file a calendar (not fiscal) year income tax return. Check below if requesting a gift or GST tax return extension, and enter your tax payment(s) in Part III:	**Part IV** Total
	9 **Total liability.** Add lines 6, 7, and 8 $ _____
	10 Amount you are paying. . . . . ▶ _____
Yourself ▶ ☐ Spouse ▶ ☐	If line 10 is less than line 9, you may be liable for interest and penalties. See page 3.

Where To File

If you live in:	And you are making a payment, send Form 4868 with your payment to IRS:	And you are NOT making a payment, send Form 4868 to Internal Revenue Service Center:
Florida, Georgia, South Carolina	P.O. Box 105073 Atlanta, GA 30348-5073	Atlanta, GA 39901
New Jersey, New York (*New York City and counties of Nassau, Rockland, Suffolk, and Westchester*)	P.O. Box 22423 Newark, NJ 07101-2423	Holtsville, NY 00501
New York (*all other counties*), Connecticut, Maine, Massachusetts, New Hampshire, Rhode Island, Vermont	P.O. Box 371410 Pittsburgh, PA 15250-7410	Andover, MA 05501
Illinois, Iowa, Minnesota, Missouri, Wisconsin	P.O. Box 970028 St. Louis, MO 63197-0028	Kansas City, MO 64999
Delaware, District of Columbia, Maryland, Pennsylvania, Virginia	P.O. Box 7990 Philadelphia, PA 19162-7990	Philadelphia, PA 19255
Indiana, Kentucky, Michigan, Ohio, West Virginia	P.O. Box 6252 Chicago, IL 60680-6252	Cincinnati, OH 45999
Kansas, New Mexico, Oklahoma, Texas	P.O. Box 970027 St. Louis, MO 63197-0027	Austin, TX 73301
Alaska, Arizona, California (*counties of Alpine, Amador, Butte, Calaveras, Colusa, Contra Costa, Del Norte, El Dorado, Glenn, Humboldt, Lake, Lassen, Marin, Mendocino, Modoc, Napa, Nevada, Placer, Plumas, Sacramento, San Joaquin, Shasta, Sierra, Siskiyou, Solano, Sonoma, Sutter, Tehama, Trinity, Yolo, and Yuba*), Colorado, Idaho, Montana, Nebraska, Nevada, North Dakota, Oregon, South Dakota, Utah, Washington, Wyoming	P.O. Box 7122 San Francisco, CA 94120-7122	Ogden, UT 84201
California (*all other counties*), Hawaii	P.O. Box 54916 Los Angeles, CA 90054-0916	Fresno, CA 93888
Alabama, Arkansas, Louisiana, Mississippi, North Carolina, Tennessee	P.O. Box 1236 Charlotte, NC 28201-1236	Memphis, TN 37501
American Samoa or Puerto Rico (*or exclude income under section 933*); are a nonpermanent resident of Guam or the Virgin Islands; have an APO, FPO, or foreign address; are a dual-status alien; or file Form 2555, 2555-EZ, or 4563	P.O. Box 7990 Philadelphia, PA 19162-7990	Philadelphia, PA 19255
Guam: Permanent residents	Send Form 4868 and payments to:	Department of Revenue and Taxation Government of Guam P.O. Box 23607 GMF, GU 96921
Virgin Islands: Permanent residents	Send Form 4868 and payments to:	V.I. Bureau of Internal Revenue 9601 Estate Thomas Charlotte Amalie St. Thomas, VI 00802

Filing Your Tax Return

You may file your tax return any time before the extension expires. But remember, Form 4868 does not extend the time to pay taxes. If you do not pay the amount due by the regular due date, you will owe interest. You may also be charged penalties.

Do not attach a copy of Form 4868 to your return.

For your convenience, we have included an extra copy of Form 4868. However, only file one.

Interest

You will owe interest on any tax not paid by the regular due date of your return. The interest runs until you pay the tax. Even if you had a good reason for not paying on time, you will still owe interest.

Late Payment Penalty

The penalty is usually ½ of 1% of any tax (other than estimated tax) not paid by the regular due date. It is charged for each month or part of a month the tax is unpaid. The maximum penalty is 25%.

The late payment penalty will not be charged if you can show reasonable cause for not paying on time. Attach a statement to your return fully explaining the reason. **Do not** attach the statement to Form 4868.

You are considered to have "reasonable cause" for the period covered by this automatic extension if at least 90% of your actual 1997 tax liability is paid before the regular due date of your return through withholding, estimated tax payments, or with Form 4868.

Late Filing Penalty

A penalty is usually charged if your return is filed after the due date (including extensions). It is usually 5% of the tax not paid by the regular due date for each month or part of a month your return is late. Generally, the maximum penalty is 25%. If your return is more than 60 days late, the minimum penalty is $100 or the balance of the tax due on your return, whichever is smaller. You might not owe the penalty if you have a good reason for filing late. Attach a statement to your return fully explaining the reason. **Do not** attach the statement to Form 4868.

How To Claim Credit for Payment Made With This Form

When you file your return, include the amount of any payment you sent with Form 4868 on the appropriate line of your tax return. If you file Form 1040EZ, the instructions for line 9 of that form will tell you how to report the payment. If you file Form 1040A, see the instructions for line 29e. If you file Form 1040, enter the payment on line 57.

If you and your spouse each filed a separate Form 4868 but later file a joint return for 1997, enter the total paid with both Forms 4868 on the appropriate line of your joint return.

If you and your spouse jointly file Form 4868 but later file separate returns for 1997, you may enter the total amount paid with Form 4868 on either of your separate returns. Or you and your spouse may divide the payment in any agreed amounts. Be sure each separate return has the social security numbers of both spouses.

Specific Instructions
How To Complete Form 4868

Skip Part III unless you are requesting an extension of time to file a gift or GST tax return.

Part I—Identification

Enter your name(s) and address. If you plan to file a joint return, include both spouses' names in the order in which they will appear on the return.

If you want correspondence regarding this extension to be sent to you at an address other than your own or to an agent acting for you, include the agent's name, if any, and enter that address instead.

If you changed your name after you filed your last return because of marriage, divorce, etc., be sure to report this to your local Social Security Administration office before filing Form 4868. This prevents delays in processing your extension request.

If you changed your mailing address after you filed your last return, you should use **Form 8822,** Change of Address, to notify the IRS of the change. Showing a new address on Form 4868 will not update your record. You can get Form 8822 by calling 1-800-TAX-FORM (1-800-829-3676).

▼ DETACH HERE ▼   (This is an extra copy. File only one Form 4868.)

Form **4868**	**Application for Automatic Extension of Time To File U.S. Individual Income Tax Return** For calendar year 1997, or other tax year beginning ,1997, ending ,19 .	OMB No. 1545-0188 19**97**
Department of the Treasury Internal Revenue Service		

Part I Identification	**Part II** Individual Taxes
1 Your name(s) (see instructions)	4 Total tax liability for 1997 . . . . . $ ____
	5 Total 1997 payments. . . . . ____
Address (see instructions)	6 **Balance.** Subtract 5 from 4 . . . . ____
City, town or post office, state, and ZIP code	**Part III** **Gift/GST Tax**—If you are not filing a gift or GST tax return, go to Part IV now. See the instructions.
2 Your social security number 3 Spouse's social security no.	7 Your gift or GST tax payment. . . $ ____ 8 **Your spouse's** gift/GST tax payment
This form also extends the time for filing a gift or generation-skipping transfer (GST) tax return if you file a calendar (not fiscal) year income tax return. Check below if requesting a gift or GST tax return extension, and enter your tax payment(s) in Part III:	**Part IV** Total
	9 **Total liability.** Add lines 6, 7, and 8 $ ____ 10 Amount you are paying. . . . . ▶ ____
Yourself ▶ ☐ Spouse ▶ ☐	If line 10 is less than line 9, you may be liable for interest and penalties. See page 3.

If you plan to file jointly, enter on line 2 the SSN that you will show first on your return. Enter your spouse's SSN on line 3.

Part II—Individual Taxes

Line 4—Total Tax Liability for 1997

This is the amount you expect to enter on Form 1040EZ, line 10; Form 1040A, line 28; or Form 1040, line 53. If you expect this amount to be zero, enter zero.

Caution: *You can estimate this amount, but be as exact as you can with the information you have. If we later find that your estimate was not reasonable, the extension will be null and void.*

Line 5—Total Payments for 1997

This is the amount you expect to enter on Form 1040EZ, line 9; Form 1040A, line 29e; or Form 1040, line 60 (excluding line 57).

Line 6—Balance

Subtract line 5 from line 4. If line 5 is more than line 4, enter zero.

If you find you cannot pay the amount shown on line 6, you can still get the extension. But you should pay as much as you can to limit the amount of interest you will owe. Also, you may be charged the late payment penalty on the unpaid tax from the regular due date of your return. See **Late Payment Penalty** on page 3.

Part III—Gift/GST Tax

Fill in this part only if you or your spouse plan to file Form 709 or 709-A **and** you are also using Form 4868 to apply for an extension of time to file your 1997 **calendar year** income tax return. **Do not** include income tax on lines 7 and 8.

Enter the amount of gift and GST tax you (or your spouse) are paying on these lines. If your spouse files a **separate** Form 4868, **do not** check the box for your spouse; enter on your form only the total gift and GST tax **you** are paying. Pay in full with this form to avoid interest and penalties.

Part IV—Total

Enter the total of line 6 (and 7 and 8, if applicable) on line 9. If you are paying your entire estimate of tax liability, both lines 9 and 10 should be the same.

Paperwork Reduction Act Notice. We ask for the information on this form to carry out the Internal Revenue laws of the United States. You are required to give us the information. We need it to ensure that you are complying with these laws and to allow us to figure and collect the right amount of tax.

You are not required to provide the information requested on a form that is subject to the Paperwork Reduction Act unless the form displays a valid OMB control number. Books or records relating to a form or its instructions must be retained as long as their contents may become material in the administration of any Internal Revenue law. Generally, tax returns and return information are confidential, as required by Internal Revenue Code section 6103.

The time needed to complete and file this form will vary depending on individual circumstances. The estimated average time is: **Recordkeeping,** 26 min.; **Learning about the law or the form,** 12 min.; **Preparing the form,** 17 min.; and **Copying, assembling, and sending the form to the IRS,** 10 min.

If you have comments concerning the accuracy of these time estimates or suggestions for making this form simpler, we would be happy to hear from you. You can write to the Tax Forms Committee, Western Area Distribution Center, Rancho Cordova, CA 95743-0001. **DO NOT** send the form to this address. Instead, see **Where To File** on page 2.

Form **4952**

Department of the Treasury
Internal Revenue Service   (99)

Investment Interest Expense Deduction

▶ **Attach to your tax return.**

OMB No. 1545-0191

1997

Attachment
Sequence No. **72**

Name(s) shown on return

Identifying number

Part I   **Total Investment Interest Expense**

1	Investment interest expense paid or accrued in 1997. See instructions	**1**	
2	Disallowed investment interest expense from 1996 Form 4952, line 7	**2**	
3	**Total investment interest expense.** Add lines 1 and 2	**3**	

Part II   **Net Investment Income**

4a	Gross income from property held for investment (excluding any net gain from the disposition of property held for investment)	**4a**	
b	Net gain from the disposition of property held for investment . . . **4b**		
c	Net capital gain from the disposition of property held for investment **4c**		
d	Subtract line 4c from line 4b. If zero or less, enter -0-	**4d**	
e	Enter all or part of the amount on line 4c that you elect to include in investment income. Do not enter more than the amount on line 4b. See instructions . . . . ▶	**4e**	
f	Investment income. Add lines 4a, 4d, and 4e. See instructions	**4f**	
5	Investment expenses. See instructions	**5**	
6	**Net investment income.** Subtract line 5 from line 4f. If zero or less, enter -0-	**6**	

Part III   **Investment Interest Expense Deduction**

7	Disallowed investment interest expense to be carried forward to 1998. Subtract line 6 from line 3. If zero or less, enter -0-	**7**	
8	**Investment interest expense deduction.** Enter the smaller of line 3 or 6. See instructions . .	**8**	

Section references are to the Internal Revenue Code unless otherwise noted.

General Instructions

Purpose of Form

Interest expense paid by an individual, estate, or trust on a loan allocable to property held for investment may not be fully deductible in the current year. Use Form 4952 to figure the amount of investment interest expense deductible for the current year and the amount, if any, to carry forward to future years.

For more details, see **Pub. 550,** Investment Income and Expenses.

Who Must File

If you are an individual, estate, or a trust, and you claim a deduction for investment interest expense, you must complete and attach Form 4952 to your tax return, unless **all** the following apply.

● Your only investment income was from interest or dividends.

● You have no other deductible expenses connected with the production of interest or dividends.

● Your investment interest expense is not more than your investment income.

● You have no disallowed investment interest expense from 1996.

Allocation of Interest Expense Under Temporary Regulations Section 1.163-8T

If you paid or accrued interest on a loan and used the loan proceeds for more than one purpose, you may have to allocate the interest. This is necessary because different rules apply to investment interest, personal interest, trade or business interest, home mortgage interest, and passive activity interest. See **Pub. 535,** Business Expenses.

Specific Instructions

Part I—Total Investment Interest Expense

Line 1

Enter the investment interest paid or accrued during the tax year, regardless of when you incurred the indebtedness. Investment interest is interest paid or accrued on a loan (or part of a loan) that is allocable to property held for investment (as defined later).

Include investment interest expense reported to you on Schedule K-1 from a

partnership or an S corporation. Include amortization of bond premium on taxable bonds purchased after October 22, 1986, but before January 1, 1988, unless you elected to offset amortizable bond premium against the interest payments on the bond. A taxable bond is a bond on which the interest is includible in gross income.

Investment interest expense **does not** include the following:

● Home mortgage interest.

● Interest expense that is properly allocable to a passive activity. Generally, a passive activity is any business activity in which you **do not** materially participate and any rental activity. See the separate instructions for **Form 8582,** Passive Activity Loss Limitations, for more details.

● Any interest expense that is capitalized, such as construction interest subject to section 263A.

● Interest expense related to tax-exempt interest income under section 265.

● Interest expense, disallowed under section 264, on indebtedness with respect to life insurance, endowment, or annuity contracts issued after June 8, 1997, even if the proceeds were used to purchase any property held for investment.

Property held for investment. Property held for investment includes property that produces income (unless derived in the ordinary course of a trade or business) from interest, dividends, annuities, or royalties; and gains from the disposition of property that produces those types of income or is held for investment. However, it does not include an interest in a passive activity.

Property held for investment also includes an interest in an activity of conducting a trade or business in which you did not materially participate and that is not a passive activity. For example, a working interest in an oil or gas property that you held directly or through an entity that did not limit your liability is property held for investment if you did not materially participate in the activity.

Part II — Net Investment Income

Line 4a

Gross income from property held for investment to enter on line 4a includes income (unless derived in the ordinary course of a trade or business) from:

● Interest,

● Dividends (except Alaska Permanent Fund dividends),

● Annuities, and

● Royalties.

If you are filing **Form 8814,** Parents' Election To Report Child's Interest and Dividends, part or all of your child's income may be included on line 4a. See Form 8814 for details.

Also, include on line 4a net income from the following passive activities:

● Rental of substantially nondepreciable property,

● Equity-financed lending activities, and

● Acquisition of certain interests in a pass-through entity licensing intangible property.

See Regulations section 1.469-2(f)(10) for details.

Also include on line 4a (or 4b, if applicable) net passive income from a passive activity of a publicly traded partnership (as defined in section 469(k)(2)). See Notice 88-75, 1988-2 C.B. 386, for details.

Include investment income reported to you on Schedule K-1 from a partnership or an S corporation. Also include net investment income from an estate or a trust.

Do not include on line 4a any net gain from the disposition of property held for investment. Instead, enter this amount on line 4b.

Line 4b

Net gain from the disposition of property held for investment is the excess, if any, of total gains over total losses from the disposition of property held for investment. When figuring this amount, include capital gain distributions from mutual funds.

Line 4c

Net capital gain from the disposition of property held for investment is the excess, if any, of net long-term capital gain over net short-term capital loss from the disposition of property held for investment. When figuring this amount, include capital gain distributions from mutual funds.

Line 4e

Net capital gain from the disposition of property held for investment is excluded from investment income. However, you may elect to include in investment income all or part of the net capital gain from the disposition of property held for investment. If you make the election, you also must reduce the amount of net capital gain eligible for capital gains tax rates by the amount of net capital gain you included in investment income. Therefore, you should consider the effect on your tax using the capital gains tax rates before making this election. You must make the election no later than the due date (including extensions) of your income tax return. Once made, the election may not be revoked without IRS consent.

To make the election, enter all or part of the amount on line 4c, but not more than the amount on line 4b, that you elect to include in investment income. Also enter this amount on line 21 of Schedule D (Form 1040), or on line 20 of Schedule D (Form 1041), if applicable.

Line 5

Investment expenses are your allowed deductions, other than interest expense, directly connected with the production of investment income. For example, depreciation or depletion allowed on assets that produce investment income is an investment expense.

Include investment expenses reported to you on Schedule K-1 from a partnership or an S corporation.

Investment expenses **do not** include any deductions taken into account in determining your income or loss from a passive activity.

If you have investment expenses that are included as a miscellaneous itemized deduction on Schedule A (Form 1040), line 22, you may not have to use the entire amount for purposes of Form 4952, line 5. The 2% adjusted gross income limitation on Schedule A (Form 1040), line 25, may reduce the amount you must enter on Form 4952, line 5.

To figure the amount to use, compare the amount of the investment expenses included on Schedule A (Form 1040), line 22, with the total miscellaneous expenses on Schedule A (Form 1040), line 26. The smaller of **(a)** the investment expenses included on Schedule A (Form 1040), line 22, or **(b)** the total on Schedule A (Form 1040), line 26, is the amount of investment expenses included as a miscellaneous itemized deduction to use when figuring Form 4952, line 5.

Example. Assume Schedule A, line 22, includes investment expenses of $3,000, and line 26 is $1,300 after the 2% adjusted gross income limitation. Investment expenses from Schedule A of $1,300 are used to figure the amount of investment expenses for line 5. If investment expenses of $800 were included on line 22 and line 26 was $1,300, investment expenses from Schedule A of $800 would be used.

Part III — Investment Interest Expense Deduction

Line 8

This is the amount you may deduct as investment interest expense.

Individuals. Generally, enter the amount from line 8 on Schedule A (Form 1040), line 13, even if all or part of it is attributable to a partnership or an S corporation. If any portion of this amount is attributable to royalties, enter that part of the interest expense on Schedule E (Form 1040). If any portion is attributable to a trade or business in which you did not materially participate and that is not a passive activity, enter that part of the interest expense on the schedule where you report other expenses for that trade or business.

Estates and trusts. Enter the amount from line 8 on Form 1041, line 10.

Form 6198. If any portion of the deductible investment interest expense is attributable to an activity for which you are not at risk, you must also use **Form 6198,** At-Risk Limitations, to figure your deductible investment interest expense. Enter the portion attributable to the at-risk activity on Form 6198, line 4. Reduce Form 4952, line 8, by the amount entered on Form 6198. See Form 6198 and its instructions for more details, especially the instructions for line 4 of that form.

Alternative minimum tax (AMT). Deductible interest expense is an adjustment for the AMT. Get **Form 6251,** Alternative Minimum Tax—Individuals, or Form 1041, Schedule I, for estates and trusts.

Paperwork Reduction Act Notice

We ask for the information on this form to carry out the Internal Revenue laws of the United States. You are required to give us the information. We need it to ensure that you are complying with these laws and to allow us to figure and collect the right amount of tax.

You are not required to provide the information requested on a form that is subject to the Paperwork Reduction Act unless the form displays a valid OMB control number. Books or records relating to a form or its instructions must be retained as long as their contents may become material in the administration of any Internal Revenue law. Generally, tax returns and return information are confidential, as required by section 6103.

The time needed to complete and file this form will vary depending on individual circumstances. The estimated average time is:

Recordkeeping . . . . . . 13 min.

Learning about the law or the form . . . . . 15 min.

Preparing the form . . . . . 21 min.

Copying, assembling, and sending the form to the IRS . . 10 min.

If you have comments concerning the accuracy of these time estimates or suggestions for making this form simpler, we would be happy to hear from you. See the instructions for the tax return with which this form is filed.

Form **4972**

Department of the Treasury
Internal Revenue Service   (99)

Tax on Lump-Sum Distributions
From Qualified Retirement Plans

▶ Attach to Form 1040 or Form 1041.   ▶ See separate instructions.

OMB No. 1545-0193

19**97**

Attachment
Sequence No. **28**

Name of recipient of distribution	Identifying number

Part I   Complete this part to see if you qualify to use Form 4972

		Yes	No
1	Was this a distribution of a plan participant's entire balance from all of an employer's qualified plans of one kind (pension, profit-sharing, or stock bonus)? If "No," do not use this form **1**		
2	Did you roll over any part of the distribution? If "Yes," do not use this form **2**		
3	Was this distribution paid to you as a beneficiary of a plan participant who died after reaching age 59½ (or who had been born before 1936)? **3**		
4	Were you a plan participant who received this distribution after reaching age 59½ **and** having been in the plan for at least 5 years before the year of the distribution? **4**		
	If you answered "No" to both questions 3 **and** 4, do not use this form.		
5a	Did you use Form 4972 after 1986 for a previous distribution from your own plan? If "Yes," do not use this form for a 1997 distribution from your own plan **5a**		
b	If you are receiving this distribution as a beneficiary of a plan participant who died, did you use Form 4972 for a previous distribution received for that plan participant after 1986? If "Yes," you may not use the form for this distribution **5b**		

Part II   Complete this part to choose the 20% capital gain election (See instructions.) Do not complete this part unless the participant was born **before** 1936.

6	Capital gain part from box 3 of Form 1099-R **6**		
7	Multiply line 6 by 20% (.20) **7**		
	If you also choose to use Part III, go to line 8. Otherwise, include the amount from line 7 in the total on Form 1040, line 39, or Form 1041, Schedule G, line 1b, whichever applies.		

Part III   Complete this part to choose the 5- or 10-year tax option (See instructions.)

8	Ordinary income from Form 1099-R, box 2a minus box 3. If you did not complete Part II, enter the taxable amount from box 2a of Form 1099-R **8**		
9	Death benefit exclusion for a beneficiary of a plan participant who died before August 21, 1996 **9**		
10	Total taxable amount. Subtract line 9 from line 8 . . . . **10**		
11	Current actuarial value of annuity (from Form 1099-R, box 8) **11**		
12	Adjusted total taxable amount. Add lines 10 and 11. If this amount is $70,000 or more, **skip** lines 13 through 16, and enter this amount on line 17 . . . . **12**		
13	Multiply line 12 by 50% (.50), but **do not** enter more than $10,000 **13**		
14	Subtract $20,000 from line 12. If the result is less than zero, enter -0- **14**		
15	Multiply line 14 by 20% (.20) **15**		
16	Minimum distribution allowance. Subtract line 15 from line 13 . . . . **16**		
17	Subtract line 16 from line 12 . . . . **17**		
18	Federal estate tax attributable to lump-sum distribution **18**		
19	Subtract line 18 from line 17 . . . . **19**		
	If line 11 is blank, skip lines 20 through 22 and go to line 23.		
20	Divide line 11 by line 12 and enter the result as a decimal **20**	.	
21	Multiply line 16 by the decimal on line 20 . . . . **21**		
22	Subtract line 21 from line 11 . . . . **22**		

For Paperwork Reduction Act Notice, see separate instructions.   Cat. No. 13187U   Form **4972** (1997)

Part III **5- or 10-year tax option—CONTINUED**

5-year tax option

23	Multiply line 19 by 20% (.20)	**23**
24	Tax on amount on line 23. Use the Tax Rate Schedule for the 5-Year Tax Option in the instructions	**24**
25	Multiply line 24 by five (5). If line 11 is blank, skip lines 26 through 28, and enter this amount on line 29	**25**
26	Multiply line 22 by 20% (.20) **26**	
27	Tax on amount on line 26. Use the Tax Rate Schedule for the 5-Year Tax Option in the instructions **27**	
28	Multiply line 27 by five (5)	**28**
29	Subtract line 28 from line 25. (Multiple recipients, see page 2 of the instructions.) . . .	**29**

Note: *Complete lines 30 through 36 ONLY if the participant was born before 1936. Otherwise, enter the amount from line 29 on line 37.*

10-year tax option

30	Multiply line 19 by 10% (.10)	**30**
31	Tax on amount on line 30. Use the Tax Rate Schedule for the 10-Year Tax Option in the instructions	**31**
32	Multiply line 31 by ten (10). If line 11 is blank, skip lines 33 through 35, and enter this amount on line 36	**32**
33	Multiply line 22 by 10% (.10) **33**	
34	Tax on amount on line 33. Use the Tax Rate Schedule for the 10-Year Tax Option in the instructions **34**	
35	Multiply line 34 by ten (10)	**35**
36	Subtract line 35 from line 32. (Multiple recipients, see page 2 of the instructions.) . . .	**36**

37	Compare lines 29 and 36. Generally, you should enter the **smaller** amount here (see instructions) . . . . ▶	**37**
38	Tax on lump-sum distribution. Add lines 7 and 37. Also, include in the total on Form 1040, line 39, or Form 1041, Schedule G, line 1b, whichever applies . . . . ▶	**38**

Form **6251**	**Alternative Minimum Tax—Individuals**	OMB No. 1545-0227

Form **6251**

Department of the Treasury
Internal Revenue Service   (99)

Alternative Minimum Tax—Individuals

▶ See separate instructions.

▶ Attach to Form 1040 or Form 1040NR.

OMB No. 1545-0227

19**97**

Attachment
Sequence No. **32**

Name(s) shown on Form 1040

Your social security number

Part I   Adjustments and Preferences

1	If you itemized deductions on Schedule A (Form 1040), go to line 2. Otherwise, enter your standard deduction from Form 1040, line 35, here and go to line 6	**1**	
2	Medical and dental. Enter the smaller of Schedule A (Form 1040), line 4 **or** 2½% of Form 1040, line 33	**2**	
3	Taxes. Enter the amount from Schedule A (Form 1040), line 9	**3**	
4	Certain interest on a home mortgage not used to buy, build, or improve your home . . .	**4**	
5	Miscellaneous itemized deductions. Enter the amount from Schedule A (Form 1040), line 26	**5**	
6	Refund of taxes. Enter any tax refund from Form 1040, line 10 or line 21	**6** ( )
7	Investment interest. Enter difference between regular tax and AMT deduction	**7**	
8	Post-1986 depreciation. Enter difference between regular tax and AMT depreciation	**8**	
9	Adjusted gain or loss. Enter difference between AMT and regular tax gain or loss	**9**	
10	Incentive stock options. Enter excess of AMT income over regular tax income	**10**	
11	Passive activities. Enter difference between AMT and regular tax income or loss	**11**	
12	Beneficiaries of estates and trusts. Enter the amount from Schedule K-1 (Form 1041), line 9	**12**	
13	Tax-exempt interest from private activity bonds issued after 8/7/86	**13**	
14	Other. Enter the amount, if any, for each item below and enter the total on line 14.		

	a Charitable contributions .		**h** Loss limitations	
	b Circulation expenditures .		**i** Mining costs	
	c Depletion		**j** Patron's adjustment . .	
	d Depreciation (pre-1987) .		**k** Pollution control facilities .	
	e Installment sales . . .		**l** Research and experimental .	
	f Intangible drilling costs .		**m** Tax shelter farm activities .	
	g Long-term contracts . .		**n** Related adjustments . .	**14**

15	**Total Adjustments and Preferences.** Combine lines 1 through 14 . . . . ▶	**15**	

Part II   Alternative Minimum Taxable Income

16	Enter the amount from **Form 1040, line 36.** If less than zero, enter as a (loss) . . . . . . ▶	**16**	
17	Net operating loss deduction, if any, from Form 1040, line 21. Enter as a positive amount	**17**	
18	If Form 1040, line 33, is over $121,200 (over $60,600 if married filing separately), and you itemized deductions, enter the amount, if any, from line 9 of the worksheet for Schedule A (Form 1040), line 28	**18** ( )
19	Combine lines 15 through 18 . . . . ▶	**19**	
20	Alternative tax net operating loss deduction. See page 5 of the instructions	**20**	
21	**Alternative Minimum Taxable Income.** Subtract line 20 from line 19. (If married filing separately and line 21 is more than $165,000, see page 5 of the instructions.) . . . . ▶	**21**	

Part III   Exemption Amount and Alternative Minimum Tax

22	**Exemption Amount.** (If this form is for a child under age 14, see page 6 of the instructions.)		

IF your filing status is . . .	AND line 21 is not over . . .	THEN enter on line 22 . . .	
Single or head of household	$112,500	$33,750	
Married filing jointly or qualifying widow(er) .	150,000	45,000	**22**
Married filing separately.	75,000	22,500	

If line 21 is **over** the amount shown above for your filing status, see page 6 of the instructions.

23	Subtract line 22 from line 21. If zero or less, enter -0- here and on lines 26 and 28 . . . . ▶	**23**	
24	If you completed Schedule D (Form 1040), and had an amount on line 25 or line 27 (as refigured for the AMT, if necessary), go to Part IV of Form 6251 to figure line 24. **All others:** If line 23 is $175,000 or less ($87,500 or less if married filing separately), multiply line 23 by 26% (.26). Otherwise, multiply line 23 by 28% (.28) and subtract $3,500 ($1,750 if married filing separately) from the result . . . . ▶	**24**	
25	Alternative minimum tax foreign tax credit. See page 7 of the instructions	**25**	
26	Tentative minimum tax. Subtract line 25 from line 24 . . . . ▶	**26**	
27	Enter your tax from Form 1040, line 39 (minus any tax from Form 4972 and any foreign tax credit from Form 1040, line 43)	**27**	
28	**Alternative Minimum Tax.** (If this form is for a child under age 14, see page 7 of the instructions.) Subtract line 27 from line 26. If zero or less, enter -0-. Enter here and on Form 1040, line 48 . . ▶	**28**	

For Paperwork Reduction Act Notice, see separate instructions.　　　　Cat. No. 13600G　　　　Form **6251** (1997)

Part IV	**Line 24 Computation Using Maximum Capital Gains Rates**					
29	Enter the amount from line 23				29	
30	Enter the amount from Schedule D (Form 1040), line 27 (as refigured for the AMT, if necessary)	30				
31	Enter the amount from Schedule D (Form 1040), line 25 (as refigured for the AMT, if necessary)	31				
32	Add lines 30 and 31	32				
33	Enter the amount from Schedule D (Form 1040), line 22 (as refigured for the AMT, if necessary)	33				
34	Enter the **smaller** of line 32 or line 33				34	
35	Subtract line 34 from line 29. If zero or less, enter -0-				35	
36	If line 35 is $175,000 or less ($87,500 or less if married filing separately), multiply line 35 by 26% (.26). Otherwise, multiply line 35 by 28% (.28) and subtract $3,500 ($1,750 if married filing separately) from the result . . . . ▶				36	
37	Enter the amount from Schedule D (Form 1040), line 36 (as figured for the regular tax)				37	
38	Enter the **smallest** of line 29, line 30, or line 37				38	
39	Multiply line 38 by 10% (.10) . . . . ▶				39	
40	Enter the **smaller** of line 29 or line 30				40	
41	Enter the amount from line 38				41	
42	Subtract line 41 from line 40. If zero or less, enter -0-				42	
43	Multiply line 42 by 20% (.20) . . . . ▶				43	
44	Enter the amount from line 29				44	
45	Add lines 35, 38, and 42				45	
46	Subtract line 45 from line 44				46	
47	Multiply line 46 by 25% (.25) . . . . ▶				47	
48	Add lines 36, 39, 43, and 47				48	
49	If line 29 is $175,000 or less ($87,500 or less if married filing separately), multiply line 29 by 26% (.26). Otherwise, multiply line 29 by 28% (.28) and subtract $3,500 ($1,750 if married filing separately) from the result				49	
50	Enter the **smaller** of line 48 or line 49 here and on line 24 . . . . ▶				50	

Form **6252**

Department of the Treasury
Internal Revenue Service

Installment Sale Income

▶ See separate instructions. ▶ Attach to your tax return.
▶ Use a separate form for each sale or other disposition of
property on the installment method.

OMB No. 1545-0228

19 97

Attachment
Sequence No. **79**

Name(s) shown on return

Identifying number

1	Description of property ▶	
2a	Date acquired (month, day, year) ▶ [/ /] **b** Date sold (month, day, year) ▶ [/ /]	
3	Was the property sold to a related party after May 14, 1980? See instructions. If "No," skip line 4 . . . ☐ Yes ☐ No	
4	Was the property you sold to a related party a marketable security? If "Yes," complete Part III. If "No," complete Part III for the year of sale and the 2 years after the year of sale . . . . ☐ Yes ☐ No	

Part I **Gross Profit and Contract Price.** Complete this part for the year of sale only.

5	Selling price including mortgages and other debts. **Do not** include interest whether stated or unstated	**5**	
6	Mortgages and other debts the buyer assumed or took the property subject to, but not new mortgages the buyer got from a bank or other source .	**6**	
7	Subtract line 6 from line 5	**7**	
8	Cost or other basis of property sold	**8**	
9	Depreciation allowed or allowable	**9**	
10	Adjusted basis. Subtract line 9 from line 8	**10**	
11	Commissions and other expenses of sale.	**11**	
12	Income recapture from Form 4797, Part III. See instructions . .	**12**	
13	Add lines 10, 11, and 12	**13**	
14	Subtract line 13 from line 5. If zero or less, **stop here. Do not** complete the rest of this form .	**14**	
15	If the property described on line 1 above was your main home, enter from Form 2119 the total of lines 14 and 22, or the amount from line 27, whichever applies. Otherwise, enter -0- . . .	**15**	
16	**Gross profit.** Subtract line 15 from line 14	**16**	
17	Subtract line 13 from line 6. If zero or less, enter -0-	**17**	
18	**Contract price.** Add line 7 and line 17	**18**	

Part II **Installment Sale Income.** Complete this part for the year of sale **and** any year you receive a payment or have certain debts you must treat as a payment on installment obligations.

19	Gross profit percentage. Divide line 16 by line 18. For years after the year of sale, see instructions	**19**	
20	**For year of sale only:** Enter amount from line 17 above; otherwise, enter -0-	**20**	
21	Payments received during year. See instructions. **Do not** include interest whether stated or unstated	**21**	
22	Add lines 20 and 21	**22**	
23	Payments received in prior years. See instructions. **Do not** include interest whether stated or unstated **23**		
24	**Installment sale income.** Multiply line 22 by line 19	**24**	
25	Part of line 24 that is ordinary income under recapture rules. See instructions	**25**	
26	Subtract line 25 from line 24. Enter here and on Schedule D or Form 4797. See instructions .	**26**	

Part III **Related Party Installment Sale Income.** **Do not** complete if you received the final payment this tax year.

27	Name, address, and taxpayer identifying number of related party ....
	....
28	Did the related party, during this tax year, resell or dispose of the property ("second disposition")? . . . ☐ Yes ☐ No
29	If the answer to question 28 is "Yes," complete lines 30 through 37 below unless one of the following conditions is met. **Check only the box that applies.**
a	☐ The second disposition was more than 2 years after the first disposition (other than dispositions of marketable securities). If this box is checked, enter the date of disposition (month, day, year) ▶ [/ /]
b	☐ The first disposition was a sale or exchange of stock to the issuing corporation.
c	☐ The second disposition was an involuntary conversion where the threat of conversion occurred after the first disposition.
d	☐ The second disposition occurred after the death of the original seller or buyer.
e	☐ It can be established to the satisfaction of the Internal Revenue Service that tax avoidance was not a principal purpose for either of the dispositions. If this box is checked, attach an explanation. See instructions.

30	Selling price of property sold by related party	**30**	
31	Enter contract price from line 18 for year of first sale	**31**	
32	Enter the **smaller** of line 30 or line 31	**32**	
33	Total payments received by the end of your 1997 tax year. See instructions	**33**	
34	Subtract line 33 from line 32. If zero or less, enter -0-	**34**	
35	Multiply line 34 by the gross profit percentage on line 19 for year of first sale	**35**	
36	Part of line 35 that is ordinary income under recapture rules. See instructions	**36**	
37	Subtract line 36 from line 35. Enter here and on Schedule D or Form 4797. See instructions .	**37**	

For Paperwork Reduction Act Notice, see separate instructions.   Cat. No. 13601R   Form **6252** (1997)

Form **8283**
(Rev. October 1995)

Department of the Treasury
Internal Revenue Service

Noncash Charitable Contributions

▶ Attach to your tax return if you claimed a total deduction
of over $500 for all contributed property.

▶ See separate instructions.

OMB No. 1545-0908

Attachment
Sequence No. **55**

Name(s) shown on your income tax return | Identifying number

Note: *Figure the amount of your contribution deduction before completing this form. See your tax return instructions.*

Section A—List in this section **only** items (or groups of similar items) for which you claimed a deduction of $5,000 or less. Also, list certain publicly traded securities even if the deduction is over $5,000 (see instructions).

Part I **Information on Donated Property**—If you need more space, attach a statement.

1	(a) Name and address of the donee organization	(b) Description of donated property
A		
B		
C		
D		
E		

Note: *If the amount you claimed as a deduction for an item is $500 or less, you do not have to complete columns (d), (e), and (f).*

	(c) Date of the contribution	(d) Date acquired by donor (mo., yr.)	(e) How acquired by donor	(f) Donor's cost or adjusted basis	(g) Fair market value	(h) Method used to determine the fair market value
A						
B						
C						
D						
E						

Part II **Other Information**—Complete line 2 if you gave less than an entire interest in property listed in Part I. Complete line 3 if restrictions were attached to a contribution listed in Part I.

2 If, during the year, you contributed less than the entire interest in the property, complete lines a – e.

a Enter the letter from Part I that identifies the property ▶ _____ . If Part II applies to more than one property, attach a separate statement.

b Total amount claimed as a deduction for the property listed in Part I: **(1)** For this tax year ▶ _____
(2) For any prior tax years ▶ _____ .

c Name and address of each organization to which any such contribution was made in a prior year (complete only if different than the donee organization above):

Name of charitable organization (donee)

Address (number, street, and room or suite no.)

City or town, state, and ZIP code

d For tangible property, enter the place where the property is located or kept ▶ _____

e Name of any person, other than the donee organization, having actual possession of the property ▶ _____

3 If conditions were attached to any contribution listed in Part I, answer questions a – c and attach the required statement (see instructions).

		Yes	No
a	Is there a restriction, either temporary or permanent, on the donee's right to use or dispose of the donated property?		
b	Did you give to anyone (other than the donee organization or another organization participating with the donee organization in cooperative fundraising) the right to the income from the donated property or to the possession of the property, including the right to vote donated securities, to acquire the property by purchase or otherwise, or to designate the person having such income, possession, or right to acquire?		
c	Is there a restriction limiting the donated property for a particular use?		

For Paperwork Reduction Act Notice, see separate instructions.   Cat. No. 62299J   Form **8283** (Rev. 10-95)

Form 8283 (Rev. 10-95)   Page **2**

Name(s) shown on your income tax return	Identifying number

Section B—Appraisal Summary—List in this section only items (or groups of similar items) for which you claimed a deduction of more than $5,000 per item or group. **Exception.** Report contributions of certain publicly traded securities only in Section A.

If you donated art, you may have to attach the complete appraisal. See the **Note** in Part I below.

Part I   **Information on Donated Property—**To be completed by the taxpayer and/or appraiser.

4   Check type of property:

☐ Art* (contribution of $20,000 or more)   ☐ Real Estate   ☐ Gems/Jewelry   ☐ Stamp Collections

☐ Art* (contribution of less than $20,000)   ☐ Coin Collections   ☐ Books   ☐ Other

*Art includes paintings, sculptures, watercolors, prints, drawings, ceramics, antique furniture, decorative arts, textiles, carpets, silver, rare manuscripts, historical memorabilia, and other similar objects.

Note: *If your total art contribution deduction was $20,000 or more, you must attach a complete copy of the signed appraisal. See instructions.*

5	(a) Description of donated property (if you need more space, attach a separate statement)	(b) If tangible property was donated, give a brief summary of the overall physical condition at the time of the gift	(c) Appraised fair market value
A			
B			
C			
D			

	(d) Date acquired by donor (mo., yr.)	(e) How acquired by donor	(f) Donor's cost or adjusted basis	(g) For bargain sales, enter amount received	See instructions	
					(h) Amount claimed as a deduction	(i) Average trading price of securities
A						
B						
C						
D						

Part II   **Taxpayer (Donor) Statement—**List each item included in Part I above that is separately identified in the appraisal as having a value of $500 or less. See instructions.

I declare that the following item(s) included in Part I above has to the best of my knowledge and belief an appraised value of not more than $500 (per item). Enter identifying letter from Part I and describe the specific item. See instructions. ▶ _____

Signature of taxpayer (donor) ▶ _____   Date ▶ _____

Part III   **Declaration of Appraiser**

I declare that I am not the donor, the donee, a party to the transaction in which the donor acquired the property, employed by, or related to any of the foregoing persons, or married to any person who is related to any of the foregoing persons. And, if regularly used by the donor, donee, or party to the transaction, I performed the majority of my appraisals during my tax year for other persons.

Also, I declare that I hold myself out to the public as an appraiser or perform appraisals on a regular basis; and that because of my qualifications as described in the appraisal, I am qualified to make appraisals of the type of property being valued. I certify that the appraisal fees were not based on a percentage of the appraised property value. Furthermore, I understand that a false or fraudulent overstatement of the property value as described in the qualified appraisal or this appraisal summary may subject me to the penalty under section 6701(a) (aiding and abetting the understatement of tax liability). I affirm that I have not been barred from presenting evidence or testimony by the Director of Practice.

Sign Here | Signature ▶ _____   Title ▶ _____   Date of appraisal ▶ _____

Business address (including room or suite no.)	Identifying number

City or town, state, and ZIP code

Part IV   **Donee Acknowledgment—**To be completed by the charitable organization.

This charitable organization acknowledges that it is a qualified organization under section 170(c) and that it received the donated property as described in Section B, Part I, above on ▶ _____
                                      (Date)

Furthermore, this organization affirms that in the event it sells, exchanges, or otherwise disposes of the property described in Section B, Part I (or any portion thereof) within 2 years after the date of receipt, it will file **Form 8282,** Donee Information Return, with the IRS and give the donor a copy of that form. This acknowledgment does not represent agreement with the claimed fair market value.

Name of charitable organization (donee)	Employer identification number

Address (number, street, and room or suite no.)	City or town, state, and ZIP code

Authorized signature	Title	Date

       ✿   *Printed on recycled paper*

Form **8332**
(Rev. June 1996)
Department of the Treasury
Internal Revenue Service

Release of Claim to Exemption
for Child of Divorced or Separated Parents

▶ **ATTACH** to noncustodial parent's return **EACH YEAR** exemption claimed.

OMB No. 1545-0915

Attachment
Sequence No. **51**

Name(s) of parent claiming exemption

Social security number

Part I   **Release of Claim to Exemption for Current Year**

I agree not to claim an exemption for_____

Name(s) of child (or children)

for the tax year 19_____ .

_____
Signature of parent releasing claim to exemption

Social security number

Date

If you choose not to claim an exemption for this child (or children) for future tax years, complete Part II.

Part II   **Release of Claim to Exemption for Future Years** (If completed, see **Noncustodial Parent** below.)

I agree not to claim an exemption for_____

Name(s) of child (or children)

for the tax year(s)_____ .
(Specify. See instructions.)

_____
Signature of parent releasing claim to exemption

Social security number

Date

General Instructions

Paperwork Reduction Act Notice.—We ask for the information on this form to carry out the Internal Revenue laws of the United States. You are required to give us the information. We need it to ensure that you are complying with these laws and to allow us to figure and collect the right amount of tax.

You are not required to provide the information requested on a form that is subject to the Paperwork Reduction Act unless the form displays a valid OMB control number. Books or records relating to a form or its instructions must be retained as long as their contents may become material in the administration of any Internal Revenue law. Generally, tax returns and return information are confidential, as required by Internal Revenue Code section 6103.

The time needed to complete and file this form will vary depending on individual circumstances. The estimated average time is: **Recordkeeping,** 7 min.; **Learning about the law or the form,** 5 min.; **Preparing the form,** 7 min.; and **Copying, assembling, and sending the form to the IRS,** 14 min.

If you have comments concerning the accuracy of these time estimates or suggestions for making this form simpler, we would be happy to hear from you. See the instructions for the tax return with which this form is filed.

Purpose of Form.—If you are a **custodial parent,** you may use this form to release your claim to your child's exemption. To do so, complete this form and give it to the **noncustodial parent** who will claim the child's exemption. Then, the noncustodial parent must attach this form or a similar statement to his or her tax return EACH YEAR the exemption is claimed.

You are the **custodial parent** if you had custody of the child for most of the year. You are the **noncustodial parent** if you had custody for a shorter period of time or did not have custody at all.

Instead of using this form, you (the custodial parent) may use a similar statement as long as it contains the same information required by this form.

Children of Divorced or Separated Parents.—Special rules apply to determine if the support test is met for children of parents who are divorced or legally separated under a decree of divorce or separate maintenance or separated under a written separation agreement. The rules also apply to children of parents who did not live together at any time during the last 6 months of the year, even if they do not have a separation agreement.

The general rule is that the custodial parent is treated as having provided over half of the child's support if:

1. The child received over half of his or her total support for the year from both of the parents, **AND**

2. The child was in the custody of one or both of his or her parents for more than half of the year.

Note: Public assistance payments, such as Aid to Families with Dependent Children, are not support provided by the parents.

If both **1** and **2** above apply, and the other four dependency tests in your tax return instruction booklet are also met, the custodial parent can claim the child's exemption.

Exception. The general rule does not apply if **any** of the following apply:

● The custodial parent agrees not to claim the child's exemption by signing this form or similar statement. The noncustodial parent **must** attach this form or similar statement to

his or her tax return for the tax year. See **Custodial Parent** later.

● The child is treated as having received over half of his or her total support from a person under a multiple support agreement (**Form 2120,** Multiple Support Declaration).

● A pre-1985 divorce decree or written separation agreement states that the noncustodial parent can claim the child as a dependent. But the noncustodial parent must provide at least $600 for the child's support during the year. This rule does not apply if the decree or agreement was changed after 1984 to say that the noncustodial parent cannot claim the child as a dependent.

Additional Information.—For more details, get **Pub. 504,** Divorced or Separated Individuals.

Specific Instructions

Custodial Parent.—You may agree to release your claim to the child's exemption for the current tax year or for future years, or both.

● Complete **Part I** if you agree to release your claim to the child's exemption for the current tax year.

● Complete **Part II** if you agree to release your claim to the child's exemption for any or all future years. If you do, write the specific future year(s) or "all future years" in the space provided in Part II.

Noncustodial Parent.—Attach Form 8332 or similar statement to your tax return for the tax year in which you claim the child's exemption. You may claim the exemption **only** if the other four dependency tests in your tax return instruction booklet are met.

Note: If the custodial parent completed Part II, you **must** attach a copy of this form to your tax return for each future year in which you claim the exemption.

Cat. No. 13910F

Form **8332** (Rev. 6-96)

Form **8582**

Department of the Treasury
Internal Revenue Service   (99)

Passive Activity Loss Limitations

▶ See separate instructions.
▶ Attach to Form 1040 or Form 1041.

OMB No. 1545-1008

1997

Attachment
Sequence No. **88**

Name(s) shown on return

Identifying number

Part I   **1997 Passive Activity Loss**

Caution: *See the instructions for Worksheets 1 and 2 on page 7 before completing Part I.*

Rental Real Estate Activities With Active Participation (For the definition of active participation see **Active Participation in a Rental Real Estate Activity** on page 3 of the instructions.)

1a Activities with net income (enter the amount from Worksheet 1, column (a)) **1a**

b Activities with net loss (enter the amount from Worksheet 1, column (b)) . . . . **1b** ( )

c Prior years unallowed losses (enter the amount from Worksheet 1, column (c)) . . . . **1c** ( )

d Combine lines 1a, 1b, and 1c **1d**

All Other Passive Activities

2a Activities with net income (enter the amount from Worksheet 2, column (a)) **2a**

b Activities with net loss (enter the amount from Worksheet 2, column (b)) . . . . **2b** ( )

c Prior years unallowed losses (enter the amount from Worksheet 2, column (c)) . . . . **2c** ( )

d Combine lines 2a, 2b, and 2c **2d**

3 Combine lines 1d and 2d. If the result is net income or zero, all losses are allowed, including any prior year unallowed losses entered on line 1c or 2c. **Do not** complete Form 8582. Take the losses to the form or schedule you normally report them on.
If this line and line 1d are losses, go to line 4. Otherwise, enter -0- on line 9 and go to line 10 . **3**

Part II   **Special Allowance for Rental Real Estate With Active Participation**

Note: *Enter all numbers in Part II as positive amounts. See page 7 of the instructions for examples.*

4 Enter the **smaller** of the loss on line 1d or the loss on line 3 . . . . **4**

5 Enter $150,000. If married filing separately, see page 7 of the instructions **5**

6 Enter modified adjusted gross income, but not less than zero (see page 7 of the instructions) **6**

Note: *If line 6 is equal to or greater than line 5, skip lines 7 and 8, enter -0- on line 9, and then go to line 10. Otherwise, go to line 7.*

7 Subtract line 6 from line 5 . . . . **7**

8 Multiply line 7 by 50% (.5). **Do not** enter more than $25,000. If married filing separately, see page 9 of the instructions **8**

9 Enter the **smaller** of line 4 or line 8 . . . . **9**

Part III   **Total Losses Allowed**

10 Add the income, if any, on lines 1a and 2a and enter the total **10**

11 **Total losses allowed from all passive activities for 1997.** Add lines 9 and 10. See page 9 of the instructions to find out how to report the losses on your tax return **11**

For Paperwork Reduction Act Notice, see separate instructions.   Cat. No. 63704F   Form **8582** (1997)

Caution: *The worksheets are not required to be filed with your tax return and may be detached before filing Form 8582. Keep a copy of the worksheets for your records.*

Worksheet 1—For Form 8582, Lines 1a, 1b, and 1c (See page 6 of the instructions.)

Name of activity	Current year		Prior years	Overall gain or loss	
	(a) Net income (line 1a)	(b) Net loss (line 1b)	(c) Unallowed loss (line 1c)	(d) Gain	(e) Loss
Total. Enter on Form 8582, lines 1a, 1b, and 1c. . . . . ▶					

Worksheet 2—For Form 8582, Lines 2a, 2b, and 2c (See page 7 of the instructions.)

Name of activity	Current year		Prior years	Overall gain or loss	
	(a) Net income (line 2a)	(b) Net loss (line 2b)	(c) Unallowed loss (line 2c)	(d) Gain	(e) Loss
Total. Enter on Form 8582, lines 2a, 2b, and 2c. . . . . ▶					

Worksheet 3—Use this worksheet if an amount is shown on Form 8582, line 9 (See page 8 of the instructions.)

Name of activity	Form or schedule to be reported on	(a) Loss	(b) Ratio	(c) Special allowance	(d) Subtract column (c) from column (a)
Total . . . . ▶			1.00		

Worksheet 4—Allocation of Unallowed Losses (See page 8 of the instructions.)

Name of activity	Form or schedule to be reported on	(a) Loss	(b) Ratio	(c) Unallowed loss
Total . . . . ▶			1.00	

Worksheet 5—Allowed Losses (See page 8 of the instructions.)

Name of activity	Form or schedule to be reported on	(a) Loss	(b) Unallowed loss	(c) Allowed loss
Total . . . . ▶				

Form 8582 (1997)   Page **3**

Worksheet 6—Activities With Losses Reported on Two or More Different Forms or Schedules (See page 8 of the instructions.)

Name of Activity:	(a)	(b)	(c) Ratio	(d) Unallowed loss	(e) Allowed loss
Form or Schedule To Be Reported on:					
1a Net loss plus prior year unallowed loss from form or schedule . ▶					
b Net income from form or schedule . . . . . . ▶					
c Subtract line 1b from line 1a. If zero or less, enter -0- ▶					
Form or Schedule To Be Reported on:					
1a Net loss plus prior year unallowed loss from form or schedule . ▶					
b Net income from form or schedule . . . . . . ▶					
c Subtract line 1b from line 1a. If zero or less, enter -0- ▶					
Form or Schedule To Be Reported on:					
1a Net loss plus prior year unallowed loss from form or schedule . ▶					
b Net income from form or schedule . . . . . . ▶					
c Subtract line 1b from line 1a. If zero or less, enter -0- ▶					
Total . . . . ▶			1.00		

Form **8606**

Department of the Treasury
Internal Revenue Service   (99)

Nondeductible IRAs
(Contributions, Distributions, and Basis)
▶ Please see What Records Must I Keep? below.
▶ Attach to Form 1040, Form 1040A, or Form 1040NR.

OMB No. 1545-1007

1997

Attachment
Sequence No. **47**

Name. If married, file a separate Form 8606 for each spouse who is required to file Form 8606. See instructions.

Your social security number

Fill in Your Address Only
if You Are Filing This
Form by Itself and Not
With Your Tax Return

Home address (number and street, or P.O. box if mail is not delivered to your home)

Apt. no.

City, town or post office, state, and ZIP code

Contributions, Nontaxable Distributions, and Basis

1	Enter your nondeductible IRA contributions for 1997, including those made during 1/1/98–4/15/98 that were for 1997. See instructions	**1**
2	Enter your total IRA basis for 1996 and earlier years. See instructions	**2**
3	Add lines 1 and 2	**3**

Did you receive any IRA distributions (withdrawals) in 1997?

No ──▶ Enter the amount from line 3 on line 12. Then, **stop** and read **When and Where To File** below.

Yes ──▶ Go to line 4.

4	Enter only those contributions included on line 1 that were made during 1/1/98–4/15/98. This amount will be the same as line 1 if all of your nondeductible contributions for 1997 were made in 1998 by 4/15/98. See instructions	**4**
5	Subtract line 4 from line 3	**5**
6	Enter the total value of **ALL** your IRAs as of 12/31/97 plus any outstanding rollovers. See instructions	**6**
7	Enter the total IRA distributions received during 1997. Do not include amounts rolled over before 1/1/98. See instructions	**7**
8	Add lines 6 and 7	**8**
9	Divide line 5 by line 8 and enter the result as a decimal (rounded to two places). Do not enter more than "1.00"	**9** ✕ .
10	Multiply line 7 by line 9. This is the amount of your **nontaxable distributions for 1997**	**10**
11	Subtract line 10 from line 5. This is the **basis in your IRA(s) as of 12/31/97**	**11**
12	Add lines 4 and 11. This is your **total IRA basis for 1997 and earlier years**	**12**

Taxable Distributions for 1997

13	Subtract line 10 from line 7. Enter the result here and on Form 1040, line 15b; Form 1040A, line 10b; or Form 1040NR, line 16b, whichever applies	**13**

Sign Here Only if You Are Filing This Form by Itself and Not With Your Tax Return

Under penalties of perjury, I declare that I have examined this form, including accompanying attachments, and to the best of my knowledge and belief, it is true, correct, and complete.

▶ Your signature

▶ Date

General Instructions

Section references are to the Internal Revenue Code.

A Change To Note

Beginning in 1997, SIMPLE IRAs are available to employees of small employers. **Do not** include contributions to a SIMPLE IRA on line 1. However, if you received any IRA distributions in 1997, you **must** include the value of your SIMPLE IRA on line 6.

Purpose of Form

Use Form 8606 to:
• Report your nondeductible IRA contributions,
• Figure the basis in your IRA(s), and
• Figure the taxable part of any distributions you received in 1997 if you have ever made nondeductible contributions.

Your **basis** is the total of all your nondeductible IRA contributions minus the total of all nontaxable IRA distributions received. It is to your advantage to keep track of your basis because it is used to figure the nontaxable part of future distributions.

Note: *To figure your deductible IRA contributions, see the Instructions for Form 1040, or Form 1040A, whichever applies.*

Who Must File

You must file Form 8606 if:
• You made nondeductible contributions to your IRA for 1997, **or**
• You received IRA distributions in 1997 **and** you have ever made nondeductible contributions to any of your IRAs.

What Records Must I Keep?

To verify the nontaxable part of distributions from your IRA, keep a copy of this form together with copies of the following forms and records until all distributions are made from your IRA(s):

• Page 1 of Forms 1040 (or Forms 1040A, 1040NR, or 1040-T) filed for each year you make a nondeductible contribution.

• Forms 5498 or similar statements received each year showing contributions you made.

• Forms 5498 or similar statements received showing the value of your IRA(s) for each year you received a distribution.

• Forms 1099-R and W-2P received for each year you received a distribution.

When and Where To File

Attach Form 8606 to your 1997 Form 1040, 1040A, or 1040NR.

If you are required to file Form 8606 but you are not required to file an income tax return, you still **must** file Form 8606. Send it to the Internal Revenue Service at the same time and place you would otherwise file Form 1040, 1040A, or 1040NR.

For Paperwork Reduction Act Notice, see back of form.

Cat. No. 63966F

Form **8606** (1997)

Penalty for Not Filing

If you are required to file Form 8606 but do not do so, you will have to pay a $50 penalty for each failure to file this form unless you can show reasonable cause.

Penalty for Overstatement

If you overstate your nondeductible contributions for any tax year, you must pay a $100 penalty for each overstatement unless it was due to reasonable cause.

Additional Information

For more details on nondeductible contributions, IRA basis, and distributions, see **Pub. 590,** Individual Retirement Arrangements (IRAs).

Amending Form 8606

After you file your return, you may change a nondeductible contribution made on a prior year's return to a deductible contribution or vice versa. To do this, complete a new Form 8606 showing the revised information and attach it to **Form 1040X,** Amended U.S. Individual Income Tax Return. Send both of these forms to the Internal Revenue Service Center for your area as shown in the Form 1040X instructions.

Specific Instructions

Caution: *If you received an IRA distribution in 1997 and you also made IRA contributions for 1997 that may not be fully deductible because of the income limits, you need to make a special computation before completing this form. For details, including how to complete Form 8606, see Tax Treatment of Distributions in Chapter 5 of Pub. 590.*

Name and Social Security Number

If you file a joint return on Form 1040 or Form 1040A, enter the name and social security number of the spouse whose IRA information is shown.

Line 1

If you used the IRA Deduction Worksheet in the Form 1040 instructions, follow these instructions to figure the amount to include on line 1 of Form 8606.

● Subtract the amount shown on line 10 of the worksheet from the **smaller** of the amount shown on line 8 or line 9 of that worksheet. Enter on line 1 of Form 8606 the part of the result that you choose to be nondeductible.

● If you choose not to deduct the full amount shown on line 10 of the worksheet, subtract the amount you are deducting from the amount on line 10. Enter the result on line 1 of Form 8606. You cannot take a deduction for the part included on line 1.

● If you are married filing a joint return and the amount on line 8 of the worksheet was less than $4,000, enter on line 1 of Form 8606 any nondeductible contributions from the appropriate lines of the IRA worksheet in Pub. 590.

If you used the IRA Deduction Worksheet in the Form 1040A instructions, follow these instructions.

● Subtract the amount shown on line 8 of the worksheet from the **smaller** of the amount shown on line 6 or line 7 of that worksheet.

Enter on line 1 of Form 8606 the part of the result that you choose to be nondeductible.

● If you choose not to deduct the full amount shown on line 8 of the worksheet, subtract the amount you are deducting from the amount on line 8. Enter the result on line 1 of Form 8606. You cannot take a deduction for the part included on line 1.

● If you are married filing a joint return and the amount on line 6 of the worksheet was less than $4,000, enter on line 1 of Form 8606 any nondeductible contributions from the appropriate lines of the IRA worksheet in Pub. 590.

If none of your contributions are deductible, you may choose to make nondeductible contributions up to $2,000 (but not more than your earned income). If you are married filing a joint return and your earned income is less than your spouse's, your nondeductible contributions cannot be more than the total of your and your spouse's earned income. Enter on line 1 of Form 8606 your contributions that you choose to make nondeductible.

Line 2

If this is the first year you are required to file Form 8606, enter zero. Otherwise, use the chart below to find the amount to enter on line 2.

IF the last Form 8606 you filed was for. . .	THEN enter on line 2. . .
A year after 1992	The amount from line 12 of the **last** Form 8606 you filed
A year after 1988 but before 1993	The amount from line 14 of the **last** Form 8606 you filed
1988	The total of the amounts on lines 7 and 16 of that Form 8606
1987	The total of the amounts on lines 4 and 13 of that Form 8606

Line 4

If you made contributions in 1997 and 1998 that are for 1997, you may choose to apply the contributions made in 1997 first to nondeductible contributions and then to deductible contributions, or vice versa. But the amount on line 1 minus the amount on line 4 cannot be more than the IRA contributions you actually made in 1997.

Example. You made contributions of $1,000 in 1997 and $1,000 in 1998 of which $1,500 are deductible and $500 are nondeductible. You choose $500 of your contribution in 1997 to be nondeductible. In this case, the $500 would be entered on line 1, but not on line 4, and would become part of your basis for 1997.

Line 5

Although the 1997 IRA contributions you made during 1/1/98–4/15/98 (line 4) can be treated as nondeductible for purposes of line 1, they are not included in your basis for purposes of figuring the nontaxable part of any distributions you received in 1997. This is why you subtract line 4 from line 3.

Line 6

Enter the total value of **ALL** your IRAs (including SIMPLE IRAs) as of 12/31/97 **plus** any outstanding rollovers. You should receive a statement by 2/2/98 for each IRA account showing the value on 12/31/97. A **rollover** is a tax-free distribution from one IRA that is contributed to another IRA. The rollover must be completed within 60 days of receiving the distribution from the first IRA. An **outstanding rollover** is any amount distributed to you from one IRA within 60 days of the end of 1997 (between Nov. 2 and Dec. 31) that you did not roll over to another IRA by 12/31/97, but that you roll over to another IRA in 1998 within the normal 60-day rollover period.

Line 7

Do not include on line 7:

● Distributions received in 1997 and rolled over to another IRA by 12/31/97,

● Outstanding rollovers included on line 6,

● Contributions under section 408(d)(4) returned to you on or before the due date of the return, or

● Excess contributions under section 408(d)(5) returned to you after the due date of the return.

Line 11

This is the total of your nondeductible IRA contributions made in 1997 and earlier years minus the total of any nontaxable IRA distributions received in those years.

Line 12

This is the total of your IRA basis as of 12/31/97 and any nondeductible IRA contributions for 1997 that you made in 1998 by 4/15/98.

This amount will be used on Form 8606 in future years if you make nondeductible IRA contributions or receive distributions.

Form **8615**

Department of the Treasury
Internal Revenue Service (99)

**Tax for Children Under Age 14
Who Have Investment Income of More Than $1,300**

▶ **Attach ONLY to the child's Form 1040, Form 1040A, or Form 1040NR.**

OMB No. 1545-0998

19**97**

Attachment
Sequence No. **33**

Child's name shown on return

Child's social security number

A   Parent's name (first, initial, and last). **Caution:** *See instructions on back before completing.*

B   Parent's social security number

C   Parent's filing status (check one):

☐ Single   ☐ Married filing jointly   ☐ Married filing separately   ☐ Head of household   ☐ Qualifying widow(er)

Part I	Child's Net Investment Income

1   Enter the child's investment income, such as taxable interest and dividends. See instructions. If this amount is $1,300 or less, **stop;** do not file this form . . . . | **1** | |

2   If the child **did not** itemize deductions on Schedule A (Form 1040 or Form 1040NR), enter $1,300. If the child **did** itemize deductions, see instructions . . . . | **2** | |

3   Subtract line 2 from line 1. If the result is zero or less, **stop;** do not complete the rest of this form but **do** attach it to the child's return . . . . | **3** | |

4   Enter the child's **taxable** income from Form 1040, line 38; Form 1040A, line 22; or Form 1040NR, line 37 . . . . ▶ | **4** | |

5   Enter the **smaller** of line 3 or line 4 . . . . ▶ | **5** | |

Part II	Tentative Tax Based on the Tax Rate of the Parent Listed on Line A

6   Enter the parent's **taxable** income from Form 1040, line 38; Form 1040A, line 22; Form 1040EZ, line 6; TeleFile Tax Record, line J; Form 1040NR, line 37; or Form 1040NR-EZ, line 13. If the parent transferred property to a trust, see instructions . . . . | **6** | |

7   Enter the total net investment income, if any, from Forms 8615, line 5, of **all other** children of the parent identified above. **Do not** include the amount from line 5 above . . . . . | **7** | |

8   Add lines 5, 6, and 7 . . . . | **8** | |

9   Enter the tax on line 8 based on the **parent's** filing status. See instructions. If **Schedule D** (Form 1040) is used to figure the tax, check here . . . . ▶ ☐ | **9** | |

10   Enter the parent's tax from Form 1040, line 39; Form 1040A, line 23; Form 1040EZ, line 10; TeleFile Tax Record, line J; Form 1040NR, line 38; or Form 1040NR-EZ, line 14. If **Schedule D** (Form 1040) was used to figure the tax, check here . . . . ▶ ☐ | **10** | |

11   Subtract line 10 from line 9 and enter the result. If line 7 is blank, enter on line 13 the amount from line 11 and go to **Part III** . . . . | **11** | |

12a   Add lines 5 and 7 . . . . | **12a** | |

  b   Divide line 5 by line 12a. Enter the result as a decimal (rounded to three places) . . . . . | **12b** | × . |

13   Multiply line 11 by line 12b . . . . ▶ | **13** | |

Part III	Child's Tax—If lines 4 and 5 above are the same, enter -0- on line 15 and go to line 16.

14   Subtract line 5 from line 4 . . . . | **14** | |

15   Enter the tax on line 14 based on the **child's** filing status. See instructions. If **Schedule D** (Form 1040) is used to figure the tax, check here . . . . ▶ ☐ | **15** | |

16   Add lines 13 and 15 . . . . | **16** | |

17   Enter the tax on line 4 based on the **child's** filing status. See instructions. If **Schedule D** (Form 1040) is used to figure the tax, check here . . . . ▶ ☐ | **17** | |

18   Enter the **larger** of line 16 or line 17 here and on Form 1040, line 39; Form 1040A, line 23; or Form 1040NR, line 38 . . . . ▶ | **18** | |

General Instructions

Section references are to the Internal Revenue Code.

Purpose of form. For children under age 14, investment income over $1,300 is taxed at the parent's rate if the parent's rate is higher than the child's rate. If the child's investment income is more than $1,300, use this form to figure the child's tax.

Investment income. As used on this form, "investment income" includes all taxable income other than earned income as

defined on page 2. It includes taxable interest, dividends, capital gains, rents, royalties, etc. It also includes pension and annuity income and income (other than earned income) received as the beneficiary of a trust.

Who must file. Generally, Form 8615 must be filed for any child who was under age 14 on January 1, 1998, had more than $1,300 of investment income, and is required to file a tax return. But if neither parent was alive on December 31, 1997, do not use Form 8615. Instead, figure the child's tax in the normal manner.

Note: *The parent may be able to elect to report the child's interest and dividends on his or her return. If the parent makes this election, the child will not have to file a return or Form 8615. For more details, see* **Form 8814,** *Parents' Election To Report Child's Interest and Dividends.*

Additional information. For more details, see **Pub. 929,** Tax Rules for Children and Dependents.

Incomplete information for parent. If the parent's taxable income or filing status or the net investment income of the parent's other children is not known by the due

For Paperwork Reduction Act Notice, see back of form.   Cat. No. 64113U   Form **8615** (1997)

date of the child's return, reasonable estimates may be used. Write "Estimated" on the appropriate line(s) of Form 8615. For more details, see Pub. 929.

Amended return. If after the child's return is filed the parent's taxable income changes or the net investment income of any of the parent's other children changes, the child's tax must be refigured using the adjusted amounts. If the child's tax changes, file **Form 1040X,** Amended U.S. Individual Income Tax Return, to correct the child's tax.

Alternative Minimum Tax. A child whose tax is figured on Form 8615 may owe the alternative minimum tax. For details, see **Form 6251,** Alternative Minimum Tax—Individuals, and its instructions.

Line Instructions

Lines A and B. If the child's parents were married to each other and filed a joint return, enter the name and social security number (SSN) of the parent who is listed first on the joint return.

If the parents were married but filed separate returns, enter the name and SSN of the parent who had the **higher** taxable income. If you do not know which parent had the higher taxable income, see Pub. 929.

If the parents were unmarried, treated as unmarried for Federal income tax purposes, or separated either by a divorce or separate maintenance decree, enter the name and SSN of the parent who had custody of the child for most of the year (the custodial parent).

Exception. If the custodial parent remarried and filed a joint return with his or her new spouse, enter the name and SSN of the person listed first on the joint return, even if that person is not the child's parent. If the custodial parent and his or her new spouse filed separate returns, enter the name and SSN of the person with the **higher** taxable income, even if that person is not the child's parent.

Note: *If the parents were unmarried but lived together during the year with the child, enter the name and SSN of the parent who had the **higher** taxable income.*

Line 1. If the child had no earned income (defined later), enter the child's adjusted gross income from Form 1040, line 33; Form 1040A, line 17; or Form 1040NR, line 33.

Child's Investment Income Worksheet—Line 1 (keep a copy for your records)

1. Enter the amount from the child's Form 1040, line 22; Form 1040A, line 14; or Form 1040NR, line 23, whichever applies   . . . . .   **1.** _____

2. Enter the child's **earned income** (defined on this page) plus any deduction the child claims on Form 1040, line 29, or Form 1040NR, line 29, whichever applies   . . . .   **2.** _____

3. Subtract line 2 from line 1. Enter the result here and on Form 8615, line 1   . . . .   **3.** _____

If the child had earned income, use the worksheet on this page to figure the amount to enter on line 1. But if the child files **Form 2555** or **2555-EZ** (relating to foreign earned income), has a net loss from self-employment, or claims a net operating loss deduction, you **must** use the worksheet in Pub. 929 instead.

Earned income includes wages, tips, and other payments received for personal services performed. Generally, it is the total of the amounts reported on Form 1040, lines 7, 12, and 18; Form 1040A, line 7; or Form 1040NR, lines 8, 13, and 19.

Line 2. If the child itemized deductions, enter the **greater** of:

• $1,300, **or**

• $650 plus the portion of the amount on **Schedule A** (Form 1040), line 28, or **Schedule A** (Form 1040NR), line 17, that is directly connected with the production of the investment income on Form 8615, line 1.

Line 6. If the parent's taxable income is less than zero, enter zero on line 6. If the parent filed a joint return, enter the taxable income shown on that return even if the parent's spouse is not the child's parent. If the parent transferred property to a trust that sold or exchanged the property in 1997 before August 6, 1997, include any gain that was taxed to the trust under section 644 in the amount entered on line 6. Enter "Sec. 644" and the amount on the dotted line next to line 6. Also, see the instructions for line 10.

Line 9. Figure the tax using the Tax Table, Tax Rate Schedules, or **Schedule D** (Form 1040), whichever applies. If any net capital gain is included on line 5, 6, or 7, Part IV of Schedule D must be used to figure the tax on the amount on line 8. See Pub. 929 for details on how to figure the net capital gain included on line 8.

Line 10. If the parent filed a joint return, enter the tax shown on that return even if the parent's spouse is not the child's parent. If the parent filed Form 8814, enter "Form 8814" and the total tax from line 8 of Form(s) 8814 on the dotted line next to line 10 of Form 8615.

If line 6 includes any gain taxed to a trust under section 644, add the tax imposed under section 644(a)(2)(A) to the tax shown on the parent's return and enter the total on line 10. Also, enter "Sec. 644" on the dotted line next to line 10.

Line 15. Figure the tax using the Tax Table, Tax Rate Schedule X, or Schedule D, whichever applies. If line 14 includes any net capital gain, use Schedule D to figure the tax. See Pub. 929 for details on how to figure the net capital gain included on line 14.

Line 17. Figure the tax as if these rules did not apply. For example, if the child has a net capital gain, use Schedule D to figure his or her tax.

Paperwork Reduction Act Notice. We ask for the information on this form to carry out the Internal Revenue laws of the United States. You are required to give us the information. We need it to ensure that you are complying with these laws and to allow us to figure and collect the right amount of tax.

You are not required to provide the information requested on a form that is subject to the Paperwork Reduction Act unless the form displays a valid OMB control number. Books or records relating to a form or its instructions must be retained as long as their contents may become material in the administration of any Internal Revenue law. Generally, tax returns and return information are confidential, as required by section 6103.

The time needed to complete and file this form will vary depending on individual circumstances. The estimated average time is: **Recordkeeping,** 13 min.; **Learning about the law or the form,** 13 min.; **Preparing the form,** 45 min.; and **Copying, assembling, and sending the form to the IRS,** 17 min.

If you have comments concerning the accuracy of these time estimates or suggestions for making this form simpler, we would be happy to hear from you. See the instructions for the tax return with which this form is filed.

| Form **8824**
Department of the Treasury
Internal Revenue Service | **Like-Kind Exchanges**
(and nonrecognition of gain from conflict-of-interest sales)
▶ See separate instructions.   ▶ Attach to your tax return.
▶ Use a separate form for each like-kind exchange. | OMB No. 1545-1190
19**97**
Attachment
Sequence No. **49** |

| Name(s) shown on tax return | Identifying number |

Part I — Information on the Like-Kind Exchange

Note: *If the property described on line 1 or line 2 is real or personal property located outside the United States, indicate the country.*

1 Description of like-kind property given up ▶ ....

2 Description of like-kind property received ▶ ....

3	Date like-kind property given up was originally acquired (month, day, year)	**3**	/ /
4	Date you actually transferred your property to other party (month, day, year)	**4**	/ /
5	Date the like-kind property you received was identified (month, day, year). See instructions . .	**5**	/ /
6	Date you actually received the like-kind property from other party (month, day, year) . . .	**6**	/ /

7 Was the exchange made with a related party? If "Yes," complete Part II. If "No," go to Part III. See instructions.

a ☐ Yes, in this tax year   **b** ☐ Yes, in a prior tax year   **c** ☐ No.

Part II — Related Party Exchange Information

8 Name of related party	Related party's identifying number
Address (no., street, and apt., room, or suite no.)	
City or town, state, and ZIP code	Relationship to you

9 During this tax year (and before the date that is 2 years after the last transfer of property that was part of the exchange), did the related party sell or dispose of the like-kind property received from you in the exchange? ☐ Yes ☐ No

10 During this tax year (and before the date that is 2 years after the last transfer of property that was part of the exchange), did you sell or dispose of the like-kind property you received? . . . . ☐ Yes ☐ No

*If both lines 9 and 10 are "No" and this is the year of the exchange, go to Part III. If either line 9 or line 10 is " Yes," the deferred gain or (loss) from line 24 **must** be reported on your return this tax year, **unless** one of the exceptions on line 11 applies. See* ***Related party exchanges*** *in the instructions.*

11 If one of the exceptions below applies to the disposition, check the applicable box:

a ☐ The disposition was after the death of either of the related parties.

b ☐ The disposition was an involuntary conversion, and the threat of conversion occurred after the exchange.

c ☐ You can establish to the satisfaction of the IRS that neither the exchange nor the disposition had tax avoidance as its principal purpose. If this box is checked, attach an explanation. See instructions.

Part III — Realized Gain or (Loss), Recognized Gain, and Basis of Like-Kind Property Received

Caution: *If you transferred **and** received **(a)** more than one group of like-kind properties, or **(b)** cash or other (not like-kind) property, see **Reporting of multi-asset exchanges** in the instructions.*

Note: *Complete lines 12 through 14 ONLY if you gave up property that was not like-kind. Otherwise, go to line 15.*

12	Fair market value (FMV) of other property given up	**12**	
13	Adjusted basis of other property given up	**13**	
14	Gain or (loss) recognized on other property given up. Subtract line 13 from line 12. Report the gain or (loss) in the same manner as if the exchange had been a sale	**14**	
15	Cash received, FMV of other property received, plus net liabilities assumed by other party, reduced (but not below zero) by any exchange expenses you incurred. See instructions	**15**	
16	FMV of like-kind property you received	**16**	
17	Add lines 15 and 16	**17**	
18	Adjusted basis of like-kind property you gave up, net amounts paid to other party, plus any exchange expenses **not** used on line 15. See instructions	**18**	
19	**Realized gain or (loss).** Subtract line 18 from line 17	**19**	
20	Enter the smaller of line 15 or line 19, but not less than zero	**20**	
21	Ordinary income under recapture rules. Enter here and on Form 4797, line 16. See instructions .	**21**	
22	Subtract line 21 from line 20. If zero or less, enter -0-. If more than zero, enter here and on Schedule D or Form 4797, unless the installment method applies. See instructions	**22**	
23	**Recognized gain.** Add lines 21 and 22	**23**	
24	Deferred gain or (loss). Subtract line 23 from line 19. If a related party exchange, see instructions .	**24**	
25	**Basis of like-kind property received.** Subtract line 15 from the sum of lines 18 and 23 . .	**25**	

For Paperwork Reduction Act Notice, see back of form.   Cat. No. 12311A   Form **8824** (1997)

Form 8824 (1997)   Page **2**

Name(s) shown on tax return. Do not enter name and social security number if shown on other side.	Your social security number

Part IV **Section 1043 Conflict-of-Interest Sales.** See instructions. Attach a copy of your certificate of divestiture.

Note: *This part is only to be used by officers or employees of the executive branch of the Federal Government for reporting nonrecognition of gain under section 1043 on the sale of property to comply with the conflict-of-interest requirements. This part can be used only if the cost of the replacement property exceeds the basis of the divested property.*

26 Description of divested property ▶ ....

27 Description of replacement property ▶ ....

28 Date divested property was sold (month, day, year) . . . .   **28**   /   /

29 Sales price of divested property. See instructions **29**

30 Basis of divested property **30**

31 **Realized gain.** Subtract line 30 from line 29 . . . .   **31**

32 Cost of replacement property purchased within 60 days after date of sale **32**

33 Subtract line 32 from line 29. If zero or less, enter -0- **33**

34 Ordinary income under recapture rules. Enter here and on Form 4797, line 10. See instructions   **34**

35 Subtract line 34 from line 33. If zero or less, enter -0-. If more than zero, enter here and on Schedule D or Form 4797. See instructions **35**

36 **Recognized gain.** Add lines 34 and 35 . . . .   **36**

37 Deferred gain. Subtract line 36 from line 31 . . . .   **37**

38 **Basis of replacement property.** Subtract line 37 from line 32 . . . .   **38**

			OMB No. 1545-1266

Form 8829

Department of the Treasury
Internal Revenue Service (99)

Expenses for Business Use of Your Home

▶ File only with Schedule C (Form 1040). Use a separate Form 8829 for each home you used for business during the year.

▶ See separate instructions.

1997

Attachment Sequence No. **66**

Name(s) of proprietor(s)   Your social security number

Part I Part of Your Home Used for Business

1	Area used regularly and exclusively for business, regularly for day care, or for storage of inventory or product samples. See instructions	1	
2	Total area of home	2	
3	Divide line 1 by line 2. Enter the result as a percentage	3	%

• **For day-care facilities not used exclusively for business, also complete lines 4–6.**

• **All others, skip lines 4–6 and enter the amount from line 3 on line 7.**

4	Multiply days used for day care during year by hours used per day	4	hr.
5	Total hours available for use during the year (365 days × 24 hours). See instructions	5	8,760 hr.
6	Divide line 4 by line 5. Enter the result as a decimal amount	6	.
7	Business percentage. For day-care facilities not used exclusively for business, multiply line 6 by line 3 (enter the result as a percentage). All others, enter the amount from line 3 ▶	7	%

Part II Figure Your Allowable Deduction

		(a) Direct expenses	(b) Indirect expenses	
8	Enter the amount from Schedule C, line 29, **plus** any net gain or (loss) derived from the business use of your home and shown on Schedule D or Form 4797. If more than one place of business, see instructions			8

See instructions for columns (a) and (b) before completing lines 9–20.

		(a) Direct expenses	(b) Indirect expenses	
9	Casualty losses. See instructions	9		
10	Deductible mortgage interest. See instructions	10		
11	Real estate taxes. See instructions	11		
12	Add lines 9, 10, and 11	12		
13	Multiply line 12, column (b) by line 7		13	
14	Add line 12, column (a) and line 13			14
15	Subtract line 14 from line 8. If zero or less, enter -0-			15
16	Excess mortgage interest. See instructions	16		
17	Insurance	17		
18	Repairs and maintenance	18		
19	Utilities	19		
20	Other expenses. See instructions	20		
21	Add lines 16 through 20	21		
22	Multiply line 21, column (b) by line 7		22	
23	Carryover of operating expenses from 1996 Form 8829, line 41		23	
24	Add line 21 in column (a), line 22, and line 23			24
25	Allowable operating expenses. Enter the **smaller** of line 15 or line 24			25
26	Limit on excess casualty losses and depreciation. Subtract line 25 from line 15			26
27	Excess casualty losses. See instructions		27	
28	Depreciation of your home from Part III below		28	
29	Carryover of excess casualty losses and depreciation from 1996 Form 8829, line 42		29	
30	Add lines 27 through 29			30
31	Allowable excess casualty losses and depreciation. Enter the **smaller** of line 26 or line 30			31
32	Add lines 14, 25, and 31			32
33	Casualty loss portion, if any, from lines 14 and 31. Carry amount to **Form 4684,** Section B			33
34	Allowable expenses for business use of your home. Subtract line 33 from line 32. Enter here and on Schedule C, line 30. If your home was used for more than one business, see instructions ▶			34

Part III Depreciation of Your Home

35	Enter the **smaller** of your home's adjusted basis or its fair market value. See instructions	35	
36	Value of land included on line 35	36	
37	Basis of building. Subtract line 36 from line 35	37	
38	Business basis of building. Multiply line 37 by line 7	38	
39	Depreciation percentage. See instructions	39	%
40	Depreciation allowable. Multiply line 38 by line 39. Enter here and on line 28 above. See instructions	40	

Part IV Carryover of Unallowed Expenses to 1998

41	Operating expenses. Subtract line 25 from line 24. If less than zero, enter -0-	41	
42	Excess casualty losses and depreciation. Subtract line 31 from line 30. If less than zero, enter -0-	42	

For Paperwork Reduction Act Notice, see page 3 of separate instructions. ✪   Cat. No. 13232M   Form **8829** (1997)

APPENDIX C
Glossary of Tax Terms

The words and phrases in this glossary have been defined to reflect their conventional use in the field of taxation. The definitions may therefore be incomplete for other purposes.

A

Abandoned spouse. The abandoned spouse provision enables a married taxpayer with a dependent child whose spouse did not live in the taxpayer's home during the last six months of the tax year to file as a head of household rather than as married filing separately.

Accelerated cost recovery system (ACRS). A method in which the cost of tangible property is recovered over a prescribed period of time. Enacted by the Economic Recovery Tax Act (ERTA) of 1981 and substantially modified by the Tax Reform Act (TRA) of 1986 (the modified system is referred to as MACRS), the approach disregards salvage value, imposes a period of cost recovery that depends upon the classification of the asset into one of various recovery periods, and prescribes the applicable percentage of cost that can be deducted each year. § 168.

Accelerated death benefits. The amount received from a life insurance policy by the insured who is terminally ill or chronically ill. Any realized gain may be excluded from the gross income of the insured if the policy is surrendered to the insurer or is sold to a licensed viatical settlement provider. § 101(g).

Accelerated depreciation. Various methods of depreciation that yield larger deductions in the earlier years of the life of an asset than the straight-line method. Examples include the double declining-balance and the sum-of-the-years' digits methods of depreciation. § 167.

Accident and health benefits. Employee fringe benefits provided by employers through the payment of health and accident insurance premiums or the establishment of employer-funded medical reimbursement plans. Employers generally are entitled to a deduction for such payments, whereas employees generally exclude the fringe benefits from gross income. §§ 105 and 106.

Accountable plan. An accountable plan is a type of expense reimbursement plan that requires an employee to render an adequate accounting to the employer and return any excess reimbursement or allowance. If the expense qualifies, it will be treated as a deduction *for* AGI.

Accounting income. The accountant's concept of income is generally based upon the realization principle. Financial accounting income may differ from taxable income (e.g., accelerated depreciation might be used for Federal income tax and straight-line depreciation for financial accounting purposes). Differences are included in a reconciliation of taxable and accounting income on Schedule M–1 of Form 1120 for corporations. Seventy-five percent of the excess of adjusted current earnings over alternative minimum taxable income is an adjustment for alternative minimum tax purposes for a corporation. See *alternative minimum tax* and *economic income*.

Accounting method. The method under which income and expenses are determined for tax purposes. Major accounting methods are the cash basis and the accrual basis. Special methods are available for the reporting of gain on installment sales, recognition of income on construction projects (the completed contract and percentage of completion methods), and the valuation of inventories (last-in, first-out and first-in, first-out). §§ 446–474. See also *accrual method, cash receipts method, completed contract method, percentage of completion method*, etc.

Accounting period. The period of time, usually a year, used by a taxpayer for the determination of tax liability. Unless a fiscal year is chosen, taxpayers must determine and pay their income tax liability by using the calendar year (January 1 through December 31) as the period of measurement. An example of a fiscal year is July 1 through June 30. A change in accounting period (e.g., from a calendar year to a fiscal year) generally requires the consent of the IRS. A new taxpayer, such as a newly formed corporation or an estate created upon the death of an individual taxpayer, is free to select either a calendar or a fiscal year without the consent of the IRS. Limitations exist on the accounting period that may be selected by a partnership, an S corporation, and a personal service corporation. §§ 441–444.

Accrual basis. See *accrual method*.

Accrual method. A method of accounting that reflects expenses incurred and income earned for any one tax year. In contrast to the cash basis of accounting, expenses do not have to be paid to be deductible nor does income have to be received to be taxable. Unearned income (e.g., prepaid interest and rent) generally is taxed in the year of receipt regardless of the method of accounting used by the taxpayer.

§ 446(c)(2). See also *accounting method, cash receipts method,* and *unearned income.*

Accumulated earnings tax. A special tax imposed on corporations that accumulate (rather than distribute) their earnings beyond the reasonable needs of the business. The tax is imposed on accumulated taxable income and is imposed in addition to the corporate income tax. §§ 531–537.

ACE adjustment. See *adjusted current earnings (ACE) adjustment* and *business untaxed reported profits.*

Acquiescence. In agreement with the result reached. The IRS follows a policy of either acquiescing (*A, Acq.*) or nonacquiescing (*NA, Nonacq.*) in the results reached in certain judicial decisions.

Acquisition indebtedness. Debt incurred in acquiring, constructing, or substantially improving a qualified residence of the taxpayer. The interest on such loans is deductible as *qualified residence interest.* However, interest on such debt is deductible only on the portion of the indebtedness that does not exceed $1,000,000 ($500,000 for married persons filing separate returns). § 163(h)(3). See also *home equity loans.*

ACRS. See *accelerated cost recovery system.*

Active income. Active income includes wages, salary, commissions, bonuses, profits from a trade or business in which the taxpayer is a material participant, gain on the sale or other disposition of assets used in an active trade or business, and income from intangible property if the taxpayer's personal efforts significantly contributed to the creation of the property. The passive activity loss rules require classification of income and losses into three categories with active income being one of them.

Active participation. A term that is relevant for both the at-risk rules and the passive activity loss rules associated with rental real estate activities. For the at-risk rules, the following factors indicate active participation: (1) making decisions involving the operation or management of the activity, (2) performing services for the activity, and (3) hiring and discharging employees. For the passive activity loss rules, the taxpayer must participate in the making of management decisions in a significant and bona fide sense.

Additional depreciation. The excess of the amount of depreciation actually deducted over the amount that would have been deducted had the straight-line method been used. § 1250(b). See also *Section 1250 recapture.*

Adjusted basis. The cost or other basis of property reduced by depreciation (cost recovery) allowed or allowable and increased by capital improvements. See also *basis* and *realized gain or loss.*

Adjusted current earnings (ACE) adjustment. An adjustment in computing corporate alternative minimum taxable income (AMTI), computed at 75 percent of the excess of adjusted current earnings and profits computations over unadjusted AMTI. ACE computations reflect longer and slower cost recovery deductions and other restrictions on the timing of certain recognition events. Exempt interest, life insurance proceeds, and other receipts that are included in earnings and profits but not in taxable income also increase the ACE adjustment. If unadjusted AMTI exceeds adjusted current earnings and profits, the ACE adjustment is negative. The negative adjustment is limited to the aggregate of the positive adjustments under ACE for prior years, reduced by any previously claimed negative adjustments. See also *alternative minimum tax* and *earnings and profits.*

Adjusted gross income (AGI). A determination peculiar to individual taxpayers. Generally, it represents gross income less business expenses, expenses attributable to the production of rent or royalty income, the allowed capital loss deduction, and certain personal expenses (deductions *for* AGI). § 62. See also *gross income.*

Adjusted sales price. The amount realized from the sale of a residence reduced by the fixing-up expenses is the adjusted sales price. An amount equal to the adjusted sales price must be reinvested in a replacement residence to defer the recognition of the realized gain on the sale of a residence. This term is not relevant for the sale of a principal residence after May 6, 1997. The Taxpayer Relief Act of 1997 (TRA of 1997) repealed § 1034. See also *amount realized, fixing-up expense,* and *realized gain or loss.*

Adoption expenses credit. The provision is intended to assist taxpayers who incur nonrecurring costs directly associated with the adoption process such as legal costs, social service review costs, and transportation costs. Up to $5,000 ($6,000 for a child with special needs) of costs incurred to adopt an eligible child qualify for the credit. A taxpayer may claim the credit in the year qualifying expenses are paid or incurred if the expenses are paid during or after the year in which the adoption is finalized. For qualifying expenses paid or incurred in a tax year prior to the year the adoption is finalized, the credit must be claimed in the year the adoption is finalized. § 23.

Ad valorem tax. A tax imposed on the value of property. The most familiar ad valorem tax is that imposed by states, counties, and cities on real estate. Ad valorem taxes can, however, be imposed upon personal property (e.g., a motor vehicle tax based on the value of an automobile). §§ 164(a)(1) and (2).

Advance payments. In general, prepayments for services or goods are includible in gross income upon receipt of the advance payments (for both accrual and cash basis taxpayers). However, Rev.Proc. 71–21 (1971–2 C.B. 549) provides guidelines for the deferral of tax on certain advance payments providing specific conditions are met.

AFTR. Published by Research Institute of America (formerly by Prentice-Hall), *American Federal Tax Reports* contains all of the Federal tax decisions issued by the U.S. District Courts, U.S. Court of Federal Claims, U.S. Courts of Appeals, and U.S. Supreme Court.

AFTR2d. The second series of the *American Federal Tax Reports.*

AFTR3d. The third series of the *American Federal Tax Reports*.

Alimony and separate maintenance payments. Alimony and separate maintenance payments are includible in the gross income of the recipient and are deductible by the payor. The payments must be made in discharge of a legal obligation arising from a marital or family relationship. Child support and voluntary payments are not treated as alimony. Alimony is deductible *for* AGI. §§ 62(10), 71, and 215. See also *child support payments*.

Alimony recapture. The amount of alimony that previously has been included in the gross income of the recipient and deducted by the payor that now is deducted by the recipient and included in the gross income of the payor as the result of front-loading. § 71(f).

All events test. For accrual method taxpayers, income is earned when (1) all the events have occurred that fix the right to receive the income and (2) the amount can be determined with reasonable accuracy. Accrual of income cannot be postponed simply because a portion of the income may have to be returned in a subsequent period. The all events test also is utilized to determine when expenses can be deducted by an accrual basis taxpayer. The application of the test could cause a variation between the treatment of an item for accounting and for tax purposes. For example, a reserve for warranty expense may be properly accruable under generally accepted accounting principles but not be deductible under the Federal income tax law. Because of the application of the all events test, the deduction becomes available in the year the warranty obligation becomes fixed and the amount is determinable with reasonable certainty. See also *economic performance test*. Reg. §§ 1.446–1(c)(1)(ii) and 1.461–1(a)(2).

Alternate valuation date. Property passing from a person by reason of death may be valued for death tax purposes as of the date of death or the alternate valuation date. The alternate valuation date is six months from the date of death or the date the property is disposed of by the estate, whichever comes first. To use the alternate valuation date, the executor or administrator of the estate must make an affirmative election. The election of the alternate valuation date is not available unless it decreases both the amount of the gross estate *and* the estate tax liability. §§ 1014(a) and 2032.

Alternative depreciation system (ADS). A cost recovery system that produces a smaller deduction than would be calculated under ACRS or MACRS. The alternative system must be used in certain instances and can be elected in other instances. § 168(g). See also *cost recovery allowance*.

Alternative minimum tax (AMT). The alternative minimum tax is imposed only to the extent it exceeds the regular income tax (in effect, the tax liability is the greater of the tax liability calculated using the AMT rules and that calculated using the regular income tax rules). The AMT rates (26 and 28 percent for the individual taxpayer and 20 percent for the corporate taxpayer) are applied to the AMT base. The AMT base is calculated by modifying taxable income as follows: (1)

add tax preferences, (2) add certain adjustments, (3) deduct certain adjustments, and (4) deduct the exemption amount. §§ 55–59. See also *adjusted current earnings (ACE) adjustment*.

Alternative minimum tax credit. The AMT can result from timing differences that give rise to positive adjustments in calculating the AMT base. To provide equity for the taxpayer when these timing differences reverse, the regular tax liability may be reduced by a tax credit for prior year's minimum tax liability attributable to timing differences. § 53.

Alternative tax. An option that is allowed in computing the tax on net capital gain. For the corporate taxpayer, the rate is 35 percent (the same as the highest regular corporate tax rate). Thus, for corporate taxpayers, the alternative tax does not produce a beneficial result. For noncorporate taxpayers, the rate is usually either 20 percent (i.e., holding period is longer than 18 months) or 28 percent (i.e., holding period is longer than 12 months but not longer than 18 months). However, if the noncorporate taxpayer is in the 15 percent tax bracket, the alternative tax rate is 10 percent if the holding period is longer than 18 months. §§ 1(h) and 1201. See also *mid-term capital gain or loss* and *net capital gain*.

Alternative tax NOL deduction (ATNOLD). In calculating the AMT, the taxpayer is allowed to deduct NOL carryovers and carrybacks. A special calculation, referred to as the ATNOLD, is required for this purpose. The regular income tax is modified for AMT adjustments and preferences to produce the ATNOLD. § 56(d).

Amortization. The allocation (and charge to expense) of the cost or other basis of an intangible asset over a statutory period of 15 years. Examples of amortizable intangibles include patents, copyrights, covenants not to compete, acquired goodwill, and leasehold interests. See also *estimated useful life* and *goodwill*. § 197.

Amount realized. The amount received by a taxpayer on the sale or other disposition of property. The amount realized is the sum of the cash and the fair market value of any property or services received, plus any related debt assumed by the buyer. Determining the amount realized is the starting point for arriving at realized gain or loss. The amount realized is defined in § 1001(b) and the related Regulations. See also *realized gain or loss* and *recognized gain or loss*.

AMT adjustments. In calculating AMTI, certain adjustments are added to or deducted from taxable income. These adjustments generally reflect timing differences. § 56.

AMT exclusions. A credit that can be used to reduce the regular tax liability in future tax years is available in connection with the AMT (*AMT credit*). The credit is applicable only with respect to the AMT that results from timing differences. It is not available in connection with AMT exclusions, which include the standard deduction, personal exemptions, medical expenses deductible in calculating the regular income tax that are not deductible in computing the AMT, other itemized deductions that are not allowable for AMT purposes, excess percentage depletion, and tax-exempt interest on specified private activity bonds.

Annuity. A fixed sum payable to a person at specified intervals for a specific period of time or for life. Payments represent a partial return of capital and a return (interest) on the capital investment. Therefore, an exclusion ratio must be used to compute the amount of nontaxable income. The exclusion ratio is used until the annuitant has recovered his or her investment in the annuity contract. Thereafter, all of the annuity payments received are included in gross income. If the annuitant dies before his or her investment is recovered, a deduction is allowed. § 72. See also *qualified pension or profit sharing plan*.

Appellate court. For Federal tax purposes, appellate courts include the Courts of Appeals and the Supreme Court. If the party losing in the trial (or lower) court is dissatisfied with the result, the dispute may be carried to the appropriate appellate court. See also *Court of Appeals* and *trial court*.

Arm's length transaction. The standard under which unrelated parties would determine an exchange price for a transaction. Suppose, for example, Cardinal Corporation sells property to its sole shareholder for $10,000. In testing whether the $10,000 is an "arm's length" price, one would ascertain the price that would have been negotiated between the corporation and an unrelated party in a bargained exchange.

Asset Depreciation Range (ADR) system. A system of estimated useful lives for categories of tangible assets prescribed by the IRS. The system provides a range for each category that extends from 20 percent above to 20 percent below the guideline class lives prescribed by the IRS.

Assignment of income. A procedure whereby a taxpayer attempts to avoid the recognition of income by assigning the property that generates the income to another. Such a procedure will not avoid the recognition of income by the taxpayer making the assignment if it can be said that the income was earned at the point of the transfer. In this case, usually referred to as an anticipatory assignment of income, the income will be taxed to the person who earns it.

Association. An organization treated as a corporation for Federal tax purposes even though it may not qualify as such under applicable state law. An entity designated as a trust or a partnership, for example, may be classified as an association if it clearly possesses corporate attributes. Corporate attributes include centralized management, continuity of life, free transferability of interests, and limited liability. When the check-the-box Regulations were finalized, the association Regulations were withdrawn. Thus, for most entities, reclassification as an association is unlikely. § 7701(a)(3). See also *check-the-box Regulations*.

At-risk limitation. Under the at-risk rules, a taxpayer's deductible losses from an activity for any taxable year are limited to the amount the taxpayer has at risk at the end of the taxable year. The initial amount considered at risk is generally the sum of the amount of cash and the adjusted basis of property contributed to the activity and amounts borrowed for use in the activity for which the taxpayer is personally liable or has pledged as security property not used in the activity. § 465.

Attribution. Under certain circumstances, the tax law applies attribution (construction ownership) rules to assign to one taxpayer the ownership interest of another taxpayer. If, for example, the stock of Gold Corporation is held 60 percent by Marsha and 40 percent by Sid, Marsha may be deemed to own 100 percent of Gold Corporation if she and Sid are mother and son. In that case, the stock owned by Sid is attributed to Marsha. See, for example, §§ 267 and 318.

Audit. Inspection and verification of a taxpayer's return or other transactions possessing tax consequences. See also *correspondence audit*, *field audit*, and *office audit*.

Automatic mileage method. See *automobile expenses*.

Automobile expenses. Automobile expenses are generally deductible only to the extent the automobile is used in business or for the production of income. Personal commuting expenses are not deductible. The taxpayer may deduct actual expenses (including depreciation and insurance), or the standard (automatic) mileage rate may be used (30 cents per mile for 1995, 31 cents per mile for 1996, 31.5 cents per mile for 1997, and 32.5 cents per mile for 1998) during any one year. Automobile expenses incurred for medical purposes or in connection with job-related moving expenses are deductible to the extent of actual out-of-pocket expenses or at the rate of 10 cents per mile (12 cents for charitable activities for 1997 and 14 cents for 1998). See also *transportation expenses*.

B

Bad debts. A deduction is permitted if a business account receivable subsequently becomes partially or completely worthless, providing the income arising from the debt previously was included in income. Available methods are the specific charge-off method and the reserve method. However, except for certain financial institutions, TRA of 1986 repealed the use of the reserve method for 1987 and thereafter. If the reserve method is used, partially or totally worthless accounts are charged to the reserve. A nonbusiness bad debt deduction is allowed as a short-term capital loss if the loan did not arise in connection with the creditor's trade or business activities. Loans between related parties (family members) generally are classified as nonbusiness. § 166. See also *nonbusiness bad debts*.

Basis. The acquisition cost assigned to an asset for income tax purposes. For assets acquired by purchase, the basis is the cost (§ 1012). Special rules govern the basis of property received by virtue of another's death (§ 1014) or by gift (§ 1015), the basis of stock received on a transfer of property to a controlled corporation (§ 358), the basis of the property transferred to the corporation (§ 362), and the basis of property received upon the liquidation of a corporation (§§ 334 and 338). See also *adjusted basis*.

Book value.　The net amount of an asset after reduction by a related reserve. The book value of accounts receivable, for example, is the face amount of the receivables less the reserve for bad debts. The book value of a building is the cost less the accumulated depreciation.

Boot.　Cash or property of a type not included in the definition of a nontaxable exchange. The receipt of boot will cause an otherwise nontaxable transfer to become taxable to the extent of the lesser of the fair market value of such boot or the realized gain on the transfer. Examples of nontaxable exchanges that could be partially or completely taxable due to the receipt of boot include transfers to controlled corporations [§ 351(b)] and like-kind exchanges [§ 1031(b)]. See also *realized gain or loss* and *recognized gain or loss*.

Bribes and illegal payments.　Section 162 denies a deduction for bribes or kickbacks, fines and penalties paid to a government official or employee for violation of law, and two-thirds of the treble damage payments made to claimants for violation of the antitrust law. Denial of a deduction for bribes and illegal payments is based upon the judicially established principle that allowing such payments would be contrary to public policy.

B.T.A.　The Board of Tax Appeals was a trial court that considered Federal tax matters. This court is now the U.S. Tax Court.

Burden of proof.　The requirement in a lawsuit to show the weight of evidence and thereby gain a favorable decision. Except in cases of tax fraud, the burden of proof in a tax case generally is on the taxpayer.

Business bad debt.　A debt created or acquired in connection with a trade or business of the taxpayer, or a debt the loss from the worthlessness of which is incurred in the taxpayer's trade or business. A business bad debt is deducted as an ordinary deduction. § 166.

Business energy credit.　See *energy tax credit—business property*.

Business expenses.　See *trade or business expenses*.

Business gifts.　Business gifts are deductible only to the extent that each gift does not exceed $25 per person per year. Exceptions are made for gifts costing $4 or less and for certain employee awards. § 274(b).

C

Cafeteria benefit plan.　An employee benefit plan under which an employee is allowed to select from among a variety of employer-provided fringe benefits. Some of the benefits may be taxable and some may be statutory nontaxable benefits (e.g., health and accident insurance and group term life insurance). The employee is taxed only on the taxable benefits selected. A cafeteria benefit plan is also referred to as a flexible benefit plan. § 125.

Cafeteria plan.　See *cafeteria benefit plan*.

Canons of taxation.　Criteria used in the selection of a tax base that were originally discussed by Adam Smith in *The Wealth of Nations*. Canons of taxation include equality, convenience, certainty, and economy.

Capital asset.　Broadly speaking, all assets are capital except those specifically excluded by the Code. Major categories of noncapital assets include property held for resale in the normal course of business (inventory), trade accounts and notes receivable, and depreciable property and real estate used in a trade or business (§ 1231 assets). § 1221. See also *capital gain* and *capital loss*.

Capital contributions.　Various means by which a shareholder makes additional funds available to the corporation (placed at the risk of the business) without the receipt of additional stock. Such contributions are added to the basis of the shareholder's existing stock investment and do not generate income to the corporation. § 118.

Capital expenditure.　An expenditure that should be added to the basis of the property improved. For income tax purposes, this generally precludes a full deduction for the expenditure in the year paid or incurred. Any capital recovery in the form of a tax deduction must come in the form of depreciation. § 263.

Capital gain.　The gain from the sale or exchange of a capital asset. See also *capital asset, mid-term capital gain or loss*, and *net capital gain*.

Capital gain net income.　If the total capital gains for the tax year exceed the total capital losses, the result is capital gain net income. Note that the term does not distinguish between the long-term, mid-term, and short-term gains. § 1222(9). See also *net capital gain*.

Capital gain or loss holding period.　The period of time that a capital asset is held by the taxpayer. To qualify for long-term treatment, the asset must be held for more than 18 months. To qualify for mid-term treatment, the asset must be held for more than 12 months. See also *holding period*.

Capital gain property.　Property contributed to a charitable organization that, if sold rather than contributed, would have resulted in long-term capital gain to the donor. See also *ordinary income property*.

Capital loss.　The loss from the sale or exchange of a capital asset. See also *capital asset*.

Cash basis.　See *accounting method* and *cash receipts method*.

Cash equivalent doctrine.　Generally, a cash basis taxpayer does not report income until cash is constructively or actually received. Under the cash equivalent doctrine, cash basis taxpayers are required to report income if they receive the equivalent of cash (e.g., property is received) in a taxable transaction.

Cash method.　See *cash receipts method*.

Cash receipts method.　A method of accounting under which the taxpayer generally reports income when cash is collected and reports expenses when cash payments are made. However, for fixed assets, the cash basis taxpayer claims deductions through depreciation or amortization in the same manner as an accrual basis taxpayer. Prepaid expenses must be capitalized and amortized if the life of the asset extends "substantially beyond" the end of the tax year. See also *constructive receipt*.

Casualty loss.   A casualty is defined as "the complete or partial destruction of property resulting from an identifiable event of a sudden, unexpected or unusual nature" (e.g., floods, storms, fires, auto accidents). Individuals may deduct a casualty loss only if the loss is incurred in a trade or business or in a transaction entered into for profit or arises from fire, storm, shipwreck, or other casualty or from theft. Individuals usually deduct personal casualty losses as itemized deductions subject to a $100 nondeductible amount and to an annual floor equal to 10 percent of adjusted gross income that applies after the $100 per casualty floor has been applied. Special rules are provided for the netting of certain casualty gains and losses. § 165. See also *disaster area loss* and *Section 1231 gains and losses*.

C corporation.   A corporation that has not elected conduit treatment under § 1361. See also *S corporation status*.

Cert. den.   By denying the Writ of Certiorari, the U.S. Supreme Court refuses to accept an appeal from a U.S. Court of Appeals. The denial of certiorari does not, however, mean that the U.S. Supreme Court agrees with the result reached by the lower court.

Certiorari.   Appeal from a U.S. Court of Appeals to the U.S. Supreme Court is by Writ of Certiorari. The Supreme Court does not have to accept the appeal and usually does not (*cert. den.*) unless there is a conflict among the lower courts that needs to be resolved or a constitutional issue is involved.

Change in accounting method.   A change in the taxpayer's method of accounting (e.g., from FIFO to LIFO) generally requires prior approval from the IRS. Generally, a request must be filed within 180 days after the beginning of the taxable year of the desired change. In some instances, the permission for change will not be granted unless the taxpayer agrees to certain adjustments prescribed by the IRS.

Change in accounting period.   A taxpayer must obtain the consent of the IRS before changing his or her tax year. Income for the short period created by the change must be annualized.

Charitable contributions.   Contributions are deductible (subject to various restrictions and ceiling limitations) if made to qualified nonprofit charitable organizations. A cash basis taxpayer is entitled to a deduction solely in the year of payment. Accrual basis corporations may accrue contributions at year-end if payment is properly authorized before the end of the year and payment is made within two and one-half months after the end of the year. § 170.

Check-the-box Regulations.   These Regulations enable taxpayers to classify the tax status of a business entity without regard to its corporate or noncorporate characteristics. An entity with more than one owner can elect to be classified either as a partnership or as a corporation. An entity with only one owner can elect to be classified as a sole proprietorship or as a corporation. These Regulations should simplify tax administration and taxpayer compliance and reduce tax litigation.

Child and dependent care expenses credit.   A tax credit ranging from 20 percent to 30 percent of employment-related expenses (child and dependent care expenses) for amounts of up to $4,800 is available to individuals who are employed (or deemed to be employed) and maintain a household for a dependent child under age 13, disabled spouse, or disabled dependent. § 21.

Child support payments.   Payments for child support do not constitute alimony and are therefore not includible in gross income by the recipient or deductible as alimony by the payor. Generally, none of the amounts paid are regarded as child support unless the divorce decree or separation agreement specifically calls for child support payments. However, if the amount of the payment to the former spouse would be reduced upon the happening of a contingency related to a child (e.g., the child attains age 21 or dies), the amount of the future reduction in the payment will be deemed child support for post-1984 agreements and decrees. § 71(c). See also *alimony and separate maintenance payments*.

Child tax credit.   A tax credit based solely on the number of qualifying children under age 17. The maximum credit available is $400 per child in 1998 ($500 per child in 1999 and after). A qualifying child must be claimed as a dependent on a parent's tax return in order to qualify for the credit. Taxpayers who qualify for the child tax credit may also qualify for a supplemental credit. The supplemental credit is treated as a component of the earned income credit and is therefore refundable. The credit is phased out for higher-income taxpayers. § 24.

Circuit Court of Appeals.   See *Court of Appeals*.

Circulation expenditures.   Expenditures of establishing or increasing the circulation of a periodical that may be either expensed or capitalized. If such expenses are expensed, an adjustment will occur for AMT purposes, since the expenses are deducted over a three-year period for AMT purposes. Over the three-year period, both positive and negative AMT adjustments will be produced. § 173. See also *AMT adjustments*.

Claim of right doctrine.   A judicially imposed doctrine applicable to both cash and accrual basis taxpayers that holds that an amount is includible in income upon actual or constructive receipt if the taxpayer has an unrestricted claim to the payment. For the tax treatment of amounts repaid when previously included in income under the claim of right doctrine, see § 1341.

Claims Court.   One of three Federal trial courts that consider Federal tax controversy. Now known as the U.S. Court of Federal Claims, appeal from this court (formerly to the U.S.

Supreme Court) now goes to the Court of Appeals for the Federal Circuit. See also *trial court*.

Clear reflection of income. The IRS has the authority to redetermine a taxpayer's income using a method that clearly reflects income if the taxpayer's method does not do so. § 446(b). In addition, the IRS may apportion or allocate income among various related businesses if income is not "clearly reflected." § 482.

Closely held corporation. A corporation where the stock ownership is not widely dispersed. Instead, a few shareholders are in control of corporate policy and are in a position to benefit personally from that policy.

Collectibles. A special type of capital asset, the gain from which is taxed at a maximum rate of 28 percent if the holding period is more than 12 months. Examples include art, rugs, antiques, gems, metals, stamps, some coins and bullion, and alcoholic beverages held for investment.

Community property. Louisiana, Texas, New Mexico, Arizona, California, Washington, Idaho, Nevada, and Wisconsin have community property systems. The rest of the states are classified as common law jurisdictions. The difference between common law and community property systems centers around the property rights possessed by married persons. In a common law system, each spouse owns whatever he or she earns. Under a community property system, one-half of the earnings of each spouse is considered owned by the other spouse. Assume, for example, Alice and Jeff are husband and wife and their only income is the $50,000 annual salary Jeff receives. If they live in New York (a common law state), the $50,000 salary belongs to Jeff. If, however, they live in Texas (a community property state), the $50,000 salary is divided equally, in terms of ownership, between Jeff and Alice. See also *separate property*.

Compensatory damages. Damages received or paid by the taxpayer can be classified as compensatory damages or as punitive damages. Compensatory damages are those paid to compensate one for harm caused by another. Compensatory damages are excludible from the recipient's gross income. See also *punitive damages*.

Completed contract method. A method of reporting gain or loss on certain long-term contracts. Under this method of accounting, gross income and expenses are recognized in the tax year in which the contract is completed. Reg. § 1.451–3. Limitations exist on a taxpayer's ability to use the completed contract method. § 460. See also *long-term contract* and *percentage of completion method*.

Component depreciation. The process of dividing an asset (e.g., a building) into separate components or parts for the purpose of calculating depreciation. The advantage of dividing an asset into components is to use shorter depreciation lives for selected components under § 167. Generally, the same cost recovery period must be used for all the components of an asset under § 168.

Condemnation. The taking of property by a public authority. The property is condemned as the result of legal action, and the owner is compensated by the public authority. The power to condemn property is known as the right of eminent domain.

Conduit concept. An approach assumed by the tax law in the treatment of certain entities and their owners. Specific tax characteristics pass through the entity without losing their identity. For example, items of income and expense, capital gains and losses, tax credits, etc., realized by a partnership pass through the partnership (a conduit) and are subject to taxation at the partner level. Also, in an S corporation, certain items pass through and are reported on the returns of the shareholders.

Constructive dividends. In addition to dividends formally declared by the board of directors of a corporation (i.e., declaration date, record date, and payment date), a shareholder may receive a distribution that does not have the formalities of a dividend but is treated as a dividend. Examples include salaries paid to shareholder-employees that are not reasonable and the shareholder use of corporate property for less than an arm's length rate.

Constructive ownership. See *attribution*.

Constructive receipt. If income is unqualifiedly available, it will be subject to the income tax even though it is not physically in the taxpayer's possession. An example is accrued interest on a savings account. Under the constructive receipt of income concept, the interest will be taxed to a depositor in the year it is available rather than the year actually withdrawn. The fact that the depositor uses the cash basis of accounting for tax purposes is irrelevant. See Reg. § 1.451–2.

Consumer interest. Interest expense of the taxpayer of a personal nature (not trade or business interest, investment interest, qualified residence interest, or passive activity interest). TRA of 1986 provided that no deduction is permitted for consumer interest. However, the provision was not fully effective until 1991. § 163(h). See also *interest on student loans* and *qualified residence interest*.

Contributions to the capital of a corporation. See *capital contributions*.

Convention expenses. Travel expenses incurred in attending a convention are deductible if the meetings are related to a taxpayer's trade or business or job-related activities. If, however, the convention trip is primarily for pleasure, no deduction is permitted for transportation expenses. Likewise, if the expenses are for attending a convention related to the production of income (§ 212), no deduction is permitted. Specific limitations are provided for foreign convention expenses. See § 274(n) for the limitations on the deductions for meals. § 274(h).

Correspondence audit. An audit conducted by the IRS by mail. Typically, the IRS writes to the taxpayer requesting the verification of a particular deduction, exemption, or credit.

The completion of a special form or the remittance of copies of records or other support is all that is requested of the taxpayer. To be distinguished from a *field audit* or an *office audit*.

Cost depletion.   Depletion that is calculated based on the adjusted basis of the asset. The adjusted basis is divided by the expected recoverable units to determine the depletion per unit. The depletion per unit is multiplied by the units sold during the tax year to calculate cost depletion. See also *percentage depletion*.

Cost recovery allowance.   The portion of the cost of an asset written off under ACRS (or MACRS), which replaced the depreciation system as a method for writing off the cost of an asset for most assets placed in service after 1980 (after 1986 for MACRS). § 168. See also *alternative depreciation system*.

Cost recovery period.   A period specified in the Code for writing off the cost of an asset under ACRS or MACRS.

Court of Appeals.   Any of 13 Federal courts that consider tax matters appealed from the U.S. Tax Court, U.S. Court of Federal Claims, or a U.S. District Court. Appeal from a U.S. Court of Appeals is to the U.S. Supreme Court by Writ of Certiorari. See also *appellate court*.

Court of Federal Claims.   See *Claims Court*.

Court of original jurisdiction.   The Federal courts are divided into courts of original jurisdiction and appellate courts. A dispute between a taxpayer and the IRS is first considered by a court of original jurisdiction (i.e., a trial court). The four Federal courts of original jurisdiction are the U.S. Tax Court, U.S. District Court, the Court of Federal Claims, and the Small Cases Division of the U.S. Tax Court. See *Court of Appeals*.

Credit for child and dependent care expenses.   See *child and dependent care expenses credit*.

D

Death benefit.   A payment made by an employer to the beneficiary or beneficiaries of a deceased employee on account of the death of the employee.

Death tax.   See *estate tax*.

Declaration of estimated tax.   A procedure whereby individuals and corporations are required to make quarterly installment payments of estimated tax. Individuals are required to make the declaration and file quarterly payments of the estimated tax if certain requirements are met. In 1998, a declaration is not required for an individual whose estimated tax is reasonably expected to be less than $1,000.

Deductions for adjusted gross income.   See *adjusted gross income*.

Deductions from adjusted gross income.   See *itemized deductions*.

Deferred compensation.   Compensation that will be taxed when received or upon the removal of certain restrictions on receipt and not when earned. Contributions by an employer to a qualified pension or profit sharing plan on behalf of an employee are an example. The contributions will not be taxed to the employee until the funds are made available or distributed to the employee (e.g., upon retirement). See also *qualified pension or profit sharing plan*.

Deficiency.   Additional tax liability owed by a taxpayer and assessed by the IRS. See also *statutory notice of deficiency*.

Defined benefit plan.   Qualified plans can be dichotimized into defined benefit plans and defined contribution plans. Under a defined benefit plan, a formula defines the benefits employees are to receive. The formula usually includes years of service, employee compensation, and some stated percentage. The employer must make annual contributions based on actuarial computations that will be sufficient to pay the vested retirement benefits. See also *defined contribution plan* and *pension plan*.

Defined contribution plan.   Qualified plans can be dichotimized into defined benefit plans and defined contribution plans. Under a defined contribution plan, a separate account is maintained for each covered employee. The employee's benefits under the plan are based solely on (1) the amount contributed and (2) income from the fund that accrues to the employee's account. The plan defines the amount the employer is required to contribute (e.g., a flat dollar amount, an amount based on a special formula, or an amount equal to a certain percentage of compensation). See also *defined benefit plan* and *pension plan*.

Defined contribution pension plan.   See *defined contribution plan*.

De minimis fringe.   Benefits provided to employees that are too insignificant to warrant the time and effort required to account for the benefits received by each employee and the value of those benefits. Such amounts are excludible from the employee's gross income. § 132.

Dependency exemption.   See *personal and dependency exemptions*.

Depletion.   The process by which the cost or other basis of a natural resource (e.g., an oil or gas interest) is recovered upon extraction and sale of the resource. The two ways to determine the depletion allowance are the cost and percentage (or statutory) methods. Under the cost method, each unit of production sold is assigned a portion of the cost or other basis of the interest. This is determined by dividing the cost or other basis by the total units expected to be recovered. Under the percentage (or statutory) method, the tax law provides a special percentage factor for different types of minerals and other natural resources. This percentage is multiplied by the gross income from the interest to arrive at the depletion allowance. §§ 613 and 613A.

Depreciation.   The deduction of the cost or other basis of a tangible asset over the asset's estimated useful life. § 167. For intangible assets, see *amortization*. For natural resources, see *depletion*. Also see *estimated useful life*. The depreciation system was replaced by ACRS for most assets placed in service after 1980 (by MACRS for most assets placed in service after 1986) but still applies for assets placed in service before 1981. See also *recapture of depreciation*.

Determination letter. Upon the request of a taxpayer, a District Director will comment on the tax status of a completed transaction. Determination letters are most frequently used to clarify employee versus self-employed status, to determine whether a pension or profit sharing plan qualifies under the Code, and to determine the tax-exempt status of certain nonprofit organizations.

Direct charge-off method. See *specific charge-off method*.

Disabled access credit. A tax credit designed to encourage small businesses to make their facilities more accessible to disabled individuals. The credit is equal to 50 percent of the eligible expenditures that exceed $250 but do not exceed $10,250. Thus, the maximum amount for the credit is $5,000. The adjusted basis for depreciation is reduced by the amount of the credit. To qualify, the facility must have been placed in service before November 6, 1990. § 44. See also *general business credit*.

Disaster area loss. A casualty sustained in an area designated as a disaster area by the President of the United States. In such an event, the disaster loss may be treated as having occurred in the taxable year immediately preceding the year in which the disaster actually occurred. Thus, immediate tax benefits are provided to victims of a disaster. § 165(i). See also *casualty loss*.

Dissent. To disagree with the majority. If, for example, Judge Brown disagrees with the result reached by Judges Charles and Davis (all of whom are members of the same court), Judge Brown could issue a dissenting opinion.

District Court. A Federal District Court is a trial court for purposes of litigating (among others) Federal tax matters. It is the only trial court where a jury trial can be obtained. See also *trial court*.

Dividends received deduction. A deduction allowed a shareholder that is a corporation for dividends received from a domestic corporation. The percentage applied in calculating the dividends received deduction varies according to the percentage of stock ownership. If the stock ownership percentage is less than 20 percent, the percentage is 70 percent of the dividends received. If the stock ownership percentage is at least 20 percent but less than 80 percent, the percentage is 80 percent. If the stock ownership percentage is at least 80 percent, the percentage is 100 percent. §§ 243–246A.

Dollar value LIFO. An inventory technique that focuses on the dollars invested in the inventory rather than the particular items on hand each period. Each inventory item is assigned to a pool. A pool is a collection of similar items and is treated as a separate inventory. At the end of the period, each pool is valued in terms of prices at the time LIFO was adopted (base period prices), whether or not the particular items were actually on hand in the year LIFO was adopted,

to compare with current prices to determine if there has been an increase or decrease in inventories.

E

Earned income. Income from personal services as distinguished from income generated by property. See §§ 32 and 911 and the related Regulations.

Earned income credit. A refundable tax credit designed to provide assistance to certain low-income individuals. To receive the most beneficial treatment, the taxpayer must have qualifying children. However, it is possible to qualify for the credit without having a child. To calculate the credit for a taxpayer with one or more children for 1998, a statutory rate of 34.0 percent for one child (40.0 percent for two or more children) is multiplied by the earned income (subject to a statutory maximum of $6,680 with one qualifying child or $9,390 with two or more qualifying children). Once the earned income exceeds $12,260, the credit is phased out using a 15.98 percent rate for one qualifying child and a 21.06 percent rate for two or more qualifying children. For the qualifying taxpayer without children, the credit is calculated on a maximum earned income of $4,460 applying a 7.65 percent rate with the phase-out beginning at $5,570 applying the same rate. § 32.

Earnings and profits. A tax concept peculiar to corporate taxpayers that measures economic capacity to make a distribution to shareholders that is not a return of capital. Such a distribution will result in dividend income to the shareholders to the extent of the corporation's current and accumulated earnings and profits.

Economic income. The change in the taxpayer's net worth, as measured in terms of market values, plus the value of the assets the taxpayer consumed during the year. Because of the impracticality of this income model, it is not used for tax purposes. See also *accounting income*.

Economic performance test. One of the requirements that must be satisfied in order for an accrual basis taxpayer to deduct an expense. The accrual basis taxpayer first must satisfy the all events test. That test is not deemed satisfied until economic performance occurs. This occurs, when property or services are provided to the taxpayer or, in the case in which the taxpayer is required to provide property or services, whenever the property or services are actually provided by the taxpayer. See also *all events test*.

Education expenses. Employees may deduct education expenses that are incurred either (1) to maintain or improve existing job-related skills or (2) to meet the express requirements of the employer or the requirements imposed by law to retain employment status. The expenses are not deductible if the education is required to meet the minimum educational standards for the taxpayer's job or if the education qualifies the individual for a new trade or business. Reg. § 1.162–5. See also *HOPE scholarship credit* and *lifetime learning credit*.

Educational savings bonds.   U.S. Series EE bonds whose proceeds are used for qualified higher educational expenses for the taxpayer, the taxpayer's spouse, or a dependent. The interest may be excluded from gross income, provided the taxpayer's adjusted gross income does not exceed certain amounts. § 135.

Employee expenses.   The deductions *for* adjusted gross income include reimbursed expenses and certain expenses of performing artists. All other employee expenses are deductible *from* adjusted gross income. § 62. See also *trade or business expenses*.

Employee stock ownership plan (ESOP).   A type of defined contribution plan that qualifies as a tax-exempt employee trust. The ESOP must invest primarily in qualifying employer securities. A major benefit of an ESOP to the employer corporation is that it can contribute stock rather than cash and receive a tax deduction equal to the fair market value of the stock.

Employment taxes.   Employment taxes are those taxes that an employer must pay on account of its employees. Employment taxes include FICA (Federal Insurance Contributions Act) and FUTA (Federal Unemployment Tax Act) taxes. Employment taxes are paid to the IRS in addition to income tax withholdings at specified intervals. Such taxes can be levied on the employees, the employer, or both. See also *FICA tax* and *FUTA tax*.

Energy tax credit—business property.   A 10 percent tax credit is available to businesses that invest in certain energy property. The purpose of the credit is to create incentives for conservation and to penalize the increased use of oil and gas. The business energy tax credit applies to equipment with an estimated useful life of at least three years that uses fuel or feedstock other than oil or natural gas (e.g., solar, geothermal). §§ 46(2) and 48(a). See also *estimated useful life* and *investment tax credit*.

Entertainment expenses.   These expenses are deductible only if they are directly related to or associated with a trade or business. Various restrictions and documentation requirements have been imposed upon the deductibility of entertainment expenses to prevent abuses by taxpayers. See, for example, the provision contained in § 274(n) that disallows 50 percent of entertainment expenses. § 274.

Estate tax.   A tax imposed on the right to transfer property by reason of death. Thus, an estate tax is levied on the decedent's estate and not on the heir receiving the property. §§ 2001 and 2002. See also *inheritance tax*.

Estimated tax.   The amount of tax (including alternative minimum tax and self-employment tax) an individual expects to owe for the year after subtracting tax credits and income tax withheld. The estimated tax must be paid in installments at designated intervals (e.g. for the individual taxpayer, by April 15, June 15, September 15, and January 15 of the following year).

Estimated useful life.   The period over which an asset will be used by a particular taxpayer. Although the period cannot be longer than the estimated physical life of an asset, it could be shorter if the taxpayer does not intend to keep the asset until it wears out. Assets such as goodwill do not have an estimated useful life. The estimated useful life of an asset is essential to measuring the annual tax deduction for depreciation and amortization. An asset subject to ACRS or MACRS is written off over a specified cost recovery period rather than over its estimated useful life. In addition, most intangibles are now amortized over a 15-year statutory period.

Excise tax.   A tax on the manufacture, sale, or use of goods or on the carrying on of an occupation or activity. Also a tax on the transfer of property. Thus, the Federal estate and gift taxes are, theoretically, excise taxes.

Extraordinary personal services.   These are services provided by individuals where the customers' use of the property is incidental to their receipt of the services. For example, a patient's use of a hospital bed is incidental to his or her receipt of medical services. This is one of the six exceptions to determine whether an activity is a passive rental activity.

F

Fair market value.   The amount at which property would change hands between a willing buyer and a willing seller, neither being under any compulsion to buy or sell and both having reasonable knowledge of the relevant facts. Reg. § 20.2031–1(b).

Federal district court.   See *district court*.

FICA tax.   An abbreviation for Federal Insurance Contributions Act, commonly referred to as the Social Security tax. The FICA tax is comprised of the Social Security tax (old age, survivors, and disability insurance) and the Medicare tax (hospital insurance) and is imposed on both employers and employees. The employer is responsible for withholding from the employee's wages the Social Security tax at a rate of 6.2 percent on a maximum wage base of $68,400 (for 1998) and the Medicare tax at a rate of 1.45 percent (no maximum wage base). The employer is required to match the employee's contribution. See also *employment taxes*.

Field audit.   An audit by the IRS conducted on the business premises of the taxpayer or in the office of the tax practitioner representing the taxpayer. To be distinguished from a *correspondence audit* or an *office audit*.

Finalized Regulation.   See *regulations*.

First-in, first-out (FIFO).   An accounting method for determining the cost of inventories. Under this method, the inventory on hand is deemed to be the sum of the cost of the most recently acquired units. See also *last-in, first-out (LIFO)*.

Fiscal year.   A fiscal year is a 12-month period ending on the last day of a month other than December. In certain circumstances, a taxpayer is permitted to elect a fiscal year instead of being required to use a calendar year. See also *accounting period* and *taxable year*.

Fixing-up expense.   An expense that is incurred to assist in the sale of a residence and is deductible in calculating the adjusted sales price. Fixing-up expenses include such items as ordinary repairs, painting, and wallpapering. To qualify, the expense must (1) be incurred on work performed during the 90-day period ending on the date of the contract of sale, (2) be paid within 30 days after the date of the sale, and (3) not be a capital expenditure. This term is not relevant for the sale of a principal residence after May 6, 1997. The Taxpayer Relief Act of 1997 (TRA of 1997) repealed § 1034. § 1034. See also *adjusted sales price.*

Flat tax.   In its pure form, it would replace the graduated income tax rates with a single rate (e.g., 17 percent). All deductions are eliminated, and a large personal exemption is allowed to remove low-income and many middle-income taxpayers from the application of the tax.

Flexible spending plan.   An employee benefit plan that allows the employee to take a reduction in salary in exchange for the employer paying benefits that can be provided by the employer without the employee being required to recognize income (e.g., medical and child-care benefits).

Foreign earned income exclusion.   The foreign earned income exclusion is a relief provision that applies to U.S. citizens working in a foreign country. To qualify for the exclusion, the taxpayer must be either a bona fide resident of the foreign country or present in the country for 330 days during any 12 consecutive months. The exclusion is limited to $70,000 per year in 1997 and $72,000 per year in 1998. § 911.

Foreign tax credit or deduction.   Both individual taxpayers and corporations may claim a foreign tax credit on income earned and subject to tax in a foreign country or U.S. possession. As an alternative to the credit, a deduction may be taken for the foreign taxes paid. §§ 27, 164, and 901–905.

Franchise.   An agreement that gives the transferee the right to distribute, sell, or provide goods, services, or facilities within a specified area. The cost of obtaining a franchise may be amortized over a statutory period of 15 years. In general, the franchisor's gain on the sale of franchise rights is an ordinary gain because the franchisor retains a significant power, right, or continuing interest in the subject of the franchise. §§ 197 and 1253.

Franchise tax.   A tax levied on the right to do business in a state as a corporation. Although income considerations may come into play, the tax usually is based on the capitalization of the corporation.

Fringe benefits.   Compensation or other benefits received by an employee that are not in the form of cash. Some fringe benefits (e.g., accident and health plans, group term life insurance) may be excluded from the employee's gross income and therefore are not subject to the Federal income tax.

Fruit and tree metaphor.   The courts have held that an individual who earns income from property or services cannot assign that income to another. For example, a father cannot assign his earnings from commissions to his child and escape income tax on those amounts.

F.3d.   An abbreviation for the Third Series of the *Federal Reporter*, the official series where decisions of the U.S. Claims Court (before October 1982) and the U.S. Courts of Appeals are published.

F.Supp.   The abbreviation for the *Federal Supplement*, the official series where the reported decisions of the U.S. District Courts are published.

FUTA tax.   An employment tax levied on employers. Jointly administered by the Federal and state governments, the tax provides funding for unemployment benefits. FUTA applies at a rate of 6.2 percent in 1998 on the first $7,000 of covered wages paid during the year for each employee. The Federal government allows a credit for FUTA paid (or allowed under a merit rating system) to the state. The credit cannot exceed 5.4 percent of the covered wages. See also *employment taxes.*

G

General business credit.   The summation of various nonrefundable business credits, including the tax credit for rehabilitation expenditures, welfare-to-work credit, work opportunity credit, research activities credit, low-income housing credit, and disabled access credit. The amount of general business credit that can be used to reduce the tax liability is limited to the taxpayer's net income tax reduced by the greater of (1) the tentative minimum tax or (2) 25 percent of the net regular tax liability that exceeds $25,000. Unused general business credits can be carried back 1 year and forward 20 years (back 3 years and forward 15 years for tax years beginning before January 1, 1998). § 38.

Gift.   A transfer of property for less than adequate consideration. Gifts usually occur in a personal setting (such as between members of the same family). Gifts are excluded from the income tax but may be subject to the *gift tax.*

Gift tax.   A tax imposed on the transfer of property by gift. The tax is imposed upon the donor of a gift and is based upon the fair market value of the property on the date of the gift. §§ 2501–2524.

Golden parachute payments.   A severance payment to employees that meets the following requirements: (1) the payment is contingent on a change of ownership of a corporation through a stock or asset acquisition and (2) the aggregate present value of the payment equals or exceeds three times the employee's average annual compensation. To the extent the severance payment meets these conditions, a deduction is disallowed to the employer for the excess of the payment over a statutory base amount (a five-year average of compensation if the taxpayer was an employee for the entire five-year period). In addition, a 20 percent excise tax is imposed on the employee who receives the excess severance pay. §§ 280G and 4999.

Goodwill.   The ability of a business to generate income in excess of a normal rate on assets due to superior managerial skills, market position, new product technology, etc. In the purchase of a business, goodwill represents the difference between the purchase price and the fair market value of the net assets acquired. Goodwill is an intangible asset that possesses an indefinite life. However, since acquired goodwill is a § 197 intangible asset, it is amortized over a 15-year statutory period. Self-created goodwill cannot be amortized. Reg. § 1.167(a)–3. See also *amortization*.

Government bonds issued at a discount.   Certain U.S. government bonds (Series E and EE) are issued at a discount and do not pay interest during the life of the bonds. Instead, the bonds are redeemable at increasing fixed amounts. Thus, the difference between the purchase price and the amount received upon redemption represents interest income to the holder. A cash basis taxpayer may defer recognition of gross income until the bonds are redeemed. For Series EE savings bonds issued after 1989, the interest otherwise taxable at redemption can be excluded if the bonds are qualified educational savings bonds. As an alternative to deferring recognition of gross income until the bonds are redeemed, the taxpayer may elect to include in gross income on an annual basis the annual increase in the value of the bonds. § 454.

Gross income.   Income subject to the Federal income tax. Gross income does not include income for which the Code permits exclusion treatment (e.g., interest on municipal bonds). For a manufacturing or merchandising business, gross income means gross profit (gross sales or gross receipts less cost of goods sold). § 61 and Reg. § 1.61–3(a).

Group term life insurance.   Life insurance coverage permitted by an employer for a group of employees. Such insurance is renewable on a year-to-year basis and does not accumulate in value (i.e., no cash surrender value is built up). The premiums paid by the employer on the insurance are not taxed to an employee on coverage of up to $50,000 per person. § 79 and Reg. § 1.79–1(a).

Guaranteed payments.   Payments made by a partnership to one of its partners for services rendered or for the use of capital, to the extent the payments are determined without regard to the income of the partnership. Such payments generally are deductible by the partnership as a business expense and are reported as ordinary income by the recipient partner. § 707(c).

H

Half-year convention.   The half-year convention is a cost recovery convention that assumes all property is placed in service at mid-year and thus provides for a half-year's cost recovery for that year.

Head of household.   An unmarried individual who maintains a household for another and satisfies certain conditions set forth in § 2(b). Such status enables the taxpayer to use a set of income tax rates [see § 1(b)] that are lower than those applicable to other unmarried individuals [§ 1(c)] but higher than those applicable to surviving spouses and married persons filing a joint return [§ 1(a)]. See also *tax rate schedules*.

Highly compensated employee.   The employee group is generally divided into two categories for fringe benefit (including pension and profit sharing plans) purposes. These are (1) highly compensated employees and (2) non-highly compensated employees. For most fringe benefits, if the fringe benefit plan discriminates in favor of highly compensated employees, it will not be a qualified plan with respect, at a minimum, to the highly compensated employees.

Hobby loss.   A nondeductible loss arising from a personal hobby as contrasted with an activity engaged in for profit. Generally, the law provides a rebuttable presumption that an activity is engaged in for profit if profits are earned during any three or more years during a five-year period. § 183. See also *vacation home*.

Holding period.   The period of time property has been held for income tax purposes. The holding period is crucial in determining whether gain or loss from the sale or exchange of a capital asset is long term, mid-term, or short term. § 1223. See also *capital gain or loss holding period*.

Home equity loans.   Loans that utilize the personal residence of the taxpayer as security. The interest on such loans is deductible as *qualified residence interest*. However, interest is deductible only on the portion of the loan that does not exceed the lesser of (1) the fair market value of the residence, reduced by the *acquisition indebtedness*, or (2) $100,000 ($50,000 for married persons filing separate returns). A major benefit of a home equity loan is that there are no tracing rules regarding the use of the loan proceeds. § 163(h)(3).

Home office expenses.   See *office-in-the-home expenses*.

HOPE scholarship credit.   A tax credit for qualifying tuition expenses paid for the first two years of postsecondary education. Room, board, and book costs are ineligible for the credit. The maximum credit available is $1,500 per year per student, computed as 100 percent of the first $1,000 of tuition expenses, plus 50 percent of the second $1,000 of tuition expenses. Eligible students include the taxpayer, taxpayer's spouse, and taxpayer's dependents. To qualify for the credit, a student must take at least one-half the full-time course load for at least one academic term at a qualifying educational institution. The credit is phased out for higher-income taxpayers. § 25A.

H.R. 10 (Keogh) plan.   See *self-employment retirement plan*.

Hybrid method.   A combination of the accrual and cash methods of accounting. That is, the taxpayer may account for some items of income on the accrual method (e.g., sales and cost of goods sold) and other items (e.g., interest income) on the cash method.

I

Imputed interest.   For certain long-term sales of property, the IRS can convert some of the gain from the sale into interest income if the contract does not provide for a minimum rate of interest to be paid by the purchaser. The application of this procedure has the effect of forcing the seller to recognize less long-term capital gain and more ordinary income (interest income). §§ 483 and 1274 and the Regulations thereunder. In addition, interest income and interest expense are imputed (deemed to exist) on interest-free or below-market rate loans between certain related parties. § 7872. See also *interest-free loans*.

Incentive stock option (ISO).   A type of stock option that receives favorable tax treatment. If various qualification requirements can be satisfied, there are no recognition tax consequences when the stock option is granted. However, the spread (the excess of the fair market value at the date of exercise over the option price) is a tax preference item for purposes of the alternative minimum tax. The gain on disposition of the stock resulting from the exercise of the stock option will be classified as long-term capital gain if certain holding period requirements are met (the employee must not dispose of the stock within two years after the option is granted or within one year after acquiring the stock). § 422. See *nonqualified stock option (NQSO)*.

Income.   For tax purposes, an increase in wealth that has been realized.

Independent contractor.   A self-employed person as distinguished from one who is employed as an employee.

Individual retirement account (IRA).   A type of retirement plan to which an individual with earned income can contribute a maximum of $2,000 ($2,000 each in the case of a married couple with a spousal IRA) per tax year. IRAs can be classified as traditional IRAs or Roth IRAs. With a traditional IRA, an individual can contribute and deduct a maximum of $2,000 per tax year. The deduction is a deduction *for* AGI. However, if the individual is an active participant in another qualified retirement plan, the deduction is phased out proportionally between certain AGI ranges (note that the phaseout limits the amount of the deduction and not the amount of the contribution). With a Roth IRA, an individual can contribute a maximum of $2,000 per tax year. No deduction is permitted. However, if a five-year holding period requirement is satisfied and if the distribution is a qualified distribution, the taxpayer can make tax-free withdrawals from a Roth IRA. The maximum annual contribution is phased out proportionally between certain AGI ranges. §§ 219 and 408A. See also *simplified employee pension plan*.

Inheritance tax.   An excise tax levied on the heir based on the value of property received from a decedent. See also *estate tax*.

Installment method.   A method of accounting enabling a taxpayer to spread the recognition of gain on the sale of property over the payout period. Under this procedure, the seller computes the gross profit percentage from the sale (the

gain divided by the contract price) and applies it to each payment received to arrive at the gain to be recognized. §§ 453 and 453A.

Intangible drilling and development costs (IDC).   Taxpayers may elect to expense or capitalize (subject to amortization) intangible drilling and development costs. However, ordinary income recapture provisions apply to oil and gas properties on a sale or other disposition if the expense method is elected. §§ 263(c) and 1254(a).

Interest-free loans.   Bona fide loans that carry no interest (or a below-market rate). If made in a nonbusiness setting, the imputed interest element is treated as a gift from the lender to the borrower. If made by a corporation to a shareholder, a constructive dividend could result. In either event, the lender may recognize interest income, and the borrower may be able to deduct interest expense. § 7872.

Interest on student loans.   The Taxpayer Relief Act of 1997 (TRA of 1997) provides for a limited ability to deduct interest on student loans used to pay qualified higher education expenses (i.e., tuition, fees, books, supplies, room and board). For 1998, the ceiling on the deduction is $1,000. The deduction is allowed only with respect to interest paid on the loan during the first 60 months in which interest payments are required. The deduction is a deduction *for* AGI. § 221. See also *consumer interest*.

Interpretive Regulation.   A Regulation issued by the Treasury Department that purports to explain the meaning of a particular Code Section. An interpretive Regulation is given less deference than a legislative Regulation. See also *legislative regulation* and *procedural regulation*. § 7805.

Investigation of a new business.   Expenditures by taxpayers who are not engaged in a trade or business incurred in the evaluation of prospective business activities (acquiring an existing business or entering into a new trade or business). If the expenditures are general, it is the position of the IRS that no deduction is permitted even if the investigation is abandoned because the taxpayer is not engaged in a trade or business. The courts, however, have permitted a loss deduction providing the expenditures were specific.

Investment income.   Gross income from interest, dividends, annuities, and royalties not derived in the ordinary course of a trade or business. Net capital gain attributable to the disposition of property producing these types of income normally is not included in investment income. However, a taxpayer may elect to include the capital gains as investment income if the net capital gain qualifying for the *alternative tax* is reduced by an equivalent amount. See also *investment interest*.

Investment indebtedness.   If funds are borrowed by noncorporate taxpayers for the purpose of purchasing or continuing to hold investment property, some portion of the interest expense deduction may be disallowed. The interest deduction is generally limited to net investment income. Amounts that are disallowed may be carried forward and treated as investment interest of the succeeding year. § 163(d).

Investment interest. Payment for the use of funds used to acquire assets that produce investment income. The deduction for investment interest is limited to *net investment income* for the tax year. See also *investment income*.

Investment tax credit (ITC). A tax credit that usually was equal to 10 percent (unless a reduced credit was elected) of the qualified investment in tangible personalty used in a trade or business. If the tangible personalty had a recovery period of five years or more, the full cost of the property qualified for the credit. Only 60 percent of cost qualified for property with a recovery period of three years. However, the regular investment tax credit was repealed by TRA of 1986 for property placed in service after December 31, 1985. §§ 46–48. See also *general business credit, recapture of investment tax credit*, and *Section 38 property*.

Involuntary conversion. The loss or destruction of property through theft, casualty, or condemnation. Any gain realized on an involuntary conversion can, at the taxpayer's election, be postponed (deferred) for Federal income tax purposes if the owner reinvests the proceeds within a prescribed period of time in property that is similar or related in service or use. § 1033. See also *nontaxable exchange*.

IRA. See *individual retirement account*.

Itemized deductions. Certain personal expenditures allowed by the Code as deductions *from* adjusted gross income. Examples include certain medical expenses, interest on home mortgages, state income taxes, and charitable contributions. Itemized deductions are reported on Schedule A of Form 1040. Certain miscellaneous itemized deductions are reduced by 2 percent of the taxpayer's adjusted gross income. In addition, a taxpayer whose adjusted gross income exceeds $100,000 ($50,000 for married filing separately) must reduce the itemized deductions by 3 percent of the excess of adjusted gross income over $100,000. For 1998, the indexed amount for the $100,000 is $124,500, and the indexed amount for the $50,000 is $62,250. Medical, casualty and theft, and investment interest deductions are not subject to the 3 percent reduction. The 3 percent reduction may not reduce itemized deductions that are subject to the reduction to below 20 percent of their initial amount. §§ 63(d), 67, and 68.

K

Keogh plan. See *self-employment retirement plan*.

Kiddie tax. To reduce the tax savings that result from shifting income from parents to children, the net unearned income of a child under age 14 is taxed at the marginal tax rate of the parent(s). For the provision to apply, the child must have at least one living parent and unearned income of more than $1,400 for the tax year. § 1(g). See also *unearned income*.

L

Last-in, first-out (LIFO). An accounting method for valuing inventories for tax purposes. Under this method, it is assumed that the inventory on hand is valued at the cost of the earliest acquired units. § 472 and the related Regulations. See also *first-in, first-out (FIFO)*.

Least aggregate deferral method. An algorithm set forth in the Regulations to determine the tax year for a partnership with partners whose tax years differ. The tax year that produces the least aggregate deferral of income for the partners is selected.

Legislative Regulation. Some Code Sections give the Secretary of the Treasury or his delegate the authority to prescribe Regulations to carry out the details of administration or to otherwise complete the operating rules. Regulations issued pursuant to this type of authority truly possess the force and effect of law. In effect, Congress is almost delegating its legislative powers to the Treasury Department. See also *interpretive regulation* and *procedural regulation*.

Lessee. One who rents property from another. In the case of real estate, the lessee is also known as the tenant.

Lessor. One who rents property to another. In the case of real estate, the lessor is also known as the landlord.

Letter rulings. Issued upon a taxpayer's request, by the National Office of the IRS, they describe how the IRS will treat a proposed transaction for tax purposes. They apply only to the taxpayer who asks for and obtains the ruling, but post-1984 rulings may be substantial authority for purposes of avoiding the accuracy-related penalties. The IRS limits the issuance of letter rulings to restricted, pre-announced areas of taxation.

Life insurance proceeds. Generally, life insurance proceeds paid to a beneficiary upon the death of the insured are exempt from Federal income tax. An exception is provided when a life insurance contract has been transferred for valuable consideration to another individual who assumes ownership rights. In that case, the proceeds are income to the assignee to the extent that the proceeds exceed the amount paid for the policy plus any subsequent premiums paid. Insurance proceeds may be subject to the Federal estate tax if the decedent retained any incidents of ownership in the policy before death or if the proceeds are payable to the decedent's estate. §§ 101 and 2042.

Lifetime learning credit. A tax credit for qualifying tuition expenses for taxpayers pursuing education beyond the first two years of postsecondary education. Individuals who are completing their last two years of undergraduate studies, pursuing graduate or professional degrees, or otherwise seeking new job skills or maintaining existing job skills are all eligible for the credit. Eligible individuals include the taxpayer, taxpayer's spouse, and taxpayer's dependents. The maximum credit is 20 percent of the first $5,000 ($10,000 beginning in 2003) of qualifying tuition expenses and is computed per taxpayer. The credit is phased out for higher-income taxpayers. § 25A.

Like-kind exchange.   An exchange of property held for productive use in a trade or business or for investment (except inventory, stocks and bonds, and partnership interests) for other investment or trade or business property. Unless non-like-kind property is received (boot), the exchange will be nontaxable. § 1031. See also *boot* and *nontaxable exchange*.

Limited expensing.   See *Section 179 expensing*.

Limited liability company.   An organization that combines the corporate characteristic of limited liability with treatment as a partnership for Federal income tax purposes.

Liquidating distribution.   A distribution of assets by a corporation associated with the termination of the business. See also *liquidation of a corporation*.

Liquidation of a corporation.   In a complete or partial liquidation of a corporation, amounts received by the shareholders in exchange for their stock are usually treated as a sale or exchange of the stock resulting in capital gain or loss treatment. § 331. Special rules apply to the liquidation of a subsidiary under § 332. Generally, a liquidation is a taxable event to the corporation. § 336. Special rules apply to a parent corporation that is liquidating a subsidiary. § 337.

Listed property.   The term listed property includes (1) any passenger automobile, (2) any other property used as a means of transportation, (3) any property of a type generally used for purposes of entertainment, recreation, or amusement, (4) any computer or peripheral equipment (with an exception for exclusive business use), (5) any cellular telephone (or other similar telecommunications equipment), and (6) any other property of a type specified in the Regulations. If listed property is predominantly used for business, the taxpayer is allowed to use the statutory percentage method of cost recovery. Otherwise, the straight-line cost recovery method must be used. § 280F.

Long-term care insurance.   Insurance that helps pay the cost of care when the insured is unable to care for himself or herself. Such insurance is generally thought of as insurance against the cost of an aged person entering a nursing home. The employer can provide the insurance and the premiums may be excluded from the employee's gross income. § 7702B.

Long-term contract.   A building, installation, construction, or manufacturing contract that is entered into but not completed within the same tax year. A manufacturing contract is a long-term contract only if the contract is to manufacture (1) a unique item not normally carried in finished goods inventory or (2) items that normally require more than 12 calendar months to complete. The two available methods to account for long-term contracts are the percentage of completion method and the completed contract method. The completed contract method can be used only in limited circumstances. § 460. See also *completed contract method* and *percentage of completion method*.

Long-term nonpersonal use capital assets.   Includes investment property with a long-term holding period. Such property disposed of by casualty or theft may receive § 1231 treatment. See also *Section 1231 gains and losses*.

Lower of cost or market.   An elective inventory method, whereby the taxpayer may value inventories at the lower of the taxpayer's actual cost or the current replacement cost of the goods. This method cannot be used in conjunction with the LIFO inventory method.

Low-income housing.   Low-income housing is rental housing that is a dwelling unit for low- or moderate-income individuals or families. Beneficial tax treatment is in the form of the *low-income housing credit*. § 42. See also *accelerated cost recovery system (ACRS)*.

Low-income housing credit.   Beneficial treatment to owners of low-income housing is provided in the form of a tax credit. The calculated credit is claimed in the year the building is placed in service and in the following nine years. § 42. See also *general business credit*.

Lump-sum distribution.   Payment of the entire amount due at one time rather than in installments. Such distributions often occur from qualified pension or profit sharing plans upon the retirement or death of a covered employee. The recipient of a lump-sum distribution may recognize both long-term capital gain and ordinary income upon the receipt of the distribution. The ordinary income portion may be subject to a special 5-year or 10-year income averaging provision. § 402(e).

M

MACRS.   See *accelerated cost recovery system (ACRS)*.

Majority interest partners.   Partners who have more than a 50 percent interest in partnership profits and capital, counting only those partners who have the same taxable year, are referred to as majority interest partners. The term is of significance in determining the appropriate taxable year of a partnership. § 706(b). See also *accounting period* and *principal partner*.

Marital deduction.   A deduction allowed upon the transfer of property from one spouse to another. The deduction is allowed under the Federal gift tax for lifetime (inter vivos) transfers or under the Federal estate tax for death (testamentary) transfers. §§ 2056 and 2523.

Marriage penalty.   The additional tax liability that results for a married couple compared with what their tax liability would be if they were not married and filed separate returns.

Material participation.   If an individual taxpayer materially participates in a nonrental trade or business activity, any loss from that activity is treated as an active loss that can be offset against active income. Material participation is achieved by meeting any one of seven tests provided in the Regulations.

Medical expenses. Medical expenses of an individual, spouse, and dependents are allowed as an itemized deduction to the extent that such amounts (less insurance reimbursements) exceed 7.5 percent of adjusted gross income. § 213.

Medical savings account. A plan available to employees of small firms (50 or fewer employees) with high-deductible health insurance. The employee can place money in the fund and then deduct the contributions (within limits) from gross income. If the employer contributes to the fund, the employee can exclude the contribution from gross income. Income earned from the fund and withdrawals for medical care are not subject to tax. §§ 106(b) and 220.

Mid-month convention. The mid-month convention is a cost recovery convention that assumes property is placed in service in the middle of the month that it is actually placed in service.

Mid-quarter convention. The mid-quarter convention is a cost recovery convention that assumes property placed in service during the year is placed in service at the middle of the quarter in which it is actually placed in service. The mid-quarter convention applies if more than 40 percent of the value of property (other than eligible real estate) is placed in service during the last quarter of the year.

Mid-term capital gain or loss. Gain or loss from the disposition of a capital asset if the holding period is longer than 12 months but not longer than 18 months.

Miscellaneous itemized deductions. A special category of itemized deductions that includes such expenses as professional dues, tax return preparation fees, job-hunting costs, unreimbursed employee business expenses, and certain investment expenses. Such expenses are deductible only to the extent they exceed 2 percent of adjusted gross income. § 67. See also *itemized deductions*.

Mitigation of the annual accounting period concept. Various tax provisions that provide relief from the effect of the finality of the annual accounting period concept. For example, the *net operating loss* provisions provide relief to a taxpayer whose business profits and losses for different taxable years fluctuate. See also *accounting period*.

Modified accelerated cost recovery system (MACRS). See *accelerated cost recovery system (ACRS)*.

Moving expenses. A deduction *for* AGI is permitted to employees and self-employed individuals provided certain tests are met. The taxpayer's new job must be at least 50 miles farther from the old residence than the old residence was from the former place of work. In addition, an employee must be employed on a full-time basis at the new location for 39 weeks in the 12-month period following the move. Deductible moving expenses include the cost of moving the household and personal effects, transportation, and lodging expenses during the move. The cost of meals during the move are not deductible. Qualified moving expenses that are paid (or reimbursed) by the employer can be excluded

from the employee's gross income. In this case, the related deduction by the employee is not permitted. §§ 62(a)(15), 132(a)(6), and 217.

Multiple support agreement. To qualify for a dependency exemption, the support test must be satisfied. This requires that over 50 percent of the support of the potential dependent be provided by the taxpayer. Where no one person provides more than 50 percent of the support, a multiple support agreement enables a taxpayer to still qualify for the dependency exemption. Any person who contributed more than 10 percent of the support is entitled to claim the exemption if each person in the group who contributed more than 10 percent files a written consent (Form 2120). Each person who is a party to the multiple support agreement must meet all the other requirements for claiming the dependency exemption. § 152(c). See also *personal and dependency exemptions*.

N

National sales tax. Intended as a replacement for the current Federal income tax. Unlike a value added tax (VAT), which is levied on the manufacturer, it would be imposed on the consumer upon the final sale of goods and services. To keep the tax from being regressive, low-income taxpayers would be granted some kind of credit or exemption.

Necessary. Appropriate and helpful in furthering the taxpayer's business or income-producing activity. §§ 162(a) and 212. See also *ordinary*.

Net capital gain. The excess of the net long-term capital gain for the tax year over the net short-term capital loss. The net capital gain of an individual taxpayer is eligible for the alternative tax. § 1222(11). See also *alternative tax* and *mid-term capital gain or loss*.

Net capital loss. The excess of the losses from sales or exchanges of capital assets over the gains from sales or exchanges of such assets. Up to $3,000 per year of the net capital loss may be deductible by noncorporate taxpayers against ordinary income. The excess net capital loss carries over to future tax years. For corporate taxpayers, the net capital loss cannot be offset against ordinary income, but it can be carried back 3 years and forward 5 years to offset net capital gains. §§ 1211, 1212, and 1221(10).

Net investment income. The excess of *investment income* over investment expenses. Investment expenses are those deductible expenses directly connected with the production of investment income. Investment expenses do not include investment interest. The deduction for *investment interest* for the tax year is limited to net investment income. § 163(d).

Net operating loss. To mitigate the effect of the annual accounting period concept, § 172 allows taxpayers to use an excess loss of one year as a deduction for certain past or future years. In this regard, a carryback period of 2 years and a carryforward period of 20 years are allowed. For NOLs in tax years beginning before August 6, 1997, the carryback period is 3 years and the carryforward period is 15 years. See also *mitigation of the annual accounting period concept*.

Net worth method. An approach used by the IRS to reconstruct the income of a taxpayer who fails to maintain adequate records. Under this approach, the gross income for the year is the increase in net worth of the taxpayer (assets in excess of liabilities) with appropriate adjustment for nontaxable receipts and nondeductible expenditures. The net worth method often is used when tax fraud is suspected.

Ninety-day letter. See *statutory notice of deficiency*.

No-additional-cost services. Services that the employer may provide the employee at no additional cost to the employer. Generally, the benefit is the ability to utilize the employer's excess capacity (vacant seats on an airliner). Such amounts are excludible from the recipient's gross income. § 132.

Nonaccountable plan. An expense reimbursement plan that does not have an accountability feature. The result is that employee expenses must be claimed as deductions *from* AGI. An exception is moving expenses, which are deductions *for* AGI. See also *accountable plan*.

Nonacquiescence. Announcement of disagreement by the IRS on the result reached in certain judicial decisions. Sometimes abbreviated *Nonacq.* or *NA*. See also *acquiescence*.

Nonbusiness bad debts. A bad debt loss not incurred in connection with a creditor's trade or business. The loss is deductible as a short-term capital loss and is allowed only in the year the debt becomes entirely worthless. In addition to family loans, many investor losses fall into the classification of nonbusiness bad debts. § 166(d). See also *bad debts*.

Nonqualified deferred compensation (NQDC) plans. Compensation arrangements that are frequently offered to executives. Such plans may include stock options, restricted stock, etc. Often, an executive may defer the recognition of taxable income. The employer, however, does not receive a tax deduction until the employee is required to include the compensation in income. See also *restricted property plan*.

Nonqualified stock option (NQSO). A type of stock option that does not satisfy the statutory requirements of an incentive stock option. If the NQSO has a readily ascertainable fair market value (e.g., the option is traded on an established exchange), the value of the option must be included in the employee's gross income at the date of the grant. Otherwise, the employee does not recognize income at the grant date. Instead, ordinary income is recognized in the year of exercise of the option. See also *incentive stock option (ISO)*.

Nonrecourse debt. An obligation on which the endorser is not personally liable. An example of a nonrecourse debt is a mortgage on real estate acquired by a partnership without the assumption of any liability on the mortgage by the partnership or any of the partners. The acquired property generally is pledged as collateral for the loan.

Nonrefundable credit. A nonrefundable credit is a credit that is not paid if it exceeds the taxpayer's tax liability. Some nonrefundable credits qualify for carryback and carryover treatment. See also *refundable credit*.

Nontaxable exchange. A transaction in which realized gains or losses are not recognized. The recognition of gain or loss is postponed (deferred) until the property received in the nontaxable exchange is subsequently disposed of in a taxable transaction. Examples are § 1031 like-kind exchanges and § 1033 involuntary conversions. See also *involuntary conversion* and *like-kind exchange*.

O

Occupational tax. A tax imposed on various trades or businesses. A license fee that enables a taxpayer to engage in a particular occupation.

Office audit. An audit by the IRS of a taxpayer's return that is conducted in the agent's office. To be distinguished from a *correspondence audit* or a *field audit*.

Office-in-the-home expenses. Employment and business-related expenses attributable to the use of a residence (e.g., den or office) are allowed only if the portion of the residence is exclusively used on a regular basis as a principal place of business of the taxpayer or as a place of business that is used by patients, clients, or customers. If the expenses are incurred by an employee, the use must be for the convenience of the employer as opposed to being merely appropriate and helpful. § 280A.

One-year rule for prepaid expenses. Taxpayers who use the cash method are required to use the accrual method for deducting certain prepaid expenses (i.e., must capitalize the item and can deduct only when used). If a prepayment will not be consumed or expire by the end of the tax year following the year of payment, the prepayment must be capitalized and prorated over the benefit period. Conversely, if the prepayment will be consumed by the end of the tax year following the year of payment, it can be expensed when paid. To obtain the current deduction under the one-year rule, the payment must be a required payment rather than a voluntary payment.

Open transaction. A judicially imposed doctrine that allows the taxpayer to defer all gain until he or she has collected an amount equal to the adjusted basis of assets transferred pursuant to an exchange transaction. This doctrine has been applied where the property received in an exchange has no ascertainable fair market value due to the existence of contingencies. The method is permitted only in very limited circumstances. See also *recovery of capital doctrine*.

Options. The sale or exchange of an option to buy or sell property results in capital gain or loss if the property is a capital asset. Generally, the closing of an option transaction results in short-term capital gain or loss to the writer of the call and the purchaser of the call option. § 1234.

Ordinary.   Common and accepted in the general industry or type of activity in which the taxpayer is engaged. It comprises one of the tests for the deductibility of expenses incurred or paid in connection with a trade or business; for the production or collection of income; for the management, conservation, or maintenance of property held for the production of income; or in connection with the determination, collection, or refund of any tax. §§ 162(a) and 212. See also *necessary*.

Ordinary and necessary.   See *necessary* and *ordinary*.

Ordinary income property.   Property contributed to a charitable organization that, if sold rather than contributed, would have resulted in other than long-term capital gain to the donor (i.e., ordinary income property and short-term capital gain property). Examples are inventory and capital assets held for less than the long-term holding period.

Organizational expenses.   A corporation may elect to amortize organizational expenses over a period of 60 months or more. Certain expenses of organizing a company do not qualify for amortization (e.g., expenditures connected with issuing or selling stock or other securities). § 248.

Original issue discount (OID).   The difference between the issue price of a debt obligation (e.g., a corporate bond) and the maturity value of the obligation when the issue price is *less than* the maturity value. OID represents interest and must be amortized over the life of the debt obligation using the effective interest method. The difference is not considered to be original issue discount for tax purposes when it is less than one-fourth of 1 percent of the redemption price at maturity multiplied by the number of years to maturity. §§ 1272 and 1273(a)(3).

Outside salesperson.   An outside salesperson solicits business away from the employer's place of business on a full-time basis. The employment-related expenses of an outside salesperson are itemized deductions unless reimbursed by the employer. If reimbursed, such expenses are deductible *for* AGI.

P

Partnerships.   A partnership is treated as a conduit and is not subject to taxation. Various items of partnership income, expenses, gains, and losses flow through to the individual partners and are reported on the partners' personal income tax returns.

Passive activity.   A trade or business activity in which the taxpayer does not materially participate is subject to limitations on the deduction of losses and credits. Rental activities (subject to exceptions) and limited partnership interests are inherently passive. Relief from passive activity limitation treatment is provided in certain situations, such as for certain rental real estate if the taxpayer actively participates in the activity. The annual ceiling on the relief is $25,000. § 469. See also *portfolio income*.

Passive investment income.   As defined in § 1362(d)(3)(D), passive investment income means gross receipts from royalties, certain rents, dividends, interest, annuities, and gains from the sale or exchange of stock and securities. Revocation of the S corporation election may occur in certain cases when the S corporation has passive investment income in excess of 25 percent of gross receipts for a period of three consecutive years.

Passive loss.   Any loss from (1) activities in which the taxpayer does not materially participate or (2) rental activities (subject to certain exceptions). Net passive losses cannot be used to offset income from nonpassive sources. Rather, they are suspended until the taxpayer either generates net passive income (and a deduction of the losses is allowed) or disposes of the underlying property (at which time the loss deductions are allowed in full). One relief provision allows landlords who actively participate in the rental activities to deduct up to $25,000 of passive losses annually. However, a phase-out of the $25,000 amount commences when the landlord's AGI exceeds $100,000. See also *portfolio income*.

Patent.   A patent is an intangible asset that may be amortized over a statutory 15-year period as a § 197 intangible. The sale of a patent usually results in favorable long-term capital gain treatment. §§ 197 and 1235.

Pension plan.   A type of deferred compensation arrangement that provides for systematic payments of definitely determinable retirement benefits to employees who meet the requirements set forth in the plan. See also *defined benefit plan* and *defined contribution plan*.

Percentage depletion.   Percentage depletion is depletion based on a statutory percentage applied to the gross income from the property. The taxpayer deducts the greater of cost depletion or percentage depletion. § 613. See also *cost depletion*.

Percentage of completion method.   A method of reporting gain or loss on certain long-term contracts. Under this method of accounting, the gross contract price is included in income as the contract is being completed. § 460 and Reg. § 1.451–3. See also *completed contract method* and *long-term contract*.

Personal and dependency exemptions.   The tax law provides an exemption for each individual taxpayer and an additional exemption for the taxpayer's spouse if a joint return is filed. An individual may also claim a dependency exemption for each dependent, provided certain tests are met. The amount of the personal and dependency exemptions is $2,650 in 1997 and $2,700 in 1998. The amount is indexed for inflation. The exemption is subject to phase-out once adjusted gross income exceeds certain statutory threshold amounts. §§ 151 and 152.

Personal casualty gain.   The recognized gain from any involuntary conversion of personal use property arising from fire, storm, shipwreck, or other casualty, or from theft. See also *personal casualty loss*.

Personal casualty loss.   The recognized loss from any involuntary conversion of personal use property arising from fire, storm, shipwreck, or other casualty, or from theft. See also *personal casualty gain.*

Personal exemption.   See *personal and dependency exemptions.*

Personal expenses.   Expenses of an individual for personal reasons that are not deductible unless specifically provided for under the tax law. § 262.

Personal property.   Generally, all property other than real estate. It is sometimes referred to as personalty when real estate is termed realty. Personal property also can refer to property that is not used in a taxpayer's trade or business or held for the production or collection of income. When used in this sense, personal property can include both realty (e.g., a personal residence) and personalty (e.g., personal effects such as clothing and furniture).

Personal residence.   See *sale of principal residence.*

Personal service corporation (PSC).   A corporation the principal activity of which is the performance of personal services (e.g., health, law, engineering, architecture, accounting, actuarial science, performing arts, or consulting), with such services being substantially performed by the employee-owners.

Personalty.   All property other than realty (real estate). Personalty usually is categorized as tangible or intangible property. Tangible personalty includes such assets as machinery and equipment, automobiles and trucks, and office equipment. Intangible personalty includes stocks and bonds, goodwill, patents, trademarks, and copyrights. See also *personal property.*

Points.   Loan origination fees that may be deductible as interest by a buyer of property. A seller of property who pays points reduces the selling price by the amount of the points paid for the buyer. While the seller is not permitted to deduct this amount as interest, the buyer may do so. See *prepaid interest* for the timing of the interest deduction.

Pollution control facilities.   A certified pollution control facility, the cost of which may be amortized over a 60-month period if the taxpayer elects. § 169.

Portfolio income.   The term is relevant in applying the limitation on passive activity losses and credits. Although normally considered passive in nature, for this purpose portfolio income is treated as nonpassive. Therefore, net passive losses and credits cannot be offset against portfolio income. Examples of portfolio income are interest, dividends, annuities, and certain royalties. § 469. See also *passive activity.*

Precedent.   A previously decided court decision that is recognized as authority for the disposition of future decisions.

Prepaid expenses.   Cash basis as well as accrual basis taxpayers usually are required to capitalize prepayments for rent, insurance, etc., that cover more than one year. Deductions are taken during the period the benefits are received.

Prepaid interest.   In effect, the Code places cash basis taxpayers on an accrual basis for purposes of recognizing a deduction for prepaid interest. Thus, interest paid in advance is deductible as an interest expense only as it accrues. The one exception to this rule involves the interest element when a cash basis taxpayer pays points to obtain financing for the purchase of a principal residence (or to make improvements thereto) if the payment of points is an established business practice in the area in which the indebtedness is incurred and the amount involved is not excessive. § 461(g). See also *points.*

Principal partner.   A partner with a 5 percent or greater interest in partnership capital or profits. § 706(b)(3). See also *majority interest partners.*

Private activity bond.   Interest on state and local bonds is excludible from gross income. § 103. Certain such bonds are labeled private activity bonds. Although the interest on such bonds is excludible for regular income tax purposes, it is treated as a tax preference in calculating the AMT. See also *alternative minimum tax (AMT).*

Prizes and awards.   The fair market value of a prize or award generally is includible in gross income. However, exclusion is permitted if the prize or award is made in recognition of religious, charitable, scientific, educational, artistic, literary, or civic achievement, and the recipient transfers the award to a qualified governmental unit or a nonprofit organization. In that case, the recipient must be selected without any action on his or her part to enter a contest or proceeding, and the recipient must not be required to render substantial future services as a condition of receiving the prize or award. § 74.

Procedural Regulation.   A Regulation issued by the Treasury Department that is a housekeeping-type instruction indicating information that taxpayers should provide the IRS as well as information about the internal management and conduct of the IRS itself. See also *interpretive regulation* and *legislative regulation.*

Profit sharing plan.   A deferred compensation plan established and maintained by an employer to provide for employee participation in the company's profits. Contributions are paid from the employer's current or accumulated profits to a trustee. Separate accounts are maintained for each participant employee. The plan must provide a definite, predetermined formula for allocating the contributions among the participants. It also must include a definite, predetermined formula for distributing the accumulated funds after a fixed number of years, on the attainment of a stated age, or on the occurrence of certain events such as illness, layoff, or retirement.

Proposed Regulation.   A Regulation issued by the Treasury Department in proposed, rather than final, form. The interval between the proposal of a Regulation and its finalization permits taxpayers and other interested parties to comment on the propriety of the proposal. See also *regulations* and *temporary regulation.*

Public policy limitation.   See *bribes and illegal payments.*

Punitive damages.   Damages received or paid by the taxpayer can be classified as compensatory damages or as punitive damages. Punitive damages are those awarded to punish the defendant for gross negligence or the intentional infliction of harm. Such damages are includible in gross income. § 104. See also *compensatory damages*.

Q

Qualified employee discounts.   Discounts offered employees on merchandise or services that the employer ordinarily sells or provides to customers. The discounts must be generally available to all employees. In the case of property, the discount cannot exceed the employer's gross profit (the sales price cannot be less than the employer's cost). In the case of services, the discounts cannot exceed 20 percent of the normal sales price. § 132.

Qualified pension or profit sharing plan.   An employer-sponsored plan that meets the requirements of § 401. If these requirements are met, none of the employer's contributions to the plan will be taxed to the employee until distributed to him or her (§ 402). The employer will be allowed a deduction in the year the contributions are made (§ 404). See also *annuity* and *deferred compensation*.

Qualified real property business indebtedness.   Indebtedness that was incurred or assumed by the taxpayer in connection with real property used in a trade or business and is secured by such real property. The taxpayer must not be a C corporation. For qualified real property business indebtedness, the taxpayer may elect to exclude some or all of the income realized from cancellation of debt on qualified real property. If the election is made, the basis of the property must be reduced by the amount excluded. The amount excluded cannot be greater than the excess of the principal amount of the outstanding debt over the fair market value (net of any other debt outstanding on the property) of the property securing the debt.

Qualified residence interest.   A term relevant in determining the amount of interest expense the individual taxpayer may deduct as an itemized deduction for what otherwise would be disallowed as a component of personal interest (consumer interest). Qualified residence interest consists of interest paid on qualified residences (principal residence and one other residence) of the taxpayer. Debt that qualifies as qualified residence interest is limited to $1 million of debt to acquire, construct, or substantially improve qualified residences (acquisition indebtedness) plus $100,000 of other debt secured by qualified residences (home equity indebtedness). The home equity indebtedness may not exceed the fair market value of a qualified residence reduced by the acquisition indebtedness for that residence. § 163(h)(3). See also *consumer interest* and *home equity loans*.

Qualified state tuition program.   A program established by the individual states that allows a resident to prepay college tuition for a beneficiary. When the tuition is used, the beneficiary must recognize income equal to the difference between the amount placed in the fund and the charges for tuition at the time it is used using an annuity-type approach. § 529.

Qualified transportation fringes.   Transportation benefits provided by the employer to the employee. Such benefits include (1) transportation in a commuter highway vehicle between the employee's residence and the place of employment, (2) a transit pass, and (3) qualified parking. Qualified transportation fringes are excludible from the employee's gross income to the extent categories (1) and (2) above do not exceed $65 per month in 1998 and category (3) does not exceed $175 per month in 1998. These amounts are indexed annually for inflation. § 132.

Qualified tuition reduction plan.   A type of fringe benefit plan that is available to employees of nonprofit educational institutions. Such employees (and the spouse and dependent children) are allowed to exclude a tuition waiver pursuant to a qualified tuition reduction plan from gross income. The exclusion applies to undergraduate tuition. In limited circumstances, the exclusion also applies to the graduate tuition of teaching and research assistants. § 117(d).

R

RAR.   A Revenue Agent's Report, which reflects any adjustments made by the agent as a result of an audit of the taxpayer. The RAR is mailed to the taxpayer along with the 30-day letter, which outlines the appellate procedures available to the taxpayer.

Realized gain or loss.   The difference between the amount realized upon the sale or other disposition of property and the adjusted basis of the property. § 1001. See also *adjusted basis* and *recognized gain or loss*.

Realty.   All real estate, including land and buildings. Permanent improvements to a building (fixtures) become realty if their removal would cause significant damage to the property. An example of a fixture is the installation of a central air conditioning or heating system to a building. Thus, personalty can become realty through the fixture reclassification.

Reasonable needs of the business.   See *accumulated earnings tax*.

Reasonableness.   The Code includes a reasonableness requirement with respect to the deduction of salaries and other compensation for services. What constitutes reasonableness is a question of fact. If an expense is unreasonable, the amount that is classified as unreasonable is not allowed as a deduction. The question of reasonableness generally arises with respect to closely held corporations where there is no separation of ownership and management. § 162(a)(1).

Recapture.   To recover the tax benefit of a deduction or a credit previously taken.

Recapture of depreciation.   Upon the disposition of depreciable property used in a trade or business, gain or loss is determined measured by the difference between the consideration received (the amount realized) and the adjusted basis of the property. Before the enactment of the recapture of depreciation provisions of the Code, any such gain recognized could be § 1231 gain and usually qualified for long-term capital gain treatment. The recapture provisions of the Code (e.g., §§ 1245 and 1250) may operate to convert some or all of the previous § 1231 gain into ordinary income. The justification for recapture of depreciation is that it prevents a taxpayer from deducting depreciation at ordinary income rates and having the related gain on disposition taxed at capital gain rates. The recapture of depreciation rules do not apply when the property is disposed of at a loss. See also *residential rental property, Section 1231 gains and losses, Section 1245 recapture,* and *Section 1250 recapture.*

Recapture of investment tax credit. When investment tax credit property is disposed of or ceases to be used in the trade or business of the taxpayer, some or all of the investment tax credit claimed on the property may be recaptured as additional tax liability. The amount of the recapture is the difference between the amount of the credit originally claimed and what should have been claimed in light of the length of time the property was actually held or used for qualifying purposes. § 50. See also *investment tax credit.*

Recapture potential. Reference is to property that, if disposed of in a taxable transaction, would result in the recapture of depreciation (§§ 1245 or 1250) and/or of the investment tax credit (§ 50).

Recognized gain or loss. The portion of realized gain or loss that is considered in computing taxable income. See also *realized gain or loss.*

Recovery of capital doctrine. When a taxable sale or exchange occurs, the seller may be permitted to recover his or her investment (or other adjusted basis) in the property before gain or loss is recognized. See also *open transaction.*

Refundable credit. A refundable credit is a credit that is paid to the taxpayer even if the amount of the credit (or credits) exceeds the taxpayer's tax liability. See also *nonrefundable credit.*

Regulations. Treasury Department Regulations represent the position of the IRS as to how the Internal Revenue Code is to be interpreted. Their purpose is to provide taxpayers and IRS personnel with rules of general and specific application to the various provisions of the tax law. Regulations are published in the *Federal Register* and in all tax services. See also *interpretive regulation, legislative regulation, procedural regulation,* and *proposed regulation.*

Rehabilitation expenditures credit. A credit that is based on expenditures incurred to rehabilitate industrial and commercial buildings and certified historic structures. The credit is intended to discourage businesses from moving from older, economically distressed areas to newer locations and to encourage the preservation of historic structures. § 47. See *rehabilitation expenditures credit recapture.*

Rehabilitation expenditures credit recapture. When property that qualifies for the rehabilitation expenditures credit is disposed of or ceases to be used in the trade or business of the taxpayer, some or all of the tax credit claimed on the property may be recaptured as additional tax liability. The amount of the recapture is the difference between the amount of the credit claimed originally and what should have been claimed in light of the length of time the property was actually held or used for qualifying purposes. § 50. See *rehabilitation expenditures credit.*

Related party. Includes certain family members and controlled entities (i.e., partnerships and corporations). §§ 267, 707(b), and 1239. See also *related-party transactions.*

Related-party transactions. The tax law places restrictions upon the recognition of gains and losses between related parties because of the potential for abuse. For example, restrictions are placed on the deduction of losses from the sale or exchange of property between related parties. In addition, under certain circumstances, related-party gains that would otherwise be classified as capital gain are classified as ordinary income. §§ 267, 707(b), and 1239. See also *related party.*

Rental activity. Any activity where payments are received principally for the use of tangible property is a rental activity. Temporary Regulations provide that in certain circumstances activities involving rentals of real and personal property are not to be *treated* as rental activities. The Temporary Regulations list six exceptions.

Research activities credit. A tax credit whose purpose is to encourage research and development. It consists of two components: the incremental research activities credit and the basic research credit. The incremental research activities credit is equal to 20 percent of the excess of qualified research expenditures over the base amount. The basic research credit is equal to 20 percent of the excess of basic research payments over the base amount. § 41. See also *general business credit.*

Research and experimental expenditures. The Code provides three alternatives for the tax treatment of research and experimentation expenditures. They may be expensed in the year paid or incurred, deferred subject to amortization, or capitalized. If the taxpayer does not elect to expense such costs or to defer them subject to amortization (over 60 months), the expenditures must be capitalized. § 174. Two types of research activities credits are available: the basic research credit and the incremental research activities credit. The rate for each type is 20 percent. § 41. See also *research activities credit.*

Reserve for bad debts. A method of accounting whereby an allowance is permitted for estimated uncollectible accounts. Actual write-offs are charged to the reserve, and recoveries of amounts previously written off are credited to the reserve. The Code permits only certain financial institutions to use the reserve method. § 166. See also *specific charge-off method.*

Reserve method. See *reserve for bad debts.*

Reserves for estimated expenses. Except in the limited case for bad debts, reserves for estimated expenses (e.g., warranty service costs) are not permitted for tax purposes even though such reserves are appropriate for financial accounting purposes. See also *all events test*.

Residential rental property.   Buildings for which at least 80 percent of the gross rents are from dwelling units (e.g., an apartment building). This type of building is distinguished from nonresidential (commercial or industrial) buildings in applying the recapture of depreciation provisions. The term also is relevant in distinguishing between buildings that are eligible for a 27.5-year life versus a 39-year (or 31.5-year) life for MACRS purposes. Generally, residential buildings receive preferential treatment. §§ 168(e)(2) and 1250. See also *recapture of depreciation*.

Residential rental real estate.   See *residential rental property*.

Restricted property plan.   An arrangement whereby an employer transfers property (usually stock) to an employee at a bargain price (for less than the fair market value). If the transfer is accompanied by a substantial risk of forfeiture and the property is not transferable, no compensation results to the employee until the restrictions disappear. An example of a substantial risk of forfeiture would be a requirement that the employee return the property if his or her employment is terminated within a specified period of time. § 83. See also *nonqualified deferred compensation (NQDC) plans* and *substantial risk of forfeiture*.

Retirement of corporate obligations.   The retirement of corporate and certain government obligations is considered to be a sale or exchange. Gain or loss, upon the retirement of a corporate obligation, therefore, is treated as capital gain or loss rather than as ordinary income or loss. §§ 1271–1275.

Return of capital doctrine.   See *recovery of capital doctrine*.

Revenue neutrality.   A description that characterizes tax legislation when it neither increases nor decreases the revenue result. Thus, any tax revenue losses are offset by tax revenue gains.

Revenue Procedure.   A matter of procedural importance to both taxpayers and the IRS concerning the administration of the tax law is issued by the National Office of the IRS as a Revenue Procedure (abbreviated Rev.Proc.). A Revenue Procedure is first published in an *Internal Revenue Bulletin* (I.R.B.) and later transferred to the appropriate *Cumulative Bulletin* (C.B.). Both the *Internal Revenue Bulletin* and the *Cumulative Bulletin* are published by the U.S. Government Printing Office.

Revenue Ruling.   A Revenue Ruling (abbreviated Rev.Rul.) is issued by the National Office of the IRS to express an official interpretation of the tax law as applied to specific transactions. It is more limited in application than a Regulation. A Revenue Ruling is first published in an *Internal Revenue Bulletin* (I.R.B.) and later transferred to the appropriate *Cumulative Bulletin* (C.B.). Both the *Internal Revenue Bulletin* and the *Cumulative Bulletin* are published by the U.S. Government Printing Office.

S

Sale of principal residence.   If a residence has been owned and used by the taxpayer as the principal residence for at least two years during the five-year period ending on the date of sale, up to $250,000 of realized gain is excluded from gross income. For a married couple filing a joint return, the $250,000 is increased to $500,000 if either spouse satisfies the ownership requirement and both spouses satisfy the use requirement. § 121.

Sale or exchange.   A requirement for the recognition of capital gain or loss. Generally, the seller of property must receive money or relief from debt in order to have sold the property. An exchange involves the transfer of property for other property. Thus, *collection* of a debt is neither a sale nor an exchange. The term *sale or exchange* is not defined by the Code.

Sales tax.   A transaction tax imposed upon the sale of goods. It usually is based on a specified percentage of the value of the property sold. A sales tax is to be distinguished from an excise tax, since a sales tax applies to a broad variety of commodities.

Salvage value.   The estimated amount a taxpayer will receive upon the disposition of an asset used in the taxpayer's trade or business. Salvage value is relevant in calculating depreciation under § 167, but is not relevant in calculating cost recovery under § 168.

Scholarships.   Scholarships are generally excluded from the gross income of the recipient unless the payments are a disguised form of compensation for services rendered. However, the Code imposes restrictions on the exclusion. The recipient must be a degree candidate. The excluded amount is limited to amounts used for tuition, fees, books, supplies, and equipment required for courses of instruction. Amounts received for room and board are not eligible for the exclusion. § 117.

S corporation.   See *S corporation status*.

S corporation status.   An elective provision permitting certain small business corporations (§ 1361) and their shareholders to elect (§ 1362) to be treated for income tax purposes in accordance with the operating rules of §§ 1363–1379. Of major significance are the facts that S status avoids the corporate income tax and corporate losses can be claimed by the shareholders. See also *C corporation*.

Section 38 property.   Property that qualified for the investment tax credit. Generally, this included all tangible property (other than real estate) used in a trade or business. § 48 prior to repeal by the Revenue Reconciliation Act of 1990. See also *investment tax credit*.

Section 121 exclusion.   See *sale of principal residence*.

Section 179 expensing.   The ability to deduct a capital expenditure in the year an asset is placed in service rather than over the asset's useful life or cost recovery period. The annual ceiling on the deduction is $18,000 for 1997 and $18,500 for 1998. The ceiling amount is increased each year until it reaches $25,000 for 2003 and thereafter. However, the deduction is reduced dollar for dollar when § 179 property placed in service during the taxable year exceeds $200,000. In addition, the amount expensed under § 179 cannot exceed the aggregate amount of taxable income derived from the conduct of any trade or business by the taxpayer.

Section 401(k) plan.   A cash or deferred arrangement plan that allows participants to elect to receive up to $10,000 in 1998 in cash (taxed currently) or to have a contribution made on their behalf to a profit sharing or stock bonus plan (excludible from gross income). The plan may also be in the form of a salary reduction agreement between the participant and the employer.

Section 1231 assets.   Depreciable assets and real estate used in a trade or business and held for the required long-term holding period. Under certain circumstances, the classification also includes timber, coal, domestic iron ore, livestock (held for draft, breeding, dairy, or sporting purposes), and unharvested crops. § 1231(b).

Section 1231 gains and losses.   If the net result of the combined gains and losses from the taxable dispositions of § 1231 assets plus the net gain from the involuntary conversion of nonpersonal use assets is a gain, the gains and losses from § 1231 assets are treated as long-term capital gains and losses. In arriving at § 1231 gains, however, the depreciation recapture provisions (e.g., §§ 1245 and 1250) are first applied to produce ordinary income. If the net result of the combination is a loss, the gains and losses from § 1231 assets are treated as ordinary gains and losses. § 1231(a). See also *recapture of depreciation*.

Section 1231 lookback.   In order for gain to be classified as § 1231 gain, the gain must survive the § 1231 lookback. To the extent of nonrecaptured § 1231 losses for the five prior tax years, the gain is classified as ordinary income. § 1231(c).

Section 1231 property.   See *Section 1231 assets*.

Section 1244 stock.   Stock issued under § 1244 by qualifying small business corporations. If § 1244 stock is disposed of at a loss or becomes worthless, the shareholders may claim an ordinary loss rather than the usual capital loss. The annual ceiling on the ordinary loss treatment is $50,000 ($100,000 for married individuals filing jointly). See also *worthless securities*.

Section 1245 property.   Property that is subject to the recapture of depreciation under § 1245. For a definition of § 1245 property, see § 1245(a)(3). See also *Section 1245 recapture*.

Section 1245 recapture.   Upon a taxable disposition of § 1245 property, all depreciation claimed on the property is recaptured as ordinary income (but not to exceed the recognized gain from the disposition). See also *recapture of depreciation*.

Section 1250 property.   Real estate that is subject to the recapture of depreciation under § 1250. For a definition of § 1250 property, see § 1250(c). See also *Section 1250 recapture*.

Section 1250 recapture.   Upon a taxable disposition of § 1250 property, some or all of the additional depreciation claimed on the property may be recaptured as ordinary income. Various recapture rules apply depending upon the type of property (residential or nonresidential real estate) and the date acquired. Generally, the additional depreciation is recaptured in full to the extent of the gain recognized. See also *additional depreciation* and *recapture of depreciation*.

Self-employment retirement plan.   A designation for retirement plans available to self-employed taxpayers. Also referred to as H.R. 10 and Keogh plans. Under such plans, a taxpayer may deduct each year up to either 20 percent of net earnings from self-employment or $30,000, whichever is less. If the plan is a profit sharing plan, the percentage is 13.043 percent.

Self-employment tax.   In 1998, a tax of 12.4 percent is levied on individuals with net earnings from self-employment (up to $68,400) to provide Social Security benefits (i.e., the old age, survivors, and disability insurance portion) for such individuals. In addition, in 1998, a tax of 2.9 percent is levied on individuals with net earnings from self-employment (with no statutory ceiling) to provide Medicare benefits (i.e., the hospital insurance portion) for such individuals. If a self-employed individual also receives wages from an employer that are subject to FICA, the self-employment tax will be reduced if total income subject to Social Security is more than $68,400. A partial deduction is allowed in calculating the self-employment tax. Individuals with net earnings of $400 or more from self-employment are subject to this tax. §§ 1401 and 1402.

Separate property.   In a community property jurisdiction, separate property is the property that belongs entirely to one of the spouses. Generally, it is property acquired before marriage or acquired after marriage by gift or inheritance. See also *community property*.

Severance tax.   A tax imposed upon the extraction of natural resources.

Short sale.   A short sale occurs when a taxpayer sells borrowed property (usually stock) and repays the lender with substantially identical property either held on the date of the short sale or purchased after the sale. No gain or loss is recognized until the short sale is closed, and such gain or loss is generally short term. § 1233.

Short taxable year (short period).   A tax year that is less than 12 months. A short taxable year may occur in the initial reporting period, in the final tax year, or when the taxpayer changes tax years.

Significant participation activity.   There are seven tests to determine whether an individual has achieved material participation in an activity, one of which is based on more than 500 hours of participation in significant participation activities. A significant participation activity is one in which the individual's participation exceeds 100 hours during the year.

Simplified employee pension (SEP) plan.   An employer may make contributions to an employee's IRA in amounts not exceeding the lesser of 15 percent of compensation or $30,000 per individual. These employer-sponsored simplified employee pensions are permitted only if the contributions are nondiscriminatory and are made on behalf of all employees who have attained age 21 and have worked for the employer during at least three of the five preceding calendar years. § 219(b). See also *individual retirement account (IRA)*.

Small business corporation.　A corporation that satisfies the definition of § 1361(b), § 1244(c)(3), or both. Satisfaction of § 1361(b) permits an S corporation election, and satisfaction of § 1244 enables the shareholders of the corporation to claim an ordinary loss. See also *S corporation status* and *Section 1244 stock*.

Small business stock.　See *small business corporation*.

Small cases division.　A subsidiary division of the U.S. Tax Court. The jurisdiction of the Small Cases division is limited to small claims (i.e., claims of $10,000 or less). The proceedings of the Small Cases Division are informal, and the findings cannot be appealed.

Specific charge-off method.　A method of accounting for bad debts in which a deduction is permitted only when an account becomes partially or completely worthless. See also *reserve for bad debts*.

Standard deduction.　The individual taxpayer can either itemize deductions or take the standard deduction. The amount of the standard deduction depends on the taxpayer's filing status (single, head of household, married filing jointly, surviving spouse, or married filing separately). For 1998, the amount of the standard deduction ranges from $3,550 to $7,100. Additional standard deductions of either $850 (for married taxpayers) or $1,050 (for single taxpayers) are available if the taxpayer is either blind or age 65 or over. Limitations exist on the amount of the standard deduction of a taxpayer who is another taxpayer's dependent. Beginning in 1989, the standard deduction amounts are adjusted for inflation each year. § 63(c). See also *zero bracket amount*.

Statute of limitations.　Provisions of the law that specify the maximum period of time in which action may be taken on a past event. Code §§ 6501–6504 contain the limitation periods applicable to the IRS for additional assessments, and §§ 6511–6515 relate to refund claims by taxpayers.

Statutory employee.　Statutory employees are considered self-employed independent contractors for purposes of reporting income and expenses on their tax returns. Generally, a statutory employee must meet three tests:
• It is understood from a service contract that the services will be performed by the person.
• The person does not have a substantial investment in facilities (other than transportation used to perform the services.
• The services involve a continuing relationship with the person from whom they are performed.
　For further information on statutory employees, see Circular E *Employer's Tax Guide* (IRS Publication 15).

Statutory notice of deficiency.　Commonly referred to as the 90-day letter, this notice is sent to a taxpayer upon request, upon the expiration of the 30-day letter, or upon exhaustion by the taxpayer of his or her administrative remedies before the IRS. The notice gives the taxpayer 90 days in which to file a petition with the U.S. Tax Court. If a petition is not filed, the IRS will issue a demand for payment of the assessed deficiency. §§ 6211–6216. See also *thirty-day letter*.

Stock bonus plan.　A type of deferred compensation plan in which the employer establishes and maintains the plan and contributes employer stock to the plan for the benefit of employees. The contributions need not be dependent on the employer's profits. Any benefits of the plan are distributable in the form of employer stock, except that distributable fractional shares may be paid in cash.

Stock option.　The right to purchase a stated number of shares of stock from a corporation at a certain price within a specified period of time. §§ 421 and 422. See also *incentive stock option (ISO)* and *nonqualified stock option (NQSO)*.

Stock redemption.　The redemption of the stock of a shareholder by the issuing corporation is treated as a sale or exchange of the stock if the redemption is not a dividend. §§ 301 and 302.

Substantial risk of forfeiture.　A term that is associated with a restricted property plan. Generally, an employee who receives property (e.g., stock of the employer-corporation) from the employer at a bargain price or at no cost must include the bargain element in gross income. However, the employee currently does not have to do so if there is a substantial risk of forfeiture. A substantial risk of forfeiture exists if a person's rights to full enjoyment of property are conditioned upon the future performance, or the refraining from the performance, of substantial services by the individual. § 83. See also *restricted property plan*.

Super-full absorption costing rules.　See *uniform capitalization rules*.

Surviving spouse.　The joint return tax rates apply for a surviving spouse. Such rates apply for the two tax years after the tax year of the death of the spouse. To qualify as a surviving spouse, the taxpayer must maintain a household for a dependent child. § 2.

T

Targeted jobs tax credit.　See *work opportunity tax credit*.

Taxable year.　The annual period over which income is measured for income tax purposes. Most individuals use a calendar year, but many businesses use a fiscal year based on the natural business year. See also *accounting period* and *fiscal year*.

Tax avoidance.　The minimization of one's tax liability by taking advantage of legally available tax planning opportunities. Tax avoidance can be contrasted with tax evasion, which entails the reduction of tax liability by illegal means.

Tax benefit rule. A provision that limits the recognition of income from the recovery of an expense or loss properly deducted in a prior tax year to the amount of the deduction that generated a tax benefit. § 111.

Tax Court. The U.S. Tax Court is one of three trial courts of original jurisdiction that decide litigation involving Federal income, estate, or gift taxes. It is the only trial court where the taxpayer need not first pay the deficiency assessed by the IRS. The Tax Court will not have jurisdiction over a case unless the statutory notice of deficiency (90-day letter) has been issued by the IRS and the taxpayer files the petition for hearing within the time prescribed.

Tax credits. Tax credits are amounts that directly reduce a taxpayer's tax liability. The tax benefit received from a tax credit is not dependent on the taxpayer's marginal tax rate, whereas the benefit of a tax deduction or exclusion is dependent on the taxpayer's tax bracket.

Tax credit for the elderly or disabled. An elderly (age 65 and over) or disabled taxpayer may receive a tax credit amounting to 15 percent of $5,000 ($7,500 for qualified married individuals filing jointly). This amount is reduced by Social Security benefits, excluded pension benefits, and one-half of the taxpayer's adjusted gross income in excess of $7,500 ($10,000 for married taxpayers filing jointly). § 22.

Tax-free exchange. Transfers of property specifically exempted from Federal income tax consequences. Examples are a transfer of property to a controlled corporation under § 351(a) and a like-kind exchange under § 1031(a). The recognition of gain or loss is postponed, rather than being permanently excluded, through the assignment of a carryover basis to the replacement property. See also *nontaxable exchange.*

Tax home. Since travel expenses of an employee are deductible only if the taxpayer is away from home, the deductibility of such expenses rests upon the definition of tax home. The IRS position is that tax home is the business location, post, or station of the taxpayer. If an employee is temporarily reassigned to a new post for a period of one year or less, the taxpayer's home should be his or her personal residence, and the travel expenses should be deductible. If the assignment is for more than two years, the IRS position is that it is indefinite or permanent and the taxpayer is therefore not in travel status. If the assignment is for between one and two years, the IRS position is that the location of the tax home will be determined on the basis of the facts and circumstances. The courts are in conflict regarding what constitutes a person's home for tax purposes. For such costs paid or incurred after December 31, 1992, the Energy Policy Act of 1992 provides that the taxpayer shall not be treated as temporarily away from home if the employment period exceeds one year. Thus, in this situation, the tax home will be the place of employment. See also *travel expenses.*

Tax preferences. Those items set forth in § 57 that may result in the imposition of the alternative minimum tax. See also *alternative minimum tax (AMT).*

Tax rate schedules. Rate schedules appearing in Appendix A that are used by upper-income taxpayers and those not permitted to use the tax table. Separate rate schedules are provided for married individuals filing jointly, head of household, single taxpayers, estates and trusts, and married individuals filing separate returns. § 1.

Tax research. The method used to determine the best available solution to a situation that possesses tax consequences. Both tax and nontax factors are considered.

Tax shelters. The typical tax shelter generated large losses in the early years of the activity. Investors would offset these losses against other types of income and, therefore, avoid paying income taxes on this income. These tax shelter investments could then be sold after a few years and produce capital gain income, which is taxed at a lower rate than ordinary income. The passive activity loss rules and the at-risk rules now limit tax shelter deductions.

Tax table. A tax table appearing in Appendix A that is provided for taxpayers with less than $100,000 of taxable income. Separate columns are provided for single taxpayers, married taxpayers filing jointly, head of household, and married taxpayers filing separately. § 3.

Technical advice memoranda (TAMs). TAMs are issued by the National Office of the IRS in response to questions raised by IRS field personnel during audits. They deal with completed rather than proposed transactions and are often requested for questions related to exempt organizations and employee plans.

Temporary Regulation. A Regulation issued by the Treasury Department in temporary form. When speed is critical, the Treasury Department issues Temporary Regulations, which take effect immediately. These Regulations have the same authoritative value as final Regulations and may be cited as precedent for three years. Temporary Regulations are also issued as Proposed Regulations. See also *proposed regulation* and *regulations.*

Theft loss. A loss from larceny, embezzlement, and robbery. It does not include misplacement of items. See also *casualty loss.*

Thin capitalization. When debt owed by a corporation to its shareholders is large relative to its capital structure (stock and shareholder equity), the IRS may contend that the corporation is thinly capitalized. In effect, this means that some or all of the debt will be reclassified as equity. The immediate result is to disallow any interest deduction to the corporation on the reclassified debt. To the extent of the corporation's earnings and profits, interest payments and loan repayments on the reclassified debt are treated as dividends to the shareholders. § 385.

Thirty-day letter. A letter that accompanies a Revenue Agent's Report (RAR) issued as a result of an IRS audit of a taxpayer (or the rejection of a taxpayer's claim for refund). The letter outlines the taxpayer's appeal procedure before the IRS. If the taxpayer does not request any such procedures within the 30-day period, the IRS will issue a *statutory notice of deficiency* (the 90-day letter).

Timber. Special rules apply to the recognition of gain from the sale of timber. A taxpayer may elect to treat the cutting of timber that is held for sale or use in a trade or business as a sale or exchange. If the holding period requirements are met, the gain is recognized as § 1231 gain and may therefore receive long-term capital gain treatment. § 631.

Top-heavy plan. A type of retirement plan that primarily benefits key employees. Such plans allocate more than 60 percent of the cumulative benefits to key employees. Special rules are imposed to discourage retirement plans from conferring disproportionate benefits on key employees.

Trade or business expenses. Deductions *for* AGI that are attributable to a taxpayer's business or profession. Some employee expenses may also be treated as trade or business expenses. See also *employee expenses*.

Transportation expenses. Transportation expenses for an employee include only the cost of transportation (taxi fares, automobile expenses, etc.) in the course of employment when the employee is not away from home in travel status. Commuting expenses are not deductible. See also *automobile expenses*.

Travel expenses. Travel expenses include meals (generally subject to a 50 percent disallowance) and lodging and transportation expenses while away from home in the pursuit of a trade or business (including that of an employee). See also *tax home*.

Trial court. The court of original jurisdiction; the first court to consider litigation. In Federal tax controversies, trial courts include U.S. District Courts, the U.S. Tax Court, and the U.S. Court of Federal Claims. See also *appellate court*.

U

Unearned income. Also referred to as investment income, it includes such income as interest, dividends, capital gains, rents, royalties, and pension and annuity income. See also *kiddie tax*.

Unearned (prepaid) income. For tax purposes, prepaid income (e.g., rent) is taxable in the year of receipt. In certain cases involving advance payments for goods and services, income may be deferred. See Rev.Proc. 71–21 (1971–2 C.B. 549) and Reg. § 1.451–5. See also *accrual method*.

Uniform capitalization rules. Under § 263A, the Regulations provide a set of rules that all taxpayers (regardless of the particular industry) can use to determine the items of cost (and means of allocating those costs) that must be capitalized with respect to the production of tangible property.

Unreasonable compensation. Under § 162(a)(1), a deduction is allowed for "reasonable" salaries or other compensation for personal services actually rendered. To the extent compensation is excessive ("unreasonable"), no deduction will be allowed. The problem of unreasonable compensation usually is limited to closely held corporations where the motivation is to pay out profits in some form deductible to the corporation. Deductible compensation, therefore, becomes an attractive substitute for nondeductible dividends when the shareholders are also employees of the corporation.

Unrecaptured § 1250 gain (25 percent gain). Gain from the sale of depreciable real estate held more than 18 months. The gain is equal to or less than the depreciation taken on such property and is reduced by § 1245 gain and § 1250 gain.

U.S. Court of Federal Claims. See *Claims Court*.

Use tax. A use tax is an ad valorem tax, usually at the same rate as the sales tax, on the use or consumption of tangible personalty. The purpose of a use tax is to prevent the avoidance of a sales tax.

U.S. Supreme Court. The highest appellate court or the court of last resort in the Federal court system and in most states. Only a small number of tax decisions of the U.S. Courts of Appeal are reviewed by the U.S. Supreme Court under its certiorari procedure. The Supreme Court usually grants certiorari to resolve a conflict among the Courts of Appeal (e.g., two or more appellate courts have assumed opposing positions on a particular issue) or when the tax issue is extremely important (e.g., size of the revenue loss to the Federal government).

U.S. Tax Court. See *Tax Court*.

USTC. Published by Commerce Clearing House, *U.S. Tax Cases* contain all of the Federal tax decisions issued by the U.S. District Courts, U.S. Court of Federal Claims, U.S. Courts of Appeals, and the U.S. Supreme Court.

V

Vacation home. The Code places restrictions upon taxpayers who rent their residences or vacation homes for part of the tax year. The restrictions may result in a scaling down of expense deductions for the taxpayers. § 280A. See also *hobby loss*.

Value added tax (VAT). A national sales tax that taxes the increment in value as goods move through the production process. A VAT is much used in other countries, but has not yet been incorporated as part of the U.S. Federal tax structure.

Vesting requirements. A qualified deferred compensation arrangement must satisfy a vesting requirement. Under this provision, an employee's right to accrued plan benefits derived from employer contributions must be nonforfeitable in accordance with one of two vesting time period schedules.

W

Wash sale. A loss from the sale of stock or securities that is disallowed because the taxpayer within 30 days before or after the sale has acquired stock or securities that are substantially identical to those sold. § 1091.

Welfare-to-work credit.   A tax credit available to employers hiring individuals who have been long-term recipients of family assistance welfare benefits. In general, long-term recipients are those individuals who are certified by a designated local agency as being members of a family receiving assistance under a public aid program for at least an 18-month period ending on the hiring date. The welfare-to-work credit is available for qualified wages paid in the first two years of employment. The maximum credit is equal to $8,500 per qualified employee, computed as 35 percent of the first $10,000 of qualified wages paid in the first year of employment, plus 50 percent of the first $10,000 of qualified wages paid in the second year of employment. § 51A. See also *general business credit*.

Wherewithal to pay.   This concept recognizes the inequity of taxing a transaction when the taxpayer lacks the means with which to pay the tax. Under it, there is a correlation between the imposition of the tax and the ability to pay the tax. It is particularly suited to situations in which the taxpayer's economic position has not changed significantly as a result of the transaction.

Withholding allowances.   The number of withholding allowances serves as the basis for determining the amount of income taxes withheld from an employee's salary or wages. The more withholding allowances claimed, the less income tax withheld by an employer. An employee may claim withholding allowances for personal exemptions for self and spouse (unless claimed as a dependent of another person), dependency exemptions, and special withholding allowances.

Working condition fringe.   A type of fringe benefit received by the employee that is excludible from the employee's gross income. It consists of property or services provided (paid or reimbursed) by the employer for which the employee could take a tax deduction if the employee had paid for them. § 132.

Work opportunity tax credit.   Employers are allowed a tax credit equal to 40 percent of the first $6,000 of wages (per eligible employee) for the first year of employment. Eligible employees include certain hard-to-employ individuals (e.g., qualified ex-felons, high-risk youth, food stamp recipients, and veterans). For an employer to qualify for the 40 percent credit, the employees must (1) be certified by a designated local agency as being members of one of the targeted groups and (2) have completed at least 400 hours of service to the employer. For employees who meet the first condition but not the second, the credit rate is reduced to 25 percent provided the employees meet a minimum employment level of 120 hours of service to the employer. The employer's deduction for wages is reduced by the amount of the credit taken. For qualified summer youth employees, the 40 percent rate is applied to the first $3,000 of qualified wages. §§ 51 and 52.

Worthless securities.   A loss (usually capital) is allowed for a security that becomes worthless during the year. The loss is deemed to have occurred on the last day of the year. Special rules apply to securities of affiliated companies and small business stock. § 165. See also *Section 1244 stock*.

Writ of certiorari.   See *certiorari*.

Z

Zero bracket amount.   A deduction that was generally available to all individual taxpayers in arriving at taxable income. It represented the equivalent of the standard deduction for taxable years before 1987. The taxpayer did not take a deduction for the zero bracket amount because it was built into the tax tables and tax rate schedules. Because the amount was built in, if the taxpayer itemized deductions, only the excess itemized deductions (amount of the itemized deductions in excess of the zero bracket amount) were deductible. TRA of 1986 repealed the zero bracket amount and replaced it with the standard deduction for 1987 and thereafter. The zero bracket amount for 1986 is currently used in the 10-year forward averaging calculation for lump-sum distributions. § 63(c). See also *standard deduction*.

APPENDIX D-1
Table of Code Sections Cited

APPENDIX D–2
Table of Regulations Cited

Appendix D–3
Table of Revenue Procedures and Revenue Rulings Cited

APPENDIX E
Citator Example

▼ ILLUSTRATION OF THE USE OF THE CITATOR

BACKGROUND

The *RIA Citator* is a separate multivolume service with monthly supplements.[1] Cases reported by the *Citator* are divided into the various issues involved. Since the researcher may be interested in only one or two issues, only those cases involving the particular issue need to be checked.

The *Citator* includes the following volumes, each of which covers a particular period of time:

- Volume 1 (1863–1941)
- Volume 2 (1942–1948)
- Volume 3 (1948–1954)
- Volume 1, Second Series (1954–1977)
- Volume 2, Second Series (1978–1989)
- Volume 3, Second Series (1990–1996)
- Annual and monthly cumulative supplements (paperback)

Through the use of symbols, the *Citator* indicates whether a decision has been followed, explained, criticized, questioned, or overruled by a later court decision. These symbols are reproduced in Figure E–1.

EXAMPLE

Determine the background and validity of *Adda v. Comm.*, 37 AFTR 654, 171 F.2d 457 (CA–4, 1948).

SOLUTION

Turning directly to the case itself (reproduced as Figure E–2), note the two issues involved (issues 1 and 2). For purposes of emphasis, these issues have been bracketed and identified by a marginal notation in the figure. The reason for the division of the issues becomes apparent when the case is traced through the *Citator*.

Refer to Volume 3 of the First Series (covering the period from October 7, 1948, through July 29, 1954) of the *Citator*. The case reference is located on page 5505, which is reproduced in Figure E–3.

Correlating the symbols in Figure E–1 with the shaded portion of Figure E–3 reveals the following information about *Adda v. Comm.*:

- Application for certiorari (appeal to the U.S. Supreme Court) filed by the taxpayer (T) on March 1, 1949.

---

[1]Features in the *RIA Citator* that do not appear in the CCH *Citator* include the following: (1) distinguishes between the various issues in the case, (2) lists all court decisions that cite the court decision being researched, (3) indicates the relationship (e.g., explained, criticized, followed, or overruled) between the court decision being researched and subsequent decisions, and (4) pinpoints the exact page on which one court decision is cited by another court decision. Prior to the acquisition of Prentice-Hall Information Services, the *Federal Tax Citator* was published by Prentice-Hall. The *Citator 2nd Series* is now published by Research Institute of America.

▼ **FIGURE E–1**

Citator Symbols*
COURT DECISIONS
Judicial History of the Case

a	affirmed (by decision of a higher court)
d	dismissed (appeal to a higher court dismissed)
m	modified (decision modified by a higher court, or on rehearing)
r	reversed (by a decision of a higher court)
s	same case (e.g., on rehearing)
rc	related case (companion cases and other cases arising out of the same subject matter are so designated)
x	certiorari denied (by the Supreme Court of the United States)
(C or G)	The Commissioner or Solicitor General has made the appeal
(T)	Taxpayer has made the appeal
(A)	decision acquiesced in by Commissioner
(NA)	decision nonacquiesced in by Commissioner
sa	same case affirmed (by the cited case)
sd	same case dismissed (by the cited case)
sm	same case modified (by the cited case)
sr	same case reversed (by the cited case)
sx	same case—certiorari denied

Syllabus of the Cited Case

iv	four (on all fours with the cited case)
f	followed (the cited case followed)
e	explained (comment generally favorable, but not to a degree that indicates the cited case is followed)
k	reconciled (the cited case reconciled)
n	dissenting opinion (cited in a dissenting opinion)
g	distinguished (the cited case distinguished either in law or on the facts)
l	limited (the cited case limited to its facts. Used when an appellate court so limits a prior decision, or a lower court states that in its opinion the cited case should be so limited)
c	criticized (adverse comment on the cited case)
q	questioned (the cited case not only criticized, but its correctness questioned)
o	overruled

*Reproduced from the *Citator 2nd Series* with the permission of the publisher, Research Institute of America, New York, NY 10011.

- Certiorari was denied (x) by the U.S. Supreme Court on April 18, 1949.
- The trial court decision is reported in 10 T.C. 273 and was affirmed on appeal (sa) to the Fourth Court of Appeals.
- During the time frame of Volume 3 of the *Citator* (October 7, 1948, through July 29, 1954), one decision (*Milner Hotels, Inc.*) has agreed "on all fours with the cited case" (iv). One decision (*Comm. v. Nubar*) has cited the first issue in *Adda* without comment and two decisions (*The Scottish American Investment Co., Ltd.* and *Zareh Nubar*) have distinguished the cited case on issue number one (g–1).

▼ **FIGURE E–2**

ADDA v. COMMISSIONER OF INTERNAL REVENUE   457
Cite as 171 F.2d 457

ADDA v. COMMISSIONER OF INTERNAL REVENUE.
No. 5796.

United States Court of Appeals
Fourth Circuit.
Dec. 3, 1948.

ISSUE 1

1. Internal revenue ⚖️792

Where nonresident alien's brother residing in United States traded for alien's benefit on commodity exchanges in United States at authorization of alien, who vested full discretion in brother with regard thereto, and many transactions were effected through different brokers, several accounts were maintained, and substantial gains and losses realized, transactions constituted a "trade or business," profits of which were "capital gains" taxable as income to the alien. 26 U.S.C.A. § 211(b).

See Words and Phrases, Permanent Edition, for other judicial constructions and definitions of "Capital Gains" and "Trade or Business".

ISSUE 2

2. Internal revenue ⚖️792

The exemption of a nonresident alien's commodity transactions in the United States provided for by the Internal Revenue Code does not apply where alien has agent in United States using his own discretion in effecting transactions for alien's account. 26 U.S.C.A. § 211(b).

———•———

On Petition to Review the Decision of The Tax Court of the United States.

Petition by Fernand C. A. Adda to review a decision of the Tax Court redetermining a deficiency in income tax imposed by the Commissioner of Internal Revenue.

Decision affirmed.

Rollin Browne and Mitchell B. Carroll, both of New York City, for petitioner.

Irving I. Axelrad, Sp. Asst. to Atty. Gen. (Theron Lamar Caudle, Asst. Atty. Gen., and Ellis N. Slack and A. F. Prescott, Sp. Assts. to Atty. Gen., on the brief), for respondent.

Before PARKER, Chief Judge, and SOPER and DOBIE, Circuit Judges.

PER CURIAM.

[1, 2] This is a petition by a non-resident alien to review a decision of the Tax Court. Petitioner is a national of Egypt, who in the year 1941 was residing in France. He had a brother who at that time was residing in the United States and who traded for petitioner's benefit on commodity exchanges in the United States in cotton, wool, grains, silk, hides and copper. This trading was authorized by petitioner who vested full discretion in his brother with regard thereto, and it resulted in profits in the sum of $193,857.14. The Tax Court said: "While the number of transactions or the total amount of money involved in them has not been stated, it is apparent that many transactions were effected through different brokers, several accounts were maintained, and gains and losses in substantial amounts were realized. This evidence shows that the trading was extensive enough to amount to a trade or business, and the petitioner does not contend, nor has he shown, that the transactions were so infrequent or inconsequential as not to amount to a trade or business." We agree with the Tax Court that, for reasons adequately set forth in its opinion, this income was subject to taxation, and that the exemption of a non-resident alien's commodity transactions in the United States, provided by section 211(b) of the Internal Revenue Code, 26 U.S.C.A. § 211(b), does not apply to a case where the alien has an agent in the United States using his own discretion in effecting the transactions for the alien's account. As said by the Tax Court, "Through such transactions the alien is engaging in trade or business within the United States, and the profits on these transactions are capital gains taxable to him." Nothing need be added to the reasoning of the Tax Court in this connection, and the decision will be affirmed on its opinion.

Affirmed.

Reference to Volume 1 of the *Citator 2nd Series* (covering the period from 1954 through 1977) shows the *Adda v. Comm.* case on page 25, which is reproduced in Figure E–4.

Correlating the symbols in Figure E–1 with the shaded portion of Figure E–4 reveals the following additional information about *Adda v. Comm.*:

- The case was cited without comment in two rulings and two cases: Rev.Rul. 56–145, Rev.Rul. 56–392, *Balanovski*, and *Liang*.
- It was followed in *Asthmanefrin Co.* (f–1).
- It was distinguished in *de Vegvar* and *Purvis* (g–1).
- It was reconciled in *deKrause* (k–1).

▼ **FIGURE E–3**

» Adamson — Adler «   5505

ADAMSON, JAMES H. & MARION C. v
U. S., — F Supp —, 36 AFTR 1529, 1946
P.-H. ¶ 72,418 (DC Calif) (See Adamson
v U. S.)
ADAMSON, R. R., MRS., — BTA —, 1934 (P.-
H.) BTA Memo. Dec. ¶ 34,370
ADAMSON v U. S., 26 AFTR 1188 (DC Calif,
Sept 8, 1939)
  iv—Coggan, Linus C., 1939 (P.-H.) BTA
  Memo. Dec. page 39—806
ADAMSON; U. S. v, 161 F(2d) 942, 35 AFTR
1404 (CCA 9)
  1—Lazier v U. S., 170 F(2d) 524, 37 AFTR
  545, 1948 P.-H. page 73,174 (CCA 8)
  1—Grace Bros., Inc. v Comm., 173 F(2d)
  178, 37 AFTR 1014, 1949 P.-H. page 72,433
  (CCA 9)
  1—Briggs; Hofferbert v, 178 F(2d) 744, 38
  AFTR 1219, 1950 P.-H. page 72,267 (CCA
  4)
  1—Rogers v Comm., 180 F(2d) 722, 39 AFTR
  115, 1950 P.-H. page 72,531 (CCA 3)
  1—Lamar v Granger, 99 F Supp 41, 40
  AFTR 270, 1951 P.-H. page 72,945 (DC Pa)
  1—Herbert v Riddell, 103 F Supp 383, 41
  AFTR 975, 1952 P.-H. page 72,383 (DC
  Calif)
  1—Hudson, Galvin, 20 TC 737, 20-1953
  P.-H. TC 418
ADAMSON v U. S., — F Supp —, 36 AFTR
1529, 1946 P.-H. ¶ 72,418 (DC Calif, Jan
28, 1946)
ADAMS-ROTH BAKING CO., 8 BTA 458
  1—Gunderson Bros. Engineering Corp., 16
  TC 129, 16-1951 P.-H. TC 72
ADAMSTON FLAT GLASS CO. v COMM.,
162 F(2d) 875, 35 AFTR 1579 (CCA 6)
  4—Forrest Hotel Corp. v. Fly, 112 F Supp
  789, 43 AFTR 1080, 1953 P.-H. page 72,856
  (DC Miss)
ADDA v COMM., 171 F(2d) 457, 37 AFTR 654,
1948 P.-H. ¶ 72,655 (CCA 4, Dec 3, 1948)
Cert. filed, March 1, 1949 (T)
No cert. (G) 1949 P-H ¶ 71,050
  x—Adda v Comm., 336 US 952, 69 S Ct 883,
  93 L Ed 1107, April 18, 1949 (T)
  sa—Adda, Fernand C. A., 10 TC 273 (No.
  33), ¶ 10.33 P.-H. TC 1948
  iv—Milner Hotels, Inc., N. Y., 173 F (2d)
  567, 37 AFTR 1170, 1949 P.-H. page 72,528
  (CCA 6)
  1—Nubar; Comm. v, 185 F(2d) 588, 39 AFTR
  1315, 1950 P.-H. page 73,423 (CCA 4)
  g-1—Scottish Amer. Invest. Co., Ltd.,
  The, 12 TC 59, 12-1949 P.-H. TC 32
  g-1—Nubar, Zareh, 13 TC 579, 13-1949
  P.-H. TC 318
ADDA, FERNAND C. A., 10 TC 273 (No.
33), ¶ 10.33 P.-H. TC 1948 (A) 1948-2 CB 1
  a—Adda v Comm., 171 F(2d) 457, 37 AFTR
  654, 1948 P.-H. ¶ 72,655 (CCA 4)
  1—Nubar; Comm. v, 185 F(2d) 588, 39 AFTR
  1315, 1950 P.-H. page 73,423 (CCA 4)
  g-1—Scottish Amer. Invest. Co., Ltd.,
  The, 12 TC 59, 12-1949 P.-H. TC 32
  g-1—Nubar, Zareh, 13 TC 579, 13-1949
  P.-H. TC 318
ADDA, FERNAND C. A., 10 TC 1291 (No.
168), ¶ 10.168 P.-H. TC 1948 (A) 1953-1
CB 3, 1953 P.-H. ¶ 76,453 (NA) 1948-2
CB 5, 1948 P.-H. ¶ 76,434 withdrawn
  1—Scottish Amer. Invest. Co., Ltd., The,
  12 TC 59, 12-1949 P.-H. TC 32
ADDA INC., 9 TC 199 (A) 1949-1 CB 1, 1949
P.-H. ¶ 76,260 (NA) 1947-2 CB 6 withdrawn
  a—Adda, Inc.; Comm. v, 171 F(2d) 367, 37
  AFTR 641, 1948 P.-H. ¶ 72,654 (CCA 2)
  a—Adda, Inc.; Comm. v, 171 F(2d) 367, 37
  AFTR 641, 1949 P.-H. ¶ 72,303 (CCA 2)
  e-1—G.C.M. 26069, 1949-2 CB 38, 1949 P.-H.
  page 76,226
  3—Koshland, Execx.; U.S. v, 208 F(2d)
  640, — AFTR —, 1953 P.-H. page 73,597
  (CCA 5)
  4—Kent, Otis Beall, 1954 (P. H.) TC
  Memo. Dec. page 54—47

ADDA, INC.; COMM. v, 171 F(2d) 367, 37
AFTR 641, 1948 P.-H. ¶ 72,654 (CCA 2, Dec
6, 1948)
  sa—Adda, Inc., 9 TC 199
  s—Adda, Inc.; Comm. v, 171 F(2d) 367, 37
  AFTR 641, 1949 P.-H. ¶ 72,303 (CCA 2) reh.
  den.
  e-1—G.C.M. 26069, 1949-2 CB 39, 1949 P.-H.
  page 76,227
  e-2—G.C.M. 26069, 1949-2 CB 39, 1949 P.-H.
  page 76,227
ADDA, INC.; COMM. v, 171 F(2d) 367, 37
AFTR 641, 1949 P.-H. ¶ 72,303 (CCA 2, Dec
6, 1948) reh. den.
  sa—Adda, Inc., 9 TC 199
  s—Adda, Inc.; Comm. v, 171 F(2d) 367, 37
  AFTR 641, 1948 P.-H. ¶ 72,654 (CCA 2)
ADDISON-CHEVROLET SALES, INC. v
CHAMBERLAIN, L. A. & NAT. BANK
OF WASH., THE, — F Supp —, — AFTR
—, 1954 P.-H. ¶ 72,550 (DC DC) (See
Campbell v Chamberlain)
ADDISON v COMM., 177 F(2d) 521, 38 AFTR
821, 1949 P.-H. ¶ 72,637 (CCA 8, Nov 3,
1949)
  sa—Addison, Irene D., — TC —, 1948
  (P.-H.) TC Memo. Dec. ¶ 48,177
  1—Roberts, Supt. v U. S., 115 Ct Cl 439,
  87 F Supp 937, 38 AFTR 1314, 1950 P.-H.
  page 72,292
  1—Cold Metal Process Co., The, 17 TC
  934, 17-1951 P.-H. TC 512
  1—Berger, Samuel & Lillian, 1954 (P.-H.)
  TC Memo. Dec. page 54—232
  2—Urquhart, George Gordon & Mary F.,
  20 TC 948, 20-1953 P.-H. TC 536
ADDISON, IRENE D., — TC —, 1948 (P.-
H.) TC Memo. Dec. ¶ 48,177
  App (T) Jan 14, 1949 (CCA 8)
  a—Addison v Comm., 177 F(2d) 521, 38
  AFTR 821, 1949 P.-H. ¶ 72,637 (CCA 8)
  1—Urquhart, George Gordon & Mary F.,
  20 TC 948, 20-1953 P.-H. TC 536
ADDITON, HARRY L. & ANNIE S., 3
TC 427
  1—Lum, Ralph E., 12 TC 379, 12-1949 P.-H.
  TC 204
  1—Christie, John A. & Elizabeth H., —
  TC —, 1949 (P.-H.) TC Memo. Dec.
  page 49—795
ADDRESSOGRAPH - MULTIGRAPH
CORP., 1945 (P.-H.) TC Memo. Dec.
¶ 45,058
  f-10—Rev. Rul. 54-71, 1954 P.-H. page
  76,453
ADDRESSOGRAPH-MULTIGRAPH CORP.
v U. S., 112 Ct Cl 201, 78 F Supp 111, 37
AFTR 53, 1948 P.-H. ¶ 72,504 (June 1, 1948)
No cert (G) 1949 P.-H. ¶ 71,041
  1—New Oakmont Corp., The v U. S., 114
  Ct Cl 686, 86 F Supp 901, 38 AFTR 924, 1949
  P.-H. page 73,181
ADELAIDE PARK LAND, 25 BTA 211
  g—Amer. Security & Fidelity Corp., — BTA
  —, 1940 (P.-H.) BTA Memo. Dec. page
  40—571
ADELPHI PAINT & COLOR WORKS,
INC., 18 BTA 436
  1—Neracher, William A., — BTA —, 1939
  (P.-H.) BTA Memo. Dec. page 39—69
  1—Lyman-Hawkins Lumber Co., — BTA —,
  1939 (P.-H.) BTA Memo. Dec. page 39—350
ADEMAN v U. S., 174 F(2d) 283, 37 AFTR
1406 (CCA 9, April 25, 1949)
ADICONIS, NOELLA L. (PATNAUDE),
1953 (P.-H.) TC Memo. Dec. ¶ 53,305
ADJUSTMENT BUREAU OF ST. LOUIS
ASSN., OF CREDIT MEN, 21 BTA 232
  1—Cook County Loss Adjustment Bureau,
  — BTA —, 1940 (P.-H.) BTA Memo. Dec.
  page 40—331
ADKINS, CHARLES I., — BTA —, 1933
(P.-H.) BTA Memo. Dec. ¶ 33,457
ADLER v COMM., 77 F(2d) 738, 16 AFTR 162
(CCA 5)
  g-2—McEuen v Comm., 196 F(2d) 130, 41
  AFTR 1172, 1952 P.-H. page 72,604 (CCA 5)

▼ **FIGURE E–4**

ADASKAVICH—ADELSON   25

ADASKAVICH, STEPHEN A. v U.S., 39 AFTR2d
77-517, 422 F Supp 276 (DC Mont) (See Wiegand,
Charles J., Jr. v U.S.)
AD. AURIEMA, INC., 1943 P-H TC Memo ¶ 43,422
  e-1—Miller v U.S., 13 AFTR2d 1515, 166 Ct Cl 257, 331
  F2d 859
ADAY v SUPERIOR CT. OF ALAMEDA COUNTY, 8
AFTR2d 5367, 13 Cal Reptr 415, 362 P2d 47 (Calif,
5-11-61)
ADCO SERVICE, INC., ASSIGNEE v CYBERMATICS,
INC., 36 AFTR2d 75-6342 (NJ) (See Adco Service,
Inc., Assignee v Graphic Color Plate)
ADCO SERVICE, INC., ASSIGNEE v GRAPHIC
COLOR PLATE, 36 AFTR2d 75-6342 (NJ, Supr Ct,
11-10-75)
ADCO SERVICE, INC., ASSIGNEE v GRAPHIC
COLOR PLATE, INC., 36 AFTR2d 75-6342 (NJ) (See
Adco Service, Inc., Assignee v Graphic Color Plate)
ADDA v COMM., 171 F2d 457, 37 AFTR 654 (USCA 4)
Rev. Rul. 56-145, 1956-1 CB 613
  1—Balanovski; U.S. v, 236 F2d 304, 49 AFTR 2013
  (USCA 2)
  1—Liang, Chang Hsiao, 23 TC 1045, 23-1955 P-H TC
  624
  f-1—Asthmanefrin Co., Inc., 25 TC 1141, 25-1956 P-H
  TC 639
  g-1—de Vegvar, Edward A. Neuman, 28 TC 1061,
  28-1957 P-H TC 599
  g-1—Purvis, Ralph E. & Patricia Lee, 1974 P-H TC
  Memo 74-669
  k-1—deKrause, Piedad Alvarado, 1974 P-H TC Memo
  74-1291
  1—Rev. Rul. 56-392, 1956-2 CB 971
ADDA, FERNAND C.A., 10 TC 273, ¶ 10,133 P-H TC
1948
  1—Balanovski; U.S. v, 236 F2d 303, 49 AFTR 2012
  (USCA 2)
  1—Liang, Chang Hsiao, 23 TC 1045, 23-1955 P-H TC
  624
  g-1—de Vegvar, Edward A. Neuman, 28 TC 1061,
  28-1957 P-H TC 599
  g-1—Purvis, Ralph E. & Patricia Lee, 1974 P-H TC
  Memo 74-669
  k-1—deKrause, Piedad Alvarado, 1974 P-H TC Memo
  74-1291
ADDA, INC., 9 TC 199
  Pardee, Marvin L., Est. of, 49 TC 152, 49 P-H TC 107
  [See 9 TC 206-208]
  f-1—Asthmanefrin Co., Inc., 25 TC 1141, 25-1956 P-H
  TC 639
  1—Keil Properties, Inc. (Dela), 24 TC 1117, 24-1955 P-H
  TC 615
  1—Saffan, Samuel, 1957 P-H TC Memo 57—701
  1—Rev. Rul. 56-145, 1956-1 CB 613
  1—Rev. Rul. 56-392, 1956-2 CB 971
  4— Midler Court Realty, Inc., 61 TC 597, 61 P-H TC
  368
ADDA, INC.; COMM. v, 171 F2d 367, 37 AFTR 641
(USCA 2)
  1—Pardee, Marvin L., Est. of, 49 TC 152, 49 P-H TC
  107
  1—Saffan, Samuel, 1957 P-H TC Memo 57-701
  2—Midler Court Realty, Inc., 61 TC 597, 61 P-H TC
  368
ADDELSTON, ALBERT A. & SARAH M., 1965 P-H TC
Memo ¶ 65,215
ADDISON v COMM., 177 F2d 521, 38 AFTR 821 (USCA
8)
  g-1—Industrial Aggregate Co. v U.S., 6 AFTR2d 5963,
  284 F2d 645 (USCA 8)
  1—Sturgeon v McMahon, 155 F Supp 630, 52 AFTR
  789 (DC NY)
  1—Gilmore v U.S., 16 AFTR2d 5211, 5213, 245 F Supp
  384, 386 (DC Calif)
  1—Waldheim & Co., Inc., 25 TC 599, 25-1955 P-H TC
  332
  g-1—Galewitz, Samuel & Marian, 50 TC 113, 50 P-H TC
  79
  1—Buder, G. A., Est. of, 1963 P-H TC Memo 63-345
  e-1—Rhodes, Lynn E. & Martha E., 1963 P-H TC
  Memo 63-1374
  2—Shipp v Comm., 217 F2d 402, 46 AFTR 1170 (USCA
  9)

ADDISON—Contd.
  g-2—Industrial Aggregate Co. v U.S., 6 AFTR2d 5964,
  284 F2d 645 (USCA 8)
  e-2—Buder, Est. of v Comm., 13 AFTR2d 1238, 330
  F2d 443 (USCA 8)
  2—Iowa Southern Utilities Co. v Comm., 14 AFTR2d
  5063, 333 F2d 385 (USCA 8)
  2—Kelly, Daniel, S.W., 23 TC 687, 23-1955 P-H TC 422
  f-2—Morgan, Joseph P., Est. of, 37 TC 36, 37, 37-1961
  P-H TC 26, 27
  n-2—Woodward, Fred W. & Elsie M., 49 TC 385, 49
  P-H TC 270
ADDISON, IRENE D., 1948 P-H TC Memo ¶ 48,177
  1—Waldheim & Co., Inc., 25 TC 599, 25-1955 P-H TC
  332
  f-1—Morgan, Joseph P., Est. of, 37 TC 36, 37, 37-1961
  P-H TC 26, 27
  1—Buder, G. A., Est. of, 1963 P-H TC Memo 63-345
  e-1—Rhodes, Lynn E. & Martha E., 1963 P-H TC
  Memo 63-1374
ADDISON, JOHN MILTON, BKPT; U.S. v, 20 AFTR2d
5630, 384 F2d 748 (USCA 5) (See Rochelle Jr., Trtee;
U.S. v)
ADDRESSOGRAPH - MULTIGRAPH CORP., 1945
P-H TC Memo ¶ 45,058
  Conn. L. & P. Co., The v U.S., 9 AFTR2d 679, 156 Ct
  Cl 312, 314, 299 F2d 264
  Copperhead Coal Co., Inc., 1958 P-H TC Memo 58-33
  1—Seas Shipping Co., Inc. v Comm., 19 AFTR2d 596,
  371 F2d 529 (USCA 2)
  e-1—Hitchcock, E. R., Co., The v U.S., 35 AFTR2d
  75-1207, 514 F2d 487 (USCA 2)
  f-2—Vulcan Materials Co. v U.S., 25 AFTR2d 70-446,
  308 F Supp 57 (DC Ala)
  f-3—Marlo Coil Co. v U.S., 1969 P-H 58,133 (Ct Cl
  Comr Rep)
  4—United Gas Improvement Co. v Comm., 240 F2d 318,
  50 AFTR 1354 (USCA 3)
  10—St. Louis Co. (Del) (in Dissolution) v U.S., 237 F2d
  156, 50 AFTR 257 (USCA 3)
ADDRESSOGRAPH - MULTIGRAPH CORP. v U.S.,
112 Ct Cl 201, 78 F Supp 111, 37 AFTR 53
  f-1—St. Joseph Lead Co. v U.S., 9 AFTR2d 712, 299
  F2d 350 (USCA 2)
  e-1—Central & South West Corp. v U.S., 1968 P-H
  58,175 (Ct Cl Comr Rep)
  1—Smale & Robinson, Inc. v U.S., 123 F Supp 469, 46
  AFTR 375 (DC Calif)
  1—St. Joseph Lead Co. v U.S., 7 AFTR2d 401, 190 F
  Supp 640 (DC NY)
  1—Eisenstadt Mfg. Co., 28 TC 230, 28-1957 P-H TC 132
  f-2—St. Joseph Lead Co. v U.S., 9 AFTR2d 712, 299
  F2d 350 (USCA 2)
  f-3—Consol, Coppermines Corp. v U.S., 8 AFTR2d
  5873, 155 Ct Cl 736, 296 F2d 745
ADELAIDE PARK LAND, 25 BTA 211
  g—Custom Component Switches, Inc. v U.S., 19
  AFTR2d 560 (DC Calif) [See 25 BTA 215]
  O'Connor, John C., 1957 P-H TC Memo 57-190
ADELBERG, MARVIN & HELEN, 1971 P-H TC Memo
¶ 71,015
ADELMAN v U.S., 27 AFTR2d 71-1464, 440 F2d 991
(USCA 9, 5-3-71)
  sa—Adelman v U.S., 24 AFTR2d 69-5769, 304 F Supp
  599 (DC Calif)
ADELMAN v U.S., 24 AFTR2d 69-5769, 304 F Supp 599
(DC Calif, 9-30-69)
  a—Adelman v U.S., 27 AFTR2d 71-1464, 440 F2d 991
  (USCA 9)
ADELSON, SAMUEL; U.S. v, 52 AFTR 1798 (DC RI)
(See Sullivan Co., Inc.; U.S. v)
ADELSON v U.S., 15 AFTR2d 246, 342 F2d 332 (USCA
9, 1-13-65)
  sa—Adelson v U.S., 12 AFTR2d 5010, 221 F Supp 31
  (DC Calif)
  g-1—Greenlee, L. C. & Gladys M., 1966 P-H TC Memo
  66-985
  f-1—Cochran, Carol J., 1973 P-H TC Memo 73-459
  f-1—Marchionni, Siro L., 1976 P-H TC Memo 76-1321
  f-2—Krist, Edwin F. v Comm., 32 AFTR2d 73-5663, 483
  F2d 1351 (USCA 2)
  f-2—Fugate v U.S., 18 AFTR2d 5607, 259 F Supp 401
  (DC Tex) [See 15 AFTR2d 249, 342 F2d 335]

Reference to the "Court Decisions" section of Volume 2, *Citator 2nd Series* (covering the period from 1978 through 1989) shows that *Adda v. Comm.* was cited in *Judith C. Connelly* and *Robert E. Cleveland*, as to the first issue in *Adda* without comment. This page (22) is reproduced in Figure E–5.

The *Citator* includes a cumulative supplement (i.e., 1990–1997), and a cumulative monthly supplement is published each month. Be sure to refer to these supplements, or very recent citations might be overlooked. No citations appear in the supplements for *Adda v. Comm.*

Except as otherwise noted, it appears that *Adda v. Comm.* has withstood the test of time.

▼ **FIGURE E–5**

22   **ADAMSON—ADELSON**

ADAMSON, LEE A., 1981 PH TC Memo ¶ 81,285 (See Petty, R. M. & Allene A.)

ADAMSON, RAY P., 1981 PH TC Memo ¶ 81,285 (See Petty, R. M. & Allene A.)

ADAMSON, ROY & CATHERINE, 1986 PH TC Memo ¶ 86,489
- f-1—Dew, James Edward, 91 TC 626, 91 PH TC 310
- e-1—Telfeyan, Louis & Lynn, 1988 PH TC Memo 88-2146
- e-1—Bullock, Kenneth & Gail, 1988 PH TC Memo 88-2706

ADAMSON, SANDRA L., 1981 PH TC Memo ¶ 81,285 (See Petty, R. M. & Allene A.)

ADAMSON; U.S. v, 161 F2d 942, 35 AFTR 1404 (USCA 9)
- e-1—Inco Electroenergy Corp., 1987 PH TC Memo 87-2295

ADAMUCCI, RICHARD, 1987 PH TC Memo ¶ 87,378 (See Batastini, Paul J. & Amelia)

ADCOCK, HOMER & DOROTHY, 1982 PH TC Memo ¶ 82,206
- e-1—Kauffman, Wilma G., 1982 PH TC Memo 82-2193
- e-1—Scallen, Stephen B. & Chacke Y., 1987 PH TC Memo 87-2134

ADDA v COMM., 171 F2d 457, 37 AFTR 654 (USCA 4)
- 1—Connelly, Judith C., 1982 PH TC Memo 82-2866
- 1—Cleveland, Robert E., 1983 PH TC Memo 83-1223

ADDA, FERNAND C.A., 10 TC 273, ¶ 10.133 PH TC 1948
- 1—Connelly, Judith C., 1982 PH TC Memo 82-2866
- 1—Cleveland, Robert E., 1983 PH TC Memo 83-1223

ADDA, INC., 9 TC 199
- e—Hodges, Irene McLaughlin & Thomas Lyman, 1985 PH TC Memo 85-2062 [See 9 TC 210-211]
- 1—Security Bancorp, Inc. v U.S., 48 AFTR2d 81-5514 (DC Mich)
- 4—Watson Land Co., 1983 PH TC Memo 83-744

ADDA, INC.; COMM. v, 171 F2d 367, 37 AFTR 641 (USCA 2)
- Security Bancorp, Inc. v U.S., 48 AFTR2d 81-5514 (DC Mich)
- Watson Land Co., 1983 PH TC Memo 83-744
- e—Hodges, Irene McLaughlin & Thomas Lyman, 1985 PH TC Memo 85-2062

ADDEO, ARTHUR J., Jr. & MARY, 1984 PH TC Memo ¶ 84,493
- e-1—Brown, Stewart L., 1986 PH TC Memo 86-1153

ADDINGTON, DOUGLAS F., 1986 PH TC Memo ¶ 86,358 (See Hoak, Roderick C. & Cornelia)

ADDINGTON, WILLIAM H. & DONNA L., 1980 PH TC Memo ¶ 80,046
- a—Court Order, 10-20-81, 663 F2d 104 (USCA 5)
- d—1981 PH 61,000 (USCA 10)

ADDISON, ALBERT I., 1979 PH TC Memo ¶ 79,317
- e-1—Ridenour, Harry P., Jr. v U.S., 52 AFTR2d 83-5589, 3 Cl Ct 134
- e-1—Reinhardt, Jules & Marilyn D., 85 TC 526, 85 PH TC 299

ADDISON INTERNAT., INC., 90 TC 1207, ¶ 90.78 PH TC
- a—Addison Internat., Inc. v Comm., 64 AFTR2d 89-5747, 887 F2d 660 (USCA 6)
- rc—Rocky Mountain Associates Internat., Inc., 90 TC 1241, 1242, 90 PH TC 637, 638
- g-1—Butka, David J. & Sabine I., 91 TC 130, 91 PH TC 66

ADDISON INTERNAT., INC. v COMM., 64 AFTR2d 89-5747, 887 F2d 660 (USCA 6, 10-10-89)
- sa—Addison Internat., Inc., 90 TC 1207, ¶ 90.78 PH TC

ADDRESSOGRAPH-MULTIGRAPH CORP., 1945 PH TC Memo ¶ 45,058
- 1—Buffalo Wire Works Co., Inc., 74 TC 938, 74 PH TC 509
- g-1—Maier Brewing Co., 1987 PH TC Memo 87-1978

ADEE, ALLEN R., TRUST NO. 1 v U.S., 52 AFTR2d 83-6437 (DC Kan, 7-19-83)

ADEE, DONALD P., TRUSTEE v U.S., 52 AFTR2d 83-6437 (DC Kan) (See Adee, Allen R., Trust No. 1 v U.S.)

ADEE, JACK R., TRUSTEE v U.S., 52 AFTR2d 83-6437 (DC Kan) (See Adee, Allen R., Trust No. 1 v U.S.)

ADELBERG, MARVIN & HELEN M., 1985 PH TC Memo ¶ 85,597
- a—Court Order, 1-21-87, 811 F2d 1507 (USCA 9)
- e-1—Chao, Wen Y. & Ching J., 92 TC 1144, 92 PH TC 577
- e-1—Nicklo, Joseph J., 1988 PH TC Memo 88-1199

ADELEKE, JOEL & CATHERINE A., 1980 PH TC Memo ¶ 80,479
- e-1—Pike-Biegunski, Maciej Jan & Denise Nadine, 1984 PH TC Memo 84-1123

ADELMAN v U.S., 27 AFTR2d 71-1464, 440 F2d 991 (USCA 9)
- e-1—Barbados #7 Ltd., 92 TC 813, 92 PH TC 409

ADELMAN v U.S., 24 AFTR2d 69-5769, 304 F Supp 599 (DC Calif)
- e-2—Barbados #7 Ltd., 92 TC 813, 92 PH TC 409

ADELSON, SHELDON G. v U.S., 54 AFTR2d 84-5428, 737 F2d 1569 (USCA Fed, 6-28-84)
- remg—Adelson, Sheldon G. v U.S., 52 AFTR2d 83-5211 (Cl Ct)
- s—Adelson, Sheldon G. v U.S., 51 AFTR2d 83-574 (Cl Ct) 535 F Supp 1082
- s—Adelson, Sheldon G. v U.S., 54 AFTR2d 84-5959, 6 Cl Ct 102
- rc—Adelson, Sheldon G. v U.S., 57 AFTR2d 86-736, 782 F2d 1010 (USCA Fed)
- rc—Adelson, Sheldon G. v U.S., 59 AFTR2d 87-993, 12 Cl Ct 231
- e-1—Larson, Roger Roy, In re, 62 AFTR2d 88-5801, 862 F2d 117 (USCA 7)
- e-1—Raab, George S. v I.R.S., 57 AFTR2d 86-715, 86-716 (DC Pa)

ADELSON, SHELDON G. v U.S., 57 AFTR2d 86-736, 782 F2d 1010 (USCA Fed, 1-29-86)
- remg—Adelson, Sheldon G. v U.S., 54 AFTR2d 84-5959, 6 Cl Ct 102
- rc—Adelson, Sheldon G. v U.S., 54 AFTR2d 84-5428, 737 F2d 1569 (USCA Fed)
- rc—Adelson, Sheldon G. v U.S., 52 AFTR2d 83-5211, 2 Cl Ct 591
- rc—Adelson, Sheldon G. v U.S., 51 AFTR2d 83-574, 1 Cl Ct 61, 553 F Supp 1082
- rc—Adelson, Sheldon G. v U.S., 59 AFTR2d 87-993, 12 Cl Ct 231

ADELSON, SHELDON G. v U.S., 51 AFTR2d 83-574, 1 Cl Ct 61, 553 F Supp 1082 (12-27-82)
- s—Adelson, Sheldon G. v U.S., 54 AFTR2d 84-5428, 737 F2d 1569 (USCA Fed)
- s—Adelson, Sheldon G. v U.S., 52 AFTR2d 83-5211, 2 Cl Ct 591
- rc—Adelson, Sheldon G. v U.S., 57 AFTR2d 86-736, 782 F2d 1010 (USCA Fed)
- rc—Adelson, Sheldon G. v U.S., 54 AFTR2d 84-5959, 6 Cl Ct 102
- rc—Adelson, Sheldon G. v U.S., 59 AFTR2d 87-993, 12 Cl Ct 231
- e-1—Mann, Guy L. Est. of, 53 AFTR2d 84-1304, 731 F2d 273 (USCA 5)

ADELSON, SHELDON G. v U.S., 52 AFTR2d 83-5211, 2 Cl Ct 591 (6-14-83)
- remd—Adelson, Sheldon G. v U.S., 54 AFTR2d 84-5428, 737 F2d 1569 (USCA Fed)
- s—Adelson, Sheldon G. v U.S., 51 AFTR2d 83-574 (Cl Ct) 553 F Supp 1082
- rc—Adelson, Sheldon G. v U.S., 57 AFTR2d 86-736, 782 F2d 1010 (USCA Fed)
- rc—Adelson, Sheldon G. v U.S., 54 AFTR2d 84-5959, 6 Cl Ct 102
- rc—Adelson, Sheldon G. v U.S., 59 AFTR2d 87-993, 12 Cl Ct 231

ADELSON, SHELDON G. v U.S., 54 AFTR2d 84-5959, 6 Cl Ct 102 (9-12-84)
- remd—Adelson, Sheldon G. v U.S., 57 AFTR2d 86-736, 782 F2d 1010 (USCA Fed)
- s—Adelson, Sheldon G. v U.S., 54 AFTR2d 84-5428, 737 F2d 1569 (USCA Fed)
- rc—Adelson, Sheldon G. v U.S., 51 AFTR2d 83-574, 1 Cl Ct 61, 553 F Supp 1082
- rc—Adelson, Sheldon G. v U.S., 52 AFTR2d 83-5211, 2 Cl Ct 591
- rc—Adelson, Sheldon G. v U.S., 59 AFTR2d 87-993, 12 Cl Ct 231

APPENDIX F
Comprehensive Tax Return Problems

PROBLEM 1

1. Dan B. and Marla R. Luce, ages 44 and 46, are married and file a joint income tax return. Dan is a specialist in horticulture and is employed by the Harlan Seed Corporation as director of research activities. Marla is a schoolteacher and is employed by the Methodist Middle School, a private institution owned and operated by a religious group. Salary and tax withholdings for 1997 were:

	Salary	Federal	State
Dan	$72,000	$6,340	$2,580
Marla	33,000	4,300	1,550

   The proper Social Security tax and Medicare tax amounts have been withheld from their salaries.

2. The Luces have always lived and worked in Des Moines, Iowa. They reside at 4010 Green Avenue, Des Moines, IA 50312. Living with them are their three children, Bo (age 13), Julius (age 15), and Mona (age 22). Also living with the Luces is Dan's widower father, Peter (age 70). Mona is a full-time student at Drake University. During the year, she earned $3,000 from a part-time job. Peter received $8,000 in Social Security benefits, which he deposited in his savings account. The Luces contributed more than 50% of the support of their children and of Peter.

3. The Luces contributed 25% of the support of Marla's aunt, Mary Lyons, who lives with Marla's sister. Mary receives the remainder of her support from Marla's sister and two brothers, 25% each. Marla's sister and brothers have each signed a multiple support agreement allowing Marla to claim the dependency exemption for Mary. As noted below, the Luces have provided their share of support by paying Mary's medical expenses.

4. Relevant Social Security numbers are:

Dan	478–12–6024
Marla	477–19–1002
Bo	479–22–6018
Julius	479–29–5025
Mona	479–31–4129
Peter	481–15–6113
Mary	480–42–1266

5. Because Peter is confined to a wheelchair due to a stroke he suffered several years ago, the Luces spent $7,200 during the year adding impairment-related improvements to their personal residence (e.g., wheelchair ramp, widening of hallways, bathtub railings). A friend who is in the real estate business estimates that these changes increased the value of the residence by $3,500.

6. During 1997, the Luces' personal residence suffered water damage. They had purchased this house on June 15, 1973, and paid $55,000 for it. A professional appraisal, for which the Luces paid $500, indicates that the value of the residence decreased by $14,000 ($120,000 before and $106,000 after) due to the water damage caused by the storm. The Luce's homeowner's insurance policy does not cover water damage.

7. On June 1, 1992, as a favor to a former college roommate, Dan loaned $4,200 to Bill Wild. Bill signed a note, maturity date of June 1, 1997, with annual interest of 10%. Dan has never recovered any of the loan or received any interest. Bill was declared bankrupt in April 1997 and is currently under investigation for mail fraud.

8. Marla has a Bachelor of Education degree that she received many years ago. Recently, the directors at her school resolved that all of its teachers must earn a Master of Education degree in order to continue in their present jobs. The teachers are allowed 10 years in which to satisfy this new requirement. During the summer of 1997, Marla enrolled at a local university and took several graduate courses in education. Marla lived at home and commuted to her classes. Her expenses were as follows:

Books and tuition	$2,100
Transportation	
Bus fares	125
Personal auto mileage (170 miles)	?
Meals while on campus (between classes)	105
Parking charges	82

When Marla did not take the bus, usually on rainy days, she drove the family auto (use the automatic mileage method—31.5 cents for 1997). When Marla drove, she had to pay for on-campus parking.

9. During 1997, the Luces sold the following stocks:

Owl Corporation	
(400 shares common) July 5	$34,000
Falcon Corporation	
(300 shares preferred) August 10	18,000

The Owl Corporation stock was received from Marla's mother as a gift on January 2, 1997, when it had a fair market value of $30,000. Her mother had purchased the stock on June 1, 1996, for $30,500. No gift tax was due or paid on the mother's gift.

Dan inherited the Falcon Corporation stock from his mother. She died on December 10, 1996, and her estate was settled on March 3, 1997 (the day Dan received the stock). The stock was worth $15,600 on December 10, 1996, and $14,900 on March 3, 1997. Dan has found a broker's statement that shows his mother purchased the stock on September 9, 1996, for $15,100 (including brokerage fee).

10. Besides any other items mentioned elsewhere, the Luces had the following receipts for 1997:

Interest on CD (Iowa State Bank)		$2,920
Interest on City of Des Moines general purpose bonds		700
Dividends		
Owl Corporation stock	$1,050	
Falcon Corporation stock	820	1,870
Garage sale of old clothes and household goods (reasonable cost estimate of items sold is $8,500)		2,100

11. As to medical expenses, the Luces had the following during 1997:

Hospital and doctor bills for Mary	$3,200
Dan's contribution toward the cost of his employer's medical insurance premiums	2,800
Insurance recovery for 1996 expenses under employment medical policy	880
Orthodontia expenses for children	4,600
Prescription drugs	500
Doctor bills for family	1,100
Tonsillectomy for Bo (surgeon and hospital)	1,700
Wheelchair and hearing aid for Peter	2,250

The $880 insurance recovery for the year 1996 was for medical expenses the Luces deducted on their 1996 Federal income tax return.

The Luces have not yet submitted any claims to the insurance company for their 1997 medical expenses. They estimate that, after the required deductible, the reimbursed amount will be $1,800.

12. Other expenditures for 1997 are summarized below:

Interest on home mortgage	$5,200
Property taxes on home	3,200
Payment of church pledge ($300 was for the 1996 remaining balance)	1,850
Additional state income tax due for 1996	130
School supplies Marla uses for her classes (not provided by her school)	205
Professional dues (Dan and Marla)	310
Professional journals (Dan and Marla)	400
Lab coats (used by Dan at work)	240
Laundry of lab coats	115
Safety goggles and shoes (used by Dan at work)	90
Riverboat casino losses (supported by adequate records)	300

13. On a timely basis, the Luces made four quarterly estimated Federal income tax payments of $300 each.

14. The Luces do not wish to designate a contribution to the Presidential Election Campaign Fund. If they have overpaid, any refund is to be applied toward their 1998 Federal income tax liability.

Requirements

You are to prepare a joint Federal income tax return for the Luces for 1997.

PROBLEM 2

1. Al P. Hart, age 44, is divorced and lives alone at 426 Latner Lane, Cincinnati, OH 45221. He provides more than half of the cost of maintaining a household for Norma Hart, who lives in an apartment nearby. Norma, age 70, is Al's widowed mother and qualifies as his dependent.

2. Al and Leona were married 18 years ago and were divorced in 1994. Leona was awarded custody of their only child, Peter, now 12 years old. Under the divorce decree, Al must pay Leona $400 each month until Peter reaches age 21 or dies (whichever occurs first). Upon the occurrence of either event, the monthly payment becomes $100. Since Al and Leona have been alternating claiming Peter as a dependent, Leona completed and sent to Al a Form 8332 for 1997. Al sent Leona the required $4,800 ($400 × 12) for 1997. Furthermore, he sent Leona an additional $400 for dental work she had done on her teeth. He also paid an optometrist/optician $300 for Peter's eye exams and prescription glasses.

3. Al is a licensed hair stylist and beautician and operates his own salon under the business name "Al's Creations." Although the number varies, Al's business consists of four to six stations operated by himself and other licensed beauticians. The beauticians who work in the salon are treated as independent contractors. In this regard, each has his or her own telephone line. They maintain their own appointment books, have their own customers, and collect and keep the fees charged. For the use of the work stations and various facilities (e.g., hair dryers, shampoo sinks, waiting area), each beautician pays Al a monthly rental. Al does not control their work hours, although most choose to follow Al's own work schedule.

4. Al's Creations is well-known for the selection and quality of its men's hairpieces (i.e., toupees) and women's wigs. The business also sells a considerable quantity of beauty

products (e.g., conditioners, shampoos, curling irons). Some of these items are sold to other beauticians, but most are sold to regular patrons and walk-in customers.

5. Al's Creations is located at 6194 Taft Street, Cincinnati, OH 45221. The employer identification number is 31–0009521; the professional activity code for beauticians is 8110.

6. The building in which the business is located is rented under a long-term lease for $1,000 each month. Al pays his own utilities. Before Al moved in, the landlord customized the facilities for its intended use. The only employee Al has is a shampoo person, who also performs light janitorial services. Al hires an outside service to do the heavier janitorial duties. Likewise, a local accounting group is on retainer to keep the financial records and prepare the tax returns for the business.

7. Al's Creations had the following receipts for 1997:

Sales of cosmetics	$18,000
Sales of hairpieces, wigs	30,000
Fees received from patrons by Al (including tips received)	35,000
Rent charged other beauticians	25,000

The amounts shown for the retail sales of cosmetics, hairpieces, and wigs include state sales tax.

8. Al's Creations had the following expenses for 1997:

Purchases of cosmetics	$ 7,980
Purchases of hairpieces, wigs	11,800
Operating supplies (shampoo, permanent wave solution, color, etc.)	4,900
Rent for building	12,000
Utilities and telephone	5,800
Payroll expense	5,200
Payroll taxes (FICA, FUTA, state unemployment)	590
Sales taxes remitted to state	2,400
Health insurance coverage for employee	810
City of Cincinnati occupation permit for 1997	400
State beautician license fee	210
Liability insurance premiums (coverage is for calendar years 1997–1999)	4,800
Casualty insurance on business furnishings and equipment for 1997	1,400
Janitorial services	2,400
Accounting services	4,100
Waiting room furniture	3,000
Magazine subscriptions for waiting room	300
Advertising	600
Fine paid to city of Cincinnati	200

9. Al decided to completely renovate the furnishings in his waiting room. Consequently, he spent $3,000 for chairs, sofa, lamps, coffee table, etc., all placed in service on April 20, 1997. The old furnishings were given to patrons or thrown away. The old furniture was completely depreciated and had a zero tax basis. Al has always followed a policy of claiming as much depreciation as soon as possible. All of his other business assets (e.g., hair dryers, work-station chairs) have been fully depreciated by 1997.

10. The fine paid to the city was assessed by the Sanitation Department. Al had failed to separate the business's trash into recyclable and nonrecyclable bins as required by a city ordinance.

11. Al maintains an inventory as to the merchandise he sells. The business inventories (based on the lower of cost or market) are as follows:

	12/31/96	12/31/97
Hairpieces and wigs	$3,000	$2,800
Cosmetics	2,100	2,000

12. In 1997, Al was audited by both the city and the state as to his 1996 income tax returns. As a result of the audits, he had to pay the city an additional $110, but he received a refund of $170 from the state.

13. Except for the inventory and purchases accounts, Al operated the business on a cash method. Customers pay for services as rendered. Sales income is recorded when the merchandise is sold.

14. Al's medical expenses for 1997, and not mentioned elsewhere, included the following:

Gallbladder operation (includes hospital and surgeon's charges) for Norma	$2,000
Annual physical for Al	500
Dentist charges for Al (includes crown, bridges, fillings, etc.)	3,100
Hernia operation (includes hospital and surgeon's charges)	2,500
Prescription medicines	400
Medical insurance premiums	800

In November 1997, Al purchased a medical insurance policy. The policy does not cover anyone but Al and his one employee (see item 6 above). The premium for the employee coverage is stated separately at item 8. Also, the policy does not apply to dental bills. Al filed a claim with the insurance company in late December. In January 1998, he received a check for $300 after the appropriate deductible.

15. Al's other expenses were as follows:

Property taxes on residence	$3,800
Interest on home mortgage	4,400
Annual dues for membership in the American Association of Beauticians	150
Professional journals	200

16. Al has always itemized his deductions because even without substantial medical expenses, his deductions from adjusted gross income have exceeded the standard deduction.

17. Al had the following stock transactions during 1997 (all are held as investments):

Stock	Date Acquired	Date Sold	Sales Price	Cost Basis
Peach Corp.	1/2/96	10/14/97	$19,000	$17,000
Orange Corp.	9/26/96	10/23/97	16,000	15,000
Tan Corp.	2/4/97	12/3/97	14,000	14,500

18. Al's other income for 1997 is summarized below:

Interest income from a savings account at United Bank	$5,100
Cash dividend from General Electric	3,300

19. Al made estimated tax payments for 1997 as follows:

City income tax	$ 650
Ohio income tax	2,600
Federal income and self-employment taxes (paid $2,500 quarterly)	10,000

20. Relevant Social Security numbers are:

Al Hart	268–01–5869
Norma Hart	301–42–2657
Leona Hart	300–52–7981
Peter Hart	302–64–1826

Requirements

You are to prepare Al's Federal income tax return for 1997. Al wants to designate that $3 be directed to the Presidential Election Campaign Fund. If he has overpaid his 1997 taxes, he wants to have the amount applied to his 1998 estimated tax.

APPENDIX G
Table of Cases Cited

Appendix H
Depreciation

Introduction

Cost recovery, amortization, and depletion are presented in Chapter 8. For most fixed assets (e.g., machinery, equipment, furniture, fixtures, buildings) placed in service after December 31, 1980, the Economic Recovery Tax Act of 1981 (ERTA) has replaced the depreciation system with the cost recovery system.[1] The general relationship between the depreciation system and the cost recovery system is summarized in Exhibit H–1.

Despite ERTA, a discussion of § 167 depreciation is still relevant for two reasons. First, assets that were placed in service prior to 1981 are still in use. Second, certain assets placed in service after 1980 are not eligible to use the cost recovery system (ACRS and MACRS) and therefore must be depreciated. They include property placed in service after 1980 whose life is not based on years (e.g., units-of-production method).

Depreciation

Section 167 permits a depreciation deduction in the form of a reasonable allowance for the exhaustion, wear and tear, and obsolescence of business property and property held for the production of income (e.g., rental property held by an investor).[2] Obsolescence refers to normal technological change due to reasonably foreseeable economic conditions. If rapid or abnormal obsolescence occurs, a taxpayer may change to a shorter estimated useful life if there is a "clear and convincing basis for the redetermination." Depreciation deductions are *not* permitted for personal use property.

The taxpayer must adopt a reasonable and consistent plan for depreciating the cost or other basis of assets over the estimated useful life of the property (e.g., the taxpayer cannot arbitrarily defer or accelerate the amount of depreciation from one year to another). The basis of the depreciable property must be reduced by the depreciation allowed and by not less than the allowable amount.[3] The *allowed*

▼ **EXHIBIT H–1**
Depreciation and Cost Recovery: Relevant Time Periods

System	Date Property Is Placed in Service
§ 167 depreciation	Before January 1, 1981, and *certain* property placed in service after December 31, 1980.
Original accelerated cost recovery system (ACRS)	After December 31, 1980, and before January 1, 1987.
Modified accelerated cost recovery system (MACRS)	After December 31, 1986.

---

[1]Depreciation is covered in § 167, and cost recovery (ACRS and MACRS) is covered in § 168.

[2]§ 167(a) and Reg. § 1.167(a)–1.
[3]§ 1016(a)(2) and Reg. § 1.167(a)–10(a).

depreciation is the depreciation actually taken, whereas the *allowable* depreciation is the amount that could have been taken under the applicable depreciation method. If the taxpayer does not claim any depreciation on property during a particular year, the basis of the property still must be reduced by the amount of depreciation that should have been deducted (the allowable depreciation).

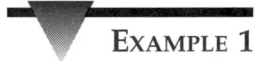

EXAMPLE 1

On January 1, Ted paid $7,500 for a truck to be used in his business. He chose a five-year estimated useful life, no salvage value, and straight-line depreciation. Thus, the allowable depreciation deduction was $1,500 per year. However, depreciation actually taken (allowed) was as follows:

Year 1	$1,500
Year 2	–0–
Year 3	–0–
Year 4	1,500
Year 5	1,500

The adjusted basis of the truck must be reduced by the amount of allowable depreciation of $7,500 ($1,500 × 5 years) even though Ted claimed only $4,500 depreciation during the five-year period. Therefore, if Ted sold the truck at the end of Year 5 for $1,000, he would recognize a $1,000 gain, since the adjusted basis of the truck is zero. ▼

QUALIFYING PROPERTY AND BASIS FOR DEPRECIATION

The use rather than the character of property determines whether a depreciation deduction is permitted. Property must be used in a trade or business or held for the production of income to qualify as depreciable.

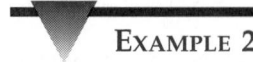

EXAMPLE 2

Carol is a self-employed CPA who maintains her office in a room in her home. The room, which is used exclusively for her business, comprises 20% of the square footage of her house. Carol is permitted a depreciation deduction only for the business use part of the house. No depreciation deduction is permitted for the 80% of the square footage of her house that is used as her residence. ▼

The basis for depreciation generally is the adjusted cost basis used to determine gain if the property is sold or otherwise disposed of.[4] However, if personal use assets are converted to business or income-producing use, the basis for depreciation *and* for loss is the *lower* of the adjusted basis or fair market value at the time of the conversion of the property.[5] As a result of this lower of basis rule, losses that occurred while the property was personal use property will not be recognized for tax purposes through the depreciation of the property.

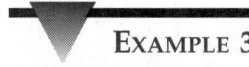

EXAMPLE 3

Hans acquires a personal residence for $130,000. Four years later, when the fair market value is only $125,000, he converts the property to rental use. The basis for depreciation is $125,000, since the fair market value is less than the adjusted basis. The $5,000 decline in value is deemed to be personal (since it occurred while the property was held for personal use) and therefore nondeductible. ▼

---

[4]§ 167(c).　　　　　　　　　　　　　　　　[5]Reg. § 1.167(g)–1.

The Regulations provide that tangible property is depreciable only to the extent that the property is subject to wear and tear, decay or decline from natural causes, exhaustion, and obsolescence.[6] Thus, land and inventory are not depreciable, but land improvements are depreciable (e.g., paved surfaces, fences, landscaping).

OTHER DEPRECIATION CONSIDERATIONS

In determining the amount of the depreciation deduction, the following additional considerations need to be addressed:

- The salvage value of the asset.
- The choice of depreciation methods.
- The useful life of the asset.

For property subject to depreciation under § 167, taxpayers generally must take into account the **salvage value** (assuming there is a salvage value) of an asset in calculating depreciation. An asset cannot be depreciated below its salvage value. However, the Code permits a taxpayer to disregard salvage value for amounts up to 10 percent of the basis in the property. This provision applies to tangible personal property (other than livestock) with an estimated useful life of three years or more.[7]

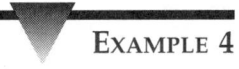
EXAMPLE 4

Green Company acquired a machine for $10,000 in 1980 with an estimated salvage value of $3,000 after 18 years. The company may disregard salvage value to the extent of $1,000 and compute the machine's depreciation based upon a cost of $10,000 less $2,000 salvage value. The adjusted basis may be reduced to $2,000 (depreciation of $8,000 may be taken) even though the actual salvage value is $3,000. ▼

This provision was incorporated into the law to reduce the number of IRS-taxpayer disputes over the amount of the salvage value that should be used.

Another consideration is the *choice of depreciation methods* from among the several allowed. The following alternative depreciation methods are permitted for property placed into service before January 1, 1981, and for the aforementioned property placed in service after December 31, 1980, for which cost recovery is not permitted:

- The straight-line (SL) method (cost basis less salvage value ÷ estimated useful life).
- The declining-balance method (DB) using a rate not to exceed twice the straight-line rate. Common methods include 200 percent DB (double-declining balance), 150 percent DB, and 125 percent DB. Salvage value is not taken into account under any of the declining-balance methods. However, no further depreciation can be claimed once net book value (cost minus depreciation) and salvage value are the same.
- The sum-of-the-years' digits method (SYD).
- Any other consistent method that does not result in greater total depreciation being claimed during the first two-thirds of the useful life than would have been allowable under the double-declining balance method. Permissible methods include machine hours and the units-of-production method.

[6]Reg. § 1.167(a)–2.

[7]Reg. §§ 1.167(a)–1(c) and (f)–1.

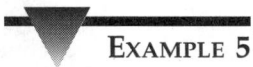

EXAMPLE 5

On January 1, 1980, Diego acquired a new machine to be used in his business. The asset cost $10,000 with an estimated salvage value of $2,000 and a four-year estimated useful life.[8] The following amounts of depreciation could be deducted, depending on the method of depreciation used:

	1980	1981	1982	1983
1. Straight-line: $10,000 cost less ($2,000 salvage value reduced by 10% of cost) ÷ 4 years	$2,250	$2,250	$2,250	$2,250
2. Double-declining balance:				
a. $10,000 × 50% (twice the straight-line rate)	5,000			
b. ($10,000 − $5,000) × 50%		2,500		
c. ($10,000 − $5,000 − $2,500) × 50%			1,250	
d. ($10,000 − $5,000 − $2,500 − $1,250) × 50%				250[9]
3. Sum-of-the-years' digits:* $10,000 cost less ($2,000 salvage value reduced by 10% of cost) or $9,000				
a. $9,000 × 4/10	3,600			
b. $9,000 × 3/10		2,700		
c. $9,000 × 2/10			1,800	
d. $9,000 × 1/10				900

*The formula for the sum-of-the-years' digits (SYD) method is

$$\text{Cost} - \text{Salvage value} \times \frac{\text{Remaining life at the beginning of the year}}{\text{Sum-of-the-years' digits of the estimated life}}$$

In this example, the denominator for SYD is 1 + 2 + 3 + 4, or 10. The numerator is 4 for Year 1 (the number of years left at the beginning of Year 1), 3 for Year 2, etc. The denominator can be calculated by the following formula:

$$S = \frac{Y(Y + 1)}{2} \text{ where } Y = \text{estimated useful life}$$

$$S = \frac{4(4 + 1)}{2} = 10$$

▼

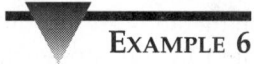

EXAMPLE 6

Using the depreciation calculations in Example 5, the depreciation reserve (accumulated depreciation) and net book value at the end of 1983 are as follows:

	Cost	− Depreciation	= Net Book Value*
Straight-line	$10,000	$9,000	$1,000
Double-declining balance	10,000	9,000	1,000
Sum-of-the-years' digits	10,000	9,000	1,000

*Note that an asset may not be depreciated below its salvage value even when a declining-balance method is used.

▼

In 1969, Congress placed certain restrictions on the use of accelerated methods for new and used realty that are subject to the depreciation rules under § 167. These restrictions were imposed to reduce the opportunities for using real estate investments as tax shelters. The use of accelerated depreciation frequently resulted in the recognition of ordinary tax losses on economically profitable real estate ventures.

---

[8] A four-year life is used to illustrate the different depreciation methods. Note that an asset placed in service in 1980 must have a useful life of at least 19 years in order for depreciation to be deducted in 1998.

[9] Total depreciation taken cannot exceed cost minus estimated salvage value ($1,000 in this example).

The following methods were permitted for residential and nonresidential real property:

	Nonresidential Real Property (Commercial and Industrial Buildings, Etc.)	Residential Real Property (Apartment Buildings, Etc.)
New property acquired after July 24, 1969, and generally before January 1, 1981	150% DB, SL	200% DB, SYD, 150% DB, or SL
Used property acquired after July 24, 1969, and generally before January 1, 1981	SL	125% DB (if estimated useful life is 20 years or greater) or SL

Congress chose to permit accelerated methods (200 percent declining-balance and sum-of-the-years' digits) for new residential rental property. Presumably, the desire to stimulate construction of new housing units justified the need for such accelerated methods.

Restrictions on the use of accelerated methods were not imposed on new tangible personalty (e.g., machinery, equipment, and automobiles). However, the 200 percent declining-balance and sum-of-the-years' digits methods were not permitted for used tangible personal property. The depreciation methods permitted for *used* tangible personal property were as follows:

	Useful Life of Three Years or More	Useful Life of Less Than Three Years
Used tangible personal property acquired after July 24, 1969, and generally before January 1, 1981	150% DB, SL	SL

Since the acquisition of used property does not result in any net addition to gross private investment in our economy, Congress chose not to provide as rapid accelerated depreciation for used property.

The determination of a *useful life* for a depreciable asset often led to disagreement between taxpayers and the IRS. One source of information was the company's previous experience and policy with respect to asset maintenance and utilization. Another source was the guideline lives issued by the IRS.[10] In 1971, the IRS guideline life system was modified and liberalized by the enactment of the **Asset Depreciation Range (ADR) system.**[11]

[10]Rev.Proc. 72–10, 1972–1 C.B. 721, superseded by Rev.Proc. 83–35, 1983–1 C.B. 745.   [11]Reg. § 1.167(a)–11.

KEY TERMS

Asset Depreciation Range (ADR) system, H–5

Salvage value, H–3

INDEX

AMT FORMULA FOR INDIVIDUALS

Regular Taxable Income

Plus or minus:	Adjustments
Plus:	Tax preferences
Equals:	Alternative minimum taxable income
Minus:	Exemption
Equals:	Alternative minimum tax base
Times:	26% and 28% graduated rates
Equals:	Tentative minimum tax before foreign tax credit
Minus:	Alternative minimum tax foreign tax credit
Equals:	Tentative minimum tax
Minus:	Regular income tax liability
Equals:	Alternative minimum tax (if amount is positive)

AMT EXEMPTION PHASE–OUT FOR INDIVIDUALS

		Phase-out	
Filing Status	**Exemption**	**Begins at**	**Ends at**
Married, filing jointly	$45,000	$150,000	$330,000
Single or head of household	33,750	112,500	247,500
Married, filing separately	22,500	75,000	165,000

AMT FORMULA FOR CORPORATIONS

Regular Taxable Income before NOL Deduction

Plus or minus:	Adjustments (except ACE adjustment)
Plus:	Tax preferences
Equals:	AMTI before ATNOL deduction and ACE adjustment
Plus or minus:	ACE adjustment
Equals:	Alternative minimum taxable income (AMTI) before ATNOL deduction
Minus:	ATNOL deduction (limited to 90% of AMTI before ATNOL deduction)
Equals:	Alternative minimum taxable income (AMTI)
Minus:	Exemption
Equals:	Alternative minimum tax base
Times:	20% rate
Equals:	AMT before AMT foreign tax credit
Minus:	AMT foreign tax credit (possibly limited to 90% of AMT before AMT foreign tax credit)
Equals:	Tentative minimum tax
Minus:	Regular income tax liability before credits minus regular foreign tax credit
Equals:	Alternative minimum tax (AMT) if positive